INDIA TOUR
LESSONS
ON LIFE AND TEACHING
OF THE MASTERS
OF THE FAR EAST

By Baird T. Spalding

Volume IV

DeVorss & Co., *Publishers*
P. O. Box 550
Marina del Rey, CA 90291

ISBN: 0-87516-087-5

Printed in the United States of America by
Book Graphics, Inc., Marina del Rey, California.

THE LIFE AND TEACHING
OF THE
MASTERS OF THE FAR EAST

by BAIRD T. SPALDING

Baird T. Spalding, whose name became legend in metaphysical and truth circles during the first half of the 20th century, played an important part in introducing to the Western world the knowledge that there are Masters, or Elder Brothers, who are assisting and guiding the destiny of mankind. The countless numbers of letters that have come in through the years, from all over the world, bear testimony of the tremendous help received from the message in these books.

Partial listing of the contents of the five volumes:

Volume I: Introduction of the Master Emil—Visit to the "Temple of Silence"—Astral projection—Walking on Water—Visit to the Healing Temple—Emil talks about America—The Snowmen of the Himalayas—New Light on the teachings of Jesus.

Volume II: Visit to the Temple of the Great Tau Cross—Visit with the Master Jesus—Jesus discusses the nature of hell; the nature of God—The Mystery of thought vibrations—Jesus feeds the multitude—An account of a healing experience—Jesus and Buddha visit the group.

Volume III: One of the masters speaks of the Christ consciousness—The nature of cosmic energy—The creation of the planets and the worlds—The trip to Lhasa—Visit at the Temple Pora-tat-sanga—Explaining the mystery of levitation—A doubter becomes convinced of the existence of Jesus.

Volume IV: This material was first presented as "The India Tour Lessons." Each chapter has text for study, as well as guides to teachers for developing and interpreting the material. Among subjects covered: The White Brotherhood—The One Mind—Basis of coming social reorganization—Prana.

Volume V: Material taken from lectures given by Mr. Spalding in California during the last two years of his life. There is also a brief biographical sketch. Partial contents: Camera of past events—Is there a God—The divine pattern—The reality—Mastery over death—The law of supply.

Each of the 5 volumes has approximately 175 pages.

Publisher's Note

Both Mr. Spalding and Mr. DeVorss (who knew Mr. Spalding personally) died in the 1950's. The people who were associated with Mr. Spalding on the tour have also passed on. We are therefore without contact with anyone who has firsthand knowledge of the work, and the books themselves are now the only source of information. To our knowledge, there is no map available of the tour, and we know of no photographs. We have tried at various times to locate additional records, as well as camera information, but without success. We sincerely regret that we have no additional information to offer.

DeVorss & Company

CHAPTER I

GREAT WHITE BROTHERHOOD AND WORLD PEACE

1. Before going further in the study of certain underlying laws and facts regarding the teachings of the Masters, it is well to consider the scope their vision covers. One must enlarge his mind and outlook upon life to that in which the Masters work in order to fully understand the full purport of their teachings. At this time we will deal chiefly with the field to be taken into consideration and the general trends of mankind in order that we may fully adapt ourselves to the work that is before us. It is necessary to know the nature and scope of a field of work before selecting the tools and laying down a plan for tending the field. We must know to what the field is adapted, what crops are to be raised, and to what end the cultivation is to be directed. There must be a purpose back of all work and it is far beyond the reaches of what we commonly call our own individual nature. Each man's nature in one way and another is vitally associated with the life and well-being of every other individual in the world and what affects one must in some degree affect the rest of humanity.

2. I rather feel that this discussion of peace should be very general because everyone is interested. The fact is that the world is becoming peace-minded and that people are saying that we have had enough of war. People are beginning to understand that war is not a natural condition and to understand that all those who assume the role of

providence by setting themselves up as the embodiment of perfect Justice—the creators of Happiness—are only deceivers. Peace and Happiness, the heart's desire of all Humanity is not a gift to be bestowed upon mankind, but has to be earned by honest effort. There is not such a thing as political miracles. Man has to realize that he alone has the power to work out his destiny with his own intelligence.

3. This sweeping tide of human interest in that which will promote and guarantee peace is the inevitable working out of the Universal Law which always moves to promote the common good. God is no respecter of persons and this awakening of men along peace lines is their response to the movement of the Spirit of Peace which is fostered by the Masters. Only as the individual identifies himself with Universal Law can he expect to find his individual good for it is inseparably united with the common good. For this reason, true progress is slow and suffering is great.

4. There is a great brotherhood throughout the world who have been working for peace for thousands of years. They are back of every movement for world peace and are becoming stronger and stronger all the time. There are now about 216 groups throughout the world. There is always one central unit as a first or centralizing body and twelve units which surround that unit, giving it more force and power. They are working also for the enlightenment of the whole world.

5. These groups are really composed of human beings who are actuated by the high thought of the White Brotherhood. All of these groups work together. There is a very strong thought coming to the whole world for peace and enlightenment as well.

6. There are many misconceptions regarding the White Brotherhood. It must first be understood that they never make themselves known as such, nor are they exclusively back of any outer organization or organizations. They are Universal in their function and purpose. They definitely work with the Universal Law to universal ends and any individual or group working toward the same ends without selfish or group motives may receive their full support. This support may be known on the part of the man but it is more likely to come in the form of an unknown stimulus. That is, the help is not likely to assume the form of that coming from any definite place or person. Those receiving this support are conscious only of the help or influence.

7. The League of Nations originally was an instrument of the White Brotherhood but it was misused in many ways by certain nations and individuals. It will, however, come back under the guidance of the Brotherhood some time in the future.

8. The birth of a new order is in process; we are witnessing right now the destruction of an old civilization. The White Brotherhood will assert itself positively on the most important issues when the time is propitious.

9. The time has come when there can be no halfway ground in this purification of the race, whether or not individuals or groups array themselves against the common good in this day. The mills of God grind swiftly at times and also finely. Only from the siftings shall the selfish and aggressively grasping rear a new life's structure. It were far better to unify oneself with purely creative motives that contribute to universal good, for thereby shall good come to the individual.

10. Often the influences working in Universal

ideas come into being without much notice. It is something that seems to germinate and move forward as a contagion while the minds of many are still so engrossed in other things that they do not notice the change. Then, all of a sudden, each individual seems to realize that it has come into being and that it is in exact accord with his own secret thoughts. Thus, he very often slips into the new order rather unknowingly. The point is to be alert to these secretly developing forces within oneself and in the race, and here one will find the key to his most rapid progress and most vital service in the universal cause.

11. India has maintained peace by using methods identical to those used by these 216 groups about which I have spoken. It was brought about originally by twelve groups which have expanded and are still expanding. The influence of these bodies has been very great, entering into the whole fabric of Indian thought. Their work from the outer point of view has been largely educational. They release information orally which is acted upon under their direction. Results prove the efficacy of this method.

12. Gandhi studied the situation of non-violence for twenty years before he began his work, becoming a very deep student of it. The principle has been in existence in India for 600 years. Because of the Untouchables it was made operative through Gandhi in this generation. Gandhi went among the Untouchables, teaching non-violence, making it an effective force. The younger generation took it up immediately. They recognized the great effect of it and it spread throughout all India. The younger generation now have brought it before the people stronger than ever. This will eventually result in the dissolution of the caste system. The Untouchables became quite an issue there as they numbered some 65,000,-000 and guidance was necessary because they had

such powerful influence. Gandhi has been almost entirely responsible for their present emancipation.

13. Those in the groups mentioned that are working for world peace are persons of a very high spiritual understanding. One man of each group is always prominent as one of spiritual attainment.

14. There are some sixty in the United States who definitely belong to this association. They are very quiet concerning their connection with it. They do not give out the place of their group meetings or any information concerning their activities.

15. This is why many people are more or less incredulous concerning the great work being done by the illumined. They are so accustomed to outer show and display that they cannot imagine any great work being done in such a quiet, simple manner. But if one will stop to think for just a moment he will realize that all the motivating forces of the Universe are silent and those who work consciously with these forces move according to motives. There will come a time, however, when they will work more openly, but that will be when there are enough illumined people to know and understand just what they are doing. Study your own experiences. Are you not aware that silent influences working underneath the surface of your own being are those forces which control your life more than the outwardly manifest things which you express in words? However, just as these silent "broodings" of your own inner nature eventually find their outer expression when you are in an environment which harmonizes with them, you do not hesitate to express them. Study yourself and you will find everything working in you just as it is in the race. "What the Father sees in secret, He will reward you openly" is not an idle statement but it reveals the manner in which all things come into being in the outer world. To understand this fact will

not only be to better understand yourself but also the manner of the universal spiritual work that is going on underneath the surface all the time. It is only through adapting oneself to this sort of conscious procedure that he will be able to clearly trace the workings of the Secret Brotherhood. Their activities are hidden only to those who do not discern the mode of accomplishment. We are accustomed to noise and display and the quiet yet most powerful forces in ourselves and the world about us go unnoticed. We follow the noisy people into bypaths and lose the path of life that moves in stillness through our own individual being.

16. This Brotherhood is not properly an organization, as anyone can belong who will work constructively either openly or silently for peace. It is rather an association of kindred spirits. They co-operate, in fact, with any association or organization that is for the benefit of mankind or the advancement of humanity.

17. The group in India works silently but it is its influence that brings these bodies together and co-ordinates their activities. It was the activity of this very group that brought the Nobel Peace Prize before the world.

18. Tolstoy was a great factor in making this principle practically effective. But it has always been presented through the nine rulers of India. Tolstoy was an advanced soul. He was working with the great Central Group all the time.

19. While no one knows its exact location, that Thirteenth Group has always been a very dominant factor in world education. That group of twelve are working in every educational center in the world.

20. These groups are not an organization here or anywhere that makes propaganda for world peace.

It was seen that the spoken word, or the silent word, when sent out to the world, was of far greater influence than the written word. The written word can be garbled. The spoken word is an ever-expanding and ever-increasing influence.

21. Here again is the wisdom of the wise which has always been in evidence. So long as constructive forces work in "secret" they grow unnoticed by those who would destroy their effect. The world does not realize the advance of the Constructive Force until it has already undermined the sordid structures of the selfish and self-seeking and then it is too late. At the time of such helpless disintegration, and only then, are the activities of the Brotherhood likely to come out into the open to strengthen the Truth in the minds of all the people. This is not done through fear of attack but through knowledge of the most powerful way to bring about any great constructive movement for world betterment. The selfish have no access to it.

22. In a sense, all those who are working for India's freedom or for the freedom and peace of the world are Avatars, as the Western World looks at the Avatars. Many of the Great Ones have been disseminating this teaching for thousands of years. Jesus has been and is working definitely for the betterment of the whole world.

23. The reason many people in the Western World do not recognize the work of Avatars is that they can conceive of them only as working on the surface, saying and doing spectacular and miraculous things in public. They do not know that the true miracles are always worked out in silence first.

24. Regarding arbitration as an instrument for world peace, this movement was started in the Punjab of India. It is a powerful instrument of world

peace. It has completely outlawed aggression. India never did use an aggressive attitude, never did encourage open warfare in that territory at all, and the Punjab was the greatest influence back of this whole movement. It has been maintained throughout India for about three thousand years. Non-aggression and arbitration have been proved practical.

25. W. J. Bryan, consciously or unconsciously actuated by the silent influence, succeeded in getting peace treaties with all but four nations. So far no national character has since dared to take up his work. It will be taken up again some day in the future with the forming of a board of men, unknown to the outer world, that will have complete authority from the peace societies and groups working unselfishly for world peace.

26. If all the financial world were to get behind this movement for unity, it would be the greatest influence for peace. There could then be no finances for war. It could be impossible to finance war and hence there could be no war. If the cooperative system should be adopted universally, there could be no booms and no more depressions. It would also be of great influence in the abolition of war. As a matter of fact, cooperation is coming into existence. The people who do not cooperate and align themselves with the new order will be outlawed completely.

27. Following this spreading tendency to outlaw war, people will have their eyes opened to the causes of war, which are in the sole promotion of group or national advantages. The practice of non-cooperation will also be outlawed as a contributing cause of war. This brings the whole thing right down to the individual and each one must outlaw his own selfishness and self-seeking at the expense of others. He as an individual will find that the best way to promote his own interest is to promote the common in-

terest and the only way to preserve his own good is to preserve the good of the whole. This silent tendency is now being awakened on a broad scale. But each individual must find its beginning in himself and one who will earnestly search his own soul will find the embryo of this movement increasing in his own nature every day. Spreading from individual to individual it will grow into a mighty world movement and will be the ultimate motive in all human activities. Just as the individual who does not obey this eternal trend of his inner nature is destroyed, so will such groups, institutions, religious organizations, races and nations be disintegrated, leaving the world for those who love the law of God and live that law in relationship to every other man and nation.

28. In all modern movements it is clearly revealed that the changes must be first in the individual for, unless his own nature is properly correlated with the movement back of outer conduct, he becomes a disintegrating factor in any movement that might otherwise accomplish untold good. One can scarcely do anything in the way of accomplishing universal peace until he has found peace within his own nature and he cannot find peace in his own nature until he has been long enough truly in touch with the unseen forces which move toward the common good.

29. There is no question but that the individual first must be at peace. Not only that but he must realize what it means to the individual as well as to the nation. If he is centralized in that idea of peace, he projects that influence and he becomes one of the great moving factors of the spiritual development of the age. The peace movement is one of the most definite factors toward spiritual enlightenment as well.

30. Politics will be broken down completely with this new system that is coming. But, so long as the

present political set-up endures, no really effective program can be launched and carried to a successful conclusion. Everyone who keeps in step with the trend of the times is receiving all the help he is capable of receiving from these higher forces. Some of them receive this help consciously, some unconsciously, but nevertheless the help is there. Some have gone so far that they know and acknowledge this help.

31. Political parties, in the working out of the underneath movement of constructive forces, will probably merge into one great party for greater simplicity of government. These changes must come through our party system, moving into single chamber legislation and not divided. "A house divided against itself shall fall." That will eradicate a great many of our political evils. This will all originate within the States due to changes brought about there. It is coming as a national movement in the United States.

32. PEACE IS HERE! When we relate ourselves definitely to that Principle, it makes us a working unit.

FOR THE TEACHER

Paragraph 1. I should be clearly developed in the beginning of this study that the people generally need a new perspective in the matter of spiritual progress. We have for the most part been pursuing the whole subject as that of bearing entirely upon the body and the things which we imagine the body should have. In reality, all the body is and has depends upon something infinitely beyond these.

Paragraph 2. Show by further illustration, if possible, how the general reaction of the people is in the direction of peace and that back of this is the coming of the purpose of the Universe, or God.

Paragraph 3. Show your students how this peace movement which is springing up is identical with their own ideals, awakening them to the fact that they are inwardly actuated by Universal movements that are the objectives of all the illumined.

Paragraphs 4 to 12. Show how brotherhood comes into being through obedience to innermost impulses toward general betterment and that the difference between one's relationship to another in a sense of unity and the relationship of the White Brotherhood to the whole is but the difference in the degree to which they are actuated by these deeper impulses.

Paragraphs 13 and 14 doubtless will stand in your presentation much as they are unless your knowledge includes much that is only referred to lightly in these paragraphs.

Paragraph 15, 16. This should make clear why it is impossible for the average individual to understand why the Masters do not appear in the open with their work. Whole volumes could profitably be written along this line. It is the very reason that you sometimes do not venture to express your opinions even within your own home. You know as long as you are silent you have no opposition but once you have spoken the whole thing is open to controversy. Then again, you feel the right time comes to speak and it is all acceptable and everyone cooperates. What moves in the Universe also moves within man. To know himself in some of these most simple things is his key to great understanding and power.

Paragraphs 17 to 26. The motive is much the same and is but further emphasis upon the importance of silent cooperative work in the positive realization that the great Creative Spirit is working through all men in some degree; and the important thing so far as we are concerned is that we make it a more vital issue in our own lives.

Paragraphs 27 to 32 afford additional opportunity for amplification along the foregoing lines and can become a vital factor in liberating the people to progress. Teach the people to expect and prepare for changes. Become sensitive to the changes now moving underneath the political and economical structure. The change that will liberate is not in any of these outer forms but is in the hearts of men.

CHAPTER II

THE ONE MIND

1. We have evidence of the control of the One Mind. In every field of action we will note the One Mind control. Even upon this boat you will note that there is one head; consequently there is one control, with many activities under that control, and all these lesser activities emanate from that centralized authority.

2. It is only through this centralization of power and authority that there is anything like harmony in the operations of any organized section of society or even within the individual. We all know what happens when there is a division of power or rather an attempt to divide authority without consideration of some central motivating source. The orders which go forth from two sources to the various centers of activity can result only in confusion and chaos. If power emanates from more than one central directive head, the authority is destroyed and the entire structure is broken down.

3. Where there is one controlling element which has dominion, power, or control of motivating action, we are brought directly to that One Element and, thereby, brought to one-pointed action which we have discussed before many times. It is through that action that we do accomplish and that action brings us into a harmony with that central control in that we do not scatter our forces but work with the One Force, or power, which is complete control.

4. You always bring yourself into accord with that to which you have delegated power. That is, if you

believe in the power of the world and its environment, you are seemingly receiving directive control from a thousand different sources and this is the source of your confusion. You do not know whether to obey the seeming demands made here, there, or some other place and this division in the consciousness breaks down the entire structure of man's nature. He must know "Whom we have believed, and become persuaded that He is able to keep that which we have committed unto Him against that day."

5. That one control does exist for every human being if he will but use it. Of course, the use of that control must be conscious; it must be consciously directed or used for the purpose which we decree or which we establish. It is through the establishment of that control that our thoughts are brought into that one power of action or one thought of expression. There they cannot help but express that which they send forth. In other words, the motivating principle we determine must come into existence. "His servants are ye, to whom you yield yourselves servants to obey," and the manifest results must be determined by the outworking of that motivating force from which you receive your direction. The results can be no greater than is the power vested in the authority.

6. This central control of the Universe is often called Principle as well as Mind. Principle does not bind it as closely perhaps as the One Mind. Still, that Principle controls and governs and it knows what it is doing; it governs with intelligence, so it must be a Mind Principle. The Hindoo always puts it as Principle, or the All-Mighty, which means that man does become that mighty, controlling element. Man stands in his all-mightiness the moment he projects his thought to that one control, that one central directive authority.

7. It is all so simple if one looks at the entire situation with an open-minded and sane approach to it. You say in your own mind that this person or that condition has power to make you sad. This is delegating authority to a definite location or form. Obeying the authority which you have thus assigned, you embody in yourself the mental and emotional state which you recognize as existing in the nature of that authority. You could not possibly think of embodying joy from a source that you decree has only the power to make you sad. Then, through your obedience to the authority you embody the sadness which you have admitted it has power to manifest in you and you say "I am sad." You become that which you embody. This is the whole secret power but, to manifest that Mighty power that is ours, we must obey that source and embody the characteristics which it possesses; then we should not hesitate to proclaim "I am that," as the Hindoos put it, when *that* becomes the thing we have embodied. This will all become perfectly clear to anyone who will dwell on the matter for a time.

8. In this state will-power is not a method of control. Will-power gives us the impetus for bringing that control into existence but it is not the motivating factor back of the control. Will may differ entirely from control. Self-will never is able to project thoughts to one central point. Definite control or mind action is capable of carrying thoughts, feelings or actions to one central control, which is a definite attribute or element that man uses always and which he has dominion to work WITH. Not Over, but to work WITH. That is the very force which man brings into activity the moment he brings his thought to that focal point of Principle which activates all conditions.

9. Let us take a very simple illustration. Man has

power to bring his mind into subjection to the principle of mathematics but he does not have the will to make the principle act. The principle acts of itself and is a single center of control within its sphere. Man may bring his will up to the point of the activity of the principle but from then on the principle is the motivating force and through this subjection of his will — to be more accurate — he finds the secret of his mathematical power. The principle of the human will is that it is to be brought into subjectivity to some higher authority and thus man becomes the embodiment of it and is possessed of the power of this higher authority. Man's weakness is brought about through making himself subject to that which in reality has no power and this should be proof to him of the immense power which is possible to him. He must now learn to apply this principle of his own will and recognize power as existing only in the One Principle.

10. Our everyday life is a concrete application of this fact in that our statements conform to the One Principle or One Mind. We vision or project an ideal. Let us say that that ideal is for perfection. We immediately come into direct accord with the One Mind control or Principle. We project an ideal for ourselves to accomplish. If it is a high ideal that Power immediately becomes active and brings that ideal into existence. The moment that ideal is projected and the force back of it becomes active through it, that ideal is complete. That is, the moment the ideal is released from the activity of our will and is projected into the activity of the One Principle, it is a completed thing.

11. So long as there is any dual sense it is difficult for anyone to see how this can be true on the manifest plane. The Masters do not take into consideration any plane outside of the Spiritual — the Spiritual

made manifest. If we do not take into consideration any plane outside of the Spiritual, it must be in existence always after the statement is made, even before the statement is made. We quite evidently withhold from ourselves the accomplishment of our ideal because we look to three planes upon which it may manifest. It is found very conclusively today that it manifests only on one plane. It manifests on the Spiritual plane always. It is always fact.

12. Now if we hold to and remain within that Spiritual plane we would see it in its true expression. We would not need to look to the material at all for when we do we speak in terms of materializations and materialization is not spiritually a fact. The *actual* thing is the fact always. That is the Spiritual made manifest. Two plus two equals four in the mathematical principle, it equals four in the mind, and likewise in manifestation. This is not three planes but it is all the mathematical fact separated or differentiated at NO point whatever.

13. After the manifestation it is said that it does no harm to name it material or physical because you cannot harm the Fact. But it is always elevated or exalted to the Spiritual. That was Jesus' meaning when He said: "If ye exalt all things to Spirit they are in existence already." Evidently He had that very thing in mind when He gave the prayer: "Father, I thank you that you have heard me, and that you do hear me always." He knew fully that that which He saw as His ideal was already accomplished. To Him it came forth instantly. Then He gave the statement that "if you go forth into the vineyard it is ready for harvest."

14. Now, if we take that definite position, there is no question but that we would be out of all of this difficulty completely. He immediately rose above every difficulty by the very attitude that He took. It

was not a long, arduous process to Him. It was instantaneous. He saw completely through the non-existence of them. That is not claiming that He denied them. It is quite evident that He never denied any condition. He always rose above it to the True Spiritual Condition and then there was no need for denial or for paying any attention to anything but the True Spiritual Condition. He said, "I live always in Spirit."

15. Our Bible says "I live always in *a* spirit," being an entirely wrong interpretation. The interpolation of "a" where it does not belong makes a lot of difference. That is where many mistakes were made in our understanding.

16. The Christian Bible says "God is *a* Spirit." The original was "God is Spirit," never confining him to one attribute to one condition. One writer said: "It is like trying to crowd God into the quart measure of our intellect." Spirit and Mind are synonymous. They are one and the same in vibratory influence. That which seems to make a difference is that we take our thoughts as indicating mind. Mind is consciousness, for mind and consciousness are inseparable. The element of consciousness is thought and when conscious of spiritual Fact there is no difference to us between mind and spirit. We are in a state of Spiritual Consciousness.

17. You are right in thinking of mind as consciousness in action but so is Spirit consciousness in action. They, too, are synonymous. Either may become quiescent or become submerged in the individual but they are not submerged in the outer condition. If the outer is like the inner, mind is never submerged in the individual but is only quiescent. The individual only thinks that it is submerged and to that person it may become non-existent because he is not conscious of it. The consciousness is always

24

there and springs into existence instantly if one projects consciousness toward that which always is, the Spiritual Fact.

18. The element of consciousness is the directive rather than the motivating agency of mind. Thus, it is indispensable in the sending forth of the emanations of mind or, as we put it, in stepping up the emanations of mind to their true state, providing the element of consciousness is true to the Spiritual Fact.

19. Today many scientists are approaching this same conclusion regarding the underlying cause of all things. They dissolve the whole structure of substance and resolve it all back to emanating energy identical with Spirit. Spirit is all-pervading; it manifests in everything. It is found that all elements, including radium, are reduced to that one primal element — emanating energy. But this energy, in the last analysis, is not blind force but intelligent force. It knows what it is doing. Scientists even admit that there is a certain form of "electricity" that seems to know what it is doing. This all-pervading, creative energy back of all things is aware of itself, aware of what it is doing, aware of how to do it, and we therefore call it Spirit or God. It is omnipresent, omnipotent, and omniscient as the Christian Bible puts it.

20. When man begins to assemble in his consciousness the activities of any principle, he begins to say "I am that." This is the centralizing of the authority of the principle in himself. "I am" renders the mind dynamic instead of letting it rest in potentiality. It becomes dynamic the moment we focus thought upon I AM. That focal point is the center always and from it emanates the authoritative commands that control and determine the entire status of manifest man. The I AM must be used to

indicate man's true estate, that which he is in fact, and not what he has seemed to himself to be in manifest form. "I am *THAT* I am," which is the embodiment of the motivating authority of the Universe. Beside THAT "I AM" there is no true existence but only delusion.

21. This name "I AM" was God to Moses. It has come down through the ages as "I AM." To the Hindoos it is AUM, which means the same. Likewise to the Aryans it is AUM. The Chinese use it as TAU.

22. The so-called "blind spots" in the ether common in our radio and scientific fields is in a sense symbolic of the blind spots in human consciousness. The radio beam crosses right through these non-magnetic fields as if they did not exist. Our layers of atmosphere, the concentric bands of atmospheric conditions, are in motion. In our earth they are stationary. When a non-magnetic field moves over a magnetic field of our concentric bands a vacuum-like condition is established. When a magnetic field passes over a non-magnetic field on the earth's surface it passes right through it and is lost. It is frequently more powerful at night than in the daytime. These non-magnetic fields are like the static states in human consciousness, more intense with greater darkness or ignorance. But the positive radiations of the Spiritual I AM, the declarations of that which man is in fact, penetrate through these static fields of his consciousness and it is as though they do not exist. The persistent declaration of Spiritual facts regarding man's nature and his place in the Universe eventually will eliminate all these static fields in human consciousness as well as in his affairs.

23. The One Mind is not constantly creating new ideas. It is manifesting Ideas that have been created from the beginning, for the One Mind is and always

has been Omniscient—all knowing. It has never been nor will it ever be more or less than ITSELF. It is all a process of reverberation. It is the same as our radio currents today. They are flooding back and forth or reverberating from one space to the other space. That is, from space to space as you might say.

24. Thought is, of course, the most potent of any radiations because it has control over the vibratory field of electricity and radio. In fact, both the vibratory field of electricity and of radio will impinge and reflect from the vibratory field of thought always. Radio follows a track in the atmosphere regardless of a conductor. It follows a true track or trend. It operates through the ether. But thought in this sense does not "travel" for thought is omnipresent. It is already there no matter to what point you refer. It is the impingement of thought upon the electrons that causes thought to appear to move. Mind is the motivating element, thought moving concurrently with mind and in striking upon the electrons produces all movement in the plane of manifest substances.

25. That which we call space is in reality the One Spiritual Mind. That is the Principle by which the human soul, which is the replica of the Spiritual mind, can overcome time and space, for there is no such thing as time and space in Spirit. In Spirit all is complete and in completeness there can be no such thing as time or space. This is what is meant by "letting the same mind be in you which was also in Christ." It is a state of complete oneness existing in fact between the individual and the Universal soul and it must become a conscious fact to the individual. That is the complete Mind, the controlling mind, functioning through the individual consciously.

26. Physical man or man conscious of himself only as a physical being that thinks he is apart from

God, the One Mind, and thinks in terms of moving from place to place, is only moving in illusion for himself and, hence, unhappiness. He really is in and of that One Mind and lives and moves and has his being in IT. In Jesus' talks His greatest statement was "Peace be still." It is never said in a loud voice, projected of the will of man, but in unison with the calm, knowing power that comes from a sense of Oneness. There is the greatest security and the greatest power. We have seen some of the greatest storms overcome by that simple statement. Likewise, the seeming "brain storms" of human mind are stilled until one can feel the controlling power of the One Mind.

FOR THE TEACHER

Paragraphs 1 and 2 give ample opportunity to conclusively point out to the individual that so long as his mind is divided he has, by that act of division, lost his sense of power and direction. Only from some definite premise can any structure be builded and until one has arrived at this premise he cannot proceed to do anything. This must have been what Jesus meant when he said, "Thou shalt worship the Lord thy God, and Him only shalt thou serve."

Paragraph 3. This one underlying principle of Life, God, is the controlling and ruling force of the Universe and man can find himself only in relationship to this principle. The only adjustment that will harmonize man's being is a realignment of his entire nature with the facts from which he came.

Paragraph 4. Man himself has assigned power to the external world for there is no power there originally, nor is power there even when he has seemed to delegate it. That power still remains within himself and that which seems to be power in environment or anything outside of his own I AM, his central identity, is the perversion of this same power within himself. The power is always within man and it works according to the direction given it. But back of it all is the controlling force of the Universe and that which I am individually must be one with the I AM which is universal. Perfect accord must exist between cause and effect for the movement of the cause is the life of the effect.

Paragraphs 5, 6 and 7 can be further extended along this same line and the lesson made of eternal benefit to every individual. Nothing else so completely tallies with the true message which Christ tried to give to the world as this. "Greater things than these shall ye do" was His estimate of man's potential capacity.

Paragraphs 8 and 9. The most helpful lesson and liberating practice can be developed from these two paragraphs. The willful attempt to force thought into the plane of manifestation is a hopeless task. It is destructive to the individual who practices it. The acceptance of Universal Power, a central executive emanation that produced heaven and earth as the already-completed manifestation of itself and the self-existent fact back of every constructive idea of man, is the way to liberation.

Paragraph 10 shows the method of procedure in so-called demonstration which is, in the last analysis, stepping aside from our sense of incompleteness and imperfection to accept the Facts.

Paragraph 11 shows more accurately what happens in this matter of manifest results. A freeing of the mind from all duality is the solution to the whole matter.

Paragraph 12 is a further extension of this same idea.

Paragraphs 13, 14 and 15 can be made to strengthen the foregoing.

Paragraph 16. Can we not once and for all make clear that the different "minds", as we call them, are but a difference in thought? Mind functioning as what we call mind is this same spiritual capacity in man functioning in its lowest capacity through perverting it to lesser purposes. When man "thinks the thoughts of God after him" his mind is then spiritualized or functioning in its true field with God thoughts, thinking as God thinks or, more accurately, knowing as God knows. The human mind thinks; the God Mind KNOWS.

Paragraphs 17, 18 and 19 give excellent opportunity to extend this idea further and to drive home the idea that man is not truly living until he consciously functions in harmony with his source.

Paragraphs 20 and 21. The true use of the "I AM" is to maintain man's original identity in and with his source, not allowing it to descend to include within his nature that which he is not. Man is not his experiences. He is what he IS. Experiences with that which seems less than himself should never be admitted into his estimate of himself. I am always that which "I AM IN SPIRIT," not what I seem to be in experience or what I have experienced in the world. No matter what I have gone through or seem to be going through, I still remain what I am in the original sense, the Image and Likeness of God.

Paragraph 22 shows the far reaching influence of spiritual fact as transcending all sense of limitation. Spirit takes no account of evil, of loss, lack, poverty, disease. These are but blind spots in human consciousness. To the mind that KNOWS there are no such things and it goes right on with that which it KNOWS and IS.

Paragraph 23. The mind which is God is the same yesterday and forever. That which seems to be a new idea to us is but our discovery of what always was.

Healing and so-called demonstrations are not bringing something into being but are an awakening to that state which has always prevailed in fact.

Paragraph 24. Power of thought, so-called, is not the power of thought. Thought is only a conveyor of power. Power is in Spirit and thought conveys or carries power only to the extent that it conforms to the standards and purposes moving in Spirit. "My words are spirit," said Jesus, meaning that his words accurately conformed to the Universal trend which he called the Will of God.

Paragraphs 25 and 26 present man as an integral part of infinite space and not an isolated being among isolated forms. "By one spirit are we baptized into one body." Finding our calm in this eternal unity of all things is our position of power where all contrary illusion is dissolved into the peace and tranquillity of illumination.

CHAPTER III

DUAL MIND

1. Many of the Western World look at duality instead of to the One Mind or Principle. That scatters the forces and one is not able to hold his mind in accord as when he sees but the One force or One Principle and himself and all things as integral parts of the One.

2. "Behold our God is One," say the Scriptures, and it is only in the preservation of this fundamental truth that man lives in harmony with his own nature. Man is not a separate being, projected away from his source, but is created within the image of God and like unto God. It is only in the *sense* of his isolation, which is the root of all unrighteousness, that he loses the beneficent influences of the Creative Cause, which are his by the natural order of things. In this sense of aloneness he has imagined all sorts of contrary actions to his well being and is often inclined to blame the Universal system for his misfortunes. In reality they are all of his own doings, for the Universe does not isolate him nor is it accountable for the difficulties that arise because of his own isolation. "Return unto me and I will return unto you, saith the Lord," is the offer of the ONE to him who will accept his rightful place in the divine order of the whole created scheme.

3. Duality is brought into existence through thought and action without regard to the whole. But, by reversing the dual thought or bringing the thoughts to One point of action, duality is eliminated completely. It is a well known fact that we cannot

accomplish with a dual purpose or even with a dual nature.

4. In reality there is not duality in nature. There is the positive and negative, good and evil, hot and cold, all the opposites, but the opposites, when related and brought together, bring the thought to one purpose, one action, one Principle. In connection with the opposites it is not necessary to recognize them as opposite or opposed. The essential recognition is the single purpose. Jesus always said that His greatest accomplishments were with the single attitude or steadfast purpose, as He related it. That steadfastness does bring us into unity where Principle exists always. That is where Principle is always immanent. Then, instead of duality, there is that "single eye" or single I AM.

5. Many Hindoos use the I, while many use the I AM. It is thought by some that that was where duality began to manifest first—between the I and the I AM—many believing that this practice involved two attitudes or purposes, where in reality, it is but one correlation or subjugation of everything to the One Purpose. There is no duality of Principle but the union of Principle in all things. They (the words "I AM") even pronounce the exact Principle or Truth. As they put it, the exaltation of the One principle allows it to work in that Principle conclusively. We do not see, either, the duality of nature and thus we do not recognize it. As duality has no recognition it becomes harmonized.

6. Summer and winter are not two things but phases of one Nature. Winter is as essential to the growth of vegetation as is summer and only depicts two phases of a single process. What we call evil contains the germ of good and, when looked through to behold the good, the sense of evil disappears and

there remains only the sense that all things are working together for good. The apparent evil surrounding conditions of poverty and pain that are shunned by human beings, if faced for the good within them, would vanish. Jesus taught that blindness was not an evil nor the result of evil but an opportunity to show forth the "glory of God." A problem is not foreign to the principle of mathematics nor is it an obstacle to one who wishes to become a mathematician. The problem is only a statement of certain conditions through which the principle may be applied to produce a desired result and is a means of growth to the individual who so faces it. Conditions in life that seem opposed to our highest good are but points of practice until we attain that strength of character to see and manifest only the perfection of the One. When life is seen in this way all unpleasantness vanishes and everything becomes a sort of practice game in which we see, live, move, and have being that the existing good may show forth in our own character and in our world. Nature then is harmonious. All is harmony. All is working under the influence of the One Purpose.

7. Just as the difference between a perfect chord and discord is apparent even to the novice, so is the individual able to know within himself that which is in harmony with the Universal Principle and that which is at variance with it. Any inharmonious condition in the nature of man is evidence that he is out of harmony with the natural order of things and the secret of his perfect progress is to always approach every condition in such a manner as to preserve his sense of inward calm. This is impossible so long as there exists any sense of separation from the innate good that runs through all things. Man's nature is eternally attuned to the good for he is the offspring

of God, and God is good. When one is conscious that his good is eternally and unvaryingly seeking to manifest itself in all things and in his own nature he is in harmony with himself and the Principle of his being. By working to uncover the good contained in every experience man is instantly in that state where that which to others seems evil becomes the source of his good.

8. Of course, with the relation of the opposites we find that we come to the same attitude. It is said that there may be many opposite manifestations but they are not opposed unless the individual allows the opposition. The individual must harmonize the opposites in his attitude toward them for, in reality, they are never out of harmony. When we come to that attitude where all is harmony, then we see the harmonious relation in all things as well as in ourselves. It becomes one simple attitude of complete harmony. Then there can be no discord. There can be no discord in life or in living. There can be no discord between the opposites for they have their perfect relationship to each other in Principle.

9. Many scientists, through their research today, are making the same statement: The only discord that exists is with the human or the individual and that discord is brought about by discordant thoughts. It is said today that the American people are the most discordant in their thinking. It is quite evident that this fact is brought about by the many attitudes of thought held by the numerous nationalities which are brought together here. These nationalities have not yet been fully assimilated. It is found, however, that the great assimilating process is going on very rapidly now.

10. The mathematical axiom that only things that are equal to the same thing are equal to each

other is, after all, the key to all harmony. It is only as the peoples of America become actuated by a common impulse that any semblance of harmony can be established. This is also true of the world generally, just as it is true of the individual. Only when all the forces involved in a single organism, or in many organisms, become animated by a single impulse and move in perfect unison toward a given objective is there complete harmony.

11. There is no question but that Jung in his work struck a very deep key in the attitude of harmony in relation to all things when he related his experience of going into a cave. In many portions of India the people retire to caves in order to become perfectly silent to work out a definite conclusion about certain determining factors. In every instance where these reports are available it is found that when they go to the place where they are perfectly silent to conditions around them they come into the greatest activity of life. They see further as they project their vision further. They see completely through the material or physical to what they say is that perfect condition wherein all activity is harmonious. Then that which they see as true universally is merely related to the world of things. It is not that the world is subjugated to the spiritual but merely related to its original state; and then the perfection of the spiritual world is immediately manifested. That activity, in harmonious accord, works perfectly under their guidance.

12. In reality this is the same procedure which all men follow in the application of any principle. It is first necessary to leave the outer forms—through which principle is expressed—alone until there is clear discernment of the movement of the principle involved. This movement of principle is then related

to the outer form and we have harmony and rhythm in music, correct answers to problems, perfect architectural structures, perfect paintings, and perfect statues. All these manifestations are brought about because of the individual's ability to identify himself with underlying reality and this reality is then brought forth through the form with the same beauty and harmony that is seen in principle.

13. Now these same people will tell you that it is not necessary for each individual to become as they are in order to get into that harmonious relation but that it can be brought about in the ordinary walks of life. They purposely take that attitude to find out what happens, to come to a definite conclusion. After that conclusion is reached they are able to teach others but they do not teach others to do as they have done. They teach that it may be made practical; that it is not necessary to spend long years in meditation to bring this about because they have found a shorter method or an easier way; that the instant you become silent you are one with harmony or accord. Thus, from that very moment you begin to progress; the attitude of thought changes from turmoil to harmony; strife is not evident; consequently you have raised your body's vibration to the vibration where strife does not exist.

14. If *one* is able to accomplish that condition, *all* can but all need not take the long and arduous way. Once a fact is revealed one needs but to accept that fact. The thought of the Masters is: We have gone through the process of making the discovery, we know what the determining factors are, and the rest of mankind need not make the discovery for themselves but may accept what has been revealed. Consequently, it is not necessary for the mass to sit in Samadhi. They express it by stating that one who

sits in Samadhi is able to teach others what he has discovered. All may go through the practice of Samadhi if they wish although it is unnecessary for this reason: Through accepting the conditions which have been revealed, that acceptance brings about a certain leveling influence, a certain vitalizing condition wherein one sees more readily. By beginning with the revealed knowledge one is more easily adjusted to the silence, or the harmonious conditions and facts about him. Therefore, by following the conclusions of those who have gone through the preliminary steps, he moves forward directly into the Samadhic state. Those who have gone through to this state are the way-showers or teachers. As they say, it is not necessary to follow the teacher step by step, because they have cleared the way. They have realized the condition which has then become general and the projection has opened the way for all.

15. This is the truth back of the vicarious atonement of Jesus. He, as the way-shower, explained that we are one with the Father even as He was one with the Father. We do not have to fight our way back to this state for He revealed it as an established fact. Our work is but to assume as being true what He proved as true. We do not have to prove that the sum of all the angles of a triangle is equal to two right angles after it has once been proved. When it is a revealed fact, all we have to do is accept it. If that were not true, each one would have to prove for himself every movement of mathematics, mechanics, art, etc. But, when others have proved these things, we vicariously enter into their labors, begin where they left off, and proceed to the next condition under that principle.

16. The larger the group or the greater the number of persons in a group, the greater the influence. The greater the influence the greater the impetus

always. Therefore, it is said that if a group of one hundred would sit in Samadhi, or complete silence, that influence created would suffice for thousands. Therefore, thousands would be elevated to a greater enlightenment by that one hundred.

17. This is where the Yogis play a very vital part. They purposely give up a certain portion of their lives to putting out that influence, especially the influence for body perfection. And it is often said that it is not necessary for all people to go through the system of Yoga to perfect the body because they have gone through and made that perfection possible for all. That is what was expressed when Jesus gave His life upon the cross. They, as well as Jesus, knew that they were not giving up their lives. They were giving that certain portion to a higher expression that all might see and follow. They became the way-showers or teachers. Therefore, the people who could progress would go further and in greater strides.

18. These are the reasons why it is said that it is not necessary to go through all the many stages of Yoga or Joga. Many accomplish these steps in just a few hours because added impetus is given by those who have given greater time to service and greater impetus for that service. There are certain select groups who are working along that line all the time. That influence can be picked up, as it is radiated out from different groups and different centers all of the time.

19. This influence is picked up on the spiritual plane just as radio music is picked up on the electrical plane. But, as radio music picked up from the electrical plane is heard and felt on the material and mental planes, so are these spiritual influences manifest upon every plane below, for it is all-inclusive. It is all a spiritual plane, One Universal Plane

working in perfect unison with itself when the individual awakens to see it as it truly is. The contact is made, not by seeking the masters or their influences, but by seeking the plane of harmonious thought and spiritual influence which permeates all time and space and in which they work.

20. A line may seemingly have two opposites but bring these opposites together and you have a circle and the opposites have thus disappeared. Extend the circle and you have a perfect sphere, which is complete, synchronized relationship of all elements. As Millikan says, "The Cosmic becomes the globe." Then you have completed the circle in every way and brought about perfect unity. The point becomes the line, the line becomes the circle, the circle becomes the globe. This is true of every line of thought and through the continual process of relating all things to the One instead of separating everything, the point of unity or oneness is established. This is One-pointedness.

21. When the individual attains concentration in thought, he enters the Samadhic condition and that is where he begins to accomplish—when he reaches that One-pointedness.

22. It should be remembered, however, that this concentration or One-pointedness is an expanded state of mind and not a contracted state. It comes through the principle of relating all things rather than through the mistaken idea of excluding anything. Samadhi permits the individual to see directly through to the whole, the Truth or Principle.

23. This eliminates what the Western World teaches about the conscious and subconscious minds. In reality there is but ONE MIND, and that, we could call the Superconscious. That is where you bring the conscious and subconscious into accord.

You are then conscious of the whole. It is complete consciousness. Then there is no division whatever and if we make no division we are in complete conscious accord.

24. The division of the mind into conscious, subconscious and so forth was first put forth as an assistance in teaching. Now, however, the reverse is true. We can best understand mind and progress consciously in spiritual unfoldment by thinking and working in terms of One Mind. The divisions were a part of the teaching of symbolism now past. It may have been a necessary classification in that period but the race has now worked through symbolism completely. We are accepting the completeness of all symbols. When we become One with that one attitude of thought, there is where we begin to accomplish.

25. I have talked with men of great achievement and find that they for the most part work with the One Mind, with the consciousness that everything is always here and always present. That has been their attitude. That very attitude is coming out so dominantly now that we will find it is going to change all of our economic system. If we could be wholly at one with that Mind there would be no cross-purposes. Consumption of energy would be 90 per cent less. That energy is rapidly and increasingly being used for higher and greater purposes instead of being dissipated in efforts to take away from the other fellow what he needs for himself. The truly Great never have to go out and take away from the other fellow in order to produce. With them everything that is here belongs to them and that which belongs to them they are free to use.

FOR THE TEACHER

Paragraphs 1 and 2. Every principle with which we deal begins from a definite premise and only through adherence to this basic premise is any structure possible. The reason man's life has seemingly gone into decay is that he has disregarded the basic fact of life. This basic fact of life is that the entire system of the Universe is one single unit and that man is an integral part of this system. He is in no sense separated from it and it is only his notion that he is an isolated being that has lost for him his rightful place and authority.

Paragraphs 3 and 4. In these paragraphs it can be clearly pointed out just how the sense of duality was developed and, thereby, we may learn how it may be overcome.

Paragraph 5 and 6. "I" in the individual is the first movement of his nature, the central point of his identity. "Am" is that which embodies, or embraces within the "I" — individual identity — whatever it encircles. The "I" is a positive assertion and the "Am" is the qualifying element. "I" is masculine and "Am" is the feminine principle. The "Am" brings forth into being whatever it embraces or conceives. The "Am" must become immaculate in its embracing power if man is to bring forth that which is in Spirit. "I," which is my identity in Spirit, "Am," that which embraces or embodies all that is in God, is the true use of these words. "I am THAT I am," which is the embodiment of God. I can never in reality be anything but THAT which it is in Spirit. "I am THAT I am, and beside me there is no other."

Paragraphs 7 and 8 afford a wonderful opportunity to show the necessity and advantage of completely harmonizing everything. It is impossible, of course, to harmonize everything with our own thought and notion but we can at least recognize that since a thing has being at all it must to some extent contain the elements of the whole. By seeing it in relationship to the whole and harmonizing it with the All, we at least escape the discord that arises in our own nature, and thereby preserve ourselves in our true relationship. "God moves in a mysterious way" and even though we do not see just how all things are working in ultimate harmony with the Universal purpose, it would not require a great stretch of the imagination to admit that it must be so because of the very nature of God.

Paragraph 9. There is no discord in the natural order of the Universe. All discord is our reaction to that which we imagine to be wrong or out of its rightful place. It is only to the degree that we are not in tune with things as they are in Fact that there is discord in our own nature. Discord is not without, it is within our own nature. To prevent this discord we must harmonize with the spiritual reality back of all appearances. The mixed thought of America is only symbolic of the mixed thought of the individual American mind and all will be harmonized as we progress toward a common goal.

Paragraph 10. Illustrative of paragraph 9.

Paragraphs 11 and 12 show clearly how harmony may be established. All who achieve let the world's thinking and doing alone and concern themselves with what ought to be done.

Paragraphs 13, 14 and 15 point out clearly the short cut to spiritual attainment and should be made clear enough to forever free the individual student from the idea that he must do a lot of overcoming before he can reach his spiritual estate. He must accept his spiritual estate as has been revealed by every illumined teacher since the beginning of time and this illumined state is in itself the over-coming.

Paragraphs 16 and 17 afford an excellent op-portunity to point out the value of individual and group meditation upon spiritual things. This is the real ground work of any center or class movement and to neglect it is to lose sight of the most potent force in the building of a spiritual ministry and individual power for accomplishing the tasks of everyday life.

Paragraphs 18 and 19 are illustrative of the same facts brought out in paragraphs 13, 14 and 15.

Paragraphs 20 and 21 are illustrative of the prin-ciple of harmonization and can be exemplified profitably.

Paragraph 22. This paragraph should forever free the student from the idea that concentration is a state of mental fixity or focusing the mind on thoughts, ideas, pictures, or objects. Concentration is that expanded state of mind to take in the One-ness of all things rather than an attempt to exclude anything from the thought. It is a process of relat-ing all things to the Source.

Paragraph 23 and 24. The so-called subcon-scious mind is but a reactionary phase of mind to intellectual thought that has cut off a person from the natural activity of Universal thought. There are no eddies in a stream unless the flow of direct cur-rent is impeded in some way and there is no sub-conscious mind, so called, when the stream of il-luminating thought is uninterrupted. When one is in the stream of life as it is, there is only radiant consciousness of reality.

Paragraph 25 is illustrative and may be enlarged upon according to the knowledge of the instructor.

CHAPTER IV

BASIS OF COMING SOCIAL REORGANIZATION

1. In taking up this subject of social reorganization we will begin with Hawaii and the situation there. There is a great similarity in the thought of the Hawaiian people and our own, especially when brought about by experiences. You can take an Hawaiian anywhere in the ocean that you want and you cannot lose him. Never have they gone out in their canoes but that there was at least one man in each canoe who could tell where they were as though they had the best compass in the world in that canoe. It was the concern of the others to work the boat and his business to pilot it at all times. They have brought this capacity down through the ages with them.

2. At one time we took one of the Hawaiians out into the Atlantic ocean where he had never been before and discovered that this sense of direction was bred in him. We put this man in a boat with sailors who knew nothing of navigation and he directed them to the Cape Verde Islands hundreds of miles away. The Hawaiians keep quiet and find a solution readily. They use this quality very definitely.

3. The great inventive capacity of the American mind is the functioning of this same sense. The difference lies chiefly in the field into which it is directed. Also we are all making use of it to a much larger extent than we realize. When we know how we naturally function and then proceed to consciously work in harmony with ourselves, we will make much greater progress in every direction. Did

you ever note how you yourself very often function in certain ways through an inner sense, or hunch, or feeling and then all the reasons develop afterwards which show the whys and wherefores? Many people try to think it all out first, then they never do anything but think, for there is no apparent solution for anything until after it has been done. The feeling that it can be done, or that it should be done, or it were better so and so is the first activity of this sense and, if one would be still, the rest of the information would come, completing his whole plan of action. Then the intellectual explanation or the thoughts defining the process would be readily formulated. The reasoning mind, as we commonly know it, only travels over the same grounds it has previously been over, but reason is never complete until this other sense is taken into account. The new social order will come just as the inventor's ideas come. It will be a flash of revelation, so to speak, and then the mind may put it together and carry it out. Man's description for this new order will be complete only as it is in operation. Reason is descriptive but this other sense sees and goes beyond reason, opening the way for larger reason.

4. This is not a phase of the super-conscious as many style it nor is it a phase of the sub-conscious. It is the power to penetrate into either. With the Hawaiians it is a perfectly conscious thing. It is brought about by involution. It is presented to them and is worked out through them. When they used to go on foot around the islands, before they had transportation at all, they were drawn to places where they were needed. I have seen forty or fifty of them go across the island to find that some of their people were in trouble there. Sometimes their friends across the island would come to them. They

never missed in those things. They were in constant touch with each other all the time. I have inquired of them and they think nothing of it. They simply function that way because they have never been given the impression that it is anything but natural.

5. Were the interest of those on one side of the island centered wholly within themselves they would not be concerned about the needs of those on the other side. They are unified through common interests and are concerned with the welfare of those about them and it is this interest that makes them sensitive to needs outside their own circle or location. Where there is need among their fellows they draw this sense of need into themselves through the bond of sympathy which makes them one and the needs of one group become instantly known by another. Selfishness and self-interest separate us, isolate us from the rest of humanity, and this sense of separateness makes people immune to their needs, thus throwing the social structure out of balance. It is in this way that greater and greater needs develop in one group while greater and greater abundance develops in another and the whole social structure is thrown out of balance. This is where war and strife develop. Can you imagine two groups going to war, each striving to meet the needs of the other? "Nature abhors a vacuum" and just as violent storms occur because of extreme differences in atmospheric pressure, so do wars develop primarily from extremes in the human status.

6. This faculty of the Hawaiians is mostly memory going back to former generations. They have never been out of it. There are no barriers put up between them and their former lives. They say, "It isn't that we have lived in this spot all the time. We see all of these places at all times from one point.

We have never been separated from it. It is only necessary to become quiet and then we know where we want to go."

7. In a sense this is the same faculty of instinct which the animal uses but, just as the man is much higher form of being than the animal, so are all his faculties comparatively enlarged. In the animal it is instinct but in man it is very much extended in its capacity, call it intuition or spiritual discernment if you will. The animal has it only to an extent but the human goes right through. He can see just what he is going to accomplish. The animal returns over the same ground it has traveled but the human being can go to any position without going over the same ground.

8. It cannot be accurately determined to what extent this faculty leads the animal into new fields but we do know that it is the primary function of this faculty that has paved the way for human advancement in every field of human progress. The only difference between men of great achievement and those who remain in mediocrity is that the great pay little attention to what has been done and what obstacles or apparent reasons may stand in the way of achievement but devote themselves to contemplating what can or ought to be done. Those who allow their mental and emotional natures to recoil, refusing to let this sense reach out into the undiscovered, destroy their own capabilities and this keeps them always in the prison house of limitation. But it should be noted that prison is only the recoil or reflex of their own nature. Genius is that which goes on through conditions and circumstances and keeps eternally in the process of expansion and extension of achieving power.

9. The ability to use this sense for unlimited progress applies to everyone. It is not for the select

individual. It is for all to use. The Hawaiians are far more conscious than any others we know of, except the Polynesians. The latter will come to Hawaii on a visit from a distance of three thousand miles. The true Polynesian and Hawaiian are true Caucasian. It seems that this faculty runs more definitely in the true Caucasian race. If they do not submerge it by doubting its existence or allowing it to stop with apparent limitations, it seems to be greater always.

10. This is what Theodore Roosevelt encountered in Africa. It is evident also in Alaska and Siberia. When I went out in 1905 to take relief to Amundsen there was no evidence of a trail at all but, when we were within thirty or forty miles of that village, the villagers came out and met us, told us how many dogs and sleds we had and generally all about our party and its equipment.

11. One reason the Americans do not possess this faculty is becaue they have too many accommodations. We have just let it slip by and have not retained it consciously. Subconsciously or unconsciously the American has this faculty to a great extent. Most Americans have had the experience of it but hesitate to use it generally or to say anything about it.

12. The average American thinks it a sign of being a bit off if something is suggested for which there is no apparent reason. Such a feeling is the result of ignorance regarding the true capacities of the individual and the most vital means he has for any degree of achievement. It is his doubt of himself and his ability that holds him back. "If ye believe and doubt not, nothing shall be impossible to you," said Jesus. This faculty is the first requisite to sound reason, while the other processes of reason commonly relied upon as the only basis of intelligent reason are secondary. Great achievements have

been accomplished from realms beyond reason and the reasons appeared after. Sound reason is brought about by first looking clear through the limitations, catching the vision of the unapparent, yet entirely possible, and then building the other processes of reason as these facts are worked out. "To faith add knowledge" say the scriptures but most of us attempt to attain faith by first knowing all about a thing objectively.

13. Then, too, we let others do our thinking for us. We rely upon them to think everything out, to give it form, and then we rely upon the thing produced. The producer becomes more and more capable and the dependent one becomes more and more dependent. Emerson said as much when he referred to the fact that what we gain on one hand we lose on the other. We have watches but have lost the ability to tell the time of day ourselves. To neglect the development of self through dependence upon anything outside yourself is to weaken your own nature.

14. The Chaldean astronomers got their information on astronomy through the use of the intuitive faculty—or the power of the mind to penetrate through to fact. They would depend on this completely and then work out all theories. These ancient Chaldeans included the workings of this faculty in their history. It has always been in evidence. The influence is still in existence. If we want it we must become one with it. That is all.

15. This is the "eye of the soul" about which the Mystics wrote. Through it men have read and will continue to read the Akashic records. Through it we may perceive things happening at a distance or envision future events with the speed of light— 186,000 miles per second. It comes to us at times during an earthquake or other extremity. "Coming

events cast their shadows before them." Everything happens first on higher planes; then reflection occurs here. It functions in the Devachan period between consciousness and form. It is the two faces of the Gargoyle at the temple gate. Looking one way it admits limitation of delusion into the temple, man's being. Looking into the realm of Spirit it admits the freedom and power of illumination.

16. The Hawaiians possess a great natural insight into things and they prophesy and prognosticate. There is a certain group of Hawaiians who will get together and tune in impending influences. If they perceive an influence that is not of benefit, they turn it over to another group who work against it, and it never manifests. The Hindus say that one man can prophesy and another God-man can stop fulfillment of the prophecy.

17. In our experience with the Hawaiians we never found an instance where they had failed to stop a negative event that had been prophesied. It is claimed that they have stopped many invasions. The ones performing that duty would lay down a certain line and the enemy could not cross it. Many times this has been included in their legends. At times the enemy could not even land on their shores.

18. The Carnegie Institute experimented some time ago with a group of Indians in Arizona. This group laid down a certain line and none could cross it except in love. Two men tried to force their way across the line and both men lost their lives.

19. The unillumined make the mistake of thinking that prophecy is inevitable, that if a thing is set to happen it must happen. "Whether there be prophecies they shall fail," say the scriptures. Prophecy comes mostly from the established mental structure immediately surrounding the earth, being the pro-

jection of man's own limited thought. The faculty of perception directed into this field may sense the trend of this mental influence and what will likely be the outworking in the material plane. This belongs to the realm of false prophecy and it can all be set aside. The scriptures warn against false prophets who turn the attention of the people away from God. True prophecy is the result of keeping this sense directed to the plane of Spirit until the individual catches the trend of the Universal Law. The law of the Universe readily sets aside any accumulations to the contrary in the minds of individuals or races. It is accomplished as easily as shadows are dispelled by the light. The sun dispels the night, a single candle will banish darkness from a room; for light, whether small or great, has unlimited power over surrounding darkness whether it be large or small. Only a little illumination on the part of the individual can dispel any amount of negation, limitation, or false prophecy around him, for they are only vague shadows with no potency within them. Do not accept prophecies of destruction and calamity. Look into the realm of Spirit and they vanish.

20. There was a group of persons in the Hawaiian Islands who came there from Japan, bringing black magic with them. They claimed they could pray a person to death; but that group no longer exists. Before one can practice black magic or become an antichrist, he must first become versed in the powers of the Christ consciousness. He gets the Christ power and uses it erroneously. The outcome of such practice is self-destruction and, with the destruction of individuals given to the practice of the black art, the art passes with them.

21. The most painful, if not the quickest, method of self-destruction is the misuse of spiritual knowledge. The individual tempted to use this spiritual

knowledge to influence, control, or gain advantage over others should remember that every edict which goes forth from his own mind or mouth passes through his own being and becomes a fiat of power within his own nature, working upon himself exactly as he had intended it for another. That is what Christ meant when He said that the Kingdom of heaven is within you. Your being is a kingdom, subject to the rulership of what you yourself decree. Whether his decree is accepted by another makes little difference to the individual sending it forth. It is received and acted upon within his own kingdom and he is sure of the most complete results in his own being. The kingdom within the individual will be heavenly only when he sends forth decrees that come from the heavenly realms, the Spirit where all things move in harmony to promote the well-being and advancement of every individual on earth. "The gift is to the giver and comes back to him," whether it be good or ill. "As you give, so you receive."

22. One denomination of Rishis in India is able to perceive an event that is set to happen. If it be evil, another group immediately takes it up and it does not happen at all. That was true also of the Hebrew race in the past. They prevented many wars among their people in that way.

23. Many are using the same method in preventing accidents today. Many people never have an accident. We worked with a group of over seven hundred people in the United States that worked definitely to prevent accidents and in the three and one-half years we were with them there was never an accident in the group. That group has now been augmented until there are about 4,000 members today. They work quietly and are not publicly known.

24. Why should not man put all the forces of his

being to work in some good purpose? By keeping his perceptive faculty, or whatever else you may wish to name it, working in the spiritual realm where everything moves in harmony toward the complete good of every being, there would be a corresponding action developed in the minds of all people. Because they were all working in obedience to the power that works toward the good of all, they could not possibly say or do anything except that which was for the good of each other. In other words, through obedience to the Great Law there could be no conflict among individuals. There could be no wars, no accidents, nor any of the other things that make for misery in the ranks of human nature.

25. This capacity can be put to varied uses. There is the case of the world war veteran, DeJong, who was treated in the Letterman Hospital at San Francisco and who, though blind, demonstrated that he had received a higher illumination by driving a car through the streets of San Francisco and Los Angeles. This particular young man had developed the faculty before and this was simply his sudden awakening. This often happens.

26. The point is that, if it can be awakened, as has been proved in so many cases, the faculty is there. If there, it can be understood, rightly directed, and awakened to proper function. We must give attention to these things and proceed intelligently to uncover the latent possibilities within our own natures, if we would arrive at the plane of mastership. No one can do this for us but ourselves.

27. This involves complete emotional control more particularly than mental control. We must be brought to one-pointedness. When our forces are centered, it works positively. Jesus said "One-pointedness is God."

28. The entire matter of our social reorganization centers around a deeper perception. People must learn how to develop this faculty. That will be the social reorganization: knowing how to do the right thing at the right time. It will help now to hold the thought of right action always. We will come to the point where we will know that everything we do is the right thing to do at the right time. This is the substance of social functioning in the future.

FOR THE TEACHER

This lesson deals with the motive from which will develop the new social order to come through these changing times and which will be reverting to man's primal faculty of discerning the spiritual trend of affairs, rather than relying upon the intellectual standards and material values of the past. Our past experiences have dulled, in a sense, this spiritual faculty and it must now be resurrected if we are to attune ourselves to the movement of Universal Laws.

Paragraphs 1 and 2 show how the more primitive races, as we call them, have a sense superior in some ways to our own and show how in some ways they fare better than we fare.

Paragraph 3 shows in what field this faculty functions most clearly with us but it must be expanded along spiritual lines if we would make the best of our own possibilities and opportunities.

Paragraphs 4, 5. This faculty might be variously named but in mystical science it is what is called the "penetrative sense" or the ability to press or lead the mind out into new fields. When directed to its highest purpose it will lead us into spiritual values just as accurately as it has led us into the fields of inventive genius.

Paragraphs 6, 7 and 8 are self-explanatory but can be developed further from the knowledge of the instructor.

Paragraphs 9, 10 and 11 afford a good opportunity for showing clearly how the mind of man is clouded through too much concern with the realm of effects and how it may be clarified by re-direction back into the realm of causes.

Paragraph 12 should be self-explanatory but affords plenty of opportunity for enlargement. Paragraph 13 may be handled in the same manner.

Paragraph 14 reverts to the same category as paragraphs 1 and 2.

Paragraphs 15 and 16 bring out to some extent the possibilities of this faculty and the fields where it may normally function. More may be said upon what the faculty really is. In its simplest form it is that phase of the mind that looks back to see what we may have done yesterday or what we hope to do to-morrow . . . the simple act of attention. If it is toward form, we discover only the complications thereof but, if into Spirit, it expands in the realm of spiritual reality.

Paragraph 17 brings out some of the possibilities arising from its use. This can be greatly enlarged upon and made of immense value to the student if he will heed the advice therein. Paragraph 18 may be handled in this connection.

Paragraph 19. The point to be clearly brought out in this paragraph is that prophecy is not accurate when based on the mental and physical plane. What is thoroughly organized on the mental plane may transpire in the physical unless set aside by a direct application of spiritual authority. True prophecy is proclaiming the constructive results which follow the authoritative application of discovered spiritual movements.

Paragraph 20. The folly of misuse of spiritual power should be self-evident to anyone but it should be clearly impressed upon the mind of every individual as a measure of self-preservation. The habit developing in many metaphysical circles of mentally influencing others to do the will of another is black magic in its embryonic form and can only lead to chaos.

Paragraph 21 should be handled in connection with paragraph 20.

Paragraphs 22 and 23 may be handled as paragraph 19 and may be developed further according to the leading of the instructor.

Paragraph 24 is self-explanatory but affords practical opportunity for showing the basis of true cooperation in ushering in the new order of things. The true motive of the spiritual aspirant is in harmony with the Universal Motive which works alike for saint and sinner, rich or poor, bond or free, and in a common motive there can not be discord and strife, hence no war. "Things equal to the same thing are equal to each other" is the basis of Universal unity.

Paragraphs 25 and 26 give opportunity to impress upon each individual student the fact that no one ever has developed or expressed any so-called unusual powers but that the same potential power is resident within him and his business is to develop his own capacities if he would know the measure of his own soul.

Paragraph 27. A whole volume might be given on the necessity of self-control. It is as essential to individual power and progress as the organization and application of energy is essential to mechanical power. Without it there is no practical power to constructive purposes in either field.

Paragraph 28 can be amplified according to the ability of the instructor.

CHAPTER V

POWER OF THE SPOKEN WORD

1. The spoken word has a great power but there is one thing certain: we must select the words and then we must give them power. There is no power in a negative word unless we do select and give the word power. It does not of itself contain power. Power must be given to the word by the one who speaks it. Of course, as the Eastern Philosophy goes, the thought which precedes the word is more important. Consequently, the thought can be the motivating force behind the spoken word and in that way it adds power and, as the Masters put it, that word must go forth and create.

2. Now, if a word is spoken idly or without force of thought, it does not accomplish. By the selection of that word, the power given to it through thought cannot help but accomplish that very thing for which it is sent. That is why they claim such selectivity for the spoken word and that is why they say the spoken word is always selective.

3. That power which we put back of the word to accomplish must be the energy that we ourselves perceive. As they put it, not the energy which you give to the word but the energy for the accomplishment of that word is what you perceive.

4. Jesus said, "My words are spirit and they are life and they do accomplish that whereunto they are sent." Spirit is the creative cause in the universe and our words are potent only as this same spirit is seen as the operative force back of them. It is the activity of the force of nature that makes the seed grow for no seed has power within itself. It is a container or

vehicle of that force. So it is with words. The Scriptures say, "The word is a seed," and the power of Spirit acts upon words as nature does upon the seed. Our consciousness or awareness of Spirit is the focal point in this matter of the power of the word. Idle words are impotent and do not create, though they, in a sense, may add to the state of hypnosis. To fear negative words is to add to their hypnotic energies and it thereby adds to the influence of the negative word. The power of ignorant or idle words is only that they may intensify the hypnotic state of man's mind but they do not alter the creative cause in the least. The power of negative words is only the modernization of the old idea of the devil and is a direct violation of the fact that there is only the power of God. There is no power opposed to the ultimate good in the universal trend. That which seems to be opposition is in our own minds, which often work contrary to the divine purpose. The creative trend of the Universe or the will and purpose of God is to dissolve ignorance just as light dissolves darkness.

5. We have seen them—"them" used in this sense always refers to the Masters—put forth a word and what the word represented would come into existence immediately. There was no time element at all. In fact, there is no way of placing a time element upon the spoken word if the energy—Spirit—is in it. As they put it, a word spoken directly with the impetus of true thought behind it must create that very condition instantly. It is quite evident that the Western World looks upon a word as less potent. That is, a word may be spoken but, with no energy behind it, it loses its potency entirely. It is often said that this is why the Western World gets into such childish prattle. It fails to put the proper value upon its words.

6. Now, the thought which possesses the proper selectivity or which possesses the force that belongs to it, should always be given to the word, not to drive that word through will or the force of the will but to give that word the power which belongs to it. That of course is the power of the Spirit and this is included in our words only through highly selected thought, thought which corresponds to the creative purposes of the Universe. In that way the will, which has directive ability, sends the word forth but it is not the will that gives power to the spoken word. The will selects or enters into the selection of thought and the speaking of the word but the power is conceded or admitted through an enlarged consciousness of the presence and power of Spirit. But, when a word is selected for its meaning or its use, it is always selected in the frequency where it belongs and is placed there.

7. This should eliminate the fear which many have of negative words and at the same time should inspire the individual to a more intelligent selection of his words and how to put them to better use. "To think the thoughts of God after him" would be the essence of spiritual power for back of such words would be the very power that created the heavens and the earth. Man's words should always be an outlet for his own innate spiritual nature and a means of establishing this spiritual nature in his outer being. To speak only in harmony with the highest and most constructive ideals would be to speak with the greatest power and, in this way, that which seems the greatest improbability would become the most probable in that such words have the greater power. In other words, the more Godlike the thought, the realization, and the consciousness, the greater the power involved in the process.

8. As the Eastern Philosophers express it, you

could not be separated from Principle one iota if you would use selective words. Therefore, every word that is put out can be selective. Then you are not energizing a negative condition. You are only giving energy to that one conclusion.

9. The Hindu, or the Aryan always put it: "Man is the creator of words; therefore, man is the selector or he has dominion over those words and he selects or places words in existence which must operate or become potent." Now, in the measure that he uses this fact rightly, there is no way of connecting that power with negative words, as they put it. Consequently, negative words do not enter into or have any consideration from the individual who wishes to manifest forms. This thought of manifest form is always that condition brought into existence wherein man is able to create. That is where man has dominion over every word spoken. The Sanskrit language in one of its phases allows for that condition. There is in that the power to manifest. By that we mean that one position of the Sanskrit language allows only four positive words, or statements. That is, words that can be made into positive statements and from these there is no deviation.

10. Naturally, everyone asks what those four positive words are. They are always words which mean the positive declaration of facts. Each one can select them. Of course, the most positive word is the first word, God. Going back to the Principle, you would formulate your statement with that as a basis; you would formulate with that word whatever positive sentence you wished. Thereby is the power of the spoken word. Your key word is always the highest, or God. Then you select the words which accompany that for your positive declaration.

11. Just as all mathematical calculation springs from the Unit symbolized by the figure 1, so must

all words emanate from a single derivative, or principle. GOD IS and, because God is, I AM. Because God is life, I am life. Because God is intelligence, I am intelligence. Because God is power, I am power. Because God is all substance, I am substance, et cetera. Father in Sanskrit means first mover and the first movement of the mind of the individual must always emanate from the One Source and it must be sustained through the consciousness of the individual. To admit anything into the individual consciousness that does not originate in the facts of God is to adulterate the process of life in himself and, to this extent, he becomes unaware of the fullness of his Divinity. He must give himself to the underlying facts of life in their entirety; he must tarry at Jerusalem — his contact with The All — until the Holy, or entire spirit of God is the motivating energy of his every thought, word, and act.

12. Man cannot express a word or thought outside of his own field of competency with any manifesting power. He cannot go outside of that field because that very word which he expresses creates the field in which he acts.

13. The average person does not really know what a word is. It is merely a vehicle used in the processes of mind to convey or extend certain processes of the mind. The word cannot convey that which is not in the mind. Webster says that a "name" implies the "essential nature" of a thing. A word is only a name for certain states of consciousness and that is something that rests with the individual himself. One person may say "I am happy" and it would convey nothing to another individual hearing the word. If his consciousness is only a bit joyous, his words would convey but little authority.

But if he were radiant with joy his words would convey complete conviction. Idle words are empty words, words which do not contain the consciousness and realization of spiritual facts. You see, a word as we use it is just what it contains and the content of the word is determined by our consciousness and our consciousness is determined by the degree of intelligent selection which we use.

14. It is not repetition that makes a word effective. Your first declaration, if it be true, is sufficient. There is nothing left to do but stand by your statement, abide in your word. Repetition, however, is often an effective means of bringing one into accord with the possibilities contained within a statement. One often repeats a sentence or rule over and over before the meaning is clearly revealed to his consciousness. Without this expansion of the mind toward the inner facts repetition is only hypnotic.

15. If man repeats words and they do not become hypnotic to him, this repetition brings him into closer accord with the facts back of the words. It effects a higher realization. It is worth while to repeat up to a certain point and then it is not worth while even to repeat because your word is established unto you. When you understand that your word is clearly established repetition is of no more value whatever. In REALITY, we come to understand that our word is always established and we never repeat it.

16. If the manifestation of your word does not appear, that is no proof of its ineffectiveness. The better policy in such a case is to give thanks that the manifestation is there. You get out of doubt completely in that way. But, by going on and repeating your word, you may very quickly begin to engender

doubt; whereas, if you give thanks, you are more closely in harmony with your word and become more easily aware that your word is established.

17. The mere repetition of a word does not establish it any more firmly. It only brings you into harmony with that which IS. It is very often possible to bring yourself into more harmonious relationship by giving thanks that it is here NOW and that it is established.

18. When one realizes that the whole problem of manifest results is more a matter of opening up the consciousness to see or include something which already exists in Fact, instead of trying to bring something that is not out into manifest form, then the matter will be much simpler. It is "the land thou seest, that will I give unto thee as an inheritance," that contains all the mystery. It is a fact in Spirit, it is a fact everywhere and on all so-called planes, for there is only one plane and that is spiritual. As the mind expands to see or grasp the spiritual fact, there can be no question whatever about the manifestation of that fact. If it is so in God, it is so everywhere for God is all. It is all a matter of awareness upon our part and our awareness must be expanded to include the reality and existence of the Spiritual fact.

19. That was Jesus' method of working. Every word was established unto Him. He exalted every word through His exalted consciousness, knowing that it was already in existence. The Hindu stands in the same position. He states his declaration and then he may say that it is finished. He takes the attitude that it is already finished; it is already in existence; it is his; and then he goes on. One accomplishes far more in that way than to go back to the repetition and it seems to always make one stronger.

20. In the matter of treatment of so-called dis-

ease, the average metaphysician makes the mistake of dealing with the opposites, disease and health. Here are two conditions, the one to replace the other. In the East they do not work in this way any more than did Jesus. When you seek for perfection, know that it is established unto you. Exalt perfection. Perfection exists independent of both the opposites of health and disease. Perfection is an eternally established fact in principle and it is complete within itself on every so-called plane. Both health and disease are delusions according to Eastern Philosophy for they are only human concepts. For instance, your own idea of health today would not suffice you in five years from now for health is a relative idea in your own consciousness. There is nothing relative in Being, all is complete, all is perfect, and the true practitioner identifies himself with reality and does not deal with delusion. Let go of the opposites altogether and put in their place the perfection. We find that Jesus did not in any instance treat with the opposites. He put into the place of both the opposites the true perfection. His great statement was perfection always and that perfection was always established unto Him.

21. If I place on the blackboard the figures two plus two equals three and then follow with two plus two equals five, would you deal with the three and five and try to establish the right answer? No, you would go right through these figures, deal with the fact that two plus two equals four, and both these extremes would vanish. That which is less or more than the correct answer has nothing to do with the fact in Principle and it is only by bringing the fact of principle to bear upon the situation that any correct answer is possible. Our ideas of health and disease are both less than the perfection which is established in the foundations of the Universe and never

can that which is less than perfection be made into perfection. You are dealing with something unrelated to either of these extremes. "Be ye perfect, even as your Father in heaven is perfect," is the correct standard of procedure here.

22. Most people fail in the so-called demonstration because they make a statement of perfection and then immediately begin to look back into the matter of the opposites. Only "if thine eye be single shall thy body be filled with light." Lot's wife turned and saw double and her body became stone or salt. "Now, henceforth and forever, see only perfection," said Jesus. The moment that we establish perfection, the Christ stands forth dominant. Each works to establish the other, for the fact in Spirit is the form of its manifestation.

23. The effect of true spiritual treatment is not dependent upon the degree of unfoldment or spiritual development of the person "treated". We need not bother about his consciousness for it is based upon the opposites else he would not be ill. The spiritual Fact IS and the moment we stand in perfection our consciousness is perfect as well.

24. Speaking the Word is never hypnotic for it is the essence of the true nature of all creation. Treatment, or speaking the Word, is not projecting our ideas of health to offset disease. This latter is hypnotic. Speaking the Word is only telling the Truth, declaring that which always has been and always will be true of any individual, condition, or circumstance, in Principle. Hypnosis is a result of speaking from the human mind with its imperfect concepts.

25. It is not necessary that the sick or needy person ask for your help nor that he be conscious that you are sending forth the Word to him. If you send it forth on the Christ Right Ray, you are merely presenting his own innate perfection to him. In this

way you liberate both yourself and him for you are not dealing with anything but fact. You are not working against the will of any individual when you work with perfection for the innate will of everyone is for perfection. This rather frees his will from its entanglements in the realm of false habits and concepts. There is no so-called "Influence" in this sort of facing the situation. It is merely calling forth that which has always existed until it arrests the attention of everyone involved and they merely see that it is so.

26. There is power in the spoken word always if we see it as Spirit, for then it can be nothing but Spirit. We are the determinator. We are both the power and the expressor of that power and we are the sole determinator of what that word shall carry with it. There is power in medicine on exactly this same basis. It is but the conveyor or means by which the mind of the patient is expanded to admit the creative authority of the Universe. God is in the doctor, the patient, or the pill. Any individual, regardless of his profession or status, need only project the perfection. Of course, if we always would work in that perfection and manifestation of perfection we soon would get out of Medicine completely. Our Word would heal.

27. There is no harm in using an agency in an attempt to minister to the needs of suffering mankind. There are many steps and many methods but only one Power. If our ideal is Perfection, we are going to arrive at a point where there are no agencies. The agency which an individual employs only indicates the progress he has made in his own mind as to the suitable and most efficient means of admitting perfection into his being. One thinks it must come through a pill, one thinks it will come through affirmations, but, through whatever it comes, it is

the Perfection of Principle that manifests. Only the highest ideals are adequate to contain the full measure of power that exists in Divine Principle, for the larger the container the more can be conveyed. When the container and the contained are one— Perfection—then it is complete in every plane.

28. In treating at a distance, or what metaphysicians call absent treatment, thought is more rapid and potent than words. Thought does not know time and space while a word or audible sound belongs on the material plane and must traverse space and endure in time in order to reach its destination. Notice how instantly your thought is at the sun, the center of the earth, or at any other place. Thought does not travel, it is already there. Every fact in Spirit is already there and, further, it is already in evidence. To see this fact is to lift yourself into this fact and to see it for another is to lift him into it. I, if I be lifted up—if the perceptive faculty is lifted up to the plane of reality it draws all things into this realm. This is the true approach, rather than to try to lift anything or anybody into the perfect state. We might as well try to make energy out of earth by using a pick and shovel.

29. We know a man in India who walks through a storm just by the presentation of perfection of that storm. He will walk through a storm and never get wet. We have seen him stop fires and storms. Man himself is the Word of God if he abides in that Word. "If ye abide in my Word and my Word abides in you, then are you in me even as I am in you," is the truth of the whole thing. When Jesus sent his Word and healed the Centurion's daughter he did not send anything as we measure it in the three dimensional world. Jesus, or Christ, WAS the Word himself and there was not anything that was made but that which was made by the same Word.

Therefore, the Word which He "sent" did not traverse space, for the Word was there as the Truth of the Centurion's daughter, just as it was with Him. He simply announced a Universally True spiritual Fact and outer minds became awakened to this Fact.

30. "Our remedies oft in ourselves do lie
Which we ascribe to Heaven." — *Shakespeare.*

FOR THE TEACHER

Paragraph 1. Was not man given dominion over all things in the beginning? If that be the case, that same power is resident within man yet and all the seeming power which anything has over man is the working out of power which he himself has assigned to that thing. But, even though the power seems to emanate from the thing or from a person, the power is really within the individual for that is where its activity moves and is felt. To govern the action and reaction of his own nature, therefore, would be one of man's primal secrets of power. To keep one's nature always working in perfect accord with the Divine Ideal of perfection would be to have all power in Heaven and in earth.

Paragraphs 2, 3 and 4. It should be clear to everyone, though it seems not to be, that the words we speak are no more power than cylinders in an automobile engine are power. They are vehicles of energy and only the kind and degree of energy moving through them determines the power. When Jesus said, "My words are Spirit," he meant to convey that he was conscious that the moving force of God was moving through what he said or thought and it was this motivating energy which did the apparent healing. The assertion of fact is infinite in its potency in the face of that which is not fact. Follow

69

this idea through with any illustration in the realm of truth and falsity, light and dark.

Paragraph 5. The important point in this paragraph is to make the student realize what tremendous opportunity he is losing in idle talk. His words might as well be conveying an infinite energy that would free him from his mediocrity if he would only proceed intelligently.

Paragraph 6 should be carefully considered and we should differentiate between the natural impetus of an accepted fact and the imposition of our wills to force a condition which we imagine to be better than the one already existing. The acceptance of a thing given never involves what we call a forceful will. Receiving an offered gift is infinitely more effective than to attempt to force one to give you something that is not already within his mind to give. Accepting a fact that is universally true involves no supreme assertion of the individual will. Perfection does not come from projecting our own ideas but from awakening to the knowledge that it is already the established order of things.

Paragraph 7. Clearly free the student from the notion that negative words have power. They are only a waste of time and add to the state of hypnosis. The higher the ideal, the more illumined is the idea, the more powerful it becomes. Your lightest word is your most illumined word.

Paragraph 8. Use right discrimination in the selection of words so they convey or project into the manifest world only that which conforms to your highest ideals.

Paragraph 9. Man's dominion is over himself. His being is supposed to be the Kingdom of Heaven. Only the law governing infinite space should govern his thoughts and feelings, his bodily and manifest conditions. His sphere of rulership is within himself, heavenly only when that rulership is exercised according to the facts of Principle.

Paragraph 10 and 11 show clearly the origin of all constructive thoughts and words and that the entire field of thought and action should be developed from this manner of procedure.

Paragraphs 12 and 13. Show what is in the Word that gives it power. Repetition versus realization.

Paragraphs 14, 15 and 16. The function of words or The Word is not to project something into being but it is to expand the mind of man until he sees that which has always been from the beginning. "Before Abraham was, I am," is just as true of every fact in Sprit as it was of Christ.

Paragraphs 17, 18 and 19 are a continuation of the same truth . . . training the mind to see through its veil of hypnotism, the veil in the temple, to see through to the other side where all things are already perfect and in evidence. It is all a matter of training the mind to SEE.

Paragraphs 20 and 21 contain practical advice not only for the metaphysician but also for the individual who wishes to help some friend in distress. So much of mental practice is purely hypnotic and only substitutes a condition that may be somewhat better for the condition that was already there. Why substitute one human state or conception for another when the Perfection of God himself is there waiting recognition?

Paragraph 22. To stand by the fact regardless of the consequences is the procedure. There can be no loss but the loss of our illusion and the gain is Truth itself, so why should we hesitate.

Paragraphs 23, 24, 25 and 26 are clearly enough defined and highly illuminating to everyone but they may be enlarged upon out of the richness of the instructor's mind.

Paragraph 27. The difference between the *conveyor* and the *thing conveyed* comprises all the difference with which we succeed in any kind of curative practice. "It is the Spirit that quickens," and the effectiveness of treatment is the amount of Spirit admitted in the practice.

Paragraphs 28 and 29 eliminate the idea that there is such a thing as absent treatment of disease for in Spirit there is no "absence". Spirit is present at all times and in all places the same and needs only recognition.

CHAPTER VI

CONSCIOUSNESS

1. Consciousness is man's state of awareness. It is the capacity of the mind to know and its knowing determines his capacities along all lines. Man may be aware of that which is true or he may develop in his mind a sense of awareness that has the semblance of reality but which is entirely false. The truth or falsity of his estate is, therefore, dependent upon his state of awareness or his consciousness.

2. Consciousness must be that which represents the highest attributes. It must be related to all high attributes. We carry our consciousness to God consciousness wherein we are aware of all things including ourselves in the highest state. That is the state where we see through all conditions and all circumstances. As the Masters say, the veil is then completely removed — the veil that hitherto seemed to exist between the mortal or physical and Spirit. There is no limitation here. The mortal and physical conceptions are abandoned completely for the true Spiritual.

3. This spiritual consciousness does not exclude sense activity. True sense activity is included in the highest consciousness always. Sense activity in its rightful function is true spiritual activity. The senses —so-called— act in a limited manner only when not under the right determining influence. When activated by the Spiritual facts the senses function properly and are then said to be opened.

4. The question is often asked in what state of consciousness is the individual when in trance. Trance is only a partial expression of sense activity.

73

We might just as well carry our consciousness to the true activity or completion always and, when this partial expression becomes one with true activity, we are never in trance and we are never under any destructive hypnotic condition.

5. This same fact applies to what we commonly classify as subdivisions of consciousness. One should not attempt to classify consciousness for it cannot be subdivided. It is ONE consciousness and in that state we cannot think in terms of divisions or separations. The subdivisions are illusions, the same as illusionary trance. They are so subtle that they can be very deceptive to one who is not using higher discrimination. It is so much easier to see it all as One. The subdivisions originated with man. Man saw the subdivisions as attributes when they are really not such at all.

6. The thought of most teachers is possibly for clarity in conveying the message but it is better for them always to make it One thing. Simplicity in the end is always the greatest clarity. The trouble with subdivisions is that they are almost always considered as attributes. It is better to keep our eye fixed on One. We get into negative conditions through using the subdivisions. They are nearly always symbolic and most of our symbols represent the subdivisions of consciousness. That is another reason why symbols no longer suffice. It is well known today that we have worked through symbolism. As the Masters say, we are in the pure light of day in consciousness. It becomes far simpler to have that consciousness, the complete Light, as our aim without any subdivisions whatever.

7. Take the matter of eating, digesting, assimilating, and the rebuilding of the body through the conversion of food into energy, muscle, bone, blood, teeth, hair, et cetera. Imagine that you

worked out a theory that each one of these is a separate function to be dealt with individually and that you had to determine with each meal just what portion of your food would be handled through each one of these particular functions and just when each would function in turn. How could you escape confusion? The fact is, you recognize it as one process with many phases and each one of these phases is a self-operative process within a single system. In a normal physical state there is not a single phase of the entire system that functions independently but every one of the various phases is but the working out of the single system.

8. The body is only a symbol of the soul or the man who lives within the body. That is, the body is a symbol of the workings of consciousness. To protect and determine that which enters into consciousness, which is through the control of one's attention, the entire system of consciousness is self-operative as a single system. There is not conscious, subconscious, superconscious but just one radiant living consciousness of reality. This is the state of complete freedom from symbols and therefore from hypnosis.

9. Some people become so interested in the psychic sense or the lower phases of consciousness that a complete earth life is given over to it to the extent that the true consciousness cannot manifest. The best solution is to simply let go of it and become one with the Whole. This is what Paul inferred when he said, "reckon ye yourself to be dead unto sin, but alive unto God." The difference is in clear knowing and influenced knowing. Clear vision is what clairvoyance intends to convey but the commonly accepted meaning of clairvoyance is partial or clouded viewing—seeing only in part.

10. There can be certain relative phenomena

brought into existence through clairvoyance and clairaudience, as practiced, or any of the five divisions of consciousness but they can never be or lead to the Whole. You see, they may become false and under a manifestation of these conditions we may get a false concept completely, which I usually refer to as a negative concept. When we stand one with the whole we cannot be either negative or false. It should be clear knowing of Truth itself. We cannot reach that state of Knowing or that One Consciousness through mediumship or any other form of hypnosis. All are distinctly detrimental to spiritual unfoldment.

11. In that high sense all senses become One. They all become One in perfect coordination. Our senses coordinate absolutely and every part and cell of our bodies coordinate and vibrate in unison. One great trouble with these other conditions is that we are likely to have one member of the body vibrating in the wrong field and then the new cells do not attach themselves properly to the organ to which they belong. Each cell that is created represents the organ to which it will attach itself. If one cell gets out of the vibratory field in which it belongs it may attach itself to the wrong organ and then you have a discordant condition.

12. This discord is often extremely intensified by the various occult methods of concentration upon the physical centers or organs. This practice only superimposes a hypnotic state more definitely into the manifest form and greater confusion results. In the first place, hypnosis is only a function of a partial consciousness, or a specialized consciousness in some particular form or direction. Therefore, the more diversified the field and departmental the consciousness, the more hypnotic it becomes. And to wilfully work in subdivisions and phases of con-

sciousness would be the most definitely hypnotic in influence. The attention should always be directed into the whole, into complete oneness, and then the distribution of vibratory energy is carried on through the mechanism of consciousness just as it is in the body. Then there is perfect synchronization or harmony throughout the entire organism.

13. The idea of an inner and an outer consciousness is also a phase of hypnosis for the theory imposes a sense of separation or division. There is in reality not an inner and an outer consciousness nor a personal consciousness and a universal one. When the Self becomes conscious in the outer it is only one attitude of consciousness and it is complete in every way and it is ONE in and with universal consciousness. I and my Father are ONE.

14. We are then not conscious of an inner for the inner and outer are one. The whole is always evident. If we see and project our vision or our Ideal, it is for that complete wholeness. The Masters call that being of "sound mind," or completely *sound* in consciousness. It is perfectly sound and whole. The body is perfectly sound and perfectly whole as well. The Knower and the thing known become One. Paul included that in his writings but it was never included in the translations. We can become the known as well as the Knower if we will complete the two and bring them together. The trouble is that we make a separation when in reality none exists.

15. The practice of denial as an effective means of liberation into this perfect state should also be intelligently considered in this light. Denial is supposed to erase from the mind or blot out of consciousness, hence out of man's being, an experience or process that is not true or that is seemingly opposed to his perfect state of completion or oneness.

77

But is the ordinary use of denial as practiced in our metaphysics an efficient means in bringing about this liberation? If the denial, as it is commonly used, produces the desired result, then well and good but, if not, let us find out what is back of it and what is the efficient practice involved.

16. Let us take a specific case of denial in its relationship to what is commonly considered the law of heredity. Denial is in no sense necessary. It has a tendency always to plunge one further into illusion because the denial keeps the mind fixed upon the condition and it is thereby more likely to intensify that condition. The mind naturally enlarges upon that condition toward which it is directed. The purpose is that the condition be eliminated entirely and, in order for this to be brought about, it must be put out of consideration altogether. It is not to be countenanced.

17. In reality there is no law of heredity. It is only a manifestation. It is not necessary to deny something that does not exist. You will find it far better to put perfection in the place of denial. You will get quicker results. Usually a denial holds it closer to the individual, whereas, by putting Perfection in the place of the denial, you realize that condition far more quickly. And it does not matter what the condition is. It has been shown by repeated experiments that it is far better to simply release the condition. Free it entirely through non-attention. Dismiss it. That was evidently Jesus' meaning when He said, "loose him and let him go."

18. There is neither race nor family heredity for the one presupposes the other. People may look alike but this is always because of some former close relationship or similarity of past experience and environment. There is an apparent chromosomatic

condition that shows processes of evolution running parallel but these processes are not in reality parallel processes or parallel evolutionary conditions. They do, of course, run parallel with the human race as well as with the animal kingdom but not with the same frequency by any means. It is a well known fact today that every frequency of the human body is above that of the animal frequency. The transmission of the acquired characteristics can be influenced through the thought but it can also be set aside through the reversal of thought.

19. It is a state of mind that causes the characteristics of form and similarity in form is due to the similarity of mental and emotional experiences of individuals in a group. Two people, not much alike in the beginning, through long association with each other and enduring the same general mental and emotional reactions ultimately develop similar characteristics. A man and a woman living together over a period of years, if they have sympathetic interests and mutual emotional reactions, begin to look alike. This is a reproduction of similar mental states.

20. Medical science today is quite reversing its former opinions regarding hereditary disease. When Jesus healed the epileptic the disciples wanted to know whether the man or his parents had sinned. This was His direct answer: "Neither this man nor his parents have sinned, unless you see the sin." It was only sin because of the thought of the parents or those surrounding him. In reality, the only sin connected with the condition was the sin of erroneous thinking.

21. The so-called law of Karma comes under the same category. It can be proved today that there is no debt of Karma, that the Soul does not bring any

of this through. Spiritual understanding takes no account of Karmic conditions or any imperfect condition. It is as foolish as to say that one must correct his mistakes in mathematics before he can study the rule. The fact is that the mistake is erased of itself when one applies himself to the rule. One's access to the rule is always direct no matter what his mistakes are and once the rule is known and followed there are no false results.

22. The leading and better Universities in India and, particularly, Dr. Bose of Calcutta University are making the statement today that there would be no appearance of what we call heredity if people would drop it out of their thought completely. Even with the plant heredity may be shown but it can be corrected by the thought of the people surrounding that plant.

23. That which is commonly accepted as inherited insanity is only a condition fastened upon the victims by other people. They are in parallel groups. It is an attraction and not an inheritance. Instead of accepting this theory of heredity, Paul's idea that we have an inheritance from God that is immutable and cannot be changed should be substituted. This is the effective denial of race heredity— the substitution of the true for the false, leaving the false entirely outside the range of our consideration. God has nothing to do with things that obsess the human mind and we, as sons of God, need not have.

24. Jesus said to call no man on earth your father for one is your Father which is in Heaven. This, then, is man's true line of inheritance and to get out of his mind these intervening mental processes he has but to return to the foundation fact of his being. In the beginning God created—that is, the beginning of all creation is in God. That does not

refer to time but to fact. With nothing in his thought between himself and his beginning there could be no other line of inheritance for nothing would have access to his being from any other source. Thought is always the determining factor and by returning always to his beginning, God, man always inherits through his own mind that which is FROM his beginning.

25. In the second chapter of Genesis we have a wrong translation that has done much toward our erroneous idea of sin and the matter of inheritance. It does not mean that man sinned and thereby became mortal and this mortality was handed on down to the rest of us. It did not intend to convey that the sin reversed man's nature but that the sin itself could have been reversed, that it could have been corrected. At that time it merely meant an error could be corrected. Jesus taught the remission of sin rather than its perpetuation with consequent results. Mistakes can be REVERSED is the teaching.

26. All the so-called human laws, or mental laws, belong in this category. They are all mistakes in that they do not define the true governing law of the Universe and all things therein. But they can be set aside at any time. They are denied by merely rejecting them in favor of the true law. Bose has proved that conclusively. He states that all so-called laws of heredity are only manifestations brought about by the thoughts of men and can be set completely aside at any time.

27. First, however, we must become one with the Christ Self. It takes a Christ consciousness to set these laws aside just as it takes true knowledge to set aside false beliefs. This Christ state must first be attained, or unfolded and, once in this state, there is, of course, nothing else.

28. Hypnosis may spring from two conditions, a partial state of consciousness or a false state of consciousness. A partial state of consciousness admits of certain capabilities and one feels limited or unable to go beyond that which his consciousness indicates. All restraint, or the sense of inability to accomplish, is only a state of partial hypnosis. The false state of consciousness is the notion that certain things are true which are not true at all. This is a state of complete ignorance of reality. It is a mental state built up of impressions that are entirely false, states of consciousness built up regarding something—if it can be so stated—that does not exist at all or, on the other hand, a set of impressions that are entirely false regarding a thing that in itself is entirely true.

29. This might be illustrated with the notion once held by man that the earth is flat. The hypnotic result was that men were held with certain restricted zones of activity, fearing to go beyond these restricted areas lest they should fall off the edges of the earth. That idea seems completely silly now that we know the earth is round. It was round all the time but the people were as limited in their activity as if the earth itself had actually been flat with a great chasm spreading beyond these edges. Adventurers who had another notion about the earth dared to venture beyond the limitations in which others lived and they sailed out across the chasm without any difficulty so far as they were concerned. To them the chasm did not exist nor did it exist in fact. However, the others knew they would fall into it. The manner in which the condition was met was not in overcoming the chasm for there was no such thing. It was simply a matter of sailing out beyond the limitations of opinions and it was found that no actual limitation existed at all. This is

exactly the manner in which the Masters meet every situation. "What appears exists not at all," they say. They are not hypnotized by the opinions held by the race nor conditions as they appear to the race, for they know Reality. Their determination is in the realm of facts and they traverse time and space just as Columbus sailed across the edges of the earth. There were no edges to the earth and there is no time or space to the Master. They are all illusions just as the flat earth with its edges was an illusion.

30. This is what Jesus meant when He said, "Get thee behind me, Satan," as it is translated. In reality He said "Get thee behind me, limitation," for there is no such thing. He put it out of the range of His consideration and conduct for in his illumined state there were no such things. He saw through the hypnotic spell, the veil in the temple, and lived wholly in reality.

31. In sleep the consciousnes becomes completely universal. It becomes Knowing, with all attributes alert. That is why we can often do in our sleep what we cannot do when awake. We submerge it because of our outer activities during the day. We go on in a great hurry during the day so that we become completely exhausted when night comes and our consciousness immediately floods back to the All-knowing condition, though we do not know it. We are not conscious of what is taking place. We should be just as conscious as in our so-called waking condition. Sleep allows that complete consciousness to come into function.

32. That is why psycho-analysis lays such stress on the dream state as being superior to the waking state when used rationally and in its right order. But the two—the sleeping and waking states— should be exactly the same. If we would turn our thoughts to this higher consciousness we would be in

that realm always. We would KNOW. The dream is more of a clairvoyant state of a very low order unless we do turn our minds to a higher condition or knowing state. If we do this our dreams are true always and are not something that has not actually happened to us at all. Dreams ordinarily are a mixture of the earthly and the higher experiences. If our thoughts were always of that higher condition, our dreams would correspond. Our days would be concluded the moment we went to sleep.

33. Some times when a man is up against a stone wall, so to speak, due to serious problems which he cannot seem to solve, his state of exhaustion appears to quiet the outer and very often the solution comes through. He has merely carried on the false practices of living until he has contracted his being as far as he can. It is just the same as if he had gone to sleep. The cessation of activity through exhaustion caused his mind to let go of the condition and then the solution came through.

34. The method of relaxation which the Masters use is to let go completely of any outer condition and always project their thoughts to a perfect activity. The physical, emotional, and mental must be stilled by directing the attention higher.

35. The difference between the ordinary dream and a nightmare is that in the nightmare you have the psychic phenomena in evidence becoming connected with an outer activity and always thus permitting anything to come in, the same as in psychism or mesmeric influence. I have seen people hypnotized and they were not themselves at all. They would act like monkeys or go about barking like dogs. This is quite similar to the nightmare.

36. When you are in the nightmare, it is possible to come out of it if you will think of what you would think if you were in the waking stage. A

patient has been known to cure himself entirely of extreme cases of nightmare by thinking while experiencing the nightmare, "Just what would I do if I were in the waking state?" He would have accomplished the same result more quickly had he thought what he would do were he in a perfect state of spiritual consciousness and would have raised himself nearer to that state. If he would ask himself what he would accomplish if he could see directly through to the Spiritual, it would become much simpler and more beneficial because it would be permanent. The breaking up of a nightmare becomes automatic if just before you go to sleep you declare that you are one with perfection. It has no chance to enter when you are in this state.

37. This same practice can be applied equally to the so-called waking state. All negative conditions and difficult problems can be corrected and solved every time by this method. You will find it very practical to ask yourself, when faced with problems or apparent negative conditions, what you would do if you were in Spiritual Consciousness. Get rid of the complexities of earthly living in this way. It is really just as simple as that.

38. To "be still and know that I am God" covers the case perfectly for that is the completion of it all. And that other phrase, "God is in His Holy Temple, let all the earth keep silent before God and rejoice," is equally applicable. And again, "In everlasting Joy all things have their birth."

39. Joy is the very highest state. It is the exaltation of Soul as physical pleasure is the exaltation of the body. But it is the true emotional state of man, born from his inner release into the truth of his being. It is only when we get out of that condition of Joy and Harmony that we begin to get separated from the Highest. You are going to hear a great

deal of that talk in the coming years in all theological schools. It is quite remarkable how that is now being brought about and how this change is manifesting even in the teaching of children to become harmonious and to let the turmoil around them go on as it pleases without becoming a part of it.

40. The moment you train children to react to constructive ideals and band together to promote harmony, developing the mass instinct in this way, you are destroying the very root of all unhappiness, misery, want, and war in the world. Our past method has been to develop the sense of strife. The moment that someone acted in a manner that aroused any resentment or resistance everyone else began to take on the same attitude and in this way we have been trained to develop the sense of strife. Only by reversing the process and getting back to the true state will we find our perfect social structure coming into the world.

FOR THE TEACHER

Paragraphs 1 and 2. To grow from the present state of awareness of himself as a material being and into the consciousness that he is a spiritual being contains the full secret of man's attainment. It is a structural change in consciousness that is to be considered for all the other changes which he has striven to effect are dependent upon it. It is merely a matter of being able to discern the difference between truth and falsity, between right knowledge and ignorance. To be aware of oneself as a spiritual being, offspring of an infinite spiritual system and one with all the powers and capacities within that spiritual system, is the very essence of attainment.

Paragraph 3. An awakened state does not do away with the outer man nor his so-called sense activities. They are lifted up and become outlets for his illumination instead of inlets for limited or false information.

Paragraph 4. Self-control and self-expression is the law of life and not the subjecting of oneself to control by outside forces or even by partial knowledge.

Paragraphs 5, 6 and 7. The consciousness becomes clouded always in partial actions of the mechanism of awareness. To be only partially aware in any so-called phase of the mind is not complete consciousness. The new psychology recognizes that the mind is and functions as a unit—that it is one process and not made up of many functions and processes. Consciousness is the function of the spiritual man, just as eating, digesting, assimilating are functions of his body, and the physical is but an outward replica of the spiritual. That is why the outer is always called the symbol.

Paragraphs 8, 9, 10. Pure knowing and pure being are the result of clairvoyance or clear vision, vision which sees through to the spiritual fact as it exists in the Divine Principle. "And he lifted his eyes unto heaven" is the practice that awakens pure vision or clear sight. What is commonly called clairvoyance is but the extension of the physical sense to see the movement of human ideas in the mental or psychic ethers. Only the radiance of Truth itself is the object of clear vision.

Paragraphs 11 and 12. To impose one idea upon the body in substitution for another, or to attempt with the mind to awaken bodily centers, is the most intense form of hypnosis for it is the wilful imposition of thought and becomes most binding. Did you ever notice how a living sense of joy functions equally and automatically over your entire being? No part of your being had to be stimulated to that state of joy. Imagine how long it would take you to become joyous if you had to proceed to concentrate upon each part of your body to awaken it to the state of joy and then proceed with each body center in this way until you finally became happy. Mental processes do not produce spirituality nor do they awaken the physical centers. Spiritual awakening immediately pervades the entire being of man and when the I is lifted up the entire man is lifted up with it.

Paragraphs 13 and 14 may be handled as above, with further development if desired.

Paragraphs 15 and 16. Denial is not a matter of dealing directly with negation but is the practice of ignoring it. The first function of the mind is attention and whatever occupies the attention develops through the mental process. Therefore, denial is putting the thing out of the range of consciousness. "Get thee behind me Satan" is putting all negation out of the realm of consideration. It is not even to be dealt with for it is but a shadow. Light is that which dispels the shadow and knowledge dispels ignorance.

Paragraphs 17, 18, 19, 20. All the so-called laws of the material world are only attempts to define the rule of behaviorism in the material system. But matter is not bound in obedience to any such laws but is always escaping beyond the so-called bounds of these laws and obeying something superior. The ultimate governing principle of matter is Spirit for all the Universe is a spiritual system. Heredity, so-called, is not the result of a law at all but is the result of imposition of false states of mind into the process of life. Heredity, so-called, is not a law but the result of counter-action to law. The law of the Spirit of Life is the true governing principle.

Paragraph 21. Karma is likewise the result of

counter-action to the law of the spirit of life. The fruits of the law are deliverance, illumination, perfection. Only so long as this law is kept from the individual consciousness is there even a semblance of Karma or the effect of some other influence. Overcoming Karma is not a matter of mastering and overcoming the results of our mistakes but correcting the mistakes. That is brought about through understanding and obeying the true law.

Paragraphs 22, 23 and 24 establish man's heritage as coming from the One Source, and not from the channels through which he passes. The stream is the flow of water descending from its source and not the banks between which it flows. It gathers water from its source but only mud from its banks.

Paragraphs 25, 26 and 27. The law of the spirit does not move to punish sin but to release man from the effects of his mistakes. The wrong procedure is to be corrected, not that man is supposed to endure the results of his error. Man's nature cannot be reversed for he always remains a spiritual being. He can only reverse his notion of himself. Instead of doing this, he should reverse his mistaken idea that he is a material being and retain the truth that he is a spiritual being created in the image and likeness of God.

Paragraphs 28 and 29. All consciousness that is limiting is hypnotic to that degree. Man is a free, omnipotent being, given power and dominion over all things from the beginning. The only limiting influence is the limitation of his own consciousness. To free the consciousness is to free the man.

Paragraph 30 is the continuation of the same idea.

The balance of the lesson is to emphasize that the important thing is to learn, whether when asleep or awake, to bridge this gap in consciousness wherein dwells all sense of human limitation. So long as we keep ourselves open at any point to anything less than the highest our nature is circumscribed just to that extent. One may just as well receive pure consciousness direct from the Source, as to receive partial knowledge from lesser planes. Why be always seeking the lesser when the greater is more easily available? Why not train ourselves and our children in the knowledge of realities and let the limitations and ignorance of the world alone?

CHAPTER VII

GOD

1. People generally are interested in the Masters' idea of God and the location of God. We shall, therefore, consider this idea in the present chapter. However, it will be impossible to consider their idea without including man for to them God and man are inseparable.

2. The Masters talk of God considerably but they consider It as One attribute of Being—Being as one attribute, or a single entity comprising the entire universal system, visible and invisible. The mind of man got its idea of God through superstition about God. Man saw then nothing but the graven image. It was then necessary to bring him back to the realization that he is God, there being no separation between the individual and the Universal; that man is an integral part of the whole and is identical in nature with the whole.

3. They teach that God is right within man always, just as Jesus Christ taught. That is always the attitude and thought of the illumined. Man is God. That statement, "I am God," is one of the most definite statements that man can use. We have never known them to give instructions in writing. But they do give oral instructions or oral talks. They do not call their talks instructions. They are simply stating facts which are obvious and they assume that the obvious should be known universally. Therefore, they do not teach, but merely confirm what all men instinctively know and which is universally true.

4. As a guide in individual progress they suggest

reading the Mahabharata, the Vedas, the Upanishads and the Gita. This reading is suggested as
preparation for one who desires to take the real inner work and for concentration. A few verses at a
time are best. They never suggest reading a whole
book through. They often read but one sentence in
a whole day. The instructions given in the Gita are
steps toward the accomplishment of individual perception of what God really is and to really bring
the individual into the consciousness of what it
means.

5. No man will actually know God until he himself experiences the realization of God within himself. "NO man knoweth the things of God except
the spirit of God which is in him reveal them." The
preparatory work prior to the discovery of the inner
or secret doctrine as it is sometimes called is the result of training the mind to grasp that which is within the statements for that is the inner work or inner doctrine. It is like studying to understand the
meaning of a mathematical rule. The thought is
that, when one has trained himself to gain the
knowledge of the inner meaning of the teachings of
the Gita or the Bible or any other Sacred book, he
is then in position to make an inner search of himself to find the inner meaning of his own being.
Man is not a physical organism, but that inner self
living through a physical organism. The inner work
is finding the Self which is the God-Self.

6. There are so many orthodox conceptions today that hold to the theory that God is made in the
image and likeness of man instead of the truth that
man is made in the image and likeness of God. But
they think of man as physical rather than that
which is back of the physical, the inner Self. Man is
really the image and likeness of God.

7. If God is the sum of all things visible and invisible, the Infinite One, the image of God embraces all time and space for there is nothing but God. Man could only be created in or within His image for there could be no outside where man could be created. He subsists within the very image of God, as your thoughts exist within and live as an integral part of your mind. Not only is man created within this image of God or contained within the allness of God but he is made of the very essence of the God nature, like unto it. If the cause is God, the effect is God in manifestation. Cause and effect must be one. Can there be thought without mind and can there be mind without thought?

8. The union of every condition brings man right back to God. He does not need to attain. He is God. That is wholeness of Principle. The materiality of illusion is that which gets us into all kinds of difficulties and strife. In that complete unification of Principle in man we rise out of objectification entirely as we know objectification. There is a pure manifestation of God but it is not a material or limited objectification. It is a state of consciousness expression of all that Principle is. But there is not the slightest degree of separation or limitation. It is like a ray of light among innumerable rays of light, which altogether make the light that is universal, but each ray IS light.

9. The statement, "I am God," accompanied by the realization of what is truly involved in it will heal any condition instantly. If you realize it and see nothing but that Truth, only that Truth can manifest. In treating yourself or another you see and declare only the eternal Unity with God. That Light comes forth instantly for it is the true light and then we know that unity is in existence within ourselves

and within everybody else. It is all accomplished. That is the Christ Light, the Christ Principle.

10. This eliminates the theory that it is necessary to do any specific work on the glands, on body centers, upon the body itself, or to treat disease, as you state it. The physical will fall into line as soon as we realize that fundamental Unity. When this state is reached the glands and all bodily functions are stimulated until they become harmonious. Every atom of the body is stimulated and aroused to action in perfect coordination with the Spirit. It is the Spirit that quickens. You cannot raise the bodily action into accord with spirit by the processes of mind for the Spirit is above the mind as the heavens are high above the earth.

11. The ten commandments are not the objectified law of God at all. In them Moses tried to lay down a law for mental and moral conduct but there is no such conduct outside the law of the Spirit and the consciousness of the activity of Spirit must be discerned as the only governing law. The statement, "As you stand one with Law, you *will not*" do these things, was the original intent, but has been translated, "Thou shalt not." If you are within the law of harmony you will not produce discords but to merely refrain from producing discords does not place you within the law of harmony. To refrain from discord merely involves doing nothing at all and surely this never would produce a musician nor would it express harmony. The active doing of the law produces effects commensurate with the law. Life is active, dynamic and not static. It is DOING TRUTH, not merely refraining from that which is not truth.

12. If you are in obedience to the Law itself you will automatically refrain from doing certain things

which are not included in the natural operations of the law. You do not do these thing if you follow the law, but in omitting these things you may not fulfill the law at all but only obey your own notions. "Thou shalt not," was the Mosaic law as Moses gave it out. These were the emanations of the Sephiroth or the Tree of Life. He veiled that fact and objectified it for the people but gave the Priests the real meaning in the Talmud.

13. When God spoke to Moses in a "loud voice" as it is given, it was not intended to convey the fact that He spoke with much noise. God is a "sound voice," which brings light into expression. That was Moses' statement. A "Sound Voice," not a "voice of sound." There is an important difference. If we have a "sound voice" that voice is One and will bring light into existence. It gives us that power. It may be out of noise completely or what we would designate as soundless. And that is what we are coming to today, the Soundlessness of sound. Then it is beyond noise completely and you pay no attention to noise because you are in Sound Voice or definite principle.

14. Soundness is wholeness and, when God spoke in a sound voice, He spoke in the completeness of Himself. It is like we often say of a person, "He put his whole self into what he said." It is only when the entire nature is aroused and operative that the voice is sound or that we speak with soundness. We do not speak partially or in any separateness but in complete oneness. When God said to Moses, "I am that I am and beside me there is no other," He was speaking in a "sound voice," for He excluded nothing from His proclamation but moved as a complete Unit. This is particularly illuminating regarding the discarded psychological idea that the

mind is a sectional or departmental thing made up of many operations. This is the hypnotism of unsoundness. The more differentiated, the more unsound becomes the mind. Study some of the people who are given to this departmental function of the mind, concentrating here and there and moving their minds about one section at a time. They are extremely unsound and are never safe within themselves nor are they safe to follow for they lead only into confusion. It may be a good way to build up a large following for a group of people who are unsound mentally are easily herded into organizations, but this ultimately becomes the greatest bondage, particularly to the one who thus deceives the people. Soundness is wholeness—Oneness. "I am God," spoken in the consciousness that you are one with the All and that the All is centered within you and that you move with and are included in the operations of the whole, is the only truly sound statement for it is complete. No structure is stable unless it becomes a unit and no man is stable until he is a complete unit in and with the Principle.

15. We cannot stop in our progress with organizations and systems either orthodox or metaphysical for they are sectional, sectarian, and teach a doctrine that is more or less involved with the idea of separations. They are only steps in the process of man's discovery of himself. We cannot stop at any point without becoming orthodox. That prevents further progress until we break away.

16. That is where so many people become mixed in affirmations and denials. Of course, many modern thought organizations become mixed up in that very thing when they begin to deny. They fasten to themselves a condition which does not exist and then, when they feel this false influence of their own mental reaction, they call it malicious-animal-mag-

netism. They begin to get into psychic influences again, being held there by their repetitions.

17. One is really not working properly when he denies. Denial separates us from Spirit for we stop to consider something that we designate as "not spirit." In Spirit there is no separation and, consequently, it is only man's separation through which he becomes involved in the psychic or phenomenal. Moses classified anything and everything in phenomena as a separation from Spirit. The orthodox churches evidently get into trouble because they allow a separation. They have built up a great image in the heavens, calling it God. There is a psychic determination there which they see, believing that this image talked to them instead of which it was their own voice talking to them through psychic influences. The voice of God speaks within man as Jesus taught. It is the Father within.

18. Christ's denial of limitation—Satan—was not a declaration of his non-existence but a simple letting go of the idea which was entirely false. He did not reckon with it at all.

19. Moses, in referring to the dividing of Heaven and Earth, evidently meant that the earth was the outer. In the Sanskrit there is a word which defines the Earth as the outer condition. That condition is to be overcome and that overcoming is in thought only. Moses meant to convey that Heaven and Earth should be complete and One always. He let go of Earth completely and then the One attitude of Principle stood forth. He knew fully that the form was a complete embodiment of Spirit as life.

20. That is what Job was trying to bring out when he said, "Yet in my flesh shall I see God." It even is expressed that way in the Upanishads. In everything bring forth the Christ Self and see reality in place of a differentiated physical body. The body

is radiant and pure spiritual substance and it will show forth this condition when the thought of its materiality is withdrawn and gives place to the truth that flesh in its true state is the radiant light of God through which and in which God is manifest in His spiritual perfection.

21. Flesh does not need to be spiritualized; it is already spirit in manifestation, just as water is oxygen and hydrogen in manifest form. The water is one in and with its source and is identical in nature with its source. To separate oxygen and hydrogen from water would be to disintegrate the water itself. "Your body is the temple of the living God" in exactly the same manner and, when reunited with its source, the body becomes pure and perfect as radiant light, the Light that was in the beginning and out of which all things were formed. That which makes the body appear to be something else is the clouded mentality that has imposed itself between the flesh and its true source. The body—Temple of the living God—has become a den of thieves, robbing the body of its true sustaining principle.

22. In the Lord's Prayer, "Our Father which art in Heaven" was not intended to convey the idea that heaven was elsewhere. Jesus meant what the original Sanskrit intended to convey, the everywhere-present inner peace and harmony. That is Heaven in its true meaning. The Kingdom of Heaven is among you. There is an inner meaning in the Lord's Prayer which cannot be given out except privately and orally. If man understood this inner meaning he would be in the Kingdom of Heaven. This involves completely surrendering what we have called the self and accepting the Self that is the only reality, which is the spiritual Self, for there is no other Self. Those who have attained follow this path and

enter into that which exalts the whole into Spirit. Such an one knows himself as God.

23. This is difficult for many to understand for they think of themselves only in terms of their conscious thought. All such thoughts must be discarded. The realization includes the conscious mind when the Christ mind has become the complete consciousness of the individual, for the conscious mind is then included in complete consciousness. All thoughts that we have embraced within our consciousness that are at variance with the Truth must be given up. That is what Christ meant when He said to "deny thyself." Give up your own estimate of yourself and accept yourself as you are in complete relationship to the whole. It is forsaking all conditions which appear outwardly in favor of the architectural design back of it all. The Christ mind is the God mind always.

24. When any individual attains to true knowledge of God his works will be completed instantly. If he would stand completely one with God, it would be finished instantly. Jesus said, "It is finished," and from then on went right on to other accomplishments. If we ourselves recognize perfection we become that perfection Itself. We need no other recognition. It is all God if we wish to put it that way.

25. That was the only thing which the people two thousand years ago had against Christ. They thought it "blasphemy" that He should consider Himself as God for their state of hypnosis could not fathom the mystery of His position, which is the true position of all men. But that was the only thing they had against Him. When we make that same statement before unillumined people, those steeped in ignorance regarding the true state of all creation, they accuse us of blasphemy today just as they did

Christ two thousand years ago. But why should we care? So long as we care what people think, just so long will we keep ourselves in subjection to the hypnotic spell of the earth. But one who is awakened never goes about making such outward statements to the profane world. One meaning of I am God is "I am silent."

26. The attempt to make God a trinity came through the idea of differentiation of the One. The reduction of all elements to the One element, or emanating energy, leads to the three in one or unity and directly to the true Trinity or Triad as one attribute of Being. This is the Holy Spirit, the Whole I, the Creative Spirit as complete action. The moment we project our thought to the Holy Ghost we are projecting our being to the complete Creative Spirit in action. It is the movement of the whole as a UNIT. When the Holy Spirit comes upon you, you are conscious that all action within and without is but the complete action of the Principle in its entirety without the slightest sense of separation or deviation. It is ONE action.

27. There can be no actual sin against the Holy Ghost. In the original text we find nothing about the expiation of sin. Man alone commits what he himself calls sin and man alone forgives sin. The son of man on earth has power to forgive sin. There could be no sin against the Holy Ghost for it is impossible for man to divide the indivisible or to actually separate the uni-action of the One. He only seems to do so. That is where the Divine Right of Kings comes from. If the King is in his Divine Right he can make no mistakes and man, as the King, could make no mistakes. This did not refer only to a certain king or family ruling over a nation but to man ruling over himself. When he rules over him-

self he becomes a King. Every man is a King when he knows himself as God and exercises his God Authority to completely subject every phase of himself to the One idea.

28. The interpretation of God speaking to individuals or groups of people as designating only that particular person or group is false. What God speaks to one man or one nation He speaks to all men and all nations, for He created of one blood all nations of men and He is no respecter of persons. But, from this false interpretation man has built up the idea of a racial or national God. This has resulted in religious wars and built up separate groups into nations. The orthodox churches, according to Dr. Lyman Abbot, have done more toward the retrogression of civilizations than any other influence because of their hatreds. The first intention in the presentation of God was that you look immediately to the Light which emanates from your own being and from the being of every individual as being ONE and the same light and that God equally manifests Himself to and through all beings in exactly the same sense without partiality or distinction. The moment you can project your vision to that light you are at once conscious completely, namely, in the Divine Consciousness, and there can be no separation there. With no sense of separation there can be no separation in creed or race or nation and hence, no strife or war.

29. Referring to the incident mentioned in *The Life and Teaching of the Masters of the Far East* where Emil separated the jackals that were fighting over the carcass of an animal, Emil said, "It is not the self that you see, but only the God-Self that does the work." He meant to convey that when you get away from the fear of the animal and project the

God-Self there is peace and harmony. And they came together and ate their meal in perfect harmony instead of fighting.

30. This is the theory back of our experience in walking through fire. The Masters told us afterward that we had raised our vibration to such an extent that there was no conflict between us and the fire. There was perfect harmony and oneness. We clearly saw the fire raging all around us but we felt no heat or discomfort. Our clothes were not even scorched. This experience has quite recently been duplicated in London by a young Hindoo Yogi under the severest scientific test conditions. Pictures of this incident were shown in America on one of the news reels and Edwin C. Hill, famous news commentator, wrote at some length upon the subject. Copies of this comment were mailed to 100 teachers conducting classes on these lessons.

31. The life of the Masters is simply the God life. They always put it, "Life is Light." "The moment we express Light, life emanates." If you live the Life, then you will Know and that knowing is complete. It is not a life of asceticism or apartness. It is a Life and Light in unity, in wholeness.

32. Anyone may break his seeming bondage to a condition that is not Godly by simply letting go of the bondage completely. That was our training from boyhood on. If a discordant condition came into our surroundings we let go of it completely. The Masters sometimes go for hundreds of days without eating. They are not bound in any way. But when they do not eat outwardly they do feed upon the Prana or spiritual substance that is all about them. They take in Pranic substance and it is assimilated for the direct and complete sustenance of the body. Plants feed upon Prana and when man uses the vegetables for food he takes in Prana also. He

can take it directly even more readily than the plants and vegetables do, if he will.

33. It would not be the part of wisdom for the Western world to discard the Bible in favor of the Bhagavad Gita. Our Bible is of greater importance to the Western world for we do not understand the Bhagavad Gita. The latter is best, however, for the East. The West could with profit read the Bhagavad Gita, as it would obviate the necessity of wading through the folklore and mistranslations of the Bible. The Bhagavad Gita has taken all that out. The Vedanta Philosophy in most instances is the best exposition of the teachings of the Masters. Many people get a more simplified thought and can assimilate these thoughts through the Vedas. Then they can go on to the Vedantic teachings.

34. The reason those of the West have difficulty in understanding spiritual things is that the Western consciousness has always been an evasion of Principle for the reason that they did not know what Principle meant. They even misled themselves, largely by the acceptance of their philosophers' teaching that Principle is an unknown quantity. The Master Mind knows what Principle is but so can we accept Principle and know what it means. We must accept the Goal toward which we are working or we do not work at all.

35. You cannot go into India with a Spirit of egotism, selfishness and design and get anything out of India any more than you can in these states get anything from these lessons, from the Bible, or any other source of Truth. There is nothing in Truth compatible with these attitudes. You get out of India whatever you take to India. It is not a matter of going into India at all. It is an ever present state is you can receive it.

36. It is not a matter of going to India, studying

the Bible, or the Bhagavad Gita. It is letting go of all these confusions that infest the mind and the up-set conditions resulting therefrom. Then one may get a great spiritual uplift from the Bible or any other source. We are beginning to see that we take from the Bible what we take to the Bible. The very determination to get the very meaning out of the book will open its secrets to us to some extent. If we read the Bhagavad Gita or any other book we must take the same attitude toward it. There is, of course, nothing in the Bible that is not interpreted in the Bhagavad Gita, the Mahabharata, and the Vedas. That is where all the knowledge that is con-tained in the Bible came from.

FOR THE TEACHER

Paragraphs 1 and 2. Perhaps the hardest thing for the average individual is to realize that God is the great Universal Scheme of creation and the point should be emphasized by the teacher and practiced by the student until this very fundamental fact in life has become a matter of individual reali-zation. Personality is an individual identity, while God is the Universal identity, the Universe as a single conscious identity, the sum of consciousness, power, love, life, and substance.

Paragraph 3. Man cannot escape the ultimate Unity that exists between himself and the Universal system for he is a part of that system. If a product of the Universal system, he must contain the potential-ities of the Universe and, by whatever name he des-ignates the Universe, he must also bear that name as well as its nature. One ray of light is just as truly light as a dozen of them, a million, a billion or all of them.

Paragraphs 4 and 5. It is not what man studies

but how he studies that is the secret of illumination; not what we know *about* a thing but *what* we know *of* it that makes the difference. As well try to classify and describe the size, shape, color, and density of seeds in an attempt to know Nature as to merely read the descriptions of God in the hope of knowing God. To know nature is to know it in its fullness, to see its growth on every hand, and to sense in some degree the force which produces it. Man must be still and know God in the same way; cease from descriptions and come to "feel after Him," if he would know the nearness, the power, the wisdom and substance that is ever moving within his own nature. This is the inner or secret doctrine.

Paragraphs 6 and 7. The same as paragraphs 4 and 5.

Paragraphs 8, 9 and 10. If God is ALL and man is created in His image and likeness, in what manner can man grow except in the enlargement of his consciousness to comprehend the greatness of his created state. He truly does not attain to anything but only in the discovery of that which already is. The point is whether he shall discover himself a little at a time or whether he shall discover the ultimate fact from the beginning. The wise of all ages have declared that the latter is the true way. "Know ye not that we are Gods and Sons of the Most High," is calling man back to his beginning, which is his perfection in and with God.

Paragraphs 11 and 12. If man is in a certain state of consciousness, he automatically does not express that which is its opposite. On the other hand, the elimination of certain modes of conduct does not produce an opposite state of consciousness. Action, and not inaction, is productive of results. It may be well, in a state of ignorance of the Truth, to refrain from error states of procedure but it is not this practice that leads to illumination. If you are not happy, you do not become so by merely refusing to act unhappy. If you are happy, on the other hand, you do not act nor look as one who is unhappy. This may be illustrated in many ways.

Paragraphs 13 and 14. Soundness is a matter of being complete, a complete unit. Soundness is without separation. A sound building or bridge is a structure that is made up of many units all bound together in a single unit. You would not think of a building made of many parts all separated as being a sound building. Soundness and wholeness are synonymous. The sound voice in this instance like the "sound" mind in a previous lesson refers to the Unified consciousness in action. No man is sound when he thinks of himself as a departmental being nor is his mind sound when it functions partially nor does he speak soundly when he voices but half the Truth. Truth is that which is true of God for God is all and God is One.

Paragraph 15. Wherever one group or race or nation segregate themselves as a chosen people, a distinct people, in some sense more directly related to or favored of God, they are not a sound people and their doctrines are never sound. God is no respecter of persons and His creation is all manifestation and they are all included impartially within himself. It cannot be that some people are not the chosen of God and others are the chosen of God. He created all men and therefore all people are the chosen of God. All people are God in manifestation just as all forms of plant life are the manifestations of nature. Equality is in the fact and outward equality is dependent upon the degree to which we have embodied through realization the universal Fact.

Paragraphs 16, 17, 18 and 19. Progress is made,

not through denial, but through the practice of habitually unifying all things with the Source. Unified with the Source, all things begin to manifest their likeness to the source and all appearance to the contrary disappears like ignorance in the presence of knowledge or shadows in the presence of light. To deal with fact is to dispel fancy. To work with fancy is to work with nothing and to accomplish nothing. To achieve something one must work with something. Something can never be made out of nothing.

Paragraphs 20 and 21. Whether your face is radiant with joy or clouded with sorrow, it is the same face but appears differently under different influences. The flesh is just as much manifest spiritual substance whether diseased or whole. Only the influence back of it needs to be changed. When the consciousness is expanded to its true state of Knowing the allness and oneness of God, the flesh automatically manifests this condition. It then is the return of the flesh to its true state as radiant Substance of the Word of God.

Paragraphs 22 and 23. The Kingdom of reality is all about us and the only trasition we need to make is to discard our notion that it is a remote place. All that God is is within, through, and around all men and man himself is included in that allness of God. There is nothing he can do about it but accept it and, in accepting it, living in harmony with it, he becomes aware of it.

Paragraphs 24 and 25. Cause and effect are one and to know the truth is to be instantly free. To know God as health is to be instantly well. To know God as supply is to be instantly supplied for the one presupposes or includes the other. There can be no separation.

Paragraph 26. We must come to the realization

that we are on the way back to the Father's house and not moving out away from it. We are progressing toward unity and not diversity. "Behold our God is One" is the song of the returning soul.

Paragraph 27. The close of the lesson should be self-explanatory but may be illustrated and enlarged upon as the leader is inclined or inspired. The whole point of the entire lesson is to get away from the formed opinions of man which have led him into the sense of separation and to bring him into the consciousness of his Oneness with the Universal whole, his likeness to the whole, and his access to all that there is in Infinite Space.

CHAPTER VIII

MAN

1. As in the preceding lesson it was impossible to study the nature of God without including man, so in this lesson it will be impossible to consider man without a further study of God. The one presupposes the other and they are inseparable. It is impossible to have a king without a kingdom and it is impossible to have a kingdom without a king. It is inconceivable to imagine a creator without his creation and certainly there could be no creation without a creator. They are but the two aspects of a single thing and without the one there could not be the other. Man is therefore an indispensable part of the Universal whole.

2. The Masters' thought of man is that he is in his true estate, always active, and is that through which Principle works or comes into manifestation. As they often put it: "Man projecting God; Man becoming God; the very Ideal of all Perfection; God selective but completely universal." Selection evidently came about through man's thought entirely. The Masters' thought is always that man must make the selection but in that he can never carry that selection out of the Whole or out of complete Principle or Spirit. And that means, of course, that man never does get away from his true Being or true origin. Every man is his own determining factor and that factor is always absolutely one with Principle, never separated and never dependent upon anything but Principle.

3. Man as man can never be a completely independent organism for he is inseparably united with

the whole. How could he remove himself out of infinity? He only imagines his isolation and that imagination is the sole source of his limitation. It is purely imaginary. The extent of his free will, or right of selection, cannot be carried beyond his imagination for, in fact, he is always united in and with his source. He only needs to rid himself of his vain imaginings and accept the inevitable and he is at once in his rightful place with the Universal system. He is king only in the sense that he has the privilege of carrying out the laws of the Kingdom and any king who disregards the laws of his kingdom does not remain king for long. Kingship is subject to the laws of the kingdom just as are the subjects and they are all units in a single system with the law superseding at all times. Only through the binding influences of the law does the kingdom remain an harmonious unit.

4. Man is triune but that trinity is never separated; it is always one. You understand all the attributes of man if you understand Man. The Greeks knew this and expressed it in their statement: "Man, know thyself." It is very evident that we have not begun to know ourselves, our importance, our Divinity; Divinity meaning, of course, that Man is a part of the whole and, as such, does know all and IS the All in manifestation.

5. There can be no triangle unless the three lines which form its sides are joined together in unity. Unless they are joined, there are only three lines and not a trinity at all. The trinity is dependent upon unity and their unity is the trinity. Man's business is not to dissect himself until he understands his trinity which would only be diversity. Man is progressing back to his Father's house and his progress in this direction is to discover himself as a unit, the

undifferentiated position which he occupies in the Universal scheme.

6. It is always possible for man to improve his consciousness to the point where he becomes God-like. That was the first thought in the Divine Right of Kings. It was not for the king to put himself up as the only Divine Ruler. All mankind should be Divine Rulers and rule as Kings but always with that expression of Love which is Service. Man stands One with his own Divinity and he is then of Service always. He never exalts himself above another. If he is an egotist, he destroys himself. He cannot be an egotist for long. Man's kingship arises from his sense of oneness with the whole and egotism arises from the sense that he is a separate ego within and of himself. Therefore, egotism is the greatest violation of the natural law of his being and produces the most disastrous results.

7. The translation of the Bible is in error where it says that man was created in the image of God. The "in" should be left out so that it reads, "Man IS the image of God." The word "in" does not appear in the original. And right here we find illustrated the major trouble with the orthodox conception. They all try to make God in the image of man and, in taking this attitude, they have created something that man cannot understand. Man can understand himself and, if he thinks of God as another personality like himself, only in larger proportions, he can never understand the true relationship that exists between himself and his source. But, if he understands that he is the universal individualized or that he is as an individual what God is universally, he has something which he can comprehend. If we leave out the "in," then man is the image of God. "I am God" is the great statement. It belongs to

man wholly. The image or likeness means the *exactness* in the old Sanskrit. The name and nature of cause and effect are always interchangeable for the one is essentially the counterpart of the other. The activity of cause is the life and form of the effect.

8. Some people quite naturally ask that, if this be true, why did Jesus always say that "I am the son of God," but never "I am God?" But this is only one of His statements. He said, "I and my Father are one." Then the translators, failing to understand the next sentence: "You are God as you present God, therefore I present God to you," left that completely out. Yet he said, "He that hath seen me hath seen the Father—God."

9. It should be remembered also that the name "I am God" was the unspeakable name to the Ancients. The theory was that it was never to be made as an audible statement. Its utterances were in the silence of their own souls and the only way it was ever to be voiced was in the natural radiation of authority, perfection, and power that emanated from this inner secret acknowledgment. "The Father who seeth in secret shall reward thee openly" is the thought. It is the Silent name of the Silent being of God, the inner and universal fact of all creation. In a previous talk we noted that another meaning to the statement, "I am God," is, "I am Silent." The "I am God" is the silent witness within the nature of man to a Universal fact. It is the name hidden within the name Jesus Christ and the secret name of every man that hath breath, and that name is the Breath.

10. It was considered blasphemous to make this audible statement and the people of Christ's time construed His statements as inferring that the unutterable NAME was applied to Himself. They condemned Him by their own inference regarding His

statements. But He was true to the law of the mystics and, though many of His statements inferred the fact, He did not utter it. "Thou hast said," "I am," "He that hath seen me hath seen the Father," all infer this same fact but, whatever He may have said in His heart, He is never credited with voicing the fact outwardly that, "I am God." The theory is that man IS the word himself and his own presence in the Universe is the spoken evidence and needs no further utterance. In the beginning was the Word— the word became flesh and when man appears in creation he IS that word unspeakable in sounds or syllables for he is the completed word as he stands. If I AM anything, the living embodiment of it, it is self-apparent and needs no further projection. Everything spoken from this consciousness is the authority of the Universe speaking with all power in heaven and in earth.

11. This was included in his statement that, "before Abraham was, I am," for man, as the formed aspect of God universal, always was and always will be God in evidence. He referred right back to the old Sanskrit law of Abraham: A-Brahm—light—a God. Then came David the Light-bearer, and one who bore the Light to all mankind, and Mary, the Preceptor of Creative Principle. You can bring it all down to the Ah Brahm, which means a Christ Child, the Union of all forces to present the Christ Ideal—man is God—to the world.

12. There should be no distinction made between Universal Man and individual man. No more can such a distinction be made than you can make a distinction between the circumference and the center of a sphere. There is where most of the trouble has arisen. You cannot divide man. Man is One, One with God. "I and my Father are one," was Jesus' true statement and He carried it still further

when He said: "When you pray, pray to the Christ of God; include yourself as the Christ."

13. The Masters do not talk of God *and* man. They are always one in their consideration. There is no separation whatever. There is no priest and a separate congregation. It is the congregation and the priest—all one.

14. Huxley and Darwin and their kind brought forth much evidence regarding mortal man and tried to establish his human or animal origin, hoping thereby to overthrow the creation theory. The Master's attitude is that of the Divinity of man; that he is of Divine origin, never separated from his Divinity in any way. Darwin and Huxley and the others built up their evidence so that there was no Head whatever and that is the reason for their failure. They failed completely to carry it through to Principle. The very last statement of Darwin was: "Beyond this which we have built up still remains Principle, which is a mystery to us." There is no effect without a cause and it is impossible to understand the effect without consideration of the cause.

15. That is why Emil says, "You can do these things just as easily as I do them," with true child-like simplicity. That was the reason for Jesus' great accomplishments, leaving out all egotism. "These and greater things shall ye do."

16. Man as a separate identity can do nothing. "I of myself can do nothing," said Jesus. In his isolated sense man is like a street car with the trolly off the wire. He has lost contact with all motivating power, which is the great underlying cause of all manifestation. The activity, which is cause, not only is the motivating power which produces but also is the effect itself and the only way man can keep going is to keep contact with that which projected him in the first place. "It is the Father within me, He doeth the

works." Cause must always be the motivating force within the effect, for the effect could not propel itself.

17. On this trip to date we have seen many races very different in appearance and custom from each other. The Masters see it all in the light of one consciousness. If we think of them as differing phases of consciousness we are apt to establish for ourselves a separation from that One. The only difference is in the outer for all are motivated by the same inner ideal, which is the Christ, or the I AM God of each one. We must evaluate all men from this point if we would escape the differences that appear outwardly. When this inner becomes the without then there can be no outward difference, hence no strife, no greed, no war. There are many seeds and bulbs but when each has fulfilled itself in outward form it is all one harmonious Nature.

18. It is from this point of view that the Masters look upon reincarnation. They say it is not necessary. It is a human hypothesis only. They say that if there is a light placed in the center of the room the best way to reach that light is to go straight to it. Why circle around it time after time? If you go directly to that light and pick it up and incorporate it, you are through with all reincarnation and karma completely. It is only man's failure to go direct to the central point or fact of life that keeps him in the "wheel of incessant grind." If he will accept that central fact, which is the light that lighteth every man that cometh into the world, he will have arrived and all his going round and round will have ceased, it will have come to an end.

19. All of these great problems that afflict the minds of man are completely overcome when he lives the life of the Masters or the life of his own mastery, the true inner Self. Jesus' firm statement

was that the Truth makes you free. Man gets rid of the idea that he is not God by refusing to accept the negative statements. The statement, "I am God," held habitually as the secret fact within his own nature, frees him from the negative statement that he is not God. It is always better to state the Truth than the untruth.

20. Even your ability to analyze the "I AM" is a direct spiritual evidence of Divinity. If it were not there to analyze you could not analyze it, nor would it occur to you to even attempt an analysis. It is only necessary to accept that Divinity with no negative thoughts or statements regarding it, to be One with it. Analysis, and all efforts to confine it to formalities, keep you from it. Even in mechanics we produce a thing and then account for it afterwards. All attempts to analyze it first only indicate its impossibility. This is true of every progressive step even in our material advancement. How much more should this same procedure apply with things entirely beyond our present system of human reason. The airplane was never accepted as a possibility by the world until it actually flew. A first analysis said it could not fly. Now we have an infinite amount of explanation as to how and why it is so. Facts must always come first and they may be accounted for later.

21. If one is overly cautious and is not fully awake to himself, this may seem like laying hold of your Divinity by means of blind faith but that is not necessary. But, if you take it wholly on blind faith, you have made a separation again and would never get to the goal. It is far better to say "I can" and then go right on to "I AM." "I can" is the potential fact, but "I am" is its fulfillment in your consciousness. Jesus said, "I am the way, the truth and the life." You can never be that which you are not nor

can you be anything but what you ARE. If you can become anything, as you put it, you ARE that. It is really not a matter of becoming, it is a matter of Being. Because you accept the "I can't" attitude in any condition or circumstance, you have accepted a division. Jesus said you could not compromise with sin, you cannot deviate from the fact and express that fact.

22. When Jesus considered the suggestion that He turn the stones into bread He realized that the stones were already in existence and in manifestation and He did not need to change the stones into bread as He could stretch forth His hand and the bread was there. "What ought to be IS," is the teaching of the Masters. If He needed bread, He did not need to concern Himself with the stones. He knew that if there was a need for bread it was already in existence and all He needed to do was to give thanks for it.

23. It would be impossible for man to need anything if it were not already in existence. Could you need air if there were no such thing in existence? The need indicates the fact and all one needs to do is to let go the sense of need and accept the fact implied in the need that it is already in existence. That which ought to be IS. This is true of what we refer to as the limitation of the physical body. This is an hypnotic influence of the mind wholly. It has no basis in fact at all. Man brought the sense of material into existence and not the body. The "mortal" body is the hypnotic body and, when man wakes from this state of hypnosis, all this experience will be to him just a nightmare. He wakes to dream no more. If he feels the need of a radiant spiritual body, void of limitation and expressing the glorious Light Body that is his perpetual dream, this is the foreshadowing in his consciousness of his fully awak-

ened state. The thought, the need, the desire is the evidence of the fact that such a state already exists for him and his only achievement is in accepting its existence. This IDEAL state IS the true estate of man.

24. This body does not need to be spiritualized. It is already spiritual but man's false beliefs about it have shut his mind to its radiance and limitlessness. Spirit is always Spirit. Man creates the materiality. There is but one body and that body is Spiritual. It is the Temple of the Living God and God is in the Temple; let all the earth rejoice before God. If you call the body material, it is denying God and profaning the Temple. If you call the body or any true condition material, you are denying God. You are worshiping a material condition more than you are worshiping God. That is how you get into hypnosis. The moment that you deny God you are in a hypnotic influence and the moment you see the body as material you are in a hypnotic influence wherein you deny God.

25. The body is an instrument through which to express God. It is the greatest known instrument to express Spirit. It is brought here definitely for you to present God every moment. Not to present materiality, or hypnosis, or psychism; not to present phenomena, but to present Spirit. We are God. We cannot make a separation and, if we refuse completely all separation, we would be out of all material conditions and all psychic phenomena. This is how man comes to know and understand the One Presence and One Power. It is all One, One Power, One Reality. And everything works and operates under that One Power and One Presence according to its own law. It is not adulterated with any other notion but moves as Itself in its own complete field.

26. You cannot make any differentiation be-

tween the individual soul and the Universal Soul or the Over-Soul. That is, you cannot draw apart. As Jesus said: "That is putting asunder God's Principle." There is a generalization under which every human being works but that is an assembly of Universal Units. There is individual identity but you are one in an assembly of Universal units. So is every human being. All are one and the same, operating under the same harmonious conditions. Always in harmony. Not differentiating from harmony but assembling in harmony.

27. A God-man is a genius, Christ standing forth, man expressing God without reserve or restraint. The reason children are often found to express what we call unusual genius is only that they have not yet been hypnotized with the idea of limitation possessed by those about them. If they continue to escape this hypnotic spell they remain geniuses, or the Divine Self, throughout the earth experience. They do not experience the earth, they experience their universality and the Christ-Self always.

28. To be the Master, the Self, is our great work always. The Masters of the East never say anything less than that America contains 130,000,000 Masters. That means that everyone is a Master. That is, of course, true of the whole world. It is worldwide to them. Every individual IS a Master. Even man's limitation is proof to them of his mastership for only a Master could make himself to appear that which he is not.

29. The greatest presentation of Principle is what the world commonly calls the appearance of an Avatar or Savior. The acclamation, "Behold the King," means that man lives closely to Principle, not that a great personage is coming but one who lives closely to Principle. Others acclaim him the

Avatar or genius. He is but one man standing forth in the character that is potentially the Kingship of every man. Only he had the courage and conviction to take himself for what he IS. "The King can do no wrong," for the moment any wrongdoing enters in, the moment a man accepts himself as less than the King, less than his Divinity, he has thereby become less than his own Kingship. The King is the Master, the Genius, expressing himself in his true nature, and therein is his Kingship. He rules himself, for he is in his own Kingdom. The Kingdom of heaven is within. This Kingship which he is is also his message to all men. Not that he is King but that every man is a King within his own kingdom, a master over himself and his own environment, for he lives in reality; he lives as he is and in a realm of things as they really are. This is the Path which He shows to others or the life He lives becomes the path of life for all mankind.

30. His appearance or reappearance upon the earth is not dependent upon any condition of spiritual unfoldment for He is that Thing in its fullness. He steps right through all unfoldment and lives one with Spirit always. The idea of unfoldment belongs to man and his own theories. The Master has only accepted the state in which he was created from the beginning, the Image and likeness of God, the embodied nature of Infinity or Divinity.

31. These illumined souls or Masters or Avatars do not write books because of the utter simplicity of their teachings. There is nothing to be said or written about "I AM," for it is complete within itself. The life they live is its own revelation, it is the book of life revealed, opened as a scroll and needs no testimony but itself. When you reach the top you pull the stairs up with you. Therefore, there is no teaching to give. There is but the fact of life, the

Truth of life revealed as itself, as it always has been and always will be. Steps as man would teach and write about are but degrees to which he lets go of falsity. He had better let it all go at once for, to "think yourself there is to be there," as the Masters say.

FOR THE TEACHER

Paragraphs 1 and 2 bring us back to the eternal Unity of all things and the inseparable relationship which exists between God and man. This point cannot be stressed too strongly for the illumined have always taught that there is not God and Man, there is only God. Man is a unit in and with the Infinite and, as such, contains within himself all the potentialities of Infinity and all of Infinity is accessible to him. Man is ONE in and with the Universe.

Paragraphs 3, 4 and 5. Man cannot be an independent organism in the Universe for his whole being is dependent upon the source from which he came and his mastership is wholly dependent upon taking his place in the Universe. This is the prodigal returning to his Father's house, that point where he dwells and lives in relationship with his source. He can be nothing of himself.

Paragraph 6. The Divine right of Kings, the divinity of man, lies in exercising the power that his position in the Universe presents; not in controlling others but ruling within his own kingdom, himself, under the law that governs all things. "Greater is he that ruleth his own spirit than he that taketh a city." Inward rulership is the Mastery of the Masters. The Master does not prate his mastership. Christ did not attempt to reveal his own divinity but to acquaint all men with their own divinity.

Paragraph 7. Man is the personification of the

Divine Principle or the individuality of the Universe. Man is the personal God or the embodiment of the Universal and Impersonal.

Paragraphs 8, 9 and 10. The "I am God" does not belong to the sense which man has of himself but the projected and ideal man of the Oversoul. For this reason the wise never have proclaimed to the world that "I am God." They knew it within themselves, acknowledged it before God, but before the world they became the expressed fact and let it stand for itself. This is the ark of the covenant, the silent acceptance of the secret relationship which exists between creator and created.

Paragraphs 11, 12 and 13. Brahm was one name for God and a Brahm means a God. Before I was God individual, I was God Universal, for the one is dependent upon the other. They are one and the same thing, always have been so and always will be so. "I am with you always."

Paragraph 14. There can be no material accounting for man, for matter does not produce intelligence, nor intelligence attain to spirit. Spirit is cause and, as cause, it endows its creation with the power of thought and being or expression. There is no determination for anything except as the expression of Spirit or cause.

Paragraphs 15 and 16. The habit of attributing certain powers to others and denying them for oneself is the practice that forever keeps man from arrival at his own mastery. The thought should always be that "if he has achieved I also may achieve, for what is potential with one is potential within all. Man's arrival at the height of achievement is only the revelation of myself." He has attained or manifested that which I AM should always be the thought.

Paragraph 17. To see all men as the embodiment

of the same potential character, to see all men as the Christ, is to instantly dissolve all differences for things equal to the same thing are always equal to each other. This is the secret of the new order of things where peace and goodwill will be established in the earth. Only in the sense of difference can greed and strife develop.

Paragraphs 18 and 19. Can we not see once and for all that this running to and fro in the earth is entirely beside the pont and that it is all due to the fact that we avoid the main issue? To accept the central fact of life is to become entirely free from all those ideas and processes which are less than the fact. If one arrives, he is free from the processes of arriving, and man must learn to begin his life at the beginning, which is God.

Paragraph 20. "What man can conceive he can achieve," is an old adage but it has a meaning even above that for what he can conceive, he IS. It is as impossible to conceive a thing that is not already a fact as it would be to breathe if there were no air. The function within the nature of man is indication of that fact with which the function deals. It would be impossible for the cry to originate in the nature of man if there were not already the supply, the completed fact in the nature of God. And the fact precedes the desire in man for the desire is the recognition of the fact and its existence.

Paragraph 21. Caution is the retardant; boldness is not presumptuous when dealing with facts. It is merely accepting that which has already been proved in the lives of others as equally true of yourself.

Paragraph 22. It is not necessary to convert one form into another for the other is already there just as truly. It is training the mind to know this, to work in the realm of reality, and not always to be trying to make something over into another form of reality. Two plus two equals four and three plus three equals six and it is not necessary to try to make one over into the other. They are both manifest facts already.

Paragraph 23. A continuation of the same truth.

Paragraph 24. You are not making your body over or changing your world, you are only recognizing reality and discarding all false notions about everything.

Paragraph 25. The body is already the temple of the living God. It needs to be freed of the money changers, dealers in comparative values, the ideas of individual profit. The Lord of Hosts and King of Kings must be admitted into the consciousness so it may express through the body what IT IS.

Paragraph 26 is obvious.

Paragraph 27. The Master, the Genius, the God man are all one and the same thing and this is but man being MAN, being Himself, void of the opinions of race experience.

Paragraph 28. There is no work for man but being the Self for when the Self appears he enters the realm of completion. He is forever busy, however, for he has only then begun to work.

Paragraph 29. The Divine self of each man is the Avatar, the Savior of his own being, but he must accept his Savior, be that SELF.

Paragraph 30 is a continuation of Paragraph 29.

Paragraph 31. Man arriving at his divine estate is the book of life opened before all men as a scroll, the seals of the book are broken and man as he is appears.

CHAPTER IX

LIFE

1. The "Life of the Masters" is Life the way they live it. They live life as it is. Their attitude toward life is that it is the action of the One Principle, never divided or separated from its source. They live life true to that Principle and thus, they show the way for all to live true to that Principle of Life. To them life is not a theory of existence, it is an actual fact, a fact with no beginning and no ending. The individual must come to this one attitude of living which comes through the one attitude of thought toward it. They say that it is God expressing through the human individual, the highest and most select channel through which life manifests. Thus life can manifest in a more select activity or complete form through the human individual.

2. They see the One Life emanating in and through all things. In fact, everything that has being is of the very essence of this one life. The human being only postulates life as beginning when this form came into existence through which life could manifest, when in reality life existed prior to the form and even produced the form. That was only the beginning of form and not the beginning of life. Life has always existed and it will always exist. If we select life, or measure it in some specific manner, we may manifest it in that select form. It, of itself, flows freely and universally without cessation or limitation. Consequently, we may select and use that life force, as we would say, in a degenerate way where we do not allow it to manifest in its greatest degree or potency. The human being can

use it in that way but it is only the fault of the individual or the group and is not in any way the fault of life itself. Life, if we will allow it to be so, is the all-knowing, all-seeing and all-being activity of Principle. If we allow it to flow through us in its highest attributes, we cannot help but live by expressing these very conditions which are in its nature.

3. When we accept life as it is, the body becomes a living, breathing unit, expressing life to its fullest degree. The reason that it does not express to its fullest degree is because of the limitation which the human unit puts upon life. We turn it in many ways whereas, in reality there is but one way and that is life in its fullest expression.

4. The Hindoo thought of the three score and ten years of man's allotted time is that this should be the time of man's greatest accomplishment. At seventy, man should reach his majority or his greatest realization of life. Then, they say that man should live five times as long as it takes him to reach his majority. The Western world has completely missed this meaning.

5. Man should not be limited even to that space of time. They do not limit man at all. If you accomplish three score years and ten, you should accomplish all life and all conditions of life. That is not putting a limitation upon it. Five times is not a limit because you can make it five thousand times if you wish. Man does, usually, after he has reached seventy, begin to think more along Spiritual lines. This tendency begins to develop after forty.

6. When Jesus said," In the midst of life ye are in death," he was not warning the people that they are always face to face with death. He expressed astonishment at the condition of death among men when they lived in the midst of life continually. Man only

needs to live life as it is, accept it as it is, and not measure it by years and material standards. You are eternal life right here and now if you would only recognize it. But life is not something that is to come; it is here at this very moment in which you live. People separate themselves from the life which IS by trying to live in the past or the future. But the past is dead and the future is only born in the eternal now. All the life of Infinite Space moves at this very moment and whosoever will may drink of that life freely. You do not even need to try to live eternally for, if you are alive at all, you are in eternal life and all you need to do is to so live it. Forget the past, do not try to project yourself into the future for NOW is the only acceptable time. You are in eternity NOW.

7. It is held as a theory that the masters often receive their enlightenment in the springtime of their thirty-seventh year. But there is no limitation except that put on it by the individual. Thirty-seven in the Sanskrit means Eternity because you can repeat the thirty-seven or the seven as many times as you wish, since it completes the octave. It does not necessarily refer to years at all but to the extension of the individual consciousness into the Life Universal or into its true spiritual expression.

8. Instead of the awakening which comes to man being a matter of years, it simply means that he becomes mature in himself and many of the ideas given him by the race are nullified in this maturity of soul. False ideas are crowded out of consciousness as the swelling bud pushes back the leaves that enfold it and then the inner character stands forth. It is not intended as a second childhood when the old man becomes childish but he becomes the child capable of entering the Kingdom. He loses the sense of importance in respect to the material world and

127

its many problems and begins to live in the realization of life as it is unfolding in him.

9. Our scientists are telling us that there is not a human body in existence over seven years old. That is, the cells are completely renewed every seven years. That is not putting a limitation on life, because life moves in cycles and not years and you cannot limit a cycle. It has no real beginning and it does not come to an end. It is the eternal process of fulfilling itself and the eternal renewing process going on within the instrument through which it expresses. Life does not end at seven nor does life ever end. Life is eternal. There is not a thing in existence that does not have life. All planets are alive. Everything has life. The rock has life.

10. When we express life in its true and unlimited natural expression, we can and will be our own books and teachers. Also, if you can appreciate the fact that all of the cells of the body are renewed every seven years, you will begin to realize the possibilities of life. If you will keep your mind continually renewed as the processes of life unfold, you will begin to see that life might just as well go on cycle after cycle, or continuously. The buds on a tree are just as young whether that tree be old or young. And the bud has the completed tree within itself. That tree does not grow old except through the limitation of years that man puts upon it. Nothing grows old except through the concept that man places upon it. The Scriptures teach that he was given dominion over all things. Life can not be measured by years and we should cease to attempt it. Life can be measured only by itself and life is eternal, everpresent, and limitless. It is the vital action of the entire system called the Universe or God. Man places the limitation on time by delineating time for his own convenience and that delinea-

tion does not restrict life or time by any means, except so far as his manifest possibilities are concerned.

11. This is, in all probability, the only plane and the only condition where death is recognized. Christ said: "Let the dead bury their dead." The true man places no limitation on time. The mortal man alone does this. We get into the mortal or physical only by the placement of time or the designation of time for man's convenience. We have gone on and built up a great world of supposition, a great barrier of supposition between ourselves and the true condition. We have been led to see that barrier as insurmountable. Consequently, many of our philosophers have said that life is unknowable and could not be solved. Of course it cannot be solved when you put up barriers against it.

12. The life of the masters is not passed in what the world would call gainful occupations. They have passed that. Their life is of Service always, many of them going about from place to place assisting in what we would look upon as material ways, with material things. We have never seen them accepting anything from anyone for themselves. We have seen them give out food and clothing and supplies of all descriptions. A Master is a servant. If he is a Master, he is above the world and the world can give him nothing. He must reverse the process and he in turn gives to the world.

13. In this service they do not seem to seek out people nor do people necessarily seek them out. The Masters come across those in need in their everyday life as they go about among the people. They also assist in a universal attitude as well through thought and the projection of thought. They also project conditions of perfection into the whole world. Of course, where an individual does appeal to them for

help there is always the assistance ready. We have seen them not only assisting the individual but great groups of individuals. But, even while they are going on with that work, they are evidently sending out emanations to the whole world which in time will cure the condition they are working on locally. They say it is necessary to work locally to assist people to a better understanding and, in many cases, a better understanding comes through the furnishing of food and clothing or a better condition in which to live.

14. The Masters do go out among the people and the people do appeal to them for help very often and the condition which they are under is corrected almost immediately. The help given is only to show a better way to accomplish than that which they are using at the time. They do not go out and preach and proselyte at all. They walk among the people and the people who recognize them may ask for assistance in any way they wish—for healing, food, raiment, or shelter and they receive it. But they are shown that they, themselves, do it and not the Masters. It is not what the Masters have that they receive but the people themselves have built up that which is brought to them through their own attitude of thought; not what someone else has but what they have and what belongs to them. It does not necessarily follow, however, that you must appeal in order to get assistance.

15. The statement that the servant is worthy of his hire does not mean that one may commercialize healing. That means that the individual who thus serves is worthy of a higher life, worthy to become a Master and not a servant. Of course the Master is the greatest servant, for his entire life is spent in service, for that is the field in which he works and expresses his mastership.

16. In the matter of food, the Masters consume far less than we do. We have known them to eat no more than three grains of rice a day but they take in enough pranic substance to support their bodies for long periods if necessary. They masticate their food thoroughly. They can chew these three grains of rice all day and, by the time they have finished, they have taken enough prana to last their bodies at least twenty-four hours. They have no set time for eating for they do not work with time as men measure it. They eat whenever they feel like it. We have never known them to recognize meal hours as we recognize them. They can go without food completely for hundreds of days.

17. As far as we know they take very little sleep, not in excess of two hours a day, and they are conscious during these two hours. It is a well known fact that you can get along without sleep, if you know how to live without wasting your energies or contracting your consciousness through separating yourself from the Universal energies. The Western world and the way they live causes sleep to become more or less a condition brought about by, as we say it, a toxic state of the body. The toxic condition overcomes to a great extent the rebuilding process of the body and thousands of people are in that toxic state instead of being in a true condition of sleep. When Jesus said, "Awake thou that sleepest," he meant to arise from that comatose condition and then you are out of the influence to which you have become subject.

18. The Western world consumes at least ten times as much food as the body needs and then consumes energy to digest that food. That energy which is used to handle this nine-tenths of the surplus food that we take unnecessarily could be used much more effectively to build up the body. It is a well

known fact that today the Western world eats at least ten times as much food as is healthful. If we would take life direct or energy direct from the ethers, we would be adding energy to our bodies all of the time instead of giving it out to assimilate food. It would go directly to every organ of the body and rebuild and renew it.

19. It is not necessary that one be with a Master or contact a Master in any sense to understand life and its possibilities. Life is perfectly understandable at every corner of the earth. It is Omnipresent and anyone may contact it if he will turn his attention in that direction and get away from the mere forms which life uses and through which life expresses.

20. If you will take the simple attitude that all the life that you can live is LIFE and begin to exalt life, you will then be doing what you would do if you were living with them. There is nothing phenomenal regarding their life at all. Usually people going to them look only for phenomena. If we live life, we cannot help but understand life. Life is a process of inward force working itself out into outward form. It is the vital principle of the Universe animating all space and all form.

21. So many people have the notion that the Masters lay down certain rules for your daily practice, a certain daily regime of mental and physical exercises, but this is not so. There are many who lead out with this sort of teaching, of course, to the point where the student recognizes that he himself is a Master. Then the way is opened to meet the actual Master. The moment that man gets into his mind that there is any life to live other than the One life, he is out of harmony completely. The difficulty is with his mental application always. Man did not fall and die spiritually, he simply got himself out of harmony with life and this resulted in all his diffi-

culty. The moment life becomes hard, it is not life. That individual is out of life just to the degree that any inharmony develops and this state should be a warning for him to get back into life as it is.

22. Children are happy because they live life abundantly. They put no limitations upon life whatever. The moment we put limitation upon life we cease to live abundantly. There is not a limiting condition in life. Life could not limit itself. It could not be kept away except through your own attitude of thought toward it. No two individuals have the same vision of life. It is quite often illustrated in this way:It is said that only children and sages are happy because the child has not developed a material sense of value and the sage knows that the material has no value. To them form is not the point of consideration but living life.

23. One man may look at life through a very narrow opening in a wall. That person says, "I see all of life." The view may face a hill where there is nothing but rocks. The next may see trees; the next one sees animated forms moving about. If we look through but one small opening, we soon hypnotize ourselves into believing that there is no other life within the great expanse of the Universe of life. If we would take this attitude alone: see the Universe as embodying and expressing the One Infinite life, then we would expand our vision to take in all of life and there would be no limitation whatever for us.

24. The Masters never take conscious life. It is not necessary to take conscious life because man can assimilate into his consciousness all of the life elements, bring them into existence in himself, live them, and be always one with them. Consequently it is not necessary to take conscious life at all.

25. Many people ask the question why it is that

the people of India are afraid of the lower forms of life. Not all people in India are masters, even though they have been taught that there is but one life. They do not see all they have been taught any more than Americans see or live all they have been taught.

There are only a few of the lower classes who are bound in this way because they have been taught to worship these conditions. It is thus that they fear them.

26. And why do the Masters not raise the people out of that condition? How could they raise you out of a condition if you would not accept that raising? They cannot inject their own minds into you. They can only show you the path which they have traveled. If you will not see that path you must make your own until you are ready for a better way. All of the higher castes, even the great Maharajas, work for the better condition in India but they cannot do the overcoming for the masses nor transform them into higher beings. That is the work of the individual always.

27. It is a misconception to think that the Masters live an ascetic life. We have never found them so living. You will find them in a loin cloth or in the highest walks of life! You will not find them isolating themselves at all. There are a few, a very few compared to the whole, living in seclusion in order to give out more fully to the whole world certain conditions for betterment. But they are only groups who come together for that specific purpose. They do not live an ascetic life at all.

28. You may see a Yogi living an ascetic life for a certain time for a certain purpose only but then, they never allow asceticism to become hypnotic. Yogi means living for a great experiment. Many of

the so-called "holy men" of India live a complete ascetic life but usually they are beggars and not Masters. A great many of them are as dirty and as filthy as anything you can imagine. They are leeches on humanity and nothing else. But they are not the Masters. Just because a man goes about saying mantrams, or sitting in Samadhi, he is not thereby a Master.

29. We have never known of one of these who has reached a high accomplishment begging of anyone but they are giving all of their time to the betterment of humanity. They do not beg anything to give away even. They have, as they put it, all that they want and to spare always. They do not go around and beg for others to give. They do not organize charitable institutions. They go out and assist all of the time, separating themselves by their accomplishments. There are thousands of people in India who are giving out continually and yet, we have never known any of them to take a penny from anyone. The beggars who call themselves "holy men" are such only by their own designation. They have nothing to do with the Masters.

30. Life is always a matter of giving. To draw on the Universal life that flows freely throughout infinite space is the privilege of anyone and his way of living life should be to receive from this source and then give it out to all who are around him, inspiring them to seek life where he has found it. This is not only the work of the Masters, but it is the work all men should be doing. This is living life as it should be lived and is really the only life there is. To merely receive from those about you is not life at all but a constantly contracting existence. To seek life from the material world is to lose it.

FOR THE TEACHER

Paragraph 1. It should become evident to the mass of humanity that life as revealed by the illumined has always been portrayed in its universal and eternal aspect. That life which is manifest in form is only the outcropping of the vital essence that fills infinite space. Life is not confined to a period of expression through form but is and forever remains the movement of the creative force that produced form in the first place and that form was produced for the sole purpose of affording it expression. No one lives truly until he knows that life is moving in and through him and eternally seeking a fuller, freer, richer expression always.

Paragraphs 2 and 3. Life being universal, it is universally expressed in every form, and when the sense of separateness disappears from the mind of man he may enter more fully into its activity and align himself more completely with its purpose. Only in the human consciousness do complications seem to develop and life and consciousness are so inseparably united that before man can realize life in its fullness he must expand his consciousness to see and live life as it is. Only his mental reactions to the appearance keep him from this fuller life.

Paragraphs 4, 5, 6, 7 and 8. The text of these paragraphs shows clearly that it is the period during life when man's outward thought, his thought developed through his material contacts, so greatly interferes not only with his life but with his capabilities generally. It is this period of false estimates of life, his world, and himself that impedes his entire existence and it is only prior to this state and occasionally following it that man seems to enter into the real joy of living. The genius is one who seems to a degree to escape this period of thought oppression;

one who has the courage or fortitude to go his own appointed course and not let the world thought of limitation hinder him. The reason man, in his later years, seems to live a more spiritual life is that the false run down like an eight-day clock and then his true nature asserts itself. Had this consciousness been preserved through the years of oppression, his body would not have been sapped of its vital forces and his greatest years of usefulness would have been extended indefinitely.

Paragraph 9. The age of the body is not designated by the span of years which we call life. The body is forever renewing itself and the cells and tissues which form the body are constantly being replaced through a perfectly natural process. It is the pattern under which this building process is forced to operate that gives the body its condition of age. We should be continually renewing our minds in accordance with the truth of life and then the pattern for the renewing processes of the body would be such that a more perfect and vital body would be the result.

Paragraph 10. Man is the book of life, the law of God. The governing principle of life is written in his inward parts, and this period of existence should be a process of self-discovery and self-expression. In the unfoldment of man's own nature he learns the secrets of his own being. Study yourself at first hand, the deepest longings of your own inner nature, watch them unfold and you will understand.

Paragraph 11. Sin, according to the Scriptures, is the cause of death. Sin is every thought and feeling that is out of harmony with the purposes of life. These thoughts and feelings make up the opposition to life as it would express itself through the flesh. To remove the obstruction would be the remedy, of course. Instead of perpetuating a consciousness that deprives the body of its sustaining power, thereby separating the body from consciousness in death, one should die to the false consciousness. "Forgetting the things which are behind, pressing forward."

Paragraphs 12, 13, 14 and 15. Life is a matter of progress and not profit as we construe it. Profit is contingent upon our progress and our progress is determined by the kind and quality of our expression. Expression should not be the constant projection of our own limited opinions but living true to the deepest impulses are always true. Only when we descend to the plane of what we call necessity or expediency do we begin to violate our inward sense of what is right.

Paragraphs 16, 17 and 18. "Man shall not live by bread alone." Only enough food is required to supply material for the natural reconstruction of man's body. What is more than this is but giving the functions of the body an excess of labor. One should feed more and more upon the substance that moves in the creative principle of his being and then he would find real nourishment. As food is supplying material for body building, sleep is consuming energies that have been wasted during our periods of false living.

Paragraphs 19, 20, 21. We must learn to contact our good at its source. What we are seeking does not come from another and it will do no good to contact Master or teacher unless we thereby are inspired to seek that in ourselves which he represents to us. "Not everyone that saith unto me Lord, Lord, shall enter in, but He that doeth the will of my Father."

Paragraph 22. The values of life are to be found in the Soul, the Real Self, the inner Master, and not in the world. The world has only the value imparted to it by the awakening of true consciousness.

Paragraphs 23, 24 and 25. Seek to find life as it is in its great universal movements which are revealed in your nature through your own highest ideals and deepest longings. Only when we measure life in our own limited ideas does it become limited in its manifestation through us. Depend upon the Life Universal for supply.

Paragraph 26. Man's individual right to expression cannot be violated in the true processes of life. It is by our own effort that we rise and not by the efforts of others. Vicarious living without effort upon our part is destructive to our own character and well-being.

Paragraphs 27 to 30. Life is action, self-expression, giving. It is as necessary to give in order to live as it is necessary to exhale in the processes of breathing. One should receive from his source and then give of that source in his highest expressions. One first receives from any principle by taking it into his consciousness and then he expresses it in outward performance. This is equally true in the processes of life. To receive without giving or to give without receiving is to make life static through surfeit or exhaustion. To receive from your source and express what you have received in manifesting your greater capabilities is the way of life.

CHAPTER X

THE UNIVERSE

1. The Universe is the sum total of all things visible and invisible that fill infinite space. The Universe is the great whole, composed of all its parts. It might be said that the Universe is another name for God for He identified himself as "I am that I am and beside me there is no other." It is the sum of all life, all substance, all intelligence, all power. In it is contained all knowledge for it is Omniscience. It is the sum of all power for it is Omnipotence. It is the sum of all substance for out of it are all visible things formed. It is all Love for it is bound together in a single system and operates as a single unit. Love is the integrity principle or the binding principle which maintains the universe as a unity and keeps all its operations moving in perfect harmony and regularity.

2. The Masters think of the Universe as the univerality of all things, with every condition and circumstance a portion of that Universe or universality. A person may become separate or he may separate himself in thought from that Universe. Then he becomes a unit which in thought only is separate or apart. But instead of being apart he is still a part of the Great Universe. One may become so separated in thought from that Great Universality that he surrounds himself with apartness or the sense of limitation. He may withdraw so far from that Universality in thought that he falls or descends in his capacities and, thus, he is in a measure separated from that Universality in which he really belongs.

3. Of course it is impossible to separate oneself

or completely exclude oneself from that Universality, for that would be to reduce himself completely to a state of non-existence. But, when he returns to that Universality of Principle in consciousness, he is one with it and is lifted up into a higher state of capability. That is illustrated in the parable of the Prodigal Son. He wandered in many lands and spent his substance but there was a welcome in the Father's house upon his return. Even the brother who had stayed at home was jealous of the reception. But the Father knew that the reception was always there. It is an allegorical picture of how one can extensively separate himself from Universality by thought and recognize that he is feeding on the husks and yet when he decides to return to the Father's house there is everything there for him. In fact, the Father was not even conscious of the separation. It did not matter how far away the son had wandered.

4. All sense of apartness, isolation, limitation is only fictitious for it is impossible for separation to be an actual fact. If it were possible the Universe could not be a whole. David illustrated this fact in his realization that it was impossible to get out of the Universal System when he said: "Whither shall I flee from thy Spirit," and whether he went to the uttermost bounds of the earth, ascended into heaven, or made his bed in hell, that same Universal relationship awaited him. You cannot divide the indivisible.

5. It is the same when death occurs. Many feel that there is a separation there, but in reality, there is no such thing. We can be just as close to those that we feel have departed as we were in what we think of as this life. It is only the separation in our conscious thought. In what we call the Superconscious there is no separation whatever. If we would

let go of that thought of separation there would be no evidence of separation for it exists only in consciousness. It might be more truly stated that separation exists only in unconsciousness when one is unconscious of the true state of being.

6. Separation is only an appearance for in reality there could be no such thing. If the Universe is a single Unit and all things within it are eternally united into a single system, how and where could any separation exist? In fact, it could be only an imagined state. Ignorance of the facts is the only kind of separation that can exist and illumination would completely eliminate that. Behold our God is One, say the Scriptures, and if God is the great ONE, all things and all people are included within him and, being included within him, they are one in and with him.

7. Our being is a complete Universe in itself and it acts in perfect harmony if we let go of every thought of inharmony or separation. The thought of harmony returns us to the unity of Principle. We can think of ourselves so far out of harmony that sickness and disease and discordant conditions come about but they are only that which is out of harmony. If we would keep in complete Universal harmony in thought there could be no inharmonious condition come into our lives . . . not one . . . because whenever we vibrate in harmonious relation with the Universal Principle no inharmony can manifest. It is perfectly possible for it to be so.

8. We make it possible ourselves for inharmony to manifest by the reduction of the vibration of our bodies and in no other way. We allow what should be the impossible to take place. When we look upon complete accord as an impossibility, we worship discord instead of worshiping harmony. That was the

very teaching that Jesus gave out when He said that you of yourself are always harmonious. He referred directly to that harmony of Principle which in reality we always manifest and which we could not help but manifest if we would let go of that personal, egotistical desire for direct service from our neighbor instead of giving Service always. Our expectancy should be from above and our attitude toward the world as giving.

9. One of the easiest ways to isolate ourselves from harmony is to demand service from another instead of giving of our service all of the time. It does not matter if we direct it to one individual or a million individuals. When demanding service from others we are always in that separation but when in service to all we are completely immersed in universality. When we give of ourselves we come nearer and nearer to that Universality where we belong.

10. It takes no energy from our bodies to give out Service, Love, and Harmony but it does take energy from our bodies to give out inharmony or discordant conditions or to give out negative thoughts or words. All positive words or words of accord add energy to our bodies every instant that we are giving them out. Not only that, but we create an influence that returns and surrounds us with emanating energy.

11. One does not need instructions from a Master nor does he need to learn from a book what is true to the processes of the Universal life in him. One knows when he violates the law of life just as easily as one knows when the principles of music have been violated. Instantly a discord is recognized by anyone, whether he has studied music or not. The moment any discord or unpleasantness arises in the nature of man, that instant he should know that he

is violating the law of his being. It is not only a violation of the law of his being but it produces inharmonious results in his body. All discordant emotional and mental states are sins against man's true nature. Everything that produces an harmonious effect in man's nature, that which gives him a sense of peace, freedom, power, and harmony, is in direct harmony with life and only harmonious results prevail.

12. Man is exactly the same as a test tube in a chemical laboratory. If we add harmonious solutions we get harmonious results. Otherwise we set up an inharmonious condition wherein we get either inharmonious results or no results at all. We might see great turbulence in a test tube but that is not inharmony if the correct chemicals are placed in that test tube. It is the same in our bodies. We never set up inharmony if we induce or give out only harmonious thoughts and feelings. It is absolutely impossible for us to set up inharmony if we give out harmony, because we surround ourselves with an influence that is completely harmonious. And, if it is all harmony, no inharmony can manifest through that influence. It is all controlled through consciousness and we become perfectly conscious of harmony, far more so than we can become conscious of inharmony, because harmony is our natural state. That is done by refusing to project our vision to inharmony.

13. If people think that they cannot properly discriminate in the matter of consciousness, they can give out Love to the best of their ability and refuse to give out anything else but Love. That will bring them accurately to harmonious conclusions. Jesus placed Love before everything else. There is a little book written by Henry Drummond entitled *Love, the Greatest Thing in the World*, which gives

the complete key to the harmonious solution of every condition that comes up. It is the simplest little book ever written and has a wide circulation. It takes only about ten minutes to read it but it takes a lifetime to live it. In the living of it there is perfect harmony and perfect freedom.

14. If one should take a negative stand and deny the Spiritual, that does not change the spiritual at all. It could not change Spirit for Spirit is eternally unchangeable, but your wrong ideas would slow up your own progress. We should not concern ourselves with what the other person does or what we think he should do, because we cannot tell when his actions or creations will bring him into direct harmony again. Jesus said, "Loose him and let him go." He thus gave him the privilege of incorporating the Christ consciousness. He saw everyone as the Christ. That very statement: "I see the Christ in every face, in every form," is indicative of His attitude.

15. Do not let the world tell you what it is like for it cannot do so. It is not what it appears to be. It appears to be limited but it is not, for it is formed out of the Universe and Science tells us that each cell is a replica of the Universe. You must learn to find out what the world is like by knowing what the Universe is like and then you will be able to tell the world what it is. Only in this manner can you be free for you are expressing only what your own consciousness is. Look through the surface until you see the inner reality and you will find that "Nothing in this world is single, All things by a law Divine with one another's being mingled," and there is perfect harmony and perfect freedom for yourself and for the world.

16. "When the first man was born, your Christ was born," is the true Christ message. "Before Abraham was I am," "The glory which I had with

145

thee in the beginning before the world was." Add love to all statements and they move in harmony with the Christ as He taught. We can so surround one with Love that that very influence floods in upon him and it may in an instant change his whole life, his whole thought. We are not dominating him when we surround him with Love for that is his native environment. We are only placing an influence that he may accept, thus changing the whole course of his life, and we may also change the whole course of our own lives and thoughts. We are but seeing him as he really is, seeing him as God sees him. This does not hinder or influence him but it frees him from hindrance and influence, because we are surrounding him with that influence in which he was created, that state in which all men live in reality.

17. It is far better to love your enemies and pray for them who persecute you because you merely exalt yourself and at the same time help to free them from those characteristics which cause them to act as your enemies. You are doing a double service both to yourself and to them. The gift is to the giver and comes back most to him. Then, too, sometimes our so-called enemies bring our thoughts out into the clear light of day more so than our friends do.

18. Should you have a supposed friend that does you a great wrong, a harm, the consciousness of perfect love can absolutely change the whole aspect of the situation. That is man's privilege, not his duty. And a privilege is the greatest motive for all of our service. It is a real privilege to love your enemies and exalt them because you are thereby exalting yourself. It is the greatest exaltation in the world to exalt your enemy and see him standing higher even than you stand.

19. This practice is the greatest sincerity for to be

sincere is to be without blemish. It is to be whole. The moment that you cut that individual out of your consciousness you have allowed that individual greater privileges than you have allowed yourself. You must exalt him and then you have finished with the matter. If you loose him and let him go before the exaltation, it is not finished, for you still have your own consciousness to mend. It is like this: you never knew that man before he came into your consciousness. Now you are perfectly conscious of him because there was some situation with which you or he needed assistance. The moment you have gained that which was needed and have finished with that person through exaltation, you can loose him and let him go back just as he was before he came into your life. Then, when your duty is finished and the exaltation is complete, you are both free. Both can go your separate ways the same as you did before. Unless this is done the blemish is still in your own consciousness.

20. You see, all imperfection exists in consciousness only. There is to you no imperfection in those whom you have not contacted. The moment you recognize any imperfect state through contact with anyone, that imperfection is thereby brought into consciousness. Before perfect harmony in your nature can be reestablished, that state must be erased and love is the only attitude that will erase it, for love is the Universal Solvent; it restores everything to its native state in the Universal Scheme. Only in this way are you free and only thus can you free the other person.

21. It is impossible to "loose them and let them go" without the element of love. Pity, either for the other person or for yourself, is not the way of release. Pity always binds you closer to the imperfection. You can pity yourself to the extent that you

will tie yourself up with them faster and faster. You can also pity them until you do exactly the same thing. Pity reduces everything to the low estate of the condition involved, while love exalts the same elements into their rightful place in the Universal. Love is the highest thought you can have. Jesus exalted himself and everyone around him through love. Love is the very essence of the Universe and, in perfect love, all things are united into the Universal Whole.

22. To the individual the universe may be large or small, just as his consciousness dictates. It may be a single atom, it may be a complete body, or it may be the one entire Universality of God completely Universal. When we say universal, if we do not limit our thought to any separate division, we are speaking truly. The thought then is all-embracing just as light surrounds and fills all space. There is a very good saying regarding that in the Mahabharata: "When I see Light, I see all universality." That is because Light is the vehicle that carries Universality into complete existence. The moment we exalt a word it becomes light. The Universe is unlimited. There is no limitation outside of the human concept. The animal never limits itself. It is only man that limits himself.

23. The theory of the expanding Universe is not accurate except in that it expands in our thoughts, or rather we expand our conception of the Universe. We are always discovering that it is larger than we imagined. The Universe is constantly expanding and contracting according to your own concept but not within itself, for the Universe is the sum of Infinity. Many people think of the Universe as referring to a single solar system but a solar system is only one cell or atom in a Universe of innumerable solar systems.

24. There is one law governing the Universe for the Universe is One. We need not obey a single law that is less than the One Law. There is but One Law and that is the only thing that we need to obey. A human being does not need to obey even the manifestation of law, which is gravitation. You need not obey even the conscious manifestation of law; you need obey only the law that controls these manifestations. The moment you become unconscious of the manifestation of law you are perfectly conscious of the Law that is All, the Allness or the Universality of Principle. Every manifestation of law then obeys us. We are in complete authority, complete dominion over every manifestation of law.

25. The thought that there are lesser laws, such as the law of matter, brought the idea of materiality or mortality into effect. It was not Adam, it was the man who followed Adam. Matter is but one attitude of consciousness, the same as thought is but one attitude of consciousness. In other words, matter is only a fixed mental habit. Thought and matter are in reality only avenues of expression and neither should be limited in the considerations of men. Adam, of course, did express consciousness but not the mortal consciousness or mortality of consciousness. That was attached to his name long after the advent of Adam.

26. To the Master there is no material universe. The visible Universe to him is the manifestation of Spirit and is, therefore, spiritual in essence and governed by the law of Spirit. It is this knowledge which gives him power and therein is the secret of all individual power. To know the law of Spirit and to live in harmony with that law is always power of unlimited degree. And that law of the Spirit is the law of Love. It is love that governs infinite space and all forms that are projected in space. That is

why the Scriptures say that if you are in love you are in God and God is in you. Love is harmony and therefore keeps all things in harmony not only with itself but with each other. When man is in a consciousness of love or a consciousness of perfect unity with all things, he is in a state of perfect harmony with all things and with all people. Love is, as it might be said, cohesion, or a binding force that keeps all things in relationship to their source. Working in harmony with their source they work in harmony with all projections of that same source. But love will dissolve that which is not in harmony with the Universal order for it demands of everything its complete adherence to the principle of its own nature, which is Spirit. For that reason love destroys hate, greed, selfishness, and self-seeking and the ego that comes from those states of consciousness.

27. Man is a replica of the complete Universe and he is a complete Universe within himself when he includes himself in that Whole. If he would let go of every thought of creed and dogma, he would be completely out of superstition. He would be completely unlimited. The moment that we unlimit ourselves, it can be shown through photographic evidence today that light emanates from every cell of our body. Light, in the same way, emanates from every cell of the Universe. The source of this Light and energy, which invigorates and fills the expanse of the Universe and the Universe of our body, is the Great Central Sun. Cosmic means great; it is the whole of which man is a part.

FOR THE TEACHER

Paragraphs 1 and 2. This lesson, like the ones just preceding, deals with the Universality of all things and shows that all manifest forms are contained within the whole and are an inseparable part of the whole. It also deals with the fact that each individual organism is in miniature what the Universe is in all its infinity. The point in these first two paragraphs is to help the student to the realization that all the immeasurable power and force that moves throughout Infinite space moves also within him and that his attainment in life is determined by the degree to which he becomes conscious of and works in harmony with these forces.

Paragraphs 3 and 4. Man is only isolating himself by ignorance and by perpetuating his own notions of separation. There is nothing in the attitude of God which separates man or relegates him to obscurity and weakness. God is intent always upon fulfilling himself and, instead of moving to exclude man from the blessings that are rightfully his, is seeking always to manifest Himself through man. Man needs but to eliminate his obstructions to the Divine purpose.

Paragraph 5. There is no death! What seems to be death is only that state where man has crowded the Divine Fact of his being so completely out that it cannot longer sustain the body. The life of the body is the Spirit that created it and, when through ignorance the body is completely dominated by false concepts about life, the body has lost all its true sustaining power and, therefore, can no longer function. That is what is called death. The spiritual man, the man that God created and the only man that God knows, lives as eternally as God is eternal.

Your ideas live on when the forms through which you have expressed them are destroyed and God's idea of man lives on when it is crowded from the vehicle designed for its expression. They remain one in and with the Father Principle and, whether in the flesh or out of the flesh, all men may be conscious of the eternal Unity that exists if the ignorance which causes the sense of separation is dropped out of consciousness.

Paragraphs 6 and 7. Ignorance is the only enemy of man. Knowledge of the facts brings him into harmony with the forces of infinite space, all of which are friendly and move constructively for his good. In principle there can be no opposition to itself. Therefore, all that there is in the Universe is moving in the very nature of man and his position is the direct point or vehicle in and through which infinite power and possibility is manifest.

Paragraphs 8, 9 and 10. It is impossible for anyone to find peace and harmony so long as they are expecting everything and everybody to do for them what they alone can do for themselves. No one can give us that which we already possess and cannot awaken in us that which we ourselves refuse to express. It is not the world or the people of the world that can give us what we need or serve us in accordance with our need. Every good gift and every perfect gift comes from above. The Law of the Universe moves from Principle, God, through the individual manifestation and then gives of itself, its true nature, to the world in service. If we reverse the process, expect the world and its people to give to us so that we in turn may become happy and harmonious, thereby attaining our Divinity, we can but meet disappointment. God is the beginning and is the Great Servant of mankind. To receive His spirit is to become the Sons of God and then, our attitude toward the world is to bestow our great gifts upon all around us, a gracious and generous service.

Paragraph 11. Man's own nature is the Book of Life and, if he will study the eternal trends of his inner nature, allow the deepest side of his nature to expand and grow, then he will understand himself, the Universe, and the law of the Universe. He will not need any man to instruct him.

Paragraph 12. This should be obvious to anyone who has known turmoil and peace within his own nature. Only when false elements are induced into his nature does this upheaval come and only when he receives into his nature that which is harmonious is he in harmony. Man is the chemist and he mixes within himself that which produces his pains and his pleasures.

Paragraphs 13, 14 and 15. It is as easy for anyone to tell what is in harmony with his nature and the purpose of God moving through him as it is easy to tell the difference between harmony and discord in music. This is as evident to the one who has never studied music as to one who is a finished musician. It is just as easy for the most ignorant to recognize discord and inharmony as it is for a Master to do so. We must learn to discriminate and refuse to let ourselves indulge in any mental or emotional reaction that dulls our sense of perfection.

Paragraph 16. It was not Adam but ignorance that caused man to forget his divinity and it is ignorance that keeps us in bondage when in reality there is no bondage. Infinity fills all time and space and our mission is to awaken to the fact that all of Infinity moves through us and our capacities are measured only by this fact.

Paragraphs 17 to 21. The greatest doctrine of Christ was Love, for love is not only the fulfillment of all law but is the solution for every problem that

153

arises in life. Love is the law of the Universe and, when it becomes the ruling passion of the individual, then he is in harmony with all the forces of infinite space. He that is in Love is in God. Love is first to be developed in the individual as an inseparable Union with the Infinite. Being one with the Infinite you are one with all the manifestations of the Infinite. This does not mean that you are to love the imperfections in the world, in your neighbor, or in yourself. Drop these out of consciousness and make your union with the Divine that is back of this outward mask in which you cannot see or know God.

Paragraphs 22 and 23. Your Universe is the one you see. "The Land thou seest, that will I give unto thee as an inheritance." Back of all things is Light for in the beginning was Light. The light became the life of man. Even our material scientists say that light is the foundation of all manifest form. Therefore, man's real body is not a body of material flesh but a body of light which includes the flesh, for light sustains the flesh in exactly the same sense that oxygen and hydrogen sustain water. When ignorance is withdrawn from consciousness we will see and manifest the light.

Paragraphs 24 and 25. If one obeys the constitution of the United States and gives everyone the right to life, liberty, and the pursuit of happiness, will he not automatically obey every other law in the country? Obedience to the Highest law automatically involves the fulfillment of every obligation to every other law. The law of the Universe is Love and, if one moves in love, conscious union, and oneness with God and man, he will not do any thing that would violate any lesser law. But, in this sense, he would move in an infinitely free and uncircumscribed manner and there would be no sense of bondage by these lesser manifestations of laws.

Paragraphs 26 and 27. The Universe and all that is contained within it is one single system and our mission is to so see it. Not that it matters to the Universe so much, but it makes all the difference to the individual. His release comes in his knowledge of things as they are.

CHAPTER XI

YOUR SELF

1. When Jesus the Christ taught "Unless you become as a little child, you can in no wise enter into the kingdom of Heaven," He gave one of the most profound truths. A child has not yet been hypnotized by the world idea of limitation and lives naturally in harmony with its source. That is why most grown people love to be with children. They radiate the natural harmony of the Universe and that is the natural environment of man. If we would only drop all the ideas that have related us to the world, we would find ourselves in that determination which comes from the Universal movement and we would perform the works that are always seeking to manifest themselves through our nature. "Wherever thou findest self, drop that self," wrote the ancient Hindus and that is still the central teaching of the Masters. Only when habits to the contrary are dropped from the primal nature of man can he hope to live the life which is the only life. Most of our attempts at living are so completely adverse to the purpose and natural trend of life that it only leads to the dissolution of the flesh. "There is a way that seemeth right unto man, but the end thereof is death," said Jesus.

2. Know this: There is nothing that really limits man and keeps him in a state of uncertainty and inefficiency but his own thought. When these thoughts are removed he may enter into the life of the universe with ease and then his life begins to give evidence of its natural possibilities. "In that day when ye think not the son of man cometh," was the

wise instruction of the great Master. All thought that comes into man's consciousness from the world is but a reflex of the impressions so received and man is not a reflector. Man is the projection of the Divine and, only as he allows the deepest impulses of his own nature to express, is he in life as it is.

3. The divine purpose of the law of life is to perfect and refine the nature of man until it is a complete and perfect expression of Itself. When life is lived in this way, without the reserve and restraint caused by the hypnotic spell of induced thought, the nature of man is continually refined. This requires the constant control of the individual until all his nature is a unit in expressing the one single purpose. The determination of this force is then perfect outwardly as it is already a fact in the Universal. Only in this way can man fulfill his destiny and receive the full support of the Universal forces. Many people wonder why God does not manifest through their own ideas and give them what they imagine they want. God no more acts through the ideas of man than the law of nature acts through infertile seeds, except to disintegrate them. God or Spirit is about his own business, fulfilling his own ideal and purpose, and man must come into harmony with this Universal purpose. Then, and only then, will he attain that state of complete childlikeness where he lives life naturally. Natural life is perfect and produces perfect results. Our ideas are either altogether imperfect or incomplete. They have not the nature or purpose of the Universal trend in them, therefore they are only to be discarded and put aside in order that the higher influences may become the determining factors in our entire being.

4. You say you have been taught that the first law of nature is self-preservation and so it is. But

that does not mean that one protects his own life at the expense of another. The law of life moves to preserve and promote life. The life of a Master is one that promotes and preserves life for he lives in harmony with the only life which is. In him there is no revenge and his whole motive is to protect life from every intrusion. That is the secret of Mastery. Until one has mastered that in his own nature which would destroy his life, he is out of life. But when he is free from that which would destroy life he is completely in life. Even Jesus did not condemn those who crucified him but released them from the karma of their own ignorance through the law of forgiveness.

5. The fact is, to hold another in blame or to attempt to place blame upon another, is only to involve yourself in that ignorance. Protect life wherever it is manifest. Guard your own life and the lives of others from all ignorant intrusion. Protect yourself and others from any thought or act which would involve them in anything but the fuller and more harmonious expression of life. To do otherwise is suicidal. Constantly refine your own life by protecting the life all around you. But, to protect others is not only to protect them from bodily violence but to protect them from their own ignorance and the ignorance of others. Free yourself and others from the hypnotism of human thought and see yourself and them as free sons of the highest. Only in this way can you enter into life and to enter into life is to become the master yourself. If someone does you an injury, free him instantly in your own mind and free him from the possibility of criticism or condemnation from others. Always hold him freely in the Universal life.

6. Many people never stop to think why artists paint a halo of light around the saints and masters.

It is because they are illumined and illumination is always there when the veil of ignorance, the cloud of hypnotism, is removed. You even see in some degree this same light around children and it is the emanation of this light that makes you feel peaceful and calm when in the presence of very small children. They are perfectly free vehicles of the Universal life. This is the influence one feels and the light one sees around a Master. He has become as a little child; he is freed from all world ideas that dim the light. Light is life and when one is completely in life he is in light—he IS that light. One who is completely in light lifts everyone into that same light to the degree that they are willing to let themselves respond to its influence. It is nothing supernatural that people should see light emanating from a Master. It is perfectly natural for that is life in its natural state. You have all potentialities within yourself and you are able to recognize life as it is in those about you if you will just let yourself see. The only thing that prevents it is your unwillingness to drop what you have come to believe is your state or condition. Drop the veil and behold, there is the light.

7. To advance, you must come to see yourself as a Master. You must conduct yourself as a Master. There is no one who can teach you mastery nor is there anyone who can give you mastership, for they are already yours. Practice is required. You must live as a Master lives, think as a Master thinks, act like a Master acts before you would know a Master if you were to meet one.

8. Just how do you think a Master would meet the situations you have to face every day? Try meeting your problems in that same way. How would a Master speak to those about him? Try speaking in the same way. What would a Master's attitude be

159

toward those about him? Try expressing the same attitude. Could you imagine a Master worrying about business? Would a Master gossip and hate and become jealous or angry? Would he flinch at some particular task? Well, there is a pattern for you, for your own idea of how a Master would face life is exactly the way you should be facing it. If you will so face life, conscious that this is the determination moving in the Universe with which you are one, you will find the seeds of your own mastership sprouting and growing into their full stature.

9. Can you not certainly see that what they have always taught is true, that it is not necessary for you to sit long hours in Samadhi or go through mystical rites and religious forms to come into illumination? They have prepared the way. They have proved that when you work outside the mind with its thoughts and just enter into life as it is, you are then in the state of mastership and, by so continuing until it is your own attitude as you face life, that you are then a Master. Drop that self which you seem to be and begin to live your life as you inherently feel you should live it and you will find that to be truly YOUR life.

10. Nor is it at all necessary for you to journey to India to find your master or teacher as many students believe. Your teacher and your master is your own SELF. The Masters and Jesus do not journey in the world for their knowledge and power. They look within themselves to that Self which is the God within and that is why they are masters. So long as you seek outside of yourself that which is to be found only within yourself, you will not find it. It is in this way that you will always be able to know the teachings of a real master. The unillumined tell you that you must find some teacher outside yourself but a Master tells you that you must find the teach-

er within. This is the main point which Christ tried to make clear to the world. "Lo here and lo there" is the anti-Christ teaching. "The Father within" is the true Christ teaching.

11. It is now seen what you find moving in your Self, that deepest side of your own nature, you must be doing outwardly. Practice makes perfect and it is by practicing your own Mastership or living life as it should be lived, doing as you instinctively feel a Master would be doing, that you will find that all you have been seeking is already here, completely manifest. All that was necessary was that you completely step out of character as you have been living and into the new character, living as life should be lived.

12. When one learns to live from the Soul, the Self, and not from the mind, everything in life is clear and understandable. You know what you should do, where you should go, and life becomes simple and harmonious. That is life as it is intended, life as it is, life as we must ultimately live it. Children only live in the realm of thought when we have taught them to do so. They live naturally in the beginning and we should become like them and not make them over like ourselves. That does not mean we shall live unintelligent lives and that we will have no thoughts. It means that we will truly live intelligently and that our thoughts will be the outcome of properly expressing the Inner Self.

13. It is true, to make this complete change from what we appear to be to what we really are, to enter into life as it is, will require some determination. Whatever the Hindu's belief is, he gives his all for it. He will walk hundreds of miles to fulfill what he believes to be his spiritual duty. When we are equally intent upon being what we instinctively feel we should be, we shall arrive without difficulty. We

must quit hoping and wishing and set about doing and being.

THE CORRESPONDENT WRITES

Note: Because of the interest and helpful suggestions which the following letter from Mrs. Grace G. Hahn will hold for the students, we are making it a part of the lesson at this time. Mrs. Hahn was a member of the party with Mr. Spalding in India.

"I will try to recount some of the experiences since writing you last.

"Mr. M. M. Ghose, a friend of Mr. Spalding's, invited us to be his guests on a river boat trip to Dacca, the Ashram of Swami Paramananda. It would be very difficult to describe the jungle through which we passed. At places the river was so narrow that it was impossible for two boats to pass. Then again the river was one-half mile in width. All was going well as we proceeded on our journey. On the evening of the third day at eight-fifteen, most of us were asleep in our bunks when we felt a terrific impact and heard loud screaming close by. We soon realized we had collided with another steamer. Suffice it to say that confusion and terror reigned for some little time and we were informed that the barge of the other steamer sank in a few moments. We were damaged but no lives were lost. It was impractical to proceed so we anchored for the night. The lights were gone and the boats were leaking badly. The small son of our host calmly entered the circle of excitement on deck and said: 'God has saved us all, Baba (father), now can I go to bed'? There was a hush for a few moments; then we all realized the lesson which this blessed Hindu boy had given us. We quietly went to our beds with the

162

assurance that all was well. Here was a potential Master, quieting a whole boatload of people by his calm assurance and simple childlike faith.

"The next morning we proceeded slowly to the next town and took the train back to Calcutta. We are meeting some very wonderful Hindu men. A Mr. Sircar presented his book to Mr. Spalding and may I quote a single paragraph from the book which appealed to me? 'Complete Truth and life in its finest flowering cannot be enjoyed unless all the forces; natural and spiritual, can be controlled and applied to the unfolding of life in its increasing fineness.' We have spent many, many hours with him and feel greatly enriched thereby.

"A story told us at the Calcutta University one afternoon is well worth mentioning for the lesson it carries. The incident occurred 600 B. C. Even in those days there were disagreements in the teachings, so part of the adherents separated from the main group and tried to persuade the teacher to change his viewpoint. After a period of time the leader of the withdrawing faction saw that it was useless and decided to take the law into his own hands. He laid in ambush and when the teacher passed him he drew his sword. As the wounded teacher fell he called the assailant to him and asked him to sit by his side for a moment as he wished with his last gasping breath to speak to him. Very kindly and lovingly he told him to go straight ahead and then no one would know what had happened and thus many people be saved from avenging his death because in reality he was going on to a greater realization, but that if he returned the way he came he would cause many others to suffer for his deed. He alone would suffer for the crime which was his. The great Master gave this lesson to the man who thought he could harm him.

"We left Calcutta last Monday and arrived at the Ashram of Swami Omkar. Such a wonderful restful place in the country thirty miles from the railroad. After a couple of days of rest, each one of us was called individually to interview the Swami. As I sat listening to him talk in his quiet, calm voice I saw the light glow all around him and back of him. I was spellbound for a few moments and was afraid it would disappear but it remained as long as I did. The room was aglow just as Mr. Spalding has told us many times. It was my first actual experience and one that I shall always cherish and remember.

"Last evening I was again privileged to spend two hours with the Swami. He explained in detail the meaning of masters, or mastership. Masters become masters of themselves first. Mastery over anger, jealousy, greed, egotism, possessions — the wife possessing the husband and the husband possessing the wife — selfishness, and a thousand other things which we have taken upon ourselves.

"We came thousands of miles to see a master, one who has accomplished that which we could and must do in our own homes and environment. Just like the cow that wants the grass on the other side of the fence even though there is abundance all around. Swami gives one word as the foundation upon which we start upon the path and that is PRACTICE. Practice daily that which you already know. Practice mastery over anger. Practice the mastery of love toward everything in the Universe. A very large order I grant you but by eternal practice hourly and daily we will soon see the results and thus be ready for another lesson in the school of life. These silent men know the value of the law of mastery over the self and thus they do not mingle with those that have not yet learned to be silent for at least some part of each day. How can we ever

164

hope to contact them in our western chaotic state of mind? Argument shuts the door. An open mind and intuition alone throw the portals wide open. This much I have so far learned in India. I thought I knew it before but, when you come into the presence of one of these Holy men, you very soon realize it was theoretical only. It requires the actual practice and the soul's sincere desire to master the self and really become that which *they* have become.

"There is a wonderful Hindu boy here twelve years of age. He is a little master in the making. He anticipates every want or desire before we are able to express it. The eyes are the windows of the soul, therefore one must see the radiance of that youngster's smile as he silently stands before you wanting to serve you. He stood at my door last night and seemed reluctant to depart. Not yet accustomed to the Hindu custom, I waited for him to make his wants known and, as he advanced toward me with that wonderful smile, he looked me straight in the eye and said, 'I love you so.' Then he turned and was gone like a flash. During the meditation class he sits immovable for an hour in the silence. Some of the older ones go to sleep but not this child.

"We spent one happy week with the Swami, then wended our way southward to Madras. Mr. Spalding went ahead to Tiruvannamali and met Paul Brunton, the author of 'The Secret Search of India.' Mr. Spalding wired us to come and after a night's journey we were met by Mr. Spalding and Mr. Brunton. We were taken to the ashram of one of the greatest living saints in India: Sri Ramana Maharishi. A great many people sit on the floor cross-legged for many hours just to be in the presence of this great man. He is one of the Holy men who gives his time to the students. He never speaks unless a question is asked and before the answer is given he remains silent until the answer comes from within. This contact alone is worth the whole trip.

"From Tiruvannamali we went to Pondicherry. A great man lives here but only appears in public three times a year. The next time will be on the twenty-fourth of February. The ashram is one to be long remembered. Many, many men students are living there and one is greatly attracted to them. Their faces radiate the life they live and there is absolutely no doubt about it. From here we learned that a Mela, or pilgrimage, would take place in Allahabad on the thirteenth of January. We went to Calcutta and then on to Allahabad. Never will I forget the sight which we saw at this Mela. Pilgrims from all over India, coming to bathe in the sacred waters of the Ganges, were there. The confluence of these two rivers, Ganges and Jumna, occurs here. The water is icy cold, yet they plunge in. They have come long distances under terrible hardships to join in this religious rite. A million people with but one thought, namely to bathe in the Ganges on this particular day. There were so many incongruous 'get ups.' Some naked, others bordering on savagery; some on elephants and camels, others in ox carts, all headed for the Ganges. I was greatly impressed by the religious zeal evidenced beyond question of doubt. What was it that would impel a million people to come to the Ganges? It was beyond my comprehension and the question seemed to revolve in my mind over and over. 'What am I seeking for in this place?' After I returned to the hotel the answer seemed to come and it was this: 'You are seeking the Primal cause of brotherhood.' How can you be one with all mankind if you see only the exterior, if you think they are psychopathic patients; if you say that black is black and white is white? Do you not observe the same love throbbing in the heart of the mother as she fondles her babe whose tiny body is filthy, diseased, and crippled, wallowing in the dirt, poverty stricken, homeless, and actually starving, walking miles under tremendous hardships merely to bathe in the 'sacred' waters of the Ganges? What but the inborn spark of Divinity could possibly urge them on to lay it all at the feet of their conception of God? We worship God in luxury; they have nothing. Their feet are weary and footsore, their energy is their all, yet they give it to come once a year and every six, twelve and twenty-four years to meet on common ground and bathe and worship in their way. Just think of it. A million people on a small area of ground, peaceable, happy, singing and joyous. No sign of confusion or interference, each one regarding the rights of his brother to worship as he pleases.

"To me the real brotherhood is expressed here under inconceivable conditions, thousands of conditions which we never thought could exist and yet, from the hearts of these pilgrims love is expressed and the eyes reveal an unfathomable depth which we might well envy. All worshiping God, God, God. Many different languages, the rich and the poor, the halt, the lame and the blind. A smile will always bring forth a smile. In fact, they seem surprised that we will deign to smile or greet them in their own fashion. I sincerely wonder if we would smile under the same environment. Could we, or would we, on hands and knees crawl to the Ganges, worshipping God with every breath, scarcely able to keep soul and body together? Could we, I ask you, could we?

"We saw Saddus with matted hair, their bodies covered with ashes, naked with the exception of a G-string, and I asked the question, 'why should anyone treat the body in such a fashion?' The answer was that they have relinquished pride and are no longer concerned with the world. That is their conception of it and, after all is said and done, we all act and think as our conscience dictates and as our individual evolution has progressed.

"We take pride in 'dolling up' the body, while they go to the other extreme and spend their entire lives in caves and in the Himalayan mountains in the contemplation of God. They must first realize these attributes in themselves before they can go into the world and teach their inner experiences to others. We have many isms, creeds, and dogmas very often theoretical and intellectual only. Thousands of these pilgrims coming in from all over India for this great Mela are actually living the God-life as they understand it. Of course there are many professional beggars and one soon learns to differentiate. The intuition is the best guide. Beggars are beggars whether they are in India or in America. Here we see them in the 'raw' and there we often meet them in the best of society.

"We witnessed a man returning from the Ganges walking with a cane, his servant just behind him carrying his crutches. You may draw your own conclusions.

"Another great day is just ahead. On Friday the twenty-fourth the Mela of the sixth year occurs, so we will remain for that. I will continue this letter after that occasion. Mr. Spalding has taken two of our party to the Ganges today. I have remained at home to get this letter off to you."

GRACE G. HAHN

FOR THE TEACHER

In presenting this chapter, the letter from Mrs. Hahn should be read to the class, as it completely illustrates the lesson. Incident by incident, which the tour party experienced, is explained in the lesson and the teacher can readily check from the lesson to the illustrations in the letter.

Paragraph 1. The age-old illustration of the child is not that we become feeble-minded or that we lack intelligence. It means that we live life as it moves out from our interior nature. That is why it is difficult for children to understand adults. They have not had their minds filled with thoughts and they only live what they inwardly feel. When these inner feelings are completely dulled by having our thoughts drilled into them children become dull and inefficient like the older people. Thought is not the leading factor in successful living but is the outcome of successful living. Every step in human progress came from some one's inner conviction and thought was evolved to describe that which has been achieved.

Paragraph 2. Man is really not limited at all for he is a replica of infinity. He only allows himself to be limited by his thought. Live life as it unfolds from within and you will find life as it is and the key to your own mastership. Thought, word, and act are the outlets or vehicles through which life is expressed and not the standard from which it is lived.

Paragraphs 3 and 4. The purpose of the Universe is to perpetuate and perfect life in all its completeness. It supports in man only that which is in harmony with life. It destroys out of man's nature that which operates against life. It is said that evil bears the seed of its own destruction and that is true but the seed of destruction in evil is the inherent good and when good manifests it destroys evil, leaving nothing but the good. And life is the good that is always present and always moving to fulfill itself.

Paragraph 5. It is not an intelligent thing to place blame upon yourself or upon others. The only true intelligent thing to do is to protect yourself and others from anything that is less than the Universal divinity. When we become as intent upon preserving the potential nature of ourselves and others as we are intent upon preserving our earthly possessions, the world will be filled with real Masters.

Paragraph 6. Look at yourself in the mirror. Is there any light in your face when you are sad? When you are radiant with joy, is there a light there? Imagine the light which would emanate from you if you were living that kind of life which you idealize and which is your life as you are capable of living it and as you should live it.

Paragraphs 7, 8 and 9. "If you want to know God, act as though God were."

If you want to know what the life of a master is like, live that life yourself. Only in this way can we really know. No man knows the things of God except the spirit of God, which is in him, shall reveal them.

Paragraphs 10 and 11. The distinct difference between the teachings of the illumined and the unillumined is that the illumined teach you to go within yourself for knowledge. All the rest go and teach others to seek, outside themselves. You are not likely to find outside of yourself what you have failed to find within yourself. The world gives back to you what you give into the world.

Paragraph 12. One should study the difference between the state of his mind and the state of his soul. The mind says thus and so and that only this and that are possible. The soul knows itself to be immortal, to be the Master, and it never changes in its activity. Your deepest desire is identical with the manner in which any Master would act.

Paragraph 13. Complete devotion to an ideal is the secret of its attainment. It is not wishing and hoping for things to break right but persistently working toward the goal of perfection.

CHAPTER XII

PRANA

1. It is a well known fact today that the Cosmic Life Force surrounds and interpenetrates every condition and every atom and that the Life Force can be drawn within our bodies with the breath we breathe. Every act can be according to that Life Force. Every thought we think can be in harmony with it.

2. Note that it is said that this Life Force may be drawn in "with the breath we breathe." It is not the mere act of breathing that draws into the body of man this Cosmic Life Force. Unless definite attention to it accompanies our physical breathing it is not definitely appropriated. It is a life force which is so much finer than our physical air that it is not affected by mere physical processes any more than one might draw electricity into his being by the mere of physical breathing. Of course there is a certain amount of electricity, or what we call electricity, that is taken into the system by every act and, likewise, with the Cosmic Life Force which is sometimes called Prana. If you will notice, everything toward which your attention is directed registers an impression on the mind. In turn, this impression is developed into an idea and the idea expressed in words. This is a sort of mental breathing, is it not? Well, there is an inner attention, a deep longing you call it, to be perfect in every department of your being. When the outer attention is linked with this inner attention or when it looks always toward the perfection of the Universe, as does what Seneca called the "eye of the soul," then

there is drawn into man's being the elements of the Cosmic forces around and about us. The mystics have always taught that attention is the secret of success in dealing with the Cosmic forces. Deep, sincere, abiding attention to the surrounding spiritual ethers, a completely relaxed body and an all-absorbing interest and complete openness of mind are the necessary attitudes in order that one may realize this "inner breath" as it is called. This is "soul breathing" or letting the Self expand into its native ethers, the interpenetrating life force or spiritual ethers, as Steinmetz called it, until through the act of attention it is drawn within the whole being of man.

3. This Life Force being Cosmic must interpenetrate all elements. This is, in reality, the force that stimulates all cellular growth, allows it to expand and become the growth of the body as well as the growth of plants. In fact, it is incorporated with all growth of every description and is the sustaining element of life. It becomes that which imbibes life as well for, like every other force, it is both positive and negative and acts and reacts within itself, just as whirling currents of air act and react within themselves. One might say that the air breathes, or moves and, at the same time, is acting within itself and upon itself.

4. The method of consciously appropriating the universal Cosmic Life Force, or Prana, is commonly called Pranayama. One might call it Prana-breathing or the practice of consciously breathing the Cosmic Life Force. The exact procedure is difficult to define and it would take too much time and space to give the entire technique of the Pranic breath. The technique for starting the operation is proper breathing, then one may with care and sincerity find his own method for the balance of the process.

As we have said above, attention is the one fundamentally important practice in the process—attention to the highest source of energy existing, that all-surrounding presence that you call God. The mind must be without strain and whatever method best relieves the mind of strain would be the next step in right procedure. In fact, the Prana or spiritual substance is so fine and sensitive that it is deflected by the least force. Did you ever try to catch a piece of lint or down floating in the air? Every tense or quick movement to grasp it only drove it away but a quietness that was like letting it come between your fingers of its own volition was the proper technique for grasping it. That is as nearly an illustration as one could give. It is also like trying to remember something you have forgotten. If you make strong mental effort you do not remember but, if you let the mind rest, become quietly reflective, then the idea comes quickly within the mind. So with the Prana, it is breathed into the nature through quietness and confidence. Every phase of the mind must be free and the body completely relaxed. One must have a sense of complete freedom and complete expansion as if the cells of the body were actually moving out from each other until they almost stood apart. This practice may be continued until one forgets the sense of physical limitation altogether, then one is in the most perfect state mentally and physically to receive this Universal Substance into his whole being. It then has access to every cell of his being; it becomes the sustaining and invigorating element of life and especially of the human body. This method of control causes the body to keep young and vibrant.

5. It is a sustaining and invigorating practice that allows the cells and tissues of the body to expand, thereby giving greater oxidation to the body.

It is a complete spiritual airing of every cell of the body to the original ethers from which it came. Just as in a ray of light you find the various colors, so in Prana do you find all the elements of life, that is the real essence of all the lesser forces. Prana is not oxygen but is that which gives life to the oxygen, the actual life within the oxygen. It is that which gives force to electricity, consciousness to mind. In other words, it is the reality existing within and standing back of and sustaining all lesser forces. It is called the Spirit of God in the Scriptures. Prana-yama—spiritual breathing—allows the proper expansion of all the elements taken into the body for the body's growth and, because of this expansion, all the elements are oxidized or "aired" as we say when we expose things to the air or sun to become freshened. Just so when the body is relaxed, when the mind and spirit are freed, when the whole nature expands to consciously allow the Prana to interpenetrate throughout the entire being, the whole nature is freshened, revived, refreshed, fed. This is Pranayama or the art of spiritual breathing. But, attention is the fundamental secret of the practice. You even have to give attention to the sun in order to gain the greatest benefit from a sun bath.

6. It is through this practice that certain Yogi are able to suspend animation for certain periods of time. This rests the whole system and renews it for the contact with its origin or source. It is restored and the original life elements are again contacted by the flesh itself. In the same way and, with the same results, they suspend respiration. It is like coming up out of the water into fresh air after one has been submerged for a period. To try to suspend animation and respiration would only be to drown yourself literally. But, to expand yourself and so relax yourself that you begin to consciously sense the

life-giving ethers, makes one so much alive, so vitally filled with life, so refreshed and fed that one has no need of the outer breath or the outer activities of the body. He becomes alive from within.

7. Just as this practice vitalizes the body, so it enlivens the mind. The reason men do not think well is because the mind is too tense, too compressed — so to speak — so that it does not function freely. Under the practice of Pranayama the whole nature is expanded and functions more freely and completely. It is like loosening bearings that are too tight on a machine and letting the oil penetrate through it. It then moves more freely. Memory, in this case, comes in from a thousand different sources and one remembers what he was in the beginning. It comes without any effort at all and anything he wants to know comes instantly and easily into his mind. Inasmuch as Prana interpenetrates all, there must be a close relationship between Prana and that function of the mind. Prana allows no division in function for it unites all the functions of the individual with the Universal. It is, of course, Universal and opens the way for all activities, thousands and thousands of activities at the same time. Prana is an emanating energy underlying all substance. Of course, substance in its original state is energy and energy is substance. What we know as energy and substance are but two aspects of a single primal energy and this primal energy is Prana, or Spirit.

8. We may more truly say that Prana is one of the elements of Spirit for spirit is not only energy but intelligence and substance. It is more subtle than ether. The Western World is defining ether as Prana, though there is a difference in the subtlety and the activity of Prana and ether. The latter is nascent while Prana is always active. Ether is Prana becoming or coming out toward manifestation. All

of the finer forces of nature such as electricity and the other moving elements of creation are divisions and mediums in which and through which Prana works.

9. When the human body or any material form disintegrates it goes back into Prana, first into the various forms of energy and thence back into Universal and primal force. If Prana were constantly received into the whole being of man, the flesh would be eternally quickened, or it would become more and more animated, more and more alive, and the last enemy would be overcome. There are those who overcome old age and death with or through an understanding of Prana right along. They rebuild the body with the Pranic influence. This happens in a slight degree every time one goes to sleep or rests but, when one adds conscious attention to the Pranic Presence, completely relaxes in mind and body, the attention breathes the ever-present Prana into and through his whole being; therefore, the greatest degree of renewal of mind and body is attained.

10. You see, intelligence is the primal attribute of being and the activity of consciousness is Prana, or vital force of creation, and substance is the form through which both act. Intelligence, Life, and Substance are the trinity of elements in the first cause as defined by the Western world. Intelligence is its KNOWING aspect. Life is its QUICKENING or vital aspect. Substance is the aspect which has the capacity of FORM. Prana is usually used as embracing both the substance and life elements and they are the vehicles or mediums through which intelligence moves to direct and determine the created forms.

11. This primal intelligence, life, and substance are just God Almighty in action but it must become

a conscious fact in every individual. It becomes selective to the individual and is of conscious use to
the individual as the individual selects it.

12. The Cosmic Ray of which Millikan speaks is
a Pranic wave. They will find nine divisions of the
Cosmic ray which are all definitely Pranic in origin.
They can be of great benefit if properly used. These
nine rays are the emanations of Pranic energy, just
as the seven colors are emanations of a ray of pure
white light. Creation is only the splitting up and re-
combining of influences or energies, as we call
them, emanating from the Pranic ethers.

13. When we go back to the center of anything,
it is pure light and this is the inner light of which
Jesus spoke. It is the light of Illumination. The
greater man's spiritual awakening, the greater the
light. Have you not noticed that one awakened in
joy has a radiance about his countenance? When
one is spiritually awake, the light is correspondingly
bright. That is why artists paint Jesus with a halo
of light about him. Light is life. This is the "light
that lighteth every man that cometh into the
world" and it is the fire through which the initiates
of the occult schools had to walk in order to be
eligible to illumination. This light is all about us
and is an emanation of the Pranic ethers. It is the
light which is the beginning and the end of creation. When you can live in the light, as you now live
in your sense of body, you will be immortal for the
light never dies. I was noticing a report of some
kind of light shining in Transjordan although ar-
chaeologists were perfectly sure that there was nothing there of an old civilization. Those following the
light found and broke into archaeological remains
very quickly. That has happened in Persia as well.
We have not yet seen it in the Gobi. There is a
history, however, that the light always showed in

that country. We have a complete history, in fact, that that light showed over the first tower of Babel, a tower that was built of actual stone in the form of a step-pyramid. However, this light is seen only through the Single Eye, such devoted attention that all the senses and faculties of man are pointed in one direction and that direction must be toward what the Scriptures call the "light of His countenance."

14. This is the light of the New Jerusalem spoken of by John in Revelations. John knew well how to use the Pranic Light. He extended his vision to take in all of it. It is, of course, much beyond what we know as clairvoyance, though clairvoyance is a phase of it and is really a step backward in evolution. It is like living in the borrowed light from another when the true light, the light that lighteth every man, is within him.

15. We must go forward to that Light and the lower senses which hold us back or away from our birthright will let go. The limited activities direct us away from the unfoldment and use of the Pranic Light by the higher sense. The psychic faculties will fall into line and become valuable instruments when the Pranic Light is unfolded. The Pranic light vibrates way beyond the psychic forces. Furthermore, mediumship and so-called psychic development are not steps toward the unfoldment of the direct Pranic Light.

16. Pranic light can always be called upon to overcome any degrading forces that oppose it, just as light can be brought into play to dispel darkness. It can be the I AM center. The statement, "I am the force of that Pranic Light and I project It and put it forth as all powerful," will break that condition of the conflicting forces or voices every time. But it must be the voice of the Christ Self, which is

the real I AM within each individual. This I AM is not above you or outside of you but at the very center of your being. That was Jesus' thought when he said, "I have nothing except that which comes in the Name and through the Power of the Christ." It involves the highest embodiment of Prana.

17. The transfiguration of Christ was when the consciousness of Jesus was merged into the realization that Intelligence, Life, and Substance were in the last analysis ONE and that One was what he called the Father, or primal cause, like all the various colors of the spectrum returning to a pure ray of white light.

18. There is but one Consciousness, One Principle, One Sense. It is only complicated when we deal too much with differentiations or apparently differing functions and attributes. To deal with the mind as functioning in many faculties is only to further dissipate yourself and draw you further and further away from your source. Behold, our God is ONE. With that one thought, or attitude, of Pranic forces always being in operation within as well as about us, we become unified, or one with the whole. John said that that which is without is really within. He carried it right to that great Pranic force which always exists and is always active and this action is the One action throughout all creation and all space.

FOR THE TEACHER

The foregoing lesson received from Mr. Spalding by the India Tour party deals with a subject most vital to every student. It reveals the close relationship which exists in the minds of the Hindoo Scientists of Calcutta University and other Eastern scientists and the religion of the Orient. We are fast approaching the time when walls of difference are to be entirely dissolved and the ultimate union of religion and science will be generally recognized as one and the same thing, though they may often approach a single fact from opposite directions.

Paragraph 1. In the matter of successful living it should be clearly understood that man is not sustained by what he has commonly considered essential. His real supply must necessarily be contained within the movement of forces which operated to create him in the beginning. Within these forces are all the elements out of which the visible creation is formed and it is only through a conscious contact with these original forces that man may hope to successfully live life to its fullest possibilities.

Paragraph 2. The "Cosmic breath" is not a matter of physical breathing but it is a matter of conscious contact with the Life forces that move in the spiritual ethers about us. Breathing is receiving into your nature the elements within the air, and then exhaling what the body does not assimilate. Spiritual breathing is receiving into the consciousness of man that which is within the spiritual ethers and that is brought about through the quiet and deep attention of the mind. People often related it to physical breathing, but it should not be confused with this process. Whatever you look upon, you receive impressions concerning it into the consciousness and everything you do is an expression of what thus impresses you. By attention to the spiritual ethers you draw their elements into your being and your whole life's expression is quickened and increased because of the very nature of that which occupies your attention.

Paragraph 3. One should contemplate the permeating presence of all the forces of Being until he becomes as conscious of these forces as he is now conscious of form. This is the secret of developing unlimited power or mastery.

Paragraph 4. Pranic breath is not something mystical or difficult and does not require a lot of instruction. One easily and readily absorbs the sunshine for it is the nature of sunlight to penetrate all objects upon which it shines. More penetrating is the vital energies of the spiritual ethers. Relaxed, quiet attention is the secret.

Paragraph 5. Physical tension is a contraction of the flesh caused by mental contractions. Mental contractions are caused by studying the apparent limitations of form and environment. A wider view of life frees the mind which in turn frees the body. Give your whole being a good pranic airing every day and watch the increase in every capacity of your being.

Paragraph 6. Suspended animation is not a matter of merely stopping the processes of bodily functions. It is identifying one's self with a superior action that meets all the requirements of the physical being; then the so-called normal functions are not necessary. The greater always supersedes the lesser and fulfills the needs of the lesser. Do not try to stop eating or breathing or cause the heart to stop. Apply yourself to the Divine presence until you find it quickening your entire being.

Paragraph 7. Vitality or living energy is not the result of food or breath. It is the activity of the life force of the Universe re-animating the being of man.

Paragraph 8. Spirit is the activity of the entire creative machinery of the Universe; it is God in action. This action involves all the elements within the nature of God and, therefore, contains all the elements involved in creation.

Paragraph 9. Death and decay is only a lack of animation from the source of one's being as is failure and poverty.

Paragraphs 10 and 11. The Universal Cause knows what it is doing and it knows what you should be doing to fulfill its purposes. Constant attentiveness to all the activities of the Spirit is to know and to have the power to do.

Paragrphs 12 and 13. Light is life but there are higher forms of light just as there are higher forms of ether and energy. Only the individual who practices the Presence of God can know exactly what that light is like but one who is given to deep meditation often catches a glimpse of it.

Paragraph 14. True clairvoyance—clear vision—is not seeing shapes and forms but is that awareness of mind that sees and knows the pure action of Spirit.

Paragraph 15. Do not wait to do what you call overcoming before you feel worthy to enter the path that leads to illumination. Go into the light and let it burn away that which is false. Drop your faults, diseases, undesirable conditions. Face the light and these conditions are not.

Paragraphs 16 and 17. Pranic light, or Spiritual light, is not something difficult to obtain any more than is physical light. It is always moving toward you and works as quickly through your highest ideals or least needs with infinite swiftness just as physical light flashes instantly through any opening large or small.

Paragraph 18. Reducing everything to oneness simplifies the entire matter of living and spiritual progress.

CHAPTER XIII

THE QUANTUM THEORY

1. Principles of physics are involved in a study of the Quantum Theory. It is the theory of distribution of energy throughout nature. It was developed in the Berlin University as an outcome of investigation into radiation from black objects. This research resulted in the conclusion that all forms radiate a definite energy and that there is nothing in the world of form that is an inert mass. Every form has within itself some degree of energy and this energy is a distinct emanation of the energy that fills infinite space. The amount of energy that each particular form radiates is in direct proportion to the relationship which it has with the Universal energy.

2. Just as a pendulum swings in a long or short arc according to the amount of force exerted to start it swinging, just so all forms retain the amount of active energy required in sending it forth. This energy is retained by the form just to the degree that it retains its relation to the energy which sent it forth. If the pendulum stops, it is because the impelling force has ceased to exert influence upon it. Matter becomes less and less active as it loses some of its contact with the original impelling force which started it into motion. When this energy ceases to act within the form, the form disintegrates.

3. Metaphysically, this has much of vital importance to those of the Western world. The movement in the United States came under the depression and all that that means is that there was no foundation

in fact. That is, it was founded on only a half truth. There is fact as a basis for our metaphysics but that fact was overlooked and misunderstood by most of its exponents in the United States. This will all be discussed in our consideration of the Quantum Theory.

4. The Eastern world, those of higher thought, have known the facts propounded in the Quantum Theory. They deal, in brief, with but one fact, that of the universality of all things and, consequently, in dealing with that one fact they have a definite basis for both science and metaphysics. The psychology of the Western world is mere child's play. It is based to a great extent upon theory. Whenever you deal with divisions of mental, material, and physical you are bound to base at least 75% of your calculations on theory. Division is not unity and unity is not division and the basis of all creation is that it is a unit. "I am that I am and beside me there is no other," is the eternal declaration of fact which is the unity of all things. The direct violation of this fundamental unity is in considering the mind as having phases or faculties, when, in reality, mind is a single unit, not only as within the individual but as existing in and of the Universe. Material form is not something isolated from and independent of the Universe but is one in and with the Universal substance. The physical body is not an isolated phase of the creative scheme but is in and one with the Universal Energy. To violate this fundamental unity is to isolate yourself in a hypnotic state where you seem to be a separate being and, therefore, you cut yourself off, devitalize yourself, and ultimately destroy your ability to further manifest in this plane. To deny the relationship of the visible with the invisible is to push yourself right out of your body and into the invisible.

185

5. The Eastern philosophy is not based upon theory at all. It is based upon a definite scientific fact or principle. That is the same idea that Einstein is bringing out in the Quantum Theory. He has brought it out in greater evidence than has any other scientist in the Western world. Many are saying that it is the gap between Science or Physics and true Religious thought.

6. The Easterner does not approach the matter of religious thought as theory at all. In fact, he proves that it is not theory. Thereby, he accomplishes that very fact and the possibilities involved in that fact. You do not see the Eastern philosophers pass out a theory of anything. Their basis is always in fact. It, of course, is not fact simply because they pronounce it so but because it has a scientific basis in fact. That fact was clearly revealed by Christ when he said, "I and my father are ONE," preserving the unity of himself with the whole. That is the basis from which all successful living must evolve and it is only to the degree that this oneness is maintained by the individual that he begins to radiate the energy that sent him into being. This is the basis of the Quantum Theory as applied from the viewpoint of pure religion or pure metaphysics. And that is why the Eastern philosophers gave so much attention to the Quantum Theory. They see the scientists of the world returning to the basis of their own religious thought held for thousands of years.

7. Einstein did not come right out and say that it is all Spirit. Consequently, it was urged that the physical or material was not a fact, but he showed that it is based upon one joint determination. He put it as one general Principle, co-relating all physics, as he said, under one head. That is exactly what

those of higher Eastern thought had determined long ago—that there is but one Principle, one scientific basis, and that basis one of Being.

8. Now the Western world does not go back and reason from that Principle. They work through to that principle from the external, consequently it is not necessarily a true form of reasoning; that is, their form of reason is not truly scientific reason. All true reason works out from principle to its manifestation and not from the manifestation back to principle. Imagine trying to work a problem by reasoning back or attempting to reason back to Principle by studying the size, shape, form and general construction of an accumulation of figures. The people of the Western world, in their attempt to solve the riddle of life, are doing that very thing. By this process they become highly mental or, as we put it, intellectual. And as we already know, their intellectual knowledge is always subject to revision for it does not prove itself. That is why one of our modern scientists has said that all written works on science prior to the last ten years should be burned. The Eastern world is carried beyond the intellectual or the ordinary intellectual. Of course, true principle and reason from the basis of the One Fact is the highest form of intellect. But the hypothesis that the Eastern world takes puts it wholly on a true intellectual basis in carrying it to a clear conception.

9. The intellect of the Western world covers a wide range but comes to no absolute conclusion in its hypotheses or theories. All of the Science of the Western world has been based upon that hypothesis or theory. The people of the Western world have progressed to the point where they know the existence of certain determining factors but they never go directly to the simple denominator of One Prin-

ciple when handling fact. The Eastern philosophers have always based their premises upon one Natural Fact. And there you have the basis of the Quantum Theory. One Universal Fact from which all form emanates and operates as the animating force of the created form — the Universal distribution of energy.

10. The difference between the Hindu conception and the theory of Monism is that the latter eliminated all but the blind force of nature or creation. The Hindu always considered it an active, intelligent force that knew what it was doing, an energetic force, and a force that did accomplish an intelligent creation that moved toward an intelligent purpose and that anyone who would work with the intelligence of that force could accomplish all things through it.

11. The crux of the whole matter is therefore right knowledge. What we have called knowledge is past. The true knowledge is outside of the senses. The true basis of knowledge is to know the motivating force and the ends toward which it moves, as it is this motivating sense or the inward sense of the trend of the motivating force of the Universe that brought all things into existence in the beginning and will bring all things into being through that individual who senses and works in harmony with its purpose.

12. The true knowledge comes through samadhi or silence. It comes through an inner feeling or an intuitive knowing. This is rightly what we call understanding. With all your getting, get understanding. When we obey what we inwardly feel the accomplishment is achieved and then we have correct knowledge for it is based on the outworking of Principle. This is the manner in which all true knowledge comes, not only in things spiritual, but in rela-

tion to the principles which we use every day. We discover certain principles, apply those principles, results are forthcoming, and from these results we formulate our knowledge.

13. When you take that knowledge completely out of the realm of hypnosis you get down to the fundamental fact or truth. Knowledge does not necessarily exist in the fundamental fact. That fact exists prior to and is greater than knowledge. Knowledge, as the Hindu puts it, comes directly from the expression of the fundamental fact.

14. When the Bible says that "the flesh profiteth nothing" it does not say that the flesh is nothing. It has no reality except that which is of the Spirit which produced it. The flesh is not a producer; it does not produce anything for it is the thing produced. It is the Spirit which produces. Flesh is Spirit in form, as they put it. They do not make any distinction between flesh and Spirit or material and spiritual. Consequently, it is all one and the same to them and that is where they accomplish. The Word made flesh is the true spiritual form.

15. When the Spirit works in manifest form it obeys a manifestation of law. If you can know that Law you can know Spirit definitely. As Paul says, "Faith is Spirit substance." It means that Faith, made knowing, is all substance. You know instead of having Faith. There is where the Sanskrit never deviates. That evidence of Spirit, which is first faith and then knowing, creates. Through that evidence men create always, not through the senses or the sense of the material or physical, but through all substance as Spirit.

16. Faith is the active principle of the mind. The mind acting upon inner knowing or understanding ripens into knowledge or becomes absolute knowl-

edge. Spiritual intuition is direct knowing; it is tapping the infinite consciousness directly at its source. This power of direct knowing is born in every individual. Some manifest it earlier in life, chiefly because they are less hypnotized. That is, the less one is subjected to the supposed knowledge of the race, which is really ignorance, the more readily does that one follow what he instinctively knows and feels to be true. It is within the individual always and must be brought out.

17. Jesus said, "I have nothing save that which comes in the name and through the power of Christ," putting himself in direct receptivity to spiritual intuition at all times. What Jesus did was really a lesson in how each man should proceed in every phase of life. That you might be one with the Father even as he was one with the Father, and his contact was always through the Christ, the Word of God, that is the inner fact of all men. "Christ is all and in all" and Christ is the inner reality of each individual.

18. There is only one kind of intuition just as there is only one kind of physical sight. You can, through your eyes, look toward and discover anything you wish. You may look for beauty and ugliness and you use the same sight. One is desirable and the other is undesirable. You may train your intuition to search out the determining principle and its operations; you can train it into psychic planes and find out what is going on there; or you can train it on your neighbor and discover his secret thought and motives. But, intuition turned in any other direction than to discover the operations of the Principle itself is perversion of this sense back of all senses and hypnosis is the result, for it clouds the clear perception of the individual. The only way to

escape any degree of hypnosis is to train the intuition into the channels of direct knowing. This is the path of light and any perversion of the intuitive sense is the path of darkness.

19. The old theory of occultism that the senses must be destroyed or killed or reversed is not in accordance with the teachings of the pure Hindu philosophy. They say that all is Spirit, that the senses are Spirit but must be so used and their true spiritual significance preserved. They become avenues of expression of that which the intuition learns as coming from the Spirit. This direct knowing is also direct manifestation. If we would accept the fact which is revealed in Principle, that fact would become immediately manifest to us. It is just that easy. The Westerner has simply submerged it in complexities.

20. When you rightly understand the nature of what you call matter as pure Spirit substance, then you can see just why this is true. The Hindu says, "Compress the cube and you have a different substance. Expand it and you have a different substance." You do not define this as material or physical substance, as in the compression or expansion you do not change its nature, but only the relative position of the atoms. Water or ice is just as much H_2O, regardless of its form, and this power of expansion and contraction is the fourth dimension of it. Likewise, the power of extending anything from one magnitude to another by the simple rearrangement of the atoms is its fourth dimension and does not change its inherent character. If all things are made of Spiritual substance, there is no dividing line between what we have called Spirit and its manifestation. Only when man is under a state of hypnosis does he imagine that there is something besides the unity of all things and the oneness of all things.

191

Through his state of hypnosis he imposes false influences into form and these distortions are the fabrications of his own ignorance.

FOR THE TEACHER

Paragraphs 1 and 2. The lesson to be found in this explanation of the Quantum Theory offers unusual opportunity to impress upon the mind of the individual the fact that all of his lack is due to separating himself from the original first cause. Just as a motor stops when it is disconnected from an electrical current or a light goes out when the switch is turned off, so does man cease to function in just that degree that he separates himself from the Spirit of God.

Paragraph 3. When it comes to a matter of merely manipulating the world with thought, trying to demonstrate by the use of affirmation, man sooner or later exhausts the ability to achieve. Only through deep meditation upon the oneness of all things, man's unity with God, is his power revived so that he again returns to the position of power that is rightfully his. Man of himself can do nothing. It is the Spirit that quickens and, when his mind and nature are reanimated with the Spirit, his words and acts become alive and then only does he move with power.

Paragraphs 4, 5, 6 and 7. It makes a vast difference to man whether he proceeds from a true or from an assumed or false hypothesis. The conclusions at which he arrives in his calculations depend upon the foundation or principle from which he moves. If that foundation is false, the conclusion must be false. As creation began in the great Universal Whole, man can find no substantial starting point for his own activities except from that same basis. One cannot adapt a principle to his own thought but he must adapt himself to the movement of principle and his thoughts must be evolved from that principle. In turn, his action must conform to that same principle and then, only, can he hope to have results forthcoming that are consistent with his fundamental nature.

Paragraphs 8 and 9. These paragraphs involve the difference between true and false reason, between intelligent logic and false logic. We get our minds completely reversed when we work from the external or when we work merely for external results that we imagine will suit our own idea of things. There is an established order in the Universe and only through aligning ourselves with that natural order of things can we hope for satisfactory results.

Paragraph 10. The force which designed and created the Universe could not be considered an unintelligent force or blind force moving without conscious direction. Electricity must be governed by intelligence in our everyday affairs, else we could not have light, heat, and power resulting from it. Electricity by itself is a blind force but, subjected to the control of intelligence, it produces constructive results. So all creative force of the Universe must be subjected to the direction of intelligence, else there never could have been an orderly creation.

Paragraphs 11, 12 and 13. Right knowledge comes through becoming so still that one feels within himself the movement of Universal forces, the Spirit of God. Its activity not only becomes a vitalizing influence but it awakens an understanding in the mind of man. "The inspiration of the Almighty giveth understanding." Just as you must first understand the operation of the principle of mathematics through quiet submission to the rule, so must you contemplate the action of Divine Principle until you understand its operations. Knowledge is the accumulation of ideas and true knowlege would be the result of seeing the spirit of God made manifest. Knowledge comes in the completion of a process. Understanding discerns the way toward results.

Paragraph 14. Neither mind nor matter have any power to create or to produce. The power to produce is in Mind or Spirit. It is the Spirit that quickens. Holding thoughts and driving the body only deplete the man. Life is renewed, power awakened through communion with Spirit.

Paragraphs 15 and 16. Faith is the means through which principle is discerned and applied. First, faith is resting the mind of its own activities to gain new impetus. Secondly, it is relying upon that impetus until it produces results. Faith is a sort of mental transformer whereby unaccomplished things or unmanifest powers are brought to manifestation.

Paragraph 17. The secret of Jesus' power was in his complete reliance upon what he felt moving in his deepest nature and which he called the Father within. The law of God is written in your inward parts and, to outwardly obey what is moving within is to bring the inner capacity into outer manifestation. That which moves in the deepest side of man's nature is the inward action of the Universal Principle.

Paragraph 18. Intuition is only another avenue through which consciousness may be increased. Through intuition one gains the inner facts of life. Trained to the Omniscience of God or the all-enfolding intellingence, man can understand anything or any situation from the viewpoint of absolute knowing.

194

Paragraph 19. The outer senses are outlets or avenues through which we express inward knowledge to the outward world. The outer senses should not be condemned or destroyed. In so doing you would destroy your outlets into the world. See to it that the function of your whole being lines up with the innermost tendencies of your nature until you express what you are in the sight of God.

Paragraph 20. To know the true nature of all things, not as separated or isolated divisions, but as one and the same thing in different stages of progression, is to be possessed of the power and dominion that belongs to you as a product of One First Cause.

CHAPTER XIV

RESUME

On our present tour, we have endeavored to give the student more of the actual teachings and practices of the Masters, rather than to recite the phenomena performed by them. We have not laid much stress upon our actual contacts in India but enough has been given of our travels and contacts to satisfy the minds of those persons who have wished to know something of the trip itself. Should we relate all the incidents and experiences thus far encountered, there would be no time nor space left in which to give that vital instruction that would help the student to live in his own experiences that which the masters live and prove. The average student is more interested in the philosophy and science which the masters employ. It is only through such knowledge that the individual may know how to proceed in attaining his own mastership. Furthermore, the miraculous feats and the manner in which the masters live has doubtless been sufficiently covered in the three volumes of *Life and Teaching of the Masters of the Far East.*

This trip has yielded us much of practical knowledge and it is our purpoe at this time to review the main points in order that they may stand out in the mind of the student. Thus he may have a clearly defined working basis from which to proceed in recasting his life in accordance with those motives through which the illumined have attained to mastership. Mastership is everyone's possibility but this state is not achieved through reading, study, or theorizing, but by actually living the life which the masters live.

It has been clearly stated that life lived by the average individual is hypnotic; that is, the majority of men and women are not living life as it was intended at all. Not one in a million feels the freedom to live what he inwardly feels he should live. He has come under the world opinion of himself and this opinion is what he obeys, rather than the law of his own being. In this respect and to this degree he is living under an hypnotic spell. He lives under the delusion that he is a mere human being, living in a merely material world, and only hopes to escape it when he dies and goes to what he calls Heaven. This is not the determination intended in the plan and purpose of life. Obedience to one's inner nature, the expression of life as he instinctively feels it ought to be expressed, is the very foundation of the life which the masters reveal as the only true mode of living.

Now, the difference between the teachings and practices of the masters and those of fakirs is that the fakir only intensifies the hypnotic condition of the mind. Further false and material pictures are so impressed upon the sensitive minds of people that they are thrown into further states of hypnosis. The masters say, "That which seems external exists not at all," by which they mean that it is not what appears that is the reality of life. The reality of life is that which moves out from the very center of one's being. They seek in every way to clarify their minds of world impressions and sit in long periods of Samadhi—Silence—in order that they may see clearly that innermost trend of their nature. Then their next attempt is to live in thought, word, and act that movement which they have discerned within themselves. True mastery is living the instruction of the inner teacher, the inner self, and not seeking the opinions of the world.

Nor does the method of the fakirs differ in any large measure from much of the teaching and practice of the metaphysical world of the West. The gathering of thoughts from teachers and books, building them into the conscious nature of one's being, is to establish a false determination which is largely hypnotic. The mere making of one's consciousness over according to thoughts evolved by other's minds is to impose a false condition upon that individual. To manipulate the body, the affairs, or to concentrate within the body to awaken its centers or functions is only to throw the individual further out of the true determination of life and the "last state of that man is worse than the first." Instruction received from the without must be taken into the mentality and assimilated, analyzed, checked with the deepest facts of one's own inner nature in order to determine if it be true to the Self. One best consult the Self first and gain his outer knowledge thus at first hand. The first method is slow and retarding to one's progress, while the latter is swift and freeing. Notice the difference when you act according to someone's instruction and when you obey what you instinctively feel to be the right thing to do. This of itself should teach us that the way of life is from within out.

The forces of life are silent and that is the main reason for the silent nature of the masters. That is the way they keep in harmony with life itself. Even our Scriptures teach in substance that a multitude of words is not without sin. Only when we speak in harmony with what we inwardly feel do we let ourselves out into complete harmony with the true determination of life. Have you not noticed that when you speak what you feel, just as when you do what you feel is right, that you are free? Also when you speak that which does not meet with the sanction of your innermost feelings, you feel you have limited or bound yourself.

This is the philosophy of non-resistance propounded by Gandhi and which is prevalent in Hindu teachings. Christ emphasized this teaching. When you speak or act in a manner that is out of harmony with yourself you create resistance and that resistance is the influence of hypnotic practices. It contracts the nature of man and keeps him from expressing what he truly is. Not only does this resistance occur in his own nature but, when brought to the notice of others, they further add to this resistance and by this practice the whole world is kept in darkness. "The Father who sees in secret rewards thee openly." No one resents the radiations of pure joy, even though they may be exceedingly sad, but try to talk them into joy and they resent it. Tell a poor man that he does not need to be poor and he is likely to resent it and will offer all sorts of excuses in defense of his poverty but bring him under the silent influence of abundance and his very soul expands. Try to separate two men who are fighting and they are likely to attack you but radiate a sense of peace from your own inner nature and they are more than likely to catch your sense of peace and cease fighting. The doctrine of non-resistance is not passive but is a dynamic radiation of the inner SELF.

Social reorganization and economic reform must emanate from the awakening consciousness of man. One cannot legislate or lay down rules that will govern man when under a spell of hypnosis. You cannot organize men's thoughts and motives until they conform to each other. It is in this realm that all differences arise. One man is selfish, another is unselfish. One is successful and another is a failure. One has unusual strength and ability, while another is weak and incapable. One thinks only of his material welfare and another thinks only of his spiritual welfare as entirely divorced from his outer nature. How can such diverging thoughts and feelings be organized into an harmonious mass? Only in man's innermost nature is he identical with his neighbor in thought and motive and only through bringing out what is within can there be peace and harmony in the earth.

It is that which moves in man's innermost nature that is identical with the great Universal Mind or God. "The law of God is written in your inward parts." Mastership is bringing to the surface what is buried within. This is brought about only through deep meditation and consulting with the SELF, which is the only master one can ever find that will lead him to the goal of life.

Overcoming is all a matter of learning to drop all seeming conditions of mind, body, and affairs and to begin life over again at its beginning. Start with the idea that you are that Self which you inwardly long to be and so devote yourself to being that Self that everything else is forgotten. Once you have found your Self and have become that Self, you are a master and a world helper. Many such working together in Silence will spread an influence over the world more powerful than any movements that originate in the machinery of organized industry, war, or social reform. The effectiveness of one's life is not so much in what he does but in how he does it and how he does it is determined by the degree of himself he has discovered.

Merely speaking words and relying upon the

power within them or the vibratory effect of the word never helps man to become a master. Words contain only that degree of power that is limited into them through the consciousness of the individual using them. The power is the depth of realization or the degree of consciousness back of them. It is not "words" that produce consciousness nor is it "words" that heal the body or change the affairs. It is a matter of awakened realization that produces words and impels outer action and the word or act is powerful only to the extent of this inner awakening.

The result of speaking or acting from outer motives not only produces an hypnotic condition of mind but gives rise to the notion that there are two opposing minds and, carried on, seems to divide the mind into many separate actions. Mind is a Unit and moves as a Unit and what seems to be dual-mindedness is only a dual set of ideas, one set evolved from outer impressions and one set originating in the natural state of mind as it originally moves. The mind is completely unified and harmonized by denial or rejection of every thought and impulse that does nto spring from one's innermost nature. This clears up the entire stream of consciousness and leaves the individual free to think and act as he should in perfect harmony with the Universal Mind. This is the very essence of mastery.

Speaking and living in this oneness without sense of division is the greatest gift of man for he was given "a sound mind", according to the Scriptures. In other words, he was started out into being in perfect oneness with his source; he was sound, whole, and Jesus said he must return to this state of sound-mindedness. "Tarry at Jerusalem until the Holy— whole—Spirit comes upon you" or until you return to that sense of oneness with the Universal Mind.

Spirit is Cause and when man returns to Cause, his Source, he becomes whole and sound. He is not only sound in mind but sound in body and his affairs become sound for his entire being is united into that great Unity which is the essential nature of all things. It is the soundness or oneness of all things in and with Source. Soundness or unity cannot mean anything less than the whole. It cannot refer to any individual or part of the whole. It must refer to the oneness of the whole. Everything is a center of unity or a center where the oneness of all things must be preserved and manifest. To localize or segregate any fact is to take it completely out of its nature and to lose its meaning altogether. When Christ spoke, "These and greater things shall ye do," or when Emil said, "You can do these things just as easily as I can do them," they were speaking from this consciousness of the only true unity, the soundness of the individual in his relationship to and with the whole.

This life of oneness is the life of the masters and anyone may live that life if he will drop his alliances with institutions and religions and races and nations and accept his alliance with the Universe. This is the "ark of the covenant" which enabled the Children of Israel to succeed but, when it was lost, they failed to gain their liberty from opposition.

All separation is purely a matter of individual hypothesis. One cannot really be separated from the whole for he is created within it, is a part of it, and is like unto it. Love is the great unifier in the consciousness of man and to keep oneself always in an attitude of love is to progress toward oneness. It is the only preserver of life and health and ability. One need not try to love everybody but he must eternally seek to keep his nature whole through the increase of love. When one's nature expands in love, he will sooner or later find himself in a loving attitude toward all men and, in this attitude, he not only lifts himself but all those around him into that same oneness. There are no divisions in an awakened sense of love.

One does not gain mastery or illumination by going to India and sitting at the feet of a master. One gains mastery by listening to the deepest facts of his own nature and by obeying what he there learns. There is no help that is needed that is not available instantly if one but turns in this direction and proceeds from this fact. All the power of the Universe is back of every high motive, every true impulse that stirs in man's inner nature. It is like the germ of life within the seed and all the forces of nature move to bring it forth into its full expression of all its potentialities. This is the manner of the masters and their instruction is always that you must be true to the Self, live the life of the Self, express what is inherently true until you are outwardly what you inwardly long to be.

When man returns to this motive of life, all that there is in the Universe begins to move in upon him, to manifest itself through him. Not only must man have the intelligence to direct him and the power to do that which is to be done, but also the substance that nourishes and supports him in the doing. There is no lack, except in the realm of hypnotic ideas that have clouded his mind from reality. Back in his native oneness, where he consciously receives what the Universe is pouring out upon him, there can be no lack in any phase of his being nor in his affairs.

The Quantum Theory is the approach of Science to this basic fact of life and there can be no true science, religion, social structure, or successful living outside the undefeatable and indissoluble oneness of all things.

This is the road to mastery, the life of the masters, and the only true life there is. It is to be found just where you are in the secret places of your own inner nature. The masters teach that liberation is to be found in this and in no other way. Christ, speaking in the man Jesus, said the same thing when he said, "No man cometh unto the Father but by me." The same Christ in you speaks the same message to you. Your only contact with a master is through the mastery in yourself.

THE ROUGH GUIDE TO

New England

written and researched by

Sarah Hull and Stephen Keeling

ROUGH GUIDES

roughguides.com

Contents

INTRODUCTION 4

Where to go 5
When to go 8
Things not to miss 10
Itineraries 16

BASICS 18

Getting there 19
Getting around 21
Accommodation 23
Food and drink 25
The media 26
Festivals 26
Culture and etiquette 28
Sports 28
Outdoor activities 30
Travel essentials 32

THE GUIDE 40

1 Boston 40
2 Eastern Massachusetts 126
3 Central and Western Massachusetts 202
4 Rhode Island 238
5 Connecticut 274
6 Vermont 326
7 New Hampshire 384
8 Maine 446

CONTEXTS 518

History 519
New England on film 528
Books 531

SMALL PRINT & INDEX 534

Introduction to
New England

The states of Massachusetts, Rhode Island, Connecticut, Vermont, New Hampshire and Maine – collectively known as New England – exemplify America at its most nostalgic: country stores that brim with cider and gourds, snow-dusted hillsides, miles of blazing autumn foliage, white-steepled churches fronting village greens, clam shacks, crimson cranberry bogs and an unruly ocean that distinguishes and defines it all. Scratch just beneath the surface, however, and you'll also uncover fiercely independent locals, innovative chefs and some of the country's best contemporary art museums. Both a marvellous time capsule and an idyllic trailblazer, New England offers visitors a captivating slice of Americana that's blessed with spellbinding terrain and a profound sense of history.

Boston especially is celebrated as the birthplace of American independence – so many of the seminal events of the **Revolutionary War** took place here, or nearby at Lexington and Concord – and the **coastal towns** of Massachusetts, Rhode Island and Maine still bear plenty of traces of the region's early settlements.

Not everything is about historical legacy, though. Indeed, above all, New England packs an enormous amount of variety into what is by American standards a relatively small area. Its attractions are many and sundry, taking in sites both cerebral – fine collections of art and Americana, the homes of numerous seminal figures of **American literature** (Emily Dickinson, Henry David Thoreau and Mark Twain, among legions of others), and the country's most influential academic institutions – and active, including excellent opportunities for **skiing**, **hiking**, **cycling** and **watersports**, not to mention eating and drinking or just watching the leaves change colour. The landscape is surprisingly diverse as well, ranging from sandy beaches and rocky bluffs to green rolling hills and even snowy mountains.

This varied **terrain**, in particular, has had a major impact on the character of the region's inhabitants. Inland, its thin soil and harsh climate have traditionally made it

ABOVE COVERED BRIDGE, NEW HAMPSHIRE **RIGHT** BOSTON HARBO

difficult to sustain an agricultural way of life, with residents instead turning to – and prospering from – **manufacturing** in the nineteenth and early twentieth centuries. Over time, these difficult circumstances produced a tough, hearty "Yankee" spirit on which locals still pride themselves. The sea has been another historic source of sustenance: **whaling** and **shipbuilding** were successful industries in the nineteenth century, and lobstering, fishing and shellfish harvesting continue the tradition today.

New England is compact, well defined and quite easy to **get around**; only Maine, the region's largest and most rural state, takes any real time to navigate. Connecticut, Massachusetts and Rhode Island are more urban and historic, and where nature intervenes, it is usually along the spectacular coastline. Further north, the lakes and mountains of Vermont, New Hampshire and particularly Maine, offer **wilderness** to rival any in the nation.

Where to go

Boston is the undisputed capital of New England, perhaps America's most historic city and certainly one of its most elegant, full of enough colonial charm, Victorian town houses, groomed greenspaces, contemporary culture and fine restaurants and bars to satisfy most appetites. Together with its energetic student-orientated neighbour, **Cambridge**, Boston merits a visit of at least a few days. It also makes a good base for day-trips out to historic Lexington and Concord, the ocean-battered North Shore, where the witch-related sights of seventeenth-century **Salem** probably hold the most interest,

and **Cape Cod** – a charming beach-laden peninsula, with delightful, quirky **Provincetown** at its outermost tip.

Ferries head from the Cape to the popular summer retreats of **Martha's Vineyard** and **Nantucket**, marked by pockets of wild heaths and moors in addition to premium stretches of sand. The former is famous for its neighbourhood of "gingerbread"-style cottages, the latter, its cedar-shingled homes, blanketed with roses.

West of Boston, there's the pretty and collegiate **Pioneer Valley**, which gives way to the **Berkshires**, a scenic retreat – all Gilded Age mansions, exceptional art museums and leafy byways – for the east coast's cultural elite. Southwest of Boston, along the coast, tiny Rhode Island's two main attractions are energetic **Providence** and the string of lavish waterfront estates that make up old-money **Newport**, beyond which you can take in the better parts of the Connecticut coast: the seaport of **Mystic**, and, further on, likeable **New Haven**, the home of Yale University and several iconic restaurants.

In Vermont, beyond relaxed, urbane **Burlington**, it's most enjoyable to simply meander the state's backroads, calling in at country inns and dairy farms – unless, of course, you're making the pilgrimage to **Ben & Jerry's Ice Cream** in Waterbury. If you've come for winter sports, you can enjoy, resorts like **Killington** and **Stowe**, which rank among the best in the Northeast. Over in New Hampshire, the rugged glory of the **White Mountains** is the state's most dramatic lure, with the highest peaks in the region; indeed, if you enjoy camping or hiking you won't want to miss this area. Back at the coast, **Portsmouth** is crammed with historic mansions and enticing restaurants.

Finally, there's Maine, which has New England's most extreme blend of seaside towns – **Portland, Bar Harbor** – and untamed interior wilderness. You can spot moose outside **Rangeley**, whitewater raft near **Moosehead Lake** and do some hiking in **Baxter State Park** along the Appalachian Trail, which runs through all three of New England's northern states.

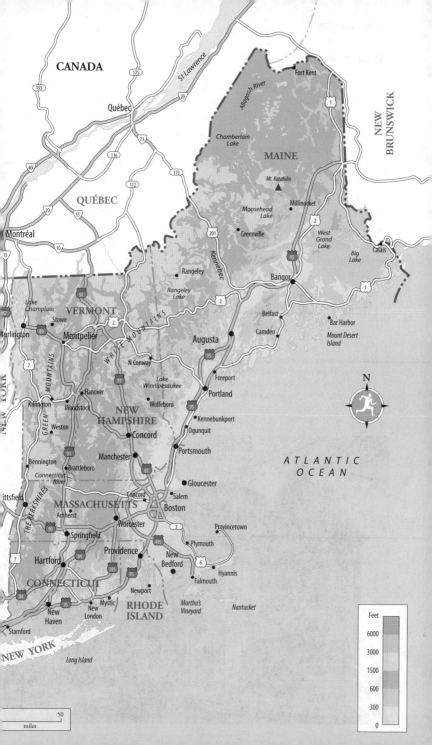

When to go

New England is at its most beautiful during **autumn**, when the foliage is magnificent (particularly in October), but this is also one of the most popular times to visit the region, so accommodation can fill up quickly and prices rise (notably, this is not the case with many coastal communities, such as Cape Cod and the islands, where shoulder season prices apply). Often overlooked as a travel month, **September** is also quite inviting: warm temperatures prevail, there's a hint of crispness in the air and summertime crowds have abated. The region gets quite cold and snowy during the **winter** months, but they're a perfect time to visit if you want to ski or take part in other winter sports. **Summer** is high season, when most tourist attractions – especially along the coasts of Cape Cod, Maine and Rhode Island, and inland in the Berkshires – really kick into high gear and things can get crowded. On balance, late **spring** is a more relaxed time to come: the temperature is generally agreeable, if a little unpredictable, the crowds are more dispersed, and prices have yet to go up for the tourist season.

LITERARY NEW ENGLAND

Perhaps fitting for a region dominated by institutions of higher education, New England has an incredibly rich literary heritage that's particularly well versed in poetry, transcendentalist and Gothic writings. You can visit many of the region's literary landmarks, including the homes where Longfellow (see p.93), Alcott (see p.132), Dickinson (see p.217), Twain (see p.308), Wharton (see p.229) and many more notables were either born, raised or spent their time writing. It's also possible to see sites made famous by the works themselves, like the House of the Seven Gables in Salem (see p.144), or the Seaman's Bethel in New Bedford, from Moby Dick (see p.157). Whether meditating by Walden Pond (see p.134) or stopping in the snowy woods near Robert Frost's farm in Derry, New Hampshire (see p.404), you're sure to feel some creative spirit move you.

Author picks

Whittling our favourite New England picks down to a brief list was a Herculean challenge. Ultimately, our authors went with the places, activities and foods for which they are the most nostalgic. If time and distance were no object, they would sample all the following on a regular basis…

Beachcomber, MA Encapsulating everything we love about Cape Cod, this sand dune shanty has stellar live music, a beer-swilling crowd and some of the world's best raw oysters. p.177

A peppermint-striped lighthouse, ME Windswept and remote, West Quoddy Head lighthouse marks the easternmost point in the country, augmented by several miles of trails along sheer cliffs and a boardwalk across a fascinating bog. p.504

Apple-picking It's an annual tradition to pick apples and enjoy freshly pressed cider in the autumn, when orchards throughout New England open their gates to visitors. p.136

A kaleidoscope of colour, VT Travel writers are notorious for waxing poetic about Vermont's autumn foliage, but we can't help it: year after year, the sheer scale of the blazing hues of the leaves here consistently take our breath away. p.326

Boston museums, MA Just down the block from one another, the one-of-a-kind Isabella Stewart Gardner Museum and the spectacular Museum of Fine Arts are not to be missed. p.85

World-famous pizza, CT To get a higher education in pizza order the famous clam pie at New Haven's *Pepe's* or *Sally's*, rival pizzerias that have been sparring it out for over seventy years. p.296

Island escape, MA We jump at any chance to visit Martha's Vineyard, which has more beaches, wild moorlands and quaint New England villages than you can shake a stick at. p.183

> Our author recommendations don't end here. We've flagged up our favourite places – a perfectly sited hotel, an atmospheric café, a special restaurant – throughout the guide, highlighted with the ★ symbol.

LEFT MARK TWAIN HOUSE **RIGHT FROM TOP** AUTUMN IN VERMONT; APPLES, NEW HAMPSHIRE; MUSEUM OF FINE ARTS, BOSTON

18

things not to miss

It's not possible to see everything that New England has to offer in one trip – and we don't suggest you try. What follows is a selective taste of the region's highlights: dramatic scenery, picturesque villages, colonial relics and unusual museums. All highlights have a page reference to take you straight into the Guide, where you can find out more.

1 ACADIA NATIONAL PARK
Page 497
Although it's petite, this national park packs a beautiful punch – rugged, varied and dramatic.

2 LITCHFIELD HILLS
Page 316
If you're looking for scenic villages and manicured town squares amidst some surprisingly rural patches, this Connecticut alternative to the Berkshires should do the trick.

3 A BASEBALL GAME AT FENWAY PARK
Page 82
The country's oldest Major League ballpark is home to the beloved Red Sox, the 37ft-tall "Green Monster", and lots of legendary baseball lore.

4 NEWPORT'S MANSIONS
Page 257
Such ostentation was called "conspicuous consumption" in Thorstein Veblen's day; in ours, you don't have to be self-conscious at all to gawk at the folly.

5 **SAINT-GAUDENS NATIONAL HISTORIC SITE**
Page 416
Exuberant sculptures set within the sculptor's tranquil former home.

6 **MASS MOCA**
Page 236
A first-class contemporary art museum in an unlikely location.

7 **BLOCK ISLAND'S INNS**
Page 272
Watch the sun set from a grand Victorian inn in Old Harbor.

8 **SUMMER FESTIVALS IN THE BERKSHIRES**
Page 231
Tanglewood is the most celebrated outdoor venue of all, but there are plenty more.

9 **EATING IN PORTSMOUTH**
Page 395
There is a raft of surprisingly smart restaurants in this seafront town.

10 **HIKING THE LONG TRAIL**
Page 344
This Vermont trek is one of the region's most rewarding.

11 **PORTLAND**
Page 460
Portland boasts tempting museums, boutiques and restaurants galore.

12 **SKIING STOWE**
Page 361
Fine slopes abound in New England, but the oldest resort of Stowe is still one of the best.

13 **TRACING COLONIAL HISTORY**
Pages 50, 132 & 328
Discover the emblems of America's birth from the Freedom Trail to the region's battlegrounds.

14 **NANTUCKET**
Page 192
A wild island with a rich whaling legacy.

15 **MYSTIC SEAPORT**
Page 280
A fascinating re-construction of an 1800s shipyard and village.

16 **CAPE COD NATIONAL SEASHORE**
Page 175
Enjoy untouched beaches and tempting clam shacks in this fragile national park.

17 **SHELBURNE MUSEUM**
Page 375
An illuminating collection of Americana from the past two centuries.

18 **BURLINGTON**
Page 369
This enjoyable town has an assured sense of vitality and a lovely lakeside setting.

Itineraries

There are many ways to approach New England, and the following itineraries are just a sampling of our favourite ways to zigzag the region. Routes can be followed point-by-point or simply used as aids for brainstorming your own fantasy road trip.

THE GRAND TOUR

This **three-week trip** covers our take on New England's greatest hits: an enticing path that ambles through historic cities, verdant farmland and coastal villages.

❶ Boston, MA Catch a baseball game in the country's oldest Major League ballpark, retrace the steps of Revolutionary War leaders and view world-class art. **See p.40**

❷ Provincetown, MA Retreat to the beach at this Cape Cod town with an arresting shoreline. Visit one of the Cape's two inviting islands – Martha's Vineyard and Nantucket. **See p.178**

❸ Block Island, RI Continue your beachcombing theme at this secluded (but never exclusive) island hideaway. Just nine miles long, it manages to pack in two lighthouses and thirty miles of trails. **See p.268**

❹ Hartford, CT It may be a little rough around the edges, but this seventeenth-century city is home to a wealth of cultural gems, including Mark Twain's house and the child-friendly Connecticut Science Center. **See p.305**

❺ MASS MoCA, MA The Berkshires' crazy, artistic lovechild, this museum of contemporary art is the perfect introduction to the area. **See p.236**

❻ Robert Frost Trail/Rte-125, VT Walk or snowshoe in the footsteps of poet Robert Frost, who so loved this forested patch that he spent his final twenty-four summers here. **See p.358**

❼ Mount Washington, NH Hike, drive or take the cog railway up the northeast's highest peak, nestled in the picturesque White Mountain Forest. **See p.441**

❽ Stonington, ME Just around the bend from Acadia National Park, this remote fishing village shares the beauty of the preserve without the inhibiting crowds. **See p.493**

REGIONAL CHOW

This **two-week trip** is a little fanciful, incorporating our top choices for eating the region's iconic and mouthwatering comestibles.

❶ JT Farnham's Seafood and Grill, MA Cape Ann is famed for its fried clams – the shellfish crown goes to *Farnham's*, where crowds are thinner and the golden shellfish is accompanied by views of a scenic marsh. **See p.151**

❷ Lobster rolls, ME Maine is justly lauded for its lobster and a good crustacean is never far here. Two notable eateries are the *Lobster Shack at Two Lights* and *Red's Eats*. **See p.466** & **p.477**

❸ Ben & Jerry's Factory, VT Perhaps the sweetest byproduct of Vermont's famous cows is this whimsical brand of ice cream, manufactured amid rolling hills. **See p.360**

❹ Connecticut Wine Trail, CT Bucolic western Connecticut is home to more than a dozen wineries, perfect for sampling local vintages on a balmy day. **See p.319**

ABOVE BIKERS ON THE KANCAMAGUS HIGHWAY

⑤ Pizza in New Haven, CT The ultimate road trip pit stops, legendary *Pepe's* and *Sally's* dish out unbeatable Neapolitan fare. **See p.296**

⑥ Coffee cabinets, RI A Rhode Island-only delicacy, made of blended ice cream, milk and coffee syrup. Pop by *Gray's Ice Cream* to sample a great one – they've been mixing up home-made batches for over eighty years. **See p.264**

⑦ Miss Worcester Diner, MA Great breakfasts in the lunch car said to be the model for the diners once made across the street. **See p.209**

AUTUMN FOLIAGE

Nothing compares to the spectacular New England foliage season (mid-Sept to Oct). The air is crisp, plump apples hang heavy and maple, poplar and birch trees turn brilliant shades of crimson, amber and gold. Get a front row seat with the following **two-week itinerary**. Leaves change colour from north to south; check ⓦ yankeefoliage.com before heading out.

① Coastal Rte-1, ME Plenty of folks favour Maine's Rte-1 in summer, which is why we prefer it in autumn. Drive all the way to Canada, or just to Ogunquit or Portland. **See p.453**

② Kancamagus Highway, NH Easily driven in a day, but pleasant enough to be savoured for weeks, "the Kanc" will satisfy even the most discerning foliage gawker. **See p.430**

③ Rte-100, VT Widely considered the region's best for leaf-spotting, easygoing Rte-100 cuts through the heart of the state and skirts the perimeter of the Green Mountain Forest. **See p.343**

④ Mount Greylock, MA Take a break from the road and summit Massachusetts' highest peak (don't worry, it's only 3491ft); the Berkshires are unbeatable for autumn colour. **See p.236**

⑤ Kent, CT Off any major circuit, this sleepy yet refined Connecticut town is near the Appalachian Trail and has smart restaurants and a small but acclaimed arts scene. **See p.320**

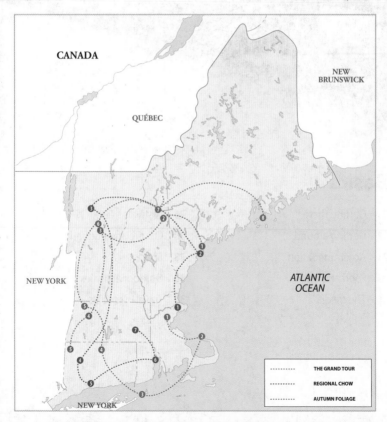

MOUNT WASHINGTON COG RAILWAY

Basics

19 Getting there

21 Getting around

23 Accommodation

25 Food and drink

26 The media

26 Festivals

28 Culture and etiquette

28 Sports

30 Outdoor activities

32 Travel essentials

Getting there

The primary point of arrival into New England is Boston, Massachusetts, the region's largest city. All the major airlines operate direct flights to Boston's Logan International Airport from the US, Canada and Europe (those coming from points west typically connect with domestic flights in California). Within North America, trains are a second (but not particularly cheap) option for getting to regional cities like Boston, Portland and Providence, while for budget travellers buses make a good alternative and are also useful for reaching smaller towns. Really, though, the best way to get to New England is by car, especially if you're looking to cover a lot of ground.

From North America

Getting to New England **from anywhere in North America** is only problematic – via any kind of transport – in the winter, when roads get icy and airports occasionally close due to inclement weather.

By air

Direct **flights** to Boston's Logan International Airport are available from all the major hubs in North America (including the Canadian cities of Toronto, Montréal, Vancouver and Ottawa), though you may find yourself connecting through Chicago, New York or another large East Coast city. Some of the discount domestic airlines use other New England cities as hubs: Southwest (**W** southwest.com) flies to Providence's T.F. Green Airport (RI) and Manchester's Manchester–Boston Airport (NH), and JetBlue (**W** jetblue.com) flies to Burlington (VT) and Portland (ME) in addition to Boston. Smaller airports in Portland (ME), Bangor (ME) and Windsor Locks (near Hartford, CT) are serviced less regularly by smaller aircraft, though some have international terminals as well. It's also worth checking flights to New York City, as these are often cheap enough to make taking a bus or train the rest of the way to New England worth the inconvenience.

East Coast arrivals have the best access to the region, as frequent **shuttle services** (JetBlue, **W** jetblue.com; Delta, **W** delta.com; US Airways, **W** usairways.com) to Boston originate from New York's LaGuardia, JFK and Newark airports, and Washington, DC's Reagan National Airport; most of these fly hourly during the week and every couple of hours on the weekend. Southwest also runs a near-hourly shuttle from Baltimore's BWI Airport (near DC) to Providence for just over $150 each way.

Generally, the most expensive time to fly is from mid-May to early September; note, though, that regional flights can continue to stay pricey well into October thanks to the popularity of the **autumn foliage** season (mid-Sept to late Oct).

The **winter season** – with the exception of Thanksgiving, Christmas and New Year's – is the cheapest time to fly. Year-round, **fares** are lowest in the heavily trafficked Northeast corridor; a return fare from New York can cost as little as $90–100, although $150–200 is more typical; from Washington, DC and Miami, the range is usually $200–300; from Chicago, $200–300. Return fares from LA, San Francisco or Seattle typically cost $250–400, though these can go as low as $350. From **Canada**, be prepared to pay around Can$305–410 from Toronto and Montréal, and closer to Can$610–760 from Vancouver.

By train

For those heading to New England from Washington, DC and New York, **train** travel is a pleasant alternative to flying, though unless you're taking local commuter services, it's not much less expensive than air travel. The **Amtrak** (**T** 1 800 872 7245, **W** amtrak.com) trains that serve the Northeast corridor are the fleet's most reliable, generally sticking to their official schedule. **Fares** from New York to Boston range from $136 to $262 return; the *Acela Express* is the most expensive, but will shave only forty minutes or so off the normal travel time (4hr 20min). From Washington, DC, the regular train runs just shy of eight hours (beginning at $180 return) while the *Acela Express* takes 6hr 30min (beginning at $304 return). Amtrak does offer several good-value **rail passes** that allow unlimited travel in certain areas, and the website also offers special **deals** and weekly sales.

Travellers headed south from elsewhere in New England can hop on Amtrak's inexpensive *Downeaster* (**W** amtrakdowneaster.com), which stops at various points in Maine and New Hampshire on its way south to Boston from Portland, Maine. Tickets from Portland to Boston's North Station are just $24, and the trip takes two and a half hours.

Visitors approaching the region **from Canada** on Via Rail (**T** 1 888 842 7245, **W** viarail.ca) can connect with Amtrak in Montréal. The rail journey can take anywhere from twelve to twenty hours from

---

A BETTER KIND OF TRAVEL

At Rough Guides we are passionately committed to travel. We feel that travelling is the best way to understand the world we live in and the people we share it with – plus tourism has brought a great deal of benefit to developing economies around the world over the last few decades. But the growth in tourism has also damaged some places irreparably, and climate change is exacerbated by most forms of transport, especially flying. All Rough Guides' trips are carbon-offset, and every year we donate money to a variety of charities devoted to combating the effects of climate change.

Toronto and Montréal, and more than three days from Vancouver. Fares start at around $250 return from the nearer points.

By bus

Considering how expensive rail travel can be in the US, getting to New England by **bus** can be an appealing option. Greyhound (☎1 800 231 2222, ⓦgreyhound.com) has an extensive network of destinations in New England. As with air and train routes, **Boston** is the best-served destination, especially if you're coming from New York or Washington, DC; trips typically take 4hr 15min from New York and 10hr 30min from DC; return fares are around $50 and $120, respectively (book online for the best deals).

Visitors from **New York City** have additional, better choices when it comes to buses, ranked here in descending order of quality (the last two being simply adequate): Bolt Bus (☎1 877 265 8287, ⓦboltbus.com; free wi-fi on board), Mega Bus (☎1 877 462 6342, ⓦmegabus.com; free wi-fi on board), Fung Wah (☎617 345 8000, ⓦfungwahbus.com) and Lucky Star (☎1 888 881 0887, ⓦluckystarbus.com). Fares average about $20–25 one-way (Fung Wah and Lucky Star have fares of $15 one-way) and arrive at South Station in Boston. If you're coming from NYC, the worst bus to take is (arguably) Greyhound, with its long queues and poor customer service; if you can, book ahead and get a seat on Greyhound's **Bolt Bus** affiliate instead. Bolt offers additional service between New York, Philadelphia, and Washington, DC, while Mega reaches more local areas, with stops in Amherst and Hyannis, MA, and Holyoke and Storrs, CT.

Coming **from Canada**, the wi-fi-enabled NeOn (ⓦneonbus.com) bus runs direct from New York City to Toronto for as little as Can$1. Several daily buses from Toronto reach Boston with at least one changeover, contributing to a minimum 14hr ride (Can$163 return). Direct buses from Montréal to Boston take around eight hours (Can$137 return). In all cases, contact Greyhound (☎1 800 661 8747, ⓦgreyhound.ca).

By car

Renting a car in North America involves the usual steps of phoning the local branch, or checking the website, of one of the major companies (see p.22); most have offices at destination airports. Also worth considering are **fly-and-drive deals**, which give cut-rate (and sometimes free) car rental when buying an air ticket; most airlines offer these deals so it is worth shopping around.

To rent a car you must be **over 21** years old, and drivers under 25 are charged a per-day surcharge of approximately $30. In general, $300 a week is a fairly standard base rate for an economy vehicle; note that renting your car at a **local branch** is often cheaper than at the airport, and returning the car in a different city from the one in which you rented it can incur a charge.

It's very easy to get to New England by car, with several **major highways** transecting the region: I-95, which runs along the Atlantic coast south from Canada and circumscribes the Boston area; I-90 (the Massachusetts Turnpike or "Mass Pike"), which approaches Massachusetts from the west; and I-91, which heads south from Québec and straddles Vermont and New Hampshire before hitting Amherst, MT and Hartford, CT. Drivers planning on hitting downtown Boston during their New England tour should be prepared for its confusing road layout, poor signage and crazy drivers. Other than that, driving should be straightforward.

A car rented in Canada can normally be driven **across the border** into the US, but you will pay a much higher fee if you do not return it to its country of origin. Most of the larger companies have offices in Canada.

From the UK and Ireland

There are plenty of direct flights **from Britain and Ireland** to Boston, fewer to other regional cities. Keep in mind that the first place the plane lands on American soil is your point of entry into the US, which means you'll have to collect your bags and go through customs and immigration, even if you're continuing on to other regional points.

Fares from the UK hover around £250 in low season (Nov to mid-Dec & Jan–March), £350 in spring and fall, and over £400 in high season (mid-May to early Sept). Flights from Dublin cost around the same, but can ring in at over €820 from Shannon.

From Australia, New Zealand and South Africa

There are no direct flights to Boston **from Australia** or **New Zealand** – most visitors from those countries reach the eastern US by way of western cities such as Los Angeles and San Francisco. However you do it, it's a long trip (about 14hr to the West Coast and another 6hr to New England).

Return fares from eastern Australian cities are usually around Aus$1400–1700, while tickets from Perth and Darwin can cost up to Aus$600 more. The best connections to the West Coast tend be with United (@united.com), Delta (@delta.com), V Australia (@virginaustralia.com) and Qantas (@qantas.com.au).

From **New Zealand**, most flights are out of Auckland, although they also run from Christchurch and Wellington. A two-tiered flight (nonstop to the West Coast and nonstop again to Boston) costs NZ$3000–3500 in high season.

Flights from Johannesburg, **South Africa**, generally have one to two layovers (in Atlanta, New York, London or Madrid), with prices hovering at around ZAR10,000.

AGENTS AND OPERATORS

Adventure World Australia ☎ 02 8913 0755, @ adventureworld .com.au; New Zealand ☎ 09 524 5118, @ adventureworld.co.nz. Agents for a vast array of international adventure travel companies that operate trips to every continent.

Airtech US ☎ 212 219 7000, @ airtech.com. Standby seat broker with great deals on plane tickets.

Bon Voyage UK ☎ 0800 316 3012, @ bon-voyage.co.uk. Tailor-made trips to the US, from short-term breaks to extended family stays.

ebookers UK ☎ 0871 223 5000; Republic of Ireland ☎ 01 4311 311; @ ebookers.com. Low fares on an extensive selection of scheduled flights and package deals.

Exodus US ☎ 1 800 843 4272; UK ☎ 020 8675 5550, @ exodus .co.uk. Adventure and activity-orientated vacation packages focusing on low-impact tourism.

Explore Worldwide UK ☎ 0845 868 6480, @ explore.co.uk. Hundreds of group tours, including everything from short weekend trips to activity-orientated family adventures.

IGLTA US ☎ 954 630 1637, @ iglta.org. A good resource for LGBT travel needs: lists destinations, tours and travel agents.

North South Travel UK ☎ 01245 608 291, @ northsouthtravel .co.uk. Friendly, competitive travel agency, offering discounted fares worldwide. Profits are used to support projects in the developing world, especially sustainable tourism.

STA Travel US ☎ 1 800 781 4040; UK ☎ 0800 819 9339; Australia ☎ 134 782; New Zealand ☎ 0800 474 400; @ statravel.com. Worldwide specialists in independent travel; also student IDs, travel insurance, car rental, rail passes and more. Good discounts for students and under-26s.

Trailfinders UK ☎ 0845 054 6060; Republic of Ireland ☎ 01 677 7888; @ trailfinders.com. One of the best-informed and most efficient agents for independent travellers.

Trek America US ☎ 1 800 873 5872, @ trekamerica.com; UK ☎ 0844 576 1400, @ trekamerica.co.uk. Road trip company geared to 18–38-year-olds, with 7 to 64-day camping, hiking and adventure tours throughout the US (from $800).

Getting around

Although rural areas can be nearly impossible to access if you don't have a car, getting from one city to another in New England on public transport is seldom much of a problem – good bus links and reasonable, though limited, train services are nearly always available. If you want to visit smaller towns, though, or to be able to travel without being tied to a schedule, renting your own car is highly recommended.

By car

Driving is the best way to get around New England. Away from the cities and major towns, many places are almost impossible to reach without your own vehicle. National and state parks and forests, especially, are served infrequently by public transport, which will usually take you only as far as the main visitors' centre.

The maximum **speed limit** in New England is 65mph, with lower signposted limits – usually around 25–35mph – in built-up areas. The default

---

HITCHHIKING

The usual advice given about hitchhiking in the US is that it's a **bad idea**; we do not recommend it, nor do we recommend picking up hitchhikers.

> ## ADVICE FOR NON-US DRIVERS
> First things first: make sure you're driving on the **right side** of the road, and note that the steering wheel is on the left side of the car. **Seat belts** are compulsory and at junctions you are allowed to turn on a red light as long as there is no prohibiting sign. Remember that 1 mile equals 1.6 kilometres. If you are from an English-speaking country, a **valid driver's licence** and **passport** should suffice for car rental; if your licence is not in English, you will also need to present an **International Driving Permit**. Keep in mind that most rental cars in the USA have automatic transmission.

speed limit in residential areas is 25mph, so if you don't see a sign, you'd probably do well to adhere to this limit.

Aside from in the most rural areas, **petrol stations** are open late and easy to find. At the time of writing, petrol prices in New England hovered at around $2.60–3.10 a gallon.

Winter driving

Driving in the **winter** is actually less perilous than you may expect. New England is well used to snow, and has learned to take care of the roads efficiently so that residents can drive to work and school all winter long. As long as you don't drive *during* a snowstorm or icestorm and take care in the mountains, there's not too much to worry about.

In general, it's smart to check road and weather conditions before setting out and keep your petrol tank two-thirds full to prevent the vehicle's fuel line from freezing. Drive slowly, and don't slam on the brakes (apply a consistent tapping motion instead), as slamming can cause your vehicle to slide if there's any ice present. Consider getting snow tires or tire chains, or carrying an **emergency car-care kit** on trips in difficult weather conditions. Such a

> ## DRIVING TIMES FROM BOSTON
> **To Burlington, VT** 3hr 40min (216 miles)
> **To Concord, NH** 1hr 15min (68 miles)
> **To Hartford, CT** 1hr 35min (101 miles)
> **To Hyannis, MA** 1hr 20min (70 miles)
> **To New Haven, CT** 2hr 10min (137 miles)
> **To Newport, RI** 1hr 15min (71 miles)
> **To Northampton, MA** 1hr 35min (103 miles)
> **To Portland, ME** 2hr (107 miles)
> **To Providence, RI** 1hr (50 miles)
> **To Provincetown, MA** 3hr (116 miles)

kit typically contains antifreeze, windshield washer fluid, shovel, ice scraper, jumper cables, flares or reflectors, blankets, non-perishable food and a first-aid kit.

CAR RENTAL AGENCIES
Alamo ☎ 1 800 522 9696, ⓦ alamo.com.
Avis ☎ 1 800 331 1212, ⓦ avis.com.
Budget ☎ 1 800 527 0700, ⓦ budget.com.
Dollar ☎ 1 800 800 3665, ⓦ dollar.com.
Enterprise Rent-a-Car ☎ 1 800 261 7331, ⓦ enterprise.com.
Hertz ☎ 1 800 654 3131, ⓦ hertz.com.
Holiday Autos ☎ 1 866 392 9288, ⓦ thrifty.com.
National ☎ 1 800 227 7368, ⓦ nationalcar.com.
Thrifty ☎ 1 800 847 4389, ⓦ thrifty.com.

MOTORING ORGANIZATIONS
American Automobile Association ☎ 1 800 222 4357, ⓦ aaa.com. Provides roadside assistance, free maps and trip planning and an array of discounts to members.
Canadian Automobile Association ☎ 1 613 247 0117, ⓦ caa.ca. Offers the same services as the American Automobile Association.

By air

New England is small enough that travelling around by **plane** is generally unnecessary. It can be useful for long trips – from Boston, MA to Burlington, VT, for example (which costs around $250). At off-peak times, flights between Boston and Portland, ME, cost around $150.

By train

Amtrak's (☎ 1 800 872 7244, ⓦ amtrak.com) four main routes in New England provide decent, though limited, **rail connections** between the few major cities in western New England, as well as some of the minor ones. Probably the prettiest route is via the *Vermonter*, which winds from Washington, DC through New York City and then western Connecticut, western Massachusetts and all the way north through Vermont. The other major north–south Amtrak routes in and around New England – the *Ethan Allen* (Washington, DC to Rutland, VT) and the *Northeast Regional* (Washington, DC to Boston, MA) – are almost as scenic, as is the *Downeaster* (Boston, MA to Portland, ME). There's also a route called the *Lake Shore Limited* that travels the length of Massachusetts (from Chicago, IL) to Boston.

Fares can be cut greatly by using one of several Amtrak **rail passes**, which give unlimited travel within certain time periods.

By bus

If you're travelling on your own, and making a lot of stops, **buses** are by far the cheapest way to get around. There are several main bus companies (see below) linking the major cities and many smaller towns in New England. Out in the country buses are fairly scarce, sometimes appearing only once a day, so you'll need to plot your route with care. As for **fares**, bus tickets are consistently less than train or airline tickets.

BUS COMPANIES

C&J Trailways ☎ 1 800 258 7111, **ⓦ** ridecj.com. Service from Logan Airport and Boston's South Station through northern MA to southern NH.

Concord Coach Lines ☎ 1 800 639 3317, **ⓦ** concordcoachlines .com. Good coverage of New Hampshire and Maine, with connecting services to Logan Airport.

Greyhound ☎ 1 800 231 2222, **ⓦ** greyhound.com. Nationwide coverage; the website can fill you in on routes, times and addresses of local terminals.

Peter Pan ☎ 1 800 343 9999, **ⓦ** peterpanbus.com. Frequent and extensive service between Boston and New York, as well as service to Cape Cod, Rhode Island, Connecticut and New Hampshire.

Plymouth and Brockton ☎ 508 746 0378, **ⓦ** p-b.com. Comprehensive service to Cape Cod and the South Shore from Boston.

BUS PASSES

One good bus deal is the **Greyhound Discovery Pass** offering unlimited travel within a set time limit: most travel agents can oblige or you can order online at **ⓦ** discoverypass.com. They come in several versions, lasting between seven days ($246) and sixty days ($556). Also, make sure to check timetables other than Greyhound's – the pass is valid on some participating lines like Peter Pan (see above).

Cycling

If you have the stamina for it, **cycling** is one of the best ways to see New England. Some of the larger cities have cycle lanes and local buses equipped to carry bikes (strapped to the outside), and many states also have **rail trails**, old railway routes that have been paved and turned into bike paths. These are great because they are scenic and tend to take steep hills gradually.

Bikes can be **rented** for around $20–30/day, or $90–100/week, from most bike stores; local visitor centres will have details (we've listed rental options where applicable).

Accommodation

Accommodation standards in New England are high and room rates are pricey. That said, there is a nice range of accommodation available throughout the region – from historic lodges and swanky resorts to hostels and scenic campsites – and, aside from in the most rural areas, a place to hang your hat is never far away.

Budget room rates start at around $70/night in the country, while mid-range rooms ring in at $100–150. In **Boston**, it can be a challenge finding a decent room for under $150/night, although they do exist (often at B&Bs). A growing number of New England hotels also provide a **complimentary breakfast**.

Most hotels require a **credit card number** to make a reservation, though this does not mean that you'll have to pay by card. Since cheap accommodation in the cities and on the popular sections of the coast is snapped up fast, **book ahead** whenever possible.

Discounts

One of the best ways to get a cheap room in New England is to come during **off-peak or shoulder seasons**. The month of **September**, in particular, makes for good accommodation deals and is often overlooked by visitors. Squeezed in between the region's busiest tourist periods – summer and autumn – September offers the lingering warmth of summer, and, come nightfall, a bit of autumn's crispness, in addition to a noticeable lack of crowds. Coastal lodgings, especially, can see their room rates drop in September as well as in **March**, **April** and the **winter months**.

When booking your trip, see if you can find a better room rate on a **search engine** beforehand (Ⓦexpedia.com or kayak.com). Staying in the same place for more than one night may bring further reductions and hotels might also make their rooms available to online booking consolidators like Ⓦhotels.com, where the rate can be much lower than even the hotel is allowed to offer. For motels in particular, note also that you might be able to get a **discount** by presenting a membership card from a motoring organization like the AAA –American Automobile Association (see p.22).

B&Bs

Bed-and-breakfast inns (B&Bs) are ubiquitous in New England – nearly every town with tourist traffic will have one. Typically, **B&Bs** are restored old buildings with fewer than ten rooms and plenty of antique furnishings, although recent years have seen a range of chic and contemporary B&Bs opening up throughout the region. **Prices** vary greatly: anywhere from $90 to $350 depending on location, season and facilities. Most fall between $125–150/night for a double.

B&B CONTACTS

B&B Cape Cod ☎ 1 800 541 6226, Ⓦbedandbreakfastcape cod.com. A good resource, but does not allow you to contact B&Bs directly.
B&B Online ☎ 1 800 215 7365, Ⓦbbonline.com. A good selection of New England lodging is organized geographically on this nationwide site.
Boston Area B&B Reservations ☎ 617 964 1606, Ⓦbbreserve.com. Includes limited listings for Boston, Cape Cod and the North Shore.
New England Inns and Resorts ☎ 603 964 6689, Ⓦnewenglandinnsandresorts.com. Represents properties all over New England.
Nutmeg B&B ☎ 1 800 727 7592, Ⓦnutmegbb.com. Connecticut listings only.
Passport to New England ☎ 1 800 981 3275, Ⓦpassportto newengland.com. A partnership of high-end regional inns.

Hostels

At an average of $25–30/night/person ($35–55 for a private room) **hostels** are the cheapest accommodation option in New England other than camping. There is a fairly good concentration of hostels in New England, at least compared with the rest of the US. A number of these, particularly the majority of hostels on Cape Cod and the islands, are wonderful places to stay. For a complete list of the hostels in the region, check out Ⓦhostels.com or Ⓦhinewengland.org.

YOUTH HOSTEL INFORMATION

IN THE US AND CANADA
Hosteling International–American Youth Hostels ☎ 301 495 1240, Ⓦhiusa.org.
Hosteling International Canada ☎ 1 800 663 5777 or ☎ 613 237 7884, Ⓦhihostels.ca.

IN THE UK AND IRELAND
Hostelling International Northern Ireland ☎ 028 9032 4733, Ⓦhini.org.uk.
Irish Youth Hostel Association ☎ 01 830 4555, Ⓦanoige.ie.
Scottish Youth Hostel Association ☎ 0845 293 7373, Ⓦsyha.org.uk.
Youth Hostel Association (YHA) ☎ 01629 592700, Ⓦyha .org.uk.

IN AUSTRALIA AND NEW ZEALAND
Australia Youth Hostels Association Ⓦyha.com.au.
Youth Hostelling Association New Zealand ☎ 0800 278 299 or ☎ 03 379 9970, Ⓦyha.co.nz.

Camping

New England **campgrounds** range from the primitive (a flat piece of ground that may or may not have a water tap) to places more like open-air hotels, with shops, pools, game rooms, restaurants and washing facilities. Naturally enough, **prices** vary accordingly, from next-to-nothing for the most basic plots to $55/night for something comparatively luxurious. Call ahead for

---

ACCOMMODATION PRICE CODES

Throughout this book, accommodation has been priced according to the average cost of the least expensive **double room** in high season. Note that the high and low seasons for tourists vary across the region, so there can be a great deal of fluctuation in room rates – for example, in areas like the Berkshires, prices can rise drastically during the popular autumn foliage season, conversely, rates can fall dramatically in winter, or during shoulder months such as September. Many establishments charge more on Friday and Saturday nights, while big-city business hotels often slash their weekend prices.

reservations at the bigger parks and during national holidays or the summer.

Kampgrounds of America (KOA; ☎406 248 7444, ⓦkoakampgrounds.com) privately oversees many **campgrounds** all over New England; although these are largely for RVs, there are also one-room "Kabins" available at almost all their sites. More tent-friendly (and aesthetically pleasing) sites can be found in the state parks and public lands. To reserve a site at a public campground, contact the individual state's division of parks and recreation: CT (☎860 424 3200), MA (☎1 877 422 6762), ME (☎207 287 3821), NH (☎603 271 3556), RI (☎401 222 2632) and VT (☎802 879 6565). The **Appalachian Mountain Club** (AMC) also has some very well-maintained camping areas and mountain huts; call their headquarters in Boston for reservation information (☎617 523 0655, ⓦoutdoors.org).

Wilderness camping

Contact the local chamber of commerce for information on land usage and **wilderness camping**. You should take the proper precautions when camping rough: carry sufficient food and drink to cover emergencies, inform a park ranger of your travel plans, and watch out for bears and the effect your presence can have on their environment. For more information on undeveloped regions – which are often protected within either national parks or national forests – contact the **US Forest Service** (☎1 800 832 1355, ⓦfs.fed.us).

Food and drink

Built on the unfussiness of the Puritan appetite and the region's proximity to the Atlantic Ocean, New England's traditional cuisine – epitomized by pot roast, seafood chowder and cream pies – is as comforting as comfort food gets.

Nowadays, this nostalgic brand of Yankee cooking is accompanied by a more diverse, contemporary range of food – burgers, steaks and salads mingle with plates of sushi, Mexican meals, Italian dishes and voguish French fare, among numerous others.

New England's coast is famed for its outstanding array of **fresh seafood** (including oysters, clams, fish and lobsters), where it is prepared in both high-end gourmet restaurants and no-frills harbourside shacks. Any of these ocean creatures can also be part of a traditional New England clambake (see box, p.477), a delicious way of enjoying the fruits of the sea. Keep an eye out, too, for the prized **lobster roll** – lobster meat mixed with a bit of mayonnaise and lemon, and served on a grilled hot-dog bun – and **clam chowder**, a thick, creamy shellfish soup. Many fishing towns in New England have large **Portuguese** and Brazilian communities – Portuguese restaurants in these areas are on the whole authentic and inexpensive.

New England also offers a vast range of **produce**: corn, apples, pears, strawberries, blueberries, peaches, plums and cranberries are all grown locally. **Maple syrup** is a big product here and every state produces at least some amount of the sweet liquid.

Rhode Island takes the prize for quirky regional specialities: it's known for "coffee milk" and "cabinets", two liquid concoctions rarely found outside its borders. The former is the official state drink, made by swirling milk through with coffee syrup; a "cabinet", really just another word for milkshake, is crafted by adding ice cream into the mix. Del's frozen lemonade, a blend of crushed ice, lemon juice and sugar, is a Rhode Island treat that traces its origins back to a humble 1940s food cart.

In addition to the Pine Tree State's lobster dishes – considered to be the best in the US – **Maine** is famed for diner-style restaurants and "whoopie pies", baseball-sized confections comprised of two pieces of cake spread with a generous dollop of frosting in-between. You'll find great seafood throughout **Massachusetts**, but its North Shore region is actually more famous for roast beef sandwiches, served hot and cheap at late-night dives. **Vermont** is probably the most culinarily distinct of the states, lauded for its quality dairy products: cow, sheep and goat's cheese, milk and yogurt – not to mention Ben & Jerry's ice cream (see p.360). Finally, New Haven, **Connecticut**, is known for its pizza pies, widely considered to be the best in the galaxy (see p.296).

Drinking

Bars and cocktail lounges are prevalent across New England. The **bars** in Boston are particularly lively, while other younger and more tourist-driven towns like Portland, ME, Portsmouth, NH, Burlington, VT and Providence, RI, hold most of New England's worthwhile pubs and microbreweries.

To buy and consume **alcohol** in the US you need to be 21, and in New England you will be asked for **ID** even if you look much older. It is sometimes permitted to take your own wine into a restaurant, where the corkage fee will be around $10. You can buy beer, wine or spirits more cheaply and easily in supermarkets, delis and liquor stores.

An alternative to drinking dens, **cafés** play a vibrant part in New England's social scene. It's worth looking beyond the ubiquitous *Starbucks* to smaller, local joints, where the ambience will be more enjoyable and the coffee most likely much better.

The media

The birthplace of America's first newspaper, *Publick Occurrences*, which was published in Boston in 1690, New England continues to have a number of well-executed, generally left-leaning media strongholds. You'll find local listings in a slew of weeklies, while the local paper of note is the liberal Boston Globe (Ⓦboston.com).

Newspapers

Boston's oldest **newspaper**, the *Boston Globe* ($1; Ⓦboston.com) remains the region's best general daily; its fat Sunday edition ($3.50) includes substantial sections on art, culture and lifestyle. The *Boston Herald* ($1; Ⓦbostonherald.com) is the *Globe*'s conservative tabloid competitor and is best for getting your fix of gossip and local sports coverage. The two stalwarts are complemented by smaller papers like the *Hartford Courant* (Ⓦcourant.com), the *Portland Press Herald* (Ⓦpressherald.com), Vermont's *Seven Days* (Ⓦ7dvt.com) and the *Providence Journal* (Ⓦprojo.com), which tend to excel at local coverage, but typically rely on agencies such as the Associated Press (AP) for foreign and even national news stories.

Radio

Radio stations are abundant on both the FM and AM dials; the latter is strong on news and talk, while the former carries some of the region's best stations, including **National Public Radio** (NPR) and college broadcasts of jazz, classical, world music and other genres neglected by mainstream radio.

Festivals

Someone, somewhere is always celebrating something in New England, although, apart from national holidays (see p.36), few festivities are shared throughout the entire region. Instead, there is a multitude of local events: arts-and-crafts shows, county fairs, cultural celebrations, music festivals, parades and more.

JANUARY

Moby Dick Marathon New Bedford, MA (first weekend) ☎ 1 508 997 0046, Ⓦ whalingmuseum.org. Non-stop read-aloud of the seaman's classic *Moby Dick*, held in the New Bedford Whaling Museum (see p.157). It takes about 25hr to complete the tome; light whale-ship fare, such as grog, propels readers through the night.

Stowe Winter Carnival Stowe, VT (third week) ☎ 1 800 4678693, Ⓦ stowewintercarnival.com. Hard-partying celebration of all things winter – also includes movie nights, ice carving and a snow volleyball tournament.

FEBRUARY

Winter Festival Burlington, VT (first weekend) ☎ 802 864 0123, Ⓦ enjoyburlington.com. Ice sculptures, a "penguin plunge" (volunteers brave an icy Lake Champlain for charity) and general merrymaking.

Winter Festival Newport, RI (third weekend) ☎ 401 847 7666, Ⓦ newportevents.com. Discounts at area shops and restaurants with the purchase of a festival button (badge), plus hayrides, concerts and ice sculpting.

MARCH

Boston Flower & Garden Show Boston, MA (mid-March) ☎ 617 933 4900, Ⓦ masshort.org. Winter-weary Bostonians turn out in droves to gawk at hothouse greenery at this five-day horticultural fest.

St Patrick's Day Parade South Boston, MA (Sun closest to March 17) ☎ 781 436 3377. Very Irish South Boston does Saint Patty proud with spectators, families and pub-crawlers alike all turning the streets into a sea of green.

Maple Syrup Open House Weekend Statewide, VT (last weekend) Ⓦ vermontmaple.org. Vermont sugarhouses open their doors for production demos, taste tests and "sugar-on-snow" – wherein the hot, fresh, first maple syrup of the season is tossed onto snowbanks, creating a promptly gobbled "taffy".

APRIL

Boston Marathon Boston, MA (third Mon) ☎ 617 236 1652, Ⓦ baa.org. Perhaps the premier running event in the US; quite fun for spectators as well.

Patriots' Day Lexington and Concord, MA (third Mon) ☎ 781 862 1450, Ⓦ nps.gov/mima. A celebration and re-creation of Paul Revere's famous ride from the North End to Lexington, as well as the "shot heard 'round the world" and ensuing Revolutionary War battle. Spectators should arrive by 4am to secure good seats.

Vermont Maple Festival St Albans, VT (last full weekend) ☎ 802 524 5800, Ⓦ vermontmaplefestival.org. Maple-related exhibits and demonstrations, food contests, and, of course, pancake breakfasts.

MAY

Moose Mainea Greenville, ME (mid-May to mid-June) ☎ 207 695 2702. Moose-watching, boat and bike races, and family activities.

Lilac Sunday Jamaica Plain, MA (third Sun) ☎ 617 524 1718, Ⓦ arboretum.harvard.edu. You can view more than three hundred lilac varieties in full bloom at the Arnold Arboretum during this early summer event. Tip: go a few days early if you want to see the flowers without the crowds.

Open Studios Statewide, VT (last weekend) ☎ 802 223 3380. Artists open their homes and studios to the public.

JUNE

Boston Pride Boston, MA (first week) ☎ 617 262 9405, Ⓦ bostonpride.org. The celebration kicks off with a rainbow flag-raising at City Hall and culminates a week later with a gay pride parade, festival and block parties.

Ethan Allen Days Manchester, VT (mid-June) ☎ 802 362 6313. Revolutionary battle enactments along Vermont's Ethan Allen Highway (Rte-7A).

JULY

Fourth of July Celebration Boston, MA ☎ 1 888 484 7677, Ⓦ july4th.org. The largest Fourth of July celebration in the country. The main attraction is a Boston Pops concert at the Hatch Shell accompanied by an awesome fireworks display. People arrive early in the morning, or even the night before, to get prime seats for the concert, while others queue up in boats along the Charles River. The Pops (see p.119) perform an identical programme (minus the fireworks and the 1812 Overture) on the evening of July 3.

Fourth of July Celebration Bristol, RI ☎ 401 253 0445, Ⓦ july4thbristolri.com. This small seaside town hosts the oldest Fourth of July festival in the country, including an impressive parade, fireworks and weeks of events leading up to the occasion.

Moxie Festival Lisbon Falls, ME (second weekend) ☎ 207 783 2249, Ⓦ moxiefestival.com. Activities, fireworks and entertainment in celebration of this old-fashioned, odd-tasting soda in a bright orange can.

AUGUST

Maine Lobster Festival Rockland, ME (first weekend) ☎ 207 596 0376, Ⓦ mainelobsterfestival.com. Twenty thousand pounds of boiled lobster. Enough said.

Newport Folk Festival Newport, RI (early Aug) Ⓦ festivalnetwork.com. This three-day festival has been drawing big names since 1959 – it's where Bob Dylan first caused an outrage by going electric. Get tickets in advance.

Narragansett Powwow Charlestown, RI (second weekend) ☎ 401 364 1100. Native American dancing, music, crafts and food.

Crane Beach Sand Blast! Ipswich, MA (late Aug) ☎ 978 356 4351. Sandcastle-building contest with astounding beach creations.

Union Fair and Blueberry Festival Union, ME (mid-Aug) ☎ 207 785 3281, Ⓦ unionfair.org. One of the oldest traditional fairs in the state, with music, rides, animals and blueberry pies.

SEPTEMBER

Windjammer Festival Camden, ME (first weekend) ☎ 207 236 4404, Ⓦ camdenwindjammerfestival.com. Maine's largest windjammer gathering, with a schooner parade, fireworks, contests and concerts in Camden's beautiful harbour.

The Big E West Springfield, MA (last two weeks) ☎ 413 737 2443, Ⓦ thebige.com. The largest fair in the northeast, with agricultural competitions, horse shows and really good cream puffs.

Oyster Festival Norwalk, CT (second weekend) ☎ 203 838 9444, Ⓦ seaport.org. Seaport Association extravaganza, featuring tall ships, a craft competition and oysters every which way.

World's Fair Tunbridge, VT (second weekend) ☎ 802 889 5555, Ⓦ tunbridgefair.com. Agricultural fair with butter-churning, cheese-making, sheep-shearing and the like.

OCTOBER

Haunted Happenings Salem, MA (through Oct) ☎ 1 877 725 3662, Ⓦ hauntedhappenings.org. Visit the haunted houses and historic waterfront of this pretty town in the foliage-filled days leading up to Halloween.

Cranberry Harvest Celebration Wareham, MA (first weekend) ☎ 508 322 4000, Ⓦ cranberryharvest.org. Harvest festival that includes helicopter rides over flooded red fields of berries, bog tours and cooking demonstrations.

Topsfield Fair Topsfield, MA (first week) ☎ 978 887 5000, Ⓦ topsfieldfair.org. The country's oldest agricultural fair (dating to 1818) with a bee-keeping show, pie-baking contest and lots of cute farm animals.

Head of the Charles Regatta Cambridge, MA (mid-Oct) ☎ 617 868 6200, Ⓦ hocr.org. One of the largest rowing events in the world, with more than six hundred teams participating and thousands of picnicking fans.

Wellfleet OysterFest Wellfleet, MA (second weekend) Ⓦ wellfleetoysterfest.org. This weekend includes concerts, art fairs, plenty of shellfish tasting, and – oddly – a spelling bee.

NOVEMBER

Antiquarian Book Fair Boston, MA (mid-Nov) ☎ 508 266 6540, Ⓦ bostonbookfair.com. Tons of old books on display and for sale, plus author panels and signings.

Thanksgiving at Plimoth Plantation Plymouth, MA (weekend before Thanksgiving) ☎ 508 746 1818, Ⓦ usathanksgiving.com. Roast turkey, gravy, mashed potatoes and all the T-day trimmings, served near the site of America's first Thanksgiving.

DECEMBER

Christmas in Newport Newport, RI (through Dec) ☎ 401 849 6454, Ⓦ christmasinnewport.org. Events all over town, including concerts, make-your-own-gifts workshops, *The Nutcracker* and a ride aboard the *Polar Express* train.

Victoria Mansion's Holiday Gala Portland, ME (first weekend; sometimes last weekend of Nov) ☎ 207 772 4841, ⓦ victoriamansion.org. Gape at the holiday finery decking out one of New England's most dazzling historic homes.

Christmas Town Festival Bethlehem, CT (first weekend) ☎ 203 266 5557, ⓦ christmastownfestival.com. Carolling, crafts and the lighting of the town tree by Santa himself.

Boston Tea Party Reenactment Boston, MA (Sun nearest to Dec 16) ☎ 617 482 6439. A re-enactment of the march from Old South Meeting House to the harbour, and the subsequent tea-dumping that helped spark the American Revolution.

First Night various cities (Dec 31). Many regional cities host First Night festivals on New Year's Eve, generally lasting all day and into the night. A button (badge) will grant you admission into venues throughout the town that have concerts and activities.

Culture and etiquette

New Englanders are often characterized as standoffish, but this perception isn't really fair. While not necessarily as exuberant as Southerners, they are a polite, hearty crew and quick to help a person in need. Small-town New England is quite community-minded – don't be surprised if strangers wave at you, or go out of their way to welcome you into the neighbourhood fold.

Smoking

Smoking is as much frowned upon in New England as in the rest of the US. Cinemas are non-smoking, smoking is prohibited on public transport and flights, and all New England states have banned smoking in restaurants and bars.

Tipping

Tipping is expected for all bar and restaurant service. Expect to tip fifteen percent of the bill before tax to waiters (unless the service is truly wretched) and twenty percent for good service. In the US, this is where most of a server's income comes from, and not leaving a fair amount is seen as an insult. When sitting at a bar, you should leave at least a dollar per round for the bartender; more if the round is more than two drinks. About fifteen to twenty percent should be added to taxi fares. A hotel porter should get $2 per bag. Housekeeping gets $2 per guest per day in a moderate hotel, $3–5 for high-end accommodation (you can leave it under the pillow); valet attendants get $2–3.

Sports

Boston is the only city in New England with major professional sports teams – excepting football, they have one team in each of the primary sports (baseball, hockey and basketball); the region's only professional football team is based slightly further afield, in Foxboro, MA.

Although Boston is undeniably a sports town, until fairly recently New England residents suffered a lot of team-related angst – the **New England Patriots** (American football) had never won a Super Bowl, and the beloved **Boston Red Sox** (baseball) had not won a World Series since 1918. All that has changed now – the Patriots were victorious in the 2002, 2004 and 2005 Super Bowls while the Sox clinched their first Series in 86 years in 2004 (and then won again in 2007). The **Boston Celtics** (basketball) have also had their share of glory lately, winning the 2008 NBA championship, and the **Boston Bruins** (hockey) snagged the Stanley Cup championship in 2011 – their first victory since 1972. Soccer is also catching on – the New England Revolution ("Revs") claimed a championship title at the 2007 US Open Cup.

Baseball

Baseball, often called "America's pastime", has a relaxed pace and seemingly Byzantine rules. Games are played (162 each season) almost every day from April to September, with the league championships and the World Series, the final best-of-seven playoff, lasting through October. Watching a game is almost always a pleasant day out, enhanced by beer drinking and hot dog eating; in the unshaded bleachers beyond the outfield, tickets are cheap ($20) and the crowds quite sociable.

Teams and tickets

All Major League Baseball (MLB) teams play in either the **National League** or the **American League**, each of which is split into three divisions, East, Central and West. New England's Major League team is the American League East **Boston Red Sox**, who play at Fenway Park (see p.82). The Sox's two "farm teams" – minor league clubs that are training grounds for future stars – are also located in New England. The Pawtucket Red Sox (known as the Pawsox) play just minutes from Providence, RI, while the Portland Sea Dogs are based out of Maine (see p.468). Tickets to farm team games are almost never sold out, and are much cheaper than Major League games, around $9. **Tickets** to see the Red Sox (☎617 267 9440, ⓦredsox.com) cost $12–165 per seat but are difficult to come by, since game viewing borders on a religious experience for many residents. If you're desperate to see a game, check local Sox blogs or ⓦboston.craigslist.org to see if any locals have tickets (be sure to meet the seller in person and ensure they have paper tickets – not just an online printout). Fenway Park also sells a small number of one-per-person tickets at Gate E on game day; be sure to get there five hours early (but no earlier – this is enforced), follow all the rules (no leaving the queue, no saving a place for your friends, etc) and hope to get lucky.

American football

American football in America attracts the most obsessive and devoted fans of any sport, perhaps because there are fewer games played – only sixteen per team in a season, which lasts through the autumn and into mid-winter. With quick skirmishes and military-like movements up and down the field, the game is ideal for television; never is this more apparent than Sunday or Monday nights, when televised games feature prominently at national bars.

Teams and tickets

All teams play in the **National Football League** (NFL), which divides the teams into two conferences, the National Football Conference (NFC) and the American Football Conference (AFC). The football season begins in early September and lasts through to the end of January. **Tickets** for New England's only team, the Patriots, who play at Gillette Stadium in Foxboro, MA (☎1 800 543 1776, ⓦgillettestadium.com), cost $75–195, but are nearly impossible to procure. When they are available, ticket sales are handled by Ticketmaster (☎1 800 745 3000, ⓦticketmaster.com); for team **information**, call or visit the Patriots' website (☎508 543 1776, ⓦpatriots.com). If you're desperate to see a live game, you can always try to buy tickets from a tout outside the stadium on game day – though be aware that you're sure to pay very inflated prices, and that buying tickets from a tout is technically illegal.

Basketball

Basketball is played by athletes of phenomenal agility – 7ft-tall giants who float through the air over a wall of equally tall defenders, seemingly change direction in mid-flight, then slam-dunk the ball in the hoop. Games last for 48 minutes of play time, around two hours total from start to finish.

Teams and tickets

While New England's National Basketball Association (NBA) team, the **Boston Celtics** (☎617 523 6050, ⓦceltics.com), had their most iconic days in the 1980s with Larry Bird and company, they have recently seen a hard-earned resurgence with an NBA championship win in 2008. Contact Ticketmaster (☎1 800 745 3000, ⓦticketmaster.com) for available seating and pricing (good seats cost $50–200, but you can snag a seat in the rafters for as little as $10). College basketball is also extremely popular in the US. In New England, the University of Connecticut, the University of Massachusetts, Boston College and Providence College all field perpetually competitive teams. Additionally, in recent years quite a lot of buzz has been generated around the University of Connecticut **women's basketball** team, the Huskies, who were the 2000, 2002, 2004, 2009 and 2010 NCAA (National Collegiate Athletic Association) champions. **Tickets** cost around $25 for college games. Call each school's athletic department for game and ticket info: UConn (☎1 877 288 2666); UMass (☎1 866 862 7849); Boston College (☎617 552 4622) and Providence College (☎401 865 4672).

Ice hockey

Ice hockey is popular in New England, not least because the cold winter weather is so conducive to the sport. Many children grow up playing it and go on to compete at the area's highly competitive colleges and universities; a very small percentage go on to play in the professional **National Hockey League** (NHL). In Boston, college hockey is huge, culminating with February's wildly popular Boston Beanpot (ⓦbeanpothockey.com), when men's and women's teams from Boston University, Boston College, Harvard University and Northeastern University all compete for city bragging rights.

Teams and tickets

New England has one NHL team, the **Boston Bruins** (ⓦbostonbruins.com), one of the most legendary teams in professional ice hockey, with six Stanley Cup titles and a history going back to the founding of the National Hockey League. **Tickets** range from $17–200; contact Ticketmaster (☎1 800 745 3000, ⓦticketmaster.com) for more information. Tickets cost around $20 for college games. In Boston, call each school's athletic department for game and ticket info: Boston University (☎617 353 4628); Harvard University (☎1 877 464 278273); Boston College (☎617 552 4622) and Northeastern University (☎617 373 4668).

Outdoor activities

New England has some fabulous backcountry and wilderness areas, and there's plenty to keep you busy. The most popular activities include skiing and snowboarding, hiking, fishing, hunting and camping, though mountain biking and kayaking fall closely behind.

Protected areas in the US fall into a number of categories. Most numerous are **state parks**, run by the individual states and centred on sites of geological or historical importance that are not necessarily in rural areas. Daily **fees** are usually less than $5, though beaches in high season can charge as much as $20 per car.

Acadia National Park in Maine (ⓦnps.gov/acad) is New England's best-known national park, administered by the federal government. New England's two **national forests**, the Green Mountain National Forest in Vermont (see p.346) and the White Mountain National Forest in New Hampshire (see p.432), are huge, covering fifty percent of all public land in Vermont and an area larger than the state of Rhode Island in New Hampshire. They are federally administered by the US Forest Service (ⓦfs.fed.us), but with much less protection than national parks. More roads run through national forests, and often there is some limited logging and other land-based industry operated on a sustainable basis.

Skiing and snowboarding

Skiing and **snowboarding** are the region's biggest participant sports, with downhill resorts all over northeastern New England. In fact, the mountains ringing the northern ends of Maine, New Hampshire and Vermont offer the best skiing in the eastern US. In **Maine**, Sugarloaf (see p.514) and Sunday River (see p.511) are good spots, while **Vermont**'s best are Killington

(see p.349), Mount Snow (see p.346), Stowe (see p.364), Stratton (see p.342) and Okemo (see p.347). Though **New Hampshire**'s mountains are less steep, you can still get a good day of skiing in at Waterville Valley (see p.428). Smaller mountains can be great learning spots and are often less crowded. You can **rent** equipment for about $80 a weekend, and lift tickets for the best locations top out at around $90 a day. Each state mentioned above has its own website with links to mountains and weather reports (ⓦskimaine.com, ⓦskivermont.com and ⓦskinh.com). A number of companies run all-inclusive ski trips (including transport, lift tickets, equipment and accommodation) from the larger cities. In addition to convenience, these outfits usually offer good deals.

A cheaper alternative to downhill is **cross-country skiing**. A number of backcountry ski lodges offer a range of rustic accommodation, equipment rental and lessons, from as little as $40 a day for skis, boots and poles, up to about $250 for an all-inclusive weekend tour. For additional information, consult ⓦnensa.net, an exhaustive reference on the sport in New England.

Hiking

Hiking is hugely popular, especially in the northern areas of New England, although you'll find good places to get out into nature just about anywhere outside of the main cities. Most state and federally operated parks maintain good trails, not least the famous **Appalachian Trail**, which originates in Georgia and winds through the backcountry of New England before traversing New Hampshire's White Mountains and terminating at Mount Katahdin in northern Maine.

Wilderness areas start close to the main areas of national parks. In peak periods, a quota system operates for the most popular paths, so if there's a hike you specifically want to do, obtain your permit well ahead of time (at least two weeks in advance, or more).

The **Appalachian Mountain Club** (AMC; ☎617 523 0655, ⓦoutdoors.org) offers a range of backcountry hikes into otherwise barely accessible parts of the wilderness, with food and guide provided. The hikes happen at all times of the year, cost anywhere from $0 to $800, last from a day to two weeks, and are heavily subscribed, making it essential to book well in advance. Club members pay around $20 less, though you'll also have to pay $50 to join. AMC also has some

OUTDOOR DANGERS AND WILDLIFE

You're likely to meet many kinds of **wildlife** and come upon unexpected **hazards** if you head into the wilderness, but with due care, many potential difficulties can be avoided.

BUGS AND PESTS

Hiking in the foothills should not be problematic but you should check your clothes frequently for **ticks** – blood-sucking, burrowing insects known to carry **Lyme disease** (especially in southern New England). One early sign of Lyme disease is a bull's-eye rash that forms around a bite – if you develop one of these, seek treatment immediately. Less harmful but more prevalent are **mosquitoes**; bring along insect repellent to keep them at bay. **Black flies** also come out in force in the warm summer months, and, with a tenacious appetite for human heads, ears and faces, and a perpetual buzz, can be tremendously annoying; again, carry insect repellent.

BEARS

You're highly unlikely to encounter a **bear** in New England, though the American black bear is native to the region, and prevalent in the northern wilderness areas. To reduce whatever likelihood there is of running into one, make noise as you walk. If you do come across a bear, keep calm, and make sure it is aware of your presence by clapping, talking or making other sounds. Black bears may **charge** with no intention of attacking when attempting to steal food or if they feel threatened. Don't run, just slowly back away.

If a bear visits your camp, it will be after your food, which should be stored in airtight containers. Some campgrounds are equipped with **bear-proof lockers**, which you are obliged to use to store food when not preparing or eating it. Elsewhere, you should hang both food and garbage from a high branch some distance from your camp. **Never feed a bear**: it will make the animal dependent on humans for food and increase the risk of attacks on humans in the future.

MOUNTAIN LIONS AND COYOTES

You probably won't run into a **mountain lion** or **coyote** in New England (and if you do, they will most likely just slink away), but there have been recent sightings in the region. While both animals generally keep pretty much to themselves, it's possible that they would take an interest in you (or more probably, your pets), as they are known to attack livestock. Keep your dogs on a leash (the cats are likely to view you as a larger animal this way); if by some small chance you run into one of these creatures and sense they are about to attack, shout, wave your arms and throw rocks at them.

MOOSE

Moose, which live in the lush, unpopulated regions near the Canadian border, seldom attack unless provoked. The largest member of the deer family, they can be up to 9ft tall and weigh as much as 1200 pounds. They are mostly active at night, but can also be seen at dusk and dawn, when they may gather to feed near lakes and streams. Though they may seem slow, tame and passive, moose can be unpredictable, especially during the **mating season** in September and October. If you happen upon one in the forest, move slowly, avoid making any loud noises and keep your distance. Drivers should be careful speeding along northern country roads, especially at night – Maine sees 700 moose-to-vehicle collisions a year. If you're planning on driving in the state's forested interior region, it is highly recommended that you reach your destination before sunset.

POISON IVY

Poison ivy is recognizable by its configuration of three leaves to a stem, which can be matte or shiny, green or, in the fall, yellow and red. Plants can be low-growing or can climb as vines to surround trees, and both forms are found in open woods or along stream banks throughout much of New England. It's highly allergenic, so avoid touching it. If you do, washing with strong soap, taking frequent dips in the sea and applying cortisone cream usually helps to relieve the symptoms; in extreme cases, see a doctor. Whatever you do, don't touch your face or eyes.

very well-maintained camping areas and mountain huts; call their headquarters in Boston for information on how to make reservations.

Hunting and fishing

Hunting and **fishing** are two of the most popular outdoor pursuits in New England. Duck, deer and sometimes even the mighty moose are all popular targets, though hunting and gun-carrying laws are strict and you'll need a **permit** (ask the local chamber of commerce how you can get one). Streams, lakes, ponds and rivers fill up with fishermen in season, though, as with hunting, permits are required and laws are strict.

Travel essentials

Costs

Accommodation is likely to be your biggest single expense in New England. Few hotel, motel or B&B rooms cost under $90 a night; you're likely to pay more than $150 for anything halfway decent in a city, and rates in rural areas are not substantially cheaper. In Boston, it may well be difficult to find anything at all for less than $150 a night. Hostels offering dorm beds – usually for $25–30 a night – are another option, but they are by no means everywhere. Camping, of course, is cheap (anywhere from free to $55 per night). As for **food**, $25 a day is enough for an adequate life-support diet – while $35–40 is more reasonable.

Crime and personal safety

New England is a very **safe** place to visit. In the more risky areas, common sense and a certain degree of caution should be enough to avoid most problems. For instance, seek local advice before exploring unfamiliar and run-down parts of a city; avoid walking along deserted streets at night, leave valuables in hotel safes, don't leave luggage clearly visible in cars (especially rental cars), and don't resist violent theft.

The **emergency number** for police is ☏911; contact your bank directly if you have a lost or stolen credit or debit card.

Identification should be carried at all times. Two pieces will satisfy any enquiry, one of which should have a photo: a driver's licence, passport and credit card(s) are your best bets.

Electricity

Electrical outlets use 120V AC, and plugs are two- or three-pronged. A good reference for all things electric is Ⓦ kropla.com.

Entry requirements

Under the **Visa Waiver Program**, citizens from more than thirty countries – the UK, Ireland, Australia, New Zealand and most of Europe – do **not** require **visas** for visits to the US of ninety days or less, so long as they have an onward or return ticket. As of 2009, however, VWP participants must obtain **Electronic System for Travel**

AVERAGE MONTHLY TEMPERATURES AND RAINFALL

	Jan	Feb	Mar	Apr	May	Jun	Jul	Aug	Sep	Oct	Nov	Dec
BANGOR, ME												
max °C/°F	-3/27	-2/28	3/37	11/52	17/63	23/73	26/79	24/75	20/68	14/57	7/45	-1//30
min °C/°F	-13/9	-12/10	-6/21	1/34	6/43	11/52	14/57	13/55	9/48	4/39	-1/30	-9/16
rain (mm)	76.2	73.7	81.3	83.8	88.9	83.8	83.8	83.8	86.4	86.4	116.8	99.1
BOSTON, MA												
max °C/°F	2/36	3/37	7/45	14/57	19/66	25/77	28/82	27/81	22/72	17/63	11/52	4/39
min °C/°F	-5/23	-4/25	0/32	5/41	10/50	15/59	18/64	18/64	14/57	8/46	4/39	-3/27
rain (mm)	91.4	91.4	94.0	91.4	83.8	78.7	71.1	81.3	78.7	83.8	106.7	101.6
BURLINGTON, VT												
max °C/°F	-4/25	-3/27	3/37	12/54	19/66	24/75	27/81	26/79	21/70	14/57	7/45	-1/30
min °C/°F	-13/9	-13/9	-6/21	1/34	7/45	12/54	15/59	14/57	9/48	4/39	-1/30	-9/16
rain (mm)	45.7	40.6	55.9	71.1	78.7	88.9	91.4	104.1	83.8	73.7	78.7	61.0

Authorization (ESTA) online before they fly (at ⓦ https://esta.cbp.dhs.gov), which involves completing a basic form on the computer for a $14 fee (paid online). ESTA authorizations are valid for **multiple entries** into the US for two years or until the passport expires. It is recommended that you submit an ESTA application as soon as you start planning your trip (it can take up to 72hr to get a response, although most authorizations are issued within minutes).

You'll also need to present a machine-readable **passport** that's valid for at least six months beyond your stay (check with your home consulate if you're unsure whether yours passes muster). Although ESTA information is stored electronically, you should bring a copy of your authorization with you when you travel; know too that you must re-register for ESTA if you obtain a new passport or have a name change. The best place for up-to-date US visa information is online at ⓦ travel.state.gov.

Canadian citizens now require a passport to cross the border, although their passports need only be valid until the day of their intended return to Canada (not for an extra six months, as with those travelling under the Visa Waiver Program).

Prospective visitors from parts of the world not covered by the Visa Waiver Program, and those without machine-readable passports, often require a valid passport and a **non-immigrant visitor's visa**. How you obtain a visa depends on what country you're in and your status when you apply; it's best to enquire directly at the nearest US embassy or consulate.

A good method for keeping track of your passport information is to email a scanned copy of the first two pages back to yourself and to someone at home before embarking on your travels abroad.

EMBASSIES AND CONSULATES

Australia 150 East 42nd St, 34th floor, New York, NY ☎ 212 351 6500.

Canada 3 Copley Place, suite 400, Boston, MA ☎ 617 247 5100.

Ireland 535 Boylston St, Boston, MA ☎ 617 267 9330.

New Zealand 222 East 41st St, Suite 2510, New York, NY ☎ 212 832 4038.

South Africa 3051 Massachusetts Ave NW, Washington, DC ☎ 202 232 4400.

UK 1 Memorial Drive, Cambridge, MA ☎ 617 245 4500.

Gay and lesbian travellers

Go to the right places, and New England can be a very enjoyable destination for **gay and lesbian** visitors. The region possesses some firm favourites

on the gay North American travel circuit, and gay-friendly accommodation can be found dotted all over the region. However, go to the wrong places – mainly rural areas – and you will find that the narrow-minded attitudes of "small town America" are still alive. Be cautious, then, with open **displays of affection**. As difficult and frustrating as this may be, it's usually the most effective way to keep the bigots at bay.

There are sizeable predominantly gay areas in almost all of the New England states. The **South End** of Boston is what Greenwich Village and Chelsea are to New York and the Marais is to Paris. "Gay" towns in Massachusetts include **Provincetown**, one of the world's premier gay beach resorts, and **Northampton**, well known for its large lesbian community. Elsewhere, the Rhode Island city of **Providence** has a vibrant gay scene, while **Ogunquit** is the quieter, Maine version of Provincetown. **Vermont** is famously liberal, and even traditionally conservative **New Hampshire** has recently joined other New England states in passing anti-discrimination laws.

In July of 2000, Vermont became the first state in the Union to legally recognize **civil unions** for same-sex couples. In 2004, this groundbreaking move was taken a step further by Massachusetts, when, at the stroke of midnight on May 17th, it became the first state in the nation to issue same-sex **marriage licences**. As of 2011, four of the six US states granting same-sex marriages were located in New England: Massachusetts, Connecticut, New Hampshire and Vermont. If you're interested in getting hitched on holiday, check in at a city or town hall located in one of these states.

Contact the International Gay & Lesbian Travel Association (☎ 954 630 1637, ⓦ www.iglta.org), for a list of gay- and lesbian-owned or -friendly **tour operators**. Meanwhile, gaytravel.com (☎ 1 800 429 8728) is a good online travel agency where you can make bookings and get help with travel planning, and Now Voyager (☎ 1 800 255 6951, ⓦ nowvoyager.com) is a gay and lesbian travel consolidator offering Boston-based package tours.

Publications

There are a number of **publications** covering New England's gay scene. *Bay Windows* (☎ 617 266 6670, ⓦ baywindows.com) is the region's largest gay and lesbian weekly, with cultural listings for all six states. The bimonthly *Metroline Magazine* (☎ 860 231 8845, ⓦ metroline-online.com) has information on the gay scene in Connecticut, with additional news pertaining to greater New England. Some tourist information centres stock the free *Pink Pages* (☎1 866 943 7465, ⊛linkpink.com), a complete listing of gay- and lesbian-friendly businesses and community organizations in the New England states – although about half of the book is devoted to Boston.

For additional research try one of many **online publications**, such as gay and lesbian travel resources like ⊛outtraveler.com, or something more specific to New England, such as ⊛edgeboston.com, ⊛vermontgaytravel.com and ⊛gayogunquit.com.

Health

Visitors from Canada, Europe, Australia, New Zealand and South Africa don't require any **vaccinations** to enter the US. For **emergencies** or ambulances, dial toll-free ☎911 from any phone. If you have medical or dental problems that don't require an ambulance, make your way a walk-in emergency room, which most hospitals have: for the nearest hospital, check with your hotel or dial information at ☎411.

Be aware that even simple medical consultations are costly, usually around $100 each visit. Keep receipts for any part of your medical treatment, including prescriptions, so that you can claim against your insurance once you're home (see opposite).

For minor ailments such as a headache or the common cold, stop by a local **pharmacy**; some are open 24hr, especially in the larger cities. Foreign visitors should note that many medicines available over the counter at home – codeine-based painkillers, for one – are available by prescription only in the US.

MEDICAL RESOURCES FOR TRAVELLERS

CDC ⊛cdc.gov/travel. Official US government travel health site.
International Society for Travel Medicine ⊛istm.org. Full listing of travel health clinics.

Insurance

Getting travel insurance is highly recommended, especially if you're coming from abroad and are at all concerned about your health – prices for medical attention in the US can be exorbitant. A secondary benefit is that most policies also cover against theft and loss, which can be useful if you're toting around an expensive camera or any high-tech gear. Before paying for a new policy, though, check to see if you're already covered: some home insurance policies may cover your possessions while overseas, and many private medical schemes include cover when abroad.

Internet

If you have a suitable laptop, you'll find free **wireless access** is plentiful in New England. Most hotels have wi-fi, as do libraries, *Starbucks* and numerous local coffee shops. If you're without a laptop, pop by one of the ubiquitous **FedEx Office** stores; these provide internet access for around 25 cents a minute, and some of them have the added benefit of 24hr service. While **libraries** and **universities** have more limited hours and time constraints (around 15min–1hr/person), their major advantage is that web access is free to all.

Laundry

Laundromats are pretty easy to find in the larger cities – check in with hotel staff or look online to see what's available. Generally, a load of laundry costs $2 (paid for in quarters – a good laundromat will have a change machine) and $1.50 for an hour of drying time.

Mail

Post offices are usually open Monday to Friday from about 8am to 5pm, and in some cases on

---

ROUGH GUIDES TRAVEL INSURANCE

Rough Guides has teamed up with WorldNomads.com to offer great travel insurance deals. Policies are available to residents of over 150 countries, with cover for a wide range of adventure sports, 24hr emergency assistance, high levels of medical and evacuation cover and a stream of travel safety information. Roughguides.com users can take advantage of their policies online 24/7, from anywhere in the world – even if you're already travelling. And since plans often change when you're on the road, you can extend your policy and even claim online. Roughguides.com users who buy travel insurance with WorldNomads.com can also leave a positive footprint and donate to a community development project. For more information, go to ⊛roughguides.com/shop.

Measurements and sizes

Measurements are in inches, feet, yards and miles; weight is in ounces, pounds and tons. American pints and gallons are about four-fifths of imperial ones. **Clothing sizes** are two figures less than their equivalent in Britain – a British women's size 12 is a US size 10 – while British shoe sizes are 1.5 sizes below American ones for women, and one size below for men.

Money

US **currency** comes in bills of $1, $5, $10, $20, $50 and $100. The dollar is made up of 100 cents with coins of 1 cent (known as a penny), 5 cents (a nickel), 10 cents (a dime) and 25 cents (a quarter). At press time, one US dollar was worth £0.61, €0.69, Can$0.94, Aus$0.91, NZ$1.15 and ZAR6.69. For current exchange rates check ⓦxe.com.

A combination of **cash** and an **ATM** or **debit card** are the best way to carry and obtain money while in New England. You'll find ATMs ("automated teller machines") on nearly every corner in big cities, and they shouldn't be too difficult to locate in rural areas, either. Any ATM or debit card issued in the US should work in all ATMs, while travellers from abroad should make sure their personal identification number (PIN) will work overseas; it's also a good idea to let your bank know you'll be out of the country before you head out (lest your purchases are flagged as "suspicious" and your card temporarily frozen). Keep in mind that you'll be charged up to $3 every time you make a withdrawal from an ATM not operated by your home bank.

Credit cards are a must for hotel reservations and car rental; the major companies (MasterCard, Visa and American Express) are widely accepted. A compromise between plastic and travellers' cheques is **Visa TravelMoney**, a disposable prepaid debit card with a PIN which works in all ATMs that accept Visa cards. You load up your account with funds before leaving home, and when they run out, you simply throw the card away. For more information, check the Visa TravelMoney website at ⓦusa.visa.com.

Banks are generally open from 9am until 5pm Monday to Thursday, and 9am to 6pm on Friday. Some have limited hours on Saturdays, and bank ATMs are accessible 24 hours a day. Most major banks change foreign travellers' cheques and currency as well. **Exchange bureaus**, found at airports, tend to charge less commission than banks: Thomas Cook and American Express are the biggest names.

Saturday from 9am to 1pm (although Saturday hours vary widely according to branch); there are also **blue mailboxes** on many street corners, into which you can deposit already-stamped mail. You can receive mail at larger post offices by having it addressed to "[your name] c/o General Delivery"; non-acquired letters are thrown out after thirty days. Hotels will also generally accept post for guests.

Ordinary mail within the US costs 44 cents for a letter weighing up to an ounce; addresses must include the five-digit zip code (postal code), and a return address should be written on the upper left corner of the envelope, postcards cost 28 cents to mail. **Air mail** between New England and Europe generally takes about a week to arrive. International postcards and letters weighing up to one ounce cost 98 cents.

Note that if you want to send any **parcels** out of the country, they must be packaged and sealed accordingly, and you'll need to fill out a green customs declaration form, available at the post office.

For all things mail, head to the **US Postal Service**'s website at ⓦusps.com; it's especially helpful for looking up zip codes.

Maps

Most of the tourist offices we've mentioned throughout this guide can supply you with good **maps**, either free or for a small charge; supplemented with the ones in the guide, these should be enough for general sightseeing and touring. For driving or cycling through rural areas, Maine-based DeLorme (ⓦdelorme .com) publishes its invaluable *Atlas & Gazetteer* for each of the New England states ($19.95 each), with marked campgrounds and national park and forest information; you can also visit their headquarters in Yarmouth, ME (see p.470). For detailed **hiking** maps, check with ranger stations in parks and wilderness areas or with camping stores.

Youth and student discounts

Various **youth/student ID cards** can offer noteworthy travel discounts. Full-time students are eligible for the International Student ID Card (ISIC; ⓦisic.org or ⓦstatravel.com), which entitles the bearer to special air, rail and bus fares, as well as discounts at museums, theatres and other attractions. There's also the added benefit of a free hotline to call in the event of a medical, legal or financial emergency. The card costs $22 for Americans, Aus$25 for Australians, NZ$25 for New Zealanders and £9 in the UK.

You have to be 26 or younger to qualify for the **International Youth Travel Card** (ⓦisic.org or ⓦstatravel.com), which costs US$22/£9 and carries the same benefits. Teachers qualify for the **International Teacher Card**, offering similar discounts and costing US$22, Aus$25 and NZ$25. All of these cards are available online or from student-oriented travel agents in North America, Europe, Australia and New Zealand.

Opening hours and public holidays

Shops and services are generally open Monday to Saturday from 8 or 9am until 5 or 6pm. Many stores are also open on Sundays, and larger towns and cities will invariably have 24hr supermarkets and pharmacies. Information on banking and post office hours is listed under "Mail" (see p.34) and "Money" (see p.35).

On the national, or federal, **public holidays** listed below, banks and offices (and many shops) are liable to be closed all day. The traditional **summer season** for tourism runs from Memorial Day to Labor Day, and some tourist attractions (such as most lobster shacks in Maine) are open only during that period.

PUBLIC HOLIDAYS

New Year's Day Jan 1
Martin Luther King Jr's Birthday Third Mon in Jan

Presidents' Day Third Mon in Feb
Easter March or April
Memorial Day Last Mon in May
Independence Day July 4
Labor Day First Mon in Sept
Columbus Day Second Mon in Oct
Veterans' Day Nov 11
Thanksgiving Fourth Thurs in Nov
Christmas Day Dec 25

Phones

With respect to calling abroad from the US, you've got several options, the most convenient of which is using your **credit card** – most pay phones now accept them. A cheaper option is using a **prepaid phone card**, sold at many convenience stores in denominations that begin at $5. Skype (ⓦskype .com) is a great service that enables users to place free phone calls via the internet or free video calls on domestic smartphones; there are good rates for international phone plans as well.

Mobile phones

If you're from overseas and you want to bring your **mobile phone** (referred to as "cell phones" in the US) with you, you'll need to check with your phone provider about whether it will work abroad and what the roaming charges will be. If you find your phone won't work in the States, you might consider renting one.

Senior travellers

For many senior citizens, **retirement** brings the opportunity to explore the world in a style and at a pace that is the envy of younger travellers. As well as the obvious advantages of being free to travel for longer periods during the quieter – and less expensive – seasons, anyone over the age of 62 (with suitable ID) can enjoy a tremendous variety of discounts. Amtrak, Greyhound, local buses and many US airlines offer (smallish) percentage reductions on fares to older passengers. In addition, museums, art galleries and even hotels offer small discounts, and since the definition of "senior" can drop to as low as 55, it is always worth asking.

The **American Association of Retired Persons** (AARP; ☎ 202 434 2277 or ☎ 1 800 424 3410, ⓦ aarp .org), organizes group travel for senior citizens and can provide discounts on accommodation, car rental, air travel and holidays with selected tour operators. Annual membership (which includes a subscription to *AARP The Magazine*) is available to

---

> ### TOP 5 KOOKY SIGHTS
>
> **Adventure Suites** Jackson, NH. See p.438
> **International Cryptozoological Museum** Portland, ME. See p.463
> **Lizzie Borden Bed & Breakfast** Fall River, ME. See p.159
> **Strolling of the Heifers** Brattleboro, VT. See p.333
> **Wilhelm Reich Museum** Rangeley, ME. See p.512

USEFUL PHONE NUMBERS AND AREA CODES

EMERGENCIES AND INFORMATION
Emergencies ☎911; fire, police or ambulance.
Phone directory ☎411
Toll free directory information ☎1 800 555 1212
Long-distance toll-free directory information ☎1 (area code) 555 1212
Operator ☎0

NEW ENGLAND AREA CODES
Connecticut northern Connecticut ☎860/959; southern Connecticut ☎203
Maine ☎207
Massachusetts Boston ☎617/857; suburban Boston ☎781/339; Cape Cod ☎508/774;
northern MA ☎978/351; western MA ☎413
New Hampshire ☎603
Rhode Island ☎401
Vermont ☎802

INTERNATIONAL CALLING CODES
Calling TO New England from abroad: your country's international access code + 1 + area
code + seven-digit number
Calling FROM New England
To Australia ☎011 + 61 + city code + local number
Canada city code + local number
To New Zealand ☎011 + 64 + city code + local number
To the Republic of Ireland ☎011 + 353 + city code
To South Africa ☎011 + 27 + city code
To the UK and Northern Ireland ☎011 + 44 + city code

---

nyone over 50, costing $16 ($43 for three years) for
S residents, $17 for Canadians and $28 for those
ving abroad.

There are a number of Boston-based **tour
perators** specializing in vacations for senior citizens.
ʔad Scholar, 11 Ave de Lafayette (☎1 800 454 5768,
ʔroadscholar.org), runs an extensive worldwide
ʔetwork of educational and activity programmes for
ʔeople over 55 (companions may be younger). Trip
ʔemes are conducted along the lines of "Curveballs,
ʔe Curse and Red Sox Legends" ($784 for four nights)
ʔd costs are on the whole in line with those of
ʔmmercial tours. There are numerous programmes
ʔfered in New England, with themes ranging from
ʔush painting in Massachusetts to sea-kayaking off
ʔe Maine coast. In the UK, Saga Holidays (☎0800 096
ʔ78, ☻saga.co.uk/travel) is the country's biggest and
ʔost established specialist in holidays aimed at older
ʔeople. New England tours include most of the major
ʔghts, and are conducted during the popular
ʔutumn foliage season.

ʔime

ʔew England runs on **Eastern Standard Time
ʔST)**, five hours behind GMT in winter and three

hours ahead of the US West Coast. East Coast
daylight savings time (5hr behind GMT) runs from
the second Sunday in March to the first Sunday in
November.

Tourist information

Advance information for a trip to New England can
be obtained by calling the appropriate state's information centre (see p.38). A publicly funded firm
called **Discover New England** (☎603 766 0606,
☻discovernewengland.org) also exists to provide
advance information on all six New England states.

Once you've arrived, you'll find most towns
have **visitor centres** of some kind – often called
the Convention and Visitors Bureau (CVB) or the
Chamber of Commerce: many are listed within
the *Guide*. The essential difference between the
two types of visitors centres is that the former
deals exclusively with tourism-related businesses,
while the latter represents all types of commerce.
Either one will give out detailed information
on the local area, however, and can often help
with finding accommodation. Additionally, free
newspapers in most places carry news of events
and entertainment. Of the several **publications**

with travel information specific to New England, check out the range of magazines published by Yankee Publishing (Ⓦyankeemagazine.com). *Yankee Magazine* is published ten times a year, and contains travel features and coverage of the latest New England trends. Their annual *Yankee Magazine Travel Guide to New England* also contains travel features, accompanied by plenty of useful practical information. Lastly, *Boston* magazine (Ⓦboston magazine.com) is a fine monthly publication which has feature articles on its title town as well as the rest of New England.

STATE INFORMATION CENTRES

Connecticut One Constitution Plaza, 2nd floor, Hartford, CT 06103 ☎ 860 256 2800 or ☎ 1 888 288 4748, Ⓦ ctvisit.com.

Maine 59 State House Station, Augusta, ME 04333 ☎ 1 888 624 6345, Ⓦ visitmaine.com.

Massachusetts 10 Park Plaza, suite 4510, Boston, MA 02116 ☎ 617 973 8500 or ☎ 1 800 227 6277, Ⓦ massvacation.com.

New Hampshire 172 Pembroke Rd, Concord, NH 03302 ☎ 603 271 2665, Ⓦ visitnh.gov.

Rhode Island 315 Iron Horse Way, Suite 101, Providence, RI 02908 ☎ 1 800 250 7384, Ⓦ visitrhodeisland.com.

Vermont Vermont Dept. of Tourism and Marketing, One National Life Drive, 6th floor, Montpelier, VT 05620 ☎ 802 828 3237 or ☎ 1 800 837 6668, Ⓦ vermontvacation.com.

WEBSITES

Though we've listed relevant websites for accommodation, organizations, major sights and so on throughout this guide, the following might help you pursue a few special areas of interest in preparation for your visit.

AlpineZone Ⓦ alpinezone.com. Check up on ski and hiking trail reports in the northeast, as well as accommodation on all the mountains.

National Park Service Ⓦ nps.gov. Provides detailed information on New England's eighteen historic national parks.

New England for Visitors Ⓦ gonewengland.about.com. Links to all sorts of fairly mainstream info, including tour operators, major ski resorts and the like.

New England History Ⓦ newenglandhistory.info. Well-organized site for limited historical background on each state, plus some good old images and notable quotes.

New England Lighthouses Ⓦ lighthouse.cc. Organized by state, with photos, history and pretty much everything you might need to find out about your favourite lighthouse.

Travellers with children

New England is a great place to bring **children**, as so many of the region's historical sights – ships, lighthouses, recreated colonial villages with character actors – are actually more fun with a wide-eyed kid to show around. In addition, there

---

BEST BOAT TOURS

Codzilla Boston, MA. See p.98
Lake Champlain ferries Burlington, VT. See p.372
Lucky Catch Cruises Portland, ME. See p.462
Mystic River Tours Mystic, CT. See p.282
Pirate Adventures Hyannis, MA. See p.166
Portland mailboats Portland, ME. See p.462
Squam Lake Holderness, NH. See p.427
Thimble Islands tours Stony Creek, CT. See p.290

are several zoos, aquariums and children's museum in the region.

Check the internet and you'll find that in additio to commercial attractions catering to children mini-golf, water slides, arcades and the like – mar states also have **apple orchards** for picking in th autumn and **farms** with strawberries an raspberries for picking in the spring and summe All destination **ski areas** in New England hav reputable and licensed ski schools for children th include lessons, lift tickets and meals.

In **Boston**, the Children's Museum (see p.60), th Museum of Science (see p.72) and the Aquariu (see p.58) are all world-class sights geared towar children. In **Connecticut** the Mystic Seaport ar Aquarium (see p.280) and Dinosaur State Park (se p.313) outstrip the area's museums in exciteme for kids. One good resource is the Association f Children's Museums website (Ⓦ childrensmuseum .org), which has a state-by-state breakdown kid-oriented museums.

Amusement parks in New England are n destination sights the way they are in Flori though the area does have a smattering of sma town carnivals. If the kids are clamouring for a roll coaster, consider Six Flags New England (Ⓦ sixfla .com), StoryLand in New Hampshire (Ⓦ storylandr .com) or Funtown/Splashtown USA in Main (Ⓦ funtownsplashtownusa.com) – though note th a day out at any of these parks can be fairly pricey.

Travellers with disabilities

Travellers with mobility problems or other physic disabilities are likely to find New England – as wi the US in general – to be much more in tune wi their needs than anywhere else in the world. public buildings must be **wheelchair-accessib** and have suitable toilets; most city street corners have dropped kerbs; subways have lifts; and most city buses are able to kneel to make access easier. Most hotels, restaurants and theatres (certainly any built in the last ten years or so) also generally have excellent wheelchair access. Most obstacles can usually be overcome – or avoided altogether – if you call 48 hours or so before your arrival at a bus or train station, airport, hotel, restaurant, park or other such facility.

CONTACTS

IN THE US AND CANADA
Mobility International USA ☎ 541 343 1284, ⓦ miusa.org. Information and referral services, offering access guides, tours and exchange programmes.

Society for the Accessible Travel and Hospitality (SATH) ☎ 212 447 7284, ⓦ sath.org. Non-profit educational organization that has actively represented travellers with disabilities since 1976.

IN THE UK AND IRELAND
Disability Action Group Belfast ☎ 028 9029 7880, ⓦ disabilityaction.org. Advocacy group for people with disabilities.

Irish Wheelchair Association Dublin ☎ 01 818 6400, ⓦ iwa.ie. Useful information provided about travelling abroad with a wheelchair.

Tourism for All Andover ☎ 0845 124 9971, ⓦ tourismforall .org.uk. Provides information on all aspects of travel for the disabled and elderly.

IN AUSTRALIA AND NEW ZEALAND
Disabled Persons Assembly ☎ 04 801 9100, ⓦ dpa.org.nz. New Zealand resource centre with lists of travel agencies and tour operators for people with disabilities.

NDS (National Disability Services) ☎ 02 6283 3200, ⓦ nds.org.au. Umbrella site listing travel agencies, tour operators and services for those with disabilities.

Boston

46 Downtown
61 South Boston
62 The North End
65 Charlestown
68 Beacon Hill
72 The West End
72 Back Bay
78 The South End
80 Kenmore Square
80 The Fenway
86 Brookline
86 Jamaica Plain
87 Roxbury
87 Dorchester
88 Cambridge
95 Arrival and departure
96 Getting around
98 Information
98 Tours
99 Accommodation
105 Eating
114 Drinking
118 Nightlife
118 Entertainment
121 Gay and lesbian
122 Shopping
125 Directory

BOSTON HARBOR

1

Boston

Boston is about as close to the Old World as the New World gets: a modern American city that proudly trades on its colonial past. Occasionally it takes things a bit too far – what's a faded relic elsewhere is a plaque-covered sight here – but nowhere else will you get a better feel for the events and personae behind the birth of a nation. This is not to say that Boston is lacking in contemporary attractions: its cafés, shops, nicely landscaped public spaces and diverse neighbourhoods are as alluring as its historic sites. The new millennium has brought a renaissance to the city, contributing to the feeling that Boston's future may be even stronger than its past.

A visit to **BOSTON** is the highlight of any trip to New England; the student hives, ethnic enclaves and courtly preserved town houses of this elegant port have much to offer its guests. Steeped in history, the city is home to many of the region's foremost cultural institutions and is famed for its venerated sports teams. Boston's relatively small size – both physically and in terms of population (twentieth among US cities) – and its provincial feel serve to its advantage. Though it has expanded since it was first settled in 1630, through landfills and annexation, it has never lost its core, a tangle of streets over old cowpaths clustered around Boston Common. Groups of Irish and Italian descent have carved out authentic and often equally unchanged communities in areas like the North End, Charlestown and South Boston, and the districts around downtown exude an almost small-town atmosphere. Even as Boston has evolved from busy port to the blighted metropolis of the 1970s and the rejuvenated place it is today, it has remained, fundamentally, a city on a human scale.

Boston may be small for an American city, but it nonetheless encompasses many diverse neighbourhoods, almost all of which are easy to explore on foot. The **downtown** area is situated on a peninsula that juts into Boston Harbor; most of the other neighbourhoods branch out south and west from here. Downtown really begins with **Boston Common**, a large public green that holds many of the city's major historical sights either on or near its grounds. A ten-minute walk east of the Common, historic Faneuil (pronounced "Fan-yoo-el") Hall, the so-called "Cradle of Liberty", and nearby Quincy Market bustle with office workers in search of lunch. Across Surface Road and the Rose Kennedy Greenway (formerly I-93) from the marketplace is the **North End**, the city's Little Italy, while just across Boston's Inner Harbor is **Charlestown**, the home of the world's oldest commissioned warship, the *USS Constitution*. Southeast

Free Boston p.47
The Freedom Trail p.50
The Boston Tea Party p.53
The Boston Massacre p.54
Downtown vistas p.57
The Harborwalk p.58
Top Dog p.61
The Battle of Bunker Hill p.67
The architecture of Charles Bulfinch p.69
The Black Heritage Trail p.70

From swamp to swank: the building of Back Bay p.73
The Curse: reversed! p.82
Frederick Law Olmsted and the Emerald Necklace p.83
364.4 Smoots (+ 1 Ear) p.94
The Boston CityPass p.96
B&B agencies and short-term accommodation p.100
North End pastries p.109
Boston Speed Dog p.113
Brewery tours p.116

BEACON HILL

Highlights

❶ The North End You'll find some of Boston's most famed sights, plus its best cannoli, in its most authentic Italian neighbourhood. **See p.62**

❷ Beacon Hill Long the neighbourhood of choice for the city's elite, with stately red-brick Federalist town houses and gaslights lining the narrow, cobblestoned streets. **See p.68**

❸ Newbury Street This swanky promenade of designer boutiques and cafés may well tempt you to break the bank. **See p.76**

❹ A Red Sox game at Fenway Park Watch Boston's legendary baseball team play in one of the country's classic ballparks. **See p.82**

❺ Isabella Stewart Gardner Museum Styled after a fifteenth-century Venetian palace, this delightful museum boasts an eclectic collection of art and a sublime central courtyard. **See p.85**

❻ Arnold Arboretum The crown jewel of Boston's "Emerald Necklace" is a botanist's delight and one of the finest arboretums in North America. **See p.86**

❼ Harvard Square The buzzing heart of Cambridge is steps from the ivy-covered walls of Harvard University and close to the colonial mansions of Brattle Street. **See p.89**

HIGHLIGHTS ARE MARKED ON THE MAP ON P.44

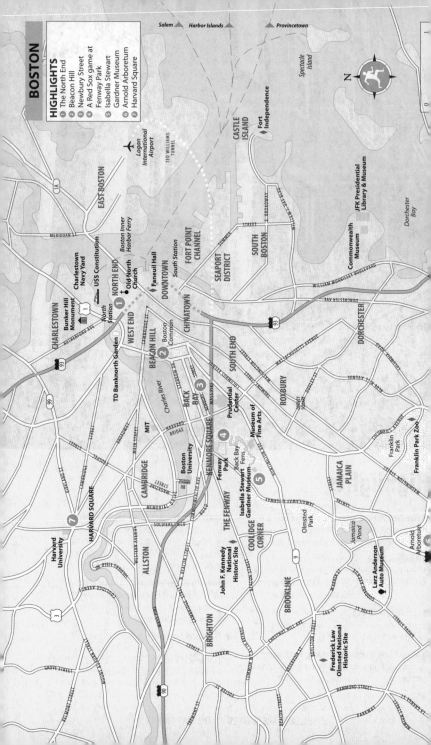

BOSTON

HIGHLIGHTS
1. The North End
2. Beacon Hill
3. Newbury Street
4. A Red Sox game at Fenway Park
5. Isabella Stewart Gardner Museum
6. Arnold Arboretum
7. Harvard Square

Salem ▲ Harbor Islands ▲ Provincetown ▲

Spectacle Island

N

Logan International Airport

TED WILLIAMS TUNNEL

CASTLE ISLAND

Fort Independence

EAST BOSTON

1A

MERIDIAN ST

Charlestown Navy Yard

USS Constitution

Boston Inner Harbor Ferry

NORTH END

North Station

Old North Church

Faneuil Hall

DOWNTOWN

South Station

FORT POINT CHANNEL

SUMMER STREET

SEAPORT DISTRICT

WILLIAM J. DAY BOULEVARD

SOUTH BOSTON

STREET

Commonwealth Museum

JFK Presidential Library & Museum

Dorchester Bay

CHARLESTOWN

Bunker Hill Monument

RUTHERFORD AVE

TD Banknorth Garden

WEST END

BEACON HILL

Boston Common

CHINATOWN

SOUTH END

MASSACHUSETTS AVENUE

WILLIAM MORRISSEY BOULEVARD

DORCHESTER

93

DORCHESTER AVE

99

93

Charles River

BACK BAY

Prudential Center

Museum of Fine Arts

ROXBURY

DUDLEY SQUARE

BLUE HILL AVENUE

WARREN STREET

MIT

HARVARD BRIDGE

MASS AVE

KENMORE SQUARE

Fenway Park

Back Bay Fens

Isabella Stewart Gardner Museum

Columbus Avenue

Franklin Park

Franklin Park Zoo

CAMBRIDGE

Boston University

BU BRIDGE

MEMORIAL DRIVE

SOLDIERS FIELD

THE FENWAY

COOLIDGE CORNER

Olmsted Park

Jamaica Pond

JAMAICA PLAIN

HUNTINGTON AVENUE

7

HARVARD SQUARE

Harvard University

ALLSTON

JFK STREET

John F. Kennedy National Historic Site

9

BROOKLINE

Larz Anderson Auto Museum

Arnold Arboretum

6

3

BRIGHTON

MARKET STREET

CHESTNUT HILL AVE

HARVARD STREET

Frederick Law Olmsted National Historic Site

BEACON STREET

BOYLSTON STREET

HAMMOND STREET

GROVE STREET

90

FAIRWAY

of the North End lies the **waterfront**, beautified since the Big Dig opened up the area by sending I-93 underground (see below). These structural changes have also inspired development on the other side of the water, in the **Seaport District** and **Fort Point** neighbourhoods; always a haven for artists' studios, they also now play host to sleek boutiques, restaurants and the Institute of Contemporary Art.

North of the Common are the vintage gaslights, dignified town houses and steep byways of **Beacon Hill**, the city's most exclusive residential neighbourhood. Charles Street runs south along the base of the hill and separates Boston Common from the Public Garden, which marks the beginning of **Back Bay**. This similarly well-heeled neighbourhood of gracious terraced houses is also home to modern landmarks like the John Hancock Tower, New England's tallest skyscraper. South of Back Bay is the gay enclave of the **South End**, known for its hip restaurants and residents. The student domains of **Kenmore Square** and the **Fenway** are west of Back Bay: the former has some of the area's best nightlife, while the latter is home to the Museum of Fine Arts, the Isabella Stewart Gardner Museum and hallowed Fenway Park, stomping ground of the beloved Red Sox baseball team. Southwest of these neighbourhoods are Boston's vast **southern districts**, including **Jamaica Plain** and **Roxbury**, which boast some links in Frederick Law Olmsted's series of parks known as the "Emerald Necklace", such as the dazzling Arnold Arboretum and Franklin Park, home to the city zoo. Across the Charles River from Boston lies **Cambridge**, a must for its excellent bookstores and funky café scene and, above all, prestigious Harvard University.

Brief history

Boston's first permanent settlement was started by British Reverend **William Blackstone**, who split off from a camp in Weymouth, Massachusetts for more isolated territory in 1625. He was rapidly joined by Puritan settlers, to whom he sold most of the land he had claimed; then called the Shawmut Peninsula, it was soon renamed by the Puritans after their hometown in England: Boston.

Early Bostonians enjoyed almost total political autonomy, but with the restoration of the British monarchy in 1660, the Crown began appointing governors to oversee the colony. The colonists clashed frequently with these appointees, their resentment growing with a series of acts over the next ninety years that restricted certain civil and commercial liberties. This culminated in such skirmishes as the Boston Massacre (1770) and the Boston Tea Party (1773), events that helped ignite the **Revolutionary War** (1775–83), which effectively started in Lexington (see p.130), just outside Boston.

Post-Revolution, Boston emerged as a leading port city, eventually moving on to prominence in textiles and other industries. Its success in these fields brought waves of **immigrants** – notably Irish, Italian and Chinese – in the nineteenth century; all three groups still have sizeable communities in the city and the region. Additionally, the city gained a reputation as the centre of the American **university system**, with more than sixty higher learning institutes in the area. This academic connection has played a key role in the city's left-leaning political tradition, which spawned, most famously, the Kennedy family.

Race relations and urban renewal

Despite a strong history of progressive thought, the city was less successful when it came to integration, and **racial tensions** flared up frequently in the twentieth century, most notoriously with the advent of public school "busing" aimed at creating racially mixed schools in the 1970s. Race relations have improved since that low-point, spurred on by community revitalization that has strengthened the business centres of African-American neighbourhoods, and more symbolically, with the election and re-election of Massachusetts's first black governor, **Deval Patrick**, in November 2006 and 2010.

The physical transformation of the city is even more apparent. Boston, always a stately town, got a facelift in 2007 with the completion of the **Big Dig** construction

1

project – wherein an unsightly elevated highway (I-93) was stowed underground – freeing up 150 acres of land for park and recreational use. The project gave Boston the skyline-altering Zakim Bridge, the manicured Rose Kennedy Greenway and a beautified HarborWalk, appealing greenspaces that are indicative of Boston's progressive present, as well as playgrounds for its future.

Downtown

Boston's compact **downtown** encompasses both the colonial heart and contemporary core of the city. An assemblage of red-brick buildings and modern office towers, the area's glamour factor doesn't quite rival that of other big-city centres in the USA, but

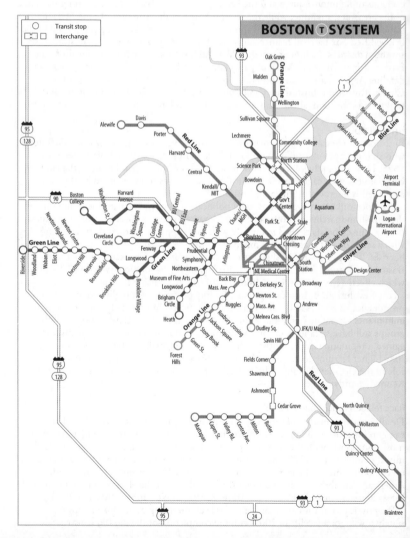

FREE BOSTON

With **no admission fee** (some ask for a small donation), the following laudable attractions are putting the "free" back into Freedom Trail. They're scattered across the city, so you're bound to find an easy-on-the-wallet activity no matter which neighbourhood you visit.

470 Atlantic Ave observation deck
  See p.58
Arnold Arboretum See p.86
Athenaeum See p.51
Boston Public Library See p.77
Bunker Hill Monument See p.67
Copp's Hill Burying Ground See p.63
Custom House observation deck
  See p.56
Faneuil Hall See p.56
Forest Hills cemetery See p.87
Granary Burying Ground See p.51
Hatch Shell See p.71

Institute of Contemporary Art Thurs
  5–9pm, families free last Sat of the
  month. See p.60
Massachusetts State House See p.69
Mount Auburn cemetery See p.94
Museum of Fine Arts By donation Wed
  after 4pm. See p.83
National Park Service tours See p.99
Old North Church See p.63
Old South Church See p.77
Public Garden See p.73
Samuel Adams Brewery tour See p.116
USS Constitution and museum See p.65

the sheer concentration of historic sites here makes up for whatever's lacking in flash. It is also home to a number of the best reasons – both historical and modern – for visiting the city.

The best place to start exploring downtown is **Boston Common**, a king-sized version of the tidy greenspace at the core of innumerable New England villages. If you want to learn about the city's past, follow the **Freedom Trail**, a self-guided walking tour (see box, p.50), out of the Common. Probably the most popular stop on the Trail is **Faneuil Hall Marketplace**, but there are other areas of interest as well: **King's Chapel**, on Tremont Street, and the nearby **Old State House**, for instance, mark the periphery of Boston's earliest town centre. The most evocative streets are those whose character has been less diluted over the years – **School Street**, **State Street** and the eighteenth-century enclave known as **Blackstone Block**, near Faneuil Hall. East of the Common is the **Financial District**, where the short streets follow the tangled patterns of colonial village lanes; south of here is the small but vibrant **Chinatown** and adjacent **Theater District**.

During the day, when the streets are full of office workers and tourists, the whole downtown area is quite lively, but come nightfall the crowds thin out substantially. Chinatown, the Theater District and Quincy Market are exceptions to this, as is the **waterfront**, which is seeing a renaissance following the completion of the Big Dig, and is particularly pleasant, illuminated by the twinkling lights of moored ships.

Boston Common

Boston's premier open space is **Boston Common**, a fifty-acre green that effectively separates historic, workaday downtown from its posh neighbours, the Beacon Hill and Back Bay districts. Established in 1634 as "a trayning field" and "for the feeding of cattell" – or so a tablet opposite the central Park Street **T** station recalls – the Common is still more of a functional space than a decorative one, used by both pedestrian commuters on their way to downtown's office towers and tourists seeking the **Boston Common Visitor Center** (see p.98), the official starting-point of the Freedom Trail. While not as manicured as the adjacent **Public Garden** (see p.73), it nonetheless offers plenty of benches and lawn space well suited for taking a breather. Along the northern side of the Common, the lovely Beacon Street (see p.68) runs from the gold-domed **State House** to Charles Street, opposite the Public Garden. Free **Shakespeare performances**, an on-the-lawn summertime tradition, take place at the Parkman Bandstand in July and August (⊛commshakes.org).

1

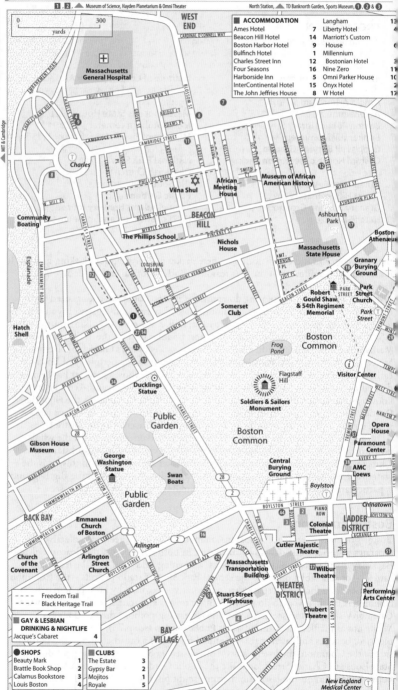

Museum of Science, Hayden Planetarium & Omni Theater

North Station, TD Banknorth Garden, Sports Museum

ACCOMMODATION			
Ames Hotel	7	Langham	13
Beacon Hill Hotel	14	Liberty Hotel	4
Boston Harbor Hotel	9	Marriott's Custom	
Bulfinch Hotel	1	House	6
Charles Street Inn	12	Millennium	
Four Seasons	16	Bostonian Hotel	3
Harborside Inn	5	Nine Zero	11
InterContinental Hotel		Omni Parker House	10
The John Jeffries House	8	Onyx Hotel	2
		W Hotel	17

WEST END

CARDINAL O'CONNELL WAY

Massachusetts General Hospital

Charles

MIT & Cambridge

Community Boating

Esplanade

Hatch Shell

BEACON HILL

Vilna Shul

African Meeting House

Museum of African American History

The Phillips School

Nichols House

Massachusetts State House

Ashburton Park

Boston Athenaeum

Granary Burying Ground

Robert Gould Shaw & 54th Regiment Memorial

Park Street Church

Park Street

Somerset Club

Boston Common

Frog Pond

Flagstaff Hill

Visitor Center

Soldiers & Sailors Monument

Ducklings Statue

Public Garden

Boston Common

Opera House

Paramount Center

Gibson House Museum

George Washington Statue

Swan Boats

Public Garden

Central Burying Ground

Boylston

AMC Loews

Chinatown

BACK BAY

Emmanuel Church of Boston

Church of the Covenant

Arlington Street Church

Arlington

Colonial Theatre

LADDER DISTRICT

Massachusetts Transportation Building

Cutler Majestic Theatre

Wilbur Theatre

Citi Performing Arts Center

Stuart Street Playhouse

THEATER DISTRICT

BAY VILLAGE

Shubert Theatre

New England Medical Center

South End

- - - Freedom Trail
- - - Black Heritage Trail

GAY & LESBIAN DRINKING & NIGHTLIFE	
Jacque's Cabaret	4

SHOPS	
Beauty Mark	1
Brattle Book Shop	2
Calamus Bookstore	3
Louis Boston	4

CLUBS	
The Estate	3
Gypsy Bar	2
Mojitos	1
Royale	5

0 ____ 300
yards

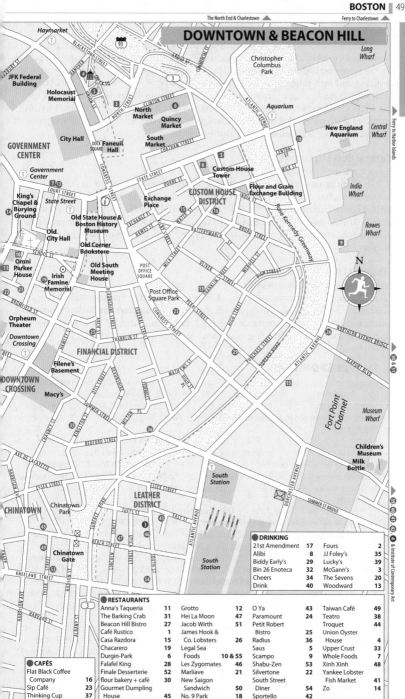

1

Brief history

Even before John Winthrop, Massachusett's first governor, and his fellow Puritan colonists earmarked the land for public use in 1634, the Common was used as pasture by the **Reverend William Blackstone**, Boston's first European settler. Not long after, it disintegrated into little more than a town gallows. Newly elected president **George Washington** made an appearance on the Common in 1789, as did his aide-de-camp, the Marquis de Lafayette, several years later. Ornate nineteenth-century iron fencing encircled the park until World War II, when it was taken down for use as scrap metal; it's now said to grace the bottom of Boston Harbor.

Central Burying Ground

Boylston St, at Tremont St • Boylston **T**

While often unnoticed by passers-by, the **Central Burying Ground** has occupied the southeast corner of the Common since 1754. The gravestones are worth a look; artist Gilbert Stuart (see p.265), best known for his portraits of George Washington, died penniless and was interred here in tomb 61. Among other notable residents are various soldiers of the Revolutionary Army and Redcoats killed in the Battle of Bunker Hill.

Flagstaff Hill

Just north of the Central Burying Ground • Boylston **T**

It's a short walk north from the Central Burying Ground to **Flagstaff Hill**, the Common's highest point, crowned with the Civil War **Soldiers and Sailors Monument**, which is topped by a bronze statue of Lady Liberty and encircled by four plaques displaying scenes of cap-wearing sailors and bayonet-toting soldiers.

THE FREEDOM TRAIL

Delineated by a 2.5-mile-long red-brick (or painted) stripe in the sidewalk, the **Freedom Trail** (w thefreedomtrail.org) stretches from Boston Common to Charlestown, linking sixteen points "significant in their contribution to this country's struggle for freedom". About half the sights on the trail are related to the Revolution itself; the other half are more germane to other times and topics.

In the Revolution-relevant column, there's the **Old North Church** (see p.63), whose lanterns warned of the British troop movements in 1775; **Faneuil Hall** (see p.56), where opposition to the Brits' proposed tea tax was voiced; the **Old South Meeting House** (see p.53), wherein word came that said tax would be imposed; the **Old State House** (see p.54), which served as the Boston seat of British government; and the site of the **Boston Massacre** (see p.54).

Other stops on the trail include the **USS Constitution** (see p.65), which failed to sink under British cannon fire in the War of 1812, earning her the nickname "Old Ironsides"; the **Park Street Church** (see p.51), site of William Lloyd Garrison's seminal oration in favour of abolition; and the **Old Corner Bookstore** (see p.53), a publishing house for American (and some British) writers. You'll also find two instances of British dominion along the trail: the **Bunker Hill Monument** (see p.67), an obelisk commemorating a British victory, albeit in the guise of a moral one for America, and **King's Chapel** (see p.52), built to serve the King's men stationed in Boston. Finally, you can check out the gilt-domed **Massachusetts State House** (see p.69) after visiting the gravesites of the Boston luminaries who fought for it – they lie interred in three separate **cemeteries**.

Though some of the touches intended to accentuate the trail's appeal move closer to tarnishing it (the costumed actors outside some of the sights, the pseudo-antique signage), the Freedom Trail remains the easiest way to orient yourself downtown, and is especially useful if you'll only be in Boston for a short time, as it does take in many "must-see" sights. Detailed National Park Service **maps** of the trail can be picked up from the visitor centre at 15 State St. Thrifty visitors take note: most stops on the Trail are either **free** or inexpensive to enter.

Frog Pond

Near the Common's Beacon St border • Park St **T**

Overlooked by Flagstaff Hill, the **Frog Pond** was once home to legions of unusually large amphibians and the site of the first water pumped into the city. These days it's a simple kidney-shaped pool, used for wading in summer and ice-skating in winter; there's also a great playground nearby.

Brewer Fountain

Tremont St, at Park St • Park St **T**

A path east of the Frog Pond leads to the elegant, two-tiered **Brewer Fountain**, an 1868 bronze replica of one from the Paris Exposition of 1855; the scantily clad gods and goddesses at its base are watched over by cherubs from above.

Northeast of Boston Common

The handful of sights radiating out from the Common's narrow northeastern corner are some of Boston's most illustrious. They include the **Park Street Church**, first in the nation to strike up *America* (a patriotic tune), **Granary Burying Ground**, place of interment for many of Boston's best-known Revolutionaries and **King's Chapel Burying Ground**, the city's oldest cemetery. The grand **Boston Athenæum**, a venerable research library, is also nearby.

Park Street Church

Park St, at Tremont St • Office hours Mon–Fri 8.30am–4.30pm • Free • ☎ 617 523 3383 • Park St **T**

Although the 1809 **Park Street Church** is a simple mass of bricks and mortar, its 217ft-tall white telescoping **steeple** is undeniably impressive. The church's reputation rests not on its size, however, but on the events that took place inside: this is where famed abolitionist William Lloyd Garrison delivered his first public address calling for the nationwide abolition of slavery, and where the song *America* ("My country 'tis of thee …") was first sung, on July 4, 1831.

Granary Burying Ground

Tremont St, between Park and School streets • Daily 9am–5pm • Free • Park St **T**

Adjacent to the Park Street Church is one of the more peaceful stops on the Freedom Trail, the **Granary Burying Ground**, final resting place for numerous Revolutionary leaders. The entrance, an Egyptian Revival arch, fronts Tremont Street, and it's from the sidewalk here that some of the most famous gravesites can be best appreciated: the boulder and plaque commemorating revolutionary James Otis; Samuel Adams's tomb; and the group grave of the five people killed in the **Boston Massacre** of 1770. From any angle you can see the stocky **obelisk** at dead centre that marks the grave of Benjamin Franklin's parents. Further inside are the graves of **Peter Faneuil**, **Paul Revere** and **John Hancock**, although, as the rangers will tell you, "the stones and the bones may not match up".

The Boston Athenæum

10 1/2 Beacon St • Mon & Wed 9am–8pm, Tues, Thurs & Fri till 5.30pm, Sat till 4pm; art and architecture tour Tues & Thurs 3pm reservations required • Free, including tours • ☎ 617 227 0270 (ext 279 for tours), ⓦ bostonathenaeum.org • Park St **T**

Around the block from the Granary Burying Ground, the venerable **Boston Athenæum** is one of Boston's most alluring and yet least-visited sights. Established in 1807, this hidden-in-plain-view national landmark stakes its claim as one of the oldest independent research libraries in the country. Best known are its special collections, including the original library of **King's Chapel** – which counts the 1666 edition of Sir Walter Raleigh's *History of the World* among its holdings – as well as books from the private library of George Washington. That said, there's more here than just sober shelves of literature. For example, the library's **ornate interior** and impressive array of **artworks**, including paintings by John Singer Sargent and Gilbert Stuart, easily rival

1

anything at the Museum of Fine Arts, but can be viewed here without the accompanying crowds. In fact, the artistic nucleus of the MFA was spun from the Athenæum's holdings when it opened in 1876; to this day, certain works continue to travel back and forth between the two establishments.

The Athenæum is not exactly welcoming to guests (perhaps explaining its lack of visitors); non-members are confined to the first floor, and everyone has to leave his or her bags and coats at the **front desk** – it's all very formal Beacon Hill. Still, if you can handle a bit of scrutiny, it's well worth popping in – sitting in one of its leather armchairs, an experience that's enhanced by knockout views of Granary Burying Ground, you'll discover an oasis of studious refinement right in the centre of honk-and-go downtown Boston.

King's Chapel and Burying Ground

58 Tremont St • **King's Chapel** June–Sept Mon–Sat 10am–4pm, Sun 1–4pm • Free **Chamber music recitals** Tues 12.15–12.50pm • $3 suggested donation • ☎ 617 523 1749 **Burying Ground** Daily during "daylight hours"; may fluctuate according to season • Free • Government Center **T**

Just a block or so east from the Athenæum is Boston's oldest cemetery, the atmospheric **King's Chapel Burying Ground** and its accompanying church. One of the chief pleasures here is examining the ancient tombstones, many beautifully etched with winged skulls and contemplative seraphim. The burying ground was one of the favourite Boston haunts of author **Nathaniel Hawthorne**, who drew inspiration from the grave of a certain Elizabeth Pain to create the famously adulterous character of Hester Prynne for his novel *The Scarlet Letter*.

The most conspicuous thing about the **chapel** that stands on the grounds is its absence of a steeple (there were plans for one, but not enough money). The grey, foreboding building was completed in 1754, with the pillar-fronted portico added in 1789; the belfry boasts the **biggest bell** ever cast by Paul Revere. The current structure replaced an earlier wooden chapel, which had been constructed amid some controversy: in 1686, King James II revoked the Massachusetts Bay Colony's charter, installed Sir Edmund Andros as governor and gave him orders to found an Anglican parish – a move that didn't sit too well with Boston's Puritan population. While hardly ostentatious, the elegant **Georgian interior**, done up with wooden Corinthian columns and lit by chandeliers, provides a marked contrast to the minimalist adornments of Boston's other historic churches. Few visitors go past the entrance, but it is worth peeking inside, ideally during one of the weekly chamber music concerts.

Washington Street shopping district

Downtown proper comes in two parts: the **Washington Street shopping district** (namely the School Street area and Downtown Crossing) and the adjacent Financial District. The former, situated east of King's Chapel, has some of the city's most historic sights – the **Old Corner Bookstore, Old South Meeting House** and **Old State House** – but it tends to shut down after business hours. The stops can be seen in half a day, though you'll need to allow more time if shopping is on your agenda; the stretch around **Downtown Crossing** is full of thrifty clothes shopping opportunities.

Omni Parker House Hotel

60 School St (across from King's Chapel) • Park St **T**

No one can compete with the **Omni Parker House Hotel** (see p.100) in the history department: it's the oldest continuously operating hotel in the US. It was in this legendary hostelry that Boston cream pie – really a layered cake with custard filling and chocolate glaze on top – was concocted in 1855. On a more bizarre note, both Ho Chi Minh and Malcolm X used to work here, the former in the kitchen and the latter as a busboy.

School Street

Just one block long between Tremont and Washington streets, School Street offers up some of the best of Boston's charms, beginning with the antique gaslights that flank the western wall of King's Chapel. Just beyond is a grand French Second Empire building that served as **Boston City Hall** from 1865 to 1969. Outside the gate, a mosaic embedded in the pavement marks the original location of the country's first public school – **Boston Latin**, founded in 1635.

Old Corner Bookstore

School St, at Washington St • Not open to the public; free to view from outside • State St **T**

The gambrel-roofed former **Old Corner Bookstore** anchors the southern end of School Street as it joins Washington Street. In the nineteenth century, the stretch of Washington from here to Old South Meeting House was Boston's version of London's Fleet Street, with a convergence of booksellers, publishers and newspaper headquarters. The bookshop itself – once home to the publishing house Ticknor & Fields – was Boston's hottest literary salon, with the likes of Emerson, Longfellow, and even Dickens and Thackeray, among their list of authors. The building was available for rent at the time of writing; perhaps the next owners will rekindle this site's passion for prose.

Irish Famine Memorial

School St, at Washington St • State St **T**

The **Irish Famine Memorial** commemorates the Irish refugees who emigrated to Boston in the 1840s as a result of the fungal potato crop and ensuing famine that claimed one million lives in their home country. Its focus is an unsettling pair of statues, one depicting an Irish family holding their hands out for food, the other a (presumably) Bostonian family that passes them by.

Old South Meeting House

310 Washington St • Daily: April–Oct 9.30am–5pm; Nov–March 10am–4pm • $6, children (6–18 years) $1 • ☎ 617 482 6439, ⓦ oldsouthmeetinghouse.org • State St **T**

Washington Street's big architectural landmark is the **Old South Meeting House**, a charming brick church recognizable by its tower – an octagonal spire. Put up in 1729, this is the second oldest church building in Boston, after Old North Church (see p.63). The venue certainly saw its share of anti-imperial rhetoric while it was still young. The day after the Boston Massacre, outraged Bostonians assembled here to demand the

THE BOSTON TEA PARTY

The first major act of rebellion preceding the Revolutionary War, the **Boston Tea Party** was far greater in significance than it was in duration. On December 16, 1773, a long-standing dispute over colonial taxation came to a dramatic head. At nightfall, a group of five thousand waited at **Old South Meeting House** to hear the Governor's ruling regarding three ships full of tea (one of many imports from England bearing a Crown-imposed tax in the colonies) moored in Boston Harbor. Upon receiving word that the Crown would not remove the ships, the civil throng converged on **Griffin's Wharf**. Around one hundred of them, some dressed in Native American garb, boarded the brigs and threw the cargo of tea overboard. The partiers disposed of 342 chests of **tea**, each weighing 360 pounds; the total amount discarded was enough to make 18.5 million cuppas, and worth more than one million dollars by today's standards. While it had the semblance of spontaneity, the event was in fact planned beforehand, and the mob was careful not to damage anything but the offending cargo. In any case, the "party" transformed protest into revolution. The ensuing **British sanctions**, colloquially referred to as the "Intolerable Acts", and the colonists' continued resistance, further inflamed the tension between the Crown and its colonies, which eventually exploded at Lexington and Concord (see p.130).

1

removal of the troops that were ostensibly guarding the town. More momentously, on the morning of December 16, 1773, nearly five thousand locals met here, awaiting word from **Governor Thomas Hutchinson** on whether he would permit the withdrawal of three ships in Boston Harbor containing taxed tea. When a message was received that the ships would not be removed, Samuel Adams announced, "This meeting can do no more to save the country!". His simple declaration triggered the **Boston Tea Party** (see box, p.53).

Before becoming a **museum**, the Meeting House served as a stable, a British riding school and even a bar. One thing lost in the transition was the famous original high pulpit, which the British tore out during the Revolution and used as firewood; the ornate one standing today is a replica from 1808. Note the exterior **clock**, installed in 1770, which you can still set your watch by.

Old State House

206 Washington St, at State St • Daily: Jan 9am–4pm; Feb–June & Sept–Dec till 5pm; July & Aug till 6pm • $7.50 • ☎ 617 720 1713,
Ⓦ bostonhistory.org • State St **T**

That the graceful, three-tiered tower of the red-brick **Old State House**, at the corner of Washington and State streets, is dwarfed by skyscrapers, amplifies rather than diminishes its colonial-era dignity. For years this was the seat of the **Massachusetts Bay Colony**, and consequently the centre of British authority for Massachusetts and Maine. Later it served as Boston's city hall, and in 1880 it was nearly demolished so that State Street traffic might flow more freely. Fortunately, the **Boston Historical Society** was formed in 1881 specifically to preserve the building, and was ultimately successful in converting it into a museum.

The building has certainly seen its share of history. An impassioned speech in the second-floor Council Chamber by James Otis, a Crown appointee who resigned to take up the colonial cause, sparked the quest for independence from Britain fifteen years before it was declared; legend has it that on certain nights you can still hear him hurling his anti-British barbs. The **balcony** overlooking State Street was the place from which the Declaration of Independence was first read publicly in Boston, on July 18, 1776, and two hundred years later, Queen Elizabeth II – the first British monarch to set foot in Boston – made a speech from the balcony as part of the American Bicentennial.

The museum

The **museum**'s permanent ground-level exhibit, titled "Colony to Commonwealth", has a number of displays chronicling Boston's role in inciting the Revolutionary War, including tea from the infamous party, a flag that the Sons of Liberty used to announce their meetings, a dapper jacket belonging to John Hancock and Paul Revere's propagandist **engraving** of the Boston Massacre.

Adjacent to the Old State House, at 15 State St, is the downtown **visitors centre** for the National Park Service (see p.98).

THE BOSTON MASSACRE

Directly in front of the Devonshire Street side of the Old State House, a circle of cobblestones embedded in a small traffic island marks the site of the **Boston Massacre**, the tragic outcome of escalating tensions between Bostonians and the British Redcoats that occupied the city. This riot of March 5, 1770, began when a young wigmaker's apprentice began heckling an army officer over a barber's bill. The officer sought refuge in the **Custom House**, which stood opposite the Old State House at the time, but a throng of people had gathered, including more soldiers, at whom the mob flung rocks and snowballs. When someone threw a club that knocked a Redcoat onto the ice, he rose and fired. Five Bostonians were killed in the ensuing fracas. Two other **patriots**, John Adams and Josiah Quincy, actually defended the offending eight soldiers in court; six were acquitted, and the two guilty were branded on their thumbs.

Downtown Crossing

1

Pedestrian-friendly **Downtown Crossing**, an outdoor mall area centred on the corner of Washington and Summer streets, brims with department stores and smaller shops that cater to budget shoppers. Its nucleus for nearly one hundred years was the original **Filene's Basement** (426 Washington St), a thrift-seeker's delight previously famous for its "Running of the Brides" event, during which frenzied brides-to-be feverishly pawed their way to marked-down gowns. Sadly, since 2007 the Basement has been left in the lurch over a botched property deal and it's not clear when or if this location will reopen. Although a portion of the corniced facade still stands (as well as its iconic clock), much of the former building is now merely a hole in the ground, and like a jilted bride, the Basement's defunct northern wall is wrapped up in dreary white sheets.

The Financial District

Boston's **Financial District** hardly conjures up the same image as those of New York or London, but it continues to wield influence and is not entirely devoid of historic interest – though this is generally more manifest in plaques rather than actual sights. The area runs on an office-hours-only schedule, and many of its little eateries and Irish pubs are closed on weekends, though some brave new restaurants are beginning to appear that have longer hours. The generally immaculate streets follow the same short, winding paths as they did three hundred years ago, though nowadays thirty- and forty-storey skyscrapers have replaced the wooden houses and churches that used to occupy the area.

Milk Street

Milk Street is the most dramatic approach to the Financial District. A bust of **Benjamin Franklin** surveys the scene from a recessed niche above the doorway at 1 Milk Street; the site marks Franklin's birthplace, although the building itself dates from 1874.

Post Office Square

Mid-way along Milk Street lies **Post Office Square**, the park's pretty triangular layout and cascading fountains popular with the area's professionals (and visitors, too). When standing in Post Office Square, see if you can identify the "Pregnant Building", just west of here at 100 Federal Street, so nicknamed because of its bulging midsection.

Government Center

Congress Street's major tenant, **Government Center**, lies northwest of Exchange Place. Passing through here is just about all there is to do, although this wasn't always the case: today's government buildings stand on the former site of **Scollay Square**, once Boston's red-light district. Scollay was razed in the early 1960s; the only thing that remains from the area's steamier days is the Oriental Tea Company's 227-gallon Steaming Kettle advertisement, which dates to 1873 and overhangs the *Starbucks* at 63–65 Court St. The plaza is now overlaid with concrete, thanks to a plan by I.M. Pei, and towered over by two monolithic edifices: Boston City Hall on the east side, and the John F. Kennedy Federal Building on the north. One pretty face stands out from all the concrete, however: the graceful nineteenth-century **Sears Crescent** building, at 100 City Hall Plaza.

Faneuil Hall Marketplace and around

Between the Financial District and the North End is **Faneuil Hall Marketplace**, a pedestrian zone popular with tourists and (less so) with locals. Built as a market during colonial times, it declined during the nineteenth century and, like the area around it, was pretty much defunct until the 1960s, when it was successfully reinvented as a restaurant and shopping mall.

1

Faneuil Hall

Faneuil Hall Square • Daily 9am–5pm • Free • ☎ 617 242 5642, ⓦ nps.gov/bost • State St **T**

Much-hyped **Faneuil Hall** doesn't appear particularly majestic from the outside: it's simply a four-storey brick building topped with a gold grasshopper weathervane. Nevertheless, this is where revolutionary firebrands such as Samuel Adams and James Otis whipped up popular support for independence by protesting British tax legislation. Head upstairs to the impressive second floor: the auditorium has been preserved to reflect modifications made by Charles Bulfinch in 1805. Its focal point is a massive canvas depicting an embellished version of "The Great Debate", during which Daniel Webster argued against South Carolina Senator Robert Hayne, in 1830, for the concept of the United States as one nation. While the debate was an actual event, the painting contains a number of nineteenth-century luminaries, such as writer Nathaniel Hawthorne and historian Alexis de Tocqueville, who certainly weren't in attendance – the artist simply thought this would help him sell his painting.

Quincy, North and South markets

In front of Faneuil Hall • Mon–Sat 10am–9pm, Sun noon–6pm • Free • ☎ 617 523 1300, ⓦ faneuilhallmarketplace.com • State St **T**

The three oblong markets just behind Faneuil Hall were built in the early eighteenth century to contain the trade that quickly outgrew the hall. The centre building, known as **Quincy Market**, holds a super-extended corridor lined with stands selling a variety of take-out treats – it's the mother of mall food courts. To either side of Quincy Market are the **North and South markets**, which hold restaurants and popular chain clothing stores, as well as specialized curiosity shops (one sells only purple objects, another nothing but vests).

Custom House Tower

3 McKinley Square • Tours of the observation deck Sat–Thurs 2pm, weather permitting • $3 donation • ☎ 617 310 6300 • Aquarium **T**

Though no longer the tallest skyscraper in New England (a status it held for 49 years), the 1847 Custom House Tower – now a Marriott hotel (see p.100) – still has plenty of character and terrific views You can check out the vista via a 360-degree observation deck.

Dock Square and around

If you walk to Faneuil Hall from Government Center you may also notice **Dock Square**, so named for its original location directly on Boston's waterfront; carvings in the pavement indicate the shoreline in 1630. The square's centre is dominated by a statue of **Samuel Adams**, notable for its hyperbolic caption: "A statesman, incorruptible and fearless". A narrow corridor known as Scott's Alley heads north from here to Creek Square and **Blackstone Street**, the eastern edge of a tiny warren of streets. The uneven cobblestones and low brick buildings stretching west from here to Union Street have remained largely untouched since the 1750s; many of them, especially those along Union, now house restaurants and pubs. If you're in the area on a Friday or Saturday afternoon, follow Blackstone Street to Hanover Street and you'll find Boston's most historic open-air market, **Haymarket**, which dates to the 1830s. Here, produce sellers heckle patrons and happy shoppers haggle right back.

Holocaust Memorial

Congress St, between Hanover and North streets • Daily 24hr • Free • ☎ 617 457 8755, ⓦ nehm.org • Haymarket **T**

At the northern end of Dock Square you'll find six tall hollow glass pillars erected as a **memorial** to victims of the **Holocaust**. Built to resemble smokestacks, the columns are etched with six million numbers, recalling the tattoos the Nazis gave their victims. Steam rises from grates beneath the pillars to accentuate their symbolism, an effect that's particularly striking at night.

DOWNTOWN VISTAS

Whether from in or out of town, people can't seem to get enough of Boston's skyline – its pastiche of brownstone churches and glass-panelled skyscrapers framing Massachusetts Bay ranks among the country's finest. You can check out Boston from every angle by ascending the **Custom House Tower** (see p.56), the **Prudential Tower** (see p.78), the office building at **470 Atlantic Ave** (see p.58) and the **Bunker Hill Monument** (see p.67). The best lay of the land, though, is had from the water – board the **Charlestown ferry** (see p.65) or visit the **Harbor Islands** (see p.60) and watch the city recede.

The Theater District

Just west of Downtown Crossing is the slightly seedy **Theater District**, the chief attractions of which are the flamboyant buildings that lend the area its name. Not surprisingly, you'll have to purchase tickets in order to inspect their interiors (see p.120), but it's well worth a quick walk along Tremont Street to admire their facades. At the corner of Washington and Avery streets, you'll find the 1928 Beaux Arts **Opera House**, recently renovated after being closed for more than a decade, alongside another rejuvenated gem, the Art Deco **Paramount**, its red-and-orange light bulb marquee looking almost garish next to its dainty sister. The **Citi Performing Arts Center** – formerly the Wang Center for the Performing Arts and the Shubert Theatre – is just around the corner from **Piano Row**, a section of Boylston Street between Charles and Tremont that was the centre of American piano manufacturing and music publishing in the nineteenth and early twentieth centuries.

Chinatown

Boston's **Chinatown** lies wedged into just a few square blocks between the Financial and Theater districts, but it makes up in activity for what it lacks in size. Lean against a pagoda-topped payphone on the corner of **Beach and Tyler streets** and watch the way life here revolves around the food trade: by day, merchants barter over the price of produce, while by night Bostonians arrive in droves to eat in the restaurants. Walk down either of those streets – the neighbourhood's two liveliest – and you'll pass most of the restaurants, bakeries and markets, in whose windows you'll see the usual complement of roast ducks hanging from hooks and aquariums filled with future seafood dinners.

At the corner of Tyler and Beach streets, a plaque marks the site where, in 1761, John Wheatley purchased eight-year old **Phillis Wheatley** to serve as his slave; twelve years later she become the first published African-American woman with *Poems on Various Subjects, Religious and Moral.* Chinatown has two noteworthy outdoor spaces: the impressive **Chinatown Gate**, a red-and-gilt monolith guarded by four Fu dogs overlooking the corner of Hudson and Beach streets; and **Chinatown Park**, a feng shui-inspired plaza on Surface Road. The latter is landscaped with smooth pebbles, streams and tall sheaves of bamboo, that sway around angular red metal posts. Chinatown is at its most vibrant during its festivals, especially **Chinese (Lunar) New Year** in January (sometimes early Feb). At the **Festival of the August Moon**, held on the second weekend in August, there's a bustling street fair; contact Chinatown Main Street, a neighbourhood cultural organization, for more info (☎617 350 6303, ⓦchinatownmainstreet.org).

The waterfront

Boston's urban renewal programme, sparked by the beginning of the Big Dig in the early 1990s, has resulted in a resurgence of its **waterfront** area, which stretches from the North End to South Station. The underground routing of I-93, which had separated the waterfront from the rest of downtown since the 1950s, has allowed the city to

THE HARBORWALK

The **Harborwalk** officially begins in Dorchester, curving eastwards into the beaches of South Boston (a whopping 47 miles in all). Though visitors shouldn't expect to see the whole thing, it's quite pleasant to walk the portion that meanders through the wharves alongside the Boston waterfront. Start at **Lewis Wharf**, in the North End (see p.62), where a gravel path leads to a pretty circular garden. Continue south, passing by Christopher Columbus Park and the Aquarium. Before arriving at the *Boston Harbor Hotel*'s breathtaking vaulted entrance, check out David von Schlegell's **Untitled Landscape** on India Wharf, two pairs of 15ft L-shaped bends of metal which seem to magnetically compel children (and adults, too) to run between them.

Throughout, there are peaceful harbour vistas, complete with drifting sailboats and bobbing birds, but the best scenery of the walk lies between Lewis Wharf and 470 Atlantic Ave, former site of the Boston Tea Party and current home to a fantastic fourteenth-floor observation deck (daily 10am–5pm; free). For more information, visit the Harborwalk's extensive website (🔴 bostonharborwalk.com).

reconnect with the sea through a series of projects such as the expansion of the New England Aquarium and the conversion of wharf buildings into housing. As you cross Surface Road, which separates Faneuil Hall Marketplace from the North End, take note of the **Rose Kennedy Greenway**, a thirteen-acre public park occupying the strip that used to be I-93. Here, what was once a car-ridden stretch is now a ribbon of greenspace, flower gardens, spouting fountains and free wi-fi.

While the waterfront that's concentrated around **Long Wharf** is quite touristy, strolling the **Harborwalk** (see box above) that edges the water affords unbeatable views of the city. You'll also find plenty of diversion at the **New England Aquarium** if you've got little ones in tow. Otherwise, you can explore on a number of **boat tours** or escape the city altogether by heading out to the **Harbor Islands**. The up-and-coming **Fort Point** neighbourhood and the **Seaport District**, meanwhile, are two spacious harbourside areas across the Congress Street Bridge from downtown. Accessible by the Silver Line **T**, these two vast enclaves are full of brick warehouse galleries and restaurants, and boast two compelling museums.

Long Wharf

Long Wharf has been the waterfront's main drag since its construction in 1710. This is also the main point of departure for **harbour cruises** (see p.98), whale-watching trips (see p.99), and ferries to Cape Cod (see p.97) and Salem (see p.97). Summer is its most active season, when the wharf comes alive with vendors selling souvenirs and ice cream. It's perhaps most enjoyable – and still relatively safe – at night, when even the freighters appear graceful against the moonlit water. Walk out to the end for an excellent view of **Boston Harbor**.

Situated between Long Wharf and Commercial Wharf, **Christopher Columbus Park** is a pretty greenspace bisected by a wisteria-laden trellis. The park also features a rose garden and kiddie-sized sprinkler fountain.

New England Aquarium

Central Wharf • **Aquarium** July & Aug Sun–Thurs 9am–6pm, Fri & Sat till 7pm; Sept–June Mon–Fri 9am–5pm, Sat & Sun till 6pm • $22.95, children (3–11 years) $15.95 • ☎ 617 973 5200, 🔴 neaq.org **Whale-watching trips** April–Oct; 3hr–4hr, call for times • $39.95, children (3–11 years) $31.95 • ☎ 617 973 5206 **3D IMAX theatre** Daily 9.30am–10.30pm • $9.95, children (3–11 years) $7.95 • ☎ 1 866 815 4629 • Aquarium **T**

Next door to Long Wharf is the waterfront's main draw, the **New England Aquarium**. Especially fun for children, the aquarium has plenty of good exhibits, including the

FROM TOP INSTITUTE OF CONTEMPORARY ART (P.60); BOSTON PUBLIC LIBRARY (P.77) >

1

penguins on the bottom floor. In the centre of the aquarium's spiral walkway is an impressive three-storey, 200,000-gallon cylindrical tank packed with sea turtles, moray eels, sharks, stingrays and other ocean exotica. Near the ticket counter, brave visitors can pat scratchy bonnethead sharks and velvety cownose rays as they swim elegantly through a mangrove-themed touch tank that opened in 2011. The Aquarium also runs **whale-watching** trips and is home to a **3D IMAX theatre**.

Boston Children's Museum

308 Congress St • Sat–Thurs 10am–5pm, Fri till 9pm • Adults and children $12; Fri 5–9pm $1 • ☎ 617 426 6500, ⓦ bostonchildrensmuseum.org • South Station **T**

It's hard to miss the larger-than-life 1930s-era **Hood Milk Bottle** model, across the Congress Street bridge from downtown. Just behind it, the expanded **Boston Children's Museum** comprises three floors of educational exhibits craftily designed to trick kids into learning about topics from musicology to the engineering of a humungous bubble. Before heading out, be sure to check out the Recycle Shop, where industrial leftovers are transformed into appealing craft fodder.

Institute of Contemporary Art

100 Northern Ave • Tues, Wed, Sat & Sun 10am–5pm, Thurs & Fri till 9pm • $15, Thurs 5–9pm Free; children (17 years and under) free; free for families last Sat of the month • ☎ 617 478 3100, ⓦ icaboston.org • Courthouse Station **T**

Looking like a glamorous ice-cube perched above Boston Harbor, the glimmering facade of the **Institute of Contemporary Art** gives you an impressive show before you've even stepped inside. Over the threshold, the permanent collection and gallery space, located on the **fourth floor**, features late twentieth- and twenty-first-century work such as photography by Nan Goldin, sculptural textiles by Mona Hatoum and figures by Louise Bourgeois. One standout piece is Cornelia Parker's *Hanging Fire*; a beguiling, suspended sculpture comprised of floating charcoal shapes that the artist uncovered at an arson site. Complementing the art is the building's dramatic cantilever shape, extending 80ft over the water; from the interior this section functions as the "Founders Gallery", a meditative ledge where, if you look down, you'll find yourself standing directly above the harbour.

The **second and third floors** house an innovative theatre whose glass walls darken from clear to opaque at the flip of a switch; shows here range from modern dance performances to screenings of *The Matrix*; check their website for details.

The Harbor Islands

Extending across Massachusetts Bay from Salem to Portsmouth, NH, the 34 bucolic **Harbor Islands** served as defence points during the American Revolution and Civil War. They were transformed into a national park in 1996, with the result that six are now easily accessible by ferry from Long Wharf (see p.58), and a seventh, Little Brewster, has a tour that leaves from 2 Northern Ave in the Fort Point Channel (near Boston Children's Museum). In the interest of preserving island ecology, no bicycles or rollerblades are allowed.

George's Island

The most popular and best-served of the Harbor Islands, **George's Island** saw heavy use during the Civil War, as evidenced by the remains of **Fort Warren** (May to mid-Oct daily dawn–dusk; free), a battle station covering most of the island. You'll get more out of a visit by taking a park ranger tour (free; no need to pre-book). George's Island often holds performances, including jazz, children's theatre and vintage baseball games; check the Harbor Islands website (see p.61) for scheduling.

Spectacle Island

In 2006, **Spectacle Island** outgrew its murky past (it was a horse rendering plant, then a city dump) to become an environmentally savvy greenspace. In cleaning up the island, engineers solved two civic headaches at once – they used the Big Dig's dirt (2.8 million cubic meters) to cap Spectacle's landfill. The island now features a small lifeguarded beach, a snack bar, clambakes (see p.477), an eco-friendly visitor centre (complete with self-composting bathrooms) and pretty walking trails.

Little Brewster

National Park Service tours leave from 2 Northern Ave in the Fort Point Channel • Late June to mid-Oct Fri–Sun; 3hr (bring lunch) reservations recommended • $39; children (3–11 years) $29 • ☎ 617 223 8666, ⓦ bostonislands.com • South Station **T**

The most intriguing of the islands is the one furthest out to sea – **Little Brewster** – home to the 1783 **Boston Light**, the oldest light station in the country, and the only one that still has a Coast Guard keeper on site. Tours visit two other harbour lighthouses, then disembark at Little Brewster for a 76-step climb to the top of Boston Light.

ARRIVAL AND DEPARTURE   THE HARBOR ISLANDS

By boat A 15min ferry ride connects Long Wharf with central George's Island or Spectacle Island (May to mid-June & Sept to mid-Oct daily on the hour 10am–4pm; late June to Aug Mon–Thurs on the hour 9am–5pm; Fri, Sat & Sun every 30min till 6pm; call to confirm times; $14, children (3–11 years) $8; ☎ 617 223 8666, ⓦ bostonislands .com; Aquarium **T**). From George's, water taxis ($3) shuttle visitors to the other four islands.

INFORMATION

Tourist information The Harbor Islands information kiosk, at the foot of Long Wharf, keeps a detailed shuttle schedule and stocks excellent maps. Visit ⓦ bostonislands .com and ⓦ nps.gov/boha for more information.

ACCOMMODATION, EATING AND DRINKING

The more remote islands lack a freshwater source, so be sure to bring **bottled water** with you. The same goes for food – if you're travelling beyond George's or Spectacle, you should also consider packing a **picnic lunch**. George's and Spectacle offer low-key snack bars and – for a small snack – you can go berry-picking on Grape and Bumpkin islands.

Camping You can camp on three of the islands (Lovells, Bumpkin and Grape; late May to mid-Oct; ☎ 1 877 422 6762); you'll need to bring your own supplies. $15

South Boston

Across the Fort Point Channel from downtown and east into Boston Harbor lies **South Boston**, often referred to as "Southie", and known for its Irish-American population. South Boston's Celtic heritage is quite evident on the main commercial boulevard, **East and West Broadway**, where seemingly every laundry, convenience store and restaurant has a sign covered with shamrocks. Southie cites the 1997 film *Good Will Hunting* as a claim to fame. In this cinematic paean to the neighbourhood, South Boston featured prominently as the backdrop for Will Hunting's path to mathematical truth and personal harmony.

TOP DOG

Sullivan's 2080 Day Blvd. Adjacent to Fort Independence (see p.62), South Boston ☎ 617 268 5685; Bus #9 or #11 from the Broadway T. *Sullivan's*, a snack bar founded in 1951, is a local institution in these parts, with a seasonal army of employees serving up tasty grilled fare; enjoying one of their $1.60 hot dogs is the perfect way to cap off a summer's day. Mid-Feb to late Nov daily 8.30am–close (fluctuates with weather; till 5pm winter, 10pm summer).

1 Castle Island

Bus #9 or #11 from the Broadway **T**

South Boston narrows to an end in Boston Harbor on a strip of land called **Castle Island**, off the end of William J. Day Boulevard, a favourite leisure spot for residents. Its appeal is easy to see: the beach runs for miles, parking is free and swimming is accompanied by spectacular views of downtown and the planes of Logan Airport. At its tip is **Fort Independence** (guided tours Sat & Sun noon–3.30pm; free), a stout granite edifice that was one of the earliest redoubts in the Americas.

The North End

Hemmed in nearly all around by Boston Harbor, the small, densely populated **North End** is Boston's **Little Italy**, where grandmothers chatter in Italian, bocce ball is a way of life, and laundry dangles from upper-storey windows. Here, narrow streets are chock-a-block with Italian bakeries and restaurants and hold some of Boston's most illustrious sights. And, despite the fact that the above-ground highway that once separated the area from downtown has been removed (replaced by the diverting Rose Kennedy Greenway), the area still has a bit of a detached feeling, making it all the more charming. In addition to the Italian cultural scene, the North End has become known for its sense of style, owing to a number of the city's best clothing and home decor **boutiques** opening their doors here within the past few years.

Hanover Street and around

Hanover Street has long been the main connection between the North End and the rest of Boston, and it is along here – and small side streets like Parmenter and Richmond (actually a continuation of each other on each side of Hanover) – that many of the area's traditional *trattorias*, *caffés* and bakeries are located. It's also where you'll find a distinctly European flavour: although there are a handful of chain stores in the neighbourhood, the majority of businesses remain refreshingly independent.

Paul Revere House

19 North Square • Mid-April to Oct daily 9.30am–5.15pm; Nov to mid-April daily 9.30am–4.15pm, Jan, Feb & March closed Mon • $3.50 • ☎ 617 523 2338, ⓦ paulreverehouse.org • Haymarket **T**

The little triangular wedge of cobblestones and gaslights known as **North Square**, one block east of Hanover between Prince and Richmond, is among the most historic and attractive pockets of the city. Here the eateries recede in deference to the **Paul Revere House**, the oldest residential address in downtown Boston. The three-storey post-and-beam structure, which dates from about 1680, stands on the site of the former home of Increase Mather, a North End minister and Puritan heavyweight known for his involvement in the Salem Witch Trials (see p.143), which burned down in the Great Fire of 1676. The property's most famous tenant, however, was silversmith Paul Revere, who lived here from 1770 to 1800. Revere gained immortality on the night of April 18, 1775, when he headed out on his now-legendary "midnight ride" to Lexington, successfully warning John Hancock and Samuel Adams (and anyone else within earshot) of the impending British march (see p.130). Examples of Revere's silverware upstairs merit a look, as do the museum's small but evocative rotating exhibits.

Paul Revere Mall

Hanover St , between Tileston and Charter streets • Haymarket **T**

A couple of blocks north of the Paul Revere House on Hanover St, the famous bronze **statue** of Paul Revere astride his borrowed horse marks the edge of the **Paul Revere**

Mall. The cobblestoned park (also known as the Prado) was carved out of a chunk of apartment blocks in 1933 and runs back to tiny Unity Street.

All Saints' Way

Between nos. 4 and 8 Battery St • Haymarket **T**

All Saints' Way sits at the northern end of Hanover Street, a reverential alley squeezed in between nos. 4 and 8 Battery St. Ingenuous and sweet, it's decked out with images of saints and peaceful cherubim.

Old North Church

193 Salem St • Jan & Feb Tues–Sun 10am–4pm; March–May daily 9am–5pm; June–Oct daily 9am–6pm; Nov & Dec daily 10am–5pm • Free **Behind the Scenes tour** Week between Christmas and New Year 10am–5pm; June Sat & Sun 9am–6pm; July–Oct daily 9am–6pm • $8, children (16 years and under) $5 • ☎ 617 523 6676, ⦿ oldnorth.com • Haymarket **T**

Few places in Boston have as emblematic a quality as the simple yet noble **Old North Church**. Built in 1723, it's easily recognized by its gleaming 191ft **steeple** – though it was a pair of lanterns that secured the structure's place in history. The church sexton, Robert Newman, is said to have hung both of them inside on the night of April 18, 1775, to signal the movement of British forces "by sea" from Boston Common (which then bordered the Charles River) to Lexington and Concord (see p.130) at the same time that Paul Revere was galloping along on his famous ride (see p.62).

The interior of the church is spotlessly white and well lit, thanks to the Palladian windows behind the pulpit. Churchgoers can check their watches by the clock at the rear; made in 1726, it's the oldest one still ticking in an American public building. Beneath your feet, the timber on which the pews rest is supported by 37 basement-level crypts. The eight bells inside the belfry – open to the public for tours from June to October ($8, children $5) – were the first cast for the British Empire in North America and have since tolled for the death of every US President.

Copp's Hill Burying Ground and around

Hull St • Daily dawn–dusk • Free • Haymarket **T**

Up Hull Street from Old North Church, the atmospheric **Copp's Hill Burying Ground**, with its eerily tilting slate tombstones and stunning harbour views, holds the highest ground in the North End. Among the ten thousand interred here are nearly a thousand men from the "New Guinea Community", a colonial enclave of free blacks. The most famous gravesite here is that of the **Mather family**, just inside the wrought-iron gates on the Charter Street side. Increase Mather and son Cotton were big players in Boston's early days of Puritan theocracy, a fact not at all reflected in the rather diminutive, if appropriately plain, tomb. You'll notice that many gravestones have chunks missing, the consequence of British soldiers using them for target practice during the 1775 Siege of Boston; the grave of one Captain Daniel Malcolm bears particularly strong evidence of this. As you exit the burying ground, keep an eye out for the **narrowest house** in Boston, at 44 Hull St. It really *is* narrow – 10ft feet wide – but that's about it, as it's a private residence and you can't go in.

The granite **Copp's Hill Terrace**, on Charter Street across from the burial ground's northern side, was the place from which British cannons bombarded Charlestown during the Battle of Bunker Hill. Just over a century later, in 1919, a 2.3-million-gallon tank of molasses exploded nearby, creating a syrupy tidal wave 30ft high that engulfed entire buildings and drowned 21 people and a score of horses. Old North Enders claim you can still catch a whiff of the stuff on exceptionally hot days.

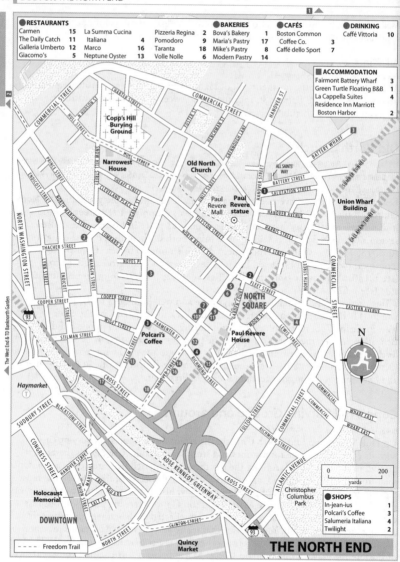

● RESTAURANTS
Carmen	15	La Summa Cucina		Pizzeria Regina	2
The Daily Catch	11	Italiana	4	Pomodoro	9
Galleria Umberto	12	Marco	16	Taranta	18
Giacomo's	5	Neptune Oyster	13	Volle Nolle	6

● BAKERIES
Bova's Bakery	1
Maria's Pastry	17
Mike's Pastry	8
Modern Pastry	14

● CAFÉS
Boston Common	
Coffee Co.	3
Caffè dello Sport	7

● DRINKING
| Caffè Vittoria | 10 |

■ ACCOMMODATION
Fairmont Battery Wharf	3
Green Turtle Floating B&B	1
La Cappella Suites	4
Residence Inn Marriott	
Boston Harbor	2

● SHOPS
In-jean-ius	1
Polcari's Coffee	3
Salumeria Italiana	4
Twilight	2

Salem street

While Old North Church is **Salem Street**'s star attraction, the lower blocks between Prince and Cross streets together make up arguably the North End's most colourful thoroughfare. The street is so narrow here that the buildings seem to lean into one another, and light traffic makes it a common practice to walk right down the middle of the road.

Along here you'll find an agreeable assemblage of Italian grocers, aromatic *pasticcerias*, *salumerias* and *caffès*. Just a couple of blocks up, the corner of **Salem and Parmenter streets** is the unofficial heart of the North End: locals typically while away the day along the pavement here on folding chairs brought from home. This corner is also home to **Polcari's Coffee** (see p.123), a North End landmark and a renowned coffee bean and spice vendor; on hot days, a serving of their $1.50 lemon slush – scooped into paper cups from an old barrel at the front door – is a must.

The Neapolitan bustle ends at Cross Street: if you continue on, you'll pass the sunbathers and fountain-jumpers of the Rose Kennedy Greenway and then reach Faneuil Hall.

Charlestown

Across Boston Harbor from the North End, historic **Charlestown** (fondly called "The Chuck" by residents) is a very pretty, quietly affluent neighbourhood that stands considerably isolated from the city, despite its annexation more than a century ago. Most visitors only make it over this way to see the historic frigate the **USS Constitution** (if at all), which is a shame, because the neighbourhood's narrow, hilly byways, lined with antique gaslights and colonial- and Federal-style terraced houses, make for pleasant exploration and offer great views of Boston. As you make the uphill climb to the **Bunker Hill Monument** – Charlestown's other big sight – look toward the water for jaw-dropping vistas of the Zakim Bridge and Boston at large.

Brief history

The earliest **Puritan settlers** had high hopes for developing Charlestown when they arrived in 1629, but an unsuitable water supply pushed them over to the Shawmut Peninsula. Charlestown grew slowly after that, and had to be completely rebuilt after the British burned it down in 1775. The mid-1800s witnessed the arrival of the so-called "lace-curtain Irish", somewhat better off than their East Boston brethren, and the district remains **Irish** at heart. Longtime locals have acquired a reputation for being standoffish, due to episodes such as their resistance to **school desegregation** in the 1970s, but relations have been vastly improved since then.

Charlestown Navy Yard and the USS Constitution

Constitution Wharf • **Charlestown Navy Yard** April–Oct Tues–Sun 10am–6pm; Nov–March Thurs–Sun till 4pm; lower deck only accessible on a 30min guided tour • Free • **Visitor centre** Daily: Sept–June 9am–5pm; July & Aug till 6pm • Free • ☎ 617 242 5601, ⓦ www.history.navy.mil/ussconstitution • Inner Harbor ferry from Long Wharf to Pier 3 in the Charlestown Navy Yard or North Station **T**

The sprawling **Charlestown Navy Yard** was one of the first and busiest US naval shipyards – riveting together an astounding 46 destroyer escorts in 1943 alone – though it owes most of its present-day liveliness to its grandest tenant, the **USS Constitution ("Old Ironsides")**. Launched in 1797 to safeguard American merchant vessels from Barbary pirates and the French and British navies, the *Constitution* earned her nickname during the War of 1812, when cannonballs fired from the British **HMS Guerrière** bounced off the hull (the "iron sides" were actually hewn from live oak, a particularly sturdy wood from the southeastern US), leading to the first and most dramatic American naval conquest of that war. The ship went on to win 33 battles – never losing one – before it was retired in 1830.

The *Constitution* has certainly taken its hits – roughly 85 percent of the ship has been reconstructed. Even after **extensive renovations**, Old Ironsides is still too frail to support sails for extended periods of time, and only makes around six to eight small trips a year (including her annual Fourth of July turnarounds in Boston Harbor).

There's often a queue to visit the ship, but it's worth the wait to get a close-up view of its physique, which is as tall as a twenty-storey building, and 341ft long. After ambling about the main deck, you can scuttle (with a guide) down to the **lower deck**, where you'll find an impressive array of **cannons**. Though these are all replicas, two functional models face downtown from the bow, where they shoot off explosive powder to mark flag-raising and -lowering daily. Were they to fire the balls for which they were originally outfitted, they'd topple the Custom House Tower across the bay.

1

Adjacent to the ship, the National Park Service runs a **visitor centre** detailing the history of the naval yard. Here, you'll find vintage photographs as well as supersized pallets of chain, nautical treasures and artefacts, such as the pleasingly named "Warner-Swaysey Twister-Winder". Used for twisting rope, the machine looks like one of Madonna's famous cone bras.

USS Constitution Museum

Building 22 • Daily: April–Oct 9am–6pm; Nov–March 10am–5pm • $5 donation • ☎ 617 426 1812, ⓦ ussconstitutionmuseum.org • Inner Harbor ferry from Long Wharf to Pier 3 in the Charlestown Navy Yard or North Station **T**

Housed in a substantial granite building across from Old Ironsides, the **USS Constitution Museum** helps contextualize the vessel and her unparalleled role in American maritime history. Downstairs galleries cover the history of the ship, including the story of how, in the 1920s, US schoolchildren contributed $154,000 in pennies toward its preservation; you can also glimpse the ship's original logbooks and examine the drafting tools used by the *Constitution*'s designer. Upstairs is perhaps more fun, with hands-on exhibits putting you in the role of a sailor: determine whether your comrades have scurvy or gout, attempt to balance yourself on a shifting footrope and ponder whether you would be willing to eat a biscuit "as hard as a brick".

USS Cassin Young

Daily 10am–4pm • Free • Inner Harbor ferry from Long Wharf to Pier 3 in the Charlestown Navy Yard or North Station **T**

Berthed in between Old Ironsides and the ferry to Long Wharf is the arresting hulk of the grey World War II destroyer **USS Cassin Young**. Wander about the expansive main deck, check out (via tour) the cramped chambers below, or attempt your best *Titanic* impression from the bow of the ship (albeit within the crosshairs of a menacing-looking anti-aircraft gun).

Ropewalk Building

Chelsea St at 5th • Closed to public; free to view the exterior • Inner Harbor ferry from Long Wharf to Pier 3 in the Charlestown Navy Yard or North Station **T**

At the northern perimeter of the Navy Yard is the **Ropewalk Building**. From 1837 to the mid-1950s, "ropewalkers" made nearly every single strand of rope used by the US Navy in this narrow, quarter-mile-long granite building, the only one of its kind still standing in the country; unfortunately it's not open to the public.

City Square and around

Towards Charlestown's centre, only a few minutes' walk northwest of the yard, there's a wealth of eighteenth- and nineteenth-century **town houses**, many of which you'll pass on your way to the Bunker Hill Monument.

Right in Charlestown's "downtown", **City Square Park** is a small, attractive plaza that preserves at its centre the outline of the first building erected by the Massachusetts Bay Colony. Built for governor John Winthrop in 1629, this house and civic meeting place was razed by fire during the battle of Bunker Hill; its foundation was rediscovered during the Big Dig excavation work of the 1980s.

Main Street extends north from the park; at no. 55 you'll find the wooden 1795 house of **Deacon John Larkin**, who lent Paul Revere his horse for his famous ride to Lexington (see p.62) and never got it back. At the corner of Main and Warren streets is the **Warren Tavern**, a small wooden structure (and still an active watering hole) built after the British burned Charlestown in the Battle of Bunker Hill. It's named for Dr Joseph Warren, who was killed in the battle.

Head up Monument Avenue toward the **Bunker Hill Monument**, passing along the way red-brick town houses that are some of Boston's most exclusive residences.

THE BATTLE OF BUNKER HILL

The Revolutionary War was at its bloodiest on the hot June day in 1775 when British and colonial forces clashed in **Charlestown**. In the wake of the battles at Lexington and Concord two months before, the British had assumed full control of Boston, while the patriots had the upper hand in the surrounding countryside. The British, under the command of generals Thomas Gage, William Howe and "Gentleman Johnny" Burgoyne, intended to sweep the area clean of "rebellious rascals". Colonials intercepted the plans and moved to fortify **Bunker Hill**, the dominant hill in Charlestown. However, when Colonel William Prescott arrived on the scene, he chose to occupy **Breed's Hill** instead, either due to confusion – the two hills were often confused on colonial-era maps – or tactical foresight, based on the proximity of Breed's Hill to the harbour. Whatever the motivation, more than a thousand citizen-soldiers arrived during the night of June 16, 1775, and fortified the hill with a 160ft-long earthen redoubt by morning.

Spotting the Yankee fort, the **Redcoats**, each carrying 125lb of food and supplies on their backs, rowed across the harbour to take the rebel-held town. On the patriots' side, Colonel Prescott had issued the now-legendary order that his troops not fire "'til you see the whites of their eyes" – such was their limited store of gunpowder. When the enemy's approach was deemed near enough, the patriots opened fire; though vastly outnumbered, they successfully repelled two full-fledged assaults. Some British units lost more than ninety percent of their men, and what few officers survived had to push their men forward with their swords to make them fight on. By the third British assault, the Redcoats had shed their gear, reinforcements had arrived and the Americans' gunpowder was dwindling – as were their chances of clinching victory. The rebels continued to fight with stones and musket butts; meanwhile, British cannon fire from **Copp's Hill** in the North End was turning Charlestown into an inferno. Despite their eventual loss, the patriots were invigorated by their strong showing, and the British, who lost nearly half of their men in the battle, became convinced that victory over the rebels would only be possible with a much larger army.

Bunker Hill Monument

Monument Square • **Monument** Daily July & Aug 9am–5.30pm; Sept–June till 4.30pm • Free • ☎ 617 242 5641 **Museum** Daily July & Aug 9am–6pm; Sept–June till 5pm • Free • ☎ 617 242 7275 • North Station **T**

Commemorating the Battle of Bunker Hill is the **Bunker Hill Monument**, a grey, dagger-like obelisk that's visible from just about anywhere in Charlestown, thanks to its position atop a butte confusingly known as Breed's Hill (see box above). It was here that the New England militia built a fort on the night of June 16, 1775, to wage what was ultimately a losing battle, but still considered a great moral victory in the fight for independence. The tower is centrally positioned in **Monument Square** and fronted by a statue of Colonel William Prescott, who commanded the Americans. Inside, 294 steps wind the 221ft to the top; hardy climbers will be rewarded with sweeping views of Boston, the harbour and surrounding towns – and, to the northwest, the stone spire of the **St Francis de Sales Church**, which stands atop the real Bunker Hill. Afterwards, you can picnic in the park encircling the monument, a favourite spot for sunbathing.

A new three-storey **museum**, housed in the former Charlestown library at the base of the monument, offers exhibits on the battle, the history of Charlestown and some interesting ephemera, such as two cannonballs from the conflict and the 1825 competition drawings submitted to determine the monument's design.

ARRIVAL AND DEPARTURE   CHARLESTOWN

On foot There are two main ways to get to Charlestown: one is to walk over the Charlestown Bridge, which affords exhilarating views of both Boston Harbor and the Zakim Bridge (follow the Freedom Trail's strip of red paint).

By boat Equally as fun as walking, and the better choice on a hot day, is to take the short ferry trip ($1.70) from Long Wharf to Pier 3 in the Charlestown Navy Yard (☎ 1 800 392 6100, ⊚ mbta.com).

1 Beacon Hill

No visit to Boston would be complete without an afternoon spent strolling around delightful **Beacon Hill**, a dignified stack of red brick rising over the north side of Boston Common. This is the Boston of wealth and privilege, one-time home to numerous historical and literary figures – including John Hancock, John Quincy Adams, Louisa May Alcott and Oliver Wendell Holmes – and still the address of choice for the city's elite. Its narrow, sloping byways are edged with brick, lit with gas lamps and lined with nineteenth-century-style town houses, all part of a historic preservation effort that prohibits architectural alterations that tamper with the neighbourhood's genteel character.

Both sides of the Hill have much to offer: on the south slope, there's the grandiose **Massachusetts State House**, attractive boulevards like **Charles** and **Beacon streets**, and the residences of past and present luminaries. The north slope is home to a wealth of African-American historical sites (owing to the free black community that lived here in the nineteenth century), including the **Black Heritage Trail** sights (see box, p.70), such as the **African Meeting House** and the stellar **Robert Gould Shaw/54th Regiment Memorial**. Bear in mind that streets here are uneven, full of cul-de-sacs and at times quite steep; lovely to behold, they're best enjoyed with comfortable shoes and a map.

Brief history

It was not always this way. In colonial times, Beacon Hill was the most prominent of three peaks known as the **Trimountain**, which formed Boston's geological backbone. The sunny south slope was settled by the city's elite, while the north slope was closer in spirit to the **West End**, a tumbledown port district populated by maritime tradesmen; indeed, the north slope was home to so much salacious activity that outraged Brahmins – Beacon Hill's moneyed elite – termed it "Mount Whoredom". By the end of the twentieth century, this social divide was largely eradicated, however.

Beacon Street

Running along the south slope of Beacon Hill above the Common, **Beacon Street** was described by Oliver Wendell Holmes as Boston's "sunny street for the sifted few". This lofty character remains today: a row of stately brick **town houses**, fronted by ornate iron grillwork, presides regally over the area. As you walk, keep an eye out for the **purple panes** in some of the town houses' windows, especially at nos. 63 and 64. The story behind the odd colouring evinces the street's long association with Boston wealth and privilege. When panes were installed in some of the first Beacon Hill mansions, they turned purple upon exposure to the sun, due to an excess of manganese in the glass. At first an irritating accident, they were eventually regarded as the definitive Beacon Hill status symbol due to their prevalence in the windows of Boston's most prestigious homes; some residents have gone so far as to shade their windows purple in imitation.

Cheers Bar

84 Beacon St • Daily 11am–midnight • Free (not including the cost of drinks) • ☎ 617 227 9605, ⓦ cheersboston.com • Arlington **T**

The basement level of no. 84 holds what might be the most famous address on the block, **Cheers** (see p.115). This ultra-touristy bar, whose setting inspired the hit TV series, unabashedly trades in on the association and even boasts a gift shop.

54th Massachusetts Regiment Memorial

Edge of Boston Common, facing the Massachusetts State House • Park St **T**

Across from the State House on Beacon Street is a majestic monument honouring the **54th Massachusetts Regiment**, the first all-black company to fight in the Civil

War, and its leader, Robert Gould Shaw, scion of a moneyed Boston Brahmin clan. Isolated from the rest of the Union army, given the worst of its resources, and saddled with menial or terribly dangerous assignments, the regiment performed bravely; most of its members, including Shaw, were killed in a failed attempt to take Fort Wagner from the Confederates in 1863. Augustus Saint-Gaudens' (see p.416) outstanding 1897 bronze sculpture depicts the regiment's farewell march down Beacon Street, with the names of the soldiers killed in action listed on its reverse side. The wistful angel that presides over the men carries both poppies and laurels, the former a symbol of death, the latter of victory.

Massachusetts State House

Beacon St, at Park • Mon–Fri 10am–4pm. Last tour at 3.30pm; call in advance for the day's tour schedule • Free • ☎ 617 727 3676 Park St **T**

Across the street from the 54th Massachusetts Regiment Memorial rises the large gilt dome of the Charles Bulfinch-designed **Massachusetts State House**. An all-star team of Revolution-era luminaries contributed to its construction: built on land purchased from John Hancock's estate, its cornerstone was laid by Samuel Adams and the copper for its dome was rolled in Paul Revere's foundry in 1802 (though it was covered over with gold leaf in the 1870s).

Once through security, head to the second floor, where 40min tours start from **Doric Hall** – though you'd do just as well to show yourself around. Best is the impressive **Memorial Hall**, a circular room surrounded by tall marble columns; it contains transparencies of the original flags carried into battle by Massachusetts soldiers and is lit by a stained-glass window bearing the state seal. On the third floor, a carved wooden fish known as the **Sacred Cod** hangs above the public gallery in the House of Representatives. The politicos take this symbol of maritime prosperity so seriously that when Harvard pranksters stole it in the 1930s, the House didn't reconvene until it was recovered.

Museum of African American History

46 Joy St • Mon–Sat 10am–4pm • $5 • ☎ 617 725 0022, ⓦ afroammuseum.org • Park St **T**

Walk north on sloping Joy Street from Beacon Street and you'll intersect with tiny **Smith Court**, once the centre of Boston's substantial pre-Civil War African-American community and now home to a few stops on Boston's Black Heritage Trail (see box, p.70). Built in 1843, the **Abiel Smith School**, at the intersection of Joy and Smith, was the first public building in the country established for the purpose of educating black children. Today, it houses the **Museum of African American History** and rotates small but well-tailored exhibits centred on abolitionism and other aspects of African-American history.

THE ARCHITECTURE OF CHARLES BULFINCH

Charles Bulfinch was America's foremost architect of the late eighteenth and early nineteenth centuries, and his distinctive style – somewhere between Federal and Classical – remains Boston's most recognizable architectural motif. Mixing Neoclassical training with New England practicality, Bulfinch built residences characterized by their rectilinear brick structure and pillared porticoes – examples remain throughout Beacon Hill, most notably at 87 Mount Vernon St and 45 Beacon St. Although most of his work was residential, Bulfinch made his name designing various government buildings, such as the 1805 renovation of **Faneuil Hall** and the **Massachusetts State House**, whose dome influenced the design of state capitol buildings nationwide.

1

African Meeting House

8 Smith Court • Free • ☎ 617 725 0022, ⓦ afroammuseum.org • Park St **T**

The **African Meeting House** is the oldest African-American church structure in the country (dating to 1806), and in its nineteenth-century heyday served as the spiritual and political centre for Boston's black community. It is also the birthplace of abolitionism: in 1832, William Lloyd Garrison founded the **New England Anti-Slavery Society** here, the first group of its kind to call for an immediate end to slavery, and in 1860 Frederick Douglass gave an anti-slavery speech on the site after being forced out of Tremont Temple. Currently being remodelled, it can only be viewed from the exterior.

Nichols House Museum

55 Mount Vernon St • Tours on the half hour: April–Oct Tues–Sat 11am–4pm; Nov–March Thurs–Sat 11am–4pm • $7 • ☎ 617 227 6993, ⓦ nicholshousemuseum.org • Park St **T**

The **Nichols House Museum**, a hidden gem, is the only Beacon Hill residence open year-round to the public. A Bulfinch design (see p.69), from 1885 until 1960 it was the home of landscape designer and suffragist Rose Standish Nichols, favourite niece of sculptor Augustus Saint-Gaudens, (see p.68). Born in 1872, Miss Rose, as she was known to posterity, had as full a life as her splendid home. A pacifist, she helped to found the Women's International League for Peace and Freedom, and made the then-radical decision to eschew the path of marriage and family in favour of single life and a successful career as a landscape architect. Tours take in heirlooms, such as striking Flemish tapestries, sculptures by Saint-Gaudens and several pieces of furniture made by Thomas Seymour (a renowned craftsman of the Federal period), in addition to giving visitors perspective on the opulent lives led by Beacon Hill's well-heeled elite.

Vilna Shul

18 Phillips St • Mid-March to late Nov Wed–Fri 11am–5pm, Sun 1–5pm • Admission by donation • ☎ 617 523 2324, ⓦ vilnashul.org • Charles/MGH **T**

Dating to 1919, the **Vilna Shul** was once one of fifty synagogues in Boston and is now the last link to a formerly thriving Jewish community. Currently a museum and cultural centre (there are also monthly Kabbalat services), the building has a spellbinding interior – all peeling paint, stained glass and antique fixtures – that makes for a delightful diversion. On the second floor, note the L-shaped **sanctuary** that, in keeping with the Orthodox tradition, provided separate seating for men and women. Three huge skylights bathe the room in light, illuminating **pews** salvaged from the 1840 Twelfth Baptist Church, once the chapel of choice for members of the Civil War's 54th Massachusetts Regiment (see p.68); 150 years ago, those famed African-American

---

THE BLACK HERITAGE TRAIL

In 1783, Massachusetts became the first state to declare slavery illegal. Not long after, a large community of free blacks and escaped slaves grew up in Beacon Hill. The **Black Heritage Trail** traces the neighbourhood's key role in local and national black history and is the most important historical site in America devoted to pre-Civil War African-American history and culture. Starting from the **54th Massachusetts Regiment Memorial** (see p.68), the 1.6-mile loop takes in fourteen sights, detailed in a **guide** available at the **Museum of African American History** and at the Boston National Historical Park **visitors centre** at 15 State St (see p.98). The best way to experience the trail is by taking a 90min National Park Service **walking tour** (late May to early Sept daily 10am, noon & 2pm; mid-Sept to mid-May 2pm only; free; ☎ 617 742 5415 or ☎ 617 242 5642, ⓦ nps.gov/boaf; Park St **T**).

soldiers sat for sermons in these very seats. Thanks to a restorative grant, visitors can begin to glimpse the sanctuary **murals**, which date to the mid-1920s, peeking out from beneath a thick beige overcoat. Other notable details include the richly carved **Ark**, curiously decorated with scallops (in Judaism, shellfish are a forbidden, non-kosher food) and a chandelier wired with an electric Star of David. Downstairs you'll find the building's community room and an exhibit on the Jewish diaspora in Boston.

Louisburg Square

A few blocks southwest of the Vilna Shul, **Louisburg Square** forms the gilded, geographic heart of Beacon Hill between Pickney and Mount Vernon streets. The central lawn, surrounded by wrought-iron fencing and flanked by statues of Columbus and Aristides the Just, is owned by local residents, making it the city's only private square. On either side of this oblong green are rows of brick town houses, though the square's distinction is due less to its architecture than to its residents. Among those to call the area home have been novelist Louisa May Alcott and members of the Vanderbilt family; current residents include former presidential candidate Senator John Kerry and his wife, ketchup heiress Teresa Heinz.

Acorn and Chestnut streets

Just south of Louisburg Square, squeezed in between Willow and West Cedar streets, narrow **Acorn Street** still has its original early nineteenth-century cobblestones. Barely wide enough to accommodate a car, it was originally built as a byway lined with servants' residences, and is often referenced for being the epitome of Beacon Hill quaint. One block south, **Chestnut Street** features some of the most intricate facades in Boston, such as Bulfinch's **Swan Houses** at nos. 13, 15 and 17; take note of this triplet's recessed arches, Doric columns and even-keeled entranceways, manipulated so that, in defiance of the street's downward slope, each of the three front doors open on the same level plane.

Charles Street

Down the hill and towards the river from Mount Vernon Street, **Charles Street** provides a pleasant flat respite from the north and south slopes. The commercial centre of Beacon Hill, this attractive byway is lined with scores of restaurants, antique shops and speciality boutiques.

The Esplanade

On the Charles River, between the Longfellow and Harvard bridges • Community Boating April–Oct Mon–Fri 1pm–sunset, Sat & Sun 9am–sunset • One-day sailboat pass $75, junior programme for children aged 10–18 only $1 • ☎ 617 523 1038, ⓦ community-boating .org • Charles/MGH **T**

Connected to Charles Street at its north end by a footbridge and spanning nine miles along the Charles River, the **Esplanade** is another of Boston's well-manicured public spaces. The nicest stretch runs alongside Beacon Hill and continues into Back Bay, providing a scenic way to appreciate the Hill from a distance. Just below the Longfellow Bridge, which connects to Cambridge (see p.88) is Community Boating, the point of departure for sailing, kayaking and windsurfing outings on the Charles.

Hatch Shell

1 David G Mugar Way • ☎ 617 227 0627, ⓦ hatchshell.com • Charles/MGH **T**

The white half-dome rising from the riverbank along the Esplanade is the **Hatch Shell**, a public performance space best known for its Fourth of July celebration, which features

1

a free concert by the Boston Pops (a pared-down, snappy version of the Boston Symphony Orchestra) and a massive fireworks display over the river (see p.119). Free movies and jazz concerts occur here almost nightly in summer.

The West End

North of Cambridge Street, the tidy rows of town houses are replaced by a more urban spread of office buildings and old brick structures, signalling the start of the **West End**. Once Boston's main port of entry for immigrants and transient sailors, this area has seen its lively character pretty much disappear, though a vestige remains in the small tangle of byways behind the buildings of **Massachusetts General Hospital**. Here you'll find urban warehouses interspersed with Irish bars that swell to a fever pitch after Celtics basketball and Bruins hockey games. Those games take place nearby at the **TD Garden** (see p.125).

Sports Museum

Levels 5 & 6 of the TD Garden, 100 Legends Way · Daily 10am–4pm; hours fluctuate according to events · $10 · ☎ 617 624 1235, Ⓦ sportsmuseum.org · North Station **T**

Located amid the box seats of the TD Garden stadium is the affable **Sports Museum**. Here, visitors can glimpse classic Boston sports ephemera like Celtic Larry Bird's locker and the Red Sox's hard-won 2004 American League Championship banner. There are also old-school uniforms and equipment, including a prim woman's basketball uniform from the 1890s. Best is the hockey penalty box from the old Boston Garden, which you are invited to climb into.

Museum of Science

1 Science Park · July to early Sept Fri 9am–9pm, Sat–Thurs till 7pm; mid-Sept to June Fri 9am–9pm, Sat–Thurs till 5pm · $22, children (3–11 years) $19; CityPass accepted **Planetarium** Call for show times · $10, children (3–11 years) $8 **3D Cinema** Call for show times · $5, children (3–11 years) $4 · ☎ 617 723 2500, Ⓦ mos.org · Science Park **T**

Situated on a bridge over the Charles, Boston's beloved **Museum of Science** consists of several floors of interactive exhibits illustrating basic principles of natural and physical science. The best exhibit is the Theater of Electricity, a darkened room full of optical illusions and glowing displays on the presence of electricity in everyday life. Here, the world's largest Van de Graaf generator utilizes 2.5 million volts of electricity and gives daily shows in which simulated lightning bolts flash and crackle. The museum also houses a five-storey IMAX theatre and the digitally advanced Charles Hayden Planetarium, while the museum's **3D Theater** provides a chance to wear those retro-cool 3D glasses.

Back Bay

Meticulously planned **Back Bay** is Boston at its most cosmopolitan. Beginning at the **Public Garden**, the neighbourhood's elegant, angular streets form a pedestrian-friendly area that looks much as it did in the nineteenth century, right down to the original gaslights and brick sidewalks. Buzzing with restaurants and chic shopping boutiques, the area is also worth visiting for its trove of Gilded Age terraced houses, liberally frosted with fanciful architectural details.

Running parallel to the Charles River in neat rows, Back Bay's east–west thoroughfares – **Beacon**, **Marlborough**, **Newbury** and **Boylston streets**, with **Commonwealth Avenue** in between – are crossed by eight shorter streets. The latter

FROM SWAMP TO SWANK: THE BUILDING OF BACK BAY

The fashioning of **Back Bay** occurred in the mid-nineteenth century, when a shortage of living space in Boston prompted developers to revisit a failed dam project on the Charles River, which had made a swamp of much of the area. **Arthur Gilman** manned the huge landfill project, which began in 1857. Taking his cue from the grand boulevards of Paris, Gilman decided on an orderly street pattern extending east to west from the Public Garden. By 1890, the cramped peninsula of old Boston was flanked by 450 new acres.

roads have been so fastidiously laid out that not only are their names in alphabetical order, but trisyllables are deliberately intercut by disyllables: Arlington, Berkeley, Clarendon, Dartmouth, Exeter, Fairfield, Gloucester and Hereford, until you get to Massachusetts Avenue. The grandest town houses are on Beacon Street and Commonwealth Avenue, though Marlborough, between the two, is more atmospheric. Boylston and Newbury are the main commercial drags, and a shopping excursion on the latter is a must-do Boston experience. In the middle of it all is a small open space, **Copley Square**, surrounded by the area's main sights: **Trinity Church**, the **Boston Public Library** and the **John Hancock Tower**.

Public Garden

Bounded by Beacon, Arlington, Boylston and Charles streets • **Swan boats** April to late June daily 10am–4pm; late June to early Sept daily 10am–5pm; early to mid-Sept Mon–Fri noon–4pm, Sat & Sun 10am–4pm • $2.75 • ☎ 617 522 1966, ⓦ swanboats.com • Arlington **T**

Boston's most beautiful outdoor space, the **Public Garden**, is a 24-acre botanical park first earmarked for public use in 1859. Of the garden's 125 types of trees, many identified by little placards, most impressive are the weeping willows that ring the picturesque man-made **lagoon**, around which you can take a fifteen-minute ride in a **swan boat**. These elegant, pedal-powered conveyances, inspired by the opera *Lohengrin*, have been around since 1877, long enough to have become a Boston institution.

Statues and monuments

The Garden has another fowl-related draw: a cluster of bronze bird sculptures (by the Charles Street entrance) collectively called **Mrs Mallard and Her Eight Ducklings**. The sculptures were installed in 1987 to commemorate Robert McCloskey's 1941 *Make Way for Ducklings*, a children's tale set in the park. Of the many other statues and monuments throughout the park, the oldest and oddest is the 30ft **Good Samaritan** monument (along the Arlington Street side), a granite and red-marble column that is a tribute to, of all things, the anaesthetic qualities of ether; controversy as to which of two Boston men invented the drug led Oliver Wendell Holmes to dub it the "Either Monument". Finally, a dignified equestrian statue of **George Washington**, installed in 1869 and the first to show the general astride a horse, watches over the Garden's Commonwealth Avenue entrance.

Commonwealth Avenue

The Public Garden leads into the tree-lined parkway of **Commonwealth Avenue**, modelled after the grand boulevards of Paris and Back Bay's showcase street. The mall here forms the first link in Frederick Law Olmsted's so-called **Emerald Necklace** (see box, p.83), which begins at Boston Common and extends all the way to Franklin Park in Dorchester. "Comm Ave", as locals call it, is at its prettiest in early May, when the magnolia and dogwood trees are in full bloom, showering the brownstone steps with their fragrant pink buds.

1

Cambridge ▲

ACCOMMODATION

40 Berkeley	21	The Colonnade	17	HI-Boston at Fenway	1
Aisling Bed and Breakfast	26	Copley Inn	18	Hotel 140	16
Back Bay Hotel	15	Copley Square Hotel	13	Hotel Commonwealth	3
Caj House	25	Eliot	6	Inn @ St. Botolph	19
Chandler Inn	20	Encore B&B	24	The Lenox	10
Charlesmark Hotel	8	Fairmont Copley Plaza	11	Mandarin Oriental	9
Clarendon Square Inn	23	Gilded Lily	22	Newbury Guest House	7
College Club	4	Gryphon House	2	Oasis Guesthouse	14
		HI-Boston	12	Taj Boston	5

The Castle

Boston University

STORROW DRIVE

Charles River

2A

COMMONWEALTH AVENUE
CUMMINGTON ST
90

Morse Auditorium

BAY STATE ROAD

Shelton Hall

Citgo Sign

Myles Standish Hall

BEACON STREET — **Kenmore**

KENMORE SQUARE

NEWBURY STREET

CLUBS
Jillian's	5

LIVE MUSIC
Church	8
Great Scott	3
House of Blues	4
Paradise Rock Club	2
Scullers	1
Wally's Café	11

BROOKLINE AVENUE

LANSDOWNE ST

Fenway Park

IPSWICH ST

IPSWICH ST

GAY & LESBIAN DRINKING AND NIGHTLIFE
Club Café	9
dbar	12
Fritz	10
Machine/Ramrod	6
Rise	7

VAN NESS STREET

BOYLSTON STREET

BOYLSTON STREET

Victory Gardens

Back Bay Fens

BOYLSTON STREET

Berklee College of Music

HAVILAND ST

PETERBOROUGH STREET

QUEENSBERRY ST

THE FENWAY

AGASSIZ ROAD

WESTLAND AVE

Mapparium

PARK DRIVE

Kelleher Rose Gardens

SYMPHONY RD

Christian Science Mother Church

GAINSBOROUGH ST

Horticultural Hall

Back Bay Fens

Muddy River

THE FENWAY

HEMENWAY ST

ST STEPHEN

Symphony Hall

Isabella Stewart Gardner Museum

Museum of Fine Arts

MUSEUM RD

HUNTINGTON AVENUE

Huntington Theatre Company

Jordan Hall

HUNTINGTON AVENUE

9

Museum

Northeastern

SHOPS
Bobby from Boston	11
Bodega	7
Dress	3
Formaggio Kitchen	10
In Your Ear!	1
Looney Tunes	6
Newbury Comics	5
Raven Used Books	2
Trident Booksellers & Café	4
Underground Hip-Hop	8
Uniform	9

PARKER ST

RAVEN ROAD

Northeastern University

RUGGLES STREET

Ruggles

TREMONT STREET

0		400
	yards	

BACK BAY, THE FENWAY & THE SOUTH END

▼ Jamaica Plain

RESTAURANTS

tlantic Fish Company	18
&G Oysters	44
urritos and Tacos to Go!	32
utcher Shop	43
afé Jaffa	12
harlie's Sandwich Shoppe	36
Douzo	33
ranklin Café	46
aaslight, Brasserie du Coin	50

Giacomo's	39
India Quality	4
L'Espalier	21
La Verdad Taqueria	8
Legal Sea Foods	20 & 29
Mike & Patty's	27
Mistral	30
Myers + Chang	47
The Other Side	
Cosmic Café	11

Parish Café & Bar	17
Petit Robert Bistro	5 & 41
Picco	40
South End Buttery	
Bistro & Bar	48
Stella	49
Toro	51
Trattoria Toscana	31
Trident Booksellers & Café	13
Upper Crust	16 & 45
Via Matta	22

CAFÉS

Berkeley Perk Café	35
Espresso Royale Caffe	1, 14 & 38
L'Aroma Café	9
Wired Puppy	15

DRINKING

Anchovies	37
Audubon Circle	2
The Beehive	42
Bleacher Bar	7
Bukowski Tavern	23
City Bar	19
The Delux Café & Lounge	34
Eastern Standard	3
Flash's	28
Lansdowne Pub	10
Lower Depths Taproom	6
minibar	25
Oak Bar	26
Top of the Hub	24

1

First Baptist Church of Boston

110 Commonwealth Ave • Tues & Thurs 1pm–4pm, Wed & Fri 11am–2pm • Free • ☎ 617 267 3148 • Copley **T**

The landmark belfry of the **First Baptist Church of Boston** was designed by architect H.H. Richardson in 1872 for a Unitarian congregation, though at bill-paying time only a Baptist congregation was able to pony up the necessary funds. The puddingstone exterior is topped off by a 176ft **bell tower**, covered by four gorgeous friezes by Frédéric-Auguste Bartholdi, of Statue of Liberty fame. Richardson's lofty plans for the interior never materialized, again for lack of money, but the Norman-style rose windows are still worth a peek if you happen by when someone's in the church office.

Newbury and Boylston streets

Newbury Street comprises eight blocks of Victorian-era brownstones housing more than three hundred upmarket boutiques, luxury shops, art galleries and restaurants, plus chain stores like Urban Outfitters and H&M. Designed as an architect's house, the flight-of-fancy at **no. 109** is more arresting for its two donjon towers than the Cole Haan footwear inside. A block down, **271 Dartmouth** houses a *Lolita Cocina* restaurant, but the building with mock battlements that hunkers over it steals the show: originally the *Hotel Victoria*, it looks like a Venetian-Moorish castle. And not everything here is shopping-related: Newbury and neighbouring **Boylston** are home to most of the old **schools** and **churches** built in the Back Bay area too.

Arlington Street Church

Corner of Boylston St, at Arlington • Mon–Fri 10am–5pm, Sun till 3pm • Free • ☎ 617 536 7050 • Arlington **T**

The **Arlington Street Church**, a minor Italianesque masterpiece designed in 1859 by Arthur Gilman; its host of Tiffany stained-glass windows, believed to be the largest assemblage of Tiffany windows unified under one roof, were added from 1898 to 1933.

Church of the Covenant and Gallery NAGA

67 Newbury St • Tues–Sat 10am–5pm, till 5.30pm in July & Aug • Free • ☎ 617 267 9060, ⓦ gallerynaga.com • Arlington **T**

On the first block of Newbury Street itself, the Gothic Revival **Church of the Covenant** boasts a soaring steeple and 30ft stained-glass windows by Tiffany. The church's chapel houses one of Boston's biggest contemporary art spaces, the **Gallery NAGA**.

Gibson House Museum

137 Beacon St • Wed–Sun 1–3pm, tours on the hour • $9, cash only • ☎ 617 267 6338, ⓦ thegibsonhouse.org • Arlington **T**

As a continuation of Beacon Hill's stately main thoroughfare, **Beacon Street** was long the province of blueblood Bostonians. One building, the Italian Renaissance town house on the first block of Beacon, holds the remarkable **Gibson House Museum**. Built in 1859, the ornate interior boasts a host of whimsical Victoriana: gold-embossed wallpaper, antique clocks and a still-functioning dumbwaiter.

Marlborough Street

Sandwiched between Beacon Street and Commonwealth Avenue is quiet **Marlborough Street**, one of the most prized residential locales in Boston. Even though the town houses here tend to be smaller than elsewhere in Back Bay, they display a surprising range of styles, especially on the blocks between Clarendon and Fairfield streets.

Copley Square and around

Bounded by Boylston, Clarendon, St James and Dartmouth streets, petite **Copley Square** makes up the heart of Back Bay. The square itself is fairly plain, but its periphery holds quite a bit of interest, including two venerated **churches** and the **Boston Public Library**.

Trinity Church

206 Clarendon St • Mon, Fri & Sat 9am–5pm, Tues–Thurs till 6pm, Sun 1–6pm • $7, includes guided tour (call for times) • ☎ 617 536 0944, ⓦ trinitychurchboston.org • Copley **T**

The star of Copley Square is **Trinity Church**, whose interior was designed to feel like "walking into a living painting". The result is H.H. Richardson's 1877 Romanesque masterpiece, a breathtaking display of chromatic eye candy fashioned by stained-glass artist John La Farge. An architectural triumph, the church's majestic central tower reaches an eye-opening ten storeys, and is attractively situated between sweeping arches and a massive gold chancel. While it's all quite lovely, Trinity's finest feature is La Farge's aquamarine *Christ in Majesty* triptych, a bold, multidimensional stained-glass window. Aim to visit while the sun is setting and the glass is at its most brilliant, or during one of the free organ recitals (Fri 12.15pm).

Boston Public Library

700 Boylston St • Mon–Thurs 9am–9pm, Fri & Sat till 5pm • Free • ☎ 617 536 5400, ⓦ bpl.org • Copley **T**

The handsome **Boston Public Library** anchors the end of Copley Square opposite Trinity Church. Architects McKim, Mead & White built the Italian Renaissance Revival structure in 1895; the massive inner bronze doors were designed by Daniel Chester French (sculptor of the Lincoln Memorial in Washington, DC). Beyond the marble staircase and signature lions are a series of murals, most impressive of which is a diaphanous depiction of the nine Muses. You can also check out the imposing **Bates Reading Room**, with its barrel-vaulted ceiling and oak panelling. The library's most remarkable facet is tucked away on the top floor, however, where the dimly lit **Sargent Hall** is covered with more than fifteen murals painted by John Singer Sargent. Entitled the *Triumph of Religion*, the panels range from the brazen *Pagan Gods* to the serene scenes of *Heaven*. After viewing, you can take a breather in the library's open-air central **courtyard**, modelled after that of the Palazzo della Cancelleria in Rome.

New Old South Church

645 Boylston St • Mon–Fri 8am–7pm, Sat 10am–4pm, Sun 8.30am–4pm • Free • ☎ 617 536 1970, ⓦ oldsouth.org • Copley **T**

Opposite the Boston Public Library is one of Boston's most attractive buildings, the **New Old South Church**, a name to which there is actually some logic: the congregation at downtown's Old South Meeting House (and church) outgrew those premises and decamped here in 1875 – hence, the "New" Old South Church. The names of former Old South members reads like a who's who of historical figures: Benjamin Franklin, Phillis Wheatley, Samuel Adams and even Mother Goose (née Elizabeth Vergoose, the famed nursery rhyme author) all worshipped here. You need not be a student of architecture to be won over by the Italian Gothic design, which is most pronounced in the ornate, 220ft bell tower, its copper roof lantern replete with metallic dragons. The interior is an alluring assemblage of dark woods set against a rose-coloured backdrop, coupled with fifteenth-century English-style stained-glass windows.

John Hancock Tower

200 Clarendon St • Closed to the public but free to view from outside • Copley **T**

At 62 storeys, the **John Hancock Tower** is Boston's signature skyscraper – first loathed, now loved and taking on startlingly different appearances depending on your vantage point. In Back Bay, the angular edifice is often barely perceptible, due to designer I.M. Pei's deference to adjacent Trinity Church and the old brownstones nearby. From Beacon Hill, it appears broad-shouldered and stocky; from the South End, taller than it really is; from across the Charles River, like a crisp metallic wafer. With such a seamless

1

facade, you'd never guess that soon after its 1976 construction, dozens of windowpanes popped out, showering Copley Square with glass, due to a design flaw that prompted the replacement of more than 10,000 panes. Next door to the tower is the *old* Hancock Tower, which cuts a distinguished profile with its truncated step-top roof.

Prudential Center

800 Boylston St • **Skywalk Observatory** Daily: April–Oct 10am–10pm; Nov–March till 8pm • $13 • ☎ 617 859 0648 • ⓦ prudentialcenter.com • Hynes or Prudential **T**

Nothing can cloak the funkiness of the **Prudential Center** ("The Pru"), just west of Copley Square, its edifice a 52-storey grey intruder on the Back Bay skyline. While it may not be as beautiful as its neighbours, the Pru's iconic outline, which dates to 1964, is a fond landmark for residents. Apart from being the starting point for a number of Boston tours (see p.98), its chief selling point is its fiftieth-floor **Skywalk Observatory**, offering the only 360-degree aerial view of Boston, which is complemented by a fun audio tour. If you're hungry (or just thirsty) you can avoid the admission charge by ascending two more floors to the *Top of the Hub* restaurant (see p.116); your bill may well equal the money you just saved, but during daytime hours it's fairly relaxed, and you can linger over coffee or a drink. The Prudential also doubles as the city's best shopping centre.

Christian Science complex

People gazing down from the top of the Prudential Center are often surprised to see a 224ft-tall Renaissance Revival basilica at its base. This structure is the central feature of the world headquarters of the **First Church of Christ, Scientist**, at 175 Huntington Ave (Mon–Sat 10am–4pm; free; ⓦchristianscience.org; Symphony T), which overshadows the earlier Romanesque **Christian Science Mother Church** just behind it, built in 1894. The centre's 670ft-long red-granite-trimmed reflecting pool makes a good spot for picnics, and children are often seen running amok in the property's fountains.

Mary Baker Eddy Library

200 Massachusetts Ave • Tues–Sun 10am–4pm • $6 • ☎ 617 450 7000, ⓦ marybakereddylibrary.org • Prudential or Hynes **T**

The highlights of a visit to the Christian Science complex are on the ground floor of the **Mary Baker Eddy Library**, in the Christian Science Publishing building. The library's original Neoclassical lobby has been transformed into the grandly named Hall of Ideas, home to a glass-and-bronze fountain that appears to cascade with words as well as water; the sayings – a collection of inspiring tidbits – are projected from above for an effect that verges on holographic. Tucked behind the Hall of Ideas is the marvellous **Mapparium**, a curious stained-glass globe whose 30ft diameter can be crossed on a glass bridge. The technicolour hues of the glass panels, illuminated from behind, reveal the geopolitical reality of the world in 1935, when the globe was constructed, as evidenced by country names such as Siam, Baluchistan and Transjordan. Intended to symbolize the worldwide reach of journalism, the Mapparium has a more immediate payoff: thanks to the spherical glass surface, which absorbs no sound, you can whisper, "What's Tanganyika called today?" at one end of the bridge and someone on the opposite end will hear it clear as a bell – and perhaps proffer the answer (Tanzania).

The South End

The residential **South End**, extending below Back Bay from Massachusetts Avenue to I-93 and the Mass Pike (I-90), has the good fortune of being both quaint and stylish in equal measure. A foodie hotspot that's given rise to a number of the city's best restaurants, it has also generated many seminal art galleries, theatres and boutiques. This posh enclave's spectacular concentration of **Victorian architecture** earned it a National Landmark District designation in 1983, which made the 500-acre area the largest historical neighbourhood of its kind in the country. The South End is also known for its well-preserved **ironwork** – a French botanical motif known as rinceau adorns many of the houses' stairways and windows. Details like these have made the area quite popular with upwardly mobile Bostonians, among them a strong gay and lesbian contingent, who began populating the area in the 1990s. The upshot has been some of the liveliest **streetlife** in town; the activity is most visible on Tremont Street and on pockets of Washington Street, a few blocks below the Back Bay **T**, although in recent years the party has started to spread: voguish restaurants, stores and bars can now be found south of Washington ("SoWa") and in the further reaches of the community.

Dartmouth Street

Dartmouth Street, anchored by the Copley Place mall, gets posher the closer it gets to Tremont Street, a few blocks southeast. Immediately below Copley Place, at no. 130, is **Tent City**, a mixed-income housing co-op that owes its name to a 1968 sit-in protest – tents included – staged on the formerly vacant lot by residents concerned about the neighbourhood's dwindling low-income housing. Their activism thwarted plans for a parking garage, and the result is a fine example of environmental planning.

Southwest Corridor Park

The pocket of land separating Tent City from Copley Place marks the start of the **Southwest Corridor Park**, a grassy 4.7-mile promenade that connects the Back Bay **T** with the Forest Hill **T** station in Jamaica Plain. The park runs parallel to the Orange MBTA line and was designed with low shrubs to increase visibility and give an "open" feeling. Part of a creative urban design project, it expertly covers the tracks of a nineteenth-century railroad corridor.

Clarendon and Tremont streets

The heart of the South End is at the intersection of **Clarendon and Tremont streets**, where a smart pseudo-triangle is flanked by some of the most renowned restaurants in Boston; Tremont Street is known as Boston's "Restaurant Row". Here you'll also find **Boston Center for the Arts**, one of the city's newest and most illustrious theatre spaces.

Boston Center for the Arts

539 Tremont St • ☏ 617 426 5000, ⓦ bcaonline.org • Back Bay **T**

Smack in the middle of Tremont Street at no. 539, lies the domed **Cyclorama** building, which was built in 1884 to house an enormous, 360-degree painting of the Battle of Gettysburg (since moved to Gettysburg itself). Later used as a carousel space and even a boxing ring, the building changed roles repeatedly until 1972, when its current tenant, the **Boston Center for the Arts**, moved in. The centre provides a home for numerous low-budget theatre troupes, and in 2000, two new theatres – the first to be built in Boston in over 75 years.

Union Park Square

Charming **Union Park Square**, east of Tremont along Union Park Street, is a tiny decorative park which, in typical English fashion, you can walk around but not through – an elegant wrought-iron fence encircles it to make sure you keep off the

1

grass. The oval-shaped park is framed by refined bowfronted terraced houses with larger windows and more elaborate cornice-work than homes on surrounding streets. Keep an eye out for the Frisbee-sized bronze discs embedded in the pavement in front of the homes – they're remnants of coal-heating days, when the stuff was delivered through portals straight into the basement. The best way to see the interior of one of these dignified residences is to take the South End Historical Society's annual October **house tour** (☎617 536 4445, ⊛southendhistoricalsociety.org).

Ramón Betances Mural

A bronze plaque at the corner of Washington and West Dedham streets commemorates the 65th infantry of World II, a largely Puerto Rican regiment, and along with two large metal "V"s, serves as the unofficial marker of the southern frontier of **Villa Victoria**, a housing project serving three thousand residents. Be sure to check out the **Ramón Betances Mural** in the enclave's central square, two blocks up on West Dedham, which occupies wall space measuring a whopping 45ft long by 14ft high. Created in 1977 by three hundred teenagers, this colourful mosaic (named after a leader in Puerto Rico's fight for independence from Spain) depicts a hodgepodge of merrily tiled images (including fish, faces and musical instruments) surrounding a massive sun; a Spanish inscription asserts "let us know how to fight for our honour and our liberty". Meticulously executed and yet unexpected, it may be Boston's best piece of public art.

The SoWa District

Around the intersection of **Harrison Avenue** and **Thayer Street**, near the eastern edge of the South End, a handful of **art galleries** have showrooms in cavernous loft spaces. Wandering around the self-styled **SoWa** ("South of Washington") district could easily distract you for an hour or so. The best time to visit is on **First Fridays** (first Fri of month 5–9pm; free; ⊛sowaartistsguild.com), when galleries ply visitors with wine and spaces are abuzz with artists and fans. On Sundays from May to October, the **SoWa Open Market** (10am–4pm; free; ⊛sowaopenmarket.com), is held just south of here at 460 Harrison Ave. Fronted by a vast warehouse edifice artists and local food vendors plying their wares from billowing white tents.

Kenmore Square

Kenmore Square, at the junction of Commonwealth Avenue and Beacon Street, is the primary point of entry to Boston University, one of the country's larger private institutions. The unofficial playground for BU students, the square is a lively stretch of youth-oriented bars and casual restaurants. Many of the buildings on its north side have been snapped up by BU, such as the six-storey Barnes & Noble bookstore at 660 Beacon St, on top of which is perched the monumental **Citgo Sign**, Kenmore's main landmark. This 60-square-foot neon advertisement, a pulsing red-orange triangle (the oil company's logo), has been a popular symbol of Boston since it was placed here in 1965.

The Fenway

The Fenway spreads out south of Kenmore Square like an elongated kite, taking in sights disparate enough to please almost any visitor. Lansdowne Street marks the northern edge of the district, where you'll find many of Boston's nightclubs. Bordering

FROM TOP FENWAY PARK (P.82); OLD STATE HOUSE (P.54) >

1

THE CURSE: REVERSED!

With the Boston Red Sox having won baseball's coveted World Series titles in both 2004 and 2007, the "curse" that once hung over the team is quickly becoming a distant memory. In 1903, the **Boston Pilgrims** (as they were then called) became the first team to represent the American League in baseball's World Series, upsetting the heavily favoured Pittsburgh Pirates to claim the championship; their continued financial success allowed them to build a new stadium, **Fenway Park**, in 1912. During their first year there, Boston won the Series again, and repeated the feat in 1915, 1916 and 1918, led in the latter years by the young pitcher **George Herman "Babe" Ruth**, who also demonstrated an eye-opening penchant for hitting home runs. The team was poised to become a dynasty when its owner, Harry Frazee, began a fire sale of the team to finance a Broadway play that was to star his girlfriend. Most of the players went for bargain prices, including Ruth, who was sold to the New York Yankees, which went on to become the most successful professional sports franchise ever, with the Babe at the forefront.

After Ruth's departure, the Red Sox embarked upon a long period in the **wilderness**, with 86 demoralizing years without a World Series win. This drought began, over the years, to be blamed on "**the Curse of the Bambino**" (aka Babe Ruth) – punishment meted out by the baseball gods for selling off one of the game's greatest players. After coming maddeningly close to the title many times – most notably in 1986, when the Sox were one strike away from clinching the Series before a ground ball rolled through the legs of first baseman Bill Buckner – the team finally broke the curse in 2004: after losing the first three games of a best-of-seven series to the Yankees, the Red Sox won four in a row, then went on to beat the St Louis Cardinals for the **World Series** crown. In 2007, the Red Sox began a new tradition of World Series sweeps, beating the Colorado Rockies in four straight games to win their second championship in four years.

Lansdowne is hallowed **Fenway Park**, where the Red Sox play ball. This is quite removed, however, from the highbrow spaces of Fenway's eastern perimeter, dotted with some of Boston's finest cultural institutions: **Symphony Hall**, the **Museum of Fine Arts** and the **Isabella Stewart Gardner Museum**. Running down the neighbourhood's spine is the **Back Bay Fens**, a monumental greenspace designed by Frederick Law Olmsted, urban landscaper extraordinaire.

Fenway Park

4 Yawkey Way • 50min tours daily 9am–4pm, on the hour but call ahead as times vary according to game schedule; $12, children (3–15 years) $10 • Tours ☎ 617 226 6666, tickets ☎ 617 267 1700, ⓦ redsox.com • Kenmore or Fenway **T**

Baseball is treated with reverence in Boston, so it's appropriate that the city's team, the Red Sox, plays in one of the country's most celebrated ballparks, **Fenway Park**. The country's oldest ballpark, Fenway was constructed in 1912 in a tiny, asymmetrical space just off Brookline Avenue, resulting in its famously awkward dimensions, which include an abnormally short rightfield line (302ft) and a fence that doesn't at all approximate the smooth arc of most outfields. The 37ft left-field wall, aka the **Green Monster**, is another quirk (it was originally built because home runs were breaking local windows); that it is so high makes up for some of the park's short distances.

Tours of the ballpark are fun and deservedly popular, but your best bet is to come for a game. The season runs from April to October, and **tickets** are fairly reasonable, though often very hard to come by: since the team clinched the 2004 and 2007 World Series titles, Red Sox hysteria has surpassed even its own mind-boggling standards for fan devotion.

The Back Bay Fens

Daily dawn–dusk • ☎ 617 522 2700, ⓦ emeraldnecklace.org • Museum **T**

The Fenway gets its name from the **Back Bay Fens**, a snakelike segment of Frederick Law Olmsted's Emerald Necklace that takes over where the prim Commonwealth Avenue greenway leaves off. The Fens were fashioned from marsh and mud in 1879, a fact reflected in the name of the waterway that still runs through them today – the **Muddy River**. In the northern portion of the park, local residents maintain small garden plots in the wonderfully jumbled **Victory Garden**, the oldest community garden in the US. Nearby, below Agassiz Road, the more formal **Kelleher Rose Garden** boasts colourful hybrid species bearing exotic names like Marmalade Skies and Climbing White Iceberg. Though pretty, the Fens get a bit dodgy at night – it's best to head onwards before it gets dark.

Berklee College of Music

1140 Boylston St • See website for concert prices • ☎ 617 747 2261, ⓦ berklee.edu • Hynes **T**

Not far from the Fens' northeastern tip, the renowned **Berklee College of Music** makes its home on the busy stretch of Massachusetts Avenue south of Boylston Street, an area with several budget-friendly restaurants. In addition to coordinating the BeanTown Jazz Festival every September, there's nearly always something musical going on here – check their website for a list of (often very inexpensive) performances.

Symphony Hall

301 Massachusetts Ave • See website for concert prices • ☎ 617 266 1492, ⓦ bso.org • Symphony **T**

A few short blocks south of Berklee College, **Symphony Hall**, home to the Boston Symphony Orchestra, anchors the corner of Massachusetts and Huntington avenues. The 1900 interior, designed by McKim, Mead & White is apparently just the right shape to provide the hall with perfect acoustics.

Museum of Fine Arts

465 Huntington Ave • Mon, Tues, Sat & Sun 10am–4.45pm, Wed–Fri till 9.45pm • $22 (good for two visits in a ten-day period), Wed after 4pm admission by donation; children (7–17 years) $10, children (under 17 years) free on weekends and after 3pm on weekdays; CityPass accepted (see p.96) • ☎ 617 267 9300, ⓦ mfa.org • Museum **T**

Rather inconveniently located in south Fenway – but well worth the trip – the **Museum of Fine Arts** has been New England's premier art space since 1870 and boasts one of the most distinctive collections in the country. The museum's highlights are outlined below.

Art of the Americas wing

In 2010, the museum completed an ambitious expansion that saw the addition of a magnificent new Art of the Americas wing, with fifty-three galleries, a state-of-the-art

---

FREDERICK LAW OLMSTED AND THE EMERALD NECKLACE

The string of urban parks that stretches through Boston's southern districts, known as the **Emerald Necklace**, grew out of a project conceived in the 1870s, when landscape architect **Frederick Law Olmsted** was commissioned to create for Boston a series of urban parks like those he had designed in New York and Chicago. A Romantic naturalist, Olmsted conceived of nature as a way to escape the ills wrought by society, and considered his urban parks a means for city-dwellers to escape the clamour of their everyday lives. He converted much of Boston's remaining open space, which was largely unappealing marshland, into a series of manicured parks beginning with the Back Bay Fens, including the Riverway along the Boston–Brookline border and proceeding through Jamaica Pond and the Arnold Arboretum to Roxbury's Franklin Park (see p.87). While Olmsted's original skein of parks was limited to these, further development linked the Fens, via the Commonwealth Avenue greenway, to the Public Garden and Boston Common, all of which now function as part of the Necklace. The **Emerald Necklace Conservancy** (☎ 617 522 2700, ⓦ emeraldnecklace.org) organizes free walking tours covering each of the Necklace's segments from Boston Common to Franklin Park.

1

auditorium and a glass pavilion for the central courtyard. The first floor's marvellously rich **American collection** features Gilbert Stuart's George Washington portraits (one famously replicated on the dollar bill) alongside Thomas Sully's towering Washington-in-action paean, *Passage of the Delaware*. There are also John Singleton Copley portraits of revolutionary figures, plus his gruesome narrative *Watson and the Shark*.

Up one floor, Romantic naturalist landscapes from the first half of the nineteenth century – such as Albert Bierstadt's quietly majestic *Buffalo Trail* – dominate several rooms; from the latter half of the century there are several seascapes by Winslow Homer, Whistler's *Harmony in Flesh Colour and Red* and works from the Boston school, notably Childe Hassam's gauzy *Boston Common at Twilight* and John Singer Sargent's spare *The Daughters of Edward Darley Boit*. Seek out the playful **Folk Art** gallery, also on the second floor, where goat, peacock and leaping stag weathervanes rub elbows with twentieth-century carousel animals.

Musical Instruments gallery

Across the hall from the Huntington Street entrance, it's worth popping into the **Musical Instruments gallery**, even if just to glimpse item #12 – one of the world's first saxophones, made by Adolphe Sax himself.

Modern Art gallery

Masterpieces from the twentieth century can be found in the first floor's **Modern Art gallery**, near the Fenway entrance. Largely populated by Europeans such as Matisse, Picasso and Mondrian, it's here that you'll also find Gauguin's sumptuous display of existential angst *Where Do We Come From? What Are We? Where Are We Going?*.

Impressionist room

The second-floor **Impressionist room** contains many of the museum's best-loved pieces, including van Gogh's *Postman Joseph Roulin* and *La Berceuse*, Monet's *Water Lilies* and *Rouen Cathedral (Morning Effect)*, although the latter's real show-stopper, his tongue-in-cheek *La Japonaise* (a riff on Parisian fashion trends) is around the corner in the Rosenberg gallery. Degas also figures prominently here, his bronze cast of the *Little Fourteen-Year-old Dancer* keeping an eye on the party in Renoir's *Dance at Bougival*.

Shapiro Rotunda

Between the second-floor Egyptian and Asian galleries is the outstanding **Shapiro Rotunda**, its dome and colonnade inset with murals and bas-reliefs by John Singer Sargent, who undertook the commission following his work on the Boston Public Library (see p.77). Created with the belief that mural painting was the key to "artistic immortality", this installation certainly guaranteed the artist a lasting place in the MFA, and some controversy to boot: when the project was completed shortly before his death in 1925, his Classical theme was falling out of vogue and his efforts were considered the "frivolous works of a failing master".

Old Masters Gallery

The rotunda leads to the **Old Masters Gallery**, which ranks among the museum's more spectacular showings. Designed to resemble a European palace hallway, its walls are capped by wood-inlaid ceilings and hung two-high with dozens of portraits, religious pieces and landscapes of varying sizes, including three pieces by El Greco.

Asian Galleries

For those in the know, the MFA's **Asian galleries** are a highlight. Best is the second floor's magnificent recreation of Japan's oldest surviving **Buddhist temple**, complete with tapered wooden columns, muted lighting and a coffered ceiling. Seven Buddhas dating to the ninth century recline inside the darkened temple; two of them represent the Buddha of Infinite Illumination. Walking into this meditative alcove, you'll feel you've stumbled upon a marvellous museum secret.

Isabella Stewart Gardner Museum

280 The Fenway • Tues–Sun 11am–5pm, till 8pm the third Thurs of each month; free tours: Tues–Fri 12.30 pm & 2.30pm (confirm time at info desk) • $12; $2 off with MFA ticket stub (within two days of use); CityPass accepted; free admission for anyone named "Isabella"; free on your birthday • ☎ 617 566 1401, ⓦ gardnermuseum.org • Museum **T**

Less broad in its collection, but more distinctive and idiosyncratic than the MFA, is the nearby **Isabella Stewart Gardner Museum**. Spirited Boston socialite Gardner collected and arranged more than 2500 objects in the four-storey mansion she designed herself, making this the country's only major museum that is entirely the creation of a single individual. It's a melange of works from around the globe, presented without much attention to period or style; Gardner's goal was to foster the love of art rather than its study, and she wanted the setting of her pieces to "fire the imagination". Your imagination does get quite a workout – there's art everywhere you look, with most of the objects unlabelled, placed in corners or above doorways, for an effect that is occasionally chaotic, but always striking. To get the most out of a visit, aim to join the hour-long **tour**, but get there early as only fifteen people are allowed, on a first-come, first-served basis.

Gardner's will stipulated that every piece in the galleries stay put, or else the entire kit and kaboodle was to be auctioned off and the proceeds given to Harvard. And therefore it ruffled some feathers when, in 2010, museum officials unveiled a grandiose plan to construct a new glass-and-copper **entrance wing**, albeit one that was to be situated a courteous 50ft from the original building. Slated to open in 2012, the addition, whose approval proceedings went all the way to Massachusetts Supreme Court, will generate a new greenhouse and concert hall in addition to an information centre called "The Living Room", dedicated to the Gardner museum's own intriguing life story.

The courtyard

The Gardner is best known for its spectacular central **courtyard** styled after a fifteenth-century Venetian palace; the snake-haired Medusa mosaic at its centre is fittingly surrounded by stone-faced statuary and fountains, and brightened up, year round, by flowering plants and trees.

Spanish Cloister

The museum's greatest success is the adjacent **Spanish Cloister**, a long, narrow corridor which perfectly frames John Singer Sargent's ecstatic representation of flamenco dance, *El Jaleo* (meaning "The Ruckus").

The second floor

Up on the second floor, a first-rate array of seventeenth-century Northern European works was diminished in 1990 by the biggest art heist in history: three Rembrandts and a Vermeer were among thirteen artworks stolen. You can spot the missing pieces by their empty frames, a homage to the works and a placeholder for their return. Also on this floor, the magnificent **Tapestry Room** is hung with rich mid-sixteenth century Brussels tapestries. Extending off the Tapestry Room, the **Short Gallery** contains a notable portrait of the hostess herself, Anders Zorn's exuberant *Isabella Stewart Gardner in Venice*.

The third floor

At the head of the stairs, the third floor's **Veronese Room** is a stunner, with ornate gold and robin's-egg blue leather panels embellishing the full length of its walls. The ceiling – hung with Paolo Veronese's massive cerulean canvas *The Coronation of Hebe* – is also

1

show-stopping. Between the stairwell and the chapel is the **Gothic Room**, a sombrely decorated chamber whose chief attraction is John Singer Sargent's *Portrait of Isabella Gardner*. Although the painting is mild by today's standards, the Gardners feared its near-erotic quality was too scandalous for public consumption, and it was not exhibited until after her death (when it did indeed cause a stir).

Brookline

The leafy, affluent town of **BROOKLINE**, south of Boston University and west of The Fenway, is centred on bustling **Coolidge Corner**, at the intersection of Beacon and Harvard streets. Of note in these parts is the **Coolidge Corner Theatre**, at 290 Harvard St, a refurbished arthouse cinema with a great selection of film offerings (see p.121).

John F. Kennedy National Historic Site

83 Beals St · Mid-May to late Oct Wed–Sun 9.30am–5pm · Free · ☎ 617 566 7937, ⓦ nps.gov/jofi · Coolidge Corner **T**

Near Coolidge Corner you'll find the **John F. Kennedy National Historic Site**, the outwardly unremarkable house where JFK was born on May 29, 1917. The inside is rather plain, too, though a narrated voiceover by the late president's mother, Rose, adds some spice to the roped-off rooms.

Frederick Law Olmsted National Historic Site

99 Warren St · Free · ☎ 617 566 1689 ext 221, ⓦ nps.gov/frla · Not accessible via public transport

Along Brookline's southern fringe is the **Frederick Law Olmsted National Historic Site**, which doubled as Olmsted's family home and office; it's currently closed for renovations until 2012.

Larz Anderson Auto Museum

15 Newton St · Tues–Sun 10am–4pm · $10; children (6–12 years) $5 · ☎ 617 522 6547, ⓦ larzanderson.org · No public transport

The **Larz Anderson Auto Museum** exhibits 21 beautifully preserved antique cars in the carriage house of a palatial nineteenth-century estate. While the museum will mainly be of interest to little ones, the displays are charming, and its grounds – with skyline views – make for a great picnic.

Jamaica Plain

Walking around **Jamaica Plain** – "JP" in local parlance – you'll probably come across a bumper sticker to the tune of "ban Republican marriage" or "Make Levees, Not War". Such is the left-leaning bent of this artsy neighbourhood, populated by a mix of students, long-time Latino and African-American communities, and young middle-class families. Located between Roxbury and Brookline, the area's activity centres on, appropriately, **Centre Street**, home to some inventive cafés and restaurants.

Arnold Arboretum

125 Arborway · Daily sunrise–sunset · Donations welcome · ☎ 617 524 1718, ⓦ arboretum.harvard.edu · Forest Hills **T**

The 265-acre **Arnold Arboretum** is Jamaica Plain's star attraction, and the most spectacular link in the Emerald Necklace. Its collection of over 15,000 flowering trees, vines and shrubs has benefited from more than one hundred years of careful grooming and ample funding, and is now one of the finest in North America. Plants are arranged along a series of paths enjoyed by everyone from dog-walkers to serious botanists, and it certainly doesn't require any expert knowledge to enjoy the grounds. The array of Asian species – considered the best in the world outside of Asia – is highlighted by the **Larz Anderson Bonsai Collection**, brilliantly concentrated towards the centre of the park. It's best to visit during spring, when magnolias, crab apples and lilacs complement the greenery with dazzling chromatic schemes. "**Lilac Sunday**", a celebration held on the third Sunday in May, sees the Arboretum at its most vibrant, when its collection of lilacs – the second largest in the US – is in full bloom.

Forest Hills Cemetery

95 Forest Hills Ave • Daily 8.30am–dusk • Donations welcome • ☎ 617 524 0128, ⓦ foresthillstrust.org • Forest Hills **T**

Just east of the arboretum, **Forest Hills Cemetery** is a 250-acre burial ground and sculpture garden created in the spirit of Cambridge's Mount Auburn (see p.94). Dotted with Victorian stone carvings and contemporary art, the park – a self-proclaimed "romantic vision of nature at its most harmonious and abundant" – was chosen as a final resting place by an intriguing roster of Bostonians: poetic powerhouses Anne Sexton and e.e. cummings, playwright Eugene O'Neill and the inventor of the fountain pen, Lewis Waterman, to name a few. But it's the cemetery's elaborately carved memorials – including five works by Daniel Chester French (best known for Washington, DC's Lincoln Memorial) that really stand out. This scenic necropolis is also known for its annual **Lantern Festival**, held in July. During this celebratory (not sombre) event, participants release hundreds of glowing lanterns, inscribed with messages to loved ones who have passed, onto Lake Hibiscus, which float away into the twilight.

Roxbury

Roxbury, a historically African-American neighbourhood, occupies much of south central Boston below the South End, between Dorchester and Jamaica Plain. This formerly pastoral region was one of the city's most coveted addresses in the seventeenth and eighteenth centuries when wealthy families built sumptuous country homes here. Around the 1950s, the area hit hard times, and the urban blight has left its scars, although attempts to restore some of the impressive properties in the area have been slowly successful. The main attraction here, especially if you have children in tow, is the **Franklin Park Zoo**.

Franklin Park Zoo

1 Franklin Park Rd in Franklin Park • April–Sept Mon–Fri 10am–5pm, Sat & Sun till 6pm; Oct–March daily 10am–4pm • $16; children (2–12 years) $10 • ☎ 617 541 5466, ⓦ zoonewengland.org • Ruggles **T**

The **Franklin Park Zoo** has little besides its backdrop to distinguish it from other zoos, though it does boast the impressively recreated African Tropical Forest, the largest indoor open-space zoo in North America, housing bats, warthogs and gorillas. Check out Bird's World, too, a charming relic from the days of Edwardian zoo design: a huge wrought-iron cage you can walk through while birds fly overhead.

Dorchester

Occupying the southeast corner of the city, **Dorchester** lies east of Roxbury and beneath South Boston, below Columbia Road. Home to a broad ethnic mix of Irish, Haitians, Latinos, Vietnamese, African-Americans and students, the area has some worthwhile restaurants and shops along "Dot" (Dorchester) Avenue, although most

1

visitors come here for the **John F. Kennedy Presidential Library & Museum**. Dorchester is rough in spots; stick to the major sights and you'll be fine, however.

John F. Kennedy Presidential Library & Museum

Columbia Point • Daily 9am–5pm • $12 • ☎ 617 514 1600, ⊕ jfklibrary.org • JFK/UMass **T**, free shuttle every 20min • Free parking

The **John F. Kennedy Presidential Library & Museum** is spectacularly situated in an I.M. Pei-designed building overlooking Boston Harbor. The campaign exhibits are most interesting for their television and radio ads, which illustrate the squeaky-clean self-image America liked to project at that time. Its section on the Kennedy administration is more serious, highlighted by a 22-minute film on the Cuban Missile Crisis that evokes the tension of the event, while possibly exaggerating Kennedy's heroics. The final section of the museum is its best: a 115ft glass atrium overlooking the harbour, with excerpts from Kennedy's *Profiles in Courage* – affecting enough to move even the most jaded JFK critic. Oddly enough, the museum is also the repository for Ernest Hemingway's original manuscripts; call to make an appointment to see them.

Commonwealth Museum

220 Morrissey Blvd • Mon–Fri 9am–5pm • Free • ☎ 617 727 9268, ⊕ sec.state.ma.us/mus/museum • JFK/UMass **T**, free shuttle every 20min • Free parking

Upon entering the **Commonwealth Museum,** just across the car park from the JFK Museum and sited inside the Massachusetts Archives building, it's easy to feel you're in the wrong place – a workaday government office rather than a gallery of exhibits. Put these misgivings aside and head straight to the **Treasures Gallery**, a dark, guarded *Mission Impossible*-esque alcove where five of the state's most priceless documents lie encased under pressure-sensitive glass. Scripted in ornate cursive, the set includes one of the fourteen original copies of the Declaration of Independence and the "Constitution of the Commonwealth of Massachusetts in 1780", the oldest written document still used for governance in the world. While the rest of the museum lacks this wow-factor, the archival reproductions on display, such as the 1637 decree banishing religious dissident Anne Hutchinson from the Massachusetts Bay Colony, are fascinating.

Cambridge

Walk down almost any street in **CAMBRIDGE** – just across the Charles River from Boston, but a world apart in atmosphere and attitude – and you will pass monuments and plaques honouring literati and revolutionaries who lived and worked in the area as early as the seventeenth century. But along its colonial-era brick footpaths and narrow, crooked roads, present-day Cambridge also vibrates with energy: starched business people bustle past punk rock kids; clean-cut college students coexist with the homeless; and tourists look on as street vendors purvey goods and buskers perform. It's all enough to make Cambridge an essential stopover on your trip.

The city is loosely organized around a series of squares – confluences of streets that are the focus of each area's commercial activity. By far the most famous of these is **Harvard Square**, location of the eponymous university. Branching out from it are many of the city's main sights, most notably the stretch of colonial mansions that make up "Tory Row" in **Old Cambridge** and **Cambridge Common**, where George Washington is said to have commandeered the Continental Army. Hip **Central and Inman squares** are less touristy but no less urban than their collegiate counterpart, while further east along the Charles is **Kendall Square**, home to the remarkable architecture of the Massachusetts Institute of Technology (MIT), one of the world's premier science and research institutions.

Brief history

Cambridge began inauspiciously in 1630, when a group of English immigrants from Charlestown founded **New Towne** village on the swampy banks of the Charles River. These Puritans hoped New Towne would become an ideal religious community; to that end, they founded a college in 1636 for the purpose of training clergy. Two years later, the college took its name in honor of a local minister, **John Harvard**, who bequeathed his library and half his estate to the nascent institution.

New Towne was eventually renamed **Cambridge** for the English university where many of its figureheads were educated, and became a publishing centre after the importation of the printing press in the seventeenth century. Its printing industry and university established Cambridge as a bastion of intellectual activity and political thought. This status became entrenched during the early years of the US, particularly during the **Revolution**, when the Cambridge population became sharply divided between the artisans and farmers who sympathized with the Revolution and the minority of moneyed Tories who supported the Crown. When fighting began, the Tories were driven from their mansions on modern-day **Brattle Street** (then called "Tory Row"), their place taken by Cambridge intelligentsia and prominent Revolutionaries.

Harvard Square

Harvard Square – a buzzing public space in the shadow of Harvard Yard – radiates out from the Harvard **T** stop along Massachusetts Avenue, JFK Street and Brattle Street. A small **tourism kiosk** (see p.98) run by the Cambridge Tourism Office faces the station exit, but most of the action is in the adjacent sunken area known as **The Pit**, a melting pot for alternative culture; moody youths spend entire days sitting here admiring each other's green hair and body piercings while homeless locals hustle for change. This is also the focal point of the city's **street music scene**, at its most frenetic on Friday and Saturday nights and Sunday afternoons, when all the elements converge – crowds mill about while performers do their thing on every corner.

Old Burying Ground

Massachusetts Ave, at Garden St • Harvard **T**

North of Harvard Square along Massachusetts Avenue lies one of Cambridge's first cemeteries, the **Old Burying Ground**, whose appearance and grounds have scarcely changed since the seventeenth century. The gravestones are adorned in a style somewhere between Puritan austerity and medieval superstition: inscriptions praise the simple piety of the Christian deceased, but are surrounded by death's-heads carved to ward off evil spirits.

Dawes Park

Massachusetts Ave, at Garden St • Harvard **T**

Dawes Park, a triangular traffic island, is named for William Dawes, one of the patriots who rode to alert residents that the British were marching on Lexington and Concord in 1775. While Longfellow chose to commemorate Revere's midnight ride, Cambridge's citizens must have appreciated Dawes' contribution just as much. Bronze hoofmarks in the sidewalk mark the event.

Cambridge Common

In **Cambridge Common**, a roughly square patch of green between Massachusetts Avenue, Garden Street and Waterhouse Street, you can retrace the old **Charlestown–Watertown path**, along which British Redcoats beat a sheepish retreat during the Revolutionary War, and which still transects the park from east to west. Safe to explore by day, the Common can be sketchy after dark – try to avoid it at night.

1

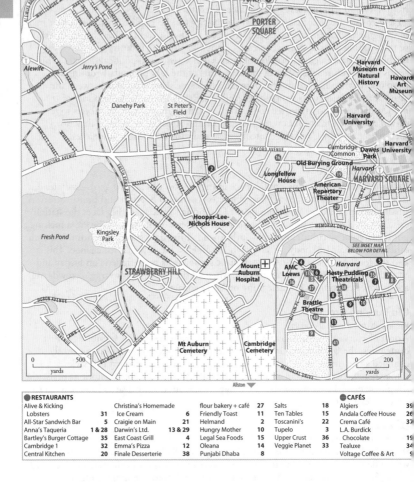

CAMBRIDGE

● RESTAURANTS							● CAFÉS	
Alive & Kicking		Christina's Homemade		flour bakery + café	27	Salts	18	Algiers	39
Lobsters	31	Ice Cream	6	Friendly Toast	11	Ten Tables	15	Andala Coffee House	26
All-Star Sandwich Bar	5	Craigie on Main	21	Helmand	2	Toscanini's	22	Crema Café	37
Anna's Taqueria	1 & 28	Darwin's Ltd.	13 & 29	Hungry Mother	10	Tupelo	3	L.A. Burdick	
Bartley's Burger Cottage	35	East Coast Grill	4	Legal Sea Foods	15	Upper Crust	36	Chocolate	19
Cambridge 1	32	Emma's Pizza	12	Oleana	14	Veggie Planet	33	Tealuxe	34
Central Kitchen	20	Finale Desserterie	38	Punjabi Dhaba	8			Voltage Coffee & Art	9

The Washington Elm

The most prominent feature on the Common is the **Washington Elm**, under which it's claimed George Washington took command of the Continental Army on July 3, 1775. The elm, located at the southern side of the park near the intersection of Garden Street and Appian Way, is actually the offspring of the original, raised from one of its branches. The city cut down the original elm in 1946 when it began to obstruct traffic; it stood at the Common's southwest corner, at the intersection of Mason and Garden streets (in fact, what looks like a manhole here bears the inscription "Here Stood The Washington Elm" – you can still view it today, just watch the traffic).

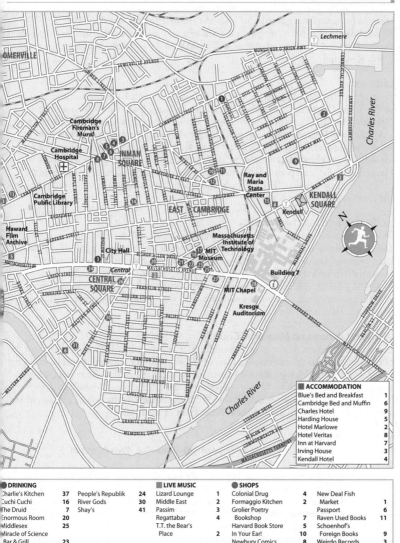

ACCOMMODATION	
Blue's Bed and Breakfast	1
Cambridge Bed and Muffin	6
Charles Hotel	9
Harding House	5
Hotel Marlowe	2
Hotel Veritas	8
Inn at Harvard	7
Irving House	3
Kendall Hotel	4

● DRINKING				■ LIVE MUSIC		● SHOPS			
Charlie's Kitchen	37	People's Republik	24	Lizard Lounge	1	Colonial Drug	4	New Deal Fish	
Cuchi Cuchi	16	River Gods	30	Middle East	2	Formaggio Kitchen	2	Market	1
The Druid	7	Shay's	41	Passim	3	Grolier Poetry		Passport	6
Enormous Room	20			Regattabar	4	Bookshop	7	Raven Used Books	11
Middlesex	25			T.T. the Bear's		Harvard Book Store	5	Schoenhof's	
Miracle of Science				Place	2	In Your Ear!	10	Foreign Books	9
Bar & Grill	23					Newbury Comics	8	Weirdo Records	3

Harvard University

Visitor information Holyoke Center Arcade, 1350 Massachusetts Ave • Tours June–Aug Mon–Sat 10am, 11.15am, 2pm & 3.15pm; Sept–May Mon–Fri 10am & 2pm, Sat 2pm • Free • ☎ 617 495 1573, ⓦ harvard.edu • Harvard **T**

As you pass through the esteemed gates on Massachusetts Avenue, the transition from Harvard Square to **Harvard Yard** – the proper centre of the university – is brief and dramatic: in a matter of only several feet, the buzz of car traffic and urban life gives way to grassy lawns, towering oaks and an aura of intellectualism. The atmosphere is more illusory than real, however, as the Yard's narrow footpaths are constantly plied by preoccupied students and camera-clicking tour groups, who make the place seem more like an amusement park than an university campus. You can join the hullabaloo by taking a free one-hour guided tour from the **Holyoke Center Arcade**, 1350 Massachusetts Ave, or by hopping on a Trademark Tour (see p.99). The Center also provides limited free internet use, as well as **maps** and brochures detailing everything Harvard-related.

Old Yard

Enter through Johnston Gate, across Massachusetts Avenue from the Common, and you're in the **Old Yard**, a large, rectangular area enclosed by freshers' dormitories. Opposite the gate, in front of marble-hued University Hall, is the Yard's trademark icon, the **John Harvard statue**, around which chipper student guides inform tour groups of the statue's oft-told three lies (it misdates the college's founding, erroneously identifies John Harvard as the college's founder and isn't really a likeness of John Harvard). While it's a popular spot for visitors to take pictures, male students at the college covet the statue as a site of public urination. You might want to avoid rubbing the toe (supposedly good luck).

Hollis Hall and Matthews Hall

The architectural contrast between modest, 1762 **Hollis Hall**, north of Johnston Gate, and its grandiose southern neighbour, **Matthews Hall**, built around a hundred years later, mirrors Harvard's transition from a quiet training ground for ministers to a cosmopolitan university. The indentations in Hollis's front steps also hold some historical interest: students used to warm their rooms by heating cannonballs, and, when it came time to leave for the summer, they would dispose of them by dropping them from their windows.

Widener Library and Memorial Church

East of the Old Yard lie the grander buildings of Tercentenary Theatre, where a vast set of steps leads up to the enormous pillars of **Widener Library**. Named after Harvard grad and *Titanic* victim Harry Elkins Widener, whose mother paid for the project, it's the centre of the largest private library collection in the US, boasting 65 miles of bookshelves. At the opposite side of the yard is **Memorial Church**, whose narrow, white spire strikes a balancing note to the pillared front of the library.

Harvard Art Museum

Currently closed for renovation; temporary exhibits at 485 Broadway • Tues–Sat 10am–5pm • $9 • ☎ 617 495 9400, ⓦ harvardartmuseums.org • Harvard **T**

Harvard's three **art museums** (the Fogg, the Arthur M. Sackler, and the Busch-Reisinger) have benefited from years of scholarly attention and donors' financial generosity. Unfortunately, all three are currently closed for a major renovation, which will merge them into one large collection at 32 Quincy St; this is not slated to reopen until 2013. Once open, the new **Harvard Art Museum** will hold over 150,000 works of art, including highlights of Harvard's substantial gathering of Western art, a small yet excellent selection of German Expressionist and Bauhaus works, and sensuous Buddhas from its Asian and Islamic art collections. During the renovation, you can check out a selection of the university's holdings at 485 Broadway, former home of the **Arthur M. Sackler Museum**.

Harvard Museum of Natural History

26 Oxford St • Daily 9am–5pm • $9, includes entry to the Peabody Museum • ☎ 617 495 3045, ⓦ hmnh.harvard.edu • Harvard **T**

North of the temporary Harvard Art Museum is the beloved **Harvard Museum of Natural History**, a nineteenth-century Victorian building that's the public front for the college's herbaria and its zoological and geological institutions. Start your visit at **Minerals, Gems and Meteorites**, a visual feast of rocks and gemstones with a spectacular 1600-pound amethyst-encrusted cavity as its centrepiece. The adjacent gallery houses the museum's *pièce de résistance*, the stunning **Ware Collection of Glass Models of Plants**. This exhibit, which began as a teaching collection in 1887 and concluded almost fifty years later, endowed the museum with an absolutely unique and visually awesome collection of flowers constructed entirely from glass. Down the hall, the **zoological galleries** are home to some gloriously huge dinosaur fossils, including a 42ft-long prehistoric marine reptile, the *Kronosaurus*, the teeth of which (as the museum proudly proclaims) "are the size of bananas". Around the corner is the *Glyptodont*, which looks like an inflated armadillo.

Peabody Museum of Archaeology and Ethnography

11 Divinity Ave • Daily 9am–5pm • $9, includes entry to the Harvard Museum of Natural History • ☎ 617 496 1027, ⓦ peabody.harvard.edu • Harvard **T**

The Museum of Natural History is connected to the **Peabody Museum**, which displays archaeological and ethnographic materials, many culled from Harvard University expeditions. The Peabody also features interesting exhibits on North American Native Americans, though the strength of the museum lies in its collection of pieces from Mesoamerica. Best are the enormous, carved Copan stelæ on which births, deaths and bloodlettings are recorded in ancient Mayan.

Old Cambridge

After the outbreak of the American Revolution, Cambridge's patriot dissidents ran their Tory neighbours out of town, but left their sumptuous houses along "Tory Row" (now **Brattle Street**, the main drag of **Old Cambridge**) more or less unharmed. The area has remained a neighbourhood of stately mansions, although only two of the houses are open to the public; the rest you'll have to view from across their expansive, impeccably kept lawns.

Longfellow National Historic Site

105 Brattle St • June–Oct Wed–Sun 10am–4.30pm, tours hourly 10.30–11.30am & 1–4pm • Free • ☎ 617 876 4491, ⓦ nps.gov/long • Harvard **T**

One house you can visit for more than just a look is the **Longfellow House**, where poet Henry Wadsworth Longfellow lived while serving as a professor at Harvard. The house was erected for **Loyalist John Vassal** in 1759, who promptly vacated it on the eve of the Revolutionary War; it was later used by George Washington as his headquarters during the siege of Boston. In 1837 it became home to Longfellow, who initially moved in as a lodger. After he married Fanny Appleton, her father purchased the house for them as a wedding gift and the poet lived here until his death in 1882. The house is preserved in an attempt to portray it as it was during his residence, and the halls and walls are festooned with Longfellow's furniture and art collection; most surprising is the wealth of nineteenth-century pieces from the Far East, amassed by Longfellow's son Charlie on his world travels. Just outside, a lovely garden features labyrinthine shrubs, snapdragons and roses, all laid out with historical accuracy from plans dating to 1904.

Hooper-Lee-Nichols House

159 Brattle St • Mon & Wed 1–5pm • $5 • ☎ 617 547 4252, ⓦ cambridgehistory.org • Harvard **T**

The second of the Brattle Street mansions open to the public, half a mile west of the Longfellow House, is the **Hooper-Lee-Nichols House**, one of the oldest residences in Cambridge. The building began as a post-medieval farmhouse, and underwent various renovations until it became the Georgian mansion it is today. Tour guides open secret panels to reveal centuries-old wallpaper and original foundations; otherwise, you'll see rooms predictably restored with period writing tables and canopy beds.

1

Mount Auburn Cemetery

580 Mount Auburn St • Daily: Oct–April 8am–5pm, May–Aug till 7pm call to confirm as hours change seasonally depending on daylight •
Free • ☎ 617 547 7105, ⓦ mountauburn.org • Harvard **T**, then #71 or #73 bus

At the terminus of Brattle Street is **Mount Auburn Cemetery**, an unexpected treasure.
Laid out in 1831 as America's first "garden cemetery", its 175 acres of stunningly
landscaped grounds, complete with ponds and fountains, provide a gorgeous contrast
with the many simple "burying grounds" in the city. Resting here are painter Winslow
Homer and art patron Isabella Stewart Gardner, among others. Pick up a **map** at the
visitor centre at the entrance to find out who's where, and get a sense of the cemetery's
scope by ascending the **tower** that lies smack in its centre – from here, you can see all
the way to downtown Boston.

Central and Inman Squares

A mile east of Brattle Street, **Central Square**, as you might expect, is located roughly in
the geographical centre of Cambridge, and is appropriately the city's civic centre, home
to its government buildings. It's a good place to shop and eat, and is home to some of
the best nightlife in Cambridge (see p.117).

Overshadowed by Cambridge's busier districts, **Inman Square** is a hip stretch directly
north of Central Square, centred on the confluence of Cambridge, Beacon and
Prospect streets. It's a pleasant, mostly residential neighbourhood where much of
Cambridge's Portuguese-speaking population resides alongside students and hipster-
types. While in the area, check out the charming **Cambridge Firemen's Mural**, at the
front of the firehouse at 1384 Cambridge St, a work of public art commissioned to
honour the men in red.

Massachusetts Institute of Technology (MIT)

77 Massachusetts Ave (aka "Building 7") • MIT Information Center Mon–Fri 9am–5pm; campus tours 10.45am & 2.45pm • Free •
☎ 617 253 4795, ⓦ mit.edu • Kendall/MIT **T**

The geography of eastern Cambridge is mostly taken over by the **Massachusetts
Institute of Technology** (MIT), which occupies more than 150 acres alongside the
Charles River, providing the area with its intellectual backbone and imbuing it with
some delightfully curious modern architecture. Originally established in Back Bay in
1861, MIT moved across the river in 1916 and has since risen to international
prominence as a major centre for theoretical and practical research in the sciences.

The campus buildings and geography reflect the quirky character of the institute,
emphasizing function and peppering it with a peculiar notion of form. Behind the
massive pillars that guard the entrance of **Building 7**, 77 Massachusetts Ave, you'll find
a labyrinth of corridors through which you can traverse the entire east campus without
ever going outside – it's known to Techies as the **Infinite Corridor**. Just inside the
entrance you'll find the **MIT Information Center**, while atop the nearby Maclaurin

---

364.4 SMOOTS (+ 1 EAR)

If you walk from Back Bay to Cambridge via the scenic **Harvard Bridge** (which leads directly
into MIT's campus), you might wonder about the peculiar marks partitioning the sidewalk.
These units of measure, affectionately known as "Smoots", represent the height of **Oliver R.
Smoot**, an MIT Lambda Chi Alpha fraternity pledge in 1958. As the shortest pledge, part of
Smoot's initiation included the use of his body as a tape measure, all down the **Harvard
Bridge** – resulting in the conclusive "364.4 Smoots + 1 Ear" at the bridge's terminus. While the
marks continue to be repainted each year by LCA, the Smoot itself has gone global: besides
the ample press devoted to Smoot and gang, the "Smoot" has made it all the way to a
conversion calculator on Google.

1

Building (aka "Building 10") is MIT's best-known architectural icon, a massive gilt hemisphere called the **Great Dome**.

MIT has drawn the attention of some major contemporary architects, who have used the university's progressiveness as a testing ground for some of their more experimental works. Two of these are located in the courtyard across Massachusetts Avenue from **Building 7**. The **Kresge Auditorium**, designed by Finnish architect Eero Saarinen, resembles a large tent, though its real claim to fame is that it rests on three, rather than four, corners; the architect allegedly designed it over breakfast by cutting into his grapefruit. In the same courtyard, another Saarinen work, the red-brick **MIT Chapel**, is shaped like a stocky cylinder with an abstract sculpture of paper-thin metal serving as a spire; inside, a delicate metal screen scatters light patterns across the floor. Looking like a set of egg timers designed by Salvador Dalí, the **Ray and Maria Stata Center**, at 32 Vassar St, is the work of renowned architect Frank Gehry.

MIT Museum

265 Massachusetts Ave • Daily: 10am–5pm • $7.50 • ☎ 617 253 5927, ⓦ web.mit.edu/museum • Central **T**

While it only takes up two small floors of galleries, the **MIT Museum**, near Central Square, packs a punch with its exhibits. The museum has a number of standout displays, including "Holography: the Light Fantastic", a collection of seriously cool visual trickery. The best exhibit, however, is Arthur Ganson's "Gestural Engineering", a collection of imaginative mini-machines, such as a walking wishbone.

ARRIVAL AND DEPARTURE BOSTON

Boston is the undisputed travel hub of New England. Conveniently, all points of arrival are located inside the city boundaries, none more than a few miles away from **downtown**, and all are well connected to **public transport**.

BY PLANE

Logan International Airport (☎ 1 800 235 6426, ⓦ massport.com/logan-airport) serves both domestic and international flights. It has four terminals (A, B, C and E), which are connected by shuttle buses. You'll find car rental desks, internet access, information booths and ATMs in all of them, and currency exchange in A, B and E. This is by far New England's busiest airport – fares are lowest and flights most frequent to and from the busy Northeast corridor (ie New York City and Washington, DC).

TO/FROM TOWN

By subway The subway, or, as it's known in Boston, the **T** (see p.96), is the cheapest way to reach downtown Boston from Logan. The Airport subway stop is a short shuttle-bus ride ($2) from the airport proper; catch the shuttle from outside the arrivals level of any of the four terminals. From the Airport station, you can take the Blue Line to State or Government Center, both in the heart of downtown, and transfer to the Red, Orange or Green lines to reach other points; the ride to downtown lasts about 15min.

By bus Another alternative is to take the Silver Line (see p.97), a speedy bus ($2) posing as subway transit that stops at the airport and continues on to South Station, the Seaport District and the South End.

By taxi Taxis from the airport are convenient but expensive – it will cost around $30 to most downtown destinations.

By water taxi Just as quick as a taxi, and a lot more fun, is the water taxi (April–Nov Mon–Sat 7am–10pm, Sun 7am–8pm; $10; ☎ 617 422 0392, ⓦ citywatertaxi.com), which whisks you across the harbour to numerous points around Boston. From the airport, courtesy bus #66 will take you to the pier. The water taxis don't run on a set schedule; if there isn't a boat waiting in the harbour, contact them via the checked call box at the Logan dock.

BY TRAIN

South Station The main terminus for trains to Boston is South Station, in the southeast corner of downtown at Summer Street and Atlantic Avenue. Amtrak trains (☎ 1 800 872 7245, ⓦ amtrak.com) arrive at one end of the station, which has an information booth, newsstands, a food court, and several ATMs. There is a subway stop (Red Line) down a level from the Amtrak station. Amtrak trains also stop at Back Bay Station, 145 Dartmouth St, on the **T**'s Orange Line.

Destinations Chicago, IL (1 daily; 23hr); New Haven, CT (15–20 daily; 2–3hr); New York City (15–20 daily; 3hr 30min–5hr); Providence, RI (15–20 daily; 35–50min); Washington, DC (15–20 daily; 6hr 30min–8hr).

North Station Located at 135 Causeway St, in the West End (near the TD Garden stadium), this station connects Boston with Portland, ME via Amtrak's Downeaster (☎ 1 800 872 7245, ⓦ amtrakdowneaster.com). Accessible from the **T**'s Orange and Green lines.

1

THE BOSTON CITYPASS

The **Boston CityPass** (available online or at the five attractions that accept it; $46; ⓦ citypass .com) is a ticket booklet that covers admission to the New England Aquarium, the Museum of Fine Arts, the Museum of Science, the Prudential Skywalk Observatory and the John F. Kennedy Presidential Library & Museum or the Harvard Museum of Natural History; if you plan to visit all or most of these sights, you'd do well to pick one up.

Destinations Dover, NH (5–8 daily; 1hr 25min); Durham, NH (5–8 daily; 1hr 20min); Exeter, NH (5–8 daily; 1hr 5min); Haverhill, MA (5–8 daily; 45min); Old Orchard Beach, ME (May–Oct only: 5–8 daily; 2hr); Portland, ME (5–8 daily; 2hr 30min); Saco, ME (5–8 daily; 2hr); Wells, ME (5–8 daily; 1hr 40min); Woburn, MA (5–8 daily; 20min).

BY BUS

South Station The main terminus for both buses and trains to Boston is South Station, in the southeast corner of downtown at Summer Street and Atlantic Avenue. Buses arrive at the clean and modern terminal next door to the train station. There is a subway stop (the Red Line) down a level from the Amtrak station, but it's a bit of a trek from the bus station; anyone with sizeable baggage will find the walk particularly awkward, as there are no porters or trolleys.

National bus companies Greyhound (ⓣ 1 800 231 2222, ⓦ greyhound.com) and Peter Pan (ⓣ 1 800 343 9999, ⓦ peterpanbus.com) offer national services, including frequent direct routes to New York City and Washington, DC; visitors headed to the former have additional (and better) options (see p.20).

New York City bus companies Ranked here in descending order of quality (the last two are just adequate): Bolt Bus (ⓣ 1 877 2659 287, ⓦ boltbus.com), Mega Bus (also covers much of the northeast corridor; ⓣ 1 877 462 6342, ⓦ megabus.com), Fung Wah (ⓣ 617 345 8000, ⓦ fungwahbus.com) and Lucky Star (ⓣ 1 888 881 0887, ⓦ luckystarbus.com).

New England bus companies Concord Coach Lines (ⓣ 1 800 639 3317, ⓦ concordcoachlines.com) serves mid-coast Maine and covers comprehensive New Hampshire

territory. Similarly, C & J (ⓣ 1 800 258 7111, ⓦ ridecj.com, travels to Portsmouth, Dover and Durham, NH, as well as Newburyport, MA. Plymouth & Brockton (ⓣ 508 746 0378 ⓦ p-b.com) provides frequent service to Cape Cod.

Destinations Concord, NH (10–12 daily; 1hr 20min) Hartford, CT (20–25 daily; 1hr 50min); Hyannis, MA (12–15 daily; 2hr); New York City (75–90 daily; 4hr 20min) Philadelphia, PA (20–25 daily; 7hr); Portland, ME (15–20 daily; 2hr); Providence, RI (8–10 daily; 1hr) Provincetown, MA (2–5 daily; 3hr 30min); Washington, DC (12–15 daily; 9hr 20min).

BY CAR

Driving into Boston is the absolute worst way to get there and will likely put a damper on your trip. Boston drivers are notorious for their aggressive, impatient style and the learning curve for navigating the city by car is so steep that ability to do so has become a source of pride and cultural identity for local residents. Two highways provide direct access to the city: I-90, known locally as the Mass Pike or The Pike, and I-93, known as the Central Artery. Once you're in Boston, Storrow Drive is the main local drag, running alongside the Charles River and providing access to the core of the city.

Parking Parking in Boston is a nightmare. The best parking secret is the Parcel 7 garage, at 136 Blackstone St (ⓣ 617 973 6954). The published rates won't mention it but if you get your ticket validated at a North End business the rates are only $1/hr for the first three hours (after that they rise steeply). The Garage at Post Office Square (ⓣ 617 423 1430) has good weekend deals ($9/day) and charges $9 for weekday nights after 4pm (out before 5am).

GETTING AROUND

Much of the pleasure of visiting Boston comes from being in a city built long before cars were invented. Walking around the **narrow streets** can be a joy; conversely, driving around them is a nightmare. If you have a car, you're best off parking it for the duration of your trip (see above) and getting around either by **foot** or **public transport** – a system of subway lines, buses and ferries run by the Massachusetts Bay Transportation Authority (MBTA; ⓣ 1 800 392 6100, ⓦ mbta.com).

BY SUBWAY (THE T)

Boston's subway (or **T**; ⓣ 1 800 392 6100, ⓦ mbta.com), is cheap, efficient, and, when you're not in a hurry, charmingly antiquated – its Green Line was America's first underground train, built in the late nineteenth century. Four train lines

transect Boston and continue out into some of its more proximate neighbours. Each line is colour-coded and passes through downtown before continuing on to other districts All trains travel either inbound (towards the quadrant made up of State, Downtown Crossing, Park Street and

Government Center stops) or outbound (away from the quadrant). The train's terminus is also designated on the train itself; for instance, trains to Harvard from South Station will be on the "Inbound" platform, and labelled "Alewife." The biggest drawback to the **T** is its hours (Mon–Sat 5.15am–12.30am, Sun from 6am–12.30am); the closing time means you'll be stuck taking a taxi home after last call at the bar.

FARES

Boston has recently installed a new and somewhat confusing system for subway fares. Within the city, the standard fare is $2, payable by the purchase of a "CharlieTicket", which can be purchased at any of the ATM-like machines in the station. If you procure a rechargeable "CharlieCard" (free) from a station agent – with more of a credit-card thickness and a longer lifespan – your fare begins at only $1.70 per ride. Your safest (and simplest) bet is the LinkPass, which covers all subway and local bus journeys (as well as the ferry to Charlestown) at a cost of $9/day or $15/week.

LINES

Red Line Runs most frequently. Serves Harvard, intersecting South Boston and Dorchester to the south and Cambridge to the north.

Green Line Stops at Back Bay, Kenmore Square, the Fenway and Brookline.

Blue Line Heads into East Boston and is most useful for its stop at Logan Airport.

Orange Line Traverses the South End and continues down to Roxbury and Jamaica Plain.

Silver Line The four subway lines are supplemented by a bus rapid transit (BRT) route, which runs above ground along Washington Street from Downtown Crossing **T** and has additional access to the airport and the Seaport District. More of a fast bus than a subway, the line cuts through the South End.

BY TRAIN

Rail travel in Boston is useful if you're making a day trip to the Revolutionary battlefields of Concord, the mills of Lowell, the witch sights of Salem, whale-watching tours in Gloucester or the Pilgrim attractions of Plymouth. All have stations on the MBTA's commuter rail (☎1 800 392 6100, ⓦmbta.com), a faster, glossier service than the **T**. Each of the aforementioned towns (except Plymouth) is north of the city, with trains leaving from the helpfully named North Station (see p.95); for Plymouth, catch a train at South Station (see p.95). Fares range from $5.75–7.75; you'll save $2 if you purchase a ticket before boarding.

Destinations Concord (8–15 daily; 45min); Gloucester (7–12 daily; 1hr); Lowell (8–25 daily; 45min); Plymouth (2–4 daily; 55min); Salem (12–25 daily; 15min).

BY BUS

The MBTA also manages a whopping 170 bus routes (☎1 800 392 6100, ⓦmbta.com), both in and around Boston. The buses run less frequently than the subway and are harder to navigate, but they have two main advantages: they're cheaper ($1.25 with CharlieCard; $1.50 in cash, exact change only) and they provide services to many more points – see ⓦmbta.com for route maps. If you're transferring from the **T**, you'll have to pay the full fare; transferring between buses is free, however, as long as you have a ticket from your original bus. Note that the **T**'s LinkPass includes unlimited bus access. Most buses run from 5.30am to 1am.

BY FERRY

Of all the MBTA transportation options, the Inner Harbor ferry (☎1 800 392 6100, ⓦmbta.com), is by far the most scenic: $1.70 gets you a 10min boat ride with excellent views of downtown Boston. The boats navigate several waterfront routes by day, though the one most useful to visitors is that connecting Long Wharf with the Charlestown Navy Yard (Mon–Fri 6.30am–8pm, Sat & Sun 10am–6pm; every 15min).

Summer-only services From May to October, Boston Harbor Cruises (☎617 227 4321, ⓦbostonharborcruises .com; Aquarium **T**) and Bay State Cruises (☎1 877 783 3779, ⓦbaystatecruisecompany.com; World Trade Center **T**) frequently make the 90min trip across Massachusetts Bay to Provincetown, MA, at the tip of Cape Cod. The Salem Ferry (May–Oct only; ☎617 770 0040, ⓦbostonsbestcruises.com; Aquarium **T**) offers a fun hour-long jaunt that leaves from Long Wharf and shuttles passengers to 10 Blaney St in Salem, MA.

BY BICYCLE

In and around Boston are some eighty miles of bike trails, making it an excellent city to explore on two wheels. A copy of *Boston's Bike Map* ($5.95) is available at any decent bike store and will help you find all the trails and bike-friendly roads in the area. Rentals are around $35/day.

BICYCLE RENTAL

Back Bay Bicycles 366 Commonwealth Ave, Hynes **T** ☎617 247 2336, ⓦbackbaybicycles.com. Near Berklee College, Back Bay will rent you a pair of wheels for $35/day. Mon–Sat 11am–6pm, Sun noon–5pm.

Community Bicycle Supply 496 Tremont St, Back Bay **T** ☎617 542 8623, ⓦcommunitybicycle .com. In the heart of the South End, this store rents bikes for $25/day.

Urban Adventours 103 Atlantic Ave, Haymarket **T** ☎1 800 979 3370, ⓦurbanadventours.com. North End company who also run fun and easy-going bike tours (see p.99). Bike rental $35/day.

1

BY TAXI

Given Boston's small scale and the efficiency of its public transport, taxis aren't as necessary – or as prevalent – as in bigger cities. You can generally hail one along the streets of downtown or Back Bay, though competition gets pretty stiff after 1am, when the subway has stopped running and bars and clubs begin to close; in this case just call the taxi company directly. In Cambridge, taxis mostly congregate around Harvard Square.

TAXI FIRMS

Chill Out First Class Cab (☎617 212 3763) has 24hr service and accepts major credit cards; Green Cab (☎617 628 0600) runs 24hr but is cash only. In Cambridge, call Yellow Ambassador Cab (☎617 547 3000) or PlanetTran (☎1 888 756 8876); the latter is powered by environmentally-friendly hybrid vehicles. As a general rule, the rate starts at $2.80 and goes up by 40 cents/seventh of a mile.

INFORMATION

For advance information, the best sources are the **Greater Boston Convention & Visitors Bureau** (GBCVB; ⓦbostonusa.com) and the **Boston Globe** (ⓦboston.com).

Boston Common Visitor Center Boston Common (daily 9am–5pm; ☎617 426 3115; Park St **T**). Boston's main public tourist office, where you'll find loads of maps and brochures, plus information on historical sights, cultural events, accommodation, restaurants and bus trips.

Boston National Historical Park Visitor Centre 15 State St, across the street from the Old State House (daily 9am–5pm; ☎617 242 5642, ⓦnps.gov/bost; State St **T**). An excellent visitor centre chock-full of maps, facts and helpful park rangers, who lead fascinating free history tours (see p.99). Also has a bookshop and toilets.

Prudential Center kiosk 800 Boylston St, in Center Court near Ann Taylor, Back Bay (daily 10am–5.30pm; ☎617 236 3100, ⓦprudentialcenter.com; Hynes or Prudential **T**).

Cambridge Office of Tourism Kiosk outside the subway station in Harvard Square (Mon–Sat 9am–5pm; ☎617 441 2884, ⓦcambridge-usa.org; Harvard **T**).

Appalachian Mountain Club Headquarters 5 Joy St, Beacon Hill (Mon–Fri 9am–5pm; ☎617 523 0636,

ⓦoutdoors.org; Park St **T**). Since 1922, this charming brownstone has served as New England's reference centre and library for outdoor enthusiasts.

Newspapers The city's oldest newspaper, The Boston Globe ($1, Sunday $3.50; ⓦbostonglobe.com), is still its principal general daily. The Boston Herald ($1; ⓦbostonherald.com) is the Globe's tabloid competitor best for local gossip and sports coverage. The Boston Phoenix (free; ⓦthephoenix.com), available at newspaper stands, offers extensive entertainment listings. Boston's Weekly Dig (free; ⓦdigboston.com) and The Improper Bostonian (free; ⓦimproper.com) have listings of new and noteworthy goings-on about town. Bay Windows (free; ⓦbaywindows.com), a small weekly catering to the gay and lesbian population, is available in the South End (the city's primary gay neighbourhood). The lone monthly publication, Boston Magazine ($4.99; ⓦbostonmagazine.com), is a glossy lifestyle magazine with good restaurant reviews and a yearly "Best of Boston" round-up in August.

TOURS

One of the best ways to orientate yourself in Boston is by taking a tour; there are many variations available. While it's always advisable to **book in advance** (particularly for the ever-popular Duck Tours), there are often last-minute tickets up for grabs. Both of Boston's two renowned **breweries** also offer tours (see box, p.116).

ON THE WATER

Boston Duck Tours ☎617 267 3825, ⓦbostonducktours.com. Excellent tours that take to the streets and the Charles River in restored World War II amphibious landing vehicles. Tours depart March to Nov every 30min from the Prudential Center (53 Huntington Ave) and the Museum of Science (1 Science Park); shorter, summer-only evening tours leave from the New England Aquarium ($28; 1 Central Wharf). Reservations advised. Tours $32.

Boston Harbor Cruises 1 Long Wharf ☎617 227 4321, ⓦbostonharborcruises.com. A nice range of options: everything from sunset cruises ($22) to lighthouse tours ($65), historic cruises ($21), weekend brunch trips ($37.50)

and even dance ($25) and "ghost cruises" ($32).

Charles Riverboat Co. 100 CambridgeSide Place, Suite 320 ☎617 621 3001, ⓦcharlesriverboat.com. Leaving from the CambridgeSide Galleria, passengers can enjoy a 1hr 55min architectural cruise ($25), a 60min Charles River tour ($14) or a 75min sunset jaunt ($16). May to Oct only.

Codzilla 1 Long Wharf ☎617 227 4321, ⓦbostonharborcruises.com. If the movie Animal House had been set on the water, this self-proclaimed "water coaster" would probably have featured heavily in the major scenes. Codzilla has a penchant for blaring AC/DC and sports a wicked shark tooth grin; expect a 40mph joyride and lots of sea spray on deck. May to early Oct only. Reservations advised. Tours $25.

Gondola di Venezia ☎617 876 2800 or ☎1 800 979 3370 (tickets), ⱳbostongondolas.com. Woo your main squeeze with a romantic gondola ride on the Charles. The company provides the chocolates and accordion player; you complete the look with champagne and your *cara bella*. Trips leave from the esplanade, by the Hatch Shell. June to mid-Oct only. Tours $99–229/couple.

Liberty Clipper 67 Long Wharf ☎617 742 0333, ⱳlibertyfleet.com. This 125ft tall ship takes visitors on exhilarating two-hour sails leaving from Central Wharf (May–Sept; $30). They also do lively Boston Tea Party re-enactment sails ($35 adults, children $24).

New England Aquarium Whale Watch 1 Central Wharf ☎617 973 5206, ⱳneaq.org. Guaranteed whale sightings or you get another trip. Late April to Oct, at least one trip per day, with additional tours scheduled in summer. Tours $40.

NARRATED TRAM TOURS

Beantown Trolley Gray Line Ticket office, 16 South Charles St ☎1 800 343 1328 or ☎781 986 6100, ⱳbrushhilltours.com. One of the oldest and most popular tours, covering the gamut from waterfront wharves to Beacon Hill Brahmins, with multiple pick-up and drop-off points around town; a 45min harbour boat tour is included in the price. *Beantown* also runs trips out to Lexington/Concord, Salem, Plymouth and the like ($37–60; late March to Nov; some tours summer only). Tours $32.

Old Town Trolley Tours ☎1 888 910 8687, ⱳtrolleytours.com. Another hop-on, hop-off tour, this one on orange-and-green trolleys with thematic routes like the "Chocolate Tour" and "Ghosts and Gravestones", in addition to the standard day tour. Tours $36; online discounts.

Upper Deck Trolley Tours 100 Terminal St, Charlestown ☎617 742 1440, ⱳbostonsupertrolleytours.com. A new fleet of trams with appealing features like double-decker seating, onboard climate control and a free boat cruise. Tours $38.

WALKING TOURS

Boston by Foot 77 North Washington St ☎617 367 2345, ⱳbostonbyfoot.org. Informative 90min walking tours that focus on the architecture and history of different Boston neighbourhoods. Also has "Boston by Little Feet" tours, geared towards the Freedom Trail's younger pedestrians. Tours $8–15.

Boston Gliders 420 Commercial St ☎1 866 611 9838,

ⱳbostongliders.com. Now you can zoom around Boston on a Segway! Beginning in the North End (420 Commercial St), tours roll amid the scenic parks and open spaces of the Seaport District and HarborWalk; longer tours take in extensive Freedom Trail sights. 1hr tour $60, 2hr tour $85, 3hr tour $125.

Boston Movie Tour ☎1 800 979 3370, ⱳbostonmovie tours.net. Take a breather on the bench made famous by *Good Will Hunting* and peek inside *The Departed*'s mobster hangouts. The 90min walking tour takes in thirty movie sights ($22); there is also a 3hr tour on wheels with forty sights ($40).

Boston National Historical Park Visitor Center Freedom Trail Tours 15 State St ☎617 242 5642, ⱳnps.gov/bost; State St T. Boston's NPS rangers are amazing – equipped with encyclopedic knowledge, they excel at presenting local history in manageable and entertaining snippets. Tours (90min) begin at the Visitor Center (15 State St) and take in a number of Freedom Trail hotspots. Mid-April to June & Sept–Nov Mon–Fri 2pm, Sat–Sun 10am & 2pm; July & Aug daily 10am, 11am & 2pm. In summer, get there 30min early – the tours are first-come, first-served. They also run the stellar Black Heritage Trail tour (☎617 725 0022). All tours are free.

Michele Topor's Boston Food Tours ☎617 523 6032 or ☎1 800 979 3370 (tickets), ⱳbostonfoodtours.com. Award-winning walking and tasting tours of Chinatown's food vendors and the North End's Italian *salumerias*. Often booked up, so reserve well in advance. Tours $50–65.

Photowalks ☎617 851 2273 or ☎1 800 979 3370 (tickets), ⱳphotowalks.com. Laidback walking tours that point out the perfect places to point and shoot. Times vary. Tours $30.

Trademark Tours ☎617 674 7788, ⱳtrademarktours .com. Boisterous 70min tour of the Harvard campus ($10) led by undergrads in humorously misspelled "Hahvahd" T-shirts. They also run a 90min "Ye Olde Boston" tour ($14), headed by collegiate guides in colonial garb.

BIKING TOURS

Urban Adventours 103 Atlantic Ave ☎617 670 0637 (office) or ☎1 800 979 3370 (tickets), ⱳurban adventours.com; Haymarket T. Leisurely 2hr 30min bike tours with themes including "City View" and "Tour de Boston", which pedal alongside the Charles River and take in sights like Fenway Park and beautiful Back Bay. Tours depart at 10am, 2pm and 6pm from their North End headquarters; bike rental is also available. Tours $50.

ACCOMMODATION

Boston has a **limited range** of well-priced accommodation. Even if the city's hotels are not suited to all budgets, they do cater to most tastes and range from chains to some excellent **independent hotels**. A surprising number of **B&Bs** are tucked into renovated brownstones in Back Bay, Beacon Hill and the South End, as well as Cambridge and Brookline. The industry is thriving, largely because it is so difficult to find hotel accommodation for less than $150/night – and many B&Bs

1

B&B AGENCIES AND SHORT-TERM ACCOMMODATION

Air BNB ⓦairbnb.com. The unchallenged international champion of short-term apartment rentals.

Bed & Breakfast Agency of Boston ⓣ617 720 3540, ⓣ1 800 248 9262 or UK ⓣ0800 895 128, ⓦboston-bnbagency.com. Can book you a room in a brownstone, a waterfront loft, or even on a yacht.

Bed & Breakfast Associates Bay Colony ⓣ781 449 5302 or ⓣ1 888 486 6018, ⓦbnbboston.com. Features some real finds in Back Bay and the South End.

Bed & Breakfast Reservations ⓣ617 964 1606, ⓦbbreserve.com. Lists B&Bs in Greater Boston, on the North Shore and on Cape Cod.

Caj House ⓣ617 803 4279, ⓦcajhouse.com. Rents premium South End apartments at economical rates (see p.78).

Inn Boston ⓣ617 236 2227, ⓦinnboston reservations.com. Offers stylish, fully furnished apartments for short term rentals. On-call telephone assistance is available 24hr.

---

offer just that. There are also numerous B&B agencies (see box above). Short-term **furnished apartments** are another option, though most have two-week minimums (see box above). There are also a handful of **hostels** for anyone who is looking for real budget accommodation.

DOWNTOWN

★ **Ames Hotel** 1 Court St ⓣ617 979 8100, ⓦameshotel.com; State St T; map pp.48–49. Currently one of Boston's "it" spots, the *Ames* is a contemporary boutique hotel located inside the city's first skyscraper. Luxurious interiors are furnished in tones of white and grey (with the occasional citrus burst), and enhanced by flat-screen TVs, iPod docks and great views of downtown. There's also a lively on-site restaurant, *Woodward* (see p.114) designed to feel like a chic museum of curios. **$305**

Four Seasons 200 Boylston St ⓣ617 338 4400, ⓦfourseasons.com; Arlington T; map pp.48–49. The tops in city accommodation, with 288 large rooms offering quiet, contemporary comfort. The penthouse-level health spa has an indoor pool that seems to float over the Public Garden. **$350**

Langham 250 Franklin St ⓣ617 451 1900, ⓦboston .langhamhotels.com; State St T; map pp.48–49. This stern granite building in the heart of the Financial District is the former Federal Reserve Bank of Boston, built in 1922. The spacious rooms are decorated in a contemporary French style with iPod docks, internet access and Italian marble bathrooms. Be sure to check out their Saturday chocolate buffet bar. **$310**

Marriott's Custom House 3 McKinley Square ⓣ617 310 6300, ⓦmarriott.com; Aquarium T; map pp.48–49. All the rooms at this downtown landmark-turned-hotel are high-end, one-bedroom suites with spectacular Boston Harbor and city views. While the exterior embodies a bygone era, the interior is modern and plush, with wi-fi, cushy linens and a small kitchen set-up. **$399**

Millennium Bostonian Hotel 26 North St ⓣ617 523 3600, ⓦmillenniumhotels.com; State St T; map pp.48–49. Right in Faneuil Hall Marketplace, the *Millennium Bostonian* completed a $24 million makeover in 2009, and the result – Frette linens, flat-screen TVs and a

funky-looking library with zebra seating – is fabulous. Rooms can be noisy, however; ask for one on a higher floor. **$234**

Nine Zero 90 Tremont St ⓣ617 772 5800, ⓦninezero .com; Park St T; map pp.48–49. Executive-class hotel with 190 polished quarters equipped with plush linens, wi-fi, CD players and a complimentary morning paper. Amazing central location. **$260**

★ **Omni Parker House** 60 School St ⓣ617 227 8600, ⓦomniparkerhouse.com; Park T; map pp.48–49. Though the present building only dates from 1927, the lobby, decorated in dark oak with carved gilt mouldings, recalls the splendour of the original nineteenth-century property (see p.52). Rooms, given their historic nature, run on the small side, but come equipped with modern amenities. **$245**

W Hotel 100 Stuart St ⓣ617 261 8700, ⓦstarwoodhotel .com; Boylston T; map pp.48–49. Smack in the Theater District, this super-trendy newcomer is spicing up Boston's hotel scene with floor-to-ceiling windows, immodest but stylish door-less bathrooms, "munchie boxes", 350-thread count sheets and a Bliss spa. **$339**

THE WATERFRONT

Boston Harbor Hotel 70 Rowes Wharf ⓣ617 439 7000, ⓦbhh.com; South Station T; map pp.48–49. Opulent accommodation in an atmosphere of studied corporate elegance, right on the water. There's a health club and pool, gracious concierge staff and rooms with harbour and city views; the former are substantially pricier. **$445**

Harborside Inn 185 State St ⓣ617 723 7500, ⓦharborsideinnboston.com; State St T; map pp.48–49. This small hotel is housed in a renovated 1890s mercantile warehouse across from Quincy Market. The rooms – with exposed brick, hardwood floors and cherry furniture – are a welcome surprise for this part of town.

They also run a great sister property, the *Charlesmark Hotel*, in Back Bay (see below). **$149**

InterContinental Hotel 510 Atlantic Ave ☎617 747 1000, ⊛intercontinentalboston.com; South Station T; map pp.48–49. New in 2006, the swanky, skyline-altering *InterContinental* offers deluxe amenities like a fitness centre with a 45ft heated pool, a tempting spa and spacious rooms overlooking the water. **$349**

THE NORTH END

★ **Fairmont Battery Wharf** 3 Battery Wharf ☎617 994 9000, ⊛fairmont.com; Haymarket T; map p.64. New in 2008, this 192-room property is superbly sited on a wharf bordering the North End. This translates to a waterfront location, plus access to all the Italian restaurants, pastries and espresso for which the North End is famed. Rooms are spacious, with huge marble bathrooms enhanced by "rain" showerheads; the *Fairmont* also stands out for its impeccable service. **$250**

★ **La Cappella Suites** 290 North St ☎617 523 9020, ⊛lacappellasuites.com; Haymarket T; map p.64. The three cosy, modern rooms at this inn in the heart of the North End come with wi-fi, cable TV and a nice public seating area. Two of the rooms have private balconies. Be prepared for a five-floor walk-up (with great views as a pay-off). **$150**

CHARLESTOWN

★ **Green Turtle Floating B&B** Shipyard Quarters Marina, 13th St ☎617 337 0202, ⊛greenturtlebb.com; North Station T; map p.64. A special place: two well-appointed rooms with kitchenettes situated on a quiet marina in Charlestown. Wake up to fresh pastries, your own harbourfront patio and the sound of waves lapping at the dock. **$260**

Residence Inn Marriott Boston Harbor 34–44 Charles River Ave ☎617 242 9000, ⊛residenceinnboston.com; Community College T; map p.64. The Marriott's *Residence Inn* is an all-suiter close to some of the main sights along the Freedom Trail. Comfortable rooms offer free wi-fi and generous kitchen amenities (stove, fridge, toaster), plus there's an amazing view of Boston's skyline over the river. **$249**

BEACON HILL

Beacon Hill Hotel 25 Charles St ☎617 723 7575, ⊛beaconhillhotel.com; Charles/MGH T; map pp.48–49. Pampered luxury in the heart of Beacon Hill, with thirteen small but sleek chambers occupying a regal mid-1800s brick building. The hotel is also home to a bistro and fireside bar (see p.110). **$225**

Charles Street Inn 94 Charles St ☎617 314 8900, ⊛charlesstreetinn.com; Charles/MGH T; map pp.48–49. One of the city's most romantic accommodation options, the *Charles Street* has nine rooms named after Boston luminaries: the "Isabella Stewart Gardner" features a Rococo chandelier, while the "Oliver Wendell Holmes" boasts a king-sized sleigh bed. All rooms come with working fireplaces. **$300**

★ **The John Jeffries House** 14 David G. Mugar Way ☎617 367 1866, ⊛johnjeffrieshouse.com; Charles/MGH T; map pp.48–49. This little gem has some of the best prices in town, and clean and tasteful rooms to match. A mid-scale spot at the foot of Beacon Hill, it offers Victorian-style decor, cable TV, wi-fi and kitchenettes in most rooms. Singles **$124**; doubles **$149**

★ **Liberty Hotel** 215 Charles St ☎617 224 4000, ⊛libertyhotel.com; Charles/MGH T; map pp.48–49. The *Liberty Hotel* has taken over the labyrinthine digs of an 1851 prison and fashioned it with stylish furniture and lush details. Prepare to be wowed by its 90ft lobby, phenomenal city views and unique architecture. The property also houses *Scampo* restaurant (see p.110) and the *Alibi* lounge (see p.115); the latter currently one of the places to see and be seen. **$315**

THE WEST END

Bulfinch Hotel 107 Merrimac St ☎617 624 0202, ⊛bulfinchhotel.com; North Station T; map pp.48–49. A fresh addition to the West End, this sleek hotel is housed in a vintage triangular – or flatiron shaped – building. The small but pretty wool-toned rooms are brightened with contemporary paintings and include internet and exercise room access. **$169**

Onyx Hotel 155 Portland St ☎617 557 9955, ⊛onyxhotel.com; North Station T; map pp.48–49. The stark, glass-panelled front of this small luxury hotel belies an opulent interior, though avoid the "Britney Spears" room – designed by her mum, it looks as you would expect the singer's childhood room to have looked, complete with pink Bible and fairy statuetts. Very pet-friendly, and the in-hotel *Ruby Room* bar is great for a nightcap. **$209**

BACK BAY

Back Bay Hotel 350 Stuart St ☎617 266 7200, ⊛doylecollection.com; Arlington T; map pp.74–75. Set in a 1920s building that used to be the Boston Police headquarters, the 220 smallish rooms here have huge beds, marble bathrooms, multi-head showers and heated towel racks. The function rooms are named after celebrated Irish writers Shaw, Yeats, Beckett, Joyce and Wilde; displays in the lobby show old police memorabilia. **$299**

★ **Charlesmark Hotel** 655 Boylston St ☎617 247 1212, ⊛thecharlesmark.com; Copley T; map pp.74–75. Forty small, contemporary rooms with cosy beechwood furniture, good rates, a lively bar and modern amenities like wi-fi and CD/DVD players (the sound system is hooked into your bathroom so you can sing as you shower). **$145**

1

College Club 44 Commonwealth Ave ☎ 617 536 9510, ⓦ thecollegeclubofboston.com; Copley T; map pp.74–75. The oldest women's club in the country, the *College Club* plays host to eleven antique-laden guest rooms (available to both men and women). A good option for solo travellers, there are five single rooms (all with shared baths), and six doubles with en-suite bathrooms and decorative fireplaces. The *Club's* smart location by the Public Garden and Newbury St goes a long way, plus the price is right. Singles $119; doubles $239

The Colonnade 120 Huntington Ave ☎ 617 424 7000, ⓦ colonnadehotel.com; Prudential T; map pp.74–75. The *Colonnade* was reinvented in 2008 to the tune of $25 million: expect contemporary rooms with deluxe bed linens, wi-fi, flat-screen HDTVs and iPod alarm clocks. Rooms are spacious, and in summer months there's access to a rooftop pool – the only one in Boston. $300

Copley Inn 19 Garrison St ☎ 617 236 0300, ⓦ copleyinn.com; Prudential T; map pp.74–75. Comfortable, clean rooms (with slightly corny decor and full kitchens), friendly staff, and a great location on the South End border. If you stay six days, the seventh night is free. $175

Copley Square Hotel 47 Huntington Ave ☎ 617 536 9000, ⓦ copleysquarehotel.com; Copley T; map pp.74–75. Situated on the eastern fringe of Copley Square, this recently renovated hotel has become a luxe hotspot with high-end amenities and *minibar*, a trendy lounge bar (see p.116). $275

Eliot 370 Commonwealth Ave ☎ 617 267 1607, ⓦ eliothotel.com; Hynes T; map pp.74–75. West Back Bay's answer to the *Four Seasons*, this independent, plush, nine-floor suite hotel has sizeable rooms with kitchenettes, Italian marble baths, huge beds with Egyptian cotton sheets, and wi-fi. Linger over a cognac at its sophisticated *City Bar* (see p.116). $250

Fairmont Copley Plaza 138 St James Ave ☎ 617 267 5300, ⓦ fairmont.com; Copley T; map pp.74–75. Built in 1912, the iconic *Fairmont* has long boasted Boston's most elegant lobby. Even if you don't stay here, you should at least have a martini in the fabulous *Oak Bar* (see p.116). $259

HI-Boston 12 Hemenway St ☎ 617 536 1027, ⓦ bostonhostel.org; Hynes T; map pp.74–75. Around the Back Bay-Fenway border, this clean and safe hostel features standard dorm accommodation, but stands out for its fun management (who plan a lot of field trips) and internet access. In summer, book ahead or check in at 8am. Dorm beds $32

Hotel 140 140 Clarendon St ☎ 617 585 5600, ⓦ hotel140.com; Back Bay T; map pp.74–75. This 65-room "discount boutique hotel" offers rates that are a welcome respite from many Back Bay prices – although with its limited amenities and location inside the YWCA

headquarters building, its budget aspect is felt. The neighbourhood – adjacent to Copley Square and near Newbury Street – is tops, however. $160

★ **Inn @ St. Botolph** 99 St. Botolph St ☎ 617 236 8099, ⓦ innatstbotolph.com; Back Bay T; map pp.74–75. Fall through the rabbit hole at this designer's dream on the western cusp of the South End. Comprised of sixteen oversized suites, *St Botolph's* guest rooms run wild with black and brown stripes, houndstooth and zebra zig-zags the work of decorating whiz Celeste Cooper. The inn's amenities are also impressive: there are kitchenettes and wi-fi throughout, an on-site laundry room, a gym and free continental breakfast. $200

The Lenox 61 Exeter St ☎ 617 536 5300, ⓦ lenoxhotel .com; Copley T; map pp.74–75. Billed as Boston's version of the *Waldorf-Astoria* when its doors first opened in 1900 *The Lenox* remains one of the most opulent hotels in the city, with a renowned staff and 212 exquisite rooms featuring high ceilings, walk-in closets, and, in some working fireplaces. $250

Mandarin Oriental 776 Boylston St ☎ 617 535 8888 ⓦ mandarinoriental.com/boston; Copley T; map pp.74–75. Boston is abuzz with the recent opening of this glamorous, extremely expensive hotel. Spacious rooms offer luxuries such as Frette linens, complimentary shoe shines, personal trainers and the city's best spa. When hunger strikes, head to *L'Espalier* (see p.111), long a darling of Boston's restaurant scene. $600

Newbury Guest House 261 Newbury St ☎ 617 670 6000, ⓦ newburyguesthouse.com; Copley T; map pp.74–75. Big, popular Victorian brownstone that fills up frequently, so be sure to call ahead. The 32 rooms were thoroughly renovated in 2009 and range from spacious bay-windowed quarters with hardwood floors to tiny digs well suited to the discerning economic traveller Continental breakfast included, wi-fi throughout and a really great location in the heart of Newbury St. Rooms can be noisy, however. $189

Taj Boston 15 Arlington St ☎ 617 536 5700 ⓦ tajhotels.com; Arlington T; map pp.74–75. Replacing (albeit lovingly) the city's historic *Ritz-Carlton* flagship, *Taj Boston* is the ultimate in luxurious, old-school Boston accommodation, with wood-burning fireplace suites gilded antique furniture and an unbeatable location across from the Public Garden. $249

THE SOUTH END

40 Berkeley 40 Berkeley St ☎ 617 375 2524 ⓦ 40berkeley.com; Back Bay T; map pp.74–75. Clean and simple hostel in a convenient South End location; full breakfast included. Singles $58; doubles $70; triples $10

Aisling Bed and Breakfast 21 East Concord St ☎ 617 206 8049, ⓦ aisling-bostonbb.com; Massachusetts Ave T

1

map pp.74–75. A three-guest room Victorian terraced house blessed with its original mouldings and marble fittings, the *Aisling*'s owners are incredibly accommodating (they'll even pick you up from the airport). The breakfasts are fabulous too. **$200**

★ **Caj House** 45 Worcester St ☎617 803 4279, ⓦcajhouse.com; Massachusetts Ave T; map pp.74–75. Ten carefully renovated apartments with polished wood floors, modern amenities (flat-screen TVs with cable, wi-fi) and full kitchens. One-week minimum stay; four weeks is the norm. They also maintain eight apartments at 677 Tremont St. **$455**

Chandler Inn 26 Chandler St ☎617 482 3450, ⓦchandlerinn.com; Back Bay T; map pp.74–75. Contemporary yet cosy, the *Chandler Inn* offers 56 petite rooms in a European-style hotel above the popular gay bar *Fritz* (see p.122); perks like satellite TV, wi-fi, iPod docks and marble bathrooms are included in the rates. **$175**

★ **Clarendon Square Inn** 198 W Brookline St ☎617 536 2229, ⓦclarendonsquare.com; Prudential T; map pp.74–75. Gorgeous three-room B&B on a residential side street with great attention paid to design details and indulgent extras like heated bathroom tiles, limestone floors, a private garden and a 24hr roof-deck hot tub. **$205**

★ **Encore B&B** 116 West Newton St ☎617 247 3425, ⓦencorebandb.com; Back Bay T; map pp.74–75. Get pampered at this cheerful three-room B&B located in a nineteenth-century Victorian town house. There's a sitting area or balcony in each guest room, wi-fi and continental breakfasts in the morning. **$140**

Gilded Lily 4 Claremont Park ☎617 877 3676, ⓦthegildedlily-boston.com; Massachusetts Ave T; map pp.74–75. Two elegant suites with a shared roof-deck are nicely sited in a terraced house with its original crown mouldings and marble mantles. **$200**

KENMORE SQUARE

Gryphon House 9 Bay State Rd ☎617 375 9003, ⓦinnboston.com; Kenmore T; map pp.74–75. This hotel-cum-B&B around the corner from Fenway has eight wonderfully appointed suites equipped with working gas fireplaces, cable TV, a handy DVD library, wi-fi, continental breakfast, and free parking (a huge plus in Boston). **$179**

HI-Boston at Fenway 575 Commonwealth Ave ☎617 267 8599, ⓦbostonhostel.org; Kenmore T; map pp.74–75. A summer-only hostel (June to mid-Aug) that functions as a BU dorm in winter months. Spacious rooms with a/c and en-suite baths, and laundry and internet access on site. Red Sox tickets available on a first-come, first-served basis. Dorms **$39**; Twin room **$99**

★ **Hotel Commonwealth** 500 Commonwealth Ave ☎617 933 5000, ⓦhotelcommonwealth.com; Kenmore T; map pp.74–75. Old-world charm paired with modern decor make this a welcome addition to Boston's luxury hotel scene, with nice touches like L'Occitane products, you'll-want-to-stay-in-bed-all-day linens and the *Eastern Standard* bar (see p.117). **$400**

Oasis Guest House 22 Edgerly Rd ☎617 267 2262, ⓦoasisgh.com; Symphony T; map pp.74–75. Sixteen comfortable, budget rooms, some with shared bathrooms, in a renovated brownstone near Symphony Hall. **$99**

BROOKLINE

Beech Tree Inn 83 Longwood Ave ☎617 277 1620, ⓦthebeechtreeinn.com; Coolidge Corner T. Just two blocks from the **T**, and around the corner from the restaurants and shops of Coolidge Corner, this welcoming Victorian B&B has ten brightly decorated rooms, scrumptious breakfasts and baked goods throughout the day. **$119**

Bertram Inn 92 Sewall Ave ☎617 566 2234, ⓦbertraminn.com; Coolidge Corner T. Sixteen luxurious rooms (and one junior suite), some with wood-burning fireplaces, in a 1907 tobacco merchant's home. They also run the *Samuel Sewall Inn*, just across the street. **$149**

On The Park B&B 88 Columbia St ☎617 277 0910, ⓦonthepark.net; Griggs St or Winchester St T. A little off the beaten path (but still near to Coolidge Corner), this 100-year-old home has three delightful guest rooms decked out in warm tones, with a nice mix of contemporary and antique furnishings. Free parking and full breakfasts in the morning. **$135**

CAMBRIDGE

Blue's Bed and Breakfast 82 Avon Hill St ☎617 354 6106, ⓦbluesbedandbreakfast.com; Porter or Harvard T; map pp.90–91. Two sunny, art-filled bedrooms in a cosy B&B that's one mile from Harvard Square and is blessed with welcoming, world-travelling innkeepers. The rate includes free wi-fi and great breakfasts. Singles **$110**, doubles **$140**

Cambridge Bed and Muffin 267 Putnam Ave ☎617 576 3166, ⓦbedandmuffin.com; Central or Harvard T; map pp.90–91. Just one block from the river and close to Harvard and Central Squares, this tranquil B&B has a friendly owner and endearing little rooms with polished pine floors. No en-suite bathrooms, and no TVs, but plenty of books and quiet. **$100**

Charles Hotel 1 Bennett St ☎617 864 1200, ⓦcharleshotel.com; Harvard T; map pp.90–91. A Harvard landmark with clean, bright rooms – some overlooking the Charles River – that come with an array of amenities: cable TV, Shaker furniture, access to the adjacent Le Pli Spa and even an ice skating rink in winter. There's also an excellent jazz club, *Regattabar* (see p.119), and two restaurants, *Henrietta's Table* and *Rialto*. **$299**

★ **Hotel Marlowe** 25 Edwin H Land Blvd ☎617 868 8000, ⓦhotelmarlowe.com; Lechmere or Kendall/MIT T; map pp.90–91. The decor at this hotel is cosy, plush and funky with leopard print rugs and bold furniture in the guest rooms. Pet friendly (they'll even order a cake for your pup), with an evening wine hour, fitness centre and complimentary kayak and bicycle rentals. **$200**

★ **Hotel Veritas** 1 Remington St ☎617 520 5000, ⓦhotelveritas.com; Harvard T; map pp.90–91. Thirty-room European-style hideaway putting the "ooh" into boutique hotel: fresh flowers, silk drapes, cocktails and access to the yoga studio across the street are all de rigueur. Classy concierges sport Brooks Brothers suits. **$269**

Inn at Harvard 1201 Massachusetts Ave ☎617 491 2222, ⓦhotelsinharvardsquare.com; Harvard T; map pp.90–91. Harvard University owns this red-brick hotel, set directly on the campus. Its four-storey atrium was inspired by a Venetian piazza, and its rooms, while small, have huge writing desks and look out onto the Square. **$179**

Irving House 24 Irving St ☎617 547 4600, ⓦirvinghouse.com; Harvard T; map pp.90–91. Sister facility: Harding House 288 Harvard St ☎617 876 2888, ⓦharding-house.com; Central T; map pp.90–91. Excellent, friendly, popular option near Harvard Square that falls somewhere between an inn, a hostel and a B&B. Laundry facilities (coin-operated), wi-fi, limited parking and generous breakfasts are included. Shared bathroom **$115**; private bathroom **$125**

Kendall Hotel 350 Main St ☎617 577 1300, ⓦkendallhotel.com; Kendall/MIT T; map pp.90–91. This independent hotel near MIT occupies a former 1894 fire station. Its 73 quaint rooms are country-chic with quilts and reproduction antiques; modern amenities include wi-fi, a full breakfast buffet and gym access. **$200**

EATING

Boston is loaded with places to **eat** – everything from cafés that serve full meals through bars and pubs that double as restaurants to higher-end dinner-only options. In most places, save certain areas of downtown, you won't have a problem finding somewhere to grab a **quick bite**. In addition to all the places listed below, many of Boston's bars (see p.114) offer food. Boston's **café** scene offers a range of places to hang out; there are a number of laptop-worthy spots around Back Bay's **Newbury Street** and over in the **South End**. Value is better in the **North End**, but the liveliest cafés are in **Cambridge**.

CAFÉS

Although the *Starbucks* invasion has done some real damage to the café scene in downtown, there are still lots of independent coffee shops in Boston or Cambridge where you can relax with a book and a hot drink. At many cafés, you can just as easily get an excellent full meal as you can a cup of coffee.

DOWNTOWN

Flat Black Coffee Company 50 Broad St ☎617 951 1440; State St T; map pp.48–49. This Australian-inspired place (in Australianese, a "flat black" is an espresso) offers up free-trade coffee to happy Financial District patrons. Not too cosy but there are excellent pastries for sale as well as free wi-fi. Mon–Fri 7am–5pm.

★ **Sip Café** 0 Post Office Square ☎617 338 3080; Downtown Crossing T; map pp.48–49. Sited in a glass house in the centre of Post Office Square, this café shines with its floor-to-ceiling windows, congenial staff, locavore sandwiches and lattes flourished with a fern or a loveheart. Mon–Fri 6.30am–6pm.

★ **Thinking Cup** 165 Tremont St ☎617 482 5555; Boylston T; map pp.48–49. Across from Boston Common, this java purveyor is serious about coffee: it's the first shop in the city to exclusively use Stumptown beans, lauded as the country's best. Mon–Thurs 7am–10pm, Fri–Sun till 11pm.

THE NORTH END

Boston Common Coffee Co. 97 Salem St ☎617 725 0040; Haymarket T; map p.64. In a neighbourhood of

historic espresso joints this mini-chain still stands out thanks to its quality beverages, sunny environs, window seating and fast, free wi-fi. Mon–Fri 6am–9pm, Sat & Sun 7am–9pm.

Caffè dello Sport 308 Hanover St ☎617 523 5063; Haymarket T; map p.64. A continuous stream of Rai Uno soccer matches is broadcast from the ceiling-mounted TV sets, making for an agreeable din amongst a very local crowd. Along with espresso, beer, wine and Sambuca are served. Cash only. Mon–Thurs 6am–11pm, Fri 6am–midnight, Sat 7am–midnight, Sun 7am–11.30pm.

BACK BAY

L'Aroma Café 85 Newbury St ☎617 412 4001; Copley T; map pp.74–75. This European-style café has friendly baristas, standout baked goods (try the "everything" cookie), and potent cappuccinos good for refuelling after browsing on Newbury St. There's outdoor seating, too, perfect for spying on the other shoppers. Mon–Fri 7am–8pm, Sat 7.30am–8pm, Sun 8am–8pm.

Wired Puppy 250 Newbury St ☎857 366 4655; Copley T; map pp.74–75. Free-trade beans are brewed by skilled baristas at this community-minded spot. Puppies are encouraged on the patio, and the café's free wi-fi invites keyboard clacking. Daily 6.30am–8pm.

THE SOUTH END

Berkeley Perk Café 69 Berkeley St ☎617 426 7375; Back Bay T; map pp.74–75. Ingenious sandwich options (vegetarians, in particular, love this place), plenty of

1

inviting booths and chairs, and big windows that peer onto an elegant tree-lined street make the *Berkeley Perk* tops for sipping coffee. Excellent baked goods as well. Cash only. Mon–Fri 6.30am–5pm, Sat 7.30am–5pm.

KENMORE SQUARE AND THE FENWAY

Espresso Royale Caffe 736 Commonwealth Ave ☎ 617 277 8737; Kenmore T; map pp.74–75. 44 Gainsborough St; Symphony T; map pp.74–75. 268 Newbury St; Hynes T; map pp.74–75. Kenmore's a little thin on coffee shops, but this funky little chain will do. Alongside traditional cups of java, original blends like a zesty orange cappuccino are served, and the shop's abstract wall paintings, free wi-fi and cosy seats are nice extras. *ERC* has an artsy little sister, *Pavement Coffeehouse* (1096 Boylston St). Mon–Fri 7am–9pm, Sat & Sun 8am–9pm.

BROOKLINE

★ **Japonaise Bakery & Café** 1020 Beacon St ☎ 617 566 7730; St. Mary's T.; 1032 Commonwealth Ave ☎ 617 738 7200; Babcock St T.; 1815 Massachusetts Ave, Cambridge ☎ 617 547 5531; Porter Square T. This life-changing café bakes exquisite French pastries with a Japanese twist. Try the An doughnut, a sugary puff filled with sweet red bean paste; the savoury curry doughnut – filled with beef, carrots and onions – is another one of the many worthy treats on offer. Mon–Thurs 8am–8pm, Fri & Sat till 8.30pm, Sun 8.30am–8pm.

CAMBRIDGE

★ **Algiers** 40 Brattle St ☎ 617 492 1557; Harvard T; map pp.90–91. There are few more atmospheric places in which to sip first-rate java than this North African café, popular with the artsy set. It has lots of cosy nooks, usually populated by Harvard bookworms powered by the signature mint coffee. Daily 8am–midnight.

Andala Coffee House 286 Franklin St ☎ 617 945 2212; Central T; map pp.90–91. Palestine-inspired brownstone café that's favoured for its inviting decor (think multicoloured lamps, Oriental rugs, hookahs and a sunny porch), Arabic coffee and authentic Mediterranean dishes like the "foole plate" – fava beans, lemon juice and parsley blended and served with warm bread. Mon–Fri 7am–11pm, Sat & Sun 8am–11pm.

Crema Café 27 Brattle St ☎ 617 876 2700; Harvard T; map pp.90–91. Popular café in the heart of Harvard Square whose clientele rally for the strong espresso drinks and standout sandwiches (don't miss the "maximillion": scrambled eggs with sweet potato, caramelized onion and rosemary goat cheese on an English muffin, $4.75). Mon–Fri 7am–9pm, Sat & Sun 8am–9pm.

★ **L.A. Burdick's** 52D Brattle St ☎ 617 491 4340; Harvard T; map pp.90–91. Simply breathing in the aromas at this fabulous *chocolaterie* is an exercise in indulgence: iced chocolate, chocolate mousse cake and little chocolate mice and penguins, all waiting to be consumed. Mon–Thurs 8am–9pm, Fri & Sat 8am–10pm, Sun 8am–9pm.

Tealuxe 0 Brattle St ☎ 617 441 0077; Harvard T; map pp.90–91. Now a chain, this is the original, and still a great spot. The place is smaller than a teacup, but they manage to stock over a hundred varieties of tea, including Crème de la Earl Grey, reported to taste like birthday cake. Mon–Thurs 8am–10pm, Fri till 11pm, Sat & Sun 8.30am–10pm.

★ **Voltage Coffee & Art** 295 3rd St ☎ 617 714 3974; Kendall/MIT T; map pp.90–91. MIT buzzes for *Voltage*, a combination slow-brew coffee shop and minimalist (white walls, exposed pipes) gallery space. Latte flavours have witty names and taste as good as their ingenious ingredients sound – the "Atticus Finch", made with vanilla and burnt sugar, does the Southern literary hero proud ($3.50). Free wi-fi, and lots of outlets. Mon–Fri 7am–7pm, Sat 9am–7pm.

RESTAURANTS

As far as the city's culinary landscape goes: Italian restaurants and bakeries cluster in the North End, mainly on Hanover and Salem streets; Chinatown packs in all types of Asian fare; and the trendiest restaurants, usually of the New American variety, tend to cluster in the South End and Back Bay. Cambridge dining life centres on Harvard, Inman and Central squares.

BOSTON COMMON AND DOWNTOWN CROSSING

★ **Chacarero** 101 Arch St ☎ 617 542 0392; Downtown Crossing T; map pp.48–49. Fabulous and fresh, the *chacarero* is a Chilean sandwich ($7) built on warm, soft bread that's filled with avocado, chicken or beef, green beans, Muenster cheese and hot sauce; there's a good veggie version ($5.70), too. Cash only. Mon–Fri 8am–4pm.

Falafel King 48 Winter St ☎ 617 338 8355; Park St T; map pp.48–49. You'll know you've found this gem, nestled within an otherwise unappealing food court, when you come across the long line of regulars waiting for cheap and tasty traditional shawarma sandwiches ($5.50; even better with pickles). Cash only. Mon–Fri 11am–8pm, Sat 11am–4pm.

Marliave 10 Bosworth St ☎ 617 422 0004; Park St T; map pp.48–49. Dating to 1875, this illustrious Boston landmark has been recently reborn by the owner of *Grotto* (see p.110). There's a bistro menu with tuna nicoise salad ($9) and steak frites ($19.50) served in an atmospheric nineteenth-century space. The second-floor dining room is entirely enclosed in glass and has great views, while the restaurant's basement level offers up coffee and home-made truffles. Downstairs: daily 11am–10pm. Upstairs: daily 5–10pm.

★ **No. 9 Park** 9 Park St ☎ 617 742 9991; Park St T; map pp.48–49. Well-loved Boston institution with serene green walls and plates busy with Southern French and Italian mains. A seven-course tasting menu ($112, with wine add $74) allows you to try almost everything. Sun & Mon 5–11pm, Tues–Sat till midnight.

Silvertone 69 Bromfield St ☏ 617 338 7887; Park St T; map pp.48–49. Nostalgia runs high at this bustling basement bar and eatery serving standout comfort foods like mashed potatoes and meatloaf ($12) and a super-cheesy macaroni cheese ($9). *Silvertone* also has cocktails and a good selection of beer on tap. Mon–Fri 11.30am–2am, Sat 6pm–2am.

FANEUIL HALL MARKETPLACE AND AROUND

Durgin-Park 340 Faneuil Hall Marketplace ☏ 617 227 2038; Government Center or State St T; map pp.48–49. A Boston landmark in operation since 1827, *Durgin-Park* has a no-frills Yankee atmosphere and staff known for their surly charm. Formerly hailed as a great place to go for iconic New England fare like roast beef, baked beans and warm Indian pudding, in recent years, the food quality has dipped; nowadays, it's best for drinks and ambience only. Mon–Sat 11.30am–10pm, Sun till 9pm.

Saus 33 Union St ☏ 617 248 8835; Government Center or State St T; map pp.48–49. A satisfying solution for cravings both savoury and sweet, *Saus* peddles pommes frites ($4.25) accompanied by fun dipping sauces (try the bacon parmesan, 75 cents) and Belgian waffles topped with toothsome pearl sugar ($3.75). They also make a mean poutine (fries topped with homemade gravy and cheese curds; $6.25) – easily the best in the city. Mon–Wed noon–10pm, Thurs till midnight, Fri & Sat till 2am, Sun till 8pm.

Union Oyster House 41 Union St ☏ 617 227 2750; Haymarket or State St T; map pp.48–49. The oldest continuously operating restaurant in America has two big claims to fame: King Louis-Philippe lived over the tavern during his youth, and the toothpick was first used here. The food is so-so, but the antiquated ambience is very cool; go for the raw bar offering superb shellfish. Sun–Thurs 11am–9.30pm, Fri & Sat till 10pm.

THE FINANCIAL DISTRICT

Casa Razdora 115 Water St ☏ 617 338 6700; State St T; map pp.48–49. This Italian newcomer is adding a much needed flavour kick to the Financial District's lunch scene. Everything, from the quattro stagioni pizza (mozzarella, artichokes and cold prosciutto; $16.99) to the tonno italiano panini (tuna in olive oil with red onion; $7.95) and the homemade pastas is made with love and pride. Mon & Tues 11am–3pm, Wed–Fri till 6pm.

Radius 8 High St ☏ 617 426 1234; South Station T; map pp.48–49. Housed in a former bank, this ultramodern French restaurant injects a dose of minimalist chic into the cautious Financial District. The tasty nouvelle cuisine is complemented by an extensive wine list, although some

would say that a trip here is wasted if you don't order (surprisingly) the burger ($19), considered to be the best in town. Mon–Thurs 11.30am–2.30pm & 5.30–10pm, Fri 11.30am–2.30pm & 5.30–11pm, Sat 5.30–11pm.

★ **Zo** 3 Center Plaza, no phone; Government Center T; map pp.48–49. A bit tricky to find (it's unfairly hidden behind the massive Center Plaza building), during weekday lunch hours *Zo* serves up Boston's best gyro sandwiches – pork, tomatoes, onion, home-made cucumber and yogurt sauce (tzatziki) on warm flatbread ($7). At press time, *Zo* was gearing up to open an additional location in Faneuil Hall, at 92 State St. Mon–Fri 11am–3pm.

THE THEATER DISTRICT

Finale Desserterie 1 Columbus Ave ☏ 617 423 3184; Arlington T; map pp.48–49. 30 Dunster St, Cambridge; ☏ 617 441 9797; Harvard T; map pp.48–49. Devilishly good desserts are the mainstay at this sweet emporium; the top-notch wines and cordials are a treat, too. There is another location in Brookline (1306 Beacon St; ☏ 617 232 3233; Coolidge Corner T). Mon & Sun 11am–11pm, Tues–Thurs till 11.30pm, Fri & Sat till midnight.

Jacob Wirth 31–37 Stuart St ☏ 617 338 8586; Boylston T; map pp.48–49. A German-themed Boston landmark, around since 1868; even if you don't like bratwurst washed down with a hearty lager, something is sure to please. There are sing-alongs on Fri. Mon 11.30am–9pm, Tues & Wed till 10pm, Thurs till midnight, Fri & Sat till 1am, Sun till 9pm.

Teatro 177 Tremont St ☏ 617 778 6841; Boylston T; map pp.48–49. Easy on the eyes, *Teatro*'s tables hold court beneath a striking vaulted ceiling – a holdover from its past life as a synagogue. Pre- and post-show patrons file in here for Italian fare, or simply antipasti ($7–14) and cocktails – be sure to order the calamari with lemon aioli ($14), considered to be some of the best squid in town. Although noisy, it's still a great date spot. Mon–Fri 5–10.30pm, Sat & Sun 5–11.30pm.

Troquet 140 Boylston St ☏ 617 695 9463; Boylston T; map pp.48–49. Breeze into *Troquet* and settle yourself in for an evening of romantic French fare overlooking Boston Common. The perfect conclusion to a night at the theatre, try the marinated beet salad with hazelnuts and goat cheese ($14), or the slow-roasted Vermont lamb with fig ($39). Hailed for its compelling wine list, *Troquet* is worth visiting for the bar alone; there's also an exquisite patisserie downstairs. Tues–Sat 5–10.30pm.

CHINATOWN

★ **Gourmet Dumpling House** 52 Beach St ☏ 617 338 6222; Chinatown T; map pp.48–49. Tables fill up quickly at this Chinese restaurant known for its dumplings (try the mini variety with pork; $6.50) and extensive, authentic menu. Daily 11am–1am.

1

Hei La Moon 88 Beach St ☎ 617 338 8813; Chinatown T; map pp.48–49. Just outside Chinatown proper, *Hei La Moon* is a local favourite for dim sum, with authentic dishes like shrimp *shumai* and barbecued pork buns served alongside more adventurous fare like chicken feet. Expect a long wait on Sunday. Daily 8.30am–11pm, dim sum till 3pm.

Les Zygomates 129 South St ☎ 617 542 5108; South Station T; map pp.48–49. Steps from South Station, this busy bistro pairs seasonal French dishes with any number of ambrosial wines (they carry more than a hundred international varieties alone). Try the roasted cod ($26) for dinner, and for dessert indulge in rhubarb and mango "crisp". Live jazz nightly. There are wine tastings on Tues at 7pm. Mon–Fri 11.30am–1am, Sat 6pm–1am.

New Saigon Sandwich 696 Washington St ☎ 617 542 6296; Chinatown T; map pp.48–49. Good Vietnamese *banh mi* sandwiches (pork paté, cold cuts, BBQ beef or tofu, served on toasted French bread; $3.25) washed down with bubble tea or an avocado shake. Daily 8.30am–6.30pm.

O Ya 9 East St ☎ 617 654 9900; South Station T; map pp.48–49. The portions here are teensy and the prices sky high, but patrons swoon over *O Ya's* exquisite sushi – try the bluefin tartare with ginger *kimchee* ($21) and roasted beet sashimi ($12). One of Boston's great foodie hangouts, in a sleek, intimate space. Tues–Thurs 5–9.30pm, Fri & Sat till 10pm.

Shabu-Zen 16 Tyler St ☎ 617 292 8828; Chinatown T; map pp.48–49. Test your culinary skills at this hot-pot eatery that lets you cook your own thinly sliced meats and veggies tableside in hot broth. Mains include rice or noodles, a side of raw vegetables and dessert; the chicken platter is $11. Mon–Wed 11am–midnight, Thurs & Sun till 1am, Fri & Sat till 2am.

South Street Diner 178 Kneeland St ☎ 617 350 0028; South Station T; map pp.48–49. The stools at the counter have been spinning since 1947. A late-night hangout, this Boston landmark is the place for burgers, sandwiches and the like. Daily 24hr.

★ **Taiwan Café** 34 Oxford St ☎ 617 426 8181; Chinatown T; map pp.48–49. Devotees swoon over this busy, authentic Taiwanese eatery serving mustard greens with edamame ($9), noodle soup with calamari and mushrooms ($5.75) and steamed pork buns done just right ($7). Cash only. Daily 11am–1am.

Xinh Xinh 7 Beach St ☎ 617 422 0501; Chinatown T; map pp.48–49. The ample "Best of Boston" awards in the window are the first clue that you're in for some superlative Vietnamese food. While the menu is huge, most people just come for the big bowls of piping-hot pho noodle soup ($6.50). Daily 10.30am–10pm.

THE WATERFRONT

The Barking Crab 88 Sleeper St, at the Northern Ave Bridge ☎ 617 426 CRAB; South Station T; map pp.48–49. This endearing, touristy seafood shack aims to please with its homey atmosphere (it looks like a circus tent) and unpretentious menu. Pretty much anything that can be pulled from the sea is served, but really, the food is passable – it's more about the prime waterfront location and ambience. Daily 11.30am–1am.

★ **flour bakery + café** 12 Farnsworth St ☎ 617 338 4333; South Station T; map pp.48–49. 190 Massachusetts Ave, Cambridge ☎ 617 225 2525; Central T; map pp.48–49. 1595 Washington St ☎ 617 267 4300; Massachusetts Ave T. An offshoot of a well-loved South End institution, this low-key café is tucked inside a brick warehouse around the corner from the Children's Museum. Bursting with fantastic pastries, sandwiches and salads, *flour* is best known for its life-changing BLTs and house-made raspberry seltzer (with carbonated water). Top off your meal with a home-made pop tart or peanut butter Oreo cookie. Mon–Fri 7am–7pm, Sat 8am–6pm, Sun 9am–4pm.

James Hook & Co. Lobsters 15–17 Northern Ave ☎ 617 423 5501; South Station T; map pp.48–49. Like a phoenix from the ashes (or a boiled lobster leaping from its shell), the seafood wholesaler James Hook survived its 2008 fire and is back to serving some of Boston's best lobster rolls (and at only $12, they're some of the city's best-priced, too). Very casual – you serve yourself at picnic tables sited by an I-93 exit ramp. Mon–Thurs & Sun 9am–5pm, Fri till 6pm, Sun till 2pm.

★ **Sportello** 348 Congress St ☎ 617 737 1234; South Station T; map pp.48–49. Step up to the counter and grab a stool at this contemporary take on a diner. Commandeered by Boston super chef Barbara Lynch (*No. 9 Park*, *Butcher Shop*), *Sportello* serves Italian-inspired dishes ranging from ricotta gnudi with black olives ($18) to a spicy tomato soup served with a grilled cheese sandwich ($9). There's also a neat little takeaway section filled with sandwiches, pastries and the like. Mon–Wed 10am–8pm, Thurs–Sat 10am–9pm, Sun 11am–5pm.

Yankee Lobster Fish Market 300 Northern Ave ☎ 617 345 9799; Silver Line Way Station T; map pp.48–49. Right by the water in the Seaport District, this casual seafood spot serves up fried fish and top-notch lobster rolls ($16) from a takeaway window. It's a hike from downtown – you might want to hop on the Silver Line. Good beer too. Mon–Thurs 10am–8pm, Fri & Sat till 9pm, Sun 11am–5pm.

THE NORTH END

Carmen 33 North Square ☎ 617 742 6421; Haymarket T; map p.64. With its intimate size, candlelit glow, and exposed brick walls *Carmen* is perhaps the North End's most romantic restaurant. No dessert, but their signature plates such as the roasted red beets with mint and ricotta ($6) or mains like the *crespelle bolognese* ($24) make sure you

NORTH END PASTRIES

One of the joys of a trip to the North End is the chance to partake of some of the city's best baked goods. While everyone else is lining up at *Mike's Pastry*, we suggest popping into *Maria's* for better pastries and a fraction of the crowds.

Bova's Bakery 134 Salem St ☎617 523 5601; Haymarket T. Satisfying all your late-night cravings, *Bova's* is a 24hr bakery that sells plain and chocolate cannoli, oven-fresh cakes and whoopie pies; famously cheap too, with most items around $5. Daily 24hr.

★ **Maria's Pastry** 46 Cross St ☎617 523 1196; Haymarket T. The best pastries in the North End, and inexplicably underrated. Maria's chocolate cannoli with fresh ricotta filling will change your life and make your day. Mon–Sat 7am–7pm, Sun 7am–5pm.

Mike's Pastry 300 Hanover St ☎617 742 3050; Haymarket T. Attended by locals and tourists alike, in

many ways *Mike's* is the North End. The full rainbow of pastries is represented here (eclairs, cannoli, marzipan, gelato et al), and lining up for one of their twine-wrapped boxes is a quintessential Boston experience. Mon & Tues 8am–10pm, Wed & Thurs till 10.30pm, Fri & Sat till 11.30pm, Sun till 10pm.

Modern Pastry 257 Hanover St ☎617 523 3783; Haymarket T. You can't miss *Modern's* glorious vintage sign out front, nor would you want to – inside is fresh torrone, cannoli and little marzipan fruits. Family-owned for eighty years. Sun–Thurs 8am–10pm, Fri till 11pm, Sat till midnight.

---

don't leave hungry. Tues 5.30–10pm, Wed & Thurs noon–3pm & 5.30–10pm, Fri & Sat noon–3pm & 5.30–11pm, Sun 3–10pm.

The Daily Catch 323 Hanover St ☎617 523 8567; Haymarket T; map p.64. Ocean-fresh seafood, notably calamari and shellfish – Sicilian-style, with loads of garlic – draws big lines to this tiny storefront restaurant. Cash only. Daily 11am–10pm.

★ **Galleria Umberto** 289 Hanover St ☎617 227 5709; Haymarket T; map p.64. North End nirvana. There are fewer than a dozen items on the menu, but the lines are consistently to the door for *Umberto's* perfect pizza slices and savoury *arancini* (fried and stuffed rice balls). Lunch only, and get there early as they almost always sell out. Cash only, very inexpensive. Mon–Sat 10.45am–2.30pm (or until they sell out).

Giacomo's 355 Hanover St ☎617 523 9026; Haymarket T; map p.64. Will you have to wait in line for an hour before getting a seat at this modest Italian restaurant? Probably. Do neighbourhood residents ever eat here? Not really. But that doesn't stop the crowds from coming, nor does it prevent *Giacomo* from turning out consistently lauded Italian classics like chicken marsala ($14) and fettucini with peas ($14). Cash only. There's another location in the South End at 431 Columbus Ave (☎617 536 5723). Mon–Thurs 4.30–10pm, Fri & Sat till 10.30pm, Sun 4–9.30pm.

La Summa Cucina Italiana 30 Fleet St ☎617 523 9503; Haymarket T; map p.64. If you simply want Italian food as good as your *nonna* used to make, without any stylish whistles or bells, then look no further than *La Summa*, named for the chef-owner's grandma, who taught her to cook while she was growing up right here in the North End. Their baked *manicotti* ($17) will make your day. Reservations recommended on weekends. Mon–Wed 4–10.30pm, Thurs–Sat noon–10.30pm, Sun noon–9.30pm.

Marco 253 Hanover St ☎617 742 1276; Haymarket T; map p.64. The hustle and bustle of Hanover Street fades away inside this secluded gem, perched on the second floor. The excellent (albeit pricey) Italian mains (such as chicken with sage and fontina; $28) are served on rustic wooden tabletops amid antique ceiling beams and exposed brick. Great date spot. Tues–Thurs 5–10pm, Fri & Sat till 11pm, Sun 4–9.30pm.

★ **Neptune Oyster** 63 Salem St ☎617 742 3474; Haymarket T; map p.64. Snazzy little raw bar filled with fans who swear by the fantastic shucked shellfish and best-in-town lobster rolls (served hot with butter or cold with mayo; $25). Mon–Fri 11.30am–10.30pm, Sat & Sun till 11.30pm.

★ **Pizzeria Regina** 111/2 Thacher St ☎617 227 0765; Haymarket T; map p.64. Visit this North End legend for tasty, cheap pizza, served in a neighbourhood feed station where the wooden booths haven't budged since the 1920s. Don't be fooled by chains bearing the *Regina* label in other parts of town – this is the original, vastly superior location. Be prepared for a wait. Mon–Thurs 11am–11.30pm, Fri & Sat 11.30am–12.30am, Sun till 11.30pm.

Pomodoro 319 Hanover St ☎617 367 4348; Haymarket T; map p.64. There are only a handful of tables at this North End treasure, but they're consistently filled with diners oohing and ahhing over the *fra diavolo* with shellfish ($23), calamari ($12) and salmon with arugula ($24). *Pomodoro's* intimate setting may appeal to couples, but the free tiramisu that often concludes meals thrills patrons from far and wide. Reservations recommended. Cash only. Mon–Fri 4–11pm, Sat 11am–11pm, Sun noon–10pm.

Taranta 210 Hanover St ☎617 720 0052; Haymarket T; map p.64. *Taranta* is a mix of Italian and Peruvian flavours, which translates into pork chops with sugar cane and giant Peruvian corn ($34) and pan-roasted mussels with

1

pancetta ($14). Located on busy Hanover Street, *Taranta* remains a bit of a secret among locals, although the folks who go once usually wind up becoming regulars. Daily 5.30–10pm.

★ **Volle Nolle** 351 Hanover St ☎617 523 0003; Haymarket T; map p.64. Chic little sandwich eatery with a handful of aluminium tables, a chalkboard menu and standout fillings, such as pesto chicken with prosciutto and fresh mozzarella ($8.95). The charismatic owner also stocks her counter with exceptional cookies and coffee. Cash only. Mon–Sat 11am–4pm.

CHARLESTOWN

Navy Yard Bistro & Wine Bar 1st Ave, at 6th St ☎617 242 0036; Inner Harbor ferry to Navy Yard (see p.65) or Community College T. Close to the USS *Constitution*, but a bit tricky to find, this neighbourhood restaurant nicely straddles the line between elegance and approachability. New American favourites like pork chops ($23) and roasted chicken with asparagus ($16.50) are served from the open kitchen amid exposed brick walls and exceptional glasses of wine. Daily 5pm–close.

Sorelle Bakery and Café 100 City Square (☎617 242 5980) and 1 Monument Ave (☎617 242 2125); Inner Harbor ferry to Navy Yard (see p.65) or Community College T. Two locations: one a welcome oasis after crossing the Charlestown Bridge, the other more tucked away, with a delightful hidden patio. Both have stellar muffins and cookies, plus lemonade and other lunch fare. Free wi-fi. 100 City Square: Mon–Fri 7am–6pm, Sat & Sun 8am–6pm; 1 Monument Ave: Mon–Fri 6.30am–3pm, Sat & Sun 8am–3pm.

Zume's 223 Main St ☎617 242 0038; Inner Harbor ferry to Navy Yard (see p.65) or Community College T. A bit out of the way from Charlestown's major sights, *Zume's* ("Zoo-mees") offers knockout doughnuts, great sandwiches (try the Greek chicken wrap with feta cheese and cucumber; $7.50), espresso drinks and free wi-fi. Mon–Fri 6am–6pm, Sat & Sun 7am–6pm.

BEACON HILL

Beacon Hill Bistro 25 Charles St, in the Beacon Hill Hotel ☎617 723 7575; Charles/MGH T; map pp.48–49. Sleek New American and French bistro with a high-end feel. Steak frites with herb and butter sauce ($29) share counter space with cod, clams and potato fondant ($26); breakfast is traditional American. They also have a gorgeous bar – go for the blood-orange Martinis and killer Mojitos. Mon–Fri 7am–11pm, Sat 7.30am–11pm, Sun till 10pm.

Grotto 37 Bowdoin St ☎617 227 3434; Government Center T; map pp.48–49. Romance is on the menu at this brick-walled, subterranean Italian spot close to Government Center. The petite dining room is suited for close conversation, and *Grotto*'s hearty offerings (such as fontina fondue with truffle oil; $10) are sure to please your date. Mon–Fri 11.30am–3pm & 5–10pm, Sat & Sun 5–10pm.

Paramount 44 Charles St ☎617 720 1152; Charles/MGH T; map pp.48–49. The Hill's neighbourhood diner serves Belgian waffles ($6) and omelettes ($5.50–8.50) to brunch regulars by day, and American standards like hamburgers ($12) and steak tips (grilled cuts of sirloin; $19) by night. Expect long waits on weekends. Mon–Thurs 7am–10pm, Fri 7am–11pm, Sat 8am–11pm, Sun 8am–10pm.

Scampo 215 Charles St (in the Liberty Hotel) ☎617 536 2100; Charles/MGH T; map pp.48–49. Set in the *Liberty Hotel* (see p.101), a sprawling, cruciform-shaped 1851 prison that was re-fashioned in 2007 as a luxury hotel, *Scampo* is an Italian restaurant helmed by star chef Lydia Shire. The imaginative menu includes a "mozzarella bar", eight different riffs on caprese salad ($14–27), handmade pasta dishes and creative pizzas. Mon–Wed & Sun 11.30am–midnight, Thurs–Sat till 1am.

Upper Crust 20 Charles St ☎617 723 9600; Charles/MGH T; map pp.48–49. Popular, thin-crust pizza joint with fresh and tasty offerings; there's generally a slice of the day (such as spinach with pesto and tomato; $3). There are other locations at 222 Newbury St (☎617 262 0090; Copley T), 683 Tremont St (☎617 927 0090; Massachusetts Ave T; map pp.74–75) and 49b Brattle St, Cambridge (☎617 497 4111; Harvard T; map pp.90–91). Mon–Wed & Sun 11am–10pm, Thurs till 10.30pm, Fri & Sat till 11pm.

THE WEST END

Café Rustico 85 Canal St ☎617 742 8770; North Station T; map pp.48–49. An inexpensive hole-in-the-wall lunch spot that's a welcome break from the West End's many sports bars. Rustico's regulars rave about the gnocchi with fresh tomatoes and basil ($9.75), the tonno (tuna) salad ($6.75), and anything made with their peerless tomato cream sauce. Cash only. Mon–Fri 11am–6pm.

Whole Foods 181 Cambridge St ☎617 723 0004; Bowdoin T; map pp.48–49. This supermarket franchise pops up like a foodie oasis on a strip that's low on good eateries. Inside, you'll find Boston's best salad bar, and casual tables standing ready for diners. Daily 8am–10pm.

BACK BAY

Atlantic Fish Company 761 Boylston St ☎617 267 4000; Copley T; map pp.74–75. Smack in the middle of busy Boylston St, the wooden dining room of this upmarket seafood restaurant feels like it was lifted from the belly of a yacht. The menu changes daily according to what's fresh; mains which cost about $28 for dinner, are stellar. Mon–Thurs & Sun 11.30am–11pm, Fri & Sat till midnight.

Burritos and Tacos to Go! 145 Dartmouth St (in the Back Bay T station), no phone; Back Bay T; map pp.74–75. This quick Mexican takeaway stand, located inside Back Bay station, serves cheap and exceptionally tasty burritos ($3.75) and tacos ($2.25) to grateful straphangers and area workers. Mon–Fri 11.30am–7pm.

Café Jaffa 48 Gloucester St ☎617 536 0230; Hynes T; map pp.74–75. Some of the city's best falafel and other Middle Eastern staples are served in this cool, inviting space with polished wood floors. A solid, inexpensive option that's just one block off of Newbury Street. Mon–Thurs 11am–10.30pm, Fri & Sat till 11pm, Sun noon–10pm.

Douzo 131 Dartmouth St ☎617 859 8886; Back Bay T; map pp.74–75. Sexy, modern decor coupled with standout sushi makes this a great new option along the Back Bay-South End border. The service can be touch and go, but the food is consistently top-notch. Daily 11.30am–3pm & 4.30pm–midnight.

Legal Sea Foods 26 Park Plaza ☎617 426 4444; Arlington T; map pp.74–75. 100 Huntington Ave, Level two, Copley Place ☎617 266 7775; Copley T; map pp.74–75. 800 Boylston St, Prudential Center ☎617 266 6800; Prudential T; map pp.74–75. 255 State St ☎617 742 5300; Aquarium T; map pp.74–75; 5 Cambridge Center ☎617 864 3400; Kendall/MIT T; map pp.74–75. The *Starbucks* of the sea: it seems you can't turn a corner in Boston without encountering one of these ubiquitous eateries. As they claim, the seafood is fresh and the clam chowder is loved by many, but the chain feel of the place may shiver your timbers. Mon–Thurs 11.30am–11pm, Fri & Sat till midnight, Sun noon–11pm.

L'Espalier 774 Boylston St ☎617 262 3023; Copley T; map pp.74–75. A ravishing French restaurant now happily situated in its new location adjacent to the *Mandarin Oriental*. A great date spot, *L'Espalier* serves a first-rate seasonal menu; the dinner *prix fixe* runs to a steep $82. Mon–Fri 11.30am–2.30pm & 5.30–10.30pm, Sat & Sun noon–1.45pm &: 5.30–10.30pm; Tea: Sat & Sun 2–3.30pm.

★ **Mike & Patty's** 12 Church St ☎617 423 3447; Arlington T; map pp.74–75. Located in Bay Village, a residential satellite of Back Bay, *Mike & Patty's* is a teensy breakfast and lunch spot serving the best sandwiches in Boston. While it's not on the road to any major sights, those who make the trek out will feel amply rewarded by *M&P's* fried green tomato BLT ($7.25) and grilled banana sandwich with cinnamon honey butter ($6.50). Wed–Fri 7.30am–3pm, Sat 8am–2pm, Sun 9am–2pm.

Mistral 223 Columbus Ave ☎617 867 9300; Arlington T; map pp.74–75. Stepping into *Mistral's* fanciful dining room is like walking into a fairy-tale creation – all arched floor-to-ceiling windows, small potted trees, high ceilings and slender wire chandeliers. Its acclaimed French menu

features Mediterranean dishes such as Atlantic swordfish with aubergine ($33). Mon–Thurs 5.30–10pm, Fri & Sat 5.30–11pm, Sun 10.30am–2pm & 5.30–9.30pm.

The Other Side Cosmic Café 407 Newbury St ☎617 536 8437; Hynes T; map pp.74–75. This ultra-casual hipster hangout on "the other side" of Newbury Street (it's across Mass Ave) offers gourmet sandwiches, creative green salads and fresh juices. They also have pitchers of quality beer. Mon–Thurs 11.30am–midnight, Fri 11.30am–1am, Sat 10am–1am, Sun 10am–midnight.

Parish Café & Bar 361 Boylston St ☎617 247 4777; Arlington T; map pp.74–75. The ambience isn't much, but who cares when you're eating one of the best sandwiches in Boston? *Parish Café* formed when a number of acclaimed Boston chefs put their heads together and created a fancy rotating sandwich menu, including Ming Tsai's "Blue Ginger" (rare tuna with teriyaki glaze and avocado wasabi aioli; $17.95). Mon–Sat 11.30am–2am, Sun noon–2am.

★ **Trident Booksellers & Café** 338 Newbury St ☎617 267 8688; Hynes T; map pp.74–75. Great little bookshop/café (see p.123), with a "perpetual breakfast", and tasty, vegetarian-friendly lunches and dinners. Pick up an obscure magazine and read it while gazing onto Newbury Street. Free wi-fi. Daily 8am–midnight.

Via Matta 79 Park Plaza ☎617 422 0008; Arlington T; map pp.74–75. This romantic Italian restaurant beckons patrons from the Theater District and offers a great range of dining environs: alfresco on the patio, inside the bright white dining room or even smack in the centre of the animated kitchen. The range of seating and the seasonal menu guarantee a different experience every visit. Mon–Fri 11.30am–midnight, Sat 5pm–1am.

THE SOUTH END

B & G Oysters 550 Tremont St ☎617 423 0550; Back Bay T; map pp.74–75. If you can manage to get a table at this tiny, pearlescent restaurant, you're in luck. The oysters (from $2.55 each) are simply the best Boston has to offer. Mon 11.30am–10pm, Tues–Fri 11.30am–11pm, Sat noon–11pm, Sun noon–10pm.

Butcher Shop 552 Tremont St ☎617 423 4800; Back Bay T; map pp.74–75. Not your grandpa's butcher shop, this sleek offspring of the Barbara Lynch empire (the woman behind *B&G Oysters* and *No. 9 Park*) offers small plates set with juicy fruits and fancy charcuterie. There's also a classy wine bar and gourmet hot dogs. An intimate neighbourhood meeting spot. Mon & Sun 11am–11pm, Tues–Sat till midnight.

Charlie's Sandwich Shoppe 429 Columbus Ave ☎617 536 7669; Back Bay T; map pp.74–75. This historic little hole-in-the-wall diner (established in 1927) was one of the first racially integrated restaurants in Boston. Standouts include the decadent banana and pecan griddlecakes and their justly famous turkey hash. Cash only, and beware – no customer toilets. Mon–Fri 6am–2.30pm, Sat 7.30am–1pm.

Franklin Café 278 Shawmut Ave ❶ 617 350 0010; Back Bay T; map pp.74–75. New American cuisine at very reasonable prices, enjoyed by a hip, unpretentious clientele. There are only eleven tables, so be prepared to wait at the bar for at least two martinis. Daily 5pm–2am.

Gaslight, Brasserie du Coin 560 Harrison Ave ❶ 617 422 0224; Broadway T; map pp.74–75. This buzzing brasserie has an authentically French white-tile-and-mirror interior. It's fun for brunch and dinner sees classic dishes like steak frites ($19.75) and steamed mussels ($16.75). Very popular – reservations recommended. Mon–Fri 5pm–1.30am, Sat & Sun 10am–3pm & 5pm–1.30am.

★ **Myers + Chang** 1145 Washington St ❶ 617 542 5200; Broadway T; map pp.74–75. This "indie diner" with an open kitchen serves Asian fusion dishes, such as braised short-rib tacos with pear ($13), nasi goreng (Indonesian fried rice with pork, pineapple and fried egg; $14) and an awesome scorpion bowl for two ($16). Bonus: your bill comes with coconut macaroons. Mon–Wed & Sun 11.30am–10pm, Thurs–Sat till 11pm. Dim sum Sat & Sun till 5.30pm.

Picco 513 Tremont St ❶ 617 927 0066; Back Bay T; map pp.74–75. Right in the heart of the South End, *Picco* serves outstanding pizza and home-made ice cream at very fair prices (a real boon in this neighbourhood of posh bistros). A red pepper, arugula and goat cheese pie will set you back $13.75. Sun–Wed 11am–10pm, Thurs–Sat 11am–11pm.

South End Buttery Bistro & Bar 314 Shawmut Ave ❶ 617 482 1015; Back Bay T; map pp.74–75. Impossible to resist, this adorable neighbourhood café (now with an adjacent bistro) offers egg sandwiches on home-made biscuits (fluffy, buttery rolls), home-made soups and sandwiches, cappuccinos and terrific cupcakes named for the owner's dogs. Mon–Wed & Sun 6.30am–10pm, Thurs–Sat till 11pm.

Stella 1525 Washington St ❶ 617 247 7747; Back Bay T; map pp.74–75. Primo Italian fare, such as mouthwatering parmesan arancini balls ($8) and home-made gnocchi ($19) served in a beautiful white interior. Nice outdoor seating in summer, and you can catch the equally good late-night menu from 11pm–1.30am. Mon–Sat 4pm–2am, Sun 10am–2am; Stella Café daily 7am–3pm.

★ **Toro** 1704 Washington St ❶ 617 536 4300; Back Bay T; map pp.74–75. We're crazy about this hip tapas bar that shakes up sassafras mojitos ($10) and dishes up mouthwatering octopus *ceviche* ($9) and grilled corn with queso ($8). Waiting times can be ridiculous on weekend nights (no reservations are taken for dinner); get there as

early as possible. Mon–Thurs noon–3pm & 5.30pm–midnight, Fri noon–3pm & 5.30pm–1am, Sun 10.30am–2.30pm & 4.30pm–midnight.

KENMORE SQUARE AND THE FENWAY

India Quality 484 Commonwealth Ave ❶ 617 267 4499; Kenmore T; map pp.74–75. The decor may be shabby, but it's the spicy Indian food – considered to be some of the best in town – and great beer selection that keeps 'em coming back to this affordable restaurant. Lunch: daily 11.30am–3pm; Dinner: Mon–Fri 5–11pm, Sat & Sun 11.30am–11pm.

La Verdad Taqueria 1 Lansdowne St ❶ 617 421 9595; Kenmore T; map pp.74–75. This Ken Oringer hangout – he also also owns *Toro* (see below) – in the shadow of Fenway Park is perfect for watching a Red Sox game or for setting up your big night after with a taco, a beer and a shot ($5 special). Mon–Thurs & Sun 11am–1am, Fri & Sat till 2am.

Petit Robert Bistro 468 Commonwealth Ave ❶ 617 375 0699; Kenmore T; map pp.74–75. 101 Arch St ❶ 617 737 1777; Downtown Crossing T; map pp.48–49. This French bistro boasts a chalkboard menu that's been priced for the little guy; mains, such as *coq au vin* with buttered noodles, cost $16–22. And one in the South End at 480 Columbus Ave (❶ 617 867 0600; Back Bay T). Daily 11am–11pm.

Trattoria Toscana 130 Jersey St ❶ 617 247 9508; Fenway or Museum T; map pp.74–75. Locals are cuckoo for this pricey Tuscan favourite, regaled for its *antipasti*, home-made pasta and lemon-drop ice cream. Great for a romantic dinner after museum hopping in the Fenway. Seating is tight. Mon–Sat 5–10pm.

BROOKLINE

Anna's Taqueria 1412 Beacon St ❶ 617 739 7300; Coolidge Corner T. Exceptional tacos, burritos and *quesadillas* are the only things on the menu at this extremely cheap Mexican eatery – but they're so good branches have opened at 446 Harvard St (Coolidge Corner T), in Beacon Hill, 242 Cambridge St (Charles/MGH T; map pp.48–49), and in Cambridge at 822 Somerville Ave (Porter T; map pp.90–91) and 84 Mass Ave (Central T; map pp.90–91). Mon–Thurs 10am–11pm, Fri–Sun 7am–11pm.

La Morra 48 Boylston St ❶ 617 739 0007; Brookline Village T. People come from all over Boston to savour this Italian gem's clam risotto ($23), seasonal *antipasti* ($9–11) and romantic, exposed brick ambience. Good for couples, or just to catch up with friends; there are nightly four-course $35 *prix fixe* menus. Mon–Thurs 5.30–10pm, Fri & Sat 5.30–10.30pm, Sun 5–9pm.

JAMAICA PLAIN

El Oriental de Cuba 416 Centre St ❶ 617 524 6464; Green St T. Popular, inexpensive, casual Cuban joint with an extensive menu and crowd-pleasing favourites like

BOSTON SPEED DOG

Boston Speed Dog 42 Newmarket Square, Roxbury (see p.87) ☎617 839 0102; Andrew Square T. Road trip aficionados will want to track down this unassuming food truck that's cranked out the city's best hot dogs since 1975. Located in a dusty, semi-sketchy part of Roxbury, *Speed*'s humongous dogs ($7) are marinated in apple cider and brown sugar, freshly grilled, stuffed into giant toasted buns, and topped with sweet Vidalia onions and special sauce. *Speed*'s has variable hours; if it's raining, call to make sure they're open, and get there early to avoid a long wait or a dog shortage. Mon–Fri 9.30am–4pm, Sat 11am–3pm.

beans, rice and plantains ($8.95), pressed Cuban sandwiches ($7.95) and paella ($17.95). Mon–Thurs 8am–9pm, Fri & Sat till 10pm, Sun till 8pm.

★ **Ten Tables** 597 Centre St ☎617 524 8810; Green St T. 5 Craigie Circle, Cambridge ☎617 576 5444; Harvard T; map pp.74–75. This inviting restaurant was designed to feel like an intimate dinner party – there really are only ten tables – although they've recently added a candlelit bar. The seasonal French and American fare ($19–27), such as local pan-seared blue fish with polenta cakes ($23), is great for wooing a beloved. Reservations recommended. Mon–Thurs 5.30–10pm, Fri & Sat 5.30–11.30pm, Sun 3–10pm.

CAMBRIDGE: HARVARD SQUARE AND AROUND

★ **Bartley's Burger Cottage** 1246 Massachusetts Ave ☎617 354 6559; Harvard T; map pp.74–75. A must-visit in Cambridge since 1960. Artery-clogging joy: Boston's best burgers, washed down with raspberry lime rickeys. The names of the dishes poke fun at politicians of the hour, and noisy staff shout out your order. Good veggie burgers, too. Sometimes they close on a whim. Cash only. Mon–Sat 11am–9pm.

Cambridge 1 27 Church St ☎617 576 1111; Harvard T; map pp.74–75. Sleek, thin-crust pizza spot in the heart of Harvard Square, which derives its name from the early 1900s brick firehouse in which it's sited. Mon–Thurs & Sun 11.30am–midnight, Fri & Sat till 1am.

★ **Darwin's Ltd** 148 Mt Auburn St (☎617 354 5233) and 1629 Cambridge St (☎617 491 2999); both Harvard T; map pp.74–75. Two locations, both offering wonderfully inventive sandwich combinations (roast beef, sprouts and apple slices) on freshly baked bread. A Harvard institution. Cash only. Mon–Sat 6.30am–9pm, Sun 7am–9pm.

Veggie Planet 47 Palmer St ☎617 661 1513; Harvard T; map pp.74–75. This casual eatery underneath *Passim* (see p.119) has creative vegetarian and vegan pizzas, soups and salads. Try the vegan peanut curry (tofu, broccoli, peanuts and Thai peanut curry sauce; $11.15) on their slow-rise organic dough. Daily 11.30am–10.30pm.

CAMBRIDGE: CENTRAL SQUARE AND AROUND

Alive & Kicking Lobsters 269 Putnam Ave ☎617 876 0451; Central T; map pp.74–75. Tricky to find, but it's worth the drive to this little fishmonger shack that's heavy on New England charm. *A&K* crafts bulging lobster sandwiches on slices of toasted bread instead of the traditional hot dog bun ($13.95 with chips). Food is served from a takeaway counter and eaten on limited outdoor picnic tables. Mon–Sat 11am–6pm, Sun noon–4pm.

Central Kitchen 567 Massachusetts Ave ☎617 491 5599; Central T; map pp.74–75. Hip bistro with a delightful chalkboard menu offering European classics (*moules frites*; $12) and contemporary American twists (mushroom ragout with ricotta dumplings; $17) in an intimate, stylish setting. Mon–Wed 5.30pm–1am, Thurs–Sat 5.30pm–2am.

★ **Craigie on Main** 853 Main St ☎617 497 5511; Central T; map pp.74–75. This family-owned, French-inspired favourite, known for its "refined rusticity", creates new menus daily based on what's available (mains begin at $22). Patrons are treated like family, and the place is perpetually packed. Reservations a must. Tues–Sat 5.30pm–midnight, Sun 10.30am–1.30pm & 5.30pm–midnight.

★ **Toscanini's** 899 Main St ☎617 491 5877; Central T; map pp.74–75. The inventive, ever-changing ice cream list here includes original flavours like "chocolate sluggo", which mixes light- and dark-chocolate ice cream, ganache, chocolate chips, almonds and Hydrox cookies. Great coffee as well. Mon–Fri 8am–11pm, Sat & Sun 9am–11pm.

CAMBRIDGE: INMAN SQUARE AND AROUND

All-Star Sandwich Bar 1245 Cambridge St ☎617 868 3065; Central T; map pp.90–91. A "wrap-free zone", the menu at this sandwich utopia crosses many borders – cubanos, muffalettas and reubens are all well represented. The meatloaf meltdown is a spicy standby ($8.95); they also make good chilli ($3.95) and fries "from hell" ($4.95). Mon–Thurs 11am–9pm, Fri & Sat till 10pm, Sun till 8pm.

★ **Christina's Homemade Ice Cream** 1255 Cambridge St ☎617 492 7021; Harvard or Central T; map pp.90–91. Inspiring well-deserved reverence among a legion of fans. People endure rush hour traffic to get their hands on a scoop of Christina's adzuki bean, burnt sugar or honey lavender flavours – ingredients procured from the owner's spice shop right next door. Daily 11am–10.30pm.

1

★ **East Coast Grill** 1271 Cambridge St ☎ 617 491 6568; Harvard or Central T; map pp.90–91. A festive and funky atmosphere – think *Miami Vice* – in which to enjoy fresh seafood and Caribbean side dishes such as grilled avocado, pineapple salsa and fried plantains. The Sunday serve-yourself Bloody Mary bar is reason enough to visit, and there's a raw bar tucked into one corner. Mon–Thurs 5.30–10pm, Fri & Sat 5.30–10.30pm, Sun 11am–2.30pm & 5.30–10pm.

★ **Oleana** 134 Hampshire St ☎ 617 661 0505; Central T; map pp.90–91. If you can, secure a table on the wisteria-laden patio, where you can linger over lamb with garlicky yogurt ($26) and warm hummus with tomato ($5). Be sure to save room for the Baked Alaska, served with coconut ice cream and passion fruit-caramel sauce ($14). Reservations recommended. Thurs & Sun 5.30–10pm, Fri & Sat till 11pm.

Punjabi Dhaba 225 Hampshire St ☎ 617 547 8272; Central T; map pp.90–91. This no-frills Indian eatery sparks almost maniacal devotion among its regulars, who trek across Cambridge for quick and cheap *palak paneer* and chicken *tikka masala*. Daily noon–midnight.

Tupelo 1193 Cambridge St ☎ 617 868 0004; Central T; map pp.90–91. Leave your diet at the door for *Tupelo's* "comfort food with a Southern drawl" – Cajun gumbo with andouille sausage, fried oysters with remoulade, cheddar grits, biscuits and sausage gravy – you name it, they've got it, and they do it good. Hard as it may be, try and save room for the pecan pie. Tues–Sat 5–10pm, Sun 11am–3pm.

CAMBRIDGE: MIT AND AROUND

Emma's Pizza 40 Hampshire St ☎ 617 864 8534; Kendall/MIT T; map pp.90–91. This tasty pizzeria has signature thin pies and slices featuring fun toppings like roasted sweet potatoes and ricotta. Consistently listed at or near the top of "best in Boston" lists. Mon–Fri 11.30am–10pm, Sat 4–10pm, Sun 3–9pm.

★ **Friendly Toast** 1 Kendall Square ☎ 617 621 1200; Kendall/MIT T; map pp.90–91. A delightful riot of '50s kitsch, bright green walls and vinyl seating, this breakfast-all-day funhouse serves pumpkin pancakes with whipped cream ($8) and "King Cakes" in honour of Elvis (banana and chocolate-chip pancakes with peanut butter in between; $10.50). Expect a long wait on weekends. Mon–Tues & Sun 8am–10pm, Wed–Sat till 11am.

★ **Hungry Mother** 233 Cardinal Medeiros Ave ☎ 617 499 0090; Kendall/MIT T; map pp.90–91. This south of the Mason-Dixon line special-occasion spot serves boiled peanut appetizers ($4), cornmeal catfish mains ($19) and cocktails shaken into mason jars. Come dessert, you'll be saying an "Amen" to the Mother. Very popular; reservations recommended. Tues–Sun 5pm–midnight.

★ **Salts** 798 Main St ☎ 617 876 8444; Kendall/MIT T; map pp.90–91. Foodies are awhirl with *Salts'* skill in merging local ingredients with exquisite French presentation and technique. The glazed duck for two ($68) is incredibly popular – you practically need to order it in advance (as many patrons do). Tues–Sat 6–10pm.

EAST CAMBRIDGE

Helmand 143 1st St ☎ 617 492 4646; Lechmere T; map pp.90–91. The interior won't win any style awards, but this treasured Afghani dinner spot is favoured by everyone from Harvard students to families and couples on a first date. Don't miss the *kaddo* (baked pumpkin seasoned with sugar and served on yogurt garlic sauce; $7.50). Mon–Thurs & Sun 5–10pm, Fri & Sat till 11pm.

DRINKING

Despite – or perhaps because of – the lingering Puritan anti-fun ethic that pervades Boston, people here seem to **drink** more than in most other American cities. The most prevalent place to nurse a pint is the **Irish pub**, of which there are high concentrations in the **West End** and downtown around **Quincy Market**. More high end are the bars and lounges of **Back Bay**, along Newbury and Boylston streets. The rest of the city's neighbourhood bars, pick-up joints, and hotspots are differentiated by their crowds: **Beacon Hill** tends to be older and a bit stuffy; **downtown**, mainly around Quincy Market and the Theater District, draws a healthy mix of tourists and locals; while **Kenmore Square** and **Cambridge** are fairly student-orientated. **Bars** in Boston stop serving at 2am (at the latest), and most strictly enforce the drinking-age minimum of 21 – you should plan on carrying **ID** even if you're well over age.

DOWNTOWN

Biddy Early's 141 Pearl St ☎ 617 654 9944; South Station T; map pp.48–49. If there's such a thing as a "classy dive", this is it; cheap beer (PBR is $1.50), inexpensive and surprisingly tasty bar food, colourful regulars, darts, a juke box and a happy after-work crowd. Mon–Fri 10am–2am, Sat 11am–2am.

JJ Foley's 21 Kingston St ☎ 617 695 2529; Downtown Crossing T; map pp.48–49. Attended by bike messengers and businessmen during the day, this little Irish gem plays host to a casual scene of locals and students by night. Barkeeps are friendly and welcoming, and the reliable pub food is served in rustic wooden booths. Good jukebox. Daily 10am–2am.

Woodward 1 Court St, in the Ames Hotel ☎ 617 979 8200; State St T; map pp.48–49. Located inside the fashionable *Ames Hotel* (see p.100), *Woodward* has two happening bars. The one on the second floor has more pronounced decor: along the dining room walls ephemera – from an old measuring cup to a vintage globe – is delicately displayed underneath glass cubes. Join the other pretty young things at an enveloping leather banquette, or if it's warm, head outside to the first-floor patio. Mon–Wed 6.30am–midnight, Thurs & Fri till 2am, Sat 8am–2am, Sun till midnight.

THE WATERFRONT

★ **Drink** 348 Congress St ☎617 695 1806; South Station T; map pp.48–49. A zigzagging bar and painstakingly constructed cocktails (they even chip their own ice) from three different centuries (the 1800s to today) are highlights at this subterranean hotspot. Don't be fooled by the limited cocktail menu – expert bartenders/therapists will lend an ear to your drinking desires and concoct the perfect customized beverage. It's a bit of a hike from downtown; take a taxi. Expect a long wait on weekends. Daily 4pm–1am.

Lucky's 355 Congress St ☎617 357 5825; South Station T; map pp.48–49. Over the water in the Fort Point neighbourhood, and quite a walk from the subway, this underground lounge is one of Boston's best-kept secrets – mainly because it's off the beaten path (there's no sign out front). Inside is a '50s pad complete with martini-swilling patrons and live jazz; on Sundays, Frank Sinatra impersonators get the locals swinging. Mon–Fri 11am–2am, Sat & Sun 10am–2am.

THE NORTH END

Caffé Vittoria 290-296 Hanover St ☎617 227 7606; Haymarket T; map p.64. A Boston institution, the *Vittoria's* atmospheric original section, with its dark-wood panelling, pressed-tin ceilings, murals of the Old Country and Sinatra-blaring Wurlitzer, is vintage North End. It's only open at night, though a street-level addition next door is open by day for excellent cappuccinos. Sun–Thurs 7am–midnight, Fri & Sat till 12.30am.

CHARLESTOWN

Tavern on the Water 1 Eighth St, Pier 6 ☎617 242 8040; Community College T. Located right on the harbour (the *USS Constitution* is anchored nearby), the *Tavern* sports what is possibly Boston's best skyline view. The food is forgettable; stick with whatever's on tap. Thurs & Sun 11.30am–11pm, Fri till midnight, Sat 10am–midnight.

Warren Tavern 2 Pleasant St ☎617 241 8142; Community College T. Paul Revere and George Washington were both regulars here, and the oldest standing structure in Charlestown is still good for a drink. Also has a generous menu of dependable tavern food. Mon–Fri 11am–1am, Sat & Sun 10am–1am.

BEACON HILL

21st Amendment 150 Bowdoin St ☎617 227 7100; Park T; map pp.48–49. This historic, friendly watering hole, which gets its name from the amendment that repealed Prohibition, is a favourite haunt of legislators from the adjacent State House (you might even spot John Kerry) and students from nearby Suffolk University. Good burgers and pub grub. Daily 11.30am–2am.

Alibi 215 Charles St, in the Liberty Hotel ☎857 241 1144; Charles/MGH T; map pp.48–49. Currently *the* place to see and be seen in Boston, and there's generally a queue out front. A young, dressed-up clientele soaks up the vibe amid lengthy leather seating, candlelight and celebrity mug shots. Daily 5pm–2am.

Bin 26 Enoteca 26 Charles St ☎617 723 5939; Charles/MGH T; map pp.48–49. This classy wine bar has up to 250 bottles in its rotation and 50–60 varieties available by the glass. Helpful servers can aid you in matching your drink up with its perfect food counterpart, perhaps a marinated olive plate ($7) or a slice of gorgonzola ($6). Mon–Thurs noon–10pm, Fri till 11pm, Sat 11am–11pm, Sun till 10pm.

Cheers 84 Beacon St ☎617 227 9605; Arlington T; map pp.48–49. If the conspicuous banners outside don't tip you off, this is the bar that served as the inspiration for the TV show *Cheers* (see p.68). If you've got to go, be warned – it's packed with tourists, the inside bears little resemblance to the NBC set, and the food, though cutely named ("eNORMous burgers"), is pricey and mediocre. Plus, it's almost certain that nobody will know your name. Daily 11am–midnight

The Sevens 77 Charles St ☎617 523 9074; Charles/MGH T; map pp.48–49. While the tourists pack into *Cheers*, you can drop by this cosy wood-panelled joint to watch the game or shoot darts in an authentic Boston neighbourhood bar. Mon–Sat 11.30am–1am, Sun noon–1am.

THE WEST END

Fours 166 Canal St ☎617 720 4455; North Station T; map pp.48–49. The classiest of the West End's sports bars, with an army of TVs broadcasting games from around the globe, as well as paraphernalia from the Celtics, Bruins and other local teams. Daily 11am–midnight.

McGann's 197 Portland St ☎617 227 4059; North Station T; map pp.48–49. An authentic Irish bar, with a smarter, restaurant-like feel. Inside its cheerful bright red exterior there's a very active world-rugby watching crowd in addition to the usual Bruins fans. Daily 11.30am–2am.

BACK BAY

Bukowski Tavern 50 Dalton St ☎617 437 9999; Hynes T; map pp.74–75. Arguably Boston's best dive bar, this

1

BREWERY TOURS

Unleash your inner Homer Simpson with a visit to one of Boston's two renowned **breweries**, both purveying high-quality beer (not the typical mass-produced swill). Note that beer samples are procured at the end; if you want to drink, be sure to bring **ID**, as breweries are quite strict on this point.

Harpoon Brewery 306 Northern Ave ☎ 1 888 427 7666 ext 522, ⓦharpoonbrewery.com; SL2 Silver Line T. Located in the outermost reaches of the Seaport District, Harpoon Brewery's silos are said to contain 3800 gallons of beer. Get up close with them on a 1hr weekend tour ($5), where you'll also chew on barley and down a couple of pints. Arrive early, as tours frequently sell out. Sat every 30min 10.30am–5pm,

Sun every 30min 11.30am–3pm.
Samuel Adams 30 Germania St, Jamaica Plain ☎ 617 368 5080, ⓦsamueladams.com; Stony Brook T. This half-pint Samuel Adams facility (used mainly for research purposes) offers extremely popular 1hr brewery tours ($2) with free samples at the end. Mon–Thurs & Sat 10am–3pm, Fri 10am–5.30pm.

watering hole has views over the Mass Pike and such a vast beer selection that a home-made "wheel of indecision" is spun by staff when patrons can't decide. Cash only. There's a smaller, equally cool location at 1281 Cambridge St in Inman Square (☎617 497 7077; Central **T**). Mon–Sat 11.30am–2am, Sun noon–2am.

City Bar 61 Exeter St, in the Lenox Hotel ☎617 933 4800; Copley T; map pp.74–75. Located inside one of Back Bay's most posh properties, *City Bar* is great for a tasteful glass of wine or cognac to begin the night. No raucous crowd here; instead, a thirty-something coterie mingles pleasantly amid expansive leather couches and candlelight. Daily 4.30pm–2am.

Flash's 310 Stuart St ☎617 574 8888; Back Bay T; map pp.74–75. A nice, laidback Back Bay alternative, with a beer-drinking crowd and lots of tempting girly drinks on offer, such as the "Summer Harvest" (strawberries, fresh cilantro and organic gin and tonic; $10). Easy to find, thanks to its blazing retro sign. Mon–Sat 11.30am–2am, Sun 5pm–2am.

minibar 51 Huntington Ave, in the Copley Square Hotel ☎617 424 8500; Copley T; map pp.74–75. Reminiscent of a European bar, this contemporary all-white lounge serves up "mini cuisine" (sandwiches and pizzettes sized for elves) to a young and stylish crowd. One of Boston's places to see and be seen. Mon–Wed 5pm–1am, Thurs–Sat till 2am.

Oak Bar 138 St James Ave, in the Fairmont Copley Plaza ☎617 267 5300; Copley T; map pp.74–75. Rich wood panelling, high ceilings and excellent martinis (including the "engaging martini", complete with diamond ring and deluxe suite; $12,750) make this a genteel spot to drink in Back Bay. Mon–Sat 11am–1am, Sun till 12.30am.

Top of the Hub 800 Boylston St ☎617 536 1775; Prudential T; map pp.74–75. The best bird's-eye views of Boston are found at this restaurant on the 52nd floor of the Prudential Center. *Top of the Hub* features a snazzy jazz

lounge, swanky cocktails and fancy food. A great date spot, although you have to go through an unromantic security check first. Mon–Sat 11.30am–1am, Sun 11am–1am.

THE SOUTH END

Anchovies 433 Columbus Ave ☎617 266 5088; Back Bay T; map pp.74–75. This dim, cosy spot welcomes a local neighbourhood crew and has standout fixings: $3 tallboys (oversized beers), kooky wall ephemera like a rubber chicken and a Virgin Mary, friendly bartenders and a kitchen serving a full menu of worthy Italian fare until 1.30am. Mon–Sat 4pm–2am, Sun 3pm–2am.

⭐ **The Beehive** 541 Tremont St ☎617 423 0069; Back Bay T; map pp.74–75. Snuggled inside the Boston Center for the Arts is this spacious newcomer to Boston's bar scene. With chandeliers dripping from the ceiling, a red-curtained stage and knock-you-down cocktails, the *Beehive* exudes a vaudeville vibe, complete with jazz, cabaret or burlesque shows nearly every night. No cover for shows, but note that they have a no under-21s admission policy. Mon–Fri 5pm–2am, Sat & Sun 10am–2am.

The Delux Café & Lounge 100 Chandler St ☎617 338 5258; Back Bay T; map pp.74–75. This retro hideaway has all the fixings for a great rendezvous point: fantastic kitschy decor, constant cartoon viewing and an Elvis shrine decorated with Christmas lights. The menu is funky American fusion blended with old standbys like grilled-cheese sandwiches and split-pea soup. Cash only. Mon–Sat 5.30pm–1am.

KENMORE SQUARE

Audubon Circle 838 Beacon St ☎617 421 1910; Kenmore T; map pp.74–75. Sleek, modern bar where a well-dressed crowd gathers for cocktails and contemporary bar food before and after games at Fenway Park. Mon–Sat 11.30am–1am, Sun 11am–1am.

⭐ **Bleacher Bar** 82A Lansdowne St ☎617 262 2424; Kenmore T; map pp.74–75. Beneath the bleachers in

1

centre field is the newest addition to Fenway Park, and you don't need a ticket to get in. Here, you'll find a pub festooned with vintage memorabilia and a window with a direct view of the diamond – quite thrilling on game night. Mon–Wed & Sun 11am–1am, Thurs–Sat till 2am.

★ **Eastern Standard** 528 Commonwealth Ave, in the Hotel Commonwealth ☎ 617 532 9100; Kenmore T; map pp.74–75. Set inside a gorgeous, high-ceilinged dining room, this Boston favourite pulls in a nice mix of clientele, both age- and style-wise. The knowledgeable bartenders are just as quick to mix up a genteel highball as they are to pull you a pint, the kitchen serves lauded comfort food, and there's a pretty patio in summer. Daily 10am–1.30am.

Lansdowne Pub 9 Lansdowne St ☎ 617 247 1222; Kenmore T; map pp.74–75. Breeze into this authentic Irish pub adjacent to Fenway Park for standout bar food like cheesy fries ($4) or fish and chips ($14) and settle in for a night of Sox-watching with a band of regulars. Frequent live music. Mon–Fri 3pm–2am, Sat & Sun 10am–2am.

Lower Depths Taproom 476 Commonwealth Ave ☎ 617 266 6662; Kenmore T; map pp.74–75. A welcome newcomer to the ballpark scene, this attractive pub is known for its extensive beer selection (16 on tap, plus plenty in bottles), pretzels and $1 hot dogs. Cash only; beer and wine only. Daily 11.30am–1am.

JAMAICA PLAIN

★ **The Haven** 2 Perkins St ☎ 617 524 2836; Stony Brook T. This authentic Scottish restaurant and bar packs a punch with its incredibly good food offerings (including haggis and neeps; $8), modern decor punctuated by eye-catching antler chandeliers, standout beer selection and charming owner. Mon–Fri noon–1am, Sat & Sun 10.30am–2.30pm & 5.30pm–1am.

CAMBRIDGE: HARVARD SQUARE

Charlie's Kitchen 10 Eliot St ☎ 617 492 9646; Harvard T; map pp.90–91. While downstairs is a well-loved burger joint, upstairs is a buzzing bar – with eighteen beers on tap, a rocking jukebox and a good mix of patrons – at its rowdiest on Tues karaoke nights. They've recently expanded to include an outdoor beer garden. Mon–Fri & Sun 11am–1am, Sat till 2am.

Shay's 58 JFK St ☎ 617 864 9161; Harvard T; map pp.90–91. Unwind with grad students over wine and quality beer at *Shay's*, a relaxed hideaway with an endearing little outdoor patio and plates overflowing with nachos. Mon–Thurs 11am–1am, Sun noon–1am.

CAMBRIDGE: CENTRAL SQUARE

Cuchi Cuchi 795 Main St ☎ 617 864 2929; Central T; map pp.90–91. Linger over cocktails at the bar to soak in *Cuchi Cuchi's* Gatsby-esque fabulousness. Staff are decked

out in vintage flapper dresses, and gilded mirrors and painted lampshades abound. It's also a restaurant serving world-travelling cuisine. Daily 5.30pm–12.30am.

Enormous Room 567 Massachusetts Ave ☎ 617 491 5550; Central T; map pp.90–91. Walking into this tiny bar tucked above *Central Kitchen* (see p.113) is tantamount to entering a swanky slumber party. The clientele lounges, sans shoes (these are discreetly placed in cubbies), on a selection of plush couches. DJs nightly. Mon–Wed & Sun 5.30pm–1am, Thurs–Sat till 2am.

Middlesex 315 Massachusetts Ave ☎ 617 868 6739; Central T; map pp.90–91. A slightly hipper-than-thou vibe, but with good reason – the gorgeous space (exposed brick, pale wood panelling) makes you want to dress to impress. Patrons enjoy creating their own drinking environs with the seats-on-wheels and moveable minimalist tables. *Middlesex* often has queues out the door for its nights of electro-retro beat dance heaven (cover ranges from free to $10). Mon–Wed 11.30am–2.30pm & 5pm–1am, Thurs & Fri 11.30am–2.30pm & 5pm–2am, Sat 5pm–2am.

★ **Miracle of Science Bar & Grill** 321 Massachusetts Ave ☎ 617 868 2866; Central T or #1 bus; map pp.90–91. Surprisingly hip despite its status as an MIT hangout, this popular bar has recently added a full restaurant. There's science-themed decor and a laidback, unpretentious crowd, though the place can get quite crowded on weekend nights. The bar stools will conjure up memories of high school chemistry class. Mon–Fri 7am–1am, Sat & Sun 9am–1am.

People's Republik 876–878 Massachusetts Ave ☎ 617 491 6969; Central or Harvard T; map pp.90–91. Smack bang between MIT and Harvard, *People's Republik* attracts a good mix of technocrats and potential world-leaders. It takes its Communist propaganda seriously – with its posters on the walls, anyway; the range of tap offerings is positively democratic. Mon–Wed & Sun noon–1am, Thurs–Sat till 2am.

River Gods 125 River St ☎ 617 576 1881; Central T; map pp.90–91. An Irish bar with a twist, *River Gods* serves good cocktails alongside Guinness, fantastic food and DJs spinning enjoyable tunes; patrons lounge in throne-like chairs and ogle the suits of armour. Mon 3pm–midnight, Tues–Sat till 1am, Sun till 11pm.

CAMBRIDGE: INMAN SQUARE

★ **The Druid** 1357 Cambridge St ☎ 617 497 0965; Central T; map pp.90–91. Smack in the centre of Inman Square, this well-loved, tightly squeezed Irish pub (complete with brogues) has reasonably priced indie beer in addition to Guinness, standout burgers ($9) and terrific fish and chips ($15). There's a popular trivia night on Wednesdays. Mon–Thurs noon–1am, Fri & Sat 11am–2am, Sun 11am–1am.

1

NIGHTLIFE

In recent years the city's **nightlife** has received something of a wake-up call. **Lansdowne Street**, adjacent to Fenway Park, and once the queen of the clubbing scene, has unfortunately quietened down after the closing of mainstays *Avalon* and *Axis*; stay tuned, however – this area has a habit of reinventing itself, and something new could pop up here at any moment. A few spots have moved into **Downtown Crossing**. Boylston Place – which links Boston Common with the Theater District and is known locally as "The Alley" – is where most of the action is found. For **club and music listings**, check Thursday's *Boston Globe* "Calendar", the *Boston Phoenix* or *Boston's Weekly Dig*; the three best websites are ⓦ boston.com, ⓦ stuffboston .com and ⓦ berklee.edu/events. Many of the Back Bay and South End venues are **gay bars** (see p.122). Otherwise, a number of the clubs below have special gay nights. **Cover charges** are generally in the $10–15 range, although they can go up to $25, and sometimes there's no cover at all (particularly if you arrive early). **Dress codes** vary according to the venue, the day of the week and the mood of the bouncer; as a general precaution, don't wear trainers or torn jeans.

CLUBS

The Estate 1 Boylston Place (in "The Alley"), Theater District ☎ 617 351 7000, ⓦ theestateboston.com; Boylston T; map pp.48–49. Go-go dancers in lingerie, chandeliers twinkling on high, a bumping ballroom and a wraparound balcony for enjoying the scene are some of the pleasures that await you at *Estate*. No cover for the ladies before 11pm, after that, it's a steep $20. There's an enforced dress code (no T-shirts, tank tops, vests, hats or sports attire…). Thursday is gay night. Thurs & Sat 10pm–2am, Fri 10.30pm–2am.

Gypsy Bar 116 Boylston St, Theater District ☎ 617 482 7799, ⓦ gypsybarboston.com; Boylston T; map pp.48–49. Very posh lounge popular with the European set; you can watch schools of jellyfish pulsing behind the bar as you order an Indulgence cocktail. Prepare to dress snappy – no sneakers or sleeveless T-shirts, as well as (weirdly) no polo shirts. DJ dance music Fri & Sat; $10 cover after 9.30pm. Wed–Sat 6pm–2am.

Jillian's 145 Ipswich St, Kenmore Square ☎ 617 437 0300, ⓦ jilliansboston.com; Kenmore T; map pp.74–75. Massive entertainment club complex housing an arcade, a raucous, spacious dance club ($5 cover) and a bowling alley. Mon–Sat 11am–2am, Sun noon–2am.

Mojitos 48 Winter St, Downtown Crossing ☎ 617 834 0552, ⓦ mojitosboston.com; Park St T; map pp.48–49. The reggaeton dance scene gets going at around 10.30pm nightly, with Latin music such as merengue, bachata and salsa thrown in. The downstairs dance floor gets cramped, but the upstairs club is roomier and lined with murals of music legends like Tito Puente and Celia Cruz. $10 cover charge. Thurs 10pm–2am, Fri & Sun 9pm–2am.

Royale 279 Tremont St, Theater District ☎ 617 338 7699, ⓦ royaleboston.com; Boylston T; map pp.48–49. This 1918 opera hall has been re-imagined as a 33,000 square foot club offering partygoers the chance to dance in a vintage ballroom. Thoroughly updated, the *Royale* features a modern sound system and stage, pricey cocktails and plenty of space (including a balcony) in which to mingle. Generally a $20 cover. Fri & Sat 10pm–2am.

ENTERTAINMENT

Boston's cultural scene is famously vibrant, and many of the city's artistic institutions are second to none. The city is arguably at its best in the **classical music** department, but its ballet and theatre groups are also world-class. **Live music** plays a major role in the city's nightlife arena, with bars and clubs catering to a young crowd, especially in Cambridge around Harvard and Central squares.

LIVE MUSIC

The strength of Boston's music scene lies in its diversity – the city's venues host superstar performers and small, experimental acts regularly. Many of the bars and clubs, especially around Central Square and Harvard Square, are just as likely, if not more, to have a scruffy garage band playing for only a nominal cover as they are to have a slick DJ spinning house tunes. Boston is also home to a number of well-loved jazz and blues joints, a scene that's anchored by the renowned Berklee College of Music; you can usually find something cheap and to your liking almost any day of the week.

ROCK AND POP

Church 69 Kilmarnock St, Fenway ☎ 617 236 7600, ⓦ churchofboston.com; Museum T; map pp.74–75.

New 225-person music lounge tucked away on a residential side street. Hosts fifteen bands a week, from rock to metal to folk (cover $7–10). Also runs an on-site comfort food restaurant with a renowned weekend brunch. Mon–Fri 5pm–2am, Sat & Sun 11am–2am.

Great Scott 1222 Commonwealth Ave, Allston ☎ 617 566 9014, ⓦ greatscottboston.com; Harvard Ave T; map pp.74–75. Popular with students and older hipsters alike, this well-loved space plays host to local and national (read: national acts you probably haven't heard of) rock and indie bands. Cheap drinks, and a pleasant patio where you can kick back and play groupie. Friday night here is "The Pill" (usually $5 cover), a mixture of live rock and a DJ-spinning dance-athon.

House of Blues 15 Lansdowne St, Kenmore Square ☎1 888 693 BLUE, ⓦhouseofblues.com; Kenmore T; map pp.74–75. The Boston icon has returned, hosting big name acts like Cyndi Lauper, BB King and She & Him in a glossy new venue next to Fenway Park.

Lizard Lounge 1667 Massachusetts Ave, Cambridge ☎617 547 0759, ⓦlizardloungeclub.com; Harvard or Porter T; map pp.90–91. This, the downstairs portion of *Cambridge Common* restaurant, is a favourite among local students. Rock and jazz acts are on stage almost nightly for a fairly nominal cover charge (usually around $8).

Middle East 472 Massachusetts Ave, Cambridge ☎617 864 3278, ⓦmideastclub.com; Central T; map pp.90–91. Local and regional bands of every sort – rock to mambo to hardcore – stop in regularly at this Cambridge institution. Bigger acts are hosted downstairs; smaller ones ply their trade in a tiny upstairs space. A third venue, the *Corner*, has shows nightly that are usually free, with belly dancing every Sunday.

Museum of Fine Arts 465 Huntington Ave, Fenway ☎1 800 440 6975, ⓦmfa.org; Museum T; map pp.74–75. Better known for hosting jazz and classical acts, the *MFA* is steadily gaining a following of indie rock fans by booking bands like The Sea and the Cake and Mates of State. Intimate, pared-down performances are held in the Remis Auditorium and outdoors in the Calderwood Courtyard; tickets cost about $30.

Orpheum Theatre 1 Hamilton Place, Boston Common ☎617 482 0106, ⓦorpheumtheatreboston.com; Park St or Downtown Crossing T; map pp.48–49. Once an old-school cinema, this is now a venue for big-name bands. The small space means you're closer to the action, and its retro environs are a refreshing change from the new, bigger box-style venues.

Paradise Rock Club 967–969 Commonwealth Ave, Allston ☎617 562 8800, ⓦthedise.com; Pleasant Street T; map pp.74–75. One of Boston's classic rocking venues. Lots of greats have played here – Blondie, Elvis Costello and Tom Waits, to name a few. It's still as popular as it was 25 years ago, only now it also has a restaurant-cum-rock lounge next door.

T.T. the Bear's Place 10 Brookline St, Cambridge ☎617 492 0082, ⓦttthebears.com; Central T; map pp.90–91. A downmarket version of *Middle East*: lesser-known bands, but in a space with a grittiness and intimacy its neighbour lacks. All kinds of bands appear, mostly rock and punk.

JAZZ, BLUES AND FOLK

Passim 47 Palmer St, Cambridge ☎617 492 7679, ⓦclubpassim.org; Harvard T; map pp.90–91. Folkie hangout where Joan Baez and Suzanne Vega got their starts. Acoustic music, folk, blues and jazz in a windowed basement setting. Covers are around $12.

Regattabar 1 Bennett St, in the Charles Hotel, Cambridge ☎617 661 5000, ⓦregattabarjazz.com; Harvard T; map pp.90–91. *Regattabar* draws top national jazz acts, although, as its location in the swish *Charles Hotel* might suggest, the atmosphere and clientele are decidedly formal. Dress nicely and prepare to pay at least a $20 cover.

Scullers 400 Soldiers Field Rd, Allston ☎617 562 4111, ⓦscullersjazz.com; Central T; map pp.90–91. Genteel jazz club in the DoubleTree hotel that draws five-star acts, including some of the stars of the contemporary jazz scene. You'll need to hop in a taxi to get here, as the walk along the river at night can be risky. The cover charge varies wildly – anything from $20 to $55.

★ **Wally's Cafe** 427 Massachusetts Ave, Roxbury ☎617 424 1408, ⓦwallyscafe.com; Massachusetts Ave T; map pp.74–75. Founded in 1947, this is one of the oldest jazz clubs around, and one of Boston's best assets. Refreshingly unhewn, they host lively jazz and blues shows nightly, drawing a diverse crowd. No cover. Daily 2pm–2am.

CLASSICAL MUSIC

Boston prides itself on being a sophisticated city, and nowhere does that show up more than in its proliferation of orchestras and choral groups. This is helped in no small part by the presence of three of the nation's foremost music academies: the Peabody and New England conservatories, and the Berklee College of Music. Paramount among Boston's first-rate artistic institutions is the Boston Symphony Orchestra, which gave its first concert in 1881, but there are also many smaller but internationally known chamber and choral music groups to shore up the city's prestigious music reputation.

SYMPHONIES AND CHAMBER MUSIC ENSEMBLES

Boston Baroque ☎617 484 9200, ⓦbostonbaroque .org. The country's first permanent baroque orchestra is now a resident ensemble at Jordan Hall and Sanders Theatre.

Boston Philharmonic ☎617 236 0999, ⓦbostonphil .org. Renowned orchestra whose conductor prefaces performances with a discussion of the evening's compositions. Performances take place at Jordan Hall (Sat) and Sanders Theatre (Sun).

Boston Pops ☎617 266 1492, ⓦbso.org. A subsection of the Boston Symphony Orchestra, the Pops are considered to be lighter and "poppier" than their more formal counterpart, and are best known for their dynamic Fourth of July performance on the Esplanade.

Boston Symphony Chamber Players ☎1 888 266 1200, ⓦbso.org. The only permanent chamber group sponsored by a major symphony orchestra and made up of its members; they perform at Jordan Hall as well as other venues around Boston.

1

Boston Symphony Orchestra ☎ 617 266 1492, ⓦ bso .org. Boston's world-renowned orchestra performs in Fenway's acoustically perfect Symphony Hall; in summer, they ship out to the Tanglewood Festival in idyllic Lenox, Massachusetts (see p.231).

Handel & Haydn Society ☎ 617 266 3605, ⓦ handelandhaydn.org. Performing chamber and choral music since 1815, these distinguished artists can be heard at Symphony Hall, Jordan Hall and the Cutler Majestic.

Pro Arte Chamber Orchestra ☎ 617 779 0900, ⓦ proarte.org. Cooperatively run chamber orchestra in which musicians have full control. Gives Sunday afternoon performances at Harvard's Sanders Theatre.

VENUES

Berklee Performance Center 136 Massachusetts Ave ☎ 617 747 2261, ⓦ berkleebpc.com; Symphony T. Berklee College of Music's main performance centre, known for its quality contemporary repertoire.

Isabella Stewart Gardner Museum 280 The Fenway ☎ 617 278 5156, ⓦ gardnermuseum.org; Museum T. Chamber and classical concerts, including many debuts, are held regularly at 1.30pm on Sundays (Sept–May) in the museum's brand-new concert hall; there are also shows on Thursday evenings, including jazz. The $27 ticket price includes museum admission.

Jordan Hall 30 Gainsborough St ☎ 617 585 1260, ⓦ necmusic.edu; Symphony T. The impressive concert hall of the New England Conservatory, just one block west from Symphony Hall, is the venue for many chamber music performances as well as those by the Boston Philharmonic (☎ 617 236 0999).

Museum of Fine Arts 465 Huntington Ave ☎ 617 267 9300, ⓦ mfa.org; Museum T. During the summer, the MFA's jazz, folk and world music "Concerts in the Courtyard" ($30) take place each Wed at 7.30pm; a variety of indoor performances are also scheduled for the rest of the year.

Sanders Theatre 45 Quincy St, Cambridge ☎ 617 496 2222; Harvard T. Dating to 1875, this 1166-seat venue has an intimate 180-degree design and excellent acoustics perfect for showing off its Boston Philharmonic and Boston Chamber Music Society performances.

Symphony Hall 301 Massachusetts Ave ☎ 1 888 266 1492 (event information) or ☎ 1 888 266 1200 (box office), ⓦ bso.org; Symphony T. This is the regal, acoustically perfect venue for the Boston Symphony Orchestra; the famous Boston Pops concerts happen in May and June; in July and Aug, the BSO retreats to Tanglewood, in the Berkshires (see p.231).

Tsai Performance Center 685 Commonwealth Ave ☎ 617 353 TSAI (event information) or ☎ 617 353 8725 (box office), ⓦ bu.edu/tsai; Boston University T. Improbably tucked into BU's School of Management, this hall is a frequent venue for chamber music performances,

prominent lecturers and plays; events are often affiliated with BU and thus can be very inexpensive.

DANCE

The city's longest-running dance company is the Boston Ballet (☎ 617 695 6950 or ☎ 1 800 447 7400, ⓦ bostonballet.org), with an unparalleled reputation in America and beyond; their biggest blockbuster, the holiday performance of *The Nutcracker*, boasts an annual attendance of more than 140,000. In addition, there are smaller dance troupes, like the curve-loving Big Moves (ⓦ bigmoves.org), which perform in less traditional venues like the Institute of Contemporary Art. The Boston Dance Alliance has an informative website centred on Boston's local dance scene (ⓦ bostondancealliance.org).

THEATRE

The theatre scene here is pretty active. Boston remains a try-out city for Broadway productions in New York City and smaller companies have increasingly high visibility. It's a real treat to see a play or musical at one of the opulent old theatres such as the Citi Performing Arts Center or the Opera House. Tickets to bigger shows range from $35 to $125 depending on the seat, and there is, of course, the potential of a pre- or post-theatre meal (see p.107) added onto the bill. Your best money-saving option is to pay a visit to BosTix, a half-price, day-of-show ticket booth with two outlets: Copley Square at the corner of Dartmouth and Boylston streets, and Faneuil Hall Marketplace (both Tues–Sat 10am–6pm, Sun 11am–4pm; ☎ 617 482 2849, ⓦ bostix.org). Useful for anyone with a valid school ID or ISIC card, a number of theatres offer cheaper student "rush" tickets on the day of the performance; call the venue in question for more information. The smaller venues tend to showcase more offbeat and affordable productions, and shows can cost under $15 – though you shouldn't bank on that.

MAJOR VENUES

American Repertory Theater 64 Brattle St, at the Loeb Drama Center, Cambridge ☎ 617 547 8300, ⓦ americanrepertorytheatre.org; Harvard T. Excellent, fairly avant-garde theatre near Harvard Square known for staging plays by the likes of Shaw, Wilde and Stoppard, and stirring contemporary performances at Oberon, their second stage. They also have a flexible performance space, Zero Arrow, at the corner of Mass Ave and Arrow St in Harvard Square.

Citi Performing Arts Center 270 Tremont St ☎ 617 482 9393, ⓦ citicenter.org; Boylston T. Formerly the Wang Center and Shubert Theatre, these two classic theatres have been rebranded under the Citi Center's moniker. The Wang is the biggest performance centre in Boston, and the city's grande dame, a movie house of palatial proportions – its original Italian marble, gold leaf ornamentation, crystal chandeliers and 3800 seats, dating to 1925 – all remain. The Shubert, dubbed the city's "Little Princess" is a 1680-seat theatre that has been restored to its pretty early 1900s appearance, with white walls and gold leaf accents.

Cutler Majestic Theatre 219 Tremont St ☎ 617 824 8000, ⊛ aestages.org; Boylston T. This lavish venue, with soaring ceilings and Neoclassical friezes, has recently had extensive renovations; it hosts productions of the Emerson Stage company and the Boston Lyric Opera.

Huntington Theatre Company 264 Huntington Ave ☎ 617 266 0800, ⊛ huntingtontheatre.org; Symphony T. The largest non-touring playhouse in Boston, known for its phenomenal sets. Productions here range from the classic to the contemporary.

The Opera House 539 Washington St ☎ 617 259 3400, ⊛ bostonoperahouse.com; Downtown Crossing T. Built in 1928, this opulent theatre hosts large-scale travelling productions (such as *Wicked*), in addition to the Boston Ballet's Christmas-time production of *The Nutcracker*.

Paramount Center 559 Washington St ☎ 617 824 8400, ⊛ aestages.org; Downtown Crossing T. Until its restoration in 2010, the Art Deco Paramount had fallen a long way from its cinema-palace heyday (its last stint, in 1976, was as a porno cinema). Today it houses two theatres – a traditional 596-seater and a flexible black-box space. Easy to spot with its blue-and-orange light-bulb marquee.

SMALL VENUES

Boston Center for the Arts 539 Tremont St ☎ 617 426 5000, ⊛ bcaonline.org; Back Bay T. Several theatre troupes, many experimental, stage productions at the BCA, which incorporates a series of small venues in a single South End property. These include the Cyclorama and the Stanford Calderwood Pavilion.

Hasty Pudding Theatricals 12 Holyoke St, Cambridge ☎ 617 495 5205, ⊛ hastypudding.org; Harvard T. Harvard University's all-male Hasty Pudding Theatricals troupe, one of the country's oldest, mounts one show per year (usually a kooky comedy performed in drag; Feb & March) at this theatre, then hits the road, after which the Cambridge Theatre Company moves in. The troupe is best known for its "Man and Woman of the Year" awards, when two big-time celebrities are chosen to lead a parade through Cambridge, and get awarded a pot of pudding.

FILM

In Boston, as in any other large American metropolis, it's easy enough to catch general release films. For foreign, independent, classic or cult cinema, you'll generally have to look to other municipalities – Cambridge is best, though Brookline has some art house movie theatres as well. Whatever you're going to see, admission will cost you about $11, though matinees (before 6pm) can be cheaper.

AMC Loews Boston Common 19 175 Tremont St ☎ 617 423 5801; Park St T. There are nineteen screens at this plush megaplex right by Boston Common; the armrests move back so you can hold hands with your honey.

AMC Loews Harvard Square 10 Church St, Cambridge ☎ 617 864 4581; Harvard T. This tiny 1926 theatre hosted the first live US performance of the *Rocky Horror Picture Show*, a beloved stage tradition which continues to this day (17+ only; Sat at midnight; prepare for a rowdy live cast in addition to the film; $10).

★ **Brattle Theatre** 40 Brattle St, Cambridge ☎ 617 876 6837, ⊛ brattlefilm.org; Harvard T. A historic indie cinema that pleasantly looks its age. Hosts a thematic film series plus occasional author appearances and readings; beer, wine and fresh popcorn are available for purchase.

★ **Coolidge Corner Theatre** 290 Harvard St, Brookline ☎ 617 734 2500, ⊛ coolidge.org; Coolidge Corner T. Film buffs flock to this classic theatre for foreign and independent movies. The Coolidge also runs ingenious programmes like "Box Office Babies", baby-friendly movie screenings where gurgling noises are just another part of the show. The interior is adorned with Art Deco murals.

Harvard Film Archive 24 Quincy St, Carpenter Center, Cambridge ☎ 617 495 4700, ⊛ hcl.harvard.edu/hfa; Harvard T. Artsy, foreign and experimental films.

Museum of Fine Arts Theater 465 Huntington Ave ☎ 617 267 9300, ⊛ mfa.org/film; Museum T. Art films and documentaries often accompanied by lectures from the filmmaker. Also hosts several showcases like the Jewish Film Festival.

★ **Somerville Theatre** 55 Davis Square, Somerville ☎ 617 625 5700, ⊛ somervilletheatreonline.com; Davis T. Wacky cinema for camp, classic, cult, independent, foreign and first-run films. Wine and beer is sold alongside the usual snacks.

Stuart Street Playhouse 200 Stuart St ☎ 617 755 3517, ⊛ stuartstreetplayhouse.com; Boylston T. Tucked away in the Theater District, this 1970s cinema reopened in 2009 with an elegant lobby and (endearingly) only one screen, generally lit up with an indie flick.

GAY AND LESBIAN

Boston is a gay-friendly city. Indeed, in 2004 Massachusetts became the first state in the nation to grant same-sex **marriage licenses** (as of 2011, the list has grown to six states and Washington, DC). The centre of the **gay scene** is the South End, a largely residential neighbourhood whose businesses, mostly restaurants and cafés, are concentrated on a short stretch of Tremont Street above Union Park. The **lesbian scene** is pretty well mixed in with the gay scene, and there

1

are few exclusively lesbian bars or clubs. Boston's free **gay newspaper** is *Bay Windows* (ⓦ baywindows.com), which is one of two good sources of **club information**, the other being the *The Boston Phoenix*. Both can be found in various venues and bookstores, notably Calamus Bookstore, 92B State St (ⓣ 617 338 1931), Boston's only gay bookshop.

DRINKING AND NIGHTLIFE

Boston has a good variety of gay bars and clubs, ranging from the sophisticated (*dbar*) to the low-key (*Fritz*) – and of course a number of bumping dance clubs (*Machine*).

Club Café 209 Columbus Ave, South End ⓣ 617 536 0966; Back Bay T; map pp.74–75. This combination restaurant/video bar popular among South End guppies ("gay urban professionals") has two back lounges, *Moonshine* and *Satellite*, showing the latest videos. They make a wide selection of martinis with fun names like "Pouty Princess" and "Dirty Birdie". Mon–Sat 4pm–2am, Sun 11am–2am.

dbar 1236 Dorchester Ave, Dorchester ⓣ 617 265 4490; Savin Hill T; map pp.74–75. Although Dorchester's *dbar* is a bit removed from the city centre, it's well worth the trip – most locals think it's the best gay bar in town. Set amid an inlaid mahogany interior, *dbar* serves fancy fusion fare from 5.30–10pm; after that it's all about pomegranate cosmos ($8.50) and getting your groove on. Mon–Thurs 5pm–last call, Fri & Sat 5pm–2am, Sun 11am–last call.

Fritz 26 Chandler St, South End ⓣ 617 482 4428; Back Bay T; map pp.74–75. South End sports bar likened to the gay version of *Cheers* because of its friendly staff and mix of casually attired locals and visitors. Daily noon–2am.

Guerrilla Queer Bar Venue changes ⓦ bostonguerrilla .com. Once a month, the *Guerrilla* kids take over a classically hetero bar, shake it up and make it queer for the evening. It's an awesome event with a splash of politics mixed in; sign up on their website if you want to get in on the action. First Fri of every month.

Jacque's Cabaret 79 Broadway, Back Bay ⓣ 617 426 8902; ⓦ jacques-cabaret.com; Arlington T; map pp.74–75. Priscilla, Queen of the Desert invades New England at this drag dream where divas lip-synch *I Love the Nightlife*. There's a nice melting pot of patrons; it's quite popular for hen parties. Showtimes nightly (check the website for times), and consult a map before you go, as it's a bit tricky to find. Cover is $6–10; bar is cash only. Mon–Sat 11am–midnight, Sun noon–midnight.

Machine/Ramrod 1254 Boylston St, Kenmore Square ⓣ 617 536 1950, ⓦ machine-boston.com; Kenmore T; map pp.74–75. A favourite on Fri and Sat when the club's large dancefloor and top-notch music has the place pumping. The adjacent pool tables, video screens and bar let you take a breather from dancing while you soak up the scene. Cover $10. In the back, *Ramrod* used to have a strictly enforced Levi/leather dress code (Fri & Sat), but seems to have loosened up into more of a *Machine* extension. Daily noon–2am.

Midway Café 3496 Washington St, Jamaica Plain ⓣ 617 524 9038, ⓦ midwaycafe.com; Green St T. Live music hangout with a popular Thursday Queeraoke Night, complete with costumes and wigs; afterwards there's a dance party till 2am. $5 cover, bar is cash only.

Milky Way 284 Amory St, Jamaica Plain ⓣ 617 524 6060, ⓦ dykenight.com; Stony Brook T. On the fourth Friday of the month the *Milky Way* hosts "Dyke Night" ($6 cover), one of the most happening lesbian dance-athons in town.

Rise 306 Stuart St, Back Bay ⓣ 617 423 7473, ⓦ riseclub.us; Arlington T; map pp.74–75. Night owls who haven't gotten their fill of dancing at closing timeshould ask around for an invite to Boston's on the down-low, after-hours private party; this members-only event for gays and straights gets going at 2am.

SHOPPING

Boston is an extremely pleasant place to shop, with attractive stores clustered on atmospheric streets like **Charles** in Beacon Hill and **Newbury** in Back Bay. Cambridge is another excellent place for browsing, with especially good **bookshops**. The **North End**, historically the go-to spot for cooking ingredients, has more recently become a magnet for clothing boutiques, while the **South End** always has something cool to seek out, be it fashion, art or home decor. There's also **Downtown Crossing**, at Washington and Summer streets, a bargain hunter's delight, albeit in slightly seedy environs.

BOOKS

Boston has a rich literary history, enhanced by its numerous universities as well as the many authors and publishing houses that have called the town home. This legacy is well reflected in the quality and diversity of bookshops to be found both in Boston and neighbouring Cambridge.

Brattle Book Shop 9 West St, Downtown Crossing ⓣ 617 542 0210; Park St T; map pp.48–49. One of the oldest antiquarian bookshops in the country. You can buy a book for $1 outside, or find one for $10,000 inside (they recently sold a first-edition *Walden* for a few grand). Mon–Sat 9am–5.30pm.

Brookline Booksmith 279 Harvard St, Brookline ⓣ 617 566 6660; Coolidge Corner T. This cosy shop with hardwood floors has friendly staff who welcome browsing; holds a good author reading series too.

Mon–Thurs 8.30am–10pm, Fri 8.30am–11pm, Sat 9am–11pm, Sun 9am–9pm.

Calamus Bookstore 92B South St, Chinatown ☎617 338 1931; South Station T; map pp.48–49. Boston's only gay bookshop, with a good selection of reasonably priced books and cards, plus a vast community bulletin board at the entrance. Mon–Sat 9am–7pm, Sun noon–6pm.

Grolier Poetry Bookshop 6 Plympton St, Cambridge ☎617 547 4648; Harvard T; map pp.90–91. With 14,000 volumes of verse, this tiny shop has gained an international following among poets and their fans. Frequent readings. Tues & Wed 11am–7pm, Thurs–Sat till 6pm.

Harvard Book Store 1256 Massachusetts Ave, Cambridge ☎617 661 1515; Harvard T; map pp.90–91. Three huge rooms of new books upstairs, a basement for used volumes and an award-winning remainder department downstairs. Academic and critical work in the humanities and social sciences dominate, with a healthy dose of fiction thrown in. Mon–Sat 9am–11pm, Sun 10am–10pm.

Raven Used Books 52B JFK St, Cambridge ☎617 441 6999; Harvard T; map pp.90–91. 263 Newbury St ☎617 578 9000; map pp.74–75. Readers rave about Raven, and rightly so. This tidy little bookshop stocks scholarly (but not pretentious) reads covering everything from anarchism and poetry to jazz and physics. Mon–Sat 10am–9pm, Sun 11am–8pm.

Schoenhof's Foreign Books 76A Mount Auburn St, Cambridge ☎617 547 8855; Harvard T; map pp.90–91. Well-stocked foreign-language bookshop that's sure to have that volume of Proust you're looking for, as well as any children's books you might be after. Mon–Wed, Fri & Sat 10am–6pm, Thurs till 8pm.

Trident Booksellers & Café 338 Newbury St, Back Bay ☎617 267 8688; Hynes T; map pp.74–75. One of the last great independent bookstores in Boston. Has a bit of an alternative vibe; buy some funky stationery and write letters home over a cup of coffee in their superb café (see p.111). Free wi-fi. Daily 8am–midnight.

FOOD AND DRINK

Eating out in Boston may prevail, but should you choose to cook your own food, or get provisions for a picnic, you won't do so badly either. Look no further than the North End for all manner of excellent pastries (see box, p.109); for gourmet-style take-home eats, Cambridge is especially strong in variety.

★ **Formaggio Kitchen** 244 Huron Ave, Cambridge ☎617 354 4750; Harvard T;map pp.90–91; 268 Shawmut Ave, South End ☎617 350 6996; Back Bay T; map pp.74–75. One of the best cheese shops in Boston; the gourmet meats, salads, sandwiches and baked goods here are also worth sampling. Mon–Fri 9am–7pm, Sat till 6pm, Sun 10am–4pm.

New Deal Fish Market 622 Cambridge St, East Cambridge ☎617 876 8227; Lechmere T; map pp.90–91. Top-notch, sashimi-grade seafood with a wide selection of fish ranging from the crowd-pleasers (crab, lobster and shrimp) to more specialized fare like maguro tuna and stickleback. Very fairly priced. Mon 3–7pm, Tues–Fri 10am–7pm, Sat 9.30am–6.30pm.

★ **Polcari's Coffee** 105 Salem St, North End ☎617 227 0786; Haymarket T; map p.64. Established in 1932, this venerated old-world coffee vendor is nicely stocked with a wide variety of blends as well as every spice you could think of. Worth going in for the aroma alone, or just to hear the local gossip from the guys behind the counter. Mon–Sat 9.30am–6pm.

Salumeria Italiana 151 Richmond St, North End ☎617 523 8743; Haymarket T; map p.64. Arguably the best Italian grocer this side of Roma, this shop stocks only the finest cheeses, meats and more. Mon–Sat 8am–7pm, Sun (summer only) 10am–4pm.

CLOTHING

Boston is a great place for clothes shopping, with options running the gamut from dollar-per-pound vintage duds to extravagant boutique and designer threads. Newbury Street remains the go-to standard for big-name designer stores such as Marc Jacobs, Armani and Chanel, while cobblestoned Charles Street is long on location charm and smart shops to match its upmarket address. The fashionable South End, arguably Boston's hippest neighbourhood, also boasts its own appealing collection of clothing stores.

★ **Bodega** 6 Clearway St, Back Bay ☎617 421 1550; Hynes T; map pp.74–75. A truly fantastic original. The front stocks your favourite corner shop mainstays (think Cheerios and toilet paper); walk towards the vending machine door to reveal a secret backroom filled with covetous designer sneakers and stylish hip-hop wear. Mon–Sat 11am–6pm, Sun noon–5pm.

Dress 221 Newbury St, Back Bay ☎617 424 7125; Copley T; map pp.74–75. A bona fide Boston best. This trendsetting yet friendly boutique has chic T-shirts, jeans, separates and droolworthy dresses to sate even the most discerning style maven. Ultra-chic but very welcoming. Mon–Thurs 11am–7pm, Fri & Sat till 6pm, Sun noon–5pm.

In-jean-ius 441 Hanover St, North End ☎617 523 5326; Haymarket T; map p.64. Stylish North End boutique filled with high-end women's denim like Rock & Republic and Goldsign; best are the helpful staffers who magically steer you toward that perfect pair of jeans. The owner also runs Twilight, around the corner (see p.124). Mon–Sat 11am–7pm, Sun noon–6pm.

Louis Boston 60 Northern Ave, Seaport District ☎617 262 6100; Courthouse Station T; map pp.48–49. A

1

Boston landmark (pronounced "Looeez"), this fashionista funhouse is loaded with perfect pieces (men's and women's clothing, shoes, jewels) by fabulous names like Zac Posen and Jason Wu. In 2010, Louis moved from its stately Back Bay digs into a glassy new home in the Seaport District. Very expensive. Mon–Wed 11am–6pm, Thurs–Sat till 7pm, Sun till 5pm.

Passport 43 Brattle St, Cambridge ☎617 576 0900; Harvard T; map pp.90–91. Possessed with wanderlust but afraid of airports? Get thee to Passport, where an inviting array of primo luggage, chic-yet-packable clothing, cashmere wraps and other delightful travel sundries stand at the ready to boost your "full body scanner" morale. At press time, Passport was headed to a new location; call for their new address. Mon–Sat 10.30am–6pm, Sun noon–5pm.

★ **Twilight** 12 Fleet St, North End ☎617 523 8008; Haymarket T; map p.64. Run by the same mastermind behind In-jean-ius (see above), Twilight opened up when trendy denim wearers started asking about things to wear for a big night out. Filled with chi-chi dresses (think Betsey Johnson), handbags and well-priced sparkly jewellery, this delightful space has friendly staffers who welcome both browsers and buyers with equal warmth. Mon–Sat 11am–7pm, Sun noon–6pm.

Uniform 511 Tremont St, South End ☎617 247 2360; Back Bay T; map pp.74–75. If you know a guy who needs a little style kick, march him into Uniform, where a kindly South End staff transforms shoppers into "after" photos sporting casually chic brands like Ben Sherman and Penguin. Tues & Wed 11am–7pm, Thurs–Sat till 8pm, Sun noon–5pm.

VINTAGE

★ **Bobby from Boston** 19 Thayer St, South End ☎617 423 9299; NE Medical or Broadway T; map pp.74–75. Long adored by rockers and professional movie stylists, Bobby's is an artful South End loft long on Union Jacks, shoes, dresses, suspenders, dapper hats and clothing from the 1920s to 1960s. It's an incredible dream world, and a must for vintage lovers. Tues–Sun noon–6pm.

HATS

Salmagundi 765 Centre St, Jamaica Plain ☎617 522 5047; Green St T. Derbys, porkpies, homburgs, straw weaves – even just the names sound fun at this modern-day milliner, known for its selection of classic hat styles in contemporary colours and stripes. Tues–Fri noon–8pm, Sat 11am–8pm, Sun 11am–6pm.

COSMETICS

★ **Beauty Mark** 33 Charles St, Beacon Hill ☎617 720 1555; Charles/MGH T; map pp.48–49. They say it's what's on the inside that counts, and if that's the case

then Beauty Mark must be feeling pretty good about itself. Decked out in hues of white and French blue, this girly-girl heaven is filled with rows of luxurious cosmetics, all enjoyably explored with the help of kindly staff. Mon–Fri 11am–7pm, Sat 10am–6pm, Sun noon–5pm.

Colonial Drug 49 Brattle St, Cambridge ☎617 864 2222; Harvard T; map pp.90–91. Family-owned since 1947, this landmark apothecary has an extensive selection of hard-to-find perfumes, colognes and high-end shaving brushes and lathers. A fragrant time capsule, it's easy to lose an hour here browsing the curious merchandise (think elm lozenges and moustache wax). Cash only. Mon–Fri 8am–7pm, Sat 8am–6pm.

MUSIC

The best places for new and used music in Boston are on Newbury Street in Back Bay, around Massachusetts Avenue near Kenmore Square, and up in Harvard Square – basically all the places students can be found hanging about.

★ **In Your Ear!** 957 Commonwealth Ave, Allston ☎617 787 9755; Pleasant St T; 72 Mount Auburn St, Cambridge ☎617 481 5035; Harvard T; map pp.90–91. Indulge in the Ear's massive collection of used CDs, records and other agreeable esoterica to sate your vintage music cravings. The Cambridge location is smaller but still appealing. Mon–Sat 11am–8pm, Sun noon–6.30pm.

Looney Tunes 1106 Boylston St, Back Bay ☎617 247 2238; Hynes T; map pp.74–75. The way a record store should be – walls festooned with vintage jazz records, a great selection of CDs and a hip staff who aren't snooty. Mon–Sat 10am–9pm, Sun noon–8pm.

Newbury Comics 332 Newbury St, Back Bay ☎617 236 4930; Hynes T; map pp.74–75. Boston's biggest alternative record store carries lots of independent labels you won't find at the national chains along with a substantial array of vinyl, posters, zines and kitschy T-shirts. There's a branch in Cambridge at the Garage mall, 36 JFK St (☎617 491 0337; Harvard **T**). Mon–Thurs 10am–10pm, Fri & Sat till 11pm, Sun 11am–8pm.

Underground Hip Hop 234 Huntington Ave, Fenway ☎617 262 0200, ⓦundergroundhiphop.com; Symphony T; map pp.74–75. One of the best selections of hip-hop in Boston or anywhere. It's well organized too – sit on a comfy stool, listen all you want to the tunes on their extensive website, and then they'll grab you what you need from the back. Mon–Sat noon–8pm.

★ **Weirdo Records** 844 Massachusetts Ave, Cambridge ☎857 413 0154; Central T; map pp.90–91. A lovingly culled mix of everything from undiscovered local bands to "squares and outsiders" and Iranian pop music. Lots of hard-to-find sounds, imports and other stuff you can't pick up anywhere else. Daily 11am–9pm.

DIRECTORY

Banks and currency exchange Bank of America is Boston's largest, with branches and ATMs throughout the city. Bureaux de change are not very prevalent; you can find locations at Logan Airport terminals A, B, Travelex, 745 Boylston St and many Bank of America branches.

Hospitals Massachusetts General Hospital, 55 Fruit St (☎617 726 2000, ⓦmgh.harvard.edu; Charles/MGH **T**); Beth Israel Deaconess Medical Center, 330 Brookline Ave (☎617 667 7000, ⓦbidmc.org; Longwood **T**); Tufts Medical Center, 800 Washington St (☎617 636 5000, ⓦtuftsmedicalcenter.org; NE Medical **T**); Brigham & Women's Hospital, 75 Francis St (☎617 732 5500, ⓦbwh .partners.org; Longwood or Brigham Circle **T**); Children's Hospital, 300 Longwood Ave (☎617 355 6000, ⓦchildrenshospital.org; Longwood **T**).

Internet Free wireless access is plentiful in Boston, and most hotels have wi-fi, as does Faneuil Hall Marketplace, the Rose Kennedy Greenway, numerous local coffee shops (see p.105) and *Starbucks*. Harvard's Holyoke Center Arcade, at 1350 Massachusetts Ave in Cambridge, has a couple of stations with 10min access maximum. The same goes for MIT's Building 7 at 77 Massachusetts Ave (also in Cambridge). Boston's main public library, at 700 Boylston St, has free internet access. You could also pop by one of the ubiquitous FedEx/Office stores; try the Government Center location, at 2 Center Plaza, which is open 24hr Mon–Thurs and has long weekend hours too (25 cents/minute; ☎617 973 9000; State St **T**).

Laundry Appleton St Laundromat, 9 Appleton St (daily 7am–6pm; ☎617 338 8887; Back Bay **T**), is a good, clean bet; drop-off service starts at $10.

Pharmacies The CVS drugstore chain has locations all over the city, though not all have pharmacies. Try the 24hr branch at 587 Boylston St, in Back Bay (☎617 437 8414; Copley **T**).

Police In case of emergency, get to a phone and dial ☎911.

Post office The most central post office downtown is at 31 Milk St in Post Office Square (Mon–Fri 7.30am–6pm; ☎617 482 1956); Cambridge's central branch is at 770 Massachusetts Ave, in Central Square (Mon–Fri 7.30am–7pm, Sat till 2pm; ☎617 575 8700). The General Post Office at 25 Dorchester Ave, behind South Station, has the best hours (daily 6am–midnight; ☎617 654 5302).

Sports Baseball: Red Sox (☎1 877 733 7699, ⓦredsox .com) play at Fenway Park, seats $12–165. Basketball: Celtics (☎1 800 4622 849, ⓦceltics.com) play at the TD Banknorth Garden, 100 Legends Way, in the West End, seats $10–200. Hockey: Bruins (☎617 624 BEAR, ⓦbostonbruins.com), also at the TD Banknorth Garden, seats $17–200.

Eastern Massachusetts

128 Around Boston

140 The North Shore

153 The South Shore

159 Cape Cod and the islands

PROVINCETOWN, CAPE COD

Eastern Massachusetts

Eastern Massachusetts has quite a bit to offer in the way of history. Just inland from Boston are the towns of Lexington and Concord, where the Revolutionary War began in 1775, and Lowell, the birthplace of America's Industrial Revolution. The coast can be divided into four sections: the North Shore, which stretches from Boston's northern suburbs to the New Hampshire border, and includes the "witch" town of Salem and rocky Cape Ann, home to the old fishing ports of Gloucester and Rockport; the South Shore, which includes Plymouth, where the Pilgrims landed in 1620 and stretches past the storied whaling port of New Bedford all the way to Rhode Island; the seventy-mile arm of sandy Cape Cod, dotted with popular resorts, none better than bohemian Provincetown; and the relaxed, upmarket holiday islands of Martha's Vineyard and Nantucket.

There are **seasonal factors** to take into consideration when visiting this part of the state. While the inland towns can be visited at any time, the coast is best experienced in the summer or early autumn, when the sun and water are at their warmest – though beautiful in winter, the beach towns can also be somewhat desolate at that time. The nicest way to holiday in this part of the state is to pick a beach town on the Cape or the islands, and plant yourself for a week of summer activities – the sights won't take more than a few days to tour, and then you can relax and enjoy the swimmable beaches, clam shacks and fun neighbourhood bars.

Around Boston

The American Revolution (see box, p.131) began at **Concord** and neighbouring **Lexington** in April 1775 with what has become known as "the shot heard round the world". These famous battles are evoked in a piecemeal but enthusiastic fashion throughout the **Minute Man National Historical Park**, with scale models, remnant musketry and the odd preserved bullet hole. Close to Concord are the towns of **Lincoln** and **Harvard**, home to some smaller museums of equal interest, while north of Boston is the industrial city of **Lowell**, now undergoing a renaissance. All these towns are best visited as day-trips from Boston.

Revolutionary history p.131
Concord and transcendentalism p.134
Cider and wine p.136
On the trail of Jack Kerouac p.139
The Salem witch trials p.143
Whale-watching off Cape Ann p.147
Audubon's Birds of America p.158
Fall River and Lizzie Borden p.159

Cape Cod Baseball league p.161
The Cape Cod Canal p.162
Cape Cod beaches p.165
Monomoy National Wildlife Refuge p.169
Cape Cod Rail Trail p.173
Cape Cod National Seashore p.175
Oyster shucking p.177
Martha's Vineyard beaches p.187
Maria Mitchell sights p.196
Nantucket beaches p.198

WALDEN POND

Highlights

❶ Walden Pond Think transcendentalist thoughts, or just take a relaxing walk and swim at this historically significant and physically beautiful spot. **See p.134**

❷ Clam shacks Fried, juicy belly clams and fresh lobster are a treat all along the Massachusetts coast. **See p.164** & **191**

❸ Cape Cod biking The Rail Trail is great for touring, while the Province Lands bike path takes a more scenic route through the dunes. **See p.173** & **p.180**

❹ Hit the beach The region's bountiful beaches make a fine excuse to laze about. **See p.165**

❺ Provincetown Perhaps the sole must-see on the Cape, a lively town with great beaches, tasty seafood, and an anything-goes mentality. **See p.178**

❻ Nantucket Leaf through Melville's *Moby Dick* while admiring the digs of one-time whaleboat captains in Nantucket Town, the *Pequod's* port of call. **See p.192**

HIGHLIGHTS ARE MARKED ON THE MAP ON P.130

Lexington and around

Buckman Tavern 1 Bedford St • Daily April–Oct 10am–4pm; guided tour every 30min • ☎ 781 862 5598 • **Hancock-Clarke House**
36 Hancock St • April–Oct, call for hours • ☎ 781 861 0928 • **Munroe Tavern** 1332 Massachusetts Ave • Daily June–Oct noon–4pm,
guided tours hourly • ☎ 781 862 0295 • All three sites can all be visited on a joint ticket for $12; otherwise admission to each one is $7 •
ⓦ lexingtonhistory.org

The main thing to see in **LEXINGTON** is the town's common, the manicured **Battle
Green**, fronted by Henry Kitson's dignified statue *The Minute Man*. This musket-
bearing figure is popularly assumed to be Captain John Parker (an American
commander at the battle). Across from the statue, the **Lexington Visitor Center** has a

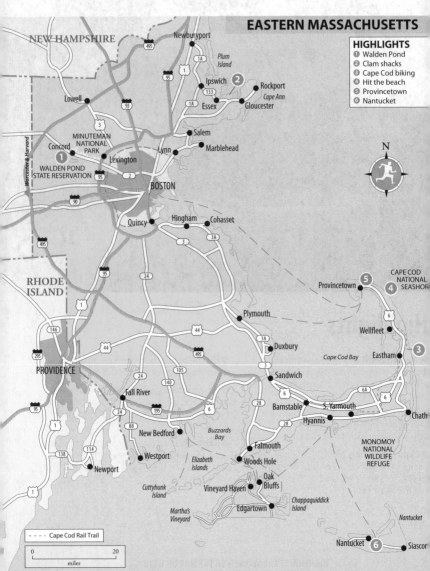

EASTERN MASSACHUSETTS

HIGHLIGHTS
1. Walden Pond
2. Clam shacks
3. Cape Cod biking
4. Hit the beach
5. Provincetown
6. Nantucket

NEW HAMPSHIRE

Newburyport

Plum Island

Ipswich

Rockport

Cape Ann

Essex

Gloucester

Lowell

Salem

Concord

Lynn

Marblehead

MINUTEMAN NATIONAL PARK

Lexington

WALDEN POND STATE RESERVATION

Worcester & Harvard

BOSTON

N

Quincy

Hingham

Cohasset

RHODE ISLAND

Provincetown 5

CAPE COD NATIONAL SEASHORE 4

Plymouth

Wellfleet

Duxbury

Eastham 3

Cape Cod Bay

Sandwich

PROVIDENCE

Fall River

Barnstable

S. Yarmouth

Chath

New Bedford

Buzzards Bay

Hyannis

Westport

Falmouth

MONOMOY NATIONAL WILDLIFE REFUGE

Woods Hole

Elizabeth Islands

Cuttyhunk Island

Oak Bluffs

Newport

Vineyard Haven

Chappaquiddick Island

Edgartown

Martha's Vineyard

Nantucket

Nantucket 6

Siascor

- - - - Cape Cod Rail Trail

0   20
miles

REVOLUTIONARY HISTORY

On April 19, 1775 the first battle of the **American Revolution** began in Lexington when British troops marched to Concord to seize American munitions. Although the British had hoped to keep their confiscation plan quiet, word of the operation had spread, and the American "**Minute Men**" – so called because they were prepared to fight at a moment's notice – were equipped with well-rehearsed plans for a British incursion. When the British set out from **Boston Common**, Paul Revere (see p.62) and William Dawes left on separate routes to sound the alarm. Within minutes, the Old Belfry (which still stands – the short path to it begins by the *Minute Man* statue) and church bells were clanging and cannons roaring throughout the countryside, signalling the rebels to head for **Lexington Green**; hundreds more converged around the North Bridge area of Concord. Revere managed to give the final alarm to a sleeping John Hancock and Samuel Adams (in town to attend the Provincial Congress) at the Hancock-Clark House (see below).

John Parker, the colonial captain, was down the street at the *Buckman Tavern* when he received word that the British were closing in on the Green. "Don't fire unless fired upon", he ordered the men, "but if they mean to have a war, let it begin here". With only 77 Americans pitted against 700 British regulars, it was more a show of resolve than a hope for victory. Who fired the **first shot** remains a mystery, but in the fracas that followed, eight Americans were killed (seven of the soldiers are buried in an affecting memorial at the northwest end of the Green). One wounded soldier crawled across the road to his home, dying at his wife's feet – the house, on the corner of Harrington Road and Bedford Street, displays a **commemorative plaque**.

The British suffered no casualties, and marched eight miles west to **Concord**. By the time they arrived, it was early morning on April 19, and hundreds more Minute Men had amassed on a farm behind **North Bridge** near where the lion's share of munitions were stored. When British officers accidentally set fire to a building, the Americans saw the smoke and thought their houses were being torched. After the British fired two warning shots, the Concord militiamen retaliated – the "**shot heard round the world**", as history books have it. The British were outnumbered four to one, and suffered heavily in the ensuing battle, which continued all the way back to **Boston**.

2

diorama showing the detail of the battle, while in the Minute Men's headquarters at the **Buckman Tavern**, facing the Green, a bullet hole from a British rifle has been preserved in an inner door near the first-floor tap room. A couple of blocks north, a plaque affixed to the exterior of the **Hancock-Clarke House** reminds us that this is where "Samuel Adams and John Hancock were sleeping when aroused by Paul Revere".

The **Munroe Tavern**, somewhat removed from the town centre, served as a field hospital for British soldiers, though only for ninety minutes. It now houses the **Museum of the British Redcoats**, which gives a British perspective on the events of April 19, 1775.

National Heritage Museum

33 Marrett Rd • Wed–Sat 10.30am–4pm • Free • ☏ 781 861 6559, ⓦ nationalheritagemuseum.org

The **National Heritage Museum**, south of downtown, is a small but intriguing American history museum founded by the Scottish Rite of Freemasonry. A nice break from Revolutionary battlegrounds, it offers rotating exhibits on varied facets of American daily life and culture, including an amusing set of cuckoo clocks (the "drunken angel" plays his organ with a jug of liquor beside him, while the "Doomsday" clock tolls with tombstones). Its display of antique pitchers and dishes may at first seem banal, but a closer look reveals mysterious Masonic symbols, such as the inverted square and compass. You'll also find a nostalgic collection of local board games and the permanent "Seeds of Liberty" exhibit, with displays on Revolutionary War events.

2

Minute Man National Historical Park

At the intersection of Rte-2A and Airport Rd, two miles west of Lexington • **Minute Man Visitor Center** Daily: mid-March to Oct 9am–5pm; Nov 9am–4pm • **Hartwell Inn** Mid-April to late May Sat & Sun 9.30am–5.30pm; late May to Oct daily 9.30am–5.30pm • Free • ☎ 978 369 6993, ⓦ nps.gov/mima

Forming a corridor between Lexington and Concord, the **Minute Man National Historical Park** preserves every inch of the **Battle Road**, along which the British forces were pushed back towards Boston on April 19, 1775.

The best place to get oriented is the **Minute Man Visitor Center**. From here Rte-2A (which becomes Lexington Rd), winds past most of the attractions, though it's far more pleasant to follow the five-mile **Battle Road Trail** from the visitor centre on bike or foot. Highlights include the monument that marks where **Paul Revere** was captured by the British, ending his famous ride, and the **Hartwell Inn**, the local hostelry in 1775 and now the site of musket-firing demonstrations, in which a costumed ranger fires off a lead ball from his trusty seventeenth-century Brown Bess.

Wayside

455 Lexington Rd, near Concord • Tours: June–Oct Wed–Sun 10am–4.30pm • $5 • ☎ 978 318 7863

The park ends at the outskirts of Concord and the seventeenth-century **Wayside**, home of Samuel Whitney, muster man for the Minute Men, but better known today as a literary landmark: Louisa May Alcott lived in the house as a teenager in the 1840s, and Nathaniel Hawthorne lived and wrote here between 1852 and 1870. Among the antique furnishings, the most evocative is the slanted desk in the fourth-floor "tower", at which Hawthorne wrote, standing up.

Orchard House

399 Lexington Rd, near Concord • Tours: April–Oct Mon–Sat 10am–4.30pm, Sun 1–4.30pm; Nov–March Mon–Fri 11am–3pm, Sat 10am–4.30pm, Sun 1–4.30pm • $9 • ☎ 978 369 4118, ⓦ louisamayalcott.org.

Alcott penned *Little Women* at **Orchard House**, next door to Wayside, where she and her family lived from 1858 to 1877. The guided tour is well worth your time; although it focuses heavily on the differences between Alcott's life and her most famous book, it is also the best way to get a good impression of the area's strong nineteenth-century literary, intellectual and liberal activist community (see box, p.134).

ARRIVAL AND INFORMATION

LEXINGTON

By bus The MBTA (☎ 617 222 3200, ⓦ mbta.com) runs buses (15min; $1.50) to Lexington from Cambridge's Alewife Station.

By car Take Rte-2 out of the city towards Arlington, then follow the signs to Lexington (11 miles from downtown Boston).

Lexington Visitor Center 1875 Massachusetts Ave, on the eastern periphery of the Green (daily: April–Oct 9am–5pm; Nov–March 10am–4pm; ☎ 781 862 2480, ⓦ lexingtonchamber.org).

GETTING AROUND

By tram Liberty Ride (June–Oct daily 10am–4pm; April & May Sat & Sun only; $25 for 2 days; ☎ 781 862 0500 ext 260, ⓦ libertyride.us), operates a hop-on, hop-off tram service between the National Heritage Museum and the North Bridge in Concord (see p.131), stopping at all the main sights.

ACCOMMODATION AND EATING

Aloft 727 Marrett Rd ☎ 781 761 1700, ⓦ starwoodhotels.com. Brainchild of the *W Hotel* with the same contemporary design and luxury accoutrements (saltwater pool, self-service car wash, flat-screen TVs, daily papers, Bliss bath products) for which the brand is known. Next door, the spacious, eco-friendly guest rooms of its sister property, *Element*, are good for long-term stays. **$150**

Rancatore's 1752 Massachusetts Ave ☎ 781 862 5090. Inventively flavoured ice cream made with impeccable ingredients – try a scoop each of gingersnap molasses and strawberry rhubarb to get hooked. Daily 10am–11pm.

Upper Crust 41 Waltham St ☎ 781 274 0089. Outpost of the popular Boston pizza chain with delicious thin-crust concoctions that move beyond basic pepperoni by using toppings like steak and gorgonzola or sundried tomato and ubergine. Mon–Thurs & Sun 11.30am–10pm, Fri & Sat 11.30am–11pm.

Via Lago 1845 Massachusetts Ave ☎ 781 861 6174. A casual counter-service spot that's good for fresh pastas,

sandwiches and salads at lunchtime; come nightfall, dinner is served by candlelight and locals unwind at the bar. Mon–Wed 7am–9pm, Thurs–Sat 7am–9.30pm.

Concord

The Revolutionary War theme continues in earnest in **CONCORD**, though the town's literary associations are just as much, if not more, of a draw. Like Lexington, it's an upscale suburb of Boston, though sleepier, and more successful at retaining the feel of a tree-filled New England country town than its urban neighbour.

Concord's business district hugs **Main Street**, which intersects Monument Street right by the historic **Colonial Inn**, an atmospheric place for high tea or lunch. Main Street crosses Lexington Road at the **Hill Burying Ground**, from the top of which you can survey much of the town. A few blocks behind the grounds, off Rte-62, lies **Sleepy Hollow Cemetery**, where Concord literati Ralph Waldo Emerson, Nathaniel Hawthorne, Henry David Thoreau and Louisa May Alcott are interred atop "Authors' Ridge".

Concord Museum

53 Cambridge Turnpike • Jan–March Mon–Sat 11am–4pm, Sun 1–4pm; April–Dec Mon–Sat 9am–5pm, Sun noon–5pm • $10 • ☎ 978 369 9763, ⓦ concordmuseum.org

A good place to learn about the town's literary and historical scene is the absorbing **Concord Museum**. Located on the former site of Ralph Waldo Emerson's apple orchard, the museum has nineteen galleries filled with prime cultural artefacts. One such prize is half of the famed pair of "one if by land, and two if by sea" signal lanterns, hung from Old North Church in Boston to warn of the impending British march at the outset of the Revolutionary War. The museum also boasts Emerson's entire study, as well as Henry David Thoreau's personal effects, including the little green desk at which he wrote *Civil Disobedience* and *Walden*.

Ralph Waldo Emerson House

28 Cambridge Turnpike • Late April to Oct Thurs–Sat 10am–4.30pm, Sun 1–4.30pm • $8 • ☎ 978 369 2236

The **Ralph Waldo Emerson House** is where the essayist and poet lived from 1835 until his death in 1882. The creaking interior – bedrooms, kitchen and dining rooms – have been preserved as they would have looked in Emerson's day, though the precious contents of his study were donated to the **Concord Museum**, across the street (see above).

North Bridge

North Bridge Visitor Center: 174 Liberty St • Daily: late March to late Oct 9am–5pm; late Oct to late Nov 9am–4pm; Dec to late March 11am–3pm • ☎ 978 369 6993, ⓦ nps.gov/mima

The most vaunted spot in Concord is the **North Bridge**, slightly removed from the town centre. This was the site of the first armed resistance to British rule in America; just before it, an inscription on the mass grave of British regulars reads: "They came 3000 miles to keep the past upon its throne." Though photogenic, the bridge itself looks a bit too groomed to provoke much patriotic sentiment – indeed, it's a 1954 replica of an earlier replacement.

Old Manse

269 Monument St • Tours hourly: mid-April to Oct Mon–Sat 10am–5pm, Sun noon–5pm • $8 • ☎ 978 369 3909, ⓦ oldmanse.org

A stone's throw from North Bridge, the grey-clapboard **Old Manse** was built by Ralph Waldo Emerson's grandfather, the Reverend William Emerson, whose wife witnessed the hostilities from the window (William, a chaplain, was at the Bridge with the

2

CONCORD AND TRANSCENDENTALISM

A half-century after independence, Concord became the centre of a revolution in American thinking known as **transcendentalism**. The transcendentalists, many of them Harvard-educated Unitarian ministers unhappy with their church's conservatism, denied the existence of miracles and stressed the conviction that insight and intuitive knowledge were the ways to enhance the relationship between man, nature and the "over-soul". These beliefs were born of a passion for rural life, liberty and intellectual freedom. Indeed, the free thinking that transcendentalism unleashed put writers at the vanguard of American literary expression.

In 1834, **Ralph Waldo Emerson** moved into the Old Manse (see p.133), the house his grandfather had built near the North Bridge; there, in 1836, he wrote the book that would signal the birth of the movement, *Nature*, in which he argued for the function of nature as a visible manifestation of invisible **spiritual truths**. His stature as an intensely pensive, learned scribe drew other intellectuals to Concord, notably Henry David Thoreau, Nathaniel Hawthorne, Bronson Alcott (father of Louisa May) and Margaret Fuller. These Concord authors formed a **close-knit group**. In 1840, Emerson and Fuller co-founded *The Dial*, the literary magazine that became the movement's semi-official journal. Nathaniel Hawthorne, a native of Salem, rented the Old Manse for three years, returned to his hometown, and then moved back to Concord permanently in 1852. Meanwhile, Emerson financed Thoreau's Walden Pond sojourn and the Alcotts lived in Orchard House, on Lexington Road. The largely wholesome literary movement spawned several short-lived utopian **farming ventures**, including Bronson Alcott's Fruitlands (see p.136). Its effects were longer lasting than these communities, however, as its proponents played an important role in the abolitionist and feminist movements.

Minute Men). The younger Emerson lived here on and off, and, in 1834, penned *Nature*, the book that signalled the beginning of the transcendentalist movement (see box above) here. The most interesting room is the upstairs study, where Nathaniel Hawthorne, a resident of the house in the early 1840s, wrote *Mosses from an Old Manse*, a collection of short stories that gave the place its name. Hawthorne passed three happy years here (although later getting evicted for non-payment of rent) shortly after getting married; his wife, Sophia, following a miscarriage, used her diamond wedding ring to etch the words "Man's accidents are God's purposes" into a window pane in the study, still visible today.

Walden Pond State Reservation

7am to sunset • Parking $5 • ☎ 978 369 3254

The tranquillity savoured by Henry David Thoreau at **Walden Pond**, just south of Concord proper off Rte-126, is still present today – although now you'll have to share it with the swimmers and hikers who pour in to retrace his footsteps. The pond itself has remained much the same since the author's famed two-year exercise in self-sufficiency began in 1845. "I did not feel crowded or confined in the least," he wrote of his life in the simple log cabin; and, though his account of the experience (documented in *Walden*) might have you believe otherwise, Thoreau hardly roughed it, taking regular walks into town to stock up on amenities and receiving frequent visitors. A reconstructed single-room hut is situated near the car park, while the site of his cabin, closer to the pond, is marked with stones. The footpath that meanders around the pond is a good spot for contemplation.

ARRIVAL AND DEPARTURE

By train The MBTA (☎ 617 222 3200, ⓦ mbta.com) operates trains from Boston's North Station to Concord Depot (40–45min; $6.25 one-way), a stiff 1.5-mile walk from the centre.
By car You'll find ample parking (free) in the centre of

Concord, behind the visitor centre on Main St, though th᷉ lot can fill up fast in the summer. Driving from Boston, yᴄ can skip Lexington and the Minute Man National Historic Park by taking Rte-2 straight to Concord.

GETTING AROUND

By tram Liberty Ride (June–Oct daily 10am–4pm; April & May Sat & Sun only; $25 for two days; ☎781 862 0500 ext 260, ⓦlibertyride.us) operates a hop-on, hop-off service between the National Heritage Museum in Lexington (see p.131) and the North Bridge stopping at all the main sights.

INFORMATION

Chamber of Commerce 15 Walden St (hours vary, call ahead; ☎978 369 3120, ⓦconcordchamberof commerce.org).

Visitor centre 58 Main St (April–Oct daily 10am–4pm).

The town's central visitor centre offers guided walking tours for $20 (1hr 30min; April–Oct Mon & Fri at 1pm, Sat & Sun 11am & 1pm).

ACCOMMODATION

Amerscot House Inn Nine miles west of Concord in Stow, 61 W Acton Rd ☎978 897 0666, ⓦamerscot.com. Offers attentive hospitality and four snugly designed rooms, three with decorative fireplaces, in a restored 1734 farmhouse. **$150**

Hawthorne Inn 462 Lexington Rd ☎978 369 5610, ⓦconcordmass.com. Esteemed, Italianate-style inn with seven richly furnished rooms, antique canopy beds and plenty of cosy nooks and crannies in which to curl up with a dog-eared copy of *Walden*. **$229**

North Bridge Inn 21 Monument St ☎1 888 530 0007, ⓦnorthbridgeinn.com. Has an unbeatable location right in Monument Square, with six New England country-style suites named after New England literati – Longfellow's lair has a stately sleigh bed and floral-print pillows; Dickinson's room is painted a cheerful lemon-yellow. Full daily breakfast included. **$190**

EATING AND DRINKING

★ **80 Thoreau** 80 Thoreau St ☎978 318 0008. While Concord may be long on Revolutionary War heroes, historically it has been short on culinary trailblazers. Enter *80 Thoreau*, an epicurean favourite drawing foodies all the way from restaurant-mad Boston. Mains $20–32. Mon–Thurs 5.30–10.30pm, Fri & Sat 5.30–11.30pm.

Bedford Farms 68 Thoreau St ☎978 341 0000. Next to the train station, this magnetic New England ice-cream purveyor has been churning out the sweet stuff since 1880. Summer Mon–Sat 11am–9.30pm, Sun noon–9.30pm; in colder months noon–6pm (call to confirm).

Cheese Shop 29 Walden St ☎978 369 5778. Take a number for made-to-order sandwiches, home-made soups and salads at this *fromagerie* in Monument Square. You'll also find deluxe picnic fixings, jams and a range of delectable cheeses. There are a handful of tables, but it's better for takeaway. Tues–Fri 10am–5.30pm, Sat 9.30am–5.30pm.

★ **La Provence** 105–107 Thoreau St ☎978 371 7428. Authentic French cooking in a colourful, casual dining room with friendly counter service. The chicken Provence sandwich ($6.75) has a tangy mustard kick, and diners wax euphoric over the red bliss potato salad ($6.95/lb). There's also an exquisite bakery on site. Mon–Fri 7am–7pm, Sat 7am–5.30pm.

Lincoln

Walden Pond straddles the border of Concord and bucolic **LINCOLN**, a quiet suburb where handwritten signs trumpet fresh produce and "downtown" consists of the town clerk's office and a nineteenth-century Victorian library. If you have little ones in tow (or are in need of yarn and fresh eggs), don't miss a visit to **Drumlin Farm** at 208 South Great Rd (Tues–Sun: March–Oct 9am–5pm; Nov–Feb 9am–4pm; $7; ☎781 259 2200, ⓦmassaudubon.org), a working farm populated by contented pigs, horses, cows, chickens and goats. The property, run by the Massachusetts Audubon Society, also has a learning garden with labelled herbs and produce, hay rides and a drumlin with walking trails.

DeCordova Museum and Sculpture Park

51 Sandy Pond Rd • Tues–Sun 10am–5pm • $12; sculpture park free when museum is closed • ☎781 259 8355, ⓦdecordova.org

At the **DeCordova Museum and Sculpture Park,** all manner of contemporary sculptures pepper the museum's expansive grounds, like Jim Dine's *Two Big Black Hearts* and Paul Matisse's *Musical Fence*, which look like they've burst through the walls of the museum and tumbled into their present positions. Matisse's piece is interactive – tap it with a wooden stick as you would a xylophone. Most of the sculptures are by American (and in particular New England) artists, and are sufficiently impressive to make the garden overshadow the small on-site museum, whose rotating exhibits are often just as eye-catching, with an emphasis on multimedia art.

Gropius House

68 Baker Bridge Rd · Guided tours on the hour 11am–4pm: June to mid-Oct Wed–Sun; mid-Oct to May Sat & Sun · $10 · ☎ 781 259 8098, ⓦ historicnewengland.org

The **Gropius House** was designed in 1937 by the German founder of the influential **Bauhaus school** of architecture, Walter Gropius, when he came to teach at Harvard University. Incorporating elements of both industrial design (a banister made from pipes, chrome factory lightbulbs) and New England quaint (white clapboard shingles – placed here unconventionally inside the entryway), this ode to contemporary aesthetics sits incongruously on a country hillside. The interior contains items belonging to the family and a valuable collection of Bauhaus-inspired furniture designed by fellow Modernist Marcel Breuer.

ARRIVAL AND DEPARTURE   LINCOLN

By train The MBTA (☎ 617 222 3200, ⓦ mbta.com) operates trains from Boston's North Station to 160 Lincoln Rd in Lincoln (35min; $5.75 one-way), from where it's a mile to Drumlin Farm, and just over two to the DeCordova Museum and Gropius House.

Harvard

Nineteen miles west of Lincoln, the small town of **HARVARD** is honeycombed with apple orchards, cow pastures and swathes of maple trees. Decidedly off the tourist circuit, visitors come here to visit the galleries of the **Fruitlands Museum** or simply to enjoy the peace and quiet this idyllic town affords.

Fruitlands Museum

102 Prospect Hill Rd · Mid-April to mid-Nov Mon–Fri 10am–4pm, Sat & Sun 10am–5pm · $12 · ☎ 978 456 3924, ⓦ fruitlands.org

The **Fruitlands Museum** was formerly the site of a nineteenth-century transcendental utopian movement headed by **Bronson Alcott**. Aiming to create a "New Eden", Alcott started the idealistic commune here with his English friend Charles Lane in 1843, espousing vegetarianism, freedom of expression and celibacy (this last after siring four daughters, including Louisa May), but talk of living off the "fruits of the land" proved much easier in theory than practice, and the experiment was short-lived. The original farmhouse now houses a **museum** with exhibits on the transcendentalist movement, including letters and memorabilia relating to Alcott, Emerson and Thoreau, and there are two hundred acres of woodlands and meadows on the site, which you can explore on four well-marked trails.

CIDER AND WINE

The Harvard area is well known for its **apples** and apple products. You can pick your own at **U-Pick Phil's Apples**, 24 Prospect Hill Rd (mid-Sept to Nov daily 8am–6pm; ☎ 978 456 3361, ⓦ philsapples.com), where you can also make **cider** at weekends. **The Nashoba Valley Winery**, on Wattaquadoc Hill Rd (daily 11am–5pm, tours at weekends 11am–5pm; $7; ☎ 978 779 5521, ⓦ nashobawinery.com), near **Bolton**, approximately fifteen miles west of Concord, offers peach-, plum-, apple- and berry-picking (seasonal), as well as samples of its award-winning wines and microbrews. Complete the experience at on-site J's *Restaurant* (closed Mon & Tues, dinner not served Sun; reservations recommended; ☎ 978 779 9816).

There are three additional galleries on the museum grounds: the **Shaker Gallery**, which displays furniture, crafts and artefacts retrieved from a Shaker community that once existed here; the **Art Gallery**, which features a collection of American art, including New England landscape paintings by Hudson River School artists Thomas Cole and Frederic Edwin Church and a large collection of vernacular portraits (painted by untrained artists); as well as a **Native American Museum** which highlights handicrafts, clothing, headdresses, pottery, dolls and carvings. Sitting atop Prospect Hill, the whole site affords spellbinding views of the surrounding countryside, best appreciated over a picnic lunch.

2

ARRIVAL AND DEPARTURE   **HARVARD**

By car There is no public transport in Harvard, and it's   easily accessed by exit 38A off Rte-2.
best to drive here. Harvard is 45min west of Boston,

Lowell

Thirty miles northwest of Boston on the Merrimack River, **LOWELL**'s downtown has been preserved as the **Lowell National Historical Park**, a powerful memorial, to the city's unparalleled role in American textile history a powerful memorial, comprised of restored mill buildings and museums, to the city's unparalleled role. As you explore, you'll also come across mentions of the city's most famous son, author **Jack Kerouac** (see box, p.139), who was born and raised here; the city makes several appearances in his novels, and Jack was buried here in 1969. Lowell was memorialized in the 2010 film *The Fighter*, which depicts local residents, professional boxers and half-brothers "Irish" Micky Ward and Dicky Eklund; Ward became World Boxing Union Champion after Eklund kicked a nasty drug habit, reinstating himself as his brother's trainer. In addition to the national park sights, there are a handful of other worthy diversions in the centre.

Brief history

The mighty red-brick mills of Lowell were once at the heart of the American Industrial Revolution. The town is named for entrepreneur **Francis Cabot Lowell**, who in 1814 established the first textile mill in America to use power looms (in Waltham, outside Boston), after memorizing the necessary technology (a secret at the time) on an earlier visit to England; Lowell, which utilized the power of the Merrimack, was a larger venture founded in 1822. By the 1840s, it was one of the most productive cities in the world, turning out almost one million yards of cotton cloth every week. The city hit hard times during the Great Depression, and the last mill closed in the 1950s; like many former industrial towns in the region, Lowell today remains proudly working-class.

National Streetcar Museum

25 Shattuck St • March–Nov Sat & Sun 11am–4pm • $3 • ☎ 978 458 5835, ⊛ trolleymuseum.org/lowell
The **National Streetcar Museum** has a small exhibition about the history of public transport in Lowell in addition to a collection of early twentieth-century trolleys. Run entirely by volunteers, the museum has limited hours, but if you pop by on a summer weekend they'll take you for a two-mile spin in a vintage streetcar.

New England Quilt Museum

18 Shattuck St • Tues–Sat 10am–4pm; May–Oct also Sun noon–4pm • $7 • ☎ 978 452 4207 ext 15, ⊛ nequiltmuseum.org
The **New England Quilt Museum** houses vintage and contemporary quilts of appeal mainly to aficionados. Even if you're not a blanket buff, the two small floors of exhibit space are charming, with poetically titled pieces (such as "A Feathered Star for Himself") and Civil War-era Americana, fabric flowers and even potholders stitched together into impressive kaleidoscopes of colour and shape.

Whistler House Museum of Art

243 Worthen St • Wed–Sat 11am–4pm • $5 • ☎ 978 452 7641, ⓦ whistlerhouse.org

The **Whistler House Museum of Art** is located in the birthplace of **James McNeil Whistler** (1834–1903). The controversial artist actually renounced his hometown, spending most of his life in London, where he became associated with the Aesthetic Movement and early Modernism. The gallery houses a small but impressive collection of nineteenth- and early twentieth-century New England artists, as well as some of Whistler's own etchings.

Lowell National Historical Park

304 Dutton St • Daily 9am–5pm, but with seasonal fluctuations, check website to confirm; March–Nov tram every 30–45min, more frequently at weekends • Free • ☎ 978 970 5000, ⓦ nps.gov/lowe

Begin your tour of the **Lowell National Historical Park** at the modern **visitor centre**, in the heart of the vast Market Mills complex. Multimedia presentations covering the history of the city (and, at 4pm on request, the life of Jack Kerouac) screen regularly in the theatre, while exhibits fill in the gaps and rangers are on hand to provide maps and advice. Walking is the best way to explore – with the exception of Wannalancit Mills, everything is within a few minutes of the visitor centre – but there's also a **tram** that runs to all the park's main sights. Illuminating tram **tours** are given daily (free), as well as boat trips along the canals ($8–10; call or see the website for schedule).

Boott Cotton Mills Museum

115 John St • Daily 9.30am–5pm • $6 • ☎ 978 970 5000, ⓦ nps.gov/lowe

The highlight of the park, the **Boott Cotton Mills Museum**, lies at the end of John Street, a fifteen-minute stroll north of the visitor centre. A beautifully restored mill building dating from the 1830s, it's one of the most memorable sights in the state. Inside, you'll find a vast room of ninety whirring looms from the 1920s. Only seven to ten run at one time, yet the noise produced is still deafening – it's hard to imagine what it would have been like to work here with all of them pounding away. Upstairs, a comprehensive history of Lowell is laid out in chronological order, enhanced by video dramatizations, testimony of actual workers (the accidents section is especially sobering) and exhibits such as a spinning frame from 1839.

Mills Girls & Immigrants Exhibit

40 French St • Daily 1.30–5pm, reduced hours in winter • Free

In addition introducing to the revolutionary power loom to the US, Francis Cabot Lowell also broke new ground with his employees: young women from New England farming communities, who became known as "mill girls". To get a deeper sense of what life was like for them, visit the Mogan Cultural Center and its poignant **Mills Girls & Immigrants Exhibit**, a re-creation of a mill boarding house for unmarried girls c.1830. Though nineteenth-century life here was grim it was nonetheless an improvement on Britain's "dark satanic mills". Things got worse after the middle of the nineteenth century, when Irish immigrants began to replace the local girls, and were treated far more poorly.

Wannalancit Mills

600 Suffolk St • Visitable by guided tour only • Free

Along Suffolk Street and the Northern Canal, **Wannalancit Mills** is home to the "River Transformed" exhibition, which showcases original nineteenth-century turbines and explains how the Merrimack River was used to power the whole city.

American Textile History Museum

491 Dutton St • Wed–Sun 10am–5pm • $8 • ☎ 978 441 0400, ⓦ athm.org

The park's industrial theme is continued at the **American Textile History Museum**, south of the visitor centre. The museum was given a jazzy makeover in 2008, including a new

ON THE TRAIL OF JACK KEROUAC

Jack Kerouac, one of America's most influential modern authors, is best known for his seminal novel *On the Road* (1957), which established him as the father of the **Beat Generation**. Though much of his adult life was spent wandering the country, Kerouac was born in Lowell in 1922 (a plaque marks the home at 9 Lupine Rd); his parents were French-Canadian immigrants from Québec and he grew up in what was known as Little Canada (east of the city centre), becoming a successful athlete at Lowell High School (still on Kirk St). Returning to Lowell in 1967, Jack wrote the last book published before his death, *Vanity of Duluoz*, and hung out at *Nicky's Bar* at 112 Gorham St (now a café). The **national historical park** commemorates the city's most famous son with documentaries shown at the visitor centre (see opposite) and a few bits and pieces displayed at the Mill Girls exhibit (see opposite), including Jack's typewriter and backpack. Fans should also check out the **Jack Kerouac Commemorative**, a collection of stones and pillars inscribed with excerpts from his writings, on Bridge Street in Kerouac Park, and Jack's simple **grave**, in the Sampas family plot at Edson Cemetery on Gorham Street, two miles south of the intersection with the Lowell Connector. Finally, if you visit in autumn, check out "**Lowell Celebrates Kerouac!**" (☎ 1 877 537 6822, 🖥 lckorg.tripod.com), a three-day festival of readings, exhibits and special events.

permanent exhibit titled "Textile Revolution: An Exploration through Space and Time". Especially fun for kids, it highlights the history of textiles with interactive spinning, weaving, design and recycling displays.

ARRIVAL AND DEPARTURE
LOWELL

By train Commuter rail trains depart frequently from Boston's North Station (45min; $6.75; ☎ 617 222 3200, 🖥 mbta.com) for 101 Thorndike St in Lowell, close to the national park.

By car Driving into Lowell from Boston is straightforward: take US-3 (N) to I-495 (N) and then the Lowell Connector; signs direct you to the visitor centre on Dutton Street, where you can park for free (although you will need to validate your ticket at the National Historical Park).

ACCOMMODATION

Courtyard by Marriott 30 Industrial Ave, East Lowell ☎ 978 458 7575, 🖥 marriott.com. Just 5min from downtown Lowell, this 120-room hotel was thoroughly renovated in 2009, and now sports new furniture and bedding, flat-screen TVs and modern bathrooms. There's a seasonal outdoor pool, and a full hot breakfast available for $10.95. $114

UMass Lowell Inn 50 Warren St Ave ☎ 1 877 886 5422, 🖥 acc-umlinnandconferencecenter.com. Run by a local university, this spacious town centre hotel is within walking distance of area attractions. Rooms are comfortably modern, with fluffy white beds, and there's biodegradable soap in the bathrooms, endearingly manufactured with a hole in the middle so as not to waste product. Ten rooms have private patios overlooking the canal, and there's a brand-new fitness centre. $120

EATING AND DRINKING

You'll find plenty of places to eat near the museums downtown, with several restaurants and Irish pubs along **Market Street** opposite the visitor centre, and alfresco dining on nearby Palmer Street.

★ **Arthur's Paradise Diner** 112 Bridge St ☎ 978 452 8647. This dilapidated dining car has inconvenient hours, no customer toilets and terrible parking, all adding to its ample charm. A Lowell landmark, it's famed for its "Boott Mill Sandwich", comprised of eggs, cheese, hash browns and bacon on a warm bread roll. Cash only. Daily 6am–noon.

Blue Taleh 15 Kearney Square ☎ 978 453 1112. Smack in the centre of downtown, this buzzing newcomer serves top-notch sushi and Thai dishes in a cheerful dining room on the canal. The chicken and shrimp mango curry will set you back $16, while sushi prices hover around $10.95 per roll. Mon 11.30am–10pm, Tues–Thurs 11.30am–10.30pm, Fri 11.30am–11pm, Sat noon–11pm, Sun noon–10pm.

★ **Life Alive** 194 Middle St ☎ 978 453 1311. Close to the visitor centre, this local favourite is part café and part health store, with a huge range of herbal teas and tasty organic and vegetarian meals like "the Goddess" wrap, a blend of carrots, beets, broccoli, tofu, ginger sauce and

2

2

brown rice ($9). Mon–Wed 10am–8pm, Thurs & Fri 10am–9pm, Sat 10am–8pm, Sun noon–6pm.
Olympia Restaurant 453 Market St ☎ 978 452 8092. Lowell has a sizeable Greek community, whose heritage is kept alive at this restaurant, depicted in *The Fighter* (see p.137). Succulent baked lamb ($15) and stuffed grape leaves ($13) are served at deep-blue booths by waiters in uniform. Tues–Sat 11am–10pm, Mon & Sun 11am–9pm.
Simply Khmer 26 Lincoln St ☎ 978 454 6700. In

addition to Greek food, Lowell is known for its authenti Cambodian restaurants, and despite its location in a slightly dodgy neighbourhood, *Simply Khmer* is the pick c the pack. Try the mouthwatering hot wings in special sauce ($7.50), beef *loc lac* (tender cubes of marinated beef on a bed of fried rice; $9.95), and hot pots, wherein mixed veggies and meats are cooked tableside in a piping hot broth ($45 for four people; call in advance so they can get i ready). Daily 8am–9pm.

The North Shore

The **North Shore**, which extends from Boston to the New Hampshire border, takes in some of Massachusetts' most disparate geography and culture. Outside the city a series of glum working-class suburbs – Revere, Saugus, Lynn – gradually yield to commuter-belt communities like Swampscott and Beverly Farms, then to the charming waterfront town of **Marblehead** and nearby **Salem**, known for its infamous witch trials. Just north of here juts scenic **Cape Ann**, the so-called "other Cape"; with its lighthouses, seafood shanties and rocky shores, it's a scaled-down version of the Maine coast. Highlights include the fishing port of **Gloucester** and the smart oceanfront village of **Rockport**. Further up the coast, the land flattens out a bit, with acres of salt marshes and some of the finest white sands in New England, particularly on **Plum Island** and near the sleepy villages of **Essex** and **Ipswich**. Closer to the New Hampshire border, the elegant old fishing burg **Newburyport** is of some historical interest, with scores of Federal mansions and a commercial district dating to the early 1800s. Any of these towns can be reached in an easy day-trip from Boston, and none should take more than a day to explore.

Marblehead

Just fifteen miles north of downtown Boston, affluent **MARBLEHEAD** sits on a peninsula thrusting out into Massachusetts Bay, its shoreline cliffs overlooking a wide natural harbour. This advantageous position has long been the town's greatest asset: founded by hardy fishermen from the English West Country in 1629, Marblehead quickly became a thriving **port**, especially in the years leading up to the Revolution. During the war, the Marblehead militia was commissioned to lease the first US warship, local schooner *Hannah*; four subsequent made-in-Marblehead vessels formed what would become the US Navy. Today boating, especially yachting, remains the lifeblood of the town, and Marblehead is at its most animated during the annual **Race Week** (last week of July).

To get a sweeping view of the port, head to the end of Front Street and **Fort Sewall**, the remnants of fortifications built by the British in 1644 and later enlarged to protect the harbour from French cruisers; these defences also shielded the USS *Constitution* (see p.65) in the War of 1812. Closer to the centre of town, but with similar views, is **Old Burial Hill** on Orne Street, the resting place of more than six hundred Revolutionary War soldiers.

Jeremiah Lee Mansion

161 Washington St • June–Oct tours Tues–Sat 10am–4pm • $5 • ☎ 781 631 0595, ⓦ marbleheadmuseum.org

The streets that wind down to the Marblehead waterfront are lined with old clapboard houses, most of them quite modest with tiny gardens – a reminder that fishermen, not farmers, lived here in the colonial period. A bit further back from the ocean, along **Washington Street**, are the larger homes of the merchants who prospered here before the Revolution. Among them is the 1768 **Jeremiah Lee Mansion**, the Georgian home of the eponymous shipping magnate, who imported all his interior decorations, including English wallpaper and South American mahogany. In fact, Lee's wallpaper is the only eighteenth-century English hand-painted paper existing in situ today.

Abbot Hall

188 Washington St • Mon, Tues & Thurs 8am–5pm, Wed 8am–6pm, Fri 8am–12.30pm, Sat 10am–5pm, Sun 11am–5pm • Free • ☎ 781 631 0000

While in Marblehead, stop by **Abbot Hall**, the town's attractive town hall, which keeps time by a still-ticking 1877 clock and houses Archibald Willard's famous painting *The Spirit of '76*, a patriotic depiction of drumming Revolutionary War soldiers.

INFORMATION	**MARBLEHEAD**

Chamber of Commerce Maintains an information booth at the corner of Pleasant and Essex streets (late May to Oct Mon–Wed noon–4pm, Thurs–Sun 11am–5pm; ☎ 781 639 8469) and an office at 62 Pleasant St (Mon–Fri 9am–5pm; ☎ 781 631 2868, ⊛ visitmarblehead.com).

ACCOMMODATION

Harbor Light Inn 58 Washington St ☎ 781 631 2186, ⊛ harborlightinn.com. The best of the central hotels, this Federal inn is decorated with plaids, antique armoires and four-poster beds. Many rooms have working fireplaces, and some have the added bonus of a double jacuzzi. There is also a heated outdoor pool, wi-fi and, come breakfast, crème brûlée French toast. $175

★ **One Kimball at Marblehead Light** 1 Kimball St, on Marblehead Neck ☎ 781 631 0010, ⊛ onekimball.com. Two beach-house-chic suites in a capacious home overlooking the ocean. The best amenity may be the view: nearly every window looks out on the Atlantic, and there's a little lighthouse close by. Full breakfast in the morning. $200

Pheasant Hill B&B 71 Bubier Rd ☎ 781 639 4799, ⊛ pheasanthill.com. On a quiet residential street, this casual B&B has three suites, one with a working fireplace and private porch. The house's patio offers water views, a great accompaniment to the complimentary continental breakfast. It's an easy walk to the beach and downtown. $140

EATING AND DRINKING

5 Corners Kitchen 2 School St ☎ 781 631 5550. Foodies rave about this French-inspired bistro that makes its own pasta, charcuterie and smoked meats in-house. Sink into a sand-hued banquette and feast on steak frites ($22.95) and greens with wild mushrooms ($5.95). Mon–Sat 5.30–11pm, Sun 10am–3pm.

Jack-Tar American Tavern 126 Washington St ☎ 781 631 2323. Friendly local joint that's good for a grilled pizza (pancetta with blue cheese; $12) and a pulled pint. The tavern-fare menu covers a wide spectrum, from burgers and pasta to steak tips and lobster cobb salad. There's a nice outdoor patio, too. Daily 5pm–late.

The Landing 81 Front St ☎ 781 639 1266. Tuck into fresh lobster (market price) and pan-roasted haddock ($20) on an outdoor deck overlooking the yacht-filled harbour. Good date spot, with frequent live music. Daily 11.30am–late.

Salem

The witch trials of 1692 put **SALEM** on the map, and the coastal town, four miles north of Marblehead, has done little since to distance itself from its macabre history; indeed, most of its attractions focus on fairly kitsch witch-related activities. Less known were the many years Salem spent as a flourishing seaport – indeed, this was where the **Massachusetts Bay Colony** was established – and the remnants from this era only add to the town's aura, with abandoned wharves, rows of stately sea captains' homes and an astounding display of riches at the **Peabody Essex Museum**.

The **Essex Street Mall** – a car-free, boutique-filled stretch of Essex Street – functions as the backbone of the town, and there's also the 1.7-mile Salem Heritage Trail (modelled after Boston's Freedom Trail, and similarly marked by a red strip of paint, which links the town's principal historic sights). Despite some of the cheesiness on offer, Halloween is a great time to visit Salem, when sights are open longer, myriad special events are held and the autumn foliage is at its most glorious; check out ⊛ hauntedhappenings.com.

2

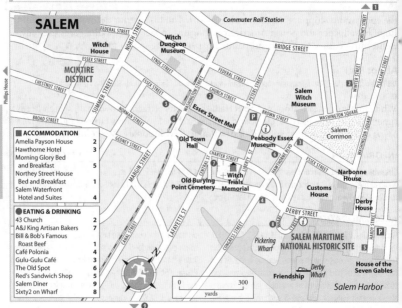

SALEM

ACCOMMODATION
Amelia Payson House	2
Hawthorne Hotel	3
Morning Glory Bed and Breakfast	5
Northey Street House Bed and Breakfast	1
Salem Waterfront Hotel and Suites	4

EATING & DRINKING
43 Church	2
A&J King Artisan Bakers	7
Bill & Bob's Famous Roast Beef	1
Café Polonia	4
Gulu-Gulu Café	3
The Old Spot	6
Red's Sandwich Shop	5
Salem Diner	9
Sixty2 on Wharf	8

Brief history

In 1626, a deep, well-protected harbour lured a handful of English settlers here, a place known by the local Native Americans as **Naumkeag**. In 1628 John Endecott arrived as the first governor of the Massachusetts Bay Colony, formally chartered the following year. When John Winthrop turned up with one thousand colonists in 1630, the focus of the colony moved south to Boston, but Salem grew steadily nonetheless. **Elias Derby**, said to be America's first millionaire, built his fortune by running privateers from the town during the Revolutionary War; afterwards, when British ports barred American vessels, he directed his ships to China and the East Indies.

Of the many goods on Salem's outbound ships, the most lucrative by far was **cod**, which found a huge market in Europe. Salem's "merchant princes" brought back everything from spices to olive oil to fine china, for a while monopolizing the luxury goods trade in the young country. But by the mid-1800s, the California Gold Rush, the Civil War, and the silting up of the harbour all conspired to rob Salem of its prosperity. Today the harbour is still home to hundreds of boats, though most are pleasure craft.

Salem Witch Museum

Washington Square North • Daily: July & Aug 10am–7pm; Sept–June 10am–5pm • $9 • ☎ 978 744 1692, ⓦ salemwitchmuseum.com

At the northwestern end of the Essex Street Mall, the **Salem Witch Museum** provides some entertaining, if kitschy, orientation on the witch trials. Though really just a sound-and-light show that uses wax figures to depict the events, it's still better than the other "museums" in town. In front of the house is an imposing statue of a caped **Roger Conant**, founder of Salem's first Puritan settlement.

Witch Dungeon Museum

16 Lynde St • April–Nov daily 10am–5pm • $8 • ☎ 978 741 3570, ⓦ witchdungeon.com

On the west side of town, the **Witch Dungeon Museum** occupies a nineteenth-century church on the site of the prison where accused witches were held. Inside, you're treated to reconstructions of key witch-trial-related events, though this time by real people.

Afterwards the actors escort you to a re-created "dungeon", where you can see that some of the cells were no bigger than a telephone booth.

The Witch House

310 Essex St • May to early Nov daily 10am–5pm, extended hours in Oct • $8.25 • ☎ 978 744 8815, ⓦ salemweb.com/witchhouse

The witch attractions pick up again at the so-called **Witch House**, one block west of the Essex Mall. The well-preserved former home of Judge Jonathan Corwin, this is where the preliminary examinations of the accused took place. Furnished with antiques, the museum focuses more on Puritan life and architecture than on the trials themselves, which are only mentioned towards the end of the half-hour tour.

The McIntire District

The Witch House is a good point of departure for exploring the **McIntire District**, a square mile of sea captains' homes west of downtown between Federal and Broad streets. The most picturesque stretch of these mansions, built after the Revolutionary War, is along **Chestnut Street**. Of these, the **Phillips House** at 34 Chestnut St (June – Oct Tues – Sun 11am–4pm; Nov – May Sat & Sun 11am–4pm; $5; ☎ 978 744 0440, ⓦ phillipsmuseum.org) is the only one open to the public, via half-hour tours. Built by Elias Derby's son-in-law in 1821, it's a welcome break from the supernatural, and worth seeing for its trove of bric-a-brac from around the world.

THE SALEM WITCH TRIALS

By their quantity alone, Salem's **witch memorials** speak of the magnitude of the hysteria that gripped the town for much of 1692 and 1693. The region's first casualties were young teenage girls, who reported as truth tales of the occult they had heard from **Tituba**, a West Indian slave. Their fun took a sinister turn when the daughter and niece of a clergyman, Samuel Parris, experienced convulsions and started barking. It's unknown if the cause of the fits was **epilepsy** or the adverse effects of eating **mouldy bread**, but other girls began to copy them, and when the village doctor failed to diagnose the problem, the accusations of witchcraft began to be taken seriously.

The trials that ensued pitted neighbour against neighbour, even husband against wife. "**Confessing**" to witchcraft spared you the gallows but meant **castigation**. Mary Lacy of Andover, for instance, reported that "me and Martha Carrier did both ride on a stick when we went to a witch meeting in Salem Village". Another accused, Giles Cory, first testified that his wife was a witch, then refused to accept the court's authority. To coerce him, he was staked to the ground under planks while stones were pressed on top of him. He lasted two days, and died without confessing.

The trials were also marked by the girls' crazed ravings: in a scene re-enacted at the Witch Dungeon Museum (see opposite), Ann Putnam claimed that Sarah Good, a pipe-smoking beggar woman, was biting her, right in front of the judge. Such "**spectral evidence**" was accepted as fact, and the trials soon degenerated into the definitive case study of guilt by association. More than 150 villagers were accused and imprisoned (this in a village of 500), nineteen were hanged and four died in jail. Tituba, who readily confessed to sorcery, was not among them.

The most grisly day in Salem's history was **September 22, 1692**, when eight villagers were hanged. Though the hysteria continued for a while unabated, with another 21 people tried in January 1693, the court's legitimacy, shaky from the start, was starting to wear thin. Appalled by the sordid state of affairs, the new royal governor, **William Phipps**, intervened after his wife was accused, and forbade the use of spectral evidence as proof. All of the accused were acquitted that May, and families of the victims eventually awarded damages. The whole affair was immortalized in the 1950s by **Arthur Miller's** play *The Crucible*, written at the height of the similarly paranoid McCarthy trials.

Witch Trials Memorial and Old Burying Point Cemetery

A respite from all the hysteria is the simple and moving **Witch Trials Memorial**, a series of elevated stone blocks etched with the names of the hanged. The memorial is wedged into a corner of the **Old Burying Point Cemetery**, at the junction of Charter and New Liberty streets, where one witch judge, **John Hathorne**, forebear of Salem's most famous son, author Nathaniel Hawthorne, is buried.

Peabody Essex Museum

161 Essex St • Tues–Sun 10am–5pm • $15 • ☎ 978 745 9500, ⓦ pem.org

It's worth a trip to Salem simply for a visit to the **Peabody Essex Museum**, the oldest continuously operating museum in the US. The vast, modern space incorporates more than thirty galleries displaying art and artefacts from around the globe that illustrate Salem's former prominence as a trading point between East and West. Founded by ship captains in 1799 to exhibit items obtained overseas, the museum boasts the biggest collection of nautical paintings in the world. Other galleries hold Chinese and Japanese art, American decorative arts and a standout collection of contemporary paintings and photography. A creatively curated whaling exhibit features not only the requisite scrimshaw but also Ambroise Garneray's 1835 painting, *Attacking the Right Whale* (blood and all), as well as the reconstructed interior salon of America's first yacht, *Cleopatra's Barge*. The Peabody's prized possession, however, is the **Yin Yu Tang**, a sixteen-room Qing dynasty house that the museum, rather incredibly, purchased, dismantled and rebuilt here. Admission is an additional $5, and you must reserve a time at the front desk to see it – advance reservations are recommended (online or at ☎ 1 877 736 8499).

Salem Maritime National Historic Site

Main visitor centre 2 New Liberty St • Daily 9am–5pm • **Salem Maritime Orientation Centre** May–Oct daily 9am–5pm; Nov–April Mon–Fri 1am–5pm, Sat & Sun 9am–5pm; daily tours $5 (Nov–April Mon–Fri afternoons only) • ☎ 978 740 1660, ⓦ nps.gov/sama

Little of Salem's original waterfront remains, although the 2000ft-long Derby Wharf is still standing, fronted by the imposing Federal-style Custom House. These two, and ten other buildings, comprise the **Salem Maritime National Historic Site**, of which the chief sights – Narbonne House, Derby House, Custom House and the *Friendship* cargo vessel – can only be visited on daily one-hour tours. Nathaniel Hawthorne worked as chief executive officer at the **Custom House** for three years, a stint which he later described as "slavery". The office-like interior is rather bland, as is the warehouse in the rear, with displays of tea chests and such.

Millionaire Elias Derby received the nearby **Derby House** in 1762 as a wedding gift from his father; its position overlooking the harbour allowed him to monitor his shipping empire. The interior has been immaculately restored in all its eighteenth-century finery. The original East Indiaman **Friendship** was launched in 1797 and captured by the British in 1812; the impressive replica on the wharf was built by the Park Service and offers a fascinating insight into life at sea in the nineteenth century. Next to Derby House, the **West India Goods Store** emulates a nineteenth-century supply shop by peddling nautical accoutrements like fishhooks and ropes, as well as supplies like molasses candy and "gunpowder tea", a tightly rolled, high-grade Chinese green tea.

The House of the Seven Gables

54 Turner St • Daily: July & Oct 10am–7pm; Nov–June 10am–5pm, closed first half of Jan • $12.50 • ☎ 978 744 0991, ⓦ 7gables.org

The most famous sight in the waterfront area is undoubtedly the **House of the Seven Gables**, a rambling mansion by the sea that served as inspiration for Hawthorne's eponymous novel. Tours of the 1668 house – the oldest surviving wooden mansion in New England – cover the building's history and architecture, including the "secret stairway" that leads to the chimney. The author's birthplace, a small, burgundy, c.1750 structure, was moved here from Union Street in 1958.

ARRIVAL AND DEPARTURE

By train MBTA commuter trains run hourly (30min; $5.25 one-way) between Boston's North Station and Salem.
By bus There's a regular MBTA bus service (50min; $3.50) from Haymarket in Boston.
By ferry A high-speed ferry (May–Oct; $19 round-trip; ☎617 770 0040, ⓦbostonsbestcruises.com), runs approximately every 2hr from Long Wharf in Boston to Salem's Blaney Street dock. Advance purchase is recommended.

By car Travelling by car from Boston, Rte-1A is the most direct but congested choice; taking I-93 I-95 and Rte-128 is usually faster. You can park in the Museum Place Garage at 1 New Liberty St, opposite the visitor centre ($1.50/hr), or in one of several signposted car parks downtown. It's advisable to take the ferry or train in October, as the roads get very congested due to the Halloween hoopla.

GETTING AROUND

On foot The Salem Heritage Trail, a painted red line on the town's pavements, links some of the key sights.
By tram Salem Trolley (April–Oct daily 10am–5pm; $15;

☎978 744 5469, ⓦsalemtrolley.com) will shuttle you round the sights; tickets are valid for a whole day, so you can jump on and off as you please.

INFORMATION

Regional Visitor Center 2 New Liberty St (daily 9am–5pm; ☎978 740 1650 or ☎1 877 725 3662, ⓦsalem.org). The National Park Service operates this

comprehensive visitor centre, which serves as the Heritage Trail's unofficial starting point.

ACCOMMODATION

Salem is full of small **B&Bs** in old historic houses with steep staircases. It is perhaps the only town in America where **hotels** are booked for Halloween months in advance; if you plan on coming any time in October, be prepared for high prices and full houses.

Amelia Payson House 16 Winter St ☎978 744 8304, ⓦameliapaysonhouse.com. A sweet little B&B in a restored 1845 Greek Revival house with friendly and accommodating owners. The rooms are clean and not too frilly, with wi-fi and snacks available. You'll eat a hearty breakfast in the morning, served on pretty floral china. May to mid-Nov. **$155**

Hawthorne Hotel 18 Washington Square W ☎978 744 4080 or ☎1 800 729 7829, ⓦhawthornehotel .com. Right in the heart of things, this full-service hotel is a Salem landmark with reasonable prices and a respectable restaurant and pub. Built in 1925, its 89 rooms are furnished with eighteenth-century reproduction furniture, iPod docks, wi-fi and flat-screen TVs. **$129**

★ **Morning Glory Bed and Breakfast** 22 Hardy St ☎978 741 1703, ⓦmorningglorybb.com. This four-room 1808 Federal town house down by the water (and the

House of the Seven Gables) has a friendly owner and a roof deck with water views. **$170**

★ **Northey Street House Bed and Breakfast** 30 Northey St ☎978 397 1582, ⓦnortheystreethouse .com. Big, blue refurbished 1809 Federal house with three comfortable guest rooms and one apartment for four. The Garden Room has modern, Asian-inspired decor and opens onto a garden with raspberries, strawberries, herbs, Japanese maples and a little koi fish pond. The affable host encourages a no-indoor-shoes policy, with complimentary slippers provided for guests. **$160**

Salem Waterfront Hotel and Suites 225 Derby St ☎978 740 8788, ⓦsalemwaterfronthotel.com. This Best Western branch has added 86 much-needed rooms to the centre of town near the water. It's a standard large hotel – minimalist design, heated indoor pool – with prices to match. **$150**

EATING AND DRINKING

Salem has a great range of places to eat and drink, some housed in **historic buildings**. Most of the top **seafood** spots are situated near the harbour.

43 Church 43 Church St ☎978 745 7665. The historic lecture hall that formerly courted Emerson, Thoreau and Hawthorne is now stylishly furnished in muted shades of moss and chocolate, with an upscale steakhouse menu that does the literary powerhouses proud. Daily 4pm–12.30am.

★ **A&J King Artisan Bakers** 48 Central St ☎978 744

4881. Hidden away on a side street with terrible parking, this to-die-for bakery has gooey sticky buns, crusty loaves of bread and plump little carrot cakes. It's worth risking a ticket for the artisanal sandwiches, such as the smoked salmon with crème fraîche and alfalfa sprouts ($7.75). Mon–Fri 7am–6pm, Sat & Sun 7am–4pm.

Bill & Bob's Famous Roast Beef 9 Bridge St (Rte-1A),

2

just south of the Essex Bridge ☎978 744 9835. The North Shore has been famous for its hot roast beef sandwiches since the 1950s, and this local chain, a short drive north of the centre, is the best place to try one ($4.75). Mon–Thurs 10am–2am, Fri & Sat 10am–2.30am, Sun 10am–1.30am.

Café Polonia 118 Washington St ☎978 745 0045. Leave your diet at the door for this Polish restaurant's scrumptious fried *kielbasa* ($12), potato pancakes with sour cream ($14), and beet soup ($6). Lunch is less expensive and just as good as dinner. Daily 11am–late.

Gulu-Gulu Café 247 Essex St ☎978 740 8882. Bohemian place named after the Czech café where the owners met and fell in love. Extensive beer selection, and a large menu with paninis, crepes, salads and cheese plates. Lots of Boston Terrier-themed decor, in honour of the owners' pup. Mon, Tues & Sun 8am–11pm, Wed–Sat 8am–1am.

The Old Spot 121 Essex St ☎978 745 5656. Cute, central English pub with sixteen craft beers on tap and worthy tavern fare like the ploughman's lunch (hardboiled eggs, three cheeses, pickle, ham, green apple and paté; $14.50).

The sweet potato fries with cheddar, bacon, sour cream and scallions are wickedly addictive ($9.50). Mon–Thurs 5pm–1am, Fri–Sun 11.30am–1am.

Red's Sandwich Shop 15 Central St ☎978 745 3527. Hearty and downright cheap breakfasts and lunches, with bigger-than-your plate pancakes and American staples (meatloaf, pasta) served in a little red house built in 1698. Very popular. Mon–Sat 5am–3pm, Sun 6am–1pm.

★ **Salem Diner** 70 Loring Ave (Rte-1A), south of the centre ☎978 741 7918. This historic diner in an original 1941 Sterling Streamliner car (one of only four remaining in the US) is a must-visit for road-trip aficionados. Try the Spanish omelette, tuna melt or "spanakopita egg roll-up", all around $5. Mon–Sat 6am–3pm, Sun 7am–2pm.

★ **Sixty2 on Wharf** 62 Wharf St ☎978 744 0062. Contemporary Italian trattoria renowned for its outstanding service; the menu offers home-made pasta dishes and small plates (try the mozzarella-stuffed *arancini*; $7) alongside pricier mains like wild stuffed bass with spicy grapefruit ($24). Be sure to save room for the warm toffee pudding ($8). Tues–Sat 5pm–midnight, Sun 5–10pm.

Cape Ann and the north coast

Beautiful **Cape Ann**, some forty miles north of Boston, draws plenty of visitors, mainly on account of its salty air, beaches and seafood restaurants. There aren't many sights per se, and the best thing about the place is its unspoiled scenery and rocky headlands. From I-95, Rte-128 (E) will take you all the way to **Gloucester**, then it's either Rte-127 or scenic Rte-127A to **Rockport**. Continuing north along the coast you come to **Essex**, notable for its fried clams, and the sleepy towns of **Ipswich** and **Newburyport**, both with compact historic districts worth exploring.

Gloucester

Founded in 1623, **GLOUCESTER** is the oldest fishing port in Massachusetts, and the fact that it remains one of the few genuine working towns on the coast makes it all the more appealing. As you'd expect, Gloucester is an excellent place for **seafood**, with several unpretentious, venerable old restaurants and diners. The town's near-legendary fishermen are at the centre of Mark Kurlansky's gripping history, *The Last Fish Tale* (2008), while the movie *The Perfect Storm* (2000) followed the true-life tragedy of local swordfishing boat *Andrea Gail*, which was caught, and lost, in the worst storm in recorded history, when three simultaneous squalls merged off the coast in 1991 and produced 100ft-high waves. Gloucester also has an artistic identity, established by the painter **Winslow Homer**, who spent summers here in 1873 and 1880, and the bevy of artists who set up a colony on **Rocky Neck**.

Driving into town on Rte-127 you'll pass one of Gloucester's sources of pride, the 1923 bronze *Man at the Wheel* – an iconic statue of a fisherman at the wheel of a ship, which commemorates the fate of all the sailors (some 10,000 in total) who have perished offshore over the centuries. Downtown Gloucester is dominated by its scruffy waterfront brightened somewhat by a handful of sights on the Harbor Loop, off Rogers Street. The best time to visit is during **St Peter's Fiesta**, held annually on the weekend closest to June 29. This three-day Italian festival pays homage to the patron saint of fishermen with parades, a boat race and "The Greasy Pole", during which participants inch their way across a slippery 45ft-long pole, poised above the water, to capture a flag.

Gloucester Maritime Heritage Center

23 Harbor Loop • Late May to mid-Oct daily 10am–5pm • $6 • ☎ 978 281 0470, ⓦ gloucestermaritimecenter.org

The **Gloucester Maritime Heritage Center** is a worthy ongoing attempt to preserve the dock area, comprising a small outdoor aquarium and marine exhibits, the main pier, boathouse, restored marine railway, gift shop and quirky **Diving Locker Museum**, with antique diving suits. Much of *The Perfect Storm* was filmed around here, though the real *Crow's Nest* bar is further up the road. Nearby you'll also find the **Whale Center of New England** (see box below).

Cape Ann Museum

27 Pleasant St • Tues–Sat 10am–5pm, Sun 1–4pm • $8 • ☎ 978 283 0455, ⓦ capeannhistoricalmuseum.org

To learn a bit more about the town's past, walk into the centre to the excellent **Cape Ann Museum**, where the history of Gloucester and Cape Ann is well documented through photographs, fishing and quarrying implements, and paintings of mostly local scenes by a variety of artists, including Winslow Homer, Milton Avery and Gloucester-born Fitz Henry Lane.

City Hall

9 Dale Ave • Usually Mon–Fri 8.30am–5pm

Across the road from the Cape Ann Museum, **City Hall** is worth a look for its sea-themed murals, and the roll of honour on the main staircase, where the names of town fishermen lost at sea are inscribed, including those depicted in *The Perfect Storm*.

Sargent House Museum

49 Middle St • Late May to early Sept Fri–Sun noon–4pm • Guided tours only • $10 • ☎ 978 281 2432, ⓦ sargenthouse.org

Two small blocks south of City Hall, **Middle Street** is home to Gloucester's oldest houses, including the **Sargent House Museum**, built in 1782 for Judith Sargent Murray, an early feminist writer. The restored interior holds a fine collection of Chinese porcelain, Revere silver, period furniture and artwork by John Singer Sargent.

Rocky Neck

ⓦ rockyneckartcolony.org • Take East Main St to Rocky Neck Ave; free parking at the base of the Neck

The **Rocky Neck Art Colony**, a two-mile drive around the southern side of the harbour, was established in the 1850s by painters, and its salt-box shacks have been attracting all types of artists – such as Fitz Henry Lane, Childe Hassam and Winslow Homer – ever

---

WHALE-WATCHING OFF CAPE ANN

One of the most popular and exhilarating activities along the north of coast is **whale-watching**: trips depart from Gloucester, Salem and Newburyport to the important feeding grounds of Stellwagen Bank and Jeffreys Ledge, where an abundance of plankton and small fish provide sufficient calories (around one million a day) to keep 50ft, 25-ton **humpbacks** happy. Most boats claim at least a 99-percent sighting record, though this does not necessarily mean that you're going to see a whale breaching just a few feet away – sometimes you may catch no more than a glimpse of a tail. Most companies also have a guarantee that if you don't see a whale you'll get a **free pass** to come back.

The best place to begin is Gloucester, home to the **Whale Center of New England**, 24 Harbor Loop, with a **museum** (July–Sept daily 11am–7pm; Oct–June Mon–Fri 9am–5pm; free; ☎ 978 281 6351, ⓦ whalecenter.org) featuring a 28ft humpback whale skeleton. Gloucester whale-watching companies include the Yankee Fleet, 37 Commercial St (☎ 1 800 942 5464, ⓦ yankeefleet.com); Captain Bill & Sons (☎ 1 800 339 4253, ⓦ captbillandsons.com) in the Whale Center building; and Cape Ann Whale Watch, at 415 Main St (☎ 1 800 877 5110, ⓦ seethewhales.com). During July and August, each company offers two daily trips (around $45; May, June & Sept just 1 daily Mon–Fri, 2 daily Sat & Sun; Oct 1 daily).

since. While the colony's quality of art varies, there are always a handful of standout galleries, and the area's unruly flowerbeds and harbour views make for pleasant browsing. Stop in at the **North Shore Arts Association** at 11 Pirates Lane (just off East Main St) for information on the thirty or so galleries in the area, and then park (free) at the causeway on Rocky Neck Avenue before exploring on foot.

Beauport

75 Eastern Point Blvd (the continuation of East Main St) • Tours hourly: June to mid-Oct Tues–Sat 10am–4pm • $10 • ☎ 978 283 0800, ⓦ historicnewengland.org

Drive down East Main Street almost to the ocean and you'll arrive at the magical **Beauport**, a 45-room mansion perched on rocks overlooking the harbour. Started in 1907 as a summer retreat for interior designer Henry Davis Sleeper (who designed Hollywood homes for Joan Crawford and Johnny Mack Brown), the house evolved over the following 27 years into a fascinating villa filled with a treasure trove of European, American and Asian *objets*. The house is a fanciful mix of styles and themes, each room strikingly different from the next; keep an eye out for one crafted to feel like the stern of a ship (with spectacular water views), hand-painted wallpaper that has no repetitions, a red and gold "octagon" room (with eight walls, eight lamps and eight-sided doorknobs) and an ingeniously illuminated collection of 130 pieces of amber glass.

Hammond Castle Museum

80 Hesperus Ave (off Rte-127) • May to early Sept Tues–Sun 10am–4pm; late Sept to mid-Oct Sat & Sun only • $10 • ☎ 978 283 2080, ⓦ hammondcastle.org

One of Gloucester's more compelling attractions is the **Hammond Castle Museum**, on the harbour's southwestern corner. It was built in the 1920s by eccentric financier and inventor John Hays Hammond Jr, who wanted to bring medieval European relics back to the US. He succeeded: the austere fortress is brimming with them, from armour and tapestries to the elaborately carved wooden facade of a fifteenth-century French bakery and the partially crushed skull of one of Columbus's shipmates. The ultimate flight of fancy, however, is the 30,000-gallon pool whose contents can be changed from fresh to salt water at the switch of a lever – Hammond allegedly liked to dive into it from his balcony.

Beaches

Good Harbor Beach Thatcher Rd (off Barn Lane via Rte-127) **Wingaersheek Beach** Atlantic Rd (off Concord St via exit 13 on Rte-128) • In summer, weekday parking at each is $20, weekends $25

With twenty miles of shoreline, it's no surprise that Cape Ann is blessed with prime beaches. The best one on the island is **Good Harbor**, a half-mile stretch with sand dunes, robust waves and, at low tide, a little island ripe for exploring. **Wingaersheek Beach** is favoured by families for its still waters and beachcombing.

ARRIVAL AND DEPARTURE
GLOUCESTER

By train Gloucester is just over an hour by commuter rail from Boston's North Station ($7.25 one-way; ☎ 617 222 3200, ⓦ mbta.com); trains arrive about half a mile from the harbour.

By car You'll find parking (free) in St Peter's Square, right on the harbour near the Cape Ann Chamber of Commerce, 33 Commercial St.

INFORMATION

Visitor centre The visitor centre is out of town at Stage Fort Park, Rte-127 (mid-May to mid-Oct daily 9am–6pm; ☎ 978 281 8865); they can give you a map detailing area beaches.

Cape Ann Chamber of Commerce 33 Commercial St (Mon–Fri 9am–5pm; ☎ 978 283 1601, ⓦ capeannchamber .com). Dispenses local information and maps.

ACCOMMODATION

Accommodations at Rocky Neck 45 Rocky Neck Ave ☎ 978 381 9848, ⓦ rockyneckaccommodations.com.

Sandwiched between the harbour and the Rocky Neck Art Colony, rooms here enjoy an utterly tranquil setting.

Accommodation is very basic but clean, with kitchens, decks and panoramic water views. **$125**

★ **Bass Rocks Inn** 107 Atlantic Rd ☎ 1 888 802 7666, ⓦ bassrocksoceaninn.com. Three beautiful properties that range from renovated suites in an 1899 house to a motel with a pool overlooking the sea. Rooms come with fridges, DVD players and satellite TV; some

have the added perk of flat-screens, jacuzzis and fireplaces. **$199**

The Harborview Inn 71 Western Ave ☎ 1 800 299 6696, ⓦ harborviewinn.com. This B&B is quiet, friendly and minutes from all of Gloucester's attractions. Rooms are vividly decorated on a Victorian theme, most with harbour views. **$139**

EATING AND DRINKING

★ **Alchemy Tapas & Bistro** 3 Duncan St ☎ 978 281 3997. Intimate, candlelit tapas restaurant with lots of comfy couches and nooks and crannies (there's even a table under the staircase). *Alchemy* buzzes with a hip clientele happily munching blue-cheese-stuffed dates ($8), corn-fried rock shrimp ($10) and grilled bruschetta ($7). Mon–Thurs 11.30am–9pm, Fri 11.30am–10pm, Sat 10.30am–10pm, Sun 10.30am–9pm.

Captain Carlo's 27–29 Harbor Loop ☎ 978 283 6342. Wharfside institution where fresh lobsters, clams, haddock, swordfish, shrimp and calamari feature prominently on the menu; the clam chowder ($6) is almost as good as the hype suggests. Live music most nights. Mid-April to Oct daily except Tues 11am–12.30am.

Duckworth's Bistrot 197 East Main St ☎ 978 282 4426. Gloucester's best upscale restaurant, housed in a snug cottage near Rocky Neck. The carefully groomed bistro menu is chock-a-block with local ingredients, and mains can be ordered as starters, making it easier to eat your heart out. Oenophiles will be quite pleased here as well. Tues–Sat 4–9.30pm, also Sat noon–2.30pm.

Lobsta Land 10 Causeway St ☎ 978 281 0415. Exquisite shellfish (the eponymous lobster takes centre stage) and a vast menu of beautifully cooked fish in a dining room overlooking a marsh. Take exit 12 off Rte-128, and head north; Causeway St is the first right. April to mid-Dec Mon–Thurs & Sun 7am–9pm, Fri & Sat 7am–9.30pm.

Rhumb Line 40 Railroad Ave ☎ 978 283 9732. Cramped local yokel bar (in the best sense) across from the train station. Short on decor but long on charm (particularly the staff), and the food – hot sandwiches, nachos, daily specials and burgers – is ridiculously good.

Insiders swear by the pressed Cuban sandwich (roast pork, salami, ham and Swiss cheese; $9.50). Frequent live music. Daily 5pm–1am.

★ **The Rudder** 73 Rocky Neck Ave ☎ 978 283 7967. On any summer night you'll find an eager group of locals, tourists, painters, sunbathers and yachters vying for a table. Overlooking a cove, the spacious deck serves "seafood chophouse" fare such as calamari ($11), steamed mussels ($14) and baked cod ($19); inside, the ceiling is decorated with twinkling lights and strands of fake ivy. A gem. Mid-June to early Sept daily 5pm–late; call for hours May & Oct.

Smokin' Jim's Bar-B-Q 121 E Main St ☎ 978 283 1055. It's worth making a trip out towards Rocky Neck to this popular roadside wood and charcoal grill with finger-licking Southern-style pulled pork, brisket and smoked chicken – most orders are $8–10, while a full rack of ribs is $21. May–Oct; closed Mon & Tues, and when it rains.

Sugar Magnolia's 112 Main St ☎ 978 281 5310. Named for a Grateful Dead ditty, this popular breakfast meeting place grills up imaginative fare such as carrot-cake pancakes with maple cream-cheese butter ($6), pineapple fritters with brown-sugar dipping sauce ($6) and Irish eggs benedict on warm cornbread ($10). Waiting times can be long (45min at weekends); aim to arrive early, or come on a weekday. Tues–Sat 7am–2.30pm, Sun 7am–1pm.

★ **Virgilio's Bakery** 29 Main St ☎ 978 283 5295. This tiny deli and bakery has been serving locals since 1961. A great place to stock up on fresh semolina loaves, Portuguese sweetbreads and fat sandwiches such as the Italian-inspired "St Joseph" and veggie "Northeaster". Mon–Sat 8.30am–5pm.

Rockport

Like Gloucester, the town of **ROCKPORT**, just five miles north, began as a fishing village. From early on, though, its picturesque harbour attracted summer holiday-makers and artists, and now the village of clapboard houses and fishing huts – many of them converted to shops, ice-cream stalls, galleries, bars and clam shacks – feels a world away from its neighbour.

Rockport Art Association and Bearskin Neck

12 Main St • Mid-May to mid-Oct Mon–Sat 10am–5pm, Sun noon–5pm; Oct–Dec & March to mid-May Tues–Fri 10am–4pm, Sat 10am–5pm, Sun noon–5pm • Free • ☎ 978 546 6604, ⓦ rockportartassn.org

Works by contemporary local artists, some of them terribly kitsch, can be seen at the **Rockport Art Association**. Main Street ends at a thin peninsula known as **Bearskin Neck**,

2

a photogenic street of old fishermen's cottages. The neck rises as it reaches the sea, and there's a dazzling view of the harbour from its end. Though squarely aimed at tourists, it's still a beguiling place to hang out and grab a bite to eat.

Paper House
Pigeon Hill St • April–Oct daily 10am–5pm • $2

Just north of Rockport on Rte-127 (turn left on Curtis St), everything inside the unique and aptly named **Paper House** is made of shellacked paper – even the desk fashioned from the *Christian Science Monitor*. It's the result of a project undertaken in 1922 by a local engineer who "always resented the daily waste of newspaper".

Halibut Point State Park
Gott Ave (off Rte-127) • Late May to mid-Oct daily 8am–9pm • $2 parking • ☎ 978 546 6604

Three miles north of Rockport on Rte-127, **Halibut Point State Park** is a former nineteenth-century granite quarry whose oceanside trails trace a craggy headland. Many a marriage proposal has been made along this rocky outcrop, from where you can see all the way to Mount Agamenticus in Maine.

ARRIVAL AND DEPARTURE   ROCKPORT

By train Rockport is the last stop on the Rockport Line from Boston's North Station ($7.75 one-way; ☎ 617 222 3200, ⊛ mbta.com).

ACCOMMODATION

Addison Choate Inn 49 Broadway (Rte-127A) ☎ 1 800 245 7543, ⊛ addisonchoateinn.com. Greek Revival house with a lovely porch, homey rooms and a complimentary breakfast buffet. Home-made cookies and tea are served in the afternoon. Open May–Oct. **$150**

Bearskin Neck Motor Lodge 64 Bearskin Neck ☎ 1 877 507 6272, ⊛ bearskinneckmotornecklodge.com. If you stay the night at this basic hotel, you'll wake up to lobstermen hauling in buoys outside your oceanfront

porch. The best location in town: it's right at the end of the spit with most of the shops and restaurants. Open late April to early Oct. **$179**

Captain's House 69 Marmion Way ☎ 978 546 3825, ⊛ captainshouse.com. Set on a corrugated shoreline a mile from downtown, the five guest rooms here are quiet, furnished with antiques and plied by ocean breezes. You can eat home-made granola and spot three lighthouses from the rambling sun porch. **$165**

EATING AND DRINKING

Fish Shack Restaurant 21 Dock Square ☎ 978 546 6667. A sister establishment to the *Roy Moore*, the *Fish Shack* has a roomier dining room, so you can have a sit-down seafood meal, but lacks that squeeze-yourself-in charm. April–Nov daily 11am–9pm.

Helmut's Strudel 69 Bearskin Neck ☎ 978 546 2824. Tempting Bavarian cottage right on the shoreline that makes piping hot strudel – cherry, apple or cheese ($7.95) – dusted with powdered sugar, and serves it to enjoy with coffee on the porch. Cash only. April to mid-Oct daily 7am–8.30pm; mid-Oct to Jan Sat & Sun only.

My Place by the Sea 68 Bearskin Neck ☎ 978 546

9667. At the culmination of Bearskin Neck, this upscale restaurant has a stupendous waterfront setting, but there have been rumblings that the food quality has started to dip; best to go for wine and appetizers. April–Nov: July & Aug daily 11.30am–3pm & 5–9pm; call for hours in other months.

★ **Roy Moore Lobster Company** 39 Bearskin Neck ☎ 978 546 6696. This 1918 fish shack on Bearskin Neck is the simplest but most inviting place, offering lobster by the pound, clam chowder ($4), stuffed clams ($1), fish cakes ($1.95) and a sunny back porch. Mid-March to Oct daily 8am–6pm.

Essex

The former shipbuilding town of **ESSEX**, seven miles northwest of Gloucester along Rte-133, is a major antiques centre these days, but should be visited primarily for the splendid **Essex Shipbuilding Museum**. This sleepy town is also famed for its fried clams; one local restaurant even claims to be the originator of the golden fried snack.

Essex Shipbuilding Museum

66 Main St • June–Oct Wed–Sun 10am–5pm; Nov–May Sat & Sun 10am–5pm • $7 • ☎ 978 768 7541, ⓦ essexshipbuildingmuseum.org

More than four thousand ships have been constructed over the years at the **Essex Shipbuilding Museum**, including schooners, steamers and yachts. The museum traces their history through models, tools and old photographs. The property also encompasses an 1835 two-room schoolhouse, an active shipyard and a seventh-century cemetery, final resting place for veterans dating back to the French and Indian War.

| ACCOMMODATION | ESSEX |

George Fuller House 148 Main St (Rte-133) ☎ 1 800 477 0148, ⓦ cape-ann.com/fuller-house. A rambling old Federal home with seven attractive, air-conditioned rooms, each styled with antiques and canopy beds, and some featuring views over the marshes. Sumptuous full breakfast included. **$150**

EATING AND DRINKING

★ **J.T. Farnham's Seafood and Grill** 88 Eastern Ave (Rte-133), just before the main village ☎ 978 768 6643. Less famous than *Woodman's*, but equally exceptional, this seafood restaurant offers a similar line-up of crisp fried clams as well as boiled lobster. March–Nov: July & Aug daily 11am–9pm; call for hours in other months.

Woodman's 121 Main St (Rte-133) ☎ 978 768 2559. This esteemed icon claims to be the first restaurant in America to serve fried clams (in 1914); order them before grabbing a table (fried plates from around $14). June–Aug daily 11am–10pm; Sept & Oct Mon–Thurs & Sun 11am–8.30pm, Fri & Sat 11am–10pm; Nov to late May Mon–Thurs & Sun 11am–8pm, Fri & Sat 11am–9pm.

Ipswich

Little **IPSWICH**, five miles northwest of Essex, is worth a stop for its pretty historical district and the stunning **Crane Beach**, four miles of enticing sands lining Ipswich Bay at the end of Argilla Road (daily 8am–sunset; ☎ 978 356 4354; $25 weekend parking in high summer, $8 rest of year). Ipswich's other claim to fame is that it has more pre-1725 houses than any other community in the country.

Castle Hill

290 Argilla Rd • **Grounds** Daily 8am–sunset • $8 per car at weekends late May to early Sept, $5 all other times • **Great House tours** Late May to early Oct Wed & Thurs 10am–4pm, Fri & Sat 10am–2pm • $10 (includes admission to grounds) • ☎ 978 356 4351, ⓦ thetrustees.org

The North Shore's own Versailles, the Great House on **Castle Hill** is a 59-room Stuart-style mansion with a half-mile lawn rippling down to the ocean. This dramatic stretch of grass, dotted with statues and dubbed the "Grand Allée", makes for a memorable picnic or walk to Crane Beach. Built in 1928 for Richard T. Crane Jr, a Chicagoan who made his fortune in pipe fittings, the house is decorated with stately antiques, but the grounds are spectacular in their own right, with four miles of trails and plenty of design delights, such as the pair of brass griffins at the back entrance.

Wolf Hollow

114 Essex Rd (Rte-133) • Sat & Sun presentations 1.30–2.30pm • $7.50 • ☎ 978 356 0216, ⓦ wolfhollowipswich.org

Close to Castle Hill, **Wolf Hollow** is an educational non-profit organization devoted to the preservation of wolves. Currently home to four captive-born wolves (with more puppies on the way), its presentations discuss the wolf's predatory role in the animal kingdom and allow visitors to view these regal creatures up close.

| ARRIVAL AND INFORMATION | IPSWICH |

By train Ipswich is a stop on the Rockport Line, which leaves from Boston's North Station ($6.75 one-way; ☎ 617 222 3200, ⓦ mbta.com).

By bus At weekends from mid-June to early Sept the

Ipswich Essex Explorer runs between the Ipswich train station, Wolf Hollow, Crane Beach and the Essex Shipbuilding Museum (one-way $1.50).

By canoe You can plunk down in the Ipswich River at the

adorable Foote Brothers canoe rental, established in 1955 (230 Topsfield Rd, ☎978 356 97710; rental is $25 Mon–Fri, $35 Sat & Sun).

Visitor centre 36 S Main St/Rte-1A (mid-May to late Oct Mon–Sat 9am–5pm, Sun noon–5pm; ☎978 356 8540). This information centre, in the red Hall-Haskell House, stocks local maps.

ACCOMMODATION

Inn at Castle Hill ☎978 412 2555, ⓦthetrustees.org. A beautiful house on the Crane Estate (two miles along Argilla Rd, just before the beach) that has been transformed into a B&B with ten spotless and TV-less rooms, each with its own character and some with water views. **$175**

Ipswich Inn 2 East St ☎978 356 2431, ⓦipswichinn .com. Centrally located, stately Victorian B&B with eight traditional guest rooms decorated in soothing neutral tones. Some rooms have the added bonus of a skylight, love seat or clawfoot tub. **$120**

EATING AND DRINKING

★ **1640 Hart House** 51 Linebrook Rd ☎978 356 9411. This delightful pub offers chicken, pasta and steak dishes in a seventeenth-century shingled house. It's north of town, off Rte-1A. Tues & Thurs 11.30am–2.30pm & 4.30–9pm, Wed 4.30–9pm, Fri 11.30am–2.30pm & 4.30–10pm, Sat 4.30–10pm, Sun 4.30–7.30pm.

Agawam Diner 166 Turnpike Rd (at the intersection of Rte-1 and Rte-133), Rowley ☎978 948 7780. Five miles west of Ipswich in Rowley, this North Shore landmark serves up egg sandwiches ($4), chilli ($4.35) and innumerable varieties of pie from inside a 1940s Fedoro dining car with formica table tops and red vinyl booths. Cash only. Mon–Fri 5am–10pm, Fri & Sat 5am–11pm.

Chick's Roast Beef 40 Central St/Rte-133 ☎978 356 5536. To try some of the North Shore's renowned hot beef sandwiches, make a stop at this affordable shop. Mon–Wed & Sun 11am–9pm, Thurs–Sat 11am–10pm.

★ **Clam Box** 246 High St ☎978 356 9707. Ipswich is lauded for its clams, so you'd be remiss not to eat at the incredible *Clam Box*, which has been knocking out fried clams ($14) and various seafood dishes since 1938; it's two miles north of town on Rte-133. Open for lunch and dinner, call ahead for hours.

Newburyport and around

Just south of the New Hampshire border, **NEWBURYPORT** is Massachusetts' smallest city and one of its most rewarding, a pleasant mix of upscale boutiques and historic homes that still functions as a fishing port. Ironically, though, while Newburyport gives off a historical air, the **Market Square Historic District**, with its brick sidewalks, old lampposts and swanky shops and restaurants, is not quite as old as you'd think – a fire destroyed the area in 1811, and everything had to be rebuilt.

To get a taste for the city, simply stroll the streets in the centre of town (especially **State** and **High**), sample some incredibly fresh seafood, and watch the boats from the Waterfront Park and Promenade, which faces the Merrimack River. You're better off skipping the town museums in favour of milling about the eerie **Old Hill Burying Ground**, adjacent to the beautiful Bartlett Mall on High Street, where many Revolutionary War veterans and prominent sea captains are interred.

Plum Island

South of Newburyport on Rte-1A • **Parker River National Wildlife Refuge** Daily dawn–dusk • $5 per car, $2 walk-in • ☎978 465 5753, ⓦfws.gov/northeast/parkerriver

Plum Island, an eleven-mile barrier beach just south of Newburyport, is mostly occupied by the remote **Parker River National Wildlife Refuge**, a birdwatching sanctuary on the migratory route of a vast number of different species. In summer the refuge is populated by great blue herons, glossy ibises and snowy egrets, though you certainly don't need to be an expert birder to enjoy the picturesque grounds. Just outside the refuge, at the end of Fordham Way, there is a nice beach (free; parking $10). It gets better, and less developed, the further south you go.

ARRIVAL AND INFORMATION   NEWBURYPORT AND AROUND

By train Newburyport is accessible by MBTA rail from Boston's North Station (1hr 5min; $7.75 one-way; ☎617 222 3200, ⓦmbta.com); the train station is less than a mile from the centre of town.

Chamber of Commerce 38R Merrimac St (Mon–Fri 9am–5pm; ☎ 978 462 6680). This outfit can help with local maps and information.

ACCOMMODATION

Blue, the Inn on the Beach 20 Fordham Way, Plum Island ☎ 978 465 7171, ⓦ blueinn.com. Get your groove back at this swish, Miami-inspired boutique hotel that sits pretty on Plum Island's beach. Encompassing six cottages and a variety of suites, its contemporary, bright-white rooms are augmented by fireplaces, a complimentary bottle of wine and beachcombing bliss. **$395**

Clark Currier Inn 45 Green St ☎ 978 465 8363, ⓦ clarkcurrierinn.com. Dating from 1803, this charming central inn features antique-laden rooms with canopy beds and plenty of common areas in which to relax, including a garden gazebo. **$145**

Compass Rose Inn 5 Center St ☎ 978 423 5914, ⓦ compassrosenewburyport.com. This all-suiter is a smart blend of New England quaint and modern luxury: beautiful guest rooms, each with a working fireplace, sitting area and a carefully renovated bathroom with heated towel racks. **$215**

EATING AND DRINKING

Fowles Diner & News 17 State St ☎ 978 463 8855. Nostalgia is on the menu at this vintage diner which doubles as a newsstand, stocking nearly every magazine imaginable. Lemon-raspberry French toast ($6.95), home-made corned beef hash with eggs ($8.95), tuna melts ($7.95) and chilli ($3.75) are served at vinyl booths and countertop stools. Mon–Fri 6.30am–3pm, Sat & Sun 7am–4pm.

Newburyport Lighthouse 6 Water St ☎ 1 800 727 2326. One of New England's most unique dining destinations: fine dining for up to four guests at the top of a 55-stair lighthouse. Patrons order dinner from one of five local menus, then watch the sun set from their panoramic perch. Reservations required. $350 per couple, plus the price of food.

★ **Plum Island Grille** 2 Sunset Blvd, Newbury ☎ 978 463 2290. On Plum Island, this buzzing restaurant serves upscale, fresh fish (mains $24–34) in a noisy dining room with stupendous views of the marsh. Even better is the bar on the porch, where easygoing bartenders pour generous measures. Mon–Wed 5–9pm, Thurs & Fri noon–9pm, Sat noon–9.30pm, Sun noon–8pm; closed Mon & Tues Nov–March.

The South Shore

The **South Shore** makes a clean sweep of the Massachusetts coast from suburban **Quincy**, home of second president **John Adams**, to the former whaling port of **New Bedford**. **Plymouth** is the only really tourist-driven place along this stretch, on account of its **Pilgrim** associations; if you're not interested in reliving the coming of the *Mayflower*, the town, while pleasant enough, will probably not merit more than a few hours' exploration. **New Bedford** has fewer sights, one of which is a well-conceived whaling museum, but they all feel a bit more authentic.

Quincy

A quick ten-mile jaunt from Boston, **QUINCY** bills itself rather imperiously as the "City of Presidents" – it was the birthplace of **John Adams** and his son **John Quincy**, the second and sixth presidents of the United States. Traditionally one of the least popular founding fathers, the elder Adams drew new attention in 2008 thanks to an HBO mini-series, with the irascible politician finally receiving some of the credit that he believed he always deserved. The Adams sights here are well worth a visit for anyone interested in the family's role in early America.

Adams National Historic Site

1250 Hancock St • Visitable on 2hr guided tour only: mid-April to mid-Nov daily 9am–5pm; last full tour 3.15pm; at 4.05pm there is a 45min mansion-only tour; only 8–12 people allowed per tour, so arrive early to ensure a spot • $5; tickets from visitor centre (see p.154) • ☎ 617 770 1175, ⓦ nps.gov/adam • **United First Parish Church** Mon–Sat 9am–5pm, Sun 1–5pm • Donations encouraged • ☎ 617 773 1290

The long Adams presence in town is recalled in the **Adams National Historic Site**, a collection of three buildings associated with the family until the 1940s, when the

2

properties and everything inside them were donated to the National Park Service. The site can only be visited on an illuminating guided **tour**; to get tickets stop by the **visitor centre**, in the centre of town (there's a fee-charging parking garage behind it, whose tickets the NPS will validate for free). A convenient **tram** runs between the visitor centre and the tour's main sites.

First you'll be taken to the **John Adams Birthplace**, a creaky wooden-frame salt-box built in 1681, and purchased by John Adams' father in 1720. Adams himself was born inside in 1735, and lived here until he married the indomitable Abigail, his great love, in 1764, when he moved into the building next door, now the **John Quincy Adams Birthplace**. The sixth president was born in this house in 1767, and it was here that John Adams ran his law practice and wrote the state constitution – it was also here that Abigail composed her now-famous letters to her husband during his long wartime absences.

In 1788 the family moved across town to the farm of Peacefield, now known as the **Old House**. Incredibly, everything you see inside once belonged to the family, and most of it dates back to the time of John and Abigail. John Quincy inherited the house after his father's death in 1826, but his greatest legacy is the magnificent **Stone Library**, in the garden. Built in 1870 to house the 14,000 -plus volumes owned by the sixth president, it contains such precious tomes as the Bible presented to John Quincy by the *Amistad* Africans in 1841 – his defence of the group to the Supreme Court, during which he condemned the institution of slavery, was dramatized in the 1997 movie *Amistad*.

After the tour, pop into the **United First Parish Church**, near the visitor centre, where both presidents are buried.

ARRIVAL AND INFORMATION   QUINCY

By subway Quincy can be reached on the **T** red line from Boston (☏ 617 222 3200, ⓦ mbta.com).
Visitor centre 1250 Hancock St (mid-April to mid-Nov daily 9am–5pm; ☏ 617 770 1175, ⓦ nps.gov/adam). This is where you buy tickets for the Adams National Historic Site tour. A convenient tram runs between the visitor centre and the tour's main sites.

EATING AND DRINKING

★ **Fat Cat** 24 Chestnut St ☏ 617 471 4363. People of all stripes pile into this hip, brick-walled tavern with a white-tiled bar. The food is excellent: fat burgers ($8), lobster mac and cheese ($18), blackened chicken pasta ($13) and four different varieties of spiced fries with a variety of addictive dipping sauces ($7) are all local favourites. Very close to the NPS visitor centre. Daily 11am–1am.
Italy's Little Kitchen 1239 Hancock St ☏ 617 479 0984. A little tricky to find (it's across from the **T** station), this inexpensive hole-in-the-wall offers meatball sub sandwiches, chicken parmigiana, and ziti cooked up behind the counter by nice Italian ladies. There are only four tables, so it's better for takeaway. Very close to the NPS visitor centre. Mon–Fri 11am–6pm.
Shabu Restaurant 397 Hancock St ☏ 617 689 0288. Sleek hot-pot haven with communal tables, contemporary decor, friendly staff and the option of alfresco dining in a tranquil Japanese garden. Dinner for two runs to about $25–30. Mon–Thurs & Sun 11am–11pm, Fri & Sat 11am–midnight.

Plymouth

PLYMOUTH, America's so-called "hometown", is best known for being the first permanent settlement established by the English **Pilgrims** in 1620. The town is mostly given over to commemorating their landing, and only needs to be visited by people with a real interest in the story. Its attractions lie in the centre, along the waterfront, or in the historic district.

Plymouth Rock

The most famous sight in town is **Plymouth Rock**, on the waterfront at North and Water streets, and sheltered by a pseudo-Greek temple on the seashore where the Pilgrims are said to have first touched land. It is really of symbolic importance only: the rock was identified in 1741, no one can be sure where exactly they did land, and the Pilgrims had in fact already spent several weeks on Cape Cod before coming here.

The Pilgrim Hall Museum

75 Court St (Rte-3A) • Feb–Dec daily 9.30am–4.30pm • $8 • ☎ 508 746 1620, ⓦ pilgrimhall.org

The 1824 **Pilgrim Hall Museum** offers a thoughtful and well-balanced introduction to the Pilgrim story, with exhibits of impressive nineteenth-century paintings, displays (including a chunk of Plymouth Rock which you are invited to touch) and artefacts, such as the last-known authentic Pilgrim hat, wampum (shell beads used by settlers to trade with Native Americans) and a 1592 Geneva bible that belonged to William Bradford.

Hedge House

126 Water St • June–Aug Wed–Sun 2–6pm • $5 • ☎ 508 746 0012

For a sense of the town's post-Pilgrim past, visit the 1809 **Hedge House**, a Federal-style mansion built by sea captain William Hammatt. The beautifully restored rooms feature period furnishings, paintings and objects from China obtained by its former merchant owners.

Sparrow House

42 Summer St • Daily 10am–5pm • $2 donation • ☎ 508 747 1240, ⓦ sparrowhouse.com

The **Sparrow House** is the oldest building in Plymouth, built in the 1630s by Richard Sparrow, who arrived from England in 1633. The ground-floor gallery contains local pottery and crafts, while the adjacent room is decorated in the threadbare style of early settlers.

Jenney Grist Mill

6 Spring Lane • Tours April–Nov Mon, Tues & Thurs–Sat 9.30am–5pm, Sun 1–5pm • $6 • ☎ 508 747 4544, ⓦ jenneygristmill.org

Just down the road from the Sparrow House and astride a small brook, the **Jenney Grist Mill** is a 1636 corn mill that proudly stakes its claim as "America's first utility". A costumed miller leads tours of the charming wooden property, whose two 5000-pound millstones continue to grind 100 pounds of corn daily (the resultant organic cornmeal is sold for $5 a pound). An added attraction are the thousands of herring that swim upstream next to the mill from mid-April to mid-May.

Mayflower II

Docked at the State Pier on Water St • Mid-March to Nov daily 9am–5pm • $10, combined ticket with Plimoth Plantation $29.50 • ☎ 508 746 1622, ⓦ plimoth.org

The best sight in Plymouth is the **Mayflower II**, a replica of the original *Mayflower*. Built in Britain by craftsmen who followed the detailed and historically accurate plans drawn up by a naval architect at MIT, the *Mayflower II* was given to America as a gesture of goodwill in 1957. This version meticulously reproduces the brown hull and red strapwork that were typical of a seventeenth-century merchant vessel – which is what the original *Mayflower* was, before being "outfitted" for passengers prior to its horrendous 66-day journey across the Atlantic. Notice the hawthorn, or English mayflower, carved into the stern; whether the original ship was so adorned is unclear. On board, modern-day crew members and

PLYMOUTH

ACCOMMODATION	
Best Western Cold Spring	1
By the Sea	3
John Carver Inn & Spa	4
Whitfield House	2

EATING & DRINKING	
Blue Blinds Bakery	4
Blue-Eyed Crab	2
Roobar	1
Water Street Café	5
Wood's Seafood	3

2

role-playing "interpreters" in period garb, meant to be representatives of the Pilgrim passengers, field questions. Below the main deck, you can have a look at the "tween decks" area, where the Pilgrims' cramped cabins would have been.

Plimoth Plantation

137 Warren Ave • Daily: mid-March to Nov 9am–5pm; July & Aug 9am–7pm • $25.50, combined ticket with Mayflower II $29.50 • ☎ 508 746 1622, ⓦ plimoth.org

Similar to the *Mayflower II* in approach and authenticity is **Plimoth Plantation**, three miles south of town off Rte-3. An introductory film and exhibitions at the **visitor centre** offer an insight into the early colonial period, beginning with the culture of the Wampanoag people; the genesis of Thanksgiving is also examined in detail.

Beyond here, a recreation of "Plimoth" c.1627, as well as a Wampanoag settlement, have been built using traditional techniques. At the English village, visitors are expected to participate in a charade – you're to pretend to have stepped back into the seventeenth century – which, depending on your level of resistance, can be quite enjoyable.

Exchanges in the Wampanoag village are less structured, with the Native American staff wearing traditional clothes (but not role-playing), and keen to chat about native customs.

ARRIVAL AND INFORMATION   PLYMOUTH

By bus Plymouth & Brockton buses (☎ 508 746 0378, ⓦ p-b.com) run from Boston ($20), stopping at the Park and Ride lot at exit 5 off Rte-3, where a local shuttle makes stops around town before heading to Plimoth Plantation (May–Aug Fri–Sun; $15 all-day re-boarding pass).

By car Driving in to Plymouth, aim for the waterfront;

there's plenty of metered parking along Water Street and near the visitor centre.

Visitor centre 130 Water St (daily: summer 8am–8pm; winter 9am–5pm; ☎ 508 747 7525, ⓦ visit-plymouth .com). Stocks plenty of local information.

ACCOMMODATION

Best Western Cold Spring 180 Court St ☎ 508 746 2222, ⓦ bestwestern.com. This appealing hotel, comprised of a set of small buildings on a leafy campus, has clean, modern rooms with flat-screen TVs, a swimming pool with views of Cape Cod bay, laundry facilities and a free breakfast buffet. It's an easy walk to town. $135

By the Sea 22 Winslow St ☎ 508 830 9643, ⓦ bytheseabedandbreakfast.com. This B&B offers three spacious, newly renovated suites with harbour views. The hosts serve a "jumpstart" in the morning (coffee and coffee cake), then offer a choice of breakfast vouchers to two area businesses, one of which is the lovely *Blue Blinds* (see below). Close enough to Plymouth Rock that the Pilgrims could have easily spent the night here instead of roughing it on shore. $175

John Carver Inn & Spa 25 Summer St ☎ 1 800 274

1620, ⓦ johncarverinn.com. The best family accommodation in Plymouth, this 79-room inn has plush rooms, a restaurant and spa. The decor was recently done in an outdated style, but the indoor pool, complete with a water slide through a *Mayflower II* replica and whirlpool tub in a faux Plymouth Rock, is a huge hit with kids. Close to the waterfront and all the downtown attractions. $200

Whitfield House 26 North St ☎ 508 747 6735, ⓦ whitfieldhouse.com. This 1782 Federal house has oodles of character and charm. There are three guest rooms, of which two are original to the house; the Patriot's room, furnished in colonial style but set in the inn's modern extension, has a fresher feel. In winter, you can warm yourself in front of a roaring fire by the living room's black marble fireplace. $120

EATING AND DRINKING

★ **Blue Blinds Bakery** 7 North St ☎ 508 747 0462. "Just a block from the Rock", and set in a bygone-era house with a wide porch, two stone fireplaces, an antique cash register and Pilgrim murals on the walls, this fragrant bakery has a small but delectable breakfast and lunch menu (pancakes, granola with yogurt, sandwiches and soups) and also peddles irresistible baked goods. Mon–Thurs 6am–9pm, Fri 6am–3pm, Sun 7am–9pm.

★ **Blue-Eyed Crab** 170 Water St ☎ 508 747 6776. By the waterfront, this merry seafood favourite has a cheerful, tropical-themed menu and ambience. The Caribbean cobb salad comes with jerk steak and crunchy plantains ($11.95), while the crab burger is topped with avocado and pickle spears ($11.95). Dinner mains are around $23. Mon–Thurs & Sun 11.30am–9pm, Fri 11.30am–10pm, Sat noon–10pm.

Roobar 10 Cordage Park ☎ 508 746 4300. Not only is this Cape Cod chain one of the best places for wood-fired pizzas in the region, but its stylish interior and popular bar also make it a great place for a drink – try the tangy martinis. It's just off Rte-3A, north of the centre. Daily 4pm–1am.

Water Street Café 25 Water St ☎ 508 746 2050. Sunny, popular breakfast and lunch nook that's close to Plymouth Rock and serves crunchy French toast stuffed with raspberry jam ($7.25), fresh fruit salad with home-made granola ($7.95) and divine chicken salad wraps ($7.95). Daily 5.30am–3pm.

Wood's Seafood 15 Town Pier ☎ 508 746 0261. Set on a rickety pier, this no-nonsense fish shanty overlooks a boat-dotted harbour and doles out great fried seafood (basket of clam strips; $9.95) from a takeaway counter. Seating is limited, and the dining room is a bit dingy, but that's all part of the charm. For dessert, duck into *Cupcake Charlie's*, just across the way at 6 Town Wharf. May–Sept daily 11am–9pm; Oct–April Mon–Thurs & Sun 11am–8pm, Fri & Sat 11am–8.30pm.

New Bedford

The famous old whaling port of **NEW BEDFORD**, 55 miles south of Boston, is still home to one of the nation's most prosperous fishing fleets. And while it has patches of grit, this working-class city has aged well. Recent preservation efforts, with an eye to the town's whaling heritage, have heightened its aesthetic appeal, and the mercantile buildings, nineteenth-century houses and cobblestone streets in its centre now more clearly conjure up the setting that inspired Herman Melville to set the early pages of *Moby Dick* here.

New Bedford Whaling National Historic Park

33 William St • Daily 9am–5pm • Free • ☎ 508 996 4095, ⓦ nps.gov.nebe

Much of the downtown area is preserved within the **New Bedford Whaling National Historic Park**, a collection of old buildings, art galleries and antique stores, the centrepiece of which is the impressive **visitor centre**. Here films and displays recount the history of the town; the emphasis is squarely on the achievements of whaling as a commercial enterprise in the eighteenth and nineteenth centuries, but other aspects of local history are also highlighted – the Underground Railroad went through here – and you can grab maps of nearby **mansions**, remnants of the town's whale-derived wealth. Chief among these are the old Federal and Victorian houses around **County Street**, of which Melville commented:

Had it not been for us whalemen, that tract of land would this day have been in as howling condition as the coast of Labrador…all these brave houses and flowery gardens came up from the Atlantic, Pacific, and Indian oceans. One and all, they were harpooned and dragged hither from the bottom of the sea.

New Bedford Whaling Museum

18 Johnny Cake Hill • Daily 9am–5pm, every second Thurs of the month open till 8pm • $14 • ☎ 508 997 0046, ⓦ whalingmuseum.org

Just around the corner from the visitor centre, the main attraction in town is the **New Bedford Whaling Museum**. This remarkable museum features the world's largest ship model as well as scrimshaw, harpoons, international artefacts retrieved by whalers and a full-size replica of a ship's forecastle. The archives of the museum contain the logbook of the whaling ship *Acushnet*, which shows Melville as one of its crew, while the entranceway showcases the 66ft skeleton of a juvenile blue whale accidentally struck and killed by a tanker in 1998, and a sperm whale skeleton that washed ashore in Nantucket in 2002.

Seamen's Bethel

Late May to mid-Oct Mon–Fri 10am–4pm • Free • ☎ 508 992 3295, ⓦ portsociety.org

Immediately opposite the whaling museum stands the **Seamen's Bethel**, the "Whaleman's Chapel" built in 1832 and described in *Moby Dick*. It features a replica of the ship-shaped pulpit described in Melville's book. More evocative are the memorials to those who died at sea lining the walls, a custom which continues to this day.

Ocean Explorium

174 Union St • Thurs–Sun 10am–4pm • $7.50 • ☏ 508 994 5400, ⓦ oceanexplorium.org

If you're travelling with children, pop by the **Ocean Explorium**, located downtown in the spectacular marble lobby of the former New Bedford Institute for Savings bank. This small, hands-on marine museum houses six aquariums filled with local and tropical sea creatures, a touch tank with starfish and crabs, and its pièce de resistance, the "Science on a Sphere" globe, a vast circle onto which curators project images and give animated presentations.

Rotch-Jones-Duff House & Garden Museum

396 County St • Mon–Sat 10am–4pm, Sun noon–4pm • $5 • ☏ 508 997 1401, ⓦ rjdmuseum.org

You can take a look inside one of the town's historic mansions, the Greek Revival **Rotch-Jones-Duff House & Garden Museum**. Built by a Quaker whaling captain in 1834, it retains many of its original decorations and furnishings, including decadent marble fireplace mantles and oriental rugs. The formal gardens, laid out in their original style, with boxwood hedges, roses and wildflowers, occupy an entire city block.

ACCOMMODATION   **NEW BEDFORD**

Orchard Street Manor 139 Orchard St ☏ 508 984 3475, ⓦ the-orchard-street-manor.com. Set in a nineteenth-century whaling captain's home, this atmospheric B&B has Moroccan accoutrements, antique chandeliers, a vintage pool table and great breakfasts. **$125**

EATING AND DRINKING

Antonio's 267 Coggeshall St ☏ 508 990 3636. If you're looking for local flavour, try the authentic Portuguese dishes at this popular restaurant, located a mile beyond downtown. Mon–Thurs & Sun 11.30am–9.30pm, Fri & Sat 11.30am–10pm.

Café Balena 24 N Water St ☏ 508 990 0061. Right in cobblestoned downtown, *Balena* offers top-notch Italian classics, enhanced by the highly gifted singing waiters. Patrons swoon over the shellfish pizza, veal ravioli and seafood risotto. Dinner for two costs around $60. Tues–Sat 5–9.30pm.

Cork Wine & Tapas Bar 90 Front St ☏ 508 994 9463. Buzzing little tapas place with exposed beams and rustic wood floors that's favoured by an older, stylish, cocktail-swilling crowd. Daily 11.30am–2pm.

Ma's Donuts 1972 Acushnet Ave ☏ 508 995 5521. you've got a car, or if you answer to a sweet-tooth addiction, head to this revered doughnut shop and dine four miles out of town. Doughnuts are only a buck apiece and some of the more popular varieties (such as glazed and chocolate frosted) can sell out by 9am – call ahead and they'll put some aside for you. Cash only. Thurs–Su 4am–noon.

No Problemo 813 Purchase St ☏ 508 984 1081. Whale sized burritos, *taquitos* and zesty sangria are served up b tattooed staff at this hip taqueria and bar with Day of th Dead decor. Mon–Wed 11am–9pm, Thurs–Sa 11am–10pm, Sun noon–8pm.

AUDUBON'S BIRDS OF AMERICA

One of New Bedford's most exceptional attractions is its **John James Audubon bird folio** (Tues & Wed 1–5pm, Thurs 1–5pm & 6–9pm, Fri 9am–12.30pm, Sat 9am–1pm & 2–5pm, also open by appointment; ☏ 508 991 6275) housed in the city's handsome nineteenth-century public library at 613 Pleasant St. Audubon, a famed ornithologist and artist, crafted this collection of 435 **engravings** between 1827 and 1839. To create his dignified artworks, Audubon developed a groundbreaking technique wherein he studied each bird's habits and positions out in the field (before shooting them); the watercolours he produced in the wild were then used as the cornerstone of an engraving process known as **intaglio**, whose resulting prints were hand-painted and the realistic images mailed in sets to paying subscribers. New Bedford's library is one of only 119 institutions in the world with a complete folio, stored here in the third-floor art room. At any given time, ten of the huge prints are out on display (viewable only with a staff member present); if there's a specific bird you'd like to see, however, **call ahead** and helpful librarians will have it ready.

FALL RIVER AND LIZZIE BORDEN

The name of **Fall River**, a glum fishing and industrial town about fifteen miles west of New Bedford, will forever be linked to the trial of **Lizzie Borden**, who was accused (and later acquitted) of the axe murders of her father and stepmother in 1892. The town plays up the associations: the **Fall River Historical Society** at 451 Rock St (❶508 679 1071, ◍lizzieborden .org) housed in a lavish 1843 mansion, contains exhibits relating to the affair, including the handle-less hatchet believed to have been the murder weapon, a bedspread spotted with Mrs Borden's blood, and Lizzie's jail stool, as well as featuring a number of architectural delights (such as 14ft-high ceilings and a mirror backed by diamond dust) that are worth a look in their own right. There are tours on the hour (April, May & Oct to mid-Nov Tues–Fri 9am–4.30pm, last tour 3pm; June–Sept Tues–Fri 9.30am–4.30pm, Sat & Sun 1–5pm, last tour 4pm; $5). There's also a **museum** at the **Lizzie Borden B&B**, 92 Second St (tours daily on the hour 11am–3pm; $12.50; ❶508 675 7333) where the deeds were actually done.

If you've had enough murder for one day, head instead for **Battleship Cove**, accessible from I-195, exit 5 at the Braga Bridge (daily: end June to Aug 9am–5pm; Sept–June 9am–4.30pm; $15; ❶508 678 1100, ◍battleshipcove.org), the site of an impressive assemblage of World War II naval craft. The *USS Massachusetts*, or "Big Mammie", as she was known to the troops, is enormous, with bunks under the deck stacking five high. Visitors are really given the run of the ship, a welcome change from tours of historic houses, and more fun for children. Of the other boats on hand, the submarine *USS Lionfish* is also worth seeing.

Cuttyhunk Island

If you're really desperate to get away from the crowds, take a one-hour boat trip from 56B State Pier in New Bedford out to minuscule **Cuttyhunk Island**, an entirely uncommercial isle with beaches lined with wildflowers. Two of the best are **Channel Beach**, just a short walk from the ferry dock, and **Church's Beach**, on the other side of the island, ideal for swimming. The outermost of the **Elizabeth Islands**, which stretch for sixteen miles from Buzzards Bay, Cuttyhunk was the site of one of the first English settlements in the northeast: a 22-day sojourn in 1602 that resulted in the building of a stockade and the planting of a medicinal garden. A small stone tower on an island in **Gosnold Pond**, at Cuttyhunk's western end, honours the event.

ARRIVAL AND GETTING AROUND

CUTTYHUNK ISLAND

By ferry Get here via the Cuttyhunk Ferry Company, which runs to the island and back at least once daily (usually 9am & 4pm, call for exact times; same-day round-trip $40; ❶508 992 0200, ◍cuttyhunkferryco.com).

By bicycle You can rent bicycles in New Bedford at Yesteryear Cyclery, 330 Hathaway Rd (closed Sun; $18/day; ❶508 993 2525, ◍yesteryearcyclery.com), and take them over on the ferry (for an extra $5) – it's the best way to get around the tiny island.

EATING AND DRINKING

There are only a couple of restaurants here, so you're best off **bringing your own lunch**. A few commercial establishments – gift shops and markets – are located at **Four Corners**, the island's hub.

Cuttyhunk Fishing Club Close to where the ferry lets off ❶508 992 5585, ◍cuttyhunkfishingclub-bb.com. An inn with clean and comfortable rooms and quilted beds in an idyllic setting. Mid-May to early Oct. **$165**

Cape Cod and the islands

One of the most celebrated slices of real estate in America, **Cape Cod** boasts a consistently stunning quality of light and some of the best beaches in New England. The slender, crooked Cape gives Massachusetts an extra three hundred miles of coastline, easily accessed from the region's snug villages, many of which have been preserved as they were a hundred or more years ago. **Provincetown**, at the Cape's very tip, is the destination of choice; known for being a vibrant gay resort, it is also an historic artists' colony, and its unique galleries, shops and restaurants make it all the more appealing The town is perched on the best stretch of the **Cape Cod National Seashore**, adding to its seemingly endless beauty, though tiny towns like **Sandwich**, **Brewster** and **Chatham** make for scenic stops along the way. In recent years local chambers of commerce have been trying to lure tourists in the off season by touting the region's "historical attractions", but for most the beaches still reign supreme.

Just off the south coast of Cape Cod, the islands of **Martha's Vineyard** and **Nantucket** have long been some of the most popular and prestigious vacation destinations in the US. Both mingle an easy-going cosmopolitan atmosphere with ornate mansions and museums harking back to the golden age of whaling. Be prepared for crowds in the summer, when day-trippers swamp both places, especially on weekends.

Brief history

Martha's Vineyard and the Cape received their English designations in 1602, when explorer **Bartholomew Gosnold** visited the area; he named the island after his daughter, while the arm's moniker was inspired by the profusion of white fish in local waters. By

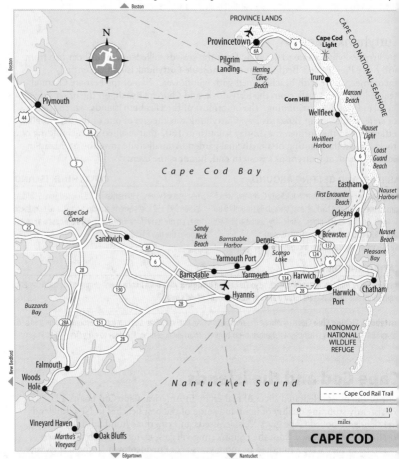

2

CAPE COD BASEBALL LEAGUE

If you're visiting the Cape in summer, consider attending a game with the **Cape Cod Baseball League**, a spectacular compilation of college baseball players (230 of their alumni are currently on Major League rosters). Set your beach chair up early by the diamond (they play locally throughout the region), and get ready for a lively night spent with an animated crowd (June to mid-Aug; no tickets, but donations are welcome; ☎ 508 432 6909, ⓦ capecodbaseball.org).

the early 1800s, **whaling** had become the Cape's primary industry, with the towns of the Outer Cape doing particularly well; fishing and agricultural ventures, including the harvesting of **cranberries**, were also lucrative.

Cape Cod's rise as a **tourist destination** is mainly attributable to the development of the railroad in the nineteenth century (Provincetown was connected to Boston by rail in 1873). Today, the Cape's population more than doubles in the summer, when more than 80,000 cars a day cross the **Cape Cod Canal**.

For the foreseeable future, however, nature will be the real arbiter of the Cape's fate. Without the rocky backbone of other parts of the coast, the land is particularly vulnerable to **erosion**: between Wellfleet and Provincetown the land is scarcely one mile wide, and narrowing all the time. The one benefit of the environmental situation is that it keeps development in check, especially in the vicinity of the protected **National Seashore**.

ARRIVAL AND DEPARTURE   CAPE COD

By plane A number of airlines fly direct to Cape Cod, including US Airways (☎ 1 800 428 4322, ⓦ usairways .com), which serves Hyannis from New York, and Cape Air (☎ 1 800 352 0714, ⓦ capeair.com), which flies to Hyannis and Provincetown from Boston several times a day, even in winter. The relevant guide sections have information on reaching Martha's Vineyard (see p.188) and Nantucket (p.198).

By bus Peter Pan Bus Lines subsidiary Bonanza (☎ 1 888 751 8800, ⓦ peterpanbus.com) operates buses from Boston (one-way $27) and New York (one-way $65) to Woods Hole and Falmouth, while Plymouth & Brockton (☎ 508 746 0378, ⓦ p-b.com) has a more complete set of Cape destinations (one-way Boston to Hyannis $25, to Provincetown $35).

By car The most direct way to reach the Cape is by car. On a fairly quiet day it takes under 2hr to get from downtown Boston to the Sagamore Bridge via Rte-3, but expect this to

double on summer weekends and holidays. Beyond the Cape Cod Canal, which marks the start of the Cape near the town of Sandwich, Rte-6 is particularly congested throughout the summer; it's also remarkably dull. If you're heading directly to Falmouth, note that it's faster to aim for the Bourne Bridge, three miles south of Sagamore, and take Rte-28.

By ferry You can take ferries to Provincetown: Bay State Cruise Company (☎ 617 748 1428, ⓦ baystatecruise company.com) runs a daily fast ferry in the summer from Boston's World Trade Center pier (90min; round-trip $83), and a standard ferry on summer Saturdays (3hr; round-trip $46); Boston Harbor Cruises (☎ 617 227 4320, ⓦ bostonharborcruises.com), offers two express services a day from Boston's Long Wharf (May–Oct; 90min; $79). The cheapest option is the Plymouth–Provincetown ferry, run by Captain John's Boats (July & Aug 10am daily; 90min; round-trip $42; ☎ 1 800 225 4000, ⓦ provincetownferry.com).

GETTING AROUND

By car Once on the Cape, the best way to get around is by car. Rentals are available through Thrifty, in Orleans (☎ 508 255 2234), or Enterprise, in Hyannis (☎ 508 778 8293).

By bus The Cape Cod Regional Transit Authority (☎ 1 800 352 7155, ⓦ capecodtransit.org) runs frequent buses connecting the Cape's outlying towns (6am–7pm; $2); simply flag them down on the side of the road.

By bicycle The Cape also has plentiful and scenic bike

paths; you can rent at Bike Zone ($20/day; ☎ 508 775 3299, ⓦ bikezonecapecod.com), which has locations in Hyannis and North Yarmouth.

By train A more touristy option is the Cape Cod Scenic Railroad (late May to Oct; $22; ☎ 508 771 3800, ⓦ capetrain.com), which runs once or twice a day from Hyannis Depot, 252 Main St, along a 2hr circuit west through cranberry bogs to the Cape Cod Canal and Sandwich.

INFORMATION

Cape Cod Welcome Center Junction of routes 6 and 132 in Centerville (May–Oct Mon–Sat 10am–5pm; Nov–April 10am–2pm; ☏ 1 888 332 2732, ⓦ capecodchamber.org).

Run by the Cape Cod Chamber of Commerce, this place has information about all the towns on the Cape.

Cape Cod's south coast

From the Bourne Bridge, **Rte-28** runs south to Falmouth then hugs the Nantucket Sound until it merges with routes 6 and 6A in Orleans. This is certainly not the most attractive route on the Cape: much of it is lined with motels and strip malls, and it can get seriously clogged with traffic during the summer. Nonetheless, it runs through a number of important hubs along the south coast, notably **Falmouth** and **Hyannis**, and at its end is the handsome town of **Chatham** and the blissfully quiet **Monomoy National Wildlife Refuge**.

Falmouth

Boasting more coastline than any other Cape Cod town, **FALMOUTH** has no fewer than fourteen harbours among its eight villages. At the centre of these is **Falmouth Village**, with a prim central green surrounded by colonial, Federal and Greek Revival homes. Typical of New England, a number of these old sea captains' houses are now B&Bs, and are dotted with a mix of T-shirt shops, ice-cream parlours and estate agencies.

Museums on the Green

55–65 Palmer Ave • Mid-June to mid-Oct Tues–Fri 10am–4pm, Sat 10am–1pm • $5 • ☏ 508 548 4857, ⓦ falmouthhistoricalsociety.org

The 1794 **Conant House**, run by the Falmouth Historical Society, contains scrimshaw, rare glass and china and sailors' memorabilia. There's also a room dedicated to local girl **Katherine Lee Bates**, who composed the song *America the Beautiful*; she was born in 1859 down the road at 16 Main St. The 1790 **Julia Wood House** next door was a doctor's home; one room is set up as a clinic, with a horrifying display of primitive dental utensils. The adjacent colonial-style flower garden, herb garden and Memorial Park are pleasant places to stroll or picnic (open year-round; free).

ARRIVAL AND INFORMATION

FALMOUTH

By bus The Falmouth bus depot occupies the old train station on Depot Ave, at the western end of Main St, around 1.5 miles from the harbour and ferry to Martha's Vineyard (see p.188); you'll find the latter clearly signposted at the eastern end of Main St.

Falmouth Chamber of Commerce 20 Academy Lane,

Rte-28 (June–Aug Mon–Fri 8.30am–5pm, Sat 10am–4pm, Sept–May Mon–Fri 8.30am–5pm, Sat 9.30am–5pm, ☏ 508 548 8500, ⓦ falmouthchamber.com). Also runs a useful visitor centre just off Main with maps covering the 10.7-mile Shining Sea Bikeway, which leads to Woods Hole and passes a salt marsh and a cranberry bog.

THE CAPE COD CANAL

Between 1909 and 1914 a **canal** was dug across the westernmost portion of Cape Cod, effectively making the Cape an island. Initial work began in 1880, under the auspices of the **Cape Cod Canal Company**. In 1899 New York businessman **Augustus Belmont** took over the project; ten years later, state-of-the-art earthmoving equipment was introduced, and the canal was finally completed in 1914. In 1928 the **federal government** purchased the waterway, and enlarged it as a WPA project during the Great Depression. By 1940 the canal was the widest in the world. You don't have to be on the water to enjoy it, though; the views of the canal from the **Sagamore** and **Bourne bridges** are some of the most dramatic on the East Coast.

FROM TOP PROVINCETOWN (P.178); NANTUCKET (P.192) >

2

ACCOMMODATION

Beach Breeze Inn 321 Shore St ☎508 548 1765, ⓦbeachbreezeinn.com. This 1858 Victorian offers heaps of character, arresting views, beautiful grounds and clean rooms, just 100 yards from Surf Drive Beach. **$219**

★ **Beach Rose Inn** 17 Chase Rd, West Falmouth, off Rte-28A ☎508 540 5706 or ☎1 800 498 5706, ⓦthebeachroseinn.com. Superb B&B dating from the 1860s, in a tranquil setting among gardens, with a koi pond, hot tub and woodlands. Exquisite breakfasts are served on a lovely outdoor deck. Also has a massage room and free wi-fi. **$175**

Cape Wind Waterfront Resort 34 Maravista Ave Ext ☎508 548 3400 or ☎1 800 267 3401, ⓦcapewind.com. Perfect for families, this waterfront resort has well-equipped cottages steps from the Great Pond inlet and a host of free attractions, including a great pool, paddleboats and even bocce. **$185**

Captain's Manor Inn 27 W Main St ☎508 388 7336, ⓦcaptainsmanorinn.com. Dating from 1849, this gorgeously restored sea captain's home is done up with Greek Revival accents – intended to please the original owner's Southern bride. The obliging hosts provide lots of pampering perks, like rain showerheads, snacks and a nightly turndown service. **$225**

★ **Inn on the Sound** 313 Grand Ave ☎508 548 3786 or ☎1 800 682 0565, ⓦinnonthesound.com. A stunning location (45ft above the bay), mesmerizing views and gourmet food make this posh B&B a real treat; luxury linens and a well-stocked library mean you may not want to venture out at all. **$225**

EATING AND DRINKING

★ **The Clam Shack** 227 Clinton Ave ☎508 540 7758. A local institution. Enjoy heaping plates of fried seafood (including the eponymous clams, of course) on outside picnic tables or the smashing rooftop deck with prime waterfront views. Late May to early Sept daily 11.30am–7.30pm.

★ **The Glass Onion** 37 North Main St ☎508 540 3730. Swish New American restaurant that's lauded as one of the Cape's best eating experiences. Order the seared sea scallops with Granny Smith apples for entry into foodie paradise ($24). Mon–Sat 5pm–late.

Liam Maguire's Irish Pub 273 Main St ☎508 548 0285. The best choice in town for a drink; it's not a great place to eat, but if you stick to basics like bangers and mash or corned beef and cabbage you can't go wrong. There's live Irish folk music most nights. Mon–Sat 11.30am–1am, Sun noon–1am.

Woods Hole

The salty drop of a town that is **WOODS HOLE** owes its name to the water passage, or "hole", between Penzance Point and Nonamesset Island, linking Vineyard Sound and Buzzards Bay. Most people come here for the ferry to Martha's Vineyard (see p.188), as it's little more than a dollop of casual restaurants clustered around the harbour and picture-perfect Nobska Point Lighthouse, on Nobska Road.

Woods Hole Oceanographic Institution

15 School St • May–Oct Mon–Sat 10am–4.30pm; Nov–Dec Tues–Fri 10am–4.30pm; twice-daily tours of research labs: July & Aug Mon–Fri 10.30am & 1.30pm; reserve in advance • $2• ☎508 289 2252, ⓦwhoi.edu

Right in the centre of town, the **Woods Hole Oceanographic Institution** houses an exhibit on the 1986 rediscovery of the *Titanic*, a project the Institution spearheaded, and some neat submarine capsules that children will enjoy. In July and August the Institution offers twice-daily **tours** of its otherwise off-limits research labs. Also worthwhile are the informative, hands-on cruises run from the harbour by **OceanQuest**: lobster and scallop traps are pulled up for inspection, and those on board can handle the marine life (July & Aug Mon–Fri 10am, noon, 2pm & 4pm, Sat noon & 2pm; $22; ☎1 800 37 62326, ⓦoceanquestonline.org).

Woods Hole Science Aquarium

Corner of Albatross and Water streets • June–Aug Tues–Sat 11am–4pm; Sept–May Mon–Fri 11am–4pm • Free • ☎508 495 2001, ⓦnefsc.noaa.gov

Examples of the marine life that lurks off the Cape's shores are kept behind glass at the National Marine Fisheries Service, which maintains America's oldest aquarium, the Woods Hole Science Aquarium. The displays are mostly limited to cod, lobster and other piscine creatures that are more appealing on a plate; the main exception, the seals, give visitors a thrill at feeding time (daily 11am & 4pm).

CAPE COD BEACHES

With over three hundred miles of coastline, Cape Cod certainly doesn't lack sand. What it does lack, however, is facilities; the few **beaches** that have services (toilets, lifeguards, snack bars) are, not surprisingly, usually busiest. **Parking** across the Cape is also a bit unreliable (day fees hover at around $20): your best bet, if you're planning on hitting the beach frequently, is to visit the local town hall and enquire about non-resident parking permits (which can range from $35 for three days to $60 for a week). In terms of water conditions, the Cape's **southern stretches** (facing Nantucket Sound) tend to be calmer and warmer than the ocean side. You'll find details of some of the best beaches in the relevant sections of the guide, but these are also worth checking out:

BREWSTER

Breakwater Beach Off Breakwater Rd. Shallow-water beach with toilets close to town. You can walk out at least a mile at low tide – kids will enjoy perusing the sea creatures in the tidal flats.

Paines Creek Beach Off Paines Creek Rd. One-and-a-half-mile-long bay beach with great body-surfing when the tide comes in.

DENNIS

Corporation Beach Off Rte-6A. One of the best-maintained beaches on the Cape, with wheelchair-accessible boardwalks, a children's play area, lifeguards and full facilities.

Mayflower Beach Off Rte-6A. Popular family spot with natural tidal pools.

FALMOUTH

Old-Silver Beach Off Rte-28A in North Falmouth. Popular, calm beach with great sunsets; college kids and young families alike gather here, the latter drawn to its natural wading pool.

Surf Drive Beach Off Shore St. Another family favourite; a shallow tidal pool between jetties is known as "the kiddie pool".

HYANNIS

Craigville Beach Off Craigville Beach Rd in Centerville, just west of Hyannis. Well-oiled and toned sun-worshippers flock to this broad expanse of sand, nicknamed "Muscle Beach".

Kalmus Beach Off Gosnold St in central Hyannis. A big windsurfing destination at the mouth of the busy harbour, with full facilities and an urban feel.

ORLEANS

Nauset Beach Off Rte-28. Over in East Orleans, this is one of the Cape's best beaches, a nine-mile-long wedge of sand at the end of Beach Road with great waves and surfing ($15 parking fee); don't miss the onion rings at *Liam's* snack bar – they're legendary. There are also regular sunset concerts.

PROVINCETOWN

Herring Cove Beach Off Rte-6. Easily reached by bike or through the dunes, and famous for sunset-watching, this beach is actually more crowded than those nearer town, though never unbearably so.

Province Lands Off Race Point Rd. Beautiful vast, sweeping moors and bushy dunes are buffeted by crashing surf.

WELLFLEET

Cahoon Hollow Beach Off Ocean View Drive. Good surfing and full facilities make this town-run beach popular with the thirty-something set. Don't miss the delicious oysters at the famous *Beachcomber* shack (see p.177).

White Crest Off Ocean View Drive. The main distinction between White Crest and neighbouring Cahoon Hollow is the clientele – here, it's a predominantly young college crowd.

ARRIVAL AND DEPARTURE

WOODS HOLE

By bus Buses arriving in Woods Hole drop off at the ferry terminal.

By ferry See information on ferries headed to Martha's Vineyard (see p.188).

ACCOMMODATION

★ **Woods Hole Inn** 28 Water St ☎ 508 495 0248, ⓦ woodsholeinn.com. In an unbeatable location just steps from the ferry terminal, this eco-smart inn has nine colourful quarters (with five additional suites on the way) artfully done up with luxury linens, wi-fi and iPod docks. $195

Woods Hole Passage 186 Woods Hole Rd ☎ 508 548 9575, ⓦ woodsholepassage.com. Brightly painted chambers in a refurbished red-shingled carriage house set on spacious grounds. The lawn is good for a round of croquet or bocce, there's a summertime outdoor shower, and a full breakfast is included in the price. $179

EATING

Fishmonger's Café 56 Water St ☎ 508 540 5376. Laid-back natural-foods restaurant with a surprising number of vegetarian dishes in addition to eclectic seafood fare; try the seafood plate loaded with fried fish, clams, shrimp and scallops ($26). Summer daily 7am–10pm; call for hours rest of year.

★ **Pie in the Sky Bakery** 56 Water St ☎ 508 540

5376. Right by the ferry terminal. Stock up here befor heading over to Martha's Vineyard: puffy popover "wonder bars" baked with chocolate, giant cookies, fres sandwiches, soups and salads are all on offer. It's a tin place, packed with glass bottles and art in a little woode alcove overlooking the harbour. Daily 5am–10pm.

Hyannis

One of the Cape's biggest and liveliest towns, **HYANNIS** is mainly visited for its transport links – the ferry to Nantucket (see below) – and commercial options. There's little in the way of sights, though there are some pleasant public beaches, quaint B&Bs and plenty of places to eat and drink, especially in summer. The town still sparkles a bi from the glamour it earned when the **Kennedy Compound**, the family's summer home in **Hyannisport**, placed it at the centre of world affairs. This private home is in an upscale residential section of town a couple of miles southwest of Hyannis proper and can only really be glimpsed from the water; Hy-Line Cruises (see below) pass by.

John F. Kennedy Hyannis Museum

397 Main St • Mid-April to late May Mon–Sat 10am–4pm, Sun noon–4pm; June–Oct Mon–Sat 9am–5pm, Sun noon–5pm; Nov Fri & Sat 10am–4pm, Sun noon–4pm; mid-Feb to mid-April Thurs–Sat 10am–4pm, Sun noon–4pm • $5 • ☎ 508 790 3077, ⓦ jfkhyannismuseum.org

If it's Kennedy legacy you've come to see, the best place to start is the **John F. Kennedy Hyannis Museum**, which displays the expected nostalgia, mainly in the form of black-and-white photographs. It's not a comprehensive history, focusing instead on Kennedy's relationship with Cape Cod.

Cape Cod Potato Chip Factory

100 Breed's Hill Rd • Mon–Fri 9am–5pm • Free • ☎ 508 775 3206, ⓦ capecodchips.com

For a welcome non-presidential diversion, take a self-guided tour of the **Cape Cod Potato Chip Factory**. The tasty crisps, once a local phenomenon but now found almost everywhere, are hand-cooked in kettles; you only get to peer in on the crisp-making process, but there are delicious free samples. You'll find the factory off Independence Drive, which leads north from Rte-132 just outside town.

Pirate Adventures

138 Ocean St • Daily cruises mid-June to early Sept; reservations required• $21 • ☎ 508 394 9100, ⓦ capecodpirateadventures.com

If you're travelling with children, the **Pirate Adventures** cruise is a must. Don your tattoo and eye-patch, then head out to find sunken treasure; en route, you'll get to launch water-spraying cannons at a rival ship.

ARRIVAL AND DEPARTURE

BY CAR

Hyannis is only twenty miles east of Falmouth along Rte-28, but is approached much faster from Boston via the north side of the Cape and Rte-6. Rte-132 into town is often heavily congested in summer.

BY BUS

Buses arrive at the Hyannis Transportation Center, at the intersection of Main and Center streets, around a 15min walk from the harbour.

BY FERRY

The ferry terminals lie around the main harbour, at th eastern end of Main St. Hyannis is the principal ferry por for Nantucket (see p.192). Both the Steamship Authorit (South Street Dock; ☎ 508 477 8600, ⓦ islandferry.com and Hy-Line Cruises (Ocean Street Dock; ☎ 508 778 260 or ☎ 1 800 492 8082, ⓦ hylinecruises.com) run year round passenger services to the island, though only th Steamship Authority's boats take cars ($140–200 pe vehicle, not including passenger tickets; make summe car reservations months in advance – spots for July an

HYANNIS

Cape Cod
Potato Chip Factory

Flint Rock
Pond

Mary Dunn
Pond

Barnstable
Municipal Airport

Cape Cod
Mall

Fawcetts
Pond

Aunt Betty's
Pond

Twin Brooks
Golf Course

Simmons
Pond

Hyannis
Transportation
Center

John F. Kennedy
Hyannis Museum

Hy-Line
Ferries

Steamship
Authority

Ferry to Nantucket & Martha's Vineyard

ACCOMMODATION	
Anchor-In	2
HI-Hyannis	3
Saltwinds B&B	4
Sea Beach Inn	5
Sea Coast Inn	1

Yarmouth, Rte-6 & Provincetown

Chatham

Nantucket & Martha's Vineyard

2

● EATING & DRINKING	
Brazilian Grill	3
Four Seas Ice Cream	5
Pain D'Avignon	1
La Petite France Café	2
Raw Bar	4

Aug fill up as early as Jan). Both companies have fast ferries (1hr; $35–39 one-way; reservations recommended). The Steamship Authority's regular car ferry (2hr 15min) costs $17.50 one-way for passengers; Hy-Line's traditional passenger ferry (around 2hr) is $22.50 per person.

Bikes Passengers can bring bikes onto fast and traditional ferries – both companies charge an additional $7 one-way.
Parking Parking at the official ferry lots is usually $12–15 per day, but if you're just heading to the island for the day, you can also leave your vehicle at the free car park behind the JFK museum, a 10min walk from the terminals.

2

INFORMATION

Visitor centre Inside the JFK museum on Main St (mid-March to mid-May Thurs–Sat 10am–4pm, Sun noon–4pm; late May to Oct Mon–Sat 9am–5pm, Sun noon–5pm; Nov & Dec Thurs–Sat 10am–4pm, Sun noon–4pm; ☎ 50 775 2201, ⓦ hyannis.com). Useful office maintained by th local Chamber of Commerce.

ACCOMMODATION

Anchor-In 1 South St ☎ 508 775 0357, ⓦ anchorin .com. Hyannis's fanciest accommodation with 42 luxury guest rooms decorated in beach tones of sand, sunshine and ocean blue. Right on the harbour, there's a heated outdoor pool, an inviting sunroom where you can take breakfast and a sitting room with fireplace for the chillier months. $269

HI-Hyannis 111 Ocean St ☎ 508 775 7990, ⓦ hiusa .org. Directly across the street from the ferry docks, this brand-new hostel has 44 dorm beds in a spacious shingled house with wi-fi. Free continental breakfast included. Late May to mid-Oct. Dorms $58

Saltwinds B&B 319 Sea St ☎ 508 771 7213, ⓦ saltwindsbb.com. Close to the beach, this pink-shuttered Victorian has three comfortabl rooms; its friendly owners usually drop guests off at th ferry. $125

Sea Beach Inn 388 Sea St ☎ 508 775 4612 ⓦ seabeachinn.net. Another solid choice close to th beach, this family-oriented B&B boasts small but nea rooms, free pick-up service, wi-fi and continenta breakfast. $90

Sea Coast Inn 33 Ocean St ☎ 1 800 466 4100 ⓦ seacoastcapecod.com. The best choice in the centr of town, offering clean and functional motel-styl accommodation close to the ferry docks; the helpfu owners throw in free breakfast and internet use. May–Oct. $128

EATING AND DRINKING

★ **Brazilian Grill** 680 Main St ☎ 508 771 0109. Be sure to indulge in the full *rodizio* ($28) at this *churrascaria* – a carnivore's paradise where mouthwatering meats are delivered straight from hand-held skewers to diners' plates. There's also an overflowing buffet with plenty of vegetarian options. Mon–Fri 11.30am–9pm, Sat & Sun 11.30am–10pm.

Four Seas Ice Cream 360 S Main St, Centerville ☎ 508 775 1394. Since 1934, this scoop shop near Craigville Beach has been the place to go for colossal ice-cream cones. Mid-May to mid-Sept daily 9am–9.30pm (until 10.30pm in July & Aug).

★ **Pain D'Avignon** 15 Hinckley Rd ☎ 508 778 8588. Beloved French restaurant by the Barnstable airport. Half bakery and half upscale bistro, with gorgeous breads and stylish-yet-understated interior (chrome lamps, sleek little black bar and decorative colour pop of red and white). Mains about $15. Mon & Tue 7am–6pm, Wed–Sun 7am–midnight. Bakery dail 7am–5pm.

La Petite France Café 349 Main St ☎ 508 775 1067 Standout coffee, tea, croissants and sandwiches wit fillings piled high on freshly baked bread. The smoke turkey sandwich with dill havarti, roasted red peppe lettuce and deli mustard will set you back $6.59. Mon–Fi 7am–3pm, Sat 8am–3pm.

Raw Bar 230 Ocean St ☎ 508 775 8800. Next to the ferr dock, this crustacean crowd-pleaser serves up plenty of ra shellfish in addition to a mean lobster roll and laudabl Jamaican jerk chicken wings. Your food comes with a view thanks to the spacious porch overlooking the harbou Daily 11am–11pm.

Chatham

A worthwhile stop on the south shore is genteel **CHATHAM**, eighteen miles east of Hyannis on Rte-28. The town's focal point is **Main Street** in **Chatham Village**, which begins on Rte-28 before branching off towards the ocean, and is home to upscale boutiques, sophisticated restaurants and charming inns. On Friday evenings in summer, the little gazebo at the centre of Kate Gould Park (on Main St) comes alive with a forty-piece band, and concertgoers – armed with blankets, picnic dinners and lawn chairs – come from all over to enjoy this nostalgic free concert.

Atwood House Museum

347 Stage Harbor Rd • June & Sept to mid-Oct Tues–Sat 1–4pm; July & Aug 10am–4pm • $6 • ☎ 508 945 2493, ⓦ chathamhistoricalsociety.org

The town's finest historical attraction, the **Atwood House Museum**, is a short walk south of Main Street. A sea captain's home dating from 1752, the house now contains eight galleries designed to highlight life on Cape Cod since the seventeenth century, with displays of seafaring artefacts, art, antique dolls, seashells and toys. The adjacent Mural Barn houses the rather gaudy *Stallknecht Murals*, a triptych painted between 1932 and 1945 by Alice Stallknecht Wight that depicts 130 Chathamites listening to a contemporarily dressed Christ.

Chatham Lighthouse

A few minutes' drive from the centre along Main Street is the 1877 **Chatham Lighthouse**, which stands guard over a windswept bluff and the "Chatham Bars", a series of sandbars. The cause of many a shipwreck, these sandbars nonetheless protected the town from Atlantic storms until January 1987, when a Nor'easter broke through, forming the **Chatham Break** and leaving the town exposed to the vagaries of the ocean. Right below the lighthouse is a nice beach, but the parking is limited to thirty minutes, so you're best off biking over from town. A mile north on Rte-28, the **Fish Pier** on Shore Road provides a spot to wait for the town's fleet to come back in the mid-afternoon.

2

ARRIVAL AND INFORMATION
CHATHAM

By bus Buses drop off at the Chatham Rotary, where Rte-28 becomes Main St, right in the middle of town.
Visitor Information Center 2377 Main St, South Chatham (Mon–Sat 10am–5pm, Sun noon–3pm). Both information outfits on Main St stock tour and bike maps of Chatham.

Information booth 533 Main St (May–Oct Mon–Sat 10am–5pm, Sun noon–5pm; ☎ 508 945 5199, ⓦ chathaminfo.com).

ACCOMMODATION

Chatham is well endowed with tasteful accommodation, with **B&Bs** that are a bit smarter (and more pricey) than those elsewhere on the Cape. Reservations are strongly advised year-round.

★ **The Captain's House Inn** 369–371 Old Harbor Rd ☎ 508 945 0127 or ☎ 1 800 315 0728, ⓦ captainshouseinn.com. Easy elegance prevails at this sumptuously renovated 1839 Greek Revival whaling captain's home; most rooms have fireplaces, and rates include delicious breakfasts and afternoon tea with freshly baked scones. **$265**

The Carriage House Inn 407 Old Harbor Rd ☎ 508 945 4688, ⓦ thecarriagehouseinn.com. This year-round B&B with young, friendly owners provides six

exquisite rooms in beachy hues of yellow and blue, each with a jar of home-made cookies, flat-screen TVs and access to spa services. **$279**

Chatham Bars Inn 297 Shore Rd ☎ 508 945 0096 or ☎ 1 800 527 4884, ⓦ chathambarsinn.com. The *grande dame* of Cape Cod's seaside resorts, with 205 rooms and cottages decorated in country-chic style spread out over a 22-acre oceanfront property. Even for this, though, the prices are high – you're really paying for the fantastic setting. **$395**

MONOMOY NATIONAL WILDLIFE REFUGE

Stretching out to sea for nine miles south of Chatham, the desolate **Monomoy National Wildlife Refuge** is a fragile barrier island and wildlife refuge that's only accessible by boat. The refuge spreads across 7600 acres of sand and dunes, tidal flats and marshes, with no roads, no electricity and, best of all, no human residents. Indeed, the only man-made buildings on the islands are the South Monomoy Lighthouse and the lightkeeper's house.

The refuge is a stopover point for almost three hundred species of shorebirds and migratory **waterfowl**, including many gulls and endangered piping plovers. In addition, the islands are home to white-tailed deer, and harbour and grey seals are frequent visitors. Several organizations conduct island **tours**, among them Monomoy Island Ferry, a small boat run by Keith Lincoln (☎ 508 237 0420, ⓦ monomoyislandferry.com); walking tours of the island are led by a naturalist (call for rates), seal-boat tours are $35, and birdwatching tours are $20. Make sure you stop in at the headquarters of the Wildlife Refuge, located on Morris Island (south of the Chatham lighthouse along Morris Island Rd), which also has a **visitor centre** (Mon–Sat 8am–4pm; ☎ 508 945 0594) offering small displays and leaflets on Monomoy.

Pleasant Bay Village Resort Motel 1191 Orleans Rd ☎ 508 945 1133, ⓦ pleasantbayvillage.com. Some of the more affordable digs in town, with spacious, clean motel rooms (suites available), a pool and jacuzzi, and stunning gardens nestled inside six acres of woodlands. June–Oct only. $155; weekly rates from $1035

EATING AND DRINKING

The Blue Coral 483 Main St ☎ 508 348 0485. Walk down a short flagstone path and transport yourself to the Caribbean at this under-the-stars restaurant and bar, long on palm fronds and frozen rum drinks. There's a pricey, seafood-oriented menu, but it's best for cocktails and alfresco ambience. June–Sept daily noon–midnight.

Chatham Bars Inn 297 Shore Rd ☎ 508 945 0096. The Gatsby-esque hotel's formal dining room offers expensive New England cuisine with wonderful ocean views; also great for breakfast or drinks on the veranda. Daily 7am–11pm.

Chatham Pier Fish Market 45 Barcliff Ave Ext ☎ 508 945 3474. Order lobster rolls and inexpensive plates of delectable fried seafood while scanning the water for seals and watching fisherman unload their catch. May–Oct daily 10am–8pm.

Chatham Squire 487 Main St ☎ 508 945 0945. This informal and affordable Chatham institution has a raw bar, a seafood menu embellished with pastas and barbecue dishes, and karaoke on Tuesdays. It's child-friendly, too. Mon–Sat 11.30am–1am, Sun noon–1am.

Corner Store 1403 Old Queen Anne Rd ☎ 508 432 1077. Think you can't find good Mexican food on the Cape? Think again. At the intersection of Rte-137 and Old Queen Anne Rd, this counter-service gem offers a cornucopia of burrito fillings accompanied by fresh salsas and toppings. The only downsides are the minimal seating and limited hours. Daily 6.30am–6.30pm.

★ **Hangar B Eatery** 240 George Ryder Rd, at the airport ☎ 508 593 3655. Watch the planes come and go at this superb little breakfast and lunch spot next to the airport. Locally roasted Chatham coffee, the chef's own jam, house-made hash and brioche French toast are specialities; lunch sees the likes of memorable fish tacos and grilled cheese and tomato soup. Daily except Tues 7am–2pm.

★ **Marion's Pie Shop** 2022 Main St (Rte-28) ☎ 508 432 9439. Popular with locals and tourists alike for delicious sweet apple pies, savoury chicken pies, and yummy breakfast cinnamon rolls. Note that "misbehaving children will be made into pies". A Chatham must-do. Tues–Sat 8am–6pm, Sun 8am–5pm.

SWEET SHOPS

★ **Chatham Candy Manor** 484 Main St ☎ 508 945 0825. This nostalgic candy shop with exquisite home-made confections, swinging screen door and pink awning tied up in a bow makes the best fudge ever – rich, buttery and frighteningly addictive. The friendly staff are generous with free samples, too. Daily 9am–5.30pm, July & Aug till 10pm.

Cape Cod's north coast

The meandering stretch of Rte-6A that parallels the Cape Cod Bay shoreline between Sandwich and Orleans is among the most scenic roads in New England, affording glimpses of the Cape Cod of popular imagination: salt marshes, crystal-clear ponds, ocean views and tiny villages. There are hundreds of historic buildings along the 34-mile stretch; the towns of **Sandwich** and **Brewster** have the highest concentration of well-preserved homes. If you're travelling by car, it's worth ditching your vehicle temporarily to bike the **Cape Cod Rail Trail**, a totally flat path running from **Dennis**, about fifteen miles past Sandwich, through Brewster to **Wellfleet**, about twenty miles up the Cape.

Sandwich

Overlooked **SANDWICH** kicks off Rte-6A with little of the commercialization common to many Cape towns, thanks in part to its position so close to the mainland. Take Rte-130 into the town's old **village centre**: a little village green, white steeped church, antiques shops and a general store.

Sandwich's attractions also include several miles of **beach**. It will cost you $10 to park at **Town Neck Beach**, accessed by a nifty boardwalk on Jarves Street off Rte-6A.

Shawme Pond and Dexter's Grist Mill

Near the junction of Main (Rte-130) and Water streets • June to mid-Oct daily 10am–5pm • $3 • ☎ 508 888 4910

The **Shawme Pond** and adjacent **Dexter's Grist Mill**, a replica of one built in 1654, make for a pleasant, peaceful stop, especially if you want to hear about (and maybe even see

n progress) the milling process. They also grind their own organic cornmeal for sale
$3.50 for a 2lb bag).

Sandwich Glass Museum

29 Main St • Feb & March Wed–Sun 9.30am–4pm; April–Dec daily 9.30am–5pm • $5 • ☎ 508 888 0251,
Ⓦ sandwichglassmuseum.org

Across the road from Dexter's Grist Mill the **Sandwich Glass Museum** contains
fourteen galleries housing artefacts from the Boston & Sandwich Glass Company,
which set up shop here in 1825. Besides thousands of functional and decorative
pieces, the museum has a working glassblowing studio, with presentations
every hour.

Heritage Museums and Gardens

7 Grove St • May–Oct daily 10am–5pm • $15 • ☎ 508 888 3300, Ⓦ heritagemuseumsandgardens.org

Recommended for those with an abiding passion for Americana; the **Heritage Museums
and Gardens** features a load of Currier & Ives prints, old firearms, a working 1912
carousel, replicas of US flags and a collection of antique cars. The 100-plus-acre
gardens are beautiful in season, especially in early June, when the rhododendrons are
in bloom.

INFORMATION   **SANDWICH**

Sandwich Chamber of Commerce 128 Rte-6A (April–Oct Mon–Fri 10am–4pm, Sun 1–4pm; ☎ 508 833 9755, Ⓦ sandwichchamber.com).

Town Hall Main St near the pond (Mon–Fri 9am–4pm). Both operations have local maps and information.

ACCOMMODATION

★ **Annabelle Bed & Breakfast** 4 Grove St ☎ 508 833 8586, Ⓦ annabellebedandbreakfast.com. This elegant, marigold-coloured house, modelled after Henry Wadsworth Longfellow's home in Cambridge, MA, is *the* place to stay in Sandwich. Its horticulturalist owner takes great care in the abundant garden, and the six divine guest rooms (two with fireplaces and private decks) offer in-suite massage services. **$170**

Belfry Inne & Bistro 8 Jarves St ☎ 508 888 8550, Ⓦ belfryinn.com. Comprises three nineteenth-century buildings, including a former Catholic church; guest rooms in the latter have a particularly imaginative architectural style, some illuminated by original stained-glass windows. There's also a restaurant and café on site. **$189**

EATING AND DRINKING

★ **Brown Jug** 155 Main St ☎ 508 888 4669. Right in the centre of town, this stylish picnic purveyor with a patio and antique wood floors peddles fancy cheeses, baguettes, good wine, salads and artisanal sandwiches. Impossible not to love. Tues–Sat 9am–5am, Sun noon–4pm; call for hours in off-season.

Twin Acres Ice Cream Shoppe 21 Rte-6A, just outside the village ☎ 508 888 0566. The best of several ice-cream shacks in these parts, set in a 1940s-era shingled cottage. Daily: April, May, Sept & Oct 11am–9pm; June–Aug 11am–10pm.

Barnstable

BARNSTABLE, ten miles east of Sandwich on Rte-6A, was, after Sandwich, the
second town to be founded on Cape Cod, in 1639. Early prosperity was attained
through the whaling industry, and Barnstable's harbour was the busiest port on
the Cape until it silted up last century. In West Barnstable, the majestic 1717
Neoclassical **West Parish of Barnstable**, at 2049 Meetinghouse Rd (Rte-149,
south of Rte-6A), is the oldest surviving Congregationalist church in the US,
and its bell tower contains a bell cast by Paul Revere. Further evidence of
Barnstable's earlier prosperity can be seen in several imposing buildings,
including many sea captains' houses, in the leafy **village centre**, another five
miles along Rte-6A.

Sandy Neck Beach Park

$20 parking late May to early Sept; free rest of year • ☎ 508 362 8300 • To get here follow Sandy Neck Rd (which splits off Rte-6A, just ove
the Sandwich line

The beautiful **Sandy Neck Beach Park**, a six-mile barrier beach which has over four
thousand acres of dunes, is probably your main reason for visiting Barnstable.
Popular with toddlers, grandparents and everyone in between, this premium stretch
of sand is perfect for laying out. It's also home to maritime forests and
complimentary walking trails.

ACCOMMODATION

⭐ **Ashley Manor** 3660 Main St ☎ 508 362 8044,
ⓦ ashleymanor.net. Dating way back to 1699, this
historic home, set on two lush acres with tennis courts and
gardens, has modern updates like wi-fi and cable TV, but
the owners have carefully preserved the building's
historical integrity. Common areas find wide-plank floors
and grandiose stone fireplaces, while the six guest rooms,
including four plush suites with jacuzzi baths, have luxur
linens and traditional decor. **$195**

⭐ **Honeysuckle Hill Bed & Breakfast** 591 Main S
(Rte-6A) ☎ 508 362 8418, ⓦ honeysucklehill.com
Another lovely option with a wraparound porch, gardens
four rooms with white wicker furniture and one suite in
quintessential Cape Cod 1810 home. **$198**

EATING

Nirvana Coffee 3206 Main St (Rte-6A) ☎ 508 744
6983. One of the Cape's best java joints, with seven
jumpstarting blends and cushy leather chairs perfect for
meditating with a newspaper. Mon–Fri 7am–6pm, Sat
8am–6pm, Sun 8am–4pm.

Osterville Fish Too 275 Millway, Barnstable Harbor

☎ 508 362 2295. Casual fish shack with outdoor picni
tables and excellent chowder ($3.99), fried seafood plate
($11.99–18.79), and the lobster "OD" – a cup of lobste
bisque with a massive lobster roll, fries and coleslav
($22.79). Daily May–Oct: July & Aug 11am–9pm
slightly shorter hours other months.

Yarmouth Port

Three miles east of Barnstable along Rte-6A is **YARMOUTH PORT**, a delightful hamlet
marked by a series of sea captains' houses that have been converted into B&Bs. Along
one two-mile stretch, no building has been constructed since 1900, which has created
something of a time-warp effect.

Hallet's

139 Hallet St (Rte-6A) • Hours have been erratic in recent years; check ⓦ hallets.com for details

Yarmouth Port's bygone-era effect is augmented by **Hallet's**, a general store that started
as a pharmacy in 1889 by the current owner's great-great-grandfather, and still boasts
its original counter and soda fountain (said to be one of the oldest in the country).

Captain Bangs Hallet House

Off Rte-6A at 11 Strawberry Lane • Tours hourly June to mid-Oct Thurs–Sun 1–3pm • $3 • ☎ 508 362 3021, ⓦ hsoy.org

Near Hallet's, on the town green, the **Captain Bangs Hallet House** is a 1740 Greek
Revival mansion built by one of the town's founders, though its name comes from the
sea captain who lived here in the late 1800s. Tours take in the original kitchen,
complete with beehive oven, and fine views from the back of the house.

Edward Gorey House

8 Strawberry Lane • Tours: mid-April to June Thurs–Sat 11am–4pm, Sun noon–4pm; July–Sept Wed–Sat 11am–4pm, Sun noon–4pm;
Oct–Dec Fri & Sat 11am–4pm, Sun noon–4pm • $5 • ⓦ 508 362 3909, ⓦ edwardgoreyhouse.org

Another historic home on the horseshoe-shaped Strawberry Lane is the **Edward Gorey
House**, former residence of the well-known artist, illustrator and costume designer.
Gorey had a delightfully imaginative, dark sense of humour, reflected in both his art
and his home – dolls are posed as if falling down staircases, miniature coffins are
displayed, and outside there's a fake cemetery (installed after his death) dedicated to the
ill-fated characters of his abecedarian book, *Gashlycrumb Tinies*. Gorey lived in the little

1820s house from 1986 until his death in 2002, and tours take in his trademark raccoon fur coat (a fervent animal-rights activist, he later eschewed it), sets he created for the famous PBS *Mystery*! television show, and a large collection of the finely wrought pen-and-ink drawings that were his hallmark. Be sure to pat the plump cat "Ombledroom" on your way out.

INFORMATION
YARMOUTH PORT

Yarmouth Area Chamber of Commerce 424 Rte-28 (Mon–Fri 9am–5pm; ☎ 508 778 1008, ⓦ yarmouthcapecod.com). An office with plenty of brochures and helpful staff.

ACCOMMODATION

Clarion Inn 1199 Rte-28, South Yarmouth ☎ 1 800 527 0359, ⓦ clarionhotel.com. Well-tended hotel with updated linens and furniture in the guest rooms, flat-screen TVs, and both an indoor and outdoor pool. **$189**

Liberty Hill Inn 77 Main St (Rte-6A) ☎ 508 362 3976, ⓦ libertyhillinn.com. This 1825 Greek Revival offers a quintessential country inn ambience in six rooms with canopy beds and fireplaces. Classical or jazz music is played frequently in the common areas, and a full breakfast is served daily in the dining room. **$210**

Village Inn 92 Old King's Hwy (Rte-6A) ☎ 508 362 3182, ⓦ thevillageinncapecod.com. Family-run for over fifty years, this friendly, well-priced B&B has four cosy guest rooms in a historic home decorated with a melange of art and colourful glass seltzer bottles. It still boasts its original window panes and an antique bread oven. **$120**

EATING AND DRINKING

Inaho 157 Main St/Rte-6A ☎ 508 362 5522. For anyone looking for a break from fried seafood, this restaurant offers the best Japanese food in town, and possibly the whole of the Cape. You'll pay for the privilege, though (dinner for two costs around $80. Daily 4pm–late, closed Sun and Mon in the off-season.

★ **Jack's Outback II** 161 Main St ☎ 508 362 5522. The best place on the Cape for breakfast, this animated restaurant retains an in-the-know quality – a result of its tricky location (set back from Rte-6A in a white country house). The house speciality is a puffy popover (hot bread roll) with scrambled ham, tomato and cheddar ($7.95), but there is also home-made hash with eggs ($8.95) and all-you-can-eat buttermilk pancakes ($5.95). Cash only. Mon–Sat 6.30am–2pm, Sun 6.30am–1pm.

Jerk Café 1398A Rte-28, South Yarmouth ☎ 508 394 1944. Renowned Jamaican jerk chicken wings ($6.99), plates of sautéed chicken and shrimp ($11.99), fresh fruit smoothies and (surprisingly) burritos, all dished up by an affable chef. Very casual ambience. Mon–Sat 10.30am–10pm, Sun 11.30am–10pm.

★ **Sweet Tomatoes** 461 Station Ave, South Yarmouth ☎ 508 394 6094. Excellent New-Haven style pizza (with a thin, bitter crust) enhanced by creative toppings such as goat's cheese, bacon and caramelized onion ($13.50). Daily 11am–9pm.

Dennis

In **DENNIS**, four miles down the road from Yarmouth Port, a trip to the beach means a visit to pristine **Scargo Lake**, just off Rte-6A. The best place for a dip is **Princess Beach**, at 184 Scargo Hill Rd (keep an eye out for the turn-off as it's not well-marked), which has toilets and a picnic area. The town itself, named after its founder, Reverend Josiah Dennis, retains a colonial feel, notably in places like the clergyman's home, at 77 Nobscusset Rd.

Cape Playhouse

On Rte-6A between Nobscusset and Corporation roads • Late June to early Sept Mon–Sat • ☎ 508 385 3911, ⓦ capeplayhouse.com • **Art cinema** ☎ 508 385 2503, ⓦ capecinema.com • Tickets $8.50 **Cape Cod Museum of Art** Jan–March Thurs 10am–8pm, Fri & Sat

---

CAPE COD RAIL TRAIL

For cycling enthusiasts, the **Cape Cod Rail Trail**, a tarred bicycle path on the bed of the Old Colony Railroad, extends 24 miles from Dennis to Wellfleet (beginning in South Dennis on Rte-134 south of Rte-6). Barbara's Bike & Sports, at 430 Rte-134 in South Dennis (☎ 508 760 4723), near the start of the trail, and also in Brewster further along, rents bikes for about $24 a day and stocks copies of trail maps. Check out ⓦ capecodbikeguide.com.

10am–5pm, Sun noon–5pm; April also Wed 10am–5pm; early May also Tues 10am–5pm; late May to early Oct Mon–Sat 10am–5pm, Thurs 10am–8pm, Sun noon–5pm; mid-Oct to Dec Tues–Sat 10am–5pm, Thurs 10am–8pm, Sun noon–5pm • $8 • ☎ 508 385 4477, ⓦ ccmoa.org

One of the most famous summer theatres in the US, the **Cape Playhouse** was a Unitarian meeting house until it was bought in 1927 by Raymond Moore, who had intended to start a theatre company in Provincetown but found that town too remote. The complex also contains an art cinema, modelled after a Congregational church. On the ceiling is a stunning astrological mural designed by Rockwell Kent and Jo Mielziner. Also on site, the **Cape Cod Museum of Art** showcases works by local artists, many of whom seem to have a penchant for seascapes and marine life portraits, though the gallery often has good contemporary fare as well.

ACCOMMODATION

DENNIS

Inn at Swan River 829 Main St, West Dennis ☎ 1 800 628 0498, ⓦ innatswanriver.com. Twenty-seven modern hotel rooms with wi-fi, flat-screen TVs and iPod docks. The staff are particularly friendly and helpful, and there is also a heated pool, fire pit and barbecue set-up on site. Pet-friendly. $179

Isaiah Hall B&B Inn 152 Whig St ☎ 508 385 9928 or ☎ 1 800 736 0160, ⓦ isaiahhallinn.com. An 1857 Greek Revival farmhouse with ten attractive rooms and two suites, all equipped with wi-fi and Waverly rose prints, within walking distance of village and beach. $160

EATING AND DRINKING

Captain Frosty's Fish & Chips 219 Rte-6A ☎ 508 385 8548. Since 1976, Cape Codders have been eating generous portions of fried clams, clam cakes and fish and chips at this adorable dairy bar right on Rte-6A. April–Sept daily for lunch and dinner.

Harvest Gallery Wine Bar 776 Main St (Rte-6A) ☎ 508 385 2444. Inviting, just-off-the-beaten-path art gallery and wine bar with a locavore menu, lots of live music and plenty of romantic nooks for tête-à-têtes. Mon–Thurs & Sun 5pm–midnight.

★ **Sesuit Harbor Café** 375 Sesuit Neck Rd ☎ 508 386 5473. Head here for terrific lobster rolls, which you can feast upon at outdoor tables off Rte-134 in East Dennis, overlooking Sesuit Harbor. The café also cooks for "Lobster Roll Cruises", which head into the bay on the SS *Lobster Roll* ($15–20; ☎ 508 385 1686, ⓦ lobsterrollcruises.com). April–Oct daily for breakfast, lunch and dinner.

Brewster

BREWSTER is yet another agreeable, if anodyne, Cape Cod town, known as a leading antiques centre. The Cape Cod Rail Trail goes through here (see box, p.173), and the town is home to a number of crystal-clear bayside beaches.

First Parish Church
1969 Main St (Rte-6A) • ☎ 508 896 5577

The 1834 **First Parish Church** has one of New England's more fascinating legends attached to (or buried within) it: one of the gravestones bears the names of two men lost at sea: Captain David Nickerson and his adopted son, Captain René Rousseau. The story goes that Nickerson was in Paris during the French Revolution when a woman handed him the infant René; locals maintain he was the son of Louis XVI and Marie Antoinette.

Cape Cod Museum of Natural History
869 Main St • July & Aug daily 9.30am–4.30pm, check website for rest-of-year hours as they fluctuate wildly • $8 • ☎ 508 896 3867, ⓦ ccmnh.org

Farther down Rte-6A, the **Cape Cod Museum of Natural History** makes for an enlightening diversion – especially for kids – with exhibits on the fragile Cape environment, whales and other marine life, and short but captivating nature trails that straddle cranberry bogs and salt marshes before continuing on to the bay.

ACCOMMODATION AND EATING   **BREWSTER**

Brewster by the Sea 716 Main St/Rte-6A ☎ 508 896 3910, ⓦ brewsterbythesea.com. An upscale, eight-room B&B with four-poster beds and fireplaces that features spa services, as well as a delicious breakfast and a summertime outdoor pool. $235

★ **Brewster Fish House** 2208 Main St (Rte-6A) ☎ 508 896 7867. A bona fide Cape Cod best, this upmarket but very approachable seafood restaurant serves local cod fish sandwiches by day ($10) and fried Cape scallops by night ($16), in a shingled cottage with hand-painted floors and nautical art. Its chowder is the chowder by which all

others must be judged. Very popular, with no reservations taken, so arrive early or expect to linger awhile at the bar. Daily 11.30–3pm & 5–9.30pm.

Chillingsworth 2449 Rte-6A ☎ 508 896 3640. For superb contemporary French cuisine, try this restaurant, which also boasts a sumptuous setting; if you're going to splurge, its seven-course table d'hôte menu (about $75) can't be beat, but the bistro menu is much cheaper. Reservations strongly recommended. May–Oct: June–Aug daily 5.30–9pm; call for hours in other months.

The Outer Cape

North of Orleans, the Outer Cape narrows considerably; beyond **Wellfleet** the land is scarcely one mile wide, and the coastline becomes increasingly wild and fragile, much of it protected within the **Cape Cod National Seashore** (see box below). Aside from the beaches and coastal attractions, lively **Provincetown**, at the very tip of the Cape, provides the biggest allure.

Eastham

Largely undiscovered **EASTHAM**, on Rte-6 as the Cape begins to curve toward Provincetown, is home to fewer than five thousand residents, most of whom are content to sit and watch the summer traffic pass by on its way north. Though the sum of the town's commercial facilities is little more than a small strip of shopping malls and gas stations along Rte-6, if you veer off the highway you will glimpse some authentic Cape flavour.

The first detour is the **Fort Hill** area (free), part of the Cape Cod National Seashore, which has a scenic overlook with views of **Nauset Marsh**, a former bay that became a marsh when **Coast Guard Beach** ($15 parking; free shuttle buses to the beach) was formed.

Nauset Light

The red-and-white **Nauset Light**, at the corner of Ocean View Drive and Cable Road, was originally located in Chatham but installed here in 1923 and moved back 350ft a decade ago when it was in danger of falling into the sea.

CAPE COD NATIONAL SEASHORE

The protected **Cape Cod National Seashore** extends along much of the Cape's Atlantic side, stretching forty miles from Chatham to Provincetown. It's a fragile environment: 3ft of the lower Cape is washed away each year. Environmentalists are hoping that a programme of grass-planting will help prevent further erosion.

It was on these shifting sands that the **Pilgrims** made their first home in the New World: they obtained their water from Pilgrim Spring near Truro, and at Corn Hill Beach they uncovered a cache of corn buried by the Wampanoag Indians, who had been living on the Cape for centuries – a discovery which kept them alive their first winter, before they moved on to Plymouth.

Displays and films at the **Salt Pond Visitor Center**, on Rte-6 just north of Eastham (daily 9am–5pm; ☎ 508 255 3421, ⓦ nps.gov/caco), trace the geology and history of the Cape. A pretty road and hiking/cycling trail head east to the sands of **Coast Guard Beach** and **Nauset Light Beach**, both of which offer excellent swimming. You can also catch a free shuttle ride there from the visitor centre in summer. Another fine beach is **Head of the Meadow**, halfway between Truro and Provincetown. Beach entrance fees are collected from late June through early September: $15 for cars and $3 for pedestrians and cyclists.

First Encounter Beach

On Eastham's bayside, at the end of Samoset Road, **First Encounter Beach** is named after the first meeting between Pilgrims and Native Americans in 1620. It was hardly a cordial rendezvous; with the *Mayflower* anchored in Provincetown, an exploration party led by Myles Standish came ashore only to meet a barrage of arrows. Things settled down after a few gunshots were returned, and since then the beach has been utterly tranquil.

ACCOMMODATION   EASTHAM

Cottage Grove 1975 Rte-6 ☎ 508 255 0500, ⓦ grovecape.com. Nestled in the woods, the eight basic but adorable cottages of *Cottage Grove* have knotty pine walls, modern bathrooms, kitchens (in all but one property), barbecue grills, picnic tables and plenty of peace and quiet. May–Oct. $135

Fort Hill Bed & Breakfast 75 Fort Hill Rd ☎ 508 240 2870, ⓦ forthillbedandbreakfast.com. By Nauset Marsh, this is *the* place to stay in Eastham. You can choose to rest

your head in either a smartly designed suite or a silvery clapboard cottage with ocean views. Sited on a former dairy farm, with a delectable organic vegetable garden. No children. Late May to mid-Oct. $245

Mid-Cape American Youth Hostel 75 Goody Hallet Drive ☎ 508 255 2785, ⓦ hihostels.com. Close to the Cape Cod Rail Trail bike path, this hostel offers dorm beds in a collection of woodsy eight-bed cabins. Mid-May to mid-Sept. Dorms $32 for non-members, cabins $135

EATING

Abba 89 Old Colony Way, Orleans ☎ 508 255 8144. In neighbouring Orleans, this Mediterranean-inspired restaurant is one of the best in the region, with the likes of lobster in yellow curry sauce with butternut jasmine rice ($29) served in a candlelit dining room with white tablecloths. Tues–Sun 5pm–late.

Arnold's Lobster & Clam Bar 3580 Rte-6 ☎ 508 255 2575. Folks are obsessed with the onion rings and fried shellfish at this wildly popular restaurant. *Arnold's* comes fully equipped with a beer garden and mini-golf course. May to mid-Sept daily 11.30am–8.30pm; rest of year Fri–Sun only.

Friendly Fisherman 4580 Rte-6, North Eastham ☎ 508 255 6770. This beloved fish market and seafood snack bar has great lobster rolls and fried clams for both lunch and dinner. BYOB; there's a liquor store nearby. May to mid-Sept daily 11.30am–late.

Sam's Deli 100 Brackett Rd ☎ 508 255 9340. As its name suggests, this is the place to go for picnic fixings and bulging beach sandwiches. The "Nauset Light" is a local favourite – roast beef, bacon, lettuce and scallion horseradish cream cheese on yummy focaccia bread. Mon–Sat 6.30am–6pm.

Wellfleet

WELLFLEET, with a year-round population of just 2500, is one of the least developed towns on the Cape. Once the focus of a thriving oyster-fishing industry, today it is a favourite haunt of writers and artists who come to seek inspiration from the unsullied landscape. Despite the fact that a number of art galleries have surfaced – most of them along **Main** and **Commercial** streets – the town remains remarkably unpretentious, with many of the galleries themselves resembling fishing shacks and selling distinctive original works.

Wellfleet Drive-In Theatre

51 Rte-6 • **Movies** Double features nightly late May to early Sept • Tickets $8.50, cash only **Flea market** Weather permitting, open weekends and holiday Mondays year-round 8am to early afternoon, July & Aug also Wed & Thurs • $1 per car Thurs & holiday Mon, $2 per car Wed & Sat; $3 per car Sun • ☎ 508 349 7176, ⓦ wellfleetcinemas.com

Wellfleet's star attraction is its 1957 drive-in theatre, which screens outdoor movies and music in summer and has the added bonus of an on-site snack bar and mini-golf course. On weekend mornings, the property doubles as a fun flea market – a major Cape destination. Both the drive-in and the flea market are summertime must-dos.

Wellfleet Historical Society Museum

266 Main St • Late June to early Sept Tues & Fri 10am–4pm, Wed, Thurs & Sat 1–4pm • Free • ☎ 508 349 9157, ⓦ wellfleethistoricalsociety.com

The **Wellfleet Historical Society Museum**, right in the heart of town, has an interesting collection of furniture, nautical artefacts and photographs as well as exhibits on the local oyster industry.

> ## OYSTER SHUCKING
>
> No visit to Wellfleet would be complete without a taste of the town's famous oysters. In fact, the little molluscs are so abundant here that the French explorer Samuel de Champlain named the town "Port aux Huîtres" (or Oyster Port) when he disembarked in 1606. One of the best places to dive into a plate of the raw variety is the rowdy *Beachcomber* (see p.177). If you're around in mid- to late October, you can also attend the annual **Wellfleet Oyster Weekend** (ⓦwellfleetoysterfest.org), complete with raw bars and shucking contests.

2

Marconi Station Site

The most scenic part of Wellfleet actually lies outside the centre, at the bluff-lined **Marconi Station Site**, east off Rte-6 in South Wellfleet, where Guglielmo Marconi issued the first transatlantic radio signal on January 18, 1903, announcing greetings from President Roosevelt to King Edward VII. Nothing remains of Marconi's radio towers, but there are some scale models beneath a gazebo-type structure overlooking the ocean. A short trail up the cliffside leads to a vantage point from where you can see across the entire Cape – just a mile wide at this point. Take the same turning off Rte-6 for sandy **Marconi Beach** (then bear right at the first junction), where you'll find facilities and parking ($15) that rarely fills to capacity.

INFORMATION   WELLFLEET

Information booth Corner of Rte-6 and LeCount Hollow Rd (June–Aug daily 9am–6pm; April, May, Sept & Oct Sat & Sun 10am–6pm; ☎ 508 349 2510). You can pick up a guide to Wellfleet's galleries at this handy information station.

ACCOMMODATION

Home Sweet Om 30 Captain Bellamy Rd ☎ 508 214 0113, ⓦhomesweetomcapecod.com. This restorative retreat with a yoga studio, colourful quarters, flower gardens and energizing breakfasts sits surrounded by lanky pine trees a few miles from downtown. **$250**

Sweet Liberty B&B 220 Holbrook Ave ☎ 508 349

1751, ⓦsweetlibertywellfleet.com. Three rooms simply furnished with antiques in a refurbished 1820s home within walking distance of downtown and Wellfleet's restaurants; one room, for singles, has a cheaper rate ($125). Free continental breakfast included. May–Oct. **$150**

EATING

★ **Beachcomber** 1120 Cahoon Hollow Rd ☎ 508 349 6055. The *Beachcomber* encapsulates everything good about Cape Cod: situated inside a former life-saving station, this lively shanty is directly on the beach, and comes with spectacular waterfront views, the area's best live music and fantastic oysters, wrested from their shells by a salty shucker. Late May to early Sept daily 11.30am–1am.

Mac's Shack 91 Commercial St ☎ 508 349 6333. Classic oyster shack that has a superb raw bar and sushi. It's easily spotted by the faux lobsterman reeling in his net on the roof of the restaurant. Daily 3pm–late.

Moby Dick's 3225 Rte-6 across from Gull Pond

Rd ☎ 508 349 9795. Order at the counter and take a seat under the buoy-lined ceiling at this longstanding family-friendly haunt. No surprises, just very good seafood. Early May to mid-Oct daily 11.30am–9pm.

PB Boulangerie & Bistro 15 LeCount Hollow Rd ☎ 508 349 1600. Finding an empty parking space at this authentic French bakery and bistro, let alone squeezing into its tiny pink house of a property, is tough. Come dinnertime, it's packed with happily dining foodies; during the daytime hours, folks come from all over to sample its exquisite pastries, like the chocolate "bombes". Wed–Sun 7am–11pm (bistro is dinner only).

Truro

Most of the sprawling town of **TRURO** falls within the boundaries of the Cape Cod National Seashore, allowing it to preserve the kind of natural beauty that has attracted artists, writers and even politicians over the years.

It was here that **Myles Standish** and his companions from the *Mayflower* found the cache of Indian corn that helped them survive their first New England winter in 1620; a plaque on **Corn Hill Road**, marks the exact spot.

Cape Cod Light

At the end of Highland Rd · Tours late May to Oct daily 10am–5.30pm · $4 to climb the lighthouse (parking is free) · ☎ 508 487 1121, ⓦ capecodlight.org

In 1797 Truro became the site of Cape Cod's first lighthouse, powered by whale oil. Today a golf course flanks the lighthouse's 1857 replacement, the **Cape Cod Light**. The interpretive centre inside has a short video about the site, but the real treat is the view from the top – you can compare it with the equally stunning views from the nearby observation deck, perched on one of the highest cliffs on the Cape.

2

ACCOMMODATION   TRURO

Places to stay in Truro are mainly confined to a strip that hugs the bay shoreline west of **Shore Road** (Rte-6A) in North Truro. The following are open only in **summer**.

HI-Hostel 111 North Pamet Rd ☎ 508 349 3889, ⓦ hiusa.org. One of the east coast's best hostels: 42 dorm beds in a capacious former Coast Guard station that's a stone's throw from the beach. Dorms $39
The Top Mast 209 Shore Rd (Rte-6A), North

Truro ☎ 508 487 1189, ⓦ topmastresort.com. This waterfront property offers clean and simple motel rooms, some self-catering, and cottages; the rooms could use a renovation but the price and beachside location are right. $100

EATING

Blackfish 17 Truro Center Rd, off Rte-6A ☎ 508 349 3399. If you're tired of fried seafood baskets and bowls of chowder, pop into this country-chic dining room with

copper tables and a candlelit glow and tuck into some fine contemporary American food (mains $19–33). Daily 5–10pm.

Provincetown

The fishing burg of **PROVINCETOWN**, at the very tip of Cape Cod, has long been a popular summer destination, with the excellent beaches, art galleries and welcoming atmosphere attracting bohemians, artists and fun-seekers alike. Over the past few decades, however, it has become known most famously as a **gay** resort destination, complete with frequent festivals and theme weekends. P-town, as the coastal community is often called, also has a drop of **Portuguese** culture, after a smallish population of fishermen began settling here in the mid-1800s. Throughout the summer, P-town's population swells into the tens of thousands, and there's often a carnival atmosphere in the bustling streets.

The town centre is essentially two three-mile-long streets, **Commercial** and **Bradford**, that follow the harbour and are connected by about forty tiny lanes of no more than two blocks each. **Fisherman's Wharf**, and the more touristy **MacMillan Wharf**, busy with whale-watching boats, yachts and colourful old Portuguese fishing vessels, split the town in half.

At Commercial Street's western end, the Pilgrim **landing place** is marked by a modest bronze plaque on a boulder. Nearby, just past the *Provincetown Inn*, is the **Breakwater Trail**, a mile-long **jetty** that cuts across to **Long Point Beach**, a great place to watch the sun set; you can also take the **shuttle** across Cape Cod Bay out here (mid-June to mid-Sept; $10 one-way, $15 round-trip; ☎ 508 487 0898), from MacMillan Wharf.

Around one and a half miles north of town along Race Point Road, the **Province Lands** form part of the Cape Cod National Seashore. The **visitor centre** (May–Oct daily 9am–5pm; ☎ 508 487 1256) has videos and displays highlighting the exceptionally fragile environment here. From the centre you can take off into the dunes; nearby **Race Point Beach** has lifeguards and miles of sand. Province Lands is also home to the best **bike path** on Cape Cod, roaming through the dunes without a building in sight.

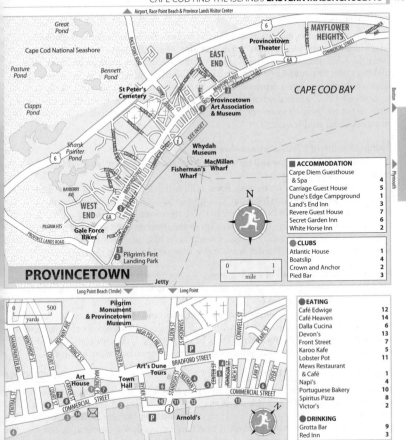

Brief history

The Pilgrims came ashore here and stayed for five weeks in 1620. They signed the **Mayflower Compact**, before sailing across Cape Cod Bay to Plymouth. Provincetown was incorporated in 1727, and soon became a thriving fishing, salt-processing and whaling port; by 1880, the town was the richest per capita in Massachusetts. Fishing retains its importance here, but the town's destiny as one of the East Coast's leading **art colonies** was assured in 1899, when painter Charles W. Hawthorne founded the **Cape Cod School of Art**. By the early 1900s, many painters had begun to ply their trade in abandoned shacks by the sea, and by 1916 there were six art schools flourishing here. The natural beauty and laidback atmosphere of the place also began to seduce young writers like Mary Heaton Vorse. She established the **Provincetown Players** theatre group in 1915 and **Eugene O'Neill** joined the company in 1916. It was in the waterfront fish house here that his *Bound East for Cardiff* premiered. Today, thanks in part to strict **zoning laws** designed to protect Provincetown's fragile environment, major development has been kept at bay. This has contributed towards preserving the flavour of the old town.

2

Whydah Museum

16 MacMillan Wharf • Daily: April, May, Sept & Oct 10am–5pm; June–Aug 10am–7pm • $10 • ☎ 508 487 8899, ⓦ whydah.com

MacMillan Wharf houses the **Whydah Museum**, which displays some of the bounty from the 1717 shipwreck of the pirate vessel *Whydah* off the coast of Wellfleet. The lifelong quest of native Cape Codder Barry Clifford to recover the treasure from the ship – holding loot from more than fifty others when it sank – paid off royally in the summer of 1984, when thousands of coins, gold bars, pieces of jewellery and weapons were retrieved, ranging from odds and ends like silver shoe buckles and flintlock pistols to rare African gold jewellery.

Pilgrim Monument & Provincetown Museum

High Pole Hill Rd • Daily: April to mid-June & mid-Sept to Nov 9am–5pm; mid-June to mid-Sept 9am–7pm • $7 • ☎ 508 487 1310, ⓦ pilgrim-monument.org

Two blocks north of the piers, atop Town Hill, is the 252ft granite tower of the **Pilgrim Monument & Provincetown Museum**. Completed in 1910 to commemorate the Pilgrims' landing here on November 21, 1620, the tower was modelled on the Torre del Mangia in Siena, Italy. It's 116 steps up to the observation deck; on a clear day you can see all the way to Boston. In the museum at its base, a series of exhibits give a fairly romantic account of the Pilgrim story and subsequent history of the town.

Provincetown Art Association and Museum

460 Commercial St • Late May to Sept Mon–Thurs 11am–8pm, Fri 11am–10pm, Sat & Sun 11am–5pm; Oct to mid-May Thurs–Sun noon–5pm • $7 • ☎ 508 487 1750, ⓦ paam.org

On the main drag, the **Provincetown Art Association and Museum** rotates works from its two-thousand-strong collection, with equal prominence given to both upcoming and well-known local artists such as Peter Busa (1914–85), though you might find the cleverly designed, eco-friendly galleries more interesting than the art on display.

ARRIVAL AND INFORMATION
PROVINCETOWN

By bus You can take a bus from Boston (☎ 508 746 0378, ⓦ p-b.com), which stops right in the middle of town near MacMillan Wharf.

By car Parking can be problematic in summer, so get here early; try the waterfront car park on MacMillan Wharf ($2.50/hr), or the Duarte Motors Parking Lot, Bradford St at Standish St (first hr $5, $1/hr thereafter; $15/day).

By ferry Taking the ferry here from Boston or Plymouth (see p.154) is a pricey but stress-free alternative to driving.

Provincetown Chamber of Commerce Next to the ferry terminal at 307 Commercial St (May–Oct daily 9am–5pm, limited winter hours; ☎ 508 487 3424, ⓦ ptownchamber.com); very useful. A good online resource is ⓦ provincetown.com; gay travellers may also want to check ⓦ ptown.gaycities.com.

GETTING AROUND

By bike Provincetown is a very walkable place, though bicycles can come in handy, especially if you want to venture a bit further afield. For rentals, Arnold's, 329 Commercial St (☎ 508 487 0844), right in the centre of town, is open from mid-April to mid-October, as is Gale Force Bikes, close to the Province Lands bike trails at 144 Bradford St Ext (☎ 508 487 4849, ⓦ galeforcebikes.com). Bikes at both places go for about $20/day.

TOURS

Tour companies abound in Provincetown, mostly of an aquatic nature – offering everything from **whale-watching** (the town claims the title of first whale-watching spot on the East Coast) to **kayaking**. Still, there's a varied range of what you can do here, with a number of landlubbing trips available as well. Some of the best operators are listed below.

4WD trips Art's Dune Tours, 4 Standish St (April–Oct 10am–dusk; ☎ 508 487 1950, ⓦ artsdunetours.com). Guided tours ramble about the dunes in a 4WD vehicle (6–8 people per car); an hour-long tour is $26.

Boat rides Viking Princess Cruises, MacMillan Wharf (☎ 508 487 7323, ⓦ capecodecotours.com), run 1hr trips round the bay several times a day in season ($17), while Flyer's Boat Rentals, 131A Commercial St (☎ 508 487 0898 or ☎ 1 800 770 0898, ⓦ flyersboats.com), rents kayaks ($50/day), Sunfish sailboats ($80/day), and powerboats (from $180/day).

Flights Race Point Aviation (☎ 508 873 2342, ⊛ racepointaviation.com) offers mesmerizing 20min flights over the Cape for just $100, from the airport on Race Point Road.

Whale-watching Dolphin Fleet, 132 Bradford St (April–Oct; $42; ☎ 508 240 3636 or ☎ 1 800 826 9300, ⊛ whalewatch.com), is the best company for whale-watching, with 3–4hr cruises leaving frequently from MacMillan Wharf.

ACCOMMODATION

Many of the most picturesque cottages in town are **guesthouses**, some with spectacular views over Cape Cod Bay – unsurprisingly, many are run by gay couples and are generally **gay-friendly**. The best area to be is the quiet West End, though anything on Bradford Street will also be removed from the summertime racket. Prices are generally very reasonable until mid-June, and off-season you can find real bargains. In addition, there are a few **motels**, mostly on the outskirts of town towards the Truro line.

★ **Carpe Diem Guesthouse & Spa** 12 Johnson St ☎ 1 800 487 0132, ⊛ carpediemguesthouse.com. You'll find friendly, accommodating owners, beautifully appointed rooms with a bit of an Eastern vibe, horseback riding, a spa and an afternoon wine and cheese hour at this lovely B&B on a quiet side street. $199

★ **Carriage Guest House** 7 Central St ☎ 1 800 309 0248, ⊛ thecarriagehse.com. Fabulously maintained rooms, some with private decks, and all with DVD and CD players; stylish breakfasts and large hot tub and sauna are soothing extras. $195

Land's End Inn 22 Commercial St ☎ 508 487 0706, ⊛ landsendinn.com. Every inch of this turreted house upon a hill has been imaginatively decorated in an extravagant Art Nouveau style. Many of the rooms and suites have sweeping ocean views, and a continental breakfast and daily wine and cheese hour is included. A truly original and very special place. $315

Revere Guest House 14 Court St ☎ 508 487 2292 or ☎ 1 800 487 2292, ⊛ reverehouse.com. This restorative B&B has a garden patio and antiques-accented rooms with iPod docks, a Vita Spa, an outdoor shower and a common room with a skylight and fireplace. It also has the entire *Sex and the City* series stocked on DVD. $235

Secret Garden Inn 300A Commercial St ☎ 1 866 786 9646 or ☎ 508 487 9027, ⊛ secretgardenptown.com. This 1830s captain's house is a relative bargain, with seven quaint rooms done up with country furnishings, but with modern touches like TVs and a/c, in a house with a veranda; country breakfast included. There's a beautiful garden just outside. $120

White Horse Inn 500 Commercial St ☎ 508 487 1790. A bright, eclectic, under-the-radar, art-strewn space in the quiet East End neighbourhood; some rooms have shared bathrooms. There are also family-sized apartments with kitchens. It's bygone-era Provincetown: no TVs and no wi-fi, but there's a private slip of beach, a delightful owner, and a beatnik vibe. Cash or cheque only. May–Sept. Singles $70; apartments $185

CAMPING

Dune's Edge Campground On Rte-6 just east of the central traffic lights ☎ 508 487 9815, ⊛ dunes-edge .com. Close to the beach, this campsite offers wooded sites. May–Sept. $40

EATING

Eating in Provincetown is fun but can be expensive; the snack bars around **MacMillan Wharf** are particularly pricey. Still, there are some real treats to be had, and they need not break your budget – look out in particular for the town's **Portuguese restaurants**. In summer, try to arrive early or make a reservation; most places close from **November to March**, though some remain open on weekends.

Café Edwige 333 Commercial St ☎ 508 487 2008. Breakfast is the thing at this popular second-floor restaurant; try the home-made Danish pastries and fresh-fruit pancakes. Creative bistro fare at dinner (mains $20–34). Daily 8.30am–10pm.

Café Heaven 199 Commercial St ☎ 508 487 9639. Massive breakfast plates (served through the afternoon), baguette sandwiches, and local art make this a popular daytime choice, but it's the juicy hamburgers that really make it stand out. Just like heaven, there's usually a wait to get in. Daily 8am–2pm & 6–10pm.

★ **Dalla Cucina** 404 Commercial St ☎ 508 487 5404. In a town filled with Italian landmarks, this newcomer shines – most residents think it's the pick of the pack. Local ingredients are used whenever possible, elevating favourites such as *caprese* in *burrata* (home-made mozzarella; $14) and day-boat cod *puttanesca* ($28) to a higher level. Reservations recommended. Daily 5.30–10.30pm.

Devon's 401 ½ Commercial St ☎ 508 487 4773. This cute fishing shack has been converted into a fine dining outpost with just 37 seats and an open kitchen by Devon Ruesch – try

2

and reserve a table by the window. The menu features French/American fusion cuisine, pairing items like local sea scallops with truffle zabaglione; the desserts and breakfasts are also stellar. Daily except Wed 8am–1pm & 5.30–10pm.

Front Street 230 Commercial St ☎ 508 487 9715. Popular Italian and continental restaurant in a Victorian house. The menu changes weekly, but you might find dishes like butternut ravioli and mojito-grilled swordfish. Mains $25–35. Daily except Tues 5.30pm–late.

Karoo Kafe 338 Commercial St ☎ 508 487 6630. Tasty, inexpensive South African fare. Order the Cape Malay stew (curry, coconut milk and veggies over rice; $14) at the counter and enjoy it on sunny, zebra-striped seating. Daily 11am–9pm.

★ **Lobster Pot** 321 Commercial St ☎ 508 487 0842. Its landmark neon sign is like a beacon for those who want ultra-fresh crustaceans. Affordable (lobster ravioli $11; clam chowder $5–6) and family-oriented, with a great outdoor deck. Daily 11.30am–10pm.

★ **Mews Restaurant & Café** 429 Commercial St ☎ 508 487 1500. Since its opening in 1961, this unassuming restaurant has served everyone from Judy Garland to Marc Jacobs, garnering rave reviews for its rotating fusion cuisine (think pork vindaloo or almond-crusted cod; both $26) and extensive vodka bar (286 and counting). Open year-round. Daily 6pm–late.

Napi's 7 Freeman St ☎ 1 800 571 6274. Popular dishes at this art-strewn spot include pastas and soups like thick Portuguese fish stew and clam chowder (from $6). There's a less expensive menu on week nights, and lots of veggie options (mains from $17). Daily 5pm–late; Oct–April also 11.30am–2.30pm.

Portuguese Bakery 299 Commercial St ☎ 508 487 1803. This old stand-by is the place to come for cheap breakfasts and baked goods, particularly the tasty fried *rabanada*, akin to French toast. Also great for an egg sandwich at breakfast; ask for it on a Portuguese muffin. Late April to Sept Mon–Fri 7am–7pm, Sat & Sun till 8pm or 9pm; call for Oct hours.

Spiritus Pizza 190 Commercial St ☎ 508 487 2808. Combination pizza place and coffee bar with an especially lively after-hours scene. Daily 11.30am–2am.

Victor's 175 Bradford St Ext ☎ 508 487 1777. Fun New American restaurant with mouthwatering small plates like blood orange grilled shrimp ($12) and deconstructed tuna napoleon ($14). *Victor's* has a raw bar happy hour ($1.25 oysters, shrimps and clams; Thurs–Sun 3–5pm) and a drag brunch on Sundays (9am–2pm). Daily 5–10pm.

NIGHTLIFE

On summer weekends, boatloads of revellers come to P-town in search of its notoriously **wild nightlife**, which is heavily geared towards a **gay** clientele. Some establishments have terrific waterfront locations, making them ideal spots to sit out with a drink at sunset. **Cover charges** will generally fall in the $5–10 range. You'll also find that many of Provincetown's restaurants have a lively bar scene. All of the following are open daily in **summer**.

Atlantic House 6 Masonic Place, behind Commercial St ☎ 508 487 3821, ⊛ ahouse.com. The "A-House" – a dark drinking hole that was a favourite of Tennessee Williams and Eugene O'Neill – is now a trendy gay dance club and bar; everyone ends up here at 12.30am.

Boatslip 161 Commercial St ☎ 508 487 1669, ⊛ boatslipresort.com. The daily tea dances (4–7pm) at this resort are legendary; you can either dance away on a long wooden deck overlooking the water, or cruise inside under a disco ball and flashing lights.

Crown and Anchor 247 Commercial St ☎ 508 487 1430, ⊛ onlyatthecrown.com. A massive complex housing several venues, including *The Vault*, a leather bar, *Wave*, a video-karaoke bar, and *Paramount*, a massive nightclub.

Pied Bar 193A Commercial St ☎ 508 487 1527, ⊛ piedbar.com. Though largely a lesbian club (it's the oldest in the country), the outdoor deck and inside dancefloor at this trendy waterfront space attract a good dose of men, too, for its long-standing "After Tea T-Dance" (daily 6.30pm).

BARS

Grotta Bar Enzo Hotel, 186 Commercial St ☎ 508 487 7555. One the newer bars in Provincetown, with campy live entertainment, bands, DJs, a 46-inch plasma TV and zesty martinis. Live piano Tues, Fri & Sun.

Red Inn 15 Commercial St ☎ 508 487 7334, ⊛ theredinn.com. For a complete change of nightlife pace, head to the *Red Inn's* teensy bar, where you can sip martinis over wide-plank wood floors in a little historic house by the sea. Stylish, with terrific ocean views.

ENTERTAINMENT

Art House 214 Commercial St ☎ 508 487 9222, ⊛ ptownarthouse.com. This landmark arts venue combines a theatre and a cinema; shows generally comprise drag acts, vaudeville, campy thrillers and comedy, while the cinema tends to feature independent films. Show tickets $15–75.

Provincetown Theater 238 Bradford St ☎ 508 487 7487, ⊛ provincetowntheater.org. A range of musicals and plays to suit all tastes. Tickets $15–30.

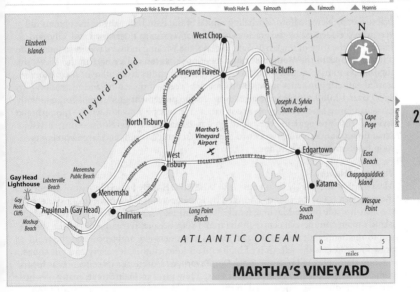

Woods Hole & New Bedford ▲   Woods Hole & ▲ Falmouth   ▲ Falmouth   ▲ Hyannis

West Chop

Vineyard Haven   Oak Bluffs

Elizabeth Islands

Vineyard Sound

Joseph A. Sylvia State Beach

Cape Poge

North Tisbury

Martha's Vineyard Airport

Edgartown

East Beach

West Tisbury

EDGARTOWN–WEST TISBURY ROAD

Chappaquiddick Island

Menemsha Public Beach

Gay Head Lighthouse   Lobsterville Beach

Katama

Wasque Point

Gay Head Cliffs

Menemsha

Aquinnah (Gay Head)   Chilmark

Long Point Beach

South Beach

Moshup Beach

ATLANTIC OCEAN

0   5
miles

MARTHA'S VINEYARD

2

Nantucket

Martha's Vineyard

The largest offshore island in New England, twenty-mile-long **Martha's Vineyard** encompasses a good deal of physical and architectural variety: hills and pasturelands provide scenic counterpoints to beaches and windswept moors, while clapboards and grey shingles are supplemented by an array of Victorian homes and colourful wooden cottages. The most genteel town on the island is **Edgartown**, with its freshly painted colonial homes and manicured gardens. The main port, **Vineyard Haven**, has a more commercial atmosphere, while **Oak Bluffs**, between the two, is best known for its gingerbread cottages. Remarkably, major development has been kept to a minimum, and though traffic can be heavy in summer (when the population swells to 100,000), the island's size means it's not too hard to escape the crowds. Indeed, it's so large that, if you want to see the whole place, travelling by bus or car is essential.

The Vineyard is basically divided into two sections, the far busier of which is "**Down-Island**", which includes the ferry terminals of **Vineyard Haven** and **Oak Bluffs**, and smart **Edgartown**. The largely undeveloped western half of the island, known as "**Up-Island**", comprises woods, agricultural land, nature reserves and a smattering of tiny villages, including **West Tisbury**, **Chilmark**, and **Aquinnah** (Gay Head). Much of the land in these areas belongs to private estates; check the Martha's Vineyard Land Bank website (Ⓦmvlandbank.com) to see what is open for public exploration.

Brief history

Wampanoags have been calling the island home for at least ten thousand years (a small community of around three hundred remains at **Aquinnah**). Wampanoag legend claims that in order to separate his tribe from enemies on the mainland, the Native American chief **Moshup** placed his cape on the ground and created Vineyard Sound. The island gained its English name in 1602, when explorer **Bartholomew Gosnold** named it after his daughter. The "vineyard" part was for its fertile store of vines – back then the island was virtually covered with wild grapes.

In 1642, one **Thomas Mayhew** bought the island from the Earl of Stirling for £40 and a beaver hat, paving the way for other Puritan farmers to settle here. They learned the **whaling industry** from the natives, and the economy flourished; the Vineyard never ousted

Nantucket or New Bedford as whaling capital of the East, but many of its captains did very nicely, evidenced by the gracious houses that remain in Edgartown and Vineyard Haven. By the time of the Civil War, however, the whaling industry was in serious decline.

It was thanks to the **Methodist camp meetings** that took place here in the 1820s that the island's tourist industry took root. Methodist families from all over the nation started gathering in tents at **Oak Bluffs** for two weeks of preaching and recreation – by 1859 over 12,000 people were attending. As the movement grew, small cottages with extraordinarily fancy facades were constructed in what is now known as "**gingerbread**" style. In 1867, recognizing the island's potential as a resort, developers constructed a separate secular community next to the original campground, and large hotels were soon built around the harbour.

Vineyard Haven

Most visitors arriving by boat come into **VINEYARD HAVEN** (officially part of **Tisbury**), at the northern tip of the island. Founded by islanders from Edgartown disillusioned with the iron-fist rule of the Mayhew family, Vineyard Haven supplanted Edgartown as the island's main commercial centre in the mid-1800s because ferries preferred the shorter run to the mainland; today the town retains a business-like ambience, and the main draw for visitors is the selection of high-end antique, clothes, jewellery and gift **shops**.

Along the way you'll pass the **Black Dog Tavern**, as famous for its souvenirs as for its comestibles (see p.190). From here, it's just a few yards to **Main Street**, many of whose original buildings were destroyed in the Great Fire of 1883, though it's rebuilt and thriving now.

Oak Bluffs

OAK BLUFFS, just across Lagoon Pond from Vineyard Haven, is the newest of the island's six towns; it was a quiet farming community until the Methodists established their campground here in the nineteenth century. This section of Oak Bluffs, centred on the Trinity Park Circle, remains filled with the brightly coloured "carpenter Gothic" or "**gingerbread**" cottages they built. During the summer, family-oriented events, Sunday-morning church services, and secular Saturday-evening concerts are still held in the **Tabernacle** in the centre. The best-known event that takes place here is **Illumination Night** (third Wed in Aug; free), when all the cottages put up Japanese lanterns. At one end of the circle, the 1867 **Cottage Museum**, 1 Trinity Park (mid-May to Oct Mon–Sat 10am–4pm, Sun 1–4pm; $2), offers a charming collection of photographs, old bibles, and other artefacts from the campground's history.

After the Civil War, speculators built up the area near the waterfront with dance halls, a skating rink, a railroad linking the town to Edgartown, and resort hotels, of which only the 1879 **Wesley Hotel**, on Lake Avenue, survives. Most of the current action focuses on **Circuit Avenue**, where shops and bars attract a predominantly young crowd. The restored **Flying Horses Carousel**, indoors on Oak Bluffs Avenue near Circuit Avenue (July & Aug daily 10am–10pm; call for hours June & Sept; $2 per ride; ☎508 693 9481), is the oldest operating carousel in the US; hand-carved in 1876, the 22 horses have real horsehair manes.

Oak Bluffs also has a few beaches worth checking out, though the **town beach**, on Sea View Avenue, can get very noisy and crowded in season. Farther south, the **Joseph A. Sylvia State Beach**, a six-mile stretch of sand, is more appealing, and it parallels an undemanding pedestrian/cycle path that leads all the way to Edgartown.

Edgartown

Six miles southeast of Oak Bluffs, **EDGARTOWN**, originally known as Great Harbor, is the oldest and swankiest settlement on the island, its elegant colonial residences glistening white and surrounded by exquisitely maintained gardens. The pageantry doesn't end there: the town brims with upmarket boutiques, smart restaurants and art galleries.

Take the bus (route #8) from the visitor centre to **South Beach** in Katama, three miles south of town, for some of the island's best public access to the Atlantic.

Vineyard Museum

59 School St • Mid-June to mid-Oct Mon–Sat 10am–5pm; rest of year Mon–Sat 10am–4pm • $7, buy tickets in the Pease House galleries; $10 with lighthouse; $15 with lighthouse, church and Vincent House Museum • ☎ 508 627 4441, ⓦ mvmuseum.org

At the **Vineyard Museum**, a complex of historical buildings, you can visit the 1740 **Thomas Cooke House**, which is decorated in the colonial style and full of absorbing displays relating to island history. Nearby, the **Carriage Shed** serves as a hodgepodge storeroom for, among other things, a peddler's cart and a whaleboat, while the **Ross Fresnel Lens Building** preserves the original lantern from Gay Head Lighthouse, made in France in 1854. The 1845 **Captain Frances Pease House** contains the gift shop and best of all, an Oral History Center, which traces the history of the island through more than 250 recorded narratives of locals. Don't miss the small collection of **Wampanoag** artefacts here, including the Burt Pot, made c.1300.

Vincent House Museum

99 Main St • May to mid-Oct Mon–Fri 10.30am–3pm; 45min tours 11am, noon, 1pm & 2pm • $10 • ☎ 508 627 8017, ⓦ mvpreservation.org

A couple of blocks to the east of the Vineyard Museum, just behind the church on Main Street, the 1672 **Vincent House Museum** is the oldest house on the island, and has the furniture to prove it. **Tours** of the museum also include the 1840 **Dr. Daniel Fisher House** and the **Old Whaling Church**, whose 92ft-high clock tower is visible for miles around. Built in 1843 and more formally known as the United Methodist Church, it's also used as a performing arts centre.

Edgartown Lighthouse

Fri–Mon 11am–5pm, Thurs 11am–sunset • $5

At the end of town, a short walk along North Water Street leads past more sea captains' homes to the **Edgartown Lighthouse** – it's a replacement of the 1828 original, destroyed in the hurricane of 1938.

Chappaquiddick

Chappaquiddick (aka "Chappy") is a strikingly beautiful and sparsely populated little island, an easy five-minute jaunt from Edgartown via the **ferry** (see p.188) that departs frequently from a ramp at the corner of Dock and Daggett streets. There are no stores, restaurants or hotels, just private residences and hundreds of acres of dunes, salt marshes, ponds and scrubland. The island is too large to walk comfortably, though easy to get around on a bike.

Mytoi (Japanese garden)

Dike Rd • Dawn–dusk • Free • ☎ 508 627 3599, ⓦ thetrustees.org

The Trustees of Reservations' small Japanese garden, **Mytoi**, is worth stopping by – it's unusual to see the typical rounded bridges and groomed trees in a pine forest. The Trustees are also the caretakers of **Wasque**, a windswept beach that is a continuation of South Beach in Edgartown, but much less crowded. In fact, you can walk between Edgartown and Chappy along this stretch of sand.

Cape Poge Wildlife Refuge

On Chappy's far east side • June to mid-Oct $3 entry; most tours run weekends May–Oct, 1hr 30min–2hr 30min • $3 entry; tours $25–40 • ☎ 508 627 3599, ⓦ thetrustees.org

The one-thousand acre **Cape Poge Wildlife Refuge** is an important habitat for thousands of birds. Half the state's scallops are harvested here, too. The best way to see it is to take various **natural history tours** run by the Trustees, which are guided by expert naturalists and involve walking, kayaking, fishing or rambling about by over-sand vehicle.

West Tisbury

WEST TISBURY, the largest of the up-island communities, also has some of the best culture on the island. The locally grown produce at the **Farmers' Market**, held at the 1859 **Grange Hall** on State Road on Saturday and Wednesday mornings in summer (9am–noon), attracts buyers from all over Martha's Vineyard. Across the street from the hall is the **Field Gallery**, 1050 State Rd (Mon–Sat 10am–5pm, Sun 11am–4pm; free; ☏ 508 693 5595), locally famous for Tom Maley's larger-than-life sculptures of ladies dancing on the grass. Also on State Road, across from the Field Gallery, is **Alley's General Store** (Mon–Sat 7am–7pm, Sun 7am–6pm; ☏ 508 693 0088), an island institution since 1858, selling everything from canned goods to mini ouija boards, and with a wide front porch where locals often gather. A short drive away at 636 Old County Rd is the picturesque **Granary Gallery** (Mon–Sat 10am–5pm, Sun 11am–4pm; free; ☏ 508 693 0455), which showcases works by notable local and regional artists.

West Tisbury has a bountiful supply of conservation areas, including the 216-acre **Cedar Tree Neck Wildlife Sanctuary**, Indian Hill Road (daily sunrise–sunset; free). Three main trails lead to a pretty but stony beach and a bluff with views to Gay Head and the Elizabeth Islands. Meanwhile, the **Sepiessa Point Reservation**, on New Lane off West Tisbury Road (daily dawn–dusk; free), surrounds West Tisbury Pond with trails ideal for birdwatching.

Chilmark

Five miles west of Tisbury, unspoiled **CHILMARK** is the land that time almost forgot, full of pastures, dense woodlands and rugged roads. That's not to say that the twenty-first century hasn't arrived: **Beetlebung Corner**, where Middle, State, South and Menemsha Cross roads meet, and which is named for the wooden mallets (aka "beetles") and stoppers ("bungs") once made from local tupelo trees, is the village's centre, heralded by the *Chilmark Store* (see p.191) and some other modern commercial concerns. Don't miss **Chilmark Chocolates** (closed Mon; ☏ 508 645 3013), halfway to Aquinnah at 19 State Rd, with a mouthwatering selection of sweets.

On South Road the tranquil **Chilmark Cemetery** is the final resting place of writer Lillian Hellman and funnyman John Belushi, who claimed that the island was the only place he could get a good night's sleep. Near the entrance, a boulder engraved with the comedian's name, a decoy to prevent fans from finding his actual unmarked grave, is where legions leave their rather unceremonious "offerings", like beer cans and condoms. Nearby, a dirt track leads to **Lucy Vincent Beach**, named after the town's librarian, who saw it as her mission to protect Chilmark residents from corruption by cutting out from the library books all pictures she deemed to be immoral. Rather ironically, the beach, which is open only to residents and their guests in the summer, doubles as a **nudist** spot in its less crowded areas. Off North Road, study the painted map at the trailhead of **Waskosim's Rock Reservation** for a three-mile hike through a variety of habitats.

Menemsha

A few miles north of Chilmark, another tiny village, **MENEMSHA**, is a picturesque collection of grey-shingled fishing shacks fronting a man-made harbour, which serves as an important commercial and sports-fishing port. Stroll past the fish markets of (see p.191) **Dutcher's Dock** for a real sense of the island's maritime heritage, or bring a picnic to pebbly **Menemsha Beach** to enjoy the spectacular sunsets. The **Menemsha Hills Reservation**, off North Road a couple of miles towards West Tisbury, is also well worth a visit, its rocky shoreline and sand bluffs peaking at **Prospect Hill**, the highest point on the Vineyard, with views of the Elizabeth Islands.

Hikers and cyclists can take the tiny **ferry** (daily 9am–5pm; $5) across the Menemsha Pond inlet from the end of North Road, and continue along tranquil Lobsterville Road for five miles to Aquinnah – even on summer weekends this part of the island hardly sees any traffic.

Aquinnah (Gay Head)

In 1997, the people of Gay Head voted to change the town's name back to its original Wampanoag one – **Aquinnah** – the culmination of a court battle in which the Wampanoags won guardianship of 420 acres of land, now known as the **Gay Head Native American Reservation**. Most people come to this part of the island (its

2

MARTHA'S VINEYARD BEACHES

The island's **beaches** vary from calm, shallow waters, predominantly on the northern and eastern sides, to long stretches of pounding surf on the southern side, where the water also tends to be a bit warmer. Unfortunately, many of the best beaches are **private**, but there are some notable exceptions. All of the beaches listed below have **lifeguards** in at least some areas during summer days.

AQUINNAH (GAY HEAD)

Lobsterville Beach Lobsterville Rd. Two miles of prime Vineyard Sound beach backed by dunes. Parking on Lobsterville Rd is prohibited, so bike or walk here via the ferry from Menemsha.

Moshup Beach (Gay Head Public Beach) State Rd/Moshup Drive. Gorgeous setting at the foot of Gay Head Cliffs, best reached by bicycle, shuttle bus or taxi. Parking costs $15 a day in season.

CHAPPAQUIDICK

Cape Poge Wildlife Refuge At the end of Dike Rd. This sandy beach is less crowded than Wasque. $3 per person.

Wasque At the end of Wasque Rd south of School Rd. Wide-open South Shore beach. $3 per person and $3 per vehicle.

CHILMARK

Lucy Vincent Beach Off South Rd. Sandy beach with access to some of the island's clay cliffs (note that bathing in the clay puddles is restricted) up to the end of September to residents and visitors with passes.

Menemsha Public Beach Next to Menemsha Harbor. The only Chilmark beach open to the public, with sparkling waters and a picturesque setting. It becomes very crowded around sunset, since it is one of the few places to see the sun sink over a beach on the East Coast.

Squibnocket Off State Rd at the end of Squibnocket Rd. This narrow, rocky beach is less attractive than the other Chilmark beaches, but the waves break farther offshore, making it the best island spot for surfing. It's a town beach, which means it's off-limits during summer days, but anyone can show up after 5pm and in September – one of the best times to catch the waves.

EDGARTOWN

Bend-in-the-Road Beach Beach Rd. Really an extension of the Joseph A. Sylvia State Beach, with similar facilities and access.

Katama Beach (South Beach) End of Katama Rd. Beautiful barrier beach backed by a protected salt pond. Known for "good waves and good bodies".

Lighthouse Beach Starbuck's Neck, off North Water St. Close to town, this harbour beach can get a bit mucked with seaweed.

OAK BLUFFS

Joseph A. Sylvia State Beach Along Beach Rd between Oak Bluffs and Edgartown. A narrow six-mile strand of sandy beach with clear, gentle waters and plenty of roadside parking.

Oak Bluffs Town Beach Between the Steamship Authority Dock and the State Beach. Narrow sliver of beach on Vineyard Sound that gets very crowded in season.

VINEYARD HAVEN

Lake Tashmoo Town Beach Herring Creek Rd. Swim in the warm, brackish water of the lake, or in the cooler Vineyard Sound.

Owen Park Beach Off Main St. A harbour beach close to the centre of town, though it's not much of a swimming hole, nor a beach.

WEST TISBURY

Lambert's Cove Beach Lambert's Cove Rd. One of the island's prettiest beaches, but open only to residents during high season.

Long Point Wildlife Refuge Beach Off South Rd. The perfect Vineyard beach: long and wide, with a freshwater pond just behind. Get there early for a parking space, on the south side of the street near the airport.

2

westernmost point), to see the **Gay Head Cliffs**, whose brilliant hues are the result of millions of years of geological work. When the Vineyard was underwater, small creatures died and left their shells behind to form the white layers. At other times, the area was a rainforest and vegetation compressed to form the darker colours. Glaciers thrust the layers of stone up to create the cliffs, dubbed "Gay Head" by English sailors in the seventeenth century on account of their brightness. The clay was once the main source of paint for the island's houses, but now its removal will incur a fine; in any case, the cliffs are eroding so fast that it's not safe to approach them too closely.

A short path from the car park runs beyond the *Aquinnah* restaurant to the **overlook**, which affords stunning views as far as the Elizabeth Islands, and, on a clear day, the entrance to Rhode Island's Narragansett Bay. Nearby, the imposing red-brick **Gay Head Lighthouse** (mid-June to mid-Sept Tues–Sat 10am–5pm; mid-Aug to mid-Sept also Fri & Sat 6–8pm; $5), built in 1854 to replace a wooden structure that dated from 1799, is well situated for sunset views. Below the lighthouse a **public beach** provides an equally impressive view of the cliffs. To reach it, take the wooden boardwalk from the **Moshup Beach** car park to the shore, then walk round towards the lighthouse.

ARRIVAL AND DEPARTURE   MARTHA'S VINEYARD

BY FERRY

The easiest way to get to Martha's Vineyard is by ferry, arriving at either Oak Bluffs or Vineyard Haven, usually from Falmouth or Woods Hole. The most frequent ferries – and the only ones that can take cars – run year-round from Woods Hole. In addition, the Woods Hole ferry is one of the few ways to get to the island in the winter. In the summer, however, leaving from somewhere else can be more convenient. Falmouth and Hyannis both have day-boats (the Hyannis boats also runs in winter). The summer ferries from New Bedford, MA and Quonset Point, RI have also become popular options. Unless otherwise specified, the ferries listed below run several times daily from mid-June to mid-Sept. Most have fewer services from mid-May to mid-June and from mid-Sept to Oct. Prices listed below are for a return trip. Be sure to reserve ahead as they do sell out.

Parking Parking at the ferries is usually $10–15/day, and most charge extra for bikes (up to $6 one-way).

FROM CAPE COD

Falmouth to Oak Bluffs (about 35min). Passengers ($18), bikes ($6), kayaks ($12). The *Island Queen* (cash or travellers' cheque only; ☎ 508 548 4800, ⓦ islandqueen.com).

Falmouth to Edgartown (1hr). Falmouth Ferry Service ($50, $10 for bikes; ☎ 508 548 9400, ⓦ falmouthferry.com).

Hyannis to Oak Bluffs. Hy-Line (☎ 1 800 492 8082, ⓦ hylinecruises.com). High-speed ferry (50min; $69) or traditional (1hr 40min; $43), both passengers only.

Woods Hole to both Vineyard Haven and Oak Bluffs (45min). Steamship Authority ($135 high season or $85 low season per car, not including passengers, who must pay $7.50 each way; ☎ 508 477 8600,

ⓦ steamshipauthority.com). Car ferry, year-round. Reservations required to bring a car on summer weekends and holidays – you can bring a car stand-by all other times, though the wait can be long.

FROM ELSEWHERE IN MASSACHUSETTS AND RHODE ISLAND

New Bedford to Vineyard Haven or Oak Bluffs (1hr). New England Fast Ferry ($70; ☎ 1 866 683 3779, ⓦ nefastferry.com). Passengers only.

Quonset Point, Rhode Island, to Oak Bluffs (1hr 30min). Vineyard Fast Ferry ($75; ☎ 401 295 4040, ⓦ vineyardfastferry.com). Passengers only. Good for those travelling from Connecticut or New York; Quonset is south of Providence and Warwick. Shuttles are provided to Kingston Amtrak station ($20) and Providence airport ($15).

TO NANTUCKET

Oak Bluffs to Nantucket. Island-hoppers can take Hy-Line's inter-island ferry ($34 one-way; pedestrians only), which makes one round-trip daily June–Sept between Oak Bluffs and Nantucket.

TO CHAPPAQUIDDICK

Edgartown to Chappaquiddick. There is a 5min ferry option ($4/person, $12 for a car and one driver; ☎ 508 627 9427, ⓦ chappyferry.net).

BY PLANE

For visitors arriving by plane, the airport (☎ 508 693 7022) is in West Tisbury. You can fly to Martha's Vineyard via Cape Air (☎ 508 771 6944 or ☎ 1 800 352 0714, ⓦ flycapeair. com) from Boston, Hyannis, Nantucket, New Bedford or Providence, RI.

BY TAXI

Taxis greet ferries and flights; all companies use the same fare sheets, and some share phone numbers. Try Jon's Taxi (☎508 627 4677), Mario's Taxi (☎508 693 8399) or All Island Taxi (☎508 693 2929).

INFORMATION

Tourist information is available in Vineyard Haven, Oak Bluffs and Edgartown. To check the internet for free, visit any of the island's public libraries.

VINEYARD HAVEN

Visitor information kiosk The bus terminal, visible as you get off the ferry, is home to a small visitors' kiosk (May–Oct daily 8am–8pm).

Chamber of Commerce 24 Beach St. (Mon–Fri 9am–5pm, Sat 10am–4pm; ☎508 693 0085, ⓦmvy.com). More helpful than the visitors' kiosk for finding information and accommodation.

OAK BLUFFS

Information kiosk Maps are available at the information kiosk (daily 9am–5pm) at Lake and Circuit avenues.

EDGARTOWN

Visitor centre Church St, next to the bus stop (late May to early Sept Mon–Sat 8.30am–10pm, Sun 9am–9pm). This seasonal visitor centre is basically just a gift and snack shop with toilets and brochures.

GETTING AROUND

BY CAR

Bringing a car over on the ferry is expensive, and often impossible on summer weekends without reserving well in advance. Another alternative is to rent a car from Budget, in Vineyard Haven, Oak Bluffs or the airport (☎508 693 1911 or ☎1 800 527 0700, ⓦbudget.com), or from Adventure Rentals in Vineyard Haven (☎508 693 1959, ⓦislandadventuresmv.com) or Oak Bluffs (☎508 696 9147); the latter rents a fleet of 4WD jeeps suitable for beach driving.

BY BUS

The island has a bus system that connects the main towns and villages (daily 7am–12.45am; $1/town, $7/day; ☎508 639 9440, ⓦvineyardtransit.com). This is the best way to get around without a car.

BY BICYCLE

In Vineyard Haven you can rent from Martha's Bike Rentals at 24 Union St, a block from the ferry (daily 9am–5.30pm; ☎1 800 559 0312, ⓦmarthasbikerentals.com); in Oak Bluffs from Anderson Bike Rentals on Circuit Ave (April–Oct daily 8am–6pm; ☎508 693 9346); and in Edgartown from R.W. Cutler Bikes at 1 Main St (☎1 800 627 2763, ⓦmarthasvineyardbike.com). A basic bike generally starts at $20/day.

BY TRAM

Martha's Vineyard Sightseeing runs narrated tram tours (2hr 30min; $29; ☎508 627 TOUR, ⓦmvtour.com); the trams run from spring to autumn from all ferry arrival points.

ACCOMMODATION

There's plenty of accommodation on the island – everything from resort hotels to B&Bs oozing charm and personality, as well as **rental cottages**, usually booked on a weekly basis and better deals for groups or families. Try ⓦislandrealestatemv.com or ⓦmvvacationrentals.com, which offer a range of properties starting at around $1400 for two bedrooms (per week). You need to reserve well in advance for **summer** visits. Prices fall dramatically in the **autumn** and **spring**. Unless otherwise noted, the hotels listed below close in **winter** (Jan & Feb).

EDGARTOWN

Edgartown Inn 56 N Water St ☎508 627 4794, ⓦedgartowninn.com. This eighteenth-century home is a quintessential New England inn with colourful rooms that evoke another era (read: none of them has a TV). The Garden House and Barn out back have shared bathrooms and the least expensive rooms). $125

The Fallon 22 N Water St ☎1 877 939 9293, ⓦthefallon.com. The 1892 home of a lauded whaling captain, this boutique inn is a smart blend of historic "bones" (high ceilings, crown mouldings) and modern comforts like iPod docks and plush linens. Great location

right in the heart of things, but this can lead to outside noise; white-noise sound machines are provided. The owner is a gem. Closed Jan–March. $325

Hob Knob Inn 128 Main St ☎508 627 9510 or ☎1 800 696 2723, ⓦhobknob.com. The place for unabashed eco-luxury, with antique-laden rooms and plenty of extras: flat-screen TVs, wi-fi, sauna, filling breakfasts, lavish afternoon teas and a spa. Just outside Edgartown's centre. $400

Winnetu Inn & Resort South Beach ☎508 627 4747, ⓦwinnetu.com. This resort hotel is just a short walk from a private stretch of South Beach. Rooms come with

2

kitchenettes, and it's not all that much more expensive than the in-town options, though you really need a car to stay here. In high season expect two- to three-night minimum stays. $245

OAK BLUFFS

Isabelle's Beach House 83 Seaview Ave ☎508 693 3955, 🌐isabellesbeachhouse.com. This B&B is a terrific option, particularly if you're planning a car-less vacation. Steps away from both the ferry terminal and the beach, rooms are simple but well dressed, and the bygone-era front porch has ocean views. Open year-round; rates fall dramatically in the off-season. $300

Madison Inn 18 Kennebec Ave ☎508 693 2760, 🌐madisoninnmv.com. Run by the masterminds behind the landmark *Nashua House* (see below), this fourteen-room inn is gussied up with floral linens, iPod docks, wi-fi, flat-screen TVs and cheerful colours. Well-priced, and within easy walking distance of the beach, the ferry terminal and restaurants. $229

Nashua House Hotel 30 Kennebec Ave ☎508 693 0043, 🌐nashuahouse.com. Small rooms, all with shared bathrooms, but this friendly, central hotel is an easy walk from the ferry, and one of the least expensive choices on the island. $129

★ **Oak Bluffs Inn** 64 Circuit Ave ☎508 693 7171, 🌐oakbluffsinn.com. One of the most inviting hotels on the island, with a convenient location, cosy, clean Victorian-style rooms, wi-fi, a wide porch, free cookies and a great host. $225

Pequot Hotel 19 Pequot Ave ☎1 800 947 8704, 🌐pequothotel.com. Friendly, mid-sized hotel in th gingerbread cottage neighbourhood with rocking chairs o the porch, fresh cookies in the afternoon, and a quick wal to town – rooms are a bit small and showing their age though. $225

ELSEWHERE ON THE ISLAND

HI-Martha's Vineyard 525 Edgartown–West Tisbury R ☎508 693 2665 or ☎1 888 901 2087, 🌐capecod.hius .org. Pleasant setting and a very neat (both clean and eclectic place to stay, with 78 beds in dormitory accommodation shared bathrooms and a full kitchen. It is a bit off the beate track, so they try to make it easy for people to stay, with bike rental deals and free bike delivery. Easily accessed by the # bus route. April to mid-Nov only. Dorms $29

★ **Menemsha Inn & Cottages and Beach Plum Inn** North Rd, Menemsha ☎508 645 2521 🌐menemshainn.com and 🌐beachpluminn.com. These adjacent properties are both beautifully maintained Within walking distance of the Menemsha beach, they als include access to private town beaches on the north shore The *Beach Plum Inn* is better for young adults, while th cottages at *Menemsha* are better for families. Open May-Nov; book early. $215; cottages from $2200/week

CAMPING

Martha's Vineyard Family Campground 56 Edgartown Rd, Edgartown ☎508 693 3772, 🌐campm .com. You can roast s'mores on an open fire at this full shade campground that's tucked inside an oak forest. Lat May to mid-Oct. $50

EATING

Eating is one of the principal pleasures of Martha's Vineyard; fresh lobster, quahogs (large clams) and day-boat fish ar particularly abundant. The **ports** have rows of restaurants to tempt tourists who've just disembarked the ferries, but hea **up-island** for the best bargains. Three of the island's six towns are dry, meaning you can only purchase **alcohol** in Oa Bluffs, Vineyard Haven and Edgartown. Note, though, that you can bring wine or beer bought there to restaurants in th other towns.

VINEYARD HAVEN

★ **Artcliff Diner** 39 Beach Rd ☎508 693 1224. Best diner on the island since the 1940s, with all the usual fry-ups supplemented by specials such as the "Bayou Bundle" (tortillas, sausage). Get there early to avoid a long wait. The food truck out front serves dinner from 5pm until late (2am or so). Thurs–Tues 7am–2pm.

The Black Dog Bakery and Tavern 3 Water St ☎508 693 4786. Though you'll see their T-shirts all over the island and the mainland (never a good sign), the original restaurant serves tasty – although inconsistent – fare. If you don't want to chance it, skip the full and "light" (less expensive) seafood dinners at the waterfront tavern, and stock up on muffins or bagels for the return ferry ride. Daily 5.30am–7pm.

Net Result 79 Beach Rd ☎508 693 6071. This revere fishmonger sells fish "so fresh it will make you blush". Alon with its raw seafood, the *Net* purveys exceptional prepare foods like sushi and heaping lobster rolls (a steal at $12) Daily 7am–7pm.

OAK BLUFFS

★ **Back Door Donuts** Kennebec Ave, behind Martha' Vineyard Gourmet Café and Bakery ☎508 693 3688 Local institution knocking out crispy doughnuts in honey dipped, Boston cream and cinnamon and sugar varieties they'll be warm and delicious (and cost $1.50 or less each) You'll see stars with their apple fritter – in the best possib way. Daily 7.30pm–12.30am.

★ **Slice of Life** 50 Circuit Ave ☎508 693 3838. Casua

afé/bakery serving breakfast, lunch and dinner. Relax on the sunny porch and enjoy a stack of buttermilk pancakes with Vermont maple syrup, or try the house speciality, a ried-green tomato BLT. The owners also run the reputable *weet Life Café*, down the block at 63 Circuit Ave (☎ 508 696 200). Tues–Sun 8am–9pm.

EDGARTOWN

Détente Nevin Square, on Winter St (between N Water St and N Summer St) ☎ 508 627 8810. Of the fancier restaurants on the island, this one's your best bet for a great meal. Seasonal menus utilize local ingredients, ranging from halibut to lamb shank – it also has a fabulous wine ist. Dinner only, mains from $33. Summer daily 5.30–10pm; call for hours rest of year.

Espresso Love 17 Church St ☎ 508 627 9211. Hidden behind the courthouse, this morning lifesaver brews a winning cup of coffee – a rarity in these parts. You can also tuck into freshly baked muffins, soups and sandwiches, lovingly made and served on a verdant garden patio. Daily 5.30am–6pm.

Right Fork Diner 12 Mattakessett Way ☎ 508 627 5522. Watch the planes come and go at this buzzing diner on the Katama airfield. While the ambience is great, it's the genuinely good food – golden pancakes, in-house corned beef hash and home-made granola – that keeps 'em coming back. Late May to mid-Oct daily 7am–2pm; until sunset in July & Aug.

WEST TISBURY AND CHILMARK

★ **Chilmark Store** 7 State Rd, Chilmark ☎ 1 866 904 0819. Another island institution, but not for seafood; queues form here for the perfectly fired slices of pizza ($4), which come in four flavours with freshly made olive oil and pesto bases – try the wholewheat. May to mid-Oct daily 7am–3pm; longer hours in July & Aug.

★ **Eileen Blake's Pies and Otherwise** State Rd, West Tisbury ☎ 508 693 0528. Eileen (who passed away in 2008) sold her sumptuous home-made fruit pies from a shack outside her house; her family is continuing the tradition. Thurs–Sat 10am–5pm; more days in summer.

Humphrey's Bakery 455 State Rd, Woodland Center, West Tisbury ☎ 508 693 6518. Fresh sandwiches on fresh bread, home-made cookies and doughnuts that are great to take to the beach. Locals claim, with some justification, that the turkey sandwiches ($7.25) are the best in the world. Cash only. There are other locations in Edgartown, at 32 Winter St (☎ 508 627 7029), and in Oak Bluffs at 1 Lake Ave (☎ 508 696 6890). Daily 5am–4.30pm.

State Road 688 State Rd, West Tisbury ☎ 508 693 8582. This classy tavern, done up with farmhouse-chic antiques and a zinc bar, makes a memorable setting for a date night, but it's even better for weekend brunch, when guests can luxuriate in the beautiful environs but enjoy more laid-back prices, as well as some of the best eggs, granola and baked goods on the island. Tues–Fri 5.30pm–late, Sat & Sun 8am–2pm & 5.30pm–late.

MENEMSHA

★ **The Bite** 29 Basin Rd ☎ 508 645 9239. Classic New England clam shack with a few outdoor tables and some of the juiciest fried belly clams you'll ever taste (from $14) – they also do mussels, fish and chips, squid and quahog chowder ($4). Cash only. Late May to Sept daily 11am–sunset.

★ **Larsen's Fish Market** 56 Basin Rd ☎ 508 645 2680. Primarily selling fresh fish and lobster to take away (great for picnics), this much-loved shack also knocks out stellar lobster rolls – freshly caught, boiled and crammed into a hot-dog bun ($11.50). May–Oct daily 9am–7pm.

DRINKING

Much of the Vineyard's evening **entertainment** comes in the form of private dinner parties, but that doesn't mean there's nothing to do if you're not invited. **Oak Bluffs** has the best nightlife, with a string of bars along the Dockside Marketplace.

BARS AND CLUBS

★ **Coop de Ville** Dockside Marketplace, Oak Bluffs ☎ 508 693 3420. People pack into this hip waterfront hangout, with a lobster fest (Tues), Red Hook ales on tap, and the house speciality – nine flavours of chicken wings ($7) – to wash down the booze. Daily 11am–10pm.

Nectar's 17 Airport Rd, Edgartown ☎ 508 693 1137, ⟡ nectarspresents.com. The biggest nightclub and live music venue on the Vineyard, blending rock, jazz, reggae and local live entertainment almost nightly during the summer. Cover typically $5–20.

★ **The Newes from America** 23 Kelley St, Edgartown ☎ 508 627 4397. Swill five hundred beers in this atmospheric pub (not necessarily all on the same night)

and they'll name a bar stool after you; New England favourites Harpoon, Smuttynose and Otter Creek are all here ($7). Decent and affordable pub grub, too. Daily 11.30am–11pm.

★ **Offshore Ale Company** 30 Kennebec Ave, Oak Bluffs ☎ 508 693 2626. Friendly local brewpub with wooden booths, toss-on-the-floor peanut shells, and live shows almost nightly in season. They also have great mains and pizzas (lunch and dinner). Daily 11.30am–late.

Ritz Café 1 Circuit Ave, Oak Bluffs ☎ 508 693 9851. This cupboard-sized bar is anything but ritzy, with live music acts (nightly in summer; weekends only rest of year) and a dark and divey setting that makes a nice escape from the island scene. Daily 11.30am–1am.

NIGHTLIFE AND ENTERTAINMENT

For current **listings** information, check the *Vineyard Gazette* (w mvgazette.com), good for cultural events, and the week▌ *Martha's Vineyard Times* (w mvtimes.com), better for nightlife listings.

Capawock Theatre Main St, Vineyard Haven ☎ 508 627 6689. First-run movies can be seen at this Art Deco theatre for $9.

Entertainment Cinemas 65 Main St, Edgartown ☎ 508 627 1076, w entertainmentcinemas.com. Shows all the latest movies for $8.50.

Vineyard Playhouse 24 Church St, Vineyard Haven

☎ 508 696 6300, w vineyardplayhouse.org. Weeken▌ cabaret and musical productions are staged in this forme▌ Masonic lodge dating from 1833.

The Yard Off Middle Rd near Beetlebung Corne▌ Chilmark ☎ 508 645 9662, w dancetheyard.org▌ Specializes in modern dance performances (May–Sept) b▌ a resident troupe.

Nantucket

The thirty-mile sea crossing to **NANTUCKET** from Cape Cod may not be an oceangoing odyssey, but it does give the "Little Gray Lady" a special, set-apart feel. Once you've landed, you can avert your eyes from the smart-money double-deck cruisers with names like *Pier Pressure* and *Loan Star* and let the place remind you that it hasn't alway▌ been a rich folks' playground. Indeed, despite the formidable prowess of its seamen, survival for settlers on the island's barren soil was always a struggle. Unlike the Vineyard, life on the island revolves around just one settlement, cobbled **Nantucket Town**. Frozen in time 150 years ago, its fine museums and restored mansions are monuments to the vast profits made in the era of *Moby Dick*. Beyond the town, Nantucket is easily navigated by bike, with a fantastic network of **paths** the best way to appreciate its natural beauty, including heaths, moorlands and mile after mile of public **beaches**. The best route follows Polpis Road seven flat miles east to the rose-covered cottages of **Siasconset** (always abbreviated to 'Sconset).

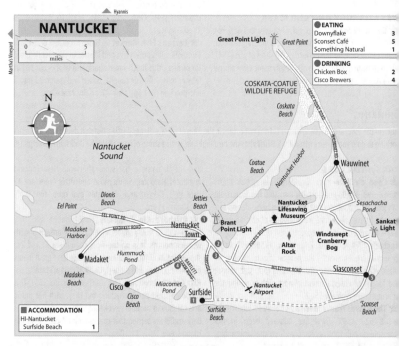

Brief history

Long before the arrival of Europeans, Nantucket was inhabited by the **Wamponoag** Indians. English settlement on the island dates from 1659, when **Thomas Mayhew**, who had been granted rights over the island, sold them on the cheap to shareholders eager to escape the repressive policies of the Massachusetts Bay Colony. The settlers, who landed at **Madaket**, were only able to survive their first winter thanks to assistance from the Wampanoag natives. In time, the number of settlers began to rival that of the natives, who were decimated by disease, and **whaling** became the business of the day. Though islanders had initially learned from the Indians to spear whales from the shore, they soon began to sail the ocean to pursue their prey.

For the next 150 years, the whaling trade flourished, as did the island; the population grew to more than ten thousand, and at its peak the harbour was base to some one hundred whaling boats. The beginning of the end came when larger ships became necessary for longer periods at sea, and Nantucket's harbour began silting in, quickly getting shallow. Whaling activity transferred to the deep-water harbours at New Bedford and Edgartown. Then, in 1846, a major **fire**, which started on Main Street, spread to the harbour, where it set light to barrels of whale oil. The harbour was almost completely destroyed, along with a third of Nantucket Town. The final blow to Nantucket's whaling business was the replacement of whale oil by kerosene as the fuel of choice.

Nantucket floundered for the next century, until a local entrepreneur revamped the **waterfront** in the 1950s; suddenly people began work to preserve the old buildings that still stood. Now the population jumps from ten thousand in winter to well over sixty thousand in the summer, and property prices are more akin to those in Manhattan than other Massachusetts shore towns.

Nantucket Town

Very much the centre of activity on the island, **NANTUCKET TOWN** boasts cobbled streets and a delightful array of eighteenth- and nineteenth-century homes, most of them concentrated around **Main Street**. Before you head there, though, you can get the salty feel of the harbour when arriving on the ferries, which dock at **Steamboat Wharf** or lively **Straight Wharf**, just to the south, dating from 1723 and lined with souvenir shops and restaurants.

Straight Wharf becomes Main Street, where, at its junction with South Water Street, you'll see the **Pacific Club**, a three-storey Georgian edifice built for William Rotch, owner of two of the three ships involved in the Boston Tea Party. It once served as a customs house, but has been used since 1861 as an elite private club for retired whaling captains.

Back on Main Street, the **Henry Coffin House**, no. 75, and the **Charles Coffin House**, no. 78, belonged to two whale merchant brothers. Their handsome homes, two of the earliest red-brick buildings on the island, were built opposite each other in the early 1830s, both designed by master mason Christopher Capen. Further up Main Street, identical numbers 93, 95, and 97, built in a transitional Federal-Greek Revival style in 1837 and 1838 by Capen for whaling tycoon Joseph Starbuck and his three sons, are known as the **Three Bricks**, and are iconic symbols of Nantucket's boom years. The Starbucks had quite an impact on the street: Joseph's daughter Eunice married William Hadwen (owner of the candle factory that is now the Whaling Museum), who built the two flamboyant Greek Revival houses at no. 94 and no. 96 in the 1840s, while daughter Eliza built the ornate Victorian at no. 73 in 1871. The only one of these grand houses you can visit is the 1845 **Hadwen House**, 96 Main St (late May to mid-Oct tours daily at 2.15pm; $10; ☎ 508 228 1894), which contains gas chandeliers, colossal pilasters and silver doorknobs, and has a lovely period garden at the back.

Nantucket Whaling Museum and Brant Point

Late May to mid-Oct daily 10am–5pm; mid- to late Oct daily 11am–4pm; Nov to late Dec Thurs–Mon 1–4pm • $17 • The Nantucket Historical Association offers a $6 Historic Sites Pass for entry to all five of its buildings open to the public (Oldest House, Old Mill, Quaker

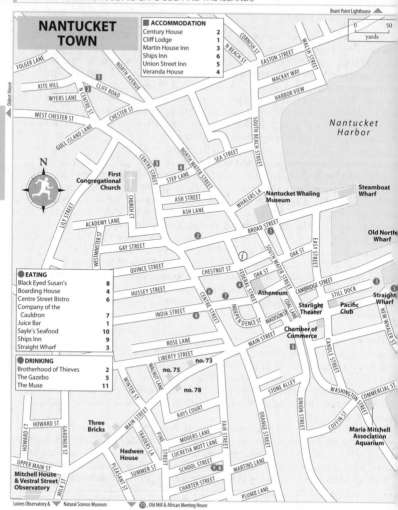

NANTUCKET TOWN

■ ACCOMMODATION
Century House	2
Cliff Lodge	1
Martin House Inn	3
Ships Inn	6
Union Street Inn	5
Veranda House	4

● EATING
Black Eyed Susan's	8
Boarding House	4
Centre Street Bistro	6
Company of the Cauldron	7
Juice Bar	1
Sayle's Seafood	10
Ships Inn	9
Straight Wharf	3

● DRINKING
Brotherhood of Thieves	2
The Gazebo	5
The Muse	11

Meeting House, Fire Hose-Cart House, Old Gaol; all late May to mid-Oct), as well as a $20 combined ticket that includes the Whaling Museum (tickets available at any of these sites) • ☎ 508 228 1894, Ⓦ nha.org

Steamboat Wharf leads directly to Broad Street, where the island's top sight, the newly refurbished **Nantucket Whaling Museum**, is housed in an old candle-making factory built just before the 1846 fire. Highlights include an exquisite scrimshaw collection carved by rough-and-tumble nineteenth-century sailors; there is also a luminous fresnel lens. A gigantic sperm whale skeleton presides over the entrance; look for the rotted tooth in its jaw – officials believe it was an infection that brought about the whale's demise. Before you leave, check out the phenomenal view over the town and harbour from the museum roof.

From the museum it's a pleasant stroll along South Beach and Easton streets up to Brant Point and the 26ft **Brant Point Lighthouse**, guarding the entrance to the harbour. Completed in 1901 (the first version was erected in 1746), the whole site is a working Coast Guard station, but the grounds are open to the public.

BRANT POINT LIGHTHOUSE (P.194) >

Maria Mitchell Association Aquarium

28 Washington St • June to mid-Sept Mon–Sat 10am–4pm • $6 • ☎ 508 228 5387

A short detour south from the Whaling Museum takes you to the **Maria Mitchell Association Aquarium**, where you can learn about Nantucket's underwater ecology via twenty small salt-water tanks and two large touch tanks, featuring scallops, whelks and baby squid.

Atheneum

1 India St • Wed, Fri & Sat 10am–5pm, Tues & Thurs 10am–7.30pm • Free • ☎ 508 228 1110, ⓦ nantucketatheneum.org

Right in the heart of downtown, the graceful 1847 **Atheneum** functions as the town library, archives, cultural centre and repository for various antiques and scrimshaw. During the nineteenth century, its elegant Great Hall hosted esteemed luminaries such as abolitionist Frederick Douglass and suffrage pioneer Lucretia Mott.

First Congregational Church

62 Centre St • Mid-June to Sept Mon–Sat 10am–4pm • $5 donation to climb tower • ☎ 508 228 0950

Built in 1834, the **First Congregational Church** is famous for its 120ft-high steeple, from which you can get a spectacular view of the island. The inside is worth a visit, too, for its trompe l'oeil ceiling, 600-pound brass chandelier and rows of old box pews.

Oldest House

Sunset Hill Rd • Late May to June daily noon–4pm; July & Aug daily noon–5pm; Sept to mid-Oct Thurs–Mon noon–4pm • $6, or as part of a $20 Historic Sites package, including the Whaling Museum • ⓦ nha.org

From the First Congregational Church, you can follow Centre and West Chester streets past Lily Pond Park to the aptly named **Oldest House** (aka the Jethro Coffin House). Built in 1686, the house is sparsely decorated, with an antique loom the most prominent feature inside.

MARIA MITCHELL SIGHTS

For a break from all things nautical, spend half a day exploring the legacy of local astronomer **Maria Mitchell** (1818–89), who discovered "Miss Mitchell's Comet" in 1847. The first professional woman astronomer in the US, she went on to reveal the cause of sunspots and later became the first female member of the American Academy of Arts and Sciences. Today her memory is kept alive by the **Maria Mitchell Association**, 4 Vestal St, which manages several attractions in town (June to mid-Oct; combined ticket $10; ☎ 508 228 9198, ⓦ mmo .org). Check the Association website for its programme of summer talks and field trips, especially good for kids.

Maria was born at the 1790 **Mitchell House**, 1 Vestal St (late May to early Sept Mon–Sat 10am–4pm; mid-Sept to mid-Oct Sat 1–3pm; $6; ☎ 508 228 2896), decorated in austere nineteenth-century Quaker style and embellished with displays covering the history of women and Quakers on Nantucket. The house contains many Mitchell family artefacts, including some of Maria's personal belongings, such as her telescope, beer mugs and opera glasses. On the same grounds, the **Vestal Street Observatory** (late May to early Sept Mon–Sat guided tours at 11am & 2pm; mid-Sept to mid-Oct 11am only; events two nights per month rest of year; $6; ☎ 508 228 9273) features an outdoor scale-model of the solar system, a planar sundial, sunspot observations (when clear) and a permanent astronomy exhibit.

The **Natural Science Museum at Hinchman House**, nearby at 7 Milk St (late May to early Sept Mon–Sat 10am–4pm; mid-Sept to mid-Oct Sat & Sun noon–4pm; late Oct to mid-May Sat 1–3pm; $6; ☎ 508 228 0898), boasts an extensive display of local flora and fauna, though the hands-on activities (shell and wildflower identification games, touch tables), live snakes and turtles will mostly appeal to kids. Finally, at the **Loines Observatory**, 59 Milk St Ext (late May to early Sept Mon, Wed & Fri 9–10.30pm weather permitting; two nights per month rest of year; $15; ☎ 508 228 9273), you can climb up to an ageing telescope and peek into space, as well as admire the association's much newer 24-inch research telescope.

Old Mill

rospect and York streets • Late May to June daily noon–4pm; July & Aug daily noon–5pm; Sept to mid-Oct Mon–Thurs & Sun noon–4pm
$6, or as part of a $20 Historic Sites package, including the Whaling Museum • ⓦ nha.org

A few blocks south of the Mitchell House, at Prospect and Tork streets, the **Old Mill** is the oldest operating windmill in the US, built around 1746. Weather permitting, millers grind corn daily and offer tours every thirty minutes.

African Meeting House

29 York St • June–Oct Mon–Fri 11am–3pm, Sat 11am–1pm, Sun 1–3pm • $5 • ☎ 508 228 9833, ⓦ maah.org

Walk down York Street and you'll come to the **African Meeting House**, a small post-and-beam shack in an area of the island once known as New Guinea. Built in 1827 by the African Baptist Society, the house is now managed by Boston's Museum of African-American History. As the only reminder of what was once a vibrant but segregated community, the house has special significance: it acted as a church, a school and a meeting house for the African-American community on Nantucket well into the twentieth century. Today it hosts cultural programmes and exhibits on the history of African-Americans on Nantucket. You can also pick up information here about the **Black Heritage Trail**, featuring nine stops in downtown and the old New Guinea area.

The rest of the island

Beyond the town, Nantucket remains surprisingly wild, a mixture of moors and marshes. Though the main draw remains the **beaches**, anyone with more time should check out the interior. Much of it is protected by the **Nantucket Conservation Foundation**; check the website for details (ⓦ nantucketconservation.com).

Polpis Road

Polpis Road, an indirect and arcing track from Nantucket Town to 'Sconset, holds a number of natural attractions both on and off its main course, all easily accessed from the **bike path** that shadows the road. Your first stop should be the **Nantucket Life Saving Museum**, off the northern side of the road at no. 158 (June to mid-Oct daily 10am–5pm; $5; ⓦ nantucketshipwreck.org), which is packed to the gills with lifesaving rescue equipment, photographs and artefacts from the *Andrea Doria*, which sank off Nantucket in 1956. Further on, an unmarked track leads south to **Altar Rock**, the island's highest point, which you'll want to walk around for views of the surrounding bogs.

Siasconset

Seven miles east of Nantucket Town, the village of **SIASCONSET**, or 'Sconset as it's universally known, is filled with venerable cottages literally encrusted with salt and covered over with roses. Once solely a fishing village, it began to attract visitors eager to get away from the foul smells of Nantucket Town's whale-oil refineries, and in the late 1800s, enough writers and actors came from big cities to give 'Sconset artistic renown.

There's not too much to see, other than the picturesque houses along Broadway and Center streets; the year-round population of 150 only supports a few commercial establishments, all close to one another in the centre of town. A few miles north of town, the red-and-white striped **Sankaty Light**, an 1849 lighthouse, stands on a 90ft bluff, though it seems only a matter of time until it falls victim to the crashing waves below.

Coskata-Coatue-Great Point

Further north still, **Coskata-Coatue-Great Point** (☎ 508 228 5646, ⓦ thetrustees.org), a five-mile-long, razor-thin slice of sand, takes in three separate wildlife refuges, and is accessible by 4WD (see p.199) or on foot. In the Coskata section, the wider beaches are backed by salt marshes and some trees: with binoculars, you may catch sight of plovers, egrets, oystercatchers, terns and even osprey. The beach narrows again as you

2

NANTUCKET BEACHES

With the majority of its fifty miles of **beaches** open to the public, Nantucket is a great place for ocean enthusiasts. The island's southern and eastern flanks, where the water tends to have rougher waves, are ideal for surfers, while the more sheltered northern beaches are good for swimming. Given the extremely limited, albeit free, **parking**, it makes sense to walk or cycle to all but the most far-flung beaches.

NANTUCKET TOWN

Brant Point Off Easton St. Very strong currents at the harbour entrance mean this beach is better for tanning and watching the comings and goings of boats than swimming.

Dionis Beach Eel Point Rd. A quiet beach with high dunes and calm waters.

Jetties Beach Off Bathing Beach Rd. Catch the shuttle bus that runs along North Water and South Beach streets in the centre of town, or simply walk it to this popular and kid-friendly beach whose facilities include lifeguards, changing room and a snack bar. The real highlight is the fabulous sandbar at low tide.

EAST OF TOWN

Sconset Beach (known also as Codfish Park) Off Polpis Rd. Sandy beach with moderate surf and a full range of facilities. Just a short walk to several eating places.

SOUTH SHORE

Cisco Beach Hummock Pond Rd. Long, sandy beach, ideal for surfing.

Madaket Beach At the end of Madaket Rd. Another long beach with strong surf and gorgeous sunsets over the water.

Surfside Beach Off Surfside Rd. Wide sands attract a youthful crowd of surfers; there's a large car park, but you'd do better to take the shuttle bus or bike from town.

approach the **Great Point Light**, at the end of the spit, put up in 1986 after an earlier light was destroyed during a 1984 storm; the new one is said to be able to withstand 240mph winds and 20ft-high waves.

Madaket and the South Shore

At the western tip of Nantucket, rural **MADAKET** is a small settlement located on the spot where Thomas Macy landed in 1659. There's nothing in the way of visitor attractions, but the area's peacefulness and natural beauty make up for that. Unspoiled **Eel Point**, a couple of miles north, sits on a spit of sand covered with all manner of plants and flowers, including wild roses and bayberries, which attract an array of birds, including graceful egrets.

ARRIVAL AND DEPARTURE
NANTUCKET

By plane Flying is an option: Island Airlines (☎ 1 800 248 7779, ⓦ islandair.net) and Nantucket Airlines (☎ 1 800 352 0714, ⓦ nantucketairlines.com) run year-round daily services from Hyannis to Nantucket (hourly in the summer); Cape Air (☎ 1 800 352 0714, ⓦ flycapeair.com) also offers daily services to and from Boston, Providence and Martha's Vineyard. Jet Blue (☎ 1 800 538 2583, ⓦ jetblue.com)

provides convenient flights from New York. The airport (☎ 508 325 5300, ⓦ nantucketairport.com) is about three miles southeast of Nantucket Town.

By ferry Most likely you'll arrive in Nantucket by ferry from Hyannis (see p.166), with Hy-Line boats pulling in at Straight Wharf and the Steamship Authority ferries docking at Steamboat Wharf.

INFORMATION

The **website** for the island's main newspaper (ⓦ ack.net), the *Inquirer and Mirror*, is a useful resource, with links to restaurant and shopping guides and other practical information. The Nantucket Historical Association (☎ 508 228 1894, ⓦ nha.org), offers a $6 **Historic Sites Pass** for entry into all five of its buildings open to the public (Oldest House, Old Mill, Quaker Meeting House, Fire Hose-Cart House, Old Gaol), as well as a $20 **combined ticket** that includes the Whaling Museum (tickets available at any of these sites). The properties are open from late May to mid-Oct.

The Chamber of Commerce Zero on Main St, second floor (Mon–Fri 9am–5pm; ☎ 508 228 1700, ⓦ nantucketchamber.org).

Nantucket Information Bureau 25 Federal St (April–Dec 9am–6pm; Jan–March Mon–Sat 9am–5pm; ☎ 508 228 0925, ⓦ nantucket-ma.gov/visitor).

GETTING AROUND

BY CAR

Once you've arrived, getting around should pose no problem. As island streets are extremely tiny, driving a car makes little sense, especially in peak season. Another alternative is to rent a 4WD jeep so that you can drive on the beach (up to Great Point, for example); rentals usually include permits. Try Nantucket Island Rent-A-Car at the airport (April–Oct only; ☎508 228 9989, ⓦnantucketislandrentacar.com) or Young's Bicycle Shop at 6 Broad St (Mon–Sat 8.30am–6pm, Sun 9am–5pm; ☎508 228 1151, ⓦyoungsbicycleshop.com). Rates are very expensive; from $150/day off season to around $200/day in June and July (including beach permits, which are $150 in peak season).

BY BICYCLE

You're best off renting a bike so you can explore the island's wonderful paths. From the moment you get off the ferry you're besieged by rental places. Try Young's Bicycle Shop (see above), just up Steamboat Wharf from the Steamship Authority dock; it should cost $30/day for a standard mountain bike.

BY BUS

There is an island bus system, with five shuttle routes operated by the Nantucket Regional Transit Authority (May–Sept 7.30am–11.30pm; $1 per in-town journey, $2 to Madaket, 'Sconset and the airport; ☎508 228 7025, ⓦnrtawave.com); you can get unlimited travel for one day ($7), three days ($12), a week ($20) or a month ($50). Hop on and off at any of the red-and-grey signposts along the routes. The buses have bike racks, so you can stick yours on the front if you get tired of pedalling. Barrett's Tours (☎508 228 0174 or ☎1 800 773 0174) also run ninety-minute narrated bus tours ($25) around the island.

BY BOAT

You might also consider taking to the water, as several beaches are best approached from the sea. Nantucket Community Sailing (mid-June to early Sept; ☎508 228 5358; ⓦnantucketcommunitysailing.org) rents kayaks ($25/hr), windsurfers ($40/hr) and sailboats (from $50/hr) from Jetties Beach, just north of Nantucket Town. The less energetic can consider renting a powerboat from Island Boat Rental at Straight Wharf (☎508 325 1001), though this will set you back at least $425/day.

BY TAXI

You probably won't need the aid of taxis while here, but they are usually available at the airport or by the ferry terminal; A-1 (☎508 228 3330) and Chief's Cab (☎508 284 8497) are both reliable.

ACCOMMODATION

There's a wide range of accommodation in Nantucket Town, from good-sized, sophisticated resorts to cosy inns and B&Bs; further afield, you can rent **private homes** by the week. One thing you won't find, however, is price diversity – it's not easy to find a room for under $200 in high season. For free, easy booking help, contact **Martha's Vineyard and Nantucket Reservations** (☎508 693 7200 or ☎1 800 649 5671, ⓦmvreservations.com). If you're stuck at the last minute with nowhere to stay, try the **Nantucket Information Bureau** (see opposite), which maintains a list of vacancies during the season. Unless otherwise indicated, all of the places listed below are in **Nantucket Town**. Note that most properties are closed from **Nov–April**.

Century House 10 Cliff Rd ☎508 228 0530, ⓦcenturyhouse.com; map p. 194. Elegant rooms with polished pine floors and country-house ambience in an 1833 late Federal home. There's an excellent complimentary breakfast buffet included. $175

Cliff Lodge 9 Cliff Rd ☎508 228 9480, ⓦclifflodgenantucket.com; map p.194. Quiet B&B in a 1771 whaling master's home, set in a residential area. They have some low-priced singles in the off season. Owned by the same proprietors as the *Martin House Inn*. $195

HI-Nantucket Surfside Beach ☎508 228 0433, ⓦhiusa.org; map p.192. Dorm beds a stone's throw from Surfside Beach in an 1873 lifesaving station, just over three miles south of Nantucket Town. Very close to a shuttle stop. Dorms $39

Martin House Inn 61 Centre St ☎508 228 0678, ⓦmartinhouseinn.com; map p.194. Thirteen lovely rooms, some with working fireplaces, offer good value in this romantic 1803 seaman's house, with inviting common areas and spacious veranda – local art and antiques feature throughout. Singles $125; doubles $220

Ships Inn 13 Fair St ☎508 228 0040 or ☎1 800 564 2760, ⓦshipsinnnantucket.com; map p.194. Three-storey whaling captain's home dating from 1831, with eleven biggish rooms and a lauded on-site restaurant (see below). Historical tidbit: abolitionist Lucretia Mott was born here. $275

★ **Union Street Inn** 7 Union St ☎1 888 517 0707, ⓦunioninn.com; map p.194. This luxurious B&B boasts a central location, hearty breakfasts and gorgeous rooms, with thick rugs, drapes and period wallpaper – it's pricey, but is much better value off season. $345

Veranda House 3 Step Lane ☎508 228 0695, ⓦtheverandahouse.com; map p.194. The theme at this boutique hotel is "retro chic", bringing a refreshingly contemporary addition to the island's traditional Victorian-style B&Bs; rooms are stylishly designed, most with harbour views, and come with free wi-fi and gourmet style breakfast. $339

EATING

Nantucket abounds in first-rate dining establishments. If you're having dinner at a restaurant, though, be prepared for the bill: **prices** are often comparable to those in Manhattan. You'll find a bevy of cheaper **takeaway** places on Broad Street near the ferry dock. **Picnics** are always an attractive option in summer; *Provisions* (on Straight Wharf) and *Something Natural* (see below) are best for sandwiches and fresh bread.

NANTUCKET TOWN: DOWNTOWN

★ **Black Eyed Susan's** 10 India St ☎ 508 325 0308; map p.194. Popular Southern-influenced breakfast and brunch place (and also dinner Mon–Sat), serving big delicious omelettes and grits with cheese for $9–10. Dinner mains from $27. Cash only. Daily 7am–1pm, Mon–Sat also 6–10pm.

Boarding House 12 Federal St ☎ 508 228 9622; map p.194. The romantic downstairs dining room here serves a range of contemporary farm-to-table meat and fish dishes; the animated bar upstairs offers lighter, cheaper bistro fare. Mon–Fri 6–10pm, Sat & Sun 10.30am–10pm.

Centre Street Bistro 29 Centre St ☎ 508 228 8470; map p.194. Intimate (seven-table) BYOB café specializing in light seafood fare – the seared salmon with lemon aioli is gorgeously fresh – with wonderful home-made desserts to top it off. Serves a mean weekend brunch, too. Daily Mon & Wed–Fri 11.30am–9pm, Sat & Sun 8am–9.30pm.

Company of the Cauldron 5 India St ☎ 508 228 4016, ⓦ companyofthecauldron.com; map p.194. A romantic, vine-covered, candlelit haven with live harp music thrice weekly. Both evening seatings of the shifting *prix fixe* menu ($65) sell out quickly, so make reservations. Check website for daily seating times and menus.

Juice Bar 12 Broad St ☎ 508 228 5799; map p.194. The fresh juices are the healthiest options on offer at this small takeaway shop near the ferry, but in summer expect long lines for the luscious home-made ice cream (try the "Crantucket"), served in cups or giant waffle cones. April to late Oct daily 11.30am–9pm.

Ships Inn 13 Fair St ☎ 508 228 0040; map p.194. Choose from artfully presented California-French-style dishes, such as sautéed halibut, served in an intimate underground space dating from the 1830s. Reservations recommended. May–June, Sept & Oct Wed–Sun 5.30–9.30pm; July & Aug daily 5.30–9.30pm.

★ **Straight Wharf** 6 Harbor Square ☎ 508 228 4499; map p.192. Superb New American restaurant serving bluefish pâté and watermelon salad in an airy, waterfront dining room. The bar shifts to more of an *Animal House* vibe come nightfall. Weekend brunch is also exceptional. Reservations recommended. Mon 5.30–10pm, Tues –Fri 11.30am–2pm & 5.30–10pm, Sat & Sun 11am–2pm & 5.30–10pm. Bar until 1am.

NANTUCKET TOWN: OUTSKIRTS

★ **Downyflake** 18 Sparks Ave ☎ 508 228 4533; map p.192. The island's best diner, a bit out of the way on the edge of town, but worth a visit for the reasonably priced plates of comfort food, and especially the fresh doughnuts (get them to go). Mon–Sat 6am–2pm, Sun 6am–noon.

Sayle's Seafood 99 Washington St Ext ☎ 508 228 4599; map p.194. The closest thing in town to a classic clam shack, serving chowder ($3.25), fresh lobster and fried clams (at market prices) – take out for a picnic or enjoy on the porch. Daily 10am–9pm (slightly shorter hours in off-season).

★ **Something Natural** 50 Cliff Rd ☎ 508 228 0504, map p.192. Handy deli-bakery on the way to Madaket, with fabulous creations like avocado, cheddar and chutney on home-made bread ($9.50). Wash down your meal with Nantucket Nectar's "Matt Fee Tea" – named for the owner. No seating per se, but there are picnic tables and blankets on offer. April to mid-Oct daily 8am–6.30pm (slightly shorter hours in April & Oct).

SIASCONSET

Sconset Café 8 Main St, facing the rotary ☎ 508 257 6365; map p.192. The best place for a sit-down lunch or dinner in 'Sconset, with a varied menu that features not only clams and chowder ($10), but also various grills, salads and sandwiches ($10–17). Cash only. May to mid-Sept. Daily 8.30am–3pm & 5.30–10pm.

DRINKING

Brotherhood of Thieves 23 Broad St ☎ 508 228 2551; map p.194. This bar is a Nantucket institution and the place to go for live folk music, year-round; huddle in the dimly lit pub or pose at the smarter bar upstairs – it also serves as a decent restaurant with outdoor deck. Daily 11.30am–1am.

Chicken Box 14 Dave St ☎ 508 228 9717; map p.192. Literally a wooden box-like shack on the outskirts of town, this local dive bar is the place to escape the tourists and see great live bands – covers usually range $7–10. Daily noon–1am.

★ **Cisco Brewers** 5 Bartlett Farm Rd ☎ 508 325 5929; map p.192. More of an alfresco bar than a tour-giving brewery (although they do offer those), *Cisco* peddles sample flights of home-made beer, wine and liquor in a pastoral courtyard; patrons are encouraged to bring comestibles. The location, 2.5 miles from town, is the only drawback – take a cab, as getting here by bike is a little hairy. Mon–Sat 10am–7pm, Sun noon–5pm.

The Gazebo 1 Harbor Square, Straight Wharf ☎ 508 228 1266; map p.194. Easy to find on summer nights, when the crowds pile around this sociable bar (literally a gazebo), right on the wharf, for potent cocktails and beers. **The Muse** 44 Surfside Drive ☎ 508 228 1471; map p.194. A mix of rock, reggae and just about anything else you can dance to, as well as a few pool tables, keep this venue popular. Daily 11am–1am.

2

NIGHTLIFE AND ENTERTAINMENT

In terms of tried-and-true **nightlife**, Nantucket is quieter than the Vineyard, but Nantucket Town still has some good options to keep you out until after midnight (though not much later). There's certainly no shortage of **live music**, especially jazz and folk, to help you kick up your heels, but if you're after a big-city nightclub, you won't find it here. Current **listings** can be found in the weekly *Yesterday's Island* (ⓦ yesterdaysisland.com) and the daily *Inquirer and Mirror* (ⓦ ack.net).

Starlight Theater and Café 1 N Union St ☎ 508 228 4435, ⓦ starlightnantucket.com. For the latest Hollywood movies, check out this small local theatre ($10). **Theatre Workshop of Nantucket** Methodist Church, 2 Centre St ☎ 508 228 4305, ⓦ theatreworkshop.com. Local theatre troupe, putting on plays and musicals throughout much of the year at the Methodist Church, and at Bennett Hall, 62 Centre St. Tickets rarely top $25.

Central and Western Massachusetts

204 Worcester

210 Sturbridge

210 Springfield

214 The Pioneer Valley

225 The Berkshires

NAUMKEAG

Central and Western Massachusetts

From Boston, most visitors speed across the state on I-90 to enjoy the forest-smothered hills and idyllic colonial villages of the Berkshires, but the once faded industrial towns of Central Massachusetts are also worth checking out: Worcester has an incredible collection of art, and Springfield is home to the Basketball Hall of Fame. The Pioneer Valley stretches north from here, home to four separate colleges and a major university supporting a year-round population of academics, artists, activists and a bevy of restaurants, cafés and bookstores – giving the area a continuous, if low-key, buzz.

3

You can base yourself in any one of three or four locations to explore this area, but **Northampton** is probably the liveliest, with a good range of places to stay and the best nightlife. **Amherst**, Northampton's eastern neighbour, is home to a museum honouring poet **Emily Dickinson**, who lived and died there. From the Pioneer Valley, most roads lead west to the **Berkshires**, as the smattering of tiny towns nestled in among the Berkshire Hills, dividing Massachusetts from New York, are collectively known. With its world-class museums, gorgeous inns and especially rich calendar of summer festivals, this region is one of the highlights of New England.

Worcester

Roughly forty miles west of Boston on I-90, **WORCESTER** is Massachusetts' second largest city, best known for its classic **diners** and world-class **art museum**. It's also notable (sort of) for birthing a mixed bag of American icons – including Abbie Hoffman, the Valentine's Day card and the yellow "smiley face", designed by Harvey Ball in 1963. Officially established in 1722, it enjoyed a century and a half of unbridled prosperity as a thriving town of textile mills before it lapsed into recession during the 1970s and 1980s. The town is only just beginning to pick itself up again; despite ongoing efforts at regeneration, much of Worcester's **downtown** remains shabby and unappealing, though development projects associated with the **Blackstone River Valley National Heritage Corridor** (☎401 762 0250, ⓦnps.gov/blac) have succeeded in revitalizing parts of the city. The most visible signs of this can be found in the **Canal District** (ⓦcanaldistrict.org) around Water Street, southeast of downtown (I-290, exit 14), which is gradually attracting new shops and restaurants.

Worcester Historical Museum

30 Elm St • Tues–Sat 10am–4pm • $5; includes entry to the Salisbury Mansion (see p.206) • ☎ 508 753 8278, ⓦworcesterhistory.org

One of the most attractive neighbourhoods in Worcester runs along Elm Street, west of downtown, where you'll also find the engaging **Worcester Historical Museum**. Worcester's industrial heritage is brought to life here through artefacts and oral

---

Worcester: Home of the Diner p.209
The quiet life of Emily Dickinson p.218
Books and beverages: the Montague Mill p.223
The Mohawk Trail p.224

Normal Rockwell: "America's best-loved artist" p.228
Summer festivals in the Berkshires p.231
Down Street Art p.237

MASS MOCA

Highlights

❶ Basketball Hall of Fame A real treat for hoops fans, the Hall of Fame resides in Springfield, the birthplace of the sport. **See p.211**

❷ Five College Consortium The college towns of Northampton, Amherst and South Hadley offer plenty in the way of arts, culture and entertainment. **See pp.214–222**

❸ Historic Deerfield Magnificently preserved colonial town, offering a hazy window into seventeenth-century life on the harsh New England frontier. **See p.223**

❹ Naumkeag This magnificent confection of architectural styles is the best of the Gilded Age summer "cottages" to be found in the Berkshires. **See p.227**

❺ Berkshires festivals Music, dance and drama junkies can get their summertime fix in the Berkshires, with many performances taking place at open-air venues in the countryside. **See p.231**

❻ MASS MoCA This fine contemporary art museum is the centrepiece of North Adams, transformed from a post-industrial eyesore to the hippest place in the region. **See p.236**

HIGHLIGHTS ARE MARKED ON THE MAP ON PP.206–207

histories; among other items, the city invented the space suit, the monkey wrench, barbed wire and the birth control pill.

Salisbury Mansion

40 Highland St • Thurs 1–8.30pm, Fri & Sat 1–4pm • $5; or free with a ticket for the Worcester Historical Museum (see p.204) • ☏ 508 753 8278, ⓦ worcesterhistory.org/salisburymansion.cfm

Half a mile north of the Worcester Historical Museum, the elegant **Salisbury Mansion** was built in 1772 for one of the city's wealthiest families. The interior has been restored in 1830s style, and houses changing exhibits on the mansion and the Salisbury family.

Worcester Art Museum

55 Salisbury St • Wed, Thurs, Fri & Sun 11am–5pm; Sat 10am–5pm; third Thurs of the month till 8pm • $14; free first Sat of the month 10am–noon • ☏ 508 799 4406, ⓦ worcesterart.org

Just across the road from the Salisbury Mansion, **Worcester Art Museum** is an absolute gem. Founded by Stephen Salisbury III in 1896, its vast holdings include a Romanesque **chapter house** from the twelfth century and a permanent gallery of American portrait miniatures. The entrance Renaissance Court is dominated by spectacular Roman

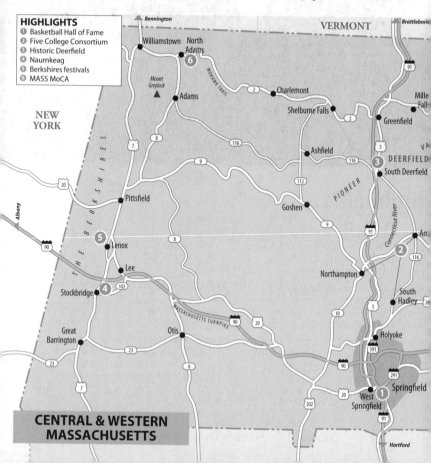

HIGHLIGHTS
1. Basketball Hall of Fame
2. Five College Consortium
3. Historic Deerfield
4. Naumkeag
5. Berkshires festivals
6. MASS MoCA

CENTRAL & WESTERN MASSACHUSETTS

Antioch mosaics (created around the third century), and it's in the galleries around here you'll find the extensive European painting collections. Highlights include a rare piece from Florentine Andrea del Sarto, *Saint John the Baptist* (1517), discovered in a local church, El Greco's *Repentant Magdalen* (1577), an early *Saint Bartholomew* by Rembrandt (1633) and a typically dark Goya portrait. Gauguin is represented by the *Brooding Woman* (1891), and there are some good pieces from Monet, including examples of his *Waterloo Bridge* and *Water Lilies* series (purchased by the museum in 1910 for just 800 francs). American art is showcased by some beguiling work from John Singer Sargent, including *Venetian Water Carriers* (1882) and *Lady Warwick* (1905), while the museum holds the country's oldest colonial portraits, dating from the 1670s. Look out also for Twachtman's *The Waterfall* (1895) and Homer's *The Gale* (1893). Other galleries contain an astonishing collection of Qing dynasty **Chinese jade**.

The EcoTarium

222 Harrington Way (I-290, exit 21 or 22) • Tues–Sat 10am–5pm, Sun noon–5pm • $12, children (2–18 years) $8 • ☎ 508 929 2703, ⓦ ecotarium.org

Two and a half miles east of downtown Worcester is the **EcoTarium**, the second oldest natural history society in the US. It's geared toward families with young ones: children

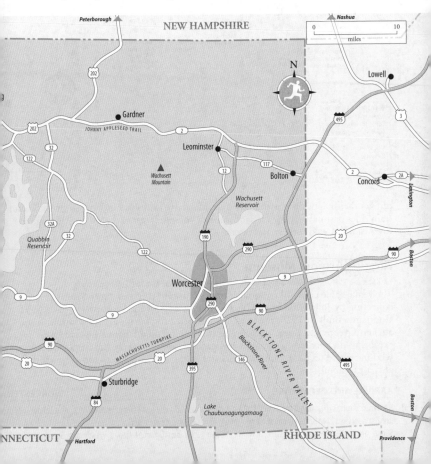

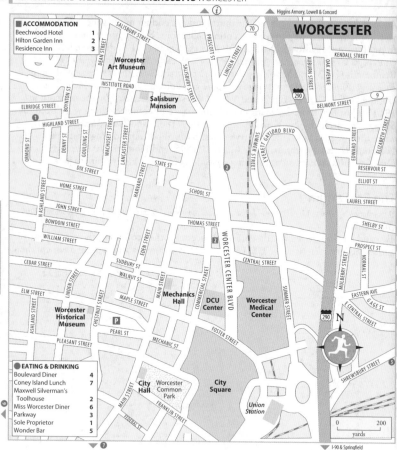

ACCOMMODATION
Beechwood Hotel	1
Hilton Garden Inn	2
Residence Inn	3

EATING & DRINKING
Boulevard Diner	4
Coney Island Lunch	7
Maxwell Silverman's Toolhouse	2
Miss Worcester Diner	6
Parkway	3
Sole Proprietor	1
Wonder Bar	5

can get their hands dirty with numerous interactive exhibits, outdoor nature walks and train rides past native New England animals you rarely see in the wild, including red foxes, skunks, wild turkeys and otters.

Higgins Armory Museum

100 Barber Ave (I-290, exit 20) • Tues–Sat 10am–4pm, Sun noon–4pm • $10 • ☎ 508 853 6015, ⓦ higgins.org

The remarkable castle-like **Higgins Armory Museum** is testament to years of collecting by John Woodman Higgins, the founder of the Worcester Pressed Steel Company. Built in 1929, the museum is chock-full of armour and weapons from ancient Greece and Rome, medieval Europe and feudal Japan. Kids will love exploring the medieval-style halls and passages and especially the Castle Quest section, where they can build a miniature castle, try on helmets and even handle ancient weapons.

ARRIVAL AND DEPARTURE

WORCESTER

By train Amtrak (ⓦ amtrak.com) and MBTA (ⓦ mbta .com) run services from Boston (around 1hr on Amtrak, 1hr 50min on MBTA), though the latter is much cheaper ($8.25) and more frequent than the Amtrak service (which runs just once a day).

By bus Union Station, 2 Washington Square, serves as

both the train and bus station. Peter Pan Bus Lines (ⓦpeterpanbus.com) shares services to Boston (11 daily; 1hr; $10) with Greyhound (ⓦgreyhound.com), and also runs to Springfield (3 daily; 1hr; $19) and Hartford (6 daily; 1hr 10min; $18).

GETTING AROUND

By bus A comprehensive local bus service is provided by the RTA (☎508 791 9782, ⓦtherta.com), though it's not especially useful for sightseeing. Fares are $1.50 (one-day pass $3.50). Buses #30 and #31 pass close to the Worcester Art Museum and Higgins Armory.

By car Worcester is spread out and can be difficult to navigate by car. I-290 cuts across the eastern edge of downtown; the easiest way to Main Street is via exit 16. There's a large multistorey car park (the Pearl/Elm Garage; $2 first hr, $1/hr thereafter, $8/day) on Elm Street, just off Main Street, which is convenient for downtown, though if you've come solely for the art museum (exit 18) simply park there and skip the city centre altogether.

INFORMATION AND TOURS

Central Massachusetts Convention & Visitors Bureau 91 Prescott St (Mon–Fri 9am–5pm; ☎508 755 7400 or ☎866 755 7439, ⓦcentralmass.org). Friendly and well-equipped. Learn more about the city at ⓦworcesterma.gov and ⓦworcestermass.org.

Preservation Worcester ☎508 754 8760, ⓦpreservationworcester.org. Worcester's historic districts are best experienced on a guided tour organized by Preservation Worcester; walking tours cost $5–10 and usually run daily in summer.

ACCOMMODATION

Beechwood Hotel 363 Plantation St ☎508 754 5789 or ☎1 800 344 2589, ⓦbeechwoodhotel.com. Even the smallest rooms at this glitzy hotel are spacious; HBO and internet are available in each one, and there are complimentary newspapers and a continental breakfast to help you start your day, as well as free transport anywhere within five miles of the hotel. **$179**

Hilton Garden Inn 35 Major Taylor Blvd ☎508 753 5700, ⓦhiltongardeninn.com. One of the newest hotels in the city, mostly catering to the conference crowd but with some great deals online. Rooms are extra-comfy, with an expansive breakfast buffet and all the standard business extras thrown in (including big desks and wi-fi). Parking $8.95/day. **$179**

Residence Inn 503 Plantation St ☎508 753 6300, ⓦmarriott.com. Fairly new, snazzy motel by Marriott, located in a quiet area; extras include free lemonade, wi-fi, breakfast and fully equipped kitchens in all rooms, making it an excellent, and popular, base. Book ahead. **$159**

WORCESTER: HOME OF THE DINER

Providence, Rhode Island, can claim the first horse-drawn diner, but it was here in Worcester that America's iconic roadside restaurants were first produced commercially, back in 1887. The **Worcester Lunch Car Company** was founded in 1906, shipping diners all over the nation; from the 1920s these had evolved to feature Art Deco or Streamline Moderne elements to make them look like stainless steel train dining cars. The company went out of business in 1957, but many classic diners remain around the city:

Boulevard Diner 155 Shrewsbury St ☎508 791 4535. Opened in 1936, this lovely old dining car is a favourite late-night hangout – it's the only one serving a full menu 24hr. Noted for its "Italian bread toast" and omelettes named after local colleges. 24hr; closed Sun 3–5pm.

★ **George's Coney Island** 158 Southbridge St ☎508 753 4362, ⓦconeyislandlunch.com. Founded back in 1918 by George Tsagarelis, this Art Deco throwback specializes in hot dogs with chilli and the works from just $1.50. Try the local pickles or home-made baked beans on the side. Mon, Wed & Thurs 10am–8pm, Fri & Sat till 9pm, Sun till 7pm.

★ **Miss Worcester Diner** 302 Southbridge St ☎508 753 5600. Opened in 1948, right across the street from the old Car Company factory, *Miss Worcester Diner* serves the biggest portions and best food of all the local diners. Highlights include the fifteen or so varieties of addictive French toast. Mon–Fri 5am–2pm, Sat 6am–2pm, Sun 7am–2pm.

Parkway 148 Shrewsbury St ☎508 753 9968. Like the *Boulevard Diner* just opposite, the *Parkway* opened in 1936. It looks modern from the outside, but the classic dining car interior features just two rows of counter seating (it's very narrow – the adjacent dining room section is roomier). The food is Italian themed – think meatball omelettes. Daily 6am–2am.

EATING AND DRINKING

Maxwell Silverman's Toolhouse 25 Union St ☎508 755 1200, ⓦmaxwellmaxine.com. One of the more atmospheric places in town: the spacious dining room is a restored factory building, and the Sunday brunch buffets are usually excellent value ($19.95). Note that it can get extremely busy, especially on club nights. Daily 4–10pm (club opens late Fri & Sat).

Sole Proprietor 118 Highland St (I-290, exit 17/18) ☎508 798 3474, ⓦthesole.com. Reliable seafood restaurant that's not especially cheap but well worth the

price (mains –$19.99–28.99). The inflatable lobster on the roof belies the joint's sophisticated atmosphere. Mon– Thurs 11.30am–10pm, Fri till 11pm, Sat 4–11pm, Sun 4–9pm. Bar daily till 1.30am.

★ **Wonder Bar** 121 Shrewsbury St ☎508 752 9909, ⓦwonderbarrestaurant.net. Get a taste of old Italian Worcester at this venerable pizza ($10–13.50) and pasta ($10–13) joint, with reasonable prices and big, tasty portions. Tues–Sat 11am–11pm.

Sturbridge

About fifteen miles southwest of Worcester, on US-20 near the junction of I-90 and I-84, the small town of **STURBRIDGE** is home to family-friendly **Old Sturbridge Village**. Sturbridge itself is a fairly typical New England town, with a smattering of old clapboard buildings and colonial churches.

Old Sturbridge Village

1 Old Sturbridge Village Rd · April to late Oct daily 9.30am–5pm; late Oct to March Tues–Sun till 4pm · $20, children (3–17 years) $7 · ☎508 347 3362 or ☎1 800 733 1830, ⓦosv.org

Made up of beautifully preserved buildings brought from all over the region, **Old Sturbridge Village** presents a somewhat idealized but engaging portrait of small-town New England life in the 1830s. Costumed actors labour in blacksmiths' shops, plant vegetables and tend cows and the like. The two-hundred-acre site, nicely landscaped and with footpaths, is also very pretty, making it a pleasant place to spend a few hours.

ACCOMMODATION AND EATING   STURBRIDGE

Publick House Historic Inn 277 W Main St (Rte-131) ☎508 347 3313, ⓦpublickhouse.com. For a bit of character, stay at this gorgeous 1771 inn with seventeen cosy rooms overlooking Sturbridge common. The *Dining Tap Room* serves lobster pie ($32), butter-crumb baked scrod ($21) and roast turkey dinners ($20),

while *Ebenezer's Tavern* serves cheaper food. $125
Sturbridge Host Hotel 366 Main St (Rte-20) ☎508 347 7993, ⓦsturbridgehosthotel.com. Smart business-orientated option, situated on nine leafy acres surrounding beautiful Cedar Lake, with an indoor heated swimming pool. $125

Springfield

In 1891 Canadian-born **James Naismith** pinned two sheets to the wall of the International YMCA Training School gym, listing the rules of a new game he'd just invented. The game was basketball, guaranteeing the fame of **SPRINGFIELD**, home of the auspicious gym and now also the site of the entertaining **Basketball Hall of Fame**. Springfield was already a booming industrial centre in the nineteenth century; founded along the banks of the Connecticut River in 1636, it became the home of the Springfield rifle, Smith & Wesson, the Indian motorcycle and the late children's author **Dr Seuss**, né Theodor Geisel. But, like so many places in this part of the state, the city was hit by recession after World War II and became rapidly depopulated.

The city has been slowly restoring its fortunes in the last ten years, though the unattractive modern centre remains eerily devoid of people outside workday hours, and was severely battered by a rare tornado in June 2011. Downtown Springfield does contain a handful of monuments to the glory years – the **Old First Church**, completed

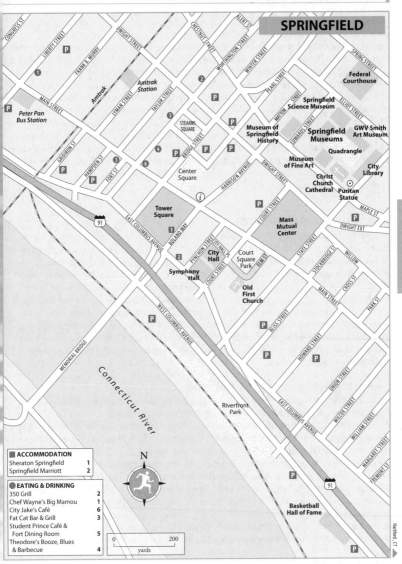

SPRINGFIELD

ACCOMMODATION

Sheraton Springfield	1
Springfield Marriott	2

EATING & DRINKING

350 Grill	2
Chef Wayne's Big Mamou	1
City Jake's Café	6
Fat Cat Bar & Grill	3
Student Prince Café & Fort Dining Room	5
Theodore's Booze, Blues & Barbecue	4

in 1819, and the nearby Greek Revival **City Hall** and **Symphony Hall** (both 1913) on Court Street, divided by a 300ft Italian-style **Campanile** (clock tower).

Basketball Hall of Fame

1000 W Columbus Ave • July & Aug daily 10am–5pm; Sept–June Mon–Fri & Sun till 4pm, Sat till 5pm • $16.99, children (5–15 years) $11.99 • ☎ 413 781 6500 or ☎ 1 877 446 6752, ⊕ hoophall.com

Springfield's premier attraction is the **Basketball Hall of Fame**, which commemorates the game's invention by Dr James Naismith, not far from this site, in 1891. The giant hollow dome is impressive, even if you're not a huge fan of sports, and the interactive games and exhibits inside are lots of fun.

Start on the **upper level**, where the **Honors Ring** marks all those players and coaches that have been inducted here (new Hall of Famers are inducted every August). **Level 2** is where the entertainment begins, with a virtual hoop game, a super shot arcade and a rebound machine, while a special gallery chronicles the history of the game with a copy of Naismith's original rules and his original wooden peach basket. The **Media Gallery** allows you to commentate on famous games, and appear as a newsreader on video. There's a special exhibit on local heroes the Boston Celtics, an image of the USA's Olympic "dream team" framed by a display of 368 Nike sneakers and one of Shaquille O'Neal's size 23 shoes. For many, the real highlight here is the display (and short video) dedicated to **Michael Jordan**. The centrepiece of **Level 1**, visible from all three floors, is a full-sized basketball court complete with suspended scoreboard. The complex also contains several chain restaurants.

The Springfield Museums

The **Springfield Museums** were established by local millionaires and voracious art collectors George and Belle Smith in 1896, and have since grown to encompass a series of five absorbing individual museums set around the city's tree-lined Quadrangle. Start at the **welcome centre** at 21 Edwards St, but before you go in, check out the famous *Puritan* statue (depicting Springfield founder Deacon Samuel Chapin), at the corner of Chestnut and State streets, an original by **Saint-Gaudens** (see p.416). In the middle of the Quadrangle, the **Dr Seuss National Memorial Sculpture Garden** (daily 9am–5pm; free) contains bronze sculptures of characters and scenes created by Springfield-born Theodor Geisel (1904–1991); note that the Museum of the Connecticut River Valley was closed in 2009 and is expected to eventually re-open as a gallery dedicated to Geisel's pen-name, Dr Seuss.

George Walter Vincent Smith Art Museum

21 Edwards St • Tues–Sat 10am–5pm, Sun 11am–5pm; July & Aug also open Mon 10am–5pm • $12.50, children (3–17 years) $6.50; tickets include access to all other Springfield Museums • ☎ 413 263 6800, ⓦ springfieldmuseums.org

The original Victorian museum building established by the Smiths in 1896 is now the **George Walter Vincent Smith Art Museum**, showcasing the eclectic collection of the museum's namesake. Smith made his fortune as a carriage manufacturer in New York City and retired when he was just 35 years old, spending the rest of his life collecting art. The holdings focus on Asian decorative arts, including a spectacular collection of **Chinese cloisonné** (the largest outside of Asia). It also boasts a gallery of now rare plaster casts of famous European sculptures by the likes of Michelangelo, a Chinese jade burial suit and some nineteenth-century American paintings by Winslow Homer and others. Don't miss the **Art Discovery Center**, targeted at children but decorated with mesmerizing **Tibetan murals** painted by the Dalai Lama's artistic team.

Museum of Fine Arts

21 Edwards St • Tues–Sat 10am–5pm, Sun 11am–5pm; July & Aug also open Mon 10am–5pm • $12.50, children (3–17 years) $6.50; tickets include access to all other Springfield Museums • ☎ 413 263 6800, ⓦ springfieldmuseums.org

Springfield's best art work is displayed in the **Museum of Fine Arts**, which is especially good on American paintings: Winslow Homer's *The New Novel* and *Promenade on the Beach*, and Frederic Church's *New England Scenery* are here, alongside lesser-known work by Georgia O'Keeffe. There's also the largest collection of **John George Brown** paintings anywhere, and masses of iconic landscapes from printmakers **Currier & Ives**. It's hard to miss the huge, fantastical work in the central gallery by **Erastus Salisbury Field**, *Historical Monument of the American Republic*, painted in the nineteenth century – Field is another one of the gallery's painters who has recently been "discovered". The

European collections are not so enticing, though almost every period is represented, and there are few gems by the likes of Tiepolo, Corot and Degas, and one of Monet's *Haystack* paintings.

Springfield Science Museum

21 Edwards St • Tues–Sat 10am–5pm, Sun 11am–5pm; July & Aug also open Mon 10am–5pm • $12.50, children (3–17 years) $6.50; tickets include access to all other Springfield Museums • ☎ 413 263 6800, ⓦ springfieldmuseums.org

The **Springfield Science Museum** is lots of fun for kids, with a life-sized replica of a *Tyrannosaurus rex*, an aquarium with Atlantic salmon, turtles and sturgeon, exhibits on Native Americans and an in-depth **African Hall**, which covers everything from animals and early man through to the slave trade. Upstairs there's an astronomy section and the **Seymour Planetarium** (July & Aug 4 shows daily; Sept–June Sat & Sun only; $3). Don't miss the hypnotic **Orb** (a representation of Jupiter that you can spin on its axis).

Museum of Springfield History

21 Edwards St • Tues–Sat 10am–5pm, Sun 11am–5pm; July & Aug also open Mon 10am–5pm • $12.50, children (3–17 years) $6.50; tickets include access to all other Springfield Museums • ☎ 413 263 6800, ⓦ springfieldmuseums.org

The newest part of Springfield's museum complex is the **Museum of Springfield History**, showcasing Springfield's remarkable (and little-known) post-Civil War industrial history. Pride of place goes to the extensive **Indian motorcycle** collection, donated by a private collector in 2006 (the bikes were made in Springfield between 1901 and 1953), but there's also an extensive collection of old carriages and vintage cars, including a couple of **Rolls-Royce** sedans: the luxury car was actually made here for the US market in the 1920s. Displays commemorate Peter Pan Buses (founded in Springfield in 1933), Friendly's ice cream (1935), Smith & Wesson (1857) and abolitionist John Brown, who worked here from 1846 to 1849.

ARRIVAL AND DEPARTURE   SPRINGFIELD

By train Amtrak trains stop at Springfield's downtown station at 66 Lyman St. There are usually two direct services a day from New York ($40; 3hr 30min), and four or five departures from New Haven ($20; 1hr 30min).

By bus Peter Pan Bus Lines (ⓦ peterpanbus.com) provides a regular daily bus service from Boston ($21; around 2hr) and New York ($25; 3–4hr) via Hartford, CT, and towns in the Pioneer Valley and the Berkshires from the bus terminal at 1776 Main St (☎ 413 781 3320).

By car I-91 cuts right through downtown Springfield, with exits 6 and 7 providing easy access to the centre. You should have no problems parking (75 cents–$1.50/hr); one of the easiest car parks to locate is Tower Square on Boland Way (exit 7).

INFORMATION

Greater Springfield Convention & Visitors Bureau Opposite Tower Square at 1441 Main St (Mon–Fri 10am–4pm; ☎ 413 787 1548 or ☎ 1 800 723 1548, ⓦ valleyvisitor.com).

ACCOMMODATION

Sheraton Springfield 1 Monarch Place ☎ 413 781 1010. Over three hundred spacious rooms with river views, opposite the *Marriott* in the heart of town. Sixteen suites come with in-room jacuzzis, while a fitness centre, indoor pool and racquetball courts are available to everyone. Internet $9.95/day. **$150**

Springfield Marriott 2 Boland Way ☎ 413 781 7111, ⓦ marriott.com. Smack in the middle of town, with easy access to I-91 and on-site parking underneath the hotel in Tower Square. On the pricey side, but comfortable and convenient with great views across the river. **$185**

EATING AND DRINKING

★ **350 Grill** 350 Worthington St ☎ 413 439 0666, ⓦ 350grill.net. Plush new restaurant set in a historic red-brick building with an outdoor patio. Specializes in eclectic "tapas" (rice balls, aubergine towers and lobster ravioli), as well as pastas, sandwiches, grills and fine seafood. Also boasts some fine steaks. Lunch plates $9–11; dinner mains $16–29. Mon–Fri 11.30am–midnight, Sat 5pm–midnight.

★ **Chef Wayne's Big Mamou** 68 Liberty St ☎ 413 732 1011, ⊛ chefwaynes-bigmamou.com. Take a break from New England food with authentic Louisiana home-cooking: pots of simmering gumbo, catfish po'boys, and addictive bread pudding. Lunch plates $6.25–9.95; dinner mains $8.95–17.95. Mon–Thurs 11am–9pm, Fri till 10pm, Sat noon–10pm.

City Jake's Café 1573 Main St ☎ 413 731 5077. The best place in Springfield for a hearty diner-style breakfast for under $5, and lunch deals (burgers, sandwiches and salads) for $5.99. Mon–Fri 7.30am–2pm.

Fat Cat Bar & Grill 232 Worthington St ☎ 413 734 0554. No-nonsense rockers' pub, especially packed when bikers hit the state in the summer, with live (mostly hard) rock Fri–Sun and open-mic nights on Wed. Also serves excellent wings and other snack food. Tues–Sat 6pm–late.

Student Prince Café & Fort Dining Room 8 Fort St ☎ 413 734 7475, ⊛ studentprince.com. This establishment has been a local favourite for German *Wiener schnitzel, goulash* and *sauerbraten* (mains $15.95–25.95) since 1935. Mon–Wed 11am–9pm, Thurs–Sat 11am–10pm, Sun noon–8pm.

Theodore's Booze, Blues and Barbecue 201 Worthington St ☎ 413 736 6000, ⊛ theobbq.com. Straightforward offerings of barbecued ribs, chicken and salmon, with a solid beer selection and live blues most nights. Mon–Fri 11am–2am, Sat 5pm–2am, Sun 4pm–2am.

3

The Pioneer Valley

A verdant corridor shaped by the Connecticut River and centuries of glacial activity, **the Pioneer Valley** is the epicentre of recreational and cultural activity in Central Massachusetts, an excellent choice for those who like to hike, bike, hang out in cafés and browse bookshops. The towns of **Northampton**, **Amherst** and **South Hadley** share between them five colleges: Smith (in Northampton), Amherst, Hampshire and the University of Massachusetts (all in Amherst), and Mount Holyoke (in South Hadley) – establishments that have formalized their relationship through the cooperative "**Five College Consortium**".

Northampton

In 1653, settlers from Springfield purchased some of the most fertile farmland in Central Massachusetts from the local Native American community, christening it **NORTHAMPTON**. In the nineteenth century Northampton blossomed as an industrial centre, though in retrospect, the town's saving grace has been its investment in education and the intellectual environment it has fostered. **Smith College**, founded in 1871 by Sophia Smith and financed with her personal inheritance, survives as a prestigious women's college. Today, liberal, progressive, and content to march to its own tune, Northampton has settled into its role as a diverse and tolerant town of artists, students, activists, independent shops, restaurants and cafés.

Historic Northampton Museum

46 Bridge St • Mon–Sat 10am–5pm, Sun noon–5pm • $3 • ☎ 413 584 6011, ⊛ historic-northampton.org

To learn about the town's history, walk or drive up to the **Historic Northampton Museum**, a small but enlightening exhibition of artefacts and displays beginning with the area's Native American inhabitants. You'll learn about colourful residents such as Mary Parsons, accused of witchcraft, and President **Calvin Coolidge**, who came to practise law in Northampton in 1895 and spent much of his subsequent life here.

Smith College Museum of Art

Smith College, Elm St, at Bedford Terrace • Tues–Sat 10am–4pm, Sun noon–4pm • $5 • ☎ 413 585 2760, ⊛ scma.smith.edu/artmuseum

Northampton's real highlight, the **Smith College Museum of Art**, lies in the grounds of the town's defining institution. The collection focuses on nineteenth- and twentieth-century art, with works by Monet (*Field of Poppies*), Georgia O'Keeffe (*Squash Flowers, no. 1*), Jean Arp (*Torso*) and Frank Stella, who is represented by the enormous *Damascus Gate* (*Variation III*). The museum also boasts an

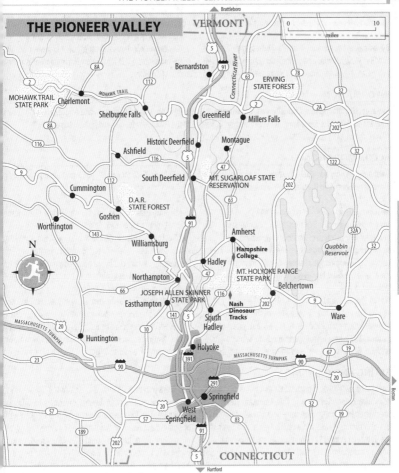

eight-thousand-strong print collection, including a large number of works by Daumier, Delacroix, Dürer, Munch, Picasso and Toulouse-Lautrec. Don't miss the killer restrooms, which local artists helped overhaul.

Mortimer Rare Book Room

Smith College • Mon–Fri 9am–noon & 1–5pm • Free • ☎ 413 585 2906, ⓦ smith.edu

Before you leave the Smith campus, take a peek inside the **Mortimer Rare Book Room**, tucked away on the third floor of the Neilson Library. This contains the precious **Sylvia Plath Collection**, four thousand pages of original manuscripts left by the poet and former student, including drafts of *Ariel* and *The Bell Jar* – a few pieces are always on display. Examples from the college's collection of letters penned by **Virginia Woolf** are also sometimes displayed here. The nearby modern **Campus Center** contains a shop (Mon–Fri 9am–4pm) selling Smith memorabilia and books.

ARRIVAL AND DEPARTURE   NORTHAMPTON

By car Northampton is just off I-91, approximately thirteen miles north of I-90; all exits marked "Northampton" lead to the centre of town, where several car parks are signposted – aim for the E. John Gare Parking Garage off

Hampton Avenue, where the first hour is free (50 cents/hr thereafter).

By bus Greyhound and Peter Pan buses from Amherst (6 daily; $6.50; 20min) and Springfield (7 daily; $8; 30min) pull in at 1 Roundhouse Plaza (bus station ☎413 586 1030); change at Springfield for Boston. The Pioneer Valley Transit Authority (PVTA; ☎413 586 5806 or ☎1 877 779 7882, ⓦpvta.com) runs shuttle bus #39 (every 30min, 6am–midnight; $1.25) between Northampton, Amherst and South Hadley.

INFORMATION

Greater Northampton Chamber of Commerce 99 Pleasant St (Mon–Fri 9am–5pm, May–Oct also Sat & Sun 10am–2pm; ☎413 584 1900, ⓦexplorenorthampton .com). Offers an array of maps and advice, as well as copies of the *Pink Pages* for gay and lesbian travellers.

ACCOMMODATION

Northampton only has a few **motels** on the fringes of town (most along US-5, off I-91) – you'll find a bigger selection along Rte-9, between Northampton and Amherst.

Autumn Inn 259 Elm St ☎413 584 7660, ⓦhampshirehospitality.com. A colonial-style inn boasting an attractive outdoor swimming pool and barbecue area surrounded by trees. Ageing but still clean, comfortable rooms, just under a mile from the centre (free bikes available). Free wi-fi and basic breakfast included. **$109**

Hotel Northampton 36 King St ☎413 584 3100 or ☎1 800 547 3529, ⓦhotelnorthhampton.com. Copious flower arrangements in the entryway of this historic 1927 hotel give an immediate sense of its – entirely deserved – self-importance. The attention to detail and charm make up for the small size of the elegant rooms. Free wi-fi. **$149**

★ **Saltbox Suites** 153 Elm St ☎413 5841790, ⓦsaltboxsuites.com. Three gorgeous suites in an eighteenth-century clapboard home downtown; it's set up for longer stays (1 week minimum), but call ahead to see if nightly rates are available. **$775**/week

Sugar Maple Trailside Inn 62 Chestnut St, Florence ☎413 575 2277, ⓦsugar-maple-inn.com. Nine antique-laden rooms in a beautifully restored 1865 colonial home, two miles west of Smith College and downtown Northampton. Free wi-fi. **$100**

EATING AND DRINKING

Caminito 7 Old South St ☎413 387 6387, ⓦcaminitosteakhouse.com. This Argentine steakhouse specializes in wood-fired Angus beef (steaks from $19), but also blends flavours from Italy, France and Spain: try the lobster ravioli ($21) or *gnocchi* pasta, served with house *marinara* ($13.50). Mon–Fri 5–10pm, Sat 4–10pm, Sun till 9pm.

FitzWilly's 23 Main St ☎413 584 8666, ⓦfitzwillys .com. Smack in the middle of it all, this local bar and restaurant (think sliders/mini hamburgers, buffalo wings) is a relaxing place to knock back a few and soak up the atmosphere. Daily 11.30am–midnight.

Haymarket Café & Juice Joint 185 Main St ☎413 586 9969, ⓦhaymarketcafe.com. Popular hangout for people looking for a cheap, healthy snack or light meal. Soups, salads and sandwiches go for around $6.75. Drinks are served in the street-level café, food in the dimly lit basement. Free wi-fi. Mon–Thurs 7am–10pm, Fri & Sat till 11pm, Sun 8am–10pm.

★ **Herrell's Ice Cream** 8 Old South St ☎413 586 9700, ⓦherrells.com. Home base for a small but illustrious regional chain of ice cream stores; original owner Steve Herrell was apparently the first to grind up candy bars and add them to his concoctions. Mon–Thurs & Sun noon–11pm, Fri & Sat till 11.30pm.

La Veracruzana 31 Main St ☎413 586 7181, ⓦlaveracruzana.com. A bright, cheerful and informal restaurant. The folks at *La Veracruzana* are credited with bringing the takeaway *burrito* ($5–7) to the Valley, but otherwise specialize in solid Tex-Mex food; *tacos*, *enchiladas*, *tamales* and the like. Daily 11am–10pm.

Northampton Brewery 11 Brewster Court, behind Thorne's Marketplace ☎413 584 9903, ⓦnorthampton brewery.com. With a reliable selection of high-quality microbrews on tap, an extensive munchies menu and a relaxing outdoor patio, this is a great place to while away a happy hour. Mon–Sat 11.30am–2am, Sun noon–1am.

Paul and Elizabeth's 150 Main St, in Thorne's Marketplace ☎413 584 4832, ⓦpaulandelizabeths .com. Vegetarian, vegan ($9.75–13) and seafood ($14.95–16.25) mains, home-made breads and desserts served in a serenely airy dining room. Mon–Thurs & Sun 11.30am–9.15pm, Fri & Sat till 9.45pm.

Pizzeria Paradiso 12 Crafts Ave ☎413 586 1468, ⓦspoletorestaurants.com. A cosy pizza place kept warm with wood-fired ovens imported from Italy (10in pizzas from $9.95). The extensive choice of toppings, drinks and desserts make this much more than just your average pizza joint. Mon–Thurs 5–9.30pm, Fri & Sat 4.30–10.30pm, Sun till 9pm.

★ **Sylvester's** 111 Pleasant St ☎413 586 5343, ⓦ sylvestersrestaurant.com. Housed in the former home of Sylvester Graham, inventor of the Graham cracker, *Sylvester's* serves up tasty fare, including delightful treats such as banana-bread French toast (two for $6) and waffles ($5.50). Daily 7am–2.30pm.

★ **Tunnel Bar** 125A Pleasant St, where Pearl St meets Strong Ave ☎413 586 5366. This old underground pedestrian walkway has been renovated into a dark martini bar with leather armchairs – a good spot for the sophisticated urbanite, or those who want to appear as such. Daily 5pm–1am.

ENTERTAINMENT

Thanks to its large artsy and student population, as well as the efforts of energetic local promoters **Iron Horse Entertainment Group**, Northampton attracts some of the biggest names in **performing arts**. You can reserve tickets for many shows at the Northampton Box Office, 76 Main St (Mon–Sat 9am–6pm, Sun noon–5pm; ☎413 586 8686 or ☎1 800 843 8425, ⓦ nbotickets.com).

Calvin Theater 19 King St ☎413 584 1444, ⓦiheg.com. The folks responsible for the *Iron Horse* (see below) have lovingly transformed this 75-year-old cinema into a beacon of the performing arts. Live theatre, music and dance performances for all ages and tastes.

Iron Horse Music Hall 20 Center St ☎413 585 0479, ⓦiheg.com. An institution in the world of folk music, this small, coffeehouse-style venue has been cheering on emerging artists for twenty years as well as pulling in big names of folk, bluegrass, jazz and blues.

New Century Theater Mendenhall Center for the Performing Arts, Smith College ☎413 585 3220, ⓦnewcenturytheatre.org. Summer-only theatre group in residence at Smith College, focusing on new works, classic dramas and comedies.

Pleasant Street Theater 27 Pleasant St ☎413 586 0935, ⓦamherstcinema.org. Though mainstream Hollywood movies increasingly show here, independent, classic and foreign films are also screened in this worthy leftover from the pre-multiplex era. Tickets $8.75.

Amherst

Settled in 1727, **AMHERST** has almost always been a college town. In 1821, its citizens opened the Collegiate Charitable Institution to educate their young men; just four years later this became the prestigious **Amherst College**. In the mid-nineteenth century, the Massachusetts Agricultural College opened to teach military, agricultural and technical skills; today, as the **University of Massachusetts at Amherst**, it is the main cog in the state's public university system. Meanwhile, **Hampshire College**, just outside town on the road to South Hadley, opened in 1970 as an experiment in true liberal arts study. Though the town maintains the feel of a small community, in fact it is a little larger than Northampton, with a mix of students, hippies, families and professionals.

Emily Dickinson Museum

280 Main St • Wed–Sun: March–May & Sept–Dec 11am–4pm; June–Aug 10am–5pm • Full tours (hourly according to season – confirm in advance; 1hr 30min) $10; Homestead tours (hourly; 40min) $8 • ☎413 542 8161, ⓦemilydickinsonmuseum.org

Former home of one of America's greatest poets, the **Emily Dickinson Museum** acts as a poignant tribute to the writer and throws light on her famously secluded life here in the nineteenth century (see box, p.218). The museum comprises **The Homestead**, the birthplace and home of the celebrated poet, and **The Evergreens** next door, home of her brother Austin and his family.

Begin your visit in the **Tour Center**, which houses the "My Verse is Alive" exhibit, highlighting the publication of Dickinson's most popular poems. The two houses can only be visited on **guided tours**: full tours usually depart on the hour, but there are also tours of just the Homestead on the half-hour. Much of the latter contains original furnishings, including an array of Dickinson's personal effects and the desk where her poems were found after her death. It's a pretty low-key display, but the tour guides are enthusiastic. The grander, Italianate Evergreens is literally frozen in time and far more evocative of the 1890s. Here you'll learn about Emily's close relationship with Austin's wife, Susan, and the efforts of niece Martha to secure the poet's legacy in later years. **Dickinson's grave** is in the nearby West Cemetery, behind Pleasant Street.

3

THE QUIET LIFE OF EMILY DICKINSON

Sometime in the 1850s, **Emily Dickinson** began to write startling, witheringly beautiful poetry; she imagined "loosened acres, lifted seas", rain that "sounded till it curved" and "felt a funeral in [her] brain, and mourners, to and fro". Virtually unpublished during her lifetime, she is now regarded as one of the greatest ever American poets. Born in Amherst in 1830, Dickinson attended nearby Mount Holyoke College, but loneliness drove her back home without finishing her studies, and she shortly afterwards began a life of **self-imposed exile** in the family home on Main Street – scholars are divided as to the cause for Dickinson's seclusion, though many believe she suffered from forms of **depression** and **agoraphobia**.

At home she read voraciously, wrote incessantly and corresponded with friends. Over the course of her life she penned some **1800 poems**, most of which mirrored her lifelong struggle between isolation and an intense search for inspiration. Despite this literary hyperactivity, she published fewer than a dozen poems during her life, and was completely unknown when she died in 1886. Her work was collected and published in 1890 by her sister, but she wasn't widely read until the 1950s. Part of the problem was that Dickinson's style differed dramatically from the **Victorian poetry** of the time; poems were untitled and characterized by short lines, unusual rhyme and unconventional punctuation. Modern audiences find her style and themes far more captivating, whether they be illness and death ("Because I could not stop for Death, He kindly stopped for me"), or meditations on immortality ("'Hope' is the thing with feathers, That perches in the soul").

Jones Library

43 Amity St • Special Collections Tues–Fri 10am–2pm & 3–5pm, Sat 2–5pm • Free • ☎ 413 259 3097, ⍟ joneslibrary.org

The Special Collections Room at the town's **Jones Library** provides Amherst with additional literary stature, notably the 12,000-item **Robert Frost Collection**, which includes original drafts of *Stopping by Woods on a Snowy Evening* and *Birches* (Frost was a professor at Amherst College for thirty years). The library also holds some seven thousand items related to **Emily Dickinson**, including original manuscript poems and letters. The exhibit room displays examples from both collections.

Mead Art Museum

Amherst College • Mid-May to early Sept Tues–Sun 9am–5pm; early Sept to mid-May Tues–Thurs & Sun 9am–midnight, Fri & Sat till 5pm • Free • ☎ 413 542 2335, ⍟ amherst.edu/~mead

Amherst's cultural attractions are rounded off by the **Mead Art Museum**, on the leafy campus of **Amherst College**. Works by Frederic Church, Thomas Cole, John Singleton Copley, Thomas Eakins and Winslow Homer dominate a collection strong on early twentieth-century American art. There's also a sprinkling of Renaissance European works, notably a seductive *Salome* by Robert Henri and a gory *Still Life with Dead Game* by Frans Snyders.

ARRIVAL AND INFORMATION   AMHERST

By train Amtrak's Vermonter train runs once a day between Burlington, VT ($35; 4hr) and New York ($52; 3hr) via Amherst, pulling into town at 13 Railroad St, just off Main St.

By bus Peter Pan buses from Northampton (6 daily; $6.50; 20min) and Springfield (9 daily; 40–50min; $8.50) drop off at 79 South Pleasant St (at the Amherst Common PVTA Shelter). Change at Springfield for Boston. The PVTA (☎1 877 779 7882, ⍟ pvta.com) runs shuttle bus

#39 (every 30min, 6am–midnight; $1.25) between Northampton, Amherst and South Hadley.

By car Amherst is easily accessible by car from I-91 exit 19, five miles along Rte-9. There is limited parking in the downtown area, with 2hr meters (40 cents/hr) and Boltwood Garage off Main Street (50 cents/hr; 4hr limit).

Amherst Area Chamber of Commerce 28 Amity St (Mon–Fri 8.30am–4.30pm; ☎413 253 0770, ⍟ amherstarea.com).

ACCOMMODATION

Your best bet for finding inexpensive **motels** is to drive along Rte-9 towards Northampton and check out some of the smaller, slightly rumpled-looking establishments along the way.

Amherst Inn 257 Main St ☎413 253 5000, ⓦ allenhouse.com. Seven cosy rooms tastefully decorated in a Victorian period style, enhanced by the gorgeous artwork of the owners. Free breakfast, wi-fi and transport to the bus or train station. **$125**

★ **Black Walnut Inn** 1184 N Pleasant St ☎413 549 5649, ⓦ blackwalnutinn.com. This attractive 1821 Federal-style B&B is shaded by tall black walnut trees, its gorgeous rooms decorated with period antiques and super-comfy beds. It's the whopping, scrumptious breakfasts, though, that really win five stars. Free wi-fi. **$125**

Delta Organic Farm 352 E Hadley Rd ☎413 253 1893, ⓦ deltaorganicfarm.com. Two miles from downtown, *Delta Organic Farm* is nirvana for health-conscious travellers (it's constructed with environmentally safe materials, and uses one hundred percent cotton linens), with special needs and requests welcomed by the accommodating owners. The plain but comfortable one- or two-bedroom private suites come with kitchenette, and air- and water-filtration systems. Organic breakfast available on request. **$100**

★ **UMass Hotel at the Campus Center** 1 Campus Center Way, University of Massachusetts ☎413 549 6000, ⓦ umasshotel.com. Situated in the heart of UMass campus, this is the most stylish digs in the area, with top-notch service and rooms with flat-screen TVs, iPod docks and free wi-fi. The hotel is a training ground for the university's hospitality students. **$125**

EATING AND DRINKING

Amherst Brewing Company 24 N Pleasant St ☎413 253 4400, ⓦ amherstbrewing.com. The brass bar and exposed brick add a touch of class to this decent brewpub. Live music – mostly jazz – and a street terrace are added attractions. Freshly brewed beers on tap. Mon–Sat 11.30am–1am, Sun 10am–1am.

Amherst Chinese Food 62 Main St ☎413 992 6181, ⓦ amherstchinesefood.com. The owners of this restaurant grow the organic vegetables they use in their dishes, adding nothing artificial as they pick, steam, sauté, fry and deliver them to your table piping hot. Daily 11.30am–10pm.

Antonio's 31 N Pleasant St ☎413 253 0808. There are just a few benches to eat at, but this is *the* pizza place in town (with pesto, veggie and chicken varieties). The good slices are always just out of the oven (pizzas from $9.75). Daily 10am–2am.

Bart's Homemade 103 N Pleasant St ☎413 253 2278, ⓦ bartshomemade.com. The street terrace is as inviting as the sundaes, smoothies and ice creams on warm days; try the local blueberry flavour, or the caramel apple.

March–Dec Mon–Thurs & Sun noon–11pm, Fri & Sat till midnight.

★ **Bistro 63 at The Monkey Bar** 63 N Pleasant St ☎413 259 1600, ⓦ bistro63.com. The lobster corn chowder, seafood *pescatore* (a blend of shellfish in tomato wine sauce, tossed over linguini), and steak *mignonette* here are so good that they even offer classes on how to make them. Mains $14.95–23.95. Daily 11.30am–10pm.

The Black Sheep 79 Main St ☎413 253 3442, ⓦ blacksheepdeli.com. Stacked sandwiches, pastries, coffee and desserts served in a down-to-earth café. Open late for coffee and occasional music, including open-mic nights, during term. Mon–Wed 7am–7pm, Thurs–Sat till 8pm, Sun till 7pm.

★ **Bub's BBQ** 676 Amherst Rd (Rte-116), Sunderland ☎413 548 9630, ⓦ bubsbbq.com. Only minutes by car from Amherst: from Rte-9, take Rte-116 (N) and look for the fluorescent pink porker on the right inviting you to "pig out in style" on delicious Southern barbecue and home-style sides ($10.50–15.95). Tues–Thurs 4–9pm, Fri 4–9.30pm, Sat 11.30am–9.30pm, Sun 11.30am–9pm.

Around Amherst

Following Rte-116 south along the **Connecticut River valley** you will find several worthwhile attractions between Amherst and South Hadley, including a couple of **absorbing museums** near Hampshire College and two **state parks**, which are especially beautiful in the autumn.

Eric Carle Museum of Picture Book Art

125 West Bay Rd • Tues–Fri 10am–4pm, Sat till 5pm, Sun noon–4pm • $9, children (under 18 years) $6 • ☎413 658 1100, ⓦ carlemuseum.org

Two miles south of Amherst, just off the main road (Rte-116) at the Hampshire College entrance, the **Eric Carle Museum of Picture Book Art** is the first museum in America devoted to children's book illustrations. Founded in part by Eric Carle, author of the classic *The Very Hungry Caterpillar*, exhibits change seasonally, but have included work from Dorothy Kunhardt's *Pat the Bunny* and Tony DiTerlizzi and Holly Black's *The Spiderwick Chronicles*.

3

National Yiddish Book Center

1021 West St · Mon–Fri 10am–4pm, Sun 11am–4pm; closed Jewish holidays · Free · ☎ 413 256 4900, ⓦ yiddishbookcenter.org

Inside the Hampshire College campus south of Amherst you'll find the enlightening **National Yiddish Book Center**, which houses one of the world's largest collections of Yiddish books in a sprawling, attractive building designed to emulate an Eastern European *shtetl*. In addition to the books, thought-provoking museum exhibitions and art displays explore the Yiddish experience in the US and Europe.

Mount Holyoke Range State Park

The Notch, 1500 West St · Daily sunrise–sunset · Notch Visitor Center daily 8am–4pm · Free; parking $2 · ☎ 413 253 2883

Four miles south of Amherst along Rte-116 is the entrance to **Mount Holyoke Range State Park**, a densely wooded reserve laced with hiking trails ranging from the easy 0.75-mile Laurel Loop to the harder 1.6-mile hike up Mount Norwottuck (1106ft). The **Notch Visitor Center**, at the entrance, can provide hiking maps and information. On the other side of Rte-116, trails lead into the east side of the Joseph Allen Skinner State Park (see below).

Nash Dinosaur Tracks

594 Amherst Rd (Rte-116) · Late May to early Sept Mon–Sat 10am–4pm, Sun noon–4pm · $3 · ☎ 413 467 9566, ⓦ nashdinosaurtracks.com

Around 6.5 miles south of Amherst, the **Nash Dinosaur Tracks** are a collection of locally excavated dinosaur bones and giant footprints in situ. Tracks were discovered near here way back in 1802, but it wasn't until the 1930s that Carlton Nash made another discovery and opened this site to the public. Somewhat controversially, you can even buy assorted fossils ($50–900) here.

Joseph Allen Skinner State Park

10 Skinner State Park Rd · Daily sunrise–sunset; auto road mid-May to Aug 9am–8pm, Sept to mid-Oct 8am–6pm · Sat & Sun parking $2 · ☎ 413 586 0350

Just off Rte-47, about seven miles south of Amherst, Mountain Road leads into the **Joseph Allen Skinner State Park**, which blankets the slopes of **Mount Holyoke** (942ft) and the forest-smothered hills of the Holyoke Range. Hiking here on clear day, especially in autumn, is wonderfully tranquil and not too strenuous, though you can also drive the 1.5 miles to the top of Mount Holyoke. Along the way you'll pass the Halfway Barn (1861) and the old steam engine (1867), which used to power the tram up here when the mountain was a major resort in the late nineteenth century. At the peak you'll find another relic of that time, the **Summit House**, a former hotel that dates from 1861. The summit offers phenomenal views of Northampton, distant Springfield and the Connecticut River valley, particularly the bend referred to as the "**Ox Bow**" – immortalized in Thomas Cole's painting of the same name. From here you can hike to the Mount Holyoke Range State Park (see above) via the **Metacomet-Monadnock Trail** (around five miles one-way; 2–3hr).

South Hadley

Located ten miles south of Amherst at the intersection of routes 116 and 47, **SOUTH HADLEY**, the home of **Mount Holyoke College**, completes the circle of towns in the Five College Consortium. Founded in 1836 by education pioneer Mary Lyon, Mount Holyoke is the oldest college for women in America and, like its neighbour Smith, is one of the most prestigious of the "Seven Sisters", a group of seven originally women-only colleges in the Northeast.

Though it's the smallest of the area's towns, South Hadley adds an exclamation point to the Pioneer Valley, mainly due to the presence of the **Mount Holyoke College Art Museum.**

Mount Holyoke College Art Museum

Lower Lake Road (adjacent to the greenhouse) • Tues–Fri 11am–5pm, Sat & Sun 1–5pm • Free • ☎ 413 538 2000, ⓦ mtholyoke .edu/artmuseum

Set in the heart of the attractive college campus, the **Mount Holyoke College Art Museum** boasts an impressive permanent collection of Asian, Egyptian and Mediterranean paintings, drawings and sculpture. Highlights include Albert Bierstadt's exuberant painting of *Hetch Hetchy Canyon*, California (1876), the precious jewel-like panel painting of an angel from Duccio's celebrated *Maestà* altarpiece (1308–11) and the only known pair of screens by Yukinobu (1643–82), the most famous female Japanese painter of the Edo Period.

ARRIVAL AND DEPARTURE   **SOUTH HADLEY**

By bus The PVTA (☎ 1 877 779 7882, ⓦ pvta.com) runs   between Northampton, Amherst and South Hadley. shuttle bus #39 (every 30min, 6am–midnight; $1.25)

3

Deerfield and around

Home to the flagship store of nationwide chain **Yankee Candle**, and the enchanting **Magic Wings Butterfly Conservatory & Gardens**, the town of **DEERFIELD** – some sixteen miles north from Northampton – is also one of the best places in the Pioneer Valley to soak up colonial history. Confusingly, modern Deerfield covers an area of more than thirty square miles, and is really an umbrella term for a handful of separate villages starting with the largely uninteresting **South Deerfield**, just off I-91 exit 24. The main attractions lie along US-5 from here, ending with **Historic Deerfield**, five miles to the north, an open-air museum that preserves much of the old town.

Brief history

Despite the sedate appearance of present-day Deerfield, its history has been punctuated by episodes of unusual violence. In September 1675, the English suffered one of their biggest defeats of **King Philip's War** (see p.521) here, when an attack by local Nipmuck tribes culminated in the death of 64 settlers and soldiers. The town saw more bloodshed in February 1704, when, in a five-hour raid, hundreds of French-led Abenaki, Huron and Mohawk warriors killed around fifty settlers and set fire to the town. Over a hundred English prisoners were marched three hundred miles to Canada; more than twenty perished en route, and even though the remainder were eventually freed, many chose to stay with their captors. By the nineteenth century, this raid had become a crucial pillar of the myth-making Colonial Revival, with its simplistic emphasis on "savages" and "pilgrims". Today, the town's museums offer a more balanced interpretation of the events.

Yankee Candle Company

25 Greenfield Rd (US-5) • Daily 10am–6pm • Free • ☎ 1 877 636 7707, ⓦ yankeecandle.com

From I-91, exit 24, the first point of interest is the sprawling **Yankee Candle Company** store, which primarily attracts hordes of shoppers for its candles, toys and home goods, but is worth a brief stop for its regular demonstrations of traditional candle-making techniques (head to the candle-making museum at the back).

Magic Wings Butterfly Conservatory & Gardens

281 Greenfield Rd (US-5) • Daily: June–Aug 9am–6pm; Sept–May till 5pm • $12, children (3–17 years) $8 • ☎ 413 665 2805, ⓦ magicwings.com

Around 2.5 miles north along US-5 from I-91, exit 24, lies **Magic Wings Butterfly Conservatory & Gardens**, a spacious greenhouse complex of tropical gardens and swarms of thousands of butterflies. The Enya-inspired soundtrack might wear you down after a while, but this remains an entrancing experience – kids will love it.

Historic Deerfield

80 Old Main St • Mid-April to Nov daily 9.30am–4.30pm • $12 • ☎ 413 775 7214, ⓦ historic-deerfield.org

Around 2.5 miles north of Magic Wings Butterfly Conservatory on US-5, **Historic Deerfield** appears frozen in time, a beautifully preserved collection of colonial houses girdled by one thousand acres of lush meadows and farmland. The museum dates back to the 1890s, when Alice Baker purchased the Frary House, restored it, and opened it to the public. Today Historic Deerfield incorporates virtually all of what was the original Deerfield settlement ("Old Deerfield"), 65 or so eighteenth- and nineteenth-century structures on either side of **The Street** (the main drag, running parallel to US-5). It includes eleven houses open to the public, in addition to a couple of museums – your ticket includes tours and entry to all of them. The best way to orientate yourself is to check in at the **Hall Tavern Visitor Center**, across from the *Deerfield Inn*. Here you'll be able to watch an introductory film and see which of the historic properties are open for guided, or self-guided tours – other houses are open by appointment only.

The houses themselves are filled with over 20,000 objects, from furniture and fabrics to silver and glass, either made or used in America between 1650 and 1850. If you don't have the patience for guided tours – and unless you have an intense interest in antique home decor – you probably don't need to visit more than one or two. The best are the **Sheldon House** (self-guided), which illustrates the life of a middle-class farming family from 1755 to 1802, and the **Frary House** (guided). Some of the most precious period pieces are displayed in the **Flynt Center of Early New England Life**, a modern timber building with a beautifully presented ensemble of furniture, textiles, dresses and powder horns.

Memorial Hall Museum

8 Memorial St • May Sat & Sun 11.30am–4.30pm; June–Oct Tues–Sun 11.30am–4.30pm • $6 • ☎ 413 774 3768, ⓦ deerfield-ma.org

Whichever houses you choose to visit in Historic Deerfield, be sure to check out the absorbing **Memorial Hall Museum**, managed separately by the local historical society. Inside you'll find exhibits depicting the history of the village, including the remnants of a wooden door from the "Indian House", which survived the 1704 attack. The most fascinating section is the Memorial Tablet, erected in 1882 to commemorate the victims, now overlain with a more sensitive translation of lines like "Mary Field, who married a savage and became one."

ACCOMMODATION AND EATING   DEERFIELD AND AROUND

Deerfield Inn 81 Main St ☎ 413 774 5587 or ☎ 1 800 926 3865, ⓦ deerfieldinn.com. The only place to stay in Historic Deerfield is this commodious country inn dating from 1884, with rooms decorated in a suitably elegant Victorian style. Tavern-style food and fine dining options are supplied by *Champney's* on site. $170

BOOKS AND BEVERAGES: THE MONTAGUE MILL

Book lovers will feel right at home at the **Book Mill** (daily 10am–6pm; ☎ 413 367 9206, ⓦ montaguebookmill.com), 440 Greenfield Rd, off Rte-63 in Montague, on the other side of the Connecticut River from Deerfield. With 40,000 used and discount books, well-seasoned armchairs and large windows overlooking the river, the mill is a magical place to spend a couple of lazy hours. Next door, in the same enchanting premises, the ★ **Lady Killigrew** pub and café (daily 8am–10pm; ☎ 413 367 9666, ⓦ theladykilligrew.com) has plenty of space to kick back with a coffee, cake and book (it also has free wi-fi and a big menu of more potent drinks). You should also consider having a meal next door at the romantic **Night Kitchen** (mains $19–24; Thurs–Sun 5.30am–10pm; ☎ 413 367 9580, ⓦ montaguenightkitchen.com), serving a high-quality blend of contemporary American and international cuisine sourced from local producers.

Shelburne Falls

Nestled in the Berkshire foothills and straddling the Deerfield River – ten miles west of the intersection of Rte-2 and I-91 (exit 26) – is the tiny town of **SHELBURNE FALLS**, a community whose buzz of artistic activity and scenic surroundings give a taste of modern New England small-town life. The most prominent thing to see here is the **Bridge of Flowers** (free), a 400ft tram bridge built in 1908 that is now festooned with foliage each spring through to late autumn – it's especially colourful in summer as you walk across.

Glacial potholes

The town's second main attraction is a series of fifty **glacial potholes** (ranging 6in to 39ft across), just east of Bridge Street along Deerfield Avenue. You can admire the potholes, the weir above them and what's left of the falls from the viewing area on the riverbank: the potholes resemble an enormous mass of once-molten stone that has now been whittled into a svelte sculpture along the riverbed.

3

INFORMATION   SHELBURNE FALLS

Village Information Center 75 Bridge St (May–Oct Mon–Sat 10am–4pm, Sun noon–3pm; ☎413 625 2544, ⊛shelburnefalls.com).

ACCOMMODATION

Dancing Bear Guest House 22 Mechanic St ☎413 625 9281, ⊛dancingbearguesthouse.com. A cosy 1852 home with antique-filled rooms, free wi-fi and full breakfast. **$119**

THE MOHAWK TRAIL

From the upper Pioneer Valley, one of most scenic routes in New England is the 63-mile **Mohawk Trail**, aka Rte-2, linking the town of Millers Falls and I-91 to the Berkshires and the Massachusetts–New York border. For more info on the trail, contact the **Mohawk Trail Association** (☎413 743 8127, ⊛mohawktrail.com).

Driving from east to west (you'll need a car to explore the trail), start at **Shelburne Falls** (see above) before moving on to Charlemont, where you'll pass the **"Hail to the Sunrise" monument**, a life-size bronze statue of a Mohawk warrior with outstretched arms (park in the Mohawk Park campsite opposite). Further along Rte-2 you can access the **Mohawk Trail State Forest**, 175 Mohawk Trail (mid-May to mid-Oct daily sunrise–sunset; parking $5; ☎413 339 5504), with hiking trails and a 56-place campground along the stunning **Cold River Gorge**.

The road drops dramatically from the ridge of the Hoosac Range into the Hoosic Valley at the **Hairpin Turn**; pull over to enjoy the scintillating views from the Western Summit at the top, or on the bend itself at the **Golden Eagle Restaurant** (see below).

Just before the route reaches **North Adams** (see p.236), look for the turn to Rte-8 and the **Natural Bridge State Park** (Mid-May to mid-Oct 9am–5pm; $2 parking; ☎413 663 6392), a former marble quarry now turned serene reserve, with the "bridge" a small arch over the narrow gushing Hudson Brook; there's also America's only marble dam and the dramatic, amphitheatre-like remains of the quarry face itself.

ACCOMMODATION AND EATING

Golden Eagle Restaurant 1935 Mohawk Trail (Rte-2), Clarksburg ☎413 663 9834, ⊛thegolden eaglerestaurant.com. The main attraction here, a spectacular perch on the Hairpin Turn overlooking the Hoosic Valley, is the view. Expect a hearty menu of steaks, roast meats and pastas (average mains $13–25). July–Oct daily noon–9pm; Nov to mid-May Fri & Sat 4–9pm, Sun 4–8pm; mid-May to June Mon–Fri 4–9pm, Sat & Sun noon–9pm.

Mohawk Trail State Forest campground 175 Mohawk Trail (Rte-2), Charlemont ☎1 877 422 6762. These rustic campsites just off the main road face the Cold River, with showers and a swimming hole on site. Note that the campground was severely damaged by Hurricane Irene in 2011 – call ahead for the latest. Mid-April to mid-Oct. **$14**/pitch

Kenburn Orchards B&B 1394 Mohawk Trail (Rte-2) ☏413 625 6116, ⓦkenburnorchards.com. Enchanting colonial B&B housed in an 1877 farmhouse, with three rooms and superb breakfasts; canopy beds and clawfoot baths adding to the Victorian ambience. **$139**

EATING AND DRINKING

Café Martin 24 Bridge St ☏413 625 2795, ⓦcafemartinsf.com. Serves international dishes with trendy ingredients, wooing patrons with home-made soups and lunch-time sandwiches (from $7.95); dinner (from steaks to coconut curry) ranges from $14.95–24.95. Tues–Thurs 5–9pm, Fri & Sat 4–9pm.

Mocha Maya's Coffee House 47 Bridge St ☏413 625 6292, ⓦmochamayas.com. Offers a great range of coffees, cakes and pastries as well as live music and free wi-fi. Mon–Sat 6.30am–7pm, Sun 7am–6pm.

West End Pub 16 State St, across the Bridge of Flowers ☏413 625 6216, ⓦwestendpubinfo.com. Has an outdoor deck overlooking the river, and pub fare such as meatloaf, burgers and fish and chips ($13.95) – it also serves Berkshire Brewing Co draught beer. Tues–Sun 11am–9pm.

The Berkshires

3

A rich cultural history, high-quality arts festivals, and a verdant landscape make the **Berkshires**, at the extreme western edge of Massachusetts, an enticing and unusually civilized region. The area has been attracting moneyed visitors since the nineteenth century, the most visible manifestations of which are sumptuous summer "cottages" hidden in the woods around the sedate villages of **Stockbridge** and **Lenox**. The latter is also home to **Tanglewood**, summer quarters of the Boston Symphony Orchestra, and the Mount, former home of novelist **Edith Wharton**. Further north, just outside the battered old mill town of **Pittsfield**, you'll find one of the best-preserved Shaker villages in the country, while art takes centre stage in the small towns of **Williamstown** and **North Adams**; the Clark and stunning MASS MoCA are world-class galleries.

Note that tourism in the Berkshires is highly **seasonal**: virtually all the big cultural events happen in summer, and in the off-season most of the museums either close or operate on skeleton schedules. Perhaps the best times to visit are late May or in September, when the foliage is changing but the "leaf peepers" have yet to arrive in force. You really need a car to get around in the Berkshires – public transport options are predictably limited.

INFORMATION

THE BERKSHIRES

Discover the Berkshires Visitor Center 3 Hoosac St, Adams (a small town just six miles south of North Adams and MASS MoCA; ☏413 743 4500, ⓦberkshires.org).

Stockbridge and around

The picture-perfect main street of **STOCKBRIDGE** is classic Berkshires, epitomized by the work of artist **Norman Rockwell**, who lived here for the last 25 years of his life. In an interesting twist, Stockbridge's other claim to fame is at quite the other end of the sociocultural spectrum: it's the setting for **Arlo Guthrie**'s 1967 classic anti-draft song/monologue *Alice's Restaurant Massacree* (the 1969 movie was also filmed here).

The actual town of Stockbridge is tiny, basically consisting of a few nineteenth-century buildings on Main Street and around the corner on Elm Street. Most visitors tend to park near the **Red Lion Inn** (see p.228) and wander from there, after having iced tea on the inn's venerable front porch. There's actually quite a lot more to see and do around town, from the **Norman Rockwell Museum** to the elegant estates of **Naumkeag** and **Chesterwood**.

Stockbridge Library and Historical Museum

46 Main St • **Museum** Tues, Wed & Fri 9am–5pm, Thurs 9am–1pm, Sat till 2pm • Free • ☏413 298 5501, ⓦstockbridgelibrary.org

The single-room **Historical Museum** in the basement of **Stockbridge Library** is worth a quick browse, with displays arranged chronologically beginning with artefacts made by

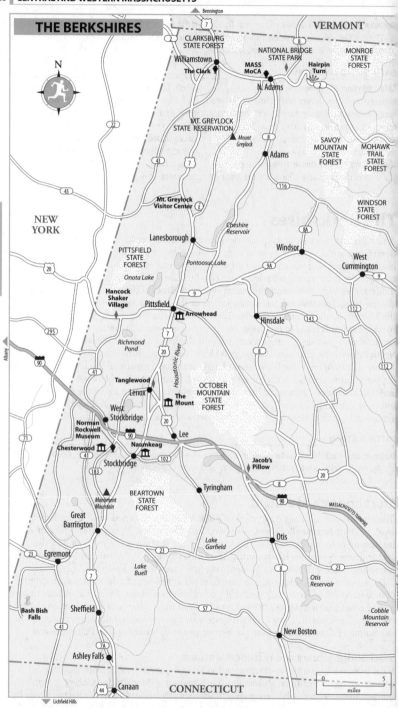

THE BERKSHIRES

N

3

VERMONT

NEW YORK

CONNECTICUT

Bennington

CLARKSBURG STATE FOREST

NATIONAL BRIDGE STATE PARK

MONROE STATE FOREST

Williamstown

The Clark

MASS MoCA

Hairpin Turn

N. Adams

MT. GREYLOCK STATE RESERVATION

▲ Mount Greylock

SAVOY MOUNTAIN STATE FOREST

MOHAWK TRAIL STATE FOREST

Adams

Mt. Greylock Visitor Center ℹ

WINDSOR STATE FOREST

Cheshire Reservoir

Lanesborough

Windsor

West Cummington

PITTSFIELD STATE FOREST

Pontoosuc Lake

Onota Lake

Hancock Shaker Village

Pittsfield

Arrowhead

Hinsdale

Albany

Richmond Pond

Housatonic River

OCTOBER MOUNTAIN STATE FOREST

Tanglewood

Lenox

The Mount

West Stockbridge

Norman Rockwell Museum

Naumkeag

Lee

Jacob's Pillow

Chesterwood

Stockbridge

Monument Mountain ▲

BEARTOWN STATE FOREST

Tyringham

MASSACHUSETTS TURNPIKE

Great Barrington

Lake Garfield

Otis

Egremont

Lake Buell

Otis Reservoir

Bash Bish Falls

Sheffield

Cobble Mountain Reservoir

Ashley Falls

New Boston

Canaan

Lichfield Hills

0   5
miles

the Mahicans (Mohicans) who once lived in the area, and the arrival of British colonists in 1735. There's also a huge collection of books to read by local authors, including *Hitty, Her First Hundred Years* by Rachel Field, a popular children's book published in 1929, which is still a bestseller.

Mission House & Native American Museum

9 Main St • Guided tours late-May to Aug Mon, Thurs & Fri 10am & 11am; Sat & Sun 10am–2pm hourly; Sept–mid-Oct Sat & Sun 10am & 11am • $6 • ☎ 413 298 3239, Ⓦ thetrustees.org

In 1734, the Mohicans of the Stockbridge area invited the British to send them missionaries in a desperate attempt to stave off disease and encroaching colonists. The **Mission House** is where their potential saviour, **Reverend John Sergeant**, planned his missionary work. Completed c.1742, it was relocated here in 1927. The exterior has a pretty, arched Connecticut River Valley-style doorway, while the inside is noteworthy mainly for its eighteenth-century chairs and a bright red Hadley chest. A grape arbour in the gardens behind the house leads to a small **Native American Museum** about the Mohicans Sergeant tried to convert; after Sergeant's death in 1749, the experiment unravelled and by 1785 most of the tribe had left the area (their ancestors live in Wisconsin).

Norman Rockwell Museum

9 Rte-183 (3 miles west of Stockbridge) • **Museum** May–June & Sept–Oct daily 10am–5pm; July & Aug daily 10am–7pm; Nov–April Mon–Fri 10am–4pm, Sat & Sun till 5pm • **Studio** May–Oct 10am–4.45pm • $16; combination ticket with Mass MoCA (see p.236) or The Clark (see p.235) $28 • ☎ 413 298 4100, Ⓦ nrm.org

Founded in 1969 with the help of the eponymous artist and former Stockbridge resident, the **Norman Rockwell Museum** is the most comprehensive of several Rockwell tributes in New England, preserving some 574 of his original paintings and drawings. Several galleries show revolving exhibits (usually including the provocative *Four Freedoms*, nostalgic *Stockbridge Main Street at Christmas* and undeniably witty *Triple Self-Portrait*). Despite Rockwell's penchant for advertising endorsements, and the idealism that infused much of his work, it's hard not be sucked in by the artist's obsessive attention to detail, and his simple but clever ideas – see *Girl Reading the Post*. The tranquil grounds include the little red building that was Rockwell's last **studio**, moved here in 1986.

Chesterwood

4 Williamsville Rd (2 miles from Stockbridge) • May Sat & Sun 10am–5pm; June to mid-Oct daily same hours • $15 • ☎ 413 298 3579, Ⓦ chesterwood.org • From town, travel west on Rte-102. Turn left on Rte-183 and follow the signs beyond the Rockwell museum

Sculptor **Daniel Chester French** (1850–1931), best known for his rendition of Abraham Lincoln at the Lincoln Memorial in Washington, DC, bought property in Stockbridge in 1897. By 1901 he had built a new summer home here (designed by Henry Bacon), dubbed **Chesterwood**, a relatively modest Colonial Revival house now open to the public. Hourly guided tours are the only way to visit the studio and residence, but you can peruse the exhibits in the visitors' centre and wander the attractive gardens at will.

Naumkeag

5 Prospect Hill Rd (1 mile from Stockbridge) • Late May to mid-Oct daily 10am–5pm • $15 • ☎ 413 298 3239, Ⓦ thetrustees.org • Take Pine St, north from the junction of US-7 and Rte-102 in central Stockbridge, and bear left onto Prospect Hill Rd

With its spectacular views of the Berkshires, distinctive gardens and whimsical style, the "cottage" of **Naumkeag** is testimony to the great wealth that flooded these hills in the Gilded Age. The mansion was built by Stanford White in 1886 as a summer home for the prosperous attorney **Joseph Hodges Choate** (1832–1917), later the US ambassador to Britain (the estate's name, pronounced "Namkeg", derives from the Native American word for Salem, Choate's birthplace). The master architect's touch is

3

evident everywhere, from the American-style shingle roof to the medieval-style brick-and-stone towers and the understated interior flourishes, including a combination of redwood, oak and mahogany panelling and a three-storey hand-carved staircase. Original furnishings and domestic accoutrements from all over the world give the impression that the Choates have just slipped out for a minute; indeed, there are even coats left hanging in the closet. You can only visit the inside on entertaining 45-minute guided tours run throughout the day, embellished with tales of life here in the nineteenth century.

As impressive as the house is, make sure you leave time for the eight acres of meticulously planned and tended **gardens**, subtly studded with contemporary sculpture; self-guided audio tours are available at the entrance.

ARRIVAL AND INFORMATION

STOCKBRIDGE

By bus BRTA buses (Mon–Sat only; $1.25; ☎ 413 499 2782 or ☎ 1 800 292 2782, ⊚ berkshirerta.com) link Stockbridge with Great Barrington, Lenox, Lee and Pittsfield.

Stockbridge Visitor Center Middle of Main Street

(summer only). Packed with information, but not always manned.

Stockbridge Chamber of Commerce 50 Main St (Mon–Fri 9am–5pm; ☎ 413 298 5200, ⊚ stockbridgechamber.org).

ACCOMMODATION

America's Best Value Inn 980 Pleasant St (Rte-102) ☎ 413 243 0501, ⊚ americasbestvalueinn.com. This appealing motel is just a short drive from central Stockbridge and a superb budget option. All rooms come with a/c, microwave, free wi-fi and cable TV, and a basic breakfast is included. **$75**

Inn at Stockbridge 30 East St (Rte-7) ☎ 888 466 7865, ⊚ stockbridgeinn.com. Ornate Georgian-style mansion built in 1906, with luxurious themed rooms featuring gas fireplaces, king-size canopy beds, flat-screen TV and DVD players. **$195**

Red Lion Inn 30 Main St ☎ 413 298 1690, ⊚ redlioninn.com. This grandmotherly inn, which also

offers accommodation in historic cottages all over town, is for many the quintessential New England hostelry with a vast range of room types. One of their properties includes Meadowlark, the smaller studio at the large Chesterwood estate (see p.227), available May–Oct. **$150**

Stockbridge Country Inn 26 Glendale Rd (Rte-183) ☎ 413 298 4015, ⊚ stockbridgecountryinn.com. Set in an 1856 country house on four acres of grounds, this seven-room B&B is close to the Rockwell Museum and offers queen-sized canopy beds, a heated pool, attractive gardens and porches from which to view them. Full country breakfast included. **$169**

NORMAN ROCKWELL: "AMERICA'S BEST-LOVED ARTIST"

Love him or hate him, if you spend any time in western New England, it's hard to avoid the work of **Norman Rockwell**. The beloved artist lived and painted in Arlington, VT, and, more famously, in Stockbridge, MA; for more than half a century, Rockwell was a fixture on the landscape of American **popular culture**, known as much for his product endorsements as for his *Saturday Evening Post* covers. Of American artists, perhaps only Warhol, sort of his spiritual opposite, is so easily recognizable.

Born in 1894 in New York City, Rockwell dropped out of high school to attend classes at the National Academy of Design, and at the age of 22 sold his first painting to the **Saturday Evening Post**; in the forty years that followed, he contributed more than three hundred paintings to that publication alone. His work presented, in the artist's own words, "**life as it should be**": children playing, adults relaxing, doctors examining healthy patients, family struggles that seemed certain to have a happy ending. His work stands in dramatic contrast to the "serious artists" of the twentieth century – the Surrealists, Dadaists, Cubists and Abstract Expressionists – much as his idyllic images stand in contrast to the often turbulent times in which he lived.

Many have questioned the **veracity** of these images, yet it seems doubtful that Rockwell saw much in the way of war, riots or lynchings during his placid small-town life. However, later in his career, working for *Look* magazine, Rockwell did take on such issues as integration of schools and neighbourhoods, and did so with the same gentle dignity that he had devoted to more insular concerns. He died in **Stockbridge** in 1978.

EATING AND DRINKING

Lion's Den 30 Main St ☎413 298 1654, ⓦredlioninn.com. Repair to the *Red Lion Inn*'s atmospheric cellar tavern to get down with the rest of the town. Live music most nights, plus tasty pub food like meatloaf with mushroom gravy and chicken pot pie (specials $9.95). Mon–Thurs 4–11pm, Fri & Sat till midnight, Sun noon–11pm.

Main Street Café 40 Main St ☎413 298 3060. The most central option and best breakfast in town ($5–9); half-pound burgers ($8) and deli-style sandwiches ($6.50) take the stage from lunch onwards. Daily 7am–4pm.

Michael's Restaurant & Pub 5 Elm St ☎413 298 3530, ⓦmichaelsofstockbridge.com. Surf, turf and pasta (mains $14.95–23.95) with a late-night menu and beers to suit every taste. Great place to watch games or shoot some pool. Mon–Thurs 9.30am–9pm, Fri & Sat till 10pm, Sun 11.30am–9pm.

Once Upon a Table 34 Main St ☎413 298 3870, ⓦonceuponatablebistro.com. Quietly tucked in the Mews off Main St, this restaurant has romantic decor and a worldly menu; Prince Edward Island mussels (from Canada; $11), sandwiches ($9–10) and more elaborate dishes like pecan-crusted rainbow trout ($22). Mon–Fri 11am–3pm & 4.30–9pm, Sat & Sun 9am–9pm.

Lenox and around

From Stockbridge, a slight detour off US-7 takes you to Rte-7A and the genteel village of **LENOX**, the cultural nucleus of the Berkshires by virtue of its proximity to the **Shakespeare Company** (see box, p.231) and **Tanglewood**, the summer home of the Boston Symphony Orchestra. It's a quiet place for most of the year, but on summer weekends traffic jams are not uncommon.

The Mount

2 Plunkett St (US-7) • May–Oct daily 10am–5pm; guided tours July & Aug 10.30am, 11am, 1pm & 3pm • $16, tours $2 extra • ☎413 551 5111, ⓦedithwharton.org

In 1902, writer **Edith Wharton** (1862–1937) joined a long list of artists summering in the Berkshires when she moved into **The Mount**, a home she designed in a sumptuous Classical Revival style. Finished in bright white stucco, the mansion was thoughtfully located on a rocky outcrop to command the most pleasing views of nearby Laurel Lake. Best known today for her later work *The Age of Innocence* (1920), the order, scale and harmony of the place are a reflection of the principles Wharton promoted in her first successful book, *The Decoration of Houses*, published a few years before she moved here. The knowledgeable guides are also a mine of information on Wharton's life, providing a biography of the author as you tour the house. Though her years at The Mount were productive – she wrote *Ethan Frome* here – they were not entirely happy; boredom with her husband and an unapologetic disgust for the turpitude of American culture ultimately sent her to France in 1911, where she lived until her death. Take time to appreciate the collection of Wharton's books in the **library**; the Mount was virtually bankrupted by their purchase from a private collector in 2006, and narrowly avoided foreclosure in 2008. Live **readings** of Wharton's work take place every Wednesday at 5pm in July and August.

Tanglewood

297 West St • **Visitors' centre** July & Aug daily 10am–4pm; June, Sept & Oct Sat & Sun same hours **Grounds** Daily 8am–dusk • Free • ☎617 266 1200, ⓦbso.org

Even if you're visiting after late August, it's well worth making a stop off West Street (Rte-183), about a mile outside Lenox, to walk around **Tanglewood**. Though its lush grounds were formerly part of the estate of a Boston banker, it was Nathaniel Hawthorne who coined the name. Today the musicians practise in a 1940s reconstruction of the red farmhouse where he lived with his wife Sophia for eighteen months between 1850 and 1851, penning *The House of the Seven Gables* on the premises and initiating a friendship with **Herman Melville** (see p.233). On summer weekends, concerts are given in the aptly named Shed, a bare-bones, indoor/outdoor hall, as well as the newer Ozawa Hall (see box, p.231).

3

ARRIVAL AND INFORMATION

By bus One or two Peter Pan buses a day from Springfield stop at Lenox (at the Village Pharmacy, 5 Walker St). BRTA buses (Mon–Sat only; $1.25; ☎413 499 2782 or ☎1 800 292 2782, ⓦberkshirerta.com) link Lenox with Great Barrington, Stockbridge, Lee and Pittsfield.

Lenox Chamber of Commerce Lenox Library, 18 Main St (June–Aug daily 10am–6pm; Sept–May Wed–Sat 10am–4pm; ☎413 637 3646, ⓦlenox.org). Has moved around over the years, so call first if you need help.

ACCOMMODATION

Blantyre 16 Blantyre Rd ☎413 637 3556, ⓦblantyre.com. A former summer "cottage", this roomy Scottish Tudor mansion with Gothic flourishes has been refurbished as one of the country's most luxurious resorts, and as such is almost a destination in itself. $675

Brook Farm Inn 15 Hawthorne St ☎413 637 3013, ⓦbrookfarm.com. The innkeepers at this twelve-room 1870 Victorian B&B are poetry aficionados, and hold readings and other entertainments in the library, often at teatime, with home-made scones and strawberry jam. In winter curl up with a book of verse in front of a fireplace, either in the common area or in your room. Also has a swimming pool. $179

★ **Garden Gables Inn** 135 Main St ☎413 637 0193, ⓦgardengablesinn.com. Stylish, luxurious B&B set in farm that dates back to 1780; all rooms come with iPod docks, free wi-fi, LCD TVs, DVD players, afternoon sherry and working fireplaces. Huge breakfast buffet included. Also boasts the largest pool in the Berkshires. $261

★ **Hampton Terrace** 91 Walker St ☎1 800 203 0656, ⓦhamptonterrace.com. This elegant 1852 Gilded Age gem offers deluxe rooms with clawfoot tubs, antique furniture and all the extras – the swimming pool is a real bonus in summer. Free wi-fi. $175

The Village Inn 16 Church St ☎413 637 0020, ⓦvillageinn-lenox.com. A 1771 country inn-style hotel whose 32 rooms boast antiques, bountiful breakfasts and afternoon English tea in the centre of Lenox. Good-value rooms if you visit during spring. $202

EATING AND DRINKING

★ **Berkshire Bagel** 18 Franklin St ☎413 637 1500. Rare budget option in the centre of town, where locals mingle with New Yorkers desperate for a bagel fix: great range of bagels (95 cents) and spreads (from $2.20), with a few tables and a small car park on site. Mon–Fri 6am–2pm, Sat & Sun 7am–noon.

★ **Bistro Zinc** 56 Church St ☎413 637 8800, ⓦbistrozinc.com. Power-lunch spot filled with diners on mobile phones gobbling up flavourful French fare at reasonable prices – dinner is considerably more expensive (mains $18–29). Daily 11.30am–3pm & 5.30–10pm (July & Aug till midnight).

Church Street Café 65 Church St ☎413 637 2745. The tasty New England fare, from sautéed Maine crab cakes to maple- and cider-glazed pork chops, wins accolades for this eatery – more restaurant than café – in the centre of Lenox. Daily 11.30am–2.30pm & 5–11pm.

Firefly 71 Church St ☎413 637 2700, ⓦfireflylenox .com. Ask the locals where they go for a night out, and they'll tell you about *Firefly*: the tavern, tapas and dinner menus offer creative, contemporary American dishes, like lobster rolls ($23) and pistachio pesto farfalle ($16). Live music most weekends. Mon–Thurs 5–9.30pm, Fri & Sat till 10pm, Sun noon–9.30pm.

Lee

During the busy summer cultural season, many last-minute travellers to Lenox end up staying in nearby **LEE**, which is just as well, for there is a genuine quality to the place altogether lacking in its ritzier neighbour. Founded in 1777, it doesn't have a lot to see, though Lee's nineteenth-century boom in paper-making and marble quarrying has left it with an attractive historic district, plenty of interesting shops and heaps of Victorian charm. It's also home to the annual **Festival Latino of the Berkshires** (ⓦfestivallatino .org), held in September, with plenty of Latin dance and salsa to enjoy.

ARRIVAL AND INFORMATION

By bus One or two Peter Pan buses a day from Springfield stop at Lee (near the Chamber of Commerce), before going on to Lenox and Pittsfield. BRTA buses (Mon–Sat only; $1.25; ☎413 499 2782 or ☎1 800 292 2782, ⓦberkshirerta.com) link Lee with Great

Barrington, Stockbridge, Lenox and Pittsfield.
Lee Chamber of Commerce 3 Park Plaza in front of the church at the end of Main St (June–Oct Mon–Sat 10am–4pm; ☎413 243 1705, ⓦleechamber.org). A good resource if you need help finding a place to sleep.

SUMMER FESTIVALS IN THE BERKSHIRES

There are several exceptional summer **cultural festivals** in the Berkshires. Tickets for the more popular events sell out far in advance, so plan accordingly.

Aston Magna Festival Simon's Rock College, Great Barrington ☎413 528 3595, ⊛astonmagna.org. The country's oldest annual summer festival, devoted to performances of Baroque music played on period instruments. Saturdays throughout July.

Berkshire Fringe Daniel Arts Center at Simon's Rock College, 84 Alford Rd, Great Barrington ☎413 298 5576, ⊛berkshirefringe.org. Contemporary theatre, music and dance at one of the region's newest festivals, established in 2004. Late July to Aug Mon–Sat.

Berkshire Theatre Festival 6 East St (Rte-102), Stockbridge ☎413 320 4175, ⊛berkshiretheatre .org). Best known for its summer productions at the Berkshire Playhouse Mainstage, but also noteworthy for Unicorn Theater readings of plays in progress. Late June –Aug Mon–Sat.

Jacob's Pillow 358 George Carter Rd (off Rte-20 between Becket and Lee) ☎413 243 0745, ⊛jacobspillow.org. The most famous contemporary dance festival in the country, founded by Ted Shawn in 1931 and improbably located in the middle of nowhere. Artists-in-residence give free performances of works in progress before the main programmes, and free guided tours of the historic premises. Mid-June to Aug Wed–Sun. Tours Fri & Sat at 5.30pm.

Shakespeare & Company 70 Kemble St, Lenox ☎413 637 1199, ⊛shakespeare.org. One of the country's biggest Shakespeare companies is based within a lovely garden property close to the centre of town. Productions are not limited to Shakespeare, and include new plays, dance and dramatizations of stories by Edith Wharton, Henry James and the like. May–Nov.

Tanglewood 297 West St (Rte-183), Lenox. For advance tickets Sept–May ☎617 266 1492; otherwise ☎413 637 1600, ⊛bso.org. Summer home of the Boston Symphony Orchestra. Full orchestral concerts take place on weekends at the Shed, while the newer Ozawa Hall is used on other days, mainly for chamber music concerts. Further musical options include open rehearsals for the BSO on Saturday mornings, plus jazz and pop performances. Tickets for the Shed and Ozawa Hall range from $21 to $105; it's cheaper ($19) and arguably more enjoyable to sit on the grass – though if you do, bring a towel or lawn chair. July to late Aug

Troubadour Series at the Guthrie Center 4 Van Deusenville Rd, Great Barrington ☎413 528 1955, ⊛guthriecenter.org. Folk singer Arlo Guthrie (Woody Guthrie's son) converted old Trinity Church into a cultural centre in the 1990s, and it now hosts this annual folk-music series. May–early Sept.

Williamstown Theatre Festival '62 Center for Theatre and Dance, Williams College, 1000 Main St (Rte-2), Williamstown ☎413 597 3400, ⊛wtfestival.org. Every summer some of the most accomplished actors from American stage and screen converge on this stately college town for a series of nearly a dozen productions, both time-tested and experimental. Mid-June to late Aug Tues–Sun.

ACCOMMODATION

Applegate 279 W Park St ☎413 243 4451, ⊛applegateinn.com. A calm, ship-shape B&B in a Southern-style Georgian colonial home. The six guest rooms have old-fashioned character but a contemporary feel; freshly baked goods contribute to great breakfasts. $275

Chambéry Inn 199 Main St, Lee ☎413 243 2221, ⊛chamberyinn.com. This 1885 French country house, built as the Berkshires' first parochial school, has nine meticulously refurbished suites with high ceilings, big windows and modern touches such as cable TV (there are also two standard double rooms). $189

★ **Historic Merrell Inn** 1565 Pleasant St (Rte-102), South Lee ☎413 243 1794, ⊛merrell-inn.com. Just south of town, between Stockbridge and Lee, this atmospheric inn has ten enticing rooms, warmly decorated with Victorian wallpaper and furnishings – four have a working fireplace in winter. Look for the vintage birdcage bar in the room where breakfast is served, a relic from its days as a stagecoach stop. $180

EATING

Cakewalk Bakery and Café 56 Main St, Lee ☎413 243 2806, ⊛cakewalkbakery.com. Offers an affordable but tasty menu of soups, sandwiches, salads, quiches and, oh yes, delicious pastries. Tues–Sun 7am–4pm.

★ **Joe's Diner** 85 Center St, Lee ☎413 243 9756. The best place to eat in Lee, whether you want a weighty corned-beef sandwich, tuna salad on rye, or scrambled eggs and waffles. Extremely popular, and with very low prices (superb sausages and eggs from $5). Mon 6am–Sat 6.30pm.

Salmon Run Fish House 78 Main St, Lee ☎413 243 3900. Boasts an informal atmosphere in which to eat a

3

variety of reasonably priced seafood and pasta dishes – salmon is cooked all ways, from the simple (chargrilled; $16.95), to the fancy (stuffed with lobster; $21). Sept–June Wed–Mon 11.30am–9pm; July & Aug daily same hours. **Sullivan Station** 109 Railroad St, Lee ☎413 243 2082,

Ⓦsullivanstationrestaurant.com. Converted 189 railroad station (you can sit in the old ticket office c caboose), serving great sandwiches and salads for lunch and hearty steaks, ribs and chops for dinner ($16.95– 24.95). Tues–Sun 11.30am–2.30pm & 4.30–9pm

Great Barrington and around

South of Stockbridge, the landscape takes on a more rustic flavour – one that definitely colours the only town of any size, **GREAT BARRINGTON**. What buzz there is here centres on Main Street near Railroad and Castle streets, where stylish home decor shops sit among a number of good eateries; in the summer the town plays host to the **Berkshire Fringe** and the **Troubadour Series at the Guthrie Center** (see p.231).

Great Barrington is also the unlikely birthplace of founding civil rights and NAACP (National Association for the Advancement of Colored People) leader **W.E.B. Du Bois** (1868–1963), the son of free black citizens – a bronze plaque commemorates his birthplace (Church St, at River St), and the site of his boyhood home (Rte-23, a quarter of a mile west of the junction with Rte-71) is marked by a five-acre park and monument. There are plans to create some sort of permanent exhibition here based on digs of the site conducted by UMass (Ⓦduboishomesite.org). In the meantime, check out the small exhibition inside the lobby of the **Triplex Cinema** (daily noon–9pm; free; ☎413 528 8885, Ⓦthetriplex.com) on Railroad Street.

Monument Mountain

US-7 • Daily sunrise–sunset • Free • ☎413 298 3239, Ⓦthetrustees.org

In 1850, authors Nathanial Hawthorne and Herman Melville met for the first time climbing **Monument Mountain** (1642ft), a forest-smothered outcrop of granite that still makes for a refreshing half-day excursion. Look for the car park four miles north of Great Barrington on US-7. From here a choice of gentle or steep trails lead up to the peak and the dramatic outcrop known as the **Devil's Pulpit,** commanding scintillating views across the Berkshires. Allow at least two hours for the round trip.

ARRIVAL AND INFORMATION

By bus BRTA (Mon–Sat only; $1.25; ☎413 499 2782 or ☎1 800 292 2782, Ⓦberkshirerta.com) buses link Great Barrington with Stockbridge, Lenox, Lee and Pittsfield.

GREAT BARRINGTON AND AROUND

Southern Berkshire Chamber of Commerce 362 Main St, US-7 (Mon & Wed 11am–5pm, Tues & Thurs–Sun 9am–5pm; ☎413 528 1510, Ⓦsouthern berkshirechamber.com).

ACCOMMODATION

Berkshire Comfort Inn & Suites 249 Stockbridge Rd (US-7) ☎1888 401 1372, Ⓦberkshirecomfortinn.com. Best of the hotels on the strip north of town, with spacious rooms (most with sofas and microwaves) and family-friendly suites. There is also a heated indoor pool and whirlpool tub – real luxuries – and an outdoor pool for the summer. Free wi-fi and decent breakfast included. $179
Wainwright Inn 518 S Main St ☎413 528 2062,

Ⓦwainwrightinn.com. Occupies a huge 1766 mansion right outside the centre of town, with comfy Victorian-themed rooms – free wi-fi but no TVs. $139
Windflower Inn 684 S Egremont Rd (Rte-23) ☎413 528 2720, Ⓦwindflowerinn.com. Relaxed country inn with thirteen rooms loaded with antiques, most with fireplaces; afternoon tea with cookies, free wi-fi and huge breakfasts are included. There's also a pool. $150

EATING AND DRINKING

Baba Louie's 286 Main St ☎413 528 8100, Ⓦbabalouiessourdoughpizzacompany.com. Does excellent wood-fired sourdough pizzas made with local organic produce. Daily 11.30am–3pm & 5–9.30pm.
Barrington Brewery 424 Stockbridge Rd ☎413

528 8282, Ⓦbarringtonbrewery.net. Family-friendly place, especially noted for its crab cakes ($16), stout chocolate cakes and pints of well-crafted ales ($4.50). Pool table upstairs. Mon–Thurs & Sun 11.30–9pm, Fri & Sat till 10pm.

SoCo Creamery 5 Railroad St ☎413 528 9420, ⓦsococreamery.com. Excellent micro-creamery (small batch ice cream maker), using local farms; the Mexicali flavour is a spicy mint treat, but everything is good. Mon–Thurs & Sun 9am–10pm, Fri & Sat till midnight.

Xicohtencatl 50 Stockbridge Rd ☎413 528 2002, ⓦxicohmexican.com. High-quality Mexican restaurant and tequila bar (over 50 types), with mains averaging $16–17. Mon–Thurs noon–9.30pm, Fri & Sat till 10.30pm.

Pittsfield and around

Once a prosperous industrial centre, **PITTSFIELD** is now one of the least attractive towns in the Berkshires, though it does boast a couple of worthy attractions in the form of the **Berkshire Museum** and Herman Melville's home, **Arrowhead**. It's also become an unlikely claimant to the title of "**birthplace of baseball**".

Berkshire Athenaeum

1 Wendell Ave, at Rte-9 • Summer Mon, Wed & Fri 9am–5pm, Tues & Thurs till 9pm, Sat 10am–9pm; winter Mon & Fri 9am–5pm, Tues–Thurs till 9pm, Sat 10am–5pm • Free • ☎ 413 499 9480, ⓦ pittsfieldlibrary.org

In 2004, historian John Thorn went public with a controversial discovery: he had uncovered a 1791 Pittsfield town ordinance that outlawed baseball nearly half a century before its "invention" in 1839 by Abner Doubleday in Cooperstown, NY. You can view a copy of the "**Broken Window Bylaw**" at the public library, the **Berkshire Athenaeum** – the original is locked away in the library vault. You'll find the copy at the entrance to the Local History section – inside is the **Melville Memorial Room**, dedicated to the author of *Moby Dick* and crammed with mementos and personal effects (books, passport and his desk).

Berkshire Museum

39 South St (Rte-7) • Mon–Wed, Fri & Sat 10am–5pm, Thurs till 10am–8pm, Sun noon–5pm • $13, children (3–18 years) $6 • ☎ 413 443 7171, ⓦ berkshiremuseum.org

Founded in 1903, the slick **Berkshire Museum** has something for everyone, though its fine art exhibits, aquarium with touch-tank and hands-on "innovation" hall will primarily appeal to kids; the dinosaurs and mummies probably will, too. The art gallery includes work from **Norman Rockwell** and the Hudson River School, including *Valley of the Santa Ysabel* by **Frederic Church**, and there's a special exhibit of nine original wooden push-and-pull toys created by **Alexander Calder** in 1927.

Arrowhead

780 Holmes Rd • Late May to Oct daily 9.30am–4pm • $13 • ☎ 413 442 1793, ⓦ mobydick.org

Hard to believe today, but when poor old **Herman Melville** sold **Arrowhead**, the eighteenth-century farmhouse where he and his family had lived for thirteen years, he was considered a failure. The author moved to Pittsfield from New York in 1850, but despite finishing *Moby Dick* here he remained best-known for his first two vaguely autobiographical novels about Tahiti – *Typee* (1846) and *Omoo* (1847). The commercial failure of *Moby Dick* brought on bouts of depression and illness – Melville moved back to New York in 1863 and died there in 1891, and it wasn't until the 1930s that his literary reputation (and that of the white whale) was restored.

Guided tours of his creaking wooden home – which dates from 1796 – add colour to his life and work. Highlights include the upstairs study where he penned the famous novel, and the adjacent bedroom where **Nathanial Hawthorne** once spent the night (the two authors met and became friends in Pittsfield in 1850).

Hancock Shaker Village

1843 W Housatonic St (Rte-20, at Rte-41) • Daily: mid-April to late May 10am–4pm; late May to Oct till 5pm • $17, children 7–12 years $4, children 13–17 years $8 • ☎ 413 443 0188, ⓦ hancockshakervillage.org

From 1790 until 1960, the **Hancock Shaker Village**, five miles west of Pittsfield, was an active **Shaker community**, and today offers an illuminating insight into this remarkable

Christian sect. The visitor centre contains temporary exhibits and an introductory eight-minute film on loop – the Shakers were a branch of the Quakers that had fled England to America in 1774, named for the convulsive fits of glee they experienced when worshipping. Best-known today for their simple but elegant furniture, they all but disappeared during the twentieth century, largely due to the members' vows of celibacy (see box, p.408).

Hancock was the third Shaker village ever established, and retains one of the biggest collections of furniture and objects. Its eighteen preserved buildings, located in fairly close proximity amid 1200 acres, include the ingenious **Round Stone Barn**, rebuilt in the 1860s and the only one of its kind. The village keeps extensive vegetable gardens and its own pigs, cows and merino sheep – you can see them in an extension to the Round Stone Barn. Other highlights include the huge **Brick Dwelling** (1830), where up to one hundred Shakers slept and ate in basic but brightly painted rooms, and the hands-on **Discovery Room**, where kids (and adults) can try working a loom, model Shaker fashions or milk a mechanical cow (aka "Mary Jane"). The free **audio guides** add plenty of detail and context. Don't miss the ice cream shop on site operated by *Soco Creamery*.

ARRIVAL AND INFORMATION

PITTSFIELD AND AROUND

By bus One or two Peter Pan buses a day from Springfield stop at Pittsfield (at the bus terminal, 1 Columbus Ave). BRTA (Mon–Sat only; $1.25; ☎ 413 499 2782 or ☎ 1 800 292 2782, ⊛ berkshirerta.com) buses link Pittsfield with Great Barrington, Stockbridge, Lenox, Lee, Williamstown and North Adams.

Pittsfield Visitors Center 179 South St, US-7 (Tues–Sun 10am–4.30pm; ☎ 413 499 9747, ⊛ pittsfield.com).

ACCOMMODATION

Berkshire Inn 150 West Housatonic St (Rte-20) ☎ 413 443 3000, ⊛ berkshireinn-ma.com. Solid budget option, offering clean motel-style rooms with microwave and cable TV, and a small pool in summer. **$80**

White Horse Inn 378 South St (Rte-20) ☎ 413 442 2512, ⊛ whitehorsebb. Enchanting colonial B&B constructed around the turn of the century; rooms have been stylishly renovated, with a simple, contemporary design. **$140**

EATING AND DRINKING

★ **Elizabeth's Restaurant Inc** 1264 East St ☎ 413 448 8244. Informal restaurant featuring home-style vegetarian cooking that you eat in the small kitchen – portions are meant to share. Try the veggie lasagne. Usually three meat options on the menu too. Mains average $20. Reservations essential. Daily 5–9pm; winter closed Sun & Mon.

Flavours 75 North St, entrance at 62 McKay St ☎ 413 443 3188, ⊛ flavoursintheberkshires.com. This wildly popular Malaysian restaurant makes a good break from the usual pub fare around here, with plenty of choices for vegetarians and live music at the weekends. Tues–Fri 11.30am–2.30pm & 4.30–9.30pm, Sat & Sun 4–9.30pm.

Patrick's Pub 26 Bank Row ☎ 413 499 1994, ⊛ patricksinpittsfield.com. Right in the centre, this no-nonsense Irish pub is the best place for a drink. Mon–Thurs & Sun 4.30–11.30pm, Fri & Sat 11.30am–12.30am.

Williamstown

Founded in 1765 at the most northwestern corner of the state, bucolic **WILLIAMSTOWN** may seem a bit remote to be one of the region's premier art destinations, but the presence of the **Clark**, with its excellent Impressionist collections, as well as the **Williams College Museum of Art**, has put it on the map. These, plus the tranquil Williams College campus – which essentially forms the centre of the town – make Williamstown a choice spot to spend a few days. Save for during the summertime **Williamstown Theatre Festival** (see box, p.231), most of the action centres on block-long Spring Street, with the requisite range of shops and restaurants, most infused with an unmistakable collegiate atmosphere.

The Clark

25 South St • July & Aug daily 10am–5pm; Sept–June Tues–Sun same hours • $15; free mid-Oct to May; combination with Norman Rockwell Museum (see p.227) or MASS MoCA (see p.236) $28 • 413 458 2303, clarknow.org

Surrounded by forest on the edge of town, **The Clark**, founded in 1955 by wealthy art collectors Sterling and Francine Clark, houses an easily digestible but incredibly rich collection of American and European art from the eighteenth to early twentieth centuries.

Highlights include an astounding ensemble of French Impressionist paintings, including some **Monet** beauties and 32 by **Renoir**; look out for *At the Concert* (1880), which established Renoir's niche of beautiful women in fashionable clothing. The Manton Collection includes some important British work by the likes of Gainsborough and **Constable**, including his early masterpiece, *The Wheatfield* (1816). **Turner**'s work includes the semi-abstract *Off Ramsgate*. Don't overlook the **Italian Renaissance** gallery, with small but precious works from Piero della Francesca, Luca Signorelli and Umbrian master Perugino. The Clark's American paintings feature classics from Sargent and Winslow Homer (*The Bridle Path* and *Undertow* among them), while Remington's *The Scout: Friends or Foes* details the anxiety and loneliness of looking into the future; his *Dismounted* is one of the most reproduced images of the American West. Take time also to check out the futuristic **Stone Hill Center** up the slope (golf carts run between the two buildings in summer, but you can also walk), designed by Japanese architect Tadao Ando and housing small but striking contemporary exhibits. Ando's **new visitor centre**, which will transform the Clark, is slated to open in 2014.

Williams College Museum of Art

15 Lawrence Hall Drive • Tues–Sat 10am–5pm, Sun 1–5pm • Free • 413 597 2429, wcma.williams.edu

The **Williams College Museum of Art** is ravishing for both its architecture and its collections; part of the museum is housed in an 1846 two-storey brick octagon, capped by a Neoclassical rotunda, while a striking three-story entrance atrium connects it to a contemporary addition. The thrust of the exceedingly well-curated collection is American visual art from the late eighteenth century to the present day, including the world's largest repository of work by brothers **Maurice** and **Charles Prendergast**. Look out also for a copy of the US **Bill of Rights** and other founding documents.

ARRIVAL AND DEPARTURE   WILLIAMSTOWN

By bus BRTA (Mon–Sat only; $1.25; 413 499-2782 or 1 800 292 2782, berkshirerta.com) buses link Williamstown with Pittsfield and North Adams.

ACCOMMODATION

1896 House 910 Cold Spring Rd (US-7) 413 458 1896, 1896house.com. Close to the centre of Williamstown, this hostelry proffers spotless rooms in three atmospheric properties—"Brookside", "Pondside" and "Barnside" – as well as a good restaurant. **$102**

The Birches 522 White Oaks Rd 413 458 8134, birchesbb.com. Three rooms (two with shared bathroom) in a 1900 cottage on fifty very scenic acres with an orchard and spring-fed pond; the breakfast is as filling as the environs are relaxing, and it's just two miles from the centre of town. **$100**

★ **The Guest House at Field Farm** 554 Sloan Rd 413 458 3135, guesthouseatfieldfarm .thetrustees.org. Six stylish bedrooms, each with private bathroom, in a 1948 Bauhaus-inspired country house littered with modern art and surrounded by more than three hundred acres of meadows and woodlands. **$175**

Maple Terrace Motel 555 Main St (Rte-2) 413 458 9677, mapleterrace.com. More like a country inn than a motel, with worldly-wise Swedish owners and comfy rooms within easy walking distance of the Williamstown Theatre Festival. **$125**

EATING AND DRINKING

Hobson's Choice 159 Water St 413 458 9101, hobsonsrestaurant.com. This country manor with beamed ceilings is a local favourite, known for locally sourced steaks, prime rib, various chicken dishes, Cajun shrimp, blackened Norwegian salmon and Alaskan king crab. Mains average $15–24. Daily 5–9pm.

★ **Mezze** 777 Cold Spring Rd (US-7) ☎413 458 0123, ⓦmezzerestaurant.com. Urban contemporary meets rural gentility. Mediterranean, Moroccan and American-influenced dishes, like braised rabbit and home-made pasta, sesame-seared organic tofu and lamb with thyme, jump off the seasonal and locally sourced menu. Dinner only; mains $19–32. July & Aug Mon & Sun 5–9pm, Tues–Thurs till 10pm, Fri & Sat till 11pm.

Pappa Charlie's Deli 28 Spring St ☎413 458 5969.

From chicken cordon bleu to the "Bo Derek" – a sandwich with peppers, onions, tomatoes, melted provolone sprouts and tomatoes – they do hot, cold and vegetarian light fare with flair ($5–6). Best place for breakfast. Mon–Sat 8am–8pm, Sun till 7pm.

The Water Street Grill 123 Water St (Rte-43) ☎41. 458 2175, ⓦwaterstgrill.com. This is a safe choice for American and Tex-Mex dining. From blackened catfish to grilled sirloin. Nothing too exciting, but it's all done well. Lunch mains $8.95–12.95. Daily noon–11pm.

North Adams and around

Settled in the 1730s, **NORTH ADAMS**, five miles east of Williamstown on the Hoosic River, was a fairly prosperous textile mill town in the nineteenth century. When Sprague Electric closed in 1985 it might have ended up being just another post-industrial eyesore were it not for the **Massachusetts Museum of Contemporary Art**, one of the region's most spectacular galleries.

Massachusetts Museum of Contemporary Art

287 Marshall St • July & Aug daily 10am–6pm; Sept–June Mon & Wed–Sun 11am–5pm • $15; combination ticket with Norman Rockwell Museum (see p.227) or The Clark (see p.235) $28 • Free guided tours run daily 11am, 1pm & 4pm • ☎413 662 2111, ⓦmassmoca.org

The vast **Massachusetts Museum of Contemporary Art** (aka MASS MoCA) is housed in a resurrected textile mill dating from the 1870s, and the setting itself is part of the attraction: exhibits are displayed in its 27 artfully refurbished red-brick and timber buildings, linked by a web of bridges, passageways, viaducts and courtyards. Most of the work is installation-oriented (displayed for up to ten months only; the museum has no permanent collection), thought-provoking and very often mind-blowing. There are some long-term installations, though, notably the **upside-down trees** at the entrance (*Tree Logic* by Natalie Jeremijenko), the stunning sound-installation in the old boiler room by Stephen Vitiello (*All Those Vanished Engines*), and the wonderfully quirky *All Utopias Fell* by Michael Oatman (involving an Airstream trailer). The real highlight, however, is the **LeWitt Retrospective** (Building 7), another long-term display that incorporates an astounding 105 drawings from the seminal conceptual artist.

LeWitt Retrospective

Sol LeWitt's mind-bending art has been installed over three massive floors and arranged, uniquely, as per the artist's instructions just before he died in 2007. There's a lot to take in here, so take it slow and start with the early work on the lower floor. His first key creation is here, *Wall Drawing No. 11* (1968), as well as the holographic peg drawing he created first in Tokyo (*Wall Drawing No. 38;* 1970). *Wall Drawing No. 46* (1970) is a touching tribute to fellow artist Eva Hesse. The next floor tackles LeWitt's middle career, beginning with the "15 bands" (*Wall Drawing 422*; 1984), a barrage of colour. The upper floor showcases his later shiny, industrial-like work and plays more with optical illusions (note the eye's inability to focus on orange/green borders). The final series of complex "scribble drawings" are magnificent – the last one was created in 2008, after Sol's death.

Mount Greylock State Reservation

30 Rockwell Rd • **Mount Greylock State Reservation** Daily sunrise–sunset; access road late May to Oct daily 9am–5pm • Parking $2 **Mount Greylock Visitor Center** 30 Rockwell Rd, Lanesborough • Daily: mid-May to early Sept 9am–5pm; early Sept to mid-May till 4.30pm • ☎413 499 4262 **Western Gateway Heritage State Park** 115 State St, Building 4, North Adams • Daily 10am–5pm • ☎413 663 6312

The densely wooded slopes of the 12,500-acre **Mount Greylock State Reservation** contain the tallest peak in Massachusetts at 3491ft, providing a mesmerizing perch

DOWN STREET ART

Each summer (late June to mid-Oct), **Down Street Art** (☎413 663 5253, ⦿downstreetart .org) brings an exciting programme of art events, exhibitions, video screenings and installations to downtown North Adams. The last Thursdays of each month all Down Street Art galleries and venues stay open late, along with shops and restaurants. However, the town is studded with galleries all year round. Some of the highlights are listed below:

Brill Gallery Eclipse Mill Studio 109, 243 Union St ☎1 800 294 2811, ⦿brillgallery109.com. High quality paintings, photography and sculptures from international and regional artists. Fri–Sun noon–6pm.

NAACO Gallery 33 Main St ☎413 664-4003, ⦿naacogallery.org. Independently member-run organization of over 35 active (primarily local) artists. Mon, Thurs–Sat 11am– 6pm, Sun noon–4pm.

MCLA Gallery 51 51 Main St ⦿mcla.edu. Run by the Massachusetts College of Liberal Arts, showing work from emerging and mid-career contemporary artists. Daily 10am–6pm.

River Hill Pottery Eclipse Mill Studio 104, 243 Union St ☎413 664 0197, ⦿riverhillpottery.com. Gallery and working studio of Gail and Phil Sellers. Daily 10am–5pm.

above three states on a clear day. The reserve is crisscrossed with scenic walking trails, but you can also drive to the top from North Adams or Pittsfield via seven-mile winding roads. The granite **War Memorial Tower**, a 92ft lighthouse erected in 1933 to honour the Massachusetts casualties of all wars, stands at the top – you can climb up for 360-degree views of the whole region. Also on the summit, **Bascom Lodge** (see below), a sturdy cottage built in 1937, offers a café and basic accommodation – perfect for hikers.

You can access the mountain from North Adams via Notch Road off Rte-2; grab a trail map at the **Western Gateway Heritage State Park** offices in North Adams, or at the **Mount Greylock Visitor Center**, 1.5 miles north of Lanesborough on North Main Road.

ARRIVAL AND DEPARTURE

NORTH ADAMS AND AROUND

By bus Berkshire Regional Transit Authority buses (Mon–Sat only; $1.25; ☎413 499 2782 or ☎1 800 292 2782, ⦿berkshireta.com) link North Adams with Pittsfield and Williamstown.

ACCOMMODATION, EATING AND DRINKING

NORTH ADAMS

Freightyard Pub Western Gateway Heritage State Park, 1 Furnace St ☎413 663 6547, ⦿freightyardpub .com. The town's best late-night drinking spot, which specializes in great live music (Fri & Sat) and excellent pub fare (try the chilli). Daily 11.30am–midnight.

Gramercy Bistro MASS MoCA, 87 Marshall St ☎413 663 5300, ⦿gramercybistro.com. Contemporary American cuisine with a focus on local produce. Dinner main dishes $18–25. Mon & Tues 5–9pm, Wed–Sat noon–2pm & 5–10pm, Sun 11am–2pm & 5–9pm.

Holiday Inn 40 Main St ☎413 663 6500, ⦿hinorthadams.com. Just minutes from the action, this is a comfortable but affordable option, with spacious rooms and free wi-fi. $144

★ **The Porches Inn** 231 River St ☎413 664 0400, ⦿porches.com. Just across the street from MASS MoCA, this is an ultramodern hotel with DVD players, free wi-fi, and nary an antique in sight. It occupies a row of houses formerly lived in by mill workers. $180

MOUNT GREYLOCK STATE RESERVATION

Boscom Lodge Mount Greylock (summit) ☎413 743 1591, ⦿bascomlodge.net. This no-frills stone-and-wood lodge on top of Mount Greylock offers basic but cosy lodgings (private rooms and co-ed dorms, all with shared bathrooms), primarily aimed at hikers. June–Oct daily 8am–10am & 11am–4.30pm (dinner 7pm for residents only). Doubles $125; dorms $35

3

Rhode Island

243 Providence and around

251 Blackstone River Valley

252 Newport

262 Around Newport

264 South County

268 Block Island

BANNISTER'S WHARF, NEWPORT

Rhode Island

Just 48 miles north to south by 37 miles east to west, Rhode Island may be the smallest state in the Union, but its influence on national life has been disproportionately large: on May 18, 1652, the territory enacted the first law against slavery in North America; just over ten years later, it was the first to guarantee religious freedom. In addition to this fruitful cultural history, the state is also surprisingly land-rich, with more than four hundred miles of spectacular coastline and thousands of acres of pristine woodlands.

In addition to mainland Rhode Island, the state is made up of over thirty tiny islands in the surrounding **Narragansett Bay**, including Hope, Despair, and Rhode Island itself (better known by its Native American title, "Aquidneck"), which gives the state its name – lore has it that in 1524 Italian explorer Giovanni da Verrazzano spotted this island from the sea, and named it for its resemblance to the Greek isle of Rhodes (one can only surmise it was foggy, or there was rum involved). The bay itself has long been a determining factor in Rhode Island's economic development, with the "**Ocean State**" prospering through sea trade, whaling and smuggling until the nineteenth century, when the focus shifted inland, and to manufacturing.

Today, the state's principal destinations are its two original ports: **Providence**, home of Brown University, and **Newport**, a town of outrageously extravagant mansions that once belonged to America's most prominent families, and still a major yachting centre. Further west, lining the coast along US-1 are the lively small towns and fishing ports of the state's **South County**, most notably **Watch Hill** and **Galilee**; ferries run from the latter to **Block Island**, a tiny, undeveloped bump of land with sandy beaches and endless ocean views. Inland, northeastern Rhode Island boasts the woodsy **Blackstone River Valley**, an important player in the Industrial Revolution, and now home to a number of old mills and some wonderful hiking.

Be sure to try Rhode Island's unique culinary specialties: **coffee milk** (milk with coffee syrup), "**coffee cabinets**" (a milkshake prepared by blending ice cream with milk and coffee syrup), the **New York System-style wiener** and **Del's frozen lemonade**, a blend of crushed ice, lemon juice and sugar that traces its origins back to a humble 1940s food cart, now sold across the state.

Brief history

In 1636, London-born **Reverend Roger Williams** was exiled from the Massachusetts Bay Colony for espousing such radical ideas as the separation of church and state and Native American rights. Moving south, he established the colony of **Providence**, on the Narragansett Bay, as a "lively experiment" in religious freedom – he finally secured a charter from Charles II guaranteeing **religious freedom** in the colony in 1663. Other Massachusetts exiles followed Williams, and Providence, Portsmouth and Newport combined as the "Colony of Rhode Island and Providence Plantations" in the 1640s. The colony soon became a safe haven for Baptists,

WaterFire p.247
Rhode Island's New York hot dogs p.249
Coffee, but not as you know it p.250
The curious case of the Newport Vikings p.254

Festive Newport p.259
White sands and surfing: South County beaches p.265
Block Island's beaches p.271

NEWPORT FOLK FESTIVAL

Highlights

❶ **Providence** Excellent food, the Waterfire Festival, Brown University and some of the finest colonial architecture in the US awaits in Rhode Island's capital. **See p.243**

❷ **RISD Museum of Art** Exceptional art and design museum with an eclectic collection that ranges from the French Impressionists to ancient buddhas from Japan. **See p.246**

❸ **Blackstone River Valley** Visit the cradle of America's Industrial Revolution, with Samuel Slater's original cotton mill and boat trips along the Blackstone River. **See p.251**

❹ **Newport** With its phenomenal mansions, fine beaches, fancy yachts and world-class summer music concerts, this coastal town has real appeal. **See p.252**

❺ **South County beaches** Welcome to endless shores, sandy dunes and lighthouses jutting out on rocky promontories. **See p.265**

❻ **Mohegan Bluffs, Block Island** Experience pure desolation at 200ft up, peering down on the Atlantic below. **See p.270**

HIGHLIGHTS ARE MARKED ON THE MAP ON P.242

Quakers and Jews, though attempts to ban slavery failed, and Newport went on to became a major **slave trade centre**.

Rhode Island flourished thanks to its growing maritime commerce and it was the first state to declare independence from Britain, in May 1776, but the last to ratify the US Constitution, in May 1790. Between the Revolution and the Civil War, the state's economic focus shifted from maritime trade to manufacturing, with the Blackstone

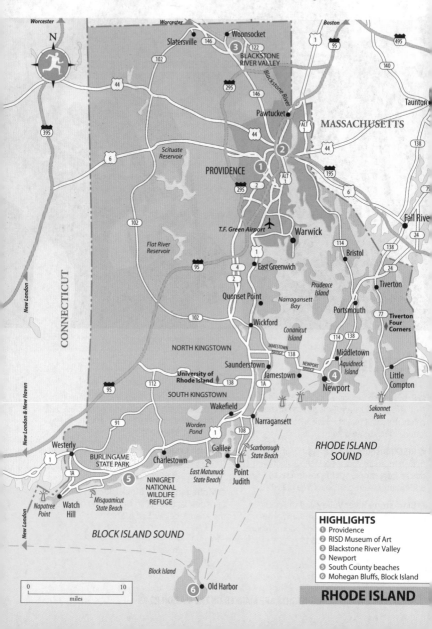

HIGHLIGHTS
1. Providence
2. RISD Museum of Art
3. Blackstone River Valley
4. Newport
5. South County beaches
6. Mohegan Bluffs, Block Island

RHODE ISLAND

Valley region playing a large role in the **Industrial Revolution**. In 1793, Pawtucket became the site of the nation's first water-powered **textile mill**, the brainchild of entrepreneur Samuel Slater. The textile industry lured thousands of immigrant workers to Rhode Island, contributing to the diverse ethnic mix that exists today; manufacturing also continues to play an important role.

Since the 1930s Rhode Island has been staunchly **Democrat** territory, with comprehensive health insurance for low-income children and a large social security net; in 2011 legislation was passed to allow the use of medical marijuana, and to allow same-sex civil unions.

INFORMATION   RHODE ISLAND

Tourist information The official website of the Rhode Island Tourism Division is ⓦ visitrhodeisland.com, loaded with all sorts of useful information. Other useful sites with current listings and information belong to the Edible Rhody magazine (ⓦ ediblecommunities.com/rhody/), ⓦ quahog .org and Motif Magazine (ⓦ motifmagazine.net).

Providence and around

Stretching across seven hills on the Providence and Seekonk rivers, **PROVIDENCE** was Rhode Island's first settlement, established "in commemoration of God's Providence" on land given to **Roger Williams** by the Narragansett Indians in 1636. The state's **capital** since 1790, today Providence is one of the three largest cities in New England, with a vibrant arts scene epitomized by the likes of multipurpose venue **AS220**, excellent restaurants and lots of students, drawn by the city's prestigious higher-education institutions. The aggressive urban renewal that took place all over Rhode Island in the late 1990s was especially effective here, utterly transforming the once bleak industrial landscape – while some grim pockets remain, the downtown area, known as **Downcity**, now gleams with new buildings, prompting Rhode Island natives the **Farrelly Brothers** to set their movie *There's Something About Mary* here in 1998.

Just as enticing are the city's historic **neighbourhoods**: west of Downcity, the vibrant Italian community on **Federal Hill** boasts some exceptional restaurants, while east of the river lies **College Hill**, the oldest part of town, home to the campuses of **Brown University** and the **Rhode Island School of Design**, one of the nation's top art schools. In this area, **Benefit Street** is particularly atmospheric, with many historic buildings – in fact, the city holds one of the finest collections of colonial and early Federal buildings in the nation.

Downtown

Providence's downtown, or **Downcity**, centres on **Kennedy Plaza**, a large public square that houses the city's transport centre. At the southwestern corner of the plaza, **City Hall** was completed in 1878, designed in the Second Empire style of the Louvre and the Tuileries palaces in Paris. Nearby **Westminster Street** is especially good for independent shops and cafés (see ⓦ shopdowncity.com).

State Capitol

82 Smith St • Mon–Fri 8.30am–4.30pm; closed holidays • Free • Call ahead for guided tours ☎ 401 222 2357

Just north of Downtown at the top of Constitution Hill, the **State Capitol** dominates the city skyline with a vast dome, purportedly the fourth largest self-supported marble dome in the world. Constructed between 1895 and 1904 by noted architects McKim, Mead & White, it's been the home of the state's General Assembly (legislature) since 1901. Tours (50min) start at the Rotunda, where you can gaze upward into the cavernous dome, decorated by *The Four Freedoms* mural by Rhode Island artist James Allen King. On the second floor you normally view the original **Rhode Island Charter** of 1663 (protected in a steel vault), the magnificent Senate and House chambers, and the State Room, the lavish formal entrance to the Governor's Office. This is where one

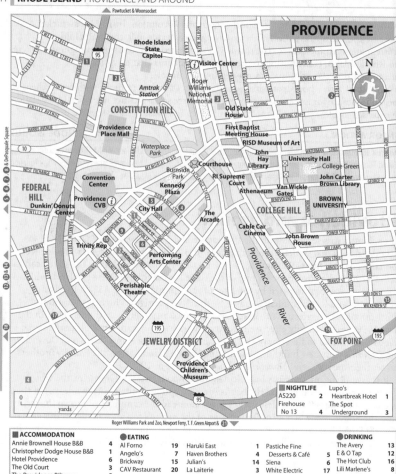

PROVIDENCE

of Gilbert Stuart's famous **paintings of George Washington** hangs, one of several copies he produced of what's known as the "Lansdowne portrait" (Stuart was born in Rhode Island in 1755).

Roger Williams National Memorial

282 N Main St • Mid-May to mid-Oct daily 9am–5pm; mid-Oct to mid-May till 4.30pm • Free • ☎ 401 521 7266, ⓦ nps.gov/rowi • Accessible on foot or via RIPTA buses #51, #52, #53, #54, #58, #72 and #99

Just across the Providence River from the State Capitol, the **Roger Williams National Memorial** was the site of the original settlement of Providence in 1636. It's now a four-acre park honouring the life of the founder of Rhode Island, also remembered for being one of colonial America's most ardent champions of religious freedom. There's not much to see in the park itself, but the small **visitor centre** at the north end includes replicas of Williams' compass and his annotated Bible – a short film provides historical context.

College Hill

Much of Providence's historic legacy can be found across the river from Downcity in the **College Hill** area, an attractive tree-lined district of colonial buildings that is also home to the historic 133-acre Ivy League campus of **Brown University**. The **Thayer Street** and the neighbouring lanes are home to bookstores, tattoo parlours and thrift stores, while at the southern end of the district, **Wickenden Street** buzzes with cafés, galleries and restaurants.

Brown University

Stephen Robert Campus Center 75 Waterman St • Term time Mon–Thurs 7.30am–11pm, Fri 7am–1am, Sat 8.30am–1am, Sun till 11pm; summer hours Mon–Fri 7.30am–4pm; guided 1hr tours Mon–Fri 9am, 11am, 1pm, 3pm & some Saturdays • Free • ☎ 401 863 1000, Ⓦ brown .edu **John Hay Library** 20 Prospect St • Term time Mon–Thurs 10am–6pm, Fri till 5pm; summer Mon–Fri 10am–5pm • ☎ 401 863 3723

The third oldest college in New England, and seventh oldest in the nation, **Brown University** was founded in 1764 in Warren as Rhode Island College; six years later it was moved to Providence, where it was renamed after graduate and donor Nicholas Brown, Jr. Brown has long been known for its creative, liberal and hip student body, attracting the likes of actress Laura Linney, actor John Krasinski (of the US version of TV show *The Office*) and most recently, Emma Watson of *Harry Potter* fame. Current faculty members include Nigerian novelist Chinua Achebe. Guided tours are offered on weekdays and select Saturdays from the Welcome Center at the **Stephen Robert Campus Center** (75 Waterman St), but you can pick up a self-guided tour map from here any day.

On Prospect Street, the huge wrought-iron **Van Wickle Gates** – opened only for incoming students in the fall and graduates in the spring (you can get in through side entrances the rest of the year) – lead onto the core of the university, the pleasant **College Green**, which is skirted by a collection of colonial and Greek Revival buildings. Among them are the 1904 Beaux Arts **John Carter Brown Library**, which holds a rich trove of early historical materials on the Americas, and nearby **University Hall**, the institution's oldest building. Dating to 1770, it was used as barracks for Continental troops during the Revolutionary War. Across the street, the English Renaissance-style **John Hay Library** houses a vast collection of rare books and special collections.

Benefit Street

Take some time to wander along **Benefit Street**, on the western edge of College Hill, a leafy thoroughfare lined with beautifully restored residences that once belonged to merchants and sea captains. This is Providence's "mile of history", with one of the most impressive collections of original colonial and Federal homes in America, most of which remain privately owned – several date from the 1780s (the oldest house in College Hill is actually the **Benjamin Cushing House**, just off Benefit at 40 N Court St, built in 1737). The Rhode Island Historical Society offers guided **walking tours** (see p.248).

John Brown House

52 Power St • April–Nov Tues–Fri 1–4pm, tours 1.30am & 3pm, Sat 10am–4pm, tours 10.30am, noon, 1.30pm & 3pm; Dec–March Fri & Sat 10am–4pm, tours 10.30am, noon, 1.30pm & 3pm • $8 • ☎ 401 273 7507, Ⓦ rihs.org

Completed in 1788, the three-story **John Brown House** is one of the grandest mansions in Providence, testimony to one of the city's most successful merchants. There's a lovely central hall and many original furnishings, as well as displays on the formidable Brown family, the slave trade and Rhode Island history. No relation to the famous abolitionist, on the contrary this **John Brown** (1736–1803) was heavily involved in the slave trade, as well as initiating US – China trade in 1787. The **Concert under the Elms** series every summer (July & Aug; $8) serves up classical, blues, jazz and pop music in the gardens.

Old State House

150 Benefit St • Mon–Fri 8.30am–4.30pm • Free • ☎ 401 222 2678, Ⓦ www.preservation.ri.gov

Facing the southeastern corner of Roger Williams National Memorial Park, the plain but dignified 1762 **Old State House**, current home of the Rhode Island Historical Preservation

& Heritage Commission, is of note for the courtroom where the Rhode Island General Assembly renounced allegiance to Britain on May 4, 1776. The lobby contains a small exhibit on the building, and during office hours, visitors can visit the famed courtroom, a simple space with original eighteenth-century bevelled panelling and mouldings.

First Baptist Meeting House

75 N Main St • Mon–Fri 10am–noon & 1–3pm • $2 • ☎ 401 454 3418, ⓦ firstbaptistchurchinamerica.org

Located between Benefit Street and North Main Street, the elegant white clapboard **First Baptist Meeting House** is home to the oldest Baptist congregation in America, established by Roger Williams himself in 1638. The current Georgian beauty, with its 185ft steeple, was completed in 1775.

RISD Museum of Art

224 Benefit St, second entrance at 20 N Main St • Tues–Sun 10am–5pm; closed Aug • $10, free Sun mornings & last Sat of the month • ☎ 401 454 6500, ⓦ risdmuseum.org

Providence's second major college is the prestigious **Rhode Island School of Design** (ⓦ risd.edu) founded in 1877, with artist Dale Chihuly and director Gus Van Sant among its alumni. The school's impressive **Museum of Art** houses more than 80,000 works in 45 galleries, a hodgepodge of five industrial buildings and houses between Benefit and Main streets skilfully melded into one museum. The collection covers everything from ancient Egypt to Asian arts and European painting from just about every period – though quality varies, everything is superbly presented and the galleries are small enough to absorb easily. Make sure you grab a floor plan at the entrance, as the museum layout can be confusing; the galleries are on floors three to six.

Third and fourth floors

Most visits start at the third and fourth floors, where highlights include the cleverly curated **Central Gallery** of twentieth-century art and design from the likes of Mark Rothko, Pollock, Rauschenberg and Matisse. Don't skip the two **nineteenth-century American galleries**, where Winslow Homer's *Fishin'* and *On a Lee Shore* are displayed with Thomas Cole landscapes and work from James Abbott McNeill Whistler, John Singer Sargent and J. Alden Weir. *Summer* by American impressionist Frank W. Benson is one of the museum's lesser-known gems.

Fifth floor

The fifth floor charts the history of European art from early Greek and Roman times. Most of the later artwork is mediocre, though the appeal of the **Main Gallery** is more about its stunning classical layout than the individual paintings on display. The museum's **Impressionists** are worth lingering over, though; there are some exquisite paintings from Monet, Cézanne and Renoir, as well as Manet's sublime *Repose*.

Sixth floor and Pendleton House

The sixth floor covers more exotic ground, with a precious wooden **Buddha** from Japan (1150–1200), opulent Indian jewellery and an astonishing bright blue hippo made out of faïence (a non-clay based ceramic), from ancient Egypt. The connected **Pendleton House** was built in 1906 as a replica of the Federal-style residence of collector and benefactor Charles L. Pendleton – each room showcases a different style of American decorative arts.

Providence Athenaeum

251 Benefit St • Sept–May Mon–Thurs 9am–7pm, Fri & Sat till 5pm, Sun 1–5pm; June–Aug closed Sat afternoon & Sun • Free • ☎ 401 421 6970, ⓦ providenceathenaeum.org

Opened in 1838, the handsome Greek Revival **Providence Athenaeum** is one of America's oldest libraries, still operating as a library and cultural centre today. It's worth a quick peek

> **WATERFIRE**
>
> Throughout the summer months, the spectacular event known as **WaterFire** (select Sat evenings May–Oct; free; ⓦ waterfire.org) enthrals visitors and locals alike with one hundred bonfires set at sunset along the centre of the Providence River. Tended by gondoliers and accompanied by music, the fires burn until just past midnight, while entertainers and food vendors keep the crowds happy. Try and book the special boat trips (see website) or a gondola journey (see p.248) along the river if you can, for an unforgettably close encounter with the fires.

inside its intimate Victorian wooden interior, overflowing with antiquated bookshelves. Edgar Allen Poe supposedly courted poet Sarah Whitman here, and it was also a favourite haunt of local writer of weird and wacky fiction, H.P. Lovecraft (1890–1937).

Federal Hill

West of Downcity, **Federal Hill** – informally considered Providence's **Little Italy** – can be entered through an arch topped with a bronze pine cone, the Italian symbol for hospitality, at Atwells Avenue. Settled by Italian immigrants in the 1910s and 1920s, this area is now one of the friendliest in the city, where you can savour the nuances of Italian culture in dozens of restaurants, bakeries and shops. For drinks, head to the bars and cafés (see p.249) around lively **DePasquale Square**, where there's a large Italianate fountain surrounded by blooming flowers in summer.

4

South of the city

South of downtown, Providence contains a handful of attractions that will especially appeal to families, starting with the **Providence Children's Museum**. **Roger Williams Park Zoo** contains plenty of exotic animals and activities for little ones, while adults (and gourmands) will have more fun at the **Culinary Arts Museum**.

Providence Children's Museum

100 South St • April–Aug daily 9am–6pm; Sept–March Tues–Sun till 6pm • $8.50, free for children under 1 • ☎ 401 273 5437, ⓦ childrenmuseum.org • RIPTA bus #1, #3, #9

Just south of Downcity, in the Jewelry District, the entertaining **Providence Children's Museum** offers interactive displays that include teeth in a giant mouth, a walk-in kaleidoscope and a time-travelling adventure through Rhode Island's history.

Culinary Arts Museum

315 Harborside Blvd • Tues–Sun 10am–5pm • $7 • ☎ 401 598 2805, ⓦ culinary.org • RIPTA bus #3

Around four miles south of downtown, off Narragansett Boulevard, the **Culinary Arts Museum** is part of the campus of Johnson & Wales University, one of the country's premier culinary colleges. The museum is a must-see for foodies, housing a wealth of food history, including ancient utensils, recipes and menus.

Roger Williams Park Zoo

1000 Elmwood Ave • Daily 9am–4pm (last admission 3.30pm) • $12, children (3–12 years) $8 • ☎ 401 785 3510, ⓦ rwpzoo.org • RIPTA bus #66 or Prairie Ave/Roger Williams Park Zoo bus ($2)

Located within Roger Williams Park, the **Roger Williams Zoo** is pretty good as zoos go, with plenty of cute-looking animals and hands-on activities to amuse young children. The grounds have been carefully laid out so that you can see everything on a long loop walk, with outdoor compounds for the bigger animals and climate-controlled indoor spaces for the smaller creatures. Though it contains some of the usual crowd-pleasers – giraffes, elephants, black bears ("moon bears"), gibbons, seals and snow leopards – be sure to seek out the more unusual wonders; the **red pandas** are almost as adorable as their giant Chinese cousins, while the rare **red wolf** is deceptively timid-looking. Other highlights include two flightless **bald eagles**, the bizarre-looking **giant anteater** and the Tropical America pavilion, where dopey **sloths** and **porcupines** share a space with frisky **tamarin monkeys**. If you visit around Halloween, be sure to check out the wonderful **Jack O Lantern Spectacular**.

ARRIVAL AND DEPARTURE

PROVIDENCE

By plane T.F. Green Airport (☎ 888 268 7222, ⓦ pvdairport .com) is served by most US carriers, with Cape Air (☎ 1 800 352 0714) also offering seasonal flights to Martha's Vineyard and Nantucket. The airport is on Post Road, I-95, exit 13 in Warwick, nine miles south of downtown Providence. RIPTA buses #14 and #20 (Mon–Fri 5.48am–11pm, Sat 5.32am–10.25pm, Sun 5.34am–7.55pm; $2) run to downtown Providence (Kennedy Plaza). Airport Taxi (☎ 401 737 2868 ⓦ airporttaxiri.com) runs a dedicated airport shuttle (daily 5am–7pm; $11) to the train station and select hotels downtown. Regular taxis should be around $32 to downtown. Cozy Cab (daily 8am–midnight; ☎ 401 846 2500, ⓦ cozytrans.com) runs a shuttle to Newport from the airport ($25).

By train The train station, 100 Gaspee St (☎ 1 800 872 7245), is served by Amtrak (☎ 1 800 872 7245, ⓦ amtrak .com) trains from Boston (50min; 20 daily; $14–43), New Haven (1hr 25min–1hr 50min; 18 daily; $36–102) and New York (around 3hr; 19 daily; $59–144), and the MBTA commuter rail from Boston (around 1hr; frequent; $8.25; ☎ 617 222 3200, ⓦ mbta.com). Taxis meet most trains.
By bus Greyhound (☎ 1 800 231 2222; ⓦ greyhound.com) and Peter Pan (☎ 1 800 443 1831, ⓦ peterpanbus.com) buses stop downtown at the city's transport centre, Kennedy Plaza. Main Greyhound destinations include Boston (1hr; 3 daily; from $10.80); and New York (5hr 25min; 3 daily; $36) via New London (1hr 45min; 3 daily; $26) and New Haven (2hr 45min; 3 daily; $28.50).

GETTING AROUND

By car You don't really need a car to explore Providence, but just in case, all the major car rental outfits are represented at the airport, including Hertz (☎ 401 738 3550) and Budget (☎ 401 739 8986); Enterprise has a location downtown at 90 Weybosset St (☎ 401 861 4408).
By taxi Taxis aren't always readily available on the street and can be arranged by calling Corporate Taxi (☎ 401 231 2228) or Yellow Cab (☎ 401 941 1122).
By bus The local RIPTA buses are easy to use and convenient (Kennedy Plaza ticket window Mon–Fri

7am–6pm, Sat 9am–noon & 1–5pm; $2/trip, $6/24hr pass; ☎ 401 781 9400, ⓦ ripta.com). Particularly useful are the two tourist-orientated "Providence Link" buses: bus #92 travels east–west from Federal Hill to Brown University, Wickendon Street and the East Side via Kennedy Plaza downtown, while bus #6 travels north–south connecting the Roger Williams Park Zoo with Washington Street and Kennedy Plaza. Buses tend to run every 20–30min from 6am–9pm weekdays, 8.30am–6.30pm Saturdays and 11am–6.30pm Sundays.

INFORMATION AND TOURS

Visitors' Information Center Rotunda lobby of the Rhode Island Convention Center, 1 Sabin St (Mon–Sat 9am–5pm; ☎ 401 751 1177 or ☎ 1 800 233 1636, ⓦ goprovidence.com). Well stocked with maps and brochures.
Walking tours The Rhode Island Historical Society leads enlightening walking tours of Benefit Street (June 15–Oct 15 Tues–Sat 11am; 1hr 30min; $12; ☎ 401 273 7507, ⓦ rihs.org), beginning at the elegant John Brown House.

Gondola tours If you're in the mood for a splurge or romantic getaway, La Gondola (☎ 401 421 8877, ⓦ gondolari.com) offers gentle rides on two authentic Venetian gondolas down the Woonasquatucket and Providence rivers, from where you have beautiful evening views of the city (May–Oct daily 5–11pm; 30–40min; $79–159 for two, $15 each for up to four additional passengers).

ACCOMMODATION

There are fairly few **budget** options downtown, though motorists will find a swath of mid-priced **motels** along I-95 towards Pawtucket, north of the city, and to the south near the airport.

Annie Brownell House B&B 400 Angell St ☎ 401 454 2934, ⓦ anniebrownellhouse.com. Four rooms in a lovely 1899 Colonial Revival clapboard house near Thayer Street, with rooms furnished in late Victorian style. Full, delicious hot breakfasts, free internet and friendly host. **$140**

Christopher Dodge House B&B 11 W Park St ☎ 401 351 6111, ⓦ providence-hotel.com. Small boutique hotel set in an Italianate town house dating from 1858, boasting 11ft ceilings, marble fireplaces and full breakfasts. Standard rooms are simply but comfortably decked out with free wi-fi and cable TV; superior rooms are a lot bigger. **$149**

Hotel Providence 139 Mathewson St ☎1 800 861 8990, ⊛thehotelprovidence.com. Newish luxury hotel with eighty plush and colourful rooms themed on classic novels from the likes of Tolstoy and Dumas, and a trendy restaurant downstairs (*Aspire*). Free wi-fi. **$199**

The Old Court 144 Benefit St ☎401 751 2002, ⊛oldcourt.com. Charming B&B in an old red-brick rectory near RISD, featuring ten Rococo Revival and Victorian-style rooms, all with private bathrooms and TV. Free wi-fi and rare free parking. **$145**

The Providence Biltmore 11 Dorrance St ☎401 421 0700, ⊛providencebiltmore.com. A Providence landmark since 1922, with a wide variety of impeccably refurbished rooms boasting enormous beds and flat-screen TVs. Free wi-fi but parking is $15/12hr, or $26/day or night. **$139**

★ **Renaissance Providence** 5 Ave of the Arts ☎401 919 5000, ⊛marriott.com. Luxurious new downtown hotel on the site of a former Masonic temple, with 272 comfortable, well-appointed rooms, some overlooking the State House. Five minutes' walk from the station. **$189**

EATING

Al Forno 577 S Main St ☎401 273 9760, ⊛alforno .com. One of the best restaurants in town. *Al Forno*'s relatively casual decor and simple menu belie the quality of the food: delicious Italian dishes, wood grills and roasts, with seasonal variations. Introduced "grilled pizza" to the US in 1980. Tues–Fri 5–10pm, Sat 4–10pm.

Angelo's 141 Atwells Ave ☎401 621 8171, ⊛angelosonthehill.com. A staple in Federal Hill since 1924, with homey, no-frills Italian fare, including pastas ($6–9) and daily specials such as braised beef ($7.75) and baked veal chops ($14). Mon–Thurs 11.30am–9pm, Fri & Sat till 10pm, Sun noon–9pm.

Brickway 234 Wickenden St ☎401 751 2477. Hip college favourite, especially on Sundays when queues form to wait for brunch and bottomless coffee. Everything is good, but the eggs Benedict ($8.95) and lemon blueberry French toast ($7.50) are tasty delights, while the burger ($7.95) and BLT ($6.75) are reliable choices for lunch. Mon–Fri 7am–3pm, Sat & Sun 8am–3pm.

CAV Restaurant 14 Imperial Place ☎401 751 9164, ⊛cavrestaurant.com. A bit out of the way in the Jewelry District, *CAV* serves an eclectic menu (everything from clam chowder to maki rolls) in an atmospheric setting (dinner mains $17.95–20.95). Mon–Wed 11.30am–10pm, Thurs till 11pm, Fri till 1am, Sat 9.30am–1am, Sun 10am–10pm.

★ **East Side Pocket** 278 Thayer St ☎401 453 1100, ⊛eastsidepocket.com. Bulging falafel sandwiches ($5), and other Middle Eastern "pockets" (wraps) served hot, fresh and cheap at this popular student hangout. Mon–Thurs 10am–1am, Fri & Sat till 2am, Sun till 10pm.

Haruki East 172 Wayland Ave ☎401 223 0332, ⊛harukisushi.com. Known as one of the best Japanese places in the city, with assorted sushi mains and unique dishes like Japanese-style crabmeat chilli *relleno* (stuffed peppers). Lunch specials from $9. Mon–Thurs noon–10pm, Fri & Sat till 11pm, Sun 4.30–10pm.

★ **Haven Brothers** Next to City Hall, Fulton St. Diner-on-wheels since 1893, with classic hot dogs, burgers and fries. Parked outside City Hall. Daily 5pm–4am.

Julian's 318 Broadway ☎401 861 1770, ⊕juliansprovidence.com. One of a new wave of innovative contemporary restaurants in the city, serving everything from house corned beef ($13.50) to Thai green curry ($20) and miso-grapefruit-rubbed sea scallops ($18). Mon–Fri 9am–11pm, Sat & Sun 9am–2.30pm & 5–11pm (bar open till 1am).

La Laiterie 184 Wayland Ave ☎401 274 7177, ⊛farmsteadinc.com/lalaiterie. Delicious seasonally changing bistro-style cuisine, with small plates (from $3) such as seared Vermont chicken livers with beer-battered onion rings, and mains like native black-back flounder in a rustic-chic dining room (mains $17–30). The amazing cheese shop next door supplies the cheese boards. Tues–Sat 5–10pm.

★ **Liberty Elm** 777 Elmwood Ave (I-95 exit 17 or 16) ☎401 467 0777, ⊛libertyelmdiner.com. Homage to locally sourced, organic foods, served in a Worcester diner car in Elmwood, south of downtown (near the zoo). Brunch often features live music, and there's free wi-fi. Most dishes range from $5–7. Tues–Fri 7am–3pm, Sat & Sun 8am–3pm.

Local 121 121 Washington St ☎401 274 2121, ⊛local121.com. Elegant restaurant serving Continental dishes with a New England touch, such as bacon-wrapped

---

RHODE ISLAND'S NEW YORK HOT DOGS

Legend has it that **hot dogs** were introduced to Rhode Island by Greek immigrants in the 1920s, trying to reproduce the snacks they'd tried at Coney Island where they were pioneered by the likes of *Nathan's Famous*.

★ **Olneyville NY System** 20 Plainfield St ☎401 621 9500, ⊛olneyvillenewyorksystem.com. This late-night joint has been serving the city's best "New York System wieners" since 1946, with "special secret sauce". Mon–Thurs 10am–2am, Fri & Sat till 3am, Sun 6pm–2am.

4

COFFEE, BUT NOT AS YOU KNOW IT

Rhode Island is the proud home of several unique (and seriously sweet) beverages, the most famous of which is the state drink, **coffee milk**, made with syrup crafted by local supplier Autocrat and served all over Providence – *White Electric* offers some of the best (see below). A **coffee cabinet** is a milkshake prepared by blending ice cream with milk and said coffee syrup – try one at *Olneyville NY System* (see p.249) or *Gray's Ice Cream* (see p.264).

quail and molasses-braised brisket. The menu focuses on fresh, local and sustainable products, with small plates from $9 and dinner mains $16–26. Mon 5–10pm, Tues–Thurs noon–4pm & 5–10pm, Fri & Sat noon–4pm & 5–11pm, Sun 10am–3pm & 5–9pm.

Pastiche Fine Desserts & Café 92 Spruce St ☎ 401 861 5190, ⓦ pastichefinedesserts.com. This relative newcomer to Federal Hill offers fabulous home-baked lemon custard tarts, mascarpone torte, banana creams and more. Tues–Thurs 8.30am–11pm, Fri & Sat till 11.30pm, Sun 10am–10pm.

★ **Siena** 238 Atwells Ave ☎ 401 521 3311, ⓦ sienari .com. Current trendsetter in Federal Hill, with a sparkling Italian menu featuring wood-fired pizzas ($12–13), superb pastas ($15–19) and luscious wood-grilled meats ($19–29). Mon–Thurs 5–11pm, Fri till midnight, Sat 4.30pm–midnight, Sun 3–9pm.

White Electric 711 Westminster St ☎ 401 453 3007, ⓦ whiteelectriccoffee.com. Great little café with fantastic coffee – the local's choice when it comes to Rhode Island's quirky speciality, coffee milk (made with coffee syrup). Mon–Fri 7am–6.30pm, Sat 8.30am–5pm, Sun 9am–5pm.

DRINKING

The Avery 18 Luongo Memorial Square, ⓦ averyprovidence.com. This small neighbourhood gem, tucked away in West Providence, is a cross between an exclusive bar and a trendy pub. Mon–Fri 4pm–midnight, Sat & Sun 5pm–midnight.

E & O Tap 289 Knight St ☎ 401 454 4827, ⓦ eandotap .com. Good music, cool drinks (with real beers on tap) and friendly locals – what more do you need? Daily 4pm–midnight.

★ **The Hot Club** 575 S Water St ☎ 401 861 9007. This is more of a bar than a club, with the major attraction the chance to sip drinks on an outdoor terrace right on the river; free popcorn but cash-only bar. Mon–Thurs & Sun noon–1am, Fri & Sat till 2am.

Lili Marlene's 422 Atwells Ave ☎ 401 751 4996. Small,

low-key bar with red leather booths and a pool table, tucked out of the way in Federal Hill; this locals' haunt draws its crowd by word of mouth. Mon–Thurs 4pm–1am, Fri & Sat till 2am, Sun till 1am.

★ **Thee Red Fez** 49 Peck St ☎ 401 272 1212. This fashionable restaurant gives way to a cool upstairs bar decorated with crazy art (think mounted deer heads with party hats) and a pinball machine. Mon–Thurs 5pm–1am, Fri & Sat till 2am.

Trinity Brewhouse 186 Fountain St ☎ 401 453 2337, ⓦ trinitybrewhouse.com. Hang out here after a Providence Bruins (minor league hockey) or Friars (college basketball) game. Everything on tap has been brewed in-house since 1995; try the Rhode Island IPA ($4.75). Mon–Thurs 11.30am–1am, Fri till 2am, Sat noon–2am, Sun till 1am.

NIGHTLIFE AND ENTERTAINMENT

Providence has a rich and varied **performing arts** and **film** scene. Major shows take place at the **Providence Performing Arts Center** (ⓦ ppacri.org) and the **Dunkin' Donuts Center** (ⓦ dunkindonutscenter.com); more cutting-edge artistic events are coordinated by **First Works** (ⓦ first-works.org). Complete **listings** can be found in the free weekly *Providence Phoenix* (ⓦ providence.thephoenix.com) and the *Providence Journal*'s (ⓦ www.projo.com) Thursday edition. On "**Gallery Night** (March–Nov third Thurs of the month; 5–9pm; ☎ 401 490 2042, ⓦ gallerynight.info), free "Art Buses" leave from the corner of Stillman and Canal streets behind Citizens Plaza (near Waterplace Park) and stop at some of the city's galleries and museums, where admission is free for the evening (and parking in the city is free).

AS220 115 Empire St ☎ 401 831 9327, ⓦ as220.org. Hip, lively, anti-establishment café/bar/gallery, with eclectic local art and diverse nightly performances; check the website to find out about their other galleries and events.

Firehouse No 13 41 Central St ☎ 401 270 1801, ⓦ fh13.com. Live music venue that encourages creative and experimental artists from almost every genre, from hip hop to folk rock. Check website for upcoming concerts.

Lupo's Heartbreak Hotel 79 Washington St ☎ 401 272 5876, ⓦ lupos.com. This is *the* spot in town to see nationally recognized bands rock out. Tickets generally $12–20 in advance, $30+ for big-name acts. Box office Wed–Fri noon–6pm, Sat 3–7pm.

Perishable Theatre 95 Empire St, ☎ 401 331 2695, ⓦ perishable.org. Founded in 1983, this is the home of edgy theatre and late night performances in the city

4

– puppetry, improv, radio plays and burlesque – as well as a lauded International Women's Playwriting Festival.
The Spot Underground 15 Elbow St ☎401 383 7133, ⓦthespotprovidence.com. Live music most days – everything from open-mic nights (Mon) to hip hop and rock (Thurs). Tues–Fri 4.30pm–close, Sat 8pm–close.

Trinity Repertory Company 201 Washington St ☎401 351 4242, ⓦtrinityrep.com. Rhode Island's Tony Award-winning theatre, with a season that runs Sept–May ($22–66), and an annual production of *A Christmas Carol*. Box office Mon–Sat noon–5pm.

Blackstone River Valley

Northwest of Providence, the gritty **BLACKSTONE RIVER VALLEY**(ⓦnps.gov/blac) has been given special status as a "Heritage Corridor" for its role in America's development as the world's leading industrial power – steps are underway to convert the area into a national park in the next few years. Rte-146 connects the main sights between Providence and Worcester, MA (p.204).

Pawtucket

Near the village of **PAWTUCKET** in 1793, **Samuel Slater**, a manufacturer's apprentice from England, used technology surreptitiously imported from his native land to build the first successful water-powered, cotton-spinning mill in North America on the banks of the Blackstone River. His mill kick-started the American Industrial Revolution, and is preserved today at the **Slater Mill Historic Site**.

Slater Mill Historic Site

67 Roosevelt Ave • March & April Sat & Sun 11am–3pm; May–Oct Tues–Sun 10am–4pm; Nov Sat & Sun 10am–4pm • $12 • ☎401 725 8638, ⓦslatermill.org • RIPTA bus #99 from Providence

The enlightening **Slater Mill Historic Site** preserves Samuel Slater's original cotton mill as it looked c.1835, with a copy of an original carding engine, a spinning frame and mule, and some rare textile machines. Also on site is the 1810 **Wilkinson Mill**, where a nineteenth-century mechanics' workshop, complete with belt-driven machine tools, still operates, and the 1758 **Sylvanus Brown House**, a worker's home furnished as it was in the early 1800s.

ARRIVAL AND DEPARTURE   PAWTUCKET

By bus RIPTA buses #99 and 42 (☎401 781 9400, ⓦripta.com) run regularly from Providence to Pawtucket (45min; daily every 10–20min; $2).

INFORMATION AND TOURS

Blackstone Valley Visitor Center 175 Main St, Pawtucket (Mon–Sat 10am–4pm, Sun 1–4pm; ☎401 724 2200, ⓦtourblackstone.com). Across the street from Slater Mill.
Blackstone Valley Explorer 45 Madeira Ave (Central Falls Landing), Central Falls ☎1 800 454 2882, ⓦrivertourblackstone.com. Runs 45min narrated wilderness riverboat tours, 1.7 miles north of the Blackstone Valley Visitor Center via Rte-114 (Broad St). Reservations advised; $10. Late May to early Oct Sun 1–4pm hourly.

EATING AND DRINKING

Connie and Nikki's Restaurant and Creamery 526 Pawtucket Ave ☎401 725 2540. Chock-full of Coca-Cola memorabilia, this is the home of traditional Rhode Island comfort food, from coffee milk and classic coffee cabinets made with Newport Creamery ice cream, to clam cakes and wieners. Mon–Fri 6.30am–4pm, Sat 7am–2pm, Sun 8am–2pm.
Modern Diner 364 East Ave ☎401 726 8390. This no-frills, 1941 Sterling Streamliner dining car serves up all sorts of crazy breakfast combos, from lobster grits and chorizo hash Benedict, to cream cheese-and-blueberry-stuffed French toast and pumpkin-walnut pancakes. Mon–Sat 6am–2pm, Sun 7am–2pm.
Stanley's Famous Hamburgers 535 Dexter St, Central Falls ☎401 726 9689, ⓦstanleyshamburgers.com. Just northwest of downtown Pawtucket in Central Falls, this unassuming place has been knocking out juicy burgers ($1.99–5.49) since 1935. Mon–Thurs 11am–8pm, Fri & Sat 11am–9pm.

4

Woonsocket

Another major manufacturing centre, **WOONSOCKET** is about fifteen miles northwest of Pawtucket and just south of the Massachusetts border. Unlike many other towns in the state, Woonsocket is a creation of the Industrial Revolution, not the colonial period, founded on the Blackstone River in 1867 as a prime location for textile mills.

Museum of Work and Culture

42 S Main St • Tues–Fri 9.30am–4pm, Sat 10am–4pm, Sun 1–4pm • $8 • ☎ 401 769 9675, ⓦ rihs.org

The absorbing **Museum of Work and Culture** traces the story of mill-workers who came from Québec to Woonsocket from the 1860s and 1920s to work in the shoe and textile factories here. A self-guided walk through their workaday world takes you from the floor of a textile mill to the porch of a tenement house.

ARRIVAL AND DEPARTURE   WOONSOCKET

By bus RIPTA bus #54 (☎ 401 781 9400, ⓦ ripta.com) runs regularly from Providence to Woonsocket (1hr; Mon–Sat   every 30min, Sun hourly; $2).

EATING AND DRINKING

Woonsocket is the proud home of the "**dynamite sandwich**" – a huge pile of beef Sloppy Joe, peppers and onions served on a torpedo-style roll.

Castle Luncheonette 420 Social St ☎ 401 762 5424. Classic dynamites (ground beef, onions and ketchup in a sandwich), with plenty of green peppers; the sauce is also smothered onto burgers and hot dogs. Mon–Sat 11am–8pm.

Moonlight House of Weiners 32 Rathbun St ☎ 401 766 5806. No-frills fast-food joint, famed for its hot dogs, dynamites and coffee milk (milk with coffee syrup). Mon & Sun 8am–8pm, Tues–Sat till 10pm.

Newport

With its gorgeous seaside location on Aquidneck Island, fleets of polished yachts, rose-coloured sunsets and long-standing association with America's fine and fabulous, **NEWPORT** is straight out of a monied American fairy tale. The Kennedys were married here in 1953 (Jackie was a local girl), and though F. Scott Fitzgerald set his novel **The Great Gatsby** in 1920s Long Island, it's no surprise that the iconic 1974 movie version was filmed in Newport. Indeed, many of the town's opulent *fin-de-siècle* mansions – former summer homes of the likes of the Astors and Vanderbilts – are still owned by America's current crop of mega-wealthy.

Newport has much more to offer than just a stroll past these extravagant facades, though – the streets are laden with history, and sights commemorate everything from the town's pioneering role in advocating religious freedom in America to the landing of French forces here during the Revolutionary War.

Newport is eminently walkable, with **Thames Street** (pronounce the "th" as in "the") being the main drag **downtown**. Colonial Newport's commercial centre, **Washington Square**, lies just east of Thames Street and **Brick Market Place** (ⓦ brickmarketnewport .com), home to a mixture of galleries and pricey souvenir shops. To the south, the converted eighteenth-century warehouses of **Bannister's and Bowen's wharves** (ⓦ bannistersnewport.com and ⓦ bowenswharf.com) are atmospheric places to browse or grab a waterside coffee.

Brief history

Newport was first settled in 1639 by refugees from Anne Hutchinson's colony in Portsmouth, Rhode Island, and others from Massachusetts seeking **religious freedom**. In the eighteenth century, Newport grew into a bustling port, with the local fleet

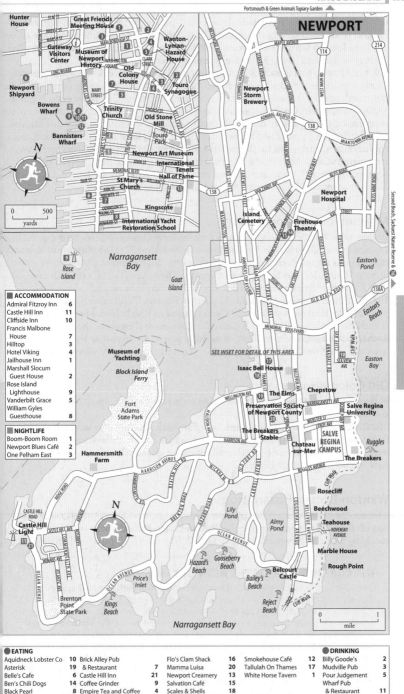

Portsmouth & Green Animals Topiary Garden

NEWPORT

Hunter House

Great Friends Meeting House

Gateway Visitors Center

Museum of Newport History

Old Colony House

Wanton-Lyman-Hazard House

Newport Shipyard

Touro Synagogue

Newport Storm Brewery

Bowens Wharf

Trinity Church

Old Stone Mill

Bannisters Wharf

Touro Park

Newport Art Museum

International Tennis Hall of Fame

St Mary's Church

Newport Hospital

Island Cemetery

Firehouse Theatre

Kingscote

International Yacht Restoration School

Narragansett Bay

Rose Island

Goat Island

Easton's Pond

Easton's Beach

Easton Bay

Museum of Yachting

Block Island Ferry

SEE INSET FOR DETAIL OF THIS AREA

Isaac Bell House

The Elms

Chepstow

Preservation Society of Newport County

Salve Regina University

The Breakers Stable

Chateau-sur-Mer

SALVE REGINA CAMPUS

The Breakers

Fort Adams State Park

Hammersmith Farm

Rosecliff

Beechwood

Teahouse

Lily Pond

Almy Pond

Marble House

Rough Point

Castle Hill Light

Hazard's Beach

Gooseberry Beach

Bailey's Beach

Belcourt Castle

Brenton Point State Park

Kings Beach

Price's Inlet

Reject Beach

Narragansett Bay

Second Beach, Sachuest Nature Reserve & 10

ACCOMMODATION

Admiral Fitzroy Inn	6
Castle Hill Inn	11
Cliffside Inn	10
Francis Malbone House	7
Hilltop	3
Hotel Viking	4
Jailhouse Inn	1
Marshall Slocum Guest House	2
Rose Island Lighthouse	9
Vanderbilt Grace	5
William Gyles Guesthouse	8

NIGHTLIFE

Boom-Boom Room	1
Newport Blues Café	2
One Pelham East	3

● EATING

Aquidneck Lobster Co	10	Brick Alley Pub		Flo's Clam Shack	16	Smokehouse Café	12
Asterisk	19	& Restaurant	7	Mamma Luisa	20	Tallulah On Thames	17
Belle's Cafe	6	Castle Hill Inn	21	Newport Creamery	13	White Horse Tavern	1
Ben's Chili Dogs	14	Coffee Grinder	9	Salvation Café	15		
Black Pearl	8	Empire Tea and Coffee	4	Scales & Shells	18		

● DRINKING

Billy Goode's	2
Mudville Pub	3
Pour Judgement	5
Wharf Pub & Restaurant	11

heavily involved in the **slave trade**. Prosperity was brought to a halt when British and Hessian troops occupied Newport in 1776: they blockaded the harbour, and forced the city's residents to burn the wharves as firewood during the brutal winter. The Brits left of their own accord in 1779, but the economy never really recovered.

While Newport's reputation as a resort town dates as back to the 1730s, when wealthy Southern merchants flocked here to escape the summer heat, it was in the latter half of the nineteenth century that it amassed its most extravagant estates. The boom really began in 1880, when socialite **Caroline Astor** (or simply "Mrs Astor") opened up house here, thereby necessitating the attendance of virtually everyone else in New York "society" (her husband, William B. Astor Jr, purchased the house as a gift). At the same time, the town acquired a reputation as a playground for the **yachting** set – from 1930 until 1983 Newport hosted the **America's Cup**. The town also benefited from the presence of the US Navy, whose departure in the 1970s was accompanied by a period of economic decline. Today, though, Newport is booming again, owing in no small part to the **tourist** economy.

Museum of Newport History

127 Thames St • Mon–Thurs 10am–6pm, Fri & Sat till 8pm, Sun till 5pm • Free; donation suggested • ☎ 401 841 8770, ⓦ newporthistory.org

Housed in the old Brick Market building completed in 1771, the **Museum of Newport History** gives a good overview of the town's past through exhibits, photographs and pithy oral histories. Inside you'll find a copy of Rhode Island's 1663 royal charter, displays on the slave trade, colonial trades such as rum-making and cabinet-making, and an original printing press owned by **James Franklin** (Benjamin's brother), purchased in England around 1717 (James moved to Rhode Island in 1725, having trained his brother in Boston). You can also learn more about how the French under **Rochambeau** landed here in 1780, destined to play a crucial part at Yorktown one year later, and the growth of Newport as a resort community in the nineteenth century.

Old Colony House

Washington Square • Tours April, May & Nov Sat 11.30am; June–Oct Mon, Wed & Fri–Sun 11.30am • Tours $12 • ☎ 401 841 8770, ⓦ newporthistorical.org

The **Old Colony House** is a handsome Georgian brick building that served as the Rhode Island state house from 1739 to 1901. Many scenes from the movie *Amistad* (1997) were shot here. The house is occasionally open for special exhibitions – otherwise you'll have to take a tour to get inside.

Wanton-Lyman-Hazard House

17 Broadway • Tours April, May & Nov Sat 11.30am; June–Oct Mon, Wed, Fri–Sun same time • $12 • ☎ 401 841 8770, ⓦ newporthistorical.org

Just up from Washington Square, the **Wanton-Lyman-Hazard House** is the oldest surviving house in Newport, dating to c.1697. The central chimney and pitched roof

---

THE CURIOUS CASE OF THE NEWPORT VIKINGS

Colonial mill or Viking ruin? Walk along Bellevue Ave to **Touro Park** and you'll spy what was once the most controversial sight in Newport. Since the nineteenth-century some commentators (including poet Longfellow) have claimed that the simple 28ft stone tower dates from the medieval period and must have been constructed by the **Vinland Vikings** (who did reach Newfoundland, Canada). Author Gavin Menzies has even argued that the tower was built by a colony of Chinese sailors. More credible experts agree that it was actually constructed around 1660 for the first governor of Rhode Island, **Benedict Arnold**. Now dubbed the "Old Stone Mill", the site has no display boards or even labels, an indication that the town wants to move on – many tour guides continue to make the old claims, however.

are typical of early settlers' homes, while inside the surviving original plasterwork is made from ground shells and molasses. **Guided tours** by the Newport Historical Society cover the lives of the house's inhabitants as well as recent restoration work.

Great Friends Meeting House

Farewell St, at Marlborough • Tours June–Oct Tues & Thurs 11.30am • $12 • ☎ 401 841 8770, ⓦ newporthistorical.org

Built by the Quakers in 1699 and used by them for the next two hundred years, the giant **Great Friends Meeting House** is the oldest religious building in town, restored to its appearance c.1807 and completely free of adornment. Tours tell the story of the Quakers in Newport, and also take in the **Seventh Day Baptist Meeting House** (1730) on nearby Barney Street (officially 82 Touro St), the oldest Baptist church building in America.

Touro Synagogue

85 Touro St • Mon–Fri & Sun: Nov & Dec, May & June 11.30am–2.30pm; July & Aug 9.30am–4.30pm; Sept–Oct 10am–2.30pm; tours every 30min • Free • ☎ 401 847 4794, ⓦ tourosynagogue.org

Rhode Island's history of religious tolerance is further revealed by the elegant **Touro Synagogue**, the oldest house of Jewish worship in America, founded by descendants of Sephardic Jews fleeing the Spanish Inquisition – the fifteen founders arrived from Barbados in 1658. The beautifully preserved building, completed in 1763 (for no charge) by English-born architect Peter Harrison, combines a blend of Georgian architecture and Sephardic sensibility – it still houses a deerskin Torah which predates the synagogue by two hundred years. The synagogue is named after its first rabbi, a Dutch Jew named Isaac Touro, recruited from Amsterdam. The other reason this place is considered so important is the letter **George Washington** wrote to the congregation in 1790 – in it, he essentially guaranteed religious freedom in the new nation of America. Though it was largely abandoned by 1800, new Jewish arrivals in the late nineteenth century revived the synagogue, and today some one hundred families worship here as part of a (mostly elderly) Orthodox congregation.

The attached **Loeb Visitors Center** features some incredibly innovative multimedia exhibits and touch-screen terminals that explore the history of the Jewish community here, as well as holographic displays that dramatize six stories associated with the site. You can only visit the synagogue as part of a tour (men are required to wear *yarmulke* or skull caps, provided), but you can spend as much time in the visitor centre as you like.

International Yacht Restoration School

449 Thames St • Wed–Sun 10am–5pm • Free • ☎ 401 848 5777, ⓦ iyrs.org • Newport Harbor Shuttle connects IYRS and the Museum of Yachting; June–Sept, every 30min, Mon–Thurs noon–6pm, Fri–Sun 11am–7pm ($6; ⓦ newportharborshuttle.com)

Newport's **International Yacht Restoration School** is a fine place to learn about maritime history, with the 1831 Aquidneck Mill Building and the 1885 schooner yacht *Coronet* under restoration on campus at the time of writing; an elevated catwalk inside the Restoration Hall allows visitors to watch IYRS craftsmen at work. You can find out more about boats at the affiliated **Museum of Yachting** at **Fort Adams State Park** (see p.259).

Newport Art Museum

76 Bellevue Ave • May–Oct Tues–Sat 10am–5pm, Sun noon–5pm; Nov–April Tues–Sat 10am–4pm, Sun noon–4pm • $10 • ☎ 401 848 8200, ⓦ newportartmuseum.org

If fancy boats don't suit your taste, check out the **Newport Art Museum** in Griswold House, a lavish mock-medieval fantasy designed by Richard Morris Hunt and completed in 1864. The museum exhibits Newport and New England art from the last two centuries, including work by George Inness, John La Farge and Gilbert Stuart, as well as contemporary pieces from the likes of Dale Chihuly and Joseph Norman.

International Tennis Hall of Fame & Museum

194 Bellevue Ave • Daily 9.30am–5pm • $11/$15 with audio guide • ☎ 401 849 3990, ⓦ tennisfame.com

The grand **Newport Casino**, an early country club designed by Stanford White, held the nation's first tennis championships in 1881 – the tournament now known as the US Open. The casino currently houses the **International Tennis Hall of Fame & Museum**, and still keeps its grass courts open to the public (mid-May to Sept; reserve ahead ☎401 846 0642; $100/hr). Exhibits at the museum include the original patent for the game granted by Queen Victoria in 1874, and a vast, comprehensive collection of tennis-related memorabilia.

Newport Storm Brewery

293 JT Connell Rd • Wed–Mon noon–5pm • Tastings & tours $7–9 • ☎ 401 849 5232, ⓦ newportstorm.com

Established in 1999 on the outskirts of town, the family-owned **Newport Storm Brewery** is Rhode Island's only real **microbrewery** and makes for an entertaining visit – just make sure you don't drive. Tastings and tour packages allow you to sample four of their superb ales, including Hurricane Amber Ale, Blueberry Beer and Summer Ale, as well as some experimental brews. You can also try their **Thomas Tew Rum**, pot-stilled and aged in oak barrels for two years – the company is the first to make rum here since the Revolutionary War. Tours of the facility are extremely enlightening – make sure you taste the samples afterwards, not before.

The Newport mansions

In the nineteenth century Newport became the summer playground of the New York elite (effectively making it the nation's summer capital), with wealthy families competing to outdo each other with a string of lavish **mansions** and annual parties. The gilded excess lasted only a few decades, though, its demise beginning with the introduction of US income tax in 1913; by the early 1940s most of the mansions had closed for good. The remainder have been converted into condos or remain private homes, owned by the likes of the Campbell soup heiress Dorrance "Dodo" Hamilton and billionaire software tycoon Lawrence Ellison, founder of Oracle Corp. Several have been converted into university buildings on **Salve Regina University**'s 75-acre campus on Ochre Point Avenue (☎401 847 6650), while the **Preservation Society of Newport County** (☎401 847 1000, ⓦnewportmansions.org) maintains the bulk of the dozen or so houses open for public viewing.

You need to visit the mansions to get a true impression of their size, but after herding into and rushing through more than one or two, the appeal rapidly begins to pall: make sure you visit The Breakers at least, the most lavish mansion of them all. A **combined ticket** to any five Society mansions is $31.50; The Breakers plus one other property is $24.50. You can easily walk between these properties, but parking is also available at all of them.

Perhaps the most pleasant (and cheapest) way to get a glimpse of nearly all the mansions' exteriors is to follow the 3.5-mile oceanside **Cliff Walk**, which winds past their immense gardens, framed on the other side by the shoreline. The trail begins on Memorial Boulevard where it meets First (Easton's) Beach, and ends at Bailey's Beach. Note that only the mansions **open to the public** are listed below; Lawrence Ellison purchased the Astor's lavish former home, **Beechwood**, for $10.5 million in 2010, and at the time of writing had closed it to the public.

Hunter House

4 Washington St • Late June to Aug daily 10am–6pm; Sept to mid-Oct Sat & Sun till 6pm; tours hourly 10.30am–4.30pm • $28 • 401 847 1000, Ⓦ newportmansions.org

Set apart from all the other houses, on the northern edge of downtown, **Hunter House** marks the era when Newport was a mercantile capital and seaport. The house was built between 1748 and 1754 for a prosperous local merchant, and had a series of owners, including US senator William Hunter of the Jackson era; at one point during the American Revolution it was also the headquarters for the French naval forces.

Kingscote

253 Bellevue Ave • May to mid-Oct daily 10am–6pm • $14.50; includes entry to Isaac Bell House (see below) • ☎ 401 847 1000, Ⓦ newportmansions.org

Kingscote is a quirky Gothic Revival cottage built in 1841 by Richard Upjohn for a rich Southern planter, but expanded in 1876 by celebrity architects McKim, Mead & White. The house's medieval exteriors are complemented by a lovely interior, with mahogany panelling and touches both exotic and colonial; there is a Tiffany glass wall in the living room.

Isaac Bell House

70 Perry St • Late June to Aug daily 10am–6pm; Sept to mid-Oct Sat & Sun same hours; tours hourly 10.30am–4.30pm • $14.50; includes entry to Kingscote (see above) • ☎ 401 847 1000, Ⓦ newportmansions.org

Tickets for Kingscote also include entry to the nearby, shingle-style **Isaac Bell House**, built by the same team in 1883, featuring Arts and Crafts interiors and even Japanese-style columns (Isaac Bell was a wealthy cotton broker).

The Elms

367 Bellevue Ave • Daily: April to mid-Nov 10am–6pm; mid-Nov to Jan till 5pm • $14.50 • ☎ 401 847 1000, Ⓦ newportmansions.org

An ornate French *maison*, **The Elms** has marble stairways, Venetian paintings and gardens fit for a king. Completed in 1901, it was designed by Philadelphia architect Horace Trumbauer after the Parisian Château d'Asnières for Pennsylvania coal magnate E.J. Berwind. Come in season to wander among those spectacular gardens and majestic drooping trees for which the mansion is named. With reservations, you can also take a rooftop and behind-the-scenes tour (April–Dec; ☎ 401 847 0478).

Chepstow

120 Narragansett Ave • Late June to early Sept; tours by reservation only 11am, 1pm & 3pm • $14.50 • ☎ 401 847 1000, Ⓦ newportmansions.org

The Italianate **Chepstow** was completed in 1861 for reclusive millionaire Edmund Schermerhorn, and showcases a fine collection of nineteenth-century American landscape paintings. The collection actually reflects the tastes of its last owner, **Alletta Morris McBean**, who died in 1986, part of a family with roots in Newport going back to the 1700s.

Chateau-sur-Mer

474 Bellevue Ave • Daily: April to mid-Nov 10am–6pm • $14.50 • ☎ 401 847 1000, Ⓦ newportmansions.org

The relatively modest **Chateau-sur-Mer** was the first of the grand Newport mansions, built in 1852 for wealthy merchant **William Shepard Wetmore** and full of his Victorian furnishings, Italian woodwork and Chinese art. During the 1870s, the Wetmores hired Richard Morris Hunt to remodel the house in French Second Empire style.

The Breakers

44 Ochre Point Ave • Daily: April to mid-Nov 9am–6pm; mid-Nov to Jan till 5pm • $19.50 • ☎ 401 847 1000, Ⓦ newportmansions.org

Tasteless vulgarity or the epitome of style? Critics have been divided ever since **Cornelius Vanderbilt II**'s four-storey Italian Renaissance-style palace **The Breakers** was completed in 1895 for a cool $15 million (at least $400 million today). It's easy to be overwhelmed by the ostentation of the interior, with several rooms that outdo Versailles for sheer opulence.

Vanderbilt, grandson of the first Cornelius (founder of the family fortune), was the president and chairman of the New York Central Railroad when he commissioned architect **Richard Morris Hunt** to build the mansion on his thirteen-acre oceanfront estate – his original clapboard summer house had just burnt down and Vanderbilt was determined to build exclusively in limestone and marble. After the "last golden summer" of 1937, the house was closed for ten years before opening to the public. Apart from being the most lavish mansion in Newport, The Breakers comes with an excellent **self-guided audio tour** that adds context, including recordings of some of the people that actually worked here.

Tours begin in the 45ft-high central **Great Hall**, with its John La Farge stained-glass skylight and faded Flemish tapestry (1619). The rest of the house is equally over the top, with the billiard room smothered in Swiss marble, a solid marble bath upstairs and gold plate liberally applied throughout.

Rosecliff

548 Bellevue Ave • Daily: April to mid-Nov 10am–6pm • $14.50 • ☎ 401 847 1000, ⓦ newportmansions.org

Lavish **Rosecliff**, built for around $2.5 million in 1902 for Nevada silver heiress **"Tessie Fair Oelrichs**, was designed by Stanford White in the style of the Grand Trianon at Versailles, complete with rose garden, heart-shaped staircase and the largest ballroom of all the mansions. Oelrichs was famous for her extravagant parties, even by Newport standards: in 1904 her *Bal Blanc* called for all-white decor and guests to wear all-white costumes. Fittingly this was the house used as the film set for *The Great Gatsby* in 1973.

Marble House

596 Bellevue Ave • Daily: April to mid-Nov 10am–6pm; mid-Nov to Jan till 5pm • $14.50 • ☎ 401 847 1000, ⓦ newportmansions.org

The **Marble House** is another Vanderbilt property, built in 1892 for **William Vanderbilt** (younger brother of Cornelius II) and his wife Alva for a trifling $11 million. The inspiration? The Petit Trianon at Versailles. Most of the house was constructed out of marble in Europe, shipped back and reassembled here. The mansion boasts an opulent golden ballroom bedecked with Greek and Roman figures, and a **Chinese teahouse** where you can still grab a drink (mid-May to mid-Oct daily 11am–5pm).

Belcourt Castle

657 Bellevue Ave • See website for tour times • $12 • ☎ 401 846 0669, ⓦ belcourtcastle.org

Still inhabited by its owner Harle Tinney, **Belcourt Castle** is another ostentatious beauty designed by the ubiquitous Richard Morris Hunt and completed in 1894. The interior was built to echo original owner Oliver Belmont's love for equines and armour; his horses slept in white linen sheets in a special stable. Various themed tours are available at different times of year, including a popular candlelit history tour (6–7pm; $25) and ghost tours (usually Fri & Sat 5.30–7pm; $25). Ms Tinney often gives the tours herself – she met her husband and castle owner, the late Donald Tinney, while working as a tour guide at the house in 1960. The house has been on the market since 2009.

Rough Point

680 Bellevue Ave • Mid-April to mid-May Thurs–Sat 10am–2pm; mid-May to Oct Tues–Sat 9.45am–3.45pm • $25 • ☎ 401 847 8344, ⓦ newportrestoration.org

At the southernmost end of Bellevue Avenue stands **Rough Point**, built in 1870 by **Fred Vanderbilt** (another younger brother of Cornelius II), but more famous as the former home of **Doris Duke**, founder of the Newport Restoration Foundation in 1968 and only child of electricity and tobacco magnate James B. Duke. Today it's one of the most entertaining mansions to visit, thanks to the rotating exhibits that focus on Duke's enigmatic personality – as well as some paintings from Gainsborough, Renoir and Reynolds.

FESTIVE NEWPORT

JUNE

Newport Flower Show ⓦnewportmansions.org. Spectacular festival of blooms held annually at Rosecliff (p.258) at the end of June. Tickets cost $25 on the day (less in advance).

JULY

Newport Music Festival ⓦnewportmusic.org. Takes place in a number of Newport's mansions and features world-class artists performing everything from chamber and orchestral music to sea shanties.

AUGUST

Newport Folk Festival ⓦnewportfolkfest.net. Founded in 1959 and famed for introducing Joan Baez and Bob Dylan to the world.

Newport Jazz Festival ⓦnewportjazzfest.net. Founded in 1954, this is now one of the top jazz dates of the year; rent a kayak or boat and see the performances in Fort Adams State Park for free (you'll have to float just off shore).

SEPTEMBER

Waterfront Irish Festival ⓦnewportwater frontevents.com. Among the country's largest Irish events, with Irish step-dance, comedy routines and nonstop Irish music. Tickets $20.

The beaches and coast

The indubitable appeal of Newport's shoreline is slightly marred by the fact that several stretches of beach are private; still, some of the best strands remain open to the public. **Ruggles** is the premier **surf** beach in Newport (keep following the road past The Breakers), best for experienced surfers only (Second Beach is best for beginners).

From the end of Bellevue Avenue, **Ocean Drive** winds west along several miles of vast, spectacular shoreline to **Brenton Point State Park** (daily sunrise–sunset; free), where panoramic views of Narragansett Bay are shadowed only by the spray from the surf below. Along the way, the calm waters of **Gooseberry Beach** (mid-May to Aug 9am–5pm; free; parking $15–20) nestled in an inlet, appeal to families.

The town beach, also known as **First** or **Easton's Beach** (mid-May to Aug 9am–6pm; free; parking $10–20; ☎401 845 5810), is a wide stretch at the east end of Memorial Boulevard with plentiful amenities, including surfboard rentals. The most attractive beach of all, though, is a couple miles east in Middletown: **Second (Sachuest) Beach** (mid-May to Aug 9am–6pm; free; parking $10–20) stretches a mile and a half, with soft sand and good surf. **Third Beach** (mid-May to Aug 9am–6pm; free; parking $10–20) lies further east (around five miles from downtown Newport) on the inner side of Narragansett Bay. The calmer waters and tidal pools here are good for children. RIPTA bus #61 (Orange Line) runs to the Middletown beaches from downtown Newport in summer only – check the visitor centre for the latest schedule.

Fort Adams State Park

90 Fort Adams Drive • Daily sunrise–sunset • Free • ☎401 847 2400, ⓦfortadams.org • Newport Harbor Shuttle connects Fort Adams with downtown; June–Sept, every 30min, Mon–Thurs noon–6pm, Fri–Sun 11am–7pm ($6; ⓦnewportharborshuttle.com)

Construction began on **Fort Adams** in 1799, but it wasn't complete for another 33 years. Today the state park includes the remains of the fort (guided tours only; late May to mid-Oct 10am–4pm, hourly; $10), a visitor centre and the **Museum of Yachting** (June–Sept Thurs–Mon 10am–5pm; $5; ☎401 847 1018, ⓦmoy.org), which hosts nautical exhibits, with a special focus on the Americas Cup and the schooner *Coronet*.

ARRIVAL AND DEPARTURE
NEWPORT

By plane The nearest airport to Newport is T.F. Green Airport at Providence (see p.248). You can take RIPTA bus #14 ($2) from here direct to Newport, or the Cozy Cab shuttle (daily 8am–midnight; ☎401 846 2500, ⓦcozytrans.com; $25), which will drop off at your hotel.

By train The nearest Amtrak station (☎1 800 872 7245, ⓦamtrak.com) is on Rte-138 at Kingston, nineteen miles west; theoretically you can take RIPTA bus #64 (Mon–Sat; $2; ☎401 781 9400) from the Kingston station to Newport, but services are infrequent – it's easier to get off the train in Providence and take a bus from there.

By car Driving to Newport is easy, but parking spaces downtown are hard to find in season. Newport is connected to the mainland by Rte-138, which crosses the impressive 1601ft Newport-Pell Bridge ($4 toll) to Jamestown, then the Jamestown Bridge to the mainland; the island is connected to Providence via Mount Hope Bridge (Rte-114). Metered parking is 25 cents for 15min (May–Oct only; free otherwise).

By bus RIPTA bus #60 from Providence (around 1hr 20min every 30–40min; Mon–Fri 4.40am–1.30am, Sat 5.35am–1.45am, Sun 6.30am–11.45pm; $2) arrives at the Gateway Center downtown. This also serves as the terminal for Peter Pan buses (☎ 1 800 443 1831, ⑩ peterpanbus .com) from Boston (1hr 40min; 5 daily; $27) and Fall River (40min; 5 daily; $12) – change at the latter for New Bedford and Cape Cod.

GETTING AROUND

By bus RIPTA bus #67 ($2) runs every 15–20min (Mon–Sat 8am–8pm, Sun 9.40am–8pm) from the Gateway Center downtown along Bellevue Avenue, past most of the mansions, ending beyond Rough Point at the end of the Cliff Walk.

By taxi For taxis, try Cozy Cab (☎ 1 800 846 1502).

By bicycle Bikes are also a great way to get around, especially if you're heading to the beaches. For bike rental, try Ten Speed Spokes, 18 Elm St (Mon–Fri 10am–6pm, Sat till 5pm; also Sun May–Oct; $35/day; ☎ 401 847 5609 ⑩ tenspeedspokes.com).

By scooter Scooters and cutesy three-wheelers are also available; try Scooter World, 9 Christie's Landing (daily 9am–7pm; scooters $30/hr, $99/day; 3-wheelers $50/hr ☎ 401 619 1349; ⑩ scooterworldri.com). They also rent bikes ($7/hr, $30/day).

INFORMATION

Gateway Visitor's Center 23 America's Cup Ave (daily 9am–5pm; ☎ 401 845 9123 ☎ 1 800 976 5122, ⑩ gonewport.com). This operation has plenty of maps, brochures and advice. Newport can be explored by a overwhelming number of tours by land and sea (see below) – a dedicated desk here offers tickets and information.

TOURS

Newport Dinner Train ☎ 401 841 8700, ⑩ newportdinnertrain.com. This makes for a very special train trip: dine in authentic Pullman carriages as the 2hr 30min ride takes you along scenic Narragansett Bay ($14.95–24.95). Trains leave from 19 America's Cup Ave June–Aug Thurs–Sat 11.30am & 6.30pm (see website for details); reserve well in advance.

Newport Historical Society ☎ 401 841 8770, ⑩ newporthistorytours.org. Runs a range of themed walking tours (from $10) through downtown.

Viking Trolley Tours ☎ 401 847 6921, ⑩ vikingtours newport.com. Bus tours (from $25), with the focus on Newport mansions and their Gilded Age owners – you'll learn a lot more about the houses closed to the public on this tour.

BOAT TOURS

Classic Cruises of Newport ☎ 401 847 0298 ⑩ cruisenewport.com. Offers trips on the beautiful 72ft schooner *Madeleine* (1hr 30min; 5 daily; $27) and *Rum Runner II* (1hr 15min; 5 daily; $18). May–Oct.

Gansett Cruises ☎ 401 787 4438, ⑩ gansettcruises .com. Offers sunset excursions 5pm & 7pm daily, leaving from Long Wharf (1hr 30min; $25). May–Oct.

Save the Bay ☎ 401 324 6020, ⑩ savebay.org Organizes seal watches leaving from Bowen's Wharf (Sat & Sun; 1hr; $20). Nov–April.

ACCOMMODATION

Newport contains almost one hundred inns and B&Bs, while cheaper chain **motels** can be found a few miles north in Middletown. If you're stuck, try **Bed & Breakfast Newport** (☎ 1 800 800 8765, ⑩ bbnewport.com), who can help find something affordable. You can also **camp** in Middletown and Portsmouth (see p.262).

Admiral Fitzroy Inn 398 Thames St ☎ 401 848 8000, ⑩ admiralfitzroy.com. Cheerfully decorated B&B in the heart of town, dating from 1854, with seventeen hand-stenciled rooms, antique beds and a roof deck. $175

Castle Hill Inn 590 Ocean Ave ☎ 401 849 3800, ⑩ castlehillinn.com. A Newport landmark overlooking Narragansett Bay from atop its own peninsula, with nine magnificent rooms in the main mansion, dating from 1874, and additional accommodation in the beach cottages nearby. Non-guests can come for Sunday brunch (May–Oct 11.30am–3pm), a much more affordable way to enjoy the views. $525

Cliffside Inn 2 Seaview Ave ☎ 401 847 1811 ⑩ cliffsideinn.com. 1880 Victorian manor house, with thirteen luxurious rooms in the main house and three in the adjacent cottage. Once the summer home of eccentric local artist Beatrice Turner, it's decorated today with more than one hundred of her works. $340

Francis Malbone House 392 Thames St ☎ 1 800 846 0392, ⑩ malbone.com. Luxurious B&B in the heart of wn, boasting twenty elegant rooms – most with flat-screen TV and DVD, iPod docking station, free wi-fi, jacuzzi bs and fireplaces. The garden-side rooms are the heapest. **$265**

★ **Hilltop** 2 Kay St, at Bellevue Ave ☎ 401 846 03902, ⓦ hilltopnewport.com. Newport's most popular B&B ccupies a gorgeous house completed in 1910. The five ooms all have comfy Victorian interiors, LCD TVs with enerous bathrooms and quality breakfasts. Enjoy the free fternoon tea (daily 3–5pm), and home-made cakes and ort left out in the evenings. Free wi-fi. **$275**

Motel Viking 1 Bellevue Ave ☎ 401 847 3300, ⓦ hotelviking.com. Grand old hotel built in 1926 to ccommodate spill-over Bellevue mansion guests – the rst real hotel in Newport, it still lures jet-setters with gyptian cotton duvets, antique furnishings and coddling t on-site Spa Terre. **$339**

Jailhouse Inn 13 Marlborough St ☎ 401 847 4638, ⓦ jailhouse.com. Few vestiges of the former Newport ounty jail remain in this restored B&B, with compact nodern rooms and occasional jailhouse trimmings. **$249**

Marshall Slocum Guest House 29 Kay St ☎ 401 841 120, ⓦ marshallslocuminn.com. Five comfortable

period-style rooms in a historic 1855 B&B near Bellevue Avenue, with gardens and gourmet breakfasts – free wi-fi but no TV. Excellent value. **$135**

★ **Rose Island Lighthouse** Rose Island, Narragansett Bay ☎ 401 847 4242, ⓦ roseislandlighthouse.org. Worth considering for the sheer novelty of staying in a lighthouse (which is a museum during the day), and for the magical sunset views across the harbour. It's a bit like camping, with an outdoor shower, bring-your-own food and limited water. Leave your car in Newport (the hotel arranges a car permit) and you'll be taken over by ferry. **$185**

Vanderbilt Grace 41 Mary St ☎ 401 846 6200, ⓦ vanderbiltgrace.com. Round out the ultimate Newport experience with a stay in this luxurious 1909 Vanderbilt mansion, where even the standard (deluxe) rooms come with kitchenette, flat-screen TV, free wi-fi and CD/DVD player. Rates halve off-season. **$595**

William Gyles Guesthouse 16 Howard St ☎ 401 369 0243, ⓦ newporthostel.com. Newport's only hostel, *William Gyles* is welcoming and comfortable, with basic breakfast, shared kitchen and free internet included. Winter rates are usually lower. Closed Jan–March. Doubles **$98**; weekday dorms **$49**; weekend dorms **$69**

4

EATING

Aquidneck Lobster Co 31 Bowen's Wharf ☎ 401 846 106. This seafood wholesaler is essentially an open shack n stilts, with huge seawater tanks filled with local hellfish and crustaceans of all types. Pick your own and ake back for a feast, or get them to cook it for no extra harge; lobsters go for as low as $4/lb and local oysters $1 ach. Daily 6am–5.30pm.

Asterisk 599 Thames St ☎ 401 841 8833, ⓦ asterisknewport.com. Elegant French bistro in a former garage, with mouthwatering breakfasts, desserts and nains like sole *meunière* and chicken *scallopini* ($21–29). Mon–Fri 4pm–1am, Sat & Sun 11am–1am.

★ **Belle's Cafe** Newport Shipyard, 1 Washington St ☎ 401 846 6000, ⓦ newportshipyard.com. At this well-kept secret, tucked away from the downtown bustle, you an grab two delicious lobster rolls for $18.75 and paninis from $9.25) in the company of the world's finest yachts. Mon–Sat 7am–3pm.

Ben's Chili Dogs 158 Broadway ☎ 401 846 8206. Best dogs in town, with Coney Island sauce, gourmet cheese auce and all the fixins for less than $5. Cash only. Mon–Sat 10am–7pm, Sun till 6pm.

Black Pearl Bannister's Wharf ☎ 401 846 5264, ⓦ blackpearlnewport.com. Harbourside institution famous for its clam chowder (bowl $8.50) and more – formal options in the Commodore's Room (*escargots bourguignon*) and less formal ones in the Tavern (*escargots* with garlic butter) are both available. Daily 11.30am–1am; closed Jan.

Brick Alley Pub & Restaurant 140 Thames St ☎ 401 849 6334, ⓦ brickalley.com. Attracts locals and tourists alike, with moderately priced American fare ($17.95–27.95) and a popular Sunday brunch. Mon–Thurs 11.30am–10pm, Fri till 10.30pm, Sat 11am–10.30pm, Sun 10.30am–10pm.

Castle Hill Inn 590 Ocean Ave ☎ 401 849 3800, ⓦ castlehillinn.com. This resort hotel and restaurant boasts the best views in town, with an outdoor bar and Adirondack chairs overlooking the water. The food is reasonable but pricey – you're paying for those gasp-inducing views. Mon–Thurs noon–2pm & 5.45–8pm, Fri noon–2pm & 5.45–9pm, Sat 11.30am–3pm & 5.45–9pm, Sun 11.30am–3pm.

Coffee Grinder Bannister's Wharf ☎ 401 841 4325, ⓦ coffeegrindernewport.com. A quiet spot amid the harbour's bustle; sip coffee or a home-made granita and watch the world go by from on the waterfront porch. Mon–Fri 7.15am–9pm, Sat & Sun 6.30am–11pm.

★ **Empire Tea & Coffee** 22 Broadway ☎ 401 619 1388, ⓦ newportbubbletea.com. Choose from bubble teas and horchata chai, *lassis*, the best coffee in Newport, or one of over 60 teas in a relaxed cafe setting. Free wi-fi. Daily 6am–10pm.

★ **Flo's Clam Shack** 4 Wave Ave ☎ 401 847 8141, ⓦ flosclamshack.net. Hugely popular joint across from First Beach. At $4.50 for a bowl of clam chowder and $5.25 for a dozen clam cakes, it's worth the wait. Cash only. Wed–Sun 11am–9pm.

Mamma Luisa ☎ 401 848 5257, ⊕ mammaluisa.com. Best Italian restaurant in Newport, with fabulous home-made pastas (from $13.95) and refreshing fruit sorbets ($6.95). Mon, Tues & Thurs–Sun 5–10pm.

Newport Creamery 181 Bellevue Ave ☎ 401 846 6332, ⊕ newportcreamery.com. Home of the patented "Awful Awful's" – a drink made from flavoured syrup, milk and iced milk – as well as the classic coffee cabinets (p.250). Mon–Thurs & Sun 7am–9pm, Fri & Sat 7am–10pm.

Salvation Café 140 Broadway ☎ 401 847 2620, ⊕ salvationcafe.com. Funky spot off the main drag, with exotic concoctions like coriander-and cumin-encrusted tuna ($21), phad Thai ($16) and coconut mojitos ($9). Mon–Thurs & Sun 5–10pm, Fri & Sat till 11pm.

Scales & Shells 527 Thames St ☎ 401 846 3474, ⊕ scalesandshells.com. Casual "fish only" restaurant serving high-quality seafood – raw, broiled or mesquite-grilled. Mon–Thurs & Sun 5–10pm, Fri & Sat 5–11pm.

Smokehouse Café 31 Scott's Wharf ☎ 401 848 980 ⊕ smokehousecafe.com. Giant BBQ combos ($28.95) ar baby back ribs ($16.95 for a half rack) in a live atmosphere. Mon–Thurs 11.30am–10pm, Fri & Sat t 11pm, Sun noon–10pm.

★ **Tallulah On Thames** 464 Thames St ☎ 401 84 2433, ⊕ tallulahonthames.com. Hot new farm-to-tab restaurant, with seasonal ingredients sourced from loc suppliers: think Block Island Sound fluke (a type of flatfis $15), Schartner Farm beets ($12) and Absolana Farm butter lettuce ($12). Feb, March & Dec Wed–Su 6–11pm; April–Nov Wed–Mon same hours.

White Horse Tavern 26 Marlborough St ☎ 401 84 3600, ⊕ whitehorsetavern.us. Dine by candlelight at on of the oldest taverns in America, open since 168 Continental cuisine with a New England touch; dinne mains $32–40. Mon–Thurs & Sun 11am–9pm, Fri & Sa till 10pm.

DRINKING

Billy Goode's 23 Marlborough St ☎ 401 848 5013. Get a feel for Newport's speakeasy days at this boisterous dive bar in the former sailors' district. Live country music Wed nights. Mon–Sat 11am–1am, Sun noon–1am.

Mudville Pub 8 W Marlborough St ☎ 401 849 1408. Irish pub and sports bar perched over Cardines baseball field, where you can sneak a seat atop the stadium where Babe Ruth used to play. Extensive beer list. Mon–Fri 4.30pm–1am, Sat & Sun 11.30am–1am.

Pour Judgement 32 Broadway ☎ 401 619 211 ⊕ pourjudgement.com. Join the locals at this friendly ba – the best place for a pint and a burger ($6). Mon–F 11am–1am, Sat 11.30am–1am, Sun 10am–1am.

Wharf Pub & Restaurant 37 Bowen's Wharf ☎ 40 846 9233. The least expensive spot in the lively Bowen Wharf area, serving a varied selection of microbrews. Liv bands on summer weekends. Mon–Thurs & Su 11am–11pm, Fri & Sat till midnight.

NIGHTLIFE AND ENTERTAINMENT

Boom-Boom Room Clarke Cooke House, Bannister's Wharf ☎ 401 849 2900. Popular disco attracting a mixed crowd with mainstream dance music, golden oldies and "top 40" songs. Cover $5–10 in summer. Fri & Sat 9pm–1am.

Newport Blues Café 286 Thames St ☎ 401 841 5510, ⊕ newportblues.com. Come watch the legends and future stars in an old bank building by the harbour; live

blues and jazz from 9.45pm nightly. Cover $5–20. Tues Sun 5pm–1am.

One Pelham East Thames St, at Pelham st ☎ 401 84 9460, ⊕ thepelham.com. Popular venue that's hosted liv bands since 1975, attracting a raucous, boozy crow throughout the summer; there's a club upstairs, with cove that ranges from $10–20. Bring ID. Mon–Fri 3pm–2am Sat & Sun 1pm–1am.

Around Newport

If you have your own transport, it's possible to make some worthwhile detours **around Newport**, including the town of **Portsmouth**, also on Aquidneck Island, **Bristol** with its bucolic Blithewold Mansion and gardens, and **Little Compton** on the **Sakonnet Peninsula**, a largely rural, agricultural area.

Portsmouth

Founded in 1638 by Anne Hutchinson, another English Puritan refugee from Massachusetts, **PORTSMOUTH** was also the location of the only major clash of the Revolutionary War in the state, the **Battle of Rhode Island** (1778). Today Portsmouth is a pleasant, tree-lined suburb about ten miles north of Newport on Rte-114.

4

Green Animals Topiary Garden

80 Cory's Lane, off Rte-11 • May to mid-Oct daily 10am–5pm • $14.50 • ☎ 401 847 1000, ⓦ newportmansions.org

The prime attraction in Portsmouth is the **Green Animals Topiary Garden**, which has eighty animal-shaped trees and shrubs set on an idyllic lawn that slopes down to Narragansett Bay.

Bristol

Fifteen miles north of Newport, back on mainland Rhode Island, the town of **BRISTOL** is home to the **Blithewold Mansion, Gardens & Arboretum**. It also holds the oldest and perhaps most enthusiastic **Fourth of July** celebration in the nation, with a massive parade and fireworks spectacle.

Blithewold Mansion, Gardens & Arboretum

101 Ferry Rd (Rte-114) • **Grounds** Daily: May–Oct 9am–5pm; Nov–April 10am–5pm • $5 **Mansion** mid-April to mid-Oct Wed–Sat 10am–4pm, Sun till 3pm • $10 • ☎ 401 253 2707, ⓦ blithewold.org

The main attraction in Bristol is the **Blithewold Mansion, Gardens & Arboretum**, one-time summer residence of Pennsylvania coal magnate Augustus Van Wickle and his wife Bessie, completed in 1907. The 45-room house is filled with knick-knacks from Bessie's globetrotting adventures, and the gardens are wonderful, spread out around the ten-acre Great Lawn overlooking Narragansett Bay, with three thousand trees and shrubs.

Little Compton

The narrow strip of mainland Rhode Island that lies between the Sakonnet River and Massachusetts, east of Newport, is anchored by tiny **LITTLE COMPTON**. The town was settled by colonists from Plymouth, Massachusetts, in the 1670s, including **Colonel Benjamin Church**, pioneer of the American Rangers (elite scout troops).

United Congregational Church

4 South of Commons Rd • Visit during office hours Tues–Fri 9am–3pm to go inside • Free • ☎ 401 635 8472, ⓦ ucclcri.org

Little Compton is dominated by the lofty, brilliant-white spire of the 1832 **United Congregational Church**. The adjacent burial ground contains the grave of Colonel Benjamin Church, who took part in the hunting down and execution of Wampanoag chief King Philip (aka Metacomet) back in 1676.

Wilbur's General Store

50 South of Commons Rd • Mon–Sat 7am–6pm, Sun till 5pm • Free • ☎ 401 635 2356, ⓦ wilbursgeneralstore.com

Opposite the church, the meandering maze that is **Wilbur's General Store**, established in 1893 by C.R. Wilbur, is a Lilliputian department store, selling everything from speciality foods to hardware, toys and clothing – buy a bottle of traditional birch beer.

Sakonnet Vineyards

162 W Main Rd (Rte-77) • Daily: late May to Sept 10am–6pm; Oct to late May 11am–5pm; free tours noon & 3pm • ☎ 1 800 919 4637, ⓦ sakonnetwine.com

The biggest draw in these parts is **Sakonnet Vineyards**, founded in 1975 and producing decent chardonnays, pinot noirs, dessert wine and even champagne. Tours shed light on the wine-making process, and the shop stocks all the major varieties.

Sakonnet Point

South Shore Rd • **South Shore Beach** Daily 8am–5pm; parking Mon–Fri $12, Sat & Sun $15 • ☎ 401 635 9974 **Goosewing Beach Preserve** ☎ 401 331 7110, ⓦ nature.org

From Little Compton, Rte-77 bends south towards the Atlantic and **Sakonnet Point**, where a broad vista is framed on one side by the restored 1884 **lighthouse** (not open to the public) and on the other by the rocky shoreline. The waters are much more welcoming on the other side of the peninsula; park at **South Shore Beach** at the end of South Shore Road, and walk to the 75-acre **Goosewing Beach Preserve**, a quiet, sandy nesting site for plovers and terns.

EATING AND DRINKING

Commons Lunch 48 Commons Way ☎ 401 635 4388. Local diner since 1966, famed for its classic Rhode Island Johnny cakes (cornmeal flatbreads), quahog (clam) chowder and Québec-style French meat pie made with minced pork and beef. Daily 8am–6pm.

★ **Gray's Ice Cream** 16 East Rd (Rte-179), Tiverton ☎ 401 624 4500, ⓦ graysicecream.com. This Rhode Island legend, open since 1923 a short drive up the road from Little Compton, knocks out some of the best ice cream and iconic coffee cabinets (ice cream, milk

and coffee syrup) on the coast. May–Sept Mon–Thu 6.30am–9pm, Fri–Sun 6.30am–10pm; Oct–Apr daily 6.30am–7pm.

DELIS

Walker's Farm Stand 261 W Main Rd ☎ 401 635 4719 A veritable kaleidoscope of colourful produce, especially i the late summer and autumn, when pumpkins and apple bask in the golden autumnal glow; there's also a deli nex door. Daily 6am–8pm.

South County

The term "**SOUTH COUNTY**" is used to describe Rhode Island's southernmost towns, mainly the coastal stretch that begins with **Wickford**, 22 miles south of Providence, which winds south past gently rolling hills and sandy beaches to **Westerly**, at the border with Connecticut. **Watch Hill** and **Narragansett** are lively resort towns, while the busy fishing port of **Galilee** is the departure point for ferries to unspoilt **Block Island**. You'll need a car to make the most of South County.

INFORMATION

Tourist information For more information on events, accommodation and tours visit the South County

Tourism Council website at ⓦ southcountyri.com.

Wickford

The harbourside village of **WICKFORD**, with its shady lanes and handsomely preserved eighteenth- and nineteenth-century homes, is the location of one of the oldest churches in the US – **Old Narragansett Church** – and one of the oldest houses, **Smith's Castle**, which dates back to the first settlement of 1637.

Old Narragansett Church

62 Church Lane • July & Aug Thurs–Mon 11am–4pm • Free • ☎ 401 294 4357

The 1707 **Old Narragansett Church** is the oldest Episcopal church north of Virginia. Among its treasures are a Queen Anne Communion set and reputedly the oldest church organ in America, dating back to 1680.

Smith's Castle

55 Richard Smith Drive • Tours May, Sept & Oct Fri–Sun 1pm, 2pm & 3pm; June–Aug Thurs–Sun noon, 1pm, 2pm & 3pm • $6; gardens free • ☎ 401 294 3521, ⓦ smithscastle.org

Just north of Wickford's centre is **Smith's Castle**, a seventeenth-century house whose origins trace back to a possibly fortified trading post (hence the "castle" in the name) established around the time of Roger Williams' arrival in the area in 1637. Burned down during King Philip's War by the Narrangansett Indians, the house was rebuilt in 1678 and the site later became one of the area's great plantations; today it houses educational exhibits on town life in the last four centuries.

WHITE SANDS AND SURFING: SOUTH COUNTY BEACHES

Many of Rhode Island's best **beaches** are in South County, though note that ocean temperatures here peak at 70–75 degrees, in August. Entry is usually free, but state beaches charge a hefty summer **parking fee** of $20 weekdays and $28 weekends, while town beach parking fees range from $12–15. Most beaches are officially open Memorial Day (late May) to Labor Day (early Sept), daily from 9am to 6pm.

Narragansett Town Beach Rte-1A, Narragansett ⓦnarragansettri.gov. A half-mile-long beach in the centre of town, popular with families and known for good surf. Admission $6 in addition to parking.

Scarborough State Beach 870–970 Ocean Rd, Narragansett ☎401 789 2324, ⓦriparks.com /scarborough.htm. One of the busiest beaches, near Point Judith some three miles south of central Narragansett; popular with students from nearby URI and day-trippers from Providence.

Roger Wheeler State Beach 100 Sand Hill Cove Rd, Narragansett ☎401 789 3563, ⓦriparks.com /wheeler.htm. A quarter of a mile of clean grey sand with excellent facilities (changing rooms, coin-operated hot showers) and expansive parking, around two miles south of Scarborough Beach.

East Matunuck State Beach 950 Succotash Rd, South Kingstown ☎401 789 8585, ⓦriparks.com /eastmatunuck.htm. Watch the boats at the port of Galilee from here. The waves are good for surfing and there's a gradual drop-off that's good for surf-casting. Two miles south of US-1 (follow the signs).

South Kingstown Town Beach Matunuck Beach Rd, South Kingstown. Beautiful beach backed by dunes, popular with families and picnickers, near the village of Matunuck (2 miles south of US-1).

Charlestown Town Beach 577 Charlestown Beach Rd (2 miles south of US-1), Charlestown. Relatively strong surf and fine sand; a popular spot with concessions, showers and restrooms.

East Beach Ninigret State Conservation Area, off E Beach Rd, Charlestown (1 mile south of US-1). Three-mile-long barrier beach with sugar-fine sand and aquamarine waters. Campsites available, but limited parking and no concessions – best wild, untouched beach in the state.

Misquamicut State Beach 257 Atlantic Ave, Westerly ☎401 596 9097, ⓦmisquamicut.org. Rhode Island's largest state beach, this seven-mile stretch can get very crowded. Amusements, fast food and amenities are close at hand. One mile south of Rte-1A via Winnapaug Road.

Napatree Point Watch Hill. Gorgeous, fragile sandy spit extending over a mile from Watch Hill, with windswept dunes and views of Watch Hill Light. Great hiking and birding. Park in Watch Hill and walk (10min).

ARRIVAL AND DEPARTURE
WICKFORD

By bus RIPTA bus #14 (☎401 781 9400, ⓦripta.com) runs regularly along Rte-1A from Providence to Wickford (1hr; Mon–Sat hourly; $2) and on to Narragansett (another 10min).

Saunderstown

More like a small village than a town, SAUNDERSTOWN lies five miles south of Wickford along Rte-1A (Boston Neck Rd). A smattering of eighteenth-century colonial clapboard houses, it's best known today as the birthplace of painter **Gilbert Stuart**.

Gilbert Stuart Birthplace and Museum

4815 Gilbert Stuart Rd • May–Sept Mon & Thurs–Sat 11am–4pm, Sun noon–4pm; tours on the hour • $7 • ☎401 294 3001, ⓦgilbertstuartmuseum.com

The **Gilbert Stuart Birthplace and Museum** preserves the childhood home of the celebrated eighteenth-century portraitist born here in 1755, with a grist mill and herb gardens thrown in. Stuart made his money (and achieved lasting fame) thanks to his beloved portraits of **George Washington**, most of which have become iconic images – he anticipated that this would happen, and spent most of his career painting reproductions.

ARRIVAL AND DEPARTURE
SAUNDERSTOWN

By bus RIPTA bus #14 (☎401 781 9400, ⓦripta.com; $2) runs regularly along Rte-1A (Boston Neck Rd) from Providence to Saunderstown via Wickford and on to Narragansett, but the Gilbert Stuart museum is over 1 mile from the bus stop.

Narragansett

Eight miles south along Rte-1A from Saunderstown, **NARRAGANSETT**, meaning "little spit of land" in Algonquin, is just that, with a rocky coastline interspersed by broad expanses of sand – a major attraction for swimmers, surfers, birdwatchers and fishermen. The centre, known as **Narragansett Pier**, had its heyday during the Victorian era, when the town competed with Newport as a major resort destination. To some extent it succeeded, luring visitors to the **Narragansett Casino Resort**, designed in 1884. Hopes of fame and prosperity came to an abrupt end in 1900, however, when a fire swept through the casino, destroying all but its turreted towers, which today are the most striking feature of the town centre, and which house the **Narragansett Chamber of Commerce**. Narragansett's long coastline boasts several outstanding **beaches** (see box, p.265) and the charmingly chaotic fishing port of **Galilee**, four miles south of the town centre, home to the **Block Island ferry** (see p.271).

South County Museum

100 Strathmore St (Rte-1A) • May, June & Sept Fri & Sat 10am–4pm; July & Aug Wed–Sat 10am–4pm • $5 • ☎ 401 783 5400, ⓦ southcountymuseum.org

For more about Narragansett's history, visit the **South County Museum**, which holds thousands of local artefacts, a replicated print shop, smithy, textile arts centre and carpentry shop. The farm exhibit, with Rhode Island Red chickens, is especially popular with younger children.

ARRIVAL AND INFORMATION

By bus You need a car to make the most of this area, but RIPTA bus #14 (☎ 401 781 9400, ⓦ ripta.com) runs regularly along Rte-1A from Providence to Narragansett (1hr 10min; Mon–Sat hourly; $2) via Wickford and Saunderstown.

Narragansett Chamber of Commerce 36 Ocean Rd (Mon–Sat 9am–5pm; ☎ 401 783 7121, ⓦ narragansettcoc.com).

ACCOMMODATION

Blueberry Cove Inn 75 Kingstown Rd ☎ 1 800 478 1426, ⓦ blueberrycoveinn.com. Gorgeous 1870s home within walking distance of the town beach, with seven guest rooms and two whirlpool suites. All come with tasty breakfast, cable TV, DVD player, free wi-fi and a guest computer with internet. $150

The Richards 144 Gibson Ave ☎ 401 789 7746, ⓦ therichardsbnb.com. This English-style manor built in 1884 has just four Victorian-style rooms, two with canopy beds. Hearty breakfasts include blueberry muffins, baked apple pancakes and mushroom strudel. $150

Tower House B&B 46 Earles Court ☎ 401 783 3787, ⓦ towerhousebandb.com. Four stylish period rooms in a handsome 1885 mansion surrounded by lush gardens a short walk from the sea. Delicious home-made breakfasts and a cocktail hour, as well as free shuttles, beach towels and picnic lunches. $170

EATING AND DRINKING

★ **Aunt Carrie's** 1240 Ocean Rd ☎ 401 783 7930, ⓦ auntcarriesri.com. A local institution sine 1920, serving traditional "Shore Dinners" (clam chowder, clam cakes, steamed clams, lobster and fish and chips) in an unpretentious, relaxed atmosphere. April–late May & Sept Sat & Sun 11.30am–9pm; late May–Aug daily same hours.

Champlin's 256 Great Island Rd ☎ 401 783 3152, ⓦ champlins.com. It's worth the wait for the fresh lobster, clambakes ($27.99) and basics like fish and chips ($12.99) from this old self-serve clam shack overlooking the water. June–Sept daily 11am–9pm; Oct–May Mon 11am–6pm, Fri–Sun till 7pm.

Iggy's Doughboys and Chowder House 1157 Point Judith Rd, ☎ 401 783 5608, ⓦ iggysdoughboys.com. Close to the Block Island Ferry, this clam shack is celebrated for its doughboys (fried, sweet dough dumplings; $3.99), chowder ($5.59), clam cakes ($3.99) and fish and chips (priced daily). April–Oct Mon–Thurs & Sun 11am–8pm, Fri & Sat till 9pm.

Charlestown

Laid-back **CHARLESTOWN**, at the heart of the southern coast, is one of the fastest-growing communities in the state, its newcomers having been seduced by an attractive oastline – miles of barrier beach backed by pristine salt ponds. The Narragansett (the ocal Native American tribe) still own plenty of land around here, and maintain a ignificant cultural impact, best observed during their **Green Corn Thanksgiving**, held he second weekend of August on tribal lands just off Rte-2 (☎401 364 1100, Ⓦnarragansett-tribe.org). Celebrations take place at the **Narragansett Indian Church**, Old Mill Rd, a humble 1994 reconstruction of the original church built to convert the Native American community. You'll need your own transport to explore Charlestown.

Ninigret National Wildlife Refuge

0 Bend Rd (off US-1) • Daily sunrise–sunset • Free • ☎401 364 9124, Ⓦfws.gov/ninigret

The **Ninigret National Wildlife Refuge** comprises four hundred acres of diverse upland and wetland habitats on the shoreline of the state's largest salt pond. More than 250 species of birds frequent the former naval landing station, with its remnants of runways, miles of trails and **Kettle Pond Visitor Center** (daily 10am–4pm), containing interactive exhibits and displays.

INFORMATION   CHARLESTOWN

Charlestown Chamber of Commerce 4945 Old Post Rd, Rte-1A (Mon–Fri 9am–4.30pm; ☎401 364 3878, ⓌcharlestownRIChamber.com). Summer only.

Westerly

WESTERLY occupies the westernmost point of Rhode Island, eleven miles from Charlestown near the Pawcatuck River. Formerly a prosperous textile and granite manufacturing centre, today the town draws crowds for its spectacular beaches, especially in the **Watch Hill** area (see below) and at **Misquamicut Beach**. Brits may be amused to learn that Westerly still celebrates **Guy Fawkes Night** in November, with bonfires and even Morris dancers commemorating the failure of the Gunpowder Plot in 1605.

ARRIVAL AND INFORMATION   WESTERLY

By train Westerly is served by Amtrak trains (☎1 800 872 7245, Ⓦamtrak.com) from Boston (1hr 20min–2hr; 6 daily; $28), New York (3hr; 5 daily; $51), New Haven (1hr 15min; 5 daily; $22) and Providence (35min; 6 daily; $15). The station lies at 14 Railroad Ave, a short walk from central Westerly but a long way from Watch Hill and the beach. Call Wright's Taxi (☎401 596 8294).

Greater Westerly Chamber of Commerce 1 Chamber Way (Mon–Fri 8.30am–4.30pm; ☎401 596 7761, Ⓦwesterlychamber.org).

ACCOMMODATION, EATING AND DRINKING

Malted Barley 42 High St, Westerly ☎401 315 2184 Ⓦthemaltedbarleyri.com. With 35 craft beers and microbrews on tap, ten variations of the baked soft pretzel and an outdoor patio on river, this is an obvious choice for a light meal or a drink. Wed–Mon 3pm–1am.

Shelter Harbor Inn 10 Wagner Rd, Westerly ☎401 322 8883, Ⓦshelterharborinn.com. Originally a farmhouse built in the early 1800s, this tranquil 24-room country inn is done up with early American fittings and has an excellent restaurant. Guests have access to a private beach in nearby Weekapaug. **$178**

Tradewinds Hotel 4 Rabbit Run, Misquamicut Beach ☎401 596 5557, Ⓦtradewindsmotel.com. This is about as good as it gets for budget options along this stretch of coast, with basic but clean and comfy rooms equipped with a fridge, microwave and a/c. **$95**

The Villa 190 Shore Rd (Rte-1A) ☎401 596 1054, Ⓦthevillaatwesterly.com. Elegant B&B with an Italian/Mediterranean theme, close to Misquamicut Beach. There's a small pool and all rooms come with jacuzzi, microwave, cable TV and DVD player. **$150**

Watch Hill

Most visitors forsake Westerly's downtown in lieu of the **WATCH HILL** (Ⓦvisitwatchhill .com) area a few miles south, which, after Newport, is Rhode Island's most select resort, with salty seaside shops and posh 1900s-era **cottages** overlooking the Atlantic. At the end of Bay Street, the 1876 **Flying Horse Carousel** (June–Aug daily 1–9pm; children 2–12 only; $1.50–2) spins out rides with twenty horses suspended from a central frame.

Watch Hill Lighthouse Museum

14 Lighthouse Rd • July & Aug Tues & Thurs 1–3pm • Free • ⓦ watchhilllighthousekeepers.org

Watch Hill's second town highlight is its old 45ft granite **lighthouse** with the small **Watch Hill Lighthouse Museum** in the adjacent oil house. The lighthouse itself is closed to the public, but you're free to meander on the grounds.

Napatree Point

ⓣ 401 348 6540, ⓦ thewatchhillconservancy.org

To the west of Watch Hill, accessible from Watch Hill Beach, the half-mile-long barrier beach of **Napatree Point** once supported a number of homes before they were destroyed by a devastating hurricane in 1938, and is today a peaceful conservation area managed by the Watch Hill Conservancy, affording birding opportunities and stunning ocean views.

ARRIVAL AND DEPARTURE

WATCH HILL

By train Unless you have your own transport you'll need to take a train to Westerly station (see p.267) and then a taxi to Watch Hill and the beach (Wright's Taxi ⓣ 401 596 8294).

EATING & DRINKING

Olympia Tea Room 74 Bay St ⓣ 401 348 8211, ⓦ olympiatearoom.com. Elegant remnant of the Gilded Age in the heart of Watch Hill, with a "wine-driven" menu based on local produce and seafood. May–Oct Mon–Sat 11.30am–9pm, Sun noon–8pm.

St Clair Annex 141 Bay St ⓣ 401 348 8407. Serves wonderful breakfasts, sandwiches and home-made ice cream (dishes $10–30). Cash only. Daily 8am–9.30pm.

Block Island

Twelve miles off Rhode Island's southern coast, **BLOCK ISLAND** somehow continues to preserve its laidback, seductive charm: inhabited by only nine hundred year-round residents, it's a small bump of gently rolling hills and broad expanses of moorland, surrounded by a sometimes angry sea. Like Martha's Vineyard and Nantucket, the island bustles with tourist activity in the summer, but doesn't attract much of the accompanying scene and is a lot less posh. With little of the history that dominates its Massachusetts island cousins, it's the **beach** that's the main focus here and the water temperature stays relatively high from June to October. Indeed, early autumn is a great time to visit, as the crowds clear and flocks of migratory birds stop here on their way south, while the quiet, wild inland is perhaps best taken in on bike, or on foot – the island has 28 miles of **walking trails.**

Brief history

In 1614, Dutch explorer Adrian Block stopped on the island and gave it the name "**Adrian's Eyelandt**", but it eventually became known as **Block Island** in his honour. A group of English settlers seeking religious freedom arrived in 1661, establishing a small farming and fishing community. A relatively quiet couple of hundred years followed until 1842, when the island's first rooming house opened and visitors began to recognize Block Island's many charms; thirty years later a new breakwater was built, meaning that larger ships could dock – bringing even more travellers. Things took a turn for the worse with the **Great Hurricane of 1938** that devastated much of the New England coast: it destroyed nearly all of Block Island's fishing fleet and caused considerable structural damage to the hotels and other buildings around Old Harbor, the island's commercial centre.

Little remains of those hard times today, as Block Island has become a highly sought-after real estate destination with many properties surpassing the million-dollar mark. In

BLOCK ISLAND

ACCOMMODATION

The 1661 Inn & Hotel	
Manisses	7
Avonlea, Jewel of the Sea	1
Blue Dory Inn	2
McCombe's Guest House	4
National Hotel	3
Rose Farm Inn	6
Spring House Hotel	8
The Upstairs	5

EATING

Atlantic Inn	12
Beachead	4
Dead Eye Dick's	2
Eli's	8
Finn's Seafood	
Restaurant	10
Hotel Manisses	11
Juice N' Java	5
The Oar	1
Payne's Killer Donuts	3
Rebecca's Seafood	9
The Tap & Grill	7
Three Sisters	6

NIGHTLIFE

Captain Nick's	1
McGovern's Yellow	
Kittens Tavern	2

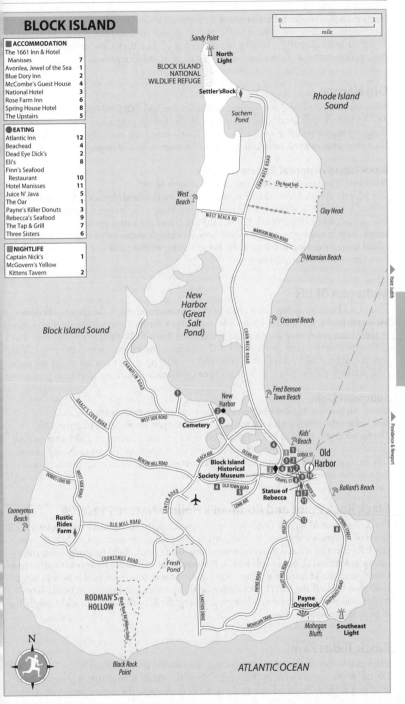

reaction to this, residents have in recent years passed a number of measures – including a camping ban – designed to preserve the island's natural environment. By 2013 Deepwater Wind (🌐dwwind.com) is planning to operate one of the nation's first **offshore wind farms** three miles southeast of the island, supplying all of its electricity needs.

Old Harbor

Most visitors' first – and last – image of Block Island is of **OLD HARBOR**, developed after 1870 when the two breakwaters were built by the federal government. To encourage the fledgling tourist industry, ornate Victorian hotels were built along **Water Street**, and their remnants can still be found today amid a touristy mix of boutiques and restaurants.

Block Island Historical Society Museum

18 Old Town Rd, at Ocean Ave • June–Sept Wed–Mon 11am–4pm • $5 • ☎ 401 466 2481

The island's eventful history is chronicled at the **Block Island Historical Society Museum**, housed in the 1871 Woonsocket House. Its rambling two floors are stuffed with ageing bric-a-brac, while display boards chart the history of the island from Native American times. Rare vintage photographs show how shockingly denuded of vegetation the island was in the nineteenth century. Enlightening **walking tours** of the town run from here (June–Sept 10am & 4pm).

Mohegan Bluffs

From Old Harbor, Spring Street trails to the southernmost tip of the island, where the **Mohegan Bluffs**, spectacular 150ft cliffs named for a Native American battle that occurred at their base, tower over the Atlantic. A trail leads down to **Bluffs Beach** right below the cliffs – it's a steep climb up and down 141 wooden steps, but well worth the effort. Make sure you at least take a moment to enjoy the scintillating views from the top of the path (the overlook platform here known as **Payne Overlook** is closed due to erosion problems).

Southeast Light

Daily July–Aug 10am–4pm • $1; $10 for hourly 15min guided tours 10.30am–3.30pm • ☎ 401 466 5009

Just before the parking area for the beach at Mohegan Bluffs you'll pass the 52ft **Southeast Light**, built in 1873 but moved to its present position in 1993 after erosion threatened its survival. Laying claim to being the highest lighthouse in New England (it's 261ft above sea level), the appealing attraction here is the trip up the sixty-odd steps of the tower for the stunning **ocean views**.

Black Rock Point and Rodman's Hollow Nature Preserve

Further west of Mohegan Bluffs on the island's southern shore, **Black Rock Point** affords views of a dramatic seascape in which many ships have met their untimely end – you can hike there in around thirty minutes along Black Rock Road (actually a dirt track), off the main road (Cooneymus Road). **Rodman's Hollow Nature Preserve** is visible from Cooneymus Road just before Black Rock Road (the hollow is accessible by a variety of trails that lead off the latter). The deep glacial depression, smothered in blackberry bushes and dense vegetation, is beautiful during the May shad bloom. It's blissfully free of people any time of year.

Rustic Rides Farm

1173 West Side Rd • Daily: May–Sept 9am–6pm; Oct–April 10am–4pm • Horseriding $40–100 • ☎ 401 466 5060

On the more remote western side of the island lies **Rustic Rides Farm**, where you can arrange a tranquil horseride along the beaches or through the nature preserves. At the farm, local eccentric Tim McCabe maintains the **Lost Manissean Indian Exhibit** (free), actually just a shed containing a video of his most impressive finds. Tim has collected many arrowheads, axe heads and knives around the island, along with ancient mortars and pestles allegedly made by the local Manissean tribe. But his most controversial claims involve the "real" holy grail (which he claims is a Native American artefact) and various relics he associates with Viking visitors to the island in the eleventh century.

New Harbor

A mile northwest of Old Harbor along Ocean Avenue, **NEW HARBOR** boasts the only other commercial area on the island: a handful of waterfront restaurants, shacks and a marina on the shores of the **Great Salt Pond**. Above the village, the atmospheric **Block Island Historical Cemetery** (daily sunrise–sunset; free) is the resting place of the island's earliest settlers.

Cow Cove

Scenic **Corn Neck Road** leads north from Old Harbor past Sachem Pond to **Cow Cove** at the northern end of the island and **Settler's Rock**, laid here in 1911 to commemorate where the English settlers first landed (with their cows) in 1661.

North Light

Interpretive centre summer daily 10am–4pm • $3

The beach at Cow Cove is often smothered in seaweed, but you can walk the half-mile up to secluded **North Light**, at Block Island's isolated northern tip (Sandy Point). The current incarnation is the fourth for this lighthouse (1867), a grim reminder of the power of nature. The old lighthouse is gradually being restored, with an **interpretive centre** inside nominally open throughout the summer, but check at the visitor centre in Old Harbor to confirm.

4

ARRIVAL AND DEPARTURE

BLOCK ISLAND

BY PLANE
New England Airlines operates up to 20 daily flights (just 12min; $49 one-way, $89 return; ☎ 1 800 243 2460) from Westerly Airport (5min off I-95) all year.

BY FERRY
Most people come to Block Island by ferry. All boats arrive at Old Harbor, close to the major hotels, bike rental outlets and restaurants.
From Point Judith, RI Interstate Navigation Co runs ferries from Point Judith to Old Harbor (summer 4–9 boats daily; winter 1–3 daily; 1hr; $11.95 one-way, $19.65 same-day return; bikes $3.15 one-way; ☎ 401

783 4613, ⓦ www.blockislandferry.com), signposted off Rte-108 some 36 miles south of Providence. RIPTA Bus #66 ($2) connects with the nearest Amtrak station at Kingston (☎ 1 800 872 7245, ⓦ amtrak.com). Passengers taking cars ($47.90 each way) must make reservations in advance, although most leave them behind at car parks near Galilee State Pier (around $10/day). The company also runs a high-speed catamaran between Point Judith and the island (mid-May to mid-Oct; 30min; $19 one way, $35.85 return).
From Newport, RI More convenient for those without a car, Interstate Navigation Co also runs daily ferries (no cars) from Newport's Fort Adams State Park from late June to

---

BLOCK ISLAND'S BEACHES

Block Island has seventeen miles of sandy, often spectacular **beaches**, all of which are free to visit. The island's eastern coast offers two and a half miles of flat sand, known as **Crescent Beach**, stretching from Old Harbor to Clay Head. The main beach here is **Fred Benson Town Beach**, with lifeguards and full amenities, popular for swimming, kayaking and surfing. At its sheltered southern tip, known as **Kid Beach**, children can play in relatively shallow water, while boisterous **Ballard's Beach** can be found just past the ferry dock. **West Beach** on the northwestern coast is a better bet for some seclusion, bordered by a bird sanctuary to the south and dunes to the north, but the cobbly shores are more suited to fishing than swimming.

September (9.15am; 2hr; $11.55 one-way, $17.15 same-day return; bicycles $3.10 one-way).

From New London, CT You can also consider the high-speed Block Island Express from New London, CT ($24 one-way, $43 same-day return; bicycles $10 one-way; ☎ 860 444 4624; ⓦ goblockisland.com), which departs close to

the Amtrak station (trips take just over 1hr).

From Long Island, NY High-speed ferries from Montauk, Long Island are operated by Viking Ferry ($40 one-way; ☎ 631 668 5700, ⓦ vikingfleet.com), while the Peconic Star Express makes trips from Greenport, Long Island (one-way $59; ☎ 631 289 6899; ⓦ peconicstarfleet.com).

GETTING AROUND

Many tourists inexplicably bring their SUVs across to Block Island, but you really don't need a car to get around (**taxis** are available if you are desperate). **Scooters** or **bikes** are easy to rent, and there are plenty of **hiking trails** to explore.

By taxis Taxis line up at the ferry dock; fares are set by the town and there are no meters. Most one-way trips will be $10–15 (plus $1 for every additional passenger), and hour-long island tours of the island are $55 for two people; add $10 for each additional person.

By bicycle/moped As you disembark from the ferry, you'll find an array of bike and moped rental agencies, with still more lurking behind the shops (the ones further from the dock tend to be cheaper). In the height of the season

(July & Aug), expect to pay around $85/4hr for moped rental, or $45/hr (petrol can add $2–8). Bikes are usually $20/5hr or $30/day. A good option is Island Moped & Bike on Chapel Street (☎ 401 466 2700).

On foot Though you could explore the island on foot, it will take a lot of time to see everything – bikes are a better option. There are some 28 miles of walking trails maintained by the Nature Conservancy (☎ 401 466 2129), though, and their map is available from the info centre at the ferry dock.

INFORMATION

Block Island Chamber of Commerce Near the ferry dock (June–Sept daily 9am–5pm; Oct–May Mon–Fri 10am–3pm; ☎ 401 466 2982, ⓦ blockislandchamber.com). Has lockers for luggage storage and sells a useful island map and cycling guide ($1 each).

Island Free Library Dodge St (Tues, Wed & Fri 10am–5pm, Thurs 11am–7pm, Sat 11am–3pm). Offers free wi-fi, computer terminals and the best collection of Block Island-related books anywhere.

ACCOMMODATION

In the **summer tourist season**, the island's limited accommodation fills up rapidly, so be sure to book well in advance if you plan on spending the night. For longer-term stays and house rentals, **Block Island Reservations** maintains a number of rental properties (☎ 1 800 825 6254, ⓦ blockislandreservations.com).

The 1661 Inn & Hotel Manisses 5 Spring St, Old Harbor ☎ 401 466 2421 or ☎ 1 800 626 4773, ⓦ blockislandresorts.com. Luxurious island institution with nine unique rooms in the *1661 Inn* and seventeen Victorian rooms in the *Hotel Manisses*. Do enquire about the other cottages and apartments on site, including the economical, contemporary guesthouse. **$125**

★ **Avonlea, Jewel of the Sea** Corn Neck Rd ☎ 1 800 992 7290, ⓦ blockislandinns.com. Renovated beach house with stellar views of the ocean and a wraparound porch just off the beach. Rooms offer a blend of modern and romantic Victorian furnishings, and rates include buffet breakfast, afternoon wine and "hors d'oeuvres hour" featuring their home-baked Blue Dory cookies. **$265**

Blue Dory Inn 68 Dodge St, Old Harbor ☎ 1 800 992 7290, ⓦ blockislandinns.com. Sister property to *Avonlea* and just as enticing, with similar amenities and just eleven lavishly furnished period rooms on the edge of town but close to the beach. **$180**

★ **McCombe's Guest House** 261 Old Town Rd ☎ 401 466 2684. One of the two-dozen or so small guesthouses

on the island, with two beautifully decorated rooms, each with private entrance – it's usually open in the summer months only, and rented by the week, but day rates are available in early September. **$140**

National Hotel Water St, Old Harbor ☎ 401 466 2901 or ☎ 1 800 225 2449, ⓦ blockislandhotels.com. Vast Victorian pile on the main drag, dating from 1888. Small but comfy rooms with flat-screen TVs and cable, many with sea views. The wraparound porch downstairs houses a popular restaurant (see opposite). **$229**

Rose Farm Inn Roslyn Rd, Old Harbor ☎ 401 466 2034, ⓦ rosefarminn.com. Seventeen rooms in two properties on twenty idyllic acres close to the water. The *Farm House* offers elegant Victorian-style rooms, while *Captain Rose House* contains comfy modern units. **$179**

Spring House Hotel 52 Spring St, Old Harbor ☎ 401 466 5844 or ☎ 1 800 234 9263, ⓦ springhousehotel.com. Stately 1852 waterfront hotel on a hill; the oldest on the island, with lovely rooms, many with ocean view. Former guests include Ulysses S. Grant and Billy Joel. **$250**

The Upstairs Connecticut Ave, Old Harbor ☎ 401 466

2627, ⓦupstairsonbi.com. Secluded suite with private deck, satellite TV and breakfast included. There is also a two-storey cottage with full kitchen, which sleeps up to four, available for weekly rental. Doubles <u>$165</u>; cottage <u>$1100</u>/week

EATING

Eating on Block Island is a lot of fun, with plenty of **seafood shacks**, cafés, a killer doughnut stall and several high-quality options. Most of these restaurants close completely or open for limited hours from November–May – call ahead if in doubt.

OLD HARBOR

Atlantic Inn 359 High St ⊕401 466 5883, ⓦatlanticinn.com. For a special night out, this hotel restaurant offers candlelight, sea views and a contemporary American menu, with lots of seafood and a fine wine list, as well as a four-course *prix fixe* menu ($49). Daily 5–10pm.

Beachead Corn Neck Rd ⊕401 466 2249, ⓦthebeachead.com. Just north of town, this old wooden bar and restaurant is the best place to be on a sunny afternoon, right off Crescent Beach. Food can be hit and miss, but stick with the fried clams or more substantial steaks and you can't go wrong. Mains from $10–29. Daily 11.30am–9pm (sometimes later in summer).

★ **Eli's** 456 Chapel St ⊕401 466 5883, ⓦelisblockisland .com. Pricey but excellent bistro, serving dishes with a little more flair than the island average – think smoked mussel spaghetti ($23), seared sea scallops ($27) and a zesty key lime pie ($10). Get there early in summer, or be prepared to wait (no reservations). May–Sept Mon–Thurs & Sun 6–9pm, Fri & Sat till 10pm, Oct–Dec Thurs–Sun 6–9pm.

Finn's Seafood Restaurant 212 Water St ⊕401 466 2473, ⓦfinnsseafood.com. Classic Rhode Island diner that's been open for over 40 years – especially good for clam chowder, moderately priced fresh fish, hot lobster salad sandwiches and strawberry-rhubarb pie, all served overlooking the harbour. May–Oct 11.30am–9.30pm.

Hotel Manisses 5 Spring St ⊕401 466 2421, ⓦblockislandresorts.com. Elegant dining in a Victorian inn or outside in the gazebo, featuring contemporary American cuisine with fresh produce from the hotel's backyard. Best place for a splurge (mains $19–36). Daily 5–10pm.

Juice N' Java 235 Dodge St ⊕401 466 5220. Tiny but popular place for a caffeine-and-bagel fix in the morning. Laidback and modern, they also sell filling egg sandwiches and muffins. Daily 6am–6pm.

Rebecca's Seafood Water St ⊕401 466 5411. Small shack on the main strip open early for breakfast plates (From $5), and extra late for tasty chowder, clam cakes and wraps. May–Sept daily 7am–2am.

The Tap & Grill National Hotel, Water St ⊕401 466 2901. Juicy steaks ($19.99–35.99) as well as the standard saltwater and American dishes – lobster roll ($21.99), local swordfish (market price) and burgers ($10.99) – served on the lively, harbourside porch of the *National Hotel*. Daily 7.30am–11pm.

★ **Three Sisters** 443 Old Town Rd ⊕401 466 9661. It's not on the waterfront, but this is a lot more authentically "island", a clam shack-style place serving classics such as Molly's Meatloaf ($8.35), "hippie chick sandwich" (vegetables and avocados) and salads. They also serve fresh fish of the day with clams. Don't skip the desserts – the choc chip cookies are sublime. Cash only. Daily 7am–10am, 11am–2.30pm & 5.30–10pm.

NEW HARBOR

Dead Eye Dick's 218 Ocean Ave ⊕401 466 2654, ⓦwww.deadeyedicksbi.com. Restaurant-come-pub that features a decent raw bar and excellent seafood. Perfect for sunset-viewing from the deck overlooking the harbour. Mains $16–24. Daily lunch and dinner.

The Oar West Side Rd, Block Island Boat Basin ⊕401 466 8820. Famed for cheap, tasty seafood (and a sushi bar), with views of the Great Salt Pond from the deck and decorated oars on their walls. Gets extra rowdy at the weekends with "yachties" over from the mainland; plastic cups and fried food, but lots of fun. May–Oct daily 8am–1am.

★ **Payne's Killer Donuts** Ocean Ave ⊕401 466 2481. Don't miss this small take-away counter in the centre of New Harbor, selling delicious doughnuts (plain, sugar or cinnamon) for just 80 cents each, a tradition started in 1963. Also does bagels and coffee, and Del's Frozen Lemonade ($2.50). May–Sept 7am–close.

NIGHTLIFE AND ENTERTAINMENT

Although Block Island is usually so quiet you can hear the grass grow, the **nightlife** picks up in **summer**. There are even two **cinemas**. Pick up a copy of the local paper, the *Block Island Times* (ⓦblock-island.villagesoup.com) for current listings.

Captain Nick's 34 Ocean Ave, Old Harbor ⊕401 466 5670, ⓦcaptainnicks.com. Live music throughout the summer (Fri–Mon 6–9pm), from national headliners to eager locals. Also celebrated for its sushi rolls ($8–10), served Thurs–Sun from 5pm till they're gone. Monday is disco night. Daily 4pm–close.

McGovern's Yellow Kittens Tavern Corn Neck Rd, Old Harbor ⊕401 466 5855, ⓦyellowkittens.net. Popular local hangout with outdoor deck; DJs play in summer. Food supplied by Mexican on the Deck (ⓦmexicanonthedeck .net). Daily 11.30am–close.

Connecticut

280 Mystic and southeast
Connecticut

290 Southwest Connecticut

304 The Connecticut River
Valley

316 The Litchfield Hills

325 The Last Green Valley

MYSTIC SEAPORT

5

Connecticut

Only ninety miles long by 55 miles wide, Connecticut is New England's southernmost state and the most influenced by New York City; thousands of commuters travel between the two each day, while many of the opulent mansions that dot the state are owned by Wall Street bankers. As a result, tourism here is of a sophisticated sort, with art galleries, vineyards, historical houses, museums and increasingly eclectic cuisine on offer, while the state's lesser-known natural offerings along the coast, and within its rural hinterland, make for some pleasant surprises.

Though the interior remains predominantly rural, the state is densely populated along the coast. The vibrant **southwest** corner is home to industrial and intellectual **New Haven**, home of **Yale University**. Further east, the coast is studded by enticing small towns, from hip **New London** to the colonial charms of **Mystic** and **Stonington**. Further inland, the state capital at **Hartford** is a real surprise, with a gradually regenerating downtown and a trio of exceptional attractions beginning with the mind-blowing Connecticut Science Center. The state's northwestern section, the **Litchfield Hills**, offers a totally different experience, more akin to the quiet roads, farms and picturesque landscapes of Vermont, but with a fraction of the tourists.

Brief history

The state was first settled by Europeans in the 1630s, when primarily **English** settlers founded several distinct colonies. The two most significant were the **Connecticut Colony** at Hartford in 1636, led by the Reverend Thomas Hooker, and the **New Haven Colony** (originally known as the Quinnipiack Colony), led by English exile John Davenport, in 1638. Hartford was the only colony that had a charter – New Haven was an unofficial colony, an experiment in severe theocratic government in its early years. To punish New Haven for harbouring three of the English judges that signed his father's death warrant, King Charles II forcibly united the two colonies in 1662. Hartford and New Haven alternated every year as capital of the state until 1873, when Hartford assumed the role full-time.

During the Revolution, Connecticut's role in supplying the war effort earned it the nickname of the **"Provisions State"**. With steady industrialization helped along by Yale graduate **Eli Whitney**, who invented the cotton gin in 1794, Connecticut prospered during the late eighteenth and nineteenth centuries. Today, like most of New England, Connecticut remains fairly liberal; it legalized same-sex marriage in 2008, and tends to favour the Democratic Party in elections.

INFORMATION
CONNECTICUT

Tourist information The Connecticut Commission on Culture & Tourism runs the state's official tourism website ⓦ ctvisit.com (call also ☎ 1888 288 4748), while the state government site at ⓦ ct.gov carries all sorts of general information.

Mystic Pizza p.283	**New Haven pizza** p.296
Gambling on Connecticut's Native american reservations p.285	**The Glass House** p.301
	After hours at the Science Center p.308
New Haven's top events p.292	**Connecticut's wine trail** p.319
The Amistad p.293	**Riding the rails at Danbury** p.324

Highlights

❶ Mystic Enchanting coastal town, home to one of North America's premier aquariums, the Mystic Seaport – and that famous pizza. **See p.280**

❷ Florence Griswold Museum Visit the spiritual home of the American Impressionists, with doors and wall panels beautifully painted. See p.287

❸ Cruise the Thimble Islands Get up close to these clumps of granite topped with lavish mansions, poking out of Long Island Sound. See p.290

❹ Yale University Breathe in the erudite air in the magnificent libraries and Classical and Gothic buildings of the nation's second oldest Ivy League college. **See p.292**

❺ Wadsworth Atheneum Marvel at world-class Dalí, Monet and Hudson School paintings at the nation's oldest continuously operating public art museum. **See p.307**

❻ Hit the wine trail Connecticut's blossoming vineyards produce surprisingly good wines. See p.319

HIGHLIGHTS ARE MARKED ON THE MAP ON PP.278–279

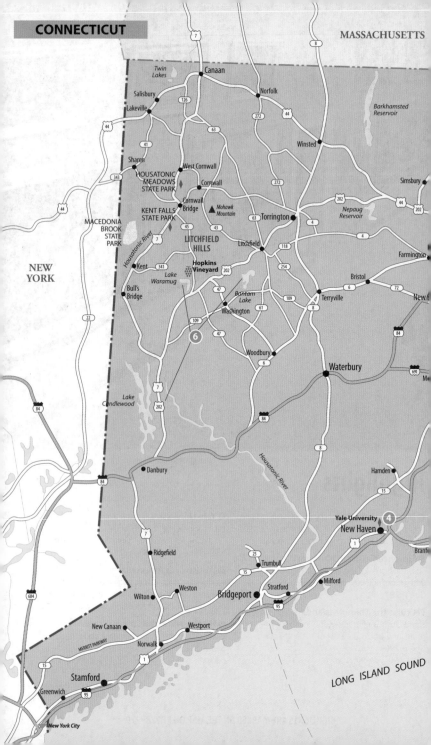

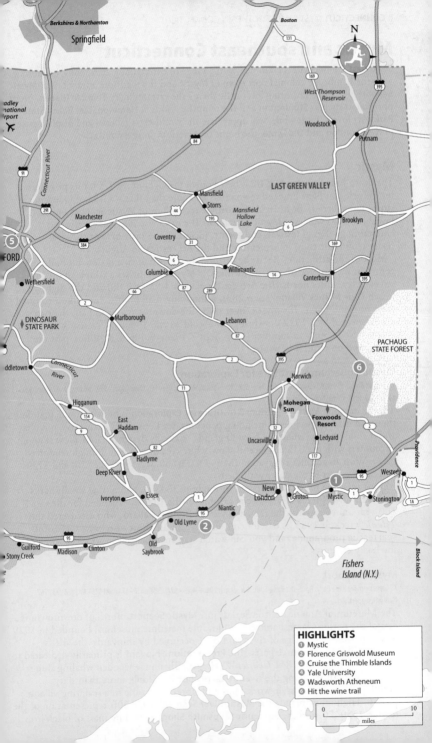

5

Mystic and southeast Connecticut

Southeast Connecticut is crammed with a range of entertaining attractions, beginning with the handsome colonial port town of **Mystic** and the maritime attractions at **Mystic Seaport**. For those favouring less bustle there's the extraordinary **Thimble Islands**, pretty port towns such as **Stonington** and the tempting sands at **Hammonasset Beach State Park**. Art lovers, meanwhile, will appreciate the world-class galleries and display spaces of **New London** and **Old Lyme**, the home of American Impressionism.

Mystic

Thanks to Julia Roberts, **MYSTIC** is best-known throughout the US for its pizza joint, but this elegant New England town offers far more than that – a host of independent stores and galleries, the intriguing maritime recreations of **Mystic Seaport** and the loveable beluga whales at **Mystic Aquarium**. The town also hosts an electric and entertaining series of **festivals and events**, including the **Taste of Mystic** festival (ⓦatasteofmystic.com) in September and the **Art Festival** in August.

Most of the attractions lie in the **historic downtown** area, a major shipbuilding centre in the nineteenth century, while **Old Mystic** comprises a couple of quaint streets a few miles north. The two are divided by I-95 (exit 90) and the slightly kitsch **Olde Mistick Village** (see p.283), a shopping mall built to look like a colonial New England town. The **Mystic River** splits the downtown area in half; the two sides are connected by a 1922 drawbridge of an old *bascule* (French: "seesaw") sort, which is still raised hourly in summer (May–Sept 7.40am–6.40pm, at 40min past the hour), and on request in winter.

Mystic Aquarium & Institute for Exploration

55 Coogan Blvd, I-95 exit 90 • Daily: April–Oct 9am–5pm; Nov–March till 4pm; Dec–Feb 10am–4pm • $29, children (3–17 years) $21 • ☏ 860 572 5955, ⓦ mysticaquarium.org

The outstanding **Mystic Aquarium & Institute for Exploration** is home to more than four thousand marine specimens, including penguins, sea lions, sharks, stingrays, piranhas and the only **beluga whales** in New England – specially designed tanks allow close-up encounters with these three graceful snow-white creatures (albeit through reinforced glass). With an advance reservation (May–Oct; ☏860 572 5955, ext 520) and $130 you can even get in the water with them.

Don't miss the **touch tanks** spread throughout the site, containing small sharks and even rays. There's also a special exhibit on the **Titanic**, expanded for the 100-year anniversary of the tragedy in 2012 (**Robert Ballard**, who discovered the *Titanic* wreck in 1985, is based here). Finally, the Institute also has a successful **seal rescue programme**, and you can watch staff members clean and feed some of the lucky creatures.

Mystic Seaport

75 Greenmanville Ave • Daily: April–Oct 9am–5pm; Nov–March 10am–4pm • $24, children (6–17 years) $15 • ☏ 1888 973 2767 ⓦ mysticseaport.org

The Museum of America & the Sea, or just **Mystic Seaport**, north of downtown, is one of the nation's largest and most enjoyable maritime museums. Founded in 1929 on a nineteen-acre wedge of riverfront once occupied by shipyards, the site is roughly divided into three parts. The **Preservation Shipyard** is primarily dedicated to the restoration of the 1841 *Charles W. Morgan*. This huge wooden whaling ship is due to offer cruises along the river by 2014. Further along, more than sixty buildings housing old-style workshops and stores reflect life in a seafaring **village** c.1876. Highlights include the **Mystic River Scale Model**, a 50ft representation of the town c.1850–70, and the authentic **Shipsmith Shop**, a jangling mass of black iron

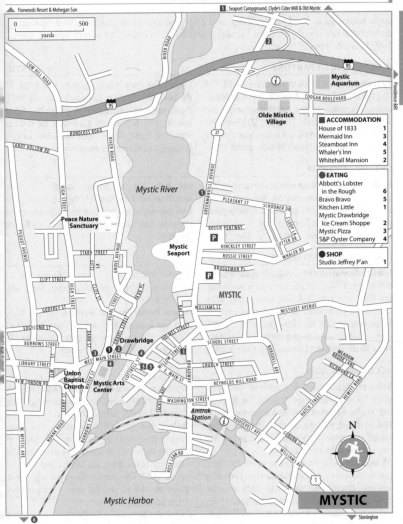

▲ Foxwoods Resort & Mohegan Sun

1 , Seaport Campground, Clyde's Cider Mill & Old Mystic ▲

0 — 500 yards

RIVER ROAD

COW HILL ROAD

95

2

95

Providence &RI ►

ℹ

Mystic Aquarium

COOGAN BOULEVARD

SANDY HOLLOW RD

BUNDLOSS ROAD

RIVER ROAD

HIGH STREET

Peace Nature Sanctuary

PEQUOT AVENUE

Mystic River

27

Olde Mistick Village

GREENMANVILLE AVENUE

PLEASANT ST

SCHOONER DR

ROSSIE PENTWAY

P

HINCKLEY STREET

ROSSIE STREET

BRUGGEMAN PL

P

SLOOP LN

CUTTER DR

WHALER RD

Mystic Seaport

STARR STREET

CLIFF LA.

GROVE AVENUE

CLIFT STREET

HIGH STREET

GODFREY ST

RANK ST

PEARL STREET

COTTRELL STREET

GRAVEL STREET

EDGECOMB ST

BURROWS STREET

LIBRARY STREET

NEW LONDON RD

WEST MAIN STREET

Union Baptist Church

Mystic Arts Center

WATER STREET

HOLMES STREET

WILLOW STREET

E. MAIN ST

JACKSON AVE

BROADWAY

WASHINGTON STREET

Amtrak Station

ℹ

ROOSEVELT AVE

MYSTIC

WILLIAMS ST

MISTUXET AVENUE

SCHOOL STREET

CHURCH STREET

REYNOLDS HILL ROAD

BONDELL AVE

RICHMOND LN

MEADOW BROOK LANE

HEWITT ROAD

MATCH STREET

COBURN ST

WILLIAMS AVE

N

Drawbridge

3

1

2

4

5 1 5

3

6

NOANK ROAD

BURROWS PL

W MYSTIC AVE

ROSSIE LN RD

Mystic Harbor

MYSTIC

Stonington ▼

■ ACCOMMODATION
House of 1833	1
Mermaid Inn	3
Steamboat Inn	4
Whaler's Inn	5
Whitehall Mansion	2

● EATING
Abbott's Lobster in the Rough	6
Bravo Bravo	5
Kitchen Little	1
Mystic Drawbridge Ice Cream Shoppe	2
Mystic Pizza	3
S&P Oyster Company	4

● SHOP
Studio Jeffrey P'an	1

blocks, hammers and anvils. The final section of the seaport contains a series of more formal **exhibit halls**, including the absorbing **Voyages** gallery, with multimedia displays covering the whole span of American maritime history. There's also the **Figureheads** exhibition, with original wooden ship figureheads displayed like ornate sculptures. If you fancy a soothing thirty-minute trip along the Mystic River, sign up for a cruise on the 1908 steamboat **Sabino** (May–Oct daily 11.30am–4.30pm; $5.50).

Clyde's Cider Mill

129 N Stonington Rd, Old Mystic • Daily: Sept–Oct 9am–6pm; Nov–Dec till 5pm • Free • ☎ 860 536 3354, ⓦ BFClydescidermill.com

Founded in 1881, **Clyde's Cider Mill** is New England's last steam-powered cider press and its oldest continuous producer of hard cider (alcoholic; most US ciders are just raw apple juices). The mill opens to the public in the autumn, when it produces ciders,

5

apple wines, jams, local honey, fudge and maple syrup. Try to take in a **cider-making demonstration**, usually held on Saturdays and Sundays only (Oct 11am, 1pm & 3pm; Nov 11am & 1pm).

ARRIVAL AND DEPARTURE

MYSTIC

By train The train station is at 2 Roosevelt Ave off US-1 (●1 800 872 7245, ⊚amtrak.com) in downtown Mystic, with Amtrak services to New York (4 daily; around 3hr; $49), Boston (4 daily; around 1hr 35min; $31), Providence (4 daily; around 45min; $17), and major towns along the Connecticut coast: New London (4 daily; around 15min;

$14); and New Haven (4 daily; around 1hr 10min; $20).

By bus Peter Pan Bus Lines (●1 800 443 1831, ⊚peterpanbus.com) runs buses to Mystic from New York (2 daily 3hr; $30). Note that the bus stops at the SEAT bus shelter near The Kite Shop in Olde Mistick Village, which is not especially convenient for downtown.

GETTING AROUND

By car Getting about is tough without your own transport; Enterprise (Mon–Fri 8am–6pm, Sat 9am–noon; ●860 536 6829, ⊚enterprise.com) rents cars at 42 Williams Ave, just down the street from the train station.

By bicycle The Mystic Community Bikes project

runs from May to October (●860 572 9578, ⊚mysticcommunitybikes.org; $10 deposit), offering free bikes (plus helmet and lock) from ten distribution centres around the town (including the train station). Valid photo ID required.

INFORMATION AND TOURS

Tourist information Mystic's main information office lies in Olde Mistick Village, off I-95 (Mon–Sat 9.30am–5pm, Sun 10am–5pm; ●860 536 1641, ⊚mystic.org), which can help with finding hotels. There's a smaller office (Mon–Fri 9am–4.30pm, Sat & Sun 10am–4pm; ●860 572 1102, ⊚mysticchamber.org) at the train station, 2 Roosevelt Ave.

Argia Mystic Cruises 15 Holmes St ●860 536 0416,

⊚ArgiaMystic.com. Runs a romantic harbour tour on the replica nineteenth-century schooner *Argia*; $42. May–Oct daily.

Historic Harbor Tours of Mystic ●860 572 1421. Offers forty-minute harbour tours from Steamboat Wharf by the drawbridge in downtown Mystic; $10, children 12 and under $5. Summer daily 11am–5pm.

ACCOMMODATION

House of 1833 72 North Stonington Rd, Old Mystic ●860 536 6325, ⊚houseof1833.com. This five-room B&B occupies a gorgeous Greek Revival mansion (built in 1833, of course), with spacious rooms decked out in an antique nineteenth-century style – extras include free sherry, cookies and a jacuzzi tub. $179

★ **Mermaid Inn** 2 Broadway Ave ●860 536 6223, ⊚mermaidinnofmystic.com. Handsome and extremely welcoming Italianate B&B (dating from 1843), where the rooms are artfully decorated in crisp, contemporary styles and the treats – cookies, popcorn, cognac and Ghirardelli chocolates – are a decadent bonus. Enjoy the healthy breakfasts on the porch. Flat-screen TVs. $225

★ **Steamboat Inn** 73 Steamboat Wharf ●860 536 8300, ⊚steamboatinnmystic.com. A luxurious

downtown option, where eleven elegant rooms overlook the water and are furnished in a modern, country inn style with cable TV and DVD players. $200

Whaler's Inn 20 E Main St ●860 536 1506, ⊚whalersinnmystic.com. Right in the heart of downtown Mystic, near the drawbridge over the river, this is the most central choice and Mystic's best hotel (as opposed to B&B). Comprises five historic buildings – *Hoxie House* rooms have the best river views. Parking and free wi-fi included. $139

Whitehall Mansion 42 Whitehall Ave ●860 572 7280, ⊚whitehallmansion.com. The most atmospheric B&B in town a 1771 shingled beauty with five rooms: each with canopy bed, working fireplace and jacuzzi tub. $189

EATING

★ **Abbott's Lobster in the Rough** 117 Pearl St, Noank ●860 536 7719, ⊚abbotts-lobster.com. Five minutes' drive south of Mystic, this is the perfect spot for a lobster picnic, serving the delicious creatures and other seafood next to the water. May–Aug daily noon–9pm; Sept to mid-Oct Fri–Sun till 7pm.

★ **Bravo Bravo** 20 E Main St ●860 536 3228, ⊚bravobravoct.com. This Italian seafood specialist is the

best place for a gourmet splurge in Mystic. Feast on lobster ravioli, linguine with clams or seafood stew (from $18). Tues–Thurs 11.30am–2pm & 5–9pm, Fri & Sat 11.30am–2pm & 5–10pm, Sun 5–9pm.

Kitchen Little 135 Greenmanville Rd (Rte-27) ●860 572 7978, ⊚kitchenlittle.org. Located right on the river, half way between downtown and Old Mystic, this classic diner serves huge breakfast plates, with a focus on eggs;

MYSTIC PIZZA

The long lines of tourists outside the otherwise ordinary **Mystic Pizza** (see below) are not really here for the food (though the pizza is genuinely good). The Zelepos family opened their simple café in 1973, but it wasn't till screenwriter Amy Jones was inspired to base her story of the lives and loves of three young waitresses here that things really took off. The movie *Mystic Pizza* (1988) starred **Julia Roberts** in her first major role, and was largely filmed in the area, though most of the pizza joint scenes in the movie were actually shot in nearby **Stonington**. Business boomed in the 1990s as a result, and though things have calmed down since then, plenty of pilgrims still make the journey to Mystic to taste a "slice of heaven". A few photos of Roberts from the film, pinned to the walls, commemorate the movie.

the menu includes omelettes ($3.95–10.95) and eggs Benedict (from $9.95), as well as a tasty clam chowder ($3.95) for lunch. Mon–Fri 6.30am–2pm, Sat & Sun till 1pm.

Mystic Drawbridge Ice Cream 2 W Main St ☎860 572 7978, ⓦmysticdrawbridgeicecream.com. The perfect spot for dessert may just be the balcony outside, where you can indulge in home-made sorbets and ice cream (from $3.75) while watching the drawbridge rise to let the boats go by. Daily: May–Oct 9am–11pm; Nov–April 10am–10pm.

Mystic Pizza 56 W Main St ☎860 536 3700, ⓦmysticpizza.com. Small, family-run restaurant that makes huge, tasty pizzas (plain $7.40–13.49; slices from $2.29) and remains a pilgrimage site for movie fanatics (see box above). Mon–Thurs & Sun 10am–10pm, Fri & Sat till 10.30pm, Sun till 10pm.

★ **S&P Oyster Co** 1 Holmes St ☎860 536 2674, ⓦsp-oyster.com. Fine seafood on the waterfront overlooking the drawbridge – the best place to enjoy Mystic in the summer. Try the incredibly fresh Stonington scallops ($16.95), lobster rolls ($17.95), chowder ($4.95) or tilapia sandwich ($8.50). No reservations. Mon–Thurs & Sun 11.30am–10pm, Fri & Sat till 11pm.

SHOPPING

Olde Mistick Village ☎860 536 4941, ⓦoldemistickvillage.com. While it's aimed squarely at tourists, this mall does at least feature some interesting independent and local stores. Mon–Sat 10am–6pm, Sun 11am–6pm; open till 8pm in summer.

★ **Studio Jeffrey P'an** 44 W Main St ☎860 536 9274, ⓦstudiojeffreypan.com. Showcases the exquisite hand-crafted work of New London-born artist Jeffrey P'an. You can also watch him blowing glass at his studio, 44 Meadow Ave, Stonington (summer Wed–Sun 11am & 2pm). Daily 10.30am–6.30pm.

Stonington

Tucked away on the coast, just south of I-95 near the state's eastern border, **STONINGTON** is a gorgeous old fishing village with a grand past, beautifully captured in Anthony Bailey's memoir *In the Village* (1971). Originally settled in 1649, the main road, **Water Street**, is dotted with restaurants and shops, while parallel **Main Street** contains some dazzling examples of colonial and Federal clapboard architecture. Water Street ends at a car park (free) on the point near the Lighthouse Museum and **duBois Beach** (daily 10am–5pm; $10 per family, $5 per individual), a small, cute patch of sand overlooking the harbour.

Old Lighthouse Museum

7 Water St • May & Sept–Oct daily 10am–6pm; June–Aug Fri–Wed till 6pm, Thurs till 8pm; April & Nov Sat & Sun till 4pm • $9, admission includes Captain Palmer House (see p.284) • ☎860 535 1440, ⓦstoningtonhistory.org/light.htm

Stonington's surprisingly eventful history is chronicled in the **Old Lighthouse Museum**, built in 1840 and active until 1889. The small galleries inside recount town life through the centuries, with exhibits on sealing and whaling, a collection of local salt-glazed ceramics from the short-lived Stonington potteries (1770s–1834) and trinkets from China brought back by the town's notable seafarers. There's also the medieval sword owned by original colonist John Mason and information on the **Battle of Stonington** (1814), when townsfolk armed with just two cannons repulsed

5

an attack by five mighty British battleships. The view from the top (via 29 steps and a short ladder) is endless on sunny days. **Historical tours** of the town run from here in July and August (Sun 2pm; $7; ☎ 860 535 8445).

Captain Nathaniel B. Palmer House

40 Palmer St • May–Nov Wed–Sun 1–5pm, tours on the hour • $9, admission includes Old Lighthouse Museum • ☎ 860 535 8445, ⓦ stoningtonhistory.org/palmer.htm

The grand Italianate **Captain Nathaniel B. Palmer House** celebrates Stonington's premier seafarer, who was credited with one of the earliest sightings of **Antarctica** in 1820 – at just 21, he had captained a 47ft sloop as part of an American sealing fleet to the South Shetland Islands, and the peninsula he discovered is still named for him. Palmer (1799–1877) and his equally adventurous brother Alexander built the house in 1852 when they were retired (and made wealthy from the clipper trade). In addition to memorabilia associated with the Antarctica voyage, there are period rooms and a chance to visit the cupola viewing tower right at the top.

ARRIVAL AND DEPARTURE   STONINGTON

By bus/train Stonington is best approached by car. The nearest bus and train stations are at Mystic, four miles and a short taxi ride via US-1 to the west (Yellow Cab ☎ 860 536 8888). Local SEAT bus #10 (☎ 860 886 2631, ⓦ seatbus.com) connects Olde Mistick Village and Mystic train station with Stonington (25min; $1.25), but it only runs five times a day (check the current timetable online).

ACCOMMODATION

Inn at Stonington 60 Water St ☎ 860 535 2000, ⓦ innatstonington.com. Right in the heart of Stonington's historic centre, this charming hotel is actually fairly new, despite appearances – all eighteen rooms come with views of the harbour or village, with fireplaces, jacuzzis and free internet. **$180**

Orchard Street Inn 41 Orchard St ☎ 860 535 2681, ⓦ orchardstreetinn.com. Five elegant rooms, some with garden patio, in a quiet clapboard cottage. The owners will pick you up for free from Mystic or New London train stations, and provide bikes once you get here. Free wi-fi. **$210**

EATING AND DRINKING

Dog Watch Café 194 Water St ☎ 860 415 4510, ⓦ dogwatchcafe.com. Excellent seafood and standard American classics, right on the harbour. Start with raw oysters ($1.25 each), then move on to the scallops ($19) or tasty bouillabaisse ($19). Mon–Thurs & Sun 11.30am–9pm, Fri & Sat till 10pm.

★ **Noah's Restaurant** 113 Water St ☎ 860 535 3925, ⓦ noahsfinefood.com. Known for its fine home-style cooking and menu of eclectic dishes – everything from Korean pancakes to surprises conjured from the local catch (dinner mains $14.95–17.95). Tues–Thurs & Sun 7.45am–9pm, Fri & Sat till 9.30pm.

Yellow House 149 Water St ☎ 860 535 4986. The best place for breakfast in town, with tasty plates of eggs and bacon, fine coffees, bagels and muffins. Mon–Fri 6.30am–2.30pm, Sat 7am–3pm, Sun 7am–noon.

New London and around

A booming **whaling port** in the nineteenth century, **NEW LONDON** is a lively, multi-cultural working city, with three absorbing attractions on the outskirts: the **US Coast Guard Academy**, **Lyman Allyn Art Museum** and **Monte Cristo Cottage**. The town relied heavily on military-base revenue in the twentieth century, but struggled in the 1990s due to spending cuts. Though parts of the town remain edgy, New London is reviving today, thanks largely to the presence of Connecticut College, the US Coast Guard Academy and pharmaceutical giant Pfizer's R&D headquarters in nearby Groton. With 275,000 residents in the metropolitan area, it is now the most populous city along this stretch of the coast.

Though the sights are spread out – you'll need a taxi or a car to get around – the **downtown** area around the station has been spruced up with a pleasant waterfront promenade along the Thames River, and **State Street**, the city's main thoroughfare, is

GAMBLING ON CONNECTICUT'S NATIVE AMERICAN RESERVATIONS

In 1988, Congress passed the Indian Gambling Regulatory Act, which recognized the rights of Native American tribes in the US to establish gambling and gaming facilities on their reservations. Connecticut has since become home to several major Native American casinos. Note that these places tend to attract locals more for their excellent **restaurants**, **nightlife** and roster of **concerts** and events than the gambling. Both casinos are open 24hr; Greyhound buses (☏1 800 231 2222, ☸greyhound.com) link New London with them three times daily (40min to *Foxwoods*; 25min to *Mohegan Sun*).

Foxwoods Resort and Casino Rte-2, Ledyard ☏1 800 369 9663, ☸foxwoods.com. Operated by the Mashantucket-Pequot Indians, 23 miles from New London, this is among the largest casinos in the world; the adjacent *MGM Grand* was opened after a $700 million expansion. The tribe also operates the fascinating Mashantucket Pequot Museum, 110 Pequot Trail (☏1 800 411 9671, ☸pequotmuseum .org), which chronicles the history of the tribe and Native Americans in general through dioramas, text panels, interactive computer programmes and films.

Mohegan Sun 1 Mohegan Sun Blvd, Rte-2A, Uncasville ☏1888 226 7711, ☸mohegansun.com. Established by the Mohegan tribe thirteen miles north of New London, this is a fashionable casino resort aimed at a younger clientele than *Foxwoods*, also boasting several celebrity-owned restaurants including Bobby Flay's *Bar Americain*, Michael Jordan's *Steak House* and Todd English's *Tuscany*.

lined with a variety of shops and restaurants. Be sure to visit **Starr Street** (a short walk south of State Street via Eugene O'Neill Drive), a handsome strip of private nineteenth-century Greek Revival and Italianate homes.

US Coast Guard Academy

31 Mohegan Ave, I-95, exit 83 • Tours Mon, Fri & Wed 1pm; self-guided tours daily 9am–4.30pm; cadet drill autumn and spring Fri 4pm • Free, ID required • Maps available from Admissions in Waesche Hall on the north end of campus • ☏ 860 444 8500, ☸cga.edu **US Coast Guard Museum** 15 Mohegan Ave • Daily, call for hours • Free • ☏ 860 444 8511

The **US Coast Guard Academy**, just off I-95 (1.5 miles north of downtown), spreads out on a leafy 103-acre red-brick campus overlooking the Thames, built in the 1930s. Visitors are welcome to explore the grounds and the **US Coast Guard Museum**, which charts two centuries of Coast Guard history and houses the figurehead from the USS *Eagle*, a 295ft barque launched in 1936. The only tall ship on active duty, the *Eagle* is now used as a training vessel and often docked at the Academy (call ☏860 444 8595 for tours).

Lyman Allyn Art Museum

625 Williams St, I-95, exit 83 (1.5 miles north of downtown New London) • Tues–Sat 10am–5pm • $8 • ☏ 860 443 2545, ☸lymanallyn.org

Founded in 1932 by Harriet Upson Allyn in memory of her father, the **Lyman Allyn Art Museum** specializes in American arts and crafts, with a special focus on New London and the surrounding area. The first floor contains the permanent collection, while the second floor hosts contemporary travelling exhibits. Highlights include a collection of Paul Revere silverware, a huge dolls house built in 1962, a rare painted tile by Winslow Homer and a fine collection of paintings from the **Connecticut Impressionists** (see p.287) and the **Hudson River School**, including work by Frederic Church. Pride of place also goes to Daniel Huntington's imagined portrait of local heroine **Abigail Dolbeare Hinman**, who tried to resist the British as they torched New London during the Revolutionary War.

Custom House Maritime Museum

150 Bank St • Jan–March Thurs–Sat 1–5pm; April–Dec Tues–Sun same hours • $5; free on Sun • ☏ 860 447 2501, ☸nlmaritimesociety.org

The Greek Revival **Custom House Maritime Museum** (1833) stands apart on Bank Street, hosting exhibits on New London history in the country's oldest continuously

5

operating custom house. A special exhibit on the *Amistad* (see p.293) commemorates the place where the ship came to port in 1839 and later, where the vessel and its cargo were auctioned after the trial.

Shaw Mansion

11 Blinman St • Summer Wed–Fri 1–4pm, Sat 10am–4pm; winter Wed–Fri 1–4pm • $5 • ☎ 860 443 1209, ⓦ newlondonhistory.org

Built in 1756 for wealthy merchant Nathaniel Shaw (who became a US naval agent in the Revolutionary War), the handsome **Shaw Mansion** is now the home of the **New London County Historical Society**, with unusual panelled-cement fireplace walls and some period furnishings. Exhibits focus on the Revolutionary War period and New London's early trade links with the West Indies.

Monte Cristo Cottage

325 Pequot Ave • June–Aug Thurs–Sat noon–4pm, Sun 1–3pm • $7 • ☎ 860 443 5378, ext 290, ⓦ theoneill.org

Overlooking the often fog-bound Thames River, two miles south of downtown, the **Monte Cristo Cottage** faithfully preserves the memory of **Eugene O'Neill** (1888–1953), one of America's most acclaimed playwrights and winner of the Nobel Prize for Literature in 1936. O'Neill was born in New York, but led an itinerant childhood thanks to his constantly travelling father James, an actor famed for performing in the *Count of Monte Cristo*. This house was a home of sorts, where the family spent their summers recovering from a life on the road. James bought it in 1884, and Eugene spent every summer here till 1927; it became the setting for two of O'Neill's most notable works, *Long Days Journey Into Night* and *Ah, Wilderness!* The house is full of period fittings and furnishings (some original), and enthusiastic guides fill in the biographical details – be warned, O'Neill's life was loaded with tragedy. Suitably inspired, take in a performance at the **Eugene O'Neill Theater Center**, 305 Great Neck Rd in nearby Waterford (☎ 860 443 5378, ⓦ theoneill.org), a lauded testing-ground for emerging playwrights and actors. Note that O'Neill's work itself is not performed here, though the theatre does organize an **O'Neill festival** every autumn.

Ocean Beach Park

98 Neptune Ave (4 miles south of downtown) • Mid-May to Aug Mon–Fri 9am–10pm, Sat & Sun 8am–10pm • $5; additional fees for activities. Parking Mon–Fri $14; Sat & Sun $18 • ☎ 860 447 3031, ⓦ ocean-beach-park.com

South of downtown, **Pequot Avenue** offers a gorgeous drive along the water, passing by the 1801 **Harbor Light** lighthouse (currently being restored by the folks at the Custom House Maritime Museum), and leading to fifty-acre **Ocean Beach Park**, an extensive bone-white beach with a half-mile boardwalk, carousel, food court, mini-golf course ($5), waterslide ($3) and Olympic-size swimming pool.

Submarine Force Museum

1 Crystal Lake Rd, Groton • May–Oct Wed–Mon 9am–5pm; Nov–April Wed–Mon 9am–4pm • Free • ☎ 1 800 343 0079, ⓦ ussnautilus.org

Industrial **Groton** faces New London across the Thames River, notable as the hometown of the US **Naval Submarine Base New London**, one of the largest submarine bases in the world. The naval base is off-limits to the public, but the **Submarine Force Museum** next door welcomes visitors to trace the history of submersibles from as early as the Revolutionary era to the **USS Nautilus** (1952), America's first nuclear-powered submarine and the first to travel under the North Pole – it's now docked at the museum for tours.

ARRIVAL AND DEPARTURE   NEW LONDON

By train Trains and Greyhound buses serve New London's Union Station, at 35 Water St (☎ 1 800 872 7245 or ☎ 860 447 3841), right in the heart of downtown and conveniently close to the ferry docks. Shore Line East trains (☎ 203 777

7433, ⓦ shorelineeast.com) connect New London with Old Saybrook, Madison and New Haven (weekdays only), while Amtrak (ⓣ 1 800 872 7245, ⓦ amtrak.com) runs to Boston (11 daily; around 1hr 45min; $34) and New York (10 daily; around 2hr 30min; $47) via New Haven (10 daily; around 50min; $16), Old Saybrook (8 daily; around 20min; $14) and Mystic (4 daily; around 15min; $14).

By boat Close to the train station, the New London Ferry Dock, 2 Ferry St, hosts a number of ferries, including one to Orient Point on Long Island via the Cross Sound Ferry (hourly; 1hr 20min; $15 one-way, $52 with vehicle; ⓣ 860 443 5281, ⓦ longislandferry.com) and one to Block Island, RI (Block Island Express; June–Sept up to 4 daily; 1hr 15min; $24.56 one-way, $44 return; ⓣ 860 444 4624, ⓦ goblockisland.com).

By bus Greyhound (ⓣ 1 800 231 2222, ⓦ greyhound.com) connects New London with Boston (3 daily; 3hr; $27) via Providence (1hr 45min; $20.50), and New York (3 daily; 3hr 40min; $36) via New Haven (1hr; $15.50). 9 Town Transit (ⓣ 860 510 0429, ⓦ estuarytransit.org) provides local bus transport between New London and Old Saybrook (1hr) and Old Lyme (6 daily; 50min). Regular fares are $1.25 (cash only, no change).

INFORMATION AND TOURS

Tourist information The Old Trolley Station (1893), on Eugene O'Neill Drive at Golden Street, serves as an information booth (May & Oct Fri–Sun 10am–4pm; June–Sept daily 10am–4pm; ⓣ 860 444 7264, ⓦ ci.new-london .ct.us, ⓦ newlondonwaterfrontdistrict.org).

Boat tours Project Oceanology runs a series of boat tours from the University of Connecticut's Avery Point Campus, I-95, exit 87, including 2hr 30min oceanographic research cruises and tours of Ledge Lighthouse (July & Aug Tues, Thurs & Sat 4pm; Sept Sat 4pm; $25, children 6–12 years $20; reservations ⓣ 860 445 9007 9am–4pm, ⓦ oceanology.org), stuck out in the middle of the river since 1909 and supposedly home to a resident ghost. New London Harbor Tours (ⓣ 860 460 6206; ⓦ newlondonharbortours.com) runs exhilarating speed boat tours ($25) along the river.

ACCOMMODATION, EATING AND DRINKING

Accommodation in New London comprises cookie-cutter **motels** along the I-95 corridor – for a bit more character consider Mystic or Stonington.

Clarion Inn 269 N Frontage Rd ⓣ 860 442 0631, ⓦ clarionhotel.com. Comfy business hotel just off I-95, with indoor pool, whirlpool and gym, and an *Outback Steakhouse* next door. Free wi-fi. **$99**

Dutch Tavern 23 Green St, at State St ⓣ 860 442 3453. For cheap drinks (pints of local ales from $3.50) and a friendly crowd, visit this small, old-fashioned pub, complete with the 100-year-old tables at which Eugene O'Neill once sat. The free newspapers are a nice touch. Mon–Sat 11am–midnight.

★ **Fred's Shanty** 272 Pequot Ave ⓣ 860 447 1301. This New London institution and classic food shack has been knocking out tasty hot dogs, fries, shakes and burgers since 1972. Overlooks the Thames River, south of downtown. March–Oct daily 11.30am–9pm.

★ **Mangetout** 140 State St ⓣ 860 444 2066, ⓦ mangetoutorganic.com. Contemporary organic and vegetarian place (though they do serve fish), with fresh breakfasts and lunches (tofu and walnut burgers from $7.65), and yummy desserts like ginger pavlova and hummingbird cake ($4.50). Mon–Fri 8am–4pm, Sat & Sun 11am–4pm.

Muddy Water Café 42 Bank St ⓣ 860 444 2232. New London's classic breakfast joint, with speciality coffees from $1.50, huge muffins for $2 and a decent range of sandwiches for lunch – try the roast beef ($7.50). Mon–Fri 7am–4pm, Sat 8am–3pm, Sun 9am–3pm (summer 8am–1pm).

Old Lyme

Fifteen miles west of New London along I-95, at the mouth of the Connecticut River, sits picturesque **OLD LYME**, founded in 1665 and the former site of a major **American Impressionist** art colony. The town is also the namesake of the dangerous tick-borne disease; a number of cases of Lyme Disease were identified here in 1975.

Florence Griswold Museum

96 Lyme St • Tues–Sat 10am–5pm, Sun 1–5pm • $9 • ⓣ 860 434 5542, ⓦ flogris.org

In 1899, Florence Griswold, an unmarried middle-aged woman saddled with a high mortgage, welcomed artist **Henry Ward Ranger** to her boarding house in Old Lyme. More artists followed, and the idyllic eleven-acre property of the **Florence Griswold**

5

Museum showcases what soon after became known as the **Lyme Art Colony**, of seminal importance in the history of **American Impressionism**.

The main attraction is the enchanting Georgian house itself, built in 1817. It's been beautifully restored to resemble its appearance c.1910, the heyday of the colony, with the upstairs rooms displaying the work of artists that spent time here: Henry Ward Ranger, who led the early groups of Tonalist artists, and Impressionists **Childe Hassam** and **William Chadwick**, whose studio is set up nearby just as it was during his lifetime. But what makes this place so unforgettable are the richly **painted doors and panels** created by the artists over the years, the best examples of which can be found in the captivating **dining room**.

ARRIVAL AND DEPARTURE	OLD LYME

By train The nearest train station to Old Lyme is Old Saybrook, four miles west across the Connecticut River.
By bus 9 Town Transit (☎ 860 510 0429, ⓦ estuarytransit

.org) provides local bus transport to Old Saybrook (6 daily; 10min) and New London (6 daily; 50min). Regular fares are $1.25 (cash only, no change).

Old Saybrook

The former shipbuilding centre of **OLD SAYBROOK**, opposite Old Lyme on the western bank of the Connecticut River, is the oldest settlement on Connecticut's coast. Massachusetts sent soldiers here in 1635 to erect a fort and the village started to take shape the following year, though little remains of that initial outpost. Instead, commercial activity bustles along US-1 and wide Main Street (Rte-154), which leads south from the town centre to the churning waters of **Saybrook Point** (where it becomes College Street).

In 1707, the town became the home of the **Collegiate School**, which later moved to New Haven and renamed itself **Yale University**; just before College Street reaches Saybrook Point you'll see a solemn stone monument marking the site on the right, now part of the town cemetery (nothing remains of the building).

Main Street

The southern section of Main Street passes through Old Saybrook's historic district, with the Greek Revival **First Church of Christ** (1840) at no. 366 the fourth incarnation of the original church established at Fort Saybrook in 1646. Next door, at 350 Main St, is the Historical Society's 1767 **General William Hart House** (June–Aug Sat & Sun 1–4pm; $5; ☎ 860 395 1635), the elegant clapboard residence of a prosperous merchant who served in the Revolutionary War.

Fort Saybrook Monument Park

150 College St • Daily sunrise–sunset • Free • ☎ 860 395 3152

Eighteen-acre **Fort Saybrook Monument Park**, at the end of College Street, commemorates the original Saybrook fort built in 1635, though nothing remains of the first or second structure (the original burnt down in 1647 and the second was demolished in 1870 to make way for a railway). Interpretive boards placed around the landscaped site explain the history and river ecology of the area – there's a romantic statue of first governor Lion Gardiner (1599–1663), and remains of the railyard that operated here from 1870 to 1922.

ARRIVAL AND DEPARTURE	OLD SAYBROOK

By train Old Saybrook's train station, at 455 Boston Post Rd (☎ 860 388 3741), is served by Amtrak (☎ 1 800 872 7245, ⓦ amtrak.com), with connections to Boston (8 daily; around 2hr 10min; $39), Mystic (4 daily; 35min; $14), New Haven (8 daily; 35min; $14), New London (8 daily; 20min; $14) and

New York (8 daily; around 2hr 15min; $44), and also by the Shore Line East rail line that connects New Haven with New London (☎ 1 800 255 7433, ⓦ shorelineeast.com).
By bus 9 Town Transit (☎ 860 510 0429, ⓦ estuarytransit .org) provides local bus transport between Old Saybrook

rain station and Madison train station (hourly; 1hr 15min); ssex (6 daily; 30min), Old Lyme (5 daily; 10min) and New London (5 daily; 50min). Regular fares are $1.25 (cash only, no change).

INFORMATION

Old Saybrook Chamber of Commerce 1 Main St, at the junction with US-1 (Mon–Fri 9am–5pm, Sat till 1pm; July & Aug also Sun 11am–1pm; ☎ 860 388 3266, ⊚ oldsaybrookchamber.com).

ACCOMMODATION

Deacon Timothy Pratt House B&B 325 Main St ☎ 860 395 1229, ⊚ pratthouse.net. Historic 1746 clapboard home with rooms furnished in period style, complete with canopy beds and jacuzzi tubs. **$120**
★ **Saybrook Point Inn & Spa** 2 Bridge St ☎ 860 395 2000 or ☎ 1 800 243 0212, ⊚ saybrook.com. Luxurious waterfront establishment right at Saybrook point, overlooking the water; rooms are decked out with eighteenth-century-style English mahogany furnishings, with views across Long Island Sound. **$299**

EATING AND DRINKING

Fresh Salt Saybrook Point Inn, 2 Bridge St ☎ 860 388 1111, ⊚ freshsalt.net. Great service, great food and superb views across Long Island Sound – the Sunday brunch is especially good. The grilled swordfish ($26) and Naragansett mussels ($12) are solid choices, while the tasty salmon burger ($15) is offered at lunch. Mon–Fri 7–10am, 11.30am–2pm & 5.30–10pm, Sat 7–10.30am, 12.15–2pm & 5.30–10pm, Sun 8am–2.15pm.

Johnny Ad's 910 Boston Post Rd (US-1) ☎ 860 388 4032, ⊚ johnnyads.com. A no-frills clam shack known for fresh fried clams and lobster rolls; order the whole belly clam platter or fresh scallops for the full experience (plates from $14.95).
★ **Tissa's Le Souk du Maroc** 2 Pennywise Lane (off Rte-154, opposite the Hart House) ☎ 860 395 1781, ⊚ tissascountrymarket.com. Serves delicious Moroccan food in an unassuming 1790 shop setting, allowing you to savour the chef's concoctions next to shelves of exotic speciality food items, also for sale. The attached *James Soda Fountain* sells great ice cream. Mon–Sat 8am–8pm, Sun 11am–5pm.

Madison

Genteel **MADISON** lies on the Connecticut coast, just fifteen miles west of Old Saybrook on US-1 or I-95. It's a pleasant place to stop for a bit, with an attractive, shady town green and broad main street (Boston Post Road, US-1) lined with chic restaurants and shops. The area's biggest draw, however, is **Hammonasset Beach State Park**, two miles east of downtown Madison off US-1.

Hammonasset Beach State Park

288 Boston Post Rd (US-1) • Daily 8am–sunset • Free. Parking Mon–Fri $15, Sat & Sun $22 **Nature Center** May–Oct Tues–Sun 10am–5pm • ☎ 203 245 8743 • No public transport

At **Hammonasset Beach State Park**, thirteen miles west of Old Saybrook, lush green meadows spread out next to two miles of sandy shoreline, backed by dunes and a salt marsh. On stormy days, when the crowds are gone, the view is truly endless. At the southernmost tip of the park, **Meigs Point** offers a nature trail and **Nature Center** with small reptilian exhibits.

ACCOMMODATION AND EATING

MADISON

Elizabeth's Cafe 885 Boston Post Rd (US-1), Madison ☎ 203 245 0250, ⊚ perfectparties.com. Fine, fresh continental and American cuisine; try the "famous chicken salad sandwich" ($9.95), home-made French onion soup ($7.50) and selection of sumptuous tarts and pies. Mon & Wed–Sat 11am–3pm & 5–9pm, Sun 8am–2pm.

Lenny & Joe's Fish Tale 1301 Boston Post Rd (US-1), Madison ☎ 203 245 7289, ⊚ ljfishtale.com. Excellent fried shrimp ($12.99), clams (market price) and other fishy delights, though it tends to gets mobbed with tourists at the weekends. The broiled or char-grilled fish (from $13.50) is always super fresh. Mon–Thurs & Sun 11am–9.30pm, Fri & Sat till 10.30pm.
★ **Scranton Seahorse Inn** 818 Boston Post Rd (US-1), Madison ☎ 203 245 0550, ⊚ scrantonseahorseinn .com. This is the area's most popular B&B for good reason – serene and cosy, rooms in this 1833 Greek Revival home come with jacuzzi tubs, DVD players and in-house masseur. Free wi-fi. **$130**

5

Thimble Islands

One of the most enchanting sights in Connecticut, the **THIMBLE ISLANDS** are a cluster of granite rocks just off the coast, crowned with 95 lavish Victorian clapboard mansions that seem to sprout precariously from Long Island Sound. The islands lie within a three-mile radius of the town of **Stony Creek**, ranging from outcroppings that vanish at high tide to larger islands worth up to $20 million – *Doonesbury* cartoonist Garry Trudeau owns one, while wealthy widow and artist Christine Svenningsen has ten, including a mock Tudor mansion on **Rogers Island**, complete with putting green, pool and tennis court.

Most of the islands are strictly off-limits to the public, but you can get a good look from one of the regular cruises from Stony Creek, and not all the islands are occupied by private homes: the largest, 17.5-acre **Horse Island**, is an ecological reserve managed by Yale University, while **Outer Island** is part of the **Stewart B. McKinney National Wildlife Refuge** (☎ 860 399 2513, ⊛ fws.gov/northeast/mckinney/) and open to the public on days when the green flag flies on the dock (call for times; visits by private boats or kayak only).

TOURS   THE THIMBLE ISLANDS

Boat tours You can hear colourful stories about the islands by taking a tour with one of several boats from Stony Creek. The *Islander* (hourly 10.40am–3.40pm; $10; ☎ 203 397 3921, ⊛ thimbleislander.net), the *Volsunga IV* ($10; ☎ 203 481 3345, ⊛ thimbleislands.com) and the *Sea Mist* (hourly 10.15am–4.15pm; $10; ☎ 203 488 8905, ⊛ thimbleislandcruise.com) offer daily 45min trips from mid-May until mid-October, departing from the Town Dock at the end of Thimble Island Rd/Indian Point Rd in Stony Creek (I-95, exit 56).

Kayak tours For a little more adventure, you can kayak around the islands with Coastal Kayaking (☎ 860 391 3837, ⊛ ctcoastalkayaking.com); 3hr tours start at $90/person.

EATING AND DRINKING

Stony Creek Market 178 Thimble Island Rd, near the dock in Stony Creek ☎ 203 488 0145. A combined restaurant, bakery, deli and (in the evenings) pizzeria, with stunning views of the Thimbles from its deck. Mon–Fri 6.30am–3pm, Sat & Sun 8am–3pm.

Southwest Connecticut

Nicknamed "the gold coast" for its exceedingly wealthy towns like **Greenwich** and **Westport**, **southwest Connecticut** has long flourished owing to its proximity to New York City, its densely populated commuter towns combining a certain cosmopolitan spirit with the moneyed sweetness of fresh country air. **New Haven** is the undoubted highlight of the region, an intriguing mix of artsy industrial hub and historic university town, but you'll find remarkable art treasures scattered all along the coast, crowned by the **Bush-Holley Historic Site** in Greenwich. Industrial vibes can be felt in the former manufacturing town of **Norwalk**, now home to a dazzling **Maritime Aquarium**.

New Haven

One of Connecticut's founding colonies, **NEW HAVEN** is best known for the idyllic Ivy League campus of **Yale University** and its two world-class (and free) **art galleries**. Yet it also offers river cruises on the *Amistad* and some of the best restaurants, exciting nightspots and diverting cultural festivals in all of New England. Tensions between the city and the university once made New Haven an uneasy place, though an active symbiosis has thrived since the 1990s under the Yale presidency of Richard Levin. Residents are encouraged to take advantage of the university's cultural and public offerings, and more than half of the student body volunteers in some sort of local outreach programme.

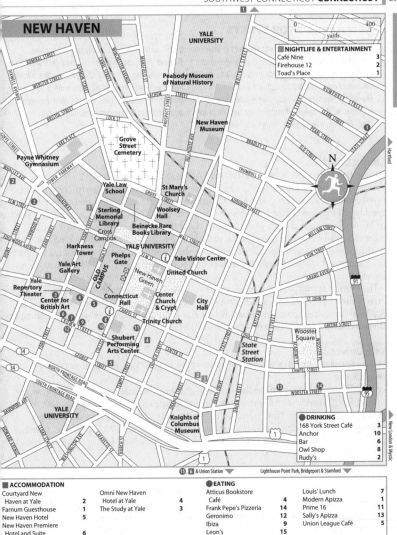

■ ACCOMMODATION			●EATING			
Courtyard New		Omni New Haven	Atticus Bookstore		Louis' Lunch	7
Haven at Yale	2	Hotel at Yale	4	Café	4	Modern Apizza	1
Farnum Guesthouse	1	The Study at Yale	3	Frank Pepe's Pizzeria	14	Prime 16	11
New Haven Hotel	5			Geronimo	12	Sally's Apizza	13
New Haven Premiere				Ibiza	9	Union League Café	5
Hotel and Suite	6			Leon's	15		

Downtown remains centred on the **Green**, the site of the city's original settlement. Surrounded by a number of stately government buildings, it borders the student-filled **Chapel Street district**, a lively area filled with bookshops, shops, cafés and bars. East of the Green, following Chapel Street past the train tracks, you'll hit New Haven's close-knit **Italian District**, with well-kept brownstones and colourful window boxes on **Wooster Street** and Wooster Square. A short walk just north of the Green, **Hillhouse Avenue**, completed in 1837, is a spellbinding thoroughfare lined with trees and handsome old buildings – Charles Dickens proclaimed it the most beautiful street in America (much of it is now occupied by Yale's administrative offices).

NEW HAVEN'S TOP EVENTS

International Festival of Arts & Ideas ⓦ artidea .org. New Haven's biggest annual cultural event sees the Green converted into a giant art gallery and music venue for two weeks. Most events are free. June.

Music on the Green ⓦ cityofnewhaven.com. Free concerts on the Green, offering everything from the likes of the New Haven Symphony Orchestra to bluesman Robert Cray. Usually late July or Aug.

Project Storefronts ⓦ projectstorefronts newhaven.com. In 2010 the city started allowing artists and entrepreneurs access to unused shop spaces downtown, free for three months. Visit the stores or attend the fun Friday open house nights. Year-round.

Center Church

311 Temple St • April–Oct Thurs & Sat 11am–1pm • Free • ☎ 203 787 0121, ⓦ newhavencenterchurch.org

Standing in the middle of the Green, **Center Church** is the successor to New Haven's original religious building, the First Church of Christ. Completed in 1814, it holds a sparkling Tiffany window over the altar depicting the New Haven Colony's first service in 1638. Below the church is the fascinating **crypt**, actually the town's first burial ground with 139 tombs dating back to 1687 – when the current church was built over it, the gravestones were simply preserved in the basement. The underground cemetery is a bizarre sight, with **Arnold Benedict**'s first wife Margaret (1744–75) among those buried here.

The church forms part of a religious trio on the Green: to the south, fronting Temple Street, the 1816 Gothic Revival **Trinity Episcopal Church**, 129 Church St (Mon–Fri 8.30am–5pm; free) contains more spectacular Tiffany windows, while to the north the **United Church** (usually closed) was built in 1813.

Yale University

Yale Visitor Information Center, 149 Elm St • Tours Mon–Fri 10.30am & 2pm, Sat & Sun 1.30pm • Free • ☎ 203 432 2300, ⓦ yale.edu/visitor

Founded in 1701, **Yale University** is one of the world's great seats of learning, with some 11,000 students and one of the largest libraries in the US. You can visit most of the major buildings (just north of the Green) on self-guided tours, but to get inside one of the twelve colleges and learn about contemporary life at Yale, take a **guided tour** from the **visitor centre** (the oldest house in New Haven, built in 1767), conducted by students.

Old Campus

Start tours of Yale at the 1896 **Phelps Gate**, 344 College St (on the west side of the Green), known as "Yale's front door". This allows access to the cobbled courtyards of **Old Campus**, whose elegant Gothic Revival buildings, many constructed in the late nineteenth century, today mostly serve as freshmen dorms. **Connecticut Hall**, completed in 1753, is the oldest surviving building in New Haven, and now houses the philosophy department. **Harkness Tower** at 74 High St, across from Old Campus, is a stunning 216ft piece of architecture completed in 1921 – come at noon and 5pm during term time to hear its **54-bell carillon** chiming out everything from classical to Beyoncé tunes.

Cross Campus and around

Further north the lawns of **Cross Campus** split **Berkeley College**, completed in 1934. This section of Yale is anchored by the cathedral-like **Sterling Memorial Library**, 120 High St, built in 1930 in neo-Gothic style, with leaded glass windows and a fifteenth-century Italian-style mural paying tribute to the exalted privilege of learning.

Nearby, at 121 Wall St, **Hewitt Quad** contains the striking 1963 **Beinecke Rare Book and Manuscript Library** (Mon–Thurs 8.30am–8pm, Fri 8.30am–5pm, Sat

0am–5pm), housing priceless ancient manuscripts, including a 1300-page Gutenberg Bible, behind its translucent Vermont marble walls. On the other side of the quad lies the **University Commons** and **Woolsey Hall** (1901), a dining hall and giant auditorium respectively.

On the other side of High Street at 127 Wall St, the Sterling Law Building (1931) is the home of **Yale Law School** (ⓦwww.law.yale.edu) consistently one of America's top law schools, and where Hillary and Bill Clinton met as students. One block north, at Grove and High streets, the **Grove Street Cemetery** (daily 9am–4pm; free; guided tours May–Nov Sat 11am; ☎203 389 5403, ⓦgrovestreetcemetery.org) opened in 1797 and is the resting place of Eli Whitney, Noah Webster, Charles Goodyear and other local luminaries.

Yale Center for British Art

1080 Chapel St • Tues–Sat 10am–5pm, Sun noon–5pm • Free • ☎ 203 432 2800, ⓦ britishart.yale.edu

The Modernist, Louis Kahn-designed **Yale Center for British Art** contains an exceptional collection of British paintings and sculpture, donated to Yale by Paul Mellon in 1966. The highlights reside in the fourth-floor galleries of pre-1850 work, with special sections on **Turner**, **Hogarth** and **Constable**. Look out in particular for Constable's romantic *Stratford Mill*, and Turner's revolutionary *Inverary Pier, Loch Shira*, precursor of the Impressionist movement. Among Hogarth's typically bawdy studies, *Beggar's Opera* and the drunken bacchanal of *A Midnight Modern Conversation* are rich snapshots of eighteenth-century reality. The gallery even has few **Canaletto** paintings of seventeenth-century London, and the Library Court on the second floor also contains giant works from animal and sport specialist **George Stubbs**. The post-1850 galleries are less crowd-pleasing, but still contain a few gems from the likes of Lucien Freud, Francis Bacon, Stanley Spencer and Henry Moore.

Yale University Art Gallery

1111 Chapel St • Tues–Sat 10am–5pm, Sun 1–6pm; guided tours Sat & Sun 1.30pm • Free • ☎ 203 432 0600, ⓦ artgallery.yale.edu

The beautifully presented work on display at the **Yale University Art Gallery** has to be one of the best bargains in New England (it's free). Founded in 1832 with **John Trumbull**'s original donation of a hundred paintings, the collection now has more than 185,000 objects from around the world, dating from ancient Egyptian times to the present. The core building is another Louis Kahn masterpiece (this was his first major commission in 1953; the Center for British Art was his last, in 1974), but by December 2012 a major renovation will see exhibition space double. Though exhibits will continue to rotate, signature pieces are likely to be on display continually.

The collection

Highlights include the exquisite **Italian Renaissance** collection, with pieces from Sienese School masters such as **Duccio**, and vivid Dutch portraits by **Frans Hals** and

---

THE AMISTAD

At the northeast corner of the Green is the **Amistad Memorial**, a three-sided bronze sculpture on the former site of the New Haven jail. The monument was erected in 1992 in memory of the 1839 revolt on the **slave ship** *Amistad*, during which 56 Africans led by Sengbe Pieh (aka Joseph Cinqué) seized control of the vessel. Intending to sail home, they instead ended up off Long Island, where they were captured by the US Navy and tried as murderers; the ensuing **Supreme Court case**, during which former president John Quincy Adams acted for the defence, took place in Hartford and New Haven. The Africans were ultimately acquitted, and were able to return home in 1842. In 1997 a Spielberg movie of the same name dramatized the incident, and today a **reproduction** of the *Amistad* offers cruises along the river (see p.295).

5

Rubens. Look out also for **Vincent Van Gogh**'s *Night Café*, the *Lion Attacking a Horse* by **George Stubbs** and thoughtful work from Impressionists **Monet** and **Cézanne**. **Picasso** is well represented and the modern and contemporary collections are pretty good too: note **Jean-Michel Basquiat**'s jarring *Diagram of the Attic*, and **Marcel Duchamp**'s *Tu'm*.

The **African Galleries** are loaded with intriguing carvings, masks and other artefacts, while the **Asian Galleries** hold a small but precious collection of pottery, statuary and lavish jewellery – don't miss the new Javanese exhibits, which include a rare gold leaf funerary mask.

Yale Peabody Museum of Natural History

170 Whitney Ave • Mon–Sat 10am–5pm, Sun noon–5pm • $7 • ☎ 203 432 5050, ⓦ peabody.yale.edu

Yale's **Peabody Museum of Natural History** is easily recognizable by the huge bronze statue of a *Torosaurus latus* out front, a good indication of what's inside – a gasp-inducing collection of complete **dinosaur fossils**. The museum was founded in 1866 by banker and philanthropist George Peabody, who also established the museum in Salem (see p.144), though the two are not related today. The impressive collection includes a 67ft **Apatosaurus** (aka *Brontosaurus*) skeleton backed by Rudolph Zallinger's stunning 110ft *Age of Reptiles* mural (1966), a full **Stegosaurus** skeleton and a series of bony **Triceratops** skulls. The museum offers plenty more, however; skeletons of giant mastodons and sabre-tooth cats, early human fossils (including a reproduction of "Lucy", a 3.2-million-year old hominid skeleton found in Ethiopia) and rare Native American artefacts, including Red Cloud's feathered headdress. Upstairs there are rooms dedicated to minerals and gems and even Egyptian mummies, but kids will especially enjoy the hands-on **Discovery Room**, with a huge leaf-cutter ant colony, snakes and poison-dart frogs.

New Haven Museum

114 Whitney Ave • Tues–Fri 10am–5pm, Sat noon–5pm • $4 • ☎ 203 562 4183, ⓦ newhavenmuseum.org

The absorbing **New Haven Museum**, housed in a purpose-built 1930 Colonial Revival building, traces local **history** through a series of art displays, industrial artefacts, rare maps and genealogical records. Permanent galleries are dedicated to the **Amistad** story, containing the famous portrait of Joseph Cinqué by Nathaniel Jocelyn (see box, p.293), and you can also see one of **Eli Whitney**'s original cotton gins (c.1803), and **Charles Goodyear**'s rubber inkwell. Look out also for **Benedict Arnold**'s original shop sign from 1760 (he was a merchant here before becoming a general/traitor in the Revolutionary War).

Knights of Columbus Museum

1 State St • May–Aug daily 10am–5pm; Sept–April Wed–Sun same hours • Free • ☎ 203 865 0400, ⓦ kofcmuseum.org

Friar Michael McGivney founded the **Knights of Columbus** in New Haven in 1882, a fraternal Catholic organization initially established to provide aid to newly arrived immigrants. The **Knights of Columbus Museum** chronicles the history of the organization, with special sections on the papacy, Christopher Columbus (explaining the name), Pope John Paul II and McGivney himself (who was the son of Irish immigrants). There are some very rare items on display (Spanish tiles from the foundation of Santo Domingo in the 1490s; the original 1613 copper-clad cross from the top of St Peter's in Rome), and the temporary art exhibits are usually of a very high standard, often coming direct from the Vatican's collection.

ARRIVAL AND DEPARTURE

NEW HAVEN

By train On Union Avenue six blocks southeast of the Yale downtown campus, Union Station serves Amtrak trains (☎1 800 872 7245, ⓦamtrak.com) to Boston (17 daily; around 2hr 30min; $49), New London (11 daily, around 50min; $16) and New York (20 daily; around 1hr 35min; $37). Metro-North trains (☎1 800 638 7646 mta.info/mnr) serve all the stations between here and New York City at 30min intervals (up to 10min intervals during rush hours): Bridgeport (20min), Westport (around 50min), South Norwalk (around 45min) and Stamford (around 1hr). A free shuttle (Mon–Fri 7.05am–10.15pm) runs every 20min between Union Station and the Green and Temple Plaza, across from the *Omni New Haven Hotel* (see below). If you arrive at night, grab a taxi to your hotel; Metro Taxi (☎ 203 777 7777) has a good reputation.

By bus Union Station is also home to Peter Pan (☎ 1 800 443 1831, ⓦ peterpanbus.com) and Greyhound bus services (☎ 1 800 231 2222, ⓦ greyhound.com) to New York (9 daily; 1hr 50min; $22), Boston (3 daily; 4hr; $33) and Hartford (6 daily; 1hr; $15).

By car New Haven lies at the junction of I-91 and I-95. Street parking downtown is hard to find, but car parks are located conveniently around the centre. The Union Station parking garage offers 24hr parking ($1/hr or $13/24 hr).

INFORMATION AND TOURS

INFO New Haven Just off the Green at 1000 Chapel St (Mon–Wed 10am–9pm, Thurs–Sat till 10pm, Sun noon–5pm; ☎ 203 773 9494, ⓦ infonewhaven.com).

Boat tours When it's in port, take a cruise on the replica of the schooner *Amistad* from Long Wharf ($30; ☎ 203 930 8061; ⓦ amistadamerica.net).

Culinary tours It's worth indulging in one of the Downtown Culinary Walking Tours from the *Omni New Haven Hotel* (once a month; no tours in May; $59; ☎ 203 777 8550, ⓦ stephenfries.com), which explore the city's culinary attractions – it's especially good during the Christmas period, when hot chocolate and carol singers (to listen to, not to eat) are added to the mix.

ACCOMMODATION

Make sure to book well in advance if you intend to visit around **Yale graduation** in June, before the **beginning of the semester** in September, and during **Parents' Weekend** in October. Cheaper **motels** are available along the I-91 corridor. Hotels in downtown New Haven tend to charge $20–25 for daily parking.

Courtyard New Haven at Yale 30 Whalley Ave ☎ 203 777 6221 or ☎ 1 888 522 1186, ⓦ courtyard.com. Conveniently located just west of campus, with 207 plush, modern rooms; some good weekend deals. Free wi-fi. **$129**

Farnum Guesthouse 616 Prospect St ☎ 203 562 7121 or ☎ 1 888 562 7121, ⓦ farnamguesthouse .com. Best B&B option, with eight charming rooms close to Yale Divinity School. Wi-fi and full breakfast included. **$109**

New Haven Hotel 229 George St ☎ 203 498 3100, ⓦ newhavenhotel.com. Stylish hotel offering luxurious, modern rooms equipped with huge flat-screen TVs, DVD players, iPod docks and free wi-fi (computers are available in the business centre). There's also a handy 24hr laundry and gym. **$120**

New Haven Premiere Hotel and Suites 3 Long Wharf Drive ☎ 203 777 5337 or ☎ 866 458 0232, ⓦ newhavensuites.com. Best of the hotels on the fringes of the city, with spacious, fully equipped condo-style suites (with kitchens) suitable for families. Free wi-fi and breakfast included. **$150**

Omni New Haven Hotel at Yale 155 Temple St ☎ 203 772 6664, ⓦ omnihotels.com. Over three hundred deluxe rooms and suites in New Haven's plushest downtown institution; the "Get Fit Guest Rooms" even include a motorized portable treadmill. Free wi-fi. **$180**

★ **The Study at Yale** 1157 Chapel St ☎ 203 503 3900, ⓦ studyhotels.com. This relatively new boutique hotel is unquestionably New Haven's top digs, with iPod docks, flat-screen TVs and large workspaces in every stylish room. Free wif-fi. **$160**

EATING

Atticus Bookstore Café 1082 Chapel St ☎ 203 776 4040, ⓦ atticusbookstorecafe.com. Artisan breads, sandwiches, scones and great breakfast plates of applewood smoked bacon, cranberry pecan toast and gruyere cheese ($5–7), all served in a relaxed bookshop. Mon–Thurs & Sun 7am–9pm, Fri & Sat till 10pm.

Geronimo 271 Crown St ☎ 203 777 7700, ⓦ geronimobarandgrill.com. Inspired Southwestern cuisine and a range of speciality cocktails and tequilas. Mains include oven-roasted sea bass and *bouillabaisse* de

Santa Fe ($14–25). Mon–Thurs noon–11pm, Fri & Sat noon till midnight, Sun 4–10pm.

Ibiza 39 High St ☎ 203 865 1933, ⓦ ibizanewhaven .com. Fine Spanish restaurant serving traditional specialities accompanied by a fine list of Spanish wines. Dinner plates – home-salted codfish, sweetbreads wrapped with almonds and breadcrumbs – cost between $26–$30, but lunch is a bit cheaper. Mon–Thurs 5–9pm, Fri noon–2.30pm & 5–10pm, Sat 5–10pm.

Leon's 501 Long Wharf Drive ☎ 203 562 5633, ⓦ leonsrestaurant.com. Great views across the bay and

NEW HAVEN PIZZA

Most people have heard of New York and Chicago pizza, but what about New Haven? The city's Italian connection goes back to the nineteenth century, when **labourers** came to work in the many factories that lined the waterfront. Almost all of them came from the **Amalfi coast**, south of Naples – as a result a very distinct community developed in New Haven (speaking its own southern Italian dialect), and a thin-crust pizza tradition was inherited direct from Naples (the home of pizza). The oldest of New Haven's existing pizzeria is **Pepe's**, founded in 1925 by Amalfi-born Frank Pepe, who emigrated to the US in 1909. Locals take the rivalry between *Pepe's* (see below) and its neighbour **Sally's Apizza**, very seriously: the latter was founded by Frank's nephew Salvatore Consiglio in 1938. Other contenders include **Modern Apizza**, dating back to 1934, while the adventurous should visit the *Bar Nightclub* (see below) on Crown Street, and order the heavenly mashed potato pizza.

★ **Frank Pepe's Pizzeria** 157 Wooster St ☎ 203 865 5762, ⓦ pepespizzeria.com. A Wooster Street institution since 1925, drawing crowds with its coal-fired pizzas. Order the white clam pizza ($12.50–25.50) for the full experience. Mon–Sat 11.30am–10pm, Sun noon–10pm.

Modern Apizza 874 State St ☎ 203 776 5306, ⓦ modernapizza.com. *Pepe's* challengers include this venerable joint, knocking out a slightly more charred pizza with slightly faster service. Basic thin-crust mozzarella pizzas range from $8.50 (12 inch) to $14 (18 inch), with specialities including clams casino (from $11) and artichoke (from $10). Tues–Thurs 11am–11pm, Fri & Sat till midnight, Sun 3–10pm.

Sally's Apizza 237 Wooster St ☎ 203 624 5271, ⓦ sallysapizza.com. *Sally's* is the connoisseurs' choice (it only serves pizza, soda and beer), with fresh, zesty sauces and perfectly baked coal-fired pizzas. The downside – you sometimes wait over an hour to get your food (join the queue before 5pm). Tues–Sat 5–10.30pm, Sun till 10pm.

excellent Italian seafood make the drive here worthwhile – it's the prime waterfront restaurant near downtown, with outdoor seating in the summer. Anything with clams is good. Mon–Sat 11.30am–10.30pm, Sun 10.30am–2.30pm & 3–10.30pm.

Louis' Lunch 261–263 Crown St ☎ 203 562 5507, ⓦ louislunch.com. Small, dark, ancient burger institution that allegedly served America's first hamburger, c.1900. It's still served on slices of toasted flat bread, with strictly no ketchup ($5.25) – cheese, tomato and onion are the only acceptable garnishes. Tues & Wed 11am–3.45pm, Thurs–Sat noon–2am; closed Aug.

Prime 16 172 Temple St ☎ 203 782 1616, ⓦ prime16.com. Temple Street hotspot with inventive gourmet burgers ($5 specials) and two dozen beers on tap (Mon $3) Daily 11am–11pm.

Union League Café 1032 Chapel St ☎ 203 562 4299, ⓦ unionleaguecafe.com. Superb but pricey French brasserie specializing in fresh, seasonal produce (some sourced from the the Yale Sustainable Garden Project). Dishes might include roasted Long Island duck, or pan-seared swordfish (mains $21–34) Mon–Thurs 11.30am–2.30pm & 5.30–9.30pm, Fri 11.30am–2.30pm & 5–10pm, Sat 5–10pm.

DRINKING

The *New Haven Advocate* (ⓦ newhavenadvocate.com), a free weekly news and arts paper, has detailed **listings** of what's on in and around the city.

168 York Street Café 168 York St ☎ 203 789 1915, ⓦ 168yorkstreetcafe.com. New Haven's oldest gay joint, also serving home-style dinners and a decent Sunday brunch. Beers $1.50–2.50. Mon–Thurs 3pm–1am, Fri till 2am, Sat 2pm–2am, Sun 11am–1am.

Anchor 272 College St ☎ 203 865 1512, ⓦ anchornewhaven.com. Authentic 1950s bar with snug plastic booths, dim lighting, frosted windows, and a jukebox. Kitchen open till midnight. Cash only. Mon–Thurs & Sun 11am–1am, Fri & Sat till 2am.

Bar 254 Crown St ☎ 203 495 8924, ⓦ barnightclub .com. A simple name for a not-so-simple spot that's a combination pizzeria, brewery, bar and stylish nightclub Mon & Tues 5pm–1am, Wed & Thurs 11.30am–1am, Fri & Sat 11am–2am, Sun 11am–1am.

Owl Shop 268 College St ☎ 203 498 2484, ⓦ owlshopcigars.com. Old-world bar and smoke shop since 1934, with an extensive list of imported cigars. Mon 4pm–1am, Tues–Thurs 10am–1am, Fri & Sat 10am–2am, Sun noon–1am.

Rudy's 1227 Chapel St ☎ 203 865 1242. A favourite local dive bar since 1934, despite being booted to this newish ocation in 2011 (the famous wood tables and wall panels, smothered in carvings, were preserved). Legendary

Belgian-style *frites*. Mon & Tues 3pm–1am, Wed & Thurs noon–1am, Fri & Sat noon–2am, Sun noon–1am.

NIGHTLIFE AND ENTERTAINMENT

New Haven's rich **cultural scene** is especially strong in **theatre**, and there are always classical music performances throughout the year on the Yale campus. One definite highlight is the **Yale Summer Cabaret Shakespeare Festival** (July & Aug), with tickets from $25 (students $12).

Cafe Nine 250 State St ☎ 203 789 8281, ⓦ cafenine.com. Intimate club with live music every night, from punk to jazz to R&B. Cover $5–10. Daily 7pm–1am.

Firehouse 12 45 Crown St ☎ 203 785 0468, ⓦ firehouse12.com. Recording studio and performance space for original, creative music, with a bar that serves speciality beers and classic cocktails. Runs an excellent jazz series every autumn. Tues–Fri 4pm–1am, Sat 6pm–2am.

Shubert Performing Arts Center 247 College St ☎ 203 562 5666, ⓦ shubert.com. Founded in 1914, this gorgeous historic theatre has been the location of many

world premieres, including Yul Brynner's *The King and I*, *Oklahoma!* and the *Sound of Music*, and it still hosts top-quality musicals and plays.

Toad's Place 300 York St ☎ 203 562 5589, ⓦ toadsplace.com. Mid-sized live music venue where Bruce Springsteen and the Stones used to "pop in" to play impromptu gigs. Hosts regular dubstep nights ($5–8). Times vary according to events (usually 6–10pm)

Yale Repertory Theater 1120 Chapel St ☎ 203 432 1234, ⓦ yalerep.org. Boasts many luminaries among its alumni, and turns out consistently good shows throughout the year.

Bridgeport

Long the state's leading industrial centre, **BRIDGEPORT**, twenty miles west of New Haven, suffered greatly during the 1960s and 1970s, a decline still evident in the abandoned factories and boarded-up stores littered throughout the city. In recent years, though, serious efforts have been made to revamp the place, and it merits a visit for the state's only **zoo**, the wonderful children's **Discovery Museum**, the **Housatonic Museum of Art** and, assuming it is open, the **Barnum Museum**.

Connecticut's Beardsley Zoo

1875 Noble Ave • Daily 9am–4pm • $12, children (3–11 years) $10 • ⓦ beardsleyzoo.org

A top draw for kids, 52-acre **Connecticut's Beardsley Zoo** is home to everything from North American mammals (the Canadian lynx, bison) to exotic species from South America. There's also a farmyard-like children's zoo and a splendid working carousel (open seasonally 10.30am–4pm) on the grounds.

Discovery Museum and Planetarium

4450 Park Ave • Tues–Sat 10am–5pm, Sun noon–5pm • $9.50, children (3–17 years) $8 • ☎ 203 372 3521, ⓦ discoverymuseum.org

A little way out of the city centre, the **Discovery Museum and Planetarium** is an interactive science and technology museum, with more than a hundred engaging exhibits on topics like electricity, nuclear energy and the science of colour. Best of all is the Challenger Learning Center, honouring the memory of the ill-fated *Challenger* space shuttle crew.

Barnum Museum

820 Main St • Tues–Sat 10am–4.30pm, Sun noon–4.30pm • $7, children (4–17 years) $4 • ☎ 203 331 1104, ⓦ barnum-museum.org

Bridgeport is home to the unique **Barnum Museum**, named after the man who changed showbiz forever with his displays of the exotic and the bizarre – **P. T. Barnum** also served as mayor of Bridgeport in 1875 and died here in 1891. The museum houses exhibits on Barnum's life and props from his circus days, but note that it was **closed to the public** following serious tornado damage suffered in June 2010 – the recovery is likely to take several years, so call ahead for the latest.

5

Housatonic Museum of Art

900 Lafayette Blvd • June–Aug Mon–Fri 8.30am–5.30pm, Thurs till 7pm; Sept–May Mon–Fri 8.30am–5.30pm, Sat 9am–3pm, Sun noon–4pm • Free • ☎ 203 332 5203, ⓦ www.hcc.commnet.edu/artmuseum

On the grounds of Housatonic Community College, the **Housatonic Museum of Art** has a superb collection of works by a dozen major twentieth-century artists, including Chagall, Picasso and Matisse, as well as contemporary local painters.

ARRIVAL AND DEPARTURE
BRIDGEPORT

By train Bridgeport train station at 525 Water St (☎ 1 800 872 7245) is served by Amtrak (☎ 1 800 872 7245, ⓦ amtrak.com) trains to New York (7 daily; around 1hr 20min; $28) and Boston (5 daily; around 3hr; $55), and frequent Metro-North (☎ 1 800 638 7646, ⓦ mta.info /mnr) services to New Haven (25min), South Norwalk (20–25min) and Westport (15–20min).

By bus Greyhound (☎ 1 800 231 2222; ⓦ greyhound.com)

serves New Haven (4 daily; 30–40min; $10), New York (5 daily; 1hr 30min–2hr 10min; $15) and Boston (3 daily; 4hr 35min–4hr 55min; $34) from the bus station at 710 Water St (☎ 203 335 1123).

By ferry A car ferry service to Port Jefferson, Long Island, NY, leaves from the ferry dock at 330 Water St (hourly 6am–9pm; 1hr 15min; $15 one-way, $53 with car; ☎ 631 473 0286 or ☎ 1 888 443 3779, ⓦ 88844ferry.com).

ACCOMMODATION

Holiday Inn 1070 Main St ☎ 203 334 1234, ⓦ hibridgeport.com. Comfy but fairly typical chain hotel – this is your best choice if you end up spending

the night in Bridgeport. Comes with gym, indoor pool and free wi-fi. **$127**

EATING AND DRINKING

Bloodroot 85 Ferris St ☎ 203 576 9168, ⓦ bloodroot .com. Legendary feminist vegetarian restaurant founded in the 1970s in Black Rock. Dishes might include spinach and potato gnocchi, or spicy Thai "chicken" (made of soy). Tues & Thurs 11.30am–2.30pm & 6–9pm, Wed 6–9pm, Fri & Sat 11.30am–2.30pm & 6–10pm, Sun 11.30am–2.30pm.

Ralph 'n' Rich's 815 Main St ☎ 203 366 3597, ⓦ ralphnrichsct.com. A downtown institution across from the Barnum Museum, serving finely crafted Italian food. Pastas from $15 and mains from $17.50. Mon–Thurs 11.30am–3pm & 5–10pm, Fri 11.30am–3pm & 5–11pm, Sat noon–3pm & 5–11pm, Sun noon–4pm & 5–9pm.

Westport and around

Roughly halfway between the urban sprawls of Stamford and Bridgeport, **WESTPORT** is an entirely different world: the country refuge of the New York art circle in the early decades of the last century, the town continues to exude both sophistication and rustic charm. Downtown, **Main Street** is lined with designer boutiques and expensive galleries, while the highly acclaimed **Westport Arts Center** lies within walking distance on the other side of the Saugatuck River.

Westport Arts Center

51 Riverside Ave • Mon–Fri 10am–4pm, Sat 10am–5pm, Sun noon–4pm • Free • ☎ 203 227 4177, ⓦ westportartscenter.org

One of the best **contemporary art galleries** in the state, the **Westport Arts Center** hosts three to four high-quality curated exhibitions each year; recent shows have included everything from paintings based on Facebook photos to the work of iconic environmental artists Christo and Jeanne-Claude. The galleries also host film screenings, concerts, literary discussions and other events.

ARRIVAL AND DEPARTURE
WESTPORT

By train The nearest Amtrak station is at Bridgeport, ten miles east. Frequent Metro-North (☎ 1 800 638 7646, ⓦ mta.info/mnr) services to New Haven (45min), South Norwalk (5–7min) and Bridgeport (17–20min) run from

Westport train station at 1 Railroad Place, two miles south of downtown. Take a taxi into town (Westport Star ☎ 203 227 5157).

EATING AND DRINKING

Acqua 43 Main St ☎ 203 222 8899, ⓦ zhospitalitygroup .com/acqua. Excellent Mediterranean seafood is the speciality and the soufflés are superb (mains $15–38), enhanced by stellar views of the Saugatuck River. On Tuesdays bottles of wine are half price. Mon–Thurs noon–2.30pm & 5.30–9pm, Fri noon–2.30pm & 5.30–10.30pm, Sat noon–3pm & 5.30–10.30pm, Sun 4.30–8.30pm.

★ **Le Farm** 256 Post Rd E ☎ 203 557 3701, ⓦ lefarmwestport.com. Top-notch farm-to-table seasonal cuisine, with produce sourced from local farms; expect creations such as black sausage with beets and goat cheese dressing, and pan roasted foie gras with huckleberry jam and granola (mains $12–22). Tues & Sat 5.30–9.30pm, Wed–Fri noon–9.30pm.

ENTERTAINMENT

Westport Country Playhouse 25 Powers Court ☎ 203 227 4177, ⓦ westportplayhouse.org. One of the oldest repertory theatres in the country. When stars like Gene Kelly and Henry Fonda first strutted their stuff here, the playhouse was little more than a rural barn, but in 2005 it re-opened after a massive renovation and is now more than comfortable while retaining its rustic charm.

Norwalk

Six miles west of Westport, saltwater cool meets beat charm in **NORWALK**, whose maritime connections can be traced back to the eighteenth century, when it was home to a flourishing oyster-fishing industry and the prolific Silvermine River mills. With its superb restaurants, bars, galleries and museums, and with the recent revamping of downtown **South Norwalk**, affectionately known as "**SoNo**", today Norwalk ranks among the most happening towns along this stretch of the coast.

Maritime Aquarium

10 N Water St • Daily 10am–5pm • $12.95, with IMAX $19.45, IMAX only $9; children (2–12 years) $9.95, with IMAX $14.45, IMAX only $6.50; Maritime Parking Garage $1 for first hr, $7 for up to 24hr • ☎ 203 852 0700, ⓦ maritimeaquarium.org

SoNo's chief attraction is the magnificent **Maritime Aquarium**, housed in an atmospheric nineteenth-century factory. The focus here is on the varied marine life of **Long Island Sound**; there's a refreshing hands-on approach to displays and an easy-to-absorb emphasis on conservation throughout. You'll need at least half a day to it justice.

Linger at the mesmerizing **shark tank**, filled with hovering rays, toothy 8ft sand tiger sharks and giant bass, or the **harbor seal** enclosure (feedings three times a day). Other highlights include a hypnotic series of **jellyfish** tanks, an illuminating **sea turtle** section (which contains one loggerhead sea turtle and two green turtles), a tank containing the monstrous **Atlantic halibut**, a collection of **seahorses**, and the frisky **otters**. **Touch-tanks** are a big part of the experience – pick up a horseshoe crab, or stroke a shark and cow-nose ray. Other galleries explain the range of habitats in the Sound, from marsh to deep water, with tanks containing the marine life found in each. It's worth splashing out for the **IMAX theatre**, which shows educational films during the day (and Hollywood movies at night).

You can also take an enlightening research **cruise** out into the Sound to get a first-hand look at local marine life (July & Aug daily; Sept–June Sat & Sun; $20.50).

Sheffield Island Lighthouse

Sheffield Island • June to early Sept Mon–Fri 11am & 3pm, Sat & Sun 11am, 2pm & 3pm • $22, children (4–12 years) $12 • ☎ 203 838 9444 • Limited parking is available in the adjacent North Water Lot ($1 first hr, $6/24hr)

Just south of Norwalk's Maritime Aquarium, the Sheffield Island Lighthouse Ferry shuttles visitors to the 1868 **Sheffield Island Lighthouse**, which warned boats off the rugged **Norwalk Islands** until 1902 – most of the islands are protected wildlife sanctuaries today. On a clear day, the Connecticut coast and even the New York City skyline is visible from the 44ft lighthouse.

5

Norwalk Museum

41 N Main St • Wed–Sun 1–5pm • Free • ☎ 203 866 0202

Norwalk's past is chronicled at the **Norwalk Museum**, a small but enthusiastic effort to commemorate key moments in the region's history. Displays focus on the once dominant **oyster industry**, redware and stoneware pottery and Norwalk's hat-makers, once the equal of those in Danbury. There's also a small display on **Raggedy Ann dolls** (creator Johnny Gruelle lived in Norwalk), and the reconstructed **Dunne Hardware Store** from across the river, a late nineteenth-century gem. The Greek Revival museum building itself was completed in 1912, and originally served as the South Norwalk Town Hall.

Lockwood-Mathews Mansion Museum

295 West Ave • Tours April to mid-Dec Wed–Sun noon, 1pm, 2pm & 3pm • $10 • ☎ 203 838 9799, Ⓦ lockwoodmathewsmansion.com

The elegant Second Empire-style **Lockwood-Mathews Mansion Museum** was constructed in 1864 for insurance and railway tycoon LeGrand Lockwood. While the impressive house predates more opulent creations of the Gilded Age, tours emphasize that technologically it was ahead of its time, with telephones, modern baths and even a burglar alarm system threading the mansion floor.

ARRIVAL AND INFORMATION

NORWALK

By train Norwalk is served by Metro-North (☎ 1 800 638 7646, Ⓦ mta.info/mnr) trains running between New York (55min–1hr) and New Haven (50min), which stop at both the South Norwalk station, 1 Chestnut St, and the East Norwalk station, 1 Winfield St. Metered parking in town is $1/hr (maximum 2hr); see Ⓦ norwalkpark.org.

Coastal Fairfield County Convention & Visitors Bureau Gatehouse of the Lockwood-Mathews Mansion (Thurs–Sun 10am–2pm; Ⓦ coastalctinc.com and Ⓦ visitfairfieldcountyct.com). The useful town website is Ⓦ norwalkct.org.

ACCOMMODATION

Norwalk Inn 99 East Ave ☎ 203 838 2000, Ⓦ norwalkinn.com. Conveniently located near I-95, with 72 immaculate rooms, free wi-fi and an outdoor pool. $95
Silvermine Tavern 194 Perry Ave ☎ 203 847 4558 or ☎ 1 888 693 9967, Ⓦ silverminetavern.com. Pleasant

accommodation of a refined Yankee sort since 1929, boasting ten delightful rooms and one suite in a nineteenth-century clapboard building next to a waterfall, along with a restaurant famous for its Sunday brunch buffet and honey buns. Each room has a jar of cracked corn to feed the local ducks. $125

EATING AND DRINKING

Brewhouse 13 Marshall St ☎ 203 853 9110, Ⓦ sonobrewhouse.com. Boasts gourmet burgers ($9.95), a tasty apple strudel ($7.50) and more than fifty beers. Mon–Thurs 11.30am–9pm, Fri till 10pm, Sat 11am–10pm, Sun 11am–9pm.
Donovan's 138 Washington St ☎ 203 354 9451, Ⓦ donovanssono.com. Cool bar and restaurant dating back to 1889, serving classic American food such as sliders (mini hamburgers; from $8.95), Cajun popcorn shrimp ($10.95) and huge burgers ($8.95). Mon–Fri 11.30am–1am, Sat till 2am, Sun 11am–2am.
Overton's 80 Seaview Ave, East Norwalk Ⓦ overtons -seafood.com. Classic clam shack across Norwalk harbour from SoNo, serving burgers, shrimp, scallops and clam belly from $7.50 on a deck sitting right on the water. Mid-March to mid-Nov daily 10am–9pm.

Valencia Luncheria 172 Main St ☎ 203 846 8009, Ⓦ valencialuncheria.com. The speciality here is Venezuelan *arepas* (pancake-like bread made of cornmeal; from $3.25), but everything on the menu is excellent – be sure to try the chocolate/avocado *batidos* (shakes; $3.50). Cash only. Mon & Tues 6am–3pm, Wed–Fri till 9pm, Sat 7am–9pm, Sun 8am–8pm.

SUPERMARKETS

Stew Leonard 100 Westport Ave ☎ 203 847 7213, Ⓦ stewleonards.com. Norwalk is home to one of only four Stew Leonard's, a marvel of a supermarket with not only fresh food (and free samples), but also animatronic displays and a tiny zoo. Daily 7am–11pm.

Stamford

Founded in 1640, **STAMFORD** today has a population of over 110,000 and a shiny new downtown that is effectively an outpost of Wall Street – Royal Bank of Scotland and UBS have trading floors here, while companies such as Thomson Reuters, Xerox, GE Capital and Clairol have also moved to the city, attracted by lower taxes and costs than in Manhattan (some thirty miles away). There's not much to see, though, and the city's main attractions are further out in North Stamford.

Stamford Museum & Nature Center

39 Scofieldtown Rd • Mon–Sat 9am–5pm, Sun 11am–5pm • $10, children (4–17 years) $5 • ☎ 203 322 1646, ⓦ stamfordmuseum.org

Families will especially enjoy the **Stamford Museum & Nature Center**, a 118-acre estate of sylvan trails and fun animal attractions. The estate was once the home of New York clothier **Henri Bendel**, and his palatial **mansion** – a Tudor and Medieval fantasy completed in 1929 – now serves as gallery for mostly rotating art exhibits. Note the extensive permanent collection of art by **Gutzon Borglum** (1867–1941) – the sculptor spent ten years working in Stamford before creating Mount Rushmore in South Dakota.

The **Heckscher Farm** is the main draw for children, with turkeys scampering around freely, a maple sugar house and special enclosures for goats, pigs, cows, sheep and horses. There are also a couple of friendly **otters** (fed at 1pm daily), and an **Animal Embassy** (summer Tues–Sun 10am–3.30pm; winter till 2pm), containing exotic animals, snakes, parrots and the like (with fearless tortoises ambling around on the floor).

Bartlett Arboretum & Gardens

151 Brookdale Rd (1.5 miles north of Merritt Parkway) • Grounds daily 8.30am–sunset; visitor centre summer daily 9am–7pm, winter daily 9am–5pm • $6 (under 12s free), Wed free • ☎ 203 322 6971, ⓦ bartlettarboretum.org

To escape the often frenetic roads in this part of Connecticut, spend half a day at the **Bartlett Arboretum & Gardens**, a tranquil 91-acre botanical garden of rare and historical trees, crisscrossed by **hiking trails**. Highlights include the boardwalk across the wetlands, and the **tropical** and **herb gardens**. The visitor centre occupies the former home of **Dr. Francis Bartlett**, founder of the Bartlett Expert Co. He bought the house in 1913, using it as home, training school and research lab – his tree collection forms the basis of the current park.

In the summer (late June to early Aug) try to visit on a Sunday – **classical soloists** from Yale serenade visitors (10–11am; free), while more lively popular music takes over later (5–7pm; $10). You can bring a picnic (and drinks).

THE GLASS HOUSE

From the 1940s to the 1960s, the pretty town of **New Canaan**, eight miles northeast of Stamford, became something of a training ground for what became known as the **Harvard Five**; architects and designers Philip Johnson, Marcel Breuer, Landis Gores, John M. Johansen and Eliot Noyes. Many of the revolutionary homes they designed still stand, with Johnson's **Glass House** (ⓦ philipjohnsonglasshouse.org) the best example. Built in 1949 of glass and charcoal-painted steel, it's regarded as one of the most thought-provoking buildings in the country and is open to the public. **Tours** (May–Nov, closed Tues; $30) are limited to ten people and begin at the Visitor Center, 199 Elm St (Mon & Wed–Sat 9.30am–5.30pm, Sun 11.30am–5.30pm; ☎ 203 594 9884) in downtown New Canaan (across from the train station). Metro-North (☎ 1 800 638 7646, ⓦ mta.info/mnr) trains connect New Canaan with New York (1hr–1hr 20min) and Stamford (around 20min).

ARRIVAL AND DEPARTURE
STAMFORD

By train Stamford is served by Amtrak (☎ 1 800 872 7245, ⓦ amtrak.com) trains to New York (20 daily; around 50min; $27) and Boston (17 daily; around 3hr 30min; $55), and frequent Metro-North (☎ 1 800 638 7646, ⓦ mta.info /mnr) trains to New Haven (50min–1hr) and South Norwalk (10–15min). The station is at 30 S State St and 490 Washington Blvd on the edge of downtown, but a long way from the main sights.

By bus Greyhound buses (☎ 1 800 231 2222; ⓦ greyhound .com) from New York (3 daily; 1hr 15min–1hr 30min; $12) and Boston (3 daily; 5hr 15min–5hr 35min; $34) run to the bus terminal next to the train station.

GETTING AROUND

By bus CT Transit (ⓦ cttransit.com) runs a network of local buses in the area: bus #31 runs from the train station up to Stamford Museum and Bartlett Arboretum every 30 minutes or so (less often at weekends) for $1.25.

By car Budget rents cars near the train station at the *Marriott Hotel*, 197 N State St (☎ 203 325 1535, ⓦ budget.com).

ACCOMMODATION

Courtyard Stamford Downtown 275 Summer St ☎ 203 358 8822, ⓦ marriott.com. Stamford has a plethora of chain business hotels, but this is one of the best. Features spacious, elegant rooms (with great views of downtown) and an on-site spa and indoor pool. Parking $10/day. **$234**

Hotel Zero Degrees 909 Washington Blvd ☎ 203 363 7900, ⓦ hotelzerodegrees.com. Stamford's hip boutique hotel just about lives up to the hype, with a chic, contemporary theme; rooms feature bold artwork, iPod docks, free wi-fi and flat-screen TVs, all apparently *feng shui* compliant. **$149**

EATING AND DRINKING

Brasitas 954 E Main St ☎ 203 353 3319. Famed for inspired Latin dishes like grilled monkfish in mango curry sauce ($23) and zesty pitchers of sangria. Mon–Thurs 11.30am–10pm, Fri & Sat till 11pm, Sun noon–9pm.
Remo's Brick Oven Pizza 35 Bedford St ☎ 203 973

0077, ⓦ remospizza.com. Easily the best pizza in the area, with 12-inch Napoletana pizzas ($8.95–14.95) – try the cherry pepper or courgette. Mon–Thurs & Sun 11am–11pm, Fri & Sat till midnight.

Greenwich

Just a short train ride or drive from Manhattan, **GREENWICH** is essentially a posh suburb of New York City – home to media celebrities and CEOs – and among the wealthiest towns in the nation. It's also the base of some major fund management companies, private equity firms and other corporate refugees from Wall Street. Soak up the scene on the main thoroughfare, walkable **Greenwich Avenue**, lined with fine shops, boutiques and restaurants.

Bush-Holley Historic Site

39 Strickland Rd, Cos Cob Harbor • Feb & March Fri–Sun noon–4pm; April–Jan Wed–Sun same hours • $10 • ☎ 203 869 6899, ⓦ hstg.org

An enchanting colonial relic that inspired the nineteenth-century **American Impressionists**, the **Bush-Holley Historic Site** lies south of Greenwich in Cos Cob, overlooking the Mianus River (but sadly overshadowed by the I-95 overpass).

Your first stop will be the **Visitor Center**, where temporary exhibits link local and national themes (recent displays have included the Civil War). **Guided tours** (the only way to visit the two-storey clapboard Bush-Holley House itself) tell the story of the two families that lived here: the Bush family purchased the home in 1738, and several rooms have been restored to c.1821. In 1884 Josephine Holley purchased the house (taking in artsy boarders), and the rest of it is filled with the relics of the "**Cobb Colony**" period (1890–1920), when painters and writers – Childe Hassam, John Henry Twachtman, Willa Cather, J. Alden Weir and Ernest Lawson among them – gathered here to create and discuss their art. The most

5

evocative room recreates the **studio of Elmer MacRae,** who eventually married Josephine's daughter. The whole house is liberally decorated with his artwork, and that of Childe Hassam.

Putnam Cottage

243 E Putnam Ave (US-1) • Jan–March by appointment only; April–Dec Sun 1–4pm and by appointment • Suggested $5 donation • ☎ 203 869 9697, ⊛ putnamcottage.org

East of downtown Greenwich along US-1, old Knapp's Tavern is better known as **Putnam Cottage,** hard to miss with its distinctive "fish-scale shingles". It's an especially well-preserved colonial home, made a bit more intriguing by some romantic history: legend has it that one day in 1779, local patriot General Israel Putnam, who was stationed at the tavern, was busy shaving when he noticed advancing British troops in his mirror. He jumped on a horse and managed to escape down a steep cliff, returning later with reinforcements to rout the enemy.

The oldest part of the cottage dates from 1680, when it was a simple one-room frontier house built for the Knapp family; it became a **tavern** in around 1738 and the main tavern room has been faithfully restored to the period 1754–90. Upstairs Putnam's bedroom contains the general's hat, and there are old spinning wheels and bits and pieces dug up from nearby (arrowheads and the like).

ARRIVAL AND DEPARTURE

GREENWICH

By train Greenwich is connected to New York (45–50min) and other towns along the coast as far as New Haven (1hr 10min–1hr 25min) by Metro-North (☎ 1 800 638 7646, ⊛ mta.info/mnr) trains. The main station is near downtown between Arch Street and Greenwich Avenue, at 1 Railroad Ave. Taxis meet most trains (Greenwich Taxi; ☎ 203 869 6000).

By bus CT Transit bus #11 (☎ 203 327 7433, ⊛ cttransit .com) runs three times an hour to Stamford ($1.25) from the train station via Putnam Cottage.

ACCOMMODATION

Cos Cob Inn 50 River Rd, Cos Cobb ☎ 203 661 5845, ⊛ coscobinn.com. Facing the water but with a view somewhat dominated by the I-95 bridge; twelve rooms in a 1870s Federal-style house, furnished in a Victorian style but with DVD players and free wi-fi. **$139**

Stanton House Inn 76 Maple Ave ☎ 203 869 2110, ⊛ shinngreenwich.com. Charming B&B dating from 1840 and redesigned by famed architect Stanford White in 1899. Its 21 individually decorated bedrooms and three suites are bright and comfy, with outdoor pool and free wi-fi in common areas. **$195**

EATING AND DRINKING

Thataway Café 409 Greenwich Ave ☎ 203 622 0947. Serving excellent burgers, pastas and sandwiches as well as some heavier fare, in a laidback, pubby atmosphere, just across from the train station – in summer eat on the outdoor terrace. Famed for its nachos ($10.95) and gut-busting "whichaway" burger ($11.95). Daily 11.30am–midnight.

Thomas Henkelmann Homestead Inn, 420 Field Point Rd ☎ 203 869 7500, ⊛ homesteadinn.com. Gourmet French restaurant where you can savour dishes like trio of Hudson Valley duck foie gras, smoked and marinated salmon and roast rabbit, in a charming setting overlooking the garden. Mon–Fri 7–9.30am, noon–2.30pm & 6–9pm, Sat & Sun 8am–10pm & 6–9pm.

Versailles Patisserie 339 Greenwich Ave ☎ 203 661 6634, ⊛ versaillesgreenwich.com. Something of a local institution, known for its heavenly cakes and tarts. Mon 7.30am–5.30pm, Tues–Fri till 9.30pm, Sat till 4pm & 5.30–9.30pm, Sun 7.30am–4pm.

The Connecticut River Valley

The **Connecticut River,** New England's longest, starts in the mountains of New Hampshire close to the Canadian border and runs 407 miles all the way down to Long Island Sound. In the state of Connecticut it's lined for the most part with tranquil small towns, the main exception being **Hartford,** the state capital and former home of Mark Twain. Farther west, gentle countryside leads to the pleasant town of **Farmington**, former clock-making centre **Bristol** and the less idyllic but still stimulating industrial city of **New Britain**, known for its hardware companies, art museum and minor league baseball.

South of Hartford the Connecticut River wends its way past historic **Wethersfield**; Rocky Hill, whose 185-million-year-old dinosaur tracks can be seen in **Dinosaur State Park**; the historic houses and gardens of **Higganum**; and **East Haddam**, site of the Goodspeed Opera House and the hilltop Gillette Castle, one of the state's leading peculiarities. **Ivoryton**, famed for its summer theatre, and quaint **Essex**, with a range of old-fashioned diversions, complete the picture near the river delta.

Hartford

The capital of Connecticut, **HARTFORD** is fast becoming one of the most alluring destinations in New England. The legacy of America's greatest writer is evocatively preserved at the **Mark Twain House and Museum**, while the **Wadsworth Atheneum** owns an astonishing collection of art – everything from the world's largest ensemble of Hudson River School paintings to major work from Salvador Dalí. Down by the river, the cutting-edge **Connecticut Science Center** is a magnet for families, with mind-boggling (and wildly entertaining) interactive exhibits.

Hartford became a **manufacturing** hub in the eighteenth century, and gradually established itself as the nation's **insurance capital** (the likes of Travelers and Aetna are still based here). Today Hartford is booming once again after years of relative decline, part of the so-called "**Knowledge Corridor**" with Springfield (see p.210), 24 miles north. There are still problems – many of the neighbourhoods around the centre remain depressed, and parts of downtown can become unsettlingly quiet at night and at weekends – but new developments include several glitzy skyscrapers, the regenerated Adriaen's Landing, State House Square and Front Street districts, and miles of new parks along the Connecticut River.

Old State House

800 Main St • July to mid-Oct Tues–Sat 10am–5pm; mid-Oct to June Mon–Fri same hours; last entry 4pm • $6 • ☎ 860 522 6766, Ⓦ ctoldstatehouse.org

Where else can you see one of the nation's oldest senate rooms, an original Gilbert Stuart portrait of George Washington and a two-headed calf? Hartford's grand Federal-style **Old State House** really does contain all three, but it's also the best place to start your tour of the city thanks to the absorbing **history museum** in the basement (don't miss **Mark Twain's bicycle**). The building was completed in 1796 as the first public commission of architect Charles Bulfinch (see box, p.69), serving as state capitol until 1878, then City Hall until 1915. You can visit the **Court Room**, which witnessed the *Amistad* trials (1839), and the second-floor **Senate Chamber** (which contains the Washington portrait), restored to c.1790s. The old **House Chamber** (where P.T. Barnum was once a legislator), has been restored to resemble its appearance in the c.1890. The highlight for many is the **Museum of Curiosities**, housed in a room on the second floor – a collection of stuffed animals and bizarre items, including the two-headed calf and a narwhal tusk, assembled by one Joseph Steward from 1797 and originally displayed in this building. Docents are usually available if you'd like a guided tour (free), and activity backpacks are provided for children.

State Capitol

210 Capitol Ave • 1hr tours hourly Mon–Fri 9.15am–1.15pm; April–Oct additional tours Sat hourly 10.15am–2.15pm; July & Aug additional tour at 2.15pm • Free • ☎ 860 240 0222, Ⓦ cga.ct.gov/capitoltours

The lawns of **Bushnell Park** surround the golden-domed **State Capitol**, an 1878 mixture of Gothic, Classical and Second Empire styles. Its ornate exterior, stained-glass

5

HARTFORD

Comcast Theater, Springfield & MA

■ **ACCOMMODATION**
Hartford Marriott Downtown	3
Holiday Inn Express	1
Mark Twain Hostel	2

● **DRINKING**
Agave Grill	1
Bin 228	8
City Steam Brewery Café	4
Vaughan's Public House	5

● **EATING**
Abyssinian	2
Black-Eyed Sally's	3
Carbone's	12
First & Last Tavern	13
Max Downtown	7
Mozzicato De Pasquale's Bakery & Pastry Shop	14
Polish National Home	11
Salute	9
Vivo	10
Woody's Hot Dogs	6

windows and lofty ceilings make it look more like a church than a place of politics, with the dome soaring 257ft up from the rotunda. Starting with a bit of history on state hero Nathan Hale and a display of historic flags, the tour takes you past the public galleries of the General Assembly, from where you can view the House and Senate when they're in session (Feb–May in even-numbered years; Jan–June in odd-numbered years). After you've had a look around, take a ride on the 1914 antique **Bushnell Carousel** in the park (May–Sept Tues–Sun 11am–5pm; $1).

Museum of Connecticut History

231 Capitol Ave • Mon–Sat 9.30am–4.30pm • Free • ☎ 860 757 6535 • ⊛ cslib.org

The most prized possession of the **Museum of Connecticut History** is the original 1662 **Connecticut Royal Charter**, framed in the wood of the **Charter Oak** (where legend claims it was hidden from Royal agents in 1687). The oak was felled in an 1856 storm, but its wood seems to turn up in an inordinate number of artefacts throughout the city (ever the cynic, Mark Twain is said to have asked if everything in the State House was made from the old tree). Displays here place the tree into a historical context. Other galleries contain an impressive collection of **Colt firearms** (made here in the nineteenth century) and other bits and pieces, from commemorative buttons to clocks and rifles constructed in Hartford.

Butler-McCook House & Garden

5

396 Main St • Wed–Sat 10am–4pm, Sun 1–4pm • $7 • ☎ 860 522 1806, ⓦ CTlandmarks.org

For a taste of old Hartford, visit the yellow clapboard **Butler-McCook House & Garden**, home to the same family for 189 years (the last descendant to live here, Francis McCook, died in 1971). Visits begin in the old medical office, added in 1897, which documents the city's history from 1750 onwards; highlights include a collection of Japanese armour acquired by a globetrotting family member. The house itself, built in 1782 by Daniel Butler, local doctor and paper manufacturer, has been faithfully restored to its appearance in the late nineteenth century, though items from earlier times remain. Guides show you around the first floor, but tours of the upstairs are self-guided, with information panels shedding light on the lives of servants, rare antique toys and memorabilia from Trinity College, Hartford and several wars.

Wadsworth Atheneum Museum of Art

600 Main St • Wed–Fri 11am–5pm, Sat & Sun 10am–5pm • $10 • ☎ 860 278 2670, ⓦ wadsworthatheneum.org

Hartford's pride and joy is the Greek Revival **Wadsworth Atheneum Museum of Art**, founded by Daniel Wadsworth in 1842 and the nation's oldest continuously operating public art museum. What makes this place so special is the way contemporary art is juxtaposed with historical pieces – the palatial **Morgan Great Hall** (1915) is a perfect example, with jarring contemporary and Modernist work from the likes of De Kooning and Warhol displayed in an elegant Victorian space with classical statuary.

A major $16-million renovation is expected to be complete by 2013, but there's plenty to see till then.

American art

Almost every school of **American art** is represented at the Wadsworth, including a precious ensemble of 160 **Hudson River School** paintings. Wadsworth was actually the patron of seminal school member **Thomas Cole**, while local heiress Elizabeth Colt aided **Frederic Church** – look out for Cole's inspiring *Mount Etna from Taormina* (1843) and *Hooker & Co* (1846) by Church. The collection of **US Impressionists** such as J. Alden Weir, Childe Hassam (*Flag Outside Her Window*) and John Henry Twachtman (*Emerald Pool, Yellowstone*), is almost as good, and there's work from John Singer Sargent (*Tents at Lake O'Hara*) and Winslow Homer.

The modern collection is well stocked with thoughtful pieces from the likes of Pollock, Clyfford Still and Sol LeWitt, but seek out in particular Georgia O'Keeffe's evocative *The Lawrence Tree* (1929), Warhol's iconic *Early Colored Jackie* (1964) and De Kooning's abstract *Montauk 1* (1969).

European art

Don't overlook the **European art galleries**, which are especially strong on modern movements, from Impressionism to Surrealism. Highlights include Monet's *Beach at Trouville* (1870) and a couple of Picasso gems, *The Painter* (1934) and one of his *Women of Algiers* series (1954). If Mondrian's *Composition in Blue and White* (1935) is confusing, try to work out what Dalí was getting at in *Apparition of a Face and Fruit Dish on a Beach* (1938), one of his most celebrated images.

The Wadsworth does own a few old masters: **Caravaggio's** *Ecstasy of St Francis* (1595), a striking night scene of St Francis being held by an angel while laying in a trance, and Spanish Baroque painter **Zurbarán**'s masterpiece *Saint Serapion* (1628), his finest painting in the Americas.

Center Church

675 Main St at Gold St • Wed & Fri 11am–2pm; call for tour information • Free • ☎ 860 249 5631

The elegant **Center Church** is home to the First Church of Christ, established by the Reverend Thomas Hooker in 1632. The current baroque structure dates from 1807 and is modelled after London's St Martin-in-the-Fields. Take a look inside to admire its six Tiffany stained-glass windows and barrel-vaulted ceiling.

Ancient Burying Ground

675 Main St • May–Oct Mon–Sat 9am–4pm, Sun till 1pm, by appointment at other times • Free • ☎ 860 522 0855, ⓦ theancientburyingground.org

The tranquil **Ancient Burying Ground** surrounding Center Church was the final resting-place for many of the city's first settlers from 1640 to 1815 (the oldest gravestone is from 1648). An eighteenth-century "tablestone" commemorates Hartford founder **Thomas Hooker**, who was buried somewhere here in 1647. Free maps are available at the entrance behind the church.

Connecticut Science Center

250 Columbus Blvd • Tues–Sun 10am–5pm; open Mon July & Aug • $17, children (4–17 years) $14; with movie $22, children $19; movie only $7, children $6 • ☎ 860 520 2116, ⓦ CTsciencecenter.org

Prepare to be blown away – and not just by the hurricane simulator and climate change theatre (where you can experience 75mph gusts and actual mist). The **Connecticut Science Center** opened in 2009, an innovative structure designed by **Cesar Pelli**. It's jam-packed with over 150 interactive exhibits that tackle everything from forensics to astronomy and test almost every scientific principle through wild and wacky games and simulations – kids go crazy for this. You can spend half a day playing **Mindball** (where your brain activity is channelled into energy that actually moves a small ball – seriously), challenging robots at basketball, pretending to be a DJ, flying over Mars or recording your own **weather report** (the local CBS-affiliated news channel films their weather report here everyday at noon). Special **3D digital movies** on a variety of themes are shown hourly (11am–4pm).

Mark Twain House and Museum

351 Farmington Ave • Mon–Sat 9.30am–5.30pm, Sun noon–5.30pm; Jan–March closed Tues • $16 • ☎ 860 247 0998, ⓦ marktwainhouse.org • CT Transit buses #60, #62, #64 & #66 from downtown Hartford

A mile or so west of downtown, the old hilltop community known as Nook Farm was home to Samuel Clemens (aka Mark Twain) and his family from 1874 to 1891. The bizarrely ornate **Mark Twain House and Museum** was where the giant of American literature penned many of his classic works, including *Huckleberry Finn*, *The Adventures of Tom Sawyer* and *The Prince and The Pauper*.

Tours of the house offer tantalizing insights into the life of the author, as well as drawing attention to the lavish and somewhat eccentric way the house was furnished – black-and-orange brickwork, elaborate woodwork and the only domestic Tiffany interior open to the public. Twain's legendary wit and ground-breaking writing style are explored in the **museum**, while the engrossing Ken Burns biographical documentary about him plays in the theatre. Twain's life itself makes for an astonishing and increasingly tragic tale: he went bankrupt in 1893, and suffered the death of three of his children and wife before he passed away in Redding, Connecticut in 1910.

AFTER HOURS AT THE SCIENCE CENTER

Four times a year the grown-ups get to play with the toys in the **Connecticut Science Center** (see above) – without the kids. **Liquid Lounge** evenings (over-21s only; 6–10pm) typically cost $10 ($15 at the door), and involve bars being set up on each floor, DJs and special "activities" like face painting, balloon art and a petting zoo. See ⓦ CTsciencecenter.org for details.

Harriet Beecher Stowe Center

5

77 Forest St (1.5 miles from downtown) • Wed–Sat 9.30am–4.30pm, Sun noon–4.30pm; June–Oct also Tues 9.30am–4.30pm • $9 • ☎ 860 522 9258, 🖥 harrietbeecherstowecenter.org • CT Transit buses #60, #62, #64 & #66 from downtown Hartford

In 1852, **Harriet Beecher Stowe** (1811–96) made history with *Uncle Tom's Cabin*, her groundbreaking and best-selling anti-slavery novel. As a woman of the nineteenth century Stowe had no right to vote, yet she was able to turn public opinion decisively against slavery, and became hugely influential – she wrote more than thirty books and was an active promoter of progressive ideas. The **Harriet Beecher Stowe Center** serves as a poignant memorial to the author, and includes her white Victorian Gothic home, next door to Mark Twain's house. Stowe moved here in 1873, and the house is a fine example of the nineteenth-century "cottage" style, with a hint of the romantic villa. You can see Stowe's writing table and some of her paintings inside the house, while the visitor centre holds exhibits on her life and work.

Cedar Hill Cemetery

453 Fairfield Ave (3 miles south of downtown) • April–Sept daily 7am–8pm; Oct–March till 5pm; office Mon–Fri 8am–4pm • Free • ☎ 860 956 3311, 🖥 cedarhillcemetery.org • Bus #61 from central Hartford

Established in 1864, the 270-acre park-like grounds of **Cedar Hill Cemetery** host a varied range of cultural programmes throughout the year, from Civil War tours to movie nights and scavenger hunts. You can also take a self-guided tour of the cemetery's famous tombs, including the 18ft pyramid marking the grave of English-born insurance king Mark Howard, and the pink granite, stately memorial for **J.P. Morgan**, the iconic New York banker buried here in 1913. Actress **Katharine Hepburn** (who was born in Hartford), artist **William Glackens** and manufacturer **Samuel Colt** are also buried here. Maps are available at the cemetery office.

ARRIVAL AND DEPARTURE

HARTFORD

By plane Just twelve miles north of the city lies Bradley International Airport (☎ 860 292 2000, 🖥 bradleyairport .com), served by the hourly CT Transit Bradley Flyer ($1.25; ☎ 860 525 9181, ☎ cttransit.com) to Union Station and Old State House in downtown Hartford. Taxis are also available outside (around $36 to downtown). Flights connect to cities all over the US (Atlanta, Baltimore, Chicago and Orlando are the busiest destinations), and also Montréal and Toronto; Southwest Airlines, Delta Air Lines and US Airways are the main carriers.

By train The city is served by Amtrak (☎ 1 800 872 7245, 🖥 amtrak.com) trains south to New Haven (6 daily; 47–58min; $12) and occasionally on to New York (2 daily; around 3hr; $38), and north to Springfield, MA (7 daily;

40–50min; $9). Union Station is at 1 Union Place, just off I-84, exit 48/49, on the western edge of downtown Hartford. Taxis tend to charge $10 for trips within the centre.

By bus Long-distance buses like Greyhound (☎ 1 800 231 2222, 🖥 greyhound.com) and Peter Pan (☎ 1 800 443 1831, 🖥 peterpanbus.com) all pull into the Union Station terminal from Boston (12 daily; 1hr 50min–2hr 40min; $28), Brattleboro, VT (1 daily; 2hr 20min; $26), Danbury (8 daily; 1hr 25min; $18), New Haven (6 daily; 1hr; $15), New York (26 daily; 2hr 30min–3hr; $41), Providence, RI (2 daily; 2hr 15min; $28), Springfield (14 daily; 35min; $10), Waterbury (8 daily; 45min; $14) and Worcester (7 daily; 1hr 5min–1hr 20min; $16.20).

GETTING AROUND

By bus CT Transit (☎ 860 525 9181, 🖥 cttransit.com; $1.25) maintains an extensive bus route serving the greater Hartford area. The Hartford Star Shuttle loops around major

tourist destinations, with frequent services and stops every 12min (Mon–Fri 7am–11pm, Sat 3–11pm; free; 🖥 ctconventions.com/visitors/star_shuttle.php).

INFORMATION AND TOURS

Greater Hartford Welcome Center 100 Pearl St (Mon–Fri 9am–5pm; ☎ 860 244 0253, 🖥 hartford.com and 🖥 letsgoarts.org), has a helpful staff and lots of information, as does the Old State House (see p.305).

Boat tours Mortensen Riverfront Plaza, 300 Columbus Blvd ☎ 860 665 9428, 🖥 hartfordbelle.com. The *Hartford Belle* is an antique-style 49-passenger riverboat (built in 1993), with a mahogany-trimmed covered cabin, open-deck section and bar – trips shuttle up and down the Connecticut River where you'll see blue herons and red-tailed hawks. Mid-May to mid-

Oct Sat & Sun 1.15pm (1hr; $14) & 3pm (90min; $20); July–Aug also Thurs & Fri, same times.

ACCOMMODATION

Hartford has a limited range of accommodation options, with only a handful of downtown hotels, catering mainly to business travellers. Budget **motels** are signposted off I-91, but for more charm, you might consider the nearby town of **Wethersfield** (see p.313).

★ **Hartford Marriott Downtown** 200 Columbus Blvd ☎ 860 249 18000 or ☎ 1 800 228 9290, ⓦ marriott.com. Luxurious contemporary hotel, overlooking the river and connected to the Convention Center (it's also next door to the Science Center). Rooms come with flat-screen TVs, plush bathrooms and workspaces, and there's a gym, pool and spa with superb views – and also great places to eat (see below). Free wi-fi in the lobby, otherwise $9.95/day. Check out the huge range of money-saving packages online. $160

Holiday Inn Express Downtown Hartford 440

Asylum St ☎ 860 246 9900, ⓦ hiexpress.com. This high-quality motel chain offers 96 good-value rooms conveniently located across from Bushnell Park and close to the train station. Free internet and basic breakfast included. $120

Mark Twain Hostel 131 Tremont St (I-84, exit 46) ☎ 860 523 7255. This hostel has seen better days, but it is a rare, genuine budget option near West Hartford, just off Farmington Ave. HI-member. Dorms $28; doubles with shared bathroom $58; en-suite $64

EATING

If you are short of time and are looking for a cheap meal in downtown Hartford, make for the **State House Square Food Court** (Mon–Fri 11am–9pm), opposite the Old State House, with a vast range of cheap eats: *Bangkok* offers the best phad Thai in the region ($8.50).

Abyssinian 535 Farmington Ave ☎ 860 218 2231. Authentic Ethiopian stews, salads, fish dishes and breads, with plentiful vegetarian options (mains $11.95–13.95); enjoy them all with the spongy *injera* bread made on site and remember Ethiopian food is designed for sharing (and eating with your right hand). Tues–Sat 11.30am–3pm & 5–10pm, Sun 5–10pm.

Black-Eyed Sally's 350 Asylum St ☎ 860 278 7427, ⓦ blackeyedsallys.com. This atmospheric restaurant and club hosts live blues bands Wed–Sat and offers hearty Cajun cooking like authentic Louisiana gumbo, jambalaya, blackened catfish and their popular Memphis-style barbecue pork ribs (mains $13.95–21.95). Mon–Thurs 11.30am–10pm, Fri & Sat till 11pm.

Carbone's 588 Franklin Ave ☎ 860 296 9646, ⓦ carbonesct.com. Superb Italian fine dining since 1938, with a classic chicken *parmigiana*, linguini with clam sauce and delicious lobster risotto; leave room for dessert, flambéed tableside (dinner mains $24–32). Mon–Fri 11.30am–10pm, Sat 4–10pm.

First & Last Tavern 939 Maple Ave ☎ 860 956 6000, ⓦ firstandlasttavern.com. A locals' favourite, no-frills Italian diner open since 1936, specializing in pastas (try the exquisite clam sauce) and brick-oven pizzas, from a tasty anchovy variety to broccoli rabe – mediums (15-inch) range from $14.50–20.25. Mon 11.30am–9pm, Tues–Thurs till 10pm, Fri till 11pm, Sat noon–11pm, Sun noon–9pm.

Max Downtown 185 Asylum St ☎ 860 522 2530, ⓦ maxrestaurantgroup.com/downtown. Hip nouveau-

American restaurant, serving an excellent duck and fig salad ($12), a sugar pie pumpkin and caramelized onion soup to start ($7) and mains like pesto-marinated chicken ($23), with a fine wine list. Mon–Thurs 11.30am–2.30pm & 5–10pm, Fri 11.30am–2.30pm & 5–11pm, Sat 5–11pm, Sun 4.30–9.30pm.

★ **Mozzicato De Pasquale's Bakery & Pastry Shop** 329 Franklin Ave ☎ 860 296 0426, ⓦ mozzicatobakery .com. Historic old-time Italian café combining the DePasquale Bakery founded in 1908 with the pastry shop opened by Italian immigrant Gino Mozzicato in 1973. Serves delicious coffee and pastries – try the whipped cream cakes. Daily 7am–9pm.

Polish National Home 60 Charter Oak Ave ☎ 860 247 1784. Venerable outpost of Hartford's Polish community, housed in a landmark 1930s Art Deco building – feast on *kielbasa* sausage, *golabki* (stuffed cabbage) and *pierogi* (dumplings). Mon & Sun 11am–3pm, Tues–Sat till 8pm, Sun till 3pm.

Salute 100 Trumbell St ☎ 860 899 1350, ⓦ salutect .com. Top-notch contemporary Italian cuisine enhanced by super-attentive, friendly service. Try the pasta *a la vodka* ($16) or spicy chicken stew ($19), but save space for the addictive cheesecake ($8). Mon–Wed 11.30am–10pm, Thurs till 11pm, Fri & Sat till midnight, Sun 4–10pm.

Vivo Hartford Marriott Downtown, 200 Columbus Blvd ☎ 860 760 2333, ⓦ vivohartford.com. Sparkling continental and contemporary American menu: the Rhode

Island-sourced scallops are always especially good ($33) as is the Atlantic swordfish ($33); meat lovers should opt for the sumptuous *osso bucco* (braised veal in a rich broth). Mon–Fri 6.30am–2pm & 5–10pm, Sat & Sun 7am–noon & 5–10pm.

Woody's Hot Dogs 915 Main St ☎860 278 5499, ⓦwoodyshotdog.com. Legendary purveyor of foot-long all-beef hot dogs ($3.50) served with the works (mustard, relish, onions and sauerkraut), founded in 1977 by locals Gary and Cindy Wood. Mon–Wed 11.30am–3pm, Thurs & Fri till 6pm, Sat noon–6pm.

DRINKING

Agave Grill 100 Allyn St ☎860 882 1557, ⓦagavehartford.com. Trendy corner bar with 60 plus tequilas; also offers fine Mexican food (tacos and enchiladas, but also Mexican-style paella and mango BBQ ribs) and live mariachi bands. The guacamole is superb. Mon 11.30am–11.30pm, Tues–Thurs till 12.30am, Fri till 1.30am, Sat 11am–1.30am, Sun till 11pm.

Bin 228 28 Pearl St ☎860 244 9463, ⓦbin228winebar .com. Choose from over 55 wines by the glass and plenty more by the bottle; Italian wines are a speciality, but the selection spans the globe. Mon–Thurs 11.30am–10pm, Fri till midnight, Sat 4pm–midnight.

City Steam Brewery Café 942 Main St ☎860 525 1600, ⓦcitysteambrewerycafe.com. This fifteen-barrel brewhouse and seven-level space serves hand-crafted and speciality beers. Also home of the *Brew Ha Ha Comedy Club* (Fri–Sat 7 & 10pm). Mon–Thurs 11.30am–midnight, Fri & Sat till 1am, Sun 4–10pm.

Vaughan's Public House 59 Pratt St ☎860 882 1560, ⓦirishpublichouse.com. Popular Irish pub with Guinness and Smithwick's on draught (pints $5–5.75) and traditional Irish dinners – think Guinness lamb stew ($9.99) and shepherd's pie ($10.99). Mon–Thurs 11.30am–1am, Fri till 2am, Sat 11am–2am, Sun till 1am.

NIGHTLIFE AND ENTERTAINMENT

There's no shortage of nightlife in Hartford, whether you want to see a play, listen to a symphony concert or bop till the wee hours. For current **listings**, check out the free arts and entertainment weekly the *Hartford Advocate* (ⓦhartfordadvocate .com) or the city's daily newspaper, the *Courant* (ⓦcourant.com).

Bushnell Center for the Performing Arts 166 Capitol Ave ☎860 987 5900, ⓦbushnell.org. Built in the 1930s with a Georgian Revival exterior and Art Deco interior (a new extension was completed in 2001), the Bushnell is now home to the Hartford Symphony Orchestra, the Hartford Ballet and the Connecticut Opera.

Comcast Theater 61 Savitt Way ☎860 548 7370, ⓦlivenation.com. This huge indoor and outdoor stadium (capacity 30,000) is a major venue for rock, pop, country, blues and jazz acts (Guns N' Roses played here in 2011).

Hartford Stage Company 50 Church St ☎860 527 5151, ⓦhartfordstage.org. Founded in 1963, this award-winning company stages classic plays and bold experimental productions at its 489-seat John W. Huntington Theatre. Main season runs Sept–May.

TheaterWorks 233 Pearl St ☎860 527 7838, ⓦtheaterworkshartford.org. This acclaimed local company presents contemporary and off-Broadway (fringe) pieces in a 1927 Art Deco gem they converted into an arts centre in the 1990s.

XL Center 225 Trumbull St ☎860 548 2000, ⓦxlcenter .com. Home of the American Hockey League (minor league NHL) Connecticut Whale hockey team and host to a variety of sports competitions and rock and pop concerts.

Farmington

Ten miles west of Hartford, lush **FARMINGTON** saw its heyday in the 1830s and 1840s, when the Farmington Canal operated between New Haven and Northampton, Massachusetts. Though today a more mundane suburb, it still merits a visit for the Hill-Stead Museum.

Hill-Stead Museum

35 Mountain Rd • Tues–Sun 10am–4pm; guided tours run for just under 1hr and are the only way to visit (apart from the first Sun of every month, when you can tour solo from noon until closing) • $12 • ☎860 677 4787, ⓦhillstead.org • Bus #66 from Hartford

A handsome Colonial Revival mansion built in 1901, the **Hill-Stead Museum** is a private art museum, set on an idyllic 152 acres. The former home of industrial magnate Alfred A. Pope, the house was designed by his daughter Theodate, one of the nation's first female architects, and holds in its original setting the family's outstanding collection of Impressionist paintings, including works by Monet, Manet, Degas and Whistler.

By bus Greyhound (☏ 1 800 231 2222, ⓦ greyhound.com) connects Farmington with Hartford (8 daily; 15min; $10), Waterbury (7 daily; 30–45min; $13), Danbury (7 daily; 1hr 10min–1hr 25min; $17) and New York (7 daily; 2hr 35min–2hr 55min; $30). Peter Pan (☏ 1 800 443 1831, ⓦ peterpanbus.com) connects Farmington with New Britain (3 daily; 25min). Buses stop at 529 Farmington Avenue. CT Transit (☏ 860 525 9181, ⓦ cttransit.com; $1.25) bus #66 also connects downtown Hartford with Farmington (frequent; 45min), while New Britain Transportation (☏ 860 828 0512, ⓦ nbt.bz; $1.25) operates bus #F between New Britain and Farmington (Mon–Sat hourly; 15min;).

New Britain

A couple of miles southwest of Farmington on I-84, industrial **NEW BRITAIN**, once one of the country's leading producers of hardware items, is the unlikely location for one of the northeast's best collections of American art. It also has a large Polish community – trawl Broad Street, officially "**Little Poland**", for the best Polish restaurants.

New Britain Museum of American Art

56 Lexington St • Tues, Wed & Fri 11am–5pm, Thurs till 8pm, Sat 10am–5pm, Sun noon–5pm • $10, free Sat 10am–noon • ☏ 860 229 0257, ⓦ nbmaa.org

The **New Britain Museum of American Art** boasts some ten thousand works spanning the colonial era to the present, including portraits by Trumbull and Stuart, works from the Hudson River School and US Impressionists, and paintings by Sargent, Homer and several twentieth-century artists such as Georgia O'Keeffe and Andy Warhol.

New Britain Industrial Museum

185 Main St • Mon, Tues, Thurs & Fri 2–5pm, Wed noon–5pm • Free • ☏ 860 832 8654, ⓦ nbim.org

With a different sort of aesthetic from the New Britain Museum, the **New Britain Industrial Museum** hosts exhibits devoted to the city's manufacturing history, with everything from tools to Art Deco kitchenware. Some of the more unusual highlights include rare nineteenth-century hinges and planes from the Stanley Works, a large photo of Buffalo Bill Cody and his Wild West show taken with local industrialists North & Judd in 1916, and a precious North & Judd document dating from 1867.

By bus Greyhound (☏ 1 800 231 2222, ⓦ greyhound.com) connects New Britain with Hartford (6 daily; 20–25min; $9.90) and New Haven (6 daily; 40min; $11.70). Buses stop outside Jimmy's Smoke Shop, 64 W Main St. Peter Pan (☏ 1 800 443 1831, ⓦ peterpanbus.com) connects Farmington with New Britain (3 daily; 25min). CT Transit (☏ 860 525 9181, ⓦ cttransit.com; $1.25) bus #41 also connects New Britain with Hartford (45min; frequent), while New Britain Transportation (☏ 860 828 0512, ⓦ nbt .bz; $1.25) operates bus #F between New Britain and Farmington (Mon–Sat hourly; 15min), and bus #PB between New Britain and Bristol (Mon–Sat hourly; 30min).

Bristol

Around seven miles west of New Britain on Rte-72, **BRISTOL** was part of the region once dubbed the "Switzerland of America" thanks to its clockmakers. It's better known today as the home of sports channel **ESPN** and the annual **Bristol Mum Festival** (Sept; ⓦ bristolmumfestival.org), a spirited celebration of chrysanthemums, another major product of the town up until the 1980s. You'll need your own transport to visit the area.

American Clock & Watch Museum

100 Maple St • April–Nov daily 10am–5pm • $5 • ☏ 860 583 6070, ⓦ clockandwatchmuseum.org

To get a sense of just how important Bristol once was, make time for the **American Clock & Watch Museum**, reputed to own the finest collection of American clocks in existence. The more than 1500 timepieces include the "Dewey", one of a series of six clocks introduced in 1899 to commemorate the Spanish-American War, with a likeness of Admiral Dewey at the top. Be prepared to cover your ears on the hour, when hundreds of chimes resonate around the museum.

New England Carousel Museum

95 Riverside Ave • March–Dec Mon–Sat 10am–5pm, Sun noon–5pm • $5, children (4–14 years) $2.50 • ☎ 860 585 5411, Ⓦ thecarouselmuseum.org

Bristol's second quirky attraction is the **New England Carousel Museum**, showcasing an enormous collection of antique carousel art and memorabilia, while a restoration department repairs old carousel pieces. The museum also runs the **Bristol Center for Arts & Culture** in the same building, which features galleries for contemporary artists.

Wethersfield

Just five miles south of downtown Hartford on I-91, **WETHERSFIELD** is Connecticut's best-preserved colonial town, with a large historic district of ageing clapboard and shingle houses. Wethersfield was founded in 1634 by Puritans from Massachusetts, which makes it older than Hartford or New Haven, though both soon superseded it in importance.

Webb-Deane-Stevens Museum

211 Main St • April Sat 10am–4pm, Sun 1–4pm; May–Oct Mon & Wed–Sat 10am–4pm; Sun 1–4pm; Nov Sat 10am–4pm, Sun 1–4pm • $10 for three-house tour • ☎ 860 529 0612, Ⓦ webb-deane-stevens.org • Bus #53 from Hartford

The **Webb-Deane-Stevens Museum** is made up of three eighteenth-century houses that each tell a different story about local society. The **Webb House**, built in 1752 by a prosperous merchant, contains a bedroom designed especially for George Washington, who came here to plan the Yorktown campaign in 1781. The 1766 **Silas Deane House** was home to lawyer-diplomat Silas Deane, who played an important role in the First Continental Congress and travelled to France to seek assistance for the Revolution. Deane was later accused of treason for dubious businesses abroad; although never convicted, he spent much of the rest of his life unsuccessfully attempting to clear his name. The more modest **Stevens House** was built in 1788 by a local leatherworker for his bride; it's charming for its simple decor.

The museum also maintains the 1711 **Buttolph-Williams House**, one of the oldest houses in town, down the road at 249 Broad St (May–Oct same hours; $5). At once medieval and romantic, it has dark clapboards, small windows and a massive open hearth.

Wethersfield Museum

200 Main St • Tues–Sat 10am–4pm, Sun 1–4pm • $5 • ☎ 860 529 7161, Ⓦ wethhist.org • Bus #53 from Hartford

The Wethersfield Historical Society maintains the **Wethersfield Museum** at the Keeney Memorial Cultural Center, hosting rotating exhibits on town history. The society also runs tours of the Georgian-style **Hurlbut Dunham House** (June–Sept Sat 11am–2pm, Sun 1–4pm; $5) at 212 Main St, built adjacent to the museum in the 1790s, and the **Cove Warehouse** (call the museum for hours) at the north end of Main Street, the lone survivor of a 1692 flood that destroyed the town's harbour.

Dinosaur State Park

400 West St, Rocky Hill • Grounds daily 9am–4.30pm, exhibition centre Tues–Sun same hours • $6, children (6–12 years) $2 • ☎ 860 529 8423, Ⓦ dinosaurstatepark.org • Bus #47 from Hartford

In 1966, the discovery of thousands of dinosaur tracks at **Rocky Hill**, two miles south of Wethersfield, led to the foundation of the bizarre attraction that is **Dinosaur State Park**, a mile east of I-91 exit 23, where you can view the largest on-site display of dinosaur

5

tracks in North America. The garishly lit display pit, with some 500 prints, housed under a gigantic geodesic dome, feels like a setting from of a Hitchcock film, but kids will enjoy the break from historic houses. Behind the exhibition centre, you can make your own dinosaur prints at the outdoor studio, and find echoes of prehistoric times along two miles of trails winding past a basalt ridge and woodland swamp.

ARRIVAL AND INFORMATION   WETHERSFIELD

By bus CT Transit (☎ 860 525 9181, ⓦ cttransit.com; $1.25) bus #53 connects downtown Hartford with Wethersfield (frequent; 20min); bus #47 connects Hartford with Dinosaur State Park (frequent; 30min).

The Keeney Memorial Cultural Center 200 Main St ☎ 860 529 7161. Serves as the town's visitor information centre; see ⓦ historicwethersfield.org for more information.

ACCOMMODATION

Chester Bulkley House Main St ☎ 860 563 4236, ⓦ chesterbulkleyhouse.com. Five Victorian-style rooms in the centre of town (two with shared bathroom), in a lovely 1830 Greek Revival home. Shared bathroom **$105**; en-suite **$165**

Silas W. Robbins House B&B 185 Broad St ☎ 860 571 8733, ⓦ silaswrobbins.com. This opulent choice occupies the lavish 1873 Second Empire mansion of entrepreneur Silas Robbins, with five luxurious period rooms equipped with flat-screen TVs and wi-fi. **$195**

EATING

Main Street Creamery 271 Main St ☎ 860 529 0509, ⓦ mainstreetcreamery.com. Wethersfield's enticing neighbourhood ice-cream parlour, with all the tempting flavours and also hot dogs and pastrami sandwiches at lunch (summer only). Daily 11am–10pm.

Village Pizza 233 Main St ☎ 860 563 1513, ⓦ villagepizzau.com. Great Greek-style pizzas (medium $12–18.50), *calzones* and Greek dishes such as gyros (kebab) platters for $11.50. Mon–Thurs & Sun 10am–10pm, Fri & Sat till 11pm.

Lower Connecticut River valley

The suburbs end and the more rustic landscapes of the **lower Connecticut River valley** reappear at Middletown, sixteen miles south of Hartford. Following the river south via routes 9 or 154 makes for a pleasant drive to the coast, with several enticing diversions along the way, notably **Gillette Castle State Park** and the **Godspeed Opera House**, both near East Haddam.

Higganum

Five miles south of Middletown on Rte-154 and the banks of the Connecticut River, the humble village of **HIGGANUM** merits a visit for its wonderfully evocative historic gardens and homes, a legacy of the great wealth created here by a booming grist- and saw-mill industry in the eighteenth and nineteenth centuries. You'll need your own transport to visit the area.

Thankful Arnold House

14 Hayden Hill Rd • Wed 9am–3pm, Thurs 2–8pm, Fri noon–3pm; late May to early Oct also Sun 1–4pm • $4 • ☎ 860 345 2400, ⓦ haddamhistory.org

The **Thankful Arnold House**, at the corner of Hayden Hill and Walkley Hill roads, is a three-storey gambrel-roofed historic house museum built in three distinct stages between 1794 and 1810. The interior has been lovingly restored, but the real highlight is the magnificent **herb and vegetable garden**, carefully researched to reflect plantings c.1830.

Sundial Herb Garden

Brault Hill Road Extension • Mid-May to mid-Oct Sat 10am–5pm, Sun noon–5pm • $2 donation • ☎ 860 345 4290, ⓦ sundialgardens.com

Higganum's premier horticultural treat is the **Sundial Herb Garden**, a series of formal gardens based on seventeenth- and eighteenth-century principles, with topiary, avenues, knot designs, statuary and sundials. The on-site teashop (Sat & Sun year-round 10am–5pm) specializes in rare and exotic teas from around the world.

East Haddam and around

About six miles southeast of Higganum, on the opposite side of the Connecticut River, the village of **EAST HADDAM** is the unlikely location for the magnificent **Goodspeed Opera House**, rising above the shore like a giant wedding cake. First settled in 1685, the village was the site of an important ferry across the river until the opening of the bridge in 1913. You'll need your own transport to visit this area.

Goodspeed Opera House

6 Main St (Rte-82) • Tours June–Oct Sat 11am–1pm • $5 • ☎ 860 873 8668, ⓦ goodspeed.org

More than six hundred people attended the opening night of the majestic **Goodspeed Opera House** in October 1877, named for local patron and shipping and banking magnate William Goodspeed. The theatre closed in 1920, but was revived in 1963, and has hosted a notable roster of plays, musicals and concerts ever since (performances April–Jan).

Gillette Castle State Park

67 River Rd (off Rte-82) • **Grounds** Daily 8am–sunset • Free **Castle** Late May to early Oct daily 10am–4.30pm • $6 • ☎ 860 526 2336

Four miles south of the centre of East Haddam, also on the east bank of the river, lies **Gillette Castle State Park**. This 24-room stone fortress was built between 1914 and 1919 by actor/playwright **William Hooker Gillette** (known for his stage portrayal of Sherlock Homes), and houses such grand features as a dining table on tracks, an enormous hall with balconies on three sides, and a replica of Sherlock Holmes' fictional London home, 221B Baker St, complete with violin, chemistry set and pipe.

ACCOMMODATION AND EATING	EAST HADDAM

Bishopsgate Inn 7 Norwich Rd (Rte-82) ☎ 860 873 1677, ⓦ bishopsgate.com. A charming 1818 clapboard house with six cosy rooms (four with open fireplaces) close to the opera house. The breakfasts are huge and guests are also provided with the inn's "Sweet Dreams" cookies at bedtime. Free wi-fi in all rooms. $145

Gelston House 78 Main St ☎ 860 873 1411, ⓦ gelstonhouse.com. Posh pre-theatre favourite serving fine American cuisine in the main dining room and on a less formal outdoor patio with spectacular river views (dinner mains $17.95–31.95). Tues–Sat 11.30am–3pm & 4.30–9pm, Sun 11.30am–8pm.

Ivoryton

The unassuming village of **IVORYTON**, together with the nearby town of Deep River, is said to have handled more than three-quarters of all the **ivory** exported from Zanzibar (off the coast of East Africa) in 1884. Phineas Pratt first manufactured ivory combs here in 1789, and the industry grew to include items like piano keys, crochet needles, brushes and organ stops. These days, though, the hamlet is best known for its **theatre**. You'll need your own transport to explore this area.

Ivoryton Playhouse

103 Main St • Parking $5 • ☎ 860 767 7318, ⓦ ivorytonplayhouse.org

Many a career has been launched from the fairly insignificant-looking wooden structure of the **Ivoryton Playhouse** since it opened in 1930, including that of local girl **Katharine Hepburn**. Today, the theatre produces seven professional shows annually, from musicals such as *The Producers* to plays such as Alan Ayckbourn's *How The Other Half Loves*.

Museum of Fife and Drum

62 N Main St • July & Aug Sat & Sun 1–5pm • $3 • ☎ 860 767 2237, ⓦ companyoffifeanddrum.org

For a generous dose of pomp and circumstance, head to the **Museum of Fife and Drum**, where the history of military music is traced through costumes, photographs and instruments. The museum sponsors free Tuesday evening concerts in the summer.

5

Essex

The Connecticut River widens noticeably as you head south towards **ESSEX**, a quaint New England town with some typically handsome colonial homes and a riverfront marina. In 1814 Essex was the scene of one of the heaviest American defeats of the **War of 1812**, when 28 ships were destroyed by the British – the disaster is commemorated on the second Saturday of May with a fife and drum corps parade down Main Street. Essex is just four miles northwest of the coast and Old Saybrook (see p.288).

Connecticut River Museum

67 Main St • Tues–Sun 10am–5pm • $8 • ☎ 860 767 8269, ⓦ ctrivermuseum.org

Housed in an atmospheric 1878 waterfront dockhouse, the absorbing **Connecticut River Museum** chronicles local maritime history, and contains a full-sized reproduction of the *American Turtle*, the world's first submarine, powered by hand cranks. The **waterfront park** outside the museum is a great place to watch boats coming and going.

Essex Steam Train & Riverboat

1 Railroad Ave • May & June Sat & Sun 11am, 12.30pm & 2pm; July & Aug daily same hours; Sept Fri–Sun same hours; Oct Thurs–Mon same hours • Train only $17, children (2–11 years) $9; train and boat $26, children (2–11 years) $17 • ☎ 860 767 0103, ⓦ essexsteamtrain.com

For something completely different, the **Essex Steam Train & Riverboat** offers narrated twelve-mile excursions into the valley on a restored steam train and riverboat (2hr 30min; train only 1hr). Trips begin at the historic 1892 Essex Station, from where steam trains chug through Chester, Deep River and untrammelled Selden Neck State Park. At Deep River Landing, passengers transfer onto the *Becky Thatcher* riverboat for a serene 75min cruise along the Connecticut River.

ARRIVAL AND DEPARTURE ESSEX

By bus CT Transit (☎ 860 525 9181, ⓦ cttransit.com; $1.25) bus #21 connects downtown Hartford and Old Saybrook with Essex. 9 Town Transit (☎ 860 510 0429, ⓦ estuarytransit.org) also provides local bus transport between Old Saybrook train station and Essex (6 daily; 30min). Regular fares are $1.25 (cash only, no change).

ACCOMMODATION AND EATING

Crow's Nest 35 Pratt St, Essex ☎ 860 767 3288. Serves fresh breakfast treats, excellent coffee, and soups and sandwiches. Eat on the deck overlooking the river. Mon–Fri 8am–3pm, Sat & Sun 7am–3pm.

Griswold Inn 36 Main St Essex ☎ 860 767 1776, ⓦ griswoldinn.com. This 1776 inn is as well known for its luxurious suites as for its sumptuous Sunday brunch (reserve ahead): chicken pot pies, braised ribs, sticky toffee pudding and the like. $145

The Litchfield Hills

The rolling, tree-clad **Litchfield Hills** in the tranquil northwest corner of the state present a rustic landscape of winding country roads, rushing brooks and picture-perfect colonial villages deep in pine-scented forests. The small town of **Litchfield**, with its maple tree-dotted green and elegant clapboard homes, serves as a fine base for exploring the area: picturesque **Washington**, antique-laden **Woodbury** and the lush green banks of **Lake Waramaug**. Due west, **Kent** remains a relaxed country town despite being "discovered" by artists from New York in the 1980s. To the north, **West Cornwall** boasts one of the area's two historic covered bridges, while close to the border of Massachusetts, **Norfolk** is home to the Yale Summer School of Music. You'll need your own transport to explore this region, as public transport is extremely limited.

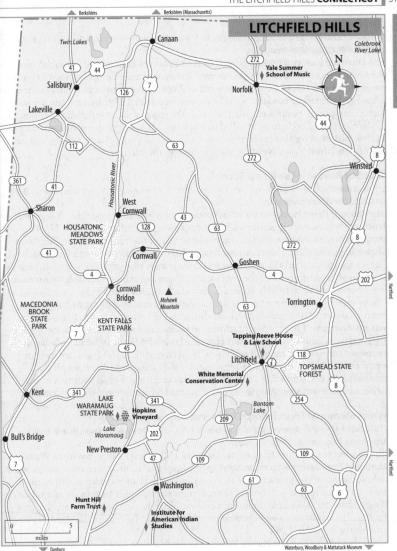

Litchfield

Founded in 1721, the town of **LITCHFIELD** spreads out around an exceptionally long and pretty village green, overlooked by the white steeple of the 1828 **Congregational Church**. During the Revolution, the town was a major manufacturer of supplies for George Washington's war effort, and soon after it became known as a centre for progressive education with the opening of the **Litchfield Law School** and the **Litchfield Female Academy**. Today, the area has become popular with gallery hoppers and cyclists, and at weekends is usually full of New Yorkers seeking peace and quiet in the town's streets and verdant hills. Much of the town's historical interest lies on **North Street**, lined with stately eighteenth-century mansions; many of these are open for tours on the annual **Open House Day** (second Sat in July 10am–5pm; ⓦlitchfieldct.com).

5

Litchfield History Museum

7 South St, at East St • Mid-April to Nov Tues–Sat 11am–5pm, Sun 1–5pm • $5; admission includes Tapping Reeve House & Law School • ☎ 860 567 4501, ⓦ litchfieldhistoricalsociety.org

The **Litchfield History Museum**, housed in the old library built in 1901, tells the story of the town from colonial days to the present. The main permanent gallery focuses on the period from 1780 to 1840, with a number of **Ralph Earl** portraits and exhibits on the law school and the female academy – the latter was founded in 1792 by local teacher Sarah Pierce. Temporary exhibits take up the rest of the space, with an especially absorbing Civil War display likely to be installed throughout 2013. Check the website for details of their **historical walking tours** of the town ($7, includes admission), usually held on the first and third Saturdays of the month through the summer.

Tapping Reeve House & Law School

82 South St (Rte-63) • Mid-April to Nov Tues–Sat 11am–5pm, Sun 1–5pm • $5; admission includes Litchfield History Museum • ☎ 860 567 4501, ⓦ litchfieldhistoricalsociety.org

The **Tapping Reeve House & Law School** preserves the former home of the College of New Jersey (now Princeton) graduate who began practising law in Litchfield in 1773 – he started taking on students (future vice-president Aaron Burr was among the first) soon after, and by the 1780s these informal lessons had evolved into **America's first law school**. Reeve's school attracted future movers and shakers from all over the new republic, but by the time of his death in 1820 the Ivy League colleges had started to establish their own law schools, and the relatively isolated Lichfield school closed in 1833.

Starting with a ten-minute movie dramatization of new students travelling to the town in about 1810, interactive exhibits bring to life a time when the practice of law was intimately tied to progressive reforms in politics and civil society; among Reeve's students were John C. Calhoun and Horace Mann, and the man himself was an avid proponent of women's rights. Each visitor is given one of 50–60 character cards on entry, containing details of a real-life student – the cards guide you through the exhibits, each one providing a slightly different experience. Finish your tour at the adjacent one-room **schoolhouse** (1784), crammed with authentic colonial-era desks.

White Memorial Foundation & Conservation Center

71 Whitehall Rd (off Rte-202) • **Reserve** Daily 24hr • Free • ☎ 860 567 0857, ⓦ whitememorialcc.org **Nature Museum** Mon–Sat 9am–5pm, Sun noon–5pm • $6; children 6–12 years $3

To get a feel for the rural heart of the Lichfield Hills, spend half a day at the **White Memorial Foundation & Conservation Center**, a pristine 4000-acre reserve that includes three-quarters of the **Bantam Lake** shoreline and more than 35 miles of well-marked trails on varied terrain – if short of time, aim for the one-mile boardwalk around Little Pond. There are also ample opportunities for cycling, horseriding, birdwatching and fishing. The whole thing was donated to the foundation by conservationist **Alain White** and his sister May in 1964.

You should also visit the **Nature Museum** housed in remnants of the White summer home ("Whitehall") built in the 1860s, to learn more about the extraordinary siblings and the environments protected here – the museum is especially fun for children, with plenty of interactive exhibits and a novel display on the art and process of **taxidermy**.

ACCOMMODATION

Abel Darling B&B 102 West St ☎ 860 567 0384, ⓦ abeldarling.com. A ravishing 1782 colonial building steps from the village green, with four bright, spotless period rooms with wood floors. Free wi-fi. **$140**

Mary Stuart House B&B 160 Sharon Turnpike (Rte-4), Goshen ☎ 860 491 2260, ⓦ marystuarthouse.com. Six charming, antique-laden rooms at bargain rates (for this area), in a restored 1798 historic colonial home a few miles north of Litchfield. **$95**

Tollgate Hill Inn 571 Torrington Rd (Rte-202) ☎ 860 567 1233 or ☎ 1 800 567 1233, ⓦ tollgatehill.com. Offers gracious rooms in a 1745 tavern, 1920 schoolhouse and an adjacent, newer building, all with cable TV and free wi-fi. **$115**

EATING

Dutch Epicure Shop 491 Bantam Rd (Rte-202) ☎860 567 5586, ☜alldutchfood.com. Tasty Teutonic treats like veal goulash, *spaetzle*, and German potato salad. Wed–Sat 9am–5pm, Sun till 2pm.

West Street Grill 43 West St ☎860 567 3885, ☜weststreetgrill.com. Centrally located and always top-quality fresh, organic food, with a small but fabulous international menu. Dinner mains $21–38.

Mon–Wed & Sun 11.30am–9pm, Thurs till 9.30pm, Fri & Sat till 10pm.

Wood's Pit BBQ & Mexican Cafe 123 Bantam Lake Rd (Rte-209) ☎860 567 9869, ☜woodspitbbq.com. This no-frills roadside diner is famed for its lip-smacking barbecued ribs and hot 'n' honey wings, and the bar features local craft beers. Side-splitting platters $13.95–15.95. Tues–Thurs & Sun 11.30am–9pm, Fri & Sat till 10pm.

Lake Waramaug

About ten miles southwest of Litchfield, just off Rte-202, lies **Lake Waramaug**, the second largest natural lake in Connecticut and easily the prettiest. The tree-lined shores are especially popular during the autumn foliage season, though visit in the summer and you can swim in the lake's pristine waters. Though the most scenic sections of shoreline tend to be in private hands, the lake loop road (an extension of Rte-42) hugs the water throughout, and there are several access points. **Lake Waramaug State Park** (daily 8am–sunset; winter weekends and year-round weekday parking free, summer weekends $15; park office ☎860 927 3238) runs a small beach and stretch of shady shoreline in the far western corner of the lake, while the **Town of Washington Beach** (late June to Aug 10am–4pm; $20 seasonal pass) is an even smaller strip at the far southern end.

Hopkins Vineyard

25 Hopkins Rd • Jan & Feb Fri & Sat 10am–5pm, Sun 11am–5pm; March & April Wed–Sat 10am–5pm, Sun 11am–5pm; May–Dec Mon–Sat 10am–5pm, Sun 11–5pm • $6 for 7 tastings • ☎860 868 7954, ☜hopkinsvineyard.com

On the northern side of Lake Waramaug, just off the loop road, the **Hopkins Vineyard** is the only Connecticut grape farm to benefit from a microclimate (yielding a longer season), with a stunning location overlooking the lake. Peruse the products (from whites and reds to a decent bubbly) or go for an informal tasting, well worth the $6. Grab lunch or spend the night at the adjacent *Hopkins Inn* (see below).

ACCOMMODATION AND EATING   LAKE WARAMAUG

Hopkins Inn 22 Hopkins Rd ☎860 868 7295, ☜thehopkinsinn.com. A moderately priced option next to the vineyard, with eleven guest rooms, some with shared bathroom, and two apartments, most with views of the lake; there is an excellent Austrian restaurant on site.

Wi-fi in the parlour only. Restaurant Tues–Fri noon–2pm & 5.30–8.45pm, Sat noon–2pm & 5–9.30pm, Sun noon–8pm. **$130**

★ **Oliva** 18 E Shore Rd (Rte-45) ☎860 868 1787. An outstanding Mediterranean eatery where flavours come

---

CONNECTICUT'S WINE TRAIL

More than a dozen wineries dot Connecticut's idyllic farmland and hills, particularly in the western part of the state. Litchfield's **Haight-Brown Vineyard**, 29 Chestnut Hill Rd (☎203 567 4045, ☜haightvineyards.com) was the first, growing Chardonnay and Riesling grapes. **Hopkins Vineyard** has a stunning location overlooking Lake Waramaug (see above), while some interesting choices are produced by the large **DiGrazia Vineyards**, 131 Tower Rd, Brookfield (☎203 775 1616, ☜digrazia.com), which add blueberries, pears or honey (eliminating the need for sulphites) to the formula. In the eastern part of the state, picturesque Rte-169 leads to Lisbon's **Heritage Trail Vineyard**, 291 North Burnham Highway (☎860 376 0659, ☜heritagetrail.com), while **Stonington Vineyards**, 523 Taugwonk Rd, Stonington (☎860 535 1222, ☜stoningtonvineyards.com), offer premium wines close to other coastal attractions. Tastings and tours are offered at many of these and other vineyards along Connecticut's Wine Trail; visit ☜ctwine.com or call ☎860 267 1399 for more info.

5

together wonderfully, even in basics like lentil soup. Wed–Sun 5.30–10pm.

The Sachem Farmhouse 15 Hopkins Rd ☎ 860 868 0359, ⓦ thesachemfarmhouse.com. Luxurious B&B in a restored 1870 farmhouse overlooking the lake and strategically positioned near the Hopkins Vineyard. Just four elegant rooms dressed with fine antiques, reading chairs, iPod docks, DVD players and free wi-fi. $195

Kent and around

In the early nineteenth century, **KENT** was a bustling industrial centre, but these days it's a refined country town and one of the top places in the country for the **autumn leaf-viewing season**. Since the 1980s an influx of boutiques and galleries have sprung up along Main Street, while the town itself remains low-key, welcoming antique-shoppers and backpackers alike to this rustic part of Connecticut.

Connecticut Antique Machinery Association

31 Kent-Cornwall Rd (US-7) • May–Oct Wed–Sun 10am–4pm • $3 • ☎ 860 927 0050, ⓦ ctamachinery.com

The **Connecticut Antique Machinery Association** maintains Kent's industrial legacy, with a sprawling collection of gigantic combustion engines, steam and diesel engines, vintage tractors and the reassembled nineteenth-century Cream Hill Agricultural School, one of the country's first. Don't forget to peek into the tiny **Museum of Mining and Mineral Science** (also on site), an earth science teacher's dream come true, with displays of fluorescent minerals, a recreated mine shaft, Connecticut bricks and educational exhibits on the history of mining in the state.

Kent Falls State Park

462 Kent-Cornwall Rd (US-7) • Daily 8am–sunset • Free • Sat & Sun parking $15 • ☎ 860 927 3238

For venturing into the great outdoors, **Kent Falls State Park**, about four miles north of downtown Kent on US-7, is an enticing option, known for its namesake 250ft falls. The most dramatic drop is a 70ft cascade that's visible from the road, not far from the car park; from there, a quarter-of-a-mile trail winds up along the water.

Macedonia Brook State Park

159 Macedonia Brook Rd • Daily 8am–sunset • Free • ☎ 860 927 3238

Near Kent Falls State Park, off Rte-341, the 2300-acre **Macedonia Brook State Park** boasts deep gorges, waterfalls and the 1350ft summit of **Cobble Mountain**, which commands views as far as the Catskills in New York.

INFORMATION   KENT

Tourist information For information call the chamber of commerce at ☎ 860 927 1463 or visit ⓦ kentct.com, which has details of local activities and events; the town website is ⓦ townofkentct.org.

ACCOMMODATION

Inn at Kent Falls 107 Kent Cornwall Rd ☎ 860 927 3197, ⓦ theinnatkentfalls.com. A gorgeous, high-end option dating from 1741– but don't be fooled by the name: the falls are more than three miles up the road. $215

Starbuck Inn 88 N Main St ☎ 860 927 1788, ⓦ starbuckinn.com. Another sensational clapboard gem (built relatively recently in 1948), with six comfy, stylish rooms; extras include a hearty breakfast and afternoon high tea and sherry. $198

CAMPING

Macedonia Brook State Park You can camp here between mid-April and October, though it's fairly primitive and alcohol is not allowed. Pitches $24

EATING AND DRINKING

★ **Belgique** 1 Bridge St ☎ 860 927 3681, ⓦ belgiqueonline.com. Boasts exquisite handmade Belgian truffles, ice cream in summer and addictive hot chocolate all year round. Thurs–Sun 10am–6pm.

Kent Coffee and Chocolate Company 8 N Main St ☎ 860 927 1445, ⓦ kentcoffee.com. Top-quality coffee and gourmet chocolate, a combination that's been winning this cosy café accolades since 1991 – they also sell pastries and crunchy *biscotti*. Mon–Thurs & Sun 7am–5pm, Fri & Sat till 5.30pm.

Fife 'N Drum Restaurant & Inn 53 N Main St ☎ 860 927 3509, ⓦ fifendrum.com. Offers fine meals like roast duck flambéed tableside. The pub-style bar features nightly piano music by proprietor Dolph Traymon, who's played with the likes of Sinatra. Mains $19–30. Mon–Thurs 11.30am–3pm & 5.30–9.30pm, Fri 11.30am–3pm & 5.30–10pm, Sat 11.30am–3pm & 5.30–10.30pm, Sun 11.30am–3pm & 3–8.30pm.

Washington and around

WASHINGTON is divided into two main parts on Rte-47, the beguiling colonial enclave of **Washington Green** on top of the hill, and the more commercial (but still attractive) **Washington Depot** in the valley. The best reason for a visit is the enlightening **Institute for American Indian Studies**, a rare tribute to Connecticut's rich Native American heritage.

Institute for American Indian Studies

38 Curtis Rd • Mon–Sat 10am–5pm, Sun noon–5pm • $5 • ☎ 860 868 0518, ⓦ birdstone.org

Just off Rte-199, the **Institute for American Indian Studies** offers a rare and fascinating window into the history and culture of Connecticut's Native American peoples. Galleries cover the history of the state, or "Quinnetukut", from a Native American perspective, beginning with the paleo-Indian era (12000–7000 BC) and ending with the disastrous encounter with European peoples in the seventeenth century. Displays chart the emergence of today's **five official tribes** – Schaghticoke, Paucatuck East Pequot, Mashantucket Pequot, Mohegan and Golden Hill Paugussett – while the interior of a sixteenth-century Algonkian longhouse is contrasted with a cramped room in a typical reservation house of the early 1900s. Behind the main building there are five nature trails and a replica of a traditional sixteenth-century **Algonkian village**; most weekends in the summer you'll find costumed interpreters up here.

Hunt Hill Farm Trust

44 Upland Rd (off US-202) • Wed–Sat 10am–5pm, Sun noon–5pm • Free • ☎ 860 355 0300, ⓦ hunthillfarmtrust.org

A short drive southwest of Washington on Rte-109, the **Hunt Hill Farm Trust** is a wonderfully atmospheric cultural centre and 130-acre nature reserve, the legacy of the late **Skitch Henderson** (1918–2005), founder and former director of the New York Pops (an orchestra specializing in popular music and show tunes). The core farm properties were constructed in the eighteenth century and purchased by the Hendersons in the 1970s – the non-profit Trust was formed in 2003 and now manages the site.

At the heart of the operation are the **Silo Gallery** and **Cooking School**. The gallery shows the work of local and nationally acclaimed artists in the cathedral-like old barn. The culinary school often hosts celebrity chefs and runs eclectic three-hour programmes ($60–90) most weekends on everything from Italian cheese-making to Russian *pierogis*. Make sure you also check the website for the latest events and concerts ($10–25) held here.

Nearby, the **Skitch Henderson Museum** houses an American music archive containing over 450 magnetic and film tape recordings, as well as plenty of memorabilia of the man himself (including his old Steinway piano, signed by the Steinway family).

Woodbury

Touted as the antiques capital of New England, **WOODBURY** has a main street lined by eighteenth- and nineteenth-century houses that have nearly all been converted into shops. First settled in 1672, Woodbury thrived as an agricultural centre through to the 1950s, after which it gradually became more suburban (folks actually commute to New York from here).

5

Glebe House Museum & Gertrude Jekyll Garden

49 Hollow Rd • May–Oct Wed–Sun 1–4pm; Nov Sat & Sun 1–4pm • $5 • ☎ 203 263 2855, ⓦ theglebehouse.org

The **Glebe House Museum & Gertrude Jekyll Garden** combines another artfully preserved colonial house with something quite unique – the only remaining garden in the US designed by the doyen of modern English landscaping, **Gertrude Jekyll** (1843–1932). The garden is a ravishing example of Jekyll's art, with waves of blossoms forming hot and cold borders, everything seemingly wild and casual, but planned with extreme detail and painstakingly maintained. Jekyll never actually came here: in 1926 she was asked to design the garden, but the plans were only enacted in 1985, after a chance discovery of her original notes in a University of California archive.

The gardens tend to overshadow the house these days, which was built in the 1740s and restored in the 1920s for its founding role in the American **Episcopal church**: the house was owned by Anglican minister John Marshall during the Revolutionary War, and it was here in 1783 that the first Episcopal bishop was elected (Samuel Seabury), signalling the continuity of Anglican practice under a new, disestablished basis. The charming interior provides a fine glimpse into life of the period, with some original china and silverware on display; there's even an old bible from 1640 and Marshall's prayer book from 1771.

ACCOMMODATION AND EATING   WOODBURY

Carmen Anthony Fishhouse 757 Main St South ☎ 203 266 0011, ⓦ carmenanthony.com. This local Connecticut chain has a seafood focus, with dishes such as potato-encrusted crab cake, swordfish and black cod. Mon–Wed 11.30am–9pm, Thurs–Sat till 10pm, Sun noon–9pm.
Curtis House 506 Main St South ☎ 203 263 2101, ⓦ curtishouseinn.com. The oldest inn in the state (1754), this atmospheric and rustic option comes with creaky, sloping floors, antique beds and a decent pub and

restaurant – the best rooms have flat-screen TVs and modern bathrooms, and there's free wi-fi, but the rooms with shared bathrooms are an excellent deal. Shared bathroom **$56**; en-suite **$89**
John's Cafe 693 Main St South, ☎ 203 263 0188, ⓦ johnscafe.com. Inspired American cuisine, with perfect steaks, home-made pasta and fresh baked desserts. Mains $22–29. Mon–Sat 11.30am–2.30pm & 5.30–9pm, Sun 4.30–8.30pm.

SHOPPING

Backcountry Outfitters 5 Bridge St ☎ 1 888 549 3377, ⓦ bcoutfitters.com. A good stop for maps of local hikes and outdoor gear. Mon–Sat 9am–6pm, Sun 10am–4pm.
Mill House Antiques 1068 Main St N ☎ 203 263 3446,

ⓦ millhouseantiques-ct.com. Of the many antique stores in town, Mill House is especially worth checking out, featuring an extensive array of French and English furniture and collectibles. Daily 10am–5pm.

Waterbury

At the very southern edge of the Litchfield Hills, and certainly not part of them in spirit, **WATERBURY** valiantly celebrates its glorious past of brass- and copper-making. Downtown is pleasing enough, with red-brick and white marble municipal buildings, including the Chase Building and the former Waterbury National Bank, both designed by **Cass Gilbert**, architect of the Woolworth Building in New York. Look, too, at 389 Meadow St, at the town's former main **railroad station**, modelled on the City Hall in Siena, Italy, with a tall campanile-style tower that is the city's most notable landmark.

Mattatuck Museum

144 W Main St • Tues–Sat 10am–5pm, Sun noon–5pm • $5 • ☎ 203 753 0381, ⓦ mattatuckmuseum.org

You'll find the requisite Waterbury history in the **Mattatuck Museum**, a haven of local art and memorabilia devoted to telling the story of the region. Highlights include a 10,000-piece button collection from all over the world – buttons have been made in Waterbury since 1812.

Timex Museum

175 Union St • Tues–Sat 10am–5pm • $6 • ☎ 203 755 8463, ⓦ timexpo.com

Like nearby Bristol (see p.312), Waterbury has a history of clock-making; the Waterbury Clock company dates back to 1854 but was renamed Timex in the 1970s, and its progression through the years is recounted in the **Timex Museum**. Hands-on activities include assembling your own clock and wrist-watch (not quite as complicated as the real thing).

ARRIVAL AND DEPARTURE   WATERBURY

By train Metro-North trains (☎ 1 800 638 7646, ⓦ mta info/mnr) serve all the stations between Waterbury and Bridgeport (8 daily; 55min), where you can transfer to trains for New York, Boston and the Connecticut coast. The station is near the centre at 333 Meadow St. For taxis, try Yellow Cab (☎ 203 754 5151).

By bus Peter Pan (☎ 1 800 443 1831, ⓦ peterpanbus.com) and Greyhound bus services (☎ 1 800 231 2222, ⓦ greyhound.com) link Waterbury with Danbury (10 daily; 40min; $13), New York (10 daily; 2hr 30min; $27), and Hartford (7 daily; 50min; $14). The bus station is at 188 Bank St (☎ 203 755 2700), just north of downtown.

Ridgefield and around

Picturesque **RIDGEFIELD**, just 22 miles from the Connecticut coast, is culturally much closer to the Litchfield Hills than to its sprawling seaside neighbours. Founded in 1708, the town was never blighted by industry, and by the nineteenth century wealthy New Yorkers were building elegant summer mansions along **Main Street** (Rte-35).

Aldrich Contemporary Art Museum

258 Main St • Tues–Sun noon–5pm • $7, free Tues • ☎ 203 438 4519, ⓦ aldrichart.org

The **Aldrich Contemporary Art Museum** is a real surprise, a cutting-edge exhibition space devoted to up-and-coming artists from all over the world. There is no permanent collection – instead, the carefully curated shows are renewed every January and June (previous exhibitors include Danish-Icelandic artist Olafur Eliasson). The twelve galleries occupy an elegant modern building completed in 2004, but the original building in front (now admin offices) is one of the gorgeous mansions on this stretch of Main Street, built around 1783.

Keeler Tavern Museum

132 Main St • Feb–Dec Wed, Sat & Sun 1–4pm; entrance to the house is by guided tour only (45min–1hr) • $5 • ☎ 203 438 5485, ⓦ keelertavernmuseum.org

Ridgefield's varied history is preserved at the **Keeler Tavern Museum**, a rambling clapboard-and-shingle property built around 1713. Tours take in the oldest, most atmospheric rooms, with their blackened fireplaces and rich aroma of old wood. Timothy Keeler turned the home into a tavern in 1772 (the original sign is on display inside), with a taproom, new bedrooms and kitchen; the tavern was a hotbed of patriotic fervour during the Battle of Ridgefield, and a British cannonball is still embedded in the wall.

In 1907 the house was purchased as a summer residence by the accomplished architect **Cass Gilbert** (designer of New York's Woolworth Building, among many others), who built the Garden House (1915) and barn, modernized the interior and added tranquil gardens and a new wing – his legacy is on show in the Dining Room, preserved in Edwardian splendour. Entrance to the house is by guided tours only (45min–1hr).

Weir Farm National Historic Site

735 Nod Hill Rd, Wilton (4 miles southeast of Ridgefield) • Grounds daily dawn–dusk; visitor centre Jan–March Sat & Sun 10am–4pm; April–Dec Thurs–Sun same hours • Free • ☎ 203 834 1896, ⓦ nps.gov/wefa • Four miles from downtown Ridgefield; take Rte-102 east from Ridgefield Main Street, then turn right along Old Branchville Road; Nod Hill Road will be on the right ahead

Hugely influential in the history of American Impressionism, the **Weir Farm National Historic Site** has been associated with art and artists since painter **J. Alden Weir**

5

RIDING THE RAILS AT DANBURY

The manufacturing town of **DANBURY**, 11 miles north of Ridgefield, was once famous as the "hat capital" of America. While there's not much of interest in the spruced up downtown these days, families with young children (and rail enthusiasts of all ages) will love the **Danbury Railway Museum** (Mid-May to Aug Mon–Sat 10am–5pm, Sun noon–5pm; Sept to mid-May Wed–Sat 10am–4pm, Sun noon–4pm; $6, children 3–12 years $4; ☎ 203 778 8337, ⓦ danbury. org/drm), 120 White St, a short walk from Main Street and the Metro-North train station. Housed in Danbury's old train station, built in 1903, exhibits include plenty of working scale model trains to play with, but the real highlight is the huge rail yard outside, jam-packed with 70 trains and carriages of all types and sizes. Most weekends the museum dusts off the engines and offers 25-minute train rides on the old locomotives. Metro-North trains (☎ 800 638 7646, ⓦ mta.info/mnr) run between Danbury and South Norwalk (50min; 11 daily), where you can transfer to trains for New York, Boston and the Connecticut coast.

(1852–1919) acquired the 153-acre property in 1882. Weir bought the clapboard gem, built in the 1760s, in exchange for a painting (not one of his own) and a measly $10. Though Weir started his painting career doing still life and portraits in the Classical or "Academic" style, by the 1890s he had started dabbling in Impressionism at his summer retreat, immersing himself in the natural beauty of the farm and its surroundings.

In 1931 **Mahonri Young** (1877–1957), the respected sculptor, married Weir's daughter **Dorothy** (who was also a talented painter) and moved to the farm, creating many of his great works here. After his death the farm passed to painters **Doris** (1920–2003) and **Sperry Andrews** (1917–2005) – the Andrews were permitted to live in the farm even after they sold the property to the National Park Service in 1990.

The park service has been working to restore **Weir House** to its late nineteenth-century heyday since the death of Sperry; it should be open for guided tours in 2014, while the **Weir Studio** (1885) and spacious **Young Studio** (1932) should also have been restored to their former appearance and opened by the end of 2012. The site owns more than 150 Weir works of art, and many of them will be on display when the restoration is complete. Until then you can watch a thirteen-minute film in the **visitor centre**, where Weir's *Truants* is also on display, before taking a ranger-guided tour of the site – tours put into context the various artists who were inspired here, with an emphasis on the surrounding landscapes.

ACCOMMODATION

RIDGEFIELD

Stonehenge Inn Rte-7, Stonehenge Rd ☎ 203 438 6511, ⓦ stonehengeinn-ct.com. This 1827 colonial inn with a pretty garden and pond has sixteen Victorian-style rooms, most with four-poster beds. Free wi-fi. **$120**

West Lane Inn 22 West Lane ☎ 203 438 7323,

ⓦ westlaneinn.com. Eighteen antique-stuffed rooms in an enchanting 1849 mansion, all with flowery Victorian-style wallpaper and free wi-fi – some rooms have fireplaces and four-posters. **$185**

EATING AND DRINKING

Bernard's 20 West Lane (Rte-35) ☎ 203 438 8282, ⓦ bernardsridgefield.com. Fine contemporary French cuisine from accomplished chef Bernard Bouissou. Dinner dishes range from $26–38 – think portobello-crusted fillet of halibut, with wild mushroom risotto and asparagus. Tues–Thurs noon–2.30pm & 6–9pm, Fri & Sat noon–2.30pm & 6–10pm, Sun noon–2.30pm & 5–8pm.

Bissell House 378 Main St ☎ 203 431 4440, ⓦ thebissellhouse.com. Contemporary American cuisine including everything from burgers to fresh fish and Cedar

River Ranch natural sirloin; small plate selection from $9.95, mains $17.95–25.95. Mon–Wed 8am–10pm, Thurs–Sat 8am–11pm, Sun 11am–10pm.

Deborah Ann's Sweet Shoppe 381 Main St ☎ 203 431 0065, ⓦ deborahanns.com. Crammed with all sorts of sweets, chocolates and fudge, as well as a tempting ice cream counter in summer – the chocolate nut malt flavour is outstanding (scoops from $3.19). Mon–Sat 10am–7am, Sun 10am–6pm.

The northwest corner

Connecticut's **northwest corner** boasts verdant hills, weathered barns and fields bursting with corn in the summer. The area has become a hotspot for Hollywood A-listers and rich New Yorkers looking for a quiet retreat, and as a result the small country towns here – **Sharon** on Rte-4 is the best example – offer exclusive galleries and superb restaurants alongside local coffeeshops and fruit stands.

Housatonic Meadows State Park and West Cornwall

Daily 8am–sunset • Free • ☎ 860 927 3238

Around eight miles north of Kent along US-7 lies **Housatonic Meadows State Park**, a densely forested two-mile stretch along the Housatonic River that's popular with picnickers and fly-fishers. **West Cornwall**, just north of the park on US-7, has a tiny main street lined with a few lively craft shops and restaurants. At the foot of the street, the Housatonic River streams giddily under the 172ft bright-red, much photographed **covered bridge**, built in 1864 of native oak and later restored.

Norfolk

To the northeast of West Cornwall, US-7 and US-44 lead to **NORFOLK**, another quaint little town whose tall church steeple stands sentinel over a lush **village green**, today best known as home to the **Yale Summer School of Music** (🖥 art.yale.edu/norfolk) and the **Norfolk Chamber Music Festival** (🖥 music.yale.edu/norfolk).

ACCOMMODATION   NORFOLK

Mountain View Inn 67 Litchfield Rd, Norfolk ☎ 860 542 6991, 🖥 mvinn.com. Best accommodation in the area – a picturesque Victorian inn with eight elegant, period rooms. Convenient for the Norfolk festivals. **$185**

The Last Green Valley

Rustic **northeastern Connecticut** is better known as "the quiet corner" or the **Last Green Valley** for good reason. Highlights include the **Nathan Hale Homestead Museum** in Coventry (2299 South St; May Sat noon–4pm, Sun 11am–4pm; June–Aug Wed–Sat noon–4pm, Sun 11am–4pm; Sept & Oct Fri & Sat noon–4pm, Sun 11am–4pm; $7; ☎ 860 742 6917, 🖥 ctlandmarks.org), birthplace of the Revolutionary War hero, and the **William Benton Museum of Art** (245 Glenbrook Rd; Tues–Fri 10am–4.30pm, Sat & Sun 1–4.30pm; free; ☎ 860 486 4520, 🖥 thebenton.org) on the University of Connecticut campus in Storrs. The museum possesses one of the most complete collections of **Reginald Marsh**'s work, as well as over one hundred Käthe Kollwitz prints and drawings, and paintings by George Bellows and Childe Hassam.

INFORMATION   THE LAST GREEN VALLEY

Tourist information Visit the Last Green Valley website at 🖥 tlgv.org, or the Coventry Visitors Center, 1195 Main St (Rte 31), in Coventry (☎ 860 742 1085) for local information.

ACCOMMODATION AND EATING

★ **Golden Lamb Buttery** 499 Wolf Den Rod, Brooklyn ☎ 860 774 4423, 🖥 thegoldenlamb.com. This place is worth making a long detour for – dinners are an event, starting with cocktails in the barn and followed by home-style food in one of three charming dining rooms lit by candles. Lunch dishes $10–15; dinner *prix fixe* $75. Tues–Thurs noon–2.30pm, Fri & Sat noon–2.30pm & 7–10pm.
Inn at Woodstock Hill 94 Plaine Hill Rd, Woodstock ☎ 860 928 0528, 🖥 woodstockhill.net. Gorgeous country inn dating back to 1816, with eighteen beautifully decorated rooms, six with four-poster beds and eight with gas fireplaces. Free wi-fi. **$160**
★ **Still River Café** 134 Union Rd (Rte-171) ☎ 860 974 9988, 🖥 stillrivercafe.com. Elegant restaurant located in a beautiful, 150-year-old barn on a 27-acre farm; seasonal, local food might include a taste of mushrooms, organic, free-range chicken and Maine lobster ($28–34). Fri & Sat 6–8pm.

Vermont

331 Southern Vermont

349 Central Vermont

369 Lake Champlain

379 Northeast Kingdom

VIEW OVER MONTPELIER

6

Vermont

With its white churches and red barns, covered bridges and clapboard houses, snowy woods and maple syrup, Vermont comes closer than any other New England state to fulfilling the quintessential image of small-town Yankee America. True, in certain areas, the bucolic image can seem a bit packaged, but exploring the state's minor roads is captivating, with myriad little villages, alluring country inns and pristine lakes and mountains. Much of the state's landscape is smothered by verdant, mountainous forests – indeed, the name Vermont supposedly comes from the French "vert mont", or green mountain.

With the occasional exception, such as the extraordinary assortment of Americana at the **Shelburne Museum** near **Burlington** (a lively city worth visiting in any case), there are few specific sights as such to seek out. Tourism here is more activity-oriented, and though the state's rural charms can be enjoyed year-round, most visitors come during two well-defined seasons: to see the **autumn foliage** in the first two weeks of October, and to **ski** in the depths of winter, when resorts such as **Killington** and **Stowe** spring to life.

Brief history

Settled early in the eighteenth century, Vermont is the youngest of New England's states. As colonists moved north in the 1740s, Benning Wentworth, the royal governor of New Hampshire, began issuing land grants for the area now known as Vermont, and settlers began to pour in. Then in 1764, King George III decided that New York state should have jurisdiction over the area, with the result that original settlers and their townships were subjected to burdensome New York fees or, worse, had their lands confiscated. In 1770 the settlers responded by forming a citizens' militia, the **Green Mountain Boys**, to protect their rights, electing **Ethan Allen** (see p.371) as their colonel. Official representatives from New York were usually sent back to Albany, bruised and humiliated.

When war with Britain broke out in 1775, the land issue was still unresolved, but Allen and the Green Mountain Boys joined the rebels, promptly capturing Fort Ticonderoga from the British and helping to win the decisive **Battle of Bennington**. But New York continued to block Vermont representatives from joining the Continental Congress, and so, in 1777, it declared independence – the **Republic of Vermont** lasted for another fourteen years.

Joining the Union

Vermont enacted the first constitution in the world to forbid slavery and grant universal (male) suffrage, yet leaders such as Ethan Allen were constantly jostling to join the new United States (even threatening to re-join the British Empire at one point). Vermont finally joined the Union in 1791.

Vermont flooding 2011 p.332	**Mount Independence** p.356
Bulls run, heifers stroll p.333	**Rte-125: Robert Frost Country** p.358
Vermont farmers' markets calendar p.341	**Summer in Stowe** p.361
A mountain for all seasons p.342	**Maple syrup and sugar on snow** p.368
The Long Trail p.344	**Ethan Allen and his Green Mountain Boys** p.371
Mount Snow: skiing and mountain biking p.346	**Vermont's cheeses** p.381

THE LONG TRAIL

Highlights

❶ **Grafton** The iconic New England village, complete with white clapboard houses, steepled church and a fast-flowing stream shaded by maples. **See p.335**

❷ **The Long Trail** Walking the length of the entire state wins serious bragging rights for competitive hikers; for others, the magnificent vistas from Vermont's highest peaks will more than justify the effort. **See p.344**

❸ **Ben & Jerry's Factory Tour** Who can resist a scoop of creamy ice-cold calories served in a cone? **See p.360**

❹ **Montpelier** Relaxed, friendly, genuine and relatively tourist-free, the only state capital without a *McDonald's* is bounded by rivers and a forest of tall trees. **See p.366**

❺ **Burlington** In complete contrast to Vermont's profusion of perfect villages, this is a genuine city, with a waterfront, a vibrant downtown and the state's best restaurants and nightlife. **See p.369**

❻ **Shelburne Museum** Two centuries of American life stuffed into fifty acres of northern Vermont. **See p.375**

HIGHLIGHTS ARE MARKED ON THE MAP ON P.330

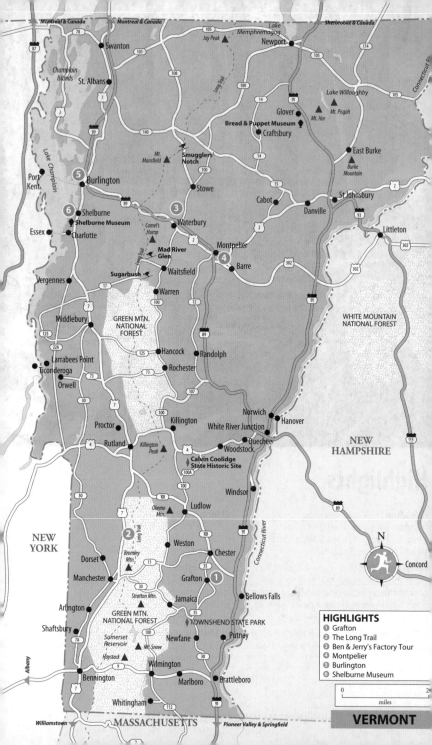

HIGHLIGHTS
1. Grafton
2. The Long Trail
3. Ben & Jerry's Factory Tour
4. Montpelier
5. Burlington
6. Shelburne Museum

VERMONT

Vermont has been a bucolic place ever since, with agriculture (particularly butter- and cheese-manufacturing) dominating the economy into the twentieth century, though since the late 1800s, when the state began to be branded as a rural paradise, the tourism industry has also played a large role.

Today, Vermont remains fairly liberal when it comes to politics: the state has been attracting a mix of hippies, environmentalists and professionals escaping the rat-race since the 1960s, most aspiring to an eco-friendly philosophy best epitomized by **Ben & Jerry's** additive-free, locally produced ice cream.

6

Southern Vermont

North of western Massachusetts, the Berkshires roll into the much higher Green Mountains of **southern Vermont**, the state's forested backbone. Most visitors begin their explorations of the area at **Brattleboro**, a lively college town with plenty of enticing stores and bars, or **Bennington**, forty miles on the other side of the hills and home to a smattering of historic attractions. From either town routes lead north through a hinterland of traditional Vermont villages, while in between, Rte-100 cuts a more central course through the **Green Mountain National Forest** to **Weston** and the **Okemo Valley**.

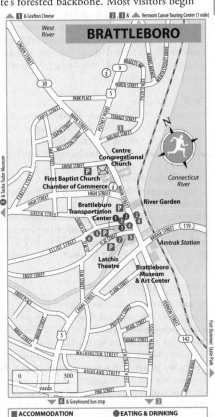

Brattleboro

Home to yoga studios, vintage record shops and bookstores catering to the town's youthful and vaguely alternative population, **BRATTLEBORO** has little in common with the clapboard villages that dominate much of Vermont. It's essentially a red-brick college town with little in the way of conventional sights – instead, it boasts cosmopolitan art and live music scenes, as well as tubing, kayaking and some crazy river skating and **ice-fishing** in winter. **Main Street** spans the length of Brattleboro's diminutive downtown, lined with hip coffee houses, art galleries and holistic apothecaries.

Sitting beside the Connecticut River, Brattleboro lies near the site of **Fort Dummer**, the first English settlement in the state, which was built in 1724 to protect Massachusetts from Indian raids (the actual site vanished under water when the Vernon Dam was built

■ ACCOMMODATION		● EATING & DRINKING	
Artist's Loft B&B and Gallery	4	Amy's Bakery Arts Café	2
Colonial Motel & Spa	2	Café a La Carte	3
Forty Putney Road B&B	3	Chelsea Royal Diner	1
Green River Bridge House	6	Flat Street Brew Pub	7
Latchis Hotel	5	McNeill's Brewery	5
Naulakha	1	Mocha Joe's	4
		TJ Buckley's	6
● SHOPS			
Brattleboro Books	3	■ ENTERTAINMENT	
Everyone's Books	1	Brattleboro Music Center	1
Vermont Artisan Designs	2	Vermont Jazz Center	2

6

VERMONT FLOODING 2011

In the aftermath of **Hurricane Irene** in August 2011, Vermont was hit with what the governor called the worst flooding in a century; many roads and bridges were completely destroyed. By the summer of 2012 everything should be back to normal, but check the **Vermont Agency of Transportation** (Ⓦ aot.state.vt.us) or **tourism websites** (Ⓦ vermontvacation.com or Ⓦ vermont.gov) for the latest.

---

in 1908). Gradually businesses and farms sprang up alongside the river and the fort, and in the 1800s Brattleboro enjoyed a modest reputation as a railroad and mill town. **Rudyard Kipling** penned his two *Jungle Book*s here in the 1890s, giving the town its sole claim to fame, one you could experience fully by staying at his former home **Naulakha** (see p.333).

Brattleboro Museum and Art Center

10 Vernon St • Thurs–Mon 11am–5pm; closed end March to end April • $6 • ☎ 802 257 0124, Ⓦ brattleboromuseum.org

The modest **Brattleboro Museum and Art Center** occupies the old railroad station building dating from 1916. The centre is more art gallery than museum, with most of the changing exhibits highlighting contemporary art in a variety of media – Vermont artists are often featured.

Grafton Cheese

400 Linden St (Rte-30) • Daily 10am–6pm • Free • ☎ 800 472 3866, Ⓦ graftonvillagecheese.com

The lauded cheese-maker **Grafton Cheese** moved its main operation from the village of Grafton to this site just outside Brattleboro in 2009. Visit the cheese and wine shop, where you can taste the products and watch cheddar being made.

Tasha Tudor Museum

2/F Jeremiah Beal House, 974 Western Ave • May Wed & Fri 10am–3pm; June–Oct Wed, Fri & Sat 10am–3pm • Free • ☎ 802 258 6564, Ⓦ tashatudormuseum.org

This temporary exhibition celebrates the life of local children's book illustrator **Tasha Tudor** (1915–2008). Tudor lived nearby in Marlboro, gaining fame for books such as *Corgiville Fair*, published in 1971. The plan is to open a much larger permanent **Tasha Tudor Museum** as soon as funds are raised – check the website for the latest.

ARRIVAL AND DEPARTURE   BRATTLEBORO

By train Amtrak trains run from Brattleboro north to Burlington, and south to New York, though there's only one or two trains in each direction daily; the "station" on Vernon Street is just a stop on the tracks (office open daily 11am–1pm & 4–6pm), though by 2013 there should be a spanking new facility here. New tracks will mean a faster service to New York City and points south. Taxis are provided by Thomas Transportation (☎ 1 800 526 8143).

By bus The Greyhound bus stop (☎ 802 254 9727) is at the Shell gas station, 429 Canal St (Rte-5), south of downtown near I-91, exit 1. Services have been cut in recent years, and most journeys involve a change at White River Junction or Springfield (Massachusetts). Brattleboro's town bus, the Brattleboro BeeLine (☎ 802 460 1195; $1), can get you to the bus terminal.

By car Driving into Brattleboro is straightforward enough, and you can park in the lots on the High Street (30 cents for 30min maximum), or in the Transportation Center on Elliot Street.

INFORMATION AND ACTIVITIES

Chamber of Commerce 180 Main St (Mon–Fri 9am–5pm; ☎ 802 254 4565, Ⓦ brattleborochamber.org). Has a wide selection of brochures on area attractions. The folks at Forty *Putney* Road *B&B* also manage the informative website Ⓦ inbrattleboro.com.

Gallery walk First Friday of the month (5.30–8.30pm; ☎ 802 257 2616, Ⓦ gallerywalk.org). Brattleboro is rich in artistic tradition and hosts a Gallery Walk once a month, when local and regional artists are spotlighted in more than forty of the town's galleries, inns and cafés.

Get maps from the Chamber of Commerce or the Brattleboro Museum (see p.332)

Vermont Canoe Touring Center 451 Putney Rd (US-5). You can hire kayaks from this place under the bridge

north of the centre, and see the town from the Connecticut River. (May–Oct daily 10am–7pm; ☎ 802 257 5008, ⓦ vermontcanoetouring.com; $25 for 2hr; $45/day; cash only).

ACCOMMODATION

Artist's Loft B&B and Gallery 103 Main St ☎ 802 257 5181, ⓦ theartistsloft.com. This tiny B&B above an art gallery offers just one suite, but its two luxurious rooms overlook the Connecticut River. Private entrance, and video and book libraries available. $158

Colonial Motel & Spa 889 Putney Rd (US-5/Rte-9) ☎ 802 257 7733, ⓦ colonialmotelspa.com. This family-owned lodge has an indoor pool, sauna and health club, though the rooms are starting to show their age. Still a good deal, considering the low rates. $65

★ **Forty Putney Road B&B** 192 Putney Rd ☎ 802 254 6268, ⓦ fortyputneyroad.com. Superb B&B in a grand French Baronial-style house dating from 1929 (when it really was no. 40), with plush, contemporary style rooms and a host of extras – free popcorn, pool table, a soothing hot tub in the garden and a small pub where the beer aficionado-owners serve drinks daily 4–7pm (with three local ales on tap). $179

Green River Bridge House 2435 Stage Rd ☎ 802 257 5771, ⓦ greenriverbridgehouse.com. This former 1830s post office has been totally gutted and restored to house high-end comfort. The three colourful rooms are

tastefully decorated and overlook a quiet lawn and a covered bridge. Geared more toward couples than families. $165

Latchis Hotel 50 Main St ☎ 802 254 6300, ⓦ latchis .com. Thirty-room restored Art Deco hotel in a good location. The centrally controlled a/c may leave you a bit chilly, though. The four-person suites are good value ($150). $95

Naulakha 481 Kipling Rd, Dummerston ☎ 802 254 6868, ⓦ landmarktrustusa.org. Rudyard Kipling designed this four-bedroom house in 1892, and today it is owned and rented by the Landmark Trust. Staying here is a magical experience for fans: you can meditate in Kipling's study, play pool in his attic or relax in his original tub. The house comes with all mod cons and is available for stays of three days to three weeks. $425

CAMPING

Brattleboro North KOA Park 1238 Rte-5, East Dummerston ☎ 802 254 5908, ⓦ brattleborokoa .com. This tranquil, super-clean park is three miles from I-91. $33

EATING & DRINKING

Amy's Bakery Arts Café 113 Main St ☎ 802 251 1071. Simple but tasty pastries, cakes, breads and some basic sandwiches. Good views from the outside tables at the back. Daily 7am–6pm.

★ **Café a La Carte** Elliot St. This tiny gourmet food cart from chef-owner Zach Corbin-Teich sells organic, local snacks such as burgers made from grass-fed Vermont farm beef for $6. April–Nov Tues–Sat 11am–5pm.

Chelsea Royal Diner Rte-9, West Brattleboro (exit 2, I-91) ☎ 802 254 8399, ⓦ chelsearoyaldiner.com. Great local diner, offering $1.99 breakfast specials, and prime ribs for just $11.99 on Friday and Saturday. Home of the "original cajun skillet". Daily 5.30am–9pm.

★ **Flat Street Brew Pub** 6 Flat St ☎ 802 257 1911, ⓦ flatstreetbrewpub.net. This bar is an ale-lover's paradise, with twenty taps in the pub upstairs, and another

thirty in the restaurant downstairs. Tues–Sat 11.30am–midnight, Sun & Mon 4pm–midnight.

McNeill's Brewery 90 Elliot St ☎ 802 254 2553, ⓦ mcneillsbrewery.com. Rough-hewn bar where you can sample eleven of their own microbrews, including Big Nose Blond, Old Ringworm and Slopbucket Brown. Mon–Thurs 4pm–2am, Fri –Sun 2pm–2am.

Mocha Joe's 82 Main St ☎ 802 257 7794, ⓦ mochajoes .com. Good caffeine-filled beverages in a stylish basement below Main St. A dark and dingy alternative to the comfy chairs and soothing music found at *Starbucks* and the like. Mon–Thurs 7am–8pm, Fri 7am–10pm, Sat 7.30am–10pm, Sun 7.30am–8pm.

★ **TJ Buckley's** 132 Elliot St ☎ 802 257 4922, ⓦ tjbuckleys.com. Just eight tables in a vintage train car, serving gourmet organic dishes such as diver scallops and crispy pork belly, mostly sourced locally. Wed–Sun 6–9pm.

BULLS RUN, HEIFERS STROLL

If you're visiting Brattleboro in early June, don't miss the annual **Strolling of the Heifers** (ⓦ strollingoftheheifers.com), the town's celebration of local farming (and tongue-in-cheek homage to Pamplona's Running of the Bulls): farmers lead a parade of one hundred young cows, covered with flowers, up Main Street, after which there is food, music and dancing.

ENTERTAINMENT

Brattleboro's **music scene** bops with talented local acts on a near-nightly basis; pick up a Thursday edition of the *Brattleboro Reformer* for listings of the week's events. The Latchis Theatre's meticulously restored **cinema** shows both studio and indie flicks (ⓦ latchis.com).

Brattleboro Music Center 38 Walnut St ☎ 802 257 4523, ⓦ bmcvt.org. Hosts a wide range of local and touring classical music groups (tickets usually $10–30), as well as folk music concerts. Home base to the Windham Orchestra and Brattleboro Concert Choir.

Vermont Jazz Center Studio #222, 2/F Cotton Mill Complex, 74 Cotton Mill Hill ☎ 802 254 9088, ⓦ vtjazz .org. Innovative centre for all things jazz, including summer jazz workshops, teacher training programmes and a monthly concert series. Jam sessions are held every Wednesday from 8–10pm.

SHOPPING

Brattleboro Books 36 Elliot St ☎ 802 257 7777. A staggering array of used volumes at incredibly low prices, though there are plenty of rare, expensive tomes. Incredibly helpful staff. Mon–Sat 10am–6pm, Sun 11am–5pm.

Everyone's Books 25 Elliot St ☎ 802 254 8160, ⓦ everyonesbks.com. Part leftist bookstore, with special sections for indie 'zines and anarchic political tracts, and part community centre. Mon–Thurs 9.30am–6pm, Fri 9.30am–8pm, Sat 9.30am–7pm, Sun 9.30am–5pm.

Vermont Artisan Designs 106 Main St ☎ 802 257 7044, ⓦ vtartisans.com. Local arts and crafts including blown glass, intricate jewellery and woodblock prints. Mon–Sat 10am–6pm, Sun 11am–5pm.

North from Brattleboro

As you drive north from Brattleboro, Rte-30 follows the picturesque **West River Valley**, past pretty **Newfane** and the serene hills of the **Townshend State Park**. From the latter area, Rte-35 provides a quieter and far more appealing route into central Vermont than I-91, passing through some of the state's most appealing small towns. **Grafton** is an enchanting white-clapboard colonial village untouched by commercial development, while **Chester**'s elegant architecture harks back to the Gilded Age.

Newfane

Thirteen miles northwest of Brattleboro on Rte-30, **NEWFANE** is a beautifully restored village, with white churches and rustic clapboard inns. There's nothing of real note to see, though it does boast a handsome town green flanked by three steepled buildings: the Union Hall, the First Congregational Church (built 1839), and the Windham County Courthouse. On Sundays, the **Newfane Flea Market** (May–Oct 6am–2pm; free) is the largest in the state, attracting up to two hundred dealers of antiques, crafts and books.

ACCOMMODATION AND EATING   NEWFANE

★ **Four Columns Inn** 21 West St ☎ 1 800 787 6633, ⓦ fourcolumnsinn.com. Smack on the green, with comfortable rooms, many with jacuzzis, as well as a gourmet restaurant serving carefully prepared New American, Asian and French cuisine. $175

Newfane Café & Creamery 550 Rte-30 ☎ 802 365 4442. Friendly place for a coffee, ice cream and tasty light meals like mac and cheese and a justly lauded steak salad wrap. Tues–Sun 7am–7pm.

Old Newfane Inn Rte-30, at Court St ☎ 802 365 4427, ⓦ oldnewfaneinn.com. Built on the green in 1787 and now offering ten charming antique-laden rooms and a restaurant serving hearty dinners. Tues–Sun 5–9pm.

West River Lodge & Stables 117 Hill Rd ☎ 802 365 7745, ⓦ westriverlodge.com. This 1820 farmhouse features eight rooms decorated with late 1800s country furnishings, and hearty breakfasts around an open fireplace. Shared bathroom $110; en-suite $140

Townshend

Five miles north of Newfane, the tiny village of **TOWNSHEND** is home to the longest wooden covered bridge in Vermont. The **Scott Covered Bridge** (277ft) over the West River was completed in 1870, and lies right on Rte-30 north of the village – you can pull over but there's not much space to park (the bridge is pedestrian only).

Townshend State Park

2755 State Forest Rd (off Rte-30) • Mid-May to mid-Oct daily 10am–sunset • $3 • ☎ 802 365 7500, ⓦ vtstateparks.com
/htm/townshend.htm

Hikers should make for **Townshend State Park**, a couple of miles north of the covered bridge. Trails include the steep 1.7-mile climb to the summit of **Bald Mountain** (1680ft), as well as plenty of less challenging walks along the valley.

Grafton

Few villages come closer to the stereotypical image of rural Vermont than **GRAFTON**, a truly gorgeous ensemble of white clapboard buildings, shady trees and a bubbling brook, the Saxtons River. Though the village centre was restored by the Windham Foundation (ⓦwindham-foundation.org), this is no theme park: with 650 permanent inhabitants and regular town hall meetings, Grafton is a vibrant, genuine community. The village lies ten miles north of Townshend on Rte-35.

Grafton Cheese Shoppe

53 Townshend Rd • Mon–Thurs 10am–5pm, Fri–Sun 10am–6pm • Free • ☎ 1 800 472 3866, ⓦ graftonvillagecheese.com

Though this cheese-maker, Grafton's biggest claim to fame, is primarily based near Brattleboro these days, the **Grafton Village Cheese Company** still sells its wares in the middle of the village. If you head a half-mile south of the village, to the original cheese factory on Rte-35 South (Townshend Rd), you can peer through windows to witness the cheese-making process (times vary, but usually Mon–Fri 8am–noon).

Nature Museum

186 Townshend Rd (Rte-35 South) • Sat 10am–4pm, Sun 1–4pm • $5, children (3–12 years) $3 • ☎ 802 843 2111, ⓦ nature-museum.org

Kids will doubtless enjoy Grafton's **Nature Museum**, a somewhat haphazard taxidermic and geological collection crammed into two floors of a creaky old house, with plenty of activities year-round.

Grafton Historical Society Museum

147 Main St • Mid-May to mid-Oct Fri–Mon & holidays 10am–noon & 2–4pm; open daily last week of Sept to first week Oct • $3 • ☎ 802
843 2584, ⓦ graftonhistory.org

If you've an interest in local history, the **Grafton Historical Society Museum** offers annually changing exhibits on everything from Grafton homes and locally quarried soapstones to textiles and the Civil War. The museum occupies the fetching Stowell/Sumner House, dating from 1843.

Grafton Ponds Outdoor Center

783 Townshend Rd (Rte-35 South) • Daily 9am–4pm • Trail passes $14–18, ski rentals $16/day • ☎ 802 843 2400, ⓦ graftonponds.com

For active pursuits, visit the **Grafton Ponds Outdoor Center**, south of the village on Townshend Road (next to Grafton Cheese), open daily for Nordic cross-country skiing in winter, and **mountain biking**, fishing and canoeing in the summer (standard bikes $30/day; $1 trail fee).

ACCOMMODATION AND EATING   **GRAFTON**

Mack's Place 56 Townshend Rd (behind the Old Tavern) ☎ 802 843 2255. Serves light (and cheap) soups, sandwiches and salads. Free wi-fi and patio dining in the summer. Mon–Sat 7.30am–4.30pm, Sun 7.30am–3pm.

★ **Old Tavern** 92 Main St ☎ 1 800 843 1801, ⓦ old-tavern.com. A smart inn and restaurant at the heart of the village. Around since 1801, it has accommodated everyone from Rudyard Kipling to Teddy Roosevelt. The old carriage house is now a cosy pub, *Phelps Barn*. **$190**

Chester

Seven miles north of Grafton, at the junction of routes 103, 11 and 35, is the tiny village of **CHESTER**, whose houses – a blend of typical Vermont clapboard and more ornate Victorian styles – are laid out charmingly along a narrow green. As in Brattleboro, there's a discernible New Age feel about the place, with plenty of "holistic wellness" on offer in the shops on Main Street (Rte-11).

Chester Historical Society Museum

230 Main St • July & Aug Sat & Sun 1–4pm • Free • ☎ 802 875 3767

Chester Historical Society Museum on Main Street is housed in the old Academy Building next to leafy Brookside Cemetery. Inside you'll find a quirky collection of curios such as a rare *carte de visite* (photographic visiting card) belonging to John Wilkes Booth (the man who killed Abraham Lincoln).

Vermont Institute of Contemporary Arts

15 Depot St • Call to confirm opening times • Free • ☎ 802 875 4808, ⓦ vtica.org

The **Vermont Institute of Contemporary Arts**, combined art school, gallery and museum, should be open in spanking new premises sometime in 2012. The focus will be on Vermont and regional artists working in paint, printmaking, drawing, photography and the visual arts.

INFORMATION
CHESTER

Chester Information Booth This tiny booth (summer only) at 218 Main St, next to the museum, is often closed, so visit Misty Valley Books (Mon–Fri 10am–6pm, Sat 10am–5pm, Sun 11am–4pm; ☎802 875 3400, ⓦmvbooks.com) across the road for maps and advice.

ACCOMMODATION

Chester House Inn 266 Main St ☎1 888 875 2205, ⓦ chesterhouseinn.com. This handsome clapboard structure was built in 1780, making it one of the oldest houses in town. It offers seven antique-laden rooms, each decorated in a different style and colour. $125

Inn Victoria 321 Main St ☎802 875 4288, ⓦinnvictoria.com. Built in 1851, this elegant B&B goes to town on the Victorian theme with its eight ornate and comfortable rooms (albeit with flat-screen TVs, DVD players, iPod docks and free wi-fi). $130

Motel-in-the-Meadow 936 Rte-11 ☎802 875 2626, ⓦmotelinthemeadow.com. About one mile west of town, a friendly "mom and pop" motel with cheap, comfortable, well-kept rooms, some with kitchenettes. Wi-fi access in gift shop and office only. $69

EATING AND DRINKING

Alice's Restaurant 90 Main St ☎802 875 4486, ⓦalicesrestaurantvermont.com. Serving heaped plates of eggs and local sausage for breakfast ($7–10) and more bistro-type steaks and grilled meats later in the day ($17–20). Wed–Fri 11.30am–3pm & 5–9pm, Sat 9am–3pm & 5–9pm, Sun 9am–3pm.

Baba-A-Louis Bakery 92 Rte-11 ☎802 875 4666. This creative bakery lies on the western edge of the village, cooking up a huge range of breads, small pies ($6), cakes and cookies ($1). Tues–Sat 7am–6pm.

Inn Victoria 321 Main St ☎802 875 4288, ⓦinnvictoria.com. Queen Victoria would probably be amused at the fabulous High Tea here, taken English style, with savoury snacks, cakes and fruit ($14.99 per person). Reservations required. Fri–Sun 3–4.30pm.

Moon Dog Café 295 Main St ☎802 875 4966. Natural and organic food store that also does fresh salads – try the Krishna Cobb Salad ($12.95) – and sandwiches from $5. Plenty of veggie options. Mon–Thurs & Sat 10am–6pm, Fri 10am–8pm, Sun 10am–5pm.

Bennington

Little has happened in **BENNINGTON** to match the excitement of the days when Ethan Allen's Green Mountain Boys were based here, two hundred years ago. Settled in 1761 on a rise by the Walloomsac River, overlooking the valley between the Green and Taconic mountains, the town became a leading nineteenth-century industrial outpost for paper mills, potteries, gristmills and the largest cotton-batting mill in the US. Today, it's most notable for its Revolutionary history, covered bridges and fine hand-crafted pottery, though the exclusive, arts-oriented

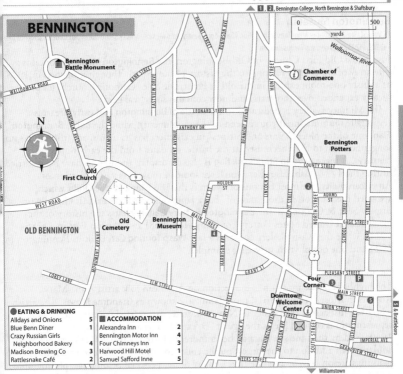

BENNINGTON

0 — 500
yards

Walloomsac River

Bennington Battle Monument

Chamber of Commerce

N

WALLOOMSAC ROAD

MONUMENT AVENUE

EASTVIEW DRIVE

BANK STREET

PAGEANT STREET

ROBINSON AVE

HUNT STREET

LEONARD STREET

ANTHONY DR

CATAMOUNT LANE

CONVENT AVENUE

BELMONT AVENUE

Bennington Potters

6

Old First Church

9

COUNTY STREET

HOLDEN ST

LINCOLN ST

DEPOT STREET

NORTH STREET

ADAMS ST

SCHOOL STREET

GAGE STREET

PARK

EAST STREET

WEST ROAD

OLD BENNINGTON

Old Cemetery

Bennington Museum

MAIN STREET

McCALL

HARRISON AVE

GRANT ST

7

Four Corners

PLEASANT STREET

MAIN STREET

P

COREY LANE

MONUMENT AVENUE

ELM STREET

Downtown Welcome Center

UNION STREET

3 & Brattleboro

STARK ST

DEWEY ST

ELM STREET

PADDOCK AVE

WASHINGTON AVE

JEFFERSON AVE

SOUTH STREET

GRANDVIEW STREET

IMPERIAL AVE

WEEKS STREET

Williamstown

● EATING & DRINKING

Alldays and Onions	5
Blue Benn Diner	1
Crazy Russian Girls Neighborhood Bakery	4
Madison Brewing Co	3
Rattlesnake Café	2

■ ACCOMMODATION

Alexandra Inn	2
Bennington Motor Inn	4
Four Chimneys Inn	3
Harwood Hill Motel	1
Samuel Safford Inne	5

Bennington College has seen the likes of authors Bret Easton Ellis and Donna Tartt pass through its halls (Tartt set her *Secret History* in a fictional version of the town). The best place to begin your exploration of Bennington is the section of town known as **Old Bennington**, one mile west of downtown and the junction known as the "Four Corners".

Bennington Battle Monument

15 Monument Circle • Mid-April to late Oct daily 9am–5pm • $3 • ☎ 802 447 0550, ⊛ HistoricVermont.org/bennington

Old Bennington is home to the town's most prominent icon, the **Bennington Battle Monument**, a 306ft limestone obelisk that commemorates the August 1777 Battle of Bennington. This pivotal conflict pitted the New Hampshire militia, led by **John Stark**, and the Green Mountain Boys, under **Seth Warner** (Ethan Allen was an English prisoner at the time), against the forces of **General Burgoyne**, who wanted to capture Bennington's arsenal. The unexpected victory of the Revolutionaries denied Burgoyne's troops of crucial supplies, contributing to their defeat at the subsequent Battle of Saratoga, the war's major turning point. You can reach the 200ft observation deck by elevator – the views of Bennington and its surroundings are magnificent.

Old First Church

Main St (Rte-9) and Monument Ave • Mid-May to June Sat 10am–noon & 1–4pm, Sun 1–4pm; July to mid-Oct Mon–Sat 10am–noon & 1–4pm, Sun 1–4pm • Free • ☎ 802 447 1223, ⊛ oldfirstchurchbenn.org

Right in the heart of Old Bennington lies **Old First Church**, a simple white pine clapboard structure erected in 1805. The abutting cemetery is the resting place of acclaimed New England poet **Robert Frost**, buried here in 1963. Signs point the way to his tombstone, which reads simply, "I had a lover's quarrel with the world".

6

Bennington Museum

75 Main St (Rte-9) • Feb–Dec Mon–Tues & Thurs–Sun 10am–5pm; Sept & Oct daily same hours • $10, children and students under 18 free
• ☎ 802 447 1571, ⦿ benningtonmuseum.org

Just below Old First Church in Old Bennington, the **Bennington Museum** contains a fine array of Americana relating to the history of the region. Though it opened in 1928 as a dusty one-room exhibit in the old St Francis de Sales Catholic Church, it's been greatly expanded over the years, and now contains some real gems.

The Military Gallery is dedicated to the **Battle of Bennington** and early firearms (especially illuminating if you've been to the monument), while the faded **Bennington Flag**, one of the oldest "Stars and Stripes" in existence, has its own space (though it's no longer believed to have been used at the battle – it dates from the early nineteenth century). A piece of **John Stark's silk flag** is also on display, thought to have been carried during the 1777 clash. Elsewhere you'll see some of museum's vast collection of American **quilts**, the most famous of which is the 1863 **Jane Stickle Quilt**, which spawned the creation of thousands of "baby Janes" all over the world (it's usually on display Sept & Oct only). The **Bennington Pottery Gallery** charts the history of the locally based United States Pottery company (1847–58) and Norton Pottery (1785–1911), while the Wasp Gallery contains a rare **Wasp Touring Car**, built in Bennington in 1924 and one of only two surviving examples.

Grandma Moses

The highlight of the museum is the section on American folk artist Anna Mary Robertson Moses (1860–1961), more familiarly known as **Grandma Moses**. The artist, who lived just across the border in New York state, first started painting her simple representations of rural life at the age of 73, experienced a meteoric rise to fame in the 1940s, and by the time she reached her hundredth birthday in 1960 enjoyed national adulation. In addition to the largest public collection of her work (twenty to thirty paintings are on view at any one time), many of her personal belongings, photographs, painting equipment and awards are displayed. A fascinating video of her 1951 interview with Edward R. Murrow plays on constant loop. The museum moved the **schoolhouse** (1834) Moses attended in upstate New York to their grounds in 1972 (fittingly, it is used as a hands-on education centre today).

Bennington Potters

324 County St • Mon–Sat 9.30am–6pm, Sun 10am–5pm • Free • ☎ 1 800 205 8033, ⦿ benningtonpotters.com

Downtown Bennington has little in the way of sights, though **Bennington Potters** remains a popular attraction for its robust, handmade New England-style pottery. You can tour the workshop, open for more than sixty years, before browsing the store.

Bennington Center for the Arts

44 Gypsy Lane (Rte-9) • June–Nov Wed–Mon 10am–5pm; mid-Jan to May Mon–Sat 10am–5pm • $9 • ☎ 802 442 7158,
⦿ benningtoncenterforthearts.org

If you have time, it's worth driving out to the **Bennington Center for the Arts**, around two miles west of the centre of town on Rte-9. Here you'll find several galleries showing the work of local artists and an engaging room of Native American (Hopi) artefacts, collected by a Colorado miner in the 1890s and discovered in a local house in 1929. The real highlight, though, is the **Covered Bridge Museum**, a small but enlightening exhibition covering just about everything connected with the iconic New England structure – there are around three hundred bridges remaining, a third of which are in Vermont.

ARRIVAL AND DEPARTURE   **BENNINGTON**

By bus Getting here by public transit is tough; there are no trains, though the Green Mountain Express bus (☎ 802 447 0477; 50 cents –$2), runs four times daily between Bennington and Manchester, with stops along Historic Rte-7A. The Bennington stop is at the Bank North car park, on Main Street one block east of the Four Corners (see p.337).

By car Bennington straddles the intersection of US-7 and Rte-9, a junction known locally as the "Four Corners." In town, Rte-9 is referred to as Main Street, while the local stretches of US-7 above and below the Corners are called North and South streets. You'll find a free car park on Main Street, east of the Four Corners.

INFORMATION

Bennington Area Chamber of Commerce 100 Veteran's Memorial Drive (US-7) Mon–Fri 9am–5pm; May–Oct also Sat & Sun 10am–4pm; ☎802 447 3311 or ☎1 800 229 0252, ⓦbennington.com. Has information on surrounding attractions and has clean public restrooms.

Downtown Welcome Center 215 South St, near the Four Corners (Mon–Sat 10am–5pm; ☎802 442 5758, ⓦbetterbennington.com). Offers a similar array of information to the Bennington Area Chamber of Commerce.

ACCOMMODATION

Budget **motels** line South and West Main streets. Anyone who prefers chain motels will be disappointed (though there is a *Best Western* on Northside Drive), but Bennington's independent motels and hotels are generally clean and reasonably priced.

★ **Alexandra Inn** 916 Orchard Rd, just off Rte-7A ☎1 888 207 9386, ⓦalexandrainn.com. Restored colonial establishment with twelve luxurious rooms featuring jet tubs, fireplaces, hearty gourmet breakfasts and a garden and beautiful views of its two green acres. $125

Bennington Motor Inn 143 Main St ☎802 442 5479, ⓦcoolcruisers.net. Family-run inn with sixteen comfortable rooms with the standard comforts, plus microwaves and data ports. $129

Four Chimneys Inn 21 West Rd (Rte-9) ☎802 447 3500, ⓦfourchimneys.com. Eleven comfortable, country rooms, most with a fireplace and sofa, in an elegant white manor on eleven acres. Full breakfast included; the restaurant is open for sumptuous dinners Wed–Sun. $149

★ **Harwood Hill Motel** 864 Harwood Hill Rd (Rte-7A) ☎802 442 6278, ⓦharwoodhillmotel.com. If you don't mind staying out of town, this friendly motel is a superb deal, with spacious and immaculate rooms equipped with free wi-fi and microwaves. $79

Samuel Safford Inne 722 Main St ☎802 442 5934, ⓦsamuelsaffordinne.com. Gorgeous B&B right in the centre with just two rooms, perfect for couples; hearty breakfast included. Reserve months in advance. $145

CAMPING

Greenwood Lodge and Campsites Prospect Mountain off Rte-9 ☎802 442 2547, ⓦcampvermont.com/greenwood. An HI/AYH-affiliated property, several miles away in Woodford, has dorm beds with kitchen and recreation access, and wooded campsites. Open mid-May to late Oct. Dorms $32; camping $25

EATING AND DRINKING

Alldays and Onions 519 Main St ☎802 447 0043, ⓦalldaysandonions.com. Creative meat and fish dishes at reasonable prices, served with bread from the in-house bakery. Mon–Wed 11am–3pm, Thurs & Fri 11am–3pm & 5–9pm, Sat 7.30–10.30am, 11am–3pm & 5–9pm, Sun 9am–1pm.

★ **Blue Benn Diner** 314 North St (US-7) ☎802 442 5140. This authentic, 1940s-era diner is a local institution that draws a diverse crowd of hard-boiled locals and artsy students. In addition to the usual diner favourites, vegetarian dishes also feature. Mon & Tues 6am–5pm, Wed–Fri 6am–8pm, Sat & Sun 6am–4pm.

Crazy Russian Girls Neighborhood Bakery 443 Main St ☎802 681 3983, ⓦcrazyrussiangirlsbakery.biz. Cool name, great bakery – freshly-baked bread, mouthwatering butter cookies, cupcakes and warm sticky buns inspired by the Russian-American co-owner's "babushka" (grandmother). Mon–Fri 7am–6pm, Sat 8am–5pm.

Madison Brewing Co 428 Main St ☎802 442 7397, ⓦmadisonbrewingco.com. Fun, stylish brewpub with hearty burgers ($7) and six varieties of in-house beer ($3.25–5). Live blues most nights. Daily until 2am.

Rattlesnake Café 230 North St ☎802 447 7018, ⓦrattlesnakecafe.com. A popular no-frills Mexican joint with a great selection of microbrews on tap. Tacos start at $6, quesadillas at $14. Tues–Sun 4.30–9pm.

North along Historic Rte-7A

US-7 and **Historic Rte-7A** parallel each other as they run from Bennington north to Manchester, though the latter is the preferable road to take – not only is it a more picturesque drive, but there are a few notable stop-offs along the way. The great spine

6

of the Green Mountains rises up to the east, with the Taconics somewhat more irregularly splayed out along the west, putting the route smack in the so-called "Valley of Vermont".

North Bennington and around

Rte-67A splits off from Rte-7A north of Bennington and continues on for five miles to **NORTH BENNINGTON**, passing three small but picturesque **covered bridges** – the Silk Road, Paper Mill Village and the Burt Henry – spanning the Walloomsac River.

Park McCullough House

1 Park St • Mid-May to late Oct daily 10am–4pm, tours hourly • $10 • ☎ 802 442 5441, ⓦ parkmccullough.org

In the centre of North Bennington, the elaborate Italianate and French Second Empire-style **Park McCullough House**, a sumptuous 1865 mansion built for local attorney and entrepreneur Trenor Park, is filled with most of its original period furnishings, including children's toys. Guided tours are the only way to get inside.

Robert Frost Stone House Museum

121 Rte-7A, South Shaftsbury • May–Nov Tues–Sun 10am–5pm • $5, children (under 18 years) $2.50 • ☎ 802 447 6200, ⓦ frostfriends.org

In the village of **South Shaftsbury**, some five miles north of Bennington, the **Robert Frost Stone House Museum** is a thoughtful memorial to one of New England's favourite poets. The museum will certainly appeal to Frost enthusiasts; though the half-stone, half-timber house dates back to 1769, the emphasis here is on poetry rather than furniture and antiques.

The main room provides biographical details on Frost and his family, as well as his time in Shaftesbury (1920–1938; he lived in this house until 1929). You can also read some of his letters. Next door is the room in which *Stopping by Woods on a Snowy Evening* was crafted in 1922 – panels bring the poem and writing process to life with discussion of metre and rhyme, a copy of the handwritten manuscript and the "controversial comma" added by one of Frost's editors.

EATING AND DRINKING   **NORTH BENNINGTON AND AROUND**

Kevin's 27 Main St, N Bennington ☎ 802 442 0122, ⓦ kevinssportspubandrestaurant.com. Locals flock to this sports bar and restaurant (with nine TVs and prime rib specials, wings, burgers and seafood on the menu) that doubles as a casual venue for live bands or karaoke on the weekends. Main courses $9–15. Daily 11am–2am.

Pangaea 3 Prospect St, N Bennington ☎ 802 442 7171, ⓦ vermontfinedining.com. Fine dining with an eclectic menu featuring such dishes as Thai curry, maple-glazed pork loin and spring rolls (main courses $19–23); the lounge menu is simpler and a bit cheaper (burgers for $9). Almost forty beers and 75 wines from all over the world. Lounge open daily. Tues–Sat 5–9pm; lounge open daily.

Arlington

About thirteen miles north of Bennington along Rte-7A (nine miles short of Manchester), the small town of **ARLINGTON** has a small but attractive centre of clapboard houses and a very English-looking church, **St James Episcopal** (this was a big Loyalist town in the Revolutionary War).

Norman Rockwell Exhibition at the Sugar Shack

Rte-7A • Mid-April to Dec daily 9am–5pm • $3, children (under 18 years) free • ☎ 802 375 6747, ⓦ sugarshackvt.com

Illustrator **Norman Rockwell** (see box, p.228) created some of his most memorable *Saturday Evening Post* covers while living in Arlington between 1939 and 1954 – his former home is now a country inn (see p.341). The modest **Norman Rockwell Exhibition**, part of the Sugar Shack complex (selling snacks and gifts), links Rockwell's art (mostly copies) with real photos of the locals that the artist used as his models – you might even meet some of them wandering around the store.

ARRIVAL AND DEPARTURE | ARLINGTON

By bus The Green Mountain Express bus (☎802 442 9458) between Bennington and Manchester stops at Stewart's store in the centre of town on Rte-7A.

ACCOMMODATION

Arlington Inn 3904 Rte-7A, at Rte-313 ☎802 375 6532, ⓦarlingtoninn.com. Gorgeous Greek Revival mansion, built in 1847 by local businessman Martin Deming in the middle of town, with luxurious rooms fitted with jacuzzi tubs, fireplaces, huge beds and free wi-fi. **$129**

Inn on Covered Bridge Green 3587 River Rd off Rte-313 ☎802 375 9489, ⓦcoveredbridgegreen.com. Norman Rockwell fans should stay at his attractive former home (an old farmhouse dating back to 1792), with the Victorian period rooms equipped with gas fireplaces, and a hearty breakfast included. **$145**

CAMPING

Camping on the Battenkill Rte-7A ☎802 375 6663, ⓦcampvermont.com/battenkill. Over a hundred sites in woods and meadows set along the Battenkill, a trout stream that is also good for swimming. April–Oct. **$23**

EATING

Arlington Dairy Bar 3158 Rte-7A ☎802 375 2546. Cool retro place (it opened in 1962), just south of the centre, serving ice cream, burgers and hot dogs in the summer months. Call to confirm opening times.

Arlington Inn 3904 Rte-7A, at Rte-313 ☎802 375 6532, ⓦarlingtoninn.com. Romantic candlelit meals – try the hazelnut-crusted chicken ($25) or grilled sea scallops ($28). Tues–Sun 5.30–9pm.

Jonathan's Table Rte-7A (at the Sugar Shack) ☎802 375 1021. Modern American food, special prime ribs, Vermont maple pork chops, veal and seafood. Don't skip the desserts. May–Dec daily 5.30–9pm.

Manchester and around

The last town on Rte-7A before it merges with US-7 is **MANCHESTER**, which has been a resort for some two hundred years. **Manchester Village** is the pristine historical section, anchored by its immaculate clapboard 1870s **First Congregational Church** (ⓦfirstcongregationalmanchester.org), the 1822 **Bennington County Court House** and *Equinox Resort* (see p.343). Park for free behind the Equinox Village Shops. Just south of here lies **Hildene**, one of the most impressive mansions in the state, while to the north, **Manchester Center** (ⓦmanchesterdesigneroutlets.com) is essentially one huge open-air shopping mall, albeit a fairly classy one.

The surrounding hills are well situated for outdoor pursuits, especially **skiing** on nearby **Bromley** and **Stratton** mountains, and **fly-fishing** in its many trout streams. It's no coincidence that **Charles Orvis**, founder of fly-rod manufacturer Orvis Company, is a Manchester native. A visit to the company's flagship store is a worthwhile excursion, even if you have no intention of buying. Finally, if you visit in summer, check out one

---

VERMONT FARMERS' MARKETS CALENDAR

The farm-to-table movement is especially strong in Vermont. Check out the local produce at these excellent farmers' markets; unless stated otherwise, they take place throughout the summer (June–Sept). See ⓦrutlandcountyfarmersmarket.org and ⓦvtfarmersmarket.org for more information.

Tuesday Rutland, Depot Park, 3–6pm. Rutland also has a winter farmers' market (Sat 10am–1pm, 77 Wales St).

Wednesday Middlebury, Marbleworks by the falls, 9am–12.30pm (mid-May to Oct) ☎802 388 0178, ⓦmiddleburyfarmersmarket.com.

Thursday Manchester, Adams Park, Rte-7A, 3–6pm (☎802 867 7080).

Friday Ludlow, 53 Main St, Okemo Mountain School, 4–7pm (May–Sept).

Saturday Brattleboro, near the Covered Bridge, 9am–2pm; Burlington, City Hall Park, Church St, 8.30am–2pm (year-round); Middlebury, Marbleworks by the falls, 9am–12.30pm; Montpelier, State St and Elm St, 9am–1pm; Rutland, Depot Park, 9am–2pm; Walloomsac (Bennington), Depot St, 10am–1pm (ⓦwalloomsac.org).

6

A MOUNTAIN FOR ALL SEASONS

Bromley Mountain Resort (one-day ski-lift tickets $65 Sat & Sun, $49 Mon–Fri; ☏ 802 824 5522, ⓦ bromley.com), six miles east of Manchester on Rte-11, is great for families in winter or summer. In summer, you can ride the Sun Mountain Flyer zipline ($20) and enjoy a 24ft climbing wall and bumper boats (all-day pass $39 Sat & Sun, $34 Mon–Fri).

Larger and slightly higher than Bromley, **Stratton Mountain Resort**, four miles off Rte-30, ranks as one of Vermont's premier **ski destinations** (one-day tickets $84 Sat & Sun, $74 Mon–Fri; ☏ 802 297 4000, ⓦ stratton.com) It's a better choice for serious skiers, with a range of plush accommodation and a Vail-like "Village" of shops, bars and restaurants to keep you entertained at night. There is also good **cross-country skiing** on the twenty-plus miles of trails at the associated Stratton Nordic Center; some of the routes weave through secluded forests and others cut across open countryside. In the summer (July–Oct) ride the Stratton gondola ($12) to the top of Stratton Mountain (3940ft) for views across four states.

of Vermont's classic **swimming holes** at **Dorset Quarry** (free access), just north of Manchester on Rte-30. The old marble quarry is filled with clean mountain water, with plenty of cliffs to jump off.

Hildene

1005 Hildene Rd (Rte-7A) • Daily 9.30am–4.30pm; free guided tours daily at noon • $13, children (6–14 years) $5 • ☏ 802 362 1788, ⓦ hildene.org

The first place of interest as you head into Manchester on Rte-7A, five miles north of Arlington, is historic **Hildene**, a 24-room Georgian Revival mansion that belonged to longtime Manchester resident **Robert Todd Lincoln** (1843–1926). Robert, the son of sixteenth US president Abraham Lincoln and a prominent diplomat and businessman in his own right, first visited Manchester in 1864, but he wasn't rich enough to build this house for another forty years – the family finally moved here in 1905.

Watch the film in the **Welcome Center** to get oriented, especially if you're not familiar with US history. Abraham Lincoln is generally regarded as America's greatest president, and since Robert was the only Lincoln child to survive into adulthood the house takes on a greater significance. The interior is made more intimate with many of the family's personal effects; exhibits include one of Abraham Lincoln's bibles and his familiar black stovepipe hat – one of just three still in existence – along with presidential portraits, while Robert's bedroom, library, books and English china set (he was a bit of an Anglophile) are all remarkably preserved. The huge, rather bizarre 1908 **Aeolian organ** set into the grand staircase and entrance lobby is a real treat – thanks to digital technology, docents can set the organ to play period tunes when you enter.

After seeing the house, stay to explore the magnificent four-hundred-acre estate and flower-filled gardens. At the self-sufficient solar-powered **Hildene Farm** you can observe a herd of playful Nubian goats, and watch how cheese is made (buy some, it's delicious). The newest exhibit, opened in 2011, is an original **Pullman Sunbeam train car** restored to its lavish appearance c.1903 (one of Robert's many jobs was president of the Pullman company).

Orvis Store

4180 Main St (Rte-7A) • Mon–Fri 10am–6pm, Sat 9am–6pm, Sun 10am–5pm • Free • ☏ 802 362 3750, ⓦ orvis.com

The flagship **Orvis Store**, a short drive beyond Manchester Village on Rte-7A, was opened in 2002, and doubles as a shrine to the company's locally born founder. The extravagantly expensive fly-fishing rods are worth a look, as are the on-site trout pond used for casting demonstrations and the beautiful handcrafted hunting rifles, yours for $10,000 (or more). Just along the road is the **Orvis Outlet** (same hours), which offers last year's models for around fifty percent less.

ARRIVAL AND INFORMATION

By bus The Green Mountain Express (☎ 802 442 9458) runs four buses daily from Arlington and Bennington ($2), while Marble Valley Regional Transit runs Commuter Connection, a similar service, north to Rutland and the Amtrak station (5 daily; $2; ☎ 802 773 3244, ⓦ thebus.com).

MANCHESTER AND AROUND

Manchester and the Mountains Chamber of Commerce 5046 Main St, Manchester Center (Mon–Fri 8.30am–5pm; ☎ 802 362 2100, ⓦ manchestervermont .net). There is also an information booth opposite (Sat 10am–5pm, Sun 10am–3pm).

ACCOMMODATION

Aspen Motel 5669 Main St (Rte-7A), north of Manchester Center ☎ 802 362 2450, ⓦ theaspenatmanchester.com. Family-run motel that's been a fixture for years, with comfortable rooms, a pool and a two-bedroom cottage available for larger groups. **$95**

Equinox Resort 3567 Main St (Rte-7A), Manchester Village ☎ 802 362 4700, ⓦ equinoxresort.com. The swankiest place in town, the sprawling *Equinox* is full of restored Victorian-era quarters, luxurious amenities and old-world New England charm. Includes the *1811 House* and the *Charles Orvis Inn*, which provides access to a billiards room, honour bar with cigars and other luxuries, in the former home of Orvis himself. **$319**

★ **Inn at Manchester** 3967 Main St (Rte-7A) ☎ 802 362 1793, ⓦ innatmanchester.com. Another justly popular choice, this fresh, spotless B&B offers a warm welcome and high standards of comfort right in the centre of town. **$165**

★ **Manchester View** 77 High Meadow Way (Rte-7A), north of Manchester Center ☎ 802 362 2739, ⓦ manchesterview.com. Not much to look at from the road, but the *View* has an unbeatable vista of the Green Mountains. Each of the 35 relaxing, great-value rooms – including some extra-spacious "speciality" rooms – comes with refrigerator and deck. Amenities include a heated pool, golf and tennis. **$125**

EATING AND DRINKING

The Bean 4201 Main St, opposite Orvis ☎ 802 362 0110, ⓦ thebeanrestaurant.com. Superb Mexican food; highlights include the crispy *chimichangas*, the platter of three giant tacos, and very potent margaritas. Vegetarian-friendly. Mon 5–9pm, Tues–Sat 11am–9pm, Sun noon–8pm.

The Perfect Wife 2594 Depot St (Rte-11/30), east of Manchester Center ☎ 802 362 2817, ⓦ perfectwife .com. Creative cooking (Peking duck with pancake starter, sesame-crusted tuna) on the expensive side (main courses $19–28), or a more traditional menu in the tavern room for the budget-conscious (main courses from $9). Mon–Sat 5–10pm.

Spiral Press Café 15 Bonnet St ☎ 802 362 9944. The

destination for excellent caffeinated drinks and wi-fi, alongside some muffins, bagels and sandwich specials. It's connected to the Northshire Books store. Daily 7am–7pm.

Up for Breakfast 4935 Main St ☎ 802 362 4204. If you crave interesting omelettes, French toast, or blueberry pancakes, this is the obvious choice. Fun and friendly, with decent portions. Mon–Fri 7am–12.30pm, Sat & Sun 7am–1.30pm.

★ **Ye Olde Tavern** 5183 Main St ☎ 802 362 0611, ⓦ yeoldetavern.net. This 1790 building is romantic and candlelit, and the perfect place for Yankee favourites like exceptional pot roast and chicken pot pie (main courses $17–29). Very extensive wine list. Daily 5–9pm.

ENTERTAINMENT

Festivals and events The summer brings a variety of events to town, including Shakespeare plays and craft fairs at Hildene (see p.342), and the Manchester Music Festival

(☎ 802 362 1956, ⓦ mmfvt.org), a series of Thursday concerts at the Southern Vermont Arts Center, 930 SVAC Drive, West Rd, Manchester (☎ 802 362 1405, ⓦ svac.org).

SHOPPING

Northshire Bookstore 4869 Main St ☎ 802 362 2200, ⓦ northshire.com. This ranks as one of the region's finest independent bookstores, with a strong

line-up of visiting authors. Mon–Wed & Sun 10am–7pm, Thurs–Sat 10am–9pm.

The Green Mountains and Rte-100

Rte-100 offers a third way into the heart of Vermont, running just to the east of the **Green Mountains**. The road is rarely busy, even in peak season, and offers unspoiled

6

THE LONG TRAIL

Running along the ridge of Vermont's Green Mountains, 272 miles from the Massachusetts border to Québec, the **Long Trail** is one of America's premier **hiking trails**. The northern section is a more strenuous and an ultimately more rewarding hike, crossing some of the highest peaks in Vermont. **The Camel's Hump** (4083ft) and **Mount Mansfield** (4393ft) are both well-trodden peaks from which you get some fine views, but not the sense of splendid isolation that kicks in farther north across the Jay Peak Range, as the trail nears its end. The Long Trail actually follows the same route as the **Appalachian Trail** for 97 miles before splitting near Rutland.

The presence of white blazes indicates that you're walking on the Long Trail. Intersections are usually marked with signs; double blazes signal important turns; and the almost one hundred side trails (totaling 175 miles) are blazed in blue and signposted. Anyone planning on hiking the entire length of the trail should count on it taking between twenty-five and thirty days. The most conventional way of accomplishing this feat is to hike from shelter to shelter (see below), although with good preparation (and some transport assistance from others) you could complete the trail by taking only day-hikes.

Accommodation on the Long Trail consists of about seventy shelters, maintained during summer and usually no more than a gentle day's hike apart. A moderate fee is charged at sites with caretakers (usually $5), and availability is on a first-come, first-served basis; if the shelter itself is full, you'll have to camp, so unless you plan to arrive early you'll need to carry a tent. All shelters are on the primitive side (no electricity or running water), and can be fully enclosed wood cabins, three-sided lean-tos, or tent sites. All sites have a water source, although this doesn't necessarily mean that the water is drinkable without treatment. For further reading, get the *Long Trail Guide* ($19), published by the caretakers of the trail, the Green Mountain Club (**☎**802 244 7037, **⊕**greenmountainclub.org).

views of evergreen slopes as well as a few charming towns as it snakes north. Note that although the Green Mountains are not as harsh as New Hampshire's White Mountains, the hills are still buried in snow for most of the winter, and the higher roads are liable to be blocked for long periods.

Pick up the route in **Wilmington**, almost halfway between Brattleboro and Bennington, where the road leads up to the unassuming ski resort at **Mount Snow**. North of here, Rte-100 weaves through the authentic villages of **Jamaica** and **Weston**, with its fun country stores, and on to more commercial **Ludlow** and **Okemo Mountain**, another of the state's top ski resorts. Beyond Ludlow, **Plymouth Notch** is one of the most absorbing presidential hometowns in the country, beautifully preserved as the **Calvin Coolidge State Historic Site**.

Wilmington

Seventeen miles west of Brattleboro, at the intersection of Rte-9 and Rte-100, you'll encounter **WILMINGTON**, a genial place situated along the North Branch Deerfield River and lined with stores full of knick-knacks, New England crafts and more than enough Vermont maple syrup and cheddar cheese. Note that Wilmington was another town devastated by **Hurricane Irene** in 2011 – check the tourist office for the latest.

INFORMATION
WILMINGTON

Mount Snow Valley Chamber of Commerce 21 W Main St (Mon 8.30am–3am, Tues–Fri 8.30am–4.30pm, Sat 10am–4pm, Sun 10am–5pm; **☎**802 464 8092, **⊕**visitvermont.com). Can help with any questions you may have about the town and surrounding area.

EATING AND DRINKING

The Anchor 8 S Main St **☎**802 464 2112 **⊕**anchorseafood.com. Top-notch seafood, lobsters and shellfish served in a maple syrup cannery dating from the 1850s. Daily 11am–3.30pm & 5–10pm.

6

MOUNT SNOW: SKIING AND MOUNTAIN BIKING

Heading north from Wilmington, Rte-100 ambles on to the resort of **Mount Snow** near the town of West Dover. Officially part of the **Green Mountain National Forest**, this is a perfectly fine place to ski, and without the crowds of other major snowbound havens such as Killington and Stowe. **Mount Snow Resort** (☎802 464-2151, ⓦmountsnow.com) offers some 130 trails (lift tickets $75 Sat & Sun, $69 Mon–Fri).

You'll also find plenty of outdoorsy stuff to occupy you here in the summer. Mount Snow has a sizeable **mountain-biking** fan base: it costs $30 for lift and trail day passes and $55 per day to rent a bike, but note that all trails accessed by lift are for advanced-level bikers only. On-site accommodation is provided at the extremely plush **Grand Summit Resort Hotel** (☎1 800 498 0479, ⓦmountsnow.com), inside the resort.

Dot's 3 W Main St (Rte-9) ☎802 464 7284, ⓦdotsofvermont.com. Casual and super-friendly lunch-counter diner at the junction in the centre of town (with parking), with award-winning chilli (bowls for $5.95) and scrumptious "berry berry" pancakes and muffins, a blend of several berries and cream cheese (from $1.95). *Dot's* was badly damaged by Hurricane Irene – call ahead. Mon–Thurs & Sun 5.30am–8pm, Fri & Sat 5.30am–9pm.

SHOPPING

Bartleby's Books 17 W Main St ☎802 464 5425, ⓦbookcellarvt.com. Great book shop with coffee. It was badly damaged by Hurricane Irene but is now re-open. Mon–Sat 10am–6pm, Sun 10am–5pm.

Young & Constantin Gallery 10 S Main St ☎802 464 2515, ⓦyandcglass.com. Though they carry an assortment of expensive handmade items (which can include ceramics and metal pieces), this gallery specializes in artisan glasswork. July 4–mid-Oct daily 11.30am.–5pm; rest of year Thurs–Mon 11.30am–5pm.

Jamaica

Some sixteen miles north of Mount Snow on Rte-100, **JAMAICA** is one of Vermont's hidden gems and about as "genuine" a village you'll find – old boys hang out on the porch, and brightly painted clapboard and grand Victorians with verandas slowly creak in the wind. Sadly, Jamaica was one of the worst hit towns during **Hurricane Irene** in 2011, with many bridges and roads destroyed – recovery was well underway at the time of writing, but check with the nearest tourist office before you visit.

ACCOMMODATION AND EATING

JAMAICA

D&K's Jamaica Grocery 3816 Rte-30 ☎802 874 4151. Family-owned grocer that also sells excellent sandwiches, cakes, hot pizza and huge calzone pies stuffed with sausage, tomato and melted cheese for $4–7. Daily 7am–8pm.

Jamaica Coffee House 3863 Rte-30 ☎802 874 4643. Small café offering fair trade and organic coffee, teas, delicious baked goods and light meals (sandwiches, wraps, soups and bagels). Tues 7am–noon, Thurs–Mon 7am–5pm.

Jamaica House B&B Rte-30, ☎802 874 4620, ⓦjamaica-house.com. This welcoming B&B, a gorgeous old property in the heart of the village; dates from 1814, it will hopefully re-open in the aftermath of Irene, but check ahead. <u>$165</u>

Weston

One of the prettier villages along Rte-100, **WESTON** spreads beside a little river on an idyllic green. In the centre Rte-100 turns into Main Street, and is lined with stores selling antiques, toys and enough fudge to sink a small ship. The spell is slightly broken when you realize that the labyrinthine **Vermont Country Store** (daily 9am–5.30pm; ⓦvermontcountrystore.com), for all its seeming quaintness, is actually part of a chain of superstores that packages and markets the state's bucolic image. The **Weston Village Store**, established in 1891 at 660 Main St (daily 9am–6pm; ⓦwestonvillagestore.com), contains a much more authentic – and cheaper – range of vaguely rural and domestic articles, such as locally produced maple syrup and cheeses.

On the other side of the village green is Weston's diminutive **Historic District**, a cul-de-sac of restored buildings managed by the Weston Historical Society.

Weston Historical Society Museums

Main St • July & Aug Wed & Sun 1–4pm, Sat 10am–4pm • Free • ☎ 832 824 5294, ⓦ westonvt.com

The primary focus of the grandly titled **Weston Historical Society Museums** is the 1795 **Farrar-Mansur House**, a former tavern that has been restored to depict lives of early Vermont settlers (Weston was founded in 1761). Inside the creaky wooden interior you'll find an array of antique houseware and some decent American folk art. Next door, the **Old Mill Museum** (same times) occupies the site of a sawmill built in 1780, though the current building was restored in the 1930s. It features an old sawmill, gristmill and an impressive assortment of vintage tinsmith, woodworking, farming and dairy tools.

Weston Playhouse

12 Park St • Box office Tues–Sun 10am–4pm • ☎ 802 824 5288, ⓦ westonplayhouse.org

Near the museums and facing the green, the **Weston Playhouse** is an elegant Neoclassical theatre, which spawned the career of the late Lloyd Bridges. The building was rebuilt in 1962 after a fire destroyed the original, a church remodelled in 1936. It puts on a mixture of standard summer-stock musicals, occasionally with more daring offerings, such as works by Brian Friel and Molière.

ACCOMMODATION WESTON

Brandmeyer's Mountainside Lodge 913 Rte-100 ☎ 802 824 5851, ⓦ brandmeyerslodge.com. Cosy modern motel with ten simply furnished rooms with cable TV, fridge and breakfast included. Free wi-fi available in the *Moose Lounge* only. $145

Colonial House Inn & Motel 287 Rte-100 ☎ 802 824 6286, ⓦ cohoinn.com. Gorgeous old house dating back to 1790, with relatively cheap motel rooms in newer wings, free wi-fi and what has to be one of the tastiest and most filling breakfasts in the state. $85

Inn at Weston 630 Main St (Rte-100) ☎ 802 824 6789, ⓦ innweston.com. This inviting, centrally located place is the best accommodation in town, with a main building dating back to 1848 and cheaper rooms in the *Coleman House* annexe; check out the greenhouse, which contains around one thousand orchids, or chill out on the deck or in the gazebo. The first-class restaurant serves divine rainbow trout, and there's a snug pub. $185

EATING AND DRINKING

Bryant House Main St ☎ 802 824 6287. A magnificent soda fountain dominates the 1885 mahogany bar of the restaurant. The menu includes such classic New England fare as "johnnycakes" of cornbread with molasses ($3.25) and chicken pie ($10.25), as well as burgers and sandwiches (from $8). Mon–Wed 11am–3.30pm, Thurs–Sun 11am–9pm.

Mildred's Dairy Bar Main St ☎ 802 776 5730. Serves lighter, cheaper fare (sandwiches, ice cream) from a window on the side of the Village Country Store; sandwiches ($4.25), hot dogs ($2.95), burgers ($4.95). June–Oct daily 11am–8pm.

Okemo Mountain Resort

Around ten miles north of Weston, Rte-100 gets slightly more built up as it nears **LUDLOW**, the access point for the family-friendly ski area of **Okemo Mountain Resort** (lift tickets $77 Sat & Sun, $72 Mon–Fri; ☎ 802 228 4041 or ☎ 1 800 786 5366 for reservations, ⓦ okemo.com). Intermediate skiers and snowboarders will find the 106 trails on Okemo Mountain and the seven trails on neighbouring **Jackson Gore** (part of the resort) challenging enough, although experts will probably get bored after a while. One thing that Okemo can guarantee at all times is snow (in season), no small thing this far south: its 95 percent snowmaking coverage is the largest of any resort in Vermont.

INFORMATION OKEMO MOUNTAIN RESORT

Okemo Valley Regional Chamber of Commerce Rte-103/100 in the Okemo Marketplace mall, opposite the turning to the resort (Mon–Thurs & Sat 8.30am–4.30pm, Fri 9am–5pm; ☎ 802 228 5830, ⓦ okemovalleyvt.org). An excellent source of information. The resort has free wi-fi, or you can check the internet at *Java Baba's* (see below). Free buses (☎1 800 786 5366) connect Ludlow to Okemo Mountain in season (Dec–March).

ACCOMMODATION

Andrie Rose Inn 13 Pleasant St ☎802 228 4846, ⓦandrieroseinn.com. Charming 1829 property at the base of the mountain, with fifteen antique-filled guest rooms and a full country breakfast included. $125

Best Western Ludlow Colonial Motel 93 Main St ☎802 228 8188, ⓦbestwesternludlow.com. Standard chain hotel just south of the centre, with 48 comfortable but ageing rooms, OK if you're just passing through. $116

Governor's Inn 45 Kingdom Rd ☎802 228 8830, ⓦthegovernorsinn.com. This former Vermont governor's home is now a luxurious bed and breakfast, with afternoon tea served on the porch and Victorian-themed rooms. $164

Inn at Water's Edge 321 Rte-103 ☎802 228 8888, ⓦinnatwatersedge.com. Spotless, charming and extremely welcoming 150-year-old Victorian inn, with elegant rooms, fun owners, a pool table and hefty breakfasts included. $125

EATING AND DRINKING

The Downtown Grocery 41 S Depot St ☎802 228 7566, ⓦthedowntowngrocery.com. Fine dining comes to Ludlow, with an incredibly varied and creative seasonal menu that might include tempura-fried squash blossoms, roast sea bass and mini chocolate soufflé. Try the amazing martinis. Daily 5.30–10pm.

Java Baba's 57 Pond St (Rte-103/100), Okemo Marketplace ☎802 228 2326, ⓦjavababas.com. For coffee, hot chocolate, soups ($3), big sandwiches ($6.95) and the like – the cosy atmosphere and comfy couches are welcome during the winter months. Daily 6am–6pm.

Sam's Steakhouse Rte-103 South ☎802 228 2087, ⓦsams-steakhouse.com. The steaks (dry-aged for fifteen to twenty days; from $35) and prime rib are worth the short drive out of town. Daily 5–9pm.

Plymouth Notch

The remote village of **PLYMOUTH NOTCH**, eleven miles north of Ludlow, was witness to of one of the most dramatic moments of American history. On a warm August night in 1923, **Calvin Coolidge** was sworn in here as the thirtieth US president – President Harding had died suddenly, a few hours earlier. The scene was pure Vermont: the oath of office was administered by his father (a notary public) by kerosene lamp, a bible was not required (as per state law) and the house had neither electricity nor a telephone. Coolidge went back to bed soon after.

Calvin Coolidge State Historic Site

3780 Rte-100A · Late May to mid-Oct daily 9.30am–5pm · $7.50 · ☎802 672 3773, ⓦhistoricvermont.org/coolidge

Calvin Coolidge was born in Plymouth Notch in 1872 (and buried in the local cemetery in 1933), and most of the village is now preserved as the immaculate **Calvin Coolidge State Historic Site**. Coolidge never lost ties to the town, conducting a "Summer White House" here during his presidency (1923–29). All of the buildings in which Coolidge's life played out have been kept more or less the way they were; the humble timber **Birthplace** (1845), the more comfortable **Homestead** (1876) where he grew up (preserved as it was on that night in 1923), and his father's general store (1855).

Other structures help fill in the details of everyday life in the late nineteenth century. The **Plymouth Cheese Factory** (daily 9am–5pm; ☎802 672 3650, ⓦplymouthcheese .com) dates back to 1890, and still knocks out high-quality granular curd cheese from a traditional recipe (you can see the old equipment upstairs). The 1840 **Union Christian Church** features a Greek Revival facade and a stunning all-wood "Carpenter Gothic" interior, crafted in the 1890s. The cavernous **Wilder Barn** (1875) contains one the largest collections of nineteenth-century agricultural equipment in the country, while the 1830 **Wilder House** (childhood home of Coolidge's mother), now serves as the site **restaurant** (try the rhubarb cobbler).

Make sure you visit the exhibition and watch the video in the **Coolidge Museum & Education Center** at the entrance – not well remembered today, Republican president

Coolidge gained praise for lowering taxes, cutting spending and reducing the national debt in the 1920s, though critics point out that his presidency was followed by the worst economic depression in modern times. T-shirts sold in the gift shop, engraved with his famous words "I do not choose to run", are apparently popular with anti-joggers.

Central Vermont

6

Central Vermont is a region of great diversity, home to the refined college town of **Middlebury**, picturesque small burgs like cultured but unstuffy **Woodstock**, and the tiny but appealing state capital, **Montpelier**. Two notable ski resorts are also here: rowdy **Killington**, the state's most popular snowy destination, and **Stowe**, a highly regarded vacation spot with a history both as a centre of cross-country skiing and as the home of the Von Trapp family (of *Sound of Music* fame). Central Vermont also holds the most visited attraction in the state: the **Ben & Jerry's Ice Cream Factory**, perhaps the most successful embodiment of Vermont activism and "green" thinking in a commercial venture.

Killington

Scenic Rte-100 eventually winds its way to **KILLINGTON**, nine miles north of Plymouth Notch, a sprawling resort that has grown out of nothing since 1958 to become the most popular ski destination in the state. Killington's permanent population is roughly one thousand, but it's estimated that in season there are enough beds within twenty miles to accommodate some ten thousand people. Like many other New England mountain areas, the region has also opened itself up to all sorts of summer activities.

Other than a small collection of stores and motels on US-4, you'll find most of the action along **Killington Road**, which starts just before the northern intersection of US-4 and Rte-100. **Killington Resort** itself sits at the top of the road, which terminates at the K-1 Lodge.

Killington Resort

4763 Killington Rd · Lift tickets $85 Sat & holidays, $80 Mon–Fri · ☎ 1 800 621 6867, ⓦ killington.com

Sometimes called the "Beast of the East", on account of its size – its two hundred trails sprawl over seven mountains – and its notoriously rowdy nightlife, **Killington Resort** sports a freewheeling and wild attitude. Indeed, Killington is often considered to be the eastern equivalent of Vail, and the resort does provide the longest ski and snowboarding season in the eastern US.

In **summer** the focus is on **hiking** and **mountain-biking**, with 45 miles of trails (basic park access $5; with K-1 Gondola rides $35 per day). Bike rentals are $70 a day. You can also take the **K-1 Express Gondola** (July, Aug & Oct daily 10am–5pm, Sept Sat & Sun 10am–5pm; $10 one-way, $15 round-trip) from the K-1 Lodge to the summit of **Killington Peak** (4241ft) and hike down. Pick up trail maps beforehand at the Bike Shop at K-1 Lodge (☎ 802 422 6232).

Pico Mountain

73 Alpine Drive, US-4 · Dec–March Thurs–Mon daily 8am–4pm · Lift tickets $49 per day · ☎ 802 422 6200, ⓦ picomountain.com

Pico Mountain, though officially part of Killington Resort, is much tamer and smaller in style and scale. Its 48 trails are best for skiers of mid-range ability, and there's not as much hot-dogging as you'll find on the other peaks. Killington lift tickets are also valid here.

In the summer Pico's **Adventure Center** (July & Aug daily 10am–5pm) offers a climbing wall, alpine slide, mini-golf and the Pico Power Jump (like a bungee jump). An all-day pass is $29 (the alpine slide can also be purchased separately for $10).

ARRIVAL AND INFORMATION

By bus Your best bet via public transport is to travel on Amtrak to Rutland (p.355) and take the Marble Valley Regional Transit bus to Killington (daily 7.15am–7.15pm; hourly; $2 one-way; ☎ 802 773 3244, ⓦ thebus.com).

Killington Chamber of Commerce On US-4, beyond the turning to Killington Road (Mon–Fri 10am–4pm; ☎ 802 773 4181, ⓦ killingtonchamber.com or ⓦ discoverkillington.com).

ACCOMMODATION

Accommodation within the resort itself is most prized (but expensive), for its proximity to the lifts. **Wise Vacations**, 405 Killington Rd (☎ 1 800 639 4680, ⓦ wisevacations.com), rents private homes and condos in and around Killington; prices vary, but are slightly higher than the average inn or B&B.

★ **Birch Ridge Inn** 37 Butler Rd ☎ 802 775 1010, ⓦ birchridge.com. This extra-cosy B&B offers classic, old-fashioned Vermont hospitality in a modern alpine ski lodge, with rooms in various styles and home-baked breads and muffins. $120

Happy Bear Motel 1784 Killington Rd ☎ 1 800 518 4468, ⓦ happybearmotel.com. Very convenient though basic digs, with refrigerators, simple breakfast, wi-fi and cable TV – it's the best deal in the region. Kids under 12 stay for free. $59

★ **Inn at Long Trail** 709 US-4, Sherburne Pass ☎ 802 775 7181, ⓦ innatlongtrail.com. After several nights spent in primitive shelters, hikers on the Long Trail will appreciate the comfort of this family-run B&B with tree-trunk beams and a stone fireplace. $105

Killington Grand Resort Hotel 228 E Mountain Rd, Killington Resort ☎ 1 800 372 2007, ⓦ killington.com.

The resort's premier hotel features luxury rooms, and a ski-bridge to the slopes. Extras include spa, health club and outdoor-heated pool. $149

Summit Lodge & Resort 200 Summit Rd ☎ 802 422 3535, ⓦ summitlodgevermont.com. Long-standing area favourite, with free wi-fi and a casual lodge feel, enhanced by the owners' two friendly St Bernards guarding the lobby. $120

★ **Vermont Inn** 78 Cream Hill Rd, Mendon ☎ 802 775 0708, ⓦ vermontinn.com. Lovely, rambling clapboard inn (built as a farmhouse in 1840), with a choice of luxurious suites with jacuzzi baths and smaller rooms with TVs; small gym, bar, restaurant, sauna, tennis court, outside hot-tub and several nooks where you can sip coffee, eat sumptuous home-made cookies and read a book. Free wi-fi, bikes and breakfast. $125

EATING

★ **Back Behind Saloon** Bridgewater Corners (southern intersection of US-4 and Rte-100) ☎ 802 422 9907, ⓦ backbehind.com. This hickory-smoke BBQ joint is a real gem (St Louis ribs full rack for $26.95), and also contains a decent bar. Tavern Thurs–Mon 4–11pm; restaurant Thurs & Mon 5–10pm, Fri–Sun noon–4pm & 5–10pm.

Casey's Caboose 1930 Killington Rd ☎ 802 422 3795, ⓦ killingtonsbest.com. This favourite train-themed family restaurant (built around two early twentieth-century railroad cars) offers free chicken wings at its daily happy hour (3–6pm), and plenty of steaks, seafood and pasta dishes. Daily 3–9pm.

The Garlic 1724 Killington Rd ☎ 802 422 5055, ⓦ thegarlicvermont.com. A tasty but not-very-Spanish version of tapas awaits in the *Olive Bar* (think hummus and fried sweet potato chips; $2–8), while in the restaurant, ravioli, chicken and seafood are liberally spiked with the

namesake seasoning. Main courses from $19. Mon–Thurs & Sun 5–9pm, Fri & Sat 5–10pm.

Pizza Jerks 1307 Killington Rd ☎ 802 422 4111, ⓦ pizzajerks.com. Choose your camp: "Tree Hugger" (all veggie) or "Carcass" (all meat), both $21.99. Otherwise, choose your own toppings for the New York-style pizzas (from $9), washed down with draught beer or wine. Mid-Oct to mid-April Mon–Thurs & Sun 11am–10pm, Fri & Sat 11am–11pm.

★ **Wobbly Barn Steakhouse** 2229 Killington Rd ☎ 802 422 6171, ⓦ wobblybarn.net. Some sort of lively entertainment every weekend, but the draw since 1963 has really been the beef and prime rib (broiled, mesquite-grilled and barbecued). Come for "Wild Game Night" on Tues (elk, venison, buffalo), or "Lynchburg Southern Barbecue Sundays" for a bit of non-regional amusement. Main courses from $25. Nov–April, daily from 4.30pm.

DRINKING

★ **Long Trail Brewing Co** 5520 US-4, Bridgewater Corners (southern intersection of US-4 and Rte-100) ☎ 802 672 5011, ⓦ longtrail.com. One of Vermont's best microbreweries offers self-guided tours and, more importantly, a bar where you can sample the freshly made suds. Pints $4–5. Daily 10am–7pm.

McGrath's Irish Pub 709 US-4, at Inn at Long Trail ☎ 802 775 7181. Warm, inviting hangout, with live Irish music on the weekends, and a tavern menu of American and Irish standards (around $10.95). Rumour has it that they sell the largest volume of Guinness in the state. Daily 11.30am–11pm, live music Sat & Sun 8pm.

Pickle Barrel 1741 Killington Rd ☏ 802 422 3035, ⓦ picklebarrelnightclub.com. A rowdy three-level bar and nightclub that gets crazy on winter weekends (opposite *Garlic*, halfway up the mountain). Sept–April Thurs–Sat 8pm–close.

Woodstock and around

Just a few miles west of the Connecticut River and the New Hampshire border, **WOODSTOCK** has long been considered a bit more refined than its rural neighbours. Much of this can be attributed to the artists and writers that have called the town home over the years, such as sculptor Hiram Powers, novelist Sinclair Lewis and painter Paul Cadmus. Don't confuse this town with the Woodstock of festival fame, though; that one is in upstate New York.

The town's centre is an oval green at the convergence of Elm, Central and Church streets, which are lined with distinguished, architecturally diverse houses that provide a genteel foreground to the landscape of rolling hills. The tiny downtown area is populated by antique shops, tearooms, galleries and smart eateries.

Dana House Museum

26 Elm St • May–Oct Mon–Sat 10am–4pm, Sun noon–4pm • $5 • ☏ 802 457 1822, ⓦ woodstockhistorical.org

The Woodstock History Center's primary attraction is the **Dana House Museum**, with well-organized multimedia displays on the history of the area, including tape recordings of older residents' reminiscences and an admirably complete town archive. The museum leads into the house itself, an 1807 clapboard gem built for local merchant Charles Dana, containing a varied collection of artefacts. Admire the assemblage of antique children's toys on display and the elegant Victorian parlour, adorned with a Carrera marble fireplace and reductions of *Greek Slave*, a statue by Hiram Powers.

Marsh-Billings-Rockefeller National Historical Park

54 Elm St (Rte-12), north of Woodstock • Late May to Oct daily 10am–5pm; tours every 30min–1hr • $8 (includes tour), children (under 15 years) free; combined ticket with Billings Farm $17 • ☏ 802 457 3368, ⓦ nps.gov/mabi

Hard to imagine today, but thanks to intensive logging, the leafy hills of Vermont were virtually stripped bare by the 1860s. The **Marsh-Billings-Rockefeller National Historical Park** encompasses the nineteenth-century mansion of three generations of ground-breaking conservationists who managed to reverse this trend. Illuminating one-hour ranger **tours** (the only way to visit the mansion) link the three and provide plenty of context. Park your car and reserve a tour at the Billings Farm and Museum (see p.352) across the road.

Brief history

The lavish Queen Anne-style house you see today was built in 1885, but its core dates back to 1806. **George Perkins Marsh** was born on the grounds five years earlier, and inherited the property from his father. Virtually unknown outside the scientific community, even today, Marsh published *Man and Nature* in 1864, a seminal work of ecological thought, inspired by the author's distress at the deforestation of his native Vermont. In 1861 Marsh was appointed US ambassador to Italy (he died there in 1882), and the house was purchased in 1869 by wealthy lawyer, businessman and admirer **Frederick Billings** (1823–90), who tried to put Marsh's ideas into practice, reseeding and replanting tracts of land with Norway spruce. Conservationist and mega-wealthy philanthropist **Laurence Rockefeller** (1910–2004), who married Billings' granddaughter, Mary, took the ethos a step further by combining the ideals of preservation with the benefits of public access; the Rockefellers opened the Billings Farm section of the property to the public in 1983 (see p.352), and donated the rest of to the National Park Service in 1992 (they had been using it as a summer home).

6

The Mansion

Today the 1895 **Carriage Barn** acts as the park visitor centre, with a small exhibition on the site. Much of the ornate interior of the **Mansion** looks exactly as it was when Billings lived here; the music room is enhanced by wonderfully florid Victorian wallpaper and a carved maple fireplace, while the library boasts a precious Tiffany stained-glass window and some exceptional paintings from the **Hudson School**, including Thomas Cole's *Niagara Falls*. You can also explore 553 acres of forest around the site, which contain a twenty-mile network of **hiking trails** across Mount Tom (1359ft).

Billings Farm and Museum

5302 River Rd (off Rte-12, north of Woodstock) • May–Oct daily 10am–5pm; Nov–Feb Sat & Sun till 4pm • $12, children 5–15 years $6; children 3–4 years $3; $3 for film only; combined ticket with Marsh-Billings-Rockefeller National Historical Park $17 • ☏ 802 457 2355, Ⓦ billingsfarm.org

Across the street from the Marsh-Billings-Rockefeller National Historical Park lies the **Billings Farm and Museum**, the working part of the former Billings and Rockefeller property (see p.351), established in 1871. Before you do anything else watch the thirty-minute screening of **A Place in the Land**, a super documentary that provides background on the three generations of conservationists who worked here. Exhibits in the barn cover various aspects of farm life, as well as the history of the site (covering the same ground as the film). In the grounds are various sheds and displays, but the real crowd-pleaser is **milking time** in the cowshed (daily 3.15–5pm), and especially for kids, the chance to pet horses and newly born Jersey calves. You can also take regular guided tours (30min) of the modest **1890 Farm House** (where Scottish farm manager George Aitken lived with his family until his death in 1910), containing authentic period rooms upstairs, and a nineteenth-century creamery below.

Sugarbush Farm

591 Sugarbush Farm Rd • Mon–Fri 8am–5pm, Sat & Sun 9am–5pm • Free • ☏ 802 457 1757, Ⓦ sugarbushfarm.com

Perhaps the most visited Woodstock attraction is **Sugarbush Farm**, which produces fourteen varieties of cheese (try the exceptional smoked cheddar), pure Vermont maple syrup and various other Vermont-made foods. Founded in 1948, the shop is open year round; March and April are the syrup-making months.

ARRIVAL AND INFORMATION
WOODSTOCK

By train/bus Getting to Woodstock is tough without your own car; Amtrak and Greyhound serve White River Junction, fourteen miles east, but you'll have to take a taxi from there (Big Yellow Taxi ☏ 802 281 8294).

Woodstock Welcome Center Mechanic St, just off the main street (daily 9am–5pm; ☏ 802 432 1100, Ⓦ woodstockvt.com). Has tons of visitor information and also has parking nearby (25 cents/30min).

ACCOMMODATION

Applebutter Inn 7511 Happy Valley Rd (just off US-4) in Taftsville, four miles east of Woodstock ☏ 802 457 4158, Ⓦ applebutterinn.com. Cosy B&B in an 1854 gabled house, with comfortable beds, personable proprietors and huge breakfasts kicking off with tasty home-made granola. $100

Braeside Motel 432 Woodstock Rd (US-4) ☏ 802 457 1366, Ⓦ braesidemotel.com. Not quite a mile east of the village, you'll find spacious, clean and simple family-owned motel digs with friendly owners and a swimming pool. Best option if you want to avoid the pricier–if more atmospheric–B&B experience around here. $98

Village Inn of Woodstock 41 Pleasant St ☏ 802 457 1255, Ⓦ villageinnofwoodstock.com. Quaint B&B, renovated in the Victorian style, with an inviting front porch and attractive gardens – the place to come for a classic New England inn experience. The tavern (open to guests only, offers cocktails, beer and espresso. $150

★ **Woodstock Inn and Resort** 14 The Green ☏ 802 457 1100, Ⓦ woodstockinn.com. The largest, fanciest and best place to stay in the area, with sumptuous rooms, beautiful grounds, an eighteen-hole golf course and four gourmet restaurants. It's also got a winter sports facility, and a health and fitness centre with a spa for the ultimate in pampering. $250

EATING AND DRINKING

Bentley's 3 Elm St ☎802 457 3232, ⓦ bentleysrestaurant.com. Superior versions of traditional bistro food (tequila and lime chicken, duck quesadillas, garlic and Guinness mussels) and a good range of microbrews. Casual and moderately priced (sandwiches from $9; main courses $17.95–23.95). Mon–Thurs 11.30am–9.30pm, Fri & Sat 11am–10pm, Sun 11am–9.30pm.

★ **Kedron Valley Inn** 10671 South Rd, Rte-106, South Woodstock ☎802 457 1473, ⓦ kedronvalleyinn .com. Eating in the tavern or on the formal front porch is more fun – and less expensive – than in the dining room, but the food, often from local sources, is superb throughout; the tender, juicy steaks and local vegetables are uniformly praised. Reservations recommended. Thurs–Mon 5.30–10pm.

Mangowood Lincoln Inn, 530 Woodstock Rd (US-4) ☎802 457 3312, ⓦ mangowood.com. New American cuisine with Asian accents from the Singaporean chef/ owner, such as pepper sesame tofu fries and penne pasta with green curry. Expect to spend $100+ per head for a full dinner. Tues–Sat 6–10pm.

Mountain Creamery 33 Central St ☎802 457 1715, ⓦ mountaincreameryvt.com. Filling country breakfasts and lunch fare served daily, as well as some fine home-made ice cream downstairs ($4–5). Try the mile-high apple pie ($11.95, slice $5.95). Daily 7am–3pm.

The Prince and the Pauper 24 Elm St ☎802 457 1818, ⓦ princeandpauper.com. Continental cuisine – braised veal, filet mignon – in an incongruously casual dining room ($49 fixed-priced dinner). There's less pricey bistro fare as well ($17–23), like linguini with meatballs and Maine crab cakes. Mon–Thurs & Sun 5–9pm, Fri & Sat 5–9.30pm.

★ **Wasp's Snack Bar** 57 Pleasant St ☎802 457 3334. This tiny roadside shack is a local institution, right on US-4 at the eastern end of town (near the motels), and specializing in home-cooked breakfasts. Tues–Sat 6am–1.30pm.

SHOPPING

F.H. Gillingham's 16 Elm St ☎802 457 2100, ⓦ gillinghams.com. Country store operating since 1886, selling just about everything "from caviar to cow manure". Mon–Sat 8.30am–6.30pm, Sun 10am–5pm.

Woodstock Folk Art Prints and Antiquities 8 Elm St ☎802 457 2012. One of the best of the many galleries in town, displaying vivid local folk art. Mon–Sat 10am–5pm, Sun 10am–4pm.

Yankee Bookshop 12 Central St ☎802 457 2411, ⓦ yankeebookshop.com. Founded in 1935, this is the oldest bookstore in Vermont, and still worth a detailed browse. Daily 10am–5pm.

Quechee

Six miles east of Woodstock, **QUECHEE** (pronounced kwee-chee) is a combination of quaint Vermont village, expensive housing developments, chic restaurants and B&Bs. The **Quechee Gorge Village shopping mall** (daily 9am–5pm) on Rte-4 offers the usual tourist kitsch, but if you need to stock up on maple syrup, cheddar cheese and local beers, it does the trick. Note that Quechee was devastated by flooding in the aftermath of **Hurricane Irene** in 2011; the Quechee Covered Bridge was destroyed. Everything should be back to normal by the summer of 2012, but check the Vermont Agency of Transportation (ⓦ aot.state.vt.us) or tourism websites for the latest.

Queechee Gorge State Park

5800 Woodstock Rd (US-4), Quechee • May–Oct daily sunrise–sunset • $3 • ☎802 295 2990, ⓦ vtstateparks.com

One of Vermont's greatest natural wonders, **Quechee Gorge** is the so-called "Grand Canyon" of the state, a narrow, 165ft tree-lined chasm that lights up with colour in the autumn. A delicate bridge takes US-4 across the Ottauquechee River here, providing the best view of the gorge (there's free parking on either side, open year-round). Hiking trails lead down through forests to its base and the surrounding **Quechee Gorge State Park** that runs along the river – pick up maps at the information centre (see p.354).

VINS Nature Center

6565 Woodstock Rd (US-4), Quechee • Daily: mid-June to Oct 10am–5.30pm; Nov to mid-April 10am–4pm; mid-April to mid-June 10am–5pm • $11 • ☎802 359 5000, ⓦ vinsweb.org

Lying between Woodstock and Quechee on US-4, the **VINS Nature Center** is operated by the **Vermont Institute of Natural Science**. View exhibits on local flora and fauna, and see how the staff rescues and treats injured birds of prey, such as falcons and owls; some of these participate in thirty-minute programmes (three times a day in summer, just once in winter), during which you can watch them in graceful, powerful action.

Simon Pearce Glass

1760 Main St • Daily 9am–9pm • Free • ☎ 802 295 2711, ⓦ simonpearce.com

If you have time, hit the town centre of Quechee (take Waterman Hill Rd off US-4 and drive across the – hopefully rebuilt – covered bridge), where a waterfall on the river turns the turbines of **Simon Pearce Glass**. Housed in a former wool mill, this is an unusual but enticing combination of **glass-blowing centre** and **restaurant** (see below).

INFORMATION   QUECHEE

Quechee Gorge Visitor Center East side of the gorge on US-4 (daily: May–Oct 9am–5pm; Nov–April 10am–4pm; ☎ 802 295 6852). Can provide local information and trail maps.

ACCOMMODATION

Parker House Inn 1792 Main St ☎ 802 295 6077, ⓦ theparkerhouseinn.com. This ravishing red-brick Victorian, built in 1857, has seven guest rooms ranging from a compact third-floor den to spacious master bedrooms with views of the river. The restaurant serves sophisticated meals utilizing local ingredients. $200

Quality Inn at Quechee Gorge 5817 Woodstock Rd, (US-4) ☎ 802 295 7600, ⓦ qualityinnquechee.com. Standard motel accommodation in the area's least expensive hotel, with indoor heated pool, free wi-fi and continental breakfast included. $99

Quechee Inn at Marshland Farm 1119 Main St ☎ 802 295 3133, ⓦ quecheeinn.com. Built in 1793 for Vermont's first lieutenant governor, this clapboard beauty offers 24 comfy rooms with Victorian-style furnishings and a fabulous setting. $150

CAMPING

Quechee Gorge State Park If you're equipped to camp, the best place to stay is in the Quechee Gorge State Park, just off US-4 (☎ 802 295 2990), which has 54 well-maintained sites in a forest of fir trees. $18

EATING AND DRINKING

Farmer's Diner Quechee Gorge Village ☎ 802 295 4600. This 1947 Worcester diner car is the best place for breakfast along US-4. The food (supplied by local farmers) is filling and inexpensive (big plates $7–9). Daily 6am–4pm.

Fire Stone's Waterman Place, US-4 (at the turning to Quechee town) ☎ 802 295 1600, ⓦ firestonesrestaurant.net. Bentley's-owned place that serves creative pasta dishes, flatbread pizzas and traditional Vermont fare, which you can enjoy on their pleasant rooftop patio. Daily 11am–9pm.

★ **Shepard's Pie Restaurant** Rte-4, at Quechee Gorge ☎ 802 295 2786, ⓦ shepards-pie.com. Excellent diner, with deals like burger and a beer for $10. Separate bar area. Also crafts mouthwatering home-made pies and sandwiches. Daily 7am–9pm.

★ **Simon Pearce Glass** 1760 Main St, Quechee ☎ 802 295 1470, ⓦ simonpearce.com. Inventive New American-type main courses starting at around $22, as well as occasional no-nonsense Irish dishes such as beef and Guinness stew and shepherd's pie. Daily 11.30am–9pm.

Windsor

About fifteen miles south of Woodstock and Quechee, the working town of **WINDSOR** sits right on the bank of the Connecticut River and the New Hampshire border. The town does have an important past: the original constitution of the Republic of Vermont was drawn up here in 1777, an event that made Windsor the "birthplace of Vermont". Its other claim to fame is the **Cornish–Windsor covered bridge**, which dates from 1866 and is open to traffic. At 460ft, it's the longest covered bridge in the US. Cross to New Hampshire for the best photo opportunities (take Bridge Street off Main Street).

Old Constitution House

16 Main St • Late May to mid-Oct Sat–Sun 11am–5pm • $2.50 • ☎ 802 674 6628, ⓦ historicvermont.org/constitution

The event that ensured Windsor's lasting fame took place at the **Old Constitution House**, at the north end of town. This was the original tavern where the

Vermont delegates met and constitutional debates took place, and it contains a well-executed re-creation of the tavern's interior plus a fascinating series of displays, featuring artefacts such as coins and newspapers from the short-lived Vermont Republic period.

Windsor House

54 Main St • Daily 9am–6pm • Free • ⓦ windsorvthistoricalsociety.com

In the centre of Windsor, take a peek inside graceful **Windsor House**, a former Greek Revival-style hotel built in the 1830s and now home to shops, galleries and displays by the **Windsor Historical Society** (usually antique photos in the lobby). The best parking in town lies behind the building (free).

American Precision Museum

196 Main St • Late May to Oct daily 10am–5pm • $6 • ☎ 802 674 5781, ⓦ americanprecision.org

At the south end of Windsor, the **American Precision Museum** focuses on what might sound a dull subject – the construction, function and historical significance of machinery. Yet the small but engaging collection incorporates antique "Mississippi" rifles, sewing machines and machine tools (many still in working condition), to illustrate not only the beauty of early technology, but also the revolutionary breakthrough made here in the early nineteenth century; the ability to make interchangeable precision machine parts. Guns manufactured on this site (an ex-gun factory) amazed and worried British observers at the **Great Exhibition of 1851** – the American guns had been made and assembled with interchangeable parts (rather than the individual guns being made by a craftsman), making mass production possible for the first time. One of Thomas Blanchard's original gun-stock lathes, responsible for the breakthrough, is on display.

Harpoon Brewery

336 Ruth Carney Drive, just off of Rte-5 • May–Oct Mon–Wed & Sun 10am–6pm, Thurs–Sat 10am–9pm; Nov–April Tues, Wed & Sun 10am–6pm, Thurs–Sat 10am–9pm • Free • ☎ 802 674 5491, ⓦ harpoonbrewery.com

Beer drinkers should follow the scent of roasting hops to the **Harpoon Brewery**, one of the state's high-quality microbreweries, 2.5 miles north of Windsor on US-5. You can grab a draught or sandwich at the **Riverbend Taps and Beer Garden**, or take a one-hour **guided tour** ($5, includes beer tasting) of the brewery on Friday (5pm, 6pm, 7pm), Saturday (11am–5pm, hourly) or Sunday (noon–4pm, hourly).

| ACCOMMODATION AND EATING | WINDSOR |

Juniper Hill Inn 153 Pembroke Rd, US-5 ☎ 802 674 5273, ⓦ juniperhillinn.com. Thirty tidy rooms dressed with period wallpaper, four-poster or canopy beds and charming antiques, set in a grand mansion built overlooking the town in 1902; the rooms, patio and gardens afford spectacular views of the surrounding hills. $175

Snap Dragon Inn 26 Main St ☎ 802 227 0008, ⓦ snapdragoninn.com. Grand Georgian red-brick mansion dating from 1815, with nine stylish rooms blending contemporary and antique styles, flat-screen TVs, DVD players and wi-fi. $180

Windsor Diner 135 Main St ☎ 802 674 5555. A traditional chrome-finished dining car that specializes in classic road food: burgers, fries, mac and cheese, tasty meatloaf and wonderful fruit pies. Daily 7am–8pm.

Rutland and around

Despite being the second largest city in Vermont, **RUTLAND**, west of Killington at the junction of US-4 and US-7, offers little in the way of traditional sights. Unlike many of the clapboard villages surrounding it, Rutland's origins lie in the nineteenth-century **marble quarrying** industry – indeed, the city was incorporated only in 1892. Rutland has struggled economically since the quarries closed in the

1980s and 1990s, and though its red-brick downtown has seen some regeneration, the main attractions lie outside the centre.

Norman Rockwell Museum

654 US-4 East · Daily 9am–4pm · $5.50 · ☎ 1 877 773 6095, ⓦ normanrockwellvt.com

Two miles east of central Rutland along US-4 sits the **Norman Rockwell Museum**, which displays more than two thousand reproductions of Rockwell paintings, including all of his *Saturday Evening Post* covers. It's a well-contextualized retrospective of the artist's work, which can be irritatingly wholesome but is nevertheless an important contribution to American graphic art (see box, p.228).

Wilson Castle

West Proctor Rd · Late-May to Oct daily 9am–5pm; guided tours only (around 1hr) · $10.75 · ☎ 802 773 3284, ⓦ wilsoncastle.com

A short drive northwest from Rutland (take US-4 and turn right onto West Proctor Road), **Wilson Castle** is the gorgeous product of a reckless spending spree and a failed marriage. The lavish mansion, a blend of Gothic arches, Romanesque curves and plain Medieval fantasy was the brainchild of one Dr John Johnson, a Vermont native who married into English nobility. He managed to blow $1.3 million of his wife's fortune fitting out the first two floors before the cash was cut off in the mid-1880s. Johnson's wife eventually left him and the state took the house in lieu of taxes in the 1890s – Herbert Lee Wilson, a radio pioneer and later a US Army colonel, bought the home for just $50,000 in 1939. His granddaughter owns the castle today.

Tours take in the best rooms and artefacts – unlike at many preserved mansions you can take pictures and even sit in some of the ageing chairs here. The rooms are littered with exceptional works of art, from Ming dynasty vases and teak silk screens, to a regal Grand Reception Room lined with rare Honduran mahogany and a fireplace constructed from bird's-eye maple (a rare speckled mutation). It all feels very real and lived in – the paint is peeling in places, and some of the carpets are worn, adding to the air of faded grandeur.

New England Maple Museum

4578 Rte-7, Pittsford · Late May to Oct daily 8.30am–5.30pm; Nov, Dec & mid-March to late May daily 10am–4pm · $2.50 · ☎ 802 483 9414, ⓦ maplemuseum.com

The history of maple sugaring is brought to life at the modest **New England Maple Museum**, principally through the 100ft of murals created by painter Grace Brigham. Antique artefacts also help chart the history of maple sugar, going back to early Native American harvesting techniques, and a tasting room allows you to sample the product.

MOUNT INDEPENDENCE

From Rutland, a forty-minute drive northwest (US-7 to Rte-73) brings you to **Mount Independence** (daily late May to mid-Oct 9.30am–5pm; $5; ☎ 802 948 2000), on the very southeastern tip of Lake Champlain, the scene of a major American defeat in the Revolutionary War. The fort was established here in 1776 to repel a British attack from Canada with Fort Ticonderoga on the opposite shore. The two forts initially proved such an intimidating sight that British general Guy Carleton aborted his invasion in October 1776. However, the following winter was brutal, and most of the troops deserted; 2500 American soldiers who remained behind fell ill or froze to death. Springtime reinforcements were insufficient to withstand an attack from General Burgoyne, and the fort was abandoned on July 5, 1777. The British occupied the fort until November of the same year, when they burned it in response to General Burgoyne's surrender across the water at Saratoga. Displays in the **Visitors Center Museum** tell the story of that dreadful winter.

ARRIVAL AND INFORMATION

By plane Rutland is a regional transport hub, with Cape Air offering three daily flights from Boston to Southern Vermont Regional Airport (⊛ flyrutlandvt.com), five miles south of the city. Budget and Hertz have car rental desks at the airport, but you'll otherwise need to take a taxi.

By train Amtrak trains arrive at the station at 25 Evelyn St; trains run once a day between New York and Albany.

By bus The bus terminal is in the centre of town at 102 West St (☎ 802 773 2774), but Greyhound no longer serves the area. Local bus company Marble Valley Regional Transit runs services ($2; ☎ 802 773 3244, ⊛ thebus.com) to Killington, Middlebury and Manchester.

Rutland Region Chamber of Commerce 256 N Main St (Mon–Fri 8am–5pm; ☎ 802 773 2747, ⊛ rutlandvermont.com). Open year-round, this is your best bet for information.

Middlebury and around

In 1800, a small group of local citizens banded together in the town of **MIDDLEBURY**, 32 miles north of Rutland, to form a "town's college", primarily intended to train young men for the ministry. Today **Middlebury College** – one of the most endowed (and expensive) liberal arts colleges in the US – is at the heart of one of Vermont's most charming towns. All roads converge at the **Middlebury Town Green**, an idyllic place with the pretty and ornate white **Congregational Church** at its northern end, and the more sombre grey **St Stephen's Episcopal Church** on the green itself. Wander down to the old mill area to view the **Otter Creek Falls**, an 18ft cascade below the Rte-125 bridge.

Henry Sheldon Museum of Vermont History

1 Park St • Mon–Sat 10am–5pm; May–Oct also Sun 1–5pm • $5 • ☎ 802 388 2117, ⊛ henrysheldonmuseum.org

Dating back to 1882, the **Henry Sheldon Museum of Vermont History** contains an endearingly quirky collection of tools, household objects and one-of-a-kind oddities, such as the remains of the "Petrified Indian Boy", actually a mid-nineteenth-century hoax. Much of the collection is displayed in the Judd-Harris House, built in 1829 by the marble merchant Eben Judd and his son-in-law Lebbeus Harris.

Middlebury College Museum of Art

Mahaney Center for the Arts, 72 Porter Field Rd • Tues–Fri 10am–5pm, Sat & Sun noon–5pm • Free • ☎ 802 443 5007, ⊛ museum.middlebury.edu

On the southeastern edge of the Middlebury College campus, the **Middlebury College Museum of Art** houses temporary art shows and a small permanent collection of nineteenth-century European and American sculpture and modern prints; highlights include three etchings by Rembrandt, prints by Piranesi, Dürer and Goya, and a portrait by William Jenny of Middlebury College founder Gamaliel Painter (c.1805). More unusually, there's a collection of decorative art by **Fabergé**, a gift to the college from a Vermont family descended from the Russian tsars.

Otter Creek Brewery

793 Exchange St • Daily 11am–6pm • Free • ☎ 802 388 072, ⊛ ottercreekbrewing.com

This being a Vermont town, Middlebury has its own microbrewer, the exceptionally good **Otter Creek Brewery**. Pop-in for self-guided tours, samples and the gift shop, where you can stock up on Black IPA and Copper Ale.

INFORMATION

Addison County Chamber of Commerce 93 Court St, Rte-7 (Mon 10.30am–5pm, Tues–Fri 9am–5pm; brochures and hiking information available at entrance Sat & Sun; ☎ 802 388 7951, ⊛ addisoncounty.com). Or look at the website ⊛ midvermont.com. Parking in town is free for 2hr.

ACCOMMODATION

Inn on the Green 71 S Pleasant St ☎ 802 388 7512, ⊛ innonthegreen.com. This aptly named B&B has eleven luxurious rooms in a light-blue 1803 Federal-style landmark building, with continental breakfast in bed included. **$159**

6

RTE-125: ROBERT FROST COUNTRY

Robert Frost spent 23 summers in Vermont on land that has since been overrun by **Rte-125** (also called the **Robert Frost Memorial Highway**). The road cuts right across the Green Mountains National Forest from Rte-7 in East Middlebury to Hancock. Just less than six miles along you'll pass the **Robert Frost Trail**, a 1.2-mile loop walk punctuated by placards quoting his work. Although it may not sound like much, it is actually quite evocative – an affecting environment in which to read his deceptively simple, old-fashioned words. Around 500 yards further on is the **Robert Frost Wayside**, a peaceful picnic area amidst red pines, right by the highway. Adjacent to this is **Frost Road**, a dirt track that leads half a mile to a white, wood-frame house known as **Homer Noble Farm**. Frost actually spent every summer here from 1939 in a log cabin nearby, still visible about a hundred yards beyond the farmhouse up a wide, grassy lane; walk until you see an opening on your left that leads into a mountain dell where the cabin, now is situated a National Historic Landmark and owned by Middlebury College. It's OK to take a look, even if no one is around.

Less than a mile west along Rte-125 is the **Bread Loaf Mountain Campus**, home of a highly regarded summer writers' conference initiated at Frost's suggestion while he was a professor at Middlebury. Rte-125 ends a few miles on at Rte-100 and Hancock, where you can continue north into the Mad River Valley.

★ **Middlebury Inn** 14 Court Square ☎ 802 388 4961, Ⓦ middleburyinn.com. Open since 1827, with 75 rooms blending modern amenities with a late nineteenth-century style, a porch with rocking chairs, a working 1926 elevator and a fine restaurant. **$139**

Waybury Inn 457 East Main St (Rte-125) ☎ 802 388 4015, Ⓦ wayburyinn.com. Sitcom junkies will want to check out this small 1810 inn, whose exterior was used on the 1980s US TV show *Newhart*. The relationship with the show ends there, but there are thirteen comfortable, well-kept rooms inside with free wi-fi and plenty of antique touches: think deep clawfoot tubs. **$125**

EATING AND DRINKING

Fire and Ice 26 Seymour St ☎ 802 388 7166, Ⓦ fireandicerestaurant.com. Cavernous steak and seafood restaurant, with a massive salad bar and enough memorabilia to fill a museum. The centrepiece is a 22ft motorboat from the 1920s. Mon–Thurs 5–9.30pm, Fri & Sat noon–9.30pm, Sun 1–9pm.

Green Peppers 10 Washington St ☎ 802 388 3164, Ⓦ greenpeppersrestaurant.com. Serves cheap pasta (from $5.75) and the best brick-oven pizza in town; slices are $3.50, special 10-inch pizzas $9.75 and up. Mon–Thurs & Sun 10.30am–9pm, Fri & Sat 10.30am–10pm.

Jackson's On the River 7 Bakery Lane ☎ 802 388 4182, Ⓦ jacksonsontheriver.com. Despite the clapboard exterior, this is more of a chic urban bistro, with sleek interior, extensive menu of salads, burgers and sandwiches, and views of the creek. Sun & Mon–Thurs 11.30am–9pm, Fri & Sat 11.30am–10pm.

Morgan's Tavern Middlebury Inn, 14 Court Square ☎ 802 388 4961, Ⓦ middleburyinn.com. If you're in the mood for a hearty meal, check out this posh restaurant, where grilled buffalo and pan-fried monkfish grace the menu (main courses $17–25). Mon & Tues 11am–2pm, Wed–Sun 11am–2pm & 5.30–8.30pm.

Sama's Café 54 College St ☎ 802 388 6408, Ⓦ samascafe.com. Cool, laid-back place, offering wholesome wraps ($6.50), wood-fired pizzas (from $13) and spicy falafel ($6). Free wi-fi. Mon–Fri 7.30am–7.30pm, Sat 8am–7.30pm, Sun 8am–5pm.

SHOPPING

Danforth Pewter 52 Seymour St ☎ 1 800 222 3142, Ⓦ danforthpewter.com. Founded in 1975, selling quality handcrafted pewter (tin alloy). View the workshop (Mon–Fri 10am–4pm) before perusing the gift store. Mon–Sat 10am–6pm, Sun 11am–4pm.

Middlebury Chocolates 52 Main St ☎ 802 349 1510, Ⓦ middleburychocolates.com. Sumptuous fair-trade chocolate, the cacao roasted, ground, conched and tempered on a marble slab in nearby Vergennes. Mon–Sat 10am–3pm.

Middlebury Mountaineer 2 Park St ☎ 1 877 611 7802, Ⓦ mmvt.com. All your outdoor needs taken care of, and a good source of camping information, fishing reports, condition of local trails and rental information. Mon–Fri 10am–5.30pm, Sat 10am–5pm, Sun 11am–4pm.

Otter Creek Used Books 20 Main St ☎ 802 388 3241, Ⓦ ottercreekusedbooks.com. Great independent store for secondhand books. Mon–Sat 10am–5pm.

Vermont Craft Center at Frog Hollow 1 Mill St ☎ 802 388 3177, Ⓦ froghollow.org. This bright space showcases

high-quality crafts from all over the state. Mon–Sat 10am–5.30pm, Sun noon–5pm.
Vermont Folklife Center Heritage Shop 88 Main St ☎ 802 388 4964, ⦿ vermontfolklifecenter.org. Sells the work of more than 25 contemporary Vermont folk artists: everything from whirligigs and handmade quilts to Native American sweetgrass and brown ash baskets. Tues–Sat 10am–5pm.

Mad River Valley

From the intersection with Rte-125, Rte-100 runs 33 miles north to Waterbury and I-89 via the untrammelled ski resorts of the **Mad River Valley**. A couple of miles beyond the town of **Warren** is the turning to **Sugarbush Resort** (☎ 802 583 6300, ⦿ sugarbush .com), with 115 trails (lift tickets $75) and year-round activities. At **Irasville**, Rte-17 leads five miles west to **Mad River Glen** (lift tickets $66 Sat & Sun, $45 Mon–Fri; ☎ 802 496 3551, ⦿ madriverglen.com), one of the least spoilt ski resorts in North America, with narrow, unforgiving trails that look pretty much as they did when they were cut fifty years ago. In keeping with tradition, no snowboards are allowed here, although **Telemark skiing** is promoted aggressively. There are 44 trails, of which nearly half are considered suitable for expert skiers.

Irasville blurs into **Waitsfield**, a good base for the area, with plenty of accommodation, stores and places to eat; it's also just twelve miles off the interstate. You can go **horseriding** at the **Vermont Icelandic Horse Farm** ($50 for 1hr; ☎ 802 496 7141, ⦿ icelandichorses.com), in an extremely tranquil location on North Fayston Road off Rte-100 a few miles north of Waitsfield. As well as day-rides, they offer two- to five-day treks stopping at country inns (May–Nov; rates start at $600).

ARRIVAL AND INFORMATION
MAD RIVER VALLEY

By bus During ski season Mad River Valley Transit (☎ 802 496 7433) has a free shuttle service from Waitsfield to Warren and the ski resorts, and runs buses to Montpelier ($2). To get to Waitsfield from Waterbury you'll have to take a taxi (around $45; try Mad Cab, ☎ 802 793 2320).

By car You really need a car to explore the Mad River Valley, especially in the summer.
Mad River Valley Visitor Center Rte-100 at the north end of Waitsfield's Main Street (Mon–Fri 8.30am–6pm; ☎ 802 496 3409, ⦿ madrivervalley.com).

ACCOMMODATION

1824 House 2150 Main St, Waitsfield ☎ 802 496 7555, ⦿ 1824house.com. A rustic ex-farmhouse inn with eight rooms dressed in a simple but crisp and contemporary style – not the classic Victoriana you might expect. The three-course breakfasts and dinners are real treats. **$140**
Mad River Inn 243 Tremblay Rd, off Rte-100 north of Waitsfield ☎ 802 496 7900, ⦿ madriverinn.com. Built c.1860, this lovely Victorian features laidback, friendly

owners and nine period rooms with hardwood floors, updated with flat-screen TVs and air-conditioning. **$130**
Slide Brook Lodge 3180 German Flats Rd, Warren ☎ 802 583 2202, ⦿ slidebrooklodge.com. Fun and cheapish wooden ski lodge one mile from Sugarbush Resort, perfect for anyone who likes to spend their days out on the slopes and their nights socializing in the bar (it can be a little noisy in the evenings). Shared bathroom **$80**, en-suite **$120**

EATING AND DRINKING

★ **Common Man** 3209 German Flats Rd, Warren ☎ 802 583 2800, ⦿ CommonManRestaurant.com. This beautifully renovated mid-1800s barn makes for a classic Vermont dining experience, with a menu based on locally-sourced, seasonal produce. Reservations strongly recommended. Tues–Sat 6–10pm.

John Egan's Big World Pub & Grill Junction of routes 17 and 100, Irasville ☎ 802 496 3033. Has an eclectic menu (rotisserie chicken, phad Thai, lamb, Hungarian goulash), which is well executed in a friendly ski-lodge atmosphere. Daily 5–9.30pm.

Waterbury

Few people paid much attention to **WATERBURY** before 1986, but since ageing hippies Ben Cohen and Jerry Greenfield opened **Ben & Jerry's Ice Cream Factory** here in that year, the city has been home to the number-one tourist destination in Vermont. There's not really much else to see in Waterbury; your best bet is to trawl the **culinary outlet shops** clustered along Rte-100, many of which offer free samples.

Ben & Jerry's Ice Cream Factory

1281 Waterbury-Stowe Rd (Rte-100) • Tours every 30min daily: July to mid-Aug 9am–8pm; mid-Aug to late Oct 9am–6pm; late Oct to June 10am–5pm; store and "scoop shop" close 1hr later • $3, children (under 12 years) free • ☎ 802 882 1240, ⓦ benjerry.com

The **Ben & Jerry's** ice cream empire, which began in 1978 as a stand at the front of a Burlington gas station, is nestled one mile north of I-89 in the village of Waterbury Center, on the way up to Stowe. The brand's rabid fans include not only those with a sweet tooth, but believers in its earth-friendly philosophy: the company has a three-part mission statement, which gives social, environmental and financial benefits equal importance. The two founders are long retired from day-to-day involvement, and corporate giant Unilever bought the company in 2000, but to its credit has maintained the philosophy and family-like ethos. Half-hour tours run by friendly locals feature a short film on the collaborators' early days, then head into the production factory where (on weekdays) machines turn cream, sugar and other natural ingredients into more than fifty flavours. Afterwards, you get a free mini-scoop of the stuff – you can buy more at the gift shop and ice cream counter outside ($3–4), while absorbing the fact that every employee gets to take a free pint of ice cream home every day (if they want it).

Cold Hollow Cider Mill

3600 Waterbury-Stowe Rd (Rte-100) • Daily 8am–6pm • Free • ☎ 1 800 327 7537, ⓦ coldhollow.com

Visit **Cold Hollow Cider Mill**, soaked in the heavenly aroma of apples and the mill's famed **cider doughnuts**, to see how cider is pressed from local McIntosh apples (two to four days a week in the summer; seven days a week beginning in early September). The shop is open year-round, selling all manner of cider products, cheeses and maple syrup. Overseas visitors should note that in North America "cider" is usually non-alcoholic, unfermented apple juice.

Green Mountain Coffee Visitor Center & Café

1 Rotarian Place, Waterbury • Daily 7am–6pm • Suggested donation $1 • ☎ 1 877 879 2326, ⓦ waterburystation.com

If you've been in Vermont for a while you'll be used to seeing the Green Mountain Coffee logo everywhere from gas stations to top hotels. The **Green Mountain Coffee Visitor Center & Café**, housed in Waterbury's old train station, is where this top-notch blend is put together, with a small exhibition on the process, a gift shop and the chance to sample the products.

ARRIVAL AND INFORMATION
WATERBURY

By train Amtrak trains pull into downtown Waterbury station at US-2 and Park Row – once in the morning heading south, and once in the evening heading north.

Tourist information For general information, check the Waterbury Tourism Council website (ⓦ waterbury.org).

ACCOMMODATION

★ **Grunberg Haus** 94 Pine St (Rte-100) ☎ 1 800 800 7760, ⓦ grunberghaus.com. Austrian-themed woodsy A-frame with great breakfasts (featuring legendary ricotta French toast) and reasonable rates; there's no TV or radio (and mobile phone signals are rare), but they do have wi-fi. **$95**

Old Stagecoach Inn 18 N Main St ☎ 1 800 262 2206, ⓦ oldstagecoach.com. Ex-tavern and stagecoach stop built in 1826, featuring eleven individually styled rooms – most stay true to the Victorian roots of the house, with antiques, old-fashioned quilts and carved wooden beds. Free wi-fi. **$120**

EATING AND DRINKING

★ **The Alchemist** 23 S Main St ☎ 802 244 4120, ⓦ alchemistbeer.com. Serves its own brews along with panini, pizzas and somewhat superior pub food like house-smoked pork sandwiches and blackened tofu burrito. Mon–Thurs 4pm–midnight, Fri–Sun 3pm–1am.

Arvad's Grill & Pub 3 S Main St ☎ 802 244 8973, ⓦ arvads.com. Fresh grill fare and what the owners call "upscale comfort food": think bacon cheddar potato skins ($8.99) and jalapeno mac and cheese ($14.99), washed down with fine pints of Vermont microbrews. Daily 11am–11pm.

SHOPPING

Cabot Annex Store 2657 Waterbury-Stowe Rd ☎ 802 244 6334. Great outlet store, where you can taste several varieties of the well-known Vermont cheddar cheese (see p.381). Daily 9am–6pm.

Lake Champlain Chocolates 2657 Waterbury-Stowe Rd ☎ 802 241 4150. Chocolate outlet for the Burlington outfit, selling cheaper "seconds" as well as the regular catalogue – also free samples. Daily 9–6pm.

Stowe and around

Unlike most of Vermont's resort towns, there is still a beautiful nineteenth-century village at the heart of **STOWE**, with its white-spired meeting house and town green. Though it has been a popular summer destination since before the Civil War, what really put the town on the map was the arrival in 1941, of the **Von Trapp family** inspiration for *The Sound of Music*. After fleeing Nazi-occupied Austria, they established a lodge here – since burned down – where Maria Von Trapp held singing camps (a rebuilt lodge and restaurant have taken its place). While most of historic Stowe village lies along Rte-100 (Main St), Rte-108 (Mountain Rd) is Stowe's primary thoroughfare, stretching from the main village on Rte-100 up to the ski areas, and on through the mountain gap known as **Smugglers' Notch**. Though Mountain Road is swamped with malls, equipment stores and condominium complexes, the setting remains spectacular, in the shadow of Vermont's highest mountain, the 4393ft **Mount Mansfield**.

Vermont Ski Museum

1 Main St • Wed–Mon noon–5pm • $3 • ☎ 802 253 9911, ⓦ vermontskimuseum.org

Housed in the 1818 clapboard Old Town Hall, the modest **Vermont Ski Museum** charts the history of skiing in the state, with a huge collection of vintage ski equipment, special exhibits on the **10th Mountain Division** (in which 260 Vermonters served in World War II), and a Hall of Fame.

Stowe Mountain Resort

5781 Mountain Rd (Rte-108) • Winter (Nov–March) daily 8am–4pm • Lift tickets $84–89/day • ☎ 802 253 3000, ⓦ stowe.com

Alpine experts hotly debate whether the **Stowe Mountain Resort** is still the "ski capital of the east", a distinction it clearly held until Killington and other eastern ski centres began to challenge its supremacy a decade or so ago. Regardless, it's an excellent mountain, and its popularity remains intact, as anyone who has driven through Stowe on winter weekends can confirm. There are 48 well-kept trails spread over two ski areas, **Mount Mansfield** and **Spruce Peak**, with excellent options for skiers of every level. In the **summer**, there's an alpine slide ($21), bungee trampolines ($27), a climbing wall

---

SUMMER IN STOWE

In summer, when the crowds thin out considerably, Stowe's cross-country skiing trails double as **mountain-bike routes**, and the Stowe Mountain Bike Club (☎ 802 253 1947, ⓦ stowemtnbike.com) sponsors group rides several times a week. They also supply a list of rental outfits, including AJ's Ski & Sports, 350 Mountain Rd (bikes from $38/day; ☎ 802 253 4593, ⓦ ajssports.com). Nearby streams and small rivers offer ample opportunity for **canoeing** and **kayaking**: Umiak Outdoor Outfitters, 849 S Main St (☎ 802 253 2317, ⓦ umiak .com), gives tours on the gentle Lamoille River (from $49) and rents full sets of equipment ($30 for 2hr) at Waterbury Reservoir. **Stowe Mountain Resort** also offers a full roster of summer activities (see above).

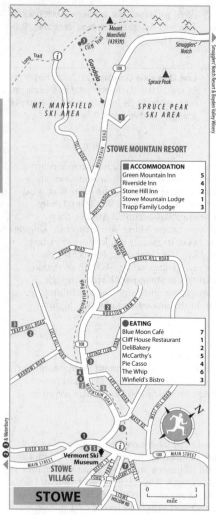

($27) and inflatable obstacle course ($21). Day passes are $76.

Mount Mansfield

Rte-108 • Gondola Skyride mid-June to mid-Oct daily 10am–4.30pm • $18, $24 round-trip • ☎ 802 253 7311, ⓦ stowe.com

Ascending to the peak of **Mount Mansfield**, the highest point in Vermont, is a challenge no matter how you do it, but the rewards are dizzying views all the way to Canada. Weather permitting, the easiest approach is to drive up the **Toll Road**, a winding 4.5-mile ascent of mostly dirt track that begins seven miles up from Stowe village on Mountain Road (June to mid-Oct daily 9am–4pm; $26 per car). Originally built in the 1850s as a carriage road, the track ends at a tiny **visitor centre** (3850ft), manned by Green Mountain Club volunteers. From here it's a short scramble to the ridge that runs along the mountain top, and around 1.5 miles to the peak, known as "the Chin" (4393ft), following the Long Trail. Alternatively, you can take the **Gondola Skyride**, which affords jaw-dropping views and ends at **Cliff House** (3660ft). Hikers can continue from here along a short but extremely strenuous 0.7-mile path up to the Chin.

If you've got the stamina, the most rewarding approach is to hike the full way to the summit; you can simply follow the Toll Road or take the steep, steady, 4.7-mile section of the Long Trail from Rte-108, halfway through Smugglers' Notch. Serious hikers should first visit the new **GMC Visitor Center** at 4711 Waterbury-Stowe Rd (Rte-100), back towards Waterbury (mid-May to mid-Oct daily 9am–5pm; rest of year Mon–Fri 9am–5pm; ☎ 802 244 7037, ⓦ greenmountainclub.org) – it's around one mile north of Cold Hollow Cider Mill (see p.360).

Smugglers' Notch State Park

6443 Mountain Rd (Rte-108) • Mid-May to mid-Oct sunrise–sunset • $3 • ☎ 802 253 4014, ⓦ vtstateparks.com

Beyond Stowe Mountain Resort lies **Smugglers' Notch State Park**, named after the illegal trading that took place here after Jefferson's 1807 Embargo Act banned exports to Canada. The road narrows considerably at the pass itself, hemmed in by 1000ft

cliffs, and is generally closed in winter. Trails lead off from the park all over the mountains, though the easiest is the short stroll down to the **Bingham Falls**, a modest series of serene rocky cascades. You can pitch a tent at the park **campsite** for $18–20.

Smugglers' Notch Resort

4323 Rte-108 South · Lift tickets $66/day · ☎ 802 644 8851, ⓦ smuggs.com

A less crowded alternative to Stowe is the family-oriented **Smugglers' Notch Resort**, on the other side of the pass, which actually has more trails (78, with about twenty "expert" runs). In summer, there are eight heated outdoor pools, four waterslides, a **zipline canopy tour** and numerous other activities, including special programmes for children.

Boyden Valley Winery

64 Rte-104, at Rte-15, Cambridge · May–Dec daily 10am–5pm; Jan–April Fri–Sun 10am–5pm · Free · ☎ 802 664 8151, ⓦ boydenvalley.com

Seven miles north of Smugglers' Notch, **Boyden Valley Winery** offers tastings ($6 per person for seven wines) of its exceptional fruit wines and Vermont ice wines (a type of dessert wine made from grapes that have been frozen while still on the vine), held in an 1878 carriage barn. Tours run most days at 11.30am and 1pm (free).

Trapp Family Lodge & Brewery

700 Trapp Hill Rd · Free · ☎ 1 800 826 7000, ⓦ trappfamily.com

Even if not staying at the **Trapp Family Lodge**, fans will especially appreciate a visit to the alpine-like grounds, Austrian-style bakery (see opposite) and gift shop, where *Sound of Music* memorabilia abounds. Having escaped the Nazis, the Trapps opened the lodge in 1950 – Maria Von Trapp died in 1987, but the family still owns the resort. **History tours** (often led by a family member) run most Tuesdays, Thursdays, Saturdays and Sundays ($10 per guest, $15 per non-guest). The **Trapp Family Brewery** opened in 2010, producing some 60,000 or so gallons of lager a year in the lower level of the *DeliBakery* (see opposite).

ARRIVAL AND INFORMATION

STOWE

By bus Green Mountain Transit Agency (☎ 802 223 7287, ⓦ gmtaride.org) provides services year-round from Montpelier and Burlington to Waterbury, from where you can take connecting buses up to Stowe ($2). Once here, you can use the free Mountain Road Shuttle that runs up and down Mountain Road, between the Town Hall in Stowe Village and the base of the ski areas (ski season only).

Visitor center 51 Main St, at Depot Rd (summer Mon–Sat 9am–8pm, Sun 9am–5pm; other months hours vary; ☎ 802 253 7321, ⓦ gostowe.com).

ACCOMMODATION

Multiple accommodation options line **Mountain Road**, ranging from luxury hotels to modest B&Bs; as always, the most convenient (and sought after) lie inside the resort itself. Make sure you reserve ahead in winter.

★ **Green Mountain Inn** 1 Main St ☎ 802 253 7301, ⓦ greenmountaininn.com. Gorgeous hotel built in 1833, centrally located in the village and amply outfitted – rooms range from opulent suites with jacuzzi tubs and fireplaces to plush rooms in the main inn. Offers two good restaurants, complimentary health club, free tea and cookies (daily 4–5pm) and a heated pool. **$159**

Riverside Inn 1965 Mountain Rd ☎ 802 253 4217, ⓦ rivinn.com. Modest, basic rooms in converted farmhouse with all the essentials, though not much more, and slightly better motel rooms with cable TV, DVD, fridge and microwave. One of the better-value options in town. **$109**

Stone Hill Inn 56 Turner Mill Lane (5.2 miles up Mountain Rd) ☎ 802 253 2062, ⓦ stonehillinn.com. Extremely popular luxury choice, despite the high cost (book ahead). This rustic-looking but modern complex was built exclusively for couples in 1998; each room boasts king beds, fireside two-person jacuzzis and flat-screen TVs. **$345**

★ **Stowe Mountain Lodge** 7412 Mountain Rd ☎ 802 253 3560, ⓦ stowemountainlodge.com. The pride of Stowe Mountain Resort opened in 2008 right next to the Spruce Peak ski area, offering real luxury; floor-to-ceiling windows make the most of the scenery, while rooms are tricked out in designer furnishings and contemporary art. TVs and stone-frame fireplaces are standard. **$199**

★ **Trapp Family Lodge** 42 Trapp Hill Rd ☎802 253 8511, ⓦtrappfamily.com. Some 2700 acres of Austrian-themed ski resort (as fancy as it is expensive) on the site of the original Trapp family house, also the first cross-country ski centre in America. Rates include cross-country ski passes and access to skiing and hiking trails. **$270**

CAMPING

It is possible to camp in Smugglers' Notch State Park from May to October (see p.362).

Gold Brook Campground 1900 Waterbury Rd ☎802 253 7683). The closest year-round campground, two miles south of town on Rte-100. **$26**

EATING

★ **Blue Moon Cafe** 35 School St, Stowe Village ☎802 253 7006, ⓦbluemoonstowe.com. Inventive, expensive New American fare featuring local game (braised venison and the like) and seafood; probably Stowe's best all-round dining choice. Good wine list. Tues–Sun 6–9pm.

Cliff House Restaurant On Mount Mansfield, at the Gondola Summit (3625ft) ☎802 253 3665, ⓦstowe .com. Fine dining near the highest point in the state, featuring regional cuisine and sandwiches ($16). 11am–2.30pm when the Gondola is in operation (winter only), and occasionally on Sat for dinner.

DeliBakery 42 Trapp Hill Rd ☎802 253 5705, ⓦtrappfamily.com. The Trapp family bakery serves up Austrian *wurst*, meat and cheese boards and all sorts of pastries from $6. Daily 7am–9pm.

★ **McCarthy's** 2043 Mountain Rd ☎802 253 8626. Irish-themed joint, but especially noted for its great heaping breakfasts, which are one hundred percent American; Mansfield Valley eggs, Vermont maple bacon,

corned beef hash and thick pancakes (plates $6–9). It's been a local favourite since 1974 – expect long lines at the weekend. Mon–Sat 9am–6pm, Sun 10am–6pm.

Pie Casso 1899 Mountain Rd ☎802 253 4411, ⓦpiecasso.com. New York-style pizzas from $13, as well as plenty of pastas and zesty wings, served up in a trendy dining room – more lounge bar than *Pizza Hut*. Live music at the weekends. Mon–Thurs & Sun at the 11am–10pm, Fri & Sat 11am–11pm.

★ **The Whip** 1 Main St ☎802 253 7301, ⓦgreenmountaininn.com. Best fine dining in town – duck cooked to absolute perfection, traditional turkey dinners piling off the plate, reasonably priced wines. Mon–Sat 11.30am–9.30pm, Sun 10.30am–9.30pm.

Winfield's Bistro 1746 Mountain Rd ☎802 253 7355, ⓦstoweflake.com. The liberal use of ingredients like "pecan dust" and "tawny port syrup" on the menu here tips this as a creative New American bistro (and also as "expensive"). Reservations recommended. Wed–Sun 6–9.30pm.

DRINKING AND NIGHTLIFE

Matterhorn 4969 Mountain Rd ☎802 253 8198, ⓦmatterhornbar.com. The region's best bands have been coming here for years – you can enjoy the live music in the nightclub on weekends most of the year, or listen from the downstairs wood-panelled dining room (specializing in, oddly, pizzas and sushi). Daily 5pm–close.

Rusty Nail 1190 Mountain Rd ☎802 253 6245, ⓦrustynailbar.com. Rotating DJs and live jazz on Thursdays fill the bill, but the *Nail* is also a sports bar with a

20ft TV screen. Check out the website for the place's entertaining history. Sun & Wed–Fri noon–10pm, Fri & Sat noon–2am.

Shed Restaurant and Brewery Pub 1859 Mountain Rd ☎802 253 4364. Hearty American fare – the speciality is the ample "Mighty Shed Burger" – but best known for the bar, which has live bands every Wednesday (no cover), from jazz to rock and country. Mon–Thurs & Sun 11.30am–10pm, Fri & Sat 11.30am–11pm.

SHOPPING

Fly Rod Shop 2703 Waterbury Rd ☎802 253 7346, ⓦflyrodshop.com. Not just fishing gear, but "Family Gone Fishing" programmes including half a day of instruction, gear and bait. Mon–Sat 9am–6pm, Sun 10am–5pm.

Laughing Moon Chocolates 78 S Main St ☎802 253 9591, ⓦlaughingmoonchocolates.com. Local

chocolatier producing delicate batches of fine choc and salted caramels. Daily 9am–6pm.

Umiak Outfitters 849 S Main St ☎802 253 2317, ⓦumiak.com. Snowshoe rentals, tours, canoe rentals and river trips. Daily 9am–6pm.

Montpelier and around

With fewer than ten thousand residents, **MONTPELIER** (mont-PEEL-yer), in a beautiful valley on the Winooski and North Branch rivers, is the smallest state capital in the country. Around the **Vermont State House**, the vital downtown area is lined exclusively

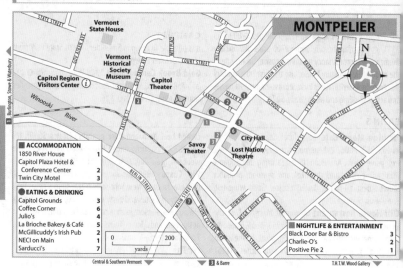

ACCOMMODATION
1850 River House	1
Capitol Plaza Hotel & Conference Center	2
Twin City Motel	3

EATING & DRINKING
Capitol Grounds	3
Coffee Corner	6
Julio's	4
La Brioche Bakery & Café	5
McGillicuddy's Irish Pub	2
NECI on Main	1
Sarducci's	7

NIGHTLIFE & ENTERTAINMENT
Black Door Bar & Bistro	3
Charlie-O's	2
Positive Pie 2	1

with nineteenth-century buildings and boasts a number of fine restaurants, museums and theatres. Despite its considerable charms, the city still bears a low tourist profile, and it is this lack of commercialism that makes Montpelier a refreshing counterpoint to the cultivated rural quaintness that pervades the rest of the state.

Vermont State House

115 State St • Mon–Fri 7.30am–4.15pm, also Sat 11am–3pm July–Oct • Free; free guided tours of the interior every 30min July to mid-Oct Mon–Fri 10am–3.30pm, Sat 11am–2.30pm • ☎ 802 828 2228, ⓦ vtstatehouse.org

The city's most visible landmark, the gilt-domed **Vermont State House**, rises high above the city centre on State Street. Most visitors just stroll around the impeccably kept exterior gardens, particularly brilliant during the autumn, and photograph the statue of **Ethan Allen** guarding the front doors – though the statue of Vermont's first governor **Thomas Chittenden**, to the left of the main entrance, is more striking. It's well worth taking a stroll through the vaulted marble hallways inside, however, especially up to the second floor, where you'll find a vast painting by Julian Scott representing the Battle of Cedar Creek, a Civil War skirmish in which Vermonters played a pivotal role. You can normally also have a peek inside the elegant Governor's Office, Senate Chamber and Representatives' Hall.

Vermont Historical Society Museum

109 State St • Tues–Sat 10am–4pm • $5 • ☎ 802 828 2291, ⓦ vermonthistory.org

The entirety of Vermont's history from the 1600s on is chronicled in the **Vermont Historical Society Museum**. The "Freedom and Unity" exhibition highlights the evolution of the state's unique character, from early settlement to the present day, with some thoughtful displays on the influence of Native Americans, the independence efforts of the Green Mountain Boys, and videos dramatizing local debates on the historically explosive issues of slavery, women's suffrage and gay civil unions.

T.W. Wood Gallery

36 College St • Tues–Sun noon–4pm • Free • ☎ 802 828 8743, ⓦ twwoodgallery.org

East of downtown, in the Vermont College campus, lies the small but distinguished **T.W. Wood Gallery**, showcasing local painter T.W. Wood's fascinating depictions of everyday New England life in the nineteenth century. Other displays include experimental American folk art and photos created for the Work Projects Administration between 1936 and 1943.

Morse Farm Maple Sugarworks

1168 County Rd • Daily 8am–8pm • Free • ☎ 1 800 242 2740, ⓦ morsefarm.com

It's worth checking out **Morse Farm Maple Sugarworks**, 2.7 miles from downtown Montpelier, one of the most traditional maple syrup farms in the state. Free tours and tastings provide an illuminating introduction to their products, best experienced in the early spring, when maple sugaring takes place. You can also check out their small outdoor **Vermont farm life museum**, sprinkled with slightly creepy carved characters created by Burr Morse.

Rock of Ages Quarry

560 Graniteville Rd, Rte-63, Graniteville (I-89, exit 6) • Mid-May to mid-Sept Mon–Sat 9am–5pm; mid-Sept to Oct daily 9am–5pm • Free; $5 for tours • ☎ 802 476 3119, ⓦ rockofages.com

Home to the world's largest deep-hole (600ft) granite mine, the **Rock of Ages Quarry**, seven miles southeast of Montpelier near the town of Barre, is testimony to the once great **granite industry** in this part of the state. You can check out the **visitor centre** (which shows videos about the mine, founded in 1885), and have a look inside the cavernous hangar-like workshop (Mon–Fri 8am–3.30pm), where stone is cut, ground and polished, all for free. It's worth shelling out a few bucks for the narrated **Quarry Tour** (40min) that takes you to the far more impressive fifty-acre working quarries, the top of the mind-blowing hole itself, and through the manufacturing centres where artisans busy themselves making fleets of **tombstones**. If this piques your interest, check out **Hope Cemetery**, just north of Barre town centre on Rte-14. While the city's stonecutters lived modestly, they knew how to die in grand style, commemorating themselves and their families with massive, elaborately wrought granite tombstones up to 10ft in height.

ARRIVAL AND INFORMATION

By train Montpelier is served by Amtrak's *Vermonter* line; the station lies two miles west of downtown near I-89, at Junction Road and Short Road. There is no public transport; you'll need to take a taxi into town.

By bus Greyhound buses from Burlington currently stop outside Bafitos, 28 Main St. Green Mountain Transit Agency runs buses (☎ 802 223 7287) to Waterbury ($2), the Mad River Valley ($2), St Johnsbury ($2) and Burlington ($4).

MONTPELIER AND AROUND

By car Montpelier is thirteen miles east of Waterbury via I-89. You should have no problem parking; try the free car park behind the Visitors Center (see below) or Blanchard Court, behind City Hall on Main Street (35 cents/hr).

Capitol Region Visitors Center Opposite the State House at 134 State St (Mon–Fri 6am–5pm, Sat & Sun 10am–5pm; ☎ 802 828 5981, ⓦ vermontvacation.com). Offers plenty of information on local and state-wide attractions.

ACCOMMODATION

1850 River House 7 Church St, Middlesex (north of Montpelier, off I-89) ☎ 802 229 0466, ⓦ 1850riverhouse.com. The top B&B choice in the area, with a hospitable host, one three-room suite, a welcome bottle of wine and some quirky touches: check out the stuffed bear outside. Cash only (skip breakfast and the rate is cheaper). **$125**

Capitol Plaza Hotel and Conference Center 100 State St ☎ 802 274 5252, ⓦ capitolplaza.com. The best hotel in downtown Montpelier offers comfortable and spacious digs across from the Art Deco Capitol Theatre, though note that you are paying a premium for the location. **$152**

Twin City Motel 1537 Barre–Montpelier Rd (Rte-302), just off I-89, exit 7 ☎ 802 476 3104, ⓦ twincitymotel .com. Probably the pick of the several old-fashioned motels southeast of town on the Barre–Montpelier Road. Rooms have the usual motel amenities, like cable TV, fridge and telephone, and the price is hard to beat. **$75**

CAMPING

Green Valley Campground 1498 Rte-2 ☎ 802 223 6217. A riverside campsite, northeast of town at the intersection of Rte-2 and Rte-302. Offers 35 pitches, showers, convenience store and laundry room. Open May–Oct. **$19**

6

MAPLE SYRUP AND SUGAR ON SNOW

Though the muddy, unpredictable and seemingly endless weeks of March in New England have few virtues, you can count on two constants: the proximity of spring and **maple syrup**. Vermont is the largest producer of maple syrup in the US, boasting small, traditional sugarhouses deep in the forest as well as large farms using the latest technology. Surrounded by ancient maples and using time-honoured methods, these low-key, often family-owned producers generally welcome visitors, give tours and sell everything from maple-coated nuts to maple lollipops and jelly, as well as high-quality maple syrup – Morse Farm (see p.367) and Sugarbush Farm (see p.352) are two of the best. One delectable treat to look out for in winter is "**sugar on snow**", where boiling hot syrup is poured onto buckets of clean snow and eaten with doughnuts, sour dill pickles and coffee.

The season starts as early as February in southern Vermont and lasts into April in the north, but many sugarhouses are open year-round. For a full list of over forty producers, contact the Vermont Maple Sugar Makers' Association (☎802 763 7435, ⓦvermontmaple.org), which also organizes the annual **Vermont Maple Open House Weekend** each March.

EATING AND DRINKING

Students from the local **New England Culinary Institute** (NECI) have lent their expertise to Montpelier's dining scene, resulting in a number of alluring, experimental restaurants. The area is blissfully resistant to fast food – it's the only state capital without a *McDonald's*, though a *Subway* and a *Quizno's* have found their way to Main Street.

Capitol Grounds 27 State St ☎802 223 7800, ⓦcapitolgrounds.com. The wooden interior of this former bank invites casual lounging over your morning coffee, which you can order from the genuinely friendly staff in four sizes: Conservative, Moderate, Liberal and Radical (20oz). Good tea selection as well. Mon–Fri 6.15am–5.30pm, Sat 7am–5.30pm, Sun 8am–10pm.

Coffee Corner 83 Main St, at State St ☎802 229 9060, ⓦcoffeecorner.com. A Montpelier standard for over sixty years, where you can scarf down cheap diner food at formica tables or rub elbows with Vermont's political potentates at the lunch counter. Daily 6.30am–3pm.

Julio's 54 State St, ☎802 229 9348, ⓦjulioscantina.com. Pretty good Tex-Mex for this area of New England, including cheap, filling burrito and enchilada dishes and zippy margaritas ($2.50 specials). Mon–Thurs & Sun 11.30am–11pm, Fri & Sat 11.30am–midnight.

★ **La Brioche Bakery & Cafe** 89 Main St ☎802 229 0443, ⓦneci.edu/labrioche. Cheerful, well-designed bakery run by NECI. The "1/2 Bag Lunch" will get you half a

sandwich, a small but interesting salad or soup and a cookie (try the "Vermont Crunchy": a peanut butter oatmeal cookie with chocolate chips and nuts). Mon–Fri 6.30am–5pm, Sat 7am–5pm, Sun 8am–2pm.

McGillicuddy's Irish Pub 14 Langdon St ☎802 223 2721, ⓦmcgillicuddysvt.com. Standard bar fare, most notable for its spicy hot wings and a wide selection of microbrews. Draws a lively, younger crowd and gets loud and busy on weekends. Daily 11am–2am.

NECI on Main 118 Main St ☎802 223 3188. The delectable, inventive specialities from NECI alumni range from $13–20 for dinner; American grill fare and shellfish are standouts. Tues–Sat 11.30am–9pm, Sun 10am–2pm.

Sarducci's 3 Main St ☎802 223 0229, ⓦsarduccis.com. Long-established, Tuscan-inspired trattoria next to the river. Pasta dishes will set you back around $9–10, or you could opt for a house speciality such as wood-roasted salmon in a white wine sauce ($17.99). Mon–Thurs 11.30am–9pm, Fri & Sat 11.30am–9.30pm, Sun 4.30–9pm.

NIGHTLIFE AND ENTERTAINMENT

Black Door Bar & Bistro 44 Main St ☎802 225 6479. Along with its trendy, moderately expensive bistro fare (mains $17–19), live music (ranging from funky jazz to zydeco) is on offer. Free. Wed–Sat 9pm.

Charlie-O's 70 Main St ☎802 223 6820. Just a tad scruffy in this pleasant city, *Charlie-O's* is simple: a pool table, wood floors and a bar. You can get your rock or blues fix here most weekends. From 2pm daily.

Positive Pie 2 22 State St ☎802 229 0453,

ⓦpositivepie.com. Live hip-hop or groove on weekends make the New York-style pizzas and Sicilian pastas available here that much better. Sometimes a $5 cover. Mon–Thurs & Sun 11.30am–9pm, Fri & Sat 11.30am–10pm.

THEATRES

Lost Nation Theatre City Hall Arts Center on Main Street ☎802 229 0492, ⓦlostnationtheatre.org. The town's main drama venue, where the resident company performs everything from Shakespearean epics through popular musicals to experimental contemporary plays. **Savoy Theatre** 26 Main St ☎802 229 0598, ⓦsavoytheatre.com. Across the street from the Lost Nation Theatre, this tiny venue shows first-rate foreign, classic and independent films. More current releases are screened at the Capitol (☎802 229 0343) on State Street.

Lake Champlain

6

Forming the boundary between Vermont and New York state, 150-mile-long **Lake Champlain** never exceeds twelve miles across at its widest point, though its area of about 490 square miles makes it the sixth largest freshwater lake in the US. The first non-native to see the lake was French explorer **Samuel de Champlain** in 1609, who humbly named it in his own honour. Today the life and soul of the valley is the French Canadian-influenced city of **Burlington**, whose long-standing trade links with Montréal have filled it with elegant nineteenth-century architecture. Within just a few miles of the centre, US-2 leads north onto the supremely rural **Champlain Islands**, covered in meadows and farmlands, while to the south, the **Shelburne Museum** is a sprawling village of historic homes and artefacts, and the **Lake Champlain Maritime Museum** offers the best insights into the history and ecology of the lake itself.

Burlington and around

With a population of around forty thousand, lakeside **BURLINGTON** is the closest Vermont gets to a big city. It's also notable as one of New England's most purely enjoyable destinations – a hip, relaxed fusion of Montréal, eighty miles to the north, and Boston, over two hundred miles southeast. In fact, from its earliest days, Burlington has looked as much to Canada as to the south – shipping connections with the St Lawrence River were far easier than the land routes across the mountains, and the harbour became a major supply centre. Burlington today is the definitive youthful university town. From its waterfront walkways to its lively brewpubs, the city is at once cosmopolitan and pleasantly manageable in scale, with a downtown you can stroll around on foot.

The waterfront

Most visitors' first stop in Burlington is the waterfront; indeed, kayaks seem to be strapped to the roof of every third car. The aptly named **Waterfront Park** stretches a couple of miles along Lake Champlain, with ample greenspaces, gorgeous swing benches, and a popular dog run. At its northern end, **Battery Park** makes a particularly good place to watch the sun go down over the Adirondacks – especially when there's a band playing, as there usually is on summer weekends.

Note, though, there is no boardwalk south of the park, and walking between cruise piers involves following the road or the 12.5-mile **Burlington Waterfront Bike Path** and connected **Island Line Trail**, which trace a former railroad bed and are a good way to see the waterfront and some of the city beaches. The bike path winds along the shoreline all the way north to Colchester, before ending past the end of Mills Point in Mallets Bay. **Local Motion** (mid-May to mid-Oct daily 10am–6pm; $30/day, $50 for two days; ☎802 652 2453, ⓦlocalmotion.org) rents bikes from its home on the path behind Union Station, at 1 Steele St. There are also **cruises** on the lake (see p.372).

ECHO Lake Aquarium and Science Center

1 College St • Daily 10am–5pm • $12.50, children (3–17 years) $9.50 • ☎802 864 1848, ⓦechovermont.org

At the end of College Street is family-favourite **ECHO Lake Aquarium and Science Center**, which affords opportunities to handle all sorts of lake-dwelling creatures. Exhibits throw light on the complex ecosystems in Lake Champlain, home to one of

6

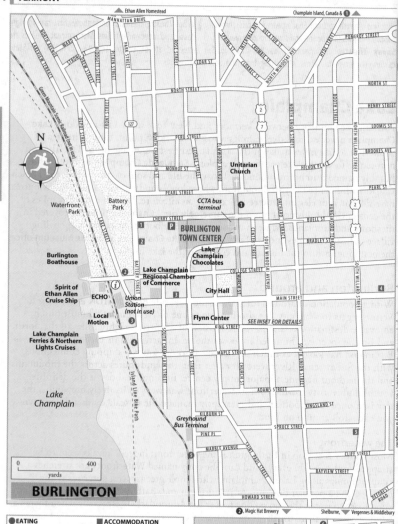

BURLINGTON

0 — 400 yards

● **EATING**		■ **ACCOMMODATION**	
American Flatbread	13	Courtyard Burlington	
Daily Planet	8	Harbor	1
Dobrá Tea Room	7	Hilton Burlington	2
Ice House	3	Lang House on	
Leunig's Bistro	10	Main Street	4
Muddy Waters	15	Sunset House B&B	3
Myer's Bagel Bakery	5	Willard Street Inn	5
Penny Cluse Café	6		
Red Onion	14		
Shanty on the Shore	4	● **NIGHTLIFE &**	
Skinny Pancake	2	**ENTERTAINMENT**	
Sneakers	1	Club Metronome	2
Sweetwaters	11	Nectar's	2
Trattoria Delia	17	Red Square	1
Zabby & Elf's			
Stone Soup	12	● **SHOPS**	
		Burton Snowboards	2
● **DRINKING**		Crow Bookshop	1
Ruben James	16	Lake Champlain	
Vermont Pub and		Chocolates	3
Brewery	9		

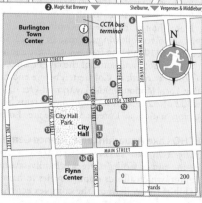

0 — 200 yards

the world's oldest coral reefs and hundreds of species of fish and plants. Special displays focus on frogs, the history of Burlington waterfront and **Champ**, the mythical Loch Ness monster of Lake Champlain. The centre's two very real 40lb lake sturgeon, as well as two gigantic channel catfish, are hand-fed on Tuesdays, Thursdays and Saturdays.

Church Street Marketplace

The **Church Street Marketplace**, a pedestrian shopping mall a few blocks from the waterfront, holds Burlington's remaining old buildings (the area in between is crammed with nondescript modern blocks), including the stately City Hall, a red-brick Victorian. The street is at its busiest at night and on weekend days, both good people-watching times. Check out the excellent **Art Market** (May–Oct Sat 9am–2.30pm), held in City Hall Park (also featuring tempting snack food).

Robert Hull Fleming Museum

61 Colchester Ave • May to early Sept Tues–Fri noon–4pm, Sat & Sun 1–5pm; early Sept to April Tues, Thurs & Fri 9am–4pm, Wed 9am–8pm, Sat & Sun 1–5pm • $5 • ☎ 802 656 2090, ⓦ flemingmuseum.org

College Street leads east from the marketplace to the sleepy campus of the **University of Vermont**, founded in 1791 by Ethan Allen's brother Ira. The university's **Robert Hull Fleming Museum** holds some intriguing European paintings and drawings from the likes of Corot, Dürer, Goya, Hogarth and Rodin, as well as a collection of precious pre-Columbian artefacts from Mexico, Central America and Peru. To catch more art, arrive on the first Friday of each month, when Burlington City Arts sponsors the free **First Friday Artwalk**, which covers more than fifteen downtown galleries (April–Oct; 5–8pm; ☎ 802 865 7166).

Magic Hat Brewing Company

5 Bartlett Bay Rd, South Burlington • Mon–Sat 10am–7pm, Sun noon–5pm • Guided tours hourly: Tues & Wed 3–4pm, Thurs & Fri 2–5pm, Sat 1–5pm, Sun 2–3pm • Free • ☎ 802 658 2739, ⓦ magichat.net

More raucous entertainment can be had at the **Magic Hat Brewing Company**, five minutes' drive south of downtown off Rte-7. The guided tours make the science of beer-making look fun, and the free beer samples enhance the experience even further.

ETHAN ALLEN AND HIS GREEN MOUNTAIN BOYS

Flamboyant and controversial, folk hero **Ethan Allen** (1738–89) typifies the independent ethos Vermont has long been known for, even if he did start out as a Connecticut farmer.

Allen's fame stems from being elected leader of the **Green Mountain Boys** in 1770, a militia created to protect local land rights from New York state officials (see p.328). Shortly thereafter, Allen and other family members formed the Onion River Land Company to speculate on the contested land grants; eventually, the Allens were selling grants purchased at 10 cents an acre for $5 an acre, a pretty profit indeed. In the meantime, Allen and his fellow settlers were developing the area, building roads and establishing a population centre on Burlington Bay.

When war with Britain broke out in 1775, Allen was behind the capture of Fort Ticonderoga, but was apprehended by the Brits in Canada later that year and took little part in the remainder of the Revolutionary War. After his release in 1778 he returned to a now independent Vermont, where his energies were directed more towards ending the old land disputes than the struggle with England.

With the coming of peace in 1783, Ethan Allen began to put together an impressive farm on the Winooski (Onion) River at Burlington, now known as the Ethan Allen Homestead (see p.372), where he settled down to become a philosopher and writer. Allen died in 1789, with Vermont yet to join the Union.

6

Ethan Allen Homestead

1 Ethan Allen Homestead, Rte-127 • Mid-May to mid-Oct Thurs–Mon 10am–4pm • $7 • ☎ 802 865 4556, ⓦ ethanallenhomestead.org

North of Burlington along Rte-127 in **Winooski**, the **Ethan Allen Homestead** is the simple rusty-red clapboard farmhouse in which the Revolutionary War hero spent the last two years of his life (see box, p.371). Allen moved here with his second wife Fanny and family in 1787, intent on living the quiet life of a philosopher-farmer. The house was lived in right up to the 1970s – today the white pine frame is all original, but the interiors have been restored to resemble frontier life in the late eighteenth century.

Though it's a site of great historical significance for Vermonters there's not much to see – two main rooms, and two small ante-rooms – and the place is really brought to life by the guides, who provide historical context as well as enlightening background on almost everything in the house, from the various stages of making linen, to basic cooking utensils. The **visitor centre** has a gift shop and small exhibit on Allen, along with a video and occasional events held in a re-created eighteenth-century tavern.

ARRIVAL AND DEPARTURE

By plane Burlington International Airport (☎ 802 863 1889, ⓦ burlingtonintlairport.com) is a few miles east of downtown along US-2 (bus #12 to downtown runs every 30min 6.30am–10pm; $1.25), with connections from Boston, Chicago, New York City, Washington, DC and several other cities. The visitor information desk is open daily 9am–midnight. Taxis downtown will be around $15.

By train Amtrak's *Vermonter* trains arrive at 29 Railroad Ave, Essex Junction, an inconvenient five miles northeast of town (connecting buses $1.25). Note that the station only opens twice a day (for the two trains) and there is no ticket office.

BURLINGTON AND AROUND

By bus Greyhound buses drop off at 19 Winooski Ave, but the main stop is at the airport, the best place to buy tickets.

By boat Lake Champlain Ferries (☎ 802 864 9804, ⓦ ferries.com) cross the lake to New York state from Burlington (to Port Kent; mid-June to mid-Oct; every 1–2hr; $17.50; 1hr), Charlotte (to Essex; year-round, as ice permits; every 30min; $9.50; 25min), and Grand Isle to Plattsburgh; year-round every 10–15min; $9.50; 12min). All of these rates are one-way for a car and driver; for additional passengers as well as for cyclists and walk-ons the rate ranges from $3.75 to $5.95.

INFORMATION AND TOURS

Lake Champlain Regional Chamber of Commerce 60 Main St (Mid-May to Aug Mon–Fri 8am–5pm, Sat & Sun 9am–5pm; Sept to mid-May Mon–Fri 8am–5pm; ☎ 1 877 686 5253, ⓦ vermont.org).

Boat tours If you're looking to get onto Lake Champlain, on board the convivial *Spirit of Ethan Allen III* (May–Oct; 1hr narrated cruises from $12.10; ☎ 802 862 8300,

ⓦ soea.com), which sets out from the Burlington Boathouse at 1 College St, or *Northern Lights* (1hr 30min $14.80; ☎ 802 864 9669, ⓦ lakechamplaincruises.com), which offers a similar service from the adjacent King Street dock. You can rent sailboats at Winds of Ireland (from $430/day for a Hunter 30; ☎ 802 863 5090, ⓦ windsofireland .net), also in the Burlington Boathouse.

GETTING AROUND

By bus The local CCTA bus ($1.25; ☎ 802 864 0211, ⓦ cctaride.org) connects points all over the downtown area, and travels to the nearby towns of Winooski, Essex and Shelburne. You can get route maps and schedules at the main downtown terminal on the corner of Cherry and Church streets. CCTA also operates a very convenient (free) shuttle along College Street between the University of Vermont and the waterfront, with stops at the Fleming Museum and the Church Street Marketplace (every 15–30min: Mon–Fri

6.30am–7pm; late May to June & Sept to mid-Oct also Sat to Sun 9am–9pm; no services July & Aug).

By bicycle You can rent bikes at Local Motion (see p.369), North Star Sports, 100 Main St (Mon–Fri 10am–7pm, Sat 10am–6pm, Sun noon–5pm; bikes $28/day; ☎ 802 863 3832, ⓦ northstarsportsvt.com), and Skirack, 85 Main St (Mon–Sat 8am–7pm, Sun 11am–5pm; bikes $28/day; ☎ 802 658 3313, ⓦ skirack.com), which also rents skis, snowboards, kayaks and in-line skates.

ACCOMMODATION

The Burlington area has no shortage of chain **motels**, though most of them are removed from the downtown area, along Williston Road (just west along US-2, off I-89, exit 14) and Shelburne Road (south of town along US-7). Downtown, there are several good places to stay within striking distance of the waterfront.

DOWNTOWN

★ **Courtyard Burlington Harbor** 25 Cherry St ☎802 864 4700, ⊛marriott.com. Best hotel downtown, with a fabulous location near the waterfront and newish, luxurious rooms and amenities; buffet breakfast, indoor pool and LCD TVs included. Parking $8/day. **$229**

Hilton Burlington 60 Battery St ☎802 658 6500, ⊛hilton.com. Not quite as plush as the *Courtyard*, the *Hilton* still provides all the requisite amenities, with a few extras (check out the Herman Miller chairs), right on the lake. **$239**

Lang House on Main Street 360 Main St ☎802 652 2500, ⊛langhouse.com. Handsome 1881 Victorian conveniently located between UVM campus and downtown, offering eleven richly furnished period rooms, many with views of Lake Champlain. **$165**

Sunset House B&B 78 Main St ☎802 864 3790, ⊛sunsethousebb.com. A good choice if you enjoy staying in family-run places with homey decor, slightly worn rooms and shared bathrooms. Prime location right in the centre of downtown. **$119**

★ **Willard Street Inn** 349 S Willard St ☎802 651 8710, ⊛willardstreetinn.com. The large rooms at this distinctive home are brilliantly restored (but not frilly). You also get a 24hr pantry, excellent home-made breakfasts and a lush, green, relaxing English garden. **$165**

OUT-OF-TOWN

Bel Aire Motel 111 Shelburne Rd ☎802 863 3116, ⊛belairevt.com. This no frills, old-fashioned roadside motel makes a cheap alternative to the numerous chains in the area, with basic but clean doubles, decent cable TV and free wi-fi. **$94**

Heart of the Village Inn 5347 Shelburne Rd, Shelburne ☎802 985 2800, ⊛heartofthevillage.com. Nine beautifully decorated rooms in a pair of Victorian houses with period antiques and delectable breakfast. Cable TV available on request. **$170**

Inn at Shelburne Farms 1611 Harbor Rd, Shelburne ☎802 985 8498, ⊛shelburnefarms.org/comevisitus /inn. If you fancy staying in something akin to a castle, this is it; a sprawling nineteenth-century mansion facing the lake on the rustic Shelburne Farms estate. Rooms are decorated in a lavish Victorian style – many of the antiques belonged to original owner Lila Vanderbilt Webb. May to mid-Oct. **$165**

CAMPING

Lone Pine Campsite 52 Sunset View Rd, Colchester ☎802 878 5447, ⊛lonepinecampsites.com. About eight miles north of town, with two hundred sites. No beach, though two swimming pools should be adequate compensation. In any case, Lake Champlain is not too far away. May to mid-Oct. **$34**

North Beach Campground 60 Institute Rd ☎802 862 0942, ⊛enjoyburlington.com. Less than two miles north of town on the shores of Lake Champlain. A total of 137 sites and various other facilities (including plenty for the kids), and access to a sandy beach. May to mid-Oct. **$26**

EATING

American Flatbread 115 St Paul St ☎802 861 2999, ⊛americanflatbread.com. Wildly popular pizza place, especially on weekends, for its organic wheat dough and all-natural toppings, including locally made cheeses and sausage (from $13 for a large). Daily 11.30am–2.30pm & 5–10pm (11pm Fri & Sat).

Daily Planet 15 Center St, behind the Church Street Marketplace ☎802 862 9647, ⊛dailyplanet15.com. This brightly coloured spot offers an eclectic menu melding Asian, Mediterranean and old-fashioned American comfort food, from chilled udon noodles ($8) to Vermont beef steak ($21). Mon–Thurs & Sun 4–11pm, Fri & Sat 4pm–midnight.

Dobrá Tea Room 80 Church St ☎802 851 2424, ⊛dobratea.com. The Burlington branch of this Czech teahouse chain is a cosy spot for a cuppa (the teas actually come from India, China and Japan, not the Czech Republic), with a huge range of seasonal teas on offer, accompanied by pastries and snacks. Daily 11am–11pm.

Ice House 171 Battery St ☎802 864 1800, ⊛theicehousevt.com. Occupying a genuine 1868 ice house, this restaurant has been knocking out tasty seafood and steaks since 1976. Eat your salmon, halibut, swordfish or crab cakes on the deck overlooking the lake. Daily 11.30am–close.

Leunig's Bistro 115 Church St ☎802 863 3759, ⊛leunigsbistro.com. Sleek, modern bistro serving contemporary continental cuisine; dinner main courses range from $19–31, but the lunch plates are better value ($10–16). Outdoor dining when weather permits, and live jazz Tues–Thurs. Mon–Thurs 11am–10pm, Fri 11am–11pm, Sat 9am–11pm, Sun 9am–10pm.

Muddy Waters 184 Main St ☎802 658 0466. A colourful, eco-friendly clientele enjoys this popular coffee house, with a crazy interior lined with used furniture, thrift-store rejects, plants and rough-hewn panelled walls. Extremely potent caffeinated beverages. Mon 9am–5pm, Tues 8am–10pm, Wed 1–11pm, Thurs–Sun 9am–11pm.

Myer's Bagel Bakery 377 Pine St ☎802 863 5013. Get a taste of brick-oven Montréal-style bagels (chewier and smaller than NY-style), at this local early morning favourite; the Montréal Spice bagel is an addictive treat (the "spice" is steak seasoning). Don't be put off by the out-of-the-way location. Plain bagels from $1, cash only. Daily 4am–1pm.

6

Penny Cluse Café 169 Cherry St ☎802 651 8834, ⓦpennycluse.com. Omelettes, pancakes, sandwiches, salads and good vegetarian lunches for under $10. Only open for breakfast and lunch – expect long lines at the weekends. Mon–Fri 6.45am–3pm, Sat & Sun 8am–3pm.

Red Onion 140 Church St ☎802 865 2563, ⓦredonioncafe.webs.com. The best sandwiches in town are made to order in this small shop. The mouthwatering menu includes breakfast and some good vegetarian options. The "red onion" sandwich is a standout, and one can easily feed two people. Mon–Fri 8am–8pm, Sat & Sun 11am–8pm.

Shanty on the Shore 181 Battery St ☎802 864 0238, ⓦshantyontheshore.com. Fresh seafood in a laidback setting with views of Lake Champlain. It has Burlington's best – if not only – raw bar, but there's also the fried whole belly clams ($11.99) and roasted scallops ($17.99). Daily 11am–9pm.

★ **Skinny Pancake** 60 Lake St ☎802 540 0188, ⓦskinnypancake.com. Facing the waterfront with outdoor seating (but not much view), this is the place for a crêpe fix ($6.50–9.95). The innovative combos – using mostly local ingredients – include the "Green Mountain" (apples and Cabot cheddar cheese) and the "Love Maker" (warm Nutella, strawberries and Vermont whipped cream). Mon–Wed & Sun 8am–8pm, Thurs 8am–10pm, Fri & Sat 8am–11pm.

Sneakers 28 Main St, Winooski ☎802 655 9081, ⓦsneakersbistro.com. This is the place for breakfast, and you should arrive early for it on weekends. Delicious waffles, home-made granola, eggs Benedict (try the smoked turkey version) and fresh juices served in a diner-like setting with Art Deco mirrors. Most plates range from $7–10. Good lunches, too. Daily 7am–3pm.

Sweetwaters 120 Church St ☎802 864 9800, ⓦsweetwatersvt.com. American grill standards in a converted bank with sidewalk dining, most notable for its sweet potato fries ($4.50), bison and Kobe beef burgers (from $12.95) and extensive Sunday brunch. Attractive raised street terrace – open in good weather. Mon–Thurs & Sun 11.30am–11pm, Fri & Sat 11.30am–midnight.

Trattoria Delia 152 St Paul St ☎802 864 5253, ⓦtrattoriadelia.com. Traditional regional Italian fare that goes beyond the usual pasta dishes – try the wild boar served over soft polenta – and a great wine list, at reasonable prices (pastas from $14.50, main courses from $20.50). Daily 5–10pm.

Zabby and Elf's Stone Soup 211 College St ☎802 862 7616, ⓦstonesoupvt.com. Excellent "mostly vegetarian" café, featuring a wide variety of sandwiches, home-made soups, cakes and the like. Mon–Fri 7am–9pm, Sat 9am–9pm.

DRINKING

Ruben James 159 Main St ☎802 864 0744, ⓦrjsburlington.com. This sports bar brings in a slightly older crowd for satisfying microbrews, loud live music, pool tournaments and football on the TV. Mon–Fri 4pm–2am, Sat & Sun noon–2am.

Vermont Pub and Brewery 144 College St ☎802 865 0500, ⓦvermontbrewery.com. Roomy and convivial brewpub, offering free tastes of its various beers – Dogbite Bitter is the best – plus an appetizing inexpensive menu (until midnight) with live music on some weekends. Mon–Wed & Sun 11.30am–1am, Thurs–Sat 11.30am–2am.

NIGHTLIFE AND ENTERTAINMENT

Though there are a handful of dance clubs in Burlington, nightlife revolves mostly around live music. Pick up a copy of the free newspaper *Seven Days* (ⓦ7dvt.com), which has listings of music and stage shows; the local band scene is a formidable presence in its own right. Downtown's Art Deco-style **Flynn Center**, 153 Main St (☎802 863 5966, ⓦflynncenter.org), plays host to a wide array of talent. Also, during the school year, UVM presents the **Lane Series** (☎802 656 4455, ⓦuvm.edu/laneseries), a collection of musical performances during which you can hear everything from folk to jazz to the occasional opera. Beware that bars and clubs are quite strict about checking IDs, as this is a college town.

Club Metronome 188 Main St ☎802 865 4563, ⓦclubmetronome.com. This very hip club above *Nectar's* (see below) hosts some live acts, but is mainly a funked-out dance venue featuring house and techno music. Eighties music dominates the dancefloor during Sat night's "Retronome" ($5). Tues–Sun 9pm–close.

Nectar's 188 Main St ☎802 658 4771, ⓦliveatnectars.com. Follow the rotating neon sign to this retro lounge lined with vinyl booths and formica tables. This was the inspiration for Phish's 1992 album title *A Picture of Nectar*, as the club hosted many of their earliest shows. Cover

charge on weekends or for bigger local acts (usually $5). Daily 5pm–2am.

Red Square 136 Church St ☎802 859 8909, ⓦredsquarevt.com. For those in the mood for a cosmopolitan experience, *Red Square* is the place to sip cocktails among a highbrow clientele. The food menu is also quite inviting and worth further investigation. Live music every night, often jazz, played outside when the weather permits. Cover on weekends. Mon–Wed & Sun 4pm–2am, Thurs 2pm–2am, Fri & Sat 1pm–2am.

SHOPPING

Burton Snowboards 80 Industrial Parkway, South Burlington (off US-7) ☎ 802 660 3200, ⓦ burton.com. Jake Burton launched the world's first snowboard factory here in Vermont in 1977, and today the flagship store is something of a pilgrimage for fans worldwide. Mon–Sat 10am–7pm, Sun 11am–6pm.

Crow Bookshop 14 Church St ☎ 802 862 0848, ⓦ crowbooks.com. This is one of the best independent bookstores downtown. Mon–Wed 10am–7pm, Thurs–Sat 10am–10pm, Sun noon–6pm.

Lake Champlain Chocolates 65 Church St ☎ 802 862 5185, ⓦ lakechamplainchocolates.com. Gourmet chocolate shop and café that tempts passersby with hot chocolate and espresso, ice cream, fudge and, of course, chocolates. You can view the candy-making process at their factory store, a short drive south at 750 Pine St (Mon–Fri on the hour 9am–2pm; free; ☎ 802 864 1807), and snag some free samples. Mon–Thurs 10am–9pm, Fri & Sat 10am–10pm, Sun 11am–6pm.

Shelburne

The strip malls along Rte-7 south of Burlington eventually fall away at the pretty village of **SHELBURNE**, best known for the exceptional **Shelburne Museum**, a vast outdoor showcase of old Vermont, and **Shelburne Farms**, a working farm especially popular with families.

Shelburne Museum

6000 Shelburne Rd • Mid-May to Oct Mon–Sat 10am–5pm, Sun noon–5pm • $20, children (5–18 years) $10 • ☎ 802 985 3346, ⓦ shelburnemuseum.org

It takes a whole day, if not more, to take in the fabulous 45-acre collection of unalloyed Americana gathered at the **Shelburne Museum**, seven miles south of Burlington on US-7. The brainchild of heiress Electra Havemeyer Webb (1888–1960), more than thirty buildings dot the beautifully landscaped grounds. Besides seven fully furnished historic houses that were moved intact from elsewhere in the region, there's a smithy, a schoolhouse, a jail, a railroad station and a general store, all of which aim to re-create aspects of everyday life over the past two centuries. Below are just a few of the highlights.

McClure Round Barn

The closest building to the entrance is the vast 80ft-diameter **McClure Round Barn**, built in 1901 three miles away in Passumpsic, and now serving as exhibition space for ornately carved carousel figures dating from the same period. The all-wood barn feels a bit like a cathedral inside, though it primarily served as a cattle-feeding silo.

Circus Building

One of the most popular structures, the horseshoe-shaped **Circus Building** (1965) lies behind the Round Barn. A homage to spectacle, the interior features temporary exhibits related to the circus, as well as the hand-carved miniature Arnold Circus Parade and the Edgar Kirk Brothers Toy Circus, a tableau of the big top made up of over 3500 wooden spectators, vendors, animal acts and trapeze artists. A vintage **carousel** operates daily (weather permitting) just outside the building.

Ticonderoga and Lighthouse

From the Circus Building you can stroll up through old railroad buildings to the museum's enormous, 892-ton steam paddlewheeler, the **Ticonderoga** (1906) which once plied the lake between Burlington and Plattsburgh, NY before being retired in 1953. Its tiny quarters have been restored to their appearance during the ship's 1923 heyday, complete with concession stand and deck chairs. A short film chronicles the mammoth effort taken to move the ship here in 1955. The park **Lighthouse**, operating between 1871 and 1933 on Lake Champlain's Colchester Reef, now stands opposite – exhibits inside include a section on the infamous "**Champ**", a Loch Ness-like monster first spotted here in the early nineteenth century.

6

Electra Havemeyer Webb Memorial Building

One of the most absorbing sections of the museum is the Greek Revival **Electra Havemeyer Webb Memorial Building**, just next door to the lighthouse, constructed between 1960 and 1967, complete with towering Ionic columns. It was built to resemble a local building dating from 1845, much loved by the museum's benefactor. Inside, six rooms were meticulously transported from Webb's luxurious 1930s Manhattan, Park Avenue apartment. Four gorgeous **Monet** paintings are displayed in the Dining Room (including *Ice Floes*), with more work from Monet, **Manet** and **Rembrandt** in the White Living Room. **Degas**' ballerinas dominate the Green Guest Room upstairs.

Webb Gallery

The **Webb Gallery** usually displays exhibits of nineteenth-century and twentieth-century American art (though "Fashion 1690–2011" was a recent show). The upper galleries are devoted to temporary exhibitions, while its rotating permanent collection occupies the basement, much of it comprising naturalist work, such as **John James Audubon**'s bird prints.

Stagecoach Inn

Another must-see at Shelburne is the 1785 **Stagecoach Inn** at the northern end of the museum grounds. The old tavern contains a wonderfully nostalgic assemblage of folk art, including weather vanes, tools, quilts, carriages and trade and tavern signs, most notably a giant copper tooth (a trade sign) forged in 1900. Nearby are some of the oldest properties on the site: the 1773 **Prentis House** (displaying seventeenth-century decorative arts) and the 1782 **Dutton House** (showcasing life in 1820s Vermont).

Shelburne Farms

1611 Harbor Rd • Daily; mid-May to mid-Oct 9am–5.30pm; mid-Oct to mid-May 10am–5pm; tours daily 9.30am, 11.30am, 1.30pm, 3.30pm •$8; with guided tour $11 • ☎ 802 985 8686, Ⓦ shelburnefarms.org

Next to the Shelburne Museum, **Shelburne Farms** is a working farm reborn as a non-profit environmental education centre. A guided tour of railroad mogul Dr Seward Webb's estate reveals his descendants' commitment to sustainable farming. The undulating landscape is punctuated by three massive buildings: the main house, which overlooks Lake Champlain and the Adirondacks, a coach barn, and a horseshoe-shaped farm barn. You can get some exercise by walking the 4.5-mile farm trail, which circles the property, or the half-mile Lone Tree Hill trail and numerous side paths diverging from the roadways.

Vergennes

Vermont's first town, sleepy **VERGENNES** was founded in 1788 (the name honours the Comte de Vergennes, negotiator of the Treaty of Paris on the French and American side). The pretty centre contains the historic 1897 **Vergennes Opera House**, 120 Main St (☎ 802 877 6737, Ⓦ vergennesoperahouse.org), restored in the 1980s to serve as an arts centre. Check the website to see what's on. Nearby riverside **Vergennes Falls Park** (daily dawn–dusk; free) is the best place to take in the roaring waterfalls on the Otter Creek, dramatically framed by old mills.

Lake Champlain Maritime Museum

4472 Basin Harbor Rd • Mid-May to mid-Oct daily 10am–5pm • $10 • ☎ 802 475 2022, Ⓦ lcmm.org

Vermont is one of the few states with designated **Underwater Historic Preserves**, where divers can see wrecks on the lake floor. There are several of these intriguing underwater "state parks", and the best place to learn about them is at the **Lake Champlain Maritime Museum** in Basin Harbor, thirty miles southwest of Burlington and seven miles west of central Vergennes. The museum comprises a collection of barns, galleries and boat sheds just up from the lake, with the **National Archaeology Center** documenting some of the three hundred shipwrecks and the technology used to research them. Ice boats take centre stage at the **Hazelett Watercraft Center**, flimsy catamarans that once flew across the iced-over lake in winter, while a life-sized replica of the 1776 gunboat *Philadelphia II* floats down at the harbour.

The museum isn't just about boats and wrecks, though. The history and culture of the lake region is brought to life by a series of hands-on exhibits and events held throughout the summer, such as the Native American encampment held in June. The **Schoolhouse Gallery** chronicles the first contact between Europeans (mostly the French) and Native Americans in the area from 1609, while the **Key to Liberty Exhibit** tells the story of the Revolutionary War in the region, with displays and a short film re-creating some of the main events.

6

ACCOMMODATION
VERGENNES

⭐ **Basin Harbor Club** 4800 Basin Harbor Rd ☏ 1 800 622 4000 or ☏ 802 622 4000, ⓦ basinharbor.com. Sprawling resort village right on the lake, dating back to the 1880s, with golf course, tennis courts, kids' camp, hikes and luxurious rooms. Get a cabin on the lake, with gasp-inducing views across the Adirondacks in New York state and fabulous sunsets. **$302**

EATING

Basin Harbor Club 4800 Basin Harbor Rd ☏ 1 800 622 4000 or ☏ 802 622 4000, ⓦ basinharbor.com. The *Basin Harbor Club* (see above) operates two excellent restaurants, both open to non-guests: the posh *Main Dining Room* with remarkable views of Lake Champlain; and the *Red Mill*, for less formal American classics. Main Dining Room mid–June to Sept daily 7–10am & 6–10pm; Oct to mid-June

Mon–Fri 7am–10pm, Sat & Sun 6–10pm; Red Mill May–Oct daily 11.30am–1am.
Black Sheep Bistro 253 Main St, Vergennes ☏ 802 877 9991. Best place to have dinner in Vergennes itself, with a creative menu featuring coriander-crusted steak with sofrito sauce and applewood smoked bacon- and brie-stuffed chicken breast. Daily 5–8.30pm.

Champlain Islands

Curling southward into Lake Champlain from Canada, the sparsely populated **Champlain Islands** comprise four narrow, oblong land masses – **North Hero**, **Grand Isle**, **Alburg** and **Isle La Motte** – that never really caught on development-wise, despite being the site of the first settlement in Vermont. With a couple of decent beaches, a handful of sights and places to eat, especially at the small village of North Hero, the islands make for a pleasant day's drive or overnight stay – and **Montréal** is just two hours' drive to the north across the Canadian border.

Isle La Motte

Samuel de Champlain stumbled upon **Isle La Motte** in 1609, but the island was named for fellow French explorer **Pierre Le Motte**, who established a short-lived settlement here in 1666. Today the eight-square-mile island has a year-round population of about five hundred, and is home to a revered Catholic shrine especially popular with French-Canadians.

St Anne's Shrine

92 St Anne's Rd (West Shore Rd) • Mid-May to mid-Oct daily 9am–5pm • Free • ☏ 802 928 3362, ⓦ sse.org
The site of Pierre La Motte's original seventeenth-century fort is now occupied by **St Anne's Shrine**, an important Catholic pilgrimage site. The worship of St Anne was associated with La Motte's fort from its earliest days and it also became the first place Mass was offered in the northeast (around 1668). The fort was abandoned a few years later, but local Catholics never forgot the connection, and a shrine was constructed in 1893. Also on the grounds is an imposing granite **statue of Champlain**, sculpted in 1967, a 15ft gold-leafed statue of Our Lady of Lourdes, a narrow sandy beach, gift shop and small history room.

6

Fisk Quarry and Goodsell Ridge preserves

3849 West Shore Rd • Reserves open 24hr • Goodsell Ridge visitor centre mid-June to early Sept Wed–Sun 11am–4pm; early Sept to mid-Oct Sat & Sun noon–4pm • Free • ☎ 802 928 3364, ⓦ ilmpt.org

Isle La Motte's principal treasure is geological; the remnants of the 450-million year-old **Chazy Fossil Reef**. Thanks to the efforts of the Isle La Motte Preservation Trust, the reef is protected within two parks: the **Fisk Quarry Preserve** is a twenty-acre wetland habitat for birds and animals, while the 81-acre **Goodsell Ridge Preserve** features interpretive paths and walking trails. An 1880s renovated farmhouse on the Goodsell Ridge serves as a visitor centre and museum.

Nearby is the former home of the once-prominent Fisk family, **Fisk Farm** (ⓦ fiskfarm.com), built in 1803. The renovated carriage barn hosts concerts and art and craft shows in the summer: there's no need to make reservations for the casual **Arts in the Garden at Fisk Farm** series (July & Aug Sun 1–5pm), when tea and snacks are accompanied by live music, but the Saturday evening **Pro-Series classical concerts** (June–Aug) cost $25.

North Hero

Originally granted to the Allens and 363 other Revolutionary War veterans in the 1780s, **North Hero** covers some fourteen square miles, most of its eight hundred residents living in and around the attractive village of the same name.

Knight Point State Park

44 Knight Point Rd • Mid-May to early Sept daily 10am–sunset • $3 • ☎ 802 372 8389

If Sand Bar (see below) is too crowded (as it often is in summer), head to **Knight Point State Park** at the southern tip of North Hero, a placid, sandy shoreline enclosing a bay. You can rent **kayaks** for $20/day.

Grand Isle

The largest of the Champlain Islands, **Grand Isle** has a population of around four thousand, divided between the towns of South Hero and Grand Isle itself, actually little more than sleepy villages.

Hyde Log Cabin

228 US-2 • July to mid-Oct Sat & Sun 11am–5pm • $2 • ☎ 802 828 3051

Grand Isle's claim to historical fame is the **Hyde Log Cabin**, built in 1783 and the oldest cabin in the state (if not the whole country). Built by one Jedediah Hyde Jr, an engineer and Revolutionary War veteran, it remained the home of the Hyde family for over 150 years before being moved here in 1946 (it was originally two miles away). Today the cedar-log one-room structure is looked after by the Grand Isle Historical Society, its restored interior testimony to the harshness of life on the frontier. Next door the society also opens up the old **Grand Isle School House #4**, built of logs and ochre clapboard in 1814, and moved here in 2003 (same times and entry price).

Sand Bar State Park

1215 US-2, Milton • July & Aug daily 10am–9pm • $3 • ☎ 802 893 2825

The area's best beach is the nearly half-mile strand at **Sand Bar State Park**, actually on a sandbar attached to the mainland just below the US-2 bridge to Grand Isle.

ARRIVAL AND INFORMATION

CHAMPLAIN ISLANDS

By car The Champlain Islands are accessible by US-2, which links Grand Isle, North Hero and Alburg by a network of bridges. Isle La Motte lies at the end of Rte-129, off US-2. US-2 loops through the islands from I-89, making the area easily accessible from Burlington. There is no public transport.

Lake Champlain Islands Chamber of Commerce US-2, North Hero (Mon–Fri 9am–4pm; ☎ 802 372 8400 or ☎ 1 800 262 5226, ⓦ champlainislands.com).

ACCOMMODATION

North Hero House 3643 US-2, North Hero ☎ 802 372 4732, ⓦ northherohouse.com. Prime lodgings in North Hero village, overlooking the lake – its comfy rooms are equipped with iPod docks and cable TV. $125

Thomas Mott Homestead 63 Blue Rock Road, Rte-78, Alburg ☎ 802 796 4402, ⓦ thomas-mott-bb.com. The superior choice, with large rooms in a Shaker-style farmhouse built in 1838; fantastic breakfasts and luxurious beds. $145

CAMPING

Grand Isle State Park 36 E Shore Rd S, Grand Isle ☎ 802 372-4300, ⓦ vtstateparks.com. Offers 156 highly developed pitches and cabins complete with restrooms, hot showers and RVs galore. May to mid-Oct. Camping $18; cabins $48

Knight Island State Park 44 Knight Point Rd, North Hero ☎ 802 524 6353, ⓦ vtstateparks.com. Secluded site with a multitude of unspoiled nature trails; you should reserve early to get one of the seven primitive campgrounds. Late May to early Sept. $18

EATING

Blue Paddle Bistro 316 Rte-2, South Hero ☎ 802 372 4814, ⓦ bluepaddlebistro.com. Fine dining in the islands – think coffee-crusted pork tenderloin and crab-stuffed ravioli. Mon–Sat 5–9pm, Sun 10am–2pm & 5–9pm.

Hero's Welcome US-2, North Hero ☎ 802 372 4161, ⓦ heroswelcome.com. Cheap pit-stop overlooking the lake, with a great range of light lunches, chocs, sweets, coffees and pastries. Mon–Sat 6.30am–6.30pm, Sun 7am–6pm.

Papa Pete's Snack Bar 35 Bridge Rd, US-2 (north end of North Hero) ☎ 802 393 9747. Summer snack van selling a cracking chicken sandwich and smoked ribs, pulled pork and beef on Saturdays. Summer only Mon–Sat 11am–8.30pm, Sun 11am–7pm.

Northeast Kingdom

Remote and rural, Vermont's **Northeast Kingdom** takes its name from a remark made by Vermont senator George Aiken in 1949, referring to the several counties that bulge out eastward in the state's uppermost corner. The only locales approaching town status in the area are **St Johnsbury** and **Newport**, at the region's southern and northern boundaries, each of which still has less than nine thousand inhabitants. Aside from its rural, idyllic character, the kingdom is home to the **Cabot Creamery** and the phenomenal **puppet museum** at Glover. In addition, two of the state's least crowded and most challenging ski areas, **Jay Peak** and **Burke Mountain**, are in this region; in the summer it's the **mountain biking** that brings in the visitors, especially from Québec – day-trips to **Montréal** are a real possibility.

St Johnsbury

The town of **ST JOHNSBURY**, estimated population 7560, is still the largest town in Vermont's sparsely populated northeast by a long stroke, though its abundance of elaborate architecture, all turrets, marble and stained glass, suggest a far grander past.

St J, as it's referred to by locals, grew from the frontier outpost of 1787 to its current size thanks to the ingenuity of resident **Thaddeus Fairbanks** (1796–1886), the "scale king", who earned his fortune and a minor place in history by inventing the **platform scale** in the 1830s. Much of the Fairbanks wealth was showered on the city in the form of funding for new municipal buildings, schools and elaborate churches.

Fairbanks Museum and Planetarium

1302 Main St • **Museum** Tues–Sat 9am–5pm, Sun 1–5pm, also Mon 9am–5pm May–Oct • $8; children (5–17 years) $6 **Planetarium** Shows July & Aug daily 1.30pm; rest of year Sat & Sun 1.30pm • $5 • ☎ 802 748 2372, ⓦ fairbanksmuseum.org

The Romanesque **Fairbanks Museum and Planetarium** is a fabulous example of the Fairbanks' largesse, a grand Victorian building with an eclectic collection of artefacts presented largely in Victorian fashion. The first floor is primarily occupied by stuffed birds and animals, while the upper gallery contains small displays on everything from Civil War pieces and Zulu war shields to Japanese handicrafts and mummified animals from ancient Egypt. The real standout – and reason enough for a visit – is the mesmerizing **Omniglobe**, a huge electronic globe that can digitally transform its surface to mimic every planet (and most of the moons) in the solar system – you can even spin the earth upside down. Downstairs is a rather more sombre exhibition of the scales that made the Fairbank millions – the museum was established by Franklin Fairbanks (1828–95), nephew of Thaddeus and a noted curio collector, in 1891.

St Johnsbury Athenaeum

1171 Main St • Mon–Fri 10am–5.30pm, Sat 9.30am–5pm • Free • ☎ 802 748 8291, ⓦ stjathenaeum.org

Just down Main Street from the Fairbanks Museum, the **St Johnsbury Athenaeum** is an elegant French Second Empire-style building, doubling as the local library and **art gallery**. This time the benefactor was Horace Fairbanks (1820–88), another nephew of Thaddeus and governor of the state, who had the library constructed in 1871 (his huge portrait hangs on the library wall). The handsome reading rooms are worth a look, but the main attraction is the art, including a number of fine paintings from the **Hudson River school**. Highlights include Albert Bierstadt's gargantuan *Domes of Yosemite*, and the crowd-pleasing *Raspberry Girl* by William-Adolphe Bouguereau.

Dog Mountain

143 Parks Rd, off Spaulding Rd • Summer Mon–Sat 10am–5pm, Sun 11am–4pm; winter Mon–Sat 10am–4pm, Sun 11am–4pm • Free • ☎ 1 800 449 2580, ⓦ dogmt.com

Dog lovers will especially enjoy this quirky but touching memorial to local artist **Stephen Huneck** (and his dogs), officially the Stephen Huneck Gallery & Dog Chapel, but better known as **Dog Mountain**. Huneck died in 2010, but his legacy remains in a series of vivid, folksy art works that decorate the "Dog Chapel" (a real chapel, and also the name of a book by Huneck). The chapel also contains his books, woodcut prints, sculptures and handmade furniture.

INFORMATION   ST JOHNSBURY

Welcome Center 51 Depot Square in the old train station (May–Oct Mon–Fri 8am–6pm, Sat 9am–6pm, Sun 10am–2pm; Nov–April Mon–Fri 8.30am–5pm, Sat 10am–5pm; ☎ 802 748 3678, ⓦ nekchamber.com).

ACCOMMODATION

Fairbanks Inn 401 Western Ave ☎ 802 748 5666, ⓦ stjay.com. One of the better-equipped motels around town, with a heated pool, putting green and cable TV. Rooms are fairly standard motel fare, but come with microwaves, fridges and free wi-fi and local phone calls. **$135**

★ **Wildflower Inn** 2059 Darling Hill Rd, off Rte-114, Lyndonville (exit 23, I-91) ☎ 802 626 8310, ⓦ wildflower.com. For a slice of rural Vermont, opt for this complex of old farm buildings (4 miles from I-91). There loads for families, courts, a pool and a ravishing view of the mountains, and hearty breakfast, home-made cookies and cider (3–5pm daily) are also thrown in. **$130**

EATING

Boxcar Bookshop & Caboose Café 394 Railroad St ☎ 802 748 3551, ⓦ boxcarandcaboose.com. Good for a simple wrap or pastry with some strong coffee; also carries a quirky collection of books. Mon–Fri 7am–7pm, Sat 9am–7pm, Sun 9am–5pm.

Elements 98 Mill St ☎ 802 748 8400, ⓔ elementsfood .com. Serves what they call "creative comfort food" in a familiar, brick-walled space, using local cheeses and strip steaks. Tues–Sat 5pm–late.

Juniper's Restaurant 2059 Darling Hill Rd, off Rte-114, Lyndonville (exit 23, I-91) ☎ 802 626 8310, ⓦ junipersrestaurant.com. One of the finest restaurants in the region, using farm-to-table produce from the Northeast Kingdom – local beef, chicken and pork and a great selection of Vermont wines and beers. Burgers and sandwiches start at $9.49, but opt for a classic meatloaf ($15.99), made with locally raised grass-fed beef, or shepherds pie. Mon–Sat 5–8.30pm.

VERMONT'S CHEESES

Something of an economic lightweight, Vermont does do a few things very well: ice cream, maple syrup and **cheese**. Nostalgic cheese historians will look back to the turn of the last century, when eighty percent of Vermont's milk was being churned into butter and cheese, and lament that things aren't what they once were, but the state still produces a very respectable seventy million pounds of cheese a year, with a significant amount coming from family farms using traditional methods. Predictably, the **tourist industry** has cashed in on the reputation of Vermont cheese, and refrigerators containing the most sought-after brands hum and rattle in gift shops statewide. If it's cheddar you're after, the best known is probably **Cabot Cheddar**, which comes in a variety of sharp flavors. Crowley Cheese (made in Healdville) is less acidic and moister than the English-style cheddars made elsewhere in Vermont (it's officially designated a colby cheese); Grafton Village Cheese is known for mature cheddars with an earthy, creamy taste; and Neighborly Farms (Randolph Center) carries the flag for organic cheddar. Cheeses made with **sheep's milk**, such as feta, camembert and brie, are produced by Peaked Mountain Farm (Townsend) and Vermont Shepherd (Putney), among others. Lazy Lady Farm (Westfield) and Vermont Butter and Cheese Company (Websterville) are the top names in **goat's milk** cheese. Such is the pull of cheese in this state, that several of the above-mentioned producers – and others not mentioned here – have formed the **Vermont Cheese Trail**, opening their doors to the paying public to reveal cheese-making methods and give away pound upon pound of free samples. For more information, contact the Vermont Cheese Council (☎ 866 261 8595, ⓦ vtcheese.com).

Cabot

Vermont is justifiably proud of its cheddar cheese (see box above), and the small town of **CABOT**, around twenty miles west of St Johnsbury, is the epicentre of the state's cheese production. It's an attractive place, but you're only really coming here for one reason.

Cabot Creamery

2878 Main St • June–Oct daily 9am–5pm; Nov–Dec & Feb–May Mon–Sat 9am–4pm; Jan Mon–Sat 10am–4pm • $2, children (under 12 years) free • ☎ 1 800 837 4261, ⓦ cabotcheese.coop

The **Cabot Creamery** churns out around fifteen million pounds of cheese a year, or approximately twenty percent of the total state production. Tours leave from the **visitor centre** every thirty minutes, starting with a ten-minute video explaining how Cabot got to where it is today, then take you through the plant itself, and end with the opportunity to gorge yourself on several different varieties of cheddar.

Craftsbury Common

CRAFTSBURY COMMON, two miles off slow, bumpy Rte-14, is just about in the middle of nowhere – which is exactly its appeal. This is one of the most enchanting villages in the state. Ignore the separate village of Craftsbury and drive two miles up the hill to the vast common, ringed by a white fence, a post office, church and the white clapboard buildings of **Sterling College**, founded in 1958 and the smallest accredited four-year college in the country. The common hosts a small **farmers' market** every Saturday (May–Oct 10am–1pm). While the main recreation here is getting away from activity, the surrounding hills are crisscrossed with a web of **trails** popular for mountain-biking and skiing.

INFORMATION   **CRAFTSBURY COMMON**

Craftsbury Outdoor Center (☎ 1 800 729 7751, ⓦ craftsbury.com). For equipment rental and more   information on walking and cross-country skiing trails in the surrounding countryside.

ACCOMMODATION AND EATING

Craftsbury Inn 107 S Craftsbury Rd ☎ 802 586 2848, ⓦ craftsburyinn.com. Gorgeous inn built c.1850 by   a prominent Craftsbury merchant, with a range of simple but cosy period rooms, the cheapest of

which have shared bathrooms. Shared bathroom $90; en-suite $115
Stardust Books and Café 1376 N Craftsbury Rd ☎ 802

586 2200, ⓦ stardustindependent.com. Pop in for a coffee and muffin, then rummage through the books and gifts. Mon–Fri 7.30am–4pm, Sat 10am–2pm.

North to Canada

From St Johnsbury, I-91 runs north up to Québec, Canada; everything east of the highway is fairly mountainous, and there are a few good diversions not too far off the main road. This part of the Kingdom is home to pristine lakes, some of the best **mountain biking** in the country and abundant wildlife, including some ten thousand **moose** (watch carefully for the enormous creatures while driving, especially at night – collisions are frequent, and most often fatal). The main outdoor attractions lie around **East Burke** and scenic **Lake Willoughby**, while **Glover** is home to the wonderful Bread & Puppet Museum and **Newport** is the area's gateway to Canada.

East Burke

In the summer, hundreds of athletic types from Québec and all over New England descend on the area around **EAST BURKE** for some serious mountain biking at the **Kingdom Trails Welcome Center**; in the winter **Burke Mountain Resort** provides the skiing action. East Burke itself, founded in 1782, is a quintessential Vermont village, containing a smattering of services and clapboard homes along the fast-flowing Dishmill Brook.

Kingdom Trails Welcome Center

478 Rte-114, East Burke • Mon–Thurs & Sun 8am–5pm, Fri & Sat 8am–6pm • Day pass $15 • ☎ 802 626 0737, ⓦ kingdomtrails.com

The majority of the area's mountain-biking action takes place at the **Kingdom Trails Welcome Center**. There are more than 120 miles of double- and single-track mountain bike trails to explore, of varying levels of difficulty.

Burke Mountain Resort

223 Sherburne Lodge Rd, East Burke • Lift tickets $64 • ☎ 802 626 3322, ⓦ skiburke.com

The nation's top young downhill skiers train at **Burke Mountain Resort**, best approached from I-91, exit 23 onto US-5, then north on Rte-114. Because of the mountain's isolation, Burke's 43 trails are virtually deserted compared to places such as Killington and Stowe, but they're all tough; three-quarters of them are intermediate and higher. In **summer**, you can drive to the top of the mountain on the **scenic toll road** ($5) and also **camp** at the Burke Mountain Campground (May–Oct; $25 tent site or $30 for a lean-to).

Lake Willoughby

It's hard to top the natural beauty of **Lake Willoughby**, nine miles east of I-91 (exit 25) near the village of **WESTMORE**, dubbed the "Lucerne of North America". The lake's southern end is surrounded by the **Willoughby State Forest** (Rte-5A), which includes two peaks that dramatically frame the waters, Mount Pisgah (2751ft) and Mount Hor (2648ft). Both mountains can be climbed via well-marked trails signposted off Rte-5A.

Glover

Bread & Puppet Museum 753 Heights Rd, Rte-122 (off Rte-16), Glover • June–Oct 10am–6pm • Free • ☎ 802 525 3031, ⓦ breadandpuppet.org

The only reason to hit tiny **GLOVER**, thirty miles north of St Johnsbury (take I-91 to exit 25) is to visit the extraordinary **Bread & Puppet Museum**. The Bread and Puppet Theatre was established by Peter Schumann in 1963 in New York City, moving to Vermont in 1970 to perform anti-Vietnam War puppet shows. There's still a left-wing vibe to the group's body of work, but whatever your politics prepare to be blown away by the museum, essentially a storehouse of old puppets housed in their rickety, two-level 1863 barn. Wandering the rows of outlandish, oversized figures – they can be as big as 18ft and require up to four people to operate – is like visiting a massive, slightly surreal contemporary art installation.

Newport

The final stop on I-91 before the Québec border, unassuming **NEWPORT** seems more French-Canadian than New England in character. Its main draw is **Lake Memphremagog**, which spans the border and was once a choice resort area. The lake area is no longer quite so exclusive, but is still popular with vacationing Québecois, who flock here to boat, jet-ski and swim – unfortunately for Newport they tend to hang out in the far more appealing towns of Georgeville and Magog, on the Québec side of the border.

The main attraction in Newport is the **MAC Center for the Arts**, 138 Main St (Mon–Sat 10am–5.30pm; also Sun 11am–4pm July–Sept; ☎ 802 505 1265, ⓦ Memphremagog ArtsCollaborative.com), a hip art space featuring the work of over 50 local artisans. Just outside the town, off Rte-105, is **Mountain Country Soap**, 322 Petit Rd (Mon–Fri 9am–5pm, Sat 9am–4pm; ☎ 1 877 665 6963, ⓦ mountaincountrysoap.com), the "home of aging hippie bath and body products", all made on site in a former dairy farm.

Jay Peak Resort

4850 Rte-242 • Lift tickets $69 • ☎ 802 988 2611, ⓦ jaypeakresort.com

The 4000ft summit of the **Jay Peak Resort**, on Rte-242, looms just south of the Canadian border, about fifteen miles west of I-91. Jay's 75 trails are some of New England's toughest, and typically only serious skiers (and Canadians, of course) venture this far out. Jay Peak consistently receives more snow than any other New England resort, an average of 351 inches a year, something which makes deep-powder skiing a distinct possibility through late April. Most skiers stay in the various snazzy accommodations on site.

INFORMATION	NORTH TO CANADA

Newport North Country Chamber of Commerce 246 The Causeway (US-5), Newport (Mon–Thurs 9am–5pm, Fri 9am–7pm, Sat 9am–4pm, Sun 1–5pm; ☎ 802 334 7782 ⓦ vtnorthcountry.org).

ACCOMMODATION AND EATING

EAST BURKE

Willy's Restaurant 570 Route 114, East Burke ☎ 802 626 9900, ⓦ willysrestaurant.net. Friendly local restaurant serving everything from burgers ($9.95) and wood-oven pizza ($12) to more unusual, German-inspired, dishes like wild mushroom strudel ($16.75) and spiced chicken with figs and pears ($17.95). Daily 2–9.30pm.

LAKE WILLOUGHBY

WilloughVale Inn & Cottages 793 Rte-5A, Westmore ☎ 802 525 4123, ⓦ willoughvale.com. Gorgeous waterside hotel on Lake Willoughby, where Robert Frost camped in 1909. Today there's a choice of luxury and standard rooms, and lakefront and lake-view wooden cottages. *Gil's Bar & Grill* (open from 3pm), is the best place to eat on the lake. Mon–Sat 6am–8pm, Sun 8am–8pm (closes 6pm in winter). Doubles $99; cottages $189

WEST GLOVER

★ **Parker Pie Co** 161 County Rd, West Glover ☎ 802 525 3366, ⓦ parkerpie.com. A pizza shop in the back of the Lake Parker Country Store, this is the best (and just about the only) place to eat in these parts. Offers excellent pizzas (try the lauded Green Mountain Special, $10), tasty craft beers and oyster nights on Fridays. Tues–Thurs & Sun 11am–9pm , Fri & Sat 11am–10pm

NEWPORT

Eastside Restaurant & Pub 47 Landing St ☎ 802 334 2340. Offers the best dining in town – grilled steaks and chicken enhanced by a wonderful view of the lake. The Sunday brunch buffet is just $10.95. There's a shop and bakery here also. Mon–Fri 11am–9pm, Sat 7.30am–10pm, Sun 7.30am–8pm.

Lago Trattoria 95 W Main St ☎ 802 334 8222, ⓦ lagotrattoria.com. The menu of Italian favourites and hand-crafted pizzas – with toppings such as fried calamari and PEI mussels – makes this a solid option for dinner. Mon–Sat 5-9pm.

Newport City Motel 444 E Main St (exit 27, I-91) ☎ 802 334 6558, ⓦ vermonter.com/ncm. Smart, if bland, option with comfy rooms and all the amenities, including indoor pool; useful as a one-night pit stop before crossing the Canadian border. $164

New Hampshire

389 Portsmouth

396 The Seacoast Region

400 The Merrimack Valley

408 The Monadnock region

412 Western New Hampshire

418 The Lakes Region

428 The White Mountains

THE WHITE MOUNTAINS

New Hampshire

"Live Free or Die" is the official motto of New Hampshire, summing up a deeply held belief in rugged individualism and independence that goes back to colonial times. The state's topography remains untamed, with forest-smothered mountains, whitewater rivers and challenging ski resorts, making the state a rustic retreat for much of the East Coast since the nineteenth century. It is arguably the premier state in the region for outdoor activities, with skiing and snowboarding in winter and kayaking, canoeing, swimming, fishing, hiking, climbing and biking in summer. Autumn is another popular time to visit, as the trees turn vibrant shades and the air temperature drops refreshingly.

New Hampshire's brief Atlantic coastline is a stretch of mellow, sun-drenched beaches capped by **Portsmouth**, a well-preserved colonial town with a crop of excellent restaurants and stylish inns. Farther inland, there are over 1300 lakes; the largest, **Lake Winnipesaukee**, is ringed with both tourist resorts and quiet villages. The magnificent **White Mountains** spread across northern New Hampshire, culminating in the highest peak in New England, formidable **Mount Washington**. Quaint communities brimming with small-town pride are scattered across the southern part of the state, connected by shaded, winding roads.

Brief history

The first European settlement in New Hampshire was established in 1623, when David Thomson brought a small group to **Odiorne Point**, at the mouth of the Piscataqua River. The colony was primarily a fishing venture, funded by **John Mason**, governor of Newfoundland, who had been ceded the area in 1622. Without ever laying eyes on the land, Mason named the region New Hampshire, for his home county in England. After he died in 1635, a small group of settlers stayed along the coast, while the interior remained the preserve of the Abenaki and Pennacook tribes. Relations with the Native Americans soured as settlers moved inland, prompting Abenaki involvement in **King Philip's War** in 1676 (see p.521). Sporadic Abenaki and French raids plagued the state for the next fifty years until the **French and Indian War** (1754–63) finally removed the French from North America. By 1700, the state's Native American population had been reduced to less than a thousand and by 1730 it had just about vanished. By this time **Portsmouth** was a thriving port, thanks mostly to the timber and shipbuilding industries. In December 1774 **Paul Revere** rode to New Hampshire to warn the locals that the

Portsmouth's historic homes p.392
Wentworth by the Sea p.394
Kate Day p.396
New Hampshire beaches p.397
Visiting the Isles of Shoals p.398
Liberty and union: the life of Daniel Webster p.406
The Shakers in America p.408
Walpole's sweet surprise p.410

Dartmouth: sports and the great outdoors p.415
Welcome Bikers p.418
Eastern shore activities p.423
The Barnstormers theatre group p.426
The Appalachian Trail – New Hampshire p.441
First-in-the-nation presidential primary p.444

LAKE WINNIPESAUKEE

Highlights

❶ Portsmouth That rare commodity: a seaside town with culture and class, displayed in historic buildings, gourmet restaurants and highbrow shows. **See p.389**

❷ Canterbury Shaker Village Tours reveal the crafts and gadgets of an eighteenth-century religious community that died out only in 1992. **See p.407**

❸ Lake Winnipesaukee Whether from its eastern or western shores, this grand expanse of blue offers a multitude of watery activities. **See p.419**

❹ Cross-country skiing, Jackson For all its mountainous terrain, New Hampshire still has

some excellent places for cross-country skiing, none finer than the pristine and varied trails at Jackson. **See p.439**

❺ Mount Washington So what if there's a road leading up to the summit of the highest mountain in the northeastern US – it's still one of the most remote, awe-inspiring and unpredictably exciting places in New England. **See p.441**

❻ Historic grand resort hotels If you can afford it, hit the luxury of the *Mount Washington* or *Balsams* up in the White Mountains. **See p.443 & p.445**

HIGHLIGHTS ARE MARKED ON THE MAP ON P.388

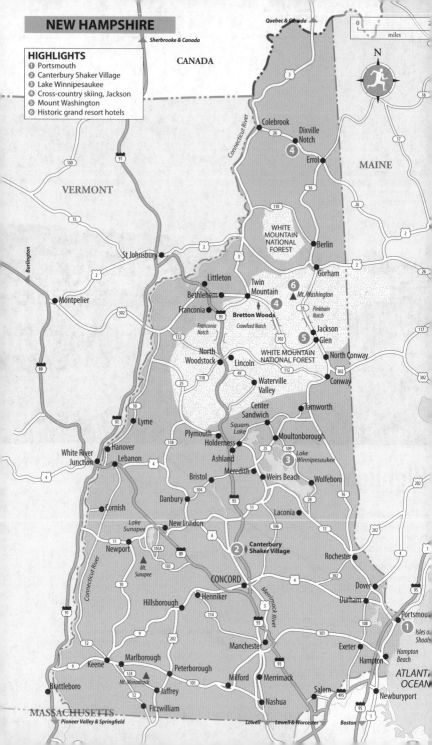

British planned to seize their stash of arms and in January 1776, New Hampshire became the first state to declare independence.

Into the modern era

Following the Revolutionary War, life remained a struggle for many settlers until the Industrial Revolution, when towns in the Merrimack Valley, such as Nashua, Concord and Manchester, became major manufacturing centres – by 1915 the enormous brick **Amoskeag Mills** in Manchester produced more cloth than any other textile facility in the world. Meanwhile, large-scale summer tourism began in the latter half of the nineteenth century, with city folk flocking to several dozen grand resort hotels. With the collapse of manufacturing after World War II, **tourism** is now the state's top money earner.

The state has also earned a degree of notoriety as the venue of the **first state primary of every presidential election**. Since 1952, the state has picked the candidates eventually nominated by both the Democrats and the Republicans about 85 percent of the time. Once safe Republican territory, New Hampshire has been something of a **swing state** since the 1990s, giving it some political clout, despite its small size.

7

INFORMATION   NEW HAMPSHIRE

New Hampshire Office of Travel and Tourism
The official site of the tourist board is ⓦ visitnh.gov, loaded with useful information.

GETTING AROUND

By train Train services are limited to Amtrak's *Downeaster* (ⓦ amtrakdowneaster.com), which connects Boston and Portland (Maine) and only stops at the towns of Exeter, Durham and Dover.

By bus You can get to a few more places by bus, but don't bank on seeing much of the northern part of the state if you don't have your own car. Bus companies serving New Hampshire include Concord Coach Lines (ⓣ 1 800 639 3317, ⓦ concordcoachlines.com), C&J Trailways (ⓣ 603 430 1100 or ⓣ 1 800 258 7111, ⓦ ridecj.com), Greyhound (ⓣ 1 800 231 2222, ⓦ greyhound.com) and Peter Pan Bus (ⓣ 1 800 343 9999; ⓦ peterpanbus.com).

Portsmouth

New Hampshire's most urbane city, **PORTSMOUTH**, just off I-95 at the mouth of the Piscataqua River, blends small-town accessibility with a hefty dose of sophistication. Having endured the cycles of prosperity and hardship typical of most New England towns, Portsmouth has found its most recent triumphs in the cultural arena, attracting artists, musicians, writers and, notably, gourmet chefs. In addition to a wealth of tantalizing restaurants, Portsmouth's unusual abundance of well-preserved colonial buildings makes for an absorbing couple of days.

Brief history

Portsmouth was officially founded in 1630 by English settlers led by Captain Walter Neal, but was known as **Strawbery Banke** until 1653, after the abundance of wild strawberries in the area. As maritime trade expanded, however, it seemed far more appropriate for it to take the name of one of England's most important ports. By then the town was one of America's leading ports (it was actually state capital 1758 to 1776). With an abundance of timber in the surrounding regions, Portsmouth's prosperous shipyards produced enormous masts, trading vessels and warships and its ships were soon carrying goods – and fighting wars – all over the world.

The city's golden age peaked in 1800, after which the combination of the 1807 Embargo Act, the War of 1812 and three devastating **fires** plunged the city into decline. The **Portsmouth Naval Shipyard** was the area's largest employer by 1900 (and is still active today, just across the Piscataqua River in Maine).

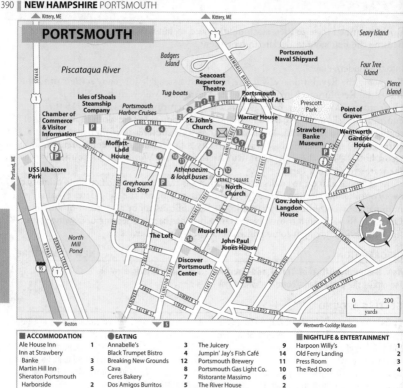

7

■ ACCOMMODATION		● EATING				■ NIGHTLIFE & ENTERTAINMENT	
Ale House Inn	1	Annabelle's	3	The Juicery	9	Harpoon Willy's	1
Inn at Strawbery		Black Trumpet Bistro	4	Jumpin' Jay's Fish Café	14	Old Ferry Landing	2
Banke	3	Breaking New Grounds	12	Portsmouth Brewery	11	Press Room	3
Martin Hill Inn	5	Cava	8	Portsmouth Gas Light Co.	10	The Red Door	4
Sheraton Portsmouth		Ceres Bakery	7	Ristorante Massimo	6		
Harborside	2	Dos Amigos Burritos	5	The River House	2		
Sise Inn	4	The Friendly Toast	13	The Wellington Room	1		

In the nineteenth century, Portsmouth became notorious as a seedy port of call, complete with a busy **red-light district**, a skyrocketing crime rate and a raucous assortment of grungy taverns. Portsmouth also became a major centre for **beer and ale** production. Angry citizens eventually drove the revellers and prostitutes from the city in the early 1900s and the beer industry collapsed after the onset of Prohibition in 1920, causing Portsmouth to settle into a long period of stagnation, heavily dependent on the government-sponsored shipyard for its well-being. It wasn't until the 1950s that the city began to actively preserve and restore its rich stock of buildings, saving the area now known as the **Strawbery Banke Museum** from demolition and creating one of the best-preserved colonial towns in New England.

Discover Portsmouth Center

15 Middle St • Late May to Oct daily 10am–5pm • Free • ☏ 603 436 8433, ⓦ portsmouthhistory.org

Get oriented at the **Discover Portsmouth Center**, housed in a Federal-style former school and library dating from 1810. Inside you can watch a twelve-minute film introducing the town's storied history and see exhibits on the main sights. There's also a display of historic paintings of the town and plenty of helpful staff members on hand.

Market Square

Once a military training site, **Market Square** has been Portsmouth's commercial centre since the mid-eighteenth century and is now surrounded by bustling cafés and gift shops. The 1854 **North Church** (open only for special church services) flanks the southwest side of the square, its towering spire the tallest point in town. A plaque nearby shows where the **State House** once stood (it was torn down around 1800).

Athenaeum

9 Market Square • Tues & Thurs 1–4pm, Sat 10am–4pm; Exhibition Gallery Tues, Thurs & Sat 1–4pm • Free • ☎ 603 431 2538, ⓦ portsmouthathenaeum.org

One of the oldest private libraries in the country, the **Athenaeum** was built around 1805 as the home of a fire insurance company. It became a library in 1817 and still boasts an **exhibition gallery**, plus the original reading rooms and leather banquettes (and a waiting list for membership).

Market Street

Scanning the chic boutiques and fashionable restaurants that line **Market Street**, it's hard to believe the brick buildings that house them were once occupied by breweries. In the late nineteenth century, when Portsmouth's **beer and ale industry** was booming, Frank Jones, founder of the Portsmouth Brewery Company, created what was once considered to be the best beer in the nation – the aptly named "Frank Jones Ale", Jones and his competitors were shut down during Prohibition and never recovered. The company's old brick warehouse, at 125 Bow St, was transformed in 1979 into a **theatre** (see p.396).

7

Moffatt-Ladd House

154 Market St • Mid-June to mid-Oct Mon–Sat 11am–5pm, Sun 1–5pm • $6 • ☎ 603 436 8221, ⓦ moffattladd.org

Of the grand old mansions in Portsmouth (see box, p.392), the **Moffatt-Ladd House** is one of the most impressive. Completed in 1763, the building is particularly notable for its Great Hall, which occupies more than a quarter of the first floor. Using inventories left by Captain John Moffatt, who designed the home and later monitored his shipping business from an office on the second floor, historians have transformed the **Yellow Chamber** (also on the second floor) into one of the best-documented eighteenth-century American rooms. Portraits of past occupants by artists such as Gilbert Stuart hang throughout the home, including a painting of William Whipple, who signed the Declaration of Independence and lived here in the late eighteenth century.

USS Albacore Park & Port of Portsmouth Maritime Museum

600 Market St • Late May to mid-Oct daily 9.30am–5pm; rest of year Thurs–Mon 9.30am–4pm • $5 • ☎ 603 436 3680, ⓦ ussalbacore.org

The **USS Albacore Park & Port of Portsmouth Maritime Museum** is anchored by the eponymous 205ft, 1200-ton **submarine**. Built in 1952, it was then the fastest electric/diesel submarine in the world. Tours of the underwater vessel offer glimpses of the cockpit, cramped living quarters and the engine room.

Prescott Park

105 Marcy St • Daily 24hr • Free • ☎ 603 436 2848, ⓦ prescottpark.org

Along the river on Marcy Street, **Prescott Park** is a welcoming expanse of grass and shrubbery that slopes gently toward the water's edge. Featuring free music and entertainment throughout the summer (the **Prescott Park Arts Festival**), the park is immaculately maintained and is a great spot for a picnic or afternoon nap. You could also check out **Point of Graves cemetery**, a creepy plot of crumbling colonial graves, opposite the park on the southeast corner of Mechanic Street (near the bridge to Pierce Island) – the oldest headstone dates from 1682.

PORTSMOUTH'S HISTORIC HOMES

Beyond the walls of Strawbery Banke, Portsmouth is home to eight restored **colonial homes**, open to the public during the summer. Hourly tours, led by scholars full of stories, can be fascinating, although after one or two, you will have probably had your fill. When you purchase your ticket, ask for a "passport" entitling you to $1 off admission at the others (and Strawbery Banke); you can print it at ⓦ portsmouthhistorichouses.org.

GOVERNOR JOHN LANGDON HOUSE

143 Pleasant St • June 1–Oct 15 Fri–Sun; tours on the hour 11am–4pm • $6 • ☎ 603 436 3205, ⓦ historicnewengland

John Langdon – three-term governor, New Hampshire Senate president and delegate to the 1787 Constitutional Convention – and his wife, Elizabeth, hosted many visitors here, including George Washington. The home, constructed in 1784, is in every way a tribute to his affluence and influence.

JOHN PAUL JONES HOUSE

43 Middle St • Daily late May to mid-Oct 11am–5pm; self-guided tours • $8 • ☎ 603 436 8420, ⓦ portsmouthhistory.org

Home to the Portsmouth Historical Society's museum, this 1758 Georgian house was where John Paul Jones, the US's first great naval commander, boarded in 1777 while his ships were outfitted in the Langdon shipyards. Inside the boxy yellow structure you can view some of his naval memorabilia and lavish period-furnished rooms (check out the wallpaper). Upstairs there's an incredibly detailed exhibit on the 1905 Portsmouth Peace Treaty, including a short version of Thomas Edison's rare film of the event.

WARNER HOUSE

150 Daniel St • Mid-June to mid-Oct Wed–Mon noon–4pm • $5 • ☎ 603 436 5909, ⓦ warnerhouse.org

Built for local merchant Captain Archibald MacPhaedris in 1716, this was the first brick house constructed in the state. It contains New Hampshire's oldest murals, painted on the staircase wall, which depict some of the earliest known images of Native Americans. Additionally, Benjamin Franklin is said to have installed the lightning rod on the west wall.

WENTWORTH-COOLIDGE MANSION

375 Little Harbor Rd, off Rte-1A • Late June to early Sept daily tours 10am, 11.30am, 12.45pm, 2pm & 3pm; Sept to mid-Oct tours Fri–Sun 1.30pm & 3pm • $7 • ☎ 603 436 6607

Home to English governor Benning Wentworth from 1753 to 1770, this rambling 42-room, mustard-yellow mansion, beautifully situated on an isolated plot overlooking Little Harbor, hosts occasional concerts and classes during the summer. It's not furnished, but the wallpaper in several of the rooms is original and there are several original Wentworth items on display.

St John's Episcopal Church

101 Chapel St • Mon–Thurs 9am–3pm • Free • ☎ 603 436 8283, ⓦ stjohnsnh.org

Completed around 1807, venerable **St John's Episcopal Church** is a worth a look, with a handful of rare artefacts on display inside. Foremost is a rare **colonial Bible** – you can see where the pages dedicated to the King have been torn out and hastily replaced with new ones for the President. There's also a rare **Vinegar Bible** (1717) and a **Brattle Organ** (pre 1708), the oldest operative pipe organ in the United States.

Strawbery Banke Museum

14 Hancock St • May–Oct daily 10am–5pm; Nov & Dec guided walking tours offered, check website for details • $15 • ☎ 603 433 1100, ⓦ strawberybanke.org

Colonial buildings are scattered all over Portsmouth, but nothing tops the condensed history of American architecture at the **Strawbery Banke Museum**, a collection of 37 meticulously restored and maintained old wooden buildings. This area began life as the home of wealthy shipbuilders and was successively the lair of privateers and a red-light district before turning into a respectable – and, in the 1950s, decaying – suburb. Restoration began in 1958, starting with the removal of all newer buildings, and the museum opened in 1965.

Start at the **Tyco Visitors Center** (buy tickets here), where introductory videos, maps and displays provide orientation. From here you can you can explore either on a guided tour or on your own (houses displaying a flag are open) – docents or costumed guides are usually on hand to add context.

In the **Shapley Drisco House** two eras collide: half of the house is outfitted as from the 1790s, the other half from the 1950s. The 1766 **Pitt Tavern** holds the most historic significance, having acted as a meeting place for patriots and loyalists during the Revolution, while the upper floors contain exhibits on the local Masonic Lodge. One of the most intriguing exhibits occupies the **Shapiro House** (1795), which in the twentieth century housed a Russian-Jewish immigrant family, while the stained-wood **Sherburne House** is a rare survivor from 1695 – its interior focuses on seventeenth-century architecture. The 1815 **Jefferson House** contains exhibits on the **gundalow**, a traditional shallow-draft cargo barge dating back to the 1600s, it's possible to take a tour on a replica (see p.394).

The site also contains the **Aldrich House** (1797), boyhood home of novelist **Thomas Bailey Aldrich** (1836–1907), which he depicted in his semi-autobiographical novel, *The Story of a Bad Boy*. Traditional crafts are studied and practised on site; the **Lowd House** (1810) contains a display on New England craftsmen and the implements they used and, in the **Dinsmore Shop**, a cooper manufactures barrels with the tools and methods of 1800. Even the **gardens** here are historically accurate, recreated from surviving plans from different time periods (Garden History Tours are offered daily at 1pm).

After 5pm you can wander around for free and observe the buildings' exteriors in the waning hours of the day (though it's hardly the same experience) – many of the houses are still rented or owned as homes today.

ARRIVAL AND DEPARTURE
PORTSMOUTH

By bus C&J Trailways (☎ 1 800 258 7111) has frequent daily services from Boston that terminate at the Portsmouth Transportation Center (☎ 603 430 1100), on the outskirts of town at I-95, exit 3A; a free Coast Trolley bus (see below) runs into the centre from here. Greyhound (☎ 603 433 3210) buses arrive from Boston three times daily, stopping outside *Mainly Gourmet* at 55 Hanover St, a short walk from Market Square.
By car The easiest way to reach downtown Portsmouth is via exit 7 (Market St) off I-95. Rte-1A, which becomes

Miller Avenue and US-1, which becomes Middle Street, both pass directly through the city centre; US-1 continues into Maine, across the Memorial Bridge. Parking near the waterfront is scarce in the summer; there's a 24hr public garage at the intersection of Hanover and High streets (75 cents/hr). You can usually find non-metered parking next to South Mill Pond, along Parrot Avenue, a short walk from Market Square. Metered parking is $1 per hour (maximum 2hr).

GETTING AROUND

By bus Portsmouth is compact and easily manageable on foot. However, the Coast Trolley (Mon–Sat 10.30am–5.30pm; ☎ 603 743 5777, ⓦ coastbus.org; 50 cents) operates two routes around the city as well as the

Downtown Loop (late June to Aug daily 10.30am–2.30pm & 3–5.30pm; every 30min; 50 cents) from Market Square, stopping at most attractions.

INFORMATION

Greater Portsmouth Chamber of Commerce 500 Market St (Mon–Fri 8.30am–5pm; ☎ 603 610 5510, ⓦ portsmouthchamber.org). A 15min walk from Market Square (parking on site), the Greater Portsmouth Chamber of Commerce houses an ample collection of brochures and can help you find a room. They also operate an information

kiosk in Market Square (May–Oct daily 10am–5pm). See also ⓦ portsmouthnh.com. Note that wi-fi is free throughout downtown Portsmouth (and in plenty of cafés and bookstores), but if you need a computer terminal you'll have to rely on your hotel.

TOURS

Walking tours The informative Portsmouth Harbour Trail walking tour guide and map ($2), available at the Chamber of Commerce or information kiosk (see above), details three walks that trace the city's history and originate in the Market Square. In the summer you can also join guided

tours (Mon & Thurs–Sat 10.30am & 5.30pm, Sun 1.30pm; $8; ☎ 603 610 5510). You can also take tours of the Music Hall (see p.395).
Kayak tours If you'd rather see the coastline up close, daily kayaking tours (1hr 30min, $45; 2hr 30min, $64) and kayak

rentals ($64/day) are offered by Portsmouth Kayak Adventures (Mon–Fri 9am–5pm, Sat & Sun 8.30am–6pm; ☎603 559 1000, ⊛portsmouthkayak.com), which originate at their store at Witch Cove Marina, south of the town centre (at 185 Wentworth Rd, aka Rte-1B).

Boat tours Several companies run cruises in Portsmouth Harbor and beyond. Portsmouth Harbor Cruises, at the Ceres Street Dock, has a full bar on every boat (90min harbour cruise $16, 1hr evening cruise $12; call ☎603 436 8084 or ☎1 800 776 0915 for departure times, ⊛portsmouthharbor .com). The Isles of Shoals Steamship Company, 315 Market St (☎603 431 5500 or ☎1 800 441 4620, ⊛islesofshoals.com), offers fun "Steamin Party Ships" (21 and over) on Fri & Sat evenings for $15 and sunset harbour tours on Fri (5.55–7.30pm) for $22. They also do trips to the Isles of Shoals (see p.398). With both companies, you need to buy your tickets in advance to guarantee a spot. Finally, the Gundalow Company at 60 Marcy St (☎603 433 9505, ⊛gundalow.org) has built two replica "gundalow" boats and by 2012 should be offering trips on the river from nearby Prescott Park.

ACCOMMODATION

Accommodation in and around Portsmouth's **historic district** can be expensive – in high season on weekends you are likely to pay $150 or more for a room in a B&B. A collection of slightly cheaper – and less pleasant – motels can be found at the **traffic circle** where I-95, the US-1 bypass and routes 4 and 16 intersect.

IN TOWN

★ **Ale House Inn** 121 Bow St ☎603 431 7760, ⊛alehouseinn.com. Portsmouth's only waterfront inn, centrally located above the theatre (free tickets for guests) is a truly luxurious treat –a contemporary, boutique hotel with each room equipped with a flat-screen TV, free wi-fi and an iPad. The ten cosy rooms occupy a remodelled brick brewery warehouse dating from 1880; room 7 is the biggest, with the best views. Snacks are available in the lounge, but otherwise there's no food on site. Free parking and free use of mountain bikes. $119

Inn at Strawbery Banke 314 Court St ☎603 436 7242, ⊛innatstrawberybanke.com. Seven bright, relaxing rooms, several with four-poster beds, in a sumptuous colonial home built in the early 1800s near the waterfront. Reservations strongly recommended. $160

Martin Hill Inn 404 Islington St ☎603 436 2287, ⊛martinhillinn.com. Meticulously furnished house built around 1815, with seven guest rooms and a shaded garden within walking distance of the city centre. Excellent full breakfast and helpful owners. $165

Sheraton Portsmouth Harborside 250 Market St ☎603 431 2300, ⊛sheratonportsmouth.com. Large chain hotel with conference facilities, indoor pool, redwood sauna and a predominantly business clientele. Comfortable and expensive and in a central location. Free wi-fi. $189

Sise Inn 40 Court St ☎603 433 1200, ⊛siseinn.com. One of the larger inns in Portsmouth, this Queen Anne-style home of 1880s shipping magnate John Sise has 34 elegant, luxurious rooms with phones and TVs. The breakfast is a delicious buffet. $199

NEAR THE TRAFFIC CIRCLE

Holiday Inn Portsmouth 300 Woodbury Ave ☎603 431 8000, ⊕holidayinn.com. Standard – yet comfortable and clean – rooms, outdoor pool and game and exercise rooms at this business hotel. Very convenient for drivers, right on the traffic circle and just off the highway. $182

Port Inn 505 US-1 Bypass, at the traffic circle ☎603 436 4378, ⊛theportinn.com. These good-value, comfortable and clean rooms, some with microwaves and refrigerators, are (depending on the season and day) among the cheapest in Portsmouth. $100

CAMPING

Camping Camping in the area is limited to crowded RV-type parks, such as the *Shel-Al Campground*, US-1, North Hampton (☎603 964 5730, ⊛shel-al.com) and the *Wakeda Campground*, Rte-88, Hampton Falls (☎603 772 5274, ⊛wakedacampground.com). *Shel-Al Campground* $32; *Wakeda Campground* pitches $36, cabins $80

WENTWORTH BY THE SEA

New Hampshire once had four hundred grand Gilded Age hotel resorts – today there are just five. The **Wentworth** – near Portsmouth in sleepy Newcastle – is one of the finest, a gorgeous beaux-arts pile with three Mansard towers and giant white clapboard frame. The current structure dates from 1888, but after lying abandoned for twenty years was re-opened in 2003 as a sparkling new member of the Marriott group. The spa packages are good value, but if you'd rather not splurge, try to visit the *Main Dining Room*, with its original murals and lavish Victorian theme and grab a table on the veranda. In January and February, the hotel runs a six-week **Winter Wine Festival**. The hotel is at 588 Wentworth Rd (Rte 1-B). Contact ☎603 373 6580, ⊛wentworth.com.

EATING

Annabelle's 49 Ceres St ☏603 436 3400, ⓦannabellesicecream.com. Highly addictive home-made ice cream, in ultra-delicious flavours like raspberry chocolate-chip and "Yellow Brick Road" (golden vanilla with roasted pecans and caramel). Daily noon–10pm (varies seasonally and according to the weather).

Black Trumpet Bistro 29 Ceres St ☏603 431 0887, ⓦblacktrumpetbistro.com. One of Portsmouth's smartest eateries, with a romantic dining room on the first floor and a wine bar upstairs. The eclectic menu features flavours from all over the Mediterranean and the Americas – with ingredients sourced from local producers – in such dishes as baby octopus sautéed with olives and fennel and house-made chorizo with black beans (small plates $6–13; main courses $18–29). Mon–Thurs 5.30–9pm, Fri & Sat 5.30–10pm.

Breaking New Grounds 14 Market St ☏603 436 9555. This friendly coffeeshop is always bustling. Grab an excellent cup of coffee and relax with a book at an indoor table, or take it outside to watch the Market Square goings-on. Mon–Fri 6.30am–11pm, Sat & Sun 6.30am–midnight.

Cava 10 Commercial Alley ☏603 319 1575, ⓦcavatapasandwinebar.com. This extremely fashionable tapas and wine bar doesn't have a sea view, but the Spanish/Catalan food is simply spectacular. Pair modern and traditional tapas ($2–10) – Spanish tortilla, Oregon spring lamb, jamon Serrano and chickpea fries – with foie gras pinchos ($18) and mezze small plates ($16–18). Mon & Tues 5–9pm, Wed, Thurs & Sun noon–3pm & 5–9pm, Fri & Sat noon–3pm & 5–10pm.

Ceres Bakery 51 Penhallow St ☏603 436 6518, ⓦceresbakery.com. Excellent fresh breads, good soups and fine pastries in this down-to-earth café with a bright blue exterior. Mon–Fri 7am–5pm, Sat 7am–4pm, Sun 7am–3pm.

Dos Amigos Burritos 107 State St ☏603 373 6001, ⓦdosamigosburritos.com. Top budget option in the centre of town, with tasty burritos (bean, fish, pork and more) from $4.95–7.75 – they also do tacos ($2.75–3.50), chilli ($3.95) and quesadillas ($5.95–7.75). Mon–Thurs & Sun 11am–11pm, Fri & Sat 11am–1.30am.

★ **The Friendly Toast** 113 Congress St ☏603 430 2154, ⓦthefriendlytoast.com. Kitschy thrift-store decor with an interesting selection of breakfasts, sandwiches and omelettes (from $4.75), a huge menu of mixed drinks, shakes, beers and coffees and an equally eclectic crowd. Try the Guinness-battered onion rings

($10). The portions are enormous. Mon–Thurs 7am–10pm, Fri 7am–Sun 9pm (24hr).

The Juicery 51 Hanover St ☏603 431 0693, ⓦportsmouthjuicery.com. The healthiest hole-in-the-wall in town. Order something fruity from the organic juice bar ($4.86–5.87), or try one of several vegan wraps. Takeaway only. Daily 8am–7pm.

★ **Jumpin' Jay's Fish Café** 150 Congress St ☏603 766 3474, ⓦjumpinjays.com. Hands down the best seafood in Portsmouth (and probably the state), with an amazing raw bar, a menu featuring dishes like lobster mac and cheese and fish tacos and a "fresh catches" menu, which might offer Florida mahi-mahi and Atlantic scallops. Main courses $11–18. Mon–Thurs 11.30am–2pm & 5.30–9.30pm, Fri & Sat 11.30am–2pm & 5–10pm, Sun 11.30am–2pm & 5–9pm.

Portsmouth Gas Light Co 64 Market St ☏603 430 8582, ⓦportsmouthgaslight.com. Large, popular restaurant with four sections; dine on juicy burgers (from $9.95) and lobster-stuffed haddock ($23.95) in the *Street Level* restaurant; take in live music on the *Deck* (lit by gas lamps and open as weather permits); or enjoy Portsmouth's favourite pizzas at *Downtown Pizza* (pizzas from $11.95, pastas $12.95). Third Floor nightclub Fri–Sat 9pm–1am. Street Level Mon–Thurs 11.30am–10pm, Fri–Sat 11am–11pm, Sun 11am–10pm; Downtown Pizza Mon–Thurs & Sun 11.30am–10pm, Fri & Sat 11.30am–2am.

★ **Ristorante Massimo** 59 Penhallow St ☏603 436 4000, ⓦristorantemassimo.com. Intimate, smart Italian restaurant, with fresh pasta ($12–24) and plenty of fish main courses ($22–34), such as olive oil-poached monkfish tail risotto. Service is exceptional. Reservations essential. Mon–Sat 5–10pm.

★ **The River House** 53 Bow St ☏603 431 2600, ⓦriverhouse53bow.com. Set right on the old wooden dock, with excellent views of the harbour and a fabulous deck in the summer. Serves possibly the best seafood chowder ($6.50–9.50) in New England. The lobster BLT is also a real treat ($20), but the fried scallops and clams, haddock sandwich ($11) and everything else is exceptional. Mon–Thurs & Sun 11am–10pm, Fri & Sat 11am–11pm.

The Wellington Room 67 Bow St, 2/F ☏603 431 2989, ⓦthewellingtonroom.com. Portsmouth's top haute cuisine experience and definitely the place to splurge. Think mussels simmered in ale broth ($12), Moroccan couscous ($22) and seared local scallops with blood orange reduction ($29). Wed–Sun 5–10pm.

NIGHTLIFE AND ENTERTAINMENT

In the summer, head to the bars and restaurants of the **Piscataqua River** decks on the back side of Bow Street: *The River House* (see above), *Harpoon Willy's* and *Old Ferry Landing*.

Music Hall 28 Chestnut St ☏603 436 2400, ⓦthemusichall.org. Boasting some nine hundred seats,

Portsmouth's largest performance space hosts well-known nationally touring folk, rock, jazz and blues bands,

7

7

KATE DAY

Once a year downtown Portsmouth is witness to an unusual sight – locals and aficionados from all over the world lining up outside the Portsmouth Brewery with "growlers" for a special one-a-year batch of "**Kate the Great Russian Imperial Stout**". The microbrewer is local legend Smuttynose Brewing Co, the folks behind the ★ **Portsmouth Brewery**, 56 Market St (daily 11.30am–12.30am; ☎603 431 1115, ⓦportsmouthbrewery.com). Check the website for the next "Kate Day" – this special beer is usually sold out by noon. The Brewery is more like a restaurant than a pub, with most of the interior taken up by wait-staffed tables – cosy up to the bar if you just want to sample their range of exceptional beers ($4.95). **Tours** of the actual brewery at 225 Heritage Ave (☎603 436 4026; ⓦsmuttynose.com) are also available, usually every Friday and Saturday at 3pm (free).

---

classical concerts, plus dance, theatre and other performances every day of the year. The beaux-arts gem dates from 1878; but the smaller, modern Loft opened in 2011 across the road at 131 Congress St, offering a more intimate line-up of events (it's managed by the same folks). You can take enlightening 75min tours of the Music Hall for $7.50, with the restrooms (seriously) some of the most lavishly decorated you've ever seen (1–2 tours/month; see website for times).

Press Room 77 Daniel St ☎603 431 5186, ⓦpressroomnh.com. Popular for its nightly live jazz, blues, folk and bluegrass performances since 1976. Also serves decent microbrews, inexpensive salads, burgers (from $8.95) and pizza ($6.95) in a casual pub-style setting. Mon–Tues & Sun 4pm–1am, Wed–Sat noon–1am.

★ **The Red Door** 107 State St ☎603 373 6827, ⓦreddoorportsmouth.com. Cool lounge with an extensive martini menu and resident DJs. Get there before 11pm – there's only room for fifty people. Tuesday is 1980s night. Look for the red door – there's no sign. Wed–Mon 7am–close.

Seacoast Repertory Theatre 125 Bow St ☎603 433 4472, ⓦseacoastrep.org. Housed in a converted brewery, this is Portsmouth's major theatrical venue, presenting mainstream professional stage productions.

The Seacoast Region

Dubbed the Seacoast Region, New Hampshire's **coastline** stretches for just eighteen miles, making it the shortest of any US state. Just across the Massachusetts border, **Hampton Beach** is a sprawling arc of sand packed in summer with giggling teenagers and lined with video arcades, ice-cream parlours and waterslides. In between here and Portsmouth, Rte-1A winds between several lovely, picturesque **beaches** (see box, p.397), where many stately homes greet the ocean from enormous bay windows – this whole stretch of coast is known as "Millionaires' Row". If you decide you'd like to take in the mansions at a more leisurely pace, you could follow the paved **walking path** along the water; the best stretch is the three miles or so between North Hampton State Beach (where you can park) and the Rye Beach Club.

Odiorne Point State Park

570 Ocean Blvd (Rte-1A) • Daily June–Aug 8am–6pm • $4, children (6–11 years) $2 • ☎603 436 7406, ⓦnhstateparks.org **Seacoast Science Center** April–Oct daily 10am–5pm; Nov–March Sat–Mon 10am–5pm • $5, children (3–12 years) $2 • ☎603 436 8043, ⓦseacoastsciencecenter.org

If you tire of the beaches, head for the 330-acre **Odiorne Point State Park**, which combines tranquil walking trails with historic ruins and the **Seacoast Science Center** for the kids, loaded with hands-on displays and interactive exhibits. Highlights include the tide pool touch tank and the giant 32ft skeleton of "Tofu", a humpback whale that was killed in 2007 after being hit by a ship. Though the park is the site of the first New Hampshire settlement in 1623, the fortifications you see today were part of Fort Dearborn in the 1940s.

Fuller Gardens

10 Willow Ave, North Hampton • Daily mid-May to mid-Oct 10am–5.30pm • $9 • ☎ 603 964 5414, 🌐 fullergardens.com

Another side-trip from the coast, the colourful **Fuller Gardens** lie at the junction of routes 1A and 111. Designed in 1939 for Massachusetts governor Alvin Fuller, the gardens include more than two thousand rose bushes and a Japanese section complete with bonsai trees.

Exeter

Eight miles west of Portsmouth on Rte-101, friendly **EXETER** was settled in 1638 by a rebellious Bostonian preacher, Reverend John Wheelwright. Sitting on the Squamscott River and an abundance of timber, Exeter thrived in the eighteenth century, selling masts and lumber to shipbuilders. It became the state capital in 1776 (Portsmouth, the previous capital, was too Loyalist) and remained so until Concord assumed the role fourteen years later. Today, Exeter's tree-shaded avenues and stately old neighbourhoods make the attractive town centre worth a quick look. The **Swasey Pavilion** stands at Front and Water streets, a circular bandstand designed by Henry Bacon, the architect of the Lincoln Memorial, in 1916 and now the town landmark.

7

Phillips Exeter Academy

20 Main St • Self-guided tours daily • Free • ☎ 603 777 3433, 🌐 exeter.edu

One of the top private schools in the US, **Phillips Exeter Academy** occupies a large portion of Exeter's attractive town centre, its regal brick buildings sprawling over well-manicured lawns. Founded in 1781 by Dr John Phillips, the school counts among its prominent alumni the great orator Daniel Webster (see box, p.406) and author Dan Brown, who also taught here before hitting the big-time with *The Da Vinci Code*. Along Front Street (Rte-111), near Elm Street south of the centre of town, is the school's boxy brick **library**, designed by architect Louis Kahn in 1971. Begin your self-guided walking tour of the campus by grabbing a free map outside the admissions office in Bissell House, on Front Street across from the Phillips Church.

American Independence Museum

1 Governors Lane • Tours hourly May–Oct Wed–Sat 10am–4pm • $5 • ☎ 603 772 2622, 🌐 independencemuseum.org

The **American Independence Museum**, in the Ladd-Gilman House, just off Water Street, houses a mildly interesting collection of artefacts documenting New Hampshire's role in the American Revolution, including a copy of the Declaration of Independence, drafts of the US Constitution and a few oddities, such as a ring containing a lock of George Washington's hair. A lot more fun is the **American**

NEW HAMPSHIRE BEACHES

It's difficult to understand why the resort town of Hampton is so popular when the beaches of **North Hampton**, a few miles north along Rte-1A, are far more pleasant. **North Beach** and **North Hampton State Beach** are usually pretty quiet, with abundant metered parking ($1.50/hr), though they still catch a bit of the slough from their brash neighbour. **Hampton Beach** itself is a mess of bad restaurants, crowded sands and ugly condominiums; unless you have a penchant for arcades, it's best avoided. Popular with families, **Jenness State Beach**, a long, curving stretch of sand with a smallish car park ($1.50/hr), is a few miles north of North Hampton. Surfers tend to congregate just to the south at **Sawyer Beach**, also known as Surfers' Beach thanks to its year-round supply of decent waves. North of Rye Harbor, **Wallis Sands State Beach** ($15/car), is the best place in New Hampshire for swimming and sunning.

VISITING THE ISLES OF SHOALS

Six miles off the New Hampshire coast are the **Isles of Shoals**, an archipelago of nine islands that became a summer resort in the 1870s. You can visit tranquil **Star Island** by ferry with Island Cruises from Rye Harbor (May–Sept daily; $19–24; ☎603 964 6446, ⓦ uncleoscar.com) or with The Isles of Shoals Steamship Company in Portsmouth (see p.394) – trips run Wed, Fri, Sat & Sun (May–Sept) and range from $33–39. Day-trips take in salt-water touch tanks, the Vaughn-Thaxter Cottage museum, remnants of the colonial village of Gosport and the Stone Chapel, built in 1800.

Oceanic Hotel Star Island ☎603 430 6272, ⓦ starisland.org. A grand establishment built on the island in 1875. The Star Island Corporation has owned and operated Star Island since 1916, founded on the "liberal spiritual" ideals of the United Church of Christ – as such the hotel is primarily a sort of hippie, Christian retreat, though programmes held here range from natural history to photography and everyone is welcome. The sunsets are mesmerizing. Mid-June to mid-Sept. **$280**

7

Independence Festival ($5; call the museum for details), which Exeter stages on the third weekend in July, when the grounds of the museum are transformed into a militia encampment, with arts and crafts, talks, parades and fireworks.

INFORMATION AND TOURS

Exeter Area Chamber of Commerce 24 Front St, Exeter (Mon–Fri 8.30am–4.30pm; ☎603 772 2411, ⓦ exeterarea .org). Park here or anywhere along Water Street and everything is within easy walking distance.

Whale-watching tours Atlantic Fleet at the State Marina in Rye Harbor, 13 miles east of Exeter (late June to early Sept daily 1pm; Sept–Oct Sat & Sun 1pm; $29; ☎603 964 5220, ⓦ atlanticwhalewatch.com).

Aerial tours Hampton Airfield, 9A Lafayette Rd, North Hampton (☎603 964 6749, ⓦ hamptonairfield.com). Enquire about exhilarating aerial tours of the coast in a helicopter or open-cockpit biplane (2-person minimum, 4-person maximum; $75 each). You'll see small signs to the airfield just south of the Rte-111 intersection (on your right heading north).

ACCOMMODATION

Exeter Elms Campground 190 Court St (Rte-108), Exeter ☎603 778 7631, ⓦ exeterelms.com. Two miles south of town and a short drive from the beach, with a decent pool, free wi-fi and plenty of family-friendly activities. May–Oct. Camping **$29**; cabins **$85**

Exeter Inn 90 Front St, Exeter ☎603 772 5901, ⓦ theexeterinn.com. Easy-going elegance and superior service in a three-storey Georgian-style building built in 1932. Rooms blend antiques with modern appliances (free wi-fi, flat-screen TVs). **$159**

Inn by the Bandstand 6 Front St, Exeter ☎603 772 6352, ⓦ innbythebandstand.com. A restored 1809 Federal-style inn where many of the elegant, antique-adorned rooms have fireplaces. Rates include breakfast, port in each room and free wi-fi. **$149**

EATING AND DRINKING

★ **Airfield Café** 9A Lafayette Rd, North Hampton ☎603 964 6749, ⓦ theairfieldcafe.com. An enticing diner based at Hampton Airfield (see above); try the grilled smoked sausage with eggs for breakfast ($6.75) or juicy burgers for lunch (from $5.50). Watch planes take off and land as you eat. Hampton Airfield lies just off Rte-1 in the centre of North Hampton town, three miles from the beach. Daily 7am–2pm.

Green Bean 33 Water St, Exeter ☎603 778 7585, ⓦ nhgreenbean.com. Serves home-made soups, salads and sandwiches ($5.50–6.50), made fresh daily, with outdoor seating in a leafy courtyard. Mon–Sat 11am–4pm.

Szechuan Taste 42 Water St , Exeter ☎603 772 8888. Best Chinese restaurant in these parts, specializing in cheap, no-frills buffets and spicy Sichuan food; try the "triple delight noodle soup", which blends shrimp, chicken and pork with noodles and vegetables ($7.50). Daily 11am–10pm.

Tavern at River's Edge 163 Water St, Exeter ☎603 772 7393, ⓦ tavernatriversedge.com. A good range of international cuisine from pan-seared haddock to five-cheese ravioli in a cosy Victorian dining room along the river (main courses $16–28). Closed Sun.

The Merrimack Valley

The financial and political heartland of New Hampshire is the **Merrimack Valley**, which – originally via the Merrimack River and now via I-93 – has always been the main thoroughfare north to the lakes, the White Mountains and Canada. Early pioneers had established a trading post near Concord by 1660 and by the 1720s large groups of English settlers were calling the area home. In the nineteenth century, the valley boomed with industry and Nashua, Manchester and Concord were all major manufacturing centres. **Concord** became the state capital in 1784 and remains the centre of New Hampshire's political life, while **Manchester** is the most populous city in the state, with ample evidence of its gritty industrial past.

Manchester

Once a prosperous mill town, **MANCHESTER**, New Hampshire's largest city (population 107,000), has been in a perpetual state of recovery ever since the **Amoskeag Manufacturing Company** went belly-up in 1935. Today, although the city remains rather rough around the edges, new apartments are slowly gentrifying the downtown area and riverfront; renovated mills are pulling in businesses, restaurants and artists; and its handful of attractions – including the world-class **Currier Art Museum** – provide a striking contrast to the state's rustic pleasures. Manchester's main commercial drag, **Elm Street**, runs north–south parallel to the Merrimack River (doubling as US-3), the best place to find shops, restaurants and bars. The **Amoskeag Millyard Historic District**, several blocks west along the banks of the river between Bridge and Granite streets, is where the city's recovery is most clearly visible. All the old red-brick mills have been converted to modern condo and office space, with the **Millyard Museum** the best place to get a sense of the city's development.

Brief history

Founded by primarily Scots and Irish settlers as **Derryfield** in the 1720s, the city was renamed in 1810 in memory of local canal builder Samuel Blodget, who had dreamed of emulating Lancashire's industrial dynamo. Though small mills had set up shop by the 1820s, the Amoskeag company – and the entire modern city, for that matter – was the brainchild of a group of Boston entrepreneurs, who purchased 15,000 acres of land around the Amoskeag Falls in 1831, acquired the rights to water power along the entire Merrimack River, built a dam and constructed the enormous Amoskeag Mills. From 1838 to 1920, the company was the world's largest textile manufacturer; at its peak, it employed 17,000 people and spewed out more than four million yards of cloth per week. After the mills closed, the establishment of **Amoskeag Industries** by local businessmen in 1936 essentially saved the city, laying the groundwork for what you see today.

Millyard Museum

200 Bedford St (entrance on Commercial St; car park on site) • Tues–Sat 10am–4pm, Sun noon–4pm • $6 • ☎ 603 622 7531, ⓦ manchesterhistoric.org

Your first stop in Manchester should be the illuminating **Millyard Museum**, housed in old Mill No. 3, which once manufactured denim, in the heart of the Amoskeag Millyard Historic District. The museum chronicles the city's history with a blend of archeological artefacts and curated exhibits, starting with the native peoples who fished at Amoskeag Falls thousands of years ago (Amoskeag means "place of many fish"). Local Revolutionary War hero **John Stark**, who had a farm near the falls, gets his own section, as does **Samuel Blodget**, builder of the canal that linked the city with Boston in 1807. The main section covers the history of the mills, with looms from the 1920s and 1930s, scale models and maps of the planned Amoskeag town and examples of linens and ginghams made here.

SEE Science Center

200 Bedford St, at Pleasant St • Mon–Fri 10am–4pm, Sat & Sun 10am–5pm • $8 (ages 3 and up) • ☎ 603 669 0400,
ⓦ see-sciencecenter.org

Kids will love the **SEE Science Center** (in the same building as the Millyard Museum,
but with the main entrance on the other side), with plenty of hands-on displays
(robots, periscopes and the like), exploring the world of science. Adults should also
take a peek for one of the most unusual sights in the state, the **LEGO Millyard Project**, a
massive but intricately detailed scale model of the old mills c.1900, said to be the
largest permanent LEGO installation in the world (it comprised three million bricks
on completion in 2006).

PSNH Energy Park and Amoskeag Overlook

PSNH Energy Park, N Commercial St • Daily April–Oct 8am–6.30pm • Free • ☎ 603 634 2228

Just before North Commercial Street meets Canal Street, at the north end of
downtown Manchester, you'll see a turning on the left into the parking area for the
Amoskeag Falls hydro-electric station. Dubbed the **PSNH Energy Park**, you can drive
through to the end of this area and park near the **Amoskeag Overlook**, right on the
Merrimack River. You'll get to see what's left of the **Amoskeag Falls** (now tumbling over
a weir and rocky area below) and fine views of the city skyline. You can also wander up
here via the **Riverwalk**, a footpath along the water that you can pick up at Granite City
Bridge (Granite Street).

Amoskeag Fishways

6 Fletcher St (exit 6, I-293) • Mon–Sat 9am–5pm (also Sun May & June) • Free • ☎ 603 626 3474, ⓦ amoskeagfishways.org

Just across the Amoskeag Bridge (on the west bank of the Merrimack), north of downtown Manchester (best approached by car; free parking), the **Amoskeag Fishways** offers an absorbing introduction to the history, flora and wildlife of the Merrimack River. It's primarily targeted at kids, with live frogs, turtles and snakes in tanks and an underwater viewing gallery at the 54-step **fish ladder** downstairs, where bewildered-looking fish get shot past the dam. The ladder usually bubbles into life during May and June when migrating shad, herring and sea lamprey power their way upriver, though since 2006 numbers have dwindled somewhat (experts are divided as to the cause). Still, it's worth checking the website for special events and the centre's fish hatchery programme, which has been successful in increasing fish numbers.

Currier Museum of Art

150 Ash St • Sun, Mon, Wed–Fri 11am–5pm, Sat 10am–5pm • $10 • ☎ 603 669 6144, ⓦ currier.org • Bus #7 (from the corner of Elm and Merrimack sts)

Featuring rotating displays of travelling shows and work from the permanent collection, ranging from Picasso and Monet to O'Keeffe, Hopper and Wyeth, the **Currier Museum of Art** is easily New Hampshire's best fine arts museum.

Pride of place in the lower level goes to *Visit of the Gypsies*, a rare 1505 Flemish tapestry; look out also for works by Constable and Tiepolo. The main level is dedicated to Contemporary, Modern and European painters, while the upper galleries focus on American art from 1680 to 1915. Highlights you might see from the permanent collection include Picasso's jarring Cubist masterpiece *Spanish Woman Seated in a Chair* and *The Seine at Bougival* by Monet, one of his most outstanding early works. Rather than paint a typical scene of the time, here he is already toying with Impressionist themes: the unifying quality of light and the use of bold patches of colour. The powerful work of O'Keeffe is wonderfully represented by the deceptively simple *Cross by the Sea, Canada*, while *The Bootleggers* is an unusually dramatic painting for Hopper. Wyeth's *Cat-O'-Nine-Tails* offers an Impressionistic view of the Maine coast – he first displayed the painting here in 1939. New Hampshire subjects are also well represented, such as Jasper Francis Cropsey's glowing *American Indian Summer Morning in the White Mountains*. The *Winter Garden Café* inside makes for a pleasant pit-stop (free wi-fi).

Zimmerman House

223 Heather St • April to early Jan; tours (1hr 30min) Mon 2pm, Thurs–Sun 11.30am & 2pm • $20 including Currier Museum entry; tickets available at the museum (tours leave by shuttle bus from here); reservations required • ☎ 603 669 6144; ⓦ currier.org

The Currier Museum also runs tours of the **Zimmerman House** (two miles north), a one-storey wooden structure designed in 1950 by **Frank Lloyd Wright** (1867–1959) that epitomizes the great American architect's vision of form in harmony with landscape. The Zimmermans left the property to the Currier in 1988 and it still contains their exceptional personal collection of modern art, pottery and sculpture – though collection lacks individual showstoppers, tours focus on the way the architecture and the artwork as a whole blends together so beautifully. Special tours are also available with specific themes such as "fabrics and furnishings". Book tours online to be sure of a place (13 people per tour maximum).

ARRIVAL AND DEPARTURE MANCHESTER

By plane Manchester-Boston Regional Airport (☎ 603 624 6556, ⓦ flymanchester.com), ten minutes south of downtown off Rte-3A at 1 Airport Rd, is served by several major carriers; take local bus #3 ($1.50; weekdays only) or a flat-fare taxi into the centre ($15–20). Shared vans (☎ 1 800 245 2525, ⓦ flightlineinc.com) to Boston and regional destinations are available if booked in advance and Greyhound buses on route between Manchester ($11; 15min), Boston ($18.50; 1hr) and Burlington ($42; 3hr 45min). All the major car rental agencies have desks at the airport.

By bus Bus services to Manchester drop off passengers at the Manchester Transportation Center, 119 Canal St. Boston Express runs frequently to Boston (1hr 40min) and Logan Airport ($14–18; ☎ 603 521 6000, ⓦ bostonexpressbus .com), while Greyhound serves various locations including Boston ($18.50), Hanover ($24) and Montreal ($63).

By car Downtown Manchester is circled by interstates I-93 and I-293, making access fairly straightforward. An easy option is to take I-295 exit 5 and drive up Granite Street into the Millyard District, where there is plenty of parking (free at the Millyard Museum). Metered parking is 50 cents/30min.

GETTING AROUND

By bus The Manchester Transit Authority (☎ 603 623 8801 ⓦ mtabus.org) runs an extensive network of buses all over town ($1.50 standard fare; exact change only), although apart from bus #3 to the airport (Mon–Fri 5.25am–6.25pm) and bus #7 to the Currier Museum, you will not have much cause to use it.

INFORMATION AND TOURS

Manchester Chamber of Commerce 54 Hanover St (Mon–Fri 8.30am–5pm; ☎ 603 666 6600, ⓦ manchester -chamber.org). Downtown office with maps and brochures. **Manchester Information Center** on Elm St at Merrimack St, next to Veteran's Park (Fri & Wed 9am–3pm, Thurs till 6pm, but call to make sure; ☎ 603 624 6465).

Segway tours The Segway was invented by Dean Kamen in Manchester in 2001, so it seems appropriate to tour the city this way. Segway of Manchester rents them out (10min for $10) and organizes 2hr guided tours (10am, 1pm, 4pm & 5.30pm; 90min; $69). Their office is at 42 Hanover St (daily 10am–5pm; ☎ 603 218 8150, ⓦ segwayofmanchester.com).

ACCOMMODATION

★ **Ash Street Inn** 118 Ash St ☎ 603 668 9908, ⓦ ashstreetinn.com. For a bit of character, try this homely Victorian B&B, built in 1885 and featuring original stained glass and bright, comfortable rooms with hardwood floors. Free wi-fi. **$159**

Hilton Garden Inn Manchester Downtown 101 South Commercial St ☎ 603 669 2222, ⓦ hgi -manchester.com. Downtown's newest hotel, perfectly located in the Millyard district (overlooking a minor league baseball stadium) with all the amenities: microwaves, LCD TVs, indoor pool, 24hr business centre and free wi-fi. **$142**

Radisson Manchester 700 Elm St ☎ 603 625 1000, ⓦ radisson.com/manchesternh. Most of the politicos stay at this otherwise standard chain hotel, which becomes a media circus during the primary season. The location is second to none – good summer rates. **$129**

EATING

Ate Doors Down 967 Elm St ☎ 603 518 5008, ⓦ atedoorsdown.com. Best budget eats downtown, with pizza slices for $2, sandwiches $5.50–7 and a small bakery in the same space. Mon–Fri 6am–9pm, Sat noon–9pm.

★ **Café Momo** 1065 Hanover St ☎ 603 623 3733, ⓦ cafemomonh.com. Cosy Nepalese restaurant giving some much-needed colour to the local dining scene; the lamb dumplings (*momos*; $8) are superb and there's an excellent choice of vegetarian dishes. Main courses $10–19. Tues–Thurs noon–9pm, Fri & Sat noon–10pm, Sun noon–8pm.

Famous Dave's 1707 S Willow St ☎ 603 668 1220, ⓦ famousdaves.com. This barbecue chain restaurant knocks out decent St Louis-style ribs ($12.99) and real fatty barbecue sandwiches (from $7.49) – try the smoked brisket and finish off with Dave's Famous Bread Pudding ($5.99), smothered in praline sauce and vanilla bean ice cream. Mon–Thurs & Sun 11am–10pm, Fri & Sat 11am–11pm.

Fratello's 155 Dow St ☎ 603 624 2022, ⓦ fratellos .com. Busy most nights for its solid menu of classic Italian dishes, pastas and pizzas. Lunch is the cheapest meal, with pizzas (from $12.99) and paninis going for under $10. Daily 11.30am–10pm.

Hanover Street Chophouse 149 Hanover St ☎ 603 644 2467, ⓦ hanoverstreetchophouse.com. This local institution is an old-fashioned steakhouse, serving Kansas City dry-aged strip steak ($38) racks of Australian lamb ($38) and NY sirloin ($34). Mon–Thurs 11.30am–2.30pm & 5–9.30pm, Fri 11.30am–2.30pm & 5–10pm, Sat 5–10pm.

Lala's Hungarian Pastry 836 Elm St ☎ 603 647 7100, ⓦ lalahungarianpastryandrestaurant.com. Offers fabulous pastries, beef goulash ($7.95), stuffed peppers ($7.50), schnitzel (from $9.50) and other Eastern European classics – lunch is a bit cheaper than dinner. Mon & Tues 7am–5pm, Wed–Sat 7am–8pm.

DRINKING

Cotton 75 Arms St ☎ 603 622 5488, ⓦ cottonfood.com. This hip bar-bistro serves superb Martinis and classic dishes such as retro meatloaf ($9) from owner Jeffrey Paige.

Mon–Fri 11.30am–2.30pm & 5–9pm, Sat 5–10pm, Sun 5–8pm.

Milly's Tavern 500 Commericial St ☎ 603 625 4444,

7

ⓦ millystavern.com. Decent brewpub offering nine varieties on tap, plus at least two seasonals under the bridge near the river, also serving justly-popular chilli and live music every Tuesday, Friday and Saturday. A local DJ spins the rest of the week. Mon–Sat 11am–1am.

★ **Strange Brew Tavern** 88 Market St ☎ 603 666 4292, ⓦ strangebrewtavern.net. Live music six nights a week (blues, jazz and rock) and 65 beers on tap (from $4) make this one of the best joints to kick back in the city, supplemented by an enticing menu of pub food. Daily 4pm–1am.

South of Manchester

South of Manchester the Merrimack River winds its way for thirty miles towards the Massachusetts border, passing old mill towns such as Merrimack and Nashua that today fall firmly within Boston's economic orbit. Along the way, the **Anheuser Busch Brewery** is a lot of fun for non-designated drivers, while the **Robert Frost Farm** is a major pilgrimage site for fans of the beloved poet.

Anheuser Busch Brewery

221 Daniel Webster Highway (Rte-3), Merrimack • Jan–April Thurs–Mon 10am–4pm; May Mon–Sat 9am–5pm, Sun 11.30am–5pm; June–Aug daily 10am–5pm; Sept–Dec daily 10am–4pm • Free • ☎ 603 595 1202, ⓦ budweisertours.com

The massive **Anheuser Busch Brewery** south of Manchester in **Merrimack**, offers free tours of its facility – one of thirteen it operates nationwide – including free tastings. Already America's biggest beer company, a 2008 merger with Belgium's InBev created the world's largest brewer.

Robert Frost Farm

122 Rockingham Rd (Rte-28), Derry • May–June & Sept to mid-Oct Wed–Sun 10am–5pm; July & Aug daily 10am–4pm • Gardens and barn free, farmhouse $5 • ☎ 603 432 3091, ⓦ robertfrostfarm.org

The **Robert Frost Farm**, on Rte-28 (take exit 4 from I-93), just south of **Derry**, is the premier New England memorial to the great poet, and the only one he himself wished to preserve. Fans should visit for the optional **free guided tours** as much as the house itself; these are entertaining hour-long introductions to the life, character and poetry of Frost, usually delivered by local poet and irascible site manager Bill Gleed.

The white clapboard farmhouse was built in 1885, but Frost's grandfather bought the property for his essentially penniless grandson in 1900. Frost lived here with his young family until 1909 (he sold the farm for $1100 in 1911). It was here he composed or drew inspiration for many of his most famous poems; *Mending Wall*, *Home Burial* and *The Death of the Hired Man* among them. Between 1942 and 1964 the property served as a junkyard before being purchased by the State. Thanks to Frost's daughter, Lesley (1899–1983), the farm was then meticulously restored over eleven years with period furniture that resembled the family originals. Start in the barn, with a thirty-minute video and small exhibit of Frost's handwritten poems and photos, before moving on to the main house. Outside there's a nature trail that takes in the remnants of Frost's apple orchard, hayfield and even the original Hyla Brook (all inspiration for his poems).

Concord and around

New Hampshire's state capital, **CONCORD** (pronounced "conquered"), is a small town with a lot of political clout, symbolized by its elegant **State House**. Famous throughout the world in the nineteenth century as the home of the "Concord" stagecoaches, the town today offers the **Museum of New Hampshire History**, the **McAuliffe-Shepard Discovery Center** and the **Pierce Manse**, once home to Franklin Pierce.

New Hampshire State House

107 N Main St • Mon–Fri 8am–4.15pm • Free • ☎ 603 271 2154, ⓦ nh.gov

Concord is all about government and the town seems to revolve, both physically and spiritually, around the gold-domed **State House** on Main Street. Designed by

Stuart J. Park, the original Greek Revival structure was completed in 1819, then expanded and twice remodelled; the handsome stone facade was quarried from local granite. The state legislature – the largest in the country, with some four hundred members – has met continuously in the same chambers since June 2, 1819, the longest such tenure in the US. On the first floor you'll find dioramas of Revolutionary War battles, including John Stark's victory at Bennington (see p.328). Portraits of more than 150 legislators hang on all three floors, including a noble-looking Daniel Webster (see box, p.406). Outside, bronze statues of New Hampshire notables, including Stark, Webster and President Franklin Pierce, strike dignified poses.

Museum of New Hampshire History

6 Eagle Square (off Main St) • Tues–Sat 9.30am–5pm, Sun noon–5pm; July–Oct 15 & Dec also open Mon 9.30am–5pm • $5.50 • ☎ 603 228 6688, ⓦ nhhistory.org

The compact but enlightening **Museum of New Hampshire History** is tucked behind the brick buildings on Main Street across from the State House, in **Eagle Square**. In the gallery on the first floor, a well-presented collection of paintings, photographs, maps and artefacts, including a restored 1855 Concord coach and a Native American canoe (used on Lake Ossipee sometime between 1430 and 1660), chronologically traces the state's history. The most famous exhibit is the "**Mystery Stone**", an egg-like object carved with symbols, dug up in 1872 near Lake Winnipesaukee – experts have been unable to decide whether it's Native American or an elaborate hoax. Upstairs are rotating displays, a replica forest fire watchtower and various hands-on exhibits for the kids.

Pierce Manse

14 Horseshoe Pond Lane • Mid-June to early Sept Tues–Sat 11am–3pm, tours on the hour • $7 • ☎ 603 225 4555, ⓦ piercemanse.org • Bus #1 (from Eagle Square)

Just off the north end of Main Street, the **Pierce Manse** stands as a memorial to 14th US president **Franklin Pierce**. Today an immaculately restored two-storey 1838 home filled with his personal effects, such as a beaver-skin top hat, Shaker-style writing table and a silver Mexican spoon (loot from the US-Mexican War), the building housed Pierce and his family between 1842 and 1848 after he had resigned his seat in the US Senate, and was working in Concord as a lawyer. The grand clapboard house was

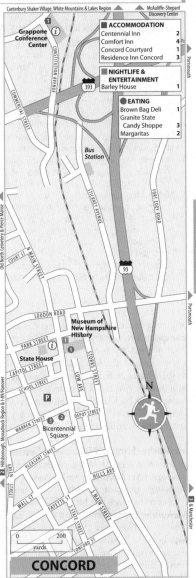

CONCORD

ACCOMMODATION
Centennial Inn	2
Comfort Inn	4
Concord Courtyard	1
Residence Inn Concord	3

NIGHTLIFE & ENTERTAINMENT
Barley House	1

EATING
Brown Bag Deli	1
Granite State Candy Shoppe	3
Margaritas	2

7

LIBERTY AND UNION: THE LIFE OF DANIEL WEBSTER

New Hampshire's best-known statesman and orator, **Daniel Webster** (1782–1852) was born in a two-room farmhouse at 131 North Rd off Rte-127 in **FRANKLIN**, eighteen miles north of Concord. Now known simply as the **Daniel Webster Birthplace** (late June to early Sept Sat & Sun 9am–5pm; free; ☎ 603 934 5057; ⓦ nhstateparks.org), the humble wooden home contains just a few pieces of period furniture and enthusiastic volunteers dressed in period costume. Built in 1781 by Webster's father, it was the most northernmost colonial farm at the time, totally dependent on good relations with the local Abenaki. The Websters moved on a few years later, but although his later life was centred around Massachusetts and Washington, DC, Daniel maintained a close relationship with the area, returning whenever he could to fish, hunt and booze in the local taverns. There's not a lot to see (and the dilapidated Sawyer House, opposite, is unlikely to be restored any time soon), but it's a tranquil, rustic place.

Webster attended Phillips Exeter Academy, graduated from **Dartmouth College** in 1801 and went on to build a successful law practice before serving in Congress from 1813 to 1817 and in the US Senate from 1827 to 1841. He loomed large on the political scene in his day, delivering persuasive speeches on topics as far-ranging as states' rights, slavery, the US-Canadian border and Dartmouth College. As secretary of state under presidents William Henry Harrison, Tyler and Fillmore, Webster remained a staunch defender of the Union. During a particularly heated discussion in 1850, in which Webster debunked the idea of states' rights, he coined the memorable phrase "Liberty and Union, now and forever, one and inseparable." In perhaps his most famous debate, the Dartmouth College Case of 1817, Webster defended his alma mater before the Supreme Court, which decided that states could not interfere with ex-royal charters.

originally located on Montgomery Street, in the centre of town, but was carefully transported to this tranquil historic district in 1971.

Known mainly as one of the US's least successful leaders, perhaps unfairly, Pierce had a tragic family life, losing all three children and eventually his wife to illness – his plan to spend time here was also cut short by the Mexican War. Illuminating free tours are provided by dedicated docents and a small exhibit and video at the entrance supply context and background. Pierce returned to Concord in 1861 and died here eight years later. He's buried in **Old North Cemetery**, near the intersection of North State Street and Keane Avenue, at the northern end of town.

McAuliffe-Shepard Discovery Center

2 Institute Drive (I-93, exit 15 E) • Daily 10am–5pm, Fri also 6.30–9pm • $12, children (3–12 years) $9; show tickets $4 • ☎ 603 271 7827, ⓦ starhop.com • Take the NHTI trolley from Eagle Square

Set within the campus of the New Hampshire Technical Institute (NHTI), between I-93 and the river, the **McAuliffe-Shepard Discovery Center** was named for Christa McAuliffe, the Concord high school teacher who perished in the Space Shuttle *Challenger* disaster in 1986 and Alan Shepard, the New Hampshire-born astronaut who became the first American in space on May 5, 1961. The 92-seat planetarium stages an impressive programme of astronomy shows, while exhibits take in everything from a full-sized replica of a Mercury-Redstone rocket and multi-sensory exhibit telling **Alan Shepard**'s story, to interactive displays on the sun, living in space and planning a trip to Mars – great fun for all ages. There is also a tribute to **Christa McAuliffe**, who was selected from a pool of 11,500 applicants to participate in the shuttle trip that ended in tragedy just 73 seconds after a seal in a rocket booster failed at lift-off.

ARRIVAL AND DEPARTURE CONCORD

By bus Concord is readily accessible via hourly buses from Boston and Logan Airport. Concord Coach Lines and Greyhound buses stop at the bus terminal (☎ 603 228 3300) at 30 Stickney Ave – it's a short walk or Concord Area Transit (CAT) bus ride into town (Mon–Fri 6am–6.30pm; 11 daily; $1.25; ☎ 603 225 1989).

By car The city is easily reached by car from I-93, which passes through the eastern side of the town (take exit 13

for downtown). Metered parking (75 cents/hr) is available on Main Street and the convenient Firehouse Parking Garage (75 cents/hr) is between Warren and School streets, just off Main Street.

GETTING AROUND

On foot Central Concord is easily explored on foot; for Pierce Manse and the McAuliffe-Shepard Discovery Center though, you'll need to drive or take a bus.

By bus Concord Area Transit (CAT) runs four main bus routes around town, with Eagle Square on Main Street acting as a central hub. Bus #1 runs past the Pierce Manse from Eagle Square (Mon–Fri 6.40am–5.50pm; 11 daily; $1.25; ☎603 225 1989), while the NHTI Trolley runs frequently past the McAuliffe-Shepard Discovery Center (Mon–Fri 8am–6pm; $1.25).

INFORMATION

Greater Concord Chamber of Commerce About a mile north of the town centre in the Grappone Conference Center, 40 Commercial St and Constitution Ave, just off I-93, exit 15; take the NHTI trolley from Eagle Square (Mon–Fri 8.30am–5pm; ☎603 224 2508, ⓦconcordnhchamber.com).

You'll also find the main visitors centre here (Mon–Fri 8.30am–5pm, Sat 9am–3pm).

Information kiosk In front of the State House (May–Oct Mon–Fri 8.30am–5pm, Sat 9am–3pm). Distributes historical walking-tour brochures.

ACCOMMODATION

Centennial Inn 96 Pleasant St ☎603 225 7102, ⓦthecentennialhotel.com. Contemporary style has been added to this Victorian landmark, supplementing its original charm with designer furniture, LCD TVs and free wi-fi. **$139**

Comfort Inn 71 Hall St ☎603 226 4100, ⓦcomfortinn .com. Smartest motel in town, with comfortable rooms, a tad more stylish than the chain's usual offerings. Extras include heated indoor pool, breakfast, free laundry and free wi-fi. **$99**

Courtyard Concord 70 Constitution Ave ☎603 225 0303, ⓦmarriott.com. Luxurious, spacious rooms with free wi-fi, flat-screen TVs and small balconies (on the third floor). There's also a pool and hot tub. Convenient for sights in the north end of the city; airport shuttle ($20) and car rentals on site. **$149**

★ **Residence Inn Concord** 91 Hall St ☎603 226 0012, ⓦmarriott.com. Relatively new Marriott property with outstanding, stylish rooms and amenities, including an indoor salt-water pool; their spacious studio-, one-bedroom- and two-bedroom-suites with full kitchen make this the best place in town, though it's also the most expensive. **$179**

EATING

Brown Bag Deli 1 Eagle Square ☎603 225 9110. Wholesome salads (from $3.75) and deli sandwiches (from $4.95) across from the History Museum. Mon–Fri 7.30am–2.30pm.

★ **Granite State Candy Shoppe** 13 Warren St ☎603 225 2591, ⓦnhchocolates.com. Get your sweet fix in this venerable chocolate and candy store, open since 1927 and selling addictive ice cream (from $3.25) and malted frappes ($4.75) in the summer. Try the butter pecan or Indian pudding (a bit like gingerbread) flavours. Mon–Sat 10am–8pm, Sun noon–5pm (reduced hours in winter).

Margaritas 1 Bicentennial Square ☎603 224 2821, ⓦmargs.com. Housed in a former police station, this popular chain serves some of the biggest Mexican dishes (main courses $13.99–19.99) around. You can sit in a former jail cell while you sip your margarita – very atmospheric. Mon–Thurs & Sun 4–10pm, Fri & Sat 4–11pm.

NIGHTLIFE AND ENTERTAINMENT

Other than a couple of basic bars, some with **live music**, there is really no nightlife to speak of – see what's on at the Capitol Center for the Arts, 44 South Main St (☎603 225 1111, ⓦccanh.com), a decent venue for live concerts and shows. The **local newspaper**, the *Concord Monitor* (ⓦconcordmonitor.com), is widely available and offers entertainment listings.

Barley House 132 N Main St ☎603 228 6363, ⓦthebarleyhouse.com. Watering hole for state legislators on lunch breaks. Good, mostly inexpensive pub-style food and live music, especially jazz. Mon–Sat 11am–1pm.

Canterbury Shaker Village

288 Shaker Rd, Canterbury (I-93 exit 18) • Mid-May–Oct daily 10am–5pm • $17, good for two consecutive days • ☎603 783 9511, ⓦshakers.org

About twenty minutes north of Concord, **Canterbury Shaker Village** is New England's premier museum of Shaker life (see box, p.408) and perhaps the most intriguing tourist

THE SHAKERS IN AMERICA

The **Shaker** church – originally an offshoot of the Quaker movement – was founded in the US by Mother Ann Lee, who arrived from England with nine followers in 1774, seeking religious freedom. The "Shaking Quakers" (so named because of their tendency to dance in church, thereby shaking off sins) lived apart from the world in communities devoted to communal living, efficiency, equality, pacifism and, perhaps most notoriously, celibacy – the sect relied upon conversion and adoption to expand. Also, believing that technology would create more time for worship, the Shakers were creative and industrious inventors and craftsmen; today the sect is probably best known for its legacy to the furniture, architecture and agriculture industries.

The first formal Shaker community was set up in **New Lebanon**, NY in 1787 and during the next century eighteen other major communities were established across Massachusetts, including the Hancock Shaker Village (see p.233), New Hampshire, Maine, Connecticut, Kentucky, Ohio and Indiana; smaller ventures were also attempted in Florida and Georgia. The sect flourished in the nineteenth century, with numbers peaking in the 1850s. Decline, when it came around the start of the twentieth century, happened quickly and was ultimately exacerbated by the denomination's self-imposed **sexual chastity**. Today only a handful of Shakers remain in the world, at the Sabbathday Lake community in New Gloucester, Maine.

destination in New Hampshire. In 1792, this tranquil village became the sixth Shaker community in the US and, at its zenith in the mid-nineteenth century, there were some three hundred people living on the grounds; the last Shaker living in Canterbury died in 1992 at the age of 96.

After watching the excellent Ken Burns documentary in the Trustees Office, next to the visitor centre at the entrance, you can take several engrossing one-hour **tours** of the site. Led by experts, these introduce the ideals, day-to-day life and architecture (there are 25 perfectly restored buildings on the site) of the Shakers as you wander from building to building – including the church, the schoolhouse and the laundry room. You are also free to wander around on your own, though only some of the buildings are open for self-guided tours; get a map at the visitor centre. It's worth a peek inside the **Carriage House** near the entrance, where precious examples of Shaker furniture are displayed.

EATING AND DRINKING · CANTERBURY SHAKER VILLAGE

Greenwood's ☎ 603 783 4238. Canterbury's full-service restaurant is housed in the old blacksmith shop, serving Shaker-inspired meals using local produce: shaker corn pudding ($5.50), shaker pot roast ($10.99) and chicken pot pie ($10.99). Mid-May to Oct daily 11am–3pm.

Shaker Box Lunch Offers cheaper snacks and drinks, including salads, soups, mouthwatering brownies and apple hand-pies (semi-circular pastries). Mid-May to Oct daily 10am–4pm.

The Monadnock region

Known as the "quiet corner" of New Hampshire, the **Monadnock region** encompasses deserted country roads and sleepy small towns, centred around the 3165ft peak of **Mount Monadnock** in the southwest part of the state. Aside from the mountain itself, which attracts plenty of outdoor enthusiasts, the region boasts no real stand-out attractions, and is probably best known for being the inspiration behind *Our Town*, the perennially popular play by Thornton Wilder. You can get a feel for the playwright's small-town New England in any of the hereabouts many picturesque communities, but several are worth highlighting, **Keene**, the area's biggest town; **Peterborough**, the region's – perhaps the state's – artistic centre; and **Hillsborough**, birthplace of the only US president to come from New Hampshire, Franklin Pierce.

Keene

With 23,000 residents, **KEENE** is the unofficial capital of the Monadnock region, its unusually wide **Main Street**, lined with cafés and trees, giving it a somewhat urbane, even European feel – at least compared to the villages around it. In recent years the calm has been occasionally shattered by **Free Keene** activists (ⓦfreekeene.com), dedicated to creating a libertarian state in New Hampshire. Unless they happen to be protesting, there's not much to do other than shop and eat and admire the picture-perfect **Keene Common** at the end of Main Street, dominated by the soaring **United Church of Christ** (1786). Note also that the town features some excellent **bike** and **hiking paths**, converted from old rail tracks.

Wyman Tavern Museum

399 Main St • June to early Sept Thurs–Sat 11am–4pm • $3 • ☎ 603 352 5161, ⓦ hsccnh.org

Keene's most historic attraction is the **Wyman Tavern Museum**, built as the local pub in 1762 by Isaac Wyman, a staunch patriot who later led a group of Minute Men (see p.522) to fight in the Revolutionary War. The tavern was also the site of the first official meeting of the trustees of Dartmouth College in 1770. The restored taproom, living quarters and ballroom are open to the public, with sections restored to reflect the periods from 1770 to 1820 and from 1820 to the 1870s.

7

ARRIVAL AND DEPARTURE
KEENE

By bus Greyhound buses going to and from Burlington and Brattleboro in Vermont and Springfield and Northampton in Massachusetts stop at *Corner News*, 67

Main St (☎ 603 352 1331).
By car Metered parking is available all along Main St (25 cents for 30min).

GETTING AROUND

On foot Keene and the Wyman Tavern museum are easily seen on foot.
By bicycle For bike rentals, visit Summers' Backcountry Outfitters, 16 Ashuelot St, at West St (Mon–Wed

10am–6pm, Thurs & Fri 10am–8pm, Sat 9am–6pm, Sun 10am–5pm; ☎ 603 357 5107, ⓦ summersbackcountry .com); bikes are $25/day and they'll also give you plenty of advice on routes.

INFORMATION

Greater Keene Chamber of Commerce 48 Central Square, at the top end of Main St (Mon–Fri 9am–5pm;

☎ 603 352 1303, ⓦ keenechamber.com).

ACCOMMODATION

Carriage Barn Bed and Breakfast 358 Main St ☎ 603 357 3812, ⓦ carriagebarn.com. Budget B&B option, offering four Victorian-style rooms with private bathroom in a cosy house just a few minutes' walk from downtown. $99
★ **Lane Hotel** 30 Main St ☎ 603 357 7070,

ⓦ thelanehotel.com. Downtown Keene is considerably enhanced by this cool boutique hotel, an 1891 conversion that features a warm contemporary style and the usual flat-screen TVs and free wi-fi. Free parking and happy hour drinks in the lobby – great value. $149

EATING AND DRINKING

Brewbakers Café 97 Main St ☎ 603 355 4844, ⓦ brewbakers.cc. A hip organic coffee joint with comfy couches and seating on the street, that also serves cheap soups, sandwiches and salads. Free wi-fi. Mon–Thurs 7am–9pm, Fri & Sat 7am–10pm, Sun 8am–8pm.
Elm City Brewery and Pub Colony Marketplace, 222 West St ☎ 603 355 3335, ⓦ elmcitybrewing.com. One of

the best places to drink in town also serves hearty American meals (main courses from $18.99) in addition to its own microbrews like Monadnock Mt. Ale ($4). Mon–Thurs 11.30am–11pm, Fri & Sat 11.30am–midnight, Sun 11am–9pm.
Lindy's Diner 19 Gilbo Ave ☎ 603 352 4273, ⓦ lindysdiner.com. This is the real deal, a no-frills diner

---

WALPOLE'S SWEET SURPRISE

Around 14 miles northwest of Keene, off Rte-12 in the tiny town of **Walpole**, you can find one of New Hampshire's most delectable stores and cafés, **L.A. Burdick Chocolates** (Mon 7am–6pm, Tues–Sat 7am–9pm, Sun 7.30am–5pm; ☎603 756 2882, 🕸burdickchocolate.com). Situated in an unassuming storefront at 47 Main St, Swiss-trained Larry Burdick makes his home-made treats from French Valrhona chocolate. If the chocolate isn't enough, you can get full meals in the adjacent restaurant.

---

since 1961 that serves up classic breakfasts, "where the politicians come to meet the real people" – the last four presidents stopped by on the way to the White House. Mon–Thurs & Sun 6am–8pm, Fri & Sat 6am–9pm. **Nicola's Trattoria** 51 Railroad St ☎603 355 5242.

Top-quality nouveau Italian cuisine in a warm setting, and not just for pasta – try the exquisite pork tenderloin stuffed with peppers, or the stuffed trout (main courses $21–30). Tues–Thurs & Sun 5–9pm, Fri 5–9.30pm, Sat 5–10pm.

Hillsborough

About 25 miles northeast of Keene on Rte-9, the tiny town of **HILLSBOROUGH** was founded in 1769. It's actually a grouping of four small villages (Bridge Village, Hillsboro Center, Lower Village and Upper Village) and the birthplace of **Franklin Pierce**, fourteenth president of the United States.

Bridge Village, just off Rte-9 on Rte-149, is home to the area's one-street downtown and some quirky places to eat. Historic **Hillsboro Center**, four miles north of Bridge Village on Center Road (Rte-149), is the oldest and prettiest part of town, a collection of clapboard buildings set around a leafy green.

Franklin Pierce Homestead

301 2nd NH Turnpike (Rte-31 at Rte-9), Hillsborough Lower Village • July & Aug Fri–Tues 10am–4pm; June, Sept & Oct Sat & Sun 10am–4pm • $7 • ☎603 478 3165

Just outside **Lower Village**, you can tour the restored boyhood home of Hillsborough's most famous son, **Franklin Pierce**, US president from 1853 to 1857. Though the docents tend to downplay Pierce's shortcomings – alcoholism, ineffective leadership – to portray him as a misunderstood hero, the building is a fine example of the Federal-style homes once common in the region. The house was built in 1804, just before Franklin was born, by his father, **Benjamin Pierce**, who came to Hillsborough after having served as a general in the Revolutionary War – Pierce senior is buried in the cemetery up the road, just outside **Upper Village**.

INFORMATION   HILLSBOROUGH

Chamber of Commerce, 25 School St, Rte-149 (Tues–Thurs 9am–3pm; ☎603 464 5858,

🕸hillsboroughnhchamber.com). Stocks local maps and information.

ACCOMMODATION

1830 House Motel 626 West Main St (Rte-9 and Rte-31) ☎603 478 3135. A rarity these days, an old-fashioned independent motel, offering basic but clean and cheap en-suite doubles. <u>$68</u>

★ **Stonewall Farm** 235 Windsor Rd ☎603 478 1947,

🕸stonewallfarmbandb.com. Wonderfully romantic B&B set in a gorgeous 1785 clapboard farmhouse and 13 acres of tranquil grounds. The five rooms feature a variety of styles, some with four-posters, and the gourmet breakfasts will set you up for the day. <u>$135</u>

EATING AND DRINKING

★ **German John's Bakery** 5 W Main St ☎603 464 5079, 🕸germanjohnsbakery.net. German-style bakery offering a vast range of fresh breads, pretzels ($1.50) and scrumptious apple strudel ($2.50). Jan to mid-June Wed

11am–3.30pm, Thurs–Sat 9.30am–5pm; mid-June to Dec Tues 11.30am–3pm, Wed–Sat 9.30am–5pm (July–Oct also Sun 11am–3pm). **Sausage Source** 3 Henniker St ☎603 464 6275,

ⓦ sausagesource.com. Fabulous food truck serving tasty hot dogs ($1.95), chilli dogs ($3.95), burgers ($3.95) and freshly made sausage subs ($6.95). Mon–Sat 11am–3pm.
Tooky Mills Pub 9 Depot St ☎ 603 464 6700,

ⓦ tookymillspub.com. Great place for a pint or a pub meal, with soups, salads, sandwiches, hand-carved beef and pasta on the menu (main courses $10.99–19.99). Mon–Thurs & Sun 11.30am–11pm, Fri & Sat 11.3am–midnight.

SHOPPING

Gibson Pewter 18 E Washington Rd ☎ 603 464 3410, ⓦ gibsonpewter.com. Artist Jonathan Gibson has been creating fine pewter products here since 1966. Mon–Sat 10am–4pm.

Well Sweep Art Gallery 584 Center Rd ☎ 603 464 6585, ⓦ galleryatwellsweep.com. Antiques, rugs and fine art in a weathered, antique barn overlooking the green. Wed–Sun 10am–5pm.

Peterborough

The riverfront town of **PETERBOROUGH**, immortalized by Thornton Wilder's play *Our Town*, is today "an entire community devoted to the arts", anchored by the **MacDowell Colony** at 100 High St (☎ 603 924 3886, ⓦ macdowellcolony.org). Founded in 1907 and now the nation's leading art colony, Mac Dowell sees resident artists open their studios to the public just once a year, usually in mid-August (call for exact date).

Peterborough's Georgian Revival downtown, centred around **Grove, Main and Depot streets**, was largely the inspiration of Boston architect Benjamin Russell, who designed the Town House (1918), as well as the Historical Society (1920) and the Guernsey Building office complex (1919). One of the finest **bookstores** in the state, the **Toadstool Bookshop**, 12 Depot Square (Mon–Fri 10am–6pm, Sat 10am–5pm, Sun 10am–4pm; ☎ 603 924 3543), has a huge selection of fiction, nonfiction and travel books.

Mariposa Museum

26 Main St • Mid-June to Aug daily 11am–5pm; Sept to mid-June Wed–Sun 11am–5pm • $5, children $3 • ☎ 603 924 4555, ⓦ mariposamuseum.org

Peterborough's artsy pretensions are nicely encapsulated by the quirky hands-on **Mariposa Museum**, with costumes, puppets, art, musical instruments and all sorts of artefacts from every corner of the world. Kids will enjoy this most, but there's also a roster of live performances that are worth checking out.

Peterborough Museum

19 Grove St • Wed–Sat 10am–4pm • $3 • ☎ 603 924 3235, ⓦ peterboroughhistory.org

History fans will enjoy the **Peterborough Museum**, a modest collection of early American furniture, decorative arts, pewter and artefacts relating to the town's industrial history. For anyone else, however, it's best saved for a rainy day.

Miller State Park

Rte-101 • Late May to Aug Sat & Sun 8.30am–sunset; Sept & Oct Mon–Fri 9am–sunset, Sat & Sun 8.30am–sunset • $4 • ☎ 603 924 3672

Three miles east of Peterborough along Rte-101, **Miller State Park** has a few excellent hikes. The **Wapack Trail** leads up to the 2290ft summit of **Pack Monadnock Mountain** (2.8 miles round-trip), from where you can sometimes see the Boston skyline and Mount Washington – you can also drive to the summit.

ARRIVAL AND DEPARTURE · PETERBOROUGH

By car The only way to reach Peterborough is by car; the town is around 20 miles east of Keene via Rte-101 and 21 miles south of Hillsborough on US-202. Once here there's plenty of free parking in the centre of town.

GETTING AROUND

On foot There is no public transport. Mariposa Museum and Peterborough Museum are downtown and can be walked.

By car Miller State Park is only accessible by car.

INFORMATION

Peterborough Chamber of Commerce 10 Wilton Rd, at the junction of Rte-101 and US-202 (mid-June to mid-Oct Mon–Fri 9am–5pm, Sat 10am–3pm; ☎ 603 924 7234, ⓦ greater-peterborough-chamber.com). Provides local maps and information.

ACCOMMODATION

Jack Daniels Motor Inn 80 Concord St (Rte-202) ☎ 603 924 7548, ⓦ jackdanielsmotorinn.com. Charming independent motel overlooking the Contoocook River, with basic but comfy rooms equipped with fridge, free wi-fi and flat-screen TV. **$114**

Little River Bed & Breakfast 184 Union St ☎ 603 924 3280, ⓦ littleriverbb.com. A renovated 1870s clapboard farmhouse close to the Nubanusit River (there's an outdoor river deck), with four homey rooms, satellite TV and free wi-fi. **$135**

EATING AND DRINKING

Harlow's Pub 3 School St ☎ 603 924 6365, ⓦ harlowspub.com. Old New England pub that offers hearty sandwiches and Tex-Mex classics as well as a healthy dose of town gossip. Mon 4–10pm, Tues noon–11pm, Wed & Thurs noon–midnight, Fri & Sat noon–1am.

Peterboro Diner 10 Depot St ☎ 603 924 6710, ⓦ peterboroughdiner.com. Cool retro diner, housed in a bright green 1950 Worcester train car – breakfast plates range $2.99–8.49, while it's hard to beat the Diner Burger at lunch ($6.75). Daily 6.30am–7pm.

ENTERTAINMENT

Monadnock Music Festival 2A Concord St ☎ 603 924 7610, ⓦ monadnockmusic.org. Annual six-week summer festival of solo, chamber and orchestral concerts, held in the historic meetinghouses and churches of seventeen towns within the Monadnock Region.

Peterborough Folk Music Society ☎ 603 827 2905, ⓦ pfmsconcerts.org. Runs annual season of folk concerts (Oct–April) featuring acts from all over North America,

usually at the Peterborough Players theatre. Tickets $18–25.

Peterborough Players 55 Hadley Rd ☎ 603 924 7585, ⓦ peterboroughplayers.com. Founded in 1933, this lauded company stages traditional and experimental theatre performances from late June through mid-September, in an eighteenth-century barn a few miles outside town.

Monadnock State Park

116 Poole Rd, Jaffrey • Daily sunrise–sunset • $4 • ☎ 603 532 8862

Reputedly the most-climbed mountain in the US, forest-smothered **Mount Monadnock** (3165ft) is the centrepiece of **Monadnock State Park**, a serene landscape of birch and pine trees. The mountain was a popular target for nineteenth-century writers and artists, including **Henry David Thoreau** who camped up here in 1858 and 1860. A small exhibit explores the connection in the basic **visitor centre** (daily 8am–sunset) above the car park, along with displays on the history of the park. It also carries information about the park's forty miles of well-marked scenic hiking trails; the **White Dot Trail** (two miles) is the most popular and direct route to the summit, taking about three and a half hours round-trip (it's quite steep in parts). If you reach the peak on a clear day, you'll be able to see all six New England states. Grab a map and plenty of water at the **park store** (Mon–Fri 9am–5pm, Sat & Sun 10am–6pm) in the car park.

ACCOMMODATION   MONADNOCK STATE PARK

Gilson Pond Campground You can camp in the park at *Gilson Pond Campground* at the base of Mount Monadnock, down the road from the park headquarters area at 585 Dublin Rd. Mid-May to early Oct. **$25**

Western New Hampshire

Divided from Vermont by the Connecticut River, the green farmland and smattering of tranquil villages in western New Hampshire form a wedge between the Monadnock region and the wilder landscapes of the White Mountains. **Hanover** is New

Hampshire's intellectual heart thanks to **Dartmouth College**, which attracts some of the country's best students and maintains an active arts scene. To the south, tiny **Cornish** was once a popular artists' colony, while **Lake Sunapee** offers a quieter alternative to the more developed lake areas further east.

Hanover

The fortunes of genteel **HANOVER**, just across the Connecticut River from Vermont, have been inextricably tied to **Dartmouth College** since the latter was founded in 1769. Dartmouth's reputation as one of the more conservative Ivy League schools is not unfounded, but stereotypes aside, it's a lively place, with all the cultural benefits you expect from a college town: an engaging museum; regular performances by international musicians, dancers and actors; inviting bookstores; and a creative selection of places to eat and drink.

The town's focal point is the grassy **Dartmouth Green**, bounded by Main, Wheelock, Wentworth and College streets. **South Main Street**, which runs south of the green, holds most of the town's eateries, bars and shops.

7

Hood Museum of Art

3 E Wheelock St, across from the Green • Tues, Thurs, Fri & Sat 10am–5pm, Wed 10am–9pm, Sun noon–5pm • Free • ☎ 603 646 2808, ⓦ hoodmuseum.dartmouth.edu

The Dartmouth-owned **Hood Museum of Art** is Hanover's main draw beyond the central campus, with paintings by Picasso and Monet, as well as works by several American artists, including Gilbert Stuart, Thomas Eakins and John Sloan. Displays from the permanent collection tend to change, but standouts include Frederic Remington's hauntingly realistic *Shotgun Hospitality*; some fine portraits, including Joseph Steward's *Portrait of Eleazar Wheelock*, the founder of Dartmouth College; and detailed etchings by Rembrandt. In addition, the museum also has a comprehensive collection of Chinese, Greek, Assyrian and African objects.

Dartmouth College

Dartmouth Green • ☎ 603 646 1110, ⓦ dartmouth.edu

Majestic **Dartmouth College**, founded by Reverend Eleazar Wheelock in 1769, is the ninth oldest college in the United States. The college was an outgrowth of a school for Native Americans that Wheelock had established in Connecticut, but few Native Americans ever studied here. Named for its initial financial backer, the Earl of Dartmouth, the Ivy League institution attracts some of the top students in the world, with particularly strong programmes in medicine, engineering and business.

The campus

The stately two-hundred-acre campus is spread out around Dartmouth Green. Flanking the north end of the green, along Wentworth Street, the looming **Baker/Berry Library**, with its 207ft bell-tower, is an imposing landmark. Inside, on the lower level, is the most arresting attraction on the campus, a series of **frescoes** by Mexican artist José Clemente Orozco. The politically rousing murals were painted between 1932 and 1934, while Orozco was an artist-in-residence and visiting professor. It's easy to see why conservative college officials and alumni viewed the violent depiction of the artist's theme, *An Epic of American Civilization*, as a direct insult: on one of the panels a skeleton gives birth upon a bed of dusty books as a group of arrogant, robed scholars look on, while on another a Jesus-like figure stands angrily next to a felled cross with an axe in his hand. Though college officials initially threatened to paint over the murals, they soon backed down, careful to avoid living up to Orozco's vision.

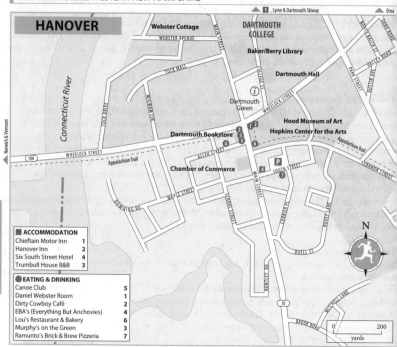

, Lyme & Dartmouth Skiway · Etna

HANOVER

DARTMOUTH COLLEGE

Webster Cottage
WEBSTER AVENUE

Baker/Berry Library

TUCK MALL

Dartmouth Hall

Connecticut River

Dartmouth Green

WHEELOCK STREET

Hood Museum of Art

Dartmouth Bookstore

Hopkins Center for the Arts

Appalachian Trail

WHEELOCK STREET

Appalachian Trail

10A

ALLEN STREET

Chamber of Commerce

SOUTH STREET

MAPLE STREET

SCHOOL STREET

MAIN STREET

LEBANON STREET

DOWNING RD

BUELL ST

HUNTLEY RD

RUELL ST.

10

N

BROOK ROAD

MITCHELL LANE

0   200
yards

Cornish & West Lebanon

ACCOMMODATION
Chieftain Motor Inn	1
Hanover Inn	2
Six South Street Hotel	4
Trumbull House B&B	3

EATING & DRINKING
Canoe Club	5
Daniel Webster Room	1
Dirty Cowboy Café	2
EBA's (Everything But Anchovies)	4
Lou's Restaurant & Bakery	6
Murphy's on the Green	3
Ramunto's Brick & Brew Pizzeria	7

On the east side of the green stands **Dartmouth Row**, a collection of four impressive old buildings that look out over the grass from a slight hill. **Dartmouth Hall**, an imposing white structure with a large "1784" on its hulking pediment, was the college's first permanent building and remains a symbol of the school's academic prowess. Although it burned to the ground in 1904, the restored structure, which today houses Dartmouth's language departments, remains on its original foundation. The other three halls in the row are **Reed** (literature, Jewish Studies and classics), **Thornton** (religion and philosophy) and **Wentworth** (undergraduate advising and research) – the latter two are the oldest original buildings on campus (1828–29).

Webster Cottage

32 N Main St · Late May to mid-Oct Wed, Sat & Sun 2.30–4.30pm · Free · ☎ 603 643 6529

North of Dartmouth College along Main Street, the memory of the school's most celebrated graduate, **Daniel Webster** (see box, p.406), is preserved in **Webster Cottage**, where he supposedly lived during his senior year in 1801.

ARRIVAL AND DEPARTURE

HANOVER

By train Amtrak's *Vermonter* train (Washington, DC to St Albans, VT), stops once a day across the river in White River Junction, less than five miles from Hanover; local buses (see p.415) can get you into town from there.

By bus One Greyhound bus a day between Boston, Manchester, Concord and White River Junction stops in Hanover at the *Hanover Inn*. There is a larger terminal in White River Junction across the river in Vermont (☎ 802 295 3011). The Concord Coach Lines-affiliated Dartmouth Coach (☎ 1 800

637 0123, ⓦ dartmouthcoach.com) has 7–8 daily services to and from Boston and Logan Airport from the *Hanover Inn* and 1–2 per day to and from New York ($74.50 one-way).

By car Hanover lies on Rte-10, close to the junction of I-91 and I-89, making it exceptionally accessible by car. Metered parking costs 25 cents for 30min (maximum 2hr); the Hanover Parking Facility on South Street and 7 Lebanon St is free for the first 30 minutes, then 50 cents for up to an hour; it's $1.25 for 2hr and $15 for the day (more than 8hr).

GETTING AROUND

By bus In and around Hanover, Advance Transit (☎ 802 295 1824, ⓦ advancetransit.com) provides a comprehensive free local bus service from Monday to Friday – schedules and route maps are available at the Chamber of Commerce.

INFORMATION

Hanover Area Chamber of Commerce 2/F Nugget Arcade, 48 S Main St (Mon–Fri 9am–noon & 1–4pm; ☎ 603 643 3115, ⓦ hanoverchamber.org). Has a vast selection of brochures and tourist information.

Information booth On the green (May–Sept daily 9.30am–5pm; ☎ 603 643 3512). Jointly maintained by Hanover and the College.

ACCOMMODATION

Chieftain Motor Inn 84 Lyme Rd (Rte-10) ☎ 603 643 2550, ⓦ chieftaininn.com. This old-style 1950s motel is the best of the few moderately priced places in the area, with access to a guest kitchen and canoes for use in the nearby river. Pool, free wi-fi and breakfast included. $119

Hanover Inn 3 S Main St ☎ 603 643 4300, ⓦ hanoverinn.com. Founded by General Ebenezer Brewster in 1780, this hotel is a local landmark, standing five storeys high with a classic brick facade. Dozens of spacious, elegantly furnished rooms overlooking Dartmouth Green. $249

★ **Six South Street Hotel** 6 South St ☎ 603 643 0600, ⓦ sixsouth.com. This relatively new hotel, opened in 2011, adds a little boutique chic to Hanover, with stylish, contemporary rooms (flat-screen TVs, iHome and free wi-fi) and a cool red-orange colour scheme blended with glass walls, black countertops and sleek furniture. $219

Trumbull House Bed and Breakfast 40 Etna Rd ☎ 603 643 2370, ⓦ trumbullhouse.com. Luxury accommodation in a quiet country inn dating from 1919, some four miles east of Dartmouth Green. Six luxurious bedrooms (cable TV, free wi-fi and DVD) and huge breakfasts included. $154

EATING AND DRINKING

Canoe Club 27 S Main St ☎ 603 643 9660, ⓦ canoeclub .us. The vibe here is more easy-going than the prices on this satisfying menu (try the shellfish stew, $22), but it's a spirited place, with live music – jazz, blues, folk – 363 days a year, and produce sourced from local farms. There's also a cheaper menu of sandwiches ($10) and salads ($8.50). Mon–Thurs & Sun 11.30–3pm & 5–9.30pm, Fri & Sat 11.30am–3pm & 5–10pm.

Daniel Webster Room Hanover Inn, 3 S Main St ☎ 603 646 3070, ⓦ hanoverinn.com. The most elegant place in town for breakfast ($9–12) and lunch ($15–19). For dinner (daily 5–10pm), next door *Zins* bistro and wine bar serves fine tapas and grilled meats ($17–28). Mon–Sat 7–10am & 11.30am–2pm, Sun 8–10.30am & 11am–1.30pm.

Dirt Cowboy Café 7 S Main St ☎ 603 643 1323, ⓦ dirtcowboycafe.com. Get your coffee drinks, as well as

---

DARTMOUTH: SPORTS AND THE GREAT OUTDOORS

Thanks to Dartmouth College, Hanover offers numerous opportunities for sports and activities, with most clubs and groups open to non-students.

Dartmouth Outing Club Robinson Hall ☎ 603 646 2429, ⓦ dartmouth.edu/~doc. Maintains hundreds of miles of hiking trails in the area and also leads group bike rides. Though it's a college club, visitors can stay at their cabins, go on their trips, rent their gear or even take their classes.

Ledyard Canoe Club ☎ 603 643 6709, ⓦ dartmouth.edu/~lcc. Paddling on the Connecticut River remains an extremely popular way to take in the scenery; rent canoes and kayaks at this college club. May–Oct Mon–Fri 10am–8pm, Sat & Sun 9am–8pm; $30–40/day.

Omer and Bob's Sportshop 20 Hanover St, Lebanon ☎ 603 448 3522, ⓦ omerandbobs.com. You can take out posh demo mountain bikes here for $45/day. Mon–Wed & Fri 9am–6pm, Thurs 9am–7pm, Sat 9am–5pm.

Dartmouth Skiway 39 Grafton Turnpike, Lyme ☎ 603 795 2143, ⓦ dartmouth.edu/~skiway. In the winter (daily 9am–4pm), Dartmouth College's very own alpine ski area costs $28–43/day (skis and snowboards $35/day).

Zimmerman Fitness Center E Wheelock St, Hanover ☎ 603 646 3284, ⓦ dartmouthsports.com. Dartmouth's enormous sports facility has a modern gym with sixty pieces of cardio equipment (32 of which have their own TVs), two pools, tennis courts, racquetball and squash courts and a basketball court. Non-students can buy an all-day guest pass for $10.

smoothies and fresh-squeezed juices, here. Daily 7am–6pm.

EBA's (Everything But Anchovies) 5 Allen St ☎603 643 6135, ⓦebas.com. Families dine on salads and burgers here, but the real deal is the pizza (28 toppings and seventeen speciality pies; large from $9.99). And yes, you can get anchovies if you want. Daily 11am–2am.

Lou's Restaurant & Bakery 30 S Main St ☎603 643 3321, ⓦlousrestaurant.net. Filling breakfasts of tasty hashbrowns, eggs and sausage for under $10, but come also for the cakes and mouthwatering pies (strawberry, seasonal). They have a tempting take-out counter on the street in summer. Bakery Mon–Fri 6am–5pm, Sat 7am–5pm, Sun 7am–3pm; restaurant Mon–Fri 6am–3pm, Sat & Sun 7am–3pm.

★ **Murphy's on the Green** 11 S Main St ☎603 643 4075, ⓦmurphysonthegreen.com. The best spot in town for a drink is also a popular restaurant serving an eclectic array of American cuisine. The good draught selection includes regional favourites Smuttynose and Magic Hat, along with Bass, Guinness and Harp. Mon–Thurs 4–11pm, Fri & Sat 11am–11pm, Sun 10am–10pm.

Ramunto's Brick 'n' Brew Pizzeria 9 E South St ☎603 643 9500, ⓦramuntospizza.com. Delicious wood-fired pizzas ($7–10), including the notorious "Philly Cheese Steak Brick" (a massive tomato, mozzarella, American cheese, beef, peppers, mushrooms and onion pizza), as well as draught beers. Watch out for lunch specials ($5 for two slices and a drink). Mon–Sat 11am–midnight, Sun noon–midnight.

ENTERTAINMENT

Hopkins Center for the Arts 2 E Wheelock St ☎603 646 2422, ⓦhop.dartmouth.edu. Screens international art and classic films year-round. It also presents globally acclaimed music, theatre and dance acts, as well as student performances. Film tickets $8.

Cornish

Other than a collection of scenic pastures and a few covered bridges, there's not much left in the town of **CORNISH**, twenty miles south of Hanover along Rte-120, which was a well-known artistic centre in the late nineteenth century. Its most famous inhabitant in recent times was **J.D. Salinger**, reclusive author of *Catcher in the Rye*, who died in 2010. Before visiting the **Saint-Gaudens National Historic Site** take some time to view or drive across the 460ft-long **Cornish–Windsor covered bridge**, a few minutes south of town off Rte-12A. Connecting New Hampshire with Vermont, it is the longest such bridge in the US and quite stunning. It was constructed in 1866 and restored in 1989.

Saint-Gaudens National Historic Site

139 Saint-Gaudens Rd, Rte-12A · Late May to Oct daily 9am–4.30pm · $5 · ☎603 675 2175, ⓦnps.gov/saga

The **Saint-Gaudens National Historic Site**, sixteen miles south of Hanover, preserves the memory of **Augustus Saint-Gaudens**, the great sculptor who lived and worked here from 1885 until his death in 1907. Saint-Gaudens is best known for his lifelike heroic bronze sculptures, including the Shaw Memorial in Boston and the General William T. Sherman Monument in New York City. Many well-known artists, writers, poets and musicians, including Maxfield Parrish, Kenyon Cox and Charles Platt followed Saint-Gaudens to Cornish, establishing the **Cornish Colony**.

The **visitor centre** on site shows an enlightening video about the life and times of Saint-Gaudens, while the surrounding grounds and houses contain all his major works; replicas or castings of his Shaw Memorial, Lincoln statue and Farragut Monument among them. The **New Gallery** displays various bas-reliefs and you can also visit Saint-Gaudens' **Little Studio**, a soaring, sun-filled barn containing more of his work. To visit his actual house, **Aspet** (built in 1800 and retaining many of the original furnishings), you'll have to join a ranger-led tour (usually 5daily; 20min). Take the time to wander around the beautiful grounds, which feature well-cared-for gardens, two wooded nature trails and a relaxing expanse of green grass. You can also check out works in progress by the artist-in-residence at the **Ravine Studio**, in the woods along the northern edge of the property.

Lake Sunapee

Easterners have been summering at **Lake Sunapee**, about 25 miles south of Hanover, since the beginning of the nineteenth century, though development has never been anything like on the scale of its huge northeastern neighbour, Lake Winnipesaukee (see p.419). The lake is still blissfully tourist-light – and you can only get there if you have your own transport – but as with most of New Hampshire's lakes, access to the water is limited – taking a boat tour is the best way to see it. Most of the action takes place in **SUNAPEE HARBOR**, though the town of **NEWBURY** on the southern shore is a pleasant alternative base. In winter **Mount Sunapee** comes alive as a ski resort, though the mountain makes a stunning viewpoint for the lake all year round.

Sunapee Harbor

A low-key, pretty village on the northern edge of the lake, **Sunapee Harbor** is the place to eat, drink, shop and take a boat tour (see p.418). The local historical society runs a small **museum** inside the old Flanders-Osborne Stable (July & Aug Tues–Sun 1–4pm, Wed 7–9pm; June & Sept Sat & Sun 1–4pm; free), crammed with bits and pieces from the eighteenth and nineteenth centuries. You can stroll from Sunapee Harbor to Rte-11 along the Sugar River via the **Riverwalk**, a bucolic trail that you'll probably have to yourself.

Newbury

Sleepy **NEWBURY**, at the southern end of the lake (Rte-103 and Rte-103A), comes alive in the summer, when families come to **swim** in the small but crystal-clear dock area (free parking) and slurp ice creams across the road (see p.418). The year-round attraction is the boxy, white clapboard **Center Meeting House** (Ⓦcentermeetinghouse .org), a gorgeous-looking church built in 1832 by Charles Bulfinch and one of the best preserved of the period in the state.

The Fells

456 Rte-103A • Grounds open daily 9am–5pm; house tours: late May to late June Sat & Sun 10am–4pm; late June to late July Wed–Sun 10am–4pm; late July to early Sept daily 10am–4pm • $8 • ☎ 603 763 4789, Ⓦ thefells.org

At the southern end of the lake, off Rte-103A, stands **The Fells**, the former Hay family estate. John Milton Hay was an adviser and friend of Abraham Lincoln and later became secretary of state under Teddy Roosevelt. He built the Colonial Revival mansion here in 1891 and passed it on to his son, Clarence, who worked on designing the grounds in a pleasing mix of Asian and European styles into the 1920s. Guided tours add context and tell Hay's story, but make time for the 84 acres of **gardens**, surrounding lake and forests.

Mount Sunapee State Park

1460 Rte-103 • Late May to early Sept Mon–Fri 9am–sunset, Sat & Sun 8.3am–sunset • $4 • ☎ 603 763 5561

Formal public access to the lake is managed through the **Mount Sunapee State Park**, which comprises a pretty lakeside **beach**, a network of well-marked hiking trails and a secluded campground above the lake ($29/night).

Mount Sunapee Resort

1398 Rte-103 • Mon–Fri 9am–4pm, Sat & Sun 8am–4pm • Lift tickets $66–70/day • ☎ 603 763 4020, Ⓦ mountsunapee.com

Winter activities in the area take place at **Mount Sunapee Resort**, at the southern end of the lake on Rte-103. With millions of dollars invested since the owners of Vermont's Okemo Mountain (see p.347) took over operations here in 1998, vast improvements have been made to lifts, snowmaking facilities and transportation to the mountain. The gentle slopes will suit learners and mildly proficient skiers more than experts. From July to October the **Sky Ride** ($7) opens on select dates to allow access to the peak – check the website for times.

INFORMATION AND TOURS
SUNAPEE HARBOR

Sunapee Welcome Center Rte-11 in Sunapee Harbor, at the intersection with Rte-103B (May–Oct daily 10am–5pm; ☎603 763 2201). Helpful but tiny. The Lake Sunapee Chamber of Commerce website at ⓦlakesunapeenh.org is also useful.

Boat tours Sunapee Cruises, 81 Main St, Sunapee Harbor,

runs tours on *MV Mt Sunapee II* (July to early Sept daily 2pm; late May–June & early Sept to mid-Oct Sat & Sun 2pm; $18; ☎603 763 4030, ⓦsunapeecruises.com) and dinner cruises on the *MV Kearsarge* (late May to mid-Oct Tues–Sun 6.30pm; $35.99; ☎603 938 6465, ⓦmvkearsarge.com).

ACCOMMODATION

1806 Inn at Mount Sunapee B&B 1403 Rte-103 ☎603 763 2040, ⓦ1806inn.com. Convenient for the ski resort and the lake, with five cosy rooms, one with a mahogany four-poster. Free wi-fi and breakfast included. $105

Blue Acorn Inn 21 Sleeper Rd, Sunapee ☎603 863 1144, ⓦblueacorninn.com. Picturesque quarters with

gorgeous mountain views, some with shared baths and a hearty country breakfast, internet and afternoon refreshments. $100

Twin Doors 49 High St, Sunapee Harbor ☎603 763 2236, ⓦtwindoors.com. A snug 1900 Cape Cod-style house a short walk from the lake, with four comfy rooms, full breakfasts and friendly hosts. $129

EATING AND DRINKING

The Anchorage 71 Main St, Sunapee Harbor ☎603 763 3334, ⓦtheanchorageatsunapeeharbor.com. A waterfront restaurant with live music at weekends and a satisfying menu of sandwiches ($9.99), steaks ($19.99), pastas ($12.99) and burgers ($8.99). Daily 11.30am–12.30pm (from 11am Sun).

Bubba's & Jolly Molly's Ice Cream 976 Rte-103, Newbury ☎603 763 3290, ⓦbubbasbarandgrille .com. Dominates eating options in Newbury, knocking out decent seafood (belly clams by the pint), sandwiches

from $4,50, soups and salads. There's an excellent ice cream annexe in summer (scoops $2.25–3.75). Daily 11.30am–9pm.

Marzelli's 899 Rte-103, Newbury ☎603 763 3290. No frills café across from the lake, with tasty hot paninis from $7, pastas ($8.95) and even takeaway lasagne. The real star is the home-made gelato ($2.95–4.95), which isn't quite Florence standard, but a noble effort and quite different to the ice cream normally served in these parts. Try the chocolate hazelnut or coconut. Daily 7am–9pm.

The Lakes Region

New Hampshire's enticing **Lakes Region**, occupying the state's central corridor east of I-93, almost doubles its population between May and September, when visitors throng the area's restaurants, hotels, lakefront cottages, beaches and crystal-clear waters. There are literally hundreds of lakes here, and the biggest by far (some 72 square miles) is **Lake Winnipesaukee**, the definitive centre of the region. The lake is dotted with 274 islands – most of which are privately owned – and its irregular shape, a seemingly endless continuum of inlets and peninsulas, resembles a giant paint splatter. The eastern and western shores of Lake Winnipesaukee are quite distinct: sophisticated **Wolfeboro** is the centre of the sparsely populated region to the east, while **Weirs Beach**, on the crowded western shore, is the epitome of summertime overkill, with enough arcades, ice-cream parlours and roadside fun-parks to keep the kids happy for weeks. Farther north, the down-to-earth nineteenth-century towns around beautiful **Squam Lake** are some of the most inviting in the region.

WELCOME BIKERS

Classic American symbols of freedom or annoying noise machines? Thanks to annual events like **Laconia Motorcycle Week** (in June), bikers (mostly of the Harley-Davidson variety) have been cruising the roads of northern New Hampshire for over eighty years and you'll see "Welcome Bikers" signs all over the state. The days of Hell's Angels are largely a thing of the past – these riders are more likely to be bankers or lawyers from New York than outlaws – but if you're here in the summer, expect to the share the road with a whole lotta 'Harleys.

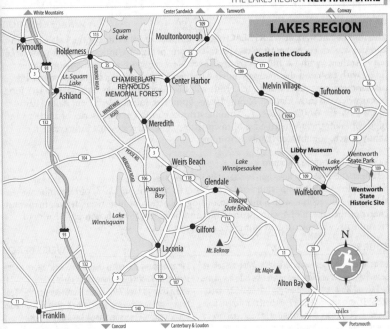

Lake Winnipesaukee

The largest lake in New Hampshire and the third largest in New England, **Lake Winnipesaukee** has been a holiday hotspot since the 1850s, when the annual Harvard-Yale boat race first took place here (it now takes place in Connecticut). Today the lakeside towns offer plenty of variety, but it's difficult to appreciate the lake's size and beauty from the road – you really need to get on the water to make the most of a trip here.

Gilford

The pleasant village of **GILFORD**, just south of the lake along Rte-11A, is worth a quick detour if you're approaching the region from the south. For excellent vistas of the lake and surrounding region, hike to the top of **Mount Belknap**, which at 2384ft is the highest peak along the west side of the lake. The easiest and shortest route up the mountain begins along Belknap Mountain Carriage Road – turn off Rte-11A at the lights in the centre of Gilford, drive through the village on Cherry Valley Road and follow the signs for the Fire Tower on Belknap. If you're feeling more sedentary, try **Ellacoya State Park**, along Rte-11 (July & Aug daily 9am–sunset; $4; ☎603 293 7821), which contains one of the finer sandy beaches – and the only one that's state-maintained – on Lake Winnipesaukee, with 600ft of sand.

ACCOMMODATION GILFORD

Belknap Point Motel 107 Belknap Point Rd ☎ 888 454 2537, ⓦ bpmotel.com. Offers no-frills accommodation, but magical views of the lake and mountains – it's tough to get closer to the lake than this. Some rooms have kitchens and can be rented by the week. $125

Inn at Smith Cove 19 Roberts Rd ☎ 603 293 1111, ⓦ innatsmithcove.com. Grand 1894 Victorian inn right on the lake, with compact nineteenth-century themed rooms and larger cottages, all with lake views and offering a wide range of prices. Free wi-fi. $90

EATING AND DRINKING

Patrick's Pub 18 Weirs Rd (Rte-11B) ☎ 603 293 0841, ⓦ patrickspub.com. This part-Irish theme pub is a decent bet for a pint or a light meal, with live music at the weekends. Daily 11.30am–midnight.

Weirs Beach

The short boardwalk at **WEIRS BEACH** is the summer social centre of the Lakes Region and the very essence of seaside tackiness – despite being fifty miles inland. The wooden jetty overflows with vacationers from all over New England, the amusement arcades jingle with cash and the roads are lined with neon signs, mini-golf courses, waterslide playland extravaganzas and motels. Kids will love **Monkey Trunks** (late May to late June & early Sept to early Oct Sat & Sun 10am–5pm; late June to early Sept daily 10am–5pm; $39–49; ☎603 367 4427, ⓦmonkeytrunks.com), a massive series of zip lines and high ropes on the northern edge of town (Rte-3) and there's even a little crescent of **sandy beach**, suitable for family swimming.

Lake Winnipesaukee Museum

503 Endicott St (US-3) • Mon–Sat 10am–2pm • Free • ☎ 603 366 5950, ⓦ lwhs.us

The modest **Lake Winnipesaukee Museum**, north of town on US-3, offers a more thoughtful diversion, with a mildly absorbing collection of historical photos, maps and charts of the lake, along with assorted bits and bobs revealing the vibrant history of steamboats, waterskiing and summer camps in the area.

TOURS   WEIRS BEACH

Boat tours The best way to take in Winnipesaukee's beautiful expanse of inlets and peninsulas is to board the *M/S Mount Washington* (mid-May to Oct; from $27; ☎ 603 366 5531, ⓦ cruisenh.com), a 230ft boat that departs from the Weirs Beach dock in the centre of town several times a day to cruise to Wolfeboro (see p.422) via Meredith. The same company also offers cruises from Weirs Beach on the smaller *M/V Doris E* (late June to early Sept hourly; $16–24) and a US mail boat, *M/V Sophie C* (mid-June to mid-Sept Mon–Sat 11am & 2pm; $24), which gives you a better opportunity to see some of the lake's many islands.

ACCOMMODATION

Cozy Inn, Lakeview House & Cottages 12 Maple St ☎ 603 366 4310, ⓦ cozyinn-nh.com. Multi-site property comprising the charming 1880s *Cozy Inn*, the hilltop 1860 *Lakeview House* and sixteen rustic cottages – shared bathrooms go for as low as $45. **$110**

Half Moon Motel & Cottages 28 Tower St ☎ 603 366 4494, ⓦ weirsbeach.com/halfmoon/motel/. It might look like an army barracks, but the rooms in this old motel were remodelled in 2011, with free wi-fi and cable TV. The views of the lake are jaw-dropping. **$109**

Meredith

MEREDITH, four miles north of Weirs Beach, is more refined than its neighbour. The pretty town centre is up the hill from the busy intersection of US-3 and Rte-25, but most of the action takes place back on US-3, where the Mill Falls Shopping Center spills into the pleasant **Meredith Marina**, on the lake itself at 2 Bayshore Drive (☎603 279 7921, ⓦmeredithmarina.com); you can rent a speedboat here from Wake Up and Ride (ⓦwakeupandride.com) from $85 for thirty minutes to $525 for six hours. The sandy town **beach**, with mountain views, is located on Waukewan Street along the shores of tiny **Lake Waukewan**. Boat cruises such as the *MS Mount Washington* also stop in Meredith (see above).

Winnipesaukee Railroad

154 Main St • Late May to early June, Sept & Oct Sat & Sun; daily mid-June to Aug • $14 for 1hr, $15 for 2hr • ☎ 603 279 5253, ⓦ hoborr.com

Using restored 1940s and 1950s diesel trains, the **Winnipesaukee Railroad** operates scenic trips along the lakeshore from Meredith to Lakeport at the end of Paugus Bay via Weirs Beach – check the website for times.

ARRIVAL AND DEPARTURE   MEREDITH

By bus Concord Coach Lines (☎1 800 639 3317, ⓦ concordcoachlines.com) runs two buses a day from Boston and Logan Airport to Berlin/North Conway via Meredith (3hr), stopping at the public car park on US-3, next to Aubuchon Hardware. Buses depart at 9.45am and 3.50pm for the return journey.

INFORMATION

Meredith Area Chamber of Commerce 272 Daniel Webster Hwy (US-3), half a mile south of the Rte-25 intersection (daily 9am–5pm; ☏603 279 6121, ⓦmeredithcc.org).

ACCOMMODATION

Harbor Hill Camping Area 189 Rte-25 ☏603 279 6910, ⓦhhcamp.com. Has tent sites and camper cabins in the woods and a swimming pool and camp store on the premises. Open late May to mid-Oct. Camping **$32**; cabins **$60**

★ **The Inns at Mill Falls** 312 Daniel Webster Hwy ☏603 279 7006, ⓦmillfalls.com. Actually a set of four lavish accommodations: the *Inn at Mills Falls* and *Chase House*, which feature plush rooms overlooking the lake, the waterside *Inn at Bay Point* and the best of the bunch, *Church*

Landing, with a polished rustic interior and huge bedrooms overlooking the lake, with free wi-fi, fireplaces and the biggest, softest beds you've ever slept in. Kayaks are available 7am–3pm for $40/day. *Inn at Mills Falls* **$119**; *Chase House* **$229**; *Inn at Bay Point* **$239**; *Church Landing* **$269**

Meredith Inn 2 Waukewan St, at Main St ☏603 279 0000, ⓦmeredithinn.com. A rose-coloured 1890s Victorian, with eight cosy, period-style rooms replete with mahogany furniture, "king plantation" wooden frame beds and flat-screen TVs. **$139**

EATING AND DRINKING

Camp 300 Daniel Webster Hwy (US-3) ☏603 279 3003, ⓦthecman.com/restaurants/camp. An entertaining trip back to summer camp, complete with log-cabin walls and casual comfort food like "Mom's meatloaf" ($14.99), baby-back ribs ($19.99), pan-fried scallops ($17.99) and BLT panini ($7.99). Tues–Sat 5–9pm, Fri & Sat 5–9.30pm.

Lago 1 Rte-25 (at US-3) ☏603 279 2253, ⓦthecman.com/restaurants/lago. Knocks out authentic Italian food, with a busy terrace on the water doubling as the town's most lively night spot – best place for cocktails or post-dinner drink. Pastas from $12, main courses $17–23. Mon–Thurs & Sun 5–9.30pm, Fri & Sat 5–10pm (lounge open from 4pm).

★ **Lakehouse Grill** Church Landing, 281 Daniel Webster Highway (US-3) ☏603 279 5221, ⓦthecman.com/restaurants/lakehouse. Best dinner option in town. Creative starters, heaping main plates of duck, pork, steak or salmon (main courses $19–24; Kobe beef burger is $15) and a

relaxed bar scene await you every night. Lunch is a bit cheaper (burgers and sandwiches $7–8). The fabulous Sunday brunch is $17.99 (kids $9.99). Mon–Thurs 7.30am–9.30pm, Fri & Sat 7.30am–10pm, Sun 9am–9.30pm.

Phu Jee 55 Main St ☏603 279 1129. A quick bite of authentic Chinese food for less than $15 (locals refer to it as "the Chinese"). Mon–Thurs & Sun 11am–9.30pm, Fri & Sat 11am–10.30pm (reduced hours in winter).

★ **Town Docks Restaurant** 289 Daniel Webster Highway (US-3) ☏603 279 3445, ⓦthecman.com/restaurants/town-docks. Best waterfront option, with a laidback deck and even "beach" section adding to the surf shack ambience. It's standard stuff – burgers, steamed and fried seafood, beers at the bar – but the location and atmosphere are unbeatable. Live bands at weekends. Mon–Thurs & Sun 11am–9pm, Fri & Sat 11am–9.30pm (reduced hours in winter).

Moultonborough and around

Other than some remote B&Bs and quiet country roads, there's not much to the sprawling town of **MOULTONBOROUGH**, north of Lake Winnipesaukee on Rte-25. If you're passing through, however, you might take a break in the **Old Country Store** at the intersection of routes 25 and 109. For some time in the sun, the **town beach** (make a right off of Rte-25 onto Moultonboro Neck Rd and follow to near the end of Long Island Rd) is an especially good spot for picnicking and swimming.

Old Country Store & Museum

1011 Whittier Hwy (Rte-25) • Daily: summer 9am–9pm; winter 9am–5pm • Free • ☏603 476 5750, ⓦnhcountrystore.com

One of the oldest of its kind (dating from 1781), the **Old Country Store & Museum** sells everything from home-made pickles and maple syrup to candles, dolls and carved wooden ducks. The bizarre "museum" has a collection of artefacts and carved Indian sculptures.

Castle in the Clouds

455 Old Mountain Rd, Rte-171 • Mid-May to mid-June Sat & Sun 10am–4pm; mid-June to mid-Oct daily same hours • $15 • ☏603 476 2352, ⓦcastleintheclouds.org

Two miles east of Moultonborough on Rte-171, **Castle in the Clouds** is the one must-see attraction in the Lakes Region. The 5200-acre mountain estate of eccentric millionaire **Thomas Plant** (1859–1941) offers some fine scenery and hiking trails, a lavish mansion on a mountain top and a truly mesmerizing view – it's the only way to really appreciate the vastness of Lake Winnipesaukee.

The winding drive up to the house takes you past several viewpoints and a worthy detour to see the **Falls of Song**, a pretty waterfall gushing through a cleft in the rock. You park at the **Carriage House** near the top (where there's a café taking in that fabulous view) and jump on a trolley bus to the house itself – after a short orientation it's a self-guided tour, but there are numerous docents on hand to add context. Half alpine lodge, half medieval fantasy, the house was completed by Italian artisans in 1914 and heavily influenced by the Arts and Crafts movement. Plant named it **Lucknow** and the lavish interior has been restored to look much as he left it (two lower floors should be finished by 2014). The view from the house and gardens, 1380ft above the lake, is worth lingering over. Plant himself was a fascinating character, a progressive-minded entrepreneur who made a $12 million fortune in the shoe manufacturing business and retired in 1910 – by the late 1920s he had spent (or given away) the whole lot and died penniless.

Allow time to **hike** some of the 45 miles of trails that crisscross the gorgeous reserve attached to the estate (buy a guidebook at the gift shop for $8). The company that bottles **Crystal Geyser** mineral water operates next door at springs that were once on Plant's land.

Loon Center

183 Lee's Mill Rd • May, June & mid-Oct to Dec Mon–Sat 9am–5pm; July to mid-Oct daily 9am–5pm; Jan–April Thurs–Sat 9am–5pm • Free • ☎ 603 476 5666, ⓦ loon.org

The Loon Preservation Committee maintains the small **Loon Center** (signposted via Blake Road off Rte-25, south of Moultonborough), which houses a collection of exhibits about the endangered and much-loved birds, focusing on environmental awareness. You can view Lake Winnipesaukee from several points along the **Loon Nest Trail**, which begins at the centre and winds through forests and marshes.

ARRIVAL AND DEPARTURE   **MOULTONBOROUGH**

By bus Concord Coach Lines (☎1 800 639 3317, ⓦ concordcoachlines.com) runs two buses a day from Boston and Logan Airport to Berlin/North Conway via Moultonborough (3hr 15min), stopping at the Hometown Market & Deli on Rte-25. Buses depart at 9.30am and 3.35pm for the return journey.

ACCOMMODATION

Olde Orchard Inn 108 Lee Rd ☎603 476 5004, ⓦ oldeorchardinn.com. A relaxing B&B in the middle of an apple orchard that dates back to the 1790s (the shingle barn is older). Some of the nine rooms feature fireplaces, iPod docking stations and jacuzzis. $110

EATING AND DRINKING

The Woodshed 128 Lee Rd ☎603 476 2311, ⓦ thewoodshedrestaurant.com. An old barn-turned-restaurant where prime rib is the speciality, but lamb chops, lobster and grilled fish are also on the menu (main courses $19–28). Ask for a table on the screened-in patio on warm summer evenings. Take the Old 109 Road from Rte-25 (first right after the Country Store, heading north) and you should see Lee Road on the right after a mile. Tues–Sun 5–9pm.

Wolfeboro

Because Governor John Wentworth built his summer home nearby in 1768, **WOLFEBORO** claims to be the oldest summer resort in America. Sandwiched between the eastern shore of Lake Winnipesaukee and smaller Lake Wentworth, at the intersection of routes 109 and 28, it's certainly the most attractive town in the region – access to the **waterfront** here, with wide, fine views of the lake, is one of the best reasons to stay. Other than admiring the lake view and taking in the shops and cafés along the short, bustling Main Street (Rte-109), there's not much to see downtown. For some exercise, stroll the half-mile **Bridge Falls Path** from behind the old station down to the Wolfeboro Falls area.

Governor John Wentworth State Historic Site
Rte-109 • Daily 24hr • Free • ☎ 603 271 3556

East of Wolfeboro, the 4300-square-foot summer mansion of Governor John Wentworth, known as the **Wentworth House Plantation**, with its own sawmill, orchards, workers' village and six-hundred-acre deer park, was, at one time, a sort of Hearst Castle of New Hampshire. Built in 1769, it burned to the ground in 1820 and was never rebuilt, but the area once occupied by the plantation, on Rte-109 three miles southeast of Rte-28 (look for the dirt road on the right) is now the **Governor John Wentworth State Historic Site**; essentially just the foundations remain. Note that **Wentworth State Park** (Wentworth State Park Rte-109; Late June to early Sept Mon–Fri 10am–6pm, Sat & Sun 9am–6pm; $4, kids 6–11 $2; ⓦnhstateparks. org)comprises a narrow beach a mile or so before the historic site, facing serene Lake Wentworth.

Libby Museum
755 N Main St (Rte-109) • June to mid-Sept Tues–Sat 10am–4pm, Sun noon–4pm • $2 • ☎ 603 569 1035

A few miles north of downtown Wolfeboro on Rte-109, the entertaining **Libby Museum** is where an early twentieth-century dentist's obsession with evolution is manifested through skeletons of bears, orangutans and humans and some ineptly stuffed animals. There's also a mastodon's tooth, a random assortment of fossils and insects, Native American artefacts and a fingernail supposedly pulled out by its Chinese owner to demonstrate his newfound Christian faith. The setting of the museum, a 1912 Historic Landmark house with superb views of the lake and a grassy park, makes the detour even more rewarding.

EASTERN SHORE ACTIVITIES
The eastern shore of Lake Winnipesaukee has enough **outdoor activities** to keep even the most avid enthusiast busy.

BEACHES
Brewster Beach (mid-June to early Sept; free; ☎ 603 569 1532). On Lake Winnipesaukee at the end of Clark Road, south of Wolfeboro. Good for sunbathing and swimming.

HIKING TRAILS
Mount Major Trail, north of Alton on Rte-11, offers excellent lake views and takes about an hour and a half to cover 1.75 miles. The trail to the top of **Bald Peak**, at the Moultonborough-Tuftonboro town line on Rte-171, is one mile long, while the **Mount Flag Trail** in Tuftonboro is a strenuous seven-mile loop. For a shorter jaunt (half a mile), with rewarding panoramic views, try the **Abenaki Tower Trail**, off Rte-109 in Tuftonboro across from Wawbeek Road, featuring an 80ft tower overlooking Lake Winnipesaukee. **Snowmobiles** and **cross-country skiers** fill the trails during the winter; call the Wolfboro Cross Country Ski Association (☎ 603 569 3151, ⓦwolfeboroxc.org) or the New Hampshire Snowmobile Association (☎ 603 224 8906, ⓦnhsa.com) for information and guidance.

WATERSPORTS
Wet Wolfe Rentals, 17 Bay St, Wolfeboro (☎ 603 569 3200, ⓦwolfetrap.com/wetwolfe.html), rents **waverunners** for a minimum of two hours ($175) or a 14ft aluminum hull with 25hp motor ($250 per day). Goodhue & Hawkins Navy Yard, 244 Sewall Rd in Wolfeboro (☎ 603 569 2371, ⓦgoodhueandhawkins.com), rents **boats** from $320 a day. You can take an all-inclusive light-tackle guided **fishing** trip with Angling Adventures, 79 Middleton Rd, Wolfeboro (☎ 603 569 6426, ⓦgadaboutgolder.com), for $300 per person ($390 for two).

7

Wolfeboro Chamber of Commerce In the old red station building on Central Avenue, just off Main Street (Rte-109) in the centre of town (Mon–Sat 10am–3pm, Sun 10am–noon; ☎ 603 569 2200, ⓦ wolfeborochamber.com).
Boat tours The best way to take in Lake Winnipesaukee's subtle beauty is aboard *MS Mount Washington* (see p.420), which departs from the dock in the centre of town and

connects with Weirs Beach across the lake. From the same place you can also take 2hr trips on former mail boat *Blue Ghost* (☎ 603 569 1114), or take a quick spin in *Millie B*, a 1928-style mahogany speedboat (July & Aug Mon–Sat 10am–7pm, Sun 10am–5pm every 45min; spring & autumn Sat & Sun 11am–2pm; $20; ☎ 603 569 1080, ⓦ millieb.net).

GETTING AROUND

By car You need a car to really see the area, though the Wolfeboro Trolley Company operates "Molly the Trolley" during the summer, which makes a 45min loop around Wolfeboro from the old railway station (July & Aug daily

10am–4pm; late May, June, Sept & Oct Sat & Sun 10am–4pm; day pass $6; children (4–12 years) $3; ☎ 603 569 1080, ⓦ wolfeborotrolley.com). You can find free parking (2hr maximum) all over the centre of the town.

ACCOMMODATION

123 North Main Bed & Breakfast 123 N Main St (Rte-109) ☎ 603 569 9191, ⓔ rbranscombe@juno.com. Cosy, 1854 colonial-style inn close to the lake and town. Rooms are tastefully furnished and full breakfast is included. $115
Lake Motel 280 S Main St (Rte-28) ☎ 603 569 1100, ⓦ thelakemotel.com. Modern accommodation, with tennis courts and even a private beach; some rooms have kitchens and stylish fireplaces for those cold autumn and winter nights. Free wi-fi. Open May–Oct. $114
Willey Brook Campground 883 Center St (Rte-28)

☎ 603 569 9493, ⓦ willeybrookcampground.com. Three miles north of Wolfeboro and only one mile from Wentworth State Beach. Open mid-May to mid-Oct; Sites from $26
★ **Wolfeboro Inn** 90 N Main St (Rte-109) ☎ 603 569 3016, ⓦ wolfeboroinn.com. Built in 1812, this historic inn is on the waterfront with its own beach and some of the best restaurants in town. It has 44 elegant rooms, ranging from plush, modern suites to vintage rooms dating back to the foundation of the inn – some have private balconies overlooking the lake. $199

EATING AND DRINKING

★ **Bailey's Bubble** 5 Railroad Ave ☎ 603 569 3612, ⓦ baileysbubble.com. Luscious ice cream in the centre of town; try "Maine Black Bear" (raspberry, chocolate chips and truffles), or "Moose Tracks" (vanilla, fudge and peanut butter cups). Summer only, daily 11am–10pm.
The Cider Press 30 Middleton Rd, off Rte-28 ☎ 603 569 2028, ⓦ theciderpress.net. Hearty American food – ribs, steak, grilled salmon ($16–20) – in a rustic, candlelit dining room. Daily 5–9pm (call ahead in winter).
Lydia's Café 33 N Main St ☎ 603 569 3991, ⓦ lydiascafewolfeboro.com. Smoothies, espresso drinks, bagels and excellent sandwiches (from just $3.50) are served in this cute café, just up from the dock on Rte-109. Daily 7am–2.30pm.
The Restaurant 37 N Main St (Rte-109) ☎ 603 569 8408, ⓦ therestaurant03894.com. Best place to splurge in town, with dishes such as roast avocado ($16) and pecan encrusted chicken ($22). Daily 11am–2pm & 5–9pm.
The Strawberry Patch 50 N Main St (Rte-109) ☎ 603 569 5523. Excellent, freshly prepared breakfasts and

lunches in a cosy and unpretentious dining room. Look out for Mon–Thurs breakfast offers such as all-you-can-pancakes-eat for $3.99. Daily 7.30am–2pm.
Wolfeboro Dockside Grill and Dairy Bar 11 Dockside ☎ 603 569 1910. Some of the best views in town, with a menu of cheap, no-frills comfort food (burgers and fried seafood from $6), plus an ice cream takeaway counter at the back. Simple deck with tables and chairs overlooking the harbour. Daily 11am–9pm.
★ **Wolfe's Tavern** 90 N Main St (Rte-109) ☎ 603 569 3016, ⓦ wolfeboroinn.com. Enticing restaurant attached to the *Wolfeboro Inn*, offering four main dining areas. The fancy *1812 Room* serves fine, expensive New England-style cuisine, while the old tavern section is a dark pub-like eatery and much better value. The *Maple Room* features a large gas fireplace and colonial decor, while the lakeside patio is the best option in summer. Enjoy one of their 72 beers on tap (and ask about the pewter beer mugs–on more than 1900 of then–the tavern room ceiling). Daily 7am–9pm.

Squam Lake

Much smaller than its sprawling neighbour, but still the second largest body of water in the state, beautiful **Squam Lake** actually holds more appeal than Lake Winnipesaukee

– the pace is slower, the roads less crowded and, thanks to a conscientious group of residents, the land is less developed. However, it's difficult to access the forested shore unless you're a local and the only way to really appreciate the lake's tranquil charm is to take a boat ride.

As you'd expect, most of the action in the area revolves around the **outdoors**: hiking, boating and swimming are all popular activities. It's easy to see why producers chose Squam Lake as the setting for the 1981 film *On Golden Pond*, starring Henry Fonda – the water is pristine and glassy and the setting sun brings a quiet calm over the lake and surrounding forests. With a population of 1700, **Holderness** is the largest town in the area, although it's really nothing more than a petrol station, a few stately old inns, a couple of restaurants and a dock, though there's a great beach and some enjoyable hikes nearby. **Center Sandwich**, to the north of the lake, also maintains its nineteenth-century quaintness.

Holderness

Named for the Earl of Holderness, a friend of Governor Wentworth's, **HOLDERNESS** was granted its original town charter in 1751. Although nothing of much historical significance ever happened here, the Holderness School has remained a prestigious preparatory school since its founding in 1879. Today, the tiny village brings together a loosely defined grouping of buildings along the shore next to a well-used public dock. Note that the water here is **Little Squam Lake**; Squam Lake itself is just to the north, connected via the Squam River but completely hidden from the road.

The **Holderness General Store** (daily 7am–9pm), at the intersection of US-3 and Rte-113 in town, is the place to come for supplies before you head out for a day on the lake (it also does sandwiches, salads and light meals). The best public **beach** is accessible along a short trail through the **Chamberlain-Reynolds Memorial Forest**, off College Road – follow US-3 south, take a left on College Road and park in the first small lot. Walk up West Fire Road for about twenty minutes to reach the beach (bring insect repellent).

The most popular **hike** in the area begins at the Rattlesnake Trailhead along Rte-113 and follows the **Old Bridle Path** to the top of **Rattlesnake Mountain** (1594ft), providing spectacular views of Squam Lake and the surrounding hills, with only half an hour of effort. Additional hiking suggestions are available at the Squam Lakes Association headquarters (see p.427).

Squam Lakes Natural Science Center

23 Science Center Rd (off Rte-113) • May–Oct daily 9.30am–4.30pm • $15, children (3–15 years) $10 • ☎ 603 968 7194, ⓦ nhnature.org

An introduction to the area's flora and fauna is provided by the **Squam Lakes Natural Science Center**, near the intersection of routes 113 and 25 in the centre of town, which features live animals – including bears, bobcats, owls and otters – housed in settings that resemble their natural habitats along a quarter-mile nature walk. Compared to a typical zoo, it's refreshingly spacious, though numerous hands-on exhibits and educational presentations tend to attract large groups of schoolchildren.

THE BARNSTORMERS THEATRE GROUP

Founded in 1931 by Francis Cleveland (son of 22nd US president Grover Cleveland), his wife Alice and Edward Goodnow, the **Barnstormers** (☎ 603 323 8661, ⓦ barnstormerstheatre.org) is the oldest professional summer theatre group in the state. It is also perhaps the only theatre company in the country in which the same actors perform a different play each week. Presenting a wide range of productions, the theatre company plays to consistently large crowds. Housed in a refurbished old store in the center of **Tamworth Village** since 1935, the company typically produces eight plays per summer. Call ☎ 603 323 8500 from late May until the end of the season in August for schedule and ticket information.

TOURS AND ACTIVITIES

Bike rental The nearest place to rent a bicycle is seven miles away, off I-93, exit 25 in Plymouth, at Rhino Bike Works, 1 Foster St (Mon, Tues, Thurs & Fri 10am–6pm, Wed & Sat 10am–5pm, Sun 10am–4pm; $30/day; ☏ 603 536 3919, ⓦ rhinobikeworksnh.com), where you can also get advice on local trails.

Boat and kayak rental If you'd rather steer your own vessel, try the Squam Lakes Association on US-3 (☏ 603 968 7336, ⓦ squamlakes.org; rentals 9am–4.30pm: late May to early Sept daily; early Sept to mid-Oct Sat & Sun only), which rents canoes and kayaks ($50/day) and sailboats ($65/day). They also run half-day kayak tours and give lessons ($50–80).

Boat tours The 90min boat trips offered by Science Center Lake Cruises (from beside *Walter's Basin* restaurant on

US-3; July to mid-Oct 11am, 1pm & 3pm, late May to June 1pm only; $22; children (3–15 years) $18; ☏ 603 968 7194) provide an absorbing tour of the lake and include a look at Thayer Cottage, where the bulk of *On Golden Pond* was filmed; guides usually embellish the tour with plenty of trivia about the film and you may also see endangered loons and bald eagles which inhabit the lake. Special tours, more focused on observing the loons, bald eagles and natural life of the lake are accompanied by the centre's naturalist (see website for times; same prices). Experience Squam (☏ 603 968 3990, ⓦ experiencesquam.com) runs more personalized excursions across the lake in smaller powerboats ($95/hr or $215/2hr) and special boats visit enigmatic Church Island on Sundays ($12–30).

7

ACCOMMODATION

Cottage Place on Squam Lake 1132 US-3 ☏ 1 877 968 7116, ⓦ cottageplaceonsquam.com. Offers cosy cottages (with up to two bedrooms), cottage suites and a six-room lodge for large groups overlooking a private 140ft sandy beach on Little Squam Lake. **$115**

Inn on Golden Pond 1080 US-3 ☏ 603 968 7269, ⓦ innongoldenpond.com. Less expensive and more down-to-earth than other lakeside hotels in the area, with eight large rooms, friendly hosts, full breakfasts and a games room. **$165**

Manor on Golden Pond US-3 ☏ 603 968 3348, ⓦ manorongoldenpond.com. An elegant mansion with crystal chandeliers, sweeping vistas and stone fireplaces. By far the ritziest and most expensive place to stay in the

area. Their award-winning dining room offers gourmet New American cuisine. **$265**

White Oak Motel 435 US-3 ☏ 603 968 3673, ⓦ whiteoakmotel.com. The cheapest lodgings in the area, with basic motel units equipped with cable TV, microwave and fridge overlooking picturesque White Oak Pond, close to Squam Lake. **$89**

CAMPING

The Squam Lakes Association maintains twelve primitive **camping sites** on Moon Island, Bowman Island and in the Chamberlain-Reynolds Memorial Forest (reservations required; ☏ 603 968 7336; May–Oct). **$60**

EATING AND DRINKING

Squam Lake Inn Lunch Café 28 Shepard Hill Rd (off US-3 at the Citgo gas station) ☏ 603 968 4417, ⓦ squamlakeinn.com. Renowned for its fresh salads and locally sourced produce, lobster rolls and ice cream. May–Oct Tues–Sat 11am–2pm.

Walter's Basin US-3 ☏ 603 968 4412,

ⓦ waltersbasin.com. The only waterfront restaurant in town serves decent rainbow trout and other fish dishes in a pleasant setting (main courses from $17) – the name alludes to the monster trout hunted by Henry Fonda in *On Golden Pond*. Mon–Thurs & Sun 11.30am–9pm, Fri & Sat 11.30am–10pm.

Center Sandwich

Thirteen miles northeast of Holderness along Rte-113, at the base of the Sandwich Range, **CENTER SANDWICH** is the most alluring town in the region, comprising a string of enchanting white clapboard buildings. There's not much in the way of sights here, but you might visit the friendly folks at the **Sandwich Historical Society** (July–Sept Wed–Sat 10am–4pm; rest of year Tues & Thurs 10am–4pm; free; ☏ 603 284 6269, ⓦ sandwichhistorical.org); they can give you local maps and have a museum of local period tools, house furnishings, textiles and the work of early local painters.

ACCOMMODATION

Strathaven Bed & Breakfast 576 North Sandwich Rd (Rte-113) ☏ 603 284 7785, ⓦ strathaveninn.com. This cosy two-room B&B is a real bargain, with private

bathroom and breakfast included. Look for the clapboard house with veranda and blue shutters. Cash only. **$80**

EATING AND DRINKING

Corner House Inn 22 Main St ☎ 603 284 6219, ⓦ cornerhouseinn.com. The best place to eat in town, an informal, historic (the structure's been around since 1849) and popular joint with both casual and more formal food – it's on the intersection of routes 113 and 109. Mon, Wed & Thurs 4.30–9pm, Fri & Sat 4.30–10pm, Sun 11.30am–9pm (also open Tues June–Sept).

SHOPPING

Sandwich Home Industries 32 Main St ☎ 603 284 6831, ⓦ nhcrafts.org. Local outlet for the League of New Hampshire Craftsmen, selling contemporary art and crafts from artisans throughout the state. Mid-May to mid-Oct Mon–Sat 10am–5pm, Sun noon–5pm.

The White Mountains

Thanks to their accessibility from both Montréal and Boston, the enchanting **WHITE MOUNTAINS** have become a year-round tourist destination, justly popular with summer hikers and winter skiers alike. It's a commercialized region, with quite a lot of development flanking the main highways, but the great granite massifs retain much of their majesty. **Mount Washington**, the highest peak in the entire Northeast (at 6288ft), claims some of the severest weather in the world – conditions are harsh enough to produce a timberline at 4000ft. Much of the region is protected within the **White Mountain National Forest**, established in 1918 and covering almost 1250 square miles today.

Piercing the range are a few high passes, called "**notches**," and the roads through these gaps, such as the **Kancamagus Highway** between **Lincoln** and **Conway**, make for predictably scenic routes. However, you won't really have made the most of the White Mountains unless you also set off on foot, bike or skis across the long expanses of thick evergreen forest that separate them. Some of the best hiking trails are in the state parks of **Franconia Notch**, straddling I-93, **Crawford Notch**, straddling US-302 and **Pinkham Notch**, along the eastern base of Mount Washington. Downhill skiing is popular at resorts such as **Waterville Valley** and **Loon Mountain**, both a few miles east of I-93, while cross-country skiing is particularly good at **Jackson**, which, along with **North Conway** and **Glen**, makes up the region's most built-up area, the **Mount Washington Valley**. Even if you don't intend to stay, check out the grand resort hotels in **Bretton Woods** and **Dixville Notch** (the first town in New Hampshire – and therefore the nation – to announce the results of its primary elections).

INFORMATION

White Mountains Recreation Pass You will need a Recreation Pass to place in your vehicle when you park and leave it unattended in the White Mountain National Forest, though not if you're just stopping briefly to take pictures or use restrooms, nor if you're staying in a National Forest campground. Passes cost $5 for seven consecutive days and you can buy them from many local stores and at all Forest Service offices. If you decide on the spur of the moment to hike to the top of a mountain or spend the afternoon at a swimming hole, you can purchase a day-pass for $3 at self-pay kiosks in car parks across the forest (bring the correct change).

Waterville Valley Resort

1 Ski Area Rd • Winter season Mon–Fri 8.30am–4.30pm, Sat & Sun 7.30am–4.30pm • Ski lift tickets $49–65/day; equipment rental $42/day • ☎ 1 800 468 2553, ⓦ waterville.com

East of I-93 along Rte-49, the sparkling **Waterville Valley Resort** was the brainchild of developer Tom Corcoran, who bought the *Waterville Valley Inn* and its surrounding land in 1965 with the intention of creating a family-oriented outdoor centre. Today, the many resort-goers enjoying all manner of summer and winter

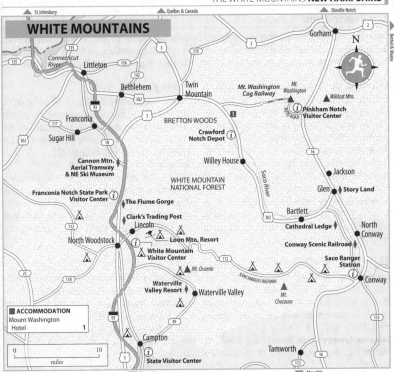

activities are evidence that he succeeded – not altogether surprising, considering the stunning tree-covered setting.

At the centre of the resort is the **Town Square**, a development of shops and restaurants alongside **Corcoran's Pond**, where you can lounge on the sand or rent a kayak, canoe or paddleboat (all $10/hr).

Though relatively active in summer, when **mountain biking** dominates the action (see below), Waterville Valley really comes to life in the winter months and the intermediate slopes of the **ski area**, a network of trails covering 2020 vertical feet on Mount Tecumseh and Snow's Mountain, are usually packed. The main ski area is three miles from the Town Square; free shuttles run in ski season.

The rugged area surrounding Waterville Valley also makes for excellent **hiking** and **camping**. Of several notable hikes that originate along Tripoli Road, the **Mount Osceola Trail** is the best, starting around 3.8 miles from the village. It's a strenuous 3.5-mile trek to the summit at 4326ft, from where you can continue for another two miles to the Greeley Ponds Trail and the Kancamagus Highway (see p.430).

INFORMATION AND ACTIVITIES

WATERVILLE VALLEY RESORT

Waterville Valley Region Chamber of Commerce 12 Vintner Rd in Campton, 10 miles west at exit 28 off I-93 (daily 9am–5pm; ☎603 726 3804 or ☎1 800 237 2307, ⓦ watervillevalleyregion.com). Your best bet for information on hiking, camping and lodging in the area; it stocks the usual brochures and has helpful attendants and good maps.

Bike rental The Adventure Center in the village (daily 9am–5pm; ☎603 236 4666), rents mountain bikes (trail passes $6/day; bikes from $32/day) and has trail maps. You can also ride the chairlift to the top of the hill at nearby Snow's Mountain with your bike (June–Sept daily 10am–5pm; $9 one-way).

ACCOMMODATION

Options in the immediate Waterville Valley area are geared to families and all-inclusive vacationers. During the **summer**, prices are surprisingly reasonable and rates at all nine of the resort's lodges, inns and condos include use of the athletic club, mountain-bike rental, golf, tennis courts and kayak rental. Be aware, though, that prices go up by as much as fifty percent in **winter**.

Best Western Silver Fox Inn 70 Packard's Rd ☎ 1888 236 3699, ⓦ silverfoxinn.com. One of the best-value lodges, and not your usual chain hotel: it's got attractive common areas and the price includes unlimited tennis-court time and two hours' bike rental. $119

Black Bear Lodge 3 Village Rd ☎ 603 236 4501, ⓦ black-bear-lodge.com. All-suite condo-style hotel targeted firmly at the skiing set, with rooms that can sleep up to six people and full kitchens. $115

Snowy Owl Inn & Resort 4 Village Rd ☎ 603 236 8383, ⓦ snowyowlinn.com. Modern lodge containing 85 rooms with cosy fireplaces and attractive furnishings, just a short walk from the Village Center. Free wi-fi. $99

CAMPING

Branch Brook Campground Rte-49, Campton ☎ 603 726 7001, ⓦ campnh.com. Seasonal tent sites and cabins along the pristine waters of the Pemigewasset River. The site was severely damaged by Hurricane Irene in 2011 – call ahead to make sure it's re-opened. $28

Osceola Vista Campground ☎ 1 877 444 6777. Thirteen tent sites managed by the White Mountain National Forest, just outside Waterville Valley on Tripoli Road and undeveloped wilderness sites with no facilities between Waterville Valley and I-93 along Tripoli Road (get a parking/camping permit at the Fee Station, I-93, exit 31). $16

EATING AND DRINKING

Coyote Grill 98 Valley Rd (above the White Mountain Athletic Club) ☎ 603 236 4919, ⓦ wildcoyotegrill.com. A smart restaurant serving creative American cuisine with a seasonally changing menu. Thurs–Sat 5–9pm.

Jugtown Country Store Town Square ☎ 603 236 3669, ⓦ jugtowncountrystore.com. With its full-service deli and wide selection of cheeses and breads, this centrally located store is a reliable stop for picnic supplies.

Mad River Tavern Rte-49 (1 mile from I-93, exit), Campton ☎ 603 726 4290, ⓦ madtav.com. Large portions of well-prepared pasta, seafood, chicken, steak, or on Wednesday evenings, Mexican food. Mon–Sat 11.30am–11pm, Sun 10am–10pm.

The Kancamagus Highway

Affording plenty of panoramic glimpses of tree-coated peaks and valleys, the **KANCAMAGUS HIGHWAY** (Rte-112) runs 34 miles from Lincoln east to Conway. The road is named for **Chief Kancamagus** ("Fearless One"), whose grandfather united seventeen Indian tribes into the Penacook Confederacy in 1627.

You can easily pass a pleasant afternoon driving the length of "the Kank", but you'll gain a better appreciation of the area if you take a hike or have a swim in the Swift River, which runs parallel to the highway for twenty miles. Better still, plan to camp at one of the many well-maintained campgrounds along the road (see p.433). No motorist services are available, so don't forget to pick up your supplies and petrol in Lincoln or Conway. Remember also to grab a **Recreation Pass** (see p.428).

INFORMATION   THE KANCAMAGUS HIGHWAY

White Mountains Visitor Center Lincoln, Rte-112, just off I-93 at exit 32 (July–Sept 8.30am–6pm; Oct–June 8.30am–5.30pm; ☎ 603 745 8720, ⓦ visitwhitemountains .com). Has a small exhibit on the region, gives lodging advice and sells parking passes (see p.428) and maps, including the excellent *White Mountains Map Book* ($24.95), which gives 400 trail descriptions and is essential

if you plan on embarking on any extended hiking expeditions.

Saco Ranger Station 33 Kancamagus Highway (on the eastern side of the highway), at the junction with Rte-16 in Conway (Mon 9am–4.30pm, Tues–Sun 8am–4.30pm; ☎ 603 447 5448; ⓦ fs.fed.us/r9/white). Staffed by friendly and knowledgeable rangers.

North Woodstock

Anchoring the western end of the Kancamagus Highway, **NORTH WOODSTOCK** is a small-town mountain retreat at the intersection of routes 3 and 112, with an attractive row of restaurants and shops and a few good places to stay.

Clark's Trading Post

110 Daniel Webster Hwy (US-3) • Mid-June to Aug daily 9.30am–6pm; May to mid-June & Sept to mid-Oct Sat & Sun 10am–5pm • $18 (ages 4–64 years) • ☎ 603 745 8913, ⓦ clarkstradingpost.com

A mile north of North Woodstock along US-3, local landmark **Clark's Trading Post** is a much-touted, family-friendly collection of tourist attractions, including a haunted house, an 1884 fire station, bumper boats, the "Old Man" climbing tower and a thirty-minute black bear show, in which a group of bears do tricks – just the ticket if you're in the mood for some hokey tourist fodder, or have kids in tow.

ACCOMMODATION   NORTH WOODSTOCK

Mt. Coolidge Motel 386 US-3 ☎ 603 745 8052, ⓦ mtcoolidgemotel.com. Excellent-value motel with eighteen spotless rooms, two three-bedroom cottages, a heated outdoor pool and free wi-fi. Open April–Nov. **$89**

Wilderness Inn 57 Main St (US-3) ☎ 603 745 3890, ⓦ thewildernessinn.com. Guests in the seven antique-furnished rooms here enjoy sumptuous

breakfasts, free wi-fi and lemonade or cider (in season) in the afternoon. **$95**

Woodstock Inn 135 Main St (US-3) ☎ 1 800 321 3985, ⓦ woodstockinnnh.com. Vast hotel complex comprising four properties in addition to the historic main house, which offers comfortable rooms, an outdoor jacuzzi and reasonable ski/lodging packages in the centre of town. **$127**

EATING AND DRINKING

★ **Clement Room** 135 Main St (US-3), Woodstock Inn ☎ 603 745 3951, ⓦ woodstockinnnh.com. Feast on duck, veal, seafood or steak. Definitely North Woodstock's most elegant dining experience (main courses $17–28). Daily 5.30–9.30pm.

Truant's Taverne 98 Main St (US-3) ☎ 603 745 2239, ⓦ truantstaverne.com. A cosy, affordable restaurant serving well-cooked American grills. Main courses $14–17.

Mon–Thurs & Sun 11.30am–9pm, Fri & Sat 11.30am–10pm.

Woodstock Station 135 Main St (US-3), Woodstock Inn ☎ 603 745 3951, ⓦ woodstockinnnh.com. A great place to go for drinks – the beer is brewed on the premises, there's an outdoor deck in summer and nearly every night there's live entertainment. The range of hearty food includes pizza, pasta, steak, seafood and burritos. Daily 11.30am–10pm.

Lincoln

A couple of miles up the highway from North Woodstock (on the other side of I-93), and far less appealing, **LINCOLN** is a continuous strip of cheap restaurants, malls and condominium-style lodgings. Like North Woodstock, the town offers little in the way of things to see, but it makes a good pit-stop on route to the western White Mountains – the real attractions lie just beyond town in the forest.

TOURS AND ACTIVITIES   LINCOLN

Alpine Adventures 41 Main St, Rte-112 ☎ 603 745 9911; ⓦ alpinezipline.com. Another popular attraction is the zipline canopy tour at the longest and highest zip in New England. Daily 9am–4pm; $89–109.

Pemi Valley Moose Tours 36 Main St ☎ 603 745 2744,

ⓦ moosetoursnh.com. Three-hour evening trips by minibus with a 97 percent success rate of seeing the giant beasts. Aug to early Oct, departing evenings; $28; children (under 12 years) $18.

ACCOMMODATION

Kancamagus Motor Lodge 11 Pollard Rd (Rte-112) ☎ 603 745 3365, ⓦ kancamaguslodge.com. An unpretentious resort motel with plenty of facilities and outdoor activities, right on the highway. *Brittany's* restaurant serves good food and there's free wi-fi and a pool. **$109**

Lost River Valley Campground 951 Lost River Rd

(Rte-112), 4 miles west of I-93, exit 32 ☎ 1 800 370 5678, ⓦ lostriver.com. Offers 125 wooded and brookfront pitches, a playground and cabin rentals . **$27**

Russell Pond Campground Off Tripoli Rd, 3.7 miles east of I-93, exit 31 ☎ 603 726 7737. The closest campsite to Lincoln, overlooking a 40-acre mountain pond. Flush toilets and coin-operated hot showers available. **$20**

EATING AND DRINKING

3 Cultures Deli Depot Mall, 260 Main St (Rte-112) ☎ 603 745 3354, ⓦ 3culturesdeli.com. Filling

sandwiches ($7–8) and deli salads, as well as decent bagels for breakfast (from $4.59). Tea and coffee is just

$1.50. The three cultures are Russian, Polish and American (reflecting the background of the owners). You'll find the Depot Mall at the eastern edge of town. Mon–Sat 9am–4pm, Sun 10am–3pm.

GH Pizza & Greek Restaurant 75 Main St (Rte-112) ☎ 603 745 6885. *GH* has the best gyros and pizza in town, right in the centre of the strip – though the

dining room's not particularly interesting. Daily 11am–11pm.

Gordi's Fish and Steak House Depot Mall, 260 Main St (Rte-112) ☎ 603 745 6635, ⓦ gordisfishandsteak.com. Catering to the jovial after-ski crowd, *Gordi's* is smarter than other Lincoln restaurants, specializing in seafood and grilled meats ($12–17). Daily noon–10pm.

Loon Mountain Resort

60 Loon Mountain Rd, Rte-112 • Winter Mon–Fri 9am–4pm, Sat & Sun 8am–4pm; late June to mid-Oct daily 9.30am–6pm • Ski lift tickets $59–76 per day • ☎ 603 745 8111, ⓦ loonmtn.com

Lincoln and North Woodstock really come to life in the winter, when enthusiastic skiers and snowboarders come to hit the slopes at nearby **Loon Mountain Resort**, two miles east of I-93 on the Kancamagus Highway. The trails here, while good for intermediate skiers, might not be challenging enough for experts. During the summer, Loon offers many of the activities you'd expect from a large full-service resort – swimming, tennis, horseriding and mountain-biking – and if you'd like a nice view of the surrounding terrain without going through the trouble of hiking or biking up the mountain, you can ride the **gondola** to the top (late June to mid-Oct daily 9.30am–6pm; $15; children (6–12 years) $10). You can rent **mountain bikes** for $33 per day at the base of the mountain ($31 for children under 12 years).

White Mountain National Forest

Beyond Lincoln and Loon Mountain, the Kancamagus Highway snakes through the scenic heart of the **White Mountain National Forest**, offering plenty of hiking, swimming and backwoods camping. The road is picturesque, but to make the most of the forest you'll need to park the car and spend the day on the trails – anyone short of time should make for the Sabbaday Falls or Rocky Gorge Scenic Area.

Lincoln Woods Scenic Area

Kancamagus Hwy (Rte-112), 5 miles east of I-93 • Daily 6am–10pm • Free with Recreation Pass • ☎ 603 536 6100, ⓦ fs.fed.us/r9/white

The **Lincoln Woods Scenic Area** is the first enticing stop on the Kancamagus Highway inside the White Mountain National Forest itself, with a small ranger station and an easy 5.8-mile round-trip hike (293ft elevation gain) to the unusual **Franconia Falls**, a large granite outcrop about an acre in size, streaked with cascading water. The path follows the Pemigewasset River, with lots of opportunities for swimming in summer. For greater exertion, drive on to the parking area for the **Greeley Ponds Trail** (9 miles east of I-93), a 4.5-mile round-trip to a dark aqua body of water.

Kancamagus Pass overlooks

Kancamagus Hwy • Daily 24hr • Free • ☎ 603 536 6100, ⓦ fs.fed.us/r9/white

Beyond Greeley Ponds, the highway rises high into the mountains through the **Kancamagus Pass** (2855ft), providing a series of stunning viewpoints. The **Pemigewasset Overlook** offers a wide panorama back to the west, while the **CL Graham Wangan Overlook** provides a more modest view northeast. A few miles further on, the Sugar Hill Overlook affords the best views of the craggy peaks to the east, including **Mount Potash** (2681ft) – you can climb it via the **Mount Potash Hike** (20 miles east of I-93), a strenuous 3.8-mile round-trip.

Sabbaday Falls

Kancamagus Hwy, 19 miles east of I-93 • Daily 6am–10pm • Free with Recreation Pass • ☎ 603 536 6100, ⓦ fs.fed.us/r9/white

The **Sabbaday Falls** are an easy half-mile hike from the main highway, a 25ft series of narrow, plunging cascades through the rocks – picturesque but not suitable for swimming.

Russell Colbath Historic Site

Kancamagus Hwy, 22 miles east of I-93 and 12.3 miles west of Conway • Daily 6am–10pm • Free with Recreation Pass • ☎ 603 447 5448, ⓦ fs.fed.us/r9/white

The **Russell Colbath Historic Site** is all that remains of the once flourishing forest community of Passaconaway, established around 1790. The village boomed on the back of the timber trade right up to 1916, but the last resident died just fourteen years later. The simple **Colbath homestead** dates back to 1832 and is open to visitors in the summer, manned by volunteers – there's also the old Town of Albany cemetery and the Rail and River Trail to explore, an easy half-mile stroll.

Mount Chocorua

About ten miles outside of Conway lies **Mount Chocorua**, whose little curved granite notch on the top makes it one of the most distinctive mountains in the area. It's a strenuous climb and will take at least six hours via the **Champney Falls Trail** (8 miles return; elevation gain 2500ft). The top – that notch you can see – is particularly dazzling, as you emerge from the forest to a stretch of pure rock. The views, including the "Presidential Range", are, of course, jaw-dropping.

Rocky Gorge and Lower Falls scenic areas

Kancamagus Hwy, 8 miles west of Conway • Daily 6am–10pm • Free with Recreation Pass • ☎ 603 536 6100, ⓦ fs.fed.us/r9/white

The **Rocky Gorge Scenic Area** covers a rugged section of the Swift River as it cuts a narrow cleft in the rocks, while one mile further on the **Lower Falls Scenic Area** is a pleasant place for a picnic or a swim (in the large, calm area below the falls). Don't miss the **Albany Covered Bridge** just beyond here (take the left fork off the highway), a charming covered bridge built in 1858.

ACCOMMODATION WHITE MOUNTAIN NATIONAL FOREST

There's not a great choice of accommodation along the mountain section of the **Kancamagus Highway** – options are limited to basic motels at either end (see p.431) and a string of campgrounds further into the forest. The six campgrounds along the highway are rather primitive affairs (many have vault toilets), and sites are allocated on a first-come, first-served basis.

Campgrounds ☎ 603 447 5448, or ☎ 1 877 444 6777 for Covered Bridge; ⓦ icampnh.com. Travelling from west to east the campgrounds are: Hancock, 5 miles east of I-93; Big Rock, 7 miles east of I-93; Passaconaway, 15 miles west of North Conway, near the historic Russell Colbath House; Jigger Johnson, 13 miles west of North Conway; Covered Bridge, 6 miles west of North Conway (the only campground that accepts reservations); Blackberry Crossing, across from Covered, bridge, 6 miles west of North Conway. Open mid-May to mid-Oct except Hancock, which is open year-round. $16–20

Franconia Notch State Park and around

North on I-93, past Lincoln and North Woodstock, the White Mountains continue to rise dramatically above either side of the freeway, boldly announcing their presence with enormous tree-covered peaks. **Franconia Notch State Park** is the highlight of the area, with miles of hiking trails and several natural wonders. Past the White Mountains, farther north along I-93, the landscape flattens into an inviting valley dotted with former resort towns turned quiet mountainside retreats, such as pleasant **Franconia**, secluded **Sugar Hill**, sleepy **Bethlehem** and the largest town in the area, **Littleton**.

Franconia Notch State Park

I-93 • ☎ 603 823 8391, ⓦ nhstateparks.org

Headed towards Canada, I-93 and the more leisurely US-3 merge briefly as they pass through **Franconia Notch State Park**. Though it's dwarfed by the surrounding national forest and split in two by the noisy interstate, the park, which features excellent hiking and camping, has several sights that are well worth a visit.

The Flume

I-93, exit 34A • May to late Oct daily 10am–5pm • $12, $24 joint ticket with Cannon Mountain Aerial Tramway • ☎ 603 745 8391, ⊕ flumegorge.com

From the **Flume Visitor Center**, where there is a helpful information desk about the whole park, a cafeteria and a gift shop, you can walk 1200 yards or ride the shuttle bus to the short trail that leads through the narrow riverbed gorge, otherwise known as the **Flume**. Formed nearly 200 million years ago and discovered in 1808 by 93-year-old "Aunt" Jess Guernsey, the 800ft-long gorge (with 70- to 90ft-high cliffs) has been fitted with a wooden walkway that weaves across cascading falls and between towering granite walls. With the rumbling water echoing through the misty crevice, it's more impressive than you might expect, though during high season the crush can be overwhelming. You can walk back to the bus stop from the top of the gorge, or return to the visitor centre on foot via a scenic trail (the whole loop is two miles). From the visitor centre car park, the 1.7-mile **Mount Pemigewasset Trail** leads up a moderate incline to the 2557ft summit of Mount Pemigewasset, affording views of the Franconia Range.

Old Man of the Mountain Historic Site

I-93, exit 34B • Daily 24hr • Free • ☎ 603 745 8391, ⓦ oldmanofthemountainlegacyfund.org

Six miles north of the Flume on I-93, exit 34B leads to the former viewing site of the **Old Man of the Mountain**, a natural rock formation known for its semblance to an old man's profile. After inspiring scores of photographs, Nathanial Hawthorne's short story *Great Stone Face* (1850), appearing on New Hampshire's license plate, and serving as the state emblem, the Old Man finally succumbed to gravity and slid off the mountain in 2003. The disaster has spawned an elaborate three-stage **memorial**, the first section opening in 2011; **Old Man of the Mountain Profile Plaza**, a short walk from the car park via the bike trail, overlooks serene Profile Lake (where the state park was opened in 1928). The plaza includes a series of sculpted metal profiles that give you some idea of what the Old Man looked like, while the final stage will involve an elaborate **monument** of five giant granite stones. You can also check out the **Mini-Museum** inside the Cannon Mountain tramway station (see below), which charts the history (and collapse) of the iconic formation.

Cannon Mountain

I-93, exit 34B • **Winter ski lift** Tickets $64 • ☎ 603 823 8800, ⓦ cannontram.com; **Aerial Tramway** Daily late May to mid-Oct 9am–5pm; every 15min • $13 return, children (6–12 years) $10; $11 one-way (children 6–12 years) $8; $24 joint ticket with the Flume

State-owned **Cannon Mountain** offers rides to the top of its 4180ft peak in an **Aerial Tramway**, displaying panoramic views of the mountains that are especially impressive – and popular – during the early autumn foliage season. In the summer you can **rent mountain bikes** at the tramway station ($20 half-day; $30 full-day). During the winter, Cannon Mountain offers some of the more challenging **alpine skiing** terrain in the state. If you'd rather hike to the top of the mountain, take the moderate, roughly two-mile **Kinsman Ridge Trail** from the southwest corner of the tramway car park. An equally rewarding, but shorter and less strenuous half-mile hike leads to **Artists Bluff** overlooking Echo Lake; the trail begins in the parking area on the north side of Rte-18, across from the Peabody Base Lodge (I-93, exit 34C). At **Echo Lake** you can swim, rent a kayak ($15/hr), or just enjoy the short stretch of sand (daily mid-June to early Sept 10am–5.30pm; $4).

New England Ski Museum

I-93, exit 34B • Daily 10am–5pm, closed April • Free • ☎ 603 823 7177, ⓦ skimuseum.org

You can learn about the history of New England skiing, browse a collection of old ski equipment and photos and watch a ski documentary at the **New England Ski Museum**, next to the Cannon Mountain tramway.

Franconia

FRANCONIA, a friendly village on I-93 just north of Franconia Notch and the White Mountains, began attracting summer vacationers including literary notables Nathaniel Hawthorne and Henry Wadsworth Longfellow soon after railroad tracks made the town accessible in the mid-nineteenth century. Today, skiers and leaf-peepers come in droves to check out the area's autumn foliage and snow-covered slopes. To get off the roads head 3.4 miles south of Franconia on Coppermine Road (off Rte-116) and hike the **Coppermine Trail** to the beautiful **Bridalveil Falls**, cascading 80ft.

Franconia Heritage Museum

553 Main St (Rte-18) • May–Oct Fri–Sat 1–4pm • Free • ☎ 603 823 5000, ⓦ franconiaheritage.org

Franconia's modest line-up of attractions includes the tiny **Franconia Heritage Museum**, proudly displaying tools, antiques and various objects scooped up locally in an 1880 farmhouse. Special exhibits tackle the Old Man of the Mountain (see opposite), the history of local guesthouses and Franconia College.

Iron Furnace Interpretive Center

Rte-18, near junction with Rte-117• Daily 24hr • Free • ☎ 603 823 5000, ⓦ franconiaheritage.org

The tiny **Iron Furnace Interpretive Center** displays iron-making objects related to the nineteenth-century brick furnace opposite, looming across the Gale River like a medieval ruin (the furnace itself is off-limits). Dating back to 1805, the furnace was abandoned by 1870. An old 1889 iron bridge lies nearby.

Frost Place

Ridge Rd, off Bickford Hill Rd, Franconia • Mid-May to June Sat & Sun 1–5pm; July to mid-Oct Wed–Mon 1–5pm • Suggested donation $5 • ☎ 603 823 5510, ⓦ frostplace.org

Franconia is best known as the one-time home of poet **Robert Frost**. After owning a small farm in Derry (see p.404) and residing for a bit in England, Frost settled here in 1915 at age 40. Now known as the **Frost Place**, this was where the poet lived with his wife and children for five years before moving to Vermont (see p.340) and where he wrote many of his best-known poems, including *The Road Not Taken*. Memorable largely for the inspiring panorama of mountains in its backdrop, the house is now a Center for Poetry and the Arts, with a poet-in-residence, readings, workshops and a small display of Frost memorabilia, such as signed first editions and photographs. There's a half-mile **Poetry Nature Trail** complete with placards displaying Frost's poetry.

INFORMATION AND ACTIVITIES

FRANCONIA

Franconia Notch Chamber of Commerce 421 Main St, Rte-18, next to the Town Offices (mid-May to mid-Oct Wed–Sun 10am–6pm; ☎ 603 823 5661, ⓦ franconianotch .org). An information booth offering 24hr access to maps and pamphlets.

Bike rentals For advice on bike routes in the area and to rent bikes ($20/day), stop in at the Franconia Sport Shop, 334 Main St, Franconia (☎ 603 823 5241, ⓦ franconiasports.com).

ACCOMMODATION

Franconia Inn 1172 Easton Rd (Rte-116) ☎ 603 823 5542, ⓦ franconiainn.com. A 31-bed inn two miles south of Franconia, with great views, a relaxing porch and an excellent restaurant; it's a good cross-country ski base, too. **$199**

Fransted Campground Rte-18 (1 mile from I-93, exit 38) ☎ 603 823 5675, ⓦ franstedcampground.com. This family-oriented campground is a developed site with private streamside tent sites. Open May to mid-Oct; $35 for a standard tent site.

★ **Gale River Motel** 1 Main St ☎ 603 823 5655, ⓦ galerivermotel.com. Offering slightly cheaper lodgings than others nearby, this sweet little ten-room motel has a heated outdoor pool, hot tub and home-made chocolate-chip cookies. Two cottages sleep four to six people. **$95**

★ **Horse & Hound Inn** 205 Wells Rd ☎ 603 823 5501, ⓦ horseandhoundnh.com. Beautifully renovated 1830 farmhouse with eight old-fashioned, cosy rooms and a pine-panelled dining room; all rooms come with private bathroom, but TV is shared in the lounge. **$95**

Lovetts Inn 1474 Profile Rd (Rte-18), Sugar Hill ☏ 603 823 7761, ⊛ lovettsinn.com. *Lovett's*, peacefully set at the foot of Cannon Mountain, is a 1794 Cape Cod-style home complete with swimming pool, a comfortable

common area, cosy rooms, an excellent restaurant and charming staff. **$129**

★ **Sugar Hill Inn** 116 Rte-117, Sugar Hill ☏ 603 823 5621, ⊛ sugarhillinn.com. This posh secluded inn is ideal for romantic getaways, with antique-filled rooms, fireplaces and mountain views (and free wi-fi). **$130**

EATING

Franconia Inn 1172 Easton Rd (Rte-116) ☏ 603 823 5542, ⊛ franconiainn.com. The inn offers elegant first-class service in its candlelit dining room and features well-prepared steak and seafood dishes. Daily 6–8.30pm.

Harman's Cheese & Country Store 1400 Rte-117, Sugar Hill ☏ 603 823 8000, ⊛ harmanscheese.com. Stock up on exquisite aged or smoked cheddar cheese at this rustic store (aged $3.95 per half pound; smoked $5.95 per half pound). The cheese actually comes from New York State, but Harman's ages it for two to three years. Free tastings. Daily 9.30am–5pm.

Lovetts Inn 1474 Profile Rd (Rte-18), Sugar Hill ☏ 603 823 7761, ⊛ lovettsinn.com. Some of the best gourmet

food in the area, including well-prepared classics such as grilled salmon and stuffed chicken breast. Main courses go for about $25 and reservations are a good idea. Daily 5.30–9pm.

★ **Polly's Pancake Parlor** 672 Rte-117 (I-93, exit 38), Sugar Hill ☏ 603 823 5575, ⊛ pollyspancakeparlor.com. *Polly's* might be in the middle of nowhere, but it's well worth the trip if you love pancakes ($7.99 for 6). Add blueberries, choc chips, coconut or walnuts and its $9.19 – all you can eat is $22.99. The original menu – around since 1938 – has since been supplemented by healthier options and there's a small bakery selling freshly baked blueberry muffins ($1.89) and whoopie pies next door. May–Oct daily 7am–3pm.

Littleton

Northwest of Franconia along I-93, **LITTLETON**, straddling the Ammonoosuc River, has a recently spruced up Main Street that's lined with attractive old brick buildings, historical plaques and new restaurants and shops. Note the bronze statue of **Pollyanna** in front of the library on Main Street – **Eleanor H. Porter**, creator of the beloved children's character, was born here in 1868. Though there's really not much else to see, the town is a good place to find reasonably priced accommodation and there's always **Chutter's**, 43 Main St (Mon–Thurs 9am–6pm, Fri & Sat 9am–8pm, Sun 10am–6pm; ☏ 603 444 5787, ⊛ chutters.com), which holds the *Guinness Book of World Record* title for Longest Candy Counter (at 111ft): grab a paper bag and start filling from the 600-odd jars of chocolate nuts, malted milk balls, fruit sours and bubble gum.

Littleton Grist Mill

18 Mill St • Tues–Sat 10.30am–3pm, Sun 11.30am–3pm • Free • ☏ 603 823 5510, ⊛ littletongristmillonline.com

Dating back to 1798 and the very beginnings of the town, the **Littleton Grist Mill** is now a working museum that still grinds its organic flour thanks to the power of the Ammonoosuc River. The mill was in use right up to the 1930s and restored in 1998. You can buy its products in the shop, see the millers at work, then climb down to the basement to see the bowels of the operation, grindstones and machinery (and a short video). Nearby is the handsome **Riverwalk Covered Bridge**, built for pedestrians only in 2004.

INFORMATION   LITTLETON

Littleton Area Chamber of Commerce Downtown across from *Thayer's Inn* (late May to mid-Oct Mon–Fri

9am–5pm; ☏ 603 444 6561, ⊛ littletonareachamber .com).

ACCOMODATION

As a general rule, nearby **Bethlehem** is the place to go for superior accommodation, while Littleton has a number of reasonably priced places to stay. **Motels** can be found around I-93, exit 42.

Adair Country Inn 80 Guider Lane, Bethlehem ☏ 1 888 444 2600, ⊛ adairinn.com. Thus grand country estate built in 1927 features deluxe antique-furnished

rooms, sweeping views and an impeccable staff; the lavish gardens were designed by the Olmsted brothers, of Central Park fame. **$195**

Mulburn Inn 2370 Main St, Bethlehem ☎603 869 3389, ⚉mulburninn.com. Completed between 1908 and 1913 in English Tudor-style by the architect of the *Mount Washington Hotel*, this inn contains seven spacious rooms with rich wood floors and elegant furnishings. **$125**

Thayer's Inn 111 Main St, Littleton ☎603 444 6469,

⚉thayersinn.com. A creaky but comfortable local landmark established in 1843, which has hosted the likes of Richard Nixon and Ulysses S. Grant. Rooms are dressed in Victorian style (with florid, period wallpaper) and there's free wi-fi and breakfast included. **$90**

EATING AND DINKING

Bishop's Homemade 183 Cottage St ☎603 444 6039, ⚉bishopshomemadeicecream.com. Thick and creamy ice cream, sundaes, cakes and pies sold from what looks like the owner's house on the road leading into town. Look out for M&M, butter crunch, amaretto and pumpkin flavours. April–Oct daily noon–9pm.

★ **Littleton Diner** 145 Main St ☎603 444 3994, ⚉littletondiner.com. This cosy diner has heaps of character. Opened in 1930, it's best-known in these parts for its delicious buckwheat pancakes and local maple syrup (the meal is supplied by the Grist Mill). It does all the other

favourites, of course, and plenty of meat and veg specials. Daily 6am–8pm.

Miller's Café & Bakery Littleton Grist Mill, 16 Mill St ☎603 444 2146, ⚉millerscafeandbakery.com. Great selection of soups, salads and sandwich deals every day, like pot roast and lamb sandwiches ($7.49), plus quiche and salads ($7.99). Summer Mon–Sat 9am–3pm, Sun 11am–2pm.

★ **Tim-Bir Alley** 7 Main St ☎603 444 6142. Haute cuisine with a New England twist; think Dijon-rubbed lamb chops ($24.95) and salmon with almonds and rhubarb and ginger sauce ($21.95). Cash only. Wed–Sun 5–9pm.

Mount Washington Valley

The eastern side of the White Mountains lines the **Mount Washington Valley**, home to New Hampshire's cross-country skiing capital of **Jackson**, which also boasts an unusual concentration of first-class lodging and eating. The valley leads up to (but doesn't include) Mount Washington itself (see p.441) and is generally thought to centre around the town of **North Conway**, a once-beautiful mountainside hamlet now overwhelmed by outlet malls and other modern encroachments. In general, the region is more congested than the western White Mountains, but if you can avoid the crowds that cram their cars onto the mile-long strip of Rte-16/US-302 south of downtown North Conway, you'll find there's plenty to do around here.

GETTING AROUND
MOUNT WASHINGTON VALLEY

By bus The AMC runs a hiker shuttle bus service daily from June through mid-September (and weekends through mid-Oct) with stops at many of the trailheads and AMC lodges throughout the Mount Washington region (call ☎603 466 2727 or visit ⚉outdoors.org for information; reservations strongly recommended). Buses depart

Pinkham Notch Visitor Center (see p.441) from 8.10am and the Highland Center at Crawford Notch Depot (see p.443) at 9am. Drivers will stop anywhere along the route if requested. One-way trips anywhere along the route cost $19 ($17 for AMC members), though there is a $10 fee for walk-ons between any stop ten minutes apart or less.

North Conway

Surrounded on all sides by shopping malls, factory outlets and fast-food chains, **NORTH CONWAY** is a major resort town and can be fairly depressing, with the strip south towards Conway particularly over-developed. Fortunately, there is some relief in the centre, a village core that manages to maintain a hint of rustic backcountry appeal – you'll also find plenty of budget accommodation and places to eat here.

Conway Scenic Railroad

38 Norcross Circle • Mid-April to late Dec, call for reservations and schedule • To Crawford Notch Depot (5hr) $48 return, children (4–12 years) $34; to Fabyan Station in Bretton Woods (5hr 30min) $53 return, children (4–12 years) $39 • ☎603 356 5251, ⚉conwayscenic.com

The centrepiece of downtown is the **North Conway Railroad Station**, a hulking brown-and-yellow 1874 Victorian structure that you can't miss along Main Street. From here, the **Conway Scenic Railroad** runs antique steam trains and old diesels to

Bartlett, the Crawford Notch Depot and the Fabyan Station in Bretton Woods. The trains are especially worth the money in early autumn, when the trees are at their peak – reservations are a must.

Echo Lake State Park and Cathedral Ledge

60 Echo Lake Rd, Conway • May to late June Sat & Sun 9am–6pm; late June to early Sept daily 9am–8pm • $4 • ☎ 603 356 2672, Ⓦ nhstateparks.org

Northwest of town along River Road, **Echo Lake State Park** (not to be confused with the Echo Lake in Franconia Notch State Park) encompasses the towering granite face of the White Horse Ledge (1470ft). The lake itself has a small beach and is great for an invigorating dip in summer, surrounded by pine forest with the awe-inspiring ledge for a backdrop. A one-mile trail circles the lake providing the best of the views.

Just to the north, via West Side Road and Cathedral Ledge Road, scores of rock climbers test their skills on the wall of the steep, sheer faces of **Cathedral Ledge** (700ft). If you'd rather not spend hours (and lots of money) tethered to the cliff's sheer face, you can simply drive the one-mile road to the top, where you're presented with scintillating views of the entire Saco River Valley and groups of climbers casually popping up over the cliff edge (there's no charge for this part of the state park).

ARRIVAL AND DEPARTURE NORTH CONWAY

By bus Concord Coach Lines (☎1 800 639 3317, Ⓦ concordcoachlines.com) runs two buses a day from Boston and Logan Airport to North Conway (4hr), stopping at Eastern Slope Inn on Rte-16. Buses depart at 8.30am and 2.35pm for the return journey.

INFORMATION AND TOURS

Mount Washington Valley Chamber of Commerce North Conway (Mon–Fri 9am–6pm; ☎603 356 3171 or ☎1 800 367 3364, Ⓦ mtwashingtonvalley.org). Small information booth on Rte-16, near the station.

Climbing tours Eastern Mountain Sports Climbing School, 1498 White Mountain Hwy, North Conway, can arrange climbs up Cathedral Ledge (☎1 800 310 4504, Ⓦ emsclimb.com).

ACCOMMODATION

1785 Inn 3582 White Mountain Hwy (Rte-16) ☎603 356 9025, Ⓦ the1785inn.com. Though it's right on the main road, the spacious rooms, gracious hosts, delicious food and mountain views here make this a good base from which to explore (or to shop). Shared bath $69, private bathroom $99

★ **Adventure Suites** 3440 White Mountain Highway (Rte-16), just north of North Conway ☎603 356 9744, Ⓦ adventuresuites.com. New Hampshire's most quirky, extravagant hotel has free wi-fi, free popcorn, over 15,000 DVDs to borrow and a communal pit-fire overlooking the mountains every evening. But it's the rooms that make this so intriguing: each one has a unique theme, from Victorian to Harley Davidson (the latter is decked out like a garage with everything from the Harley factory). All come with flat-screen TVs, Kuerig coffee machines and lavish jacuzzi tubs. Breakfast is included. $109

★ **North Conway Grand Hotel** 72 Common Court, off Rte-16 in Settlers' Green Outlet Village ☎603 356 9300, Ⓦ northconwaygrand.com. This vast, modern hotel has 200 rooms and is a good bet for late arrivals with no reservations. Rooms are spacious and equipped with microwave, cable, free wi-fi and fridge – you also get two pools, jacuzzi and all sorts of sports rentals on site. $189

Saco River Camping Area 1550 White Mountain Hwy (Rte-16) ☎603 356 3360, Ⓦ sacorivercampingarea .com. Camping in the area (from $32) is available at this wooded and open site, nicely located along the Saco River and well enough away from the highway. Open early May to mid-Oct. $32

School House Motel 2152 White Mountain Hwy (Rte-16) ☎603 356 6829, Ⓦ schoolhousemotel.com. Probably the cheapest in town, with basic but adequate rooms, all with cable TV and free morning coffee. $78

Spruce Moose Lodge 207 Seavey St ☎1 800 600 6239, Ⓦ sprucemooselodge.com. Another good base, this time for rock climbers and other outdoor types, occupying a quiet spot well off the main drag, with nine conservatively decorated rooms and five cottages. $119

White Mountains Hostel 36 Washington St, Conway ☎603 447 1001, Ⓦ whitemountainshostel .com. Nearby Conway boasts a great HI/AYH hostel, which has particularly clean dorm lodging. Dorms $23; doubles $58

EATING AND DRINKING

1785 Inn & Restaurant 3582 White Mountain Hwy (Rte-16) ☎ 603 356 9025, ⓦ the1785inn.com. Probably the best place to eat in North Conway, with highly praised gourmet food, such as apple-wood smoked rabbit, and fine wines, with prices to match (main courses $18–30). Served in a dark, romantic dining room. Daily 5.30–10pm.

Bellini's 1857 Main St (Rte-16), Willow Place Mall ☎ 603 356 7000, ⓦ bellinis.com. You can get big portions of freshly prepared Italian dishes here, all served in an attractively decorated dining room. Mon & Wed–Sun 4–11pm.

Chef's Market 2724 Main St (Rte-16) ☎ 603 356 4747, ⓦ chefsmarketnorthconway.com. This cosy café has great sandwiches ($7), pasta salads and smoothies for lunch, with more substantial main courses for dinner like pesto scallops ($28.95). Mon & Wed–Sun 11am–11pm.

Horsefeathers 2679 Main St (opposite the station on Rte-16) ☎ 603 356 2687, ⓦ horsefeathers.com. Top choice for a meal, drink or entertainment, with live rock or Irish music at the weekends, in addition to what many consider to be the best burgers in town. Mon–Thurs & Sun 11.30am–11pm, Fri & Sat 11.30am–midnight.

Met Coffee House and Art Gallery 2680 White Mountain Hwy (Rte-16) ☎ 603 356 2332, ⓦ metcoffeehouse.com. The best place for a casual cup of coffee, pastry, light meal and free wi-fi, in the centre of town. Mon–Thurs & Sun 7am–9pm, Fri & Sat 7am–10pm.

Shalimar 2197 White Mountain Hwy (Rte-16) ☎ 603 356 0123, ⓦ shalimarofindianh. For something a little spicier, check out this huge menu of reasonably priced authentic Indian dishes ($11–13), with a good selection of vegetarian specialities. Mon 4.30–10pm, Tues–Sun 11am–2.30pm & 4.30–10pm.

Jackson

With a high concentration of first-class lodgings and restaurants and hundreds of miles of trails within easy reach, **JACKSON** is one of the premier **cross-country ski** centres in the country. Indeed, the **Jackson Ski Touring Foundation** has frequently been rated the number-one cross-country ski area in the eastern US. On summer days, a great place to cool off is at **Jackson Falls**, which tumble down a stretch of boulders in the riverbed along Rte-16B. You can also admire the **Jackson Covered Bridge**, built in 1876 in the now rare Paddleford-truss style.

Jackson Ski Touring Foundation

53 Main St • Day memberships $19; equipment $16 a day (snowshoes for $12) • ☎ 603 383 9355 or ☎ 1 800 927 6697 • ⓦ jacksonxc.org

The **Jackson Ski Touring Foundation** manages some 98miles of **ski trails**, running over rolling countryside, woodland terrain, mountain descents and race-course areas, all perfectly maintained. In order to use them, though, you have to be a member.

Story Land

850 Rte-16 • Mid-June to early Sept daily 9am–6pm; early June & early Sept to mid-Oct Sat & Sun 9am–5pm • $27.99 (ages 3 and above) • ☎ 603 383 9776, ☎ storylandnh.com

If you're travelling with children, you might want to splash out and visit New Hampshire landmark **Story Land**, on Rte-16 south of Jackson, a colourful theme park, akin to a miniature Disneyland, with immaculately maintained grounds, rides such as the "Turtle Twirl" and "Bamboo Chutes", and lots of places for climbing.

ARRIVAL AND DEPARTURE   JACKSON

By bus Concord Coach Lines (☎ 1 800 639 3317, ⓦ concordcoachlines.com) runs one bus a day from Boston and Logan Airport to Berlin via Jackson (4hr 10min), stopping at the Covered Bridge on Rte-16. Buses depart at 8.20am for the return journey.

INFORMATION

Jackson Area Chamber of Commerce Jackson Falls Marketplace at the intersection of routes 16A and 16B (Mon–Fri 10am–4pm; ☎ 603 383 9356, ⓦ jacksonnh.com).

ACCOMMODATION

Bernerhof Inn 342 US-302, Glen ☎ 603 383 9132, ⓦ bernerhofinn.com. Nine comfortable and elegant guest rooms in a grand inn dating back to the 1880s (the name relates to previous Swiss owners). There's also a pub and a gourmet restaurant on the first floor. **$183**

★ Christmas Farm Inn & Spa 3 Blitzen Way, Rte-16B ☎603 383 4313, ⓦchristmasfarminn.com. The gorgeous 1778 farmhouse on the road gives way to a plush, tranquil resort that climbs up the forested hill, complete with spa and indoor pool. Rooms vary, but opt for the Carriage House, where large suites have balconies, jacuzzi tubs and four-poster beds. **$119**

Inn at Thorn Hill 40 Thorn Hill Rd, Jackson ☎603 383 4242 or ☎1 800 289 8990, ⓦinnatthornhill.com. A luxurious hillside inn with wraparound porch, designer furnishings, whirlpool tubs and private cottages out back.

Rates include breakfast, afternoon tea and a three-course dinner at the inn's gourmet restaurant. **$169**

Village House 49 Main St (Rte-16A), Jackson ☎603 383 6666, ⓦvillagehouse.com. A pleasant B&B just beyond the covered bridge, with private bathrooms and a great big porch. **$130**

★ Wildcat Inn & Tavern 94 Main St (Rte-16A), Jackson ☎603 383 4245, ⓦwildcattavern.com. Cosy and unpretentious, the *Wildcat* is right in the centre of town and has a comfortable ski-cabin feel. Especially popular in winter (as is the tavern). **$89**

EATING, DRINKING AND NIGHTLIFE

Plum Pudding Christmas Farm Inn & Spa, 3 Blitzen Way, Rte-16B ☎603 383 4313, ⓦchristmasfarminn .com. Top-notch restaurant open to non-guests. Dishes include honey soy-glazed salmon ($24) and herb-crusted rack of lamb ($31). They also run a congenial pub on site. Daily 7.30am–10am & 5.30–9pm.

Red Parka Pub 3 Station St at Rte-302, Glen ☎603 383 4949, ⓦredparkapub.com. A favourite place for a few drinks, some sports on the TV and excellent steaks (from $15.95), spare ribs (from $16.95) and sirloin burgers ($8.95). The place hops especially during ski season and at weekends, when there's live music. No reservations. Mon– Fri 3.30pm–late, Sat & Sun 3pm–late.

Shannon Door Rte-16 at Rte-16A, Jackson ☎603 383 4211, ⓦshannondoor.com. The town's long-standing Irish pub, with a suitably dark bar, plenty of Guinness and live entertainment. Thurs–Sun. Daily 4–11pm.

White Mountain Café & Bookstore Jackson Falls Marketplace, 18 Black Mountain Rd (Rte 16-B), Jackson ☎603 383 6425, ⓦwhitemountaincafe.com. Great home-made coffee cake, cookies, pies and bread, plus deli sandwiches and panini ($3–7). Daily 7am–4pm.

★ Wildcat Inn & Tavern 94 Main St (Rte-16A), Jackson ☎603 383 4245, ⓦwildcattavern.com. Gourmet country cuisine in the dining room and garden, and cheaper sandwiches and appetizers served in the less-formal couch-filled tavern, which often hosts a lively après-ski scene; Tues night is Hoot Night (8pm), when locals take to the mic — some are pretty good. Daily 5–11pm.

Yesterday's 100 Main St (Rte-16A, next to Wildcat), Jackson ☎603 383 4457, ⓦsarahsyesterdays.com. Big, cheap American breakfasts are the order of the day here, from pancakes slathered with maple syrup to prime rib and eggs. Daily 7am–3pm.

Pinkham Notch

Roughly ten miles north of Jackson along Rte-16, **PINKHAM NOTCH**, along the eastern base of towering Mount Washington, is the most jaw-dropping mountain pass in the White Mountains, with a reputation for serious outdoor activity. The Appalachian Trail and a number of other remote wilderness trails converge here, which means the Notch is overrun with adventurers during the summer. Luckily, the crowds don't detract too much and they're easy to forget once you've made your way into the forest.

Wildcat Mountain

Rte-16 • Mid-June to early Sept daily 9am–6pm; early June & early Sept to mid-Oct Sat & Sun only 9am–5pm • ☎603 383 9776, ⓦskiwildcat.com

A half-mile up the road from the Pinkham Notch visitor centre, local favourite **Wildcat Mountain** (☎603 466 3326 or ☎1 800 255 6439, ⓦskiwildcat.com) offers some of the best and most challenging **skiing** (lift tickets $63–70 per day) in the state during the winter. In summer there's a **zipline** ($20), **mountain-biking** and **gondola rides** to the 4062ft summit of Wildcat Mountain (daily: mid-June to mid-Oct 10am–5pm; late May to mid-June Sat & Sun only; $15, children 6–12 years $10).

ARRIVAL AND DEPARTURE   PINKHAM NOTCH

By bus Coach Lines (☎1 800 639 3317, ⓦconcordcoachlines.com) runs one bus a day from Boston and Logan Airport to Berlin via Pinkham Notch (4hr

35min), stopping at the Covered Bridge on Rte-16. Buses depart at 8.07am for the return journey.

THE APPALACHIAN TRAIL – NEW HAMPSHIRE

The Appalachian Mountain Club (AMC) operates eight delightfully remote **mountain huts** in New Hampshire along a 56-mile stretch of the **Appalachian Trail**, each about a day's hike apart. Generally offering full service in season (June to mid-Oct; exceptions noted below), including two hot meals per day, for $98; on Saturdays and $89 on other nights (Lonesome Lake is $79 Mon–Fri & Sun), they are a fairly popular choice – reservations are required (call ☏ 603 466 2727). All the huts except Lakes and Madison offer **self-service lodging** (without sheets, heat, or food) for $30, but only out of season (Carter Notch is the exception). For additional information, contact the Appalachian Mountain Club, 5 Joy St, Boston, MA 02108 (☏ 617 523 0655, ⓦ outdoors.org).

INFORMATION

Pinkham Notch Visitor Center Rte-16 (daily 6.30am–10pm). The best place to get information on hiking, camping and a whole range of other outdoor activities, where you can also buy the indispensable and exhaustive *AMC White Mountain Guide* ($24.95), good hiking maps, supplies and basic camping/mountaineering equipment. The centre organizes workshops, guided trips and programmes that cost anywhere from a couple of dollars to a couple of hundred dollars.

ACCOMMODATION AND EATING

Dolly Copp Campground Rte-16, 5 miles south of Gorham ☏ 603 466 2713, ⓦ icampnh.com. Some 177 campsites at $20 per site, with restrooms and fire rings; open from mid-May through mid-October. $20

Joe Dodge Lodge Pinkham Notch, Rte-16 ☏ 603 466 2727, ⓦ outdoors.org. The AMC maintains the *Joe Dodge Lodge* at Pinkham Notch, where you can get double rooms with private bathroom and meals, or bunks with a shared bathroom. Doubles $84; dorms $72

Pinkham Notch Visitor Center Rte-16 ☏ 603 466 2727. The centre serves three hearty family-style meals per day in a huge, noisy dining room at the visitor centre; the fixed-price dinner ($17) includes salad, soup, vegetables, home-made breads and dessert, a main course and plenty of conversation. Daily 6.30–8.30am, 11am–4pm & 6–7.30pm.

Mount Washington

At 6288ft, lofty **MOUNT WASHINGTON** is the highest peak in the northeastern US. On a clear day, you can see all the way to the Atlantic and into Canada from the top, once called the "second greatest show on earth" by P.T. Barnum, but the real interest lies in the extraordinary severity of the weather up here. The wind exceeds hurricane strength on more than a hundred days of the year and in 1934 it reached the highest speed ever recorded anywhere in the world – 231mph.

You can ascend the mountain via a number of hiking trails (see p.442), but most visitors opt for the easier option of driving via **Mount Washington Auto Road**, or taking the train along the **Mount Washington Cog Railway** (see p.442).

Auto Road trips start at Great Glen Trails Outdoor Center on Rte-16, where you can grab some food and buy tickets for bus rides. Next door the **Red Barn Museum** (daily 10am–4pm; free) preserves the actual vehicles that took visitors to the top in yesteryear, from the earliest mountain wagons to classic cars of the 1950s. The road was completed in 1861, a mammoth project that took seven years – even today, engineers cannot improve upon the eight-mile route taken to the summit.

The summit

Sherman Adams Summit Building • Mid-May to mid-Oct 8am–6pm • ☏ 603 466 3347, ⓦ mountwashington.org

Assuming the weather cooperates (and be prepared to be disappointed), the views from the summit of Mount Washington are predictably gasp-inducing, but look closer and you'll see the remarkable spectacle of buildings actually held down with great chains. The utilitarian **Sherman Adams Summit Building** serves as the headquarters of Mount Washington State Park and contains a cafeteria, restrooms and a gift shop, as well as the

Mount Washington Weather Observatory. Scientists here have researched the effects of wind, ice and fog since 1932; members can take a tour of the station (every hour; minimum membership $45). The observatory's various findings, exhibits on the environment and history of the mountain, videos and an electronic "weather wall" are displayed at the **Mount Washington Museum** downstairs (daily 9am–6pm; free for Auto Road or Cog Railway users, otherwise $3). You can also climb the few remaining feet to the actual (and humble-looking) summit point, or visit nearby **Tip Top House**; erected in 1853, this is the only original building to survive the devastating fire of 1908. Its saloon-like interior has been preserved, frozen in time (usually open June–Oct daily 10am–4pm; free).

ARRIVAL AND DEPARTURE MOUNT WASHINGTON

BY TRAIN

A three-hour return trip on the Mount Washington Cog Railway (with a scant twenty minutes at the summit) costs $59 and trains leave hourly late May to late Oct; call for other dates and times (☎603 278 5404 or ☎1 800 922 8825, ⊚thecog.com). It's a truly momentous experience, inching up the steep wooden trestles while avoiding descending showers of coal smut, though anyone who's not a train aficionado might not find it worth the money. The Cog also runs uphill in the winter season (Nov–March) to access one-mile-long groomed downhill ski trails ($31).

BY BUS

Specially adapted minibuses, still known as "stages" in honour of the twelve-person horse-drawn carriages that first used the road, give narrated tours (daily 8.30am–5pm; $30, children (5–12 years) $12; 90min round-trip; ☎603 466 3988, ⊚mtwashingtonautoroad.com) as they carry groups of tourists up the mountain. Driving takes thirty or forty minutes under normal conditions. Get tickets at the Great Glen Trails Outdoor Center on Rte-16.

BY CAR

The drive up the Mount Washington Auto Road (three miles north of Pinkham Notch) from Rte-16 (early May to late Oct – weather permitting – 7.30am–6pm in peak season; call ☎603 356 0300 to check weather conditions; ⊚mtwashingtonautoroad.com), is not quite as hair-raising as you may expect, although the hairpin bends and lack of guard-rails certainly keep you alert. There's a $25 toll

for private cars and driver (plus $8 for each additional adult and $6 for children 5–12 years), which includes a "This car climbed Mt. Washington" bumper sticker and a short audio-tour DVD. It takes around 25min going up.

ON FOOT

Some fifteen hiking trails – in addition to the Appalachian Trail itself – lead to the summit of Mount Washington. Whichever path you choose, take warm clothing (temperatures above the treeline can be fifty degrees colder than at the base), plenty of water and food and do not hesitate to turn back if the weather turns foul; several hikers die of exposure to the harsh weather atop the mountain every year.

Tuckerman Ravine Trail The most direct route on the eastern side of the mountain is the Tuckerman Ravine Trail, which originates at the AMC Pinkham Notch Visitor Center (see p.41) and traverses the often snow-filled Tuckerman Ravine, a popular place for backcountry skiing. If you're in good condition, the 4.1-mile trail can be completed in about four and a half hours and it is possible to hike up and back in one day.

Ammonoosuc Ravine Trail On the western side of the mountain the Ammonoosuc Ravine Trail starts in the Cog Railway car park, hooking up with the Crawford Path (built in 1819 and the oldest in the US), at the AMC's Lakes of the Clouds hut. If you're in good physical shape, the 4.5-mile trip takes roughly four and a half hours one-way. This hike is not for the faint-hearted, however, due to the extremely unpredictable weather once you near the peak.

INFORMATION

Great Glen Trails Outdoor Center At the foot of the Auto Road (daily 8.30am–5pm; ☎603 466 2333, ⊚greatglentrails.com). Family-oriented centre that can provide information about trails and conditions, as well as

renting bikes ($30 for 4hr) and arranging whitewater trips ($65); it becomes a ski centre in winter (trail pass $18/day; ski rentals $20/day).

ACCOMMODATION

Camping Unless otherwise posted, you can camp anywhere on Mount Washington below the treeline, 200ft

from the trail and water sources and a quarter-mile from any road or facility.

Crawford Notch and around

The ease with which US-302 now crosses the mountains west of Mount Washington belies the effort that went into cutting a road through **Crawford Notch**, a twisty and awe-inspiring pass halfway between the Franconia area and Conway. The main man-made attraction on route is the magnificent **Mount Washington Hotel**, which stands in splendid isolation in the wide valley known as **Bretton Woods**. A few miles east lies the **Mount Washington Cog Railway**, probably the most romantic way of getting to the summit of Mount Washington (see p.442).

Crawford Notch State Park

2057 US-302, Harts Location • Late May to late Oct Mon–Fri 9am–sunset, Sat & Sun 8.30am–sunset • $4 • ☎ 603 374 2272 • Ⓦ nhstateparks.org

Within White Mountain National Forest, **Crawford Notch State Park** is split in two by US-302, which winds through the dramatic gap formed by the steep slopes of Mount Field to the west and Mount Jackson to the east. Discovered in 1771 by hunter Timothy Nash the notch was soon recognized as a viable route through the White Mountains. A railroad was completed at great expense in 1857.

As you drive up from North Conway, the first stop of interest is the **Arethusa Falls Trail**, a steep 1.5-mile hike to the highest falls in the state (200ft). Three miles north, in the shadow of Mount Willey (4285ft), the **Willey House Historic Site** is named for a family who lived here and died in a terrible landslide in 1826 – the ruins are still visible. Next door a shack serves as the tiny park **visitor centre** and there's also a small café.

The best **hike** in the area is the **Mount Willard Trail**, a 1.6-mile (1hr) jaunt up to dizzying views of Crawford Notch at Mount Willard (2865ft), starting at the Crawford Notch Depot.

Mount Washington Hotel

310 Mt Washington Hotel Rd, Bretton Woods • ☎ 603 278 1000 or ☎ 1 800 258 0330, Ⓦ mountwashingtonresort.com

At the grand opening of the **Mount Washington Hotel** – now the **Omni Mount Washington Resort** (see p.444) – in the summer of 1902, Joseph Stickney reputedly exclaimed, "Look at me gentlemen … for I am the poor fool who built all this!" Its glistening white Spanish Revival facade, capped by red cupolas and framed by Mount Washington rising behind it, has barely changed since then. In its heyday, a stream of horse-drawn carriages brought families up from the train station, deliberately located at a distance to increase the sense of grandeur.

Restoration by a group of investors who purchased the decaying building and surrounding property in 1991 has ensured that the cruise-ship-sized hotel remains marvellously – if somewhat eerily – evocative of past splendour, with its quarter-mile terrace, white wicker furniture, grand dining room and 24-carat views. In the 1990s the resort opened its doors to the winter ski crowd for the first time and in the summer there are weekend golfing, tennis and spa packages, along with an equestrian centre and miles of hiking trails. The latest attraction is the **Bretton Woods Canopy Tour** ($110; ☎ 603 278 4947, Ⓦ brettonwoods.com), comprising ten ziplines ranging from 120ft to 830ft.

More sedate displays in the hotel lobby commemorate the **Bretton Woods Conference** of 1944, which laid the groundwork for the postwar financial structure of the capitalist world, by setting the gold standard at $35 an ounce and creating the International Monetary Fund and the World Bank.

ARRIVAL AND DEPARTURE

CRAWFORD NOTCH

By train The Conway Scenic Railroad (see p.437) cuts through the heart of Crawford Notch, stopping at Crawford Notch Depot where the visitor centre can help with hiking information.

By car You'll need a car to visit the *Mount Washington Hotel*.

INFORMATION

Macomber Family Information Center Along US-302, three miles south of *Mount Washington Hotel* and across from tiny Saco Lake (late May to mid-June Fri–Sun 9am–5pm; mid-June to mid-Oct daily 9am–5pm; ☎ 603 278 5170). The Crawford Notch Depot is now the helpful AMC-maintained Macomber Family Information Center and store selling backcountry necessities. Go to the nearby Highland Center if it's closed (see below).

Crawford Notch State Park visitor centre Willey House Historic Site, Rte-302 (mid-May to mid-Oct daily 10am–4pm; ☎ 603 374 2272). Tiny visitor centre selling maps and trail guides and offering advice on camping; they also maintain a small café.

ACCOMMODATION

AMC Highland Center Crawford Notch Depot ☎ 603 278 4453 ⓦ outdoors.org. Great choice year-round: an environmental education centre that also offers lodging in dorms or double rooms (cheapest with shared bathroom). Hearty alpine breakfasts and family-style dinners are included, as are a full roster of activities like guided hikes and game nights and free L.L. Bean gear for use in AMC programmes (at a small fee for your private use). Doubles **$137**; shared bathroom **$92**; dorms **$47**

Dry River Campground 2059 US-302 ☎ 603 271 3628. Thirty-six wooded sites, thirty of which are by reservation only; flush toilets and showers available, but note that there is no water after mid-October. May to mid-Dec. **$25**

Omni Mount Washington Resort 310 Mt Washington Hotel Rd ☎ 603 278 1000, ⓦ omnihotels.com. One of the grandest hotels in the state, with lavish rooms to match (see p.443). **$229**

Great North Woods region

The far northern section of New Hampshire is known as the **Great North Woods region**, a far less visited land of small towns and untouched wilderness. Wedged between Vermont, Maine and Québec across the Canadian border, the area could be visited on a long day trip from Jackson or Littleton, though there is little see in terms of sights. Heading north along Rte-16 from the White Mountains you'll pass through the pretty town of **GORHAM**, probably the best place to eat. Seven miles up the road lies **BERLIN**, a once prosperous logging town that has fallen on hard times. North of here Rte-16 hugs the mostly placid **Androscoggin River**, popular with fishermen – it's a scenic drive with plenty of places to pull over. At Errol take Rte-26 up to **DIXVILLE NOTCH**, the highlight of the north, with a craggy gorge and the romantic **Balsams** resort overlooking a small lake. From here you can drive down to Colebrook on the Vermont border and head south along Rte-3 and the Connecticut River Valley.

Northern Forest Heritage Park

961 Main St (Rte-16), Berlin • Mon–Fri 9am–4pm • $6 • ☎ 603 752 7202 • ⓦ northernforestheritage.org

On the northern edge of Berlin, on the banks of the Androscoggin River, the **Northern**

FIRST-IN-THE-NATION PRESIDENTIAL PRIMARY

The mountains of the "Presidential Range" might have made the state's name in tourist guides, but New Hampshire and the tiny mountain village of **DIXVILLE NOTCH** are really famous for a quite different presidential connection: the primary election. Since 1952, New Hampshire has been the first state in the US to hold its presidential primary, which more or less marks the start of the winnowing process to see who each party's presidential candidates will be, and Dixville Notch has had the privilege of being the first place in the state – and therefore the nation – to report its results. Every four years, the tiny electorate of Dixville Notch (year-round population: 75) files into the Ballot Room at the *Balsams* (guest rooms: 202) on election day, to cast votes at the stroke of midnight. Since 1968, Dixville Notch has never failed to predict the Republican nominee and the state as a whole has a good record for picking the candidates eventually nominated by both Democrats and Republicans to run for president. Due to the high media profile of the primary, as well as the state's compact size, campaigning is based very much on knocking on doors and actually meeting the people.

Forest Heritage Park is a worthy attempt to capture the spirit of the region with a recreated logging camp c.1900. Also on site, the 1853 Brown Company House, once a boarding house for sawmill workers, hosts a small exhibit on logging and a gift shop. You can take 90-minute narrated river tours (June–Oct Tues–Sat 1pm; $15) from here and there are other special events.

Dixville Notch State Park
Rte-26 • Daily 24hr • Free • ☎ 603 538 6707

Dixville Notch may officially be a "town", but there's no centre and no Main Street – today it's more a loosely affiliated group of farms and homesteads scattered over the central mountains. The main attraction is the "notch" itself, a narrow, dramatic pass (1871ft) through a cleft in the mountains and protected within 127-acre **Dixville Notch State Park**.

Balsams Hotel
Rte-16 • ☎ 603 255 3400, ⓦ thebalsams.com

One of the last grand White Mountains resort hotels, beautifully framed by mountains and Lake Gloriette, the **Balsams Hotel** (see below) is most evocative of the nineteenth century – even if you're not staying, pop in for a drink, a meal or just to look around. The first hotel here was a rustic guesthouse built in 1866 and known as *Dix House*. In 1895, wealthy industrialist Henry S. Hale renamed it the *Balsams* and started building the enormous clapboard palace with turrets you see today, complete by 1918. Inside, visit the celebrated **Ballot Room** with its blue star-spangled carpet, where the "first in the nation" voters cast their ballots at midnight (see box, p.444), and the **Captain's Study**, full of all sorts of bric-a-brac from the hotel's past. As you drive in to the hotel, look for the **cold springs** on the right – the water here is clean enough to bottle.

7

INFORMATION

North Country Chamber of Commerce US-3 north of Colebrook, just across the Connecticut River from Vermont, at the end of Rte-26 (daily 8am–6pm; ☎ 603 237 8939, ⓦ northcountrychamber.org)

Gorham information booth In the centre of town on

GREAT NORTH WOODS REGION

Rte-16, 69 Main St (Mon–Sat 10am–7pm, Sun 10am–4pm; ☎ 603 466 3103). Offers detailed information on other lodging and eating options in these farthest reaches of the state.

ACCOMMODATION

Balsams Hotel 1000 Cold Spring Rd (Rte-26) ☎ 800 255 0600, ⓦ thebalsams.com. Get a taste of old-world charm and vacationing at this grand resort hotel (see opposite), with its own lake, golf course and ski area. Rooms feature frilly Victorian decor, floral wallpaper and period furnishings; rates include all meals and use of facilities. **$209**

Moose Brook State Park Campground Jimtown Rd, off Rte-2 in Gorham ☎ 603 466 3860. There are 62 secluded tent sites in the tranquil confines of this gorgeous state park; the Moose Brook flows through the park and feeds the swimming area. Late May to mid-Oct. **$25**

EATING AND DRINKING

La Bottega Saladino's 152 Main St, Gorham ☎ 603 466 2520, ⓦ saladinositalianmarket.com. Reasonably priced home-made Italian food like meatball panini ($6.95), spaghetti and meatballs ($8.95) and pizzas from $6.95. Tues–Thurs 10am–6pm, Fri & Sat 10am–9pm.

★ **Libby's Bistro** 111 Main St, Gorham ☎ 603 466 5330, ⓦ libbysbistro.net. This Victorian mansion is a pleasant surprise up here, serving up a finely crafted bistro menu with Asian, American and Mediterranean influences (main courses $19.95–27.95). Grab a drink in their *Saalt* Pub. Wed–Sat 5.30–10pm.

Maine

451 The southern coast

471 The Mid-Coast

491 Down East Maine

506 Inland Maine

MONUMENT COVE, ACADIA NATIONAL PARK

Maine

Maine more than lives up to its unofficial motto of being "the way life should be". Filled with lobster shacks, dense forests, scenic lakes and seaside enclaves, the state offers ample opportunities for exploring, or just for lounging in Adirondack chairs and watching the leaves change colour – there's a little something for everyone here. As large as the other five New England states combined, Maine has a year-round population that barely equals that of Rhode Island. In theory, therefore, there's plenty of room for all the visitors who flood the state in summer; in practice, most people head straight for the coast.

At the southern end of the coastline, the beach towns of **Ogunquit** and **Old Orchard Beach** quickly lead up to Maine's most cosmopolitan city, **Portland**. The **Mid-Coast**, between Brunswick and Bucksport, is characterized by its craggy shores, windswept peninsulas and sheltered inlets, though the towns of **Boothbay Harbor** and **Camden** are certainly busy enough. Beyond the idyllic Blue Hill Peninsula, **Down East** Maine is home to **Acadia National Park**, the state's most popular outdoor escape, in addition to the bustling summer retreat of **Bar Harbor**. Farther north, you'll find foggy weather and exhilarating, increasingly uninhabited scenery, capped by the candy-striped lighthouse at **Quoddy Head**, the easternmost point in the United States.

You can only really begin to appreciate the size and space of the state, however, farther north or inland, where vast tracts of mountainous forest are dotted with lakes and barely pierced by roads. This region is ideal territory for hiking and canoeing, particularly in **Baxter State Park**, site of the northern terminus of the Appalachian Trail. In the northwestern part of the state, closer to the New Hampshire border, a cluster of ski resorts are scattered about the mountains, including **Sugarloaf USA**, one of New England's finest ski areas.

Seasonal Maine: when to visit p.451
Finding your way in Maine p.453
Surfing Maine's southern coast p.455
Ogunquit boat cruises p.456
Portland tours p.462
Winslow Homer's studio p.463
Sweet teeth p.467
Brewery tours p.467
Soakology Foot Sanctuary and
  Teahouse p.469
DeLorme Map Headquarters p.470
Harriet Beecher Stowe p.473
Maine Eastern Railroad p.473
AMC huts on Georgetown Island p.475
Maine's best lobster roll p.477
Clambakes p.477
Boat trips from Boothbay Harbor p.478
Renys: the Harrods of Maine p.480
Maine lighthouses p.481
Boats to Monhegan Island p.484
Rockland boat trips p.485

St George peninsula p.486
Windjammer trips p.487
Edna St Vincent Millay p.488
Bucksport p.490
Aquatic activities in Blue Hill p.493
En route to Mount Desert Island:
  Ellsworth p.495
Out to sea p.497
Hiking on Mount Desert Island p.499
Kayaking and rock climbing p.500
Camping on Mount Desert Island p.501
Maine's wild blueberries p.503
Inland Maine: when not to visit p.507
Making whoopie p.509
Skiing and outdoor activities p.511
AMC mountain huts in western
  Maine p.512
Loony tunes p.513
Hiking and biking around Moosehead
  Lake p.515
Whitewater rafting p.516

8

Highlights

❶ Portland As cosmopolitan as the state gets, coastal Portland has everything to offer, save big-city aggravation and high prices. **See p.460**

❷ Rockland With its incredible arts scene and working harbour, this hip little enclave is a great spot for viewing a Wyeth or sailing a windjammer. **See p.484**

❸ Stonington harbour Among Maine's most beautiful inlets, Stonington is filled with boats and offers exploratory kayaking, biking and puffin-sighting trips. **See p.493**

❹ Acadia National Park Bike, boat, hike, climb or simply commune with nature in the state's recreational mecca. **See p.497**

❺ Bethel Close to the White Mountains, remote Bethel is the quintessential New England small town and a hub for winter and summer outdoor adventures. **See p.510**

❻ Katahdin In the deepest heart of Maine, the beginning of the Appalachian Trail sits atop this 5300ft peak. **See p.516**

HIGHLIGHTS ARE MARKED ON THE MAP ON P.450

Brief history

Although in many ways inhospitable – the **Algonquin** called it the "Land of the Frozen Ground" – Maine has been in contact with Europe since around 1000 AD, when the **Vikings** first explored its shores. European fishermen began setting up summer camps here about five hundred years later.

North America's first agricultural **colonies** were also in Maine: Samuel de Champlain's **French** Protestants near Mount Desert Island in 1604, and an **English** group that

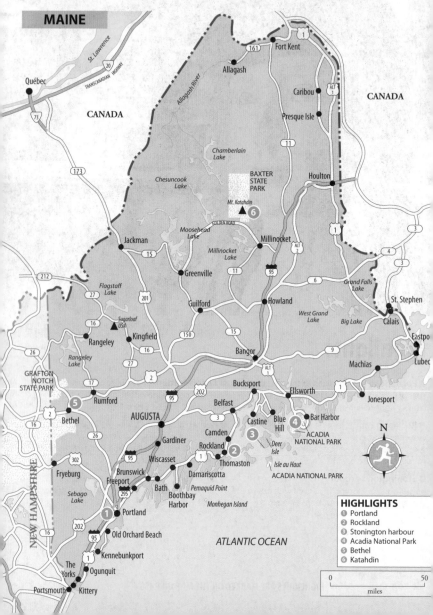

MAINE

St. Lawrence

Québec

CANADA

Fort Kent

Allagash

Caribou

Presque Isle

Houlton

CANADA

Allagash River

Chamberlain Lake

Chesuncook Lake

BAXTER STATE PARK

Mt. Katahdin ▲ ❻

GOLDEN ROAD

Jackman

Moosehead Lake

Millinocket

Millinocket Lake

Greenville

Howland

Grand Falls Lake

St. Stephen

Calais

Flagstaff Lake

Guilford

West Grand Lake

Big Lake

Eastport

Lubec

Rangeley

Sugarloaf USA ▲

Kingfield

Bangor

Machias

Rangeley Lake

GRAFTON NOTCH STATE PARK

Rumford

Bucksport

Ellsworth

Jonesport

Bethel ❺

Belfast

Castine

Blue Hill ❹

Bar Harbor

ACADIA NATIONAL PARK

AUGUSTA

Camden

❸

Deer Isle

Gardiner

Rockland ❷

Thomaston

Isle au Haut

ACADIA NATIONAL PARK

Wiscasset

Damariscotta

Brunswick

Freeport

Bath

Pemaquid Point

Boothbay Harbor

Monhegan Island

Sebago Lake

Fryeburg

Portland ❶

NEW HAMPSHIRE

Old Orchard Beach

Kennebunkport

ATLANTIC OCEAN

N

The Yorks

Ogunquit

Portsmouth   Kittery

HIGHLIGHTS
❶ Portland
❷ Rockland
❸ Stonington harbour
❹ Acadia National Park
❺ Bethel
❻ Katahdin

0 ──────── 50
miles

> ### SEASONAL MAINE: WHEN TO VISIT
>
> Maine's climate is famously harsh. In **winter**, the state is covered in snow, and often ice. Officially, **summer** is spread between two long weekends – Memorial Day (the last Mon in May) and Labor Day (the first Mon in Sept) – though temperatures don't really start to rise until June or even July. This is nonetheless Maine's most popular season, its start heralded by sweet corn and the re-opening of lobster shacks, and its end marked by the wild blueberry harvest. Brilliant **autumn colours** begin to spread from the north in late September, when, unlike elsewhere in New England, off-season prices apply, and the cool weather is great for apple-picking, leaf-peeping or simply curling up with a blanket and a book.

survived one winter at the mouth of the Kennebec River three years later. In the face of the unwillingness of English settlers to let them farm in peace, local Indians formed alliances with the French and, until as late as 1700, regularly drove out streams of impoverished English refugees.

At first considered part of Massachusetts, Maine became a separate entity only in 1820, when the Missouri Compromise made Maine a free, and Missouri a slave, state. Maine flourished in the nineteenth century, owing to its thriving lumber and shipbuilding industries. Today, the **economy** remains heavily based on the sea, although many of those who fish also farm. Lobster fishing in particular has defied gloomy predictions and continued to boom, as evidenced by the many thriving **lobster pounds**.

The southern coast

Stretching between the two shopping hubs of **Kittery** and **Freeport**, Maine's **southern coast** is the state's most settled region. Blessed with its best **beaches** – indeed, most of its beaches – this area was already a popular summer holiday spot by the mid-nineteenth century, when trains began bringing city-dwellers up from Boston and New York or down from Canada. The eleven-mile strip of sand at **Old Orchard Beach** is still one of the finest in the country, attracting huge crowds in July and August, while more attractive **Ogunquit**, the other popular resort town in the area, is only slightly less overrun in summer, with a long-established artistic community, a gay and lesbian scene and a collection of excellent restaurants. Though commercial development has definitely had an impact on the region, you can still find attractive old towns with plenty of historical interest, such as **York**, the first chartered city in America, and beautiful **Kennebunkport**, best known as the summer residence of former presidents George Bush and George W. Bush. Further north, the coast becomes more varied and prone to peninsulas, harbours, inlets and islands. At the mouth of the Fore River, Maine's largest city, **Portland**, has a hip, twenty-something population, a cobblestoned downtown and a dynamic restaurant and arts scene.

Kittery

KITTERY is just barely in Maine, right across the Piscataqua River from Portsmouth, NH. It's best known for its outlet stores – you'll find deep discounts here on everything from trainers and radios to diamonds and dishware. If you'd prefer to steer clear of the commercialism, however, the small bit of land south along Rte-103 called Kittery Point makes for a pleasant drive. It also brings you past the 1714 **First Congregational Church**, Maine's oldest house of worship, to a rocky cliff overlooking the Portsmouth Naval Shipyard on **Seavey Island**, where the treaty ending the Russo-Japanese War of 1905 was signed. Kittery was a major shipbuilding centre in the mid-eighteenth century, when the *Ranger* sailed out of a Kittery shipyard under the command of Revolutionary War hero John Paul Jones. For a detailed look at the

8

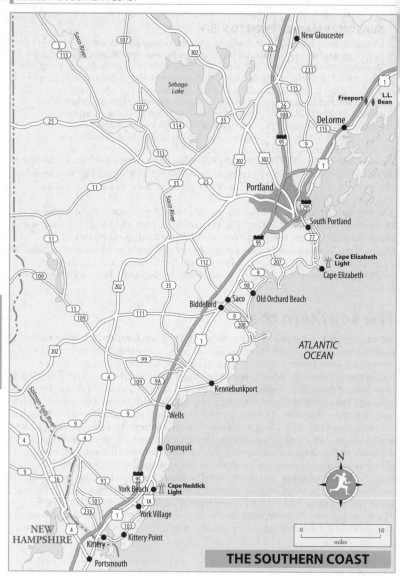

THE SOUTHERN COAST

city's maritime and cultural history, including a 14ft model of the *Ranger*, stop off at the **Kittery Historical and Naval Museum**, on Rogers Road near the intersection of routes 1 and 236 (June to mid-Oct Tues–Sat 10am–4pm; $5; ☎207 439 3080, ⓦkitterymuseum.com).

INFORMATION   KITTERY

Main State Visitor Information Center Intersection of I-95 and Rte-1 (summer Mon–Thurs & Sun 8am–6pm, Fri & Sat till 8pm; rest of year 9am–5.30pm; ☎207 439 1319). This comprehensive information centre has brochures, weather information and volunteers who can give insiders' tips and help make reservations.

FINDING YOUR WAY IN MAINE

With public transport generally nonexistent, you'll most likely want to **drive** to Maine. The most enjoyable route to follow is **Rte-1**, which runs within a few miles of the coast all the way from the border with New Hampshire to Canada. In each town, Rte-1 usually becomes a named street; sometimes several names are used. You should be prepared for traffic backups in the height of summer, particularly in Ogunquit, Wiscasset and Camden, where Rte-1 doubles as the town's main drag. If you're in a hurry, take **I-95**, which offers speedy (though tolled in parts) access to the Portland area and beyond. In the interior, roads are quiet and views spectacular; many of the northernmost routes are graveled and belong to the lumber companies.

Whatever your destination, be sure to pick up a **DeLorme Maine Atlas** (sold state-wide in bookstores, or online at Ⓦdelorme.com) – this gazetteer is a lifesaver when trying to orient yourself along local roads. DeLorme's headquarters, in Yarmouth, are also worth a visit (see box, p.470).

ACCOMMODATION

Portsmouth Harbor Inn & Spa 6 Water St ☎ 207 439 4040, Ⓦinnatportsmouth.com. After a day at the outlets, retreat to the spa at this five-room B&B with patterned wallpaper and four-poster beds overlooking the Piscataqua River. The inn is outfitted with a hot tub, a/c and wi-fi, and most rooms have water views. Full breakfast included. **$155**

EATING AND DRINKING

Anneke Jans 60 Wallingford Square ☎ 207 439 0001. This trendy *boîte* with a loyal clientele turns out some of the state's most delectable bistro dishes. The locavore menu changes frequently; seared sea scallops with potato puree ($27) is typical. Daily 5pm–late.

★ **Beach Pea Baking Co.** 59 State Rd. (Rte-1) ☎ 207 439 3555. Everything-from-scratch sandwiches, salads and soups can be had at this local favourite with a pea-green interior. Tucked inside a stand-alone house with well-tended gardens, seating is limited, but there is a sweet shaded patio. Mon–Sat 7.30am–6pm.

Bob's Clam Hut 315 Rte-1 ☎ 207 439 4233. This campy fish joint has been a favoured haunt for whole-belly clams (basket with fries; $18.95) and lobster rolls ($13.95) since 1956. It also runs the more upscale *Robert's Maine Grill* (☎ 207 439 0300), across the street. Mon–Thurs 11am–9.30pm, Fri & Sat till 10pm, Sun till 9pm.

★ **Chauncey Creek Lobster Pier** 16 Chauncey Creek Rd ☎ 207 439 1030. *Chauncey's* fair-priced seafood menu is served on colourful picnic tables overlooking picturesque Pepperrell Cove. It's BYOB and then some – patrons bring beer, salad, dessert, anything not on the menu – it's all part of the experience. Mid-May to early Sept daily 8am–11pm; mid-Sept to mid-Oct Tues–Sun 11am–7pm.

Loco Coco's Tacos 36 Walker St (Rte-103) ☎ 207 438 9322. Satisfy your Mexican cravings at this spacious hangout where you can order takeaway at the counter or get sit-down service in the big dining room out back. The hefty burritos ($6.95), quesadillas ($6.50) and piquant margaritas ($6.50) are all excellent. Daily 11am–9pm.

SHOPPING

If you follow Rte-1 through Kittery, you'll pass a string of some 120 **outlet shops** (☎ 1 888 548 8379, Ⓦthekitteryoutlets .com), which offer good deals on clothing from companies like Banana Republic and J. Crew, although the atmosphere lags behind that of rival outlet hotspot Freeport, about 75min up the road.

The Yorks

The pleasant **YORKS**, a few miles north of Kittery on routes 1 and 103, are actually five separate entities: York, York Village, Cape Neddick, scenic York Harbor and York Beach. This cumulative network of villages – sometimes referred to as "York" – bears the distinction of being America's first chartered city, incorporated in 1642 (though it was demoted to the status of "town" in 1670). A summer tram (trolley) service travels along coastal Rte-1A and stops between the beaches of Long and Short Sands ($1.50; ☎ 207 363 9600, Ⓦyorktrolley.com).

As well as its historical attractions, the Yorks boast several fine beaches, a vintage arcade (York Beach's endearing Fun-O-Rama) and a number of invigorating cliff walks. **Nubble Light**, at the end of Shore Road, off Rte-103 at York Beach, is one of Maine's most striking lighthouses, situated on an island of its own. If you have little ones in tow, or if you're simply interested in jumping up and down, be sure to visit the **Wiggly Bridge**, a local landmark just off Rte-1A on Lilac Lane (Rte-103) in York Harbor. This flexible bridge enables you to jump wildly while watching the tide go in or out beneath your feet.

Museums of Old York

3 Lindsay St • Mid-June to early Oct Mon–Sat 9.30am–4pm • Buy tickets at the Remick Barn Visitor Center; guided tours $12 for all buildings, $6 for one • ☎ 207 363 4974, ⓦ oldyork.org

The town's past is well preserved in the eight buildings that comprise the **Museums of Old York** in York Village. Foremost among the structures is the **Old Gaol**, which really is old – it's the earliest British colonial public structure still standing on its original site, dating from 1719. It was used as Maine's primary prison until the Revolution, then continued to confine York prisoners until the Civil War. Inside, the museum reconstructs the jailer's quarters and has displays on some of the prison's more colourful criminals. The museums also include the **Old Schoolhouse**, which has exhibits on education in the eighteenth century; the **John Hancock Warehouse and Wharf**, which has maritime displays in the original Customs House; and the **Old Burying Ground**, where it's rumoured that a grave covered with a stone slab was thus protected to prevent its occupant, reputedly a witch, from escaping. In fact, the slab was actually placed there by her husband to prevent pigs from foraging on her grave.

8

ACCOMMODATION   THE YORKS

Dockside Guest Quarters 22 Harris Island Rd, York Harbor ☎ 207 363 2868, ⓦ docksidegq.com. Situated on a private peninsula, the *Dockside* is a quintessential old Maine property where the porch is taken up with plenty of Adirondack chairs and the front lawn slopes down to the sea. The decor is a bit dated, but you can't beat the location, and the on-site restaurant, *Dockside*, is divine. April to mid-Nov. **$159**

Katahdin Inn 11 Ocean Ave Ext, York Beach ☎ 207 363 1824, ⓦ thekatahdin.com. Easy to spot by its canary-yellow exterior, this nine-room beach house has been pleasing guests for 125 years. Rooms are simple and small, with fridges and wi-fi; the former is for beer, the latter for ignoring, as you spend your time on Short Sands Beach, just off the porch. Shared bathroom **$95**; en-suite **$145**

Morning Glory Inn 120 Seabury Ave, York ☎ 207 363 2062, ⓦ morninggloryinnmaine.com. This 200-year-old post-and-beam B&B boasts three modern rooms decorated with lemon-yellows, stripes and silks. Nestled amid tall pine trees and overlooking a bountiful garden, guest rooms come with wi-fi and a private patio. Mid-May to Oct. **$175**

York Harbor Inn Rte-1A, York Harbor ☎ 207 363 5119 or ☎ 1 800 343 3869, ⓦ yorkharborinn.com. Incorporates five beautiful properties – four of which are seaside – decorated with crisp white linens, dignified antique dressers, and (in some) wood-burning fireplaces. *York Harbor* also has a fine dining restaurant and the *Ship's Cellar Pub*, whose portholes and wooden joinery evoke the belly of a yacht. **$149**

EATING AND DRINKING

Blue Sky 2 Beach St at the Atlantic House, York Beach ☎ 207 363 0050. Opposite *The Goldenrod* (see below) and yet light years away, style-wise, is star chef Lydia Shire's capacious *Blue Sky*, located on the second floor of the *Atlantic House* hotel. Here, steak and seafood mains are beautifully presented, but don't live up to the price ($27–35); instead, go for the freshly squeezed pineapple martinis ($10) that are shaken up behind the long marble bar. Daily 11am–3pm & 5.30pm–10pm; bar until 11pm.

Brown's Ice Cream 232 Nubble Rd, York Beach ☎ 207 363 1277. Nothing says summer better than a huge ice-cream cone eaten by a lighthouse. *Brown's* has been scooping some of the state's best flavours for over forty

years (head straight for the cookie dough). May to mid-Oct noon–late (9.30pm in July & Aug).

Cape Neddick Lobster Pound 60 Shore Rd (Rte-1A), Cape Neddick ☎ 207 363 5471. Poised on a river, this loveable seafood restaurant serves boiled lobster dinners and baked haddock in its casual dining room or on the waterfront deck. Lunch and dinner March–Nov.

Flo's 1359 Rte-1, Cape Neddick. People have loved lining up for *Flo's* hot dogs since 1959. Be sure to get the special sauce. Daily except Wed 11am–3pm.

The Goldenrod 2 Railroad Ave, York Beach ☎ 207 363 2621. This institution, a family restaurant located by the Fun-O-Rama, has been churning out saltwater taffy for

---

SURFING MAINE'S SOUTHERN COAST

Every year a small number of hardy souls brave the North Atlantic to pursue the unlikely pastime of **surfing** off Maine's coast. If you're used to surfing anywhere else, beware: the water here in January can dip below 40°F, daunting even with the newest developments in wet-suit technology. Though wave and tide conditions are usually best in autumn and winter, on certain warm summer days the waves come up and the crowds swell with the tides. The best spots are at **Higgins Beach**, south of Portland in Scarborough, **Fortune Rocks** in Biddeford, **Gooch's Beach** in Kennebunk, **Long Sands** in York and **Old Orchard Beach**. For equipment **rentals** and **lessons**, contact Aquaholics, 166 Port Rd (Rte-35) in Kennebunk (☎ 207 967 8650), or Liquid Dreams Surf, 731 Main St (Rte-1) in Ogunquit (☎ 207 641 2545).

---

more than a hundred years. Watch the hypnotizing taffy machine pull and wrap the "Goldenrod Kisses". Late May to early Sept daily 8am–10pm; mid-Sept to mid-Oct Thurs–Sun 8am–4pm.

★ **Stolen Menu Café** 127 Long Sands Rd, York ☎ 207 363 0298. It's not hard to see why M.J. Bailey, the cook and owner of *Stolen Menu*, is a self-proclaimed "artist in the kitchen" – her sticky-bun French toast ($11.95), "farmers' market benedict" (with spinach and portobello mushrooms

on warm focaccia bread; $13.95) and home-made granola ($6.95) are all exquisitely prepared and brimming with flavour. Tues–Fri 6.30am–2pm, Sat & Sun 7am–1pm.

Stonewall Kitchen 2 Stonewall Lane, just off Rte-1 ☎ 207 351 2712. Not to be missed is this branch of the condiment purveyor, which serves lobster BLTs and salads alongside its signature displays of mustards, jams and chocolate sauces. Café: Mon–Sat 8am–4pm, Sun 9am–4pm; store Mon–Sat 8am–8pm, Sun 9am–6pm.

Ogunquit

8

Approaching **OGUNQUIT** from the south, it's easy to understand why the Abenakis named the small oceanside town "beautiful place by the sea". In the nineteenth and twentieth centuries, Ogunquit enjoyed fame as the vacation spot of choice for such folks as Bette Davis and Tommy Dorsey; today it's also known for its gay and lesbian scene, arguably the best in New England outside of Provincetown, Massachusetts. The town also has a reputation as an artists' colony, and is home to a scenic art museum and a handful of galleries. Ogunquit has a little bit of a privileged attitude, but streets with names like "Whistling Oyster Lane" and "Ho Hum Hill" point to the playful character underneath. **Ogunquit Square**, along Main Street (Rte-1), is the centre of town, home to most of the town's restaurants, coffeehouses and quirky shops.

Ogunquit Beach

The Beach Street leads over the Ogunquit River to **Ogunquit Beach**, one of Maine's finest, with three miles of sugary sand. The water is always freezing, but the sun is mellow and the sand great for sunbathing. Parking near the pier costs $25, but there's a better way to access the beach: take Rte-1 north of Ogunquit Square and go right on Ocean Street, which leads to a less populated area of the beach – and cheaper parking ($20).

Perkins Cove and Marginal Way

A pleasant knot of restaurants and shops a few miles south of Ogunquit Square, **Perkins Cove** is best reached by walking along **Marginal Way**, a windy path that traces the crescent shoreline from Ogunquit Beach. The 1.5-mile trail offers unspoilt views of the Atlantic coast, particularly stunning in autumn. The folk art, pottery and jewellery shops in and around the cove warrant an hour's browse, and there are a few places to indulge in a lobster roll or some saltwater taffy.

Ogunquit Museum of American Art

543 Shore Rd • May–Oct daily 10am–5pm • $10 • ☎ 207 646 4909, ⊕ ogunquitmuseum.org

A half-mile south of Perkins Cove is the stellar **Ogunquit Museum of American Art**, called "the most beautiful little museum in the world" by a former director of the

Metropolitan Museum of Art in Manhattan. This tiny sanctuary is endowed with a strong collection of nineteenth- and twentieth-century American art, such as seascapes by Marsden Hartley and Rockwell Kent, enhanced by the building's spectacular ocean views. In the garden, grinning animal sculptures mingle with serene marble women.

ARRIVAL AND DEPARTURE

By train Amtrak's *Downeaster* pulls into neighbouring Wells 5 times daily from Boston's North Station (one-way $19; ☎ 1 800 872 7245, ⊕ amtrakdowneaster.com); call a cab to ferry you downtown (Brewster's Taxi; $18; ☎ 207 646 2141).

GETTING AROUND

By tram Traffic can be terrible, so it may be a good idea to use the tram ($1.50, exact change only; ☎ 207 646 1411), which connects with the York tram to the south as well as Perkins Cove, Ogunquit Square, and the beach, continuing north to connect with the Wells/Kennebunkport trolley.
By bike Wheels and Waves (☎ 207 646 5774), in Wells, two miles north of Ogunquit Square at 365 Post Rd (Rte-1) rents bikes and has maps of local cycling trails.

INFORMATION

Ogunquit Chamber of Commerce Just south of Ogunquit Village at 36 Main St (Rte-1; summer daily 9am–5pm; rest of year Mon–Fri 10am–4pm, Sat 11am–3pm; ☎ 207 646 2939 or ☎ 1 800 639 2442, ⊕ ogunquit.org). Stocks brochures and operates as a fully staffed information centre.

ACCOMMODATION

Beachmere Inn 62 Beachmere Place, off Shore Rd ☎ 207 646 2021, ⊕ beachmereinn.com. Newly refurbished rooms in a turreted old wooden hotel overlooking the ocean. The inn also operates a few more modern, motel-style buildings nearby. $180
Dunes on the Waterfront 518 Main St (Rte-1) ☎ 207 646 2612, ⊕ dunesonthewaterfront.com. Situated on twelve beautiful acres, the hotel rooms here – decorated in hues of sand and blue – offer water views. There are also twelve two-bedroom cottages that sleep four or five. May–Oct. Rooms $150; cottages $355
★ **Gazebo Inn** 527 Main St (Rte-1) ☎ 207 646 3733, ⊕ gazeboinnogt.com. Within walking distance of Footbridge Beach, this Ogunquit favourite has fourteen modern rooms – including four suites in a renovated barn – that seem to overflow with amenities: rain showers, heated floors, fireplaces and posh linens are a sampling of what awaits. There is also a pool, hot tub, library with two internet stations and massage room. Full breakfast included. $149
The Nellie Littlefield House 27 Shore Rd ☎ 207 646 1692. Just off Main St, this 1899 Victorian is located smack-dab between the beach and Ogunquit's best restaurants. Eight charming guest rooms exhibit an appreciation for floral prints without seeming frilly, and the owners are quick to lend you a bicycle or umbrella to take to the beach. Full breakfast included. $230
Ogunquit Beach Inn 67 School St ☎ 207 646 1112, ⊕ ogunquitbeachinn.com. On a quiet side street close to all the action, the five rooms in this gay-friendly B&B date to the 1920s and are lined with knotted pine and Ogunquit art. Sample the owner's addictive chocolate chip banana bread. April–Oct. $149
Wells-Ogunquit Resort Motel 203 Post Rd (Rte-1), Moody ☎ 207 646 8588. If you stay at the *Wells-Ogunquit Resort Motel*, located 1.5 miles north of Ogunquit in Moody and run by the same owners for 27 years, you'll end up becoming part of a cheerful summer family. The vast majority of guests here are regulars – some even date back three generations. Impeccably kept modern motel rooms have cable TV and refrigerators, and there's a pool and barbecue set-ups. Breakfast showcases great-grandma's recipe for sugar-baked beans. May–Oct. $108

CAMPING

Pinederosa Campground 128 N Village Rd in Wells ☎ 207 646 2492, ⊕ pinederosa.com. The best camping in the area, surrounded by woodlands and enhanced by an enjoyable swimming pool. June–Oct. $30

OGUNQUIT BOAT CRUISES

If you're looking to get out on the water, check out a number of sailing cruises that depart from Perkins Cove. Both *Finestkind* (☎ 207 646 5227) and *The Silverlining* (☎ 207 646 9800) run several cruises daily from May to October, while the *Bunny Clark* caters to deep-sea fishing enthusiasts ($50 half-day, $85 full day; ☎ 207 646 2214).

EATING

★ **98 Provence** 262 Shore Rd ☎ 207 646 9898. Inside this country cottage with French blue shutters lies a Provencal hideaway. Burgundy escargots in butter ($14) and fisherman's soup ($13) are served seasonally; a flock of metal roosters overlooks the scene. March–Nov daily 7am–noon & 5.30pm–late.

Amore Breakfast 309 Shore Rd ☎ 207 646 6661. Popular breakfast nook with an Americana kitsch vibe and Banana Foster French toast ($9). April to mid-Dec daily 7am–1pm.

Arrows Restaurant 41 Berwick Rd ☎ 207 361 1100, ⓦ arrowsrestaurant.com. This modest eighteenth-century farmhouse is considered to be one of the best restaurants in the northeast. Loosely New American, the *prix fixe* menu ($85 and up) is determined by what's ripe in the resplendent organic garden. Reservations are a must, and dressing up is advised. July to early Sept Tues–Sun 6–9pm; hours fluctuate wildly rest of year, check website for specifics.

Barnacle Billy's 50–70 Perkins Cove ☎ 207 646 5575. An Ogunquit stand-by, the food here (lobster dinners, rum punch) is unremarkable – the real draw is the unbeatable view of Perkins Cove. April to mid-Oct daily 11am–9pm.

★ **Bread and Roses Bakery** 246 Main St ☎ 207 646 4227. A sweet-tooth oasis with mouthwatering displays: eclairs, "mousse bombs", whoopie pies, fruit tarts and cupcakes; the gang's all here and just begging to be sampled. Daily 7am–11pm.

Caffe Prego 44 Shore Rd ☎ 207 646 7734. Excellent cappuccinos, gelato, panini sandwiches and inventive pizzas (the *al funghi* comes with seasoned mushrooms and Italian sausage; $13.75) served on a handsome outdoor patio. April to mid-Oct daily 11.30am–9pm.

★ **Fisherman's Catch** 134 Harbor Rd, Wells Harbor ☎ 207 646 8780. Ten miles north in Wells Harbor, get the best fried seafood platters in the area – scallop, shrimps, whole-belly clams and haddock ($22.99) – as well as boiled lobster, clam chowder and blueberry pie. Avoid the wait for the porch overlooking the marsh by eating takeaway at the picnic tables. April to mid-Oct daily 11.30am–9pm.

★ **Joshua's Restaurant** 1637 Post Rd (Rte-1), Wells ☎ 207 646 3355. Inside this unassuming chocolate-coloured house, chef Joshua Mather grills, sears and sautés some of Maine's best cuisine. Many of the dishes use ingredients from his own farm (mains start at $21). Reservations recommended. Mon–Sat 5pm–late.

Maine Diner 2265 Rte-1, Wells ☎ 207 646 4441. Serving diner food with a regional twist, this place is famed for its lobster pie ($20.95) and warm Indian pudding ($3.50). The vinyl booth ambience is somewhat dampened by the long waits and beeper system, however. Daily 7am–9pm (earlier in off-season).

MC Perkins Cove 111 Perkins Cove ☎ 207 646 6263. Run by the same owners as *Arrows Restaurant* (see above), but with a much more affordable menu and magnificent views of the Atlantic. Once the go-to place for an exceptional Ogunquit seafood experience, but food and service standards are rumoured to have slipped. Play it safe and enjoy the view just with drinks and appetizers. Daily 11.30am–late.

NIGHTLIFE AND ENTERTAINMENT

There are a couple of **bars** and **gay clubs** in town, offering occasional live musical acts, piano bar sing-alongs and tea dances. For more serious entertainment, the **Ogunquit Playhouse**, along Rte-1 south of town (May–Oct; tickets ☎ 207 646 5511, ⓦ ogunquitplayhouse.org), has been called "America's foremost summer theatre" for most of its seventy years, and usually attracts a few big-name performers each season.

North to Portland

North of Ogunquit, the coastal route meanders on a bit, with distances between towns lengthening. In the thirty-or-so-mile drive up to Portland, the main points of interest are in **Kennebunkport** and **Old Orchard Beach**.

The Kennebunks

There's a reason former presidents **George Herbert Walker Bush** (known locally as "41") and **George "W" Bush** summer in **Kennebunkport** – it's beautiful, historical and full of places to eat that even Barbara applauds. Maybe it's because of these political bigwigs, but **THE KENNEBUNKS** – comprised of Kennebunkport ("the Port") and **Kennebunk** – often get dismissed as a playground for the rich. While you can easily step it up here with martinis and heels, it's just as acceptable to kick back on the beach with flip-flops and a parcel of fried clams. **Dock Square** in Kennebunkport is where most of the action is – it's here that you'll find gift shops, art galleries and the bulk of the area's restaurants.

The beaches

The best beach in Kennebunkport is **Goose Rocks**, about three miles north of Dock Square on King's Highway (off Dyke Rd via Rte-9). It's a premium stretch of expansive sand, though you will need a permit to park here ($12 daily, $50 weekly; call the Kennebunkport police ☎ 207 967 2454). **Kennebunk** is home to a trio of attractive beaches: Kennebunk, Mother's and Gooch's, all located on Beach Avenue. Permits for these ($16 daily, $52 weekly) can be purchased at HB Provisions (15 Western Ave, Kennebunk ☎ 207 967 5762), which also has a deli. If you want to get beyond the beach, try *First Chance* (☎ 207 967 5507) for whale-watching and lobster trips; the majestic 55ft schooner *Eleanor* offers voyages of a more romantic nature (☎ 207 967 8809).

Seashore Trolley Museum

195 Log Cabin Rd, Kennebunkport • Daily late May to mid-Oct 10am–5pm • $8 • ☎ 207 967 2712, ⓦ trolleymuseum.org

The engaging **Seashore Trolley Museum** holds the largest collection of electric railway cars in the world. Take a thirty-minute ride on a vintage car through the Maine woods and see an international assembly of old trams, including one from the New Orleans cable car system, made famous by the Tennessee Williams play *A Streetcar Named Desire*.

Brick Store Museum

117 Main St, Kennebunk • Tues–Fri 10am–4.30pm, Sat 10am–1pm • $5 suggested donation • ☎ 207 985 4802, ⓦ brickstoremuseum.org

The quaint 1825 **Brick Store Museum** showcases artefacts related to the town's heritage. Head to the second floor to glimpse elegant oil paintings of Kennebunk notables, sea captains and ships. In particular, look for the portrait of Captain James Fairfield, which has an astonishing back-story. Lost at sea in 1822, the painting amazingly made it back home because of the letter addressed to Kennebunk, ME that's depicted in the piece. Fairfield's former residence is now a beautiful B&B (see below).

Wedding Cake House

105 Summer St (Rte-35), Kennebunk • Closed to the public

Six gorgeous carved buttresses and innumerable gingerbread swirls adorn the 1825 **Wedding Cake House**, which, although closed to the public, makes for a great photo on the way to Dock Square in downtown Kennebunkport.

ARRIVAL AND DEPARTURE   THE KENNEBUNKS

By train Amtrak's *Downeaster* pulls into neighbouring Wells five times daily from Boston's North Station (one-way $19; ☎ 1 800 872 7245, ⓦ amtrakdowneaster.com).

GETTING AROUND

By tram You may want to utilize the tram ($1); which stops around town and also continues south, providing access to Ogunquit and the Yorks.

By car There is an Enterprise Rent-A-Car at 1299A Main St (Rte-109) in Sanford (☎ 207 324 8122), which picks renters up for free from the *Downeaster* station in Wells (see above).

ACCOMMODATION

While the places listed below are more **reasonably priced**, there are a number of prohibitively expensive Kennebunkport inns that deserve a mention: *White Barn Inn, Cottages at Cabot Cove, Hidden Pond* and *Captain Lord Mansion*, all with rates starting at $325 and beyond and all outstanding.

★ **Bufflehead Cove Inn** Bufflehead Cove Rd (off Rte-35), Kennebunk ☎ 207 967 3879, ⓦ buffleheadcove .com. Accessed by a private woodland road, this 1880s inn is notable for its blissful scenery: only a mile from Dock Square (as the crow flies) the tranquil Kennebunk River winds right in front of the house. Five guest rooms have nice perks like private balconies, fresh cut flowers and an afternoon wine and cheese hour; the hosts are famed for their breakfasts. A very special place. May–Oct. **$165**

Captain Fairfield Inn 8 Pleasant St, Kennebunkport

☎ 207 967 4454, **ⓦ** captainfairfield.com. Just off Dock Square, this stylish 1813 sea captain's home has been revamped with bold, contemporary furniture – think zebra-striped headboards, chaise longues and oversized bed frames. An easy walk from both downtown and the beach. **$289**

The Colony Hotel 140 Ocean Ave, Kennebunkport **☎** 207 967 3331, **ⓦ** thecolonyhotel.com. This rambling old resort dates from 1914, with 125 guest rooms spread between three buildings and two houses. Rooms are delightfully old-fashioned – because of their historic nature, the ones in the main property do not have TVs or

a/c – with spectacular ocean views and access to the hotel's heated saltwater pool, eighteen-hole putting green and private slip of beach. Very pet-friendly. Mid-May to Oct. **$199**

Franciscan Guest House 26 Beach Ave, Kennebunk **☎** 207 967 4865, **ⓦ** franciscanguesthouse.com. Situated in the gardened grounds of a monastery (of all things), the *Franciscan's* rates simply cannot be beat. Guest rooms, located in what were once school classrooms, are basic, with no daily maid service. Still, the property is pleasant, with a saltwater pool, full breakfasts and a fun return crowd. **$89**

EATING AND DRINKING

★ 50 Local 50 Main St, Kennebunk **☎** 207 985 0850. Singlehandedly revving up Kennebunk's culinary scene, this chrome bistro dishes up French classics like *moules frites* ($10) with a New American twist, such as mac and cheese with truffle oil ($10). A chalkboard at the entrance trumpets the local origin of the ingredients. Mains $10–39. Reservations recommended. Mon–Thurs 5–9.30pm, Fri & Sat till 10.30pm, Sun till 9pm.

★ Bandaloop 2 Dock Square, Kennebunkport **☎** 207 967 4994. You can choose your own dining adventure at *Bandaloop*, where one of eight proteins – free-range chicken, hormone-free steak, tofu etc – is paired with your pick of sauces, such as a garlicky gravy or a fruity balsamic reduction ($17–29). *Bandaloop* emphasizes organic produce, and vegetarians will be quite pleased with the menu here. Daily 5–10pm.

Cape Arundel Inn 208 Ocean Ave, Kennebunkport **☎** 207 967 2125. Though it doubles as a fancy restaurant and historic inn, *Cape Arundel* is better as a place to drink cocktails – from the wide oceanfront porch, you can sip a martini and spy on the Bush family compound. Daily 5.30–9pm.

★ Clam Shack Just before the Kennebunkport Bridge, Kennebunk **☎** 207 967 3321. The mighty, mini *Clam Shack* lives up to the hype, with fried clames endorsed

by Barbara Bush and celebrity chef Rachael Ray, whoopie pies favoured by Martha Stewart and takeaway fried fish and lobster rolls. May–Oct daily 11am–9pm.

Henry VIII Carvery 3 Union St, Kennebunkport **☎** 207 967 8882. Mouthwatering, hand-carved roast-beef, turkey and ham sandwiches built on toasted French baguettes and topped with plenty of fixings. The roast beef with creamy horseradish sauce ($7.25) is particularly tasty, but there are a good variety of veggie and gluten-free wraps as well. Daily 11am–7pm.

Nunan's Lobster Hut 9 Mills Rd (Rte-9), Cape Porpoise **☎** 207 967 4362. Two miles from Dock Square, this loveable wooden sea shanty with buoys dangling from the ceiling has been the place to tie on your lobster bib since 1953. Cash only. Late May to mid-Oct daily 5–9pm.

The Ramp 77 Pier Rd, Cape Porpoise **☎** 207 967 8500. Head below deck to this lively little bar with ocean views and a decor that evokes the belly of a ship. Daily 11.30am–9pm in summer; call for hours rest of year.

White Barn Inn 77 Pier Rd, Cape Porpoise **☎** 207 967 8500. A Maine landmark where rotating *prix fixe* ($98) items like olive-crusted veal loin and champagne sorbet are served in a refurbished barn. Reservations, and sport coats, are a must. Summer Mon–Thurs 6–9.15pm, Fri, Sat & Sun 5.30–9.15pm; call for hours rest of year.

Old Orchard Beach

During the late nineteenth and early twentieth centuries, **OLD ORCHARD BEACH** ("OOB", in local parlance) stood alongside Ogunquit as a classic New England resort town, drawing upper-crust citizens from all over the eastern seaboard to stay in its massive seafront hotels. After World War II, its popularity and property values declined steadily, and in 1980 the town attempted to rectify the situation by refurbishing its decaying, carnivalesque pier. Almost overnight, OOB regained its status as a hotspot, though it resembled the spring break town of Fort Lauderdale more than the posh resort of old. Things have calmed down a bit, even if a slightly corny party atmosphere remains.

The main draw here is the **beach**, a fantastic seven-mile strip of white sand. Unfortunately, its beauty means it can get extremely crowded during summer and at holiday weekends. The beach itself is free, but **parking** can be pricey; car parks that charge $5–7 per day are reasonable. Just off the beach is the **pier**, which does a fireworks show on Thursdays at 9.45pm, and Palace Playland (**☎** 207 934 2001), with classic amusement-park rides such as a Ferris wheel, bumper cars and a vintage carousel dating from 1906. The entirety of **Old Orchard Street** (which leads down to the pier and beach) and **Grand Avenue** (which runs parallel to the ocean), are dotted with attractions, including instant-photo booths, candy-floss vendors and stores where you can design your own souvenir T-shirt. It's hopelessly tacky, but its campy carnival vibe does make an alternative to its sedate neighbours.

ARRIVAL AND INFORMATION
OLD ORCHARD BEACH

By train In season (May–Oct), Amtrak's *Downeaster* pulls into OOB five times daily from Boston's North Station (one-way $23; ☎ 1 800 872 7245, ⓦ amtrakdowneaster.com); the station is a 2min walk from the beach.
Old Orchard Beach Chamber of Commerce 11 First St

(mid-May to early Sept Mon–Fri 8.30am–4.30pm, Sat 9am–5pm, Sun 10am–5pm; rest of year Mon–Fri only; ☎ 207 934 2500, ⓦ oldorchardbeachmaine.com). The town's Chamber of Commerce operates an information centre and can help arrange accommodation.

ACCOMMODATION

Although the town is packed with **places to stay**, it can fill to capacity; definitely call ahead for reservations. The seafront is dotted with pricey motels, though they sometimes have the advantage of owning a small strip of private beach – an invaluable respite from the crowds.

Echo Motel 8 Traynor St ☎ 207 934 5174, ⓦ echomotel .com. A good, clean option that's smack-dab on the beach. *Echo* rooms have standard motel decor enhanced by flat-screen TVs, fridges and (in the majority of the units) kitchenettes. The owners also administer four furnished, oceanfront cottages. May–Oct. **$140**
Royal Anchor Resort 203 E Grand Ave ☎ 207 934 4521, ⓦ royalanchor.com. Spacious rooms, bocce ball and a tempting heated pool make this a solid seaside option.

Family-owned and operated since 1968, the *Royal* has a longstanding dedication to its property that wins many repeat customers. May to mid-Sept. **$185**
White Lamb Cottages 3 Odessa Ave ☎ 207 934 1081, ⓦ whitelambcottages.com. Comprises a series of eight standalone beach cottages done up in a 1940s-era style. Also rents an adjacent 1876 Victorian inn that sleeps fourteen ($5040/wk). Cottages May to mid-Oct only, house rental year-round. **$229**

EATING AND DRINKING

Eating in OOB is not such a treat. You'll find an overabundance of **pizza and burger joints** crowding the main thoroughfares (in addition to the overrated *Pier Fries*), although there are a few nearby exceptions. There are plenty of fun **watering holes** on the pier.

Joseph's by the Sea 55 W Grand Ave ☎ 207 934 5044. The deservedly expensive menu includes – but thankfully does not focus exclusively on – seafood, and the great ocean views are a bonus. Mains $19–32. Late May to mid-Oct daily 7–11am & 5–8.45pm; rest of year weekends only.
The Landmark Restaurant 28 E Grand Ave ☎ 207 934 0156. A stone's throw from the pier, this place does simple Maine fare like haddock with crumb topping. April–Oct daily 5pm–late.

Ocean Side Grille at The Brunswick 39 W Grand Ave ☎ 207 934 4873. Right on the beach, this is the place to go for drinking and dancing to live music. Mid-May to early Sept daily 11am–1am.
Rocco's 4 W Grand Ave ☎ 207 934 7552. Serves tasty New York-style pizza slices (with a thin, bitter crust) from a take-away counter close to the pier and the beach. Mid-April to early Sept daily 11am–2am.

Portland

The largest city in Maine, with a population hovering around 64,000, **PORTLAND** was founded in 1632, in a superb position on the Casco Bay Peninsula, and quickly prospered, building ships and exporting great inland pines for use as masts. A long line of wooden **wharves** stretched along the seafront, with merchants' houses on the hillside above.

From its earliest days, Portland was a cosmopolitan city. When the **railroads** came in the 1840s, the Canada Trunk Line had its terminus right on Portland's quayside, bringing the produce of Canada and the Great Plains one hundred miles closer to Europe than it would have been at any other major US port. **Custom House Wharf**

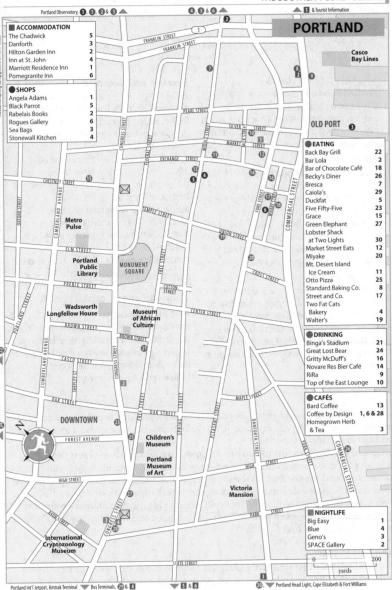

Portland Observatory, ❶ ❶ ❷ & ❸ ▲   ❹ ❺ & ❻ ▲   ▲ ❶ & Tourist Information

PORTLAND

Casco Bay Lines

OLD PORT ❸

■ ACCOMMODATION

The Chadwick	5
Danforth	3
Hilton Garden Inn	2
Inn at St. John	4
Marriott Residence Inn	1
Pomegranite Inn	6

● SHOPS

Angela Adams	1
Black Parrot	5
Rabelais Books	2
Rogues Gallery	6
Sea Bags	3
Stonewall Kitchen	4

● EATING

Back Bay Grill	22
Bar Lola	2
Bar of Chocolate Café	18
Becky's Diner	26
Bresca	7
Caiola's	29
Duckfat	5
Five Fifty-Five	23
Grace	15
Green Elephant	27
Lobster Shack at Two Lights	30
Market Street Eats	12
Miyake	20
Mt. Desert Island Ice Cream	11
Otto Pizza	25
Standard Baking Co.	8
Street and Co.	17
Two Fat Cats Bakery	4
Walter's	19

● DRINKING

Binga's Stadium	21
Great Lost Bear	24
Gritty McDuff's	16
Novare Res Bier Café	14
RiRa	9
Top of the East Lounge	10

● CAFÉS

Bard Coffee	13
Coffee by Design	1, 6 & 28
Homegrown Herb & Tea	3

■ NIGHTLIFE

Big Easy	1
Blue	4
Geno's	3
SPACE Gallery	2

Metro Pulse

Portland Public Library

MONUMENT SQUARE

Wadsworth Longfellow House

Museum of African Culture

DOWNTOWN

Children's Museum

Portland Museum of Art

Victoria Mansion

International Cryptozoology Museum

8

0   200
yards

Portland Int'l Jetport, Amtrak Terminal ▼ Bus Terminals, ❷⑨ & ❹   ▼ ❺ & ❻   ❸⓪, ▼ Portland Head Light, Cape Elizabeth & Fort Williams

remains much as it must have looked when novelist Anthony Trollope passed through in 1861 and said, "I doubt whether I ever saw a town with more evident signs of prosperity."

As with much of New England, the good times didn't last through the mid-twentieth century. Grand Trunk Station was torn down in 1966, and downtown Portland appeared to be in terminal decline – until, that is, a group of committed residents undertook the energetic redevelopment of the area now known as the **Old Port**. Their success has revitalized the city, keeping it at the heart of Maine life – though you

PORTLAND TOURS

The city offers a number of worthwhile **tours** good for getting oriented, getting out on the water or a bit of both. Several breweries offer free tours (see p.467).

NARRATED TRAM TOURS

Portland Discovery 170 Commercial St ☏ 207 774 0808, ⊛ portlanddiscovery.com. Entertaining land and sea tours that combine a tram ride with a "lighthouse lover's cruise", where you'll spot up to seven of the coastline's iconic beacons. May–Oct; 90min; $35.

WALKING TOURS

Greater Portland Landmarks ☏ 207 774 5561, ⊛ portlandlandmarks.org. Tours of the Old Port and nineteenth-century historic homes. Mid-June to early Oct; 90min; $10.

Wicked Walking Tours ☏ 207 730 0490, ⊛ wickedwalkingtours.com. Get your spook on with one of these very popular, hour-long Old Port ghost tours. Reservations required. Cash only; $15.

ON THE WATER

Casco Bay Lines 56 Commercial St ☏ 207 774 7871, ⊛ cascobaylines.com. A ferry and a twice-daily mail boat run all year, with additional cruises in summer, to eight of the scenic Calendar Islands in Casco Bay. Long, Peaks and Chebeague islands all have accommodation. Return fares to one island $7.70–11.55, scenic cruises $13.25–24.

Downeast Duck Adventures 94 Commercial St ☏ 207 774 3825, ⊛ downeastducktours.com. Amphibious World War II vehicles cavort through the Old Port and then plunk into Casco Bay for a glimpse of the Calendar Islands. Reservations recommended. May–Oct; 1hr; $24.

Lucky Catch Cruises 170 Commercial St ☏ 207 761 0941, ⊛ luckycatch.com. Throw on some bright orange gear and head out to catch your very own lobster. Late May to Oct; 1hr; $25.

Maine Sailing Adventures 56 Commercial St ☏ 207 749 9169, ⊛ mainesailingadventures.net. *Frances*, a 74ft windjammer, sails from the Maine State Pier. May–Oct; 2hr. $30.

Portland Schooner Co. 56 Commercial St ☏ 207 766 2500, ⊛ portlandschooner.com. Two majestic schooners sail from the Maine State Pier on Commercial St. May–Oct. 2hr trip $35, overnight trips $240.

HOT AIR BALLOONS

Hot Fun ☏ 207 799 0193, ⊛ hotfunballoons.com. Take to the skies in an hour-long piloted balloon ride. Trips are 3hr 30min door-to-door, and run by a 28-year balloon-flying veteran. Cash or cheque only. April–Oct. $300 per person (up to three people).

shouldn't expect a hive of energy. Portland is simply a pleasant, sophisticated and very attractive town, where you can experience the benefits of a large city at a lesser cost and without the hassle of crowds.

Central Portland consists of two main districts: the self-proclaimed **Arts District**, where you'll find several museums, the Civic Center and a smattering of good restaurants, and the **Old Port**, to the southeast, which hums with lively shops, bars and restaurants. Commercial Street runs along the water's edge, but cobblestoned Wharf Street, just inland, is the most picturesque. Aim to visit the Arts District on the first Friday of the month, when galleries open to the public and museums are free (5–8pm; ⊛ firstfridayartwalk.com).

The Arts District

Portland's **Arts District** runs along Congress Street and is dotted with the city's best cultural attractions and a handful of happening art galleries. Most of the action is bound between High and Elm streets; the latter merges with Monument Square.

Wadsworth-Longfellow House

485–489 Congress St • Guided tours on the hour: May–Oct Mon–Sat 10.30am–4pm, Sun noon–4pm • $12 • ☏ 207 774 1822, ⊛ hwlongfellow.org

Due to some massive fires, not all that much of old Portland survives, though grand mansions can still be seen along Congress and Danforth streets. The most notable of these is the **Wadsworth-Longfellow House**, which was Portland's first brick residence when it was built in 1785 by Revolutionary War hero Peleg Wadsworth. More famously, it was the boyhood home of Wadsworth's grandson, the poet Henry Wadsworth Longfellow. Now a museum, the house is furnished with antiques that belonged to the Longfellow family.

Museum of African Culture

13 Brown St • Tues–Fri 10.30am–4pm, Sat noon–4pm • Free • ☎ 207 871 7188, Ⓦ museumafricanculture.org

Well worth a look is the **Museum of African Culture**, the only museum in New England devoted exclusively to sub-Saharan African art and culture. It houses an eye-catching collection of masks with complete ceremonial regalia, as well as a rotating contemporary gallery.

Children's Museum

142 Free St • Tues–Sat 10am–5pm, Sun noon–5pm; June–Aug also open Mon 10am–5pm • $9, first Fri of the month 5–8pm admission $1 • ☎ 207 828 1234, Ⓦ childrensmuseumofme.org

Portland's **Children's Museum** is a great spot for little ones, with hands-on exhibits that include a lobster boat, a fire truck and – everyone's favourite – an interactive miniature grocery store.

Portland Museum of Art

7 Congress Square • Tues–Thurs, Sat & Sun 10am–5pm, Fri 10am–9pm; June to mid-Oct also Mon 10am–5pm • $10, Fri free 5–9pm • ☎ 207 775 6148, Ⓦ portlandmuseum.org

Portland's single best destination, the **Portland Museum of Art**, was designed in 1983 by I.M. Pei and Partners. Modernist works, scenes of Maine and stirring seascapes are prevalent, exemplified by Winslow Homer's *Weatherbeaten*, the majestic centrepiece of PMA's collection. An earthy alternative to the maritime pieces is *Woodsmen in the Woods of Maine* by Waldo Peirce. Rich and dark, it was commissioned by the Westbrook Post Office in 1937 and is displayed here with the clouded-glass mailroom door still intact. Many parts of the museum afford superb views – on a clear day you can see all the way to Mount Washington in New Hampshire.

International Cryptozoology Museum

11 Avon St • Wed–Sat 11am–4.30pm, Sun noon–3.30pm • $5 • ☎ 207 518 9496, Ⓦ cryptozoologymuseum.com

The **International Cryptozoology Museum** has 2300 items related to "cryptids" – creatures that loom large in the popular imagination, but whose existence is unconfirmed by science, for example the Loch Ness monster, Bigfoot and gang. On

---

WINSLOW HOMER'S STUDIO

In 2006, the Portland Museum of Art acquired **Winslow Homer's** studio in Prouts Neck – a coastal summer colony located in Scarborough, twelve miles south of Portland. Lauded as one of America's greatest nineteenth-century painters, Homer was born in Boston, Massachusetts in 1836, and kicked off his art career at 21 by working as an illustrator for *Harper's Weekly* magazine. Homer moved into Prouts Neck in 1883, where he completed many of the majestic seascapes that are the hallmarks of his work, such as *Weatherbeaten* and *The Gulf Stream*. Homer died in the studio in 1910.

Set to open in September 2012 after extensive renovations, the refurbished studio will give visitors an intimate peek into the life of a master painter. At research time, the museum had not finalized what would be on show in the cottage, and it was unclear whether any of Homer's artworks would be on view. One artefact that's sure to be displayed is his cantankerous "Snakes, Snakes and Mice" sign, hung to discourage unwanted visitors and "old ladies" from knocking on his door. Visitors will also enjoy the view of the pounding Atlantic from the studio's porch, gallery-worthy in its own right. The **Portland Museum of Art** houses an outstanding Homer collection, including the massive *Weatherbeaten*. For more information on tours of the studio, contact PMA (see above).

display are hair samples from the Abominable Snowman, a spooky mermaid movie prop and an enormous pterodactyl that surveys the scene from on high. The museum's highlight is its knowledgeable director, who has written scores of books on cryptozoology and is very open to questions.

Victoria Mansion

109 Danforth St • May–Oct Mon–Sat 10am–4pm, Sun 1–5pm; rest of year call for hours • $15 • ☎ 207 772 4841, ⓦ victoriamansion.org

Victoria Mansion, grande dame of house museums, is an Italianate brownstone constructed in 1859 as a summer home for hotelier Ruggles S. Morse. The exquisite interior includes fresco-ornamented walls and ceilings, a freestanding staircase made of Santo Domingo mahogany, and floor-to-ceiling gold-leaf mirrors. The best time to come is during the festive season, when the mansion is bedecked in Christmas finery.

The Old Port and the Eastern Promenade

For relaxed wandering, the restored **Old Port** near the quayside, between Exchange and Pearl streets, is quite entertaining, with all sorts of red-brick antiquarian shops, bookstores and clothing boutiques (especially on Exchange St). Several companies operate **boat trips** from the nearby wharves (see box, p.462).

If you follow Portland's waterfront to the end of the peninsula, you'll come to the **Eastern Promenade**, a scenic two-mile waterfront trail that culminates in a small beach. Once the bastion of the town's wealthy families (who've since moved to the **Western Promenade** and the **West End**), this neighbourhood became almost exclusively residential after the last major fire (in 1866) and is remarkably peaceful for being so close to downtown.

Portland Observatory

138 Congress St • Late May to mid-Oct daily 10am–4.30pm • $8 • ☎ 207 772 5561, ⓦ portlandlandmarks.org/observatory

Just above the headland, at the top of Munjoy Hill, is the shingled, eight-sided 1807 **Portland Observatory**, the oldest remaining signal tower in the country. You can climb its 103 steps for an exhilarating view of the bay and the city.

Cape Elizabeth

Five miles south of Portland via Rte-77, the stately homes in the town of **CAPE ELIZABETH** make for a scenic drive. **Two Lights State Park,** at 7 Tower Drive, has easy shoreside trails and picnic areas (day-use fee $3; ☎ 207 799 5871), although most people come this way for Two Lights' legendary lobster shack (see p.466).

Portland Head Lighthouse

1000 Shore Rd, Cape Elizabeth • Museum June–Oct daily 10am–4pm; April, May & Nov Sat & Sun only; park open year-round • $2 • ☎ 207 799 2661, ⓦ portlandheadlight.com

The **Portland Head Lighthouse** on Cape Elizabeth is the oldest in Maine, commissioned in 1790 by George Washington. Still an active light, it houses a small but intelligent **museum** on the history of lighthouses. Best are the displays combining lighthouse literature and art, such as Longfellow's paean *The Lighthouse* and reproductions of Edward Hopper's forlorn watercolours, both of which were inspired by Portland Head.

ARRIVAL AND DEPARTURE
PORTLAND

BY PLANE

Both I-95 and Rte-1 skirt the peninsula of Portland, quite near the city centre, while I-295 goes through it. Portland International Jetport (☎ 207 774 7301, ⓦ portlandjetport .org) abuts I-95. Most major carriers serve the airport, which is connected with downtown by the city bus (#5; limited Sunday service; $1.50; ☎ 207 774 0351, ⓦ gpmetrobus.com).

BY TRAIN

Amtrak's *Downeaster* pulls into the Portland Transportation Center, located three miles from the city centre at 100 Thompson's Point Rd (exit 5A off I-295; ☎ 207 828 1151) five times daily from Boston's North Station (one-way $24; ☎ 1 800 872 7245, ⓦ amtrakdowneaster.com).

BY BUS

Also arriving at the Portland Transportation Center is Concord Coach (☎ 207 828 1151 or ☎ 1 800 639 3317, ⓦ concordcoachlines.com), the principal bus operator along the coast, with frequent service from Boston and Bangor. From the terminal, city buses and taxis can ferry you downtown. Greyhound (☎ 207 772 6587, ⓦ greyhound.com) runs to Montréal, New Hampshire and Vermont as well as to points throughout Maine from 950 Congress St, on the eastern edge of downtown.

BY CAR

Car rental is available from the airport offices of National and Alamo (☎ 207 773 0036, ⓦ nationalcar.com), Avis/ Budget (☎ 207 874 7501, ⓦ avis.com), Enterprise (☎ 207 615 0030, ⓦ enterprise.com) and Hertz (☎ 207 772 1658, ⓦ hertz.com).

Parking Parking can be a hassle in Portland. If you get a space, the parking meters charge 25 cents for fifteen minutes (2hr maximum). Parking garages are numerous and inexpensive ($3/hr is average), and you can often get your ticket validated at an area store for two free hours. The Fore Street Garage at no. 427, and the Casco Bay Parking Garage at 54 Commercial St are centrally located. If you don't mind a 10min walk, you can use the free parking alongside the Eastern Cemetery on Mountfort St, near the intersection of Congress St and Washington Ave.

GETTING AROUND

By bus Downtown Portland and the Old Port are each compact enough to stroll around, though they're served by a comprehensive bus system ($1.50; ☎ 207 774 0351); stop by the METRO Pulse, the hub of the bus system, on Elm and Congress streets for a detailed route map. All manner of details concerning public transport within the area, whether by bus, boat or train, can be found at ⓦ transportme.org.

By bicycle CycleMania, 59 Federal St (☎ 207 774 2933), rents bicycles for $25 a day, which you can ride around the city's hundreds of acres of undeveloped land. Call Portland Trails (☎ 207 775 2411, ⓦ trails.org) for more information on the city's biking or walking trails.

INFORMATION

CVB of Greater Portland Gateway Terminal, where Commercial St turns into Thames, past Franklin St (May–Oct Mon–Fri 9am–5pm, Sat & Sun 9am–4pm; ☎ 207 772 5800, ⓦ visitportland.com). They also staff an information office at the Jetport (☎ 207 775 5809).

Portland Public Library 5 Monument Square, at the corner of Congress and Elm streets (☎ 207 871 1700, ⓦ portlandlibrary.com). Offers free internet access.

8

ACCOMMODATION

Finding a room in Portland is no problem if you book in advance – but you *should* **book in advance**, especially in summer and autumn. You'll generally pay more for accommodation in town than at one of the **budget motels** that cluster around exit 48 off I-95. The extra cost can be worth it, however: Portland has some great old mansions-turned-B&Bs, and the city is quite walkable.

The Chadwick 140 Chadwick St ☎ 207 774 5141, ⓦ thechadwick.com. Tucked away in Portland's West End, the four guest rooms at this 1891 Victorian offer a handsome blend of antique furniture and modern design elements. There are also excellent breakfasts, a garden with a hammock for two, wi-fi, a welcoming host and happy guests. $185

★ **Danforth** 163 Danforth St ☎ 207 879 8755, ⓦ danforthmaine.com. This 1823 Federal-style mansion overflows with architectural delights: nineteenth-century galleries filled with fresh flowers, opaqued windows in the billiard room (a holdover from Prohibition days) and a rooftop cupola with harbour views. The ten guest rooms, completely renovated in 2009, are no less pleasing – many have working fireplaces, and all feature richly patterned textiles, luxurious soaps and original art. Centrally located, and with a full breakfast in the morning. $195

Hilton Garden Inn 65 Commercial St ☎ 207 780 0780, ⓦ hiltongardeninn.com. Fitness centre, saltwater pool, flat-screen TVs and wi-fi, all in a snappy location overlooking the harbour. A bit overpriced, but a good spot. $289

Inn at St John 939 Congress St ☎ 207 773 6481, ⓦ innatstjohn.com. Just outside downtown, in a slightly dodgy area near the Greyhound bus station, this creaky yet charming 1897 Victorian offers reasonably priced, comfortable rooms, some with shared bathrooms. Breakfast included, no elevator to upper floors. Shared bathroom $109; en-suite $139

Marriott Residence Inn 145 Fore St ☎ 207 761 1660, ⓦ marriott.com. A slinky, brand-new hotel garnering rave reviews for its smart waterfront location and 179 suites well-stocked with a fridge, microwave and dishwasher. On-site laundry facilities, a pool, jacuzzi, fitness centre and free continental breakfast are among the litany of other perks. $279

Pomegranate Inn 49 Neal St ☎ 1 800 356 0408, ⓦ pomegranateinn.com. Another beloved West End B&B, this one with an exuberant colour scheme – all whimsical, hand-painted walls, graphic bedding and contemporary artworks – in an eight-room mansion. $185

EATING

Portland is packed with outstanding **restaurants**, most with a keen eye on what's local and in season. The **Farmers' Market** in Monument Square (May–Nov Wed 7am–2pm) offers the perfect opportunity to sample regional produce. **Cafés** are popular with Portland's youthful population, and frequently offer internet access.

RESTAURANTS

Back Bay Grill 65 Portland St ☎ 207 772 8833. Don't sweat the crummy neighbourhood, *BBG* is a treasure – some residents think it's Portland's best restaurant (which is quite a declaration considering the number of worthy competitors). Underneath an ebullient mural, diners feast on seasonal New American cuisine like "duck two ways" ($30) and Maine crab cakes with arugula ($14). Tues–Sat 5.30pm–late.

Bar Lola 100 Congress St ☎ 207 775 5652. Off the beaten path in Portland's East End, this tapas gem utilizes lots of local ingredients in its seasonal menu. The "feed me" option ($44) procures seven courses chosen by the kitchen. Wed–Sat 5–10pm.

Becky's Diner 390 Commercial St ☎ 207 773 7070. Vintage Maine breakfast spot serving hearty portions, including home-made muffins and pies. Open daily at 4am (for the fishermen) to 10pm.

Bresca 111 Middle St ☎ 207 772 1004. The darling of national food writers, *Bresca* is perpetually filled with diners cooing over the braised kale topped with a "six-minute egg" ($12), in-house pasta (around $22) and otherworldly desserts ($9). It seats just twenty and reservations are essential. Tues–Sat 5.30pm–late.

★ **Caiola's** 58 Pine St ☎ 207 772 1110. Cosy West End restaurant with a rotating menu of upscale comfort food – think orange-marinated swordfish, juicy burgers, paella with chicken and chorizo, and excellent desserts. Sunday brunch is more affordable but displays the same good taste. Reservations recommended. Tues–Thurs 5–9pm, Fri & Sat 5–10pm, Sun 9am–2pm.

Duckfat 43 Middle St ☎ 207 774 8080. Unassuming panini storefront where local spuds are cut and fried in duck fat, salted, poured into cones ($5) and served with a choice of dipping sauces. Singing with flavour, these humble pommes frites have elevated an outwardly modest restaurant to best-in-town status. Mon–Thurs & Sun 11am–9pm, Fri & Sat till 10pm.

Five Fifty-Five 555 Congress St ☎ 207 761 0555. A longstanding foodie favourite, *Five Fifty-Five* has a signature tasting menu ($60) with organic delights like strawberry salad with house ricotta and hanger steak with cumin-scented black beans. Mon–Thurs & Sun 5–9.30pm, Fri & Sat 5–10.30pm, Sun 9am–2pm.

Grace 15 Chestnut St ☎ 207 828 4422. Spectacularly sited in a restored 1856 Gothic Revival church, *Grace* serves a small but worthy New American menu (mains $18–34) amid giant wooden pillars, sweeping arches, and a brilliant stained-glass window. The food is good, but it's more about the experience; a seat at the bar lets you soak up the architectural grandeur for less. Tues–Sat 5am–10.30pm.

★ **Green Elephant** 608 Congress St ☎ 207 347 3111. Avid carnivores and veggie-lovers alike are crazy about this vegetarian bistro serving peanut curry with coconut milk ($14) and spinach noodles in a shiitake-ginger sauce ($12). Even the most meat-and-potatoes types will be pleased. Tues–Sat 11.30am–2.30pm & 5–9.30pm, Sun 5–9pm.

★ **Lobster Shack at Two Lights** 225 Two Lights Rd, 9 miles south of town in Cape Elizabeth ☎ 207 799 1677. Perhaps the best seafood-eating scenery in all of Maine – lighthouse to the left, unruly ocean to the right, and a scrumptious lobster roll on the plate in front of you. Daily: April–June, Sept & Oct 11am–8pm; July & Aug 11am–8.30pm.

★ **Market Street Eats** 36 Market St ☎ 207 773 3135. This unfussy sandwich joint turns out memorable lunch fare like the "Red Rooster" wrap (chicken, bacon, provolone, spicy mayo and red onion; $6.95). Mon–Fri 8am–6pm, Sat till 3pm.

★ **Miyake** 468 Fore St ☎ 207 871 9170. Formerly an insider hole-in-the-wall, this Portland favourite has moved into stylish new digs on Fore St. Featuring renowned sushi with French flair, the menu garners quite a buzz for its tasting menu (five courses $50), fresh *uni* (sea urchins) and scallop rolls with spicy mayonnaise ($15). The chef-owner is so devoted to freshness that he harvests his own clams and has a farm with pigs, chickens and veggies. Mon–Sat 11.30am–2.30pm & 5.30–10pm, Sun 1–9pm.

★ **Otto Pizza** 576 Congress St ☎ 207 773 7099. New York-style, thin-crust pizzas made with flatbread dough, their own sauce and creative ingredients (such as mashed potatoes and bacon; $21) in a hip storefront right by Portland's Museum of Art. There's another branch at 225 Congress St (☎ 207 358 7870). Mon–Thurs & Sun 11.30am–11pm, Fri & Sat till 2am.

★ **Street and Co.** 33 Wharf St ☎ 207 775 0887. A special-occasion seafood spot where the cuts are grilled, blackened or grilled to perfection and served in an intimate, noisy dining room. Reservations recommended. *Fore Street*, their land-focused brother (288 Fore St, ☎ 207 775 2717), is another top-notch eatery. Mon–Wed & Sun 5–9.30pm, Thurs–Sat till 10pm.

Walter's 2 Portland Square ☎ 207 871 9258. Local favourite *Walter's* continues to serve lauded New American fare, only now the food is prepared in a capacious new location near the Old Port. Dinner mains $23–36, but it's even better for an elegant lunch ($10–14). Mon–Sat 11.30am–2pm & 5–9pm (9.30pm at weekends).

8

SWEET TEETH

Sure, Portland is famed for its excellent restaurants, but what about dessert? Rest assured, these toothsome outlets have it covered.

★ **Bar of Chocolate Café** 38 Wharf St ☎ 207 773 6667. With its discreet signage and in-the-know clientele, *Bar of Chocolate* has a speakeasy feel (albeit one devoted to another indulgence – dessert). Head here after dinner in the Old Port for an espresso martini and a slice of chocolate-caramel cake. Mon–Thurs & Sun 4pm–midnight, Fri & Sat till 1am.

★ **Mount Desert Island Ice Cream** 51 Exchange St ☎ 207 210 3432. Ice cream lovers watch out: after sampling *MDIIC's* exquisite Nutella or chocolate coconut flavour, everything else will taste like plain old vanilla. Their original location is in Bar Harbor (see p.502). Mon–Thurs & Sun 11am–10pm, Fri & Sat till 11pm.

★ **Standard Baking Co.** 75 Commercial St ☎ 207 773 2112. Allegiance to this French-inspired bakery is so strong that you should call ahead to ensure your favourite chocolate croissant is put aside for your arrival. Sticky buns, olive bread, macaroons, madeleines, butter cookies and more. Mon–Fri 7am–6pm, Sun 7am–5pm.

Two Fat Cats Bakery 47 India St ☎ 207 347 5144. This homegrown little bakery is famed for its whoopie pies and also crafts cupcakes, fruit pies and chocolate-chip cookies. Mon–Fri 9am–6pm, Sat 9am–5pm, Sun 1–4pm.

CAFÉS

★ **Bard Coffee** 185 Middle St ☎ 207 899 4788. Residents wax poetic about the beans at *Bard*, a stylish Old Port fixture where lattes are flourished with a fern or a love heart. Free wi-fi, and plenty of outlets. Mon–Fri 7am–9pm, Sat 8am–9pm, Sun 9am–6pm.

Coffee by Design 67 India St ☎ 207 780 6767; 620 Congress St ☎ 207 772 5533; 43 Washington Ave ☎ 207

879 2233. This local chain roasts its own beans and stocks a wide assortment of teas and pastries. Mon–Fri 6am–7pm, Sat 6.30am–7pm, Sun 7am–6pm.

Homegrown Herb & Tea 195 Congress St ☎ 207 774 3484. Like something out of *Harry Potter*, the owner at this teeny storefront handcrafts your cup of tea with herbs selected from wooden drawers. If you're in need, ask for the hangover cure. Tues–Sat noon–5pm.

8

DRINKING

There are a good many **bars** scattered throughout the Old Port, of which a number feature live rock music; note, though, that **ID policies** are strict and bars aren't allowed to serve after 1am.

BARS

Binga's Stadium 77 Free St ☎ 207 347 6072. Generally, rhyming menu items are a red flag. Not so with *Binga's* "wingas" – these breaded and fried chicken munchies are delightfully addictive. *Binga's* is a fun, clean sports bar with plenty of TVs and an enthusiastic crowd. Tues–Sat 11.30am–1am.

Great Lost Bear 540 Forest Ave ☎ 207 772 0300. Outside downtown, this beer mecca has 69 varieties on tap,

including fifteen state microbrews. Decent pub grub, too. Mon–Sat 11.30am–11.30pm, Sun noon–11pm.

Gritty McDuff's 396 Fore St ☎ 207 772 2739. Portland's first brewpub, making Portland Head Pale Ale and Black Fly Stout. Food, folk music, long wooden benches and a friendly atmosphere, which can get rowdy on Saturday nights. Daily 11am–late.

★ **Novare Res Bier Café** 4 Canal Plaza, Suite 1 (enter through alleyway on lower Exchange St, by Keybank

BREWERY TOURS

Portland is at the forefront of the American **microbrew revolution**, and many of its breweries offer **free tours**.

Allagash Brewing 50 Industrial Way ☎ 207 878 5385, ⓦ allagash.com. Tours (45min) year-round: Mon–Fri 11am, 1pm & 3pm; late May to mid-Oct also Sat 1pm & 3pm. The Saturday tours are very popular; get there early to ensure a spot.

DL Geary 38 Evergreen Drive ☎ 207 878 2337,

ⓦ gearybrewing.com. Tours (30min) by appointment only, generally at 2pm.

Shipyard Brewery 86 Newbury St ☎ 207 761 0807, ⓦ shipyard.com. Hop on the website to reserve a spot on this popular Tuesday-night tour (5.30–7pm).

sign) ☎207 761 2437. A little tricky to find, this very cool Old Port beer spot has over 500 brews with 25 on tap, outdoor and indoor picnic tables and tasty charcuterie and cheese plates. Mon–Thurs 4pm–1am, Fri 3pm–1am, Sat & Sun noon–1am.

RíRa 72 Commercial St ☎207 761 4446. Authentic Irish pub with great food and an inviting waterfront location. Mon–Sat 11.30am–1am, Sun 11am–midnight.

Top of the East Lounge In the Eastland Park Hotel, 157 High St ☎207 775 5411. Sophisticated rooftop lounge, with swanky martinis and great views of the city. Mon–Wed & Sun 4pm–midnight, Thurs–Sat 4pm–1am.

NIGHTLIFE

The **Portland Music Foundation** gives a great overview of local venues and live-music events (ⓦportlandmusicfoundation.org). Big-name bands come to the State Theatre (☎207 956 6000, ⓦstatetheatreportland.com) and Port City Music Hall (☎207 899 4990, ⓦportcitymusichall.com), while the Portland Symphony Orchestra plays at Merrill Auditorium (☎207 842 0800, ⓦporttix.com).

Big Easy 55 Market St ☎207 775 2266, ⓦbigeasyportland.com. All sorts of musicians ply their trade in this intimate venue: rock, soul, blues, jazz and Grateful Dead cover bands, to name a few. Minimal cover ($3), if any. Daily 9pm–late.

Blue 650A Congress St ☎207 774 4111, ⓦportcityblue.com. Welcoming little space with jazz, Celtic, Middle Eastern, old time and, of course, the blues. Wine, beer and strong coffee, and there's a great food menu as well. No cover. Wed–Sat 6pm–late.

Geno's 625 Congress St ☎207 221 2382. Rock venue featuring mostly local indie acts. Occasional cover ($5–12). Daily 5pm–1am.

★ **SPACE Gallery** 538 Congress St ☎207 828 5600, ⓦspace538.org. Cool artsy space that displays contemporary artworks and always has something interesting going on, whether it's films, music, art shows or local bands. There's sometimes a cover ($7–18).

ENTERTAINMENT

PERFORMING ARTS

There are several options for the performing arts in Portland. The free *Portland Phoenix* (ⓦportland.thephoenix.com) has listings of all local events. Chamber music, opera, dance, and touring theatre productions are often featured as part of the Portland Ovations series, which is held at Merrill Auditorium (20 Myrtle St; tickets ☎207 842 0800, ⓦporttix.com); the Portland Stage Company puts on larger-scale productions at 25A Forest Ave (☎207 774 0465, ⓦportlandstage.org). Portland Parks and Recreation (☎207 756 8130, ⓦci.portland.me.us) sponsors free outdoor concerts at various locations throughout the city during the summer.

FILM

You can find both first-run and art-house films at Nickelodeon Cinema, 1 Temple St (☎207 772 9751, ⓦpatriotcinemas.com).

SPORTS

The Maine Red Claws (☎207 210 6655, ⓦmaineredclaws.com), an NBA Development League basketball team that's an affiliate of the Boston Celtics, play at the Expo Building (239 Park Ave; ☎207 874 8200). Other sporting choices include Portland Pirates hockey (☎207 828 4665, ⓦportlandpirates.com) and horse racing in nearby Scarborough Downs (☎207 883 4331, ⓦscarboroughdowns.com). Baseball fans should take a trip to the intimate Hadlock Field stadium on Park Avenue where the minor league Portland Sea Dogs, a Boston Red Sox affiliate (☎207 879 9500, ⓦseadogs.com), play from April to September. Tickets are wildly inexpensive (prices top out at $9).

SHOPPING

Angela Adams 273 Congress St ☎207 774 3523. A Portland landmark in the East End, Angela Adams designs imaginative wool and cotton rugs inspired by the Maine landscape. Mon–Sat 10am–6pm.

Black Parrot 131 Middle St ☎207 221 6991. This beautiful Portland boutique has carefully chosen racks of women's clothing that give real meaning to the word "design". Pricey but amazing. Mon–Sat 10am–6pm.

Rabelais Books 86 Middle St ☎207 774 1044. This captivating bookstore stocks titles devoted exclusively to food and wine, quite fitting for this city of exceptional restaurants. Mon–Thurs 11am–5.30pm, Fri & Sat 11am–7pm, Sun 11am–4pm.

Rogues Gallery 41 Wharf St ☎207 553 1999. If you want your boyfriend to look like a stylish seafarer (who doesn't?) get thee to Rogues Gallery, a small space loaded with artful sailor-meets-rocker wares. The designs have a Manhattan look, but the shop's seaside roots lend a loving legitimacy to the brand. Tues–Thurs & Sun noon–5pm, Fri & Sat 11am–6pm.

Sea Bags 24 Custom House Wharf ☎207 780 0744. This is the warehouse where sea bags – stylish totes crafted from recycled sails, now on sale from coast to coast – get

SOAKOLOGY FOOT SANCTUARY AND TEAHOUSE

It's worth a visit to Portland for a **Soakology** appointment alone (30 City Center; ☎ 207 879 7625, ⓦ soakology.com; reservations advised; Mon–Wed 11am–7pm, Thurs–Sat till 9pm, Sun till 5pm). Downstairs at this day-spa, guests place their feet into clay pots filled with river stones and hot water scented with essential oils. Tempting add-ons, such as **massages** and **facials**, are also on offer. While soaking, order tea and home-made shortbread dipped in chocolate. It makes for a good sibling outing; note that men-folk will not feel out of place here.

made. Stop by to pick up an original design, or just to see how the magic happens. Mon–Sat 9am–5pm.

Stonewall Kitchen 182 Middle St ☎ 207 879 2409. Less harried and more personable than the flagship York location, this Stonewall sells all the signature jams, mustards and grilling sauces for which these flavour kings are known. Great for take-home gifts. Mon–Sat 10am–8pm, Sun 10am–6pm.

Freeport

Sixteen miles north of Portland along Rte-1 and the coast, **FREEPORT** is simply one huge shopping mall, though the town was once one of Maine's primary shipbuilding centres. Huge logs were brought here that would ultimately be used for masts; this past is still evident in the wide shape of the town square at Main and Bow streets, which was fashioned to give the gigantic logs plenty of room to swing as the carts turned on the way to the mast landing. Freeport's prominence was such that the town's **Jameson Tavern** is believed (though not without dispute) to have been the place where the treaty separating Maine from Massachusetts was signed in 1820.

The shipping industry fell into decline following the Civil War, but Freeport managed a big comeback fifty years later when a fishing-boot maker by the name of **Leon L. Bean** planted the seeds of what has become an unbelievably successful outdoors-wear manufacturer. L.L. Bean's store stood alone along Freeport's Main Street for decades until the 1980s, when it was joined by factory outlets, with chic fashion stops (Cole Haan, Brooks Brothers, J.Crew) alongside ones geared towards outdoorsmen (Patagonia, Timberland, North Face), and the town developed its current discount-shopping character.

L.L. Bean

95 Main St • Open 24hr • ☎ 207 552 6879, ⓦ llbean.com

Freeport owes virtually all of its current prosperity to the invention by Leon Leonwood Bean, in 1912, of a funky-looking, rubber-soled fishing boot, now favoured by everyone from seasoned Mainers to Manhattan hipsters. The boot is still available (indeed, there's a huge replica stationed at the entrance), and **L.L. Bean** has grown into a multinational clothing conglomerate, housed in an enormous 90,000-square-foot factory outlet building on Main Street that literally never closes. In theory, this is so that hunters can stock up in the pre-dawn hours; all the relevant equipment is available for rent or sale, and the store runs regular workshops from its Outdoor Discovery School (ⓦ llbean.com/ods). In practice, though, the late-night hours seem more geared toward local high school students, who attempt to fall asleep in the tents without being noticed by store personnel. It's worth a spin through just to gawk at the four storeys, which are packed with camping supplies and puffy outerwear; there's also a full café and even a trout pond with a waterfall.

Frost Gully Gallery

1159 Rte-1 • Mon–Fri noon–5pm • ☎ 207 773 2555, ⓦ frostgullygallery.com

The **Frost Gully Gallery** usually has a fine display of oil paintings by both local and nationally known artists, including frequent shows by the renowned Maine artist Dahlov Ipcar, and provides a respite from the commercialism found elsewhere in town.

DELORME MAP HEADQUARTERS

If you're driving north on I-295 from Portland to Freeport, you might notice an enormous illuminated globe just by the highway at exit 17. That's Eartha, the largest rotating globe in the world, and lodestar of the **DeLorme Map Headquarters**. Worth a stop for its seemingly endless selection of maps (including the indispensable Maine Atlas & Gazetteer) you can also watch Eartha's spellbinding turns, which simulate the planet's actual rotation (year-round: Mon–Sat 9am–6pm, April–Oct also Sun 9am–5pm; T 1 800 642 0970, W delorme.com).

Soldiers and Sailors Monument

On Bow Street, the **Soldiers and Sailors Monument**, a lone reference to the city's life before Bean, was dedicated by Civil War general Joshua Chamberlain, and boasts cannons that were used at the Battle of Bull Run.

Wolfe's Neck State Park

Wolfe's Neck Rd via Bow St • Daily 9am–sunset • $3 • T 207 865 4465

To get even further from the shops, head a mile south of Freeport to the sea, where the green cape visible just across the water is **Wolfe's Neck State Park**. In summer, you can follow hiking and nature trails along the unspoiled fringes of the headland.

Desert of Maine

95 Desert Rd, exit 20 off I-295 • Guided tours: May to mid-Oct daily 9am–5pm, last tour at 4.30pm • $8.75 • T 207 865 6962, W desertofmaine.com

8

For a bizarre change of pace, head ten minutes west of downtown to the **Desert of Maine**, a vast expanse of privately owned sand deposited here by a glacier that slid through the area eleven thousand years ago. This tiny, self-contained desert spread, ultimately engulfing the surrounding homes and trees; you can still see them, half-buried in the sand.

ARRIVAL AND DEPARTURE

FREEPORT

By train At research time, Amtrak's *Downeaster* was scheduled to extend its service to Freeport in the autumn of 2012 (trains twice daily; T 1 800 872 7245, W amtrakdowneaster.com). Until then, the nearest train station is in Portland, eighteen miles south.

By bus/taxi The closest buses come to Portland, from where you'll need to take a taxi the rest of the way. Try ABCab (T 207 865 2222).

By car The best way to get to Freeport is by car – there is currently no public transport, though this may change (see opposite). There's plenty of parking behind L.L. Bean, although this can fill to capacity on busy holidays.

INFORMATION

Freeport Merchants' Association Tourist Information 23 Depot St (Mon–Fri 9am–5pm; T 207 865 1212). This incredibly well-stocked operation, housed in a restored old tower, has reams of area information as well as public toilets.

ACCOMMODATION

There's no shortage of quality **B&Bs** in town, but if you're low on cash, try the cheap motels lining Rte-1 south of town. (Better still, stay in Portland and make a quick trip through Freeport.)

★ **Applewood Inn** 8 Holbrook St T 207 865 9705, W applewoodusa.com. Welcoming B&B with artful decor in a great location just behind L.L. Bean (next door to Mr. Bean's former house, no less). Some rooms are fancier and have jacuzzis, and there is one lovely suite that sleeps eight. The charming hosts moonlight as hot-dog vendors. $165; suite $300

Brewster House 180 Main St T 207 865 4121, W brewsterhouse.com. Dignified B&B set in a beautifully restored Queen Anne home with antique furnishings. Three rooms boast working fireplaces. $159

Harraseeket Inn 162 Main St T 207 865 9377, W harraseeketinn.com. After a day spent chasing sales at the outlets, retreat to this renowned clapboard B&B inn with some eighty rooms, two good restaurants (see opposite) and an indoor pool. Its genteel quarters are spruced up with high-thread-count sheets, canopy beds and antiques; deluxe rooms include fireplaces and jacuzzi tubs. **$195**

Hilton Garden Inn 5 Park St, downtown Freeport ☎ 207 865 1433, ⓦ hiltongardeninn.com. Well-situated new *Hilton* with sleek high-end hotel decor, microwaves and fridges in each guest room, a fitness centre, heated pool and wi-fi. **$250**

★ **Maine Idyll Motor Court** 1411 Rte-1 ☎ 207 865 4201, ⓦ maineidyll.com. Basic but romantic cottage quarters in a woodsy area a few miles north of town, with blueberry muffins in the morning. Family-owned and maintained since the 1930s. May–Oct. **$71**

CAMPING

Recompense Shores 134 Burnett Rd ☎ 207 865 9307, ⓦ freeportcamping.com. Near Casco Bay, with 115 well-kept and -spaced campsites. **$25**

EATING AND ENTERTAINMENT

Freeport is a little thin on good eats, but its restaurant exteriors certainly look nice – the buildings are all done up to match the town's strict aesthetic **zoning laws**; even the *McDonald's* is disguised by a clapboard motif. For entertainment, L.L. Bean runs a fun, free Saturday **concert series** in summer; check ⓦ llbean.com for a calendar of events.

Broad Arrow Tavern 162 Main St, in the Harraseeket Inn ☎ 207 865 9377. Gourmet pizzas, pulled-pork sandwiches and a great lunch buffet served in a lodge-style dining room with an open kitchen and a roaring fire. Daily 11.30am–10.30pm.

★ **Conundrum Wine Bistro** 117 Rte-1 (by the wooden Indian sculpture) ☎ 207 865 0303. Three miles south of downtown, *Conundrum* dishes up the best food in Freeport. Most people come for the swanky martinis, then get hooked on the fresh, eclectic mains ($12–20), such as butternut squash ravioli with sage cream sauce. Tues–Thurs 4.30–10pm, Fri & Sat 4.30pm–midnight.

★ **Harraseeket Lunch & Lobster Co.** 36 Main St, South Freeport ☎ 207 865 4888. Extending on a wooden jetty into a peaceful bay, the *Harraseeket* makes a great outdoor lunch spot for seafood baskets and sandwiches. Cash only. May–Oct daily 11am–7.45pm, July & Aug till 8.45pm.

Jacqueline's Tea Room 201 Main St ☎ 207 865 2123. Girly to the max, this tempting tea spot, all white wicker and rose prints, serves a scrumptious two-hour, four-course tea service (reservations required; $29.50), or a more casual cream tea ($12) with lemon curd and fresh scones. Cash only. Tues–Fri 11am–1pm and alternate weekends.

Mediterranean Grill 10 School St ☎ 207 865 1688. Authentic Mediterranean cuisine such as *spanakopita* (spinach pie; $15.95) and chicken *sarma* stuffed with rice and pistachios ($17.95) two blocks from L.L. Bean. Mon–Thurs & Sun 11am–9pm, Fri & Sat 11am–10pm.

The Mid-Coast

Maine's central coast, which stretches roughly from the quiet college town of **Brunswick** to blue-collar **Bucksport**, is a study in geographic, economic and cultural contrasts. The shore here is physically different from the southern coast, with peninsulas such as the **Harpswells** and **Pemaquid Point** providing divergent alternatives to well-travelled Rte-1. Much of this region prospered in the late nineteenth century through shipbuilding and trading, as evidenced by its wealth of attractive old captains' homes; today, only **Bath** remains as a ship manufacturer. Throughout, though, the focus is still unquestionably the sea, be it for livelihood, sustenance or recreation. Consequently, one of the best ways to see the area is by boat. Indeed, remote **Monhegan Island**, a lobstermen's hub and artists' retreat eleven miles offshore, is accessible only by ferry. **Lobstering** is also especially important to **Rockland**, home of the most active lobster industry in the state. Busy **Camden**, just beyond Rockland, is known for its fleet of recreational **windjammers**, while picturesque fishing villages such as **Round Pond** and **Tenants Harbor** – tiny windows into rustic Maine – can be found all along this stretch, somehow coexisting with summer resorts like **Boothbay Harbor**, which is all but deserted in the winter.

Brunswick

A few miles north from Freeport is **BRUNSWICK**, home since 1794 to Bowdoin College, which counts among its alumni Henry Wadsworth Longfellow, Nathaniel Hawthorne

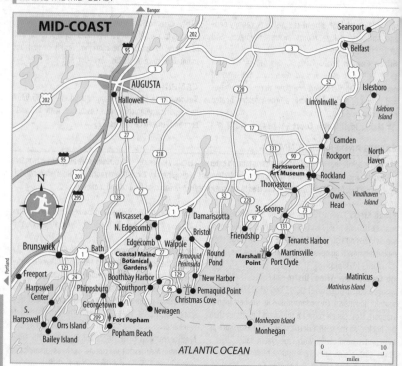

and Franklin Pierce. The town is attractive enough, with a concentration of old brick and clapboard homes and buildings, but apart from the small campus itself – at the south end of Maine Street – and a couple of unobtrusive cafés, there's little evidence of student life here. South of Brunswick, the scenic peninsulas that comprise the Harpswells make a worthy detour.

Peary-MacMillan Arctic Museum

9500 College Station, Bowdoin College • Tues–Sat 10am–5pm, Sun 2–5pm • Free • ☎ 207 725 3416, Ⓦ bowdoin.edu/arctic-museum

After decades of disagreement, experts now generally conclude that former Bowdoin student Admiral Robert Peary was the first man to reach the North Pole in 1909; whatever the truth, his sledge and other ephemera, found at the **Peary-MacMillan Arctic Museum**, will captivate anyone who longs to experience ice floes.

Bowdoin College Museum of Art

9400 College Station, Bowdoin College • Tues–Sat 10am–5pm, Thurs till 8.30pm, Sun 1–5pm • Free • ☎ 207 725 3275, Ⓦ bowdoin.edu /art-museum

Bowdoin's **Museum of Art**, housed in an 1894 brick building adjoined by a swish glass entranceway, is well worth a look, with an intriguing collection of moody nineteenth-century paintings (including a lovely one by Albert Bierstadt), modern masters like Rockwell Kent and rotating contemporary art.

General Joshua L. Chamberlain Museum

226 Maine St • May–Oct Tues–Sat 10am–4pm • Guided tours on the hour • $7.50 • ☎ 207 725 6958

One distinguished alumnus of Bowdoin College, Civil War hero General Joshua Chamberlain, graduated in 1852 and became a professor at the school in 1855. At the

HARRIET BEECHER STOWE

Harriet Beecher Stowe (1811–96), a native of Litchfield, Connecticut, moved to Brunswick with her family from Ohio in the spring of 1850 when her husband, Calvin, took a position as professor of religion at Bowdoin College. It was here that Stowe formulated and wrote *Uncle Tom's Cabin*, the anti-slavery novel that would go on to become the bestseller of the century. The passage of the 1850 **Fugitive Slave Act**, which stipulated that it was illegal for citizens to assist escaped slaves, and demanded that escapees be apprehended and deported back to their "rightful" owner, outraged Stowe, who conceived of the death of Uncle Tom while sitting at worship in Brunswick's **First Parish Church**, 223 Maine St (pew no. 23; ☎ 207 729 7331). Encouraged by her husband, she published her story serially in the *National Era*, an abolitionist weekly. The book is credited with bringing respectability to the abolitionist cause, and when Abraham Lincoln met Stowe years later he reportedly remarked, "So you're the little lady who wrote the book that started the war." The **Harriet Beecher Stowe House** in Brunswick, at 63 Federal St, is privately owned.

onset of the Civil War, and with no military training, he volunteered to serve, then went on to fight in 24 battles and receive the Congressional Medal of Honor; at the end of the war he was selected by Ulysses S. Grant to accept the formal surrender of the Confederate troops. He later became governor of Maine and, in 1871, president of Bowdoin College. The general's career is documented at the **General Joshua L. Chamberlain Museum**, his former home.

ARRIVAL AND DEPARTURE

BRUNSWICK

8

By train At research time, Amtrak's *Downeaster* was scheduled to extend its service to Brunswick in the autumn 2012 (trains twice daily; ☎ 1 800 872 7245, ⓦ amtrakdowneaster.com).

By bus Buses to and from Brunswick are fairly frequent: Greyhound stops at the depot at 152 Maine St (☎ 1 800 231 2222, ⓦ greyhound.com), from where you can catch buses to most other parts of New England. Concord Coach (☎ 1 800 639 3317, ⓦ concordcoachlines.com) stops at 16 Station Ave before continuing north to Bangor or south to Boston.

INFORMATION

Southern Midcoast Maine Chamber of Commerce 2 Main St, Topsham (Mon–Fri 8.30am–5pm) ☎ 207 725 8797, ⓦ midcoastmaine.com). The Chamber of Commerce office in neighbouring Topsham is particularly helpful, with an array of brochures and a knowledgeable staff.

ACCOMMODATION

Brunswick B&B 165 Park Row ☎ 207 729 4914, ⓦ brunswickbnb.com. A gracious old inn decorated with antiques and quilts, in the town centre within walking distance of the college. **$155**
Captain Daniel Stone Inn 10 Water St ☎ 207 725 9898, ⓦ captaindanielstoneinn.com. Elegant, Federal-style rooms and suites supplied with modern amenities. There is also an upmarket restaurant with dining on the veranda in summer. **$232**

EATING AND DRINKING

For its small size, Brunswick has an impressive number of excellent **restaurants**. In addition to what's listed here, there are also a few good Indian, Thai and Japanese spots downtown, so you won't go short of a decent meal.

MAINE EASTERN RAILROAD

If you're moving on from Brunswick to Rockland, consider hopping aboard the **Maine Eastern Railroad** (June Sat & Sun only; July–Oct Wed–Sun; $42 round-trip; ☎ 1 866 637 2457, ⓦ maineeasternrailroad.com), which runs scenic trips between the two towns (with stops in Bath and Wiscasset) in restored Art Deco cars. The train is equipped with a lounge and dining area; in the latter you can sip wine and watch the coast go by.

★ **Back Street Bistro** 11 Town Hall Place ☎ 207 725 4060. Fine dining as well as inexpensive options in a side street off the square. Easily one of Brunswick's best restaurants, with the likes of blue-cheese-crusted steak and creative seasonal salads. Daily 5pm–late.

★ **El Camino** 15 Cushing St ☎ 207 725 8228. While the exterior looks like it was lifted from the bad side of Tijuana, the interior is quirky and hip, with Day of the Dead decor and Mexican streamers. The locavore food is top-notch – cornmeal-fried fish tacos ($11.50) and pork and sweet-potato nachos ($11.50) – are washed down with killer margaritas ($9.50). Tues–Thurs 5–9pm, Fri & Sat 5–9.30pm.

Fat Boy Drive-In 111 Bath Rd (Rte-24) ☎ 207 729 9431. A beloved summer tradition since 1955, *Fat Boy* dishes up burgers, frappes and lobster rolls; just turn your lights on for service at your car. Late March to mid-Oct Mon–Thurs & Sun 11am–8pm, Fri & Sat till 8.30pm.

★ **Frontier Café** 14 Maine St (in the Fort Andross Mill) ☎ 207 725 5222, ⊕ explorefrontier.com. Foodies are abuzz for this creative newcomer – a café, cinema, live music venue and gallery all in one beautiful mill space.

Order a market plate – charcuterie, cheeses, spreads and breads served on square planks – and feast beside the mighty Androscoggin. Free wi-fi. Mon–Thurs 9am–9pm, Fri & Sat till 10pm.

Gelato Fiasco 74 Maine St ☎ 207 607 4002. Life-changing gelato in creative flavours that range from a pudding-rich chocolate through pineapple to wasabi. Good coffee, too. Daily 11am–11pm.

Lilee's Public House 148 Maine St ☎ 207 729 9482. This sister restaurant to the *Back Street Bistro* (see opposite) is more affordable and equally good. You'll find juicy burgers, French dip sandwiches with melted Swiss cheese, finger foods and an extensive beer list in a relaxed, traditional English pub setting. Mon–Sat 11am–11pm.

Scarlet Begonias 16 Station Ave ☎ 207 721 0403. This long-time Brunswick haunt is favoured by everyone from Bowdoin students to young families and tourists. Over the years, it has continued to serve creative home cooking – soups, salads, pizza and pasta – but it's now moved into an expanded new location at the Brunswick Station. Mon–Fri 11am–10pm, Sat noon–10pm.

Harpswells

South of Brunswick, a set of narrow, forested peninsulas, collectively known as the **HARPSWELLS** make for a welcome escape from the bustle of Rte-1. The only problem is that once you get to the end of one of the thrusts of land, you have to turn around and retrace your tracks. Rte-123 weaves down the Harpswell Neck past Maine's **oldest meeting house** (1757) in Harpswell Center, then clear down to South Harpswell, where the Basin Cove Falls, created by tidal flows, are popular with canoeists and kayakers. Rte-24 heads down another long, finger-like strip to **Bailey Island** (one of Casco Bay Cruise Line's stops; ☎ 207 774 7871, ⊕ cascobaylines.com), first crossing Orr's Island and then the **Cribstone Bridge**, which allows tides to flow right through it. Bailey Island's highlight is the **Giant Staircase**, off Rte-24 on the eastern shore of the island, a massive waterfront stone stairway good for exploring. On Orr's Island, H2Outfitters (☎ 207 833 5257, ⊕ h2outfitters.com) leads **kayak** trips of varying lengths.

ACCOMMODATION
THE HARPSWELLS

Captain's Watch B&B 926 Cundy's Harbor Rd ☎ 207 725 0979, ⊕ home.gwi.net/~cwatch. An 1862 cupola-topped mansion with four guest rooms and panoramic

vistas overlooking a cove. One room has a working fireplace, and a sumptuous daily breakfast is included in the rate. **$155**

EATING

★ **Dolphin Marina** 515 Basin Point Rd, South Harpswell ☎ 207 833 6000. While in the Harpswells, don't miss a chance to sample the fish chowder at this nearly hidden restaurant that overlooks a working harbour. From your dining-room table, you'll spot bobbing birds, a lighthouse and a handful of small islands. Daily: June–Aug 11.30am–9pm; May & Sept–Nov till 8pm.

Morse's at Estes Lobster House ☎ 207 833 6340; 1906 Harpswell Neck Rd, at the end of Rte-123, South Harpswell. Another longstanding seafood-on-the-water gem. Run by the same family since 1963, *Estes* satisfies your lobster cravings and boasts a panoramic view of Casco Bay. May–Oct Tues–Sun 11.30am–8.30pm.

8

Bath

Crossing the bridge into **BATH** on Rte-1, it's hard to miss the enormous industrial cranes of the massive **Bath Iron Works** shipyard jutting into the skyline. The town has an exceptionally long history of **shipbuilding** – the first vessel to be constructed and launched here was the *Virginia* in 1607. Shipbuilding continued to be a major industry in the region throughout the eighteenth century, and between 1800 and 1830, nearly 288 ships set sail out of Bath's port. Smaller trading vessels eventually gave way to larger ships, and in 1841, Clark & Sewall, one of the major builders at the time, launched the 1133-ton *Rappahannock*, at the time the world's largest ship. Despite changes in the shipbuilding market over the centuries, Bath's military contracts have never been in short supply, and during World War II more destroyers were built here than in all Japan. Today, it's worth a visit for its stellar **Maine Maritime Museum** and quaint main street, with turn-of-the-century buildings and a bowfronted city hall that epitomizes the charm of this hard-working town.

Bath Iron Works

Tram tours run May–Oct via the Maine Maritime Museum • $30; Reservations strongly recommended (can be booked online) • ☏ 207 443 1316, ⓦ bathmaine.com

With more than five thousand employees, **Bath Iron Works**, two miles south of the town centre, is the largest private employer in the state – and, thanks to a continuous stream of government contracts, the only shipbuilder remaining in Bath. Workers keep the factory running around the clock, so you should aim to avoid driving anywhere in Bath around 3.30pm, when shifts change and traffic slows. You can take a tram tour of the Works via the **Maine Maritime Museum** (see below).

Maine Maritime Museum

243 Washington St • Daily 9.30am–5pm • $12 for 2 days • ☏ 207 443 1316, ⓦ bathmaine.com

At the stellar **Maine Maritime Museum**, next to the Iron Works, you can tour the old Percy & Small shipyard, explore several historic vessels and browse the Maritime History Building, where galleries house an interesting range of ship-related paintings, photographs and artefacts. Outside, there's an intriguing, 426ft steel sculpture of the *Wyoming* – the largest wooden vessel ever built in the US, made here in 1909 – that delineates the shape of the ship. There's also a mini-pirate vessel for little buccaneers to climb around on. The museum runs a number of appealing **boat trips** and cruises (call for schedule and prices).

Popham Beach

Daily 9am–sunset • $6 for non-Maine residents, $4 residents • ☏ 207 389 1335

A pretty fourteen-mile drive south along Rte-209 leads to lovely **Popham Beach**, at the end of the Phippsburg Peninsula, and part of a 529-acre state park. In addition to its scenic sands, you can explore **Fort Popham**, a nineteenth-century granite fort.

Reid State Park

Daily 9am–sunset • $6.50 for non-Maine residents, $4.50 residents • ☏ 207 371 2303

Georgetown Island, just southeast from Bath down Rte-127, contains another superior beach at **Reid State Park**, where the dunes flatten out into three miles of seashore. While beachcombing, see if you can locate the area's four lighthouses.

AMC HUTS ON GEORGETOWN ISLAND

The **Appalachian Mountain Club** (☏ 603 466 2727, ⓦ outdoors.org) maintains a couple of excellent low-budget **accommodation options** on Georgetown Island. At the *Knubble Bay Camp*, a friendly riverfront cabin with a nice porch and kitchen, there's bunk space for up to fifteen people (1–8 people $160 per night, 9–15 people $210). A much more primitive option is the secluded wilderness campground at Beal Island (April–Nov only; $12 per night), which is accessible only by canoe or kayak.

ARRIVAL AND DEPARTURE

By train At the time of writing, Amtrak's *Downeaster* was scheduled to extend its service to Brunswick, eight miles west of Bath, in the autumn of 2012 (trains twice daily; ☎ 1 800 872 7245, ⓦ amtrakdowneaster.com). The Maine Eastern Railroad (see box, p.473) also makes a stop in Bath.
By bus Concord Coach (☎ 1 800 639 3317, ⓦ concordcoachlines.com) stops at the Mail It 4 U, 10 State Rd, before continuing north to Bangor or south to Boston.

INFORMATION

Bath Visitor Information Center 15 Commercial St (May–Oct 9am–7pm, rest of year 9am–5pm; ☎ 207 443 1513, ⓦ visitbath.com). Useful office with loads of area information.

ACCOMMODATION

1774 Inn 44 Parker Head Rd, 7 miles south in Phippsburg ☎ 207 389 1774, ⓦ 1774inn.com. This outstanding eighteenth-century property, once the home of Maine's first US congressman, houses eight gracious rooms furnished with antiques on four acres on the banks of the Kennebec River. Guests spot frequent seals and occasional bald eagles from the manicured lawn. $150

★ **Coveside B&B** 6 Gotts Cove Lane, 13 miles south in Georgetown ☎ 207 371 2807, ⓦ covesidebandb.com. This idyllic hideaway, tucked between a boat-filled cove and a beautiful garden, has seven stylish rooms, friendly hosts, kayaking opportunities and phenomenal breakfasts. Late May to Oct. $145

Hampton Inn 140 Commercial St ☎ 207 386 1310, ⓦ hamptoninn.com. New in 2010, this luxe hotel has a saltwater pool and hot tub, plus wi-fi, flat-screen TVs, fridges and microwaves in all of its 94 rooms. Full breakfast buffet included. $189

Inn at Bath 969 Washington St ☎ 207 443 4294, ⓦ innatbath.com. An 1840 Greek Revival house with friendly service and tastefully decorated rooms, some with wood-burning fireplaces and jacuzzis. $170

★ **Kismet Inn** 44 Summer St ☎ 207 443 3399, ⓦ kismetinnmaine.com. A unique retreat for tranquillity and rejuvenation. Sink into one of *Kismet*'s luxurious soaking tubs and let the world fall away. Yoga classes, body scrubs and spa services are also on offer at this turreted Queen Anne house with five brightly painted rooms and organic meals. $255

CAMPING

★ **Hermit Island** At the end of Rte-216, farther south along the Phippsburg Peninsula ☎ 207 443 2101, ⓦ hermitisland.com. You can rent small boats here and camp near a white-sand beach. $35

Meadowbrook Camping Area 33 Meadowbrook Rd, Phippsburg ☎ 207 443 4967, ⓦ meadowbrookme.com. More than one hundred campsites south of town along the water in Perry Cove. Hot showers, a heated pool and karaoke at the weekends. May–Sept. $29

EATING AND DRINKING

Admiral Steakhouse 798 Washington St ☎ 207 443 2555. Sinatra on the stereo, hot, cheese-topped loaves of bread, ridiculously good twice-baked potatoes and, of course, excellent steaks ($17–35), served in a wood-panelled dining room hung with maritime art. Mon–Thurs & Sun 4.30–9pm, Fri & Sat till 10pm.

Beale Street Barbeque and Grill 215 Water St ☎ 207 442 9514. Hickory-smoked Memphis barbecue in an airy, modern dining room. Mon–Sat 11am–10pm, Sun noon–10pm.

The Cabin 552 Washington St ☎ 207 443 6224. Near the museum, the *Cabin* dishes out some of Maine's best pizza in dark, wooden booths. Cash only. Mon–Thurs & Sun 10am–10pm, Fri & Sat till 11pm.

★ **Five Islands Lobster Co.** 1447 Five Islands Rd (off Rte-127), 14 miles south in Georgetown ☎ 207 371 2990. One of the most picturesque settings in Maine to eat lobster or great fried clams: the picnic tables have spectacular views that take in sailboats, forested islands and a lighthouse. Early May to Oct. July & Aug daily 11.30am–7pm, call to confirm hours at other times.

Mae's Café & Bakery 160 Centre St ☎ 207 442 8577. Neighbourhood café with inventive breakfast sandwiches and egg benedicts; lunch serves up salads, sandwiches and fresh flatbreads over greens. The bakery case overflows with goodies. Daily 8am–3pm; bakery until 4pm.

Montsweag Roadhouse 942 Rte-1, north of Bath in Woolrich ☎ 207 443 6563. If you're headed north on Rte-1, try this fun stop – the *Roadhouse* seamlessly ranges from fine dining to biker hangout and has a menu (think sandwiches, seafood, pizza and steak) almost as big as its premises, a sprawling old house. Frequent live music. Daily 11am–1am.

Robinhood Free Meetinghouse Robinhood Rd, Georgetown, south of Bath along Rte-127 ☎ 207 371 2188. This is one of Maine's premier restaurants, and worth the detour. Housed in Georgetown's former town hall, the creative American bistro integrates touches of Cajun, Italian and Szechuan cuisine into its $25-and-up mains. Reservations recommended. Summer daily 5.30–9pm; call for hours rest of year.

MAINE'S BEST LOBSTER ROLL

There is a healthy amount of debate about where to find the "best" lobster roll in Maine. Eating at **Red's Eats** (Rte-1, Wiscasset; ☎ 207 882 6128) is certainly a culinary rite of passage – people line the block to get their hands on his lip-smacking, using-an-entire-lobster roll – but some locals blak at the waiting. Scenery is also a factor, and for this, **Two Lights** in Cape Elizabeth (see p.466), **Five Islands Lobster Co.** in Georgetown (see p.476), and **Shaw's Fish & Lobster Wharf** in New Harbor (see p.482), are perhaps the strongest contenders, with outstanding rolls complemented by panoramic water views. At the end of the day, though, you can't go too wrong anywhere in the state. Just make sure the lobster is **fresh** – and that means straight from the boat (anything advertised as "handpicked" is a good sign). You shouldn't stand for any tomfoolery with the ingredients, either: look for a roll that is dressed simply with mayo, salt and pepper, and a perfectly grilled hot dog bun – remember that lobster should be the star flavour.

Solo Bistro Bistro 128 Front St ☎ 207 443 3373. Very hip bistro with colourful, contemporary seating, exposed brick and dangling lamps. Dinner is a seasonal, upscale affair with the likes of spiced pork tenderloin and gorgonzola polenta (mains $16–25). There's a cute wine bar downstairs. Daily 5pm–late.

Boothbay Harbor

Less than fifteen miles south of Rte-1 along Rte-27, several villages cluster near the end of the Boothbay Peninsula. The most active of these is **BOOTHBAY HARBOR**, a crowded, yet undeniably pretty, resort town on the peninsula's western edge. Much of the town's history as a prosperous fishing and shipbuilding centre has been obscured by tourism, which has been active here since the late nineteenth century, resulting in a wealth of predictable shops and restaurants. Nevertheless, the village is beautifully situated on a harbour, and has a lively town centre, some good inns and ample opportunities to explore the sea and surrounding coast. For a more genuine Maine experience, however, you might try the less popular neighbouring Pemaquid Peninsula or even the Blue Hill Peninsula, closer to Bar Harbor.

The town centre runs along **Commercial Street** and **Townsend Avenue**, while the rest of the settlement spreads out around a tiny cove, thinning into residential neighbourhoods southwest on Southport Island and southeast towards Ocean Point.

The footbridge

The most immediate view of the harbour is from the 1000ft-long wooden **footbridge** that connects downtown to the east side of town. If you venture across, head south along Atlantic Avenue to the pretty **Our Lady Queen of Peace** church (at no. 82), which holds its holy water in clam shells.

Coastal Maine Botanical Gardens

Barters Island Rd, Boothbay; call for directions as it's tricky to find • Daily 9am–5pm • $12 • ☎ 207 633 4333, ⓦ mainegardens.org

One of the state's most beloved attractions, the 248-acre **Coastal Maine Botanical**

CLAMBAKES

"Clambake" is not just the title of a particularly bad Elvis Presley movie, it's a local tradition older than New England itself. Long before the first European settlers arrived, Native Americans had perfected the ritual of cooking plentiful amounts of **clams** by what now seems like a rather unconventional method. First, a deep pit is dug in the sand and lined with **rocks**. Wood is added and ignited; its ashes are eventually swept away, with the rocks left hot enough to cook on. **Seaweed** is piled on these rocks, followed by layers of potatoes, onions, corn, clams and lobsters. Then comes another layer of seaweed, and finally a **wet canvas**, which traps the steam. The result is an unforgettable, and messy, meal.

Gardens curve alongside the Sheepscot River and are honeycombed by well-tended trails and twelve winsome gardens. In the Garden of the Five Senses, you can walk a meditative stone labyrinth, sample fresh herbs and lettuce, shake hands with a fuzzy salvia plant and listen for messages from the "sound stone" – a carved granite pillar that reverberates with noise. The two-acre Children's Garden, depicting scenes from classic Maine picture books, is another highlight.

Ocean Point and Southport Island

There's plenty of less crowded land to explore in the area surrounding Boothbay Harbor. At the end of the pretty fifteen-minute drive south along Rte-96 to desolate **Ocean Point**, you are rewarded with views of the horizon across the ocean, interrupted only by Squirrel, Fisherman and Ram islands (look out for Ram's prominent lighthouse). A few miles north on the same peninsula, the **Linekin Preserve** (☎207 633 4818) maintains extensive **hiking trails** on nearly a hundred acres of wilderness between Rte-96 and the coast. On relatively deserted **Southport Island**, south on Rte-27, you can drive all the way to Newagen, with its views of the Cuckolds Lighthouse, half a mile out to sea.

ARRIVAL AND DEPARTURE
BOOTHBAY HARBOR

By bus Concord Coach (☎1 800 639 3317, ⓦconcordcoachlines.com) stops in nearby Wiscasset twice daily, from where you can catch a taxi on to Boothbay; try Bobo's Coastal Taxi (☎207 380 4182; $30). Courtesy trams run frequently from the *Rocktide Inn* at 35 Atlantic Ave (10am–5pm in summer), to various points in town.

By car Though it's quite likely you'll have arrived by car, note that Boothbay Harbor's windy, narrow streets are packed in summer and parking can be a hassle. It's a good idea to park farther out, along West, Howard or Sea streets, or take the shuttle into town from the *Rocktide Inn*.

GETTING AROUND

By bicycle/kayak If you want to explore the coast under your own power, contact the Tidal Transit Company (☎207 633 7140, ⓦkayakboothbay.com), which offers kayak rentals ($40/half-day) and tours ($45–80) and also rents bikes ($40/day).

INFORMATION

Chamber of Commerce Rte-27 (Mon–Fri 8am–5pm, June–Aug also Sat & Sun 9am–5pm; ☎207 633 2353). A very good source of information, with binders on local accommodation and a reservation service.

ACCOMMODATION

You can always find some sort of **place to stay** in Boothbay Harbor, but in the summer, try to book at least a month in advance. Prices are considerably lower at the beginning and end of the tourist season, and many places close down by mid-October.

Five Gables Inn Murray Hill Rd, East Boothbay ☎207 633 4551, ⓦfivegablesinn.com. Fifteen of the sixteen guest rooms in this restored nineteenth-century hotel offer views of balmy Linekin Bay; five include working fireplaces. Famed for its breakfasts, and the trained chef-innkeeper does a mean tomato frittata. May to mid-Oct. **$160**

BOAT TRIPS FROM BOOTHBAY HARBOR

Aside from taking a quick stroll around the town's hilly, shop-lined streets, Boothbay Harbor's main attraction lies in the number of **boat trips** on offer from the harbour behind Commercial Street. Some depart for Monhegan Island (see p.482), while others circle the coast, taking in the dramatic scenery. Balmy Days Cruises (☎207 633 2284, ⓦbalmydayscruises.com) is as good as any of the outfits on the waterfront, with all-day trips to Monhegan Island costing $32 and harbour tours for $16. The windjammer **Eastwind** departs from the wharf four times daily (May–Oct; 2hr round-trip; $28; ☎207 633 6598, ⓦschoonereastwind.com). **Cap'n Fish's whale-watch tours** guarantee sightings of the majestic sea creatures (May–Oct; 3hr 30min round-trip; $38; ☎207 633 3244, ⓦmainewhales.com).

8

★ **Hodgdon Island Inn** 374 Barters Island Rd, Boothbay ☎ 207 633 7474, ⊚ boothbaybb.com. Close to the Botanical Gardens, the nine guest rooms at this waterfront Italianate mansion have a fresh, modern look – some, a glorious riot of colour with watermelon pink walls, others less wild but equally fun. You'll also find a heated pool, full breakfasts and home-made desserts in the evening. **$134**

Inns at Greenleaf Lane 65 Commercial St ☎ 207 633 3100, ⊚ greenleafinn.com. Right in the centre of town, this fun, friendly B&B has an international crowd, a sociable breakfast hour, a book and movie library, an outdoor jacuzzi and eight appealing guest rooms with a traditional look. They also own the adjacent *Admiral's Inn*. **$225**

★ **Topside Inn** 60 McKown St ☎ 207 633 5404, ⊚ topsideinn.com. Perched on top of a steep hill, this former sea captain's home has Boothbay's most spectacular vantage point for surveying the harbour. The impeccably stylish guest rooms are the best in town; breakfast is served in a sunny dining room. May to mid-Oct. **$155**

Welch House Inn 56 McKown St ☎ 1 800 279 7313, ⊚ welchhouseinn.com. This gabled clapboard house on a hill affords excellent views from its deck. The light and airy rooms are tastefully furnished and a buffet breakfast is included. **$130**

EATING AND DRINKING

Baker's Way 89 Townsend Ave (Rte-27) ☎ 207 633 1119. This unassuming storefront belies a marvellous culinary hybrid: a doughnut shop that moonlights as a Vietnamese restaurant. Early morning sees muffins and croissants; after 11am, bowls of piping hot *pho*, tofu curry and steamed dumplings make their way to tables in the back garden. Daily 6am–9pm.

Boathouse Bistro 12 The By-Way (Pier 1) ☎ 207 633 0400. Excellent tapas – like Maine maple scallops ($6) or bacon-wrapped dates with pecans ($5) – in a fun, sunny, rooftop bar setting. May–Oct daily 11.30am–10pm.

★ **Cabbage Island Clam Bakes** Pier 6 at the Fisherman's Wharf Inn ☎ 207 633 7200. Lobster nirvana: head out on a scenic harbour cruise (complete with full bar), then disembark at 5.5-acre Cabbage Island for an authentic clambake (see box, p.477) comprised of steamed shellfish, chowder, corn on the cob and blueberry cake. Afterwards, play horseshoes and badminton with newfound friends. $59.95. Daily departures late June to early Sept.

Ebb Tide 43 Commercial St ☎ 207 633 5692. Cheap, utilitarian breakfasts are served all day at this vintage blue-collar joint in the centre of town. If you're here in summer, don't miss the fresh peach shortcake. July & Aug daily 7am–10pm; call for hours rest of year.

Lobster Dock 49 Atlantic Ave ☎ 207 633 7120. Across the footbridge, the waterfront *Lobster Dock* has a beer-and-picnic-table vibe and dishes up ultra-fresh lobster rolls and seafood dinners at low prices. Late May to mid-Oct daily 11.30am–8.30pm.

McSeagull's Pier 1 (14 Wharf St) ☎ 207 633 5900. Right in the centre of town, this casual restaurant has a large and tasty menu ranging from seafood fettucine ($24) to pizza ($12) to pork quesadillas ($12) and fried fish sandwiches ($12) served in a harbourside porch or spacious dining room. Daily 11.30am–10pm.

★ **Ports of Italy** 47 Commercial St ☎ 207 633 1011. Excellent, authentic Northern Italian fare like home-made fettuccine with local scallops and veal milanese served in a candlelit second-floor dining room. There's also a polished wooden bar, just right for swilling one of *Ports'* perfect cabernets. Mains $18–23. Reservations recommended. Late May to mid-Oct Mon–Thurs 4.30–9pm, Fri–Sun noon–3pm & 4.30–9pm.

NIGHTLIFE AND ENTERTAINMENT

1894 Opera House ☎ 207 633 5159, ⊚ boothbayoperahouse.com. For live music, lectures and theatre performances, look no further than the 1894 Opera House, which always has something interesting going on.

8

Damariscotta

The compact town of **DAMARISCOTTA**, just off Rte-1 across the Damariscotta River from Newcastle, is a quaint entrance point into Maine's region of lakes and loons (see box, p.513), with a nineteenth-century Main Street that's a good place to stop for lunch or a stroll. From town, River Road leads south to **Dodge Point**, where you can **hike** along several miles of trails or hang out on the sandy **beach** along the Damariscotta River. It's also a popular spot for **fishing**, where anglers fish for striped bass, bluefish and mackerel. You can dig for clams in the offshore tidal flats – contact the Newcastle Town Office (☎ 207 563 3441) for rules and regulations. Damariscotta is also a pleasant place to stay while exploring the Pemaquid Peninsula.

RENYS: THE HARRODS OF MAINE

Feather-down sleeping bag? Check. Hardworking pair of jeans? Check. Beach towels? Board games? Barbecue sauce? Check, check, check. **Renys**, the humble discount store that could, lives by a slogan: "If Renys doesn't have it, I don't need it!". The store was established in Damariscotta in 1949 (116 Main St, ☎ 207 563 5757, ⓦ renys.com) – owner R.H. Reny sold merchandise out of an old truck to keep his business afloat during the business's first winter. Since then, Renys has grown into a chain of fourteen, becoming a Maine institution. In 2003, love for Renys hit the stage with *Renys: the Musical*, first performed in Newcastle. Take that, retail giants!

ARRIVAL AND DEPARTURE   DAMARISCOTTA

By bus Concord Coach (☎ 1 800 639 3317, ⓦ concordcoachlines.com) stops at the Waltz Pharmacy, at 167 Main St, before continuing north to Bangor or south to Boston.

INFORMATION

Chamber of Commerce 15 Courtyard St (Mon–Fri 9am–3pm; ☎ 207 563 8340). The region's friendly office, with lots of useful information.

ACCOMMODATION

★ **Blue Skye Farm** 1708 Friendship Rd (Rte-220), Waldoboro (follow the signs from Rte-1) ☎ 207 832 0300, ⓦ blueskyefarm.com. Open year-round, this 1775 Federal-style B&B is favoured for its surrounding acres of woodlands (great for hiking and snowshoeing), well-priced, appealing accommodation furnished with white bedspreads and clawfoot tubs, and fantastic proprietors. **$125**

EATING AND DRINKING

Damariscotta River Grill 155 Main St ☎ 207 563 2992. Damariscotta is famed for its oysters, and this comfortably upscale restaurant on Muscongus Bay is a great place to sample them. The seafood-focused menu has fun divergences like artichoke fondue ($9) and latkes ($7). Mains $17–21. Daily 11am–9.30pm.

Larson's Lunch Box 430 Main St ☎ 207 563 5755. Little blue-trimmed house with delicious lobster rolls ($14.95), crab rolls ($10.95) and cheeseburgers ($3.80) ordered from a takeaway window. You can also call ahead for picnic baskets, filled with your favourite rolls and sides ($17.50 per person, minimum of four people). Cash only. Daily except Wed: May–Oct 11am–4pm; July & Aug till 7pm.

★ **Moody's Diner** East of town on Rte-1 in Waldoboro ☎ 207 832 7785. A Maine institution for more than eighty years, *Moody's* is the real deal, open late and oozing nostalgia, with spinning vinyl stools, inexpensive daily specials, soups and fourteen types of pie – the four-berry is a must-have. Mon–Wed 5am–9pm, Thurs–Sat 5am–10pm, Sun 6am–9pm.

★ **Morse's Kraut House** 3856 Washington Rd (Rte-220), Waldoboro ☎ 207 832 5569. Another local landmark, this one peddles chocolates, jams, cheeses and home-made sauerkraut from its endearing German foodstuffs store dating to 1918. The wooden booths fill up quickly for breakfast and lunch. Mon & Tues 10.30am–4pm, Thurs–Sun 8am–4pm; store daily except Wed 9am–6pm.

The Pemaquid Peninsula

From Damariscotta, the **PEMAQUID PENINSULA** (Pemaquid means "long finger" in the native language) points some fifteen miles south along routes 129 and 130, culminating in the rocky **Pemaquid Point**. Visitors to the area, many of them painters, come to muse over this corrugated outcrop, considered to be one of the handsomest in the state – particularly when you factor in the lighthouse.

Colonial Pemaquid

Rte-130 to Huddle Rd then Colonial Pemaquid Rd • Late May to early Sept daily 9am–5pm • $3 • ☎ 207 677 2423, ⓦ friendsofcolonialpemaquid.org

Archeological studies have concluded that **Colonial Pemaquid** was the site of an English settlement in 1626, making it the country's northernmost British colonial settlement. Within the nineteen-acre historical site, which houses a small museum, stands a 1908 replica of **Fort William Henry**, the original built in 1677 by English settlers to ward off pirates, the French, and Native Americans, who are believed to have inhabited the peninsula as early as two thousand years ago. There are good **ocean views** from the top of the massive citadel.

Pemaquid Beach

Snowball Hill Rd • $4 • ⓦ bristolparks.org

The sands of **Pemaquid Beach** are some of the most inviting in the state, and correspondingly crowded on hot summer weekends. Nevertheless, it's a great place to catch some rays, and even though the water can be cold, swimming is not impossible.

Pemaquid Point Lighthouse

At the end of Rte-130 • $2; second floor of keeper's house available for weekly rental, $950.

At the tip of Pemaquid Point, the iconic **Pemaquid Point Lighthouse** sits on a dramatic granite outcrop constantly battered by the violent Atlantic surf. You can wander around the small park and craggy tidepools for a good view of the salt-stained light, built in 1827 and still operational, but be careful not to get too close to the rocks at the water's edge. Pemaquid's beauty is commemorated on the Maine state quarter coin.

Thompson Ice House

Rte-129 South Bristol • July & Aug Mon, Wed, Fri & Sat 1–4pm • Donations accepted; ice blocks $1 apiece • ☎ 207 644 8808, ⓦ thompsonicehouse.com

A potential diversion on the Pemaquid Peninsula is the **Thompson Ice House**, north of South Bristol. Although modern refrigeration has eliminated the ice industry, this house was in operation for 150 years, harvesting ice from a nearby pond and shipping it to points as far away as South America. Business mostly halted here in 1986, but the building, which sports ten-inch-thick sawdust-insulated walls, has been turned into a museum and working ice-harvesting facility. This ice is used to make hand-cranked ice cream for a "social" (open to the public) here in July, and in February, townspeople gather ice from the pond using old-fashioned tools, burying the blocks in hay to keep them cold until summer, when they are sold to local fishermen.

8

GETTING AROUND   THE PEMAQUID PENINSULA

By boat Just north of Pemaquid Beach, in quaint New Harbor, Hardy Boat Cruises (☎1 800 278 3346, ⓦ hardyboat.com) runs daily boat trips in summer (9am & 2pm; check website for rest-of-year schedule) out to Monhegan Island for $32 return (reservations required), in addition to seal watches ($14), puffin watches ($24) and lighthouse cruises ($14).

ACCOMMODATION

Bradley Inn 3063 Bristol Rd, New Harbor ☎207 677 2105, ⓦ bradleyinn.com. Near Pemaquid Point Lighthouse, the fourteen posh guest rooms (and two suites) at this secluded waterfront B&B exhibit good design

---

MAINE LIGHTHOUSES

There are few better places to observe **lighthouses** than on Maine's coast, where some 68 of the structures direct ships along the rocky shoreline. For centuries, Maine's economy has centred on the sea, and its lighthouses are symbols of this dependence (not to mention the saving grace of many a vessel). A series of museums serves to illustrate their history, none more prominent than the **Maine Lighthouse Museum** in Rockland's Chamber of Commerce (see p.485). Some of Maine's most dramatic lighthouses include the lonely **West Quoddy Head Lighthouse** (see p.504), a candy-striped beauty in Lubec and the easternmost point in the US; the scenic **Pemaquid Point Lighthouse**, south of Damariscotta (see below); and the **Portland Head Lighthouse** near Portland (see p.464), commissioned by none other than George Washington.

sense and plenty of character. There's also a restaurant, tavern and spa onsite. $195

The Inn at Round Pond 1442 Rte-32, Round Pond ☏ 207 809 7386, ⓦ theinnatroundpond.com. Adjoined by a lush garden, this 1830s colonial B&B has three spacious suites, all prettily designed with original art, mattresses piled high with pillows and plenty of quiet. Steps from the harbour, and with a bright rainbow of Adirondack chairs on the lawn. Great breakfasts. $165

Sherwood Forest Campsite 9 Campground Circle, near Pemaquid Beach in New Harbor ☏ 1 800 274 1593, ⓦ sherwoodforestcampsite.com. This woodland campsite offers two aquatic options: the ocean is only 800ft away, plus it has its own pool. Also administers several two-bedroom log cabins with full kitchens. Camping May–Oct, cottages year-round. Camping $33; cottages weekly $800

EATING AND DRINKING

Anchor Inn Anchor Inn Rd, Round Pond ☏ 207 529 5584. A good bet for lunch and dinner, with esteemed crab cakes, stuffed lobster, pastas and succulent steaks in a rustic dining room or screened-in porch overlooking the harbour. Mid-May to early Sept daily 11.30am–3pm & 5–9.30pm; call for Oct hours.

★ **Cupboard Café** 137 Huddle Rd, New Harbor ☏ 207 677 3911. A must for breakfast, famed far and wide for its fat, gooey cinnamon rolls. Chowders, overstuffed

sandwiches on home-made bread and robust salads are served in a cavernous log cabin close to Pemaquid Light. Tues–Sat 8am–3pm, Sun till noon.

★ **Shaw's Fish & Lobster Wharf** 129 State Rd (Rte-32), New Harbor ☏ 207 677 2200. A summertime tradition: chowders, sandwiches and, of course, boiled lobsters, which are cracked open and dipped in butter dockside here in the working harbour. For lobster, *Shaw's* is one of the best. Mid-May to Oct daily 11am–9pm.

Monhegan Island

Deliberately low-key **MONHEGAN ISLAND**, eleven miles from the mainland, has long attracted a hardy mix of artists and fishermen. It also attracts its fair share of tourists, but for good reason: it's the most worthwhile jaunt away from the mainland along the entirety of the Maine coast. Not much has changed since artist Robert Henri first came here in the early 1900s looking for tranquillity and solitude – credit cards are not readily accepted, and there are only two public toilets. Though there were already a few artists residing on the island at the time, Henri introduced the place to George Bellows and Rockwell Kent, establishing it as a genuine artists' colony. Edward Hopper also spent time here.

The small village – occupying only twenty percent of the island – huddles around the tiny harbour, protected by Manana and Smutty Nose islands. Other than a few old hotels (book well in advance) and some good restaurants, there's not much here. Some seventeen miles of **hiking trails** crisscross the eastern half of the island, leading through dense stands of fir and spruce to the headlands, 160ft above the island's eastern shore. Monhegan Associates publishes a reliable **trail map**, available at most island stores.

In summer, some of the artists in residence on the island open their **studios** to visitors. For times and locations, check the bulletin boards around town. You can also see works by local artists at one of several **galleries** – the Lupine Gallery (☏ 207 594 8131) at the end of Wharf Hill Road has a consistently good grouping of local works on display.

Monhegan Island Lighthouse and Museum

Museum Daily: July & Aug 11.30am–3.30pm; Sept 1.30–3.30pm • $4 donation • ☏ 207 596 7003, ⓦ monheganmuseum.com

The **Monhegan Island Lighthouse**, on a hill overlooking the village (and a great place to watch the sunset), was erected in 1824 and automated in 1959. You can check out the **Monhegan Museum** inside the former keeper's house, where there's also a building to house rotating works of Monhegan artists, including a few paintings by Rockwell Kent and George Bellows. Other rooms display artefacts, photographs and documents relating to island history and natural features.

BOATS TO MONHEGAN ISLAND

You can access Monhegan from four different towns: Port Clyde, Boothbay Harbor, New Harbor and Muscongus. To ensure a spot with one of the four **boat carriers** connecting the mainland with Monhegan, make sure you reserve in advance. Boats depart from Port Clyde for Monhegan three times daily during the summer and less often during the winter, arriving about an hour later, depending on which boat is in service ($20 one-way, $32 return; ☎ 207 372 8848, ⓦ monheganboat.com).

From Boothbay Harbor you can take the *Balmy Days III* (end of May to mid-Oct; $32 return; ☎ 207 633 2284, ⓦ balmydayscruises.com), which departs once daily at 9.30am and takes ninety minutes. The *Hardy Boat* takes seventy minutes to get from Shaw's Wharf in New Harbor (see p.482) to Monhegan (late May & early Oct departs Wed, Sat & Sun at 9am; June–Sept daily at 9am & 2pm; $32 return; ☎ 1 800 278 3346, ⓦ hardyboat.com). Finally, the 35ft sloop *Friendship* makes six-hour voyages to the island from Muscongus (June–Sept by appointment only; $500 return for up to six people; ☎ 207 380 5460, ⓦ sailmuscongus.com).

ACCOMMODATION

MONHEGAN ISLAND

★ **Island Inn** ☎ 207 596 0371, ⓦ islandmonhegan .com. This sea-salted 1816 summer property is the quintessential Maine hotel. Twenty-eight updated guest rooms (and four spacious suites) have painted floors, oak furniture and bright white beds, but the best amenity is the view – windows look out onto Manana Island and a postcard-perfect harbour. Late May to Oct. Shared bathroom **$165**; en-suite **$220**

★ **John Sterling Harbor House** 5 Wharf Hill Rd ☎ 207 596 2475, ⓦ monhegan.net. Bucolic little property with a range of accommodation: one three-level guesthouse with two bedrooms and a full kitchen, a spacious apartment for four, and single and double rooms with "semi-private" bathrooms. It's a darling space, with fresh pine panelling and harbour views from every room. Rates drop if you rent by the week. May–Oct. Guesthouse **$350**; apartment **$300**; singles **$120**; doubles **$200**

Shining Sails B&B ☎ 207 596 0041, ⓦ shiningsails .com. A stone's throw from the water, this beloved inn comprises five apartments with decks and two simple guest rooms brightened by Monhegan art. Continental breakfast included, and there's a common room with a crackling wood stove. **$145**

Trailing Yew ☎ 207 596 6194. Eclectic but well-regarded, old-fashioned abode, with 33 rooms (some of them singles) spread out among several buildings; many rooms do not have heat or electricity. Cash only. May–Oct. Doubles **$210**; singles **$120**

EATING AND DRINKING

Barnacle Overlooking the wharf. The neighbourhood nucleus, the *Barnacle* is good for light snacks and espresso, with salads, sandwiches and baked goodies. Late May to mid-Oct 8am to late afternoon or early evening.

Fish House Market Fish Beach. Worthy fishmonger doling out top-notch lobster rolls and chowder from a takeaway window. Dig in on picnic tables overlooking the beach. Late May to mid-Oct daily 11.30am–7pm.

Island Inn Overlooking the wharf (see above) ☎ 207 596 0371, ⓦ islandmonhegan.com. Comfortably upscale breakfast, lunch and dinner options (such as seafood stew and sage-roasted chicken) are served in a pastel-pink dining room with the island's best water views. Reservations required for dinner. Mains $19–32. May–Oct Mon–Wed 7.30–9.30am & 6–8pm, Thurs–Sun also 11.30am–1.30pm.

Rockland

Driving down Main Street in seaside **ROCKLAND**, you might observe a rusty old truck to your left and, a minute later, a shiny Mercedes-Benz to your right. Such is the mix of communities that make up the town, one of the more hip settlements in Maine. Rockland has historically been Maine's largest lobster distributor, and boasts the busiest working harbour in the state. In addition to the blue-collar vibe, there is also a strong arts and cultural scene: the town is endowed with some remarkable museums and a happening Art Deco theatre. In the first weekend in August, up to 100,000 visitors descend on Harbor Park for the annual **Maine Lobster Festival** (☎ 1 800 562 2529, ⓦ mainelobsterfestival.com), partly to watch the coronation of the "Maine Sea Goddess" but mainly to feast on sweet shellfish meat – some 20,000 pounds of lobster is consumed over the course of the five-day celebration. The **North Atlantic Blues Festival** (mid-July; ☎ 207 596 6055, ⓦ northatlanticbluesfestival.com) is another popular event.

Farnsworth Art Museum

16 Museum St • Jan–May Wed–Sun 10am–5pm; June–Oct daily 10am–5pm, Wed till 8pm; Nov & Dec Tues–Sun 10am–5pm
• $12, $17 combined ticket with Olson House; June–Oct free 5–8pm on Wed & first Fri of month • ☎ 207 596 6457,
ⓦ farnsworthmuseum.org

The town's centrepiece is the outstanding 1935 **Farnsworth Art Museum**, which comprises several buildings, including the **Wyeth Center**, a converted old church that holds two floors' worth of works by Jamie and N.C. Wyeth. Across the street (at the museum proper), an impressive collection spans two centuries of American art. The focal point is the "Maine in America" exhibit, which displays landscapes and seascapes by Fitz Henry Lane, watercolours by Winslow Homer, and dramatic canvases from the Wyeths. The museum does not own *Christina's World*, Andrew Wyeth's most famous work (it's at the MoMA in New York City), but you can visit the farmhouse depicted in the painting at the **Olson House**, Hathorne Point Road, just outside of town in Cushing (guided tours on the hour: June Wed–Sun noon–5pm; July to mid-Oct Tues–Sun 11am–5pm; $10, or $17 combined with museum admission; ☎ 207 354 0102).

Strand Theatre

345 Main St • Movie tickets $8.50 • ☎ 207 594 0070, ⓦ rocklandstrand.com

Rockland's other star attraction is the Art Deco **Strand Theatre**. Locals frequently step across its threshold in black tie for live Metropolitan Opera broadcasts. Shows here run the gamut from theatre performances and comedy acts to art-house films and live bands.

Maine Lighthouse Museum

1 Park Drive, in the same building as the Chamber of Commerce • May–Oct Mon–Fri 9am–5pm, Sat & Sun 10am–4pm; Nov–April Thurs &
Fri 9am–5pm, Sat 10am–4pm • $5 • ☎ 207 594 3301, ⓦ mainelighthousemuseum.com

Another worthwhile Rockland attraction, the **Maine Lighthouse Museum** allows you to peruse one of the largest collections of lighthouse memorabilia and artefacts in the country. It's fun to press the buttons that trigger various foghorns and bells, but the real attraction is the curator, who probably knows more about lighthouses than anyone in existence.

ROCKLAND BOAT TRIPS

From Rockland's enormous **harbour**, a number of powerboat and **windjammer** companies compete for your business with everything from morning breakfast cruises to week-long island-hopping charters. The majority set sail for three to six days at a time, costing a little more than $175 per night, including all meals. You really can't go wrong with any of the options, but a few boats to try include the luxurious 68ft **Stephen Taber** (☎ 1 800 999 7352, ⓦ stephentaber.com), the three-masted **Victory Chimes**, featured on the Maine state quarter coin (☎ 1 800 745 5651, ⓦ victorychimes.com), or the 95ft **Schooner Heritage** (☎ 1 800 648 4544, ⓦ schoonerheritage.com). If you're having trouble finding what you want, stop by the Chamber of Commerce at 1 Park Drive, or call the Maine Windjammer Association (☎ 1 800 807 9463, ⓦ sailmainecoast.com).

As a fun alternative, **Captain Jack Lobster Boat Adventure** lets you rendezvous with a lobsterman as he pulls up his traps ($30; ☎ 207 542 6852, ⓦ captainjacklobstertours.com). Down the road at 517A Main St, the **Maine State Ferry Service** (☎ 207 596 5400) runs modern vessels out to the summer retreats of Vinalhaven (75min; $17.50) and North Haven (1hr; $17.50), both of which make for relaxing day-trips.

ST GEORGE PENINSULA

South of Rockland, the lovely **St George Peninsula**, in particular the village of Tenants Harbor, inspired writer Sarah Orne Jewett's classic Maine novel *Country of the Pointed Firs*. Jewett describes the landscape so deftly that you can still pick out many of the sites depicted in the book, much of which was written in a tiny schoolhouse in Martinsville, since rebuilt. Boats sail from the hamlet of Port Clyde, at the tip of the peninsula, to **Monhegan Island** (see p.482) You may recognize Port Clyde's picturesque 1857 Marshall Point Lighthouse from the movie *Forrest Gump*; there's a small historical museum in the old keeper's house.

Owls Head Transportation Museum

117 Museum St, Owls Head • Daily 10am–5pm • $10 • ☎ 207 594 4418, ⊛ ohtm.org

The **Owls Head Transportation Museum**, three miles south of Rockland on Rte-73 at Owls Head, is a delightful niche-oriented spot, with a vintage (mostly working) collection of cars, motorcycles and planes from a bygone era, including a full-scale replica of the Wright Brothers' 1903 *Flyer*. In summer, it also has very popular live airplane shows.

ARRIVAL AND DEPARTURE   ROCKLAND

By plane Thanks to Cape Air (☎ 1 800 352 0714, ⊛ flycapeair.com), you can fly to Owls Head's Knox County Regional Airport direct from Boston, for a mere $89 each way.
By train The Maine Eastern Railroad (see box, p.473) pulls in at 4 Union St.

By bus Both Greyhound (☎ 1 800 231 2222, ⊛ greyhound .com) and Concord Coach (☎ 1 800 639 3317, ⊛ concordcoachlines.com) stop at 517A Main St, which doubles as the Maine State Ferry building (see box, p.485).

INFORMATION

Chamber of Commerce 1 Park Drive (May–Oct daily 9am–5pm; Nov–April Mon–Fri 9am–5pm; ☎ 207 596

0376). In the same building as the Lighthouse Museum (see p.485), with comprehensive brochures and information.

ACCOMMODATION

Captain Lindsey House Inn 5 Lindsey St ☎ 207 596 7950, ⊛ lindseyhouse.com. Nine snugly decorated guest rooms in a Federal-style 1835 sea captain's home. A generous English breakfast is included in the rate. $188
★ **LimeRock Inn** 96 Limerock St ☎ 207 594 2257, ⊛ limerockinn.com. Elegant rooms with striped wallpaper and antique cherry furniture in a mint-green Queen Anne mansion. Chat with the lovely hosts on the

wraparound porch. Excellent breakfasts. $159
Ripples Inn at the Harbor ☎ 207 594 5771, ⊛ ripplesinnattheharbor.com. Endearing little Victorian with five cheerfully decorated rooms and nice design details like antique wash stands, wainscoting and hand-painted walls. Run by a gem of a proprietor. Daily breakfast and tea. $150

EATING AND DRINKING

Café Miranda 15 Oak St ☎ 207 594 2034. Eclectic and perennially crowded bistro serving some of the best food in town – an appetizing array of international main dishes ranges from sea scallops with bacon and pasta ($27.50) to veg "wowie" in a curry spice mix ($20.50). Daily 5pm–late.
★ **Home Kitchen Café** 650 Main St ☎ 207 596 2449. Mouthwatering breakfast-all-day joint with wittily named menu items – the "pig's boogie" omelette is made with bacon and red peppers ($8.95). Don't miss the justly famous lobster tacos ($9.75) and cinnamon buns. Mon–Sat 7am–3pm, Sun 8am–2pm.
Lily Bistro 421 Main St ☎ 207 594 4141. Locavore bistro with ten tables and turnip-shaped lightbulbs overhanging

a casual dining room. Mains change daily, but seared sea scallops with sweet-corn risotto ($25) was a recent summer offering. Mon–Fri 11am–2pm & 5–9pm, Sat 5–9pm, Sun 5–8pm.
★ **Miller's Lobster Co.** 83 Eagle Quarry Rd (off Rte-73), Spruce Head ☎ 207 594 7406. Nine miles south of Rockland, this lobster landmark cooks its crustaceans in seawater and serves them on a dock that's bounded by water on three sides. Family-owned since 1977. Mid-June to early Sept daily 11am–7pm.
★ **Primo** 2 S Main St (Rte-73) ☎ 207 596 0770. This fittingly named farm-to-table superstar is one of Maine's top-rated restaurants. The menu is dictated by what's fresh outside – all of its veggies and animals are raised on site – and served

8

in a rambling Victorian house. There's fine dining downstairs, but the second floor, with its copper bar and velvet banquettes, is livelier. Reservations required. Mains $26–41. July & Aug daily 5.30–9.30pm; call for hours rest of year.

Wasses 2 N Main St ☎ 207 594 7472. A Maine favourite, *Wasses* grills its hot dogs in peanut oil, giving them an unbeatable snap, and stuffs them inside freshly steamed buns. Polish your meal off with a cold milk.

Camden

The adjacent communities of Rockport and **CAMDEN** split into two separate towns in 1891 over a dispute as to who should pay for a new bridge over the Goose River, which runs between them; since then, Camden has clearly won the competition for tourists. Today the essential stop in town is **Camden Hills State Park**, which affords beautiful coastal views and has good camping. Camden's other highlight is its huge fleet of schooners known as **windjammers**, many of which date back to the late nineteenth century, when the town was successful in the shipbuilding trade.

Camden's downtown is compact enough to be explored **on foot**. In the centre of town, the immaculately maintained **Harbor Park**, right where the Megunticook River spills into the sea, is a good spot to relax after wandering the town's small shopping district, which runs south from Main Street along the water. Farther down Bayview Street, which holds many of the shops, tiny **Laite Beach** looks out onto the Penobscot Bay.

Camden Hills State Park

280 Belfast Rd (Rte-1) • $4.50 • ☎ 207 236 3109

Just north of town, Rte-1 leads towards **Camden Hills State Park**, the best spot around for **hiking** and camping. Rather than driving up, amble along the **Nature Trail** (1hr) that begins at the visitor centre, which will take you to the top of 790ft Mount Battie. The panoramic views here of the harbour and Maine coastline are hard to beat; on the summit, you can climb to the top of a circular World War I memorial for the best vantage point. It was here that poet Edna St Vincent Millay (see box, p.488) penned part of her poem, *Renascence*, which is commemorated with a small plaque.

8

ARRIVAL AND INFORMATION

CAMDEN

By bus Concord Coach's (☎1 800 639 3317, ⓦconcordcoachlines.com) closest bus stop is in Rockport at the Maritime Farms Convenience Store on Rte-1.

By car Parking can be a problem, but with patience you can usually find something on Chestnut Street or by the police station on Washington St.

Penobscot Bay Regional Chamber of Commerce 2 Public Landing (Mon–Sat 9am–5pm, June–Aug also Sun; ☎ 207 236 4404, ⓦcamdenme.org). This office is usually a big help with finding a place to stay; it also stocks a dizzying array of brochures.

ACCOMMODATION

While accommodation in Camden is plentiful, it is not cheap – it is difficult to find a room for less than $175. The **budget spots** congregate along Rte-1 farther north in Lincolnville. There are innumerable **B&Bs** in the immediate area, but you'd still be well advised to call in advance.

WINDJAMMER TRIPS

Camden's speciality is organizing sailing expeditions of up to six days in large schooners known as **windjammers**. Daysailers, which tour the seas just beyond the harbour, include the *Appledore* (☎ 207 236 8353, ⓦappledore2.com), the *Surprise* (☎ 207 236 4687, ⓦcamdenmainesailing.com) and the *Olad* (☎ 207 236 2323, ⓦmaineschooners.com). Scenic sails on these boats cost around $35 and can often be booked on the same day. Longer **overnight trips**, including all meals, can cost from $595 to $1100 (for 3–6 days) and should be booked in advance; the ships stop at various points of interest along the coast, such as Castine, Stonington and Mount Desert Island. Contact the Maine Windjammer Association (☎1 800 807 WIND, ⓦsailmainecoast.com) for information.

★ **The Belmont** 6 Belmont Ave ☎207 236 8053, ⓦthebelmontinn.com. Decorated with conservative elegance, this stately 1891 Victorian with a wraparound porch sits on a residential street just beyond the commercial district. Guest rooms are gussied up in crisp white and forest green, rich floral prints bedeck the curtains and beds, and window seats, wingback chairs and the occasional working fireplace are tasteful extras. Breakfast (included in the rate) is an event. $179

Camden Maine Stay Inn 22 High St ☎207 236 9636, ⓦcamdenmainestay.com. Beautiful, three-storey white-clapboard 1802 inn, with eight inviting rooms that have polished pine floors, wallpapered walls and decorative flower wreaths. Out back, you can meander in the vast garden or sip lemonade on the lawn. $160

Cedarholm Garden Bay Inn 2159 Atlantic Hwy (Rte-1), Lincolnville ☎207 236 3886, ⓦcedarholm.com. Secluded seaside cottages built for two, some with whirlpool tubs and stone fireplaces, and all with private decks and lots of peace and quiet. The garden is a visual feast. $265

Ducktrap Motel Rte-1, Lincolnville ☎207 789 5400, ⓦducktrapmotel.com. Cute, basic budget option north of town. It also has an ocean-view cottage as well as two larger, family-sized rooms. $85; family rooms $99; cottage $115

The Hawthorn 9 High St ☎1 866 381 3647, ⓦcamdenhawthorn.com. Well situated by the harbour and with nice views of Mount Battie, this Camden favourite has lush gardens, traditional decor, a veranda and a lovely, helpful proprietor. Sited in a rambling Queen Anne Victorian, whose shape leads to fun design details, such as the spacious guest room that's tucked inside a three-storey turret. $140

Inn at Sunrise Point Fire Rd 9 (off Rte-1), Lincolnville ☎207 236 7716, ⓦsunrisepoint.com. This luxurious B&B tends to grace the pages of glossy travel magazines, as well it should – the ten modern rooms, with a touch of vintage Maine charm, all come with private decks, fireplaces and soaking tubs or jacuzzis. Romantic and rejuvenating, the inn overlooks the ocean and a slip of pebbled beach. $395

Lord Camden Inn 24 Main St ☎207 236 4325, ⓦlordcamdeninn.com. If you can, spring for a harbour-view room at this downtown hotel – the windows overlook a postcard-perfect Maine vista. It was once a Masonic temple, but today its 36 rooms are enjoyably modern, with flat-screen TVs and DVD players. Breakfast buffet included. Pet-friendly. $179

★ **Whitehall Inn** 52 High St (Rte-1) ☎207 236 3391, ⓦwhitehall-inn.com. It's tough to beat the 1901 *Whitehall* in the history department: in 1957, the movie classic *Peyton Place* was filmed here, and in 1912, Pulitzer prize winner-to-be Edna St Vincent Millay was "discovered" when she read a poem to partygoers in its lobby. The piano Millay played that night is still on view. A gracious old clapboard inn, it has forty guest rooms with Frette linens and flat-screen TVs that still retain a vintage Maine look. Mid-May to late Oct. $189

CAMPING

Camden Hills State Park 280 Belfast Rd (Rte-1) ☎207 624 9950 or ☎1 800 332 1501; see p.487. Easily the most beautiful campground around, sited on a forested hill near Mount Battie. Campgrounds are well tended and equipped with hot showers and flush toilets. June to mid-Oct. Non-Maine residents $25; Maine residents $15

EATING AND DRINKING

Camden has a good array of eating and drinking spots, from **gourmet restaurants** to **casual seafood joints** to busy bars. One thing is for sure: on **summer weekends**, they're all going to be full, so plan on waiting for a table.

40 Paper 40 Washington St ☎207 230 0111. Belly up to the chrome bar at this contemporary Italian bistro for a muddled mint fizz with gin ($10) or a Caiparinha (made with sugarcane rum and lime; $10). While the mains here

($23–29) are well regarded, it's even nicer just to linger over drinks at happy hour, sampling the antipasti and heavenly grilled flatbread pizzas ($14). Daily 5–9pm.

Boynton-McKay 30 Main St ☎207 236 2465. This

EDNA ST VINCENT MILLAY

Edna St Vincent Millay came to Camden with her divorced mother and two sisters in 1900, when she was 8 years old. Her mother encouraged all the sisters in the arts, and Edna (she insisted on being called "Vincent") excelled in writing. As a young child, she had poems published in *St Nicholas*, a children's magazine, and by age 20 she had won international recognition for her poem, **Renascence**, which she first recited at the *Whitehall Inn* (see above). Today, the inn maintains a small collection of her writings and photos depicting her Camden childhood. Millay reputedly had a rather carefree adulthood: an acknowledged bisexual, she had many **affairs** with women, and when she finally did marry a man, it was on open terms.

one-time soda fountain and apothecary still has its original tiles and old-fashioned wooden booths, and is famed for its breakfasts: order a tall stack of pancakes or eggs over-easy. Tues–Sat 7am–5pm, Sun 8am–4pm; July & Aug also Mon.

Cappy's Chowder House 1 Main St ☎ 207 236 2254. This nautical-themed, wood-panelled, child-friendly bar and restaurant is the place to go in town for a casual drink or meal. It also has an adjacent bakery. Mon–Thurs & Sun 11am–9pm, Fri & Sat 11am–9pm.

★ **Francine** 55 Chestnut St ☎ 207 230 0083. Elegant, candlelit French bistro with aubergine walls. The menu changes daily, but seasonal fare such as haddock with mint and tomato chutney ($23) and melon salad with goat's cheese, cucumbers and crispy prosciutto ($8) are emblematic of its offerings. Reservations recommended. Tues–Sat 5.30–10pm.

Fresh 1 Bayview Landing ☎ 207 236 7005. The name fits the bill at this straight-from-the-farm favourite where mains ($15–24) are prepared simply, allowing the superb ingredients to shine. The dining room has white tablecloths, but the vibe is neighbourly and casual. Lunch is very affordable. Mon, Thurs & Sun 11am–10pm, Tues & Wed 5–10pm, Fri & Sat 11am–11pm.

★ **Long Grain** 31 Elm St ☎ 207 236 9001. *Long Grain's* casual pink-and-gold dining room belies its remarkable Asian cuisine – a sampling of Thai, Vietnamese and Korean fare – that's very well priced (mains $8.50–14). While the ambience is laidback, the kitchen skill level is serious – the chef was a James Beard semi-finalist. Don't skip dessert. Tues–Sat 11.30am–9pm.

Smoothie Shack! 46 Elm St ☎ 207 975 1155. Fresh fruit smoothies and mouthwatering sandwich wraps, like grilled salmon with jasmine rice, served from a takeaway food cart. May–Sept daily 10.30am–4pm.

Rockport

Just over the town line from Camden, **ROCKPORT**'s picturesque Marine Park (off Rte-1), astride the harbour, has a granite statue of the town's most famous former citizen, André the Seal. André was adopted in 1961 after Rockport resident Harry Goodbridge found the little seal pup abandoned in the water. In his lifetime, André spent his winters at the Boston aquarium, and come autumn, would find his way back home to the Goodbridge residence in Rockport (a distance of 150 miles). At one point he was made honorary harbour-master, and in 1978, helped to unveil this statue of himself.

The tiny town centre holds a couple of intriguing galleries, such as the **Center for Maine Contemporary Art**, 162 Russell Ave ($5 donation; ☎ 207 236 2875, ⓦ cmcanow.org), where regional artists display their works, and the **Maine Media Workshops**, at 70 Camden St (☎ 207 236 8581, ⓦ mainemedia.edu), well known for its school of photography.

Aldermere Farm

70 Russell Ave • Tours July & Aug Fri 10–11am • Free • ☎ 207 236 2739, ⓦ aldermere.org

Don't underestimate the magnetism of the Belted Galloway cows at **Aldermere Farm**, on Russell Avenue. These endearing "Oreo cows" (so named for their black-white-black stripe pattern) have been amusing passers-by for ages. The farm gives tours in summer, but most people just pop by for a glimpse of the belties, who are nearly always in view of their camera-snapping fans.

ARRIVAL AND DEPARTURE

ROCKPORT

By bus Concord Coach (☎ 1 800 639 3317, ⓦ concordcoachlines.com) pulls into the Maritime Farms Convenience Store on Rte-1.

EATING AND DRINKING

Shepherd's Pie 18 Central St ☎ 207 236 8500. Run by the masterminds behind *Francine* (see above), this neighbourly pub with a pressed-tin ceiling is currently *the* place to dine or drink in Rockport. Don't expect low-grade bar food either – the renowned chef cranks out upscale delights like roast duck breast with pears ($22) and chicken liver toasts ($5). Daily 4–11.30pm.

8

Belfast

Cosy **BELFAST** feels like the most liveable of the towns along the Maine coast. Here the shipbuilding boom is long since over, but the inhabitants have had the waterfront declared a historic district, sparing it from over-commercialization. As you stroll around, look out for the town's Greek Revival houses, particularly prevalent along the wide avenues between Church and Congress streets. Belfast was a lively centre in the 1960s, and its allegiance to its local food co-op, in addition to its many art galleries and festivals, attest to its continued vibrancy.

Penobscot Marine Museum

40 E Main St (Rte-1), Searsport · Late May to Oct Mon–Sat 10am–5pm, Sun noon–5pm · $8 · ☎ 207 548 0334, ⊛ penobscot marinemuseum.org

Searsport, five miles north of Belfast on Rte-1, is home to the atmospheric **Penobscot Marine Museum**, which displays marine artworks and nautical artefacts spread amongst a campus of historic buildings. Keep an eye out for the nineteenth-century sea captain's home, which counts among its furnishings a very cool vintage record player and a piano with mother-of-pearl keys.

ARRIVAL AND DEPARTURE
BELFAST

By bus Concord Coach (☎1 800 639 3317, ⊛ concordcoachlines.com) stops at the Dead River convenience store (Shell gas station) at 22 Belmont Ave (Rte-3).

INFORMATION

Belfast Area Chamber of Commerce At the foot of Main St by the bay (June–Sept daily 9am–6pm; rest of year Mon–Fri 10am–6pm; ☎ 207 338 5900). A convivial local office where you can pick up a copy of the *Belfast Historic Walking Tour*.

ACCOMMODATION

Alden House 63 Church St ☎ 207 338 2151, ⊛ thealdenhouse.com. A beautiful 1840 Greek Revival house run as a B&B by two genial hostesses. Guest rooms are an alluring mix of old and new, with original marble sinks rubbing shoulders with antique cherry furniture and contemporary loveseats. April to mid-Jan. **$149**

BUCKSPORT

Named after founder Colonel Jonathan Buck, quiet **BUCKSPORT** (twenty miles north from Belfast on Rte-3) was first settled as a trading post in 1762. These days, it's known for the **Penobscot Narrows Observatory** on the bridge (daily: July & Aug 9am–6pm; May, June, Sept & Oct till 5pm; $7; ☎ 207 469 7719), which whisks gazers up inside a 420ft viewing station. On a clear day you can see out to Mount Desert Island and Katahdin, but even if it's cloudy, it's a thrill to look down and see ant-sized traffic moving below.

The hulking **Fort Knox**, adjacent to the observatory (and where you buy your tickets; May–Oct daily 9am–sunset; admission included with observatory fee; ☎ 207 469 6553), merits a wander round its castle-like structure. You can climb up and down circular stairways, stagger through tunnels that disappear into total darkness, investigate officers' quarters, and clamber to the top of the fort's thick granite walls, from where you can admire Bucksport's paper mill skyline. With all the cannon mounts – there are over 130 in all – it's hard to believe this place never saw any action.

Northeast Historic Film, in the restored 1916 Alamo Theater building at 85 Main St in Bucksport (☎ 207 469 0924 or ☎ 207 469 6910 for event info, ⊛ oldfilm.org), is also worth a look. NHF collects and screens film and video related to the history and heritage of northern New England; this even includes your old family films, which they'll edit and store for free. Call in advance and ask about tours – they'll take you into their amazing (and freezing) climate-controlled film storage room, and show you the ins and outs of their equipment setup.

Belfast Bay Inn 72 Main St ☎207 338 5600, ⓦ belfastbayinn.com. You'll want for naught in one of these eight stately suites: rooms come complete with snug sitting areas, smart decor and modern amenities like HDTV, the daily paper and breakfast in bed. Convenient location right in the heart of downtown. **$268**

★ **Carriage House Inn** 120 E Main St (Rte-1), 7 miles east of Belfast in Searsport ☎207 548 2167, ⓦ carriagehouseinmaine.com. Rambling 1874 "Painted Lady" Victorian with three colourfully wallpapered, high-ceilinged guest rooms. An original mural by one-time resident Waldo Peirce, Ernest Hemingway's best friend and portrait artist, was recently uncovered in an upstairs hall. Great breakfasts, and its very own ghost. **$110**

EATING AND DRINKING

Bay Wrap Daily 20 Beaver St ☎207 338 9757. Healthy, inventive wrap sandwiches with fun names like "To 'Thai' For" – grilled chicken, spicy peanut sauce and jasmine rice in a flour tortilla. Mon–Wed 7am–6pm, Thurs & Fri until 8pm, Sat until 7pm.

★ **Chase's Daily** 96 Main St ☎207 338 0555. Lunchtime bliss: a dining room bathed in sunlight, walls bedecked with oil paintings, an innovative menu and an on-site farmstand that sells bouquets of flowers and fresh herbs. *Chase's* terrific vegetarian fare consists of robust salads, sandwiches and more eclectic offerings like pizza with turnip greens ($11) and soft corn tacos ($11). Tues–Thurs & Sat 11am–2.30pm, Fri also 5.30pm–late, Sun 8am–1pm.

Darby's 155 High St ☎207 338 2339. Dishes out delicious food such as pecan haddock, *phad Thai* and filet mignon; they also have an adjoining pub that specializes in Scotch whiskies. Mon–Thurs 11.30am–3.30pm & 5pm–close, Fri–Sun 7.30am–11pm.

Three Tides 2 Pinchy Lane ☎207 338 1707. Hip, harbourside tapas spot that brews its own beer (with seventeen on tap) and runs its own lobster pound on site; the small dining room is lit by lampshades, and in summer, there's bocce ball and nightly fires in the beer garden. Tues–Sun 4pm–late.

Young's Lobster Pound 3 Fairview St, East Belfast ☎207 338 1160. Across the bay, *Young's* serves up fresh-boiled lobster dinners with sunset views. Daily 7.30am–8pm.

8

Down East Maine

So called because sailors heading east along the coast were also usually heading downwind, **Down East Maine** has engendered plenty of debate over its boundaries – some wish to draw its western line at Ellsworth, or Belfast, or even include the entire state in their definition. It's all a matter of pride, of course; to be a "downeaster" means to be tough and fiercely independent. For the purposes of this guide, we've defined "Down East" as the Maine coast east of Bucksport, including the **Blue Hill Peninsula**, home to several idyllic, secluded seaside towns; the extremely popular **Mount Desert Island**; and the one hundred miles of nearly deserted shoreline stretching from Ellsworth to **West Quoddy Head**, the point farthest east in the US.

As you make your way up the coast – particularly once you pass Mount Desert Island and **Acadia National Park** – the terrain and the population become more rugged and less prone to tourism. Also noteworthy are the area's mesmerizing fogs – the coast near the Canadian border is enshrouded in a wispy pouf on and off for a good half of the year.

The Blue Hill Peninsula

It used to be that the **Blue Hill Peninsula**, extending south from Bucksport, was a sleepy expanse of land, too far off the primary roads to attract much attention. But word is slowly getting out about this beautiful area, blanketed with wild blueberry bushes and dotted with both dignified old towns like **Castine** and **Blue Hill** and fishing villages like **Stonington** and **Deer Isle**. Even farther off the established tourist trail, **Isle au Haut** is a remote outpost accessible only by mail boat. In the smaller towns between, you'll find close-knit communities that can trace their ties to the peninsula back for several generations. As you might expect, the main draw down here is the tranquillity that comes with isolation, and while the area presents ample opportunities for exploration, you might find yourself content with a good book, an afternoon nap, a gourmet meal and a night in a posh B&B.

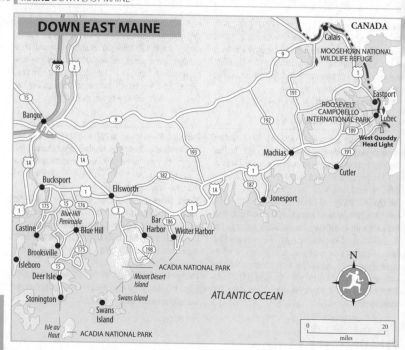

8

Blue Hill

Plenty of folks come to **BLUE HILL**, at the intersection of routes 172, 176 and 15 adjacent to the Blue Hill Harbor, simply to relax, but you could get involved with the lively music scene – it runs a popular **chamber music festival** every summer (ⓦkneisel .org), and is the self-proclaimed "Steel Drum Capital of Downeast Maine" (ⓦflashin thepans.org). Also in town, the Bagaduce Music Lending Library, at 5 Music Library Lane (ⓞ207 374 5454), loans out over 215,000 pieces of sheet music from its big, red barn of a building. The best time to visit Blue Hill is Labor Day weekend, when oxen pulling, sheep dog trials, fireworks and carnival rides are all part of the **Blue Hill Fair** ($5; ⓦbluehillfair.com), which served as inspiration for E.B. White's *Charlotte's Web*.

Several well-known writers, including E.B. White, have made their homes in the Blue Hill Peninsula. Blue Hill proper boasts two excellent **bookstores**: North Light Books, 58 Main St (ⓞ207 374 5422), is a great source for **travel books** and maps as well as fiction, speciality titles and art supplies; the larger Blue Hill Books, 26 Pleasant St (ⓞ207 374 5632), is a more comprehensive independent bookseller.

It's a thirty- to 45-minute walk up to the top of **Blue Hill Mountain**, from where you can see across the Blue Hill Bay to the dramatic ridges of Mount Desert Island. The trailhead is not difficult to find, halfway down Mountain Road between routes 15 and 172.

Castine

CASTINE, nearly surrounded by water on the northern edge of the Penobscot Bay, is one of New England's most quietly beautiful towns, with nicely kept gardens, enormous elm trees and a peaceful sophistication. The town's small population is a mix of summer residents, a number of well-known poets and writers (Elizabeth Hardwick, founder of *The New York Review of Books*, lived here until her death in 2007) and year-round locals, many of whom are employed by the **Maine Maritime Academy**, with buildings both along the water and back on Pleasant Street. It's pretty tough to miss the *State of Maine*,

AQUATIC ACTIVITIES IN BLUE HILL

South on Rte-175, **Blue Hill Falls** is a good spot to give kayaking a try: the Activity Shop in Blue Hill at 61 Ellsworth Rd (Rte-172; ☎207 374 3600, ⓦtheactivityshop.com) has canoe and kayak rentals that it will even deliver to your door ($25/day and up; reservations recommended). In summer, the Marine Environmental Research Institute (**MERI**) at 55 Main St (☎207 374 2135, ⓦmeriresearch.org) runs eco-cruises ($40, children $20) and island excursions ($60, children $40) where you might spot a seal, examine a tidepool or pull up lobster traps. Castine Kayak (☎207 866 3506, ⓦcastinekayak.com) also runs various **sea-kayaking** tours ($55–105, includes equipment and instruction) from Eatons Wharf at the public boat landing. Captain Bill at Old Quarry Ocean Adventures (see p.494) in Stonington (☎207 367 8977, ⓦoldquarry.com) runs excellent kayaking, boating and camping trips as well as lobster bakes and lighthouse cruises.

the huge ship that's usually docked at the landing (except in May and June) and is used to train the academy's students, who give tours in the summer (call ☎207 326 4311 for schedules, or simply walk up the plank and ask). Take a stroll down **Perkins Street** to check out the string of enormous mansions looking out over the water. Between these ostentatious summer retreats are a number of old historic buildings, such as the 1665 **John Perkins House**, the town's earliest, which is occasionally open to the public.

Deer Isle

DEER ISLE – all scenic inlets, hilly byways and woodlands – is one of the most idyllic regions in this state that's known for its beauty. Head over the narrow, elevated suspension bridge and sample the preserves at **Nervous Nellie's Jams and Jellies**, set in a quirky sculpture garden at 600 Sunshine Rd (☎1 800 777 6845, ⓦnervousnellies.com). Nearby, you can stroll the waterfront campus of the **Haystack Mountain School of Crafts** (☎207 348 2306, ⓦhaystack-mtn.org), and contemplate whether to sign up for a blacksmithing or bookbinding class.

Stonington

Few places are more remote than beguiling **STONINGTON**, a fishing village whose residents have long had a reputation for superior seamanship. Over the past hundred years, the place, all the way at the end of Rte-15, has found hard-earned prosperity in the sardine-canning and granite-quarrying businesses; now it has turned to lobstering. Aside from its hundred-year-old main street, the draw here is the harbour – which is as beautiful as anything you'll see in Acadia National Park. For nightlife, the restored **Opera House** (☎207 367 2788, ⓦoperahousearts.org) always has something interesting going on, be it a first-run movie or a Shakespeare performance. During the Opera House's annual jazz festival, New Orleans bands parade with dancing crowds beside the town's scenic waterfront.

Isle au Haut

Mail boats headed for **ISLE AU HAUT** (pronounced "I'll ah hoe") depart from the Stonington landing several times daily ($37 round-trip; ☎207 367 5193). On this lonely island, you can explore the trails of the less-visited part of **Acadia National Park**, highlighted by the rocky shoreline, bogs and stands of spruce trees. Alternatively, you can charter your own boat for a reasonable price from Captain Bill in Stonington (see above) who, in addition to Isle au Haut, will take you anywhere on the Maine coast.

ARRIVAL AND GETTING AROUND	BLUE HILL PENINSULA

The Blue Hill Peninsula is deceptively large and, with somewhat indirect roads, it can take well over an hour to reach its southernmost point. It's a good idea to pick up a detailed **DeLorme gazetteer** (see p.470) or locally produced map before you set out, as the streets around here are quite confusing (some even have the same name).

By car Driving is the best way to get to and around the Blue Hill Peninsula, as there is no public transport.

By bike Cycling is a good way to get around. Your best bet for renting is the Activity Shop (☎ 207 374 3600, ⓦ theactivityshop.com), which also offers kayak and canoe rentals.

INFORMATION

Blue Hill Peninsula Chamber of Commerce 107 Main St, in Blue Hill proper (☎ 207 374 3242). Most inns and shopkeepers are also well equipped to provide just about all the information you need, including regional maps.

ACCOMMODATION

There's a nice variety of **accommodation** on the Blue Hill Peninsula, ranging from B&Bs to motels. Plan to spend $135 or more per night in summer. *Old Quarry Ocean Adventures*, in Stonington (see box, p.493), has a bunkhouse and a number of off-shore island rentals.

BLUE HILL AND AROUND

★ **Barncastle Hotel** 125 South St ☎ 207 374 2330, ⓦ barn-castle.com. This grandiose 1880s hotel, originally built as the summer mansion for a nineteenth-century opera manager, is full of delightful architectural twists and turns, such as a steepled ceiling in one of its guest rooms. Come dinnertime, emerge from one of the four lavish guest rooms for pizza in the downstairs pub. May–Aug. $135

Blue Hill Inn 40 Union St ☎ 207 374 2844, ⓦ bluehillinn.com. Romantic 1830 inn with inviting rooms and decor. Guests are treated to outstanding gourmet meals. A small apartment, Cape House, is available in winter for $195 per night, two-night minimum. May–Oct. $175

Oakland House 435 Herrick Rd, Brooksville ☎ 207 359 8521, ⓦ oaklandhouse.com. Stay in one of ten well-maintained cottages strewn about the property, all with kitchens or kitchenettes, fireplaces and lake access, in a remote area along the Eggemoggin Reach. Family owned for generations. Longer stays encouraged. Six nights $702

CASTINE

Manor Inn 76 Battle Ave ☎ 207 326 4861, ⓦ manor-inn.com. Constructed as a summer home for a yachting commodore, the *Manor* looks a little incongruously like a sort of castle. The inn offers fourteen rooms decorated in eclectic lodge style, plus immediate access to trails, yoga classes, fine dining and pub fare. Pet-friendly. $125

★ **Pentagöet Inn** 26 Main St ☎ 1 800 845 1701, ⓦ pentagoet.com. A welcoming 1894 Victorian inn with sixteen rooms restored by the antique-buff owners. There is also a quiet and sophisticated pub, *Passports*, a wraparound porch and great fine dining. They'll even lend you a bicycle. May–Oct. $165

DEER ISLE

Deer Isle Homestead Hostel 65 Tennis Rd ☎ 207 348 2308, ⓦ deerislehostel.com. Set amid spruce trees and an organic garden, this woodsy six-bed hostel was crafted from scratch by its owners. There's a woodstove for cooking, solar showers, an indoor composting toilet and access to three miles of shoreline trails. $25

Pilgrim's Inn 20 Main St ☎ 207 348 6615, ⓦ pilgrimsinn.com. Dating way back to 1793, the twelve rooms (and three cottages) at this barn-like post-and-beam inn are tastefully decorated with antique headboards and floral bedding. The *Whale's Rib Tavern*, one of the island's best restaurants, is also on-site. Mid-May to mid-Oct. $149

STONINGTON

Boyce's Motel 44 Main St ☎ 207 367 2421, ⓦ boycesmotel.com. Centrally located, basic, clean rooms complemented by a very cool owner. There are also full apartments with kitchens and living rooms. Doubles $69; apartments $95

★ **Inn on the Harbor** 45 Main St, ☎ 207 367 2420, ⓦ innontheharbor.com. Stonington's fanciest accommodation, with plush bedding and good amenities (wi-fi, TVs, binoculars). It also has the best location – you could practically do a cannonball into the harbour from your room. Breakfast included. $145

★ **Pres du Port B&B** W Main St, at Highland Ave ☎ 207 367 5007. Cheerfully furnished 1849 B&B with a great view from the rooftop crow's nest and a berry-filled breakfast in the morning. Also has one endearing little room for just $50. Vintage Maine. Cash or cheque only. June–Oct. $150

EATING AND DRINKING

There's a lot of good **food** to be had on the peninsula, but keep in mind that distances between towns are deceptively large. The Blue Hill **farmers' market** is held Saturday mornings in summer (June–Aug 9–11.30am) at the Blue Hill Fairgrounds on Rte-172.

BLUE HILL AND AROUND

Arborvine 33 Tenney Hill (upper Main St/Rte-172) ☎ 207 374 2119. Contemporary fare like mushroom and leek risotto and Damariscotta River oysters, served in an

1800s-style home. There's also a more casual attached wine bar, *The Vinery*. Reservations recommended. Tues–Sun 5.30–9pm in July & Aug; call for hours rest of year.
Bagaduce Lunch Frank's Flat Rd (Rte-176), Penobscot ☎ 207 326 4197. After a God-like voice calls your order out over the speakers, head to pick up baskets of delicately fried shellfish and feast by a little bridge with rushing falls. May–Sept Mon, Tues & Thurs–Sun 11am–7pm, Wed 11am–3pm.
El El Frijoles 41 Caterpillar Hill Rd (Rte-15), Sargentville ☎ 207 359 2486. Worth visiting for the name alone (it's a riff on L.L. Bean), this casual, California-style taqueria serves up brilliant burritos, fresh salsas and house-made *agua fresca*. Wed–Sun 11am–8pm.

CASTINE

Bah's Bakehouse and Stella's Jazz Nocturnal 26 Water St ☎ 207 326 9510 (Stella's ☎ 207 326 9710). Upstairs is a morning and lunch spot, with coffee, breakfast sandwiches, baked goods, and eclectic deli offerings like Thai noodles and shepherd's pie; downstairs is a fun night-time hangout, with live music on weekends and elegant mains like lobster cobb salad and brick-oven pizza. June–Aug: Bah's daily 7am–3pm; Stella's Mon–Wed 4–11pm, Thurs–Sun 4pm–midnight.
The Breeze On the waterfront ☎ 207 326 9200. It doesn't get much better than takeaway pints of fried clams and haddock, lobster rolls, burgers and ice cream eaten on picnic tables by the water and the hulking *State of Maine*. May–Oct 8am–8pm.
The Pentagoet Inn Main St ☎ 207 326 8616. Lobster

bouillabaisse, warm asparagus salad with prosciutto crisps, and pistachio-dusted diver scallops, served on mismatched china in an elegant dining room. Call for hours and reservations.

DEER ISLE

Whale's Rib Tavern In the Pilgrim's Inn (see p.494), 20 Main St ☎ 207 348 5222, ⓦ pilgrimsinn.com. Exceptional dinner mains ($12–28) in a wood-panelled, historic barn with water views. The menu ranges from haddock chowder to ribs to sticky toffee pudding. Reservations recommended. Mid-May to mid-Oct. July & Aug daily 5–8.30pm; call for hours at other times.

STONINGTON

Harbor Café Main St ☎ 207 367 5099. A salty ambience – it's where the fishermen come in the morning – with sandwiches, coffee and muffins; right in the centre of town.
Lily's Café and Wine Bar 450 Airport Rd, at Rte-15 ☎ 207 367 5936. Everything about *Lily's* is wonderfully local – the ingredients, the diners – it's not even open at the weekend. No matter where you're from, however, you'll feel right at home ordering her just-like-mum's sandwiches and soups. Mon–Thurs Fri 9am–4pm, Fri 5–8pm.
Seasons 27 Main St, Stonington ☎ 207 367 2600. Pristine café with 250 wines complementing its New American menu. You'll also find espresso, striped banquettes and spectacular views of the harbour. A real local favourite, *Seasons* is hopping in winter. Daily 11.30am–2.30pm, Wed–Sun also 5–8.30pm; call ahead to confirm winter hours.

8

Mount Desert Island

Considering that **Mount Desert Island** boasts not only a genuine fjord but also the highest headland on the entire Atlantic coast north of Rio de Janeiro, it is an astonishingly small place, measuring just fifteen by twelve miles. The most accessible of Maine's three hundred islands (it's been linked to the mainland by bridge since 1836), it also has the best facilities and offers water- and land-based activities galore.

EN ROUTE TO MOUNT DESERT ISLAND: ELLSWORTH

Aside from a short strip of quaint brick cafés along the old part of Main Street (Rte-1), most of **Ellsworth** has been overdeveloped into a sprawl of parking lots and chain stores. There's predictably little to see, although you might check out the **Woodlawn Museum**, on Rte-172 just south of Rte-1 (June–Sept Tues–Sat 10am–5pm, Sun 1–4pm; May & Oct Tues–Sun 1–4pm; $10; ☎ 207 667 8671) a splendid 1820s Federal house with original furnishings amidst a pleasant park and two miles of trails. Also in town, antiques peddler **Big Chicken Barn Books** (1768 Bucksport Rd/Rte-1 ☎ 207 667 7308), is a godsend on rainy days, with everything from beach reads and kooky vintage lamps to jewellery and antique maps crammed inside its colossal post-and-beam structure. Otherwise, stop only for provisions or a quick bite to eat before you head south to Mount Desert Island; foodies rave about the tapas at **Cleonice**, 112 Main St (☎ 207 664 7554).

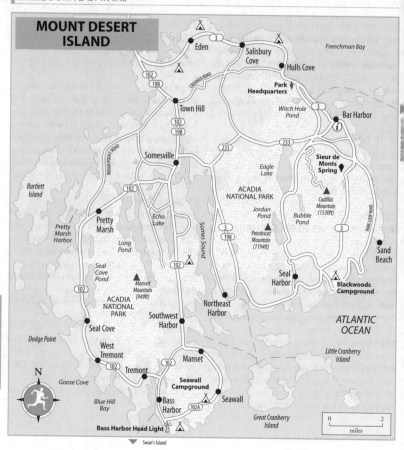

After painters Thomas Cole and Frederic Church depicted the island in mid-nineteenth-century works, word spread about its barren beauty, and by the end of the century, tourism was a fixture here. America's wealthiest families – among them the Rockefellers, Pulitzers and Fords – erected palatial estates in **Bar Harbor**, and established the organization that would later work to create Acadia National Park, the first national park donated entirely by private citizens. In 1947, a fire destroyed many of the grand cottages, including Bar Harbor's "Millionaires' Row". The fire didn't tarnish the island's lustre, however, and the place now attracts holidaying middle-class families and outdoor enthusiasts in addition to the rich.

Somes Sound roughly divides the island in half; the east side is more developed and ritzy, holding the island's social centre and travel hub, **Bar Harbor**, as well as **Northeast Harbor**, the site of huge summer homes. The west side, known to some as the "quiet side", is less harried, with a few fishing villages and year-round settlements like **Southwest Harbor**, fast catching on as a popular destination in its own right (and in many ways preferable to Bar Harbor). **Acadia National Park**, which covers much of the island, has great opportunities for camping, cycling, canoeing, kayaking, hiking and birdwatching, though you're hardly ever very far from civilization.

Bar Harbor

The town of **BAR HARBOR** began life as an exclusive resort – it was the summer home of both Vanderbilts and Astors – but a great fire in October 1947 destroyed their opulent "cottages" and changed the direction of the town's growth. Many of the old-money families rebuilt their summer estates in hyper-rich **Northeast Harbor**, southwest along Rte-3, and Bar Harbor is now firmly geared towards tourists – though it's by no means downmarket. To take in the scene, stroll around the village green and walk along the **Shore Path** past the headland of the *Bar Harbor Inn* and up the coast for views of the ocean and Frenchman Bay.

Robert Abbe Museum

26 Mount Desert St • Late May to early Nov daily 10am–5pm; Nov, Dec & Feb–May Thurs–Sat 10am–4pm • $6; admission includes Sieur de Monts location • ☎ 207 288 3519, ⓦ abbemuseum.org

One of the town sights in its heyday was the "Indian Village", a summer encampment to which Native Americans came to sell pottery, necklaces and trinkets to tourists. Nowadays, Wabanaki heritage – and current happenings – are preserved in a far more inspiring place: the **Robert Abbe Museum**. Although the opening displays on Wabanaki culture are well put together, the Abbe's knockout piece is the "Circle of the Four Directions", a contemplative space built of cedar panels that span upward into an arced skylight. If that's not enough to wow you, they even have an original artwork from glass wizard Dale Chihuly. The museum's original building, which shows Maine archeological finds and relates the history of the institution, is included in the admission price, and is just a couple of miles south of Bar Harbor at Sieur de Monts Spring, right off the Park Loop Road (daily late May to mid-Oct 10am–5pm).

Acadia National Park

Open 24hr (weather permitting) • $20/car for a 7-day pass • ☎ 207 288 3338, ⓦ nps.gov/acad

Acadia National Park, which covers most of Mount Desert Island, the Schoodic Peninsula to the east, and Isle au Haut (see p.493) to the south, is the most visited natural place in Maine. It's visually stunning, with dramatic rolling hills carving smooth silhouettes into the misty horizon. Dense stands of fir and birch trees hide over 120 miles of **hiking trails** (see box, p.499) that pop into view on the island's 26 summits. In fact, there's all you could want here in terms of mountains and lakes for secluded rambling, and sightings of **wildlife** such as seals, beavers and bald eagles are not uncommon. The two main geographical features are the narrow fjord of **Somes Sound**, which almost splits the island in two, and **Cadillac Mountain**, an unbelievable place to watch the sunrise, though the summit of the 1530ft mount offers tremendous ocean views at any time of the day (assuming clear weather). It can be reached either by a moderately strenuous climb – more than you'd want to do before breakfast – or by a very leisurely drive, winding up a low-gradient road. Many visitors do nothing more than drive the length of the 27-mile Park Loop Road, which admittedly winds through some of the park's most arresting areas, but you should also make the effort to get onto the trails.

8

OUT TO SEA

In high season, over twenty different **sea trips** set off each day from Bar Harbor, for purposes ranging from deep-sea fishing to cocktail cruises. Among the most popular are the **whale-watching**, puffin and seal trips run by Bar Harbor Whale Watch Company, 1 West St (3hr; $58; ☎ 207 288 2386, ⓦ barharborwhales.com). With Downeast Windjammer Cruises, you can enjoy a two-hour trip on the **schooner** *Margaret Todd* (leaving from the *Bar Harbor Inn* pier daily June–Oct; $37.50; ☎ 207 288 4585, ⓦ downeastwindjammer.com). Lulu Lobster Boat Rides ($30; ☎ 207 963 2341, ⓦ lululobsterboat.com) offers authentic **lobstering** trips with Captain John, who raises traps and charms riders with nautical folklore.

BAR HARBOR

ACCOMMODATION
2 Cats	5
Bar Harbor Inn	1
Bass Cottage Inn	4
Manor House Inn	2
Seacroft Inn	6
Ullikana	3

EATING & DRINKING
2 Cats	6
Atlantic Brewing Company	5
The Burning Tree	4
Café this Way	10
Carmen Verandah's	7
Dog & Pony Tavern	2
Havana	11
Jordan Pond	13
Lompoc Café & Brew Pub	3
Mâche Bistro	1
Mount Desert Island Ice Cream	8 & 12
Reel Pizza Cinerama	9

Abbe Museum (Sieur de Monts location) & Rte-3 ▼

The most enjoyable way to explore is to rent a **bicycle** (see p.500) and cycle around the 45 miles of gravel-surfaced "**carriage roads**," built by John D. Rockefeller, Jr as a protest against the 1913 vote that allowed "infernal combustion engines" onto the island. Keep an eye out for the ornate **granite bridges**, commissioned by Rockefeller and built by architects William Welles Bosworth and Charles Stonington.

Southwest Harbor and Bass Harbor

The western half of Mount Desert Island was for many years unflatteringly called the "Backside" by the well-heeled residents of Bar Harbor. These days, though, as Bar Harbor gets more and more touristy, the "quiet side" of Mount Desert is often a better place to be, with a less harried downtown and (arguably) better restaurants and scenery.

SOUTHWEST HARBOR, along Rte-102 across from Northeast Harbor, is the centre of this side's action, so to speak. The small "downtown" is graced with a couple of top-notch places to eat and the surrounding area has a smattering of cosy, out-of-the-way accommodation. Convenient for visiting neighbouring Swans Island or Long Island, the state ferry is only a couple of miles away in Bass Harbor, and both Southwest and Northeast Harbor provide access to the Cranberry Islands.

South along Rte-102, **BASS HARBOR** is even further removed, the simple homes that line its streets reflecting the modest lifestyle of its residents. At the southernmost tip of the island, just off Rte-102A, you'll find **Bass Harbor Head Light**, perched on the rocks and tucked behind the trees. Though the 1858 structure is not open to visitors, you can walk down a short seaside path for a good view of the lighthouse and the ocean. If you prefer to explore the water itself, take a three-and-a-half-hour **cruise** from Island Cruises ($29; ☎207 244 5785), to the fishing village of Frenchboro on Long Island, or a two-hour nature cruise aboard the 40ft *R.L.Gott* (mid-June to mid-Oct; $25). The Maine State Ferry also runs **boats** between Bass Harbor, Swans Island and Frenchboro several days a week (☎207 244 3254).

ARRIVAL AND DEPARTURE

MOUNT DESERT ISLAND

BY PLANE

Mount Desert is accessible by airplane. Flights into Bar Harbor are relatively infrequent and expensive – Bar Harbor/Hancock County Airport (☎207 667 7329), on Rte-3 in Trenton, has a limited service run by Colgan Air. Flights are more feasible via Bangor International Airport, 45 miles away, which is served by Delta, US Airways and Allegiant Air, and there is a shuttle bus that links Bar Harbor and Bangor ($35, cash only; ☎207 479 5911).

BY BUS

West's Coastal Connections buses ($11 one-way; ☎207 546 2823 or ☎1 800 596 2823, ⓦwestbusservice .com) travel between Bangor and the border town of Calais via Ellsworth.

BY CAR

If you're driving, Mount Desert is easy enough to get to from Rte-1 via Rte-3, although in summer roads on the island itself get congested. Public transport is minimal beyond Bar Harbor, though once there, you can take advantage of the free Island Explorer shuttle buses (ⓦexploreacadia.com), which have eight routes traversing Acadia that loop back to Bar Harbor.

8

HIKING ON MOUNT DESERT ISLAND

It's no secret that Mount Desert Island offers some of the most exhilarating **hiking** in New England. Though by no means exhaustive, the following list highlights some of the best hikes. If you plan on exploring extensively, get your hands on a copy of the detailed guide *A Walk in the Park*, published locally ($15) and available at the park visitor centre. Rangers can also provide you with decent free maps of the trails.

EASY

Flying Mountain Trail 5min north of Southwest Harbor, just off Rte-103 on Fernald Point Rd. This 0.7-mile hike affords beautiful views at the top of 284ft Flying Mountain (1hr).

Jordan Pond Shore Trail From the Jordan Pond parking area. A 3.3-mile loop that roughly follows the water's edge (2hr).

Ship Harbor Nature Trail At the southern end of the park off Rte-102A near the Bass Harbor Head Light. An easy 1.3-mile trail that loops out along the coast and back (45min).

MODERATE

Bubble Rock Trail Starting at Bubble Rock parking area. Two one-mile forest loop trails, with some vistas of Jordan Pond (1hr).

Great Head Loop Beginning at Sand Beach on the Park Loop Rd. Scenic 1.5-mile trail leading along towering cliffs right above the sea (45min).

South Ridge Trail Departing from Rte-3, near the Blackwoods Campground. This trail is the best way to get to the top of Cadillac Mountain, the highest point on the island (1530ft). The 7.4-mile round-trip is not particularly strenuous, and very rewarding (5hr).

STRENUOUS

Acadia Mountain Trail A few miles south of Somesville, on the east side of Rte-102. A relatively steep ascent to the top of the 700ft mountain, with fine views of the Somes Sound. 2.5 miles round-trip (1hr 30min).

The Beehive Just north of the Sand Beach parking area. A short one-mile trip up iron rungs on exposed ledges. There's a swimming pond near the top called the Bowl (45min).

Mansell Mountain At the south end of Long Pond, near Southwest Harbor. Trees impede the views from the 950ft summit, but the two-mile hike along the Perpendicular Trail features stairways carved into the rock and unparalleled seclusion (2hr).

Penobscot Mountain Departs near the Jordan Pond House. This 2.6-mile trail (round-trip) affords panoramic views, second only perhaps to those from Cadillac Mountain (3hr).

GETTING AROUND

ACADIA NATIONAL PARK

By bike Three companies rent bikes for less than $30/day: Bar Harbor Bicycle Shop, at 141 Cottage St on the edge of town (☎ 207 288 3886), and Coastal Kayak & Acadia Bike, across from the post office at 48 Cottage St (☎ 207 288 9605); Southwest Cycle does the same at 370 Main St in Southwest Harbor (☎ 207 244 5856). All provide excellent maps and are good at suggesting routes. Be sure to carry water, as there are very few refreshment stops inside the park.

INFORMATION

Acadia Information Center 1201 Bar Harbor Rd (Rte-3) in Trenton just before you cross the bridge to Mount Desert Island (July & Aug daily 8am–8pm; Sept to mid-Oct daily 8am–6pm; late Oct to April Mon–Fri 8am–5pm; May & June daily 8am–6pm; ☎ 1 800 345 4617, ⓦ barharborinfo .com). An advisable stop for lodging and camping information if you don't already have a reservation. It also has free maps of the island.

Acadia National Park There are numerous information outlets at Acadia during the summer, the best being the Hulls Cove Visitor Center, just off Rte-3 at the entrance to the Park Loop Road (daily: July & Aug 8am–6pm; mid-April to June & Oct till 4.30pm, Sept till 5pm; ☎ 207 288 3338); here you can enquire about hiking routes and buy maps. You can also obtain more information about the park by calling the National Park Service Headquarters at 20 McFarland Hill Drive, off Rte-233 (Nov to mid-April daily 8am–4.30pm; mid-April to Oct Mon–Fri only; ☎ 207 288 3338, ⓦ nps.gov/acad).

Bar Harbor Chamber of Commerce Summer information centre at 2 Cottage St (late May to Oct daily 9am–9pm; ☎ 207 288 5103, ⓦ barharborinfo.com).

ACCOMMODATION

Rte-3 into and out of Bar Harbor is lined with **budget motels**, which do little to improve the look of the place but satisfy an enormous demand for accommodation. In season, it's difficult to find a room for less than $150 in Bar Harbor; elsewhere, prices are a little less exorbitant. Rates increase drastically in July and August, and sea views will cost a whole lot more. Many places book up early, so call ahead to check for availability. For help with **reservations**, call or stop in at the Acadia Information Center (see above). **Camping** in Acadia itself is a pleasant option (see box, p.501) but spaces are in short supply; if possible, call well in advance for July and August.

BAR HARBOR

2 Cats 130 Cottage St ☎ 207 288 2808, ⓦ 2catsbarharbor.com. If you stay the night at *2 Cats*, your dreams will be filled with the scent of muffins baking – the inn doubles as the best breakfast spot in town (see p.501). There are three spacious rooms, sweetly furnished with four-poster beds, sitting areas, hardwood floors and big bathtubs. $165

Bar Harbor Inn Newport Drive ☎ 207 288 3351, ⓦ barharborinn.com. The grandest hotel in town, the inn has 153 rooms in three attractively decorated buildings with modern amenities, a spa and heated pool. The eight-acre property is right on Frenchman Bay, and has excellent views from many rooms. Mid-March to Nov. $209

Bass Cottage Inn 14 The Field ☎ 207 288 1234, ⓦ basscottageinn.com. On a quiet private side street steps from downtown, this luxury B&B has lovely trimmings: whirlpool tubs, fireplaces, crisp linens and decadent breakfasts. Mid-May to Oct. $230

Manor House Inn 106 West St ☎ 207 288 3759, ⓦ barharbormanorhouse.com. Eighteen rooms in a quaint old Victorian with antique furniture and polished wood floors as well as three cottages near the centre of town. The wraparound porch is nicely suited for afternoon tea. Mid-April to Oct. $125

Seacroft Inn 18 Albert Meadow ☎ 207 288 4669, ⓦ seacroftinn.com. No-frills B&B with welcoming hosts and affordable rooms, one with a detached bathroom (and a cheaper rate). Great location, and a continental breakfast in the morning. Mid-May to Oct. $129; detached bathroom $89

★ **Ullikana** 16 The Field ☎ 207 288 9552, ⓦ ullikana .com. The place to go in town for a romantic splurge, *Ullikana* has artfully decorated rooms that pop with colour and character. The location – on a private byway just off

---

KAYAKING AND ROCK CLIMBING

If you'd like to get out on the water, you can take a four-hour guided **kayak tour** ($48) from late May to early October with National Park Sea Kayak Tours, 39 Cottage St (☎ 207 288 0342, ⓦ acadiakayak.com). Just up the street at no. 48, Coastal Kayaking Tours offers similar trips, including overnight camping packages (☎ 207 288 9605, ⓦ acadiafun.com). Due to the abundance of cliffs and overhangs, in the area **rock climbing** is popular here; Acadia Mountain Guides (☎ 207 288 8186) conducts half- and full-day climbs, with prices at $60–140 a head.

CAMPING ON MOUNT DESERT ISLAND

There are three **campgrounds** in Acadia National Park, two public and one private. **Blackwoods**, near Seal Harbor (☎207 288 3274), is open all year, with reservations taken up to a year in advance (through the National Park Service ☎1 877 444 6777, ✆recreation.gov; $20). At **Seawall**, off Rte-102A near Bass Harbor (mid-May to Sept; walk-in tent site $14; ☎1 877 444 6777), campsites are available on a first-come, first-served basis. The Appalachian Mountain Club maintains the private **Echo Lake Camp** (July to early Sept; $625/wk; ☎207 244 3727 or ✆978 448 2871, ✆amcecholakecamp.org), an extremely popular lakefront camp in Acadia National Park between Somesville and Southwest Harbor, with tent sites, cots, a dining room, kitchens, shared bathhouses with hot showers, canoes, and kayaks; rates here include three family-style meals a day. The following list of **privately owned campgrounds** on the island is not exhaustive but it should be sufficient; for a more complete guide, contact the information centre (see p.500). Most charge about $30/night, or more for a waterfront location. Also, the months they are open vary – call before setting out.

Bar Harbor Campground 409 Rte-3, Bar Harbor ☎207 288 5185

Bar Harbor KOA 136 County Rd, Bar Harbor ☎207 288 3520

Bar Harbor Woodlands KOA 1453 Rte-3, Bar Harbor ☎207 288 5139

Bass Harbor 342 Harbor Drive, Bass Harbor ☎207 244 5857

Mt Desert Rte-198, Somesville ☎207 244 3710

Mt Desert Narrows 1219 Rte-3, Bar Harbor ☎207 288 4782

8

Main Street – is tops, and the sumptuous breakfasts are served on a terrace overlooking the water. They also run *A Yellow House*, across the street. Late May to Oct. **$195**

SOUTHWEST HARBOR AND THE WEST SIDE

★**The Claremont** 22 Claremont Rd, Southwest Harbor ☎207 244 5036, ✆theclaremonthotel.com. One of Maine's most beautiful properties, this classic old-fashioned hotel has tennis and croquet, boating and an excellent shorefront. On Friday nights, fine dining is accompanied by live piano-playing. They also have a number of cottages. Mid-May to mid-Oct. **$200**

★**Harbourside Inn** 48 Harborside Rd (Rte-198), Northeast Harbor ☎207 276 3272, ✆harboursideinn .com. Nineteenth-century woodland inn with patterned wallpaper, clawfoot tubs, framed antique maps and working fireplaces. The inn is right on the edge of azalea gardens and hiking trails, and there's an organic breakfast to jump-start your day. No TVs, but lots of tranquillity. Family-owned and operated. A gem. June to mid-Sept. **$130**

The Inn at Southwest 371 Main St, Southwest Harbor ☎207 244 3835, ✆innatsouthwest.com. Brilliant inn in the centre of town with a cosy living room, cheery bedrooms, hearty breakfasts and attentive proprietors. Cheaper off-season rates. **$150**

Lindenwood Inn 118 Clark Point Rd, Southwest Harbor ☎207 244 5335, ✆lindenwoodinn.com. This first-class inn offers tastefully decorated rooms and African accents in a stylish turn-of-the-century captain's home. Breakfast included. April–Oct. **$195**

EATING AND DRINKING

BAR HARBOR

★**2 Cats** 130 Cottage St ☎207 288 2808. Pancake buffs and omelette aficionados will be pleased with their meals here, considered to be the best breakfast spot in town. All the baked goods are made in-house, the herbs are home-grown, and the coffee – which comes in enormous mugs – is fair trade. Nice outdoor patio, but expect to queue. The owners also run the adjacent inn (see p.500). Daily 7am–1pm.

Atlantic Brewing Company 15 Knox Rd ☎207 288 2337 and ☎207 288 9200 (BBQ). A 20min drive from downtown, this esteemed brewery gives complimentary tours of its facilities (late May to mid-Oct daily 2pm, 3pm & 4pm), with free samples at the end. You'll also find *Mainely Meats*, a BBQ shack with all the classics (pulled pork, ribs, baked beans, barbecued chicken) well represented. Late May to mid-Oct 11.30am–7pm.

The Burning Tree 69 Otter Creek Drive (Rte-3), Otter Creek ☎207 288 9331. A few miles south of Bar Harbor, this outwardly unimpressive seafood restaurant spices up its brilliant mains ($21–31) with tasty Southwestern and Caribbean touches. Reservations a must in July and Aug. Mid-June to mid-Oct daily except Tues 5–9.30pm; Sept also closed Mon.

Café This Way 14 Mt Desert St ☎207 288 4483. Creative breakfast options like the "Café Monte Cristo" (a French toast

8

sandwich with eggs, ham, cheddar cheese and syrup on the side; $7.95), freshly squeezed orange juice, and eight varieties of eggs benedict. Expect a wait in summer. Mid-April to Oct Mon–Sat 7–11.30am & 5.30–9pm, Sun 8am–1pm.

Carmen Verandah's 119 Main St ☎207 288 2766. Above the less exciting *Rupununi* bar, this fun-loving drinkery generally dissolves into a dance party that lasts till the wee hours. There's also pool, video games and occasionally karaoke and live music. Sometimes a cover of around $5. April–Oct daily noon–1am.

Dog & Pony Tavern 4 Rodick Place ☎207 288 0900. At the heart of Bar Harbor and yet difficult to find (it's tucked between trees and a car park), this local hangout has plenty of beers on tap and a pleasant outdoor garden. Daily 11.30am–1am.

Havana 318 Main St ☎207 288 2822. Latin-inspired New American cuisine, which translates into tuna with passionfruit vinaigrette ($28) and local halibut steamed in banana leaves ($25). Cool modern ambience, sometimes with understated live music. May–Dec daily 5pm–late.

★**Jordan Pond** Park Loop Rd, Acadia National Park ☎207 276 3316. Light meals, ice cream and popovers (puffy egg muffins) in the heart of the park, between Bar Harbor and Northeast Harbor. Afternoon tea, an Acadia tradition, is served in the lakeside garden (11.30am–5.30pm; reservations recommended). May to late Oct daily 11.30am–9pm.

★**Lompoc Café & Brew Pub** 36 Rodick St ☎207 288 9392. Eclectic, affordable menu in a woodsy outdoor dining room with bocce ball. Order the bang bang sandwich (fried chicken, spicy slaw, hot sauce and honey; $9) and wash it down with a regional beer. Live music every Fri and Sat. May to early Sept daily 11.30am–1am; mid-Sept to mid-Oct dinner only.

Mâche Bistro 135 Cottage St ☎207 288 0447. This Bar Harbor favourite wows patrons with its sophisticated take on dishes inspired by both land and sea. Recent offerings included pumpkin seed-dusted scallops ($24) and duck with creamy polenta ($21). Reservations recommended (there are only ten tables). May–Oct Mon–Sat 5.30pm–late; rest of year call for hours.

★**Mount Desert Island Ice Cream** 325 Main St ☎207 801 4006. Not your average scoop – foodies wax poetic about the ultra-fresh varieties here: salt caramel, blueberry basil sorbet and Thai chilli are tops among a long list of exceptional and ever-changing flavours. Known for their sustainability, *MDIIC* recently won accolades from

Food & Wine magazine. There's another location at 7 Firefly Lane (☎207 801 4007) and one in Portland (see p.467). June–Aug daily 11am–10.30pm; call for hours April, May, Sept & Oct.

Reel Pizza Cinerama 35 Kennebec Place, right on the Village Green ☎207 288 3828 takeaway, ☎207 288 3811 movie info. Eat pizza, drink beer and watch arty or blockbuster films on the big screen – it's fun when your order comes up on the bingo board. Movie tickets $6. Daily 4.30pm–late.

SOUTHWEST HARBOR AND AROUND

Beal's Lobster Pier 182 Clark Point Rd, Southwest Harbor ☎207 244 7178. Fresh seafood for under $12 on a rickety wooden pier. You can pick out your own lobster from a tank, or choose from a small menu of other seafood choices. May–Oct daily 9am–8pm.

Eat a Pita & Café 2 326 Main St, Southwest Harbor ☎207 244 4344. A great casual, cosy and affordable spot with healthy gourmet food (pastas, veggie mains, paninis, burgers, seafood), candlelit tables (at dinner), and friendly service. Breakfast, lunch and dinner served; there's also a full bar. May–Oct daily 8am–late.

Maine-ly Delights 48 Granville Rd, Bass Harbor ☎207 244 3656. Don't sweat the corny name – this takeaway spot has incredibly good (and affordable) crab sandwiches, seafood baskets and grilled sandwiches on waterfront picnic tables. Located by the Swans Island ferry dock. May to early Sept daily 7am–9pm.

Red Sky 14 Clark Point Rd, Southwest Harbor ☎207 244 0476. Understated New American bistro with a very loyal following. Emphasis is placed on what's local and in season, with mains ranging from braised ribs ($23) to tagliatelle with roasted squash ($20). Oenophiles will be pleased here. Reservations highly recommended. July–Sept daily 5.30–9pm; rest of year call to confirm hours.

Thurston's Lobster Pound Steamboat Wharf Rd, Bernard ☎207 244 7600. Dine on your lobster of choice in a cafeteria-style layout overlooking Bass Harbor. Late May to early Sept daily 11am–8.30pm.

XYZ Restaurant Bennett Lane, off Seawall Rd (Rte 102-A), Manset ☎207 244 5221. Slamming, legitimate Mexican dishes served in a colourful, folk-artsy interior that will make you long for the southlands. Reservations (and the margaritas) strongly recommended. Late May to early Oct dinner only; call for hours.

NIGHTLIFE AND ENTERTAINMENT

BAR HARBOR

For nightlife, people head to Bar Harbor, which is home to diversions like the Art Deco Criterion cinema at 35 Cottage St (☎207 288 3441), showing current favourites, and ImprovAcadia, on the second floor at 15 Cottage St ($15; ☎207 288 2503), with nightly comedy shows in summer.

More unusual is the Great Maine Lumberjack Show (on Rte-3 in Trenton; mid-June to Aug nightly 7pm; $10.25; ☎207 667 0067, ⊛mainelumberjack.com). Hosted by Timber Tina, an international logging sports champion, it's campy family fun, with bits of history, humour, axes and sawdust flying through the air.

MAINE'S WILD BLUEBERRIES

Maine is the undisputed international **wild blueberry** king, with the world's highest production rate. Most of its 60,000 acres of barrens (patchy growing fields) are in Washington County, which starts in Steuben (south of Machias) and stretches all the way to Canada. In May, these remote fields are blanketed in pinkish-white flowers; in **August**, the berries are harvested, finding their way into everything from pies to pancakes to chicken dishes. Don't be alarmed by the small girth of the berry in your dessert, however – wild blueberries are about half the size of the cultivated ones.

East to Canada

Few travellers venture into the hundred miles of Maine lying east of Acadia National Park, mainly because it is sparsely populated, windswept, and remote. In summer though, the weather is marked by mesmerizing fogs, the air is crisp and the coastal drive is exhilarating – it runs next to the Bay of Fundy, which has the highest tides in the nation. Tourism is not big business in these parts, but each village has a B&B or two and some low-priced restaurants. In addition to the rugged scenery, highlights include picturesque **West Quoddy Head Light**, the easternmost point in the United States; the seaside town of **Eastport**; and wild **blueberries** – ninety percent of the nation's crop comes from this part of Maine.

Machias

MACHIAS, right on Rte-1, sports a little waterfall smack in the middle of town, and was the unlikely location of the first naval encounter of the Revolutionary War: in 1775, the townsfolk, brandishing pitchforks, swords and firearms, commandeered the British schooner *Margaretta* after refusing to supply it with provisions. The attack was planned in the still-standing gambrel-roofed **Burnham Tavern**, Rte-192 just off Rte-1 (mid-June to early Sept Mon–Fri 9.30am–4pm; ☎ 207 255 6930), which has been restored to approximate the tavern's original colonial setup.

Neighbouring Machiasport is the site of a unique attraction: Jasper Beach (eight miles from downtown, near the end of Rte-92/Machias Rd) is comprised entirely of smooth red pebbles that continue as far as the eye can see. Aim to visit Machias on the third weekend in August, when it has its annual **blueberry festival** (ⓦmachiasblueberry.com), with craft fairs, fireworks and blueberry feasting.

ACCOMMODATION · MACHIAS

Inn at Schoppee Farm 21 Schoppee Dairy Rd (off Rte-1) ☎ 207 255 4648, ⓦschoppeefarm.com. Run by the owners of *Helen's* restaurant, the *Inn at Schoppee Farm* has two tastefully decorated rooms with plenty of sunlight and character overlooking the Machias River. **$95**

★ **Micmac Farm** 47 Micmac Lane, Machiasport ☎ 207 255 3008, ⓦmicmacfarm.com. Set amid apple orchards and a heavenly birch grove, this farmhouse dates all the way back to 1776. Its three inviting cedar cabins are only twenty years old, however, with modern amenities like fridges and microwaves. The house itself has one adorable guest room with a warm quilt on the bed, polished wood floors, a whirlpool tub and a deck overlooking the river. May–Sept. **$95**

EATING

Fat Cat Deli 291 Main St ☎ 207 255 6777. This blues-loving deli fires up oven-fresh pizza and made-to-order sandwiches. Mon–Sat 8am–11pm, Sun 4–8pm.

★ **Helen's** 111 Main St/Rte-1 ☎ 207 255 8433. Make sure you don't leave town without trying the blueberry pie at this landmark restaurant – it's considered to be the best in the state, and possibly the world. The comfort food-filled menu is delicious as well. Mon–Sat 6am–8pm, Sun till 7.30pm.

Cutler

East of Machias, Rte-191 heads along a regal and desolate portion of shoreline known as the **Bold Coast**. From the parking lot on Rte-191, four miles east of **CUTLER**, two hiking loops head out to the windswept coast. There's a small beach at Long Point Cove, and you can sometimes catch a glimpse of humpback whales from the cliffs. The Cobscook Trails Coalition (☎207 733 5509, ☻downeastcoastalconservancy.org) has information on the trails and campsites along the way. Also in Cutler, the Bold Coast Charter Co. runs spectacular puffin-sighting trips ($100 May–Aug only; ☎207 259 4484, ☻boldcoast .com), on the 40ft *Barbara Frost,* which docks and actually lets passengers disembark onto tiny Machias Seal Island, home to thousands of the brightly beaked birds. Even if birding is not your thing, this is a unique and highly recommended experience.

West Quoddy Head
Quoddy Head Rd, off Rte-191 • $3

With its distinctive red-and-white-striped lighthouse, **WEST QUODDY HEAD** is the easternmost point of the United States, jutting defiantly into the stormy Atlantic. You can see Canada just across the Bay of Fundy, though for a better view, take the three-mile trail east in **Quoddy Head State Park** that traces a winding line along precipitous cliffs and also diverges onto a fantastic bog boardwalk.

Lubec

Tiny **LUBEC** was once home to more than twenty sardine-packing plants. They're all gone now, but the restored **McCurdy's Smokehouse**, on Water Street, gives tours (mid-June to mid-Oct Thurs–Sun 10am–3pm; $3); you might spy a seal as you stroll along the main drag. Lubec also hosts the popular adult music camp Summer Keys (☻summerkeys.com).

ACCOMMODATION | LUBEC

Home Port B&B 45 Main St ☎207 733 2077. An 1880 house with seven guest rooms, decorated with a nice mix of antiques, folk art and cheerful colours. Best is the "Library" room, with its massive floral headboard and built-in bookshelves – stocked with great reads – that span the length of the walls. Mid-May to mid-Oct. $95

Inn on the Wharf 69 Johnson St ☎207 733 4400. Contemporary white rooms with occasional bright pops of colour in a renovated sardine factory overlooking the ocean. At the on-site restaurant, you can sit amid lobstermen hauling in their catch, then order those same crustaceans right to your table. Kayak and bike rental available too. $100

Peacock House 27 Summer St ☎207 733 2403, ☻peacockhouse.com. A fantastic place to stay: charming proprietors, country-chic guest rooms, quilts and patterned wallpaper in a rambling wooden clapboard house. May–Oct. $95

Sunset Point RV Park At the west end of town ☎207 733 2272, ☻sunsetpointrvpark.com. Scenic campsites overlooking Johnson Bay that come complete with showers, laundry and a friendly office and store. Pitch your tent, then wake up early to be one of the first people in the country to see the sunrise. Open mid-May to mid-Oct. $25

West Quoddy Station 838 South Lubec Rd, by the lighthouse ☎1 877 535 4714, ☻quoddyvacation.com. One cottage, four apartment units and five guest rooms located in the former Coast Guard station of West Quoddy Head Lighthouse. The *Station's* renovated digs all have satellite TVs and full kitchens; the wood-panelled cottage is the nicest option. A fascinating setting, with impressive ocean views. $140

EATING AND DRINKING

Uncle Kippy's Rte-189 ☎207 733 2400. You know you've found *Uncle Kippy's* when you spot the miniature lighthouse with a big bunch of locals out front. Overlooking Johnson Bay, the plaid-wallpapered dining room is a favourite for oven-fresh pizza, chicken dinners, seafood and steak. July & Aug daily 11am–8pm, rest of year call to confirm hours.

Campobello Island

Lubec is the gateway to **Campobello Island**, in New Brunswick, Canada, where Franklin D. Roosevelt summered from 1909 to 1921, before he became president, and to where he occasionally returned while in office. His barn-red cottage is now open to the public, furnished just as the Roosevelts left it. The rest of **Roosevelt Campobello International Park** (mid-May to mid-Oct daily 9am–5pm; free; ☎1 877 851 6663, ☻fdr.net), located on Canadian soil but held jointly with the United States, is good for a couple of hours' wandering. There are several coastal trails and picnic areas, and the drive out to **Liberty Point** is worth the effort. You will need a valid passport to cross the border.

Eastport

EASTPORT is incredible. Perched on Moose Island, between Cobscook and Passamaquoddy bays at the end of Rte-190, the town is quite a way off the beaten track, but if you have the driving stamina, it's one of the most fascinating places you'll ever experience, with frequent fogs and a cusp-of-America charm. **Canada** is only a few miles away, but the closest border crossing is 28 miles north in Calais, and the bridge to Campobello Island in Lubec is forty miles from here by car – you have to drive all the way around Cobscook Bay or take the ferry (☎506 747 2159) to get there. The quiet town maintains the air of a remote outpost, with spotty weather, hills that slope towards a collection of Canadian islands across the bay, and lots of old brick and clapboard buildings. Eastport can also claim the largest **whirlpool** in the western hemisphere, ignobly dubbed the "Old Sow". You can view the rushing waters safely from the terminus of Clark Street.

Galleries

A result of an active local arts community, the **Commons Gallery**, 51 Water St (☎207 853 4123), is worth a spin, usually housing an interesting collection of works by Maine artists. The esteemed **Tides Institute & Museum of Art** (☎207 853 4047), across the street at no. 43, is an 1887 bank building that displays a rotating range of artworks – from photography and seascapes to basketry and contemporary paintings. Just up the hill at no. 11, the owner-artist of **Crow Tracks gallery** (☎207 853 2336) carves wooden seagulls, puffins and, if his blade guides him, more eclectic creations like mermaids and asparagus farmers.

8

TOURS EASTPORT

Boat tours If you're looking to get out on the water, the romantic windjammer *Sylvina W. Beal* (used in the film version of *The Age of Innocence*) and the *Halie Matthew* offer whale-watching, sunset, and overnight cruises (☎207 853 2500, ⊛eastportwindjammers.com).

ACCOMMODATION

Chadbourne House 19 Shackford St ☎207 853 2727, ⊛chadbournehouse.com. An elegant Federal home with four spacious rooms decorated in warm hues (except for the third-floor suite, which is a crisp white). There are four-poster beds in each, and one suite has a toasty fireplace. $135

Cobscook Bay State Park Halfway between Eastport and Lubec off Rte-1 ☎207 726 4412. Some of the best camping around, with over a hundred beautifully situated campsites, good facilities and access to clam beds ($5 day fee). Mid-May to mid-Oct. $24

★ **The Commons** 51 Water St ☎207 853 4123, ⊛thecommonseastport.com. These two refurbished suites above an art gallery make for one of Maine's best

stays; each comes with two bedrooms decorated in soothing ocean colours (think tan and pale blue), a modern kitchen, a snug dining room, internet access, laundry and a front porch with barbecue setups and jaw-dropping views of the harbour into Canada. Weekly rental $775

Weston House 26 Boynton St ☎207 853 2907. An 1810 Federal-style house with oodles of New England charm – brass pots hanging in the kitchen, walls painted in rich hues of burgundy and evergreen, and a sitting area dotted with carved sea birds. There are three delightful guest rooms, one of which was used in 1833 by painter John James Audubon while awaiting a ferry to Labrador. Cash or cheque only. $96

EATING AND DRINKING

★ **The Pickled Herring** 32 Water St ☎207 853 2323. Dishes up inviting options like lobster cakes with red pepper cream sauce ($11), stuffed haddock with spinach ($20), wood-fired pizzas and creative salads in a handsome pub ambience with a pressed-tin ceiling and a charming little bar at the back. Tues–Sat 5pm–late.

Quoddy Bay Lobster 7 Sea St ☎207 853 6640. Feast on ultra-fresh lobster rolls, chowder and clams at this seaside favourite, owned by lobstermen and with a picnic-table

ambience. July & Aug daily 10am–6pm; call for hours May, June, Sept & Oct.

FOOD SHOPS

★ **Katie's on the Cove** 9 Katie Lane, Robbinston (eight miles north of town on Rte-1) ☎207 454 8446, ⊛katiesonthecove.com. A local institution that doles out unbelievably good confections from a little canary-yellow house. Try the "needhams" – an old-fashioned Maine delicacy crafted from chocolate and mashed potatoes. While they may sound strange, you'll be hooked after one bite. June–Sept Mon–Fri 10am–5pm, Sat noon–3pm, call for hours rest of year.

★ **Raye's Mustard** 83 Washington St ☎ 207 853

4451. *Raye's* has been producing its "liquid gold" for over one hundred years – it's the country's last surviving stone mustard mill. Pick up one of its 25 varieties for friends back home (or for your own signature tuna salad recipe). Mon–Fri 9am–5pm, Sat & Sun 10am–5pm.

Calais

The border between the United States and Canada weaves through the centre of **Passamaquoddy Bay**; the towns to either side get on so well that they refused to fight in the US–UK War of 1812, and promote themselves jointly to visitors as the **Quoddy Loop**. It's perfectly feasible to take a two-nation vacation, but each passage through customs between **CALAIS** (pronounced "callous") in the States and **St Stephen** in Canada does take a while – and remember that they're in different time zones. No trace now remains of Samuel de Champlain's 1604 attempt to found a colony on the diminutive St Croix Island, but there is an International Historic site commemorating the explorer on Rte-1.

Moosehorn National Wildlife Refuge

Between Rte-191 and Charlotte Rd · Daily sunrise to sunset · Free · ☎ 207 454 7161

Fourteen miles south of downtown Calais, the Baring division of the **Moosehorn National Wildlife Refuge** is a good place to catch a glimpse of a bald eagle or woodcock; they also maintain some fifty miles of hiking trails, well-suited for cross-country skiing in winter.

ARRIVAL AND INFORMATION   **CALAIS**

By bus West's Coastal Connections (☎ 207 546 2823 or ☎ 1 800 596 2823, ⓦ westbusservice.com) runs a once-daily bus linking Calais with Ellsworth and Bangor.

Visitor centre The visitor centre, 39 Union St (daily 9am–5.30pm; ☎ 207 454 2211), has loads of information on activities and accommodation, and helpful staff.

Inland Maine

The vast expanses of the **Maine interior**, stretching up into the far north, consist mostly of forests of pine, spruce and fir, interspersed by white birches and maples responsible for the spectacular autumn colours. Distances here are large. Once you get away from the two major cities – **Augusta**, the capital, and **Bangor** – it's roughly two hundred miles by road to the northern border at **Fort Kent**, while the trip between the two most likely inland bases, **Greenville** and **Rangeley**, takes two and a half hours or more. Driving (there's very little public transport) through this mountainous scenery can be a great pleasure, but you do need to know where you're going. There are few places to stay, even fewer gas stations, and beyond Millinocket many roads are tolled access routes belonging to the lumber companies: gravel-surfaced and vulnerable to bad weather.

This is great territory in which to **hike** – the **Appalachian Trail** starts its two-thousand-mile course down to Georgia at the top of Mount Katahdin – or **raft** on the swift **Penobscot** or **Kennebec** rivers. **Skiing**, too, is a popular activity, particularly at **Sugarloaf** or in the area around **Bethel**, near the New Hampshire border.

Especially around beautiful **Baxter State Park** and enormous **Moosehead Lake**, the forests are home to deer, beaver, a few bears, some recently introduced caribou and plenty of **moose**. These endearingly gawky creatures (they look like badly drawn horses and are virtually blind) tend to be seen at early morning or dusk; in spring they come to lick the winter's salt off the roads, while in summer you may spot them feeding in shallow water. They do, however, cause major havoc on the roads, particularly at night.

Aim to be at your destination before the sun sets – each year there are a significant number of moose-related collisions.

Augusta and around

The capital of Maine since 1831, **AUGUSTA**, thirty miles north of Brunswick, is much quieter and less visited now than it was a hundred years ago. The lumber industry took off here after the technique of making paper from wood was rediscovered in 1844, and Augusta also had a lucrative ice-making business at the time: each winter hundreds of thousands of tons of ice, cut from the Kennebec River, were shipped as far as the Caribbean.

Maine State Museum

230 State St • Tues–Fri 9am–5pm, Sat 10am–4pm; May–Nov also Sun 1–4pm • $2 • ☎ 207 287 2301, ⓦ mainestatemuseum.org

Just south of the impressive capitol building, the **Maine State Museum** has exhibits devoted to inventions and industries that helped build the state. At the entrance, an enormous 1846 steam engine train segues into displays on the lumber industry, replete with massive saws and log cutters. The hallways of "Back to Nature" feel like an enlarged diorama – here, preserved animals ranging from moose, lynx, black bears and deer peek out at museum-goers from behind glass enclosures. Downstairs is a functional water-powered mill and a fantastic collection of old looms and antique forms of transport.

Maine State House

210 State St • Mon–Fri 9am–5pm • Self-guided tour or free guided tours can be arranged by calling the museum at ☎ 207 287 2301

The 180ft dome of the imposing **Maine State House**, a Charles Bulfinch design (see p.69), is visible from nearly anywhere in Augusta. The impressive granite structure, completed in 1832, has been subject to several renovations that have nearly doubled its size.

Hallowell

Just two miles south of Augusta beside the gently sloping banks of the Kennebec River, the quaint haven of **HALLOWELL** is far more pleasant than its governmentally focused neighbour, especially along its main drag, **Water Street**, lined with some excellent **restaurants** and a couple of diverting bookstores and antique shops. Once a major port for lumber and granite, as well as a shipbuilding centre, the place boasts a number of stately homes left over from those prosperous times, mostly perched in the hills above town. A small population of artists and craftsmen has arrived in recent years; for **information** on visiting the many studios in the area, contact the Kennebec Valley Chamber of Commerce (☎ 207 623 4559, ⓦ augustamaine.com).

ACCOMMODATION

AUGUSTA AND AROUND

Maple Hill Farm 11 Inn Rd (off Outlet Rd), Hallowell ☎ 207 622 2708, ⓦ maplebb.com. Set on 62 acres, this bucolic inn has eight cosy rooms decorated with wicker armchairs and paisley bedspreads; many have the added perk of whirlpool tubs and fireplaces. You can feed the farm animals in the morning before enjoying a delicious breakfast. Cheaper single rates. **$115**

Senator Inn & Spa 284 Western Ave, Augusta ☎ 207 622 5804, ⓦ senatorinn.com. This 124-room hotel is *the* place to stay in Augusta. Modern rooms with flat-screen TVs and iPod docks, plus perks like a stunning, atrium-enclosed saltwater pool, fitness classes, the

stellar *Cloud 9* restaurant and access to one of the state's best spas. $149

EATING AND DRINKING

★**A1 Diner** 3 Bridge St/Rte-9/Rte-201, in neighbouring Gardiner, 6 miles south of Augusta ☎207 582 4804. Serves traditional New England fare (think pork chops with apple sauce; $15.99) alongside more adventurous dishes like spicy noodles with shrimp ($11.99) in a vintage diner car that hasn't budged since 1946. A charming, old-fashioned setting. Mon—Thurs 7am—8pm, Fri & Sat till 8.30pm, Sun 8am—1pm.

Liberal Cup 115 Water St, Hallowell ☎207 623 2739. Enjoyable pub grub (everything down to the tartare sauce is made from scratch) and six of the *Cup's* own beers on tap, swilled on wooden church pews. There are 24 beer varieties rotated throughout the year. Daily 11.30am—1am.

★**Riverfront Barbeque** 300 Water St, Augusta ☎207 622 8899. Addictive Memphis ribs ($14.99), pulled pork sandwich plates ($8.79) and (surprisingly) garlic cream penne ($11.99) eaten in dark leather booths. There's frequent live music in the bar, a former Prohibition-era gin mill, upstairs. Mon—Wed 11am—9pm, Thurs—Sat 11am—10pm, Sun noon—9pm.

Slates Restaurant 167 Water St ☎207 622 9575. A friendly atmosphere, fair prices and original mains like shrimp and scallops with coconut pie sauce over jasmine rice. *Slates* has expanded to include a delectable bakery and deli next door. Mon 5.30—9pm, Tues—Fri 11am—9pm, Sat 10am—2.30pm & 5.30—9.30pm, Sun 10am—2pm.

Bangor

BANGOR, 120 miles northeast of Portland at the intersection of Rte-1A and I-95, is not a place to spend much time, although its plentiful motels make it a good last stop before the interior. As Maine's third largest city (35,000 people), the place is noticeably more urban and rough around the edges (for Maine, at least) than the state's smaller towns, serving as a major source of goods and services for the stretch of coast twenty miles south.

A few miles north of Bangor, the Maine Center for the Arts (☎207 581 1755), at the University of Maine in **Orono**, runs a series of big-name concerts each summer.

Brief history

In its prime, Bangor was the undisputed "**Lumber Capital of the World**". Every winter its population of "River Drivers" went upstream to brand the felled logs, which they then manoeuvred down the Penobscot River as the thaw came in April, reaching Bangor in time to carouse the summer away in the grog shops of Peppermint Row. Bangor also exported **ice** to the West Indies – and got rum in return. The forests were thinning and the prosperous days were coming to an end, however, in 1882, when Oscar Wilde addressed a large crowd at the new Opera House and spoke of "such advancement… in so small a city". A devastating **fire** in 1911 levelled much of Bangor, although a fair number of the lumber barons' lavish mansions survived.

Stephen King's residence

One of the mansions that survives along West Broadway, complete with a spider-web-shaped iron gate, is now the suitably Gothic residence of horror author **Stephen King**, a Maine native who relocated here in 1980.

Paul Bunyan statue and around

After Stephen King, Bangor's other claim to fame, the 31ft **Paul Bunyan** statue along Main Street south of downtown, is perhaps the largest such statue in the world – excepting one or two in Minnesota – though it looks more like a brightly painted model airplane kit than a statue. Bunyan was allegedly born here in 1834, though several other prominent logging towns across the US dispute that claim. From mid-May until the end of July there's **harness racing** (☎207 561 6068) and a year-round casino with **Hollywood slot machines** (☎1 877 779 7771) at Bass Park on Main Street just behind the statue; admission is free but the potential to lose money is unlimited.

Maine Discovery Museum

74 Main St • Tues–Sat 9.30am–5pm, Sun noon–5pm • $7.50 • ☎ 207 262 7200, ⓦ mainediscoverymuseum.org

Let your kids loose at the **Maine Discovery Museum**, one of the foremost children's museums in New England, and they'll be thrilled to learn about everything from art and literature to paleontology and astronomy, albeit disguised by super-fun hands-on exhibits, like the "Body Journey" that lets you floss enormous fake teeth.

Cole Land Transportation Museum

405 Perry Rd (from I-95 follow signs to War Memorials) • May to mid-Nov daily 9am–5pm • $7, children (under 19 years) free • ☎ 207 990 3600, ⓦ colemuseum.org

The **Cole Land Transportation Museum** is packed with a fantastic collection of antique fire trucks, trains and frighteningly large snowploughs; these last look like they could plough your house up along with the snow.

ARRIVAL AND DEPARTURE   BANGOR

By plane Many of the major airlines service Bangor International Airport (☎ 207 992 4600, ⓦ flybangor.com), on the western edge of town.

By bus Frequent bus service is available from Bangor to most other parts of the state. Concord Coach, which docks at the Transportation Center, 1039 Union St across from the airport (☎ 1 800 639 3317, ⓦ concordcoachlines.com), can take you to Portland, Belfast and a number of smaller coastal cities. The CYR Bus Line (☎ 1 800 244 2335, ⓦ cyrbustours.com) stops at both the Coach and the

Greyhound terminals and then heads north to Caribou, stopping in several small towns along the way. Greyhound has a terminal at 158 Main St (☎ 207 945 3000, ⓦ greyhound.com), from where you can travel to Boston via Portland and Portsmouth, NH or connect with Greyhound routes to other destinations. West's Coastal Connections buses (☎ 207 546 2823 or ☎ 1 800 596 2823, ⓦ westbusservice.com) travel between Bangor and the border town of Calais via Ellsworth.

GETTING AROUND

By bus If you're spending any time at all in Bangor, you'll find Community Connector ($1.25, five tickets $5; ☎ 207

992 4670) to be a handy means of getting around. Pick up a route map from any bus driver.

INFORMATION

Bangor Region Chamber of Commerce 208 Main Ave; call to confirm the address, as it was scheduled to move

(Mon–Fri 8.30am–5pm; ☎ 207 947 0307, ⓦ bangorregion .com). There's also an information centre in Hollywood Slots.

ACCOMMODATION

Hollywood Slots Hotel 500 Main St ☎ 1 877 779 7771, ⓦ hollywoodslots.com. After a day hitting the slots, retreat to one of the 148 sleek chambers in this brand-new

hotel adjacent to the casino. Amenities include flat-screen TVs, high-thread-count bedding and access to the horse tracks across the way. <u>$149</u>

EATING AND DRINKING

Bagel Central 33 Central St ☎ 207 947 1654. Locals rally for *Central's* fresh bagels and huge selection of kosher foods. Mon–Thurs 6am–6pm, Fri till 5.30pm, Sun till 2pm.

Bahaar 23 Hammond St ☎ 207 945 5979. Excellent, aromatic Pakistani food, such as *daal* (lentil) dishes, golden curries and hot *naan* (flat bread drizzled with butter and

---

MAKING WHOOPIE

A softball-sized, cake-and-frosting confection, the humble **whoopie pie** snagged Maine's official "state treat" title in 2011 (blueberry pie won for dessert). Traditionally, whoopies are crafted from two cake-like chocolate cookies and held together by a generous dollop of marshmallow frosting. In recent years, however, bakeries have been firing off a lot of flavour riffs – pumpkin, red velvet, even orange creamsicle whoopies have been spotted. The origin of this sweet-tooth sandwich is hotly disputed – both **Pennsylvania** and **Maine** vie for the originator crown. *Friars' Bakehouse* (see p.510) and *2 Fat Cats* (in Portland, see p.467) are generally lauded as best-in-state, but you'll be well satisfied at any reputable Maine bakery.

garlic) served in a small, noisy dining room with patterned lampshades and jars of bright legumes. Thurs & Fri 5–9pm, Sat 4–9pm.

Dysart's Exit 180 off I-95 S in Hermon ☎ 207 942 4878. Beloved 24hr truck stop that's been a Maine institution for over forty years. There's a roomy diner with great road food, showers and even a barber shop. Open 24hr.

★ **Fiddlehead** 84 Hammond St ☎ 207 942 3336. With its impressive locavore menu, perpetually filled dining room and hopping bar scene, *Fiddlehead* would be right at home in Manhattan's west village. Its personable atmosphere and doting staff are refreshingly Maine-like, however. Mains $11–22. Reservations recommended. Tues–Fri 4–9pm, Sat 5–10pm, Sun 5–9pm.

★ **Friars' Bakehouse** 21 Central St ☎ 207 947 3770. With a vibe that falls somewhere between Monty Python and Martha Stewart, baked goods here must answer to a higher power. Crafted by brothers of a Catholic order, the food consists of heaping sandwiches, fresh muffins and scones, and the best whoopie pies in the whole darn state. No mobile phones, cash only. Tues–Fri 8am–2pm.

Massimo's 96 Hammond St ☎ 207 945 5600. Amazing, authentic Italian food (the chef-owner learned to bake bread standing beside his *nonna* in Rome); the rigatoni *alla bolognese* ($13) is a standout. At lunchtime, head two doors up to *Massimo's Breads* to sample the pizza *romana* with thinly sliced potatoes, Fontina and olive oil ($2.95 a slice). Mon–Thurs 5–8.45pm, Fri & Sat 5–9.15pm.

Whig & Courier 18 Broad St ☎ 207 947 4095. This neighbourly, straightahead pub is *the* place to drink in town. Really good cheesesteaks, burgers and a wide variety of beers on tap. Mon–Wed 11am–10pm, Thurs 11am–11pm, Fri & Sat 11am–midnight.

Bethel

The remote, quintessentially New England town of **BETHEL**, nestled in the mountains about seventy miles north of Portland, may appear rather sleepy, but it's an excellent year-round base from which to explore the outdoors, most notably in the **White Mountains** and **Grafton Notch State Park**. Bethel has long attracted a rather academic and prosperous population; the prestigious Gould Academy is here, and the town was once home to the clinic of famous neurobiologist Dr John Gehring. Bethel also holds the record for the world's tallest snowman and snowwoman – 113ft and 122ft, respectively.

GETTING AROUND AND INFORMATION

By bus Bethel is not accessible via public transport, though the Sunday River Stagecoach (☎ 207 357 5783, ⓦ srstage.com) makes local and out-of-town trips, going as far as Fort Kent. In winter, the Mountain Explorer runs a free shuttle service between Sunday River and downtown.

Chamber of Commerce 8 Station Place (Mon–Fri 9am–5pm; ☎ 207 824 2282, ⓦ bethelmaine.com). This helpful outfit can assist with accommodation reservations.

ACCOMMODATION

★ **Bethel Hill Bed & Breakfast** 66 Broad St ☎ 207 824 2461, ⓦ bethelhill.com. Three freshly renovated guest rooms with jacuzzi tubs, great for unwinding after a cold day on the slopes. The ski teacher-owner is an expert on the area, and can also take you out on the mountain. There's a roaring fire in the library almost every evening. Full breakfast included. $129

Briar Lea Inn 150 Mayville Rd (Rte-2 east of Bethel Village) ☎ 207 824 4717, ⓦ briarleainn.com. Refurbished 150-year-old Georgian farmhouse with six traditional guest rooms and a full-service English pub. $105

Telemark Inn 591 Kings Hwy, Mason Township ☎ 207 836 2703, ⓦ telemarkinn.com. Mingle with huskies, horses and llamas on a private land-holding within the White National Forest. This rustic 120-year old hunting lodge is a base for dog-sledding, horseback riding, llama trekking, hiking and canoeing adventures. All meals included. Two-day dog-sledding package $525

CAMPING

Bethel Outdoor Adventures 121 Mayville Rd/Rte-2 ☎ 207 824 4224, ⓦ betheloutdooradventure.com. Family-oriented campsite with both RV and tent sites on the banks of the Androscoggin River.

Crocker Pond Campground Off Songo Pond Rd (Rte-5) just south of town ☎ 603 466 2713. Seven secluded and rather primitive campsites (first-come, first-served) maintained by the US Forest Service. Mid-May to mid-Oct. $14

EATING AND DRINKING

★ **22 Broad Street** 22 Broad St ☎ 207 824 3496. Top-notch Italian restaurant in a remarkable 1848 Greek Revival house. The bright pink dining room, which looks onto the town common, is capped off by a dramatic white-tin

SKIING AND OUTDOOR ACTIVITIES

Just a few miles north of Bethel off Rte-2 on Sunday River Road, the **Sunday River Ski Resort** (lift tickets $80; ☎ 207 824 3000, ⓦ sundayriver.com), is one of the major alpine ski areas in New England, with eighteen lifts servicing eight mountain peaks.

Bethel is also known for its **cross-country skiing**, and there are several privately owned centres in addition to the trails maintained for snowmobiles (to which skiers have access) in the White Mountain National Forest and Grafton Notch State Park (see p.512). Some 40km of cross-country ski trails penetrate the wilderness at the beginner-oriented Sunday River Inn & Cross Country Ski Center, on Sunday River Road (☎ 207 824 3000). Don't miss the trail that leads to the 1872 Artist's Covered Bridge, off Sunday River Road, which is a good spot for swimming during the summer. You can also cross-country ski at Carter's Farm & Cross-Country Ski Shop, with eighteen miles of trails at its location off Rte-26 in Oxford, and forty miles of groomed trails in Bethel on Intervale Road (☎ 207 539 4848). For warm-weather activities, stop by Bethel Outdoor Adventures, on Rte-2 just east of Bethel Village (☎ 207 824 4224). They have **bike rentals** ($25/day) and route advice; they also rent **canoes** and **kayaks** and do guided trips. Bethel is known for its precious and semi-precious **rock** quarries, and the region is honeycombed with retired mines. Maine Mineralogy Expeditions, a partner of Bethel Outdoor Adventures, offers three-hour exploratory tours into the tunnels of an 80-year-old mine (May–Sept, reservations recommended; $25; ☎ 207 824 4224). At the trip's finish, you can try your luck digging for rose quartz and feldspar in an old mining sluice. **Fishing** is another popular pastime; contact outdoor sports specialist Sun Valley Sports (☎ 1 877 851 7533) for fly-fishing, snowmobiling, kayaking and canoeing trips.

ceiling. In winter, there's a toasty fire; in summer, you can feast in the sunroom. Daily 5pm–late.

DiCocoa's 119–125 Main St ☎ 207 824 5282. Bold vegetarian and creative specialities, wraps, soups and espresso in a quirky dining room. Opening hours can be spotty – call first. Daily 7am–6pm.

★ **Cho Sun** 141 Main St ☎ 207 824 7370. People come from all around for *Cho Sun's* rejuvenating Korean and Japanese dishes. The *bibimbap* (shiitake mushrooms, beef and rice topped by a golden fried egg; $17.99) will give you a glow on a winter's day. Wed–Sun 5pm–late.

Hot Taco 7 Mechanic St ☎ 207 381 6001. Tiny, Kermit-green Mexican place with just a handful of aluminium tables and a small but delectable menu: tacos (beef, pork or chicken; two for $2.99), burritos ($6.99) and cheese quesadillas ($4.49). In summer, there's home-made

strawberry lemonade ($2.39). Mon, Wed & Thurs 11.30am–3pm & 4.30–7pm, Fri & Sat 11.30am–3pm & 4.30–9pm, Sun noon–6pm.

★ **Smokin' Good BBQ/Good Food Market** Rte-2 ☎ 207 824 4744 or ☎ 207 824 3754. Outside is a down-to-earth orange trailer dishing out Bethel's best BBQ, inside the adjacent store an adorable New England food purveyor sells made-to-order sandwiches, home-made heat-and-eat options like mac and cheese, and pumpkin whoopie pies. BBQ Thurs–Sun 11.30am–7pm; store daily 9am–8pm.

Sudbury Inn & Suds Pub 151 Main St ☎ 207 824 6558. The best of both worlds: fine dining upstairs, drinking den downstairs, with live entertainment five nights a week and a good selection of microbrews until 1am. Tues–Sun 5.30–9pm; longer hours at the pub.

White Mountain National Forest

Bethel sits just on the edge of the fifty thousand acres of the **White Mountain National Forest** that fall within Maine's borders, the centre of which is **Evans Notch**. Contact the Bethel Chamber of Commerce, (see p.510) for maps, hiking suggestions and information on campsite and shelter availability. There are a number of **backcountry shelters** in the forest. All are at least a couple of miles from the trailheads (accessible only on foot), and are either free or have a nominal fee on a first-come, first-served basis. Particularly good **hikes** through the birch, maple and pine stands include the moderately difficult seven-mile (about 5hr 30min) **Caribou Mountain Loop**, starting at the trailhead on Rte-113, following the Mud Brook Trail, and ending at the summit of Caribou Mountain, and the easier 1.8-mile (about 1hr 30min) loop that begins on Rte-113, across the bridge just north of *Hastings Campground* and leads up to the **Roost**, a granite overlook providing views of the Wild River Valley and Evans Notch.

8

AMC MOUNTAIN HUTS IN WESTERN MAINE

The Appalachian Mountain Club (ⓦoutdoors.org) maintains a number of **mountain huts** and **camps**, of which there's a concentration in western Maine near the White Mountains. If you have your own tent and stove, these well-kept facilities are excellent options, especially if you're kayaking or canoeing. If you have questions or want to make reservations, call the Pinkham Notch Visitor Center (ⓣ603 466 2727). Other AMC mountain huts in Maine are on Mount Desert Island and near Georgetown Island, south of Bath (see box, p.475). One such is **Cold River Camp**, North Chatham, NH (late June to late Aug, weekly member rate $520; late Aug to mid-Sept $60/day). Situated in the beautiful and undeveloped Evans Notch area of the White Mountain National Forest, this hundred-plus-acre site offers a full range of facilities such as cabins, electricity, hot showers, linens, a recreation hall and a screened tea house. Rates include meals and firewood.

Grafton Notch State Park

1941 Bear River Rd (Rte-26), Newry • Mid-May to mid-Oct • $3 • ⓣ 207 824 2912

North of Bethel, Rte-26 bisects beautiful **Grafton Notch State Park**, a patch of rugged mountains, gurgling streams, cascading waterfalls and bizarre geological formations. Among these, **Screw Auger Falls**, where the Bear River has carved out a gorge through the solid granite, is good for wading. Just north, easy trails lead to **Moose Cave Gorge** and through the 45ft-deep **Mother Walker Falls Gorge**, which features several natural bridges. More difficult trails head up **Old Speck Mountain**, Maine's third highest. Follow the 3.9-mile (one-way) **Old Speck Trail**, which traces the Appalachian Trail from the Grafton Notch trailhead parking area up numerous switchbacks, past the Cascade Brook Falls to the Mahoosuc Trail, which eventually affords sweeping views at the summit. A somewhat shorter option is the **Table Rock Loop** (a 2hr jaunt with some very steep sections) that also departs from the main trailhead parking area up **Baldpate Mountain** to Table Rock, where you are treated for your efforts with mountain views. The Bethel Area Chamber of Commerce (see p.510) can provide you with maps and other necessary information. There are no campgrounds in Grafton Notch State Park.

Rangeley

RANGELEY is only just in Maine, a little way east of New Hampshire and fewer than fifty miles from the Canadian border, at the intersection of routes 4 and 16. And, as the sign on Main Street boldly declares, it is equidistant from the North Pole and the Equator (3107.5 miles), though that doesn't mean it's on the main road to anywhere. It has always been a resort, served in 1900 by two train lines and several steamships, with the attraction then being the fishing in the spectacularly named Mooselookmeguntic Lake. Today this picturesque one-street town, nestled amid a complex system of lakes and waterways, serves as a base for summer explorations.

Wilhelm Reich Museum

Dodge Pond Rd, 3.6 miles south of Rangeley • July & Aug Wed–Sun 1–5pm; Sept Sun only • $7 • ⓣ 207 864 3443, ⓦ wilhelmreichtrust.org

Rangeley has one unorthodox indoor attraction, the remote **Wilhelm Reich Museum**, where Wilhelm Reich eventually made his home after fleeing Germany in 1933. Although he was an associate of Freud in Vienna and the author of the acclaimed *Mass Psychology of Fascism*, Reich is best remembered for developing the orgone energy accumulator. He claimed it could concentrate atmospheric energy; sceptical authorities focused on the way in which it was said to collect and harness human sexual energy. In a tragic end to his career, Reich was imprisoned after a student broke an injunction forbidding the transportation of his accumulators across state lines, and he died in prison in Lewisburg, PA, in November 1957. He is buried here, amid the neat lawns and darting hummingbirds, and his house remains a museum for the reflection of his work.

Angel Falls

South of town along Rte-17, it's worth seeking out **Angel Falls**, which, at 90ft, are the highest in Maine. There's a good **swimming** spot at the base. Nearby, in the old mining town of Byron, you can also swim in the clear waters of **Coos Canyon**, just off Rte-17. **Rangeley Lake State Park** has 869 acres where you can swim, fish and hike; there are also barbecue grills (mid-May to early Sept; $4.50).

ARRIVAL AND DEPARTURE

RANGELEY

Northeast Charter & Tour Lewiston (☎ 1 888 593 6328, ⓦ northeastchartertour.com). Rangeley is not accessible on public transport; Northeast Charter & Tour can take you anywhere in the state on its full-size buses and limos.

INFORMATION AND TOURS

Rangeley Lakes Chamber of Commerce 6 Park Rd (Mon–Fri 10am–4pm; July–Sept also Sat 10am–4pm; ☎ 207 864 5364, ⓦ rangeleymaine.com). Has details of various activities, including snowmobiling, moose-watching and canoeing expeditions.

Rangeley Region Lake Cruises (late May to mid-Oct; $25; ☎ 207 864 2038) offers hour-long wooden boat cruises on the little 1947 *Oquossoc Lady*.

ACCOMMODATION

The **Chamber of Commerce** (see p.510) can provide lists of private home/condo rentals and "remote campsites" around the lake – which really are remote, several of them inaccessible by road.

8

Grant's Camps 20 miles north of Rangeley, beside Kennebago Lake ☎ 1 800 633 4815. Peaceful spot with fishing, canoeing and windsurfing. Accommodation is in comfortable cabins overlooking the lake, and includes all meals. Lower rates for weekly stays. **$190**/person

Hunter Cove Cabins 33 Hunter Cove Rd ☎ 207 864 3383, ⓦ huntercove.com. Refined rusticity: seven lakeside, two-bedroom cabins with simple decor but modern perks like satellite TV, DVD players and microwaves. Old-fashioned amenities like porches, fireplaces and fishing access ensure you stay connected to nature. **$150**

★ **Kawanhee Inn** 12 Anne's Way, off Rte-142, Weld ☎ 207 585 2000, ⓦ maineinn.net. Classic waterfront lodge with plenty of Adirondack chairs, board games, swimming, hiking and rustic guest rooms overlooking Lake Webb. Eight cabins also on site, and the area's best restaurant. Late May to mid-Oct. **$110**

Loon Lodge Inn & Restaurant 16 Pickford Rd ☎ 207 864 5666, ⓦ loonlodgeme.com. This swish-looking log cabin has two types of accommodation: classic lodge-style in the upstairs 100-year-old section, with quilts, antler lamps and some shared bathrooms; downstairs has two new, more upscale rooms, with entrances that open onto the lawn and the lake. The dining room bakes a mean pumpernickel loaf, and there are frequent roaring fires in the oversized fireplace. **$90**

Pleasant Street Inn Bed & Breakfast 104 Pleasant St ☎ 207 864 5916, ⓦ pleasantstreetinnbb.com. Charming burgundy clapboard house run as a B&B by two caring hosts. Although you'll find quilts on the beds, the five guest rooms have a modern feel and are very well tended. Ask for room no. 5, which comes with a bubbling whirlpool tub and heated tile floors. **$140**

LOONY TUNES

If you stay lakeside in Maine, don't be surprised if you're awakened by the mournful cry of the **Common Loon** signaling to its mate. An iconic state creature that holds its own alongside the moose and lobster, this beloved water bird is an excellent swimmer that can dive up to 200ft and remain submerged for ten minutes, and, remarkably, will migrate back to the very same lake year after year. Quite the noisemaker, it has another famous call – the **tremolo** – that sounds like unhinged laughter (it's actually made in times of irritation, such as when a boat comes too close to its nest). A symbol of untamed wilderness, loons are a threatened species. Help preserve their habitat by using non-lead fishing tackle (even one lead sinker can kill a loon), and respect "slow, no-wake" zones when boating. For more information, head to ⓦ loon.org.

EATING AND DRINKING

Moosely Bagels 2588 Main St ☎207 864 5955. This friendly café serves home-made muffins, eggs benedict, sandwiches with a sense of humour (there's one dubbed "the frost heave" in honour of the area's crackly winter roads) and salads to a happy band of regulars. Over 25 daily varieties of coffee. Daily 6.30am–8pm.

★ **The Shed** 2647 Main St ☎207 864 3030. Pit boss Martin gets up early to smoke his pulled pork and ribs in a little wooden roadside shack – "it's done when it's ready". May to late Sept Mon–Sat 11.30am–9pm, Sun 4–8pm.

Sugarloaf USA and Kingfield

The road east of Rangeley cuts through prime moose-watching territory – in fact, locals call Rte-16 "Moose Alley". After about fifty miles, in the Carrabassett Valley, looms the huge mountain of **SUGARLOAF USA**, Maine's biggest ski resort (lift tickets $78; ☎1 800 843 5623, ⓦsugarloaf.com). A spectacular place for skiers of all abilities, with over 130 trails, this condo-studded centre would be a more popular destination if it weren't for the fact that the nearest airport is a two-hour drive away in Portland. Summer activities include a **zipline** over the woods and Gondi Brook ($39; details as above). There's also a full complement of hiking, canoe trips and cookouts, plus a **golf** course designed by Robert Trent Jones, Jr.

Kingfield

A good base for Sugarloaf is fifteen miles south in the tiny town of **KINGFIELD**. The town was the birthplace of twins Francis and Freelan Stanley, who invented, among other things, the famous Stanley Steamer car and the dry-plate photographic process (which they sold to Kodak).

Stanley Museum

40 School St • June–Oct Tues–Sun 1–4pm; Nov–May Tues–Fri only • $4 • ☎207 265 2729, ⓦstanleymuseum.org

The **Stanley Museum** celebrates the Stanley twins' story. Part of the main room is given over to their sister Chansonetta, a remarkable photographer whose studies of rural and urban workers have been widely published. Other exhibits include working steam cars from the early 1900s – if you're lucky, they might have one fired up when you arrive.

ACCOMMODATION

The Herbert Grand Hotel 246 Main St ☎207 265 2000, ⓦherbertgrandhotel.com. Nearly 100 years old, this stately hotel cuts an impressive figure on Main Street. Rooms are functional and pet-friendly. $129

Mountain Village Farm B&B 164 Main St ☎207 265 2030, ⓦmountainvillageinn.com. This bucolic farmhouse has wood-panelled floors, puffy pillows with tasteful linens, striped wallpaper, fresh eggs for breakfast (there's a barn out back) and terrific views of Sugarloaf Mountain from the dining room. $89

EATING AND DRINKING

★ **Bag & Kettle** Sugarloaf Mountain ☎207 237 2451. Refuel after a morning on the slopes at this quintessential apres-ski pub. Outstanding "Bag" burgers with special sauce, great pizza, salads, curly fries and a number of their own beers on tap. Early Oct to April daily 11am–9pm.

★ **Orange Cat Café** 329 Main St ☎207 265 2860. Groovy lunchtime hangout with fresh wraps, salads, espresso and wi-fi. Mon–Sat 7am–3pm, Sun 8am–3pm.

Tufulio's 10 miles north in the Carrabassett Valley on Rte-27 ☎207 235 2010. A good year-round Italian spot with the likes of chicken marsala, pizza and tiramisu served at sunlit wooden booths illuminated by stained-glass windows. Daily 4pm–late.

Moosehead Lake and around

Serene waters lap gently at the miles of deserted, thickly wooded shores around **Moosehead Lake**, which at 117 square miles is the largest lake in Maine. **Greenville** is the sole settlement of any size, and it makes a good base from which to explore the

HIKING AND BIKING AROUND MOOSEHEAD LAKE

One good hiking spot is **Kineo**, an isolated nature preserve in the middle of the lake. Island trails lead to the top of dramatic **Mount Kineo**, whose flint-like cliff face rises some 800ft above the lake's surface. Shuttle boats here leave from Rockwood (late May to mid-Oct daily 8am–5pm; $10 round-trip; ☎207 534 9012). Other good **hikes** in the area include the trip to **Gulf Hagas**, a 300ft gorge fifteen miles east of town off Greenville Road; the walk to an old B-52 crash site on nearby Elephant Mountain; and difficult climbs to the summits of 3196ft **Big Moose Mountain** and 3230ft **Big Spencer Mountain**. A good way to explore the area is on a **mountain bike**; you can rent them ($25/day), along with canoes, kayaks and camping equipment at Northwoods Outfitters, at 5 Lily Bay Rd in Greenville (☎1 866 223 1380, ⊛maineoutfitter.com).

area, especially if you want to see moose or go whitewater rafting, though **The Forks**, a settlement along the **Kennebec River** and US-201, has emerged as the centre of the whitewater industry (see box, p.516). West of the lake, along Rte.15, gritty **Jackman**, big with the **snowmobile** crowd in winter, is the last stop before the Canadian border.

Greenville

With a population of 1600, **GREENVILLE**, at the southern end of Moosehead Lake, is a nineteenth-century lumber town that now makes its living primarily from tourism. People come from all over to see wild **moose**, indigenous to the area, and there is nary a business around here that doesn't somehow incorporate the animal into its name. The *Birches Resort* (☎1 800 825 9453, ⊛birches.com) offers, for $35 and up, moose-spotting safaris, where you're also likely to see eagles, otters and blue herons.

This idyllic little town is well positioned for exploration within the Maine woods. The real attraction here, however, is the **lake**: a seamless, inky blot that, come nightfall, takes on the appearance of an enormous moonlit mirror. You can get out on the water via the restored **steamboat**, *Katahdin*, which tours the lake and serves as the floating Moosehead Marine Museum – no high heels or smoking on the ship (call for cruise times; $32–37; ☎207 695 2716). Near the dock, tiny **Thoreau Park** has a couple of picnic tables and a sign commemorating the writer's 1857 visit to Moosehead Lake, of which he remarked "looking into which the beholder measures the depth of his own nature". Greenville is the largest **seaplane** base in New England; contact Currier's Flying Service (☎207 695 2778, ⊛curriersflyingservice.com) or Jack's Air Service (☎207 695 3020).

8

INFORMATION
GREENVILLE

Chamber of Commerce Just south of town on Rte-6/15 (Mon–Sat 10am–4pm; ☎207 695 2702). Has lots of information about area activities and accommodation. As an alternative, the Maine Forest Service (☎207 695 3721) can provide information on their many free campsites in the area.

ACCOMMODATION

★ **Blair Hill Inn** 351 Lily Bay Rd ☎207 695 0224, ⊛blairhillinn.com. You can't help but fall in love with this inn, certainly one of the most beautiful properties in the state, and perhaps all of New England. An 1891 "gentleman's farm" perched on a hilly pedestal, it has expansive front lawn that slopes down to Moosehead Lake, creating a spectacular view. The eight guest rooms are posh and modern, yet the owners have taken care to maintain the historical integrity of the building. Dinner in its restaurant (lit with original Tiffany lamps) is the best in the area, the bar is hopping, and there's even an excellent summer concert series. May–Oct. $295

★ **Little Lyford Pond Camps** ☎603 466 2727. At the other end of the luxury scale from the *Blair Hill Inn*, yet no less beloved, this remote AMC lodge and set of rustic cabins, accessible via the logging roads, offers showers, flush toilets, hiking, biking and outdoor activities galore. Prices include lunch and dinner. Jan–March & mid-May to mid-Oct. $84

EATING AND DRINKING

The Rod & Reel 44 Pritham Ave ☎207 695 0388. Given this restaurant's name, the type of food that's served here may not surprise you, but you will be pleased to discover the quality and care that's put into your meal – be it surf, turf or home-made dessert. A local favourite, just across from the lake. Mains $11–23. April–Oct Wed–Sat 4–8.30pm, Jan & Feb Sat & Sun only.

Stress Free Moose Pub & Café 65 Pritham Ave ☎ 207

695 3100. Filling pub grub and deli sandwiches, but it's more about the bar's ambience and lakeside outdoor patio. Inside there's a good selection of beers amid placards with fun sayings such as "beauty is in the eye of the beer holder". Open late (for Greenville). Daily 11am–10pm.

Jackman

Fifty miles west of Greenville, gritty **JACKMAN** is a small frontier border town that was once a centre for logging. Situated next to deserted Wood Pond, less than twenty miles from the Canadian border, its main attraction is as a haven for **snowmobiles**, which take over the parking lots and surrounding lumber roads in winter. You can rent one of the noisy crafts at Dana's Rentals on Main Street (☎ 207 668 7828) for about $180–270. **Ice-fishing** is also popular in winter and several local businesses sell non-resident licences, bait and tackle. In summer, a forty-mile circuit known as the Moose River **Bow Trip** is one of the better flat-water **canoe trips** in the state, with good fishing and several **campsites** scattered along the way.

INFORMATION

JACKMAN

Jackman Moose River Chamber of Commerce Main St (☎ 207 668 4171, ⓦ jackmanmaine.org). This place can

help you locate a guide, if you so desire.

ACCOMMODATION

Bishop's Motel 461 Main St ☎ 1 888 991 7669, ⓦ bishopsmotel.com. Basic, very clean motel rooms right in the centre of town with brand-new mattresses, flat-screen TVs and coffee-makers. The proprietors are lovely. $99

Sally Mountain Cabins 9 Elm St ☎ 207 668 5621. Rustic cabins along Bigwood Lake with full kitchens and private bathrooms. $35/person

EATING AND DRINKING

Big Wood Steakhouse 1 Forest St ☎ 207 668 5572. This little chocolate-coloured lodge with colossal moose antlers above its front door cooks up bounteous pasta dishes, ribs and lumberjack-sized steaks for a very contented crowd. Thurs & Sun 4–8.30pm, Fri & Sat till 9pm.

Mama Bear's 420 Main St ☎ 207 668 4222. Casual all-day diner with egg breakfasts, veggie burgers, basic steak dinners and some Québécois fare. The BLT is stellar, and it's a steal at $4. Daily 5am–8pm.

Baxter State Park

On a clear day in unspoilt **Baxter State Park**, the 5268ft peak of imposing and beautiful **Katahdin** is visible from afar. Entrance to the park, collected at the Togue Pond Gate on Park Tote Road, costs $14 per car, and you should plan to arrive early in the day, as

---

WHITEWATER RAFTING

The **Penobscot** and the **Kennebec** are the two most popular rivers in Maine for the exhilarating sport of **whitewater rafting**. Along Rte-201 between Bingham and Jackman, **The Forks** (population: 35), is the undisputed rafting centre and the majority of the outfitters are based there, along with the deluxe lodges and camps they've built to house eager outdoors enthusiasts. Run from May to mid-October, most trips depart in the early morning and return by mid-afternoon and require advance reservations. Levels of difficulty vary, but the rafting companies insist that people of all athletic abilities are welcome on most trips, which, as dictated by state law, are all led by certified "Maine guides". However, many companies do have **age requirements**. Raft Maine (☎ 1 800 723 8633, ⓦ raftmaine.com) is an association comprised of several outfitters that can answer your questions. Several whitewater rafting companies have set up lodgings and **campsites** next to Millinocket Lake, ten miles northwest, as bases for their trips down the Penobscot River.

only a limited number of visitors are permitted access to Katahdin trailheads. The enormous park – covering over 200,000 acres – was the single-handed creation of former Maine governor Percival P. Baxter, who, having failed to persuade the state to buy the imposing Katahdin and the land around it, bought it himself between the 1930s and 1960s and deeded it bit by bit to the state on condition that it remain "forever wild". A 4000-acre parcel was recently added which includes Katahdin Lake and a wildlife sanctuary, best accessed by Katahdin Lake Wilderness Camps (wkatahdinlakewildernesscamps.com) on the eastern side, a privately owned site that dates to 1885. The park's majestic green peaks (48 in all) and deserted ponds remain tremendously remote and pristine, and sightings of bears, bald eagles, and (of course) moose are not uncommon.

Hiking and camping

Hiking is the major pursuit here; indeed, the northern terminus of the **Appalachian Trail** is at the top of Katahdin, and in summer, many champagne-popping family and friends join hikers here to celebrate their completion of the circuit. Among the park's 186 miles of trails, don't miss the **Knife Edge**, a thrilling walk across a narrow path that connects Katahdin's two peaks. The higher and typically more crowded of these, **Baxter Peak**, can also be reached via the **Hunt Trail** (5.2 miles, from Katahdin Stream), the **Cathedral Trail** and the **Saddle Trail** (both around two miles, originating at Chimney Pond). For a less crowded but equally rewarding jaunt, head to the top of Hamlin Peak on the two-mile **Hamlin Ridge Trail**, which starts at Chimney Pond. Wherever you plan to hike, stop beforehand at any of the visitor centres or at any of the park's campgrounds for a detailed **hiking map**. Water in the park is not treated.

8

INFORMATION	BAXTER STATE PARK

Tourist information Visitor centre headquarters are in Millinocket, 64 Balsam Drive, next to *McDonald's* (☎ 207 723 5140, wbaxterstateparkauthority.com). There is another centre at Togue Pond, the southern entrance to the park.

ACCOMMODATION	

Baxter Park Inn 935 Central St/Rte-11, Millinocket ☎ 1 866 633 9777, wbaxterparkinn.com. Standard, yet jacuzzi-enhanced, hotel rooms, which include free continental breakfasts and an accompanying newspaper. Pet-friendly. **$130**

Camping There are ten designated campgrounds in Baxter (☎ 207 723 5140), providing an array of options from basic tent sites to cabins equipped with beds, heating stoves, and gas lighting. **$10–27**

North to Canada

The northernmost tip of Maine is taken up by **Aroostook County**, which covers an area larger than several small states. Although its main activity is the large-scale cultivation of potatoes, it is also the location of the **Allagash Wilderness Waterway**, where several whitewater rafting companies put in boats (see box, p.516). If you're driving along Rte-1 between Presque Isle and Houlton, keep an eye out for the forty-mile long **solar system** built entirely by local residents that appears in scaled intervals here beside the highway. Early March is a fun (albeit Arctic) time to visit "The County", when the Can-Am Crown International Sled Dog Races take place in Fort Kent. Exhilarating for mushers and spectators alike, one of the races is an astounding 250 miles long, and in years past, contestants have battled everything from blizzards, thinning ice and -32°F temperatures for the thrill of crossing the finish line.

DUTCH MAP OF NEW ENGLAND

Contexts

519 History
528 New England on film
531 Books

History

New England has been inhabited by humans for at least ten thousand years, though little is known about its earliest peoples. By the time Europeans started arriving in the region it was populated by an estimated 100,000 Algonquian-speaking Native Americans, including the Abenaki, Narragansett, Niantic, Penobscot, Pequot, Wampanoag and many others. Columbus may have "discovered" America in 1492, but it's often forgotten that European colonization of North America didn't get going for another 120 years. During that time seasonal cod fishermen from England and Spain sometimes visited the New England coast (especially up in Maine), and in 1524 Giovanni da Verrazzano met local Native American *sachems* (leaders) at Narragansett Bay, Rhode Island, but no attempt was made at permanent settlement.

The Pilgrims

The permanent European settlement of New England began with the establishment of Plymouth (or "Plimoth"), by the English **Pilgrims** in 1620. The settlers were a motley bunch of religious separatists known as **Puritans**, exiles from England, plus hired help such as Myles Standish, professional soldier, and John Alden, cooper. In all, just over one hundred passengers set sail aboard the *Mayflower* from Southampton, England, on September 16, 1620. After two months at sea, they reached the North American coast at **Provincetown**, Cape Cod, on November 19. The same day, 41 men signed the **Mayflower Compact**, in which they agreed to establish a "Civic Body Politic" (temporary government) and to be bound by its laws. The Compact became the basis of government in the **Plymouth Colony**.

The new arrivals had landed on a virtually barren stretch of the coast, and soon resettled across the bay, arriving at what is now **Plymouth**, Massachusetts, on December 26, 1620. Only half the colonists survived their first winter on American soil. Unaccustomed to the **extreme cold**, many died from pneumonia; scurvy and other infections killed many more. It would have been even worse but for **Squanto** (see box, p.520), a Native American who had spent time in England. He managed to enlist the support of **Massasoit**, the local Wampanoag *sachem*, who signed a Treaty of Friendship, and plied the visitors with food (in part because he wanted their help dealing with a rival tribe, the Narragansett). Exactly a year after their arrival in Plymouth, the surviving colonists sat down with the Wampanoag to enjoy a feast – an occasion still celebrated in America today, at the end of November, as **Thanksgiving**.

1524	1602	1614	1616–19
Giovanni da Verrazzano explores Narragansett Bay, Rhode Island.	Bartholomew Gosnold names Cape Cod and Martha's Vineyard.	John Smith charts the New England coast.	Great epidemic (probably hepatitis) wipes out hundreds of Native American communities along the New England coast.

THE AGE OF EXPLORATION AND DISEASE

With the **Spanish** focusing almost exclusively on the southern regions of what is now North America in the sixteenth century, the Dutch, English and French were left to explore the cooler and less hospitable shores of New England. Italian explorer **Giovanni da Verrazzano**, sailing for Francis I of France, travelled as far north as Rhode Island's Narragansett Bay in 1524. In 1602 Englishman **Bartholomew Gosnold** visited the region, naming Cape Cod and Martha's Vineyard (he was to be one of the first colonists of Virginia in 1607). In 1603 fellow Englishman **Martin Pring** spent two months on Cape Cod, exploring the New England coast before returning home, while beginning in 1605 French explorer **Samuel Champlain** began extensive exploration of the same area. Finally, in 1614 **John Smith** sailed along the Massachusetts coast and named the region "New England". One of Smith's captains, **Thomas Hunt**, abducted many Native Americans as slaves, souring relations on the coast for years to come; one of those taken became known as Squanto, who eventually returned to help the Pilgrims. Worse was to follow for the **native tribes** along the coast, though: between 1616 and 1619 it is estimated that up to ninety percent of them died in a terrible **epidemic**, most likely viral hepatitis A carried over by European sailors. Those further inland, like the Narragansett, were spared, only to be decimated by a smallpox epidemic in 1633.

The early colonies

By 1624 Plymouth had become a thriving village of thirty cottages. News of the community's success reached England, and in 1629 another group, led by London lawyer **John Winthrop**, obtained a royal charter as the "Company of the Massachusetts Bay in New England". Winthrop had lofty goals for the colony, aspiring that it would be a "city upon a hill" – a model Christian town that others would look to as an example. That summer Winthrop and more than three hundred settlers arrived at Salem and founded Boston the following year; thousands more followed in the 1630s, as the persecution of Puritans in England intensified. By 1640, the **Massachusetts Bay Company** comprised around ten thousand colonists.

The colonies spread

New arrivals in the colonies were not limited to Massachusetts. In **Connecticut**, the Reverend Thomas Hooker established the community that would become Hartford in 1636, while Theophilus Eaton and John Davenport founded New Haven in 1638. But friction was already developing among the settlers, many of whom were proving to be even less tolerant than their oppressors in England. The **Reverend Roger Williams**, hounded out of the Massachusetts Bay Colony for his liberal views, established a settlement at Providence, in 1638, on land made available by two Narragansett *sachems*. The new **State of Rhode Island and Providence Plantations** guaranteed **religious freedom** for all Jews, Huguenots and even Quakers, in its 1663 charter. Communities were also established in New Hampshire in the 1620s, and Maine in the 1640s.

As the colonial population grew, so did the perceived need for clergy, preferably trained in New England. In 1636, **Harvard College** was established for that specific purpose. Several Native Americans were sent to Harvard to train as **Christian clergy** – although only one completed the training – and by the 1660s, one fifth of all Native Americans were nominally Christian.

1620	1629	1634–38	1636
The Pilgrims establish Plymouth, the first permanent English colony in New England.	Massachusetts Bay Colony established; Governor John Winthrop arrives in 1630 and founds Boston.	Pequot War: Conflict between the Pequot tribe and the Massachusetts colonies.	Rhode Island and Connecticut Colony founded. Harvard College is established in Cambridge, MT.

Conflict

At first, the new settlers and the Native Americans had been able to coexist peacefully, though a series of **epidemics** introduced by the colonists were responsible for decimating the local population. As the colonists expanded, they met growing resistance, particularly from the proud Pequot tribe, with whom war erupted in 1636, at Fort Mystic and Fairfield; many lives were lost on both sides. Then, in 1675, Narragansett leader Metacom, also known as Philip, persuaded feuding tribes, principally the Nipmuck, Narragansett and Wampanoag, to bury their differences and join in a concerted campaign against the settlers. Known as **King Philip's War**, hostilities culminated in the **Great Swamp Fight** in Kingston, Rhode Island. More than two thousand Native Americans were killed, including Metacom himself. More significantly, the outcome of the conflict signaled the destruction of independent Native American society in most of New England.

The road to revolution

Until the middle of the seventeenth century, the colonies were largely left to take care of themselves, as England was preoccupied with domestic concerns (including a bloody civil war, the beheading of Charles I and the establishment of Oliver Cromwell's parliamentary republic). To a certain extent, though, the colonists retained intimate cultural and economic ties to Great Britain, a relationship complicated further by often hostile dealings with the Native Americans and the **French**. The latter group maintained an active presence throughout North America up until the end of the **French and Indian War** (1754–63), when they ceded all land east of the Mississippi to Great Britain, with the exception of New Orleans. The exit of the French and the gradual decline of the Native American tribes set the stage for separatism, as the colonists no longer relied on Great Britain for defense. Defiance against an increasingly domineering Crown, fueled by unpopular laws and taxes, quickly escalated.

In 1686, King James II revoked the northern colonies' charters and attempted to create a **Dominion of New England** stretching from Maine to New Jersey. Allegedly a security measure to protect the English communities from the French and the Indians, it was in reality an attempt to keep tabs on an increasingly defiant populace. The king's first gubernatorial appointees were staunch **Anglicans**, which only increased the colonists' frustration.

A new respect between the Crown and colonies was temporarily forged in 1689, when the "Glorious Revolution" brought Protestants William and Mary to the British throne, but conditions reverted in 1760 with the crowning of King George III. In a move designed not so much to raise revenue as to remind the colonists who was boss, he imposed the **Revenue Act of 1764**, which taxed sugar, silk and wine. In reaction, colonists instituted a boycott of British goods and supplies. The situation deteriorated further in 1765, with the introduction of the **Stamp Act** and the imposition of taxes on commercial and legal documents, newspapers and even playing cards. Protests erupted throughout New England. The bulk of the demonstrations were peaceful, but in Boston the houses of stampman Andrew Oliver and Governor Thomas Hutchinson were plundered. British prime minister William Pitt **repealed** the act in March 1766.

1675–76	**1692**	**1706**	**1770**	**1773**
King Philip's War: Devastating conflict between colonists and local Native American tribes.	Salem Witch Trials: nineteen people were hanged (and one crushed to death) by 1693.	Benjamin Franklin born in Boston.	Boston Massacre: five colonists killed by British troops.	Boston Tea Party: 350 chests of tea dumped into Boston Harbor.

The Boston Massacre

In the summer of 1767, new British chancellor of the exchequer Charles Townshend arrogantly taunted the colonies with the remark, "I dare tax America". The subsequent **Townshend Acts**, which introduced harsh levies on imports such as paper, glass and tea, prompted the dispatch to Boston of two regiments of British soldiers, called "Redcoats" for their bright red uniform jackets. On March 5, 1770, a crowd of several hundred Bostonians gathered to ridicule a "lobster-back" guard outside the customs house. The scene turned ugly as stones and rocks were thrown, and seven nervous reinforcements arrived, one firing on the crowd without orders. In the panic, more shots followed. Three colonists were pronounced dead at the scene and two were mortally wounded in the event that was to become known as the **Boston Massacre**.

The Boston Tea Party

Eventually the Townshend acts were repealed, though not the tax on **East Indian tea**, which was boycotted by the colonists. Dutch blends were smuggled in, and a special brew called "Liberty Tea" was concocted from sage, currant or plantain leaves. Britain responded in September 1773 by flooding the market with half a million pounds of its own subsidized blend. Resistance to the British tea focused on Boston, where the **Massachusetts Committee of Correspondence**, an unofficial legislature, and the local chapter of the **Sons of Liberty**, a pseudo-secret society, organized the barricading of the piers and wharves and demanded Governor Hutchinson send home the tea-filled ship *Dartmouth*. When Hutchinson refused, sixty men disguised as Mohawk Indians, Samuel Adams and John Hancock among them, surreptitiously climbed aboard and dumped 350 crates of the tea into Boston Harbor. The date was December 16, 1773, and the event captured the world's imagination as the **Boston Tea Party**.

This blatant act of defiance rattled Parliament, which introduced the so-called "**Coercive Acts**", among them the Boston Port Act, which sealed off the city with a massive naval blockade. Meanwhile, American patriots from Massachusetts, Rhode Island and other states gathered in Philadelphia for the **First Continental Congress**, convened on September 5, 1774. Though British garrisons still controlled the major towns, such was the antagonism in rural areas that policing them was becoming virtually impossible. All the while locals continued to stockpile arms and munitions.

The Revolution

In April 1775, London instructed its Boston-based commander, **General Thomas Gage**, to put down rebellion in rural Massachusetts, where the provincial congress had assumed de facto political control. On the night of April 18, Gage dispatched seven hundred soldiers to destroy the arms depot in Concord, while at nearby Lexington seventy colonial soldiers, known as **Minute Men** (because they were prepared to fight at a moment's notice), lay in wait, having been warned of the plan by Paul Revere and William Dawes. On Lexington's town common, British musket fire resulted in the deaths of eight Americans. The British moved on to Concord, where they were repelled, and were eventually pushed back to Boston, losing 273 men on the way to the colonists' ambushes.

1775	**1776**	**1783**	**1786**
Warned by Paul Revere, colonial "Minute Men" fend off British troops at Concord – Revolutionary War begins.	Declaration of Independence; British evacuate Boston.	Treaty of Paris formally ends war with Britain and gives the colonies independence.	Shays' Rebellion: disgruntled Massachusetts citizens mount short-lived rebellion against central government.

The Battle of Bunker Hill

A couple of months later, the war intensified with the **Battle of Bunker Hill**, on Boston's Charlestown peninsula, which General Artemus Ward of the Continental Army had ordered to be fortified – though it was actually on nearby Breed's Hill, not Bunker, where the American forces were stationed. On June 17, the Redcoats attacked twice, and were twice rebuffed. The third attempt succeeded because the Americans ran out of ammunition – the much-celebrated order "don't fire until you see the whites of their eyes" was given (some say by Colonel William Prescott, others by General Isaac Putnam) specifically to save bullets. Bunker Hill, with a thousand British casualties, was an expensive triumph for the Crown. Worn down by lack of manpower, low morale and growing American resistance, less than a year later an embattled General Gage ordered a **British withdrawal** to Halifax, Nova Scotia.

Independence

The **Declaration of Independence** – with fifty-six signatories, fourteen of whom were from **Massachusetts**, **Connecticut**, **New Hampshire** and **Rhode Island** – was adopted by the Continental Congress on July 4, 1776. The war, however, was far from over; hostilities between the colonists and the British continued for another five years, though New England was mostly untouched by the conflict. In the fall of 1781, General George Washington, with significant French naval support, led a decisive victory against the British at the port of Yorktown, Virginia, essentially quashing British hopes for victory. In 1783 the **Treaty of Paris** formally ended the war and established the independence of the colonies from Great Britain.

The thirteen colonies had hammered out an integrated union in 1781, though not without the concern that a **centralized federal system** would be just as bad as British rule. For that reason, heroes Sam Adams and John Hancock gave only grudging support to the Constitution, and representatives from Rhode Island consistently voted against it, relenting only after the Bill of Rights was added. **Vermont** remained an independent republic until 1791, when it was admitted to the Union as the **fourteenth state**. In 1796, John Adams of Massachusetts became the second president of the US, but was defeated by Thomas Jefferson in 1800 – John's son, John Quincy Adams, was the next New England president (1825–29). In 1820, Maine voted to secede from Massachusetts. Following the Missouri Compromise of 1820, Maine was admitted to the Union as a free (anti-slavery) state (the 23rd state), balanced by Missouri, a slave state.

LOYALISTS AND SHAYS' REBELLION

Not everyone was happy in the colonies at the end of the Revolutionary War. Some 15 to 20 percent of the population (though much less in New England) were known as **Loyalists** and had supported the British Crown; thousands left after the war, many settling in New Brunswick, Canada, across the border from Maine.

In Massachusetts, cash was a more pressing issue; when farmers here started losing their property to creditors looking to recover war debts in 1786, Daniel Shays led hundreds of his compatriots to the county courthouse in Northampton before attacking the federal arsenal in Springfield in what would later be known as **Shays' Rebellion**. The rebels were dispersed in January 1787 by the state militia, and Shays was later pardoned.

1791	1793	1797–1801	1812–14	1820
Vermont joins the Union.	Samuel Slater opens first mechanized textile mill in Pawtucket, RI; Eli Whitney invents the cotton gin.	Boston lawyer John Adams becomes second US president.	War of 1812 pits the United States against the British Empire once more.	Maine joins the Union.

Nineteenth-century development

New England began as a predominantly **agricultural region**. However, apart from some parts of Vermont, the soil was generally rocky, making ploughing difficult, and long, cold winters meant that the ground was frozen solid for a large part of the year. The land really lent itself to little more than subsistence farming, with small farms, wheat, corn, pigs and cattle.

The region's true prosperity came first as a result of its **connection with the sea**: fishing, especially for cod, was important, as was **whaling** for whale oil, used for heating and lighting, and based in Nantucket and New Bedford, Massachusetts. More adventurous sea captains, many of them based in Boston or Salem, Massachusetts, ventured farther afield, and brought back great treasures from India and China, including tea, spices, silk and opium. Several communities, including Newport and Providence, Rhode Island, flourished through the so-called **Triangular Trade**: ships unloaded West Indian molasses, reloaded with rum, then sailed to Africa, where the rum was exchanged for slaves, in turn shipped to the West Indies and traded for molasses. **Shipbuilding** industries flourished, particularly in places such as Essex, Massachusetts. But the first two decades of the nineteenth century showed how volatile maritime trade was, especially with so many political uncertainties, notably the Napoleonic Wars, Thomas Jefferson's **Embargo Acts** (which prohibited all exports to Europe and restricted imports from Great Britain – a response to British and French interference with American ships), and the **War of 1812**, during which Stonington and Essex in Connecticut were attacked.

The Industrial Revolution

In 1789, **Samuel Slater**, a skilled mechanic from England, sailed to New York disguised as a labourer (the emigration of skilled mechanics was forbidden by the British government, and there were also serious penalties against smuggling drawings of industrial machinery). Undaunted, Slater memorized the specifications, and with financial backing provided by Moses Brown, a Providence Quaker, he set up the nation's first successful **cotton mill** in Pawtucket, Rhode Island.

Another entrepreneur determined to duplicate British weaving feats was Bostonian **Francis Cabot Lowell**, a self-styled "industrial tourist" who set up a small mill with a power loom in Waltham, Massachusetts. Lowell's **Merrimack Manufacturing Company** proved extremely profitable, with sales at $3000 in 1815 and reaching $345,000 in 1822. In 1826, having already moved once to Chelmsford, the business relocated again, to a purpose-built community named "Lowell" after its founder.

New England was fast becoming the **industrial centre** of the US, home to some two-thirds of the nation's cotton mills, half of which were in Massachusetts. Tiny Rhode Island processed twenty percent of the nation's wool, and in Connecticut Hartford-born **Samuel Colt** manufactured the first firearms with interchangeable parts. Massachusetts native and Yale graduate **Eli Whitney** also popularized and perfected interchangeable parts, and invented the cotton gin in the 1790s. Connecticut also became home to a thriving watch- and clock-making industry. And in the fields of paper and shoe manufacture and metalworking, New England, in particular New Hampshire, was unsurpassed.

1831	1836	1838	1839–42
The Liberator, an abolitionist newspaper, is founded by William Lloyd Garrison in Boston.	Publication of Ralph Waldo Emerson's *Nature* considered the beginning of the Transcendentalist movement.	Escaped slave Frederick Douglass settles in New Bedford, MA.	The Amistad trials take place in New Haven, CT.

THE BIRTH OF AN AMERICAN CULTURE

New England, particularly Boston, was a pioneer in American culture and education. The nation's first secondary school, Boston Latin, opened here in 1635, while the first **university**, Harvard, was established in 1636. Yale University was founded in 1701 in Connecticut, while Brown University, originally Rhode Island College, came into being in 1764 in Providence. Farther north, New Hampshire's Dartmouth College dates from 1769, and Bowdoin College in Maine from 1796.

In 1639, America's first **printing press** was set up in Cambridge, where the *Bay Psalm Book* and *New England Primer* were among the first published works. The colonies' first newspaper came into being in 1690, succeeded by the popular *Boston News-Letter* in 1704. By the 1850s, more than four hundred periodicals were in print. **Libraries** such as Hartford's famous Wadsworth Atheneum and the Providence Athenaeum both came into existence in the mid-nineteenth century, while in 1854 the Boston Public Library, with 750,000 volumes, became the world's first free municipal library.

With these developments, New England came to occupy a prominent place in the American cultural landscape. Easily recognized names include Henry David Thoreau, the **transcendentalist** philosopher and essayist; the poet Emily Dickinson; writers Ralph Waldo Emerson, Louisa May Alcott, Nathaniel Hawthorne, Mark Twain and Harriet Beecher Stowe; and numerous others. In Boston, the 1871 founding of the **Museum of Fine Arts** was followed a decade later by the Boston Symphony Orchestra and the Boston Pops. New Haven also became an important focus for **theatre**, with the establishment of the Long Wharf, Shubert, and Yale Repertory stages.

Abolition and the Civil War

By the 1850s most New Englanders actually held ambivalent views about slavery, even though all the region's states had abolished the practice (Vermont was the first, way back in 1777) and the region was a major component of the **Underground Railway** (helping escaped slaves to freedom). Indeed, the American **abolitionist movement** was largely based in Boston and New England – **William Lloyd Garrison**, **Wendell Phillips** and escaped-slave come New Bedford resident **Frederick Douglass** were leaders of the movement. Connecticut-born **John Brown** helped fan the flames of war with his failed raid on **Harpers Ferry** in 1859. When the **Civil War** began in earnest in 1861 the region sent thousands of men to bolster the Union cause, many of whom never returned. The **54th Massachusetts Volunteer Infantry Regiment** was one of the first official black units in the war, almost wiped out at Fort Wagner in 1863. By then Abraham Lincoln had issued the **Emancipation Proclamation**, ennobling what would otherwise have been just a nasty, brutal conflict. In the end, it was sheer economic power as much as the brilliance of the generals that won the war for the Union. It was the North, with New England leading the way, which was able to maintain full trading with the rest of the world while diverting spare resources to the production of munitions. Other than losing an egregious amount of soldiers, New England was physically untouched by the war.

Into the twentieth century

The Industrial Revolution and the Civil War created a sea of change for New England in the latter half of the nineteenth century. Meanwhile, the US frontier moved west,

1845	1850–1910	1851	1861–65
Henry David Thoreau embarks on his two-year experiment in simple living at Walden Pond.	New England develops as a major summer destination for the Gilded Age elite.	Herman Melville completes *Moby Dick* in Lenox, MA; it is a commercial failure.	US Civil War; thousands of men from New England are killed.

and other regions also began to play their part in the development of the nation. Despite a **diminishing influence** on the national stage, New England nonetheless maintained a strong tradition of social reform, paving the way in the fields of prison reform and health and mental health provision.

Meanwhile, the ethnic and religious make-up of New England was changing rapidly. No longer was it the preserve of white Anglo-Saxon Protestants; in the 1840s, following the potato famine, **Irish immigrants** began arriving. Soon more than a thousand Irish immigrants a month were landing in Boston, while Catholics from Italy, French Canada, Portugal and Eastern Europe accounted for two-thirds of the total population growth during the nineteenth century. Indeed, by 1907, seventy percent of Massachusetts' population could claim to be of non-Anglo-Saxon descent, and immigrants gradually found their way into the political system. In 1881, John Breen from Tipperary became the first Irishman to take up an establishment position, as mayor of Lawrence, Massachusetts. This had a profound motivating effect on his fellow countrymen, and three years later, Hugh O'Brien won the Boston mayorship, while Patrick Andrew Collin represented Suffolk County with a congressional seat in the nation's capital. By the turn of the twentieth century, immigrants were represented at all levels of government.

But political scandal and **corruption** were never far away. "Boss" Charlie Brayton and the *Providence Journal* ring bought their way to office in Rhode Island, with individual votes costing $2 to $5, and up to $30 in hotly contested elections. Others abused the support they enjoyed: **James Michael Curley**, elected Boston mayor four times, and governor of Massachusetts from 1934 to 1938, did much to improve the welfare of the poor, but also doled out jobs and money to community leaders who carefully manipulated the electorate.

With the huge influx of poor immigrants, especially from Catholic countries, a "**New Puritanism**" began to take hold. Encouraged by Boston-based Catholic leader William Cardinal O'Connell and the closely associated **Watch and Ward Society**, moralists lobbied for the prohibition of, among other things, Hemingway's *The Sun Also Rises* and a variety of plays and books.

The southern exodus

As time passed, other regions began to challenge New England's claim to be the manufacturing capital of the US. Many companies **moved south**, where costs were much lower, and by 1923 more than half of the nation's cotton goods were being woven there. Industrial production in Massachusetts alone fell by more than $1 billion

---

THE KENNEDYS

Few New England families had such an impact on the twentieth century as the Kennedys, led by Boston-based Irish American businessman **Joseph P. Kennedy**. His sons all became politicians: John F. Kennedy became senator and 35th US president in 1961; **Robert F. Kennedy** was a senator, US attorney general and presidential candidate before his assassination in 1968; and **Ted Kennedy** was a much-loved Massachusetts senator from 1962 until his death in 2009. Daughter Eunice Kennedy Shriver was a co-founder of the Special Olympics.

1915	**1930s**	**1960s**	**1961–63**
Amoskeag Mills in Manchester, NH, becomes most productive textile mill in the world.	The Great Depression hits New England especially hard.	US basketball is dominated by the Boston Celtics.	John F Kennedy becomes the third US president to hail from Massachusetts.

LIBERAL OR LIBERTARIAN?

In the age of Tea Parties and partisan politics in **Washington**, New England appears to be a bastion of progressive values, though it's not as liberal as the national press often makes it out to be. Indeed, New Hampshire's motto "**Live Free or Die**" is taken very seriously in a state that is often more libertarian than liberal – New Hampshire citizens often consider Vermont a socialist state in comparison. Having said that, Connecticut, Massachusetts, New Hampshire and Vermont have legalized **same-sex marriage**, and Maine, Vermont, and Rhode Island have flouted federal statutes by making **medical marijuana** legal.

during the 1920s, while unemployment skyrocketed in some towns. The **Great Depression** hit New England particularly hard and, with few natural resources to draw upon and human resources relocating, industry here never really recovered. By 1980, the region that had given birth to America's Industrial Revolution was headquarters to only fourteen of the nation's top five hundred companies.

Recent history

In the 1980s New England began to experience something of a **resurgence**. New industries, such as the production of biomedical machinery, computer hardware and software, and photographic materials, sprang up throughout the region, but especially along Rte-128 west of Boston. During this period, Boston became the country's mutual fund capital, Hartford's insurance industry continued to flourish and tourism asserted itself as the region's second largest source of income. New England became known for its **political stability** and, at the same time, for leading the way with anti-pollution laws, consumer rights, handgun controls and civil rights legislation.

Though the nationwide **economic slump** in the late 1980s and early 1990s caused problems in those larger urban centres that had failed to address the social consequences of the demise of traditional manufacturing industries, the area managed to rebound again. Almost unparalleled prosperity accompanied by low unemployment, especially in the latter half of the 1990s, meant that more money was freed up for the benefit of long-neglected areas that needed attention: roads and infrastructure, crime prevention, schools and social provision. At the same time **urban regeneration**, sometimes on a spectacular scale (in Providence, Rhode Island, for example), and the continued development of new industries have put the region more or less back on track. New England now lays claim to nearly thirty of the top five hundred companies in the US. Since the turn of the century New England has also cemented its reputation as the **most liberal region** of the US (see box above).

2001–05	2004	2008	2011
New England Patriots win three Super Bowls (American football championships) in four years.	Boston Red Sox break "the Curse of the Bambino" by winning the World Series after 86 years. They win again in 2007.	Boston Celtics win a record 17th NBA championship.	Boston Bruins win ice hockey's Stanley Cup.

New England on film

From rip-roaring comedies to slow-burning crime films the following movies are all set in New England, though many are filmed elsewhere. When it comes to TV, producer and New Englander David E. Kelley has put Boston on the map since the 1990s with shows such as *Ally McBeal, The Practice, Boston Legal* and *Boston Public*. Films marked with a ★ are especially recommended.

The Actress George Cukor, 1953. A unique portrait of Boston in the early 1910s, based on a play by Ruth Gordon about her early life in nearby Wollaston. Stars Jean Simmons as Gordon and a deliciously cantankerous Spencer Tracy as her father.

★ **Affliction** Paul Schrader, 1998. Brooding tale of violence shattering the placid surface of a snowbound New Hampshire town. Nick Nolte is superb as the divorced small-town cop stumbling through middle age, whose father's legacy of abuse is too heavy a load to bear.

Alice's Restaurant Arthur Penn, 1969. Built around Arlo Guthrie's hit song of the same name, this quizzical elegy for counterculture brought the hippie nation to the Berkshire town of Stockbridge. Guthrie plays himself, as does Stockbridge police officer William Obanhein.

All That Heaven Allows Douglas Sirk, 1955. Recounting the forbidden romance of a middle-aged widow (Jane Wyman) and her strapping, Thoreau-quoting gardener (Rock Hudson), this devastating portrait of the small-minded local country-club set served to show seventeenth-century Puritanism alive in postwar New England.

Beetlejuice Tim Burton, 1988. Early Burton comedy in which a recently deceased couple (Geena Davis and Alec Baldwin) decide to haunt their historic New England home until its new tenants decide to leave; the couple gets some unwanted "help" from Beetlejuice (Michael Keaton). Shot in Vermont.

Between the Lines Joan Micklin Silver, 1977. Shot on location, this comedy-drama documents the dying throes of counterculture in late 1970s Boston by focusing on the ragtag staff of an underground newspaper (based on the real-life *Real Paper*).

The Bostonians James Ivory, 1984. In 1875 Boston, New England women's libbers and a Southern male chauvinist battle for the soul of one very pliable young woman in the drawing rooms of Cambridge, on the lawns of Harvard and on the beaches of Martha's Vineyard.

Christmas in Connecticut Peter Godfrey, 1945. Barbara Stanwyck plays a Manhattan magazine writer who has faked her way to being the Martha Stewart of her day. When her publisher asks her to invite a war hero to her Connecticut farm for Christmas, Stanwyck has to conjure up the idyllic New England existence she'd only written about.

Cider House Rules Lasse Hallström, 1999. Adaptation of John Irving's novel starring Tobey Maguire and Michael Caine, in which a shifting Maine backdrop sets the stage for a somewhat didactic, if winning, meditation on love, suffering and the thorny issue of abortion.

The Crucible Nicholas Hytner, 1996. Riveting adaptation of Arthur Miller's allegory of McCarthyism, set in 1692 Salem. Winona Ryder and her friends are spied dancing by firelight and accused of witchcraft; to save themselves they start naming names.

The Departed Martin Scorsese, 2006. Star-studded Oscar-winner – Leonardo DiCaprio, Matt Damon, Jack Nicholson and Alec Baldwin all appear – set in Boston's criminal underworld, as the Massachusetts State Police is infiltrated by the Irish-American mob.

Dolores Claiborne Taylor Hackford, 1995. On a dreary island off the coast of Maine, Kathy Bates is suspected of killing her wealthy employer. Gothic sleeper adapted from a Stephen King novel.

The Europeans James Ivory, 1979. Shot against the gorgeous autumn foliage of New Hampshire and Massachusetts, Merchant-Ivory's genial adaptation of Henry James's novella pits New England sobriety against the dizzy charms of a couple of European visitors.

Gone Baby Gone Ben Affleck, 2007. Based on the novel by Dennis Lehane, this gritty drama centres on the hunt for an abducted four-year-old girl from the Boston neighbourhood of Dorchester, and was filmed in the area. Ben's brother Casey Affleck and Amy Ryan star.

Good Will Hunting Gus Van Sant, 1997. This Oscar-winner for Best Screenplay tells of a South Boston townie (Matt Damon) who is a closet maths wizard, and his transformation, with the help of a therapist friend (Robin Williams).

The House of the Seven Gables Joe May, 1940. Fusty superstition battles liberal enlightenment in eighteenth-century Massachusetts in this histrionic adaptation of Nathaniel Hawthorne's Gothic family saga, starring George Sanders and Vincent Price.

The Ice Storm Ang Lee, 1997. Suburban living in 1970s Connecticut – alcoholic excess, adultery, alienation – is laid bare in all its formica-covered splendour in this disturbing adaptation of Rick Moody's novel. Starring Kevin Kline, Sigourney Weaver and Joan Allen.

In the Bedroom Todd Field, 2001. Against the backdrop of Maine's small harbour-town lobster docks, a college-age boy begins seeing a local divorcee with an angry ex-husband. Tom Wilkinson wins the "best Maine accent by a foreigner" award in this intense drama.

Jaws Steven Spielberg, 1975. Godfather of the summer blockbuster, based on Peter Benchley's 1974 novel in which a man-eating great white shark wreaks havoc on the shores of Martha's Vineyard (known here as Amity Island). John Williams composed the spine-tingling shark attack theme tune.

★ **John Adams** Tom Hooper, 2008. Finely rendered TV mini-series about second US president John Adams (Paul Giamatti) and the birth of the nation, with an award-winning performance by Laura Linney as Adams's beloved wife Abigail, and vivid portrayals of other Founding Fathers.

Leave Her to Heaven John M. Stahl, 1945. A stunning, too-little-known gem, in which Gene Tierney plays a woman who loves too much. Gorgeously colourful, with some indelible scenes set in Maine.

★ **Little Women** George Cukor, 1933; Gillian Armstrong, 1994. Louisa May Alcott's timeless classic, set in Concord, MA, has not one but two wonderful Hollywood adaptations. The first, Cukor's in 1933, stars a rambunctious Katharine Hepburn as Jo; the second, made some sixty years later by Gillian Armstrong, has Winona Ryder in the lead role and Susan Sarandon as the ever-wise Marmee.

Love Story Arthur Hiller, 1970. The Harvard preppie (Ryan O'Neal) and the working-class Radcliffe wiseacre (Ali McGraw) fall for each other against a backdrop of library stacks, falling leaves and tinkling pianos, while tragedy makes its way into the air.

Malice Harold Becker, 1993. In a small college town in Massachusetts (the film was shot at Smith College in Northampton) the blissful life of newlyweds Bill Pullman and Nicole Kidman is rocked by the arrival of diabolically charismatic Harvard doctor Alec Baldwin.

Mermaids Richard Benjamin, 1990. Single mum Cher relocates her two daughters (Winona Ryder and Christina Ricci) to a small Massachusetts town. Elder daughter Winona decides she wants to become a nun, and suffers various other growing pains, while Cher finds love with Bob Hoskins and becomes a better mother.

Mystic Pizza Donald Petrie, 1988. The film that put both Julia Roberts and Mystic, Connecticut, on the national map. Shot on location in Stonington and Mystic, CT and nearby Rhode Island, this film tells of the romantic travails of three young waitresses at a local pizza joint.

★ **Mystic River** Clint Eastwood, 2003. Dark, poignant indie classic based on Dennis Lehane's novel, telling of three childhood friends (Sean Penn, Kevin Bacon, Tim Robbins) in working-class Boston, reunited when the daughter of one is brutally murdered.

Next Stop Wonderland Brad Anderson, 1998. The title of this indie romance refers to the final stop of Boston's Blue Line subway, where luckless nurse Hope Davis finally crosses paths, after many a false start, with the man of her dreams.

★ **On Golden Pond** Mark Rydell, 1981. The setting for this tearjerker is really Squam Lake in New Hampshire, where, one summer, a crabby Boston professor (Henry Fonda in his final film) and his wife (Katharine Hepburn) come to rediscover their marriage.

The Perfect Storm Wolfgang Petersen, 2000. George Clooney, Diane Lane and Mark Wahlberg star in this adaptation of Sebastian Junger's bestseller about a Gloucester swordfishing boat's doomed journey into the heart of the "storm of the century".

Reversal of Fortune Barbet Schroeder, 1990. Opening with an aerial sequence of the mansions of Newport strung along the Rhode Island coastline, this witty film dramatizes the case of Claus von Bülow, who was convicted of attempting to murder his heiress wife.

The Scarlet Letter Victor Seastrom, 1926; Wim Wenders, 1973; Roland Joffe, 1995. Hawthorne's masterpiece has been treated about as well by Hollywood as Hester Prynne was treated by the people of Salem. The first, silent, adaptation of the book, starring Lillian Gish, is the best, though it reduces Hawthorne's work to a tragic pastoral romance. The 1973 version – filmed in Spain with German actors – is about as much fun as Salem on the Sabbath, while the 1995 Demi Moore vehicle includes some racy sex scenes and a rewritten ending.

Splendor in the Grass Elia Kazan, 1961. Though the handful of scenes set at Yale University are confined to studio sets, Kazan's Kansas melodrama bears mention for the pivotal role that New Haven's legendary pizza pie plays in the protagonists' romantic proceedings.

Starting Over Alan J. Pakula, 1979. Burt Reynolds leaves his marriage and swanky Manhattan pad to move to a cold-water Boston flat for a new start. A wonderful, little-known comedy romance shot by Ingmar Bergman's cinematographer Sven Nykvist.

State and Main David Mamet, 2000. A slick Hollywood film crew lands in uptight small-town Vermont after having been run out of New Hampshire for unknown, but undoubtedly lurid, reasons. Screwball comedy with some winning performances.

The Swimmer Frank Perry, 1968. A splendid curio adapted from John Cheever's short story of the same name, in which rural Connecticut is imagined as a lush Garden of Eden through which broad-chested Burt Lancaster makes his allegorical way home one summer afternoon.

There's Something About Mary Farrelly Brothers, 1998. If Rhode Island is to go down in the annals of cinema history it would have to be as the site of Ben Stiller's notorious pre-prom mishap in this funny opus.

Tough Guys Don't Dance Norman Mailer, 1987. Set in Provincetown, Mailer's bizarre retelling of his novel is a convoluted affair involving an intoxicated writer, a gay-bashing sheriff, a Southern millionaire, a gold-digger, drug-dealing lobster men and a severed head.

The Town Ben Affleck, 2010. Another critically acclaimed homage to Boston from local boy Affleck, this crime-thriller is focused on a professional thief and the FBI crew trying to bring him down. Affleck stars as well as directs.

The Trouble with Harry Alfred Hitchcock, 1955. A black comedy painted in the reds and golds of a Vermont autumn. The trouble with Harry is that he keeps turning up dead and everybody, including his young wife (Shirley MacLaine), thinks they may have killed him.

★ **Vermont is for Lovers** John O'Brien, 1993. A charming, semi-documentary comedy about a New York couple who come to Vermont to get married, are hit with a bad case of cold feet and turn to the locals – all real Vermonters and neighbours of O'Brien – for advice. Scene-stealing septuagenarian sheep farmer Fred Tuttle had a spin-off in O'Brien's spoof of Vermont politics, *Man with a Plan* (1995).

White Christmas Michael Curtiz, 1954. Singing and dancing army buddies Bing Crosby and Danny Kaye take the train up to Vermont for a skiing holiday, only to find there hasn't been snow all year. One of the very few musicals to be set in New England, beloved for its Irving Berlin score and that magical snowy finale.

The Witches of Eastwick George Miller, 1987. An arch, handsome, but ultimately hollow adaptation of John Updike's novel about three love-starved women who conjure up a rather unwelcome visitor to their sleepy Massachusetts town.

Books

New England is home to a rich literary tradition that ranges from Nathanial Hawthorne to Stephen King. The region has been especially strong when it comes to female authors, with pioneers Emily Dickinson, Louisa May Alcott, Sylvia Plath and Edith Wharton all hailing from the region. Titles with a ★ symbol are especially recommended.

Poetry, prose and drama

Emily Dickinson *The Complete Poems*. The ultimate New England poet, who spent all her life in the same town (Amherst) – indeed the same house – and quietly recorded the seasons and her own inner contemplations.

Robert Frost *The Collected Poems* (Henry Holt). The master poet, who spent most of his life in Vermont and New Hampshire, skilfully evokes the New England landscape with classics such as *Birches* and *Stopping by Woods on a Snowy Evening*.

Donald Hall *Old and New Poems* (Mariner Books); *Life Work* (Beacon Press); *The Ox-Cart Man* (Puffin). Hall is a New England poet's poet; he lives in New Hampshire and was married to Jane Kenyon (see below). He has also written non-fiction about New England, and even a few children's books, including the much-loved *Ox-Cart Man*.

Jane Kenyon *Collected Poems* (Graywolf). Kenyon was New Hampshire's poet laureate when she died of leukaemia in 1995. Her poems have New England themes, but also deal wisely with depression, a disease she fought since childhood.

Maxine Kumin *Selected Poems; The Long Marriage; Inside the Halo* (W.W. Norton). Living on a horse farm in New Hampshire, Kumin is deeply rooted in the New England landscape, with these last two collections coming after her recovery from a near-fatal riding accident.

Henry Wadsworth Longfellow *Poems and Other Writings* (Library of America). Longfellow celebrated both common and heroic New Englanders in his sometimes whimsical verse; perhaps a bit light for some, but central to mid-nineteenth-century New England society.

Robert Lowell *Life Studies; For the Union Dead* (Noonday Press). Affecting stuff from arguably New England's greatest twentieth-century poet (who was born in Boston), tackling family and social issues in the 1960s with poems such as *Beyond the Alps* and *For the Union Dead*.

Arthur Miller *The Crucible* (Penguin). This compelling play about the 1692 Salem witch trials is peppered with quotes from actual transcripts and loaded with appropriate levels of hysteria and fervour – a must for witch fanatics everywhere.

Wallace Stevens *The Palm at the End of the Mind* (Vintage). Aspiring to create a distinctly American idiom, Stevens used simple language, but is still considered difficult. Despite growing success, he never quit his job as a lawyer for an insurance firm in Connecticut.

Henry David Thoreau *Cape Cod; The Maine Woods; Walden* (Penguin US). Thoreau put his Transcendentalist philosophy into practice by living a life of self-reliance in his cabin by Walden Pond, near Concord, Massachusetts. *Cape Cod* and *The Maine Woods*, published after his death, recount the writer's walks in nature.

Thornton Wilder *Our Town* (Perennial Classics). Classic play depicting life in small-town New Hampshire from 1901 to 1913, loosely based on towns in the Mount Monadnock region. It's not conventional theatre: the narrator, the Stage Manager, breaks the "fourth wall" and addresses the audience directly.

History, culture and society

James Chenoweth *Oddity Odyssey* (Henry Holt US). Fun little book that points out the more intriguing and humorous episodes and myths surrounding the sights and major players in New England's history.

David Hackett Fischer *Paul Revere's Ride* (University of Massachusetts Press/Oxford University Press). An exhaustive account of the patriot's legendary ride to Lexington, related as a historical narrative.

Mark Kurlansky *Cod* (Penguin). Does a fish merit this much obsessive attention? Only in New England. Kurlansky makes a good case for viewing the cod as one of the more integral commodities of the region. See also his gripping history of Gloucester, MA, *The Last Fish Tale*.

J. Anthony Lukas *Common Ground: a Turbulent Decade in the Lives of Three American Families* (Vintage US). A Pulitzer Prize-winning account of three Boston families – one Irish-American, one black, one white middle-class – against the backdrop of the 1974 race riots sparked by court-ordered "busing" to desegregate public schools.

★ **David McCullough** *John Adams* (Simon & Schuster). Bestselling 2002 biography of the country's second president and lesser-known Founding Father, who spent much of his life in Boston and Quincy, Massachusetts. Made into an equally lauded TV series (see p.529).

CHILDREN'S LITERATURE

Perhaps because its rich history is taught in schools across the country, or maybe for more romantic reasons, New England has served as a muse for **children's book authors** throughout the years. Some of the best titles are by **Robert McCloskey**, who wrote and illustrated the timeless *Make Way for Ducklings*, *Blueberries for Sal*, *One Morning in Maine* and *Time of Wonder*, all of which employ New England's landscape and wildlife. The poet **Donald Hall** has written several New England-based children's books, each beautifully illustrated: *The Ox-Cart Man*; *Lucy's Summer*; *Lucy's Christmas* and *The Man Who Lived Alone*.

For slightly older readers, Vermonter **Robert N. Peck** is famed for his *Soup* series, published in the 1970s about a small-town Vermont boy named Soup. One-name author **Avi** lived in the historic part of Providence for many years, a locale that inspired *Something Upstairs*, in which a 13-year-old boy befriends the ghost of a slave who lived in his attic hundreds of years ago. **Lois Lowry** wrote the much-loved series of books about Anastasia Krupnik, a spirited Boston adolescent, while another remarkable girl, Kit, is the protagonist of *The Witch of Blackbird Pond*, by **Elizabeth Speare**, set in rural, dark, seventeenth-century Puritan Connecticut.

★ **Louis Menand** *The Metaphysical Club* (Farrar, Straus and Giroux USA). Engaging study of four Boston literary heavyweights, this Pulitzer Prize-winning biography reveals the effect of their pragmatic idealism on American intellectual thought.

★ **Nathaniel Philbrick** *Mayflower* (Viking Books). Gripping story of the Pilgrims' arrival in Massachusetts in 1620 and especially their dealings with the local Wampanoags, through to King Philip's War in the 1670s. Massasoit comes across as a particularly adroit and sophisticated leader in this balanced rendering of New England's origins.

Dan Shaughnessy *The Curse of the Bambino* (Penguin); *Reversing the Curse* (Houghton Mifflin). Shaughnessy, a Boston sportswriter, exams the Red Sox's "curse" – no championships since 1918, until their triumphant 2004 win – that began just after they sold Babe Ruth to the Yankees.

Architecture and design

Mona Domosh *Invented Cities: the Creation of Landscape in Nineteenth-Century New York and Boston* (Yale University Press US). Fascinating historical account of how these very different cities were shaped according to the values, beliefs and fears of their respective societies.

Naomi Miller and Keith Morgan *Boston Architecture 1975–1990* (Prestel). Contextualizes Boston's transformation into a modern city, with emphasis on the building boom of the 1980s, but also detailing the early development and architectural trends of the centuries before.

Fiction

★ **Louisa May Alcott** *Little Women* (Puffin). A semi-autobiographical work drawing on family experiences in Concord, Massachusetts, Alcott's novel charting the lives and loves of four sisters remains a classic to this day. First published in 1868, it led to the equally successful sequels *Good Wives* and *Little Men*.

Brunonia Barry *The Lace Reader* (William Morrow). Debut novel by a Salem local, introducing the town with a twist – it's inhabited by modern-day witches whose human activities include dealing with tourists and going to therapy.

Gerry Boyle *Lifeline* (Berkley). Hard-hitting suspense novel about an ex-big-city reporter Jack McMorrow looking for solace in small-town Maine, only to find that crime exists there, too. Boyle lives in China, Maine and continues to knock out crime novels with McMorrow at the centre.

James Casey *Spartina* (Vintage). Set in the fishing world of Rhode Island, this memorable, spare work on a man's inner struggles captured the National Book Award in 1989. Inspired in part by Casey's four-year stint living on a four-acre island off the Rhode Island mainland.

John Cheever *The Wapshot Chronicle* (Vintage). Cheever's first novel documents the weird doings of the Wapshot family of St Botolph's, Massachusetts. The sequel, *The Wapshot Scandal*, continues the saga.

Bret Easton Ellis *The Rules of Attraction* (Picador UK; Vintage US). A sex-drug-and booze-driven narrative, charting the romantic progress of a few students through Vermont's fictional Camden College.

Mary Eleanor Freeman *A New England Nun and Other Stories* (Penguin). Relatively unknown these days, Massachusetts-native Freeman enjoyed great success about a century ago for her tales of rural New England life.

Elizabeth Graver *Unravelling* (Hyperion). In distinct and compelling fashion, Graver – who has been a professor at Boston College since 1993 – charts a fiercely independent young woman's progress on the bleaker edges of nineteenth-century New England life: its farms and the Lowell textile mills.

Nathaniel Hawthorne *The House of the Seven Gables*; *The Scarlet Letter* (Bantam). Born in Salem, Massachusetts, in 1804, Hawthorne was descended from a judge at the famous witch trials, which provide the setting for his two classic novels.

John Irving *The Cider House Rules* (Black Swan UK; Vintage US). Irving writes huge, sprawling novels set all over New England. This one, suitably Dickensian in scope, is neither his most popular (*The World According to Garp*) nor beloved (probably *A Prayer for Owen Meany*). But it is perhaps his best – a fascinating meditation on the moral dilemmas of abortion.

Henry James *The Bostonians*; *The Europeans* (Penguin). The first is a satire tracing the relationship of two fictional feminists in the 1870s, the second is an early James novella about Europeans who travelled to New England, and found the area's puritanical culture astounding.

Sarah Orne Jewett *A Country Doctor* (Bantam US). Late nineteenth-century account of life in rural Maine, about a woman who refuses marriage so she can pursue her ambitions to become a doctor. Jewett set most of her work in and around her home of South Berwick, Maine.

Jack Kerouac *Maggie Cassidy* (Penguin). The proto-beatnik grew up in Massachusetts; here, he traces the arc of a youthful romance in a small Massachusetts mill town to fine effect.

Stephen King *Different Seasons*; *Dolores Clainborne* (Penguin). Born in Maine, horror-master King is incredibly prolific. These are two of his better books, which manage to evoke his home state and region quite well.

Dennis Lehane *Darkness, Take My Hand* (Avon). Lehane sets his mysteries on the working-class streets of South Boston; they are all excellent and evocative, but this is probably the cream of the crop. His *Mystic River* (William Morrow) is highly recommended, too.

H.P. Lovecraft *The Best of H.P. Lovecraft: Bloodcurdling Tales of Horror and the Macabre* (Ballantine). The best stories from the Providence-born author whom Stephen King called "the twentieth century's greatest practitioner of the classic horror tale."

★ **Herman Melville** *Moby Dick* (Penguin). The incomparable story of a man's obsession with a great white whale, with descriptions of the whaling industry evocative of old New Bedford and Nantucket. Melville wrote the book at Arrowhead, in the Berkshires (see p.233).

Susan Minot *Folly* (Washington Square Press); *Monkeys* (Vintage). This obvious nod to Edith Wharton's *Age of Innocence* is set in 1917 Boston instead of New York, and details the proclivities of the Brahmin era.

Robert B. Parker *A Triple Shot of Spenser* (Berkley Trade). Parker, a prolific mystery author with more than forty novels behind him, is best known for his Spenser series, about the adventures of a Boston private eye.

Sylvia Plath *The Bell Jar* (Harper Perennial US). Angst-ridden, dark, autobiographical novel about a girl's mental breakdown. The second half is set in a mental hospital in the Boston suburbs. Boston-born Plath studied at Smith College in Northampton, but tragically committed suicide in England at the age of 30.

Annie Proulx *Heartsongs* (Fourth Estate UK; Macmillan US). Finely crafted, gritty stories of life in rural and blue-collar New England from the Connecticut-born author. Proulx lived in Vermont for more than thirty years, and published this book, her first novel, in 1988.

Richard Russo *Empire Falls* (Vintage). In the failing blue-collar town of Empire Falls, Maine, Miles Roby runs the town's most popular diner, which he hopes someday to inherit from its controlling owner.

George Santayana *The Last Puritan* (MIT Press). The philosopher's brilliant "memoir in the form of a novel", set around Boston, chronicles the short life and education of protagonist Oliver Alden coming to grips with Puritanism.

John Steinbeck *The Winter of Our Discontent* (Penguin). A late work by Steinbeck, published in 1961, examining the moral collapse of Ethan Hawley and his family in small-town New England in the 1950s.

Donna Tartt *The Secret History* (Penguin UK; Ballantine US). A small group of students at a fictional Vermont college in the 1980s (modelled after Bennington College, where Tartt was a student) discover the murderous turns of their elite cadre.

John Updike *The Witches of Eastwick* (Ballantine). Satirical witchy tale set in rural 1960s Rhode Island and chock-full of hypocrisy, adultery and wickedness; a fun read that was made into a movie starring Jack Nicholson (see p.530). Updike's last novel was a sequel, *The Widows of Eastwick*, published in 2008.

David Foster Wallace *Infinite Jest* (Little, Brown US). A whopping 1088-page hilarious opus, with some parts set at a tennis academy outside Boston and other nuggets involving a Cambridge store-owner in a Canadian separatist terrorist plot.

Dorothy West *The Wedding* (Anchor). A 1995 re-appearance for the 1940s author, with a touching family saga that takes place among a wealthy black community vacationing on Martha's Vineyard.

Edith Wharton *Ethan Frome* (Penguin). A distilled portrait of stark, icy New England that belies the fiery emotions blazing underneath, set in rural Massachusetts – Wharton lived in the Berkshires from 1902 to 1911 (see p.229).

Small print and index

535 Small print

536 About the author

538 Index

548 Map symbols

A ROUGH GUIDE TO ROUGH GUIDES

Published in 1982, the first Rough Guide – to Greece – was a student scheme that became a publishing phenomenon. Mark Ellingham, a recent graduate in English from Bristol University, had been travelling in Greece the previous summer and couldn't find the right guidebook. With a small group of friends he wrote his own guide, combining a highly contemporary, journalistic style with a thoroughly practical approach to travellers' needs.

The immediate success of the book spawned a series that rapidly covered dozens of destinations. And, in addition to impecunious backpackers, Rough Guides soon acquired a much broader readership that relished the guides' wit and inquisitiveness as much as their enthusiastic, critical approach and value-for-money ethos.

These days, Rough Guides include recommendations from budget to luxury and cover more than 200 destinations around the globe, as well as producing an ever-growing range of eBooks and apps.

Visit **roughguides.com** to see our latest publications.

Rough Guide credits

Editor: Alison Roberts
Additional editors: Ros Belford, Ann-Marie Shaw
Layout: Anita Singh
Cartography: Rajesh Mishra
Picture editor: Mark Thomas
Proofreader: Samantha Cook
Managing editor: Mani Ramaswamy
Assistant editor: Dipika Dasgupta
Production: Rebecca Short
Cover design: Nicole Newman, Anita Singh

Editorial assistant: Eleanor Aldridge
Senior pre-press designer: Dan May
Design director: Scott Stickland
Travel publisher: Joanna Kirby
Digital travel publisher: Peter Buckley
Reference director: Andrew Lockett
Operations coordinator: Becky Doyle
Publishing director (Travel): Clare Currie
Commercial manager: Gino Magnotta
Managing director: John Duhigg

Publishing information

This 6th edition published June 2012 by
Rough Guides Ltd,
80 Strand, London WC2R 0RL
11, Community Centre, Panchsheel Park,
New Delhi 110017, India
Distributed by the Penguin Group
Penguin Books Ltd,
80 Strand, London WC2R 0RL
Penguin Group (USA)
375 Hudson Street, NY 10014, USA
Penguin Group (Australia)
250 Camberwell Road, Camberwell,
Victoria 3124, Australia
Penguin Group (NZ)
67 Apollo Drive, Mairangi Bay, Auckland 1310,
New Zealand
Penguin Group (South Africa)
Block D, Rosebank Office Park, 181 Jan Smuts Avenue,
Parktown North, Gauteng, South Africa 2193
Rough Guides is represented in Canada by Tourmaline
Editions Inc. 662 King Street West, Suite 304, Toronto,
Ontario M5V 1M7
Printed in Singapore by Toppan Security Printing Pte. Ltd.

MIX
Paper from
responsible sources
FSC www.fsc.org   FSC™ C018179

Help us update

We've gone to a lot of effort to ensure that the sixth
edition of **The Rough Guide to New England** is accurate
and up-to-date. However, things change – places get
"discovered", opening hours are notoriously fickle,
restaurants and rooms raise prices or lower standards. If
you feel we've got it wrong or left something out, we'd like
to know, and if you can remember the address, the price,
the hours, the phone number, so much the better.

Please send your comments with the subject line
"**Rough Guide New England Update**" to ✉ mail
@uk.roughguides.com. We'll credit all contributions and
send a copy of the next edition (or any other Rough Guide
if you prefer) for the very best emails.

Find more travel information, connect with fellow
travellers and book your trip on ⓦ roughguides.com

ABOUT THE AUTHOR

Sarah Hull grew up in Massachusetts, which means she can use expressions like "wicked awesome" without getting embarrassed. She has been a contributor to Rough Guides since 2005, working on the USA, Florida and Boston guides as well as a number of the *25 Ultimate Experiences* books. When she's not on the hunt for the world's best cupcake, she's in New York State Supreme Court reporting on corporate shenanigans and celebrity lawsuits.

Stephen Keeling worked as a financial journalist and editor for seven years before writing his first travel guide and has written several titles for Rough Guides, including New York, Puerto Rico, Florida and Canada. He's been covering New England for Rough Guides since 2008, and lives in New York City.

Acknowledgements

Sarah Hull would like to thank: Stephen Keeling for the mental health meet-ups, his dedication to the cause and his restorative sense of humour. Alison Roberts, for her kindness, thoroughness and sharp editorial eye. The hilarious Annie Shaw steered the course with panache. Lisa de Kooning lent me the most spectacular writing space imaginable, and everyone at the studio doted on me, brought me firewood and let me feed the pigs. Priscilla Morgan, my great aunt, for being my lifeline and muse. A million thanks go to Molly Hamill for her friendship, the daily dispatches, and for the (equally life-saving) use of her house and car. Isabella Koen was a Cape Ann game-changer and a great partner-in-crime. Bill Girdner and Adam Angione generously supported the venture. Sue Norrington-Davies at Discover New England and Nancy Gardella in Martha's Vineyard. Team Johnson/ Zedek encouraged, counselled and provided home-cooked meals. But my most fervent thanks go to Michael McLaughlin, who stayed up late and got up early, cooked steak, poured wine, edited nearly every sentence and offered unwavering support – through bright points and dark. Every lobster roll I eat, I eat it for you.

Stephen Keeling would like to thank: Sue Norrington-Davies, Kathy Scatamacchia and all the wonderful team at Discover New England; Pamela Ruggio at the Aldrich; Eric Berger in Arlington; Barbara Rossi at the Bartlett Arboretum; Deana Mallory in Bennington; Jessica Willi on Block Island; Tim & Amy Brady in Brattleboro; Don Konen

and the team at Danbury Railway Museum; Barbara Bishop at the Greenwich Historical Society; Tammi Flynn at the Florence Griswold Museum; Margery Reynolds, Anne Lee and Sally Whipple in Hartford; Paula Maynard at Hildene; Gary and Sandra Plourde in Jackson; Angela Liptack at the Keeler Tavern; Mollie Clarke at the Lyman Allyn Art Museum; Robin Comstock and Aurore Eaton in Manchester; Erin Merz, Janice Putnam, Karin Burgess and Dan McFadden in Mystic County; Errol Saunders, Tangier Pritchett, Peter Sonski, Adrienne Webb, Nancy Franco, Kaci Bayless and Melanie Brigockas in New Haven; Andrea McHugh in Newport; Tai Freligh and Lori Harnois at the NH Division of Travel and Tourism Development; Dave Sigworth and Susan Gunn Bromley in Norwalk; Doug Palardy, Valerie Rouchon, Joan Chawziuk, Stephanie Seacord in Portsmouth and the good folks at Portsmouth Kayak Adventures; Brian Hodge in Providence; the indomitable Bill Gleed at the Robert Frost Farm; Carole Thompson at the Robert Frost Stone House Museum; Sara Orr at Springfield Museums; Erica Houskeeper, Linda Seville and Megan Smith at the Vermont Department of Tourism; Kim Reynolds at the Wadsworth Atheneum; Linda Cook at Weir Farm; Jim O'Reilly at the Wildflower Inn; Rebecca Rudnicki for the tour of Wilson Castle; Allison Berkeley at Worcester Art Museum; fellow author Sarah Hull; Ros Belford and Alison Roberts for all their hard work and editing; and lastly Tiffany Wu, whose love and support made this possible.

Readers' letters

Thanks to all the readers who have taken the time to write in with comments and suggestions (and apologies if we've inadvertently omitted or misspelt anyone's name):

Susan Duncan, Christopher Eaton, Keith Gabriel, Bettina Lange.

Photo credits

The publisher would like to thank the following for their kind permission to reproduce their photographs:
(Key: a-above; b-below/bottom; c-centre; f-far; l-left; r-right; t-top)

p.1 Getty Images/Glen Allison
p.2 Alamy/Jon Arnold Images Ltd
p.4 Alamy/imagebroker (tr)
p.5 Getty Images/Walter Bibikow
p.8 Alamy/Philip Scalia
p.9 Alamy/LOOK Die Bildagentur der Fotografen GmbH (b), Alamy/Della Huff (c), Getty Images/Ron and Patty Thomas (t)
p.10 Getty Images/James Randklev
p.11 Getty Images/James Lemass (b), Getty Images David Madison (c)
p.12 Alamy/Frank Vetere (t), Getty Images/Steve Dunwell (br)
p.13 Alamy/Jeff Greenberg (tl), Alamy/Andre Jenny (br)
p.14 Getty Images/Robert Harding (tr), Getty Images/Frank Siteman (tl), Getty Images/Altrendo Travel (b)
p.15 Alamy/George H.H. Huey (c), Getty Images/Michael Melford (t)
p.16 Alamy/Chris Cameron
p.18 Alamy/America
p.41 Getty Images/Walter Bibikow
p.59 Getty Images/Eunice Harris, Getty Images/Wendell Metzen (b)
p.81 Getty Images/Glenn Leblanc, Getty Images/David Madison (t)
p.126 Getty Images/Walter Bibikow
p.129 Getty Images/James Lemass
p.163 Getty Images/Walter Bibikow (t), Getty Images /Danita Delimont (b)

p.195 Alamy/Mira
p.221 Alamy/Philip Scalia (t), Corbis/Reuters (b)
p.238 Alamy/LOOK Die Bildagentur der Fotografen GmbH
p.241 Getty Images/Douglas Mason
p.274 Alamy/Danita Delimont
p.277 Alamy/Randy Duchaine
p.326 Alamy/David R. Frazier
p.345 Alamy/Noble Images (b)
p.354 Alamy/INTERFOTO (t)
p.363 Alamy/Stuart Kelly (b), Getty Images/Paul Hawthorne (t)
p.384 Alamy/Jerry and Marcy Monkman
p.387 Alamy/Chris Cameron
p.425 Alamy/Daniel Dempster Photography (b) Alamy /Chad Ehlers (t)
p.446 Getty Images/Danita Delimont
p.483 Getty Images/Abrahm Lustgarten (t), Getty Images /Rob Nunnington (b)
p.518 Getty Images/Historic Map Works

Front cover Restaurant, Cape Cod, Superstock/Raymond Forbes
Back cover Nantucket Harbour, Getty Images/Jon Hicks; Androscoggin River, Getty Images/Stephen Gorman; Beacon Hill, Getty Images/Chuck Pefley

All other images © Rough Guides

INDEX

Maps are marked in grey

A

AAA...22
Abbot Hall..................................141
Acadia National Park
.... **497–499**
accommodation.............**23–25**
price codes.................................24
Acela Express..............................19
Adams National Historic Site
....153
Adams, John...............54, 153, 154,
529
Adams, John Quincy......153, 154
Adams, Samuel.......51, 54, 56, 77,
131, 522
airlines...19
airports..19
alcohol...26
Alcott, Louisa May............71, 132,
133, 134, 136, 532
Aldrich Contemporary Art
Museum...................................323
Allen, Ethan ...328, 336, 366, 371,
372
American Clock & Watch
Museum...................................312
American football......................29
American Independence
Museum...................................397
American Precision Museum
....355
American Textile History
Museum...................................138
Amherst........................ **217–219**
Amistad, the...156, 254, 286, 293,
305
Amoskeag Falls..........................401
Amoskeag Fishways 402
Amoskeag Mills................389, 400
Amtrak.................................19, 22
Anheuser Busch Brewery........404
Appalachian Mountain Club
....30
Appalachian Trail...............30, 441
apple–picking.............................136
Aquinnah (Gay Head) 187
area codes...................................37
Arlington....................................340
Arostook County.......................517
Arrowhead..................................233
Aston Magna Festival...............231
Augusta 507
autumn foliage.....................8, 17

B

Balsams Hotel 445
Bangor **508–510**
banks...35
Bar Harbor..................................497
Bar Harbor **498**
Barnstable..................................171
Barnstormers..............................426
Barnum, P.T..................................297
Barnum Museum.......................297
Bartlett Arboretum & Gardens
....301
baseball.......28, 82, 125, 161, 233
basketball.........29, 125, 210, 211
Basketball Hall of Fame...........211
Bass Harbor.................................498
Bath **475–477**
Bath Iron Works.........................475
Battle of Bennington.....328, 337,
338
Battle of Bunker Hill...........67, 523
Baxter State Park.......................516
bears...31
Beauport......................................148
bed and breakfasts 24
Belfast..490
Ben & Jerry's Ice Cream............360
Bennington................... **336–339**
Bennington **337**
Bennington Center for the Arts
....338
Bennington Potters 328
Berkshire Athenaeum 233
Berkshire Museum 233
Berkshire Summer Festivals...231
Berkshires, the............. **225–229**
Berkshires, the **226**
Bethel..510
Billings Farm and Museum 352
black flies.....................................31
Blackstone, William 45, 50
Blackstone River Valley National
Heritage Corridor 204, 251
Blithewold Mansion..................263
Block Island................... **268–273**
Block Island **269**
Blue Hill......................................492
Blue Hill Peninsula....... **491–495**
blueberries.................................503
Bolt Bus......................................20
books **531–533**
Boothbay Harbor.......................477
Borden, Lizzie.............................159

BOSTON............................**40–125**
Boston **44**
Back Bay **74–75**
Boston T system (the subway)
.... **46**
Cambridge..................... **90–91**
Downtown & Beacon Hill
.... **48–49**
North End **64**
54th Massachusetts Regiment
Memorial..................................68
Abiel Smith School.......................69
accommodation 99–105
Acorn Street................................71
African Meeting House...............70
airport...............................19, 95
All Saints' Way.............................63
Arlington Street Church.............76
Arnold Arboretum.......................86
arrival and departure 95
Back Bay 72–78
Back Bay Fens.............................82
banks...125
bars.....................................114–117
Beacon Hill..............................68–72
Beacon Street.............................68
bed and breakfasts....................100
Berklee College Of Music...............83
Big Dig, the..................45, 57, 61, 66
bikes...97
Black Heritage Trail.....................70
Blackstone Street........................56
bookstores.................................122
Boston Athenaeum.....................51
Boston Bruins...........................29, 125
Boston Celtics.........................29, 125
Boston Center for the Arts............79
Boston cream pie.........................52
Boston Common..........................47
Boston Globe.............................26
Boston Herald............................26
Boston Light................................61
Boston Marathon.......................26
Boston Massacre 51, 53, 54, 522
Boston Public Library 77
Boston Pride...............................27
Boston Red Sox 28, 82, 125
Boston Speed Dog.......................113
Boston Tea Party..............28, 53, 522
Boston University.........................80
Brewer Fountain...........................51
brewery tours..............................116
Brookline....................................86
Bunker Hill Monument 67
buses 95, 96, 97
cafés...105
Cambridge....................................88–95
Cambridge Common.....................89
Castle Island...............................62
Central Burying Ground 50
Central Square.............................94

Charles Street 71
Charlestown 65–67
Charlestown Navy Yard 65
Cheers Bar 68
Chestnut Street 71
Children's Museum 60
Chinatown 57
Christian Science complex 78
Christopher Columbus Park 58
Church of the Covenant 76
cinemas 121
CityPass 96
City Square 66
Clarendon Street 79
classical music 119
clubs 118
Commonwealth Avenue 73
Commonwealth Museum 88
Copley Square 76
Copp's Hill Burying Ground 63
Curse of the Bambino 82
Custom House Tower 56
Cyclorama 102
dance 120
Dartmouth Street 79
Dawes Park 89
directory 125
Dock Square 56
Dorchester 87
Downtown 46–61
Downtown Crossing 55
drinking 114–117
eating 105–114
Emerald Necklace 83
entertainment 118–121
Esplanade, the 71
Faneuil Hall 56
Fenway, the 80–86
Fenway Park 82, 125
ferries 97
Filene's Basement 55
film 121
Financial District 55
First Baptist Church 76
Flagstaff Hill 50
Forest Hills Cemetery 87
Fort Independence 62
Fort Warren 60
Franklin Park Zoo 87
Frederick Law Olmsted National
    Historic Site 86
free attractions 47
Freedom Trail 50
Frog Pond 51
gay and lesbian 27, 121
George's Island 60
getting around 96–98
Gibson House Museum 76
Government Center 55
Granary Burying Ground 51
guided tours 98
Hanover Street 62
Harbor Islands 60
Harborwalk 58
Harvard Square 89
Harvard University 91–93
Harvard University museums 92
Harvard Yard 113

Hatch Shell 71
Haymarket 56
history 45
Holocaust Memorial 56
Hooper–Lee–Nichols House 93
hospitals 125
hostels 67
hotels 62–67
information 98
Inman Square 94
Institute of Contemporary
internet 125
Irish Famine Memorial 53
Isabella Stewart Gardner Museum
    85
Jamaica Plain 86
John F. Kennedy National Historic
    Site 86
John F. Kennedy Presidential
    Library & Museum 88
John Hancock Tower 77
Kenmore Square 80
King's Chapel Burying Ground 52
Larz Anderson Auto Museum 86
laundry 125
Little Brewster 61
Little Italy 62
live music 118
Logan International Airport 19, 95
Long Wharf 58
Longfellow House 93
Louisburg Square 71
Mapparium 78
Marlborough Street 76
Mary Baker Eddy Library 78
Massachusetts Institute of
    Technology 94
Massachusetts State House 69
Milk Street 55
MIT 94
Mount Auburn Cemetery 94
Museum of African–American
    History 69
Museum of Fine Arts 83
Museum of Science 72
New England Aquarium 58
New England Patriots 29
New Old South Church 77
Newbury Street 76
Nichols House 70
nightlife 118
North End 62–65
North End pastries 109
North Square 84
Old Burying Ground 89
Old Cambridge 93
Old Corner Bookstore 53
Old North Church 63
Old South Meeting House 53
Old State House 54
Omni Parker House 52
Park Street Church 51
parking 96
Paul Revere House 62
Paul Revere Mall 62
Peabody Museum of Archaeology
    and Ethnography 93
pharmacies 125

Piano Row 57
police 125
post offices 125
Post Office Square 55
Prescott House 90
Prudential Center 78
Public Garden 73
Quincy Market 56
Ramón Betances Mural 80
restaurants 106–114
Rose Kennedy Greenway 58
Roxbury 87
Sacred Cod, the 69
Salem Street 64
School Street 53
Sears Crescent building 55
Shaw Monument 68
shopping 122–124
South Boston 61
South End 78–80
Southwest Corridor Park 79
SoWa 80
sports 125
Sports Museum 72
Spectacle Island 61
subway (the T) 95, 96
Sullivan's 61
swan boats 73
Swan Houses 71
Symphony Hall 83
taxis 95, 98
Tent City 79
theatre venues 120
Theater District 57
tourist information 98
tours 98
train station 95, 97
Trinity Church 77
Union Park Square 79
USS Cassin Young 66
USS Constitution 65
Vilna Shul 70
Warren Tavern 115
Washington Elm 90
Washington Street 52
water taxi 95
waterfront 57
West End 72
whale-watching 58, 99

Bowdoin College Museum of Art
    472
Boyden Valley Winery 364
Brattleboro 331–334
Brattleboro 331
Bread and Puppet Museum
    382
Bread Loaf Mountain Campus
    358
Bretton Woods 442
Brewster 174
Bridge of Flowers 224
Bridgeport 297
Bristol (CT) 312
Bristol (RI) 263
Broken Window Bylaw 233
Bromley 342

Brown, John (abolitionist).....213, 525
Brown University 245
Brunswick.....................................471
Buckman Tavern 131
Bucksport.....................................490
Bulfinch, Charles 56, 69, 70, 71, 417, 507
Bunyan, Paul................................508
Burdick Chocolates 410
Burke Mountain Resort 382
BURLINGTON 369–375
Burlington 370
accommodation..................................372
airport..372
arrival and departure 372
Art Market..371
Artwalk..371
bars..374
bikes..372
boat tours...372
buses...372
Church Street Marketplace 371
Crow Bookshop...................................375
drinking...374
eating..373
ECHO Lake Aquarium and Science Center 369
entertainment....................................374
Ethan Allen Homestead...................372
ferries...372
First Friday Artwalk...........................371
getting around 372
information 372
Lake Champlain Chocolates 375
Magic Hat Brewing Company 371
nightlife...374
restaurants...373
Robert Hull Fleming Museum.......371
sailing...372
shopping...375
tours..372
trains...372
waterfront...369
bus passes 23
buses 20, 23
Bush–Holley Historic Site 302
Butler–McCook House & Garden
....307

C

Cabot 381
Cabot Creamery.........................381
Calais..506
Calvin Coolidge State Historic Site 348
Cambridge 88–95
Cambridge............................. 90
Camden 487–489
Camden Hills State Park..........487
camping...24

camping on Mt Desert Island
....501
Campobello Island....................504
Cannon Mountain......................434
Canterbury Shaker Village.......407
Cape Ann...................... 146–150
Cape Ann Museum 147
Cape Cod 159–182
Cape Cod 160
beaches...165
Cape Cod Baseball League...........161
Cape Cod Canal 161, 162
Cape Cod Light....................................178
Cape Cod Museum of Natural History..174
Cape Cod National Seashore.......175
Cape Cod Potato Chip Factory
....166
Cape Cod Rail Trail...........................173
Cape Elizabeth....................................464
Cape Playhouse...................................173
Cape Poge Wildlife Refuge
....185
car rental............................... 20, 22
casinos...285
Castine..492
Castle Hill (MA)...........................151
Castle in the Clouds..................421
Cedar Hill Cemetery 309
cell phones................................... 36
Center Sandwich.......................427
Central and western Massachusetts 202–237
Central and western Massachusetts 206–207
Champlain Islands....... 377–379
Chappaquiddick 185
Charlestown (MA).............65–67
Charlestown (RI)..........................266
Chatham...................... 168–170
Chazy Fossil Reef 378
cheddar cheese...........................381
Cheers Bar 68
cheese...381
Cheste (VT)...................................335
Chesterwood...............................227
children, travelling with............38
children's literature 532
Chilmark.......................................186
chocolate
Bar of Chocolate Café.....................467
Belgique..320
Chilmark Chocolates........................186
Chutter's...436
Granite State Candy Shoppe 407
Kent Coffee and Chocolate 320
L.A. Burdick's (MA).............................106
L.A. Burdick's (NH)..............................410
Lake Champlain Chocolates 361, 375
Laughing Moon Chocolates 365
Middlebury Chocolates 358
Chutter's.......................................436

cider...........................136, 281, 360
cigarettes...................................... 28
clam chowder 25
clambakes.............................25, 477
Clark, The.....................................235
Clark's Trading Post...................431
climate..8
climate change............................ 22
Clyde's Cider Mill........................281
Coastal Maine Botanical Gardens.....................................477
coffee cabinet....................25, 250
coffee milk 25, 250
Cold Hollow Cider Mill.............360
Cole Land Transportation Museum.....................................509
Concord (MA)............. 133–135
Concord (NH)............. 404–407
Concord (NH)........................ 405
Concord Museum.......................133
Connecticut Antique Machinery Association.................................321
Connecticut River Museum
....316
Connecticut Science Center
....308
Connecticut Wine Trail.............319
Connecticut 274–325
Connecticut 278–279
Connecticut's Beardsley Zoo
....297
Conway Scenic Railway...........437
Coolidge, Calvin 214, 348
Cornish..416
Cornish–Windsor covered bridge 354, 416
Cornwall Bridge 325
Coskata–Coatue–Great Point
....197
Coventry (CT)..............................325
Covered Bridge Museum........338
coyote.. 31
Craftsbury Common..................381
Cranberry Harvest Celebration
.... 27
Crane Beach 151
Crawford Notch State Park.....443
crime.. 32
culture & etiquette.................... 28
Currier Museum of Art............402
Cutler...503
Cuttyhunk Island 159
cycling... 23

D

Damariscotta...............................479
Danbury..324

Danbury Railway Museum.....324
Daniel Webster Birthplace 406
Dartmouth College..................413
Dawes, William 89, 131
DeCordova Museum and
    Sculpture Park.......................135
Deer Isle 493
Deerfield 222
DeLorme Headquarters 470
Dennis...173
Derby, Elias 142, 144
Desert of Maine 470
Dickinson, Emily..............217, 218,
    531
Dinosaur State Park 313
disabilities, travellers with........38
discounts, student.....................36
Discovery Museum 297
Dixville Notch 445
Dodge Point 479
Dog Mountain 380
Douglass, Frederick 70, 525
Down East Maine **491–506**
Down East Maine **492**
Dr Seuss 210, 212
drinking 25
driving 21
Drumlin Farm..............................135
Du Bois, W.E.B............................232

E

East Burke....................................382
East Haddam 315
Eastern Massachusetts
    .... **126–201**
Eastern Massachusetts...... **130**
Eastham 175
Eastport......................................505
ECHO Lake Aquarium and
    Science Center.......................369
Echo Lake State Park 438
EcoTarium...................................207
Edgartown 184
electricity.....................................32
Ellsworth.....................................495
email..34
embassies.....................................33
emergency services...................34
Emerson, Ralph Waldo..........133,
    134, 136
Emily Dickinson Museum.......217
Eric Carle Museum of Picture
    Book Art.................................219
Essex (CT) 316
Essex (MA) 150
ESTA..33
Ethan Allen Homestead 372

Eugene O'Neill Theater Center
   286
Exeter 397

F

Fairbanks Museum....................379
fall foliage...........................8, 17
Fall River.....................................159
Falmouth **162–164**
Faneuil, Peter...............................51
farmers' markets........................341
Farmington..................................311
Farnsworth Art Museum..........485
Fells, The.....................................417
ferries to Martha's Vineyard
   188
ferries to Nantucket..................166
festivals...............................26–28
films...............................528–530
First Encounter Beach..............176
fishing...32
Fisk Quarry Preserve.................378
flights 19, 20, 21, 22
Florence Griswold Museum
   287
Flume, the..................................434
food and drink.............................25
Fort Dummer 331
Fort Knox.....................................490
Fort Saybrook Monument Park
   288
Fort Sewall 140
Fourth of July...............................27
Foxwoods Resort & Casino 285
Franconia.....................................435
Franconia Notch State Park
   433
Franklin 406
Franklin, Benjamin 55, 77
Franklin Pierce Homestead....410
Freeport......................... 469–471
French, Daniel Chester 77, 87,
    227
Frost, Robert............218, 340, 358,
    404, 435, 531
Frost Gully Gallery....................469
Frost Place...................................435
Fruitlands Museum....................136
Fuller Gardens............................397
Fung Wah bus...............................20

G

Galilee..266
gambling......................................285

Garrison, William Lloyd......51, 70,
    525
gay and lesbian travellers 33
General Joshua L. Chamberlain
    Museum 472
Gilbert Stuart Birthplace.........265
Gilford...419
Gillette Castle............................315
Gilman, Arthur.............................73
Glass House, the 301
Glebe House Museum 322
Gloucester 146–149
Gloucester Maritime Heritage
    Center 147
Glover..382
Good Will Hunting..............61, 528
Goodsell Ridge Preserve.........378
Goodspeed Opera House.......315
Gorham..444
Gosnold, Bartholomew 160,
    183, 520
Governor John Wentworth State
    Historic Site............................423
Grafton 335
Grafton Cheese 332, 335
Grafton Notch State Park........512
Grafton Ponds Outdoor Center
   335
Grand Isle 378
Grandma Moses.........................338
Great Barrington........................232
Great North Woods region.....444
Green Animals Topiary Garden
   263
Green Mountain Boys ... 328, 337,
    366, 371
Green Mountain Coffee Visitor
    Center 360
Green Mountain National Forest
    ....346, 358
Green Mountains............340, 343,
    344
Greenville 515
Greenwich...................................302
Greyhound buses 20, 23
Gropius House............................136
Groton 286

H

Hale, Nathan......................306, 325
Halibut Point State Park..........150
Hallowell......................................507
Hammonasset Beach State Park
   289
Hammond Castle Museum.....148
Hampton Beach...............396, 397
Hancock–Clarke House 131

Hancock, John 51, 54, 131, 522
Hancock Shaker Village...........233
Hanover...................... 413–416
Hanover................................ **414**
Harpoon Brewery......................355
Harpswells, the.......................474
Harriet Beecher Stowe Center
....309
Hartford........................ 305–311
Hartford................................. **306**
Hartwell Inn............................132
Harvard Five 301
Harvard...................................136
Harvard University **91–93**
Hawthorne, Nathaniel 52, 56,
132, 133, 144, 229, 232, 233,
533
Head of the Charles Regatta ... 27
health.. 34
Henderson, Skitch...................321
Higganum.................................314
Higgins Armory Museum........208
hiking.. 30
hiking on Mt Desert Island 499
Hildene.....................................342
Hill–Stead Museum 311
Hillsborough............................410
Historic Deerfield 223
history........................ **519–527**
hitchhiking................................. 21
hockey.................................29, 125
Holderness...............................426
Homer, Winslow.........84, 94, 146,
147, 207, 212, 218, 235, 246,
463
Homer Noble Farm 358
Hood Museum of Art...............413
Hope Cemetery........................367
Hopkins Vineyard 319
hostels.. 24
hotels.. 23
Housatonic Meadows State Park
....325
Housatonic Museum of Art ...298
House of the Seven Gables....144
Hunt Hill Farm Trust...............321
hunting 32
Hutchinson, Gov. Thomas 54,
522
Hyannis........................ **166–168**
Hyannis................................. **167**
Hyde Log Cabin........................378

I

immigration................................ 33
Indian motorcycles..................213
information................................ 37

Institute for American Indian
Studies.................................321
insurance.................................... 34
internet....................................... 34
Ipswich.....................................151
Isle au Haut..............................493
Isle La Motte............................377
Isles of Shoals................. 394, 398
itineraries................................... 16
Ivoryton....................................315
Ivy League colleges.........**91–93,
256, 298, 301, 418**

J

Jackman....................................516
Jackson.....................................439
Jackson Gore............................347
Jacob's Pillow...........................231
Jamaica....................................346
Jay Peak Resort........................383
Jenness State Beach.................397
Jeremiah Lee Mansion.............140
JFK.............................86, 88, 526
John F. Kennedy Hyannis
Museum.................................. 66
John F. Kennedy National
Historic Site........................107
John F. Kennedy Presidential
Library & Museum................108
John James Audubon bird folio
....158
Jones Library............................218
Joseph Allen Skinner State Park
....220

K

Kancamagus Highway
......................................**430–433**
Kate Day....................................396
Keeler Tavern Museum.............323
Keene..409
Kennebunkport 457
Kent...320
Kent Falls State Park 320
Kerouac, Jack.................. 137, 139,
533
Kerry, John F.............................. 71
Killington...................... **349–351**
King, Stephen 508, 533
King Philip's War.............. 222, 521
Kingfield....................................514
Kipling, Rudyard 332, 333,
335
Kittery.......................................451
Knight Point State Park 378

Knights of Columbus Museum
....294

L

L.L. Bean...................................469
La Farge, John............ 77, 256, 258
Laconia Motorcycle Week 418
Lake Champlain **369–379**
Lake Champlain Maritime
Museum.................................376
Lake Memphremagog...........383
Lake Sunapee...........................417
Lake Waramaug 319
Lake Willoughby......................382
Lake Winnipesaukee ... **419–424**
Lake Winnipesaukee Museum
....420
Lakes Region **418–428**
Lakes Region **419**
Larkin, Deacon John.................. 66
Last Green Valley 325
laundry....................................... 34
Lee **230–232**
Lenox..229
LeWitt, Sol...............................236
Lexington 130–133
Libby Museum.........................423
Lilac Sunday 27, 87
Lincoln (MA) 135
Lincoln (NH) 431
Litchfield..................................317
Litchfield Hills............... **316–325**
Litchfield Hills **317**
literature............................. 8, 532
Little Compton 263
Littleton 436
lobster roll....................... 25, 477
Lockwood–Mathews Mansion
Museum.................................300
Logan International Airport ... 19,
95
Long Trail, the 344
Long Trail Brewing Co.............350
Longfellow, Henry Wadsworth
....93, 531
Loon Center.............................422
Loon Mountain.........................432
Lost Manissean Indian Exhibit
....271
Lovecraft, H.P................. 246, 533
Lowell............................ **137–140**
Lowell National Historical Park
....138
Lubec..504
Lucky Star bus 20
Ludlow......................................347
Lyman Allyn Art Museum.......285
Lyme disease............................. 31

M

MAC Center for the Arts..........383
MacDowell Colony.....................411
Macedonia Brook State Park
....320
Machias.....................................503
Mad River Valley........................359
Madaket....................................198
Madison.....................................289
Magic Hat Brewing Company
....371
Magic Wings Butterfly
Conservatory...........................222
mail.. 34
Maine 446–517
Maine 450
Maine Discovery Museum......509
Maine Eastern Railroad 473
Maine Lighthouse Museum...485
Maine lighthouses 481
Maine Maritime Museum 475
Maine State House....................507
Maine State Museum................507
Manchester (NH) 400–404
Manchester (NH) 401
Manchester (VT) 341–343
maple syrup...352, 353, 356, 360,
367, 368
maps..35
Marblehead 140
Marconi Station Site 177
Mariposa Museum 411
Mark Twain House.....................308
Marsh–Billings–Rockefeller
National Historical Park.......351
Martha's Vineyard........ 183–192
Martha's Vineyard............... 183
accommodation.................189
arrival and departure 188
Aquinnah (Gay Head).......187
bars 191
beaches...............................187
Chappaquiddick................185
Chilmark.............................186
Edgartown..........................184
entertainment...................192
getting around..................189
history.................................183
information.........................189
Menemsha...........................186
nightlife...............................192
Oak Bluffs..........................184
restaurants........................190
Vineyard Haven.................184
West Tisbury 186
Mass MoCA.................................236
Massachusetts.................40–237
Massachusetts Bay Colony......54,
66, 141, 520
Massachusetts Institute of
Technology 94

Massachusetts Museum of
Contemporary Art.................236
Massasoit....................................519
Mather, Cotton 63
Mather, Increase.................... 62, 63
Mattatuck Museum 322
Mayflower II.................................155
Mayflower..................155, 179, 519
Mayflower Compact.......179, 519
McAuliffe–Shepard Discovery
Center...................................406
Mead Art Museum 218
measurements............................ 34
media 26
Mega Bus.................................... 20
Melville, Herman....157, 229, 232,
233, 533
Menemsha.................................186
Meredith.....................................420
Merrimack Valley 400–408
microbreweries
Allagash Brewing......................467
Atlantic Brewing Co 501
Barrington Brewery..................232
City Steam Brewery Café........311
DL Geary...................................467
Elm City Brewery and Pub........409
Harpoon Brewery (Boston)........116
Harpoon Brewery (VT)............355
Long Trail Brewing Co 350
Magic Hat Brewing Company 371
McNeill's Brewery....................333
Newport Storm Brewery 256
Northampton Brewery............216
Otter Creek Brewery 357
Portsmouth Brewery...............396
Samuel Adams.........................117
Shipyard Brewery....................467
Trapp Family Brewery..............364
Trinity Brewhouse...................250
Mid-Coast Maine............... 472
Middlebury.................................357
Millay, Edna St Vincent 488
Miller State Park........................411
Millyard Museum.......................400
Minute Man National Historical
Park.......................................132
Misquamicut State Beach......265,
267
MIT... 94
Mitchell, Maria...........................196
mobile phones 36
Moby Dick 26, 157, 233, 533
Mohawk Trail.............................224
Mohegan Bluffs........................270
Mohegan Sun 285
Monadnock region...... 408–410
Monadnock State Park 412
money.. 35
Monhegan Island 482
Monomoy National Wildlife
Refuge 169
Montague Mill 223

Monte Cristo Cottage 286
Montpelier 365–369
Montpelier 366
Monument Mountain 232
moose... 31
Moosehead Lake 514
Moosehorn National Wildlife
Refuge 506
Morse Farm Maple Sugarworks
....367
Moultonborough......................421
Mount, the 229
Mount Belknap.........................419
Mount Desert Island ... 495–503
Mount Desert Island.......... 496
Mount Greylock 236
Mount Holyoke 220
Mount Holyoke College 220
Mount Holyoke Range State
Park.......................................220
Mount Independence..............356
Mount Katahdin........................516
Mount Mansfield 362
Mount Monadnock...................412
Mount Norwottuck..................220
Mount Snow...............................346
Mount Sunapee State Park 417
Mount Washington 441
Mount Washington Cog Railway
....442
Mount Washington Hotel.......443
Mount Washington Valley
.... 437–440
Mountain Country Soap 383
mountain lion 31
Moxie Festival 27
MS Mount Washington 420
Museum of Connecticut History
....306
Museum of Fife and Drum 315
Museum of New Hampshire
History 405
Museum of the British Redcoats
....131
Museum of Work and Culture
....252
Mystic Aquarium 280
Mystic Pizza 283, 529
Mystic Seaport...........................280
Mystic.............................. 280–283
Mystic 281

N

Naismith, James........................210
Nantucket...................... 192–201
Nantucket............................ 192
Nantucket Town 194

accommodation............................199
arrival and departure 198
bars 200–201
beaches 198
Coskata–Coatue–Great Point......197
entertainment.............................201
getting around 199
history 193
information 198
Madaket 198
Nantucket Town 193–197
nightlife..201
Polpis Road...................................197
restaurants...................................200
Siasconset....................................197
Napatree Point 268
Narragansett 266
Narragansett Indian Church
....267
Narragansett Powwow................ 27
Nash Dinosaur Tracks...............220
Nathan Hale Homestead
Museum..325
National Heritage Museum...131
National Public Radio 26
National Streetcar Museum...137
National Yiddish Book Center
....220
Natural Bridge State Park 224
Naulakha 332, 333
Naumkeag......................................227
Nauset Light...............................175
NeOn bus... 20
New Bedford 157
New Britain 312
New Canaan 301
New England Carousel Museum
....313
New England Maple Museum
....356
New England Patriots 29
New England Quilt Museum
....137
New England Ski Museum.....434
New Hampshire 384–445
New Hampshire 388
New Hampshire State House
....404
New Haven.................... 290–297
New Haven 291
New Haven Museum...................294
New Haven pizza 296
New London 284–286
Newbury...417
Newburyport 152
Newfane 334
NEWPORT (RI) 252–262
Newport (RI) 253
accommodation................................260
arrival and departure 259
Bannister's Wharf 252
bars 262
beaches 259

Beechwood 256
Belcourt Castle..............................258
bikes 260
Bowen's Wharf..............................252
Breakers, The.................................257
Brick Market Place 252
buses 260
Chateau-sur-Mer...........................257
Chepstow..257
Cliff Walk..256
Dinner Train 260
drinking...262
eating 261
Elms, The...257
entertainment................................262
festivals..259
Fort Adams State Park..................259
getting around 260
Great Friends Meeting House
....255
Hunter House 257
information 260
International Tennis Hall of Fame
....256
International Yacht Restoration
School..255
Isaac Bell House.............................257
Kingscote 257
Marble House 258
Museum of Newport History.......254
Museum of Yachting.....................259
music festivals................................259
Newport Art Museum 255
Newport Folk Festival.............27, 259
Newport Jazz Festival...................259
Newport Storm Brewery 256
nightlife...262
Old Colony House..........................254
restaurants......................................261
Rosecliff 258
Rough Point 258
Salve Regina University 256
scooters 260
seal watches 260
Seventh Day Baptist Meeting
House...255
Touro Synagogue...........................255
tours...260
trains..259
Viking Tower 254
Wanton-Lyman-Hazard House
....254
Washington Square........................252
Newport (VT) 382
newspapers 26
Ninigret National Wildlife
Refuge 267
Norfolk...325
Norman Rockwell Exhibition
(VT)...340
Norman Rockwell Museum (MA)
....227
Norman Rockwell Museum (VT)
....356
North Adams..................................236
North Bennington....................340
North Bridge 133

North Conway.................................437
North Hampton State Beach
....397
North Hero 378
North Shore 140–153
North Woodstock 430
Northampton 214–217
Northeast Historic Film 490
Northeast Kingdom 379–383
Northeastern Connecticut.....325
Northern Forest Heritage Park
....444
Norwalk 299

O

O'Neill, Eugene..........87, 179, 286
Oak Bluffs 184
Ocean Beach Park.........................286
Ocean Point 478
Odiorne Point State Park 396
Ogunquit..................... 455–457
Okemo Mountain 347
Old Constitution House 354
Old Harbor 270
Old Lyme 287
Old Man in the Mountain.......434
Old Manse 133
Old Narragansett Church 264
Old Orchard Beach.......................459
Old Saybrook 288
Old Sturbridge Village 210
Olmsted, Frederick Law......83, 86
On Golden Pond................ 426, 427
opening hours...............................36
Orchard House 132
Orvis Store......................................342
Otis, James 51, 54, 56
Otter Creek Brewery....................357
outdoor activities 30–32
Owls Head Transportation
Museum..486
oyster shucking...........................177

P

package tours................................21
Parker, John 130, 131
Parker River National Wildlife
Refuge 152
Park McCullough House 340
Patrick, Deval 45
Pawtucket 251
Peabody Essex Museum 144
Peabody Museum of Natural
History..294

Peary-MacMillan Arctic Museum 472

Pemaquid Peninsula 480–482

Penobscot Marine Museum 490

Penobscot Narrows Observatory 490

Peterborough 411
pharmacy 34
Phillips Exeter Academy..........397
phones 36
Pico Mountain 349
Pierce, Franklin 405, 410
Pierce Manse 405
Pilgrim Monument..................180
Pilgrims, the... 155, 156, 175, 179, 180, 519
Pinkham Notch.....................440
Pioneer Valley............... 214–225
Pioneer Valley 215
Pittsfield...............................233
Plath, Sylvia............ 215, 533
Plimoth Plantation 156
Plum Island 152
Plymouth...................... 154–157
Plymouth 155
Plymouth Notch.......................348
Poe, Edgar Allen......................246
poison ivy 31
Polpis Road.............................197
PORTLAND 460–469
Portland............................ 461
accommodation...................465
airport.................................464
arrival and departure 464
Arts District..........................462
bars.....................................467
bikes....................................465
buses...................................465
cafés....................................467
Cape Elizabeth......................464
car rental..............................465
Children's Museum.................463
clubs....................................468
drinking................................467
eating...................................466
entertainment......................468
films.....................................468
getting around 465
information 465
International Cryptozoology Museum..............................463
Museum of African Culture.........463
nightlife................................468
Old Port................................464
performing arts......................468
Portland Head Lighthouse.........464
Portland Museum of Art............463
Portland Observatory...............464
Portland Stage Company...........468
restaurants...........................466
shopping..............................468
Soakology.............................469

sports...................................468
tours....................................462
trains....................................464
Two Lights State Park...............464
Victoria Mansion 464
Wadsworth–Longfellow House ...462
Winslow Homer's studio 463
Portland Museum of Art.........463
PORTSMOUTH (NH)..... 389–396
Portsmouth (NH)................ 390
accommodation...................394
arrival and departure 393
Athenaeum..........................391
bars.....................................395
buses...................................393
Coast Trolley.........................393
Discover Portsmouth Center 390
eating...................................395
entertainment......................395
getting around 393
Governor John Langdon House 392
harbor cruises.......................394
information 393
John Paul Jones House.............392
Kate Day...............................396
kayaking...............................393
Market Square.......................390
Market Street........................391
Moffatt–Ladd House...............391
nightlife................................395
North Church.........................391
Point of Graves cemetery.........391
Prescott Park.........................391
restaurants...........................395
St John's Episcopal Church........392
Seacoast Repertory Theatre......396
Strawbery Banke Museum 392
tours....................................393
USS Albacore Park 391
Warner House.........................392
Wentworth–Coolidge Mansion ...392
Portsmouth (RI)........................262
post.....................................34
Prescott, William 67
PROVIDENCE................. 243–250
Providence 244
accommodation...................248
airport.................................248
arrival and departure 248
bars.....................................250
Benefit Street.......................245
Brown University....................245
buses...................................248
Children's Museum.................247
College Hill...........................245
Concert under the Elms 245
Culinary Arts Museum.............247
Downcity..............................243
drinking................................250
eating...................................249
entertainment......................250
Federal Hill...........................247
First Baptist Meeting House........246
Gallery Night.........................250

gondola tours........................248
information 248
John Brown House...................245
Kennedy Plaza.......................243
Little Italy.............................247
nightlife................................250
Old State House......................245
Providence Athenaeum............246
restaurants...........................249
RISD Museum........................246
Roger Williams National Memorial 244
Roger Williams Zoo 247
State Capitol.........................243
taxis.....................................248
theatre.................................250
tours....................................248
trains....................................248
Waterfire festival...................247
Westminster Street.................243
Provincetown 178–182
Provincetown 179
Provincetown Players..............179
public holidays........... 26–28, 36
Putnam Cottage.......................304

Q

Quechee 353
Queechee Gorge State Park 353
Quincy 153

R

radio 26
rafting...................................516
Raggedy Ann dolls...................300
rail passes 19, 23
Ralph Waldo Emerson House 133
Rangeley............................512–514
Rattlesnake Mountain 426
Renys....................................480
Revere, Paul 51, 52, 54, 62, 63, 66, 131, 132, 386
Revolutionary War... 45, 128, 131, 356, 387, 522
Rhode Island................. 238–273
Rhode Island 242
Ridgefield..............................323
RISD Museum of Art................246
Robert Abbe Museum..............497
Robert Frost Farm, NH............404
Robert Frost Memorial Highway 358
Robert Frost Stone House Museum..................................340

Robert Hull Fleming Museum 371
Rock of Ages Quarry..............367
Rockland..................... 484–487
Rockport (MA) 149
Rockport (ME) 489
Rockwell, Norman.........227, 228, 233, 340, 356
Rocky Neck Art Colony..........147
Roger Williams National Memorial 244
Rutland...................................355

S

St Anne's Shrine 377
Saint-Gaudens, Augustus........69, 70, 212, 416
Saint-Gaudens National Historic Site..416
St George Peninsula................486
St Johnsbury 379
St Patrick's Day Parade 26
Sakonnet Point.......................263
Sakonnet Vineyards................263
Salem 141–146
Salem 142
Salem Maritime National Historic Site..........................144
Salem Witch Museum 142
Salem Witch Trials...................143
Salisbury Mansion...................206
Sand Bar State Park.................378
Sandwich.................................170
Sandy Neck Beach Park..........172
Sargent, John Singer..........51, 77, 84, 147, 207, 246, 307
Sargent House Museum 147
Saunderstown 265
Scarborough State Beach.......265
Scargo Lake 173
Seacoast Region, the
.... 396–398
Seacoast Science Center.........396
SEE Science Center 401
senior travellers.......................36
Shakers, the 233, 407, 408
Shakespeare & Company........231
Sharon 325
Shaw, Robert Gould.................69
Shay's Rebellion.......................523
Sheffield Island Lighthouse
....299
Shelburne Falls 224
Shelburne Farms......................376
Shelburne Museum 375
Siasconset 197
Simon Pearce Glass.................354

skiing...............................30
Bromley Mountain Resort............342
Burke Mountain Resort..................382
Cannon Mountain 434
Grafton Ponds Nordic Ski Center
....335
Jackson Gore (VT)........................347
Jackson (NH)................................439
Jay Peak Resort............................383
Killington Resort 349
Loon Mountain 431
Mad River Glen 359
Mount Snow 346
Mount Sunapee............................417
Okemo Mountain Resort...............347
Pico Mountain 349
Smugglers' Notch Resort...............367
Stowe Mountain Resort................364
Stratton Mountain Resort.............342
Sugarbush Resort 359
Sugarloaf USA..............................514
Sunday River 511
Waterville Valley...........................428
Slater, Samuel 243, 251, 524
Slater Mill Historic Site.............251
Sleepy Hollow Cemetery 133
Smith College 214
Smith College Museum of Art
....214
Smith's Castle 264
smoking 28
Smugglers' Notch Resort........364
Smugglers' Notch State Park
....362
snowboarding 30
South County, the (RI)
.... 264–268
South County Museum 266
South Deerfield........................222
South Hadley 220
South Shore................. 153–159
Southern coast, the (ME).....452
Southern coast, the 452
Southport Island......................478
Southwest Harbor....................498
sports 28–30, 125
Springfield 210–214
Springfield 211
Springfield Museums................212
Squam Lake 424–428
Squanto....................................519, 520
Stamford 301
Stamford Museum & Nature Center......................................301
Star Island...............................398
Stark, John 337, 338
Sterling College........................381
Stockbridge 225–239
Stonington (CT) 283
Stonington (ME)......................493
Stony Creek..............................290
Storrs.......................................325
Story Land...............................439

Stowe, Harriet Beecher..........309, 473
Stowe 361–365
Stowe 362
Stowe Mountain Resort 361
Stratton 342
Strawbery Banke Museum.....392
Strolling of the Heifers.............333
Stuart, Gilbert 50, 51, 84, 243, 256, 265, 305
student discounts 36
Sturbridge...............................210
Submarine Force Museum.....286
"sugar on snow"........................368
Sugarbush Farm......................352
Sugarbush Resort 359
Sugarloaf USA.........................514
Sunapee Harbor.......................417
Sunday River 511

T

T.W. Wood Gallery 366
Tanglewood.....................229, 231
Tapping Reeve House & Law School..318
Tasha Tudor Museum..............332
telephones................................ 36
temperature...............................8
Thimble Islands.......................290
Thompson Ice House 481
Thoreau, Henry David... 133, 134, 136, 412, 531
Timex Museum........................323
tipping 28
tour operators..........................21
tourist information.....................37
Town Neck Beach 170
Townshend 334
Townshend State Park.............335
trains 19, 22
transcendentalism 134, 136, 525
Trapp Family Lodge & Brewery
....364
travel agents.............................21
travel insurance........................34
Truro.......................................177
Twain, Mark 308

U

US Coast Guard Academy 285
USS Albacore.............................391

V

Vergennes 376
Vermont.......................... 326–383
Vermont............................... 330
Vermont Canoe Touring Center
....333
Vermont Historical Society
Museum 366
Vermont Institute of
Contemporary Arts 336
Vermont Ski Museum 361
Vermont State House................366
Via Rail 19
Vineyard Haven 184
VINS Nature Center....................353
visas..32
visitor centres 37
Von Trapp family......361, 364, 365

W

Wadsworth Atheneum Museum
of Art 307
Waitsfield....................................359
Walden Pond...............................134
Wallis Sands State Beach........397
Wampanoags..........156, 175, 183,
185, 187, 193, 519
Warner, Seth 337
Warren 359
Washington (CT)........................321
Washington, George ...50, 73, 90,
93, 255, 313
Watch Hill 267
Waterbury (CT)..........................322
Waterbury (VT) 359–361
Waterville Valley........................428
Wayside.......................................132
weather..8
Webb-Deane-Stevens Museum
....313
Webster, Daniel 56, 397, 405,
406, 414

Webster Cottage........................414
Weir, J. Alden............246, 302, 324
Weir Farm National Historic Site
....323
Weirs Beach 420
Wellfleet......................................176
Wentworth, Benning................328
Wentworth State Park..............423
West Cornwall............................325
West Quoddy Head 504
West Tisbury...............................186
Westerly 267
Westmore 382
Weston, ...346
Westport 298
Wethersfield...............................313
Whale Center of New England
....147
whale-watching 58, 99, 147
Wharton, Edith 229, 533
Wheatley, Phillis 57, 77
Whistler, James McNeil...........138,
246
Whistler House Museum of Art
....138
White Memorial Foundation &
Conservation Center 318
White Mountain National Forest
(ME)...511
White Mountain National Forest
(NH)..432
White Mountains 428–445
White Mountains 429
whitewater rafting 516
Whitney, Eli 276, 524
whoopie pie 25, 25, 509
Whydah Museum 180
Wickford......................................264
Wildcat Mountain......................440
Wilder, Thornton 408, 411, 531
Wilhelm Reich Museum 512
William Benton Museum of Art
....325
Williams, Roge 240, 243, 244,
246, 520
Williams College Museum of Art
....235

Williamstown................ 234–236
Wilmington..................................344
Wilson Castle...............................356
Windham Foundation.............335
Windjammer Festival 27
Windsor.......................................354
Wine Trail 319
Winnipesaukee Railroad.........420
winter festivals 26
Winthrop, John...........50, 66, 142,
520
Witch Dungeon Museum 142
Witch House, the 143
Wolf Hollow 151
Wolfe's Neck State Park 470
Wolfeboro 422
Woodbury 321
Woods Hole.................. 164–166
Woodstock 351–353
Woonsocket................................252
Worcester 204–210
Worcester 208
Worcester Art Museum 206
Worcester diners........................209
Worcester Historical Museum
....204
Wyman Tavern Museum 409

Y

Yale Center for British Art.......293
Yale Summer School of Music
....325
Yale University 288, 292
Yale University Art Gallery 293
Yankee 5, 25, 328
Yankee Candle Company 222
Yarmouth Port 172
Yorks, the...................... 453–455

Z

Zimmerman House...................402

Map symbols

The symbols below are used on maps throughout the book

✈ Airport	✚ Hospital	⚱ Waterfall	▢ Market
★ Bus/taxi	◆ Place of interest	⊤ Gardens	▦ Church
Ⓣ Tram stop	☉ Statue	�▽ Viewpoint	▢ Park
✡ Synagogue	🏛 Monument	⚠ Campsite/ground	🏖 Beach
🅿 Parking	🏛 Stately home	⌃⌃ Mountain range	▢ Glacier
@ Internet café/access	⛷ Skiing	▲ Mountain peak	▢ Cemetery
✉ Post office	☼ Lighthouse	⋟⋞ Swamp	━ Wall
ⓘ Information office	⌂ Monastery	⁓ Bridge	●–●– Cable car
☎ Telephone office	ᚚᚚ Spring/spa	▨ Building	– – Ferry route
♣ Museum	⚓ Swimming pool/area		

Listings key

■ Accommodation
● Eating and drinking
■ Nightlife
● Shop